THE INTERNATIONAL COOKS' CATALOGUE

OTHER BEARD GLASER WOLF BOOKS:

The Cooks' Catalogue

The Great Cooks' Cookbook

Pennywise Party Perfect Dinners

The Garden-to-Table Cookbook

Where to Eat in America

The Great Cooks' Library

- Breads
- Clay Cookery
- Crêpes & Soufflés
- Fish Cookery
- Salads
- Woks, Steamers & Fire Pots

THE INTERNATIONAL COOKS' CATALOGUE

A critical selection of the best, the authentic—and the special—in available kitchen equipment from around the world. Over 800 items, including more than 100 extraordinary recipes. Plus cooking folklore and hundreds of illustrations. Produced with the assistance of the world's leading food authorities. Introduction by James Beard.

A BEARD GLASER WOLF BOOK

Random House New York

For
Ray Merritt, Bud Lowenthal
Andrew, James and Stephen

And our very special appreciation to:
Joseph M. Cohen, Arthur Cowen, Jr.,
Judy A. Cowen, Walter Farber,
H. Lowenthal, Joseph Mula, Anthony
F. Phillips, Arthur Weinberg

CAUTION

Retail prices are intended as general guidelines and for comparative purposes only. They should not be relied on for purchasing. Prices will change in time and may also vary according to the outlet through which the item is purchased.

 Published in the United States by Random House, Inc., New York, and simultaneously in Canada by Random House of Canada Limited, Toronto.

Library of Congress Cataloguing in Publication Data

Main entry under title:

The International cooks' catalogue.

Includes index.
1. Kitchen utensils — Catalogs. 2. Cookery, International. I. Beard, James Andrews, 1903-
TX656.I57 683'.82'0216 77-5976
ISBN 0-394-41768-2

Manufactured in the United States of America

98765432

First Edition

Contents

James Beard   Milton Glaser   Burton Wolf

Executive Editors:
Wendy Afton Rieder   Kate Slate

Art Director:
Kaye Sherry Hirsh

Associate Editors:
Lois Bloom   Susan Lipke

Special Consultant:
Barbara Poses Kafka

Historical Consultant/Picture Researcher:
Elizabeth Colchie

Consultants:
Giuliano Bugialli, Grace Zia Chu, Janet V. Crisler, Rona Deme, Rajeev Deshmukh, Eric Friberg, Edward Giobbi, Hank Harjodimulyo, Agnes Freudenberg Hostettler, Madhur Jaffrey, Diana Kennedy, Paul Kovi, Maria Odete Laia, Leon Lianides, Florence Lin, Toshio Morimoto, Elisabeth Lambert Ortiz, Elia Padilla, Elena Pastor, Jacques Pépin, Isabel Rivas, Ramón San Martin, Satish Sehgal, Michael Tong, Alfredo Viazzi, Margaret A. Walter, Paula Wolfert

Senior Writer:
Irene Sax

Writers:
Helen Barer, Diana Childress, Sheila Cole, Florence Fabricant, Sally French, Pat Mancini, Mary McGurn, Marjorie Morton, Jane Opper, Helen Scott-Harman, Lyn Stallworth, Sandra Streepey, Ann Weissberg

Researchers:
Vicky Apt, Susan Hearn, Penny Hinkle, Michael Sears, Barbara Spiegel

Photographer:
Ed Fitzgerald

Editorial Staff:
Emily Aronson, Christopher Carter, Leo Fuller, Mardee Haidin, Ray Razee, Marilyn Smith, Pat Thomas

Acknowledgements

The editors of *The International Cooks' Catalogue* wish to express their deep appreciation to the following:

Susan Lipke, for collecting and editing recipes from restaurants and food specialty shops around New York City.

Lois Bloom, for being our tireless, irrepressible equipment sleuth.

Marjorie P. Katz and Vivien Fauerbach, for laying the groundwork.

Raymond Sokolov, for moral support.

Richard Rieder and Stephen Smith, for their endurance.

And:

Maija Leena Aho-Frayer
Saleem Ali at *Spice & Sweet Mahal*
The Bank Restaurant
Ellen Barr
Estaban Barroso
Robert Berarducci
Lucille Bernhardt at *HOAN Products, Ltd.*
Vijay Bhatla at *Madras Woodlands*
Daniel Bloom
Donna Bogdanowich at *Vantage Art, Inc.*
Daniel Bolle at *Spring Brothers*
Hans Booge at *Nyborg & Nelson, Inc.*
Herman Bosboom at *H. Roth & Son*
Diljit Brijnath
Bob Casey at *Block China Corp.*
James Chichester at *La Cuisinière Cook's Corner, Inc.*
Naomi Cutner
Rona Deme
Kunie Dorman
Faye Eng
Marge Fahlin at *Maid of Scandinavia Co.*
Walter Farber
Lucille and Walter Fillin
Eric Friberg
Joe Harada at *Otagiri Mercantile Co.*
Osmo Heila
George and Arthur Herbst at *Mrs. Herbst's*
Frederick Hill
Karl Hipp at *Spring Brothers*
Gisele Huff
Krishna Karanth at *Madras Woodlands*
Joanne Kelly at *Vantage Art, Inc.*
Peter Kump
Charles F. Lamalle
Peter Lambiase at *Bremen House*
George Lang
Gunnar Lie at *Nor-Pro, Inc.*
David Loble at *Taylor & Ng*
Annie Maliszewski at *H. A. Mack & Co., Inc.*
Jane McIntosh at *Boston Warehouse Co.*
The Metropolitan Museum of Art
The Museum of Contemporary Crafts
New York Public Library Picture Collection
Tad Ogawa at *Otagiri Mercantile Co.*
S. Paleewong at *Siam Grocery*
Charles Patteson at *Hammacher Schlemmer*
Irene Pereira
Anthony F. Phillips
Jean-Jacques Rachou at *Le Lavandou*
Vera Randall at *Scandicrafts, Inc.*
Robert Renaud at *Le Jacques Coeur*
Seppi Renggli at *The Four Seasons*
Maro Riotrancos
Laszlo Roth at *H. Roth & Son*
Jaroslav Ruc at *Ruc*
Nelson Saldana at *Charles F. Lamalle*
Ramón San Martin
Gino Sermoneta
Mimi Sheraton
Mintari Soeharjo at *Beng-Solo Trading Corp.*
André Soltner at *Lutèce*
Lucia and Miguel Soto
Katie Sparling
Thai Tourist Office
John Umbach at *P.R.S. Foods*
Gary Valenti
Blanca Velasquez
Ed Weiss at *Paprikás Weiss*
Masaru Yamada and Akira Yoshida at *N.Y. Mutual Trading Co.*

Additional photography by Jerry Darvin

Introduction

As American cooks graduate from the techniques of French and Italian cuisines, they are investigating the delights of preparing Chinese, Japanese, Indian and Middle Eastern foods. Our shops are brimming with appliances and tools specially designed for foreign cookery. Although it is often possible to improvise with whatever equipment you have on hand, chances are you will get better results and have more fun if you cook *couscous* in an authentic *couscousière* or poach a bass in a real fish poacher.

Among the newer appliances on the market, my favorite — after the Cuisinart food processor — is an electric pasta machine, made in Italy by Bialetti. Working on the same principle as the familiar hand-cranked pasta machines, it kneads the pasta dough smoothly and cuts it in either of two widths. It is efficient, clean and compact, and one of the best additions I have ever made to my *batterie de cuisine*. I use it constantly — even in dieting, since I can make salt-free pasta. From the mixing of the dough, which can be done in the Cuisinart, to the pasta pot, is only a matter of twenty minutes.

I also value my array of Chinese cleavers, which are now available in several sizes, thicknesses and weights. Once you have mastered the skill of using one, it can produce beautifully shaped slices and strips of food. From Italy, again, I've added a new truffle cutter, which slices those magnificent white fungi to paper thinness and is ideal for shaving truffle curls for pasta or *fonduta*. I've tried the cutter on one or two vegetables, too — notably potatoes — and have gotten rather pleasing results. While most of us do not need a truffle cutter for everyday use, it is a classy object to have hanging in one's kitchen.

Other imports that intrigue me are the myriad international baking devices: brioche molds, tart pans and flan rings from France; *krumkake* irons and *aebleskiver* pans from Scandinavia; *Kugelhopf* and *Christstollen* pans from Germany; *pizzelle* irons and *cannoli* forms from Italy. The variety is without end and should motivate any serious pastry maker or baker. One specialized baking pan that has particularly captivated me is a tin for making loaves of *pain de mie* (sometimes called sandwich or pullman bread). This pan produces a loaf with a light, soft crust, about seven inches long and three inches high, suitable for making canapés, melba toast or miniature sandwiches.

Of all the ethnic kitchen utensils that have been absorbed into what I generously term American cookery, none is more widely enjoyed than the wok, that fundamental implement of Chinese cookery. It has been at the heart of the stir-fry craze and has even been put to use for deep-frying, American style. What is more, an eminent food authority has used the electric wok to turn out a splendid paella.

One of the great pleasures of my travels has always been the exploration of foreign food markets and shops where kitchen equipment is sold. Over the years, I have amassed a sizeable collection of tools, ranging from a rotating vertical spit called a *doner kebab* to simple knives; and it also includes copper molds for every conceivable purpose, beautiful enough to be looked at as sculpture. You needn't travel the world to start your own collection of kitchen equipment. *The International Cooks' Catalogue* has searched out the most functional, the most aesthetic, the best for the money and put it all within your reach.

James Beard

About Using This Book

It's a known fact that our palates are becoming more sophisticated. Travelers speed from one country to another, venturing with real curiosity into three-star restaurants, mama-papa *trattorie*, Japanese *sushi* bars — even into the hangouts of Moroccan camel drivers! Diners whose Chinese was once limited to chow mein now look into the eyes of inscrutable waiters and firmly order the same dishes as the Chinese family at the corner table. We know there is a marvelous world of food out there, and we demand to sample it. What's more, we want to cook it — all that holds us back is lack of information about the ingredients and the equipment used in its preparation.

The International Cooks' Catalogue gives the reader an overview of the food and cooking equipment in five individual countries, and five broadly defined ethnic areas — in which countries have been grouped according to similarities of food, language or history. The introductions will bring you into the heart of a variety of kitchens, giving you a glimpse of the ethnic cooking customs and equipment in many regions of the world. General essays describe food resources and their effects upon a people's eating patterns and the development of certain specialized kitchen utensils.

With a view to making our cultural tour as complete as possible, our equipment experts have sought out items that are in every way authentic. You'll find, however, that certain areas of the world — Russia, Africa, Korea, Southeast Asia and parts of Eastern Europe, for example — are lightly represented. That's because at present not much equipment from these countries is available in America. Various factors are responsible for this: politics, lack of demand, or merely questions of weight or fragility. For example, stone mortars from India are too heavy to transport economically, and large earthenware pots from the Middle East very often do not survive long journeys intact. However, the supply picture changes from day to day, mostly for the better.

Wherever possible, we have given both wholesale sources and retail prices, so that you can compare prices as well as locate, through the wholesaler, the retail source nearest you. When two sources are listed, the first is retail and the second is wholesale. The numbers in parentheses following the sources for each utensil are wholesale (or retail) style numbers, which have been included for easy indentification. (You will find the addresses for both wholesale and retail sources listed in the back of the book, on page **405**.) Prices are pegged to the time of writing, and should be taken as an indication of general cost, subject to change. Esoteric items may be more difficult to obtain from small stores with variable stocks. In instances where a particular item is available in a range of sizes, the sizes have usually been indicated to give you a choice.

A number of typical (and delicious) recipes have been chosen as helpful indications of how you might use the equipment. (Page numbers for the various recipes appear in the index in heavy type for easy identification.) The catalogue is studded with illustrations of food, people with food and places with food to bring each country graphically alive and to add an historical perspective. Amusing, historical and informative anecdotes have also been included: some will delight you, others will expand your understanding of a people and their ways.

As you travel through these pages, we hope you will make discoveries that will prove of lasting reward in your culinary life.

Two Chinese Kitchens

by Florence Lin

Life is full of surprises. In this country I am a teacher of cooking and writer of cookbooks, but if I had stayed in my native China, I would probably never have learned to cook at all. That's because women in old-fashioned middle-class Chinese families didn't have to cook: there were plenty of servants to take care of such things.

It's even more surprising that you have asked me to describe a typical Chinese kitchen, because in my home near Shanghai, my mother herself rarely went into the kitchen. Occasionally, she would send word that she wanted to try out some special new recipe, and the servants would make sure that everything was prepared for her. Then she would walk over to the kitchen, which was near the servants quarters, rapidly combine some ingredients and quickly leave.

Because the kitchen was the province of the servants and not of the family members, it was most often an exceedingly rough and untidy room. Food was cooked over fires of coal and wood in stoves that looked like pails standing on the cement floor. Not only were these stoves extremely crude, but they were terrible grease and smoke producers; it was as if you barbecued in your kitchen twice every day! The walls and floor of the room had to be scrubbed down thoroughly every year to remove the traces of the fires.

Early in the day, one of the servants made a fire with a few pieces of coal. Fuel was always scarce, even in relatively well-to-do families like ours. This fire was used for cooking lunch. In the afternoon it was allowed to die down, but not to go out completely. When the cook needed to have more heat again for dinner, he would simply shove in a piece of wood, creating lively flames. That was the equivalent of turning up the gas jets or pressing the "High" button on an electric stove.

Food that was prepared in this kitchen was very good, but very simple. By working all day, the servants provided four or five dishes for the family lunch and the same number of dishes for dinner (always including rice). And they did all this with only two stoves and some rather simple tools. What the household lacked in cooking equipment, it made up for in inexpensive help and plenty of time. But if my mother wanted to order a banquet or a special meal, the cook would call in a banquet chef, who would set up his stoves out-of-doors and work with his staff for a whole day making complicated and exotic dishes for the party.

Our tableware, of course, could not be compared to the simplicity of the kitchen equipment. We always used porcelain serving platters, bowls and spoons and ate with ivory chopsticks. For formal dinners there was a complete set of more elaborate dishes and, of course, a tea set was always handy. Sometimes, too, we would eat from a Mongolian fire pot or chrysanthemum pot, especially during the cold months of winter.

When I look back, I have to thank my father for my real introduction to cooking. In the ordinary course of events, I would have lived much as other girls from old-fashioned families did: guarded from the world. But my father was a busy silk merchant, who traveled three or four times a year up and down the Yangtze river. Although I was neither a boy nor the oldest in the family, I was, for some

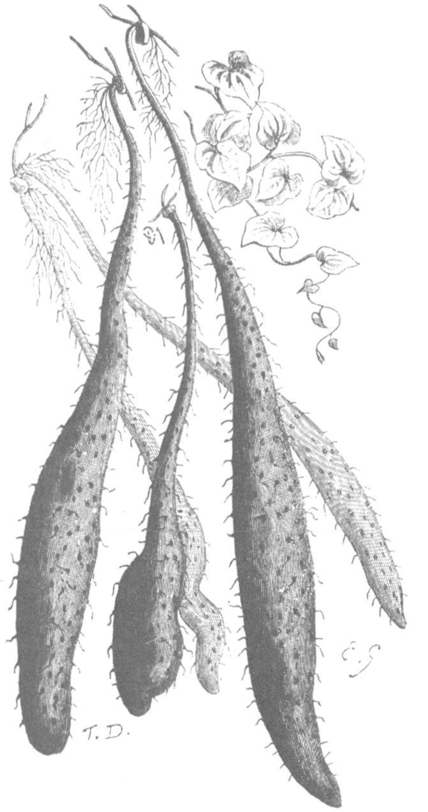

Chinese yam.

Chinese curled mustard.

Bamboo.

Litchis.

reason, his favorite child, and often he would take me with him on his business trips. Twice a day he would stop for a meal at an inn or a restaurant, and there, while my father sipped his rice wine at the beginning of the meal, we would be served wonderful foods that were quite different from the simple fare we had at home. Inevitably, I found myself watching, sometimes for hours, how these delicious foods were prepared. Chinese restaurant kitchens are open to the dining rooms, and I would stand at the edge of the kitchen, watching with interest while the cooks formed dumplings, chopped vegetables or stir-fried dishes, making a nuisance of myself by asking questions of the cooks.

Still, it was the war that changed everything. I lived in Szechwan for a while, and was even in the army—but that is another story. Finally, in 1947, I found myself in New York City, living in a fifth floor walk-up apartment near Columbia University and confronted with the task of feeding a hungry husband. At that time, there were few good Chinese restaurants in the city, mostly a lot of chop suey and egg foo yung places, so I decided that it was time to learn how to cook.

I had only a tiny kitchenette with a four-burner stove and a minute refrigerator, but to me it was a palace. I went to the five-and-ten and bought myself a couple of inexpensive frying pans. They were much too thin to be used successfully in preparing American food, but they worked just fine with my rapidly-cooked Chinese dishes—until I was able to get a proper wok. The one piece of equipment to which I gave any thought was a cleaver. I took a trip down to Chinatown and bought myself a really good heavy-weight cleaver with a carbon-steel blade. I knew that one knife would answer all my cutting needs—chopping, slicing, dicing and shredding. By the way, this concept of simplicity and frugality is central to Chinese cooking techniques: with one implement you perform many operations.

After a few years of practice—remembering what I had seen in China, reading and asking a lot of questions—I was skillful enough to come to the notice of someone who asked me to teach cooking at the China Institute. That was seventeen years and 5000 students ago. During that time there has been not only an enormous increase in interest in Chinese cooking and a great flowering of excellent Chinese restaurants in this country, but all the best Chinese cooking equipment is now available, too.

At the beginning of my course, I always advise my students on what equipment to buy; and, as you might expect, I think the first and most essential tool is the cleaver. If they are going to buy only one, it should be like mine, a small, heavy cleaver with a blade made of carbon steel or the new, easily-sharpened, high-carbon stainless steel. Then I tell them to get a medium-weight wok, one which is either 12″ or 14″ in diameter. If they become adept, they will certainly learn to cook with chopsticks, so I tell them to buy a few pairs of bamboo chopsticks and to practice, practice, practice until they can use them as easily as they do a fork. Finally, I tell them to get a Chinese spatula to use with the wok, since the curved surface of a cooking spoon is not really adapted to the gentler curve of the wok.

And that's basically all that they need. In my own kitchen, which is quite simple, I have an excellent gas range and, in addition to the equipment that I tell my students to buy, I have two tiered steamers, one of bamboo and one of aluminum, a hard plastic chopping board, and an electric rice cooker. I even have a French food processor. A recent visitor to my apartment was shocked to see it sitting on my

Continued from preceding page

counter. She thought that Chinese cooking demanded more careful preparation than could be done in a machine. I assured her that the food processor was used only in preparing certain dishes that require a great deal of tedious chopping, in which the ingredients nearly become a paste. For these dishes, such as velvet chicken, shrimp and fish balls, and the fillings for dumplings, it works wonderfully, and I am grateful to have it.

Actually, when I see the food processor next to my simple chopsticks, I am always reminded of how far I have come from my mother's kitchen in Ningpo. At the same time, I marvel at how perfectly functional Chinese cooking implements are and at how few of them are needed to make all the wonderful dishes I have learned.

The Cuisine of China

Necessity often spawns diversity. Nowhere is this truer than in China where people eat anything edible, from birds' nests, sharks' fins and fish maws, to tiger lily buds, tree ears and bean sprouts. This eclectic taste developed for good reason. Only 10 percent of China's giant land mass is arable; so, for centuries, millions of Chinese have had to depend on their ingenuity in foraging to survive. This explains why vegetables predominate and why large animals, such as cattle, are rare. Pork, poultry, fish, and especially soybeans (the beef of the East) are the principal sources of protein in the Chinese diet.

Food preparation was dramatically influenced by a scarcity of fuel and raw materials. To economize, the Chinese cut most of their food into small pieces of uniform size and stir-fried it quickly on small braziers. Thus, they saved both fuel and the need for cutlery, other than the basic cleaver and chopsticks. And because stoves were and still are, for the most part, simple braziers, and pans were hard to come by, the round-bottomed wok became the most versatile of all cooking pans. It is used for almost all cooking, including all kinds of frying and steaming.

Given the adversities associated with the procurement and preparation of food in China, it is all the more remarkable that the Chinese developed one of the great cuisines of the world. The only country whose food is at all comparable in sophistication and variety is France. Although there are many dissimilarities between the countries, both share a long culinary history, a leisure class tradition, and people who generally seem to value the pleasures of eating among life's great experiences.

"Balance" is probably the word that best describes the Chinese philosophy of eating. While each food is valued for its own taste, aroma, color and texture, it is the way in which different foods are combined that is most critical. Chinese dining customs are very particular. Meat and vegetables are usually combined in the same dish, and all the courses of a meal are brought to the table at once. Each dish is served on a platter from which the diners help themselves. Therefore every preparation must not only complement all the others on the table, but the ingredients in each one must also be carefully blended. For example, a spicy Szechwan dish should be offset by a bland one; and a crisp, deep-fried dish should be balanced with a soft, moist one of, say, bean curd and mushrooms. The colors of different

The edible nests of the salagane (swallows), with their inhabitants.

STIR-FRIED FLANK STEAK SLICES IN BLACK BEAN SAUCE

INGREDIENTS
- 2 cloves garlic, crushed and chopped
- 4 tablespoons fermented black beans, chopped coarsely
- 2 tablespoons peanut or vegetable oil
- 2 green peppers, cut into 1″ pieces

MASTER SAUCE
- 1 tablespoon dark soy
- 1 teaspoon cornstarch dissolved in ½ cup water

- 1 lb. flank steak, sliced ⅛″ thick
- 2 tablespoons dark soy
- 1 teaspoon Chinese rice wine or sherry
- ½ teaspoon sugar
- 1 tablespoon cornstarch
- 2 tablespoons peanut or vegetable oil

TO PREPARE
1. Chop garlic and black beans.
2. Remove seeds from green peppers and cut into 1″ squares.
3. Make master sauce in a cup by combining dark soy and cornstarch solution.
4. Cut flank steak in half lengthwise; then cut crosswise into ⅛″ slices. Mix together dark soy, wine, sugar,

and cornstarch; mix well with meat and marinate ½ hour.

TO COOK (*cooking time about 15 minutes*)

1. Heat 2 tablespoons oil in wok over medium flame. Add garlic and black beans, sizzle 1 minute.
2. Add green peppers, stir-fry 1 minute.
3. Add master sauce, cover wok, and simmer 5 minutes. Transfer sauce to a bowl and set aside.
4. In the same wok, heat 2 tablespoons oil over high flame. Add beef and stir-fry quickly for 2 minutes. Mixture should be sizzling all the time.
5. Add the sauce from the bowl, stir-fry to mix for ½ minute. Serve.
6. To serve: Dish up in a plate and serve hot.
7. Yield: Serves 2 alone or 6 in a 4-course dinner.

(From EIGHTY PRECIOUS CHINESE RECIPES by May Wong Trent. Copyright 1973 by May Wong Trent. Reprinted by permission of Macmillan Publishing Co., Inc.)

dishes should likewise provide pleasing contrast. To illustrate the complexity within a single preparation: deep-fried *wontons* with a filling of pork, shrimp, water chestnuts and scallions combine the qualities of freshness, crispness, tenderness and complementary colors and flavors.

China's cuisine, like that of all large countries, is marked by regional differences. In the north, where Peking is the culinary capital, wheat is the staple, and noodles, dumplings and buns are part of the daily diet. Cooking tends to be light and mild, and lamb, introduced by the Mongolians, is popular. Crisp-skinned Peking duck served with scallion brushes, Mandarin pancakes and sweetened bean sauce is perhaps the most famous dish from the area.

In the western region that includes Szechwan and Hunan food is characterized by hot and spicy flavoring, particularly derived from the well-known Szechwan pepper.

Southern, or Cantonese-style cooking is the most varied of all, reflecting the availability of many foods. It is certainly the lightest, with stir-frying the predominant cooking technique of the region.

Along the coast, in the eastern region, seafood and vegetables are abundant and cooking is characterized by the use of soy sauce (red-cooking) and salt.

Chinese food is perhaps the most well-traveled cuisine of all. In fact, it has been so easy for the whole world to eat at Chinese restaurants that only recently, with the increasing availability of both the proper cooking equipment and ingredients, has it seemed worthwhile for anyone to learn to cook Chinese food at home. But now we all can gain, firsthand, an insight into one of the great cuisines of the world.

Chinese teapot, late 18th century (from The Metropolitan Museum of Art).

The Versatile Cleaver

Confucius said that one "must not eat what has been crookedly cut." For centuries his words have been heeded, knowingly or not, by the Chinese, who value the look of food almost as much as they do its taste.

Of course, the actual reason for cutting food into small pieces before cooking is more practical than aesthetic. China has long been a fuel-starved nation, and one of the best solutions to this problem has been the tradition of cooking small pieces of food together quickly. It is a great economy that has lead to wonderful refinement. Not only must the colors and textures of a dish be complementary to each other, but all the pieces of food on a platter must be about the same size and shape. No mixing of cubes with shreds, please. In roast pork *lo mein* (noodles), for example, the pork and Chinese mushrooms are cut into thin strips to correspond more closely to the shape of the noodles.

Carried to its conclusion, the quest for proportion and balance requires that no two dishes on a table look alike. If one platter has diced food on it, all the other platters on the table should contain food in different shapes. With so much attention paid to the look of food, it's no wonder a Chinese apprentice cook must spend two to three years wielding a knife until he is qualified to take on other responsibilities.

The versatile implement that solves all these cutting tasks is the Chinese cleaver. It is used to slice, shred, dice, chop and mince all types of meats and vegetables. It will fillet a fish, bone a chicken breast, mash ginger or garlic and even grind spices. (To grind spices put them in a ladle or small bowl and pulverize them with the handle of the cleaver.) And, after you have finished slicing or chopping, you can use the broad blade of the cleaver to transport food to the wok or cooking pot.

Cleavers come in three sizes: #1, the largest; #2, medium; and #3, the smallest; and each size is usually available in two weights, light and heavy. The blade should be either of tempered carbon steel or high-carbon stainless steel that will keep a sharp edge and can be easily honed. Although a cleaver is usually associated with the chopping of large bones, the Chinese cleaver (with the exception of the very heaviest type) is mainly suited to slicing or chopping food. You may also use it to cut through light poultry or rib bones. First try holding the cleaver against the bone and use the palm of your hand or a rubber mallet to push or knock the blade through it. You may hack a light bone, if necessary; but be very careful, the bone may splinter and the blade of the knife may become knicked.

Although one good cleaver is usually sufficient for most tasks, cleavers of different shapes are made for special types of cutting. A long, thin rectangular blade is best for mincing; a wide rectangular blade, the most popular of all, is ideal for all slicing jobs and is also good for chopping; and a wide rectangular cleaver with a slightly curved cutting edge is particularly good for chopping because the blade can be rocked slightly. A round-bladed cleaver is also made for boning and chopping, but it is not very common.

To slice or chop food with a cleaver, the cutting edge of the blade should be at a slight angle to the cutting board. Grasp the cleaver with one hand. Hold the food with the other hand so that your fingers are arched over it but the ends of your fingers are slightly curled under. The knuckle of the middle finger should touch the side of the blade acting as a guide for it. The correct cutting motion consists of letting

Chinese butcher.

F. T. Cheng, Chinese ambassador to the Court of St. James, describes a chef: "But the Chinese cook . . . knows his art. To watch him mincing meat on the chopping-board is to witness the performance of a knife-dance accompanied with music. You will see a pair of shining chopping knives moving up and down swiftly and gracefully making continuous a noise that in tone is quite musical, e.g. 'Dig Dog, Dig Dog; Dig Dog, Dig Dog, Dog Dog, Drig Drog, Drig Drog,' occasionally varied by a 'Ding Dong' brought about by knocking one knife against the other."

Musings of a Chinese Gourmet *by F. T. Cheng. Hutchinson, 1954.*

the cleaver blade drop downward and forward repeatedly. The weight of the cleaver will do most of the cutting, while the edge of the blade remains well below your knuckle. You really don't have to lift the cleaver more than about ⅛″ above the food as you cut. It takes practice to operate a cleaver skillfully, but once accustomed to its weight and efficiency, you may find yourself reaching for this tool for all your chopping and slicing chores.

Slicing Cleaver A:1

No knife is more highly prized for the preparation of Chinese food than the indispensable cleaver. Although cleavers are made in several shapes, this medium-weight, broad, rectangular-bladed knife is the best for slicing, shredding and cutting through the light bones of fish, spare ribs and poultry. The long blade is especially easy to control on a large piece of meat or on a vegetable like lettuce or cabbage. And it makes a perfect scoop for transferring cut food to the wok. Like many other Cantonese knives this one is two-toned: the upper half of the blade is black, the natural color of the metal, and the lower half is a silvery color from grinding and polishing. Made of tempered carbon steel, ground to a fine edge and measuring 3⅜″ wide and 7¾″ long, this cleaver is every bit as effective as it looks. Strongly constructed, the blade has a long, tapering rattail tang that pierces the 4½″-long, naturally-finished wood handle, and a metal collar that reinforces the joint. Like all carbon-steel knives, this one will hold a sharp edge for a long while, and it can easily be rehoned. When new, the cleaver is covered with a protective film that must be scrubbed off in hot soapy water. Never put it in a dishwasher, and give it a thorough drying after every use to avoid rust. Although a cleaver may seem quite strange compared to its Western counterpart, it is a well-balanced precision implement that works beautifully and will last for years with the proper care.

Taylor & Ng (10620) $9.00

Slicing Knife A:2

Once you have used this versatile Chinese knife with its broad blade and wooden handle, its virtues will be obvious. Not only is it ideal for mincing, shredding and slicing; but it is also perfect for crushing a garlic clove, for tenderizing meat with the blunt edge of the blade and for grinding peppercorns in a bowl, using the end of the wooden handle as a pestle. And, best of all, when the ingredients have reached the desired consistency, they can be easily swept up on the broad, flat blade and transported to plate or pot. This excellent lightweight knife, which is 8″ long by 3¼″ wide and has a 4″-long handle, is for slicing meats and vegetables and cutting through joints of poultry, but not for severing bones, which would require a heavier weight. The Chinese have traditionally used and preferred a carbon-steel blade to any other since it can be sharpened to the keenness they require. But carbon steel has to be protected from rust. This Dexter knife, however, is made of high-carbon stainless steel that can be easily sharpened and will not rust. It is a favorite of Chinese cooking experts. Once you get used to using it, you will be amazed at how manageable this large implement becomes.

Russell Harrington (S5198) $12.95

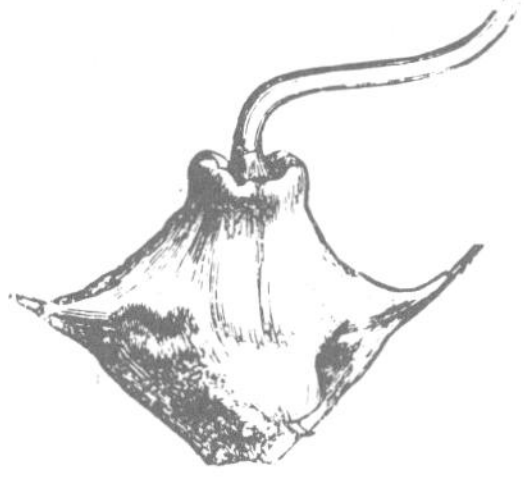

Water chestnut.

Vegetable Slicer A:3

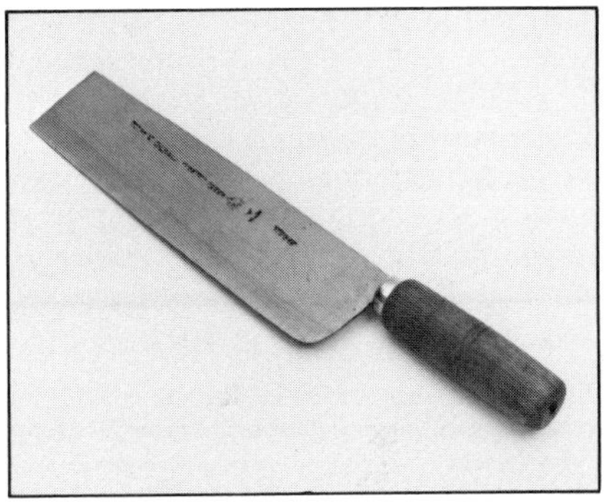

Most vegetable cutting can be done with a large cleaver, but the shorter, narrower blade of this knife makes it easier and faster to handle light jobs like slicing Peking duck or small vegetables like water chestnuts. Made of high-carbon steel, the blade measures 7½″ long by 2″ wide; the wooden handle is 3¾″ long. Water chestnuts add crunchy texture and a subtle, slightly sweet flavor to Chinese dishes. In the U.S. they have become so popular that they are grown in Florida, so you can buy them fresh. To peel one with this knife, cut a thin slice off the top and bottom of the water chestnut as you would an onion. Then hold it between thumb and forefinger, and peel halfway down, from top to middle, on the side away from you, turning the water chestnut as you work. Turn it over and peel the other half.

Kam Man Food Products $5.50

Chopping Cleaver A:4

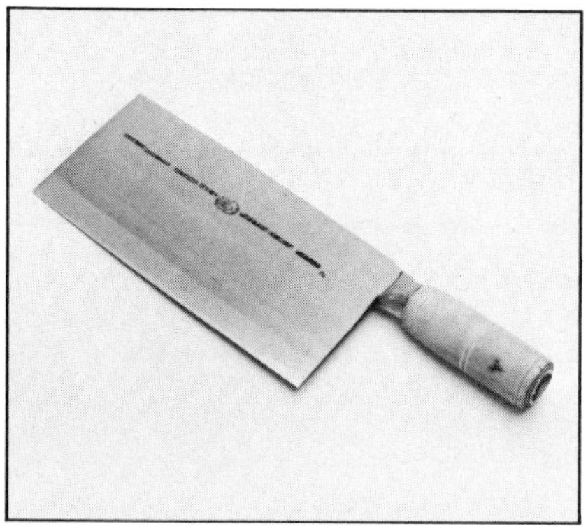

A basic chopping cleaver should have a good heavy blade whose weight is an advantage in cutting quickly through food. And its blade should take and hold a sharp edge. This cleaver is perfectly suited to the task. Its blade is large—8½″ long and 3⅞″ wide—and made of tempered carbon steel, which is second to none in quality. As with all steel cleavers, this one is coated with a moisture-resistant product that must be scrubbed off in hot water with soap before use. To preserve the life of the cleaver, always dry it well after each use to prevent rust, and never put it in a dishwasher.

Taylor & Ng (10640) $12.50

STEAMED CHICKEN WITH SAUSAGE

Hsiang Ku La Ch'ang Cheng Chi

6 dried mushrooms
2 Chinese sausages
6 thin slices fresh ginger root
1 3-pound (approximately) broiler or fryer chicken

Marinade:
1 teaspoon salt
2 teaspoons cornstarch
2 tablespoons light soy sauce
1 tablespoon peanut or corn oil

Preparation:
Wash and soak the mushrooms in ½ cup warm water for 30 minutes. Cut off and discard the stems, then cut the mushrooms into halves. Cut each sausage diagonally into 5 or 6 pieces. Set aside on a plate along with the mushrooms and ginger slices.

Clean and wash the chicken. Cut through the chicken's skin and small bones and cut the chicken into 1-inch pieces. Put the chicken pieces in a mixing bowl. Reserve the backbone, wing tips, and neck (minus its skin) for making soup stock.

In a bowl, combine and mix the marinade ingredients and then add the marinade to the chicken. Mix and toss to coat chicken pieces evenly.

Cooking:
Take a plate with a rim or a pie plate 1 inch smaller in diameter than a steamer. Place the chicken pieces in not more than two layers on the plate. Set the mushrooms, sausages, and ginger in between the chicken pieces.

Set plate in a preheated steamer, cover, and steam over high heat for 30 minutes. Serve hot on the same plate on top of a large platter.

Yield: 6 servings or up to 10 when served with other dishes.

(From FLORENCE LIN'S CHINESE REGIONAL COOKBOOK by Florence Lin. Copyright 1975 by Florence Lin. Reprinted by permission of Hawthorne Books, Inc.)

Stainless-Steel Chopping Cleaver A:5

This heavy cleaver, new in the last couple of years, is an all-in-one tool of stainless steel that will do all the bone-cutting, chopping and slicing called for in barbecued spare ribs, braised thin-sliced star anise beef, or stir-fried vegetables. It is a #2 heavy duty chopper—a good foot long with a 3¾″-wide blade that will need frequent sharpening. The handle has deep indentations to give it a surer grip. They also serve to allay our fears that a metal handle is prone to being slippery. But we suggest the cleaver be handled with care and dry hands. Chinese characters on the handle tell who made it and where. Ours had the name Ching Keelee and Hong Kong —which are also imprinted in English on the blade.

Eur-Asian Imports (M-224/L) $6.80

Curved Chopping Cleaver A:6

Most cleavers are rectangular in shape, but this one has been rounded to make it particularly suitable for chopping small amounts of food. It would make easy work of chopping scallions for an egg and pork roll or of mincing water chestnuts for a steamed ground pork dish. Greater control in deboning meats is also gained with the rounded blade. The point of the knife can work in between bones more easily than that of a square-cornered cleaver. Overall, this wooden-handled knife is 10¼″ long, and its carbon-steel blade measures 6½″ long by 3½″ at its widest point.

Sindoori Imports $7.00

"In cookery the Chinese hold a middle position, below the French and above the English. There is a certain degree of philosophy in a Chinaman's smallest act—he never does anything for which he cannot give a reason. He sees a special connection between cookery and civilization—and he conceives that the English must be very low in the intellectual scale and must hold their high rank only by brute force. An Englishman's mode of feeding is, says John Chinaman, the nearest approach to that of the savages of For-

mosa. He does the chief work of the slaughter-house upon the dinner-table and he remits the principal work of the kitchen to his stomach. In remote ages, before we became civilized, a polite Chinaman once informed me: 'we used knives and forks, as you do, and had no chopsticks. We still carry a knife in our chopstick case; but it is a remnant of barbarism,—we never use it. We sit down to table to eat, not to cut up carcases.' "

"Special Correspondence from China in the Years 1857–58" *by George Wingrove Cooke, from the* London Times.

Paring Knife A:7

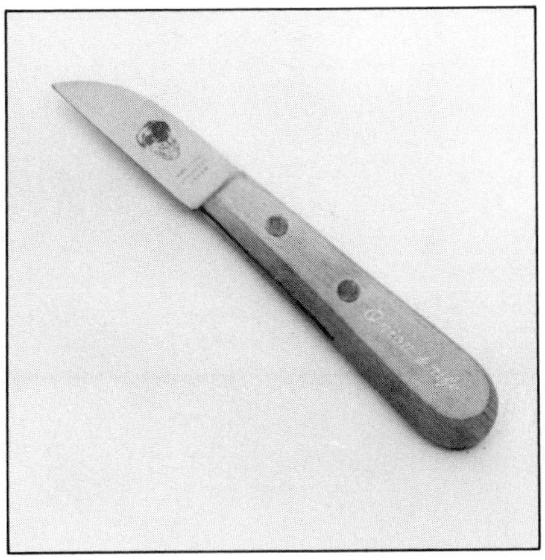

This short-bladed knife is used to peel and shape raw vegetables such as icicle radishes, bamboo shoots and carrots into decorative fans, flowers, trees or birds. It could also be used to carve fanciful decorations into the outside of a hollowed out winter melon. Winter melon soup—flavored with Chinese mushrooms and ham—is traditionally poured into the melon shell where it is cooked. The melon then makes a lovely serving dish at the table. Although the knife is actually made in Japan, which explains its unusual shape in the Chinese kitchen, it is quite strong and useful and has gained favor with Chinese cooks. The back of its short 2½″-long stainless steel blade is curved, and the tang extends half-way into the 4½″ wooden handle. Two brass rivets hold the blade and handle together.

Town Food Service Equipment Co., Inc. (24) **$1.70**

WINTER MELON AND HAM SOUP

Time: 20 minutes

For 4 Persons

INGREDIENTS
1 pound winter melon
¼ cup ham slices, 1″ × 1″ × ¼″
4 dried Chinese mushrooms
4 cups chicken broth
1 teaspoon salt
¼ teaspoon monosodium glutamate

PREPARATION
Peel and wash the winter melon. Drain. Cut into 1″ × 1″ × ¼″ slices.

Soak the dried mushrooms in ½ cup warm water for 20 minutes. Cut each into 2 to 4 pieces.

COOKING PROCEDURES
Add the melon slices to the broth and bring to boil over high flame.

Add mushrooms, salt and monosodium glutamate.

Cover and cook over medium flame for 10 minutes.

Add ham and bring to boil once more. Serve hot.

TIPS
Winter melon is very much like summer squash. It is a large green melon (as large as a basketball) with a frostlike outside layer. The seeds are found in the white spongy material in the center of the melon. Chinese grocery stores will cut winter melons into 1- or 2-pound pieces on request.

Boiled ham may be used for the ham slices, but the Chinese prefer Smithfield ham, which is nearest in texture and taste to the King Hwa ham produced in King Hwa, in Chekiang province. To keep ham for future use, clean away the skin and fat; wash, dry, and boil in water for 20 minutes. Store in the refrigerator and it will be ready for recipes calling for ham, whether it be sliced, shredded or minced.

(From THE PLEASURES OF CHINESE COOKING by Grace Zia Chu. Copyright 1962 by Grace Zia Chu. Reprinted by permission of Simon & Schuster, Inc.)

When sabers are rusty and spades gleaming, prisons empty and granaries filled, the temple steps worn by the feet of the faithful and the courts of law overgrown with grass, doctors on foot and bakers riding horseback, then the empire is well governed.

Chinese Proverb, from Le Boire et Le Manger *by Armand Dubarry, 1884.*

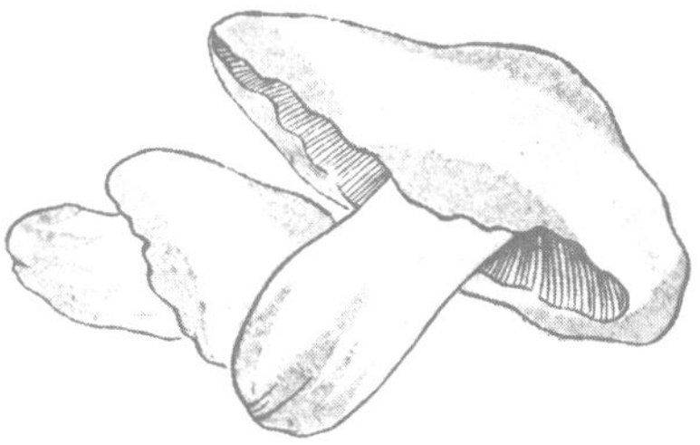

Rubber Cutting Board A:8

Although the cross-section of a tree has been long favored in China as a cutting surface, this modern successor is durable and more sanitary. You may still see a tree-trunk section in many restaurants, but this type of cutting board is now selling in the Chinese community for family use. Because the Chinese do some kind of cutting for every meal—whether it's mincing water chestnuts, chopping scallions or shredding chicken breasts —the popularity of the board is a good sign. In addition to this 10″ size, the board comes in diameters of 12″ and 16″; all are about 1″ thick. Ease of care is one of its main attractions, since stains can be removed with chlorine bleach; and the board can be run through a dishwasher to rid it of odors. Also, it won't chip or dull the cleaver's edge.

Kam Man Food Products **$9.75**

Polyethylene Cutting Board A:9

Because all Chinese cooking calls for some kind of slicing, dicing, mashing, mincing, or chopping, the choice of a cutting surface is critical. Of the various alternatives available, this board of opaque white polyethylene is favored by many on grounds of sheer practicality and hygiene. It is easier to keep clean than any wooden board because it is non-absorbent, and it will not discolor. Smells, stains and grease wash away with scouring powder or bleach or in the dishwasher, which will not cause the board to warp. The ½″ thick board measures 17″ by 10″ and has a hole at one end for hanging. It is also available in smaller sizes: 16″ by 9″, or 14″ by 8″. As with any plastic material, avoid contact with extremely hot objects that might cause melting or scorching.

Joyce Chen (JCC401) $15.00

"The priests of the Buddhist religion are not allowed to eat animal food at any of their meals. Our dinner therefore consisted entirely of vegetables, served up in the usual Chinese style, in a number of small, round basins, the contents of each—soups excepted—being eaten with chopsticks. The Buddhist priests contrive to procure a number of vegetables of different kinds, which, by a peculiar mode of preparation, are rendered very palatable. In fact, so nearly do they resemble animal food in taste and in appearance, that at first we were deceived, imagining that the little bits we were able to get hold of with our chopsticks were really pieces of fowl or beef."

Wanderings in China *by Robert Fortune, 1847.*

Vegetable Peeler A:10

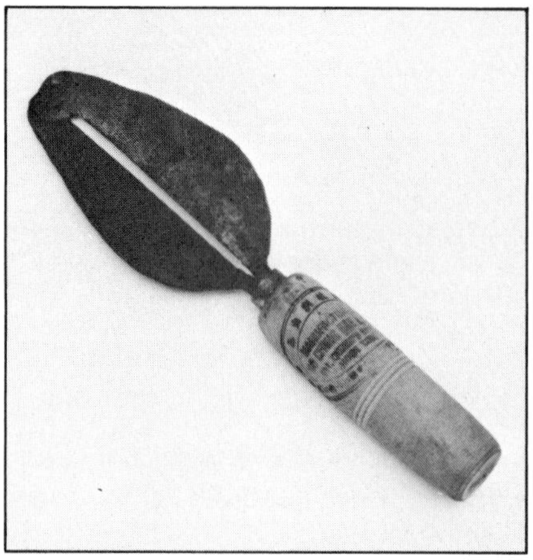

This trowel-shaped instrument from the Chinese mainland is the counterpart to our dime store vegetable peeler. It works on the same principle, but it has only one cutting edge (in the center) and its construction is quite different. The peeler is made of two pieces of iron that come together and are fixed securely in a sturdy wooden handle; at the other end, they overlap slightly and are joined by a rivet. Overall, it is 7″ long, and the blade is 3½″ long and 2″ wide. The blade is set at an angle to catch the peeling of any firm vegetable you might want to prepare. Sliced cucumber or lacy lotus root are particularly refreshing with a sweet-sour dressing of soy sauce, sugar, vinegar and sesame seed oil. One disadvantage to the peeler that should be pointed out is its tendency to rust if not dried thoroughly. Otherwise it is an intriguing and efficient artifact.

Eur-Asian Imports (M-262) $1.25

STUFFED BONELESS EIGHT-JEWEL DUCK

8 to 10 servings

PREPARATION OF INGREDIENTS

1 duckling, 4 to 5 pounds (if frozen, allow 10 to 12 hours to thaw at room temperature)
3 tablespoons oil
⅓ cup soaked Chinese dried mushrooms: discard stems, cut caps into ¼-inch squares
½ cup chopped lean pork: in pea-sized pieces
1 Chinese pork sausage or ½ cup Cantonese barbecued pork: cut into pea-sized pieces
1 tablespoon dried shrimp: soak in very hot water to soften, mince
1 cup shelled chestnuts (dried or fresh): boil in water until soft
¼ cup water chestnuts: cut into pea-sized pieces
¼ cup shelled ginkgo nuts (canned may be used): split into halves
¼ cup dried lotus seeds: cook in water until tender

SAUCE MIXTURE (mix in a bowl)
1 tablespoon black soy sauce
1 tablespoon thin soy sauce
2 tablespoons sesame seed oil
⅛ teaspoon white pepper
¼ teaspoon MSG (optional)
½ teaspoon sugar
1 tablespoon pale dry sherry

¾ cup glutinous rice: soak overnight until plump, steam over water for 10 minutes or until done, loosen and put aside
2 teaspoons salt
Soy-Sesame Oil Dip
Five-Fragrance Salt Dip

DIRECTIONS FOR COOKING

1. Scald boned duck. Hang duck to air-dry for at least 8 hours.
2. Heat wok until it is hot. Add 3 tablespoons oil. When oil is hot, add mushrooms and lean pork, and cook until pork is done. Add sausage or barbecued pork and shrimp; stir-fry for about 2 minutes. Put in chestnuts, water chestnuts, ginkgo nuts, and lotus seeds. Stir in sauce mixture. Add rice and mix until all of it is glazed with sauce. Put this stuffing in a bowl to cool in the refrigerator.
3. When duck is air-dried, rub it inside with 2 teaspoons of salt. If it is a frozen duck and the head has been removed, sew together neck skin with thread. Stuff duck with stuffing (do not pack it too tightly or it might burst). Close the cavity with thread and skewer.
4. Place a big roasting pan, containing an inch of water, on the bottom of a gas oven or the lowest rack of an electric oven to catch the drippings and prevent them from burning.
5. Preheat oven to 400 degrees.
6. Put duck directly on oven rack with breast side up. (If a gas oven, put duck on middle rack. If electric, put

duck on upper rack.) Roast duck for 1½ hours. Remove from oven.

7. Put duck on a big oval serving platter. Remove thread and skewer. Cut off wings and legs. Cut duck into ½-inch pieces crosswise and then cut it down the middle lengthwise. (Cut carefully, disturbing the stuffing as little as possible.) Serve hot with dips.

(From THE CLASSIC CHINESE COOK BOOK by Mai Leung. Copyright 1976 by Yuk Mai Leung Thayer. Reprinted by permission of Harper & Row, Publishers, Inc.)

Kitchen Shears A:11

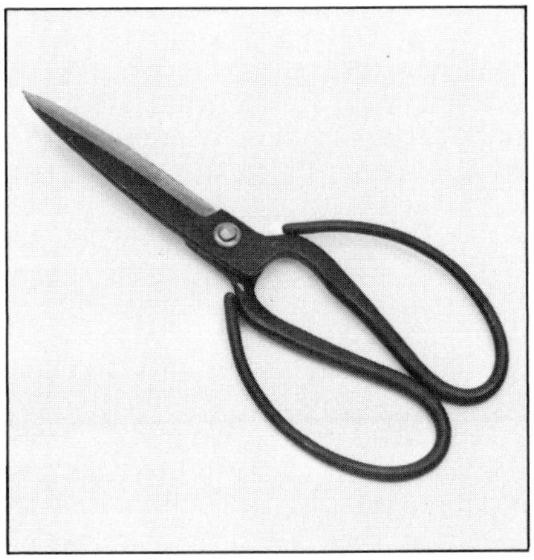

Ducks and chickens are frequently boned and stuffed in China, especially for festive occasions. The quickest way to bone a large bird (it will take about half an hour) is with a pair of kitchen scissors that has good strong blades with sharp points. This one certainly qualifies. The blades are finely ground and, unorthodox as it may look, the grip is very comfortable. A steel pin and brass ring hold the blades securely together. Scissors are particularly useful for boning a whole bird because two blades are at work instead of a single-edged knife, and they are working toward one another: this gives you good leverage in cutting, and means you are less likely to pierce the skin of the bird while you are working. Cutting through joints and small bones is also easy work for this 9″-long pair of scissors. It comes in lengths of 7″ and 8″, too. One of our favorite Chinese poultry stuffings combines glutinous rice with Chinese sausage, water chestnuts, ginkgo nuts, Chinese mushrooms and soy sauce. It's tempting enough to put scissors to work.

Oriental Country Store $3.95

Ginger Grater A:12

Creative use of bamboo is evident in this ginger grater. Roughly 5″ square, it is composed of 16 bamboo strips that are notched on both sides in a sawtooth pattern. All the notches on a single strip are slanted either to the left or to the right, and the strips are then alternated to make the surface as rough as possible. Along the ends the strips were left smooth so they could be firmly joined together. A flat piece of bamboo frames the top and is the anchor for a large, wide handle that has a good grip. Another flat piece across the bottom frames that edge and provides a surface to which two short legs are fastened. The legs keep the grater far enough off a counter top to make the lowest sawtoothed strip effective. Ginger may be even more indispensable to the Chinese kitchen than bamboo. Szechwan cooking depends on it, and many seafood, meat and vegetable dishes would not be the same without it. And there is simply no substitute for fresh ginger. Before grating, peel the ginger root. If you have some left over, you can store it for weeks in plastic wrap in the vegetable drawer of your refrigerator. To keep ginger for several months, peel the root and seal it in a jar of dry sherry in the refrigerator.

Albert Kessler & Co. $1.50
(DK 187)

Rice plough.

The Wok and Its Care

The most efficient pan for the brazier-type Chinese stove would be made of iron to conduct and hold heat well. It would have a wide rim to keep it from slipping through the hole, and its sides would be deep and sloping so that the bottom of the pan would be as close as possible to the heat and food would fall naturally toward its hot center. That pan is the wok. Whether you are cooking on a brazier or on a Western stove, it is the pan best-suited for stir-frying, the most popular of all Chinese cooking techniques. Of course, the Chinese use a wok in many other ways as well, but for the Westerner the greatest rationale for having a wok is for stir-frying.

Woks are made of iron, carbon steel, stainless steel and aluminum, but the best are of iron or carbon steel. Both of these metals distribute and hold a very intense heat. And both require seasoning before use.

To season an iron or steel wok, scrub it well with detergent in hot water to remove the moisture resistant film that usually covers it. Dry the wok and set it on medium heat. Rub the inside with a piece of toweling soaked in vegetable oil. After three minutes, rub the oil off with some clean paper toweling and then reoil the wok. Leave the wok on the fire while you do this. Repeat the rubbing and oiling process two more times at intervals of about three minutes. The wok should now be ready for use.

To clean a wok, use only hot water and a non-metallic scrubbing pad or brush. Avoid detergents and scouring powder. Always make sure the wok is as dry as possible to prevent rust; to dry it thoroughly, place it on a hot burner for about 15 seconds. Don't be dismayed if your wok blackens with use; it will.

Because a wok should come in direct contact with the heat source, a flat-bottomed wok is best for an electric stove. Obviously it can also be used on a gas stove, but a round-bottomed wok with a ring stand to hold it stable is also suitable for a gas stove. To gain greater flexibility when cooking with electricity, heat two burners at different settings so that you can quickly regulate the heat from high to low, as needed.

Classic Steel Wok and Ring Stand A:13

Here is a classic Chinese wok: a wide steel bowl with flared sides and two "ears" for handles. The versatile wok is both a pot and a pan, used for all cooking techniques: stir-frying, deep-frying, braising and steaming. In stir-frying, used for about three-quarters of Chinese cooking, the wok is heated and a small amount of peanut or vegetable oil is then poured into it. When the oil is hot, the ingredients are added in order of their cooking times. Often, a piece of garlic or ginger is cooked in the oil to flavor it and then removed before the other foods are added. Because food must circulate rapidly around the hot center of the wok, best results are obtained with limited amounts. Therefore, if a dish contains many ingredients, the vegetables may be cooked together first, and then removed from the wok; next, the meat will be added and when it is almost done, the vegetables will be returned to the wok to reheat briefly with the meat. A pound of meat is about all that can be cooked effectively; if you have to double a recipe, cook two batches and combine them. Woks for family use range from 10″ to 14″ in diameter; those used in restaurants may be 20″ or more across. And all blacken with use. This one is 12″ across and 3½″ deep. The round-bottomed wok was originally designed to rest on the circular walls of a primitive brazier. Thus, flat-topped American stoves require a ring stand to hold the wok steady over a burner. The wok rests comfortably in the stand, which is perforated on the sides with large holes to let oxygen feed the flame inside, and to let heat out. This steel ring stand is 10″ in diameter across the bottom, 8″ across the top and 2″ high. (A ring stand does not work very well on an electric stove, even if it is inverted as manufacturers suggest, because a wok should have contact with the heat source.) If you have an electric kitchen you should use a flat-bottomed wok or an electric one. But if you have a gas stove, nothing should, or can, take the place of a classic wok. Follow the instructions that come with the wok to season it correctly before use.

Taylor & Ng
Wok (10230) $9.00
Ring stand (10250) $4.00

Wok Set A:14

For someone just getting started with wok cookery, the perfect answer to his needs is an all-in-one package, or, as this set is described, a "complete Chinese kitchen." It contains nine implements: a wok, ring adaptor, cover, spatula, ladle, skimmer, steaming rack, cooking chopsticks and a bamboo scrub brush. For extra measure, and wisdom, a recipe booklet is also enclosed. All of this equipment is well constructed. The two-handled steel wok is 14″ in diameter and 3½″ deep. It is a perfect family size and is more than adequate for any stir-frying, deep-frying, steaming or braising you might want to do. For steaming, you will need to cover the wok with its 11″-diameter lid. An easy-to-grip wooden knob on the top will keep your fingers from getting burned. Together, the wok and lid are 8½″ tall. Before you can even use the wok on a Western stove you must have a ring that will fit around the burner to hold the wok steady. This one of steel is well ventilated (an important feature), and it measures 10″ in diameter and 2″ deep. To deep-fry such delicacies as ginger-flavored shrimp balls with water chestnuts, you will certainly need the classic brass-wire skimmer, too. It has a heavy wire frame and a generous wooden handle. Overall, it is 15½″ long with a basket that is 5¾″ in diameter. To stir-fry, use the spatula, which is specially designed to conform to the shape of the wok. To serve foods, especially those with a lot of liquid, use the ladle. The ladle is 14¾″ long with a 4″-wide, 1¼″-deep bowl, and the spatula is 13½″ long with a 3¾″-wide working surface. If you want to steam a whole sea bass or flounder, place the fish on a plate and then set the plate on the stainless-steel steaming rack. When unfolded, the 10″-wide rack resembles a tic-tac-toe diagram, or a parallelogram with its sides extended. The collapsible feature makes the rack easy to store. Last of the cooking utensils is a long pair of chopsticks, which the Chinese use for stirring or lifting pieces of food. Between recipes or after cooking, scrub the wok quickly with the bamboo brush under hot water. Do not use strong abrasive. With such a fine array of equipment, there's no reason why you can't become a proficient cook of Chinese food in no time.

Taylor & Ng (10020) $28.50

Flat-Bottomed Wok A:15

Western stoves and Eastern woks did not make a perfect marriage until flat-bottomed woks were developed. Florence Lin cleverly designed a wok that is flat enough to be stable on a gas or electric burner, yet round enough so that a traditional Chinese spatula can be run smoothly over it in any direction. With this wok a ring stand or collar is unnecessary. Another clever modification is the flared and rounded lip of the wok that makes it possible to scoop food or pour liquid over the edge into a serving dish without spilling it all over the floor. The wok is about ¼″ shallower than most (3¼″ deep), but it has a generous 14″ diameter, an excellent size for stir-frying and steaming. It is made of cold-pressed carbon steel that is more rust resistant than most non-stainless steel; and, of course, it is an excellent conductor of heat for fast, high-temperature, stir-fry cooking. The large domed lid of spun aluminum, topped by a wooden knob, is deep enough to cover a whole chicken with ease. As with most woks, this one still requires seasoning. Wash it well with soap and hot water; then rub the inside with vegetable oil and set it over low heat for 10 minutes. Every three minutes wipe off the oil with paper toweling and then quickly reoil the wok without removing it from the heat. Always wash it with hot water after cooking—avoid using soap—and put it on a burner just long enough to make sure it is completely dry.

Cook's Corners, Inc. $12.00

BRAISED SOY SAUCE BEEF

Hung Shao Niu Jou

This dish has a concentrated flavor and should always be accompanied by mildly flavored dishes, such as salad dishes or vegetables with meat. It is also a good idea to put half of the dish away for another meal. If stored in the refrigerator, use within the week, or if stored in the freezer, it may be kept up to a month.

2 pounds boneless shin of beef or chuck
2 scallions, cut into 2-inch-long sections
4 thin slices fresh gingerroot
1 whole or 8 pods star anise
1 tablespoon sugar
½ teaspoon salt
3 tablespoons soy sauce
2 tablespoons dry sherry
1 cup water

Preparation and cooking:
Trim the beef and save the fat. Cut the beef into 1-inch chunks. Heat a heavy pot until very hot, add the cut-up beef fat, and let brown over moderate heat. About 2 tablespoons beef drippings should be rendered. If there is no fat on the beef, use 2 tablespoons peanut oil. Add half of the beef chunks,

Continued from preceding page

stir to seal well on all sides, and remove. Stir and seal the remaining beef. Put all the beef back into the pot and add the scallions, ginger, star anise, sugar, salt, soy sauce, sherry, and water. Mix well together and bring to a boil. Cover and cook over medium-low heat for 30 minutes. Reduce the heat to low and let simmer for about 1½ hours or until the meat is tender. Stir a few times.

There should be about ¾ cup liquid left with the beef. If there is more liquid, uncover the pot, turn heat up to high, and reduce it. Discard the star anise. Serve the meat on a platter with its sauce. Serve hot, with rice or steamed buns.

Yield: 6 servings or up to 12 when served with other dishes.

Variations: Add 2 to 3 roll-cut peeled carrots to the beef for the last 20 minutes of cooking. Add 2 to 3 dried whole red chili peppers to give this dish a peppery flavor.

For Star Anise Beef, the beef may be cooked in one piece with 2 whole star anise 1 hour longer. Let cool and keep in the refrigerator until firm, then thinly slice and serve as an appetizer with the jellied sauce.

(From FLORENCE LIN'S CHINESE REGIONAL COOKBOOK by Florence Lin. Copyright 1975 by Florence Lin. Reprinted by permission of Hawthorne Books, Inc.)

Wok with Handle A:16

For those who prefer the convenience of being able to hold a wok without having to first pick up a pot holder, here's a steel one with a wooden handle. The handle is about 8″ long and has a ring at the end by which to hang the wok if space is a problem. If you want to use a Chinese steamer to make ground pork with water chestnuts, or you are simply stir-frying broccoli or making shrimp-fried rice, this 14″ wok is the right size. It is 4½″ deep and will comfortably hold a large steamer or a good-sized portion of food. Accompanying the wok, and to hold it securely on a Western stove, is a nickel-plated steel ring stand that is 10″ in diameter and 2¼″ deep. The stand is adequately ventilated and notched on the bottom so it can be used either on a gas or electric stove. Just remember to season the wok properly before assembling the ingredients for your favorite Chinese recipe.

Atlas Metal Spinning Co.
Wok (89W14) $10.00
Ring stand (113RR1) $ 4.00

An example of the long-lost art of savoring: "Chinese mushrooms can be almost perfect in shape, texture and flavor. . . . They should be left whole or cut in half, juicy, fragrant and smooth. Do not add other things to them, for it takes away from the pure enjoyment of the mushrooms. Do not talk when eating the mushrooms, or you spoil the flavour. Chew a mushroom as little as possible. Only press out its hidden juices between tongue and teeth."

Chinese Gastronomy *by Hsiang Ju Lin and Tsuifeng Lin. Pyramid Publications, 1972.*

Electric Wok A:17

At present, this is the only electric wok on the market. With a bright Mandarin-red porcelain exterior, black baked-on, non-stick interior, and heavy aluminum construction, it is a far cry from its simple iron or steel progenitor. The wok is a generous 14″ in diameter. Its matching, shallow lid is made of acrylic on aluminum. The detachable heat control can be accurately adjusted between 150 F. and 425 F.; and, with the heat control removed, the wok becomes fully immersible, even dishwasher safe. Stir-frying, deep-frying, steaming and stewing are all possible with this 5½-quart wok. But we have a reservation about electric wok-ery based on electric heat in general. Namely, it lacks the temperature flexibility necessary for stir-frying. An electric wok will not reach extremely high temperatures or switch instantly from high to low heat. Its inability to attain high heat is a particular problem if you're cooking for a crowd; it simply will not get hot enough to handle the amount of food possible in a standard wok of the same diameter. Therefore, you must cook in small batches. But for anyone determined to cook at the table or on the patio, this is *the* wok to own. And, after all, noted Chinese cooks, Grace Chu and Florence Lin, use it when giving cooking demonstrations around the country. For additional inspiration, a 22-page recipe book accompanies every wok.

West Bend Co. (5109) $35.00

Ring Stand A:18

There is a basic incompatibility between a Chinese wok and a Western stove: the wok has a round bottom and the stove has a flat top. To get the twain to meet in a stable fashion, you need a ring stand. This one of steel is 10″ in diameter across the bottom, 8″ in diameter across the top and 2½″ high. It is large enough to fit around any ordinary gas burner, thus permitting the wok to easily touch the flames. On an electric stove, always use the largest burner and invert the ring to lower the wok as close as possible to the heat. The holes in the side of the stand permit heat to escape and allow air through to feed the flame on a gas stove. With a ring around your wok, you can happily stir-fry some snow peas or deep-fry some shrimp without risking disaster.

Atlas Metal Spinning Co. (113RR1) **$4.00**

Cooking Chopsticks A:19

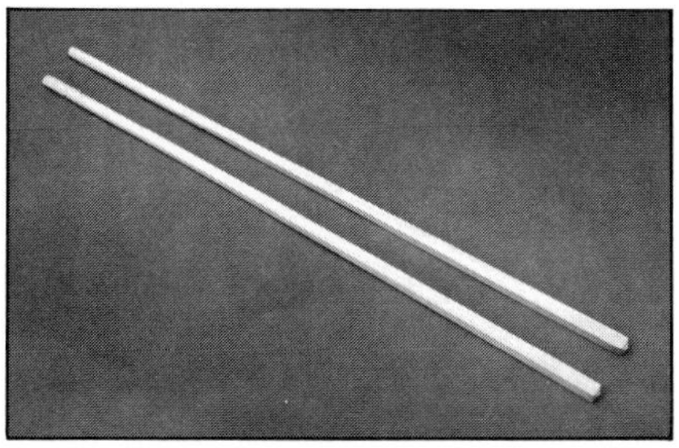

The Chinese do not use a wide variety of utensils in their kitchens. A ladle, a spatula, a strainer and an extra-long pair of chopsticks are all that is needed to stir and serve a superb meal. These 18″-long bamboo chopsticks are versatile cooking tools. You can use them to stir shrimp with lobster sauce or to beat an egg or two and then stir it into egg drops in hot soup. Or use them to fluff rice—after it has rested, of course. The Chinese let rice sit, covered, for 10 to 20 minutes after steaming so that it will have the texture they like. In Mao Tse Tung's hometown in Hunan, people even eat with these giant chopsticks, a custom that seems awkward to other Chinese. Notice, however, that Chinese chopsticks, whatever the length, are blunt at both ends, and that the wider end may be squared off. Japanese chopsticks, by contrast, are tapered evenly their whole length and are pointed at the eating end.

Albert Kessler & Co. (MK 128) **$0.40**

STIR-FRIED EGGS WITH CRABMEAT

INGREDIENTS
4 scallions, cut into 2″ × ⅛″ strips
2 tablespoons peanut or vegetable oil
one 6-oz. package frozen crabmeat, drained and coarsely shredded
4 eggs, beaten thoroughly
1 tablespoon light soy
1 teaspoon sesame oil
dash of salt and white pepper

TO PREPARE
1. Cut scallions into 2″ lengths, then into 2″ × ⅛″ strips.
2. Defrost crabmeat, drain, and shred meat coarsely.
3. Beat 4 eggs well. Add light soy, sesame oil, salt, and white pepper. Beat to mix.

TO COOK (cooking time about 5 minutes)
1. Heat 2 tablespoons oil in wok over medium flame, add scallions, and sizzle ½ minute.
2. Add crabmeat to egg mixture, stir to mix, pour mixture into wok and stir-fry till eggs are soft, but not runny, about 2 minutes. Use an under-and-over stir-fry sweep to scramble the eggs.
3. To serve: Dish up in a plate and serve hot.
4. Yield: Serves 2 alone or 6 in a 4-course dinner.

(From EIGHTY PRECIOUS CHINESE RECIPES by May Wong Trent. Copyright 1973 by May Wong Trent. Reprinted by permission of Macmillan Publishing Co., Inc.)

Iron Ladle and Spatula A:20

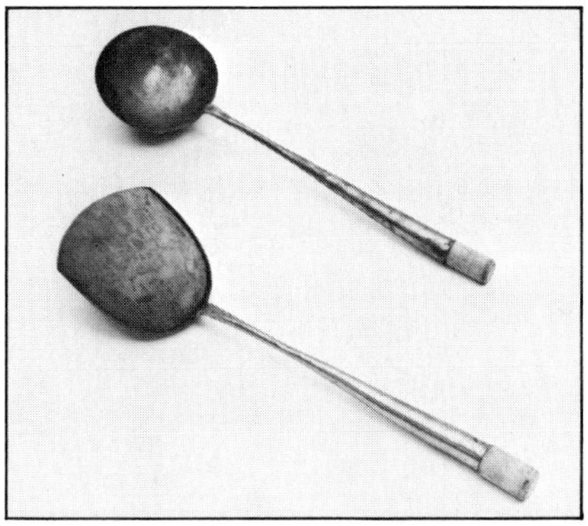

To stir-fry food, it must be moved very quickly and constantly in a wok. No implement is better suited to this task than the Chinese spatula. First, the spatula is short and curved slightly to fit the sloping sides of a wok perfectly; food will not slip under it. Second, its leading edge curves outward to scoop up the maximum amount of food possible. Last, a slight lip around the sides and back of the spatula either helps to push food forward for stir-frying, or to hold it in place for serving. Companion to the spatula is a ladle, a necessity for dishing out the soup that is part of every Chinese meal, or for other dishes with liquid. This one has a good 4½″-wide bowl that is 1½″ deep, large enough for handling soups with large garnishes like *wontons* (filled dumplings). The ladle may also serve as a small mixing bowl for the cornstarch-and-liquid thickener that is added to so many stir-fried dishes, such as stir-fried crabmeat with bean curd or stir-fried chicken with fresh mushrooms and snow peas. Both of these implements are made of iron, which is traditional, and they are about 16″ long. The wooden handles are too short to really protect your fingers and may be loose-fitting when new. Heat is not a problem, however, if the implements are kept busy, as they should be. And, after use, the wood absorbs moisture and should swell to tightly fill the surrounding metal sheath. As with anything made of iron, be sure to clean and dry these utensils immediately after using to prevent rust.

Taylor & Ng
Spatula (10300) **$2.50**
Ladle (10310) **$3.00**

Stainless-Steel Ladle and Spatula A:21

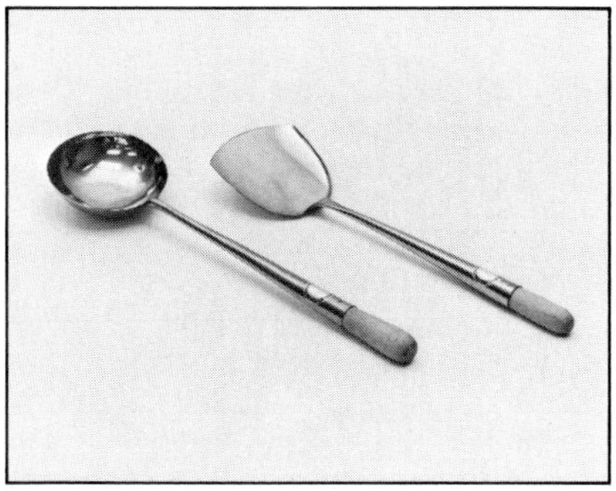

Here are modern stainless-steel versions of the classic Chinese spatula and ladle. They won't rust if left damp like their iron counterparts, and they work every bit as well. The spatula, curved to conform to the shape of a wok, accomplishes the quick, constant

Continued from preceding page

stir-frying of food in that vessel, and the ladle is used to serve or handle juicy dishes or soups. The Cantonese sometimes use both implements simultaneously to stir-fry. This type of spatula is especially critical to wok cookery. It is 17″ long, 1″ shorter than the ladle, and both the end of the spatula and the bowl of the ladle are about 4½″ across. A short wooden handle fits tightly into the metal shaft of each handle to prevent heat from reaching your fingers.

Bonjour Imports Corp.
Ladle (914) $3.50
Spatula (915) $3.00

Perforated Ladle A:22

Meat or fish dumplings are essential to a number of Chinese soups. To make them, minced meat or fish paste flavored with seasonings is formed into balls that are poached gently in water. Fish might be flavored with scallions and fresh ginger, pork with soy sauce and sherry. The dumplings are then transferred to another pot or a serving dish where they are rewarmed with hot soup stock and other ingredients. The perfect implement for handling dumplings so that they will drain and not break is a smooth perforated ladle like this one. It has a good, long (14″) handle for reaching down into a deep pot; and its bowl—about 4½″ across and 1½″ deep—is roomy enough to handle any size dumpling. The ladle is a solid piece of stainless steel with a hollow shaft into which a 4½″-long wooden handle is secured.

Town Food Service Equipment Co., Inc. (119) $4.70

Perforated Strainer A:23

Performance on a grand scale is offered by this well-made stainless-steel strainer. Its 8″-wide shallow bowl will lift several egg rolls at a time from hot oil, or transfer noodles and vegetables from a large pot of simmering Chinese noodle soup to a serving dish with great efficiency. At the same time, its large drain holes let the fat or broth escape quickly back into the pot. Because there is little angle to its handle, the strainer is most suited to a wide and relatively shallow pot like the wok. The handle is 9¾″-long, and includes a 5″-long, sturdy wooden grip section with a loop on the end for hanging. Next time you are making *wonton* (pastry folded around a ground meat or seafood filling) soup you would be happy to have the assistance of this Taiwanese strainer. You can also set it over a bowl and use it as a colander.

Oriental Country Store $7.50

Bamboo-Handled Strainer A:24

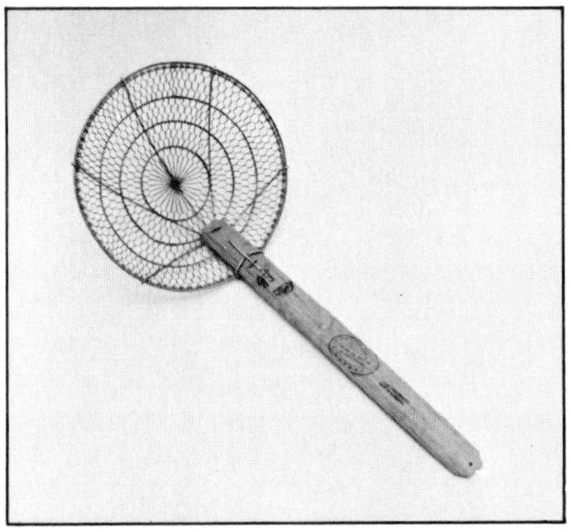

Here is the quintessential Chinese strainer for deep-frying. It is handsomely made of twisted woven brass wire, reinforced with steel wire, and has a long, broad bamboo handle that will not conduct heat and will keep your hand a safe distance from hot oil. To hang the strainer, loop a piece of string through the small hole at the end of the handle. Five spokes that extend from the other end of the handle, and a circle of heavy-gauge steel wire, frame and hold the shape of the basket. For extra strength the wire around the rim is doubled. The light, wire-mesh construction and slight scoop shape of the basket makes this the best type of strainer to use for deep-frying. With this large 7½″ strainer you can pick up a number of phoenix-tailed shrimp or deep-fried *wontons* at once and the excess oil will drain quickly back into the wok. Phoenix-tailed shrimp are slit partially down the back, flattened and dipped into batter before frying, then served with roasted salt and pepper. *Wontons* might be filled with a tasty mixture of pork, shrimp and water-chestnuts flavored with soy, sherry and scallions. Both would make perfect hors d'oeuvres for your next cocktail or dinner party.

Taylor & Ng (10570) $3.50

PHOENIX-TAIL SHRIMP

Cha Ta Hsia

1 pound raw shrimp with shells (about 24 to 28)
1 teaspoon salt
⅛ teaspoon white pepper
1 teaspoon dry sherry

Batter:
¾ cup flour
¾ cup cold water
2 teaspoons baking powder

2 cups peanut or corn oil
Sweet-and-Sour Sauce or Roasted Salt and Szechuan Peppercorns

Preparation:
Remove all but the tail sections of the shells of the shrimps. Split the back sides with a knife and remove the sandy veins. Rinse, drain, and dry well. In a small bowl combine the salt, pepper, and sherry. Add the shrimps and blend well. Set aside in the refrigerator.

Combine the batter ingredients in a bowl and mix until smooth. To test the consistency, dip a shrimp into the batter; it should be covered with a thin coating. Set aside.

Cooking:
Heat a wok or a deep fryer. Add the oil and heat until a haze forms above it or it registers about 350°. Add 1 tablespoon of the hot oil to the batter and mix well. Now hold the shrimps by the tail and dip them one by one into the batter, but leave the tail parts uncovered. Then place them in the hot oil and fry on both sides for about 2 minutes or until golden brown. Fry about 6 to 8 at a time. Drain. Keep warm in the oven while you fry the remaining shrimps. Serve hot. Accompany with Sweet-and-Sour Sauce or Roasted Salt and Szechuan Peppercorns as dips.

Yield: 8 servings as an appetizer.

Note: The shrimps may be reheated in a 400° oven for about 7 to 8 minutes.

(*From FLORENCE LIN'S CHINESE REGIONAL COOKBOOK by Florence Lin. Copyright 1975 by Florence Lin. Reprinted by permission of Hawthorne Books, Inc.*)

Bamboo Strainer Set A:25

If you don't have a teapot, or your teapot doesn't have a built-in strainer, one of these bamboo tea strainers is just the thing for you. Simply put some tea leaves in the basket, set the basket in a cup, and pour in boiling water. The basket will make better tea than a small, closed holder like a tea ball because the leaves can swell and move freely in the water to fully release their flavor and aroma. And the leaves can be put aside while you are drinking. If you want to use the strainers for company you will be in keeping with the Chinese tradition of treating each guest with their own fresh tea leaves. Many Chinese teacups are made with lids for just this purpose. Some tea leaves are put in the cup, a little boiling water is added, and the cup is covered to let the tea steep for a minute or so. Then more boiling water is added so the tea will be piping hot on the first sip. Reuse of the tea leaves is permitted for at least three cups because, as any self-respecting tea drinker knows, fresh tea leaves are that potent. The strainers in this set come in three sizes: 5¾″ long with a 2″-deep basket; 6″ long with a 2⅜″-deep basket; and 7″ long with a 3″-deep basket. Like all objects made of natural materials they have a charm of their own.

Jane Products (235) $3.00

Bamboo Strainer A:26

Close inspection of this charming bamboo strainer is warranted, because its construction is exceedingly clever. Essentially, it is made from a single piece of bamboo. The 4″-long handle retains the natural form of the hollow bamboo stalk, but at one end part of the bamboo has been cut away and the rest slit into strips to form the warp and frame of the 5″ by 4¼″ woven strainer basket. Narrower strips of bamboo are woven across the foundation strips to form the woof, or filler, of the basket, and wide strips of the light colored bamboo wrap the rim. Use the strainer to lift vegetables or noodles from a pot, or to strain food from clear broth. As with all bamboo implements, avoid strong soaps and extremely hot water. Brush out any food particles that collect between the strips of bamboo, and make sure the strainer is dry and kept in a ventilated area to prevent mildew.

Jane Products (236) $3.00

Bamboo Colander A:27

Shaped like an inverted dome, this handsome colander is a bit tipsy on a flat surface, but it is remarkably stable otherwise. The basket, made of stiff, slender, bamboo strips woven closely together across 10 ribs of wider bamboo, is rigid to the touch. To obtain this strength the six centermost ribs have been doubled. The rim of the basket, also very sturdy, is composed of six ½″-wide strips of bamboo that are placed side by side and covered inside and out with a band of thinner bamboo; all the strips are then lashed together at 1½″ intervals by narrow, pliable strips of bamboo. In China, this type of colander is often used for washing rice. The rice grains are shaken back and forth against the rough surface of the basket to clean them and to remove excess starch. In this country only Japanese or pearl rice really needs rinsing, though some people still prefer to eliminate any possibility of scum on their rice by washing it. The colander is also ample enough—12½″ in diameter and 4¾″ deep—to drain a large batch of cellophane or egg noodles, or to wash vegetables or fruit. Because bamboo survives very well and won't crack or split like some other woods exposed frequently to water, this colander should provide years of satisfactory use.

New Frontier Trading Corp. $2.45

Bamboo Wok Brush A:28

The Chinese clean their woks with a simple bamboo brush. Stiff enough to detach stubborn food particles without scratching a well-seasoned cooking surface, this 12″-long brush with a braided bamboo handle is ideally suited to its job. The brush may require more cleaning than a plastic version, but what pot scrubber ever had this much charm?

Taylor & Ng (10520) $1.70

Metal Steaming Rack A:29

A cleverly contrived steam rack like this will convert any deep, wide-bottomed pan into a steamer. It is made of a 3/8″-wide, stainless-steel band curved into a ring that is 6″ in diameter. Two long, 3/8″-wide strips of stainless steel cross each other at right angles in the center of the ring, pierce its sides and are then bent down, to make four 3¼″-high legs. The strips are riveted together where they cross to give the rack stability. It would easily hold a plate of spare ribs marinated in sweetened soy sauce with Szechwan peppers and sprinkled with ground rice and scallion shreds.

Eur-Asian Imports (M239/L) $1.50

STEAMED FISH WITH GINGER SAUCE

Yu Lin Yü

Although this fish is steamed, it has a fried flavor.

1 2-pound (approximately) gray sole, with head and tail
1 tablespoon dry sherry
2 scallions
2 tablespoons finely shredded gingerroot
3 tablespoons peanut or corn oil
3 tablespoons light soy sauce
½ teaspoon sugar

Preparation:
Ask the fish dealer to trim off the fins and part of the side fat of the sole. Cut the whole fish into 5 or 6 pieces through the backbone. Wash the fish and pat dry with paper towels. Arrange the fish pieces into a fish shape in a dish with a rim and sprinkle the sherry on top.

Split the scallions and cut into 2-inch-long sections. Set the scallions and ginger aside on a plate.

Cooking:
In a steamer bring water to a boil. Place fish with dish on steaming rack. Cover tightly and steam over medium high heat for about 10 minutes.

Heat a wok until hot. Add the peanut oil and the shredded ginger. Turn heat to moderate and let the ginger cook in the oil for 1 minute, then add shredded scallion; stir-fry for 10 seconds. Add the soy sauce and sugar and remove from heat.

Take the fish and plate out. If a lot of liquid has accumulated in the plate, pour off so that about 2 to 3 tablespoons remain. Pour the hot ginger and scallion sauce over the fish. Serve hot.

Yield: 2 to 3 servings or up to 6 when served with other dishes.

Variation: For Steamed Fish, Hunan Style, use as seasonings 1 tablespoon salted black beans, 4 dried chili peppers, 1 tablespoon soy sauce, 1 teaspoon sugar, ¼ teaspoon monosodium glutamate, and the same amounts of gingerroot, scallions, and sherry. Fry the chili peppers until dark, add the shredded ginger, black beans, and scallions, and then cook in the same manner.

(From FLORENCE LIN'S CHINESE REGIONAL COOKBOOK by Florence Lin. Copyright 1975 by Florence Lin. Reprinted by permission of Hawthorne Books, Inc.)

Round Metal Steaming Rack A:30

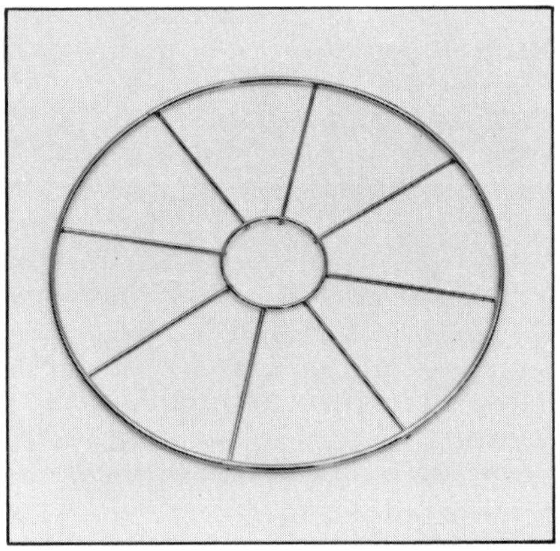

Shaped like a wheel, this sturdy chrome steaming rack is made to fit within the sloping sides of a wok. It is 10″ in diameter, a good size for a 12″ to 14″ wok, and is constructed of two concentric circles joined by eight spokes. All open racks of this kind are meant to hold plates of food for wet-steaming. In wet-steaming, water boils in the wok below the rack and steam circulates completely around the food. (In dry-steaming, a covered casserole is set into a deep water bath in a large pot; the ingredients inside the casserole cook in the steam of their own juices and are not directly affected by steam from the water.) A cover is always placed over the wok to concentrate both heat and steam. The resulting dish, like marinated chicken steamed with sausages and scallions, will be moist and tender, and the flavors will blend deliciously in a very natural way.

Taylor & Ng (10671) $1.50

Bamboo Steaming Rack A:31

In China, the most traditional material used to make steaming implements is bamboo. It is inexpensive and seldom cracks. On a 9¼″ circular rack like this one you could easily cook stuffed cucumbers Szechwan style. The cucumbers are quartered and filled with a mixture of ground pork flavored with ginger, scallions, soy sauce, and, of course, Szechwan pepper. A lovely piece of sea bass set on a deep plate and flavored with chopped, salted black beans, scallions, ginger, sherry and soy sauce would also cook very nicely on the rack; that is, if the plate is an inch narrower than the rack. Always leave an inch around any dish in a steamer to allow the water vapor to circulate freely around the food. With its simple construction—eight parallel strips of bamboo nailed at right angles to two thicker strips—the rack is quite sturdy. But the handle is attached in a rather flimsy manner. If it should come apart, a fine strand of copper or stainless-steel wire or a piece of string will quickly set it right. Smaller versions of the rack are made in diameters of 8″ or 6″, but the largest one is really the most practical for a wide variety of dishes, or for serving a number of people.

Oriental Country Store $1.50

Aluminum Steaming Tray A:32

This tray does away with the need for a plate when you steam foods in a wok. Foods, such as a boned and stuffed chicken, may be placed directly on the tray in a wok, and then covered with the wok lid. For a tray of this size (13¼″), a 14″ wok is suggested. And unlike a more traditional bamboo tray this one of aluminum is very easy to clean. While practical in some respects, it is not in others, however. Depending on the shape of the food being cooked, the steam holes may not be adequate. Also, the tray does not sit very deeply in a wok, which may limit the height of food that can be cooked on it, especially if the wok lid is shallow. However, the tray is available in several sizes.

Eur-Asian Imports (232) $4.30

Tiered Bamboo Steamer A:33

Many specialties—like the famous Cantonese *dim sum* (steamed dumplings filled with minced pork, chicken, seafood or sweet pastes) whose delicate flavors and fragile textures must be preserved—require the gentle cooking of steam. Forever frugal with their fuel, the Chinese devised multi-tiered steamers like this one that will cook more than one dish at once. You might arrange a different type of *dim sum* in each basket; or you might cook pearl balls (ground pork and water chestnuts flavored with soy sauce, ginger and scallions rolled in rice) in one basket and a lovely bass with fermented black bean sauce in the other. In addition, with a beautiful, handwoven bamboo steamer like this one, each basket makes a perfect serving dish for the cooked food. Bamboo steamers are available in a variety of diameters, from 4″ across to the 16″ size used for large fish or poultry. Our 10″ steamer is just about right for most needs. It has two tiers, each 3½″ high and it is topped by a slightly domed 2″-deep basketry lid. The secret in choosing a steamer is to make sure it is at least 2″ smaller in diameter than your wok. It will then be stable and trap enough steam beneath it to cook food effectively. To use the steamer, place enough water in the bottom of the wok to reach about an inch below it. No more than two baskets should be stacked to cook food—intense heat will not reach much higher—but as many as three or four baskets will do a good job of reheating or keeping food warm. Whether you are actually cooking or just reheating food in the steamer, always keep the lid on to get the full effect of the steam. The only drawbacks to bamboo, charming as it is, are that the wood will darken with age and use, and food particles will lodge between its woven strips. To solve this last problem, wash and brush the steamer carefully after each use, or as the Chinese do, place a plate or some Chinese cabbage leaves between the bamboo and the food. To preserve the life of the bamboo, do not use hot water or strong detergents on it, dry it thoroughly after every use, and keep it in a dry, well-ventilated spot. Rubbing with vegetable oil also helps.

Bonjour Imports Corp. (924/926) $14.00

Family making rice flour balls.

CANTONESE STEAMED DUMPLINGS WITH PORK AND SHRIMP FILLING

SHAO-MAIS

Makes About 24

PREPARATION OF INGREDIENTS

24 wonton skins

FILLING (Mix in a bowl. Keep refrigerated before use)
½ pound ground pork
3 Chinese dried mushrooms: soak in hot water until spongy, discard stems, mince caps
½ pound fresh shrimp: shell, devein, clean with running cold water, pat dry, cut into peanut-sized pieces
½ teaspoon sugar
2 teaspoons sesame seed oil
⅛ teaspoon ground pepper
½ teaspoon salt
1 tablespoon thin soy sauce
1 teaspoon pale dry sherry

Soy-Sesame Dip

DIRECTIONS FOR COOKING

1. Cut wonton skins into round circles. Put about 1 tablespoon of filling in the center of each circle. Gather sides around filling to form pleats. Squeeze the center of the dumpling. Press down the top to firm up the filling. Tap shao-mai gently to flatten bottom so it can stand up. You may make the shao-mais in advance and refrigerate them before steaming.

2. Grease the bottom of a steamer or a heatproof plate with oil. Arrange shao-mais on it. Cover and steam over boiling water for 15 minutes. Serve hot with dip.

(From THE CLASSIC CHINESE COOK BOOK by Mai Leung. Copyright 1976 by Yuk Mai Leung Thayer. Reprinted by permission of Harper & Row, Publishers, Inc.)

Tiered Aluminum Steamer A:34

If you prefer to work with the most modern, efficient cooking equipment like Grace Chu, a noted Chinese cook, you'll have an aluminum steamer like this one. It consists of two identical 4½″-deep, 12″-diameter steam trays with perforated bottoms, that are set, one above the other, atop a 12″-diameter, 6″-deep steaming pot. Each section has a pair of handles, so that the whole steamer or just part of it may be lifted. The steamer has a slightly domed lid topped with a plastic handle. Additional trays can be purchased separately. Although food can only be cooked efficiently on two trays at a time, as many as five levels may be used to reheat food. The advantage of aluminum over the traditional bamboo steamer is threefold: there is less heat loss from layer to layer, because the metal is non-porous and the sections fit tightly together; aluminum conducts heat much faster; and it is much easier to clean. Try steaming dumplings with roast pork filling on one level, and ginger-flavored bass with mushrooms on the other.

Kam Man Food Products $15.50

Large Earthenware Casserole A:35

The Chinese do not have ovens in their home kitchens, but they do have earthenware casseroles that sit directly over the fire. You can use them over a low gas flame or electric burner, adding an asbestos pad both for security and to aid in distributing the heat evenly. These pots are sturdier than you might think; we have seen them blackened on the outside with use and still in service. Casserole dishes are particularly popular during cold winter months when one usually appears at every meal. Food remains warm longer in the casserole, and the dish may be brought right to the table. Outside, this casserole has an unglazed white earthenware finish, but inside it is glazed a deep brown; the treatment is reversed on the lid to give it a more striking appearance. What is so pleasing about the casserole is the aesthetic appeal of its elemental, even primitive, appearance and its superbly functional design. The lid, for example, has a flat, disc-like, upper surface that not only fits the palm to serve as a handle, but also becomes a base on which the lid, inverted on the table, can stand. Another advantage to the vessel is its hollow handle that remains cool to the touch even when its contents are bubbling hot; the pocket of air in the center acts as an excellent insulator. A wire cage around the outside of the casserole provides support for the earthenware. The casserole is of generous proportions: 11½″ in diameter, 5½″ deep (with a lid that rises 3½″ higher), and a 4-quart capacity. It could be used for a dish of pork and salt pork cooked with bamboo shoots and pressed bean curd. Or, you might make a hot-sour soup in it with thin strips of pork, mushrooms and such intriguing ingredients as tiger lily buds, and tree ears. And, of course, boiled rice is traditionally suitable.

Kam Man Food Products **$10.95**

Small Earthenware Casserole A:36

Here is a casserole of remarkable contrasts—a bright white, unglazed earthenware pot with a deep, green-brown glazed lid. Inside, it is just the reverse; the pot is glazed avocado green and the top is naturally white. The casserole measures 8½″ in diameter, 3″ deep and it holds 1½ quarts. For long, slow cooking, like red-cooking (with soy sauce), a casserole like this would be very suitable. Red-cooked duck, for example, takes at least two hours. First, the duck is marinated in soy sauce; then it is cooked in the soy sauce together with such ingredients as scallions, star anise, sugar and sherry. Although the casserole is flameproof, it is still a good idea to place an asbestos pad under it to prevent cracking.

Kam Man Food Products **$3.95**

"Nowadays, common cooks will put chickens, geese, ducks and pork all in one pot, so that all taste the same. I am afraid that their ghosts must be filing their complaints in the city of the dead."

Yuan Mei (*1716–1799*)

Small Stoneware Casserole A:37

Cradled in a tinned-steel frame with wire handles, this satiny, deep brown-glazed stoneware casserole is meant for slow simmering or stewing in a water bath. The interior of the casserole is beige and is covered with brush strokes of caramel-colored glaze. The handles of the stand are useful for lifting the casserole out of the water bath and carrying it to the table—where you will surely want it in full view for serving. Following Chinese custom, guests should serve themselves. This casserole is the larger of two sizes, 8½″ high overall and roughly 7″ in diameter with a 3-quart capacity. A small one is 6½″ high and 5½″ in diameter.

Kam Kuo Food Inc. **$10.50**

Steamer Casserole A:38

An elegant, long-legged crane in a subtle shade of gray-blue, represents longevity and happiness on this beautiful glazed, ivory stoneware steamer pot. A simple border design in the same blue decorates the edge of the lid and the top of the pot. The steamer is about 6″ in diameter, 3½″ deep and holds 5 cups. The 7″-wide, gently-domed lid has an easy-to-grasp flat knob accented with a simple blue flower. Like Westerners, the Chinese have a double-boiler cooking technique that is called dry-steaming. A heat-proof vessel such as this one is filled with food, perhaps some chicken, mushrooms and scallions. The vessel is then placed on a rack in the bottom of a deep pot. The pot is filled with water to about two-thirds the height of the vessel and set over the fire where it remains for several hours. Additional boiling water is added from time to time as necessary. Dry-steaming can be used to cook soups and casseroles that require long, slow cooking to concentrate the flavors of food. Rice seasoned and flavored with some sausage or other ingredients may also be cooked in this manner. Dry-steamed food retains its texture; it does not fall apart, yet it is as tender as it could possibly be. And the juices remain clear and flavorful.

Quong Yuen Shing & Co. **$6.50**

Yunnan Pot A:39

Instead of stewing or simmering food, this unusual pot steams it. Called a Yunnan pot, the steamer makes one or more versions of a noted dish called Yunnan chicken. The pot is most attractive, made of reddish earthenware adorned with incised cream-colored Chinese characters and the design of a bird with cherry blossoms. But what sets it apart from other casseroles is its distinctive steam "chimney," a curved cone or funnel, open at the top and rising up in the center of the pot. Chicken, mushrooms, ham, scallions and perhaps a bit of broth are placed in the pot around the cone. The lid is then put on, and the whole thing is set like a double boiler into a slightly narrower pan filled with 2″ to 3″ of boiling water. Steam rises up through the cone and condenses on the underside of the lid, dripping down over the chicken with doubly flavorful results: delicious chicken and delicious broth. The chicken may be eaten separately as a first course with soy sauce as a dip—in which case, the broth would be served later as a soup—or chicken and broth may be served together. If you don't have a pot that will hold the steamer firmly, a metal or bamboo steaming rack in a larger pan will work, as long as the steamer is kept clear of the water. The water will need replenishing with more boiling water, since the dish takes at least 1½ hours to reach perfection. This pot is 3¼″ deep, 8″ in diameter and holds 6 cups, or 1 cut-up chicken with vegetables. Smaller versions—5″ and 7″ in diameter—are also available.

Kam Man Food Products **$9.50**

YUNNAN CHICKEN

Yunnan Ch'i Kuo Chi

A round earthenware pot with a cone in the center is the secret of this recipe. It is called a Yunnan pot. The cone tapers to a small hole at the top on the same level as the top rim. A heavy lid fits over all and the pot is placed over a large saucepan of boiling water. As the steam rises, it is forced through the small opening of the cone and disperses on the underside of the lid, dropping gently onto the chicken in the pot. The result: a superbly flavored chicken broth and chicken meat that is tender, moist, and flavorful.

Yunnan chicken is nice for company meals as it requires no last-minute attention. It can be cooked in advance and reheated for about 15 minutes. Serve it from the cooker: The chicken can be served first, with soy sauce as a dip, and with other meat and vegetable dishes as an entrée. Then ladle the clear broth into soup bowls and serve later.

1 3- to 4-pound chicken, preferably freshly killed
6 dried mushrooms
6 2 × 1 × ¼-inch slices Smithfield ham
1 scallion, cut into 2-inch-long sections
2 cups chicken broth

Preparation:
Wash the chicken. Pat dry. Cut each leg and thigh into 3 uniform pieces. Then cut remainder of carcass into similar-size pieces. (Remove backbone, neck, and wing tips to use for broth.)

Wash and soak the mushrooms in ½ cup warm water for 30 minutes. Remove and discard the stems. Reserve the mushroom water to add to the soup instead of water. Set aside on a plate with the ham and scallion.

Cooking:
Arrange the chicken evenly around the cone of a Yunnan pot. Add mushrooms, ham, scallion, chicken broth, the reserved mushroom water, and enough additional water to make 1 cup. Cover the pot and place it over a large saucepan (so that it rests on the saucepan's rim) of boiling water over medium-high heat. Check the water level every half hour. Have a kettle of hot water on low heat so the water can be replenished if necessary.

The cooking time may be 1 to 2 hours, depending on the maturity of the chicken and flow of steam. Test the chicken after 1 hour. It should be tender but firm. It should not fall off the bones.

Yield: 4 servings or up to 8 when served with other dishes.

Note: As a substitute for a Yunnan pot use a deep bowl. Fit the bowl into a large pot with a rack. The water level should be 1½ inches below the bowl's rim. Cover the pot and steam the chicken over medium-low heat for about 2 hours.

Variation: ½ cup dried flat-tip bamboo shoots can be used instead of chicken and ham; just wash and soak them with the mushrooms until soft. Save the soaking water to use in the soup and cook in the same manner.

(From FLORENCE LIN'S CHINESE REGIONAL COOKBOOK by Florence Lin. Copyright 1975 by Florence Lin. Reprinted by permission of Hawthorne Books, Inc.)

Ironstone Steamer A:40

More Americans are learning what the Chinese long knew: steam cooking preserves natural flavor and texture. And, although we can't taste them, it also saves vitamins and minerals. Here is a modern, American-made adaptation of a Yunnan pot. It is made of hand-thrown ironstone pottery that is completely glazed—except for the bottom, top rim and rim of the lid. And it is very handsome, a soft beigy gray with deep-brown speckles. Two large bands of clay-like ribbons, with a large groove in the center, form solid loop handles on opposite sides of the pot, and a similiar handle graces the lid. The capacious 3-quart size pot is 7½″ high and 9″ in diameter and will hold two chickens, enough for eight people. The Chinese dish most commonly associated with this type of pot combines chicken, mushrooms, ham, scallions and, sometimes, a little chicken broth. For as long as two hours the ingredients are cooked together, until they are tender but still hold their shape perfectly. By this time the clear juices are concentrated and the flavors are fully intermingled. Inside the pot is a 4″-high central chimney shaped like a funnel curved at both ends; it allows considerably more steam to rise than does the smaller funnel of the traditional Yunnan pot. But otherwise this California product performs like its Chinese counterpart. Steam rises through the funnel, condenses and creates additional broth. Never put the pot directly on a burner or submerge it in water. It should be placed on a rack that is 2″ to 3″ above boiling water in a saucepan. Or it can be set in the top of a narrow pan over boiling water just like the top part of a double boiler. Replenish the water as needed with boiling water. For variation, stock, wine or beer may replace water; and beef, fish or rice may take the place of chicken. The steamer can also be purchased in 2- and 5-quart sizes, and it comes with a recipe booklet.

Ironstone Pottery **$25.00**

Ginseng

Ginseng

Ginseng Steamer A:41

Truffles may be the black diamonds of France, but ginseng is the subterranean gem of China. For thousands of years the Chinese have treasured the white tendrilled root that sometimes resembles human form. They have consumed it as a powder, a tea, or whole in pieces to cure or prevent every kind of ill from anemia to impotence. Outrageous as it may seem, it is said that a large, old, man-shaped root—the more humanoid the better—from Manchuria or Korea can command a price of $10,000. But Westerners share the passion, too. A North American variety of ginseng was even appreciated by the Iroquois and great quantities of it are grown in New York State, so perhaps it is worth a try. This blue and white pot with its tranquil scene of clouds, mountains, trees on a shoreline and a sailing boat is an appealing vehicle for brewing yourself a tonic. It is about 6″ tall, 3¾″ in diameter and 3¾″ deep. Place some ginseng root in the pot and cover it well with cold water. Then place the lid on the pot and immerse the whole thing, rack and all, in a pan of water to about 1½″ below the lid of the steamer. Cook slowly for several hours and then lift the pot from the pan. Dip into the pot whenever the spirit moves or needs moving.

Quong Yuen Shing & Co. **$7.50**

Medicine Pot A:42

To chase away a headache, stomach-ache or other malaise, the Chinese have long sought comfort in homemade herbal brews. A Chinese doctor's prescription might well be for some kind of plant that is obtained from a druggist. Such concoctions are made in a special pot like this one and they vary with the malady. Whatever the combination, the flavor of a medicinal brew is powerful from long hours of concentrated steeping, and it is likely to be very bitter. This tan, rough-textured earthenware medicine pot is 7½″ tall and 8″ across at its pot-bellied girth. Outside, the pot is completely unglazed; inside, it is covered with a brown glaze. The pot is supported by a wire cage and has a stubby hollow handle that serves as a steam spout. The lid nestles down inside the top edge of the vessel and is perforated with a hole to allow some heat and moisture to escape. Although

Continued from preceding page

we doubt you'll want to brew your own medicine, the pot would be useful for any small recipe, Chinese or otherwise, requiring long, slow, stove-top cooking; because it's designed to concentrate the flavors of food. Use an asbestos mat underneath the pot to prevent cracking, and keep the flame low.

Kam Man Food Products **$5.75**

Brass Fire Pot A:43

This splendid brass fire pot exemplifies an ancient utensil first used by the nomadic tribes of the Asian Steppes. It is heated by charcoal that is placed on a removable grate in the bottom. A separate cooking pot (with large handles) fits over the chimney and rests just above the grate. The flared base catches the ashes, and perforations in its sides let in air to create a draught. The pot stands 12¼″ high overall, and the tin-lined cooking container is 11″ in diameter and holds up to 3 quarts of broth. The chimney in the center, which is just over 8″ high, gives the pot its distinctive appearance. It carries heat up through the broth and allows smoke to escape. Since ashes fall to the bottom of the vessel you must remember to put a fireproof plate and an insulating mat (preferably asbestos) underneath the pot if you use it indoors. And always make sure the cooking area is extremely well ventilated. Three sets of handles assist in handling the hot metal fire pot: a pair of sturdy brass ones with plastic rollers on the cooking container itself, a pair of thick brass wire handles on the base, and two wooden knobs on the cover at opposite sides of the chimney. The cover has a terraced dome shape and a hole in the center so that it can be slipped over the chimney. Fire-pot cookery is a kind of do-it-yourself cooking, like Western *fondue*. Guests pick up raw ingredients with chopsticks and put them in small metal strainers to cook in the bubbling hot broth. Several fire-pot meals are traditional in China. In the North the Mongolian Fire Pot is made with lamb as the only meat. Thinly-sliced lamb is cooked in stock flavored with scallions, ginger and garlic and eaten with a dipping sauce of soy sauce, sesame seed oil, wine, sugar, fermented red bean curd and pepper. Next, cellophane noodles, spinach and celery cabbage are added to the broth, cooked for a few minutes, and eaten as a soup with a touch of dipping sauce for flavoring. The Cantonese make a Chrysanthemum Fire Pot in which all kinds of meat (except lamb), vegetables and fish are cooked. Then there is also a winter specialty of eastern China called Ten Varieties Hot Pot (the number varies according to how many ingredients you use). It is usually served toward the end of a meal and is made up of ready cooked foods, such as parboiled cabbage, cellophane noodles, shrimp balls, meatballs and fish balls, star anise beef, and ham. The ingredients are carefully layered in the pot and then hot chicken broth is poured over them to reheat and keep them warm. Traditionally, each pot is shaped somewhat differently; but with this single, stunning fire pot you could make any fire- or hot-pot dish that struck your fancy.

Hammacher Schlemmer/ Albert Kessler (RX119) **$55.00**

MONGOLIAN FIRE POT

Shuan Yang Jou

3 pounds partially frozen leg of lamb, with bones, tendons, and gristle removed
2 ounces cellophane noodles, soaked in boiling water for 20 minutes, then drained and cut into 4-inch-long pieces
½ pound fresh spinach (tender parts only), well washed
½ pound celery cabbage, cut into 2 × 1-inch pieces and parboiled
2 pieces fresh tender bean curd, cut into 2 × 1-inch pieces
6 to 8 cups lamb broth, made from scraps and bone from the leg of lamb

Sauce:
2 tablespoons sesame paste, diluted with 4 tablespoons warm water
1 tablespoon red fermented bean curd
¼ cup light soy sauce
2 tablespoons sesame oil
2 tablespoons dry sherry
2 tablespoons wine vinegar
1 tablespoon sugar
2 teaspoons Hot Pepper Oil
1 scallion, finely chopped
1 teaspoon finely minced garlic
1 teaspoon fresh ginger juice (use garlic press)
¼ cup finely chopped coriander leaves
¼ cup water

12 baked Sesame Seed Pings heated in the oven before serving

Preparation:
Have the lamb partially frozen so that it is easy to slice. Slice the meat into 2 × 4 × ⅛-inch pieces and arrange in 1 layer with pieces partly overlapping on 6 plates. Put soaked cellophane noodles, spinach, celery cabbage, and bean curd in 2 serving bowls.

Pour the broth into either a traditional fire pot or an electric casserole or skillet on the dining table. Bring the broth to a boil. The broth must continue to simmer during the time the dish is served and eaten.

In a bowl mix the sauce ingredients well. Place 2 to 3 tablespoons mixed sauce in each of 6 individual rice bowls. Put the lamb plates, vegetables, and buns on the table and allow each person to serve himself, holding chopsticks in one hand and the sauce bowl in the other.

Cooking at dining table:
The method of cooking is for each person to use the chopsticks to dip a thin slice of lamb into the boiling broth and let the lamb cook to the desired

degree. The cooked meat is then dipped into one's own sauce bowl and eaten while hot. Serve the baked Sesame Seed Buns during the meal. After all the lamb has been eaten, drop the vegetables, noodles, and bean curd into the broth, cook briefly, and eat while hot. This ends the meal with a tasty hot soup with vegetables.

It is more comfortable if not more than 6 persons share a pot at one table.

Yield: 6 servings.

Note: For easy slicing, have the butcher remove the lamb bone, tendons, and gristle. Tie the meat with strings as for a roast. Freeze it until it is firm enough to cut with an electric slicer. Remove the strings and cut into paper-thin slices. One half pound of lamb is a good-size portion for each serving.

(From FLORENCE LIN'S CHINESE REGIONAL COOKBOOK by Florence Lin. Copyright 1975 by Florence Lin. Reprinted by permission of Hawthorne Books, Inc.)

Fire Pot Cooking Baskets A:44

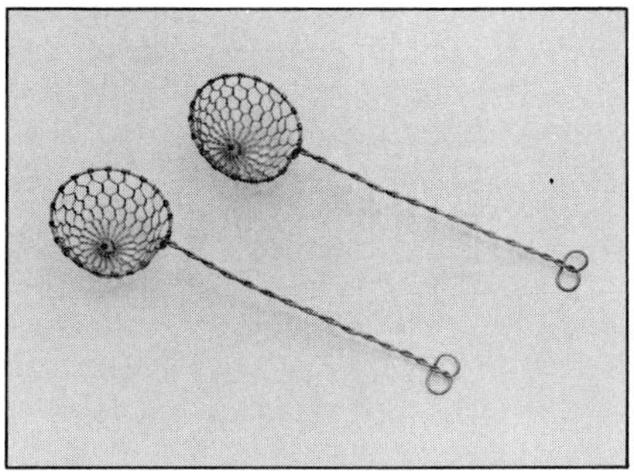

Decorative, yet completely functional, these small strainer baskets are intended for all kinds of fire-pot cookery. Each diner fills a basket with a piece of raw food, perhaps a slice of lamb or a shrimp, and balances it on the edge of a fire pot so the basket rests in the bubbling hot broth. When cooked, the food is lifted from the basket with chopsticks, dipped in a tasty sauce and then savored. You could use chopsticks to hold food in the broth, but with a basket you can let go and your food will not be retrieved by someone else. These small strainer baskets measure 2½″ across the bowl and are 9″ long overall. The baskets are made of lightweight twisted brass wire, and a thicker twisted brass wire forms the rim and handle. Only allow the food to cook for a few moments; if the handle of the strainer becomes too hot to hold, you know that the food is over-cooked. One cook we know uses the baskets to boil eggs in but is cautious to use a pot holder when removing them from boiling water.

Taylor & Ng (10550) $1.50

Chrysanthemum Pot A:45

For centuries the Cantonese have used festive utensils similar to this one to cook their elaborate chrysanthemum fire pot dish that makes a full meal. Once you have the pot, it is easy to prepare this exciting and unusual meal since the method is do-it-yourself. The stainless-steel pot commands a central position on the table and is half filled with chicken broth that is kept bubbling hot. At the base of the pot, a kerosene burner is contained in a 2″-high, broad-lipped cup that sits on a round stainless-steel tray. Encircling the burner is a 6″-wide stainless-steel ring stand with decorative petal-shaped perforations through which the blue flames curve and curl up the sides of the fire pot like the petals of a chrysanthemum. Hence, the delightful name the Chinese have given this splendid invention. The chrysanthemum is a symbol of well-being, and its petals are sometimes eaten and also made into a fragrant tea. The actual cooking pot that fits above the heat source measures just under 10″ in diameter, is 3¼″ deep and holds 2½ quarts of liquid. It has convenient moveable handles attached about an inch below the rim on each side. Diners pick up their own raw ingredients with chopsticks and place them in individual metal strainers that hold the food in the chicken broth to cook. The raw ingredients may include chicken, beef, pork or liver; sole, shrimp or oysters; and bean curd, celery cabbage or spinach. All or any combination of these, with some transparent cellophane noodles, would be traditional. When the food is cooked it is dipped into a sauce made of beaten egg, soy sauce, sesame seed oil and rice wine (dry sherry can be substituted), and then eaten. When all the meats and fish are gone, some of the enriched broth is ladled into each person's bowl. Then the vegetables and noodles are put in the rest of the broth and the pot is covered until they are heated through. They are served as the last course, sometimes with rice. Lamb is never used for this dish; it is only eaten in the North where it is the basis of the Mongolian fire pot, otherwise known as rinsed lamb.

Cook's Corners, Inc. $20.00

Chrysanthemum.

CHRYSANTHEMUM POT

Chü Hua Kuo

1 whole chicken breast, skinned and boned, then cut into 1 × 2 × ⅛-inch slices
1 pound tender beef, cut into 1 × 2 × ⅛-inch slices
½ pound raw shrimps, shelled, deveined, and split laterally in halves
½ pound fillet of gray sole or yellow pike, sliced into 1 × 2 × ¼-inch pieces
1 dozen shucked clams or oysters
¼ pound chicken livers, sliced into 1 × 2 × ⅛-inch pieces
1 teaspoon salt
¼ teaspoon white pepper
2 teaspoons dry sherry
2 teaspoons peanut or corn oil
1 large chrysanthemum flower
½ cup coriander leaves and tender stems
2 ounces cellophane noodles, boiled in water for 5 minutes, left soaking until cool, and cut into 4-inch-long pieces
½ pound fresh spinach or romaine lettuce, washed and drained
2 pieces fresh tender bean curd, sliced into 2 × 1 × ½-inch pieces
8 cups chicken broth

Sauce:
2 eggs
½ teaspoon sugar
3 tablespoons light soy sauce
2 tablespoons dry sherry
2 tablespoons sesame oil

Preparation:
On two platters or four plates arrange the chicken, beef, shrimps, sole, clams, and chicken livers in one layer with pieces partially overlapping. Sprinkle the salt, white pepper, sherry, and oil on top and decorate with chrysanthemum petals and coriander. Cover with clear plastic wrap and refrigerate until ready to serve.

Put drained cellophane noodles, spinach, and bean curd in 2 serving bowls.

Sauce:
Beat the eggs thoroughly, then add the sugar, soy sauce, sherry, and sesame oil.

Pour the chicken broth into either a traditional fire pot or an electric casserole or skillet on the dining table. Bring the broth to a boil. The broth must continue to simmer during the time the dish is served and eaten.

Place 2 to 3 tablespoons mixed sauce in each of 6 individual rice bowls. Put the meat, fish, and vegetables on the table and allow each person to serve himself, holding chopsticks in one hand and the sauce bowl in the other.

Cooking at dining table:
The method of cooking is for each person to use the chopsticks to dip a thin slice of meat, fish, or vegetable into the boiling broth and let it cook to the desired degree. It is then dipped into one's own sauce bowl and eaten while hot. You may serve steamed or baked rolls with the meal. The sauce should be used a little at a time as you eat. The vegetables may be added at any time.

Yield: 6 servings

(From FLORENCE LIN'S CHINESE REGIONAL COOKBOOK by Florence Lin. Copyright 1975 by Florence Lin. Reprinted by permission of Hawthorne Books, Inc.)

Rolling Pin A:46

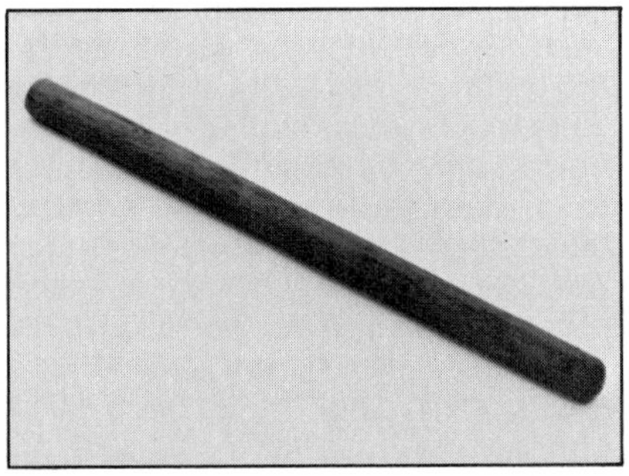

For a rolling pin that looks light, this one of dark red wood is surprisingly hefty. It is fairly short (12″), narrow (¾″ in diameter) and untapered. One end of the pin has been drilled, so a hook may be screwed in, if desired. You might want a rolling pin like this to make *po-ping* (mandarin pancakes), the delectable little pancakes served with Peking duck (duck meat, crisp duck skin, scallion bushes, and *hoisin* sauce), or to make egg roll or *wonton* wrappers.

Oriental Country Store $1.50

DOILIES FOR CASSIA PORK

Makes About 16 Doilies

INGREDIENTS
2 cups sifted all-purpose flour
⅘ cup boiling water
2 tablespoons vegetable oil

PREPARATION
Place sifted flour in a mixing bowl. Gradually stir in the boiling water with chopsticks or wooden spoon. When cool enough to touch, knead with your hands until smooth and silky, about 8 minutes. Add 1 tablespoon oil and knead for another minute. Cover with a damp cloth and let sit for 15 minutes.

Knead the dough for another 2 minutes. Roll out evenly on a lightly floured board until a large sheet about ¼ inch in thickness is formed. Using a cookie cutter or glass about 2½ to 3 inches in diameter, cut the dough into rounds. Brush one side of each round with a little oil. With oiled sides facing, lay one round over another. Slowly roll out from the center, to about 5 to 6 inches in diameter.

COOKING PROCEDURES
Heat an ungreased heavy skillet or griddle on top of stove. Cook one pair of doilies over low flame for about 2 minutes, or until bubbles form. Turn over and cook other side, then remove from the pan and pull the two pieces apart. Continue until all are cooked, piling them up and covering them to keep warm.

TIPS
These pancakes are really quite easy to make. However, allow plenty of time to make them the first time you try. They can be made ahead of time and frozen. When ready to use, keep them at room temperature for an hour. Then wet steam for 3 to 5 minutes, or until soft.

To eat with the pork dish, spread a doily on a clean plate. Scoop up a rounded spoonful of the pork mixture and place on the doily. Fold one side over and then fold the right side over at a 90-degree angle. Roll up the doily and eat with your fingers, keeping open side of doily up.

(From MADAME CHU'S CHINESE

COOKING SCHOOL by Grace Zia Chu. Copyright 1975 by Grace Zia Chu. Reprinted by permission of Simon and Schuster.)

Pastry Molds A:47

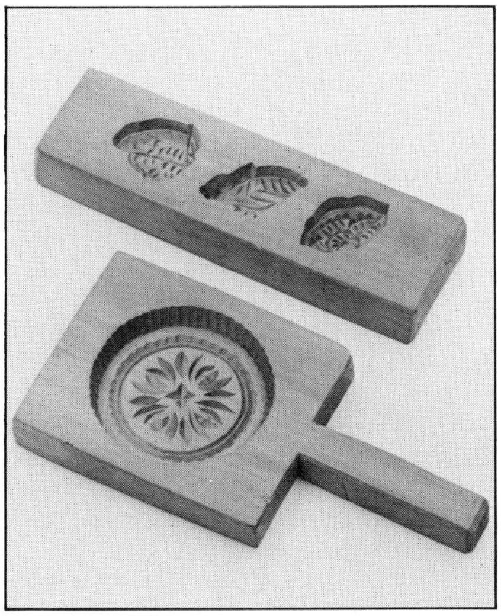

Every year special round cakes are made for the Moon Festival which falls on the 8th full moon of the lunar year. This night, of the brightest moon, was thought to be the birthday of the moon goddess. To celebrate, people would gather at moon-watching parties where poets waxed eloquent—helped by generous amounts of rice wine—and everyone exchanged gifts that always included moon cakes. In China, the cakes are baked commercially—since ovens are not common—and shaped before cooking in attractively carved wooden molds such as these. The chrysanthemum, centered within the notched 2½″ circle of the large mold, symbolizes well-being, a sense that is no doubt imparted on tasting the delectable confection shaped by it. Cut from a single piece of wood, the rectangular mold is 6½″ long, 3½″ wide and has a 2¾″-long handle. To make a moon cake, a sweet filling of red bean paste, lotus seeds and sesame seeds, or fruits, nuts and spices is covered with dough made from glutinous rice flour. It is then pressed into the mold, and the surface smoothed over with the fingers. When the mold is turned upside down and tapped firmly, the embossed cake tumbles out ready for baking. Though originally these cakes could only be found at the time of the festival, Chinese bakeries now sell them year-round. If you had such a mold, you, too, could break tradition and fête any full moon you please. The second wooden mold makes three small cakes in flower and animal shapes for the New Year or other special celebrations. Like moon cakes, these are also filled—with nuts, dates or other delectables. The mold is 6½″ long by 2″ wide, turning out cakes that are smaller, but no less delicious.

Oriental Country Store
Moon cake mold $1.95
New Year's mold $2.50

Fortune Cookie Iron A:48

Be the master of your fortune, make your own fortune cookies. Now you can devise witty, apropos sayings or jokes to surprise your family and friends for birthdays or other celebrations. Although the tradition of inserting messages in sweet cakes or cookies is an old one in China, especially for birth announcements and amusing games, the fortune cookie, as we know it, is acknowledged to be the invention of George Jung, who immigrated to Los Angeles in 1911. This sturdy iron consists of a cast-aluminum cookie sheet with four shallow 3″-diameter indentations. It is 7½″ square and attached to a 6½″-long handle. A metal top that fits exactly over the bottom sheet at one side is decorated on the outside with various Chinese inscriptions. Fortune cookie batter resembles a pancake batter and has to be spooned into each heated and greased cup. The top and bottom parts are then closed and the handles squeezed together for about 45 seconds to allow the steam to escape. Then the cookies are baked over a low heat for about 3 minutes till they are golden brown. One at a time, they are quickly removed and held in one hand while the fortune is inserted, then folded over into the familiar shape and set aside to cool and harden. The procedure is amazingly simple and will provide endless fun. A recipe and illustrated instructions accompany the fortune cookie iron.

N.Y. Mutual Trading Co. $16.50

Watering rice paddies.

Transplanting rice.

Rice for Every Meal

For at least five millennia, rice has been grown in China where its importance has made it synonymous with food, and therefore with life. For example, rice is called *fan,* the same word for "meal"; one eats *zaofan* (morning rice); *zhongfan* (noon rice) and *waufan* (evening rice). Although the thought of eating a pound of rice a day may be staggering to a Westerner, it is quite normal for any Chinese who lives in the southern two-thirds of the country were rice is the staple. In colder, northern areas, wheat, millet and other grains are basic to the diet.

But rice is not only of central importance to daily life and work; it fullfills an aesthetic function. Its color, texture and flavor contrast and complement the other foods it accompanies. It is one side of the *yin* and *yang* principle which pervades Chinese life and thought. It is therefore no surprise that it has been endowed over the years with symbolic qualities. Leaving one's job is called breaking one's rice bowl; it is considered bad luck to upset a rice bowl; and the worst of insults is to take another's bowl of rice and empty it onto the ground. For the New Year, in some parts of China, a bowl of rice is offered up on the altar dedicated to the family ancestors to give thanks for the past year and to ask favors for the year to come.

Aware of the back-breaking manual labor that goes into rice cultivation—almost unchanged for hundreds of years—and always haunted by the spectre of hunger, the Chinese respect rice too much to waste it. Children are told to eat every grain in their bowls since each one that is left represents a pock mark on the face of their future spouse—no empty threat when smallpox was prevalent. Rice represents well-being and fertility, and it is from the East that we have taken the custom of throwing rice at weddings for good luck.

While rice is indispensable to every meal, it is never eaten without some flavoring from a little meat, fish or vegetable. And it is not

BOILED RICE, THE CHINESE WAY

Time: 50 minutes

For 4 persons

INGREDIENTS
1 cup long-grain rice
1 3/4 cups cold water

PREPARATION
Place rice in strainer and rinse thoroughly in cold running water. Drain.

COOKING PROCEDURES
Place rice in a 2-quart saucepan and add 1 3/4 cups cold water. Bring to boil over high flame (about 5 minutes).

Turn flame to low, cover and let simmer for 20 minutes, until dry. Turn off flame.

Allow the rice to stand, covered, for another 20 minutes.

Stir well while rice is still hot so that it will be flaky and each grain will be separate. Makes 3 cups of cooked rice.

TIPS
Rice must be rinsed before cooking to get rid of any excess starch so that it does not burn while cooking. Do not stir the rice during cooking or it will stick to the bottom of the pan. The Chinese do not add salt or butter when cooking rice.

If rice other than long-grain is used, decrease the amount of water to 1 1/2 cups. Long-grain rice, which most Chinese prefer, absorbs more water and yields a larger quantity of cooked rice from the same amount of raw rice than the shorter-grained varieties.

Cooked rice can be kept warm in the oven. Cold cooked rice can be used to make fried rice. This will keep for a few days in the refrigerator and can be reheated with good results.

(From THE PLEASURES OF CHINESE COOKING by Grace Zia Chu. Copyright 1962 by Grace Zia Chu. Reprinted by permission of Simon & Schuster, Inc.)

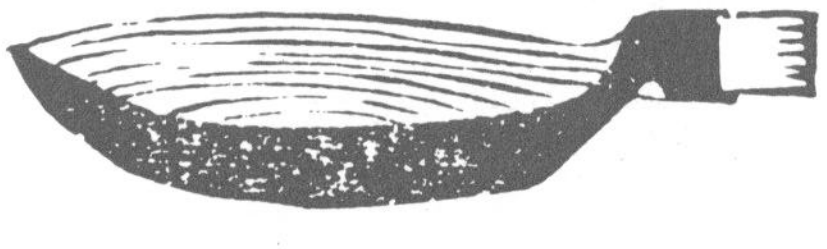

served until the end of a Chinese banquet for fear the guests will not be able to sample all the exotic courses. Apart from the plain rice that accompanies every family meal, rice does make its appearance in other forms. Leftover rice is always saved to be stir-fried for another meal with egg and morsels of seafood, pork or ham and some vegetables. "Sizzling rice" is deep-fried as a thin cake and then dropped still hot into soup where it makes the noise that gives it its name. A glutinous, or sticky, round-grain rice is used to make stuffings for poultry and desserts such as the eight treasure rice pudding. And *congee*, a thick rice gruel, is often given to babies or invalids and relished as a light breakfast or a snack. *Congee* is either cooked plain and accompanied by small dishes of meat and some highly seasoned food like preserved vegetables, or it is cooked with meat, seafood or vegetables.

As to the preparation of boiled rice, easy and specific directions abound and there is no longer any mystery surrounding it. Just make sure to let it stand, covered, for about 10 minutes after cooking, and then fluff it with chopsticks or a fork to prevent the grains from sticking. If you do have a problem, an electric rice cooker is infallible and simple to use. Regardless of how you cook rice, don't fail to serve it with every Chinese meal, for as an old proverb says, "A meal without rice is like a beautiful girl with one eye."

Electric Rice Cooker A:49

According to Chinese cooking experts, this rice cooker from Taiwan is exceptional because it steams and boils rice at the same time. This method produces a grain of excellent moist texture and taste, which matters a great deal to rice lovers. The attractive looking pot is made of anodized aluminum, with a white enameled exterior and two black plastic handles. Its stainless-steel lid also has a large black plastic handle. The pot is 11″ across and 11″ high, with the lid on. An inner aluminum container, that holds about 15 cups of cooked rice fits into the outer pot; it measures 4½″ deep and 9½″ across. To prepare rice, first put rice and cooking water together into the inner container. Then pour about half a cup of water into the outer pot. Set the inner container into the outer pot and cover with the stainless-steel lid. Plug in the cooker and push down the lever on the side. A red light will go on and will stay on until the rice is cooked, about 25 minutes, at which time the lever will snap up and the electricity will be cut off automatically. Let the pot sit for about 10 minutes before removing the lid to let the steam have its full effect on the rice. Then lift the container of rice from the pot with the detachable aluminum handle that accompanies the cooker. And, if you wish, cover it with the small aluminum lid that also comes with the cooker. For many people, the greatest feature of this cooker is that it is virtually scorch-proof. Shallow depressions in the bottom of the inner container prevent it from sitting flat against the outer pot and allow water under the container at all times. And steam from the water in the outer pot circulates around the rice continually to keep it moist. Other attachments that are included with the cooker are: two white plastic half-cup measures; a 7½″-long white plastic rice serving paddle; a ⅝″-high perforated steam rack that can be used for cooking food in the bottom of the outer pot; and a 1¾″-deep steam tray that fits into the top of the rice container. The steam tray can be used to steam cold food or soup while the rice is cooking below it. The detachable handle will also fit into brackets on the steam tray to lift it from the pot. For a family that eats rice often, or for cooking large quantities, this rice cooker would be a splendid asset.

New Frontier Trading Corp. $37.50

Husking rice.

Bamboo Rice Paddle A:50

When a common greeting in a country is "Have you eaten rice yet?" you might expect to find rice on the menu. In China, it is on every menu, at least in the southern two-thirds of the country. Red-cooked pork (cooked in soy sauce) or lobster Cantonese (with fermented black beans, soy sauce and scallions) would simply taste incomplete without the color, texture and taste of rice. And if you are making rice, you should have the proper server for it. This almost flat, 9″-long paddle, made of a solid piece of satin-smooth bamboo, is hollowed slightly and carved away at the end until it is similar to a spatula. The paddle's soft rounded edge will not cut the rice grains, but it is thin enough to separate portions of rice, sticky or not, efficiently. One side of the handle is stained dark brown.

Taylor & Ng (10500) $1.00

Wooden Rice Spoon A:51

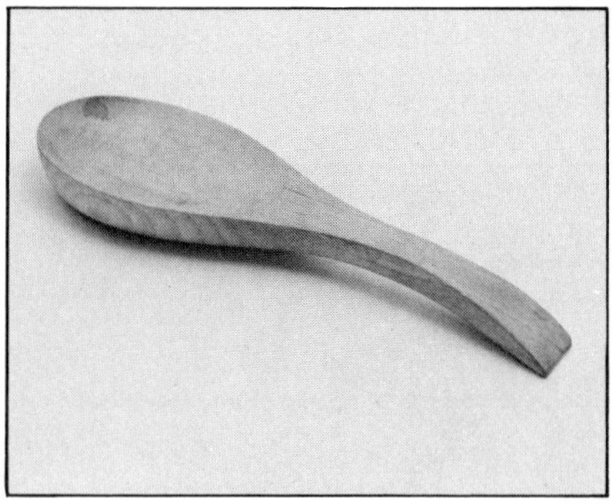

A meal without rice is not a true meal, at least not for most Chinese. And, if you want to get a good grip on rice, it's a good thing to have a spoon that will dish out large portions. This gracefully curved, natural wood rice spoon will do just that. Its bowl—3″ in diameter and 3/4″ deep—will cradle enough rice for one complete serving. The spoon is sturdy enough to last a lifetime—at least 1/2″ thick along its entire length of almost 9″.

Oriental Country Store $1.50

Chinese rice mill.

Chopsticks

"Busy little boys," is a well-earned sobriquet for chopsticks. Not only are they indispensable for eating in China, but extra long ones serve as important cooking utensils. In the kitchen, chopsticks are used for stirring, for nimbly turning or separating pieces of food as they cook, or for lifting individual pieces of food from a wok.

All Chinese chopsticks are tapered, narrow but blunt at the eating end, wider and often squared where they are held. (The Japanese variety tapers evenly its whole length and is pointed at the eating end.) Eating chopsticks may be made of elegant materials—silver, ivory or lacquerware—or of mundane plastic or bamboo. But only bamboo should be used for cooking. Metal conducts heat too quickly (unless the ends are made of wood), lacquer will chip, ivory will turn yellow, and plastic will melt.

Bamboo Chopsticks A:52

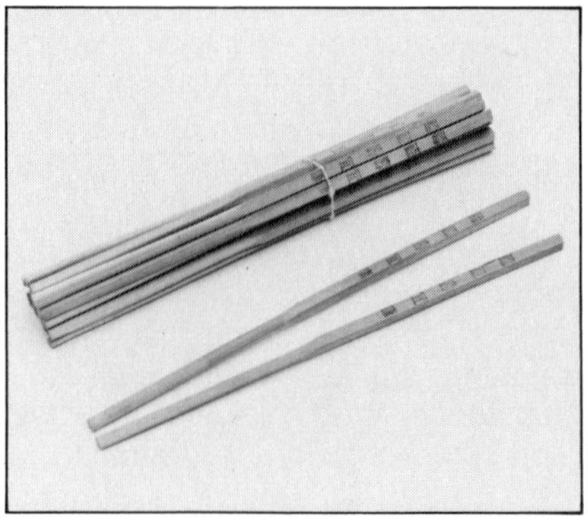

Bamboo is the traditional material used for everyday chopsticks. It is inexpensive, and it will not conduct heat. Fancy lacquered wood, ivory or silver chopsticks are only brought out for company or special celebrations. In ancient times, silver chopsticks were a particular boon to the rich who, constantly fearing treachery on the part of their servants, took solace in the belief that the silver tips of their chopsticks would instantly and visibly discolor in the presence of poison. Since we are all wiser now, everyone can relax and use plain bamboo. For added well-being, these chopsticks—like many others—are stamped with characters meaning, "Good luck, happiness, longevity and health." The only drawback to bamboo is that, with use, it absorbs flavors; so these 10½″-long chopsticks should be considered semi-disposable. Washed and dried thoroughly after each meal, and used only occasionally in an American household, one package of ten pairs should last quite a while. And, after all, they are very reasonable.

Albert Kessler & Co. (MK106) $1.25

"The points [of the chopsticks] are next to be brought carefully together, just leaving as much room as will allow the coveted morsel to go in between them; the little bit is then to be neatly seized; but alas; in the act of lifting the hand, one point of the chopstick too often slips past the other, and the object of all our hopes drops back again into the dish, or perhaps even into another dish on the table. Again and again the same operation is tried, until the poor novice loses all patience, throws down the chopsticks in despair,

and seizes a porcelain spoon, with which he is more successful."

Wanderings in China *by Robert Fortune, 1847.*

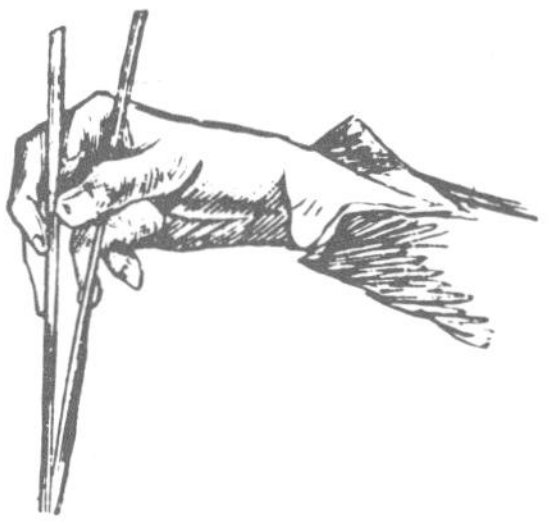

Bamboo Chopsticks with Metal Caps A:53

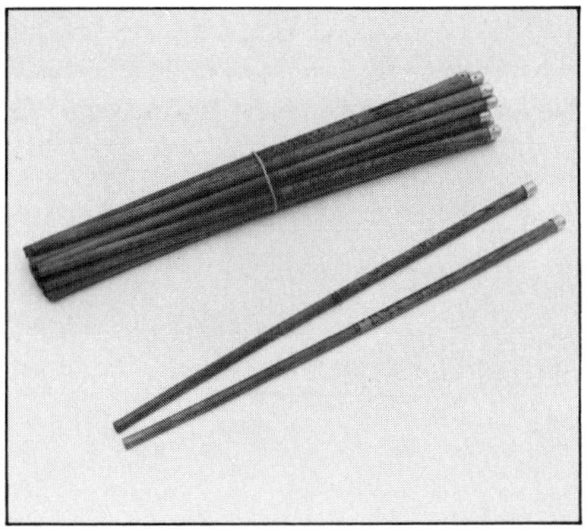

Natural beauty makes these 10″-long chopsticks distinctive. They are cut from the stalks of a species of bamboo found only in certain areas of China. This particular variety of bamboo attains only a limited height, and its stalks are solid, instead of hollow like those of the larger, tree-like form of the plant. If you look closely at the tips of the chopsticks, you can see the individual round fibers that make up the plant. The stalks were cut and polished into a mellow shade of brown. They were then decorated at one end with a graceful, burned-in design, of fish and reeds, or perhaps bamboo, and topped with silvery aluminum caps. Each package contains 10 pairs. If you believe in superstitions, take note that the Chinese consider it bad luck to drop a chopstick.

Albert Kessler & Co. (MK 127) **$1.25**

Lacquered Chopsticks A:54

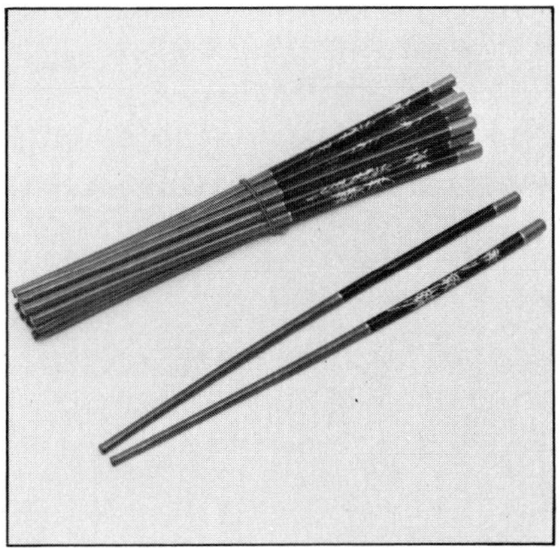

Chinese chopsticks frequently come in bundles of 10 pairs because 10 is the largest number of people that would be comfortably seated around a table at a Chinese banquet. These are 10″ long and covered with the burnt-orange lacquer that is typical of so many Chinese products. Although the design in gold on black at one end depicts the bamboo plant, the wood under the lacquer is not bamboo. As with any lacquerware, these chopsticks should not be put in the dishwasher and no abrasives should be used to clean them.

Kam Kuo Food Inc. **$1.50**

SHRIMPS IN LOBSTER SAUCE

Time: 40 minutes

INGREDIENTS
1 pound fresh uncooked shrimps
½ cup (¼ pound) ground pork
2 eggs
2 teaspoons fermented black beans
2 cloves garlic
2 scallions
2 tablespoons peanut or corn oil
1 tablespoon soy sauce
1 tablespoon dry sherry
½ teaspoon salt
½ teaspoon sugar
1 tablespoon cornstarch

PREPARATION
Shell and devein the shrimps. Wash and drain.

Beat the eggs.

Crush the black beans and the garlic with the side of a Chinese cleaver.

Wash scallions and cut into 2″ pieces.

Dissolve tablespoon of cornstarch in 2 tablespoons water.

COOKING PROCEDURES
Heat 2 tablespoons oil in a frying pan over a high flame. Add the black beans and the garlic. Stir a few times.

Add pork and continue stirring until the pork turns white, about 3 minutes.

Add shrimps and stir until they turn pink.

Add 1 tablespoon sherry, 1 tablespoon soy sauce, ½ teaspoon salt and ½ teaspoon sugar. Mix well.

Add scallion. Mix again.

Add ½ cup water. Bring to boil. Cover and cook over medium flame for 3 minutes.

Add the pre-dissolved cornstarch and stir slowly until it thickens.

Stir in the eggs. Turn off flame immediately and serve.

TIPS
Make certain that pork is well cooked over a high flame.

When making the sauce, it is important that the flame be turned off immediately after the beaten eggs have been added. This is necessary if you want to achieve a smooth, flowing sauce. It is called "lobster sauce" not because it contains lobster meat or juice—it doesn't—but because it is one of the sauces used to cook lobster. It is especially good when served very hot with boiled rice.

The fermented black beans can be purchased from Chinese food stores. Stored in a jar they will keep for a long time.

(From THE PLEASURES OF CHINESE COOKING by Grace Zia Chu. Copyright 1962 by Grace Zia Chu. Reprinted by permission of Simon & Schuster, Inc.)

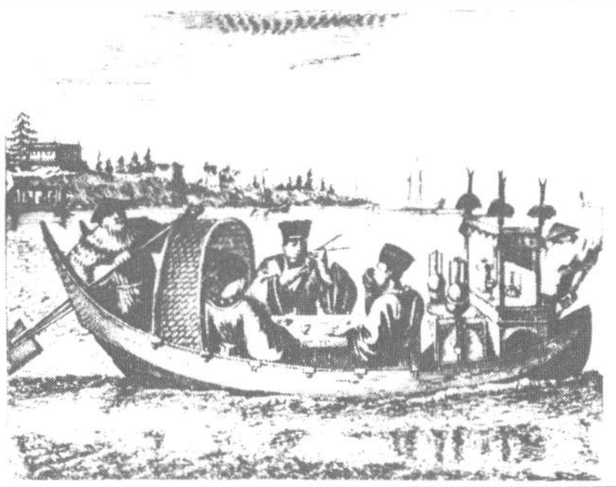

Plastic Chopsticks A:55

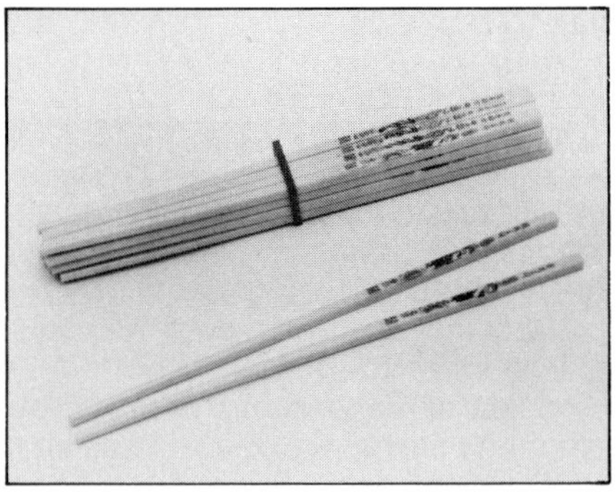

Ivory chopsticks are traditionally presented as wedding gifts and, along with silver, were once the prized possessions of the rich. Now, anyone can pretend to riches with these plastic imitations. In fact, plastic chopsticks are common in Taiwan, nowadays; and on the Chinese mainland they are highly prized as products of modern technology. But they are not modern enough to put in a dishwasher. These 10 pairs of 10½″-long chopsticks are decorated in red, blue and green with the romantic messages that are commonly exchanged at a wedding party. According to Chinese folklore, if a young girl first picks up her chopsticks near their end, her husband will come from a faraway place.

Albert Kessler & Co. (MK122) **$2.50**

Disposable Chopsticks A:56

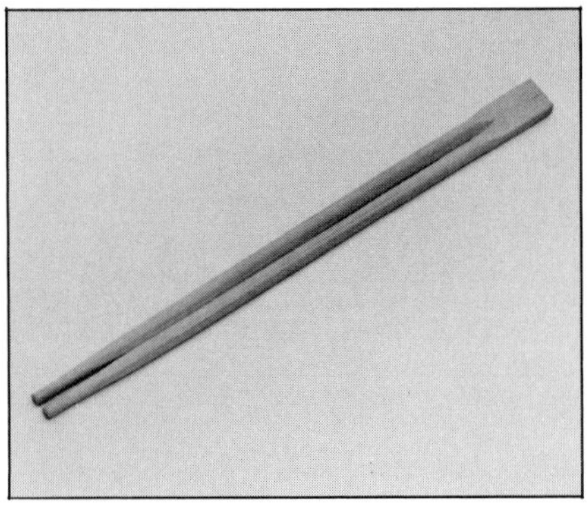

These especially short (8″), restaurant-style chopsticks are made of extremely light bamboo and are meant to be used only once. They are manufactured in Taiwan out of a single piece of wood. Although the two shafts at one end have been rounded and separated, the chopsticks are still attached. When you are ready to eat, simply pull them apart; and when you have finished, lay them across your rice bowl to signal that you can eat no more.

Lucky Gift Shop **$0.15**

In China, birthdays are celebrated with noodles, which for this occasion remain uncut. Guests are compelled to hold their chopsticks aloft and rise up on tiptoe in order to have the noodles clear their bowls. But all contortions are for a worthwhile cause, because long noodles ensure long life.

Dinner party at a Mandarin's house.

Serving a Chinese Meal

The average Chinese meal consists of four dishes that are brought to the table simultaneously: one of meat (usually pork) or poultry, one of seafood, one of soy bean products or eggs and one of vegetables, plus rice or buns and soup. Soup, not tea, is the liquid refreshment of a meal; tea is served after eating or between meals. And desserts are relatively non-existent, except for an occasional piece of fresh fruit. (Banquets are another story, but most banquet dining is done in restaurants.)

Several essential dishes are required for serving such a meal. First, you should have several platters and a large soup bowl. Then, each place setting should have a soup bowl and spoon; a rice bowl; a sauce dish or two, depending on the menu; and a pair of chopsticks. A plate may also be set at each place to make Westerners feel more comfortable, although normally the Chinese hold food over their rice bowl while eating. In fact, the Chinese often use just one bowl interchangeably for rice and soup. Last, a tea pot and cups should be handy for the proper finish to a good meal.

Serving Spoon A:57

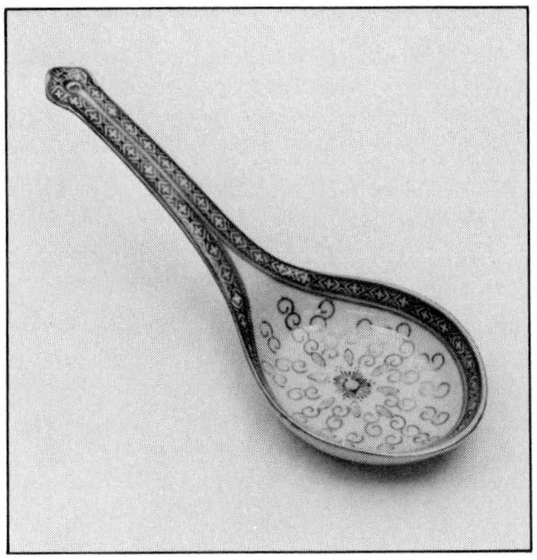

A large version of the individual spoon is used as a serving spoon for soup, *congee* (rice gruel), soupy noodle dishes, or any other dish with a lot of liquid. The porcelain spoon is about 9″ long, 3″ across at its widest point, and it has a flat bottom so that it can rest on the side of a serving bowl without sliding in. A geometric blue pattern borders the spoon, and its rim is outlined in gold. In the center is a design of orange and blue on white as well as the familiar translucent rice pattern that gives a lacy delicate feeling to this most practical of utensils. There is a hole in the end of the handle so that you can hang the spoon as a decoration when it's not in use.

Quong Yuen Shing & Co. $3.00

NOODLES IN CHICKEN BROTH WITH HAM AND LETTUCE

INGREDIENTS:
6 oz. dry egg noodles
8 cups water
one 12-oz. can clear chicken broth
1 can water
2 scallions, cut into 2″ lengths
4 thin slices cooked ham, cut into strips
1 small lettuce, cut into strips
salt and white pepper to taste

TO PREPARE:
1. Cook noodles and keep warm.
2. Cut scallions into 2″ pieces.
3. Cut ham into 2″ × ½″ strips.
4. Wash and separate stalks of lettuce. Cut crosswise into ½″ strips.

TO COOK: (cooking time about 10 minutes)
1. Bring chicken broth, water, and scallions to boil in a pot.
2. Add ham and lettuce and boil uncovered 1 minute. Season soup with salt and white pepper.
3. To serve: Divide warm noodles in 2 large bowls. Pour soup over them, arrange ham and lettuce on top and serve hot.
4. Yield: Serves 2.

Notes: This is a quick meal with everything included in one bowl. You can use other soups from the soup section—choose the kinds which are quickly boiled, with meat and vegetables in them, rather than the thick and spicy ones.

(From EIGHTY PRECIOUS CHINESE RECIPES by May Wong Trent. Copyright 1973 by May Wong Trent. Reprinted by permission of Macmillan Publishing Co., Inc.)

"A certain prefect once served large bowls of plain boiled bird's nest. It was completely tasteless. Others praised it, but I said with a smile; 'I just came to eat bird's nest, not to get it wholesale.' We were each served several ounces of it, to do us honour. Had he given us each a bowlful of pearls we would have valued them as much, and found them quite as inedible."

Yuan Mei (1716–1799)

Celadon Bowl A:58

Celadon green is a famous color known from the greatest periods of china making. It gives this bowl a classic elegance that is hard to improve upon. In contrast to most straight-sided rice or soup bowls with which we are familiar, this one has a graceful flared lip, a style that is just as typical but a little harder to make. A design of light green, almost cream-colored, clouds and cranes with wings outstretched wraps the bowl, symbolizing longevity and happiness. With a capacity of one cup, the bowl is 2″ high and 4½″ across. Ordinarily a rice bowl appears at every family meal and is considered indispensable, but it would not be seen at a Chinese banquet where there are too many other courses to eat. Soup, on the other hand, is a must for every meal and this bowl would do credit to any recipe.

Quong Yuen Shing & Co. $1.00

"I once went to a merchant's house. There were three separate tables, sixteen kinds of pastries, and a total of forty-odd dishes. The host was very pleased with himself. When I returned home I cooked congee [rice gruel] to ease my hunger."

Yuan Mei (1716–1799)

Large Serving Bowl A:59

The size of this yellow porcelain bowl suggests at once that it is too big for an individual soup bowl and too small for a serving bowl. It holds 3 cups and is 2½″ deep and 6¼″ in diameter. It would, in fact, most often be used as a noodle bowl for a meal of fresh egg noodles in chicken broth garnished with some shredded ham or roast pork, or some salted vegetables or dried shrimp. You could also use the dish for a *congee,* usually made from glutinous rice. This is a thick porridge-like cereal made with rice and water that have been cooked for a long time. It has a neutral flavor and, like its Western equivalent, is perfect food for invalids and babies. However, it is also a popular light meal or snack for the Chinese at almost any time of the day from waking to sleeping and as such it is always accompanied by a bit of meat, fish or vegetable. In northern China, *congee* is made from other grains like millet or barley. A lotus blossom for purity, butterflies, a chrysanthemum for well-being and the red character for happiness on a bright yellow background combine to make an old, highly favored china pattern that would grace any table.

Quong Yuen Shing & Co. $4.00

PEKING SOUR AND PEPPERY SOUP

6 servings

This soup comes from Peking, where the climate gets colder than in other parts of China. Therefore, this is a particularly popular soup for winter meals.

The use of either black or white pepper earmarks any dish as belonging to the northern school of Chinese cooking.

INGREDIENTS
¼ pound fresh lean pork
¼ cup dried Chinese mushrooms
12 tiger-lily buds
1 tablespoon dried cloud ears
1 cake fresh bean curd
1 egg
5 cups chicken or pork broth
¼ cup bamboo shoots in shreds
1 tablespoon salt
½ teaspoon sugar
2 tablespoons light soy sauce
2½ tablespoons wine vinegar
⅛ teaspoon black pepper
2½ tablespoons cornstarch, dissolved in 2 tablespoons of cold water
1 tablespoon Oriental sesame seed oil

PREPARATION
Cut the pork into matchstick-sized shreds.

Soak Chinese mushrooms, lily buds, and cloud ears in 1 cup of hot water for 20 minutes. Rinse, drain, and shred the mushrooms and cloud ears. Cut the tiger-lily buds into 1-inch lengths.

Cut fresh bean curd into shreds.

Beat the whole egg until white and yolk are thoroughly mixed.

COOKING PROCEDURES
Heat broth in a large saucepan until boiling. Add pork strips and mix a few times with two chopsticks. Keep the soup boiling as you add bean curd, bamboo shoots, mushrooms, lily buds, and cloud ears. Add salt, sugar, soy sauce, wine vinegar, and black pepper. Boil for 2 more minutes; stir a few times with chopsticks. Thicken with predissolved cornstarch first stirring to recombine. Pour in egg. Turn off flame immediately. Stir gently a few times with chopsticks. Dish into casserole and sprinkle sesame seed oil on top. Serve hot.

TIPS
Partially freeze the pork, then slice it first before cutting into shreds.

Chinese mushrooms, cloud ears, lily buds, and bean curd can be bought in Chinese and Oriental stores. Certain gourmet stores also carry some of these ingredients.

The cooking takes a very short while, and preparation, as always, can be done ahead of time.

In China beef broth is not used, but if desired, it can be substituted. Veal shreds can also be used in place of pork shreds, but the genuine ingredients are always the tastiest.

(From MADAME CHU'S CHINESE COOKING SCHOOL by Grace Zia Chu. Copyright 1975 by Grace Zia Chu. Reprinted by permission of Simon and Schuster.)

Soup Bowl and Spoon A:60

Perhaps the most popular of all Chinese porcelains, at least among Westerners, is the traditional blue and white rice pattern represented by this soup bowl and spoon. A ½″ blue geometric band decorates the inside and outside edges of the bowl and the interior edge of the spoon. The bowl is 4½″ in diameter, just over 1¾″ deep and sits on a small raised base. When the contents of the bowl are very hot, it is customary for the diner to hold the bowl with the thumb on the top edge and the index finger on the base to avoid getting burned. The soup spoon is 5½″ long and has a flat-bottomed bowl that will prevent the spoon from slipping completely into the soup. Originally the translucent quality of the rice pattern was achieved by cutting holes in the clay before glazing it. After it was glazed and fired the hardened glaze over the holes formed semi-opaque, rice-shaped patterns in the china. Today, in mass-produced china, a similar effect is created by simply making indentations in the clay with a mold so that the patterned areas have a translucent quality after firing. Soups may be rich and thick like bird's nest soup (based on the gelatinous saliva with which certain swiftlets build their nests) or shark's fin soup, in which case they are eaten at only one point in a meal. Or they may be clear, thin, palate-cleansing soups that are eaten throughout the meal in place of the wine or water that accompanies meals in other countries.

Continental Crafts Co., Inc.
Soup bowl (CH400) $2.00
Soup spoon (CH401) $0.70

Sauce Dish A:61

On the inside, this enchanting little porcelain sauce dish is painted dark blue and covered with mauve and yellow flowers with green leaves. Plain white sets off the underside. The dish is conveniently small and shallow, about 3/4″ deep and 3¾″ wide so that many of them will fit comfortably on a dinner table. Although most of the great sauces of Chinese cooking are combined with the other ingredients of a dish during the cooking process, there are many occasions when a dipping sauce is required on the table. For instance, *hoisin* sauce (a dark, sweet sauce made with soybeans, sugar, spices, chili and garlic) is indispensable for Peking duck and other poultry and seafood dishes. A pungent mixture of salt and crushed Szechwan peppercorns is eaten with crisp and delicious Szechwan duck. Soy and vinegar are mixed for wonderful northern pork dumplings (*chiao-tzu*) and a combination of soy sauce, wine, sesame seed oil and beaten egg is a must for the famous Chrysanthemum Fire Pot, in which meats and seafood are cooked in broth and then dipped into a sauce.

Quong Yuen Shing & Co. $0.85

"The tables were now covered with a profusion of small dishes, which contained all the finest fruits and vegetables of the season, besides many of the most expensive kind of soups, such as the celebrated bird's-nest and others, many of which were excellent even to the palate of an Englishman. The servants were continually employed in removing the centre dishes and replacing them by others of a different kind. . . . Our maiden efforts with the chop-sticks must have been a great source of amusement to our Chinese friends, but they were polite enough not to laugh at us, and did everything in their power to assist us."

Wanderings in China *by Robert Fortune, 1847.*

Stainless-Steel Serving Dish A:62

You won't see this type of stainless-steel serving dish in a Chinese home, but it's a common item in Chinese restaurants where it keeps individual orders piping hot at the table. The 6″-wide bowl of the dish is rather shallow, but large enough for one portion; and the lid stays on tightly and conserves heat. With the lid on, the dish is 5¼″ tall, and its overall diameter is 8½″. One advantage to a metal dish is that you can keep it in the oven before bringing it to the table. So have fun creating your own Chinese "restaurant" with a practical and fanciful serving dish like this one.

Bloomingdale's/ Lion General (978/978c) $12.00

CASSIA PORK

Kwei-Hwa Ro

4 servings

Pork is prepared in this manner in northern China, especially Peking. It is called Cassia Pork because the eggs added are firmly scrambled and broken into bits resembling the Chinese cassia flower. This dish is similar to the Mo-Shu-Ru Pork often served in Chinese restaurants. It contains tiger-lily buds, which, because they are orange and pointed before opening, are called "golden needles." In August they can be gathered in the morning dew from roadside clumps of tiger lilies and dried in the sun or in a warm, turned-off oven.

The dish is often served with "doilies" or thin pancakes.

INGREDIENTS
½ pound fresh lean pork butt
¼ cup dried cloud ears (tree ears)
24 dried tiger-lily buds
¼ cup dried Chinese mushrooms
½ cup canned bamboo shoots
4 eggs
3 tablespoons vegetable oil
1 tablespoon dry sherry
1 tablespoon light soy sauce
1 teaspoon salt
1 teaspoon sugar
1 teaspoon Oriental sesame seed oil

PREPARATION
Cut the pork, half frozen or half thawed, into matchstick-sized shreds, to make 1 cup. Set aside to allow

Continued from preceding page

shreds to reach room temperature before cooking.

Soak the cloud ears, tiger-lily buds, and mushrooms in 1 cup warm water for 30 minutes. Rinse and drain. Cut each tiger-lily bud into 1-inch pieces and the mushrooms and cloud ears into shreds, first removing the stems from the mushrooms.

Beat eggs. Scramble in 1 tablespoon oil for 3 minutes, tossing with spoon and breaking the eggs into little pieces. Remove from the skillet and set aside.

COOKING PROCEDURES
Heat the remaining vegetable oil in a wok or frying pan. Add pork and stir fry quickly for about 3 minutes, or until all pork strips turn grayish. Add dry sherry, soy sauce, salt, and sugar. Mix well. Add the tiger-lily buds, mushrooms, cloud ears, and bamboo shoots. Stir and cook for a minute. Add scrambled eggs. Mix for a few seconds longer. Add sesame seed oil, stir and remove to a serving platter. The dish may be eaten as is or served with doilies.

TIPS
Although it is fun to gather fresh tiger-lily buds, it is time consuming to dry them at home. It is preferable to buy them already dried at Chinese food stores. They are inexpensive and can be kept for many months on the shelf. The taste is as good as freshly gathered ones.

Oriental sesame seed oil is made from toasted sesame seeds. Dark in color and nutty in flavor, it is sold in Oriental and health food stores.

All Chinese, except the Cantonese, refer to "tree ears," rather than "cloud ears." However, in a *Cantonese* grocery, if you ask for "tree ears," you will get something quite different. As most Chinese groceries in this country are Cantonese, we indicate "cloud ears" when we want this specific type of tree ear.

Important: The eggs must be scrambled until dry and flaky.

(From MADAME CHU'S CHINESE COOKING SCHOOL by Grace Zia Chu. Copyright 1975 by Grace Zia Chu. Reprinted by permission of Simon and Schuster.)

Pedestal Cup A:63

At a festive meal this wonderfully decorative blue and white cup would be used to hold some sweet or salty tidbit to nibble on before the meal, some sauce or pickle during the meal, or something sweet like candied ginger served with tea after the meal. It stands 4″ high, is 4″ in diameter and holds ¾ cup. The sturdy 2″-high white pedestal rises out of a dense blue border of abstract leaves, which all point upward, to support the small cup that is made in the traditional rice pattern. Around the rim of the cup, both inside and out, is a soft blue geometric border.

Quong Yuen Shing & Co. $4.75

"Guests are arranged in parties of eight at tables on which there are not cloths. They help themselves with their chopsticks and little porcelain spoons from the dishes placed in the centre of the tables. When the host would compliment a guest, he selects a tidbit with his own chopsticks and puts it into the guest's bowl and the guest does the same in return. Guests also exchange elegant extracts in this manner. Those to the manner born can do wonders with chopsticks. A certain courtier was so expert that once a grain of rice fell from the Emperor's lips he caught it between his chopsticks as it fell. For this feat he was appointed to high office."

John Chinaman At Home: Sketches of Men, Manners and Things in China *by Reverend E. J. Hardy. Scribners, 1905.*

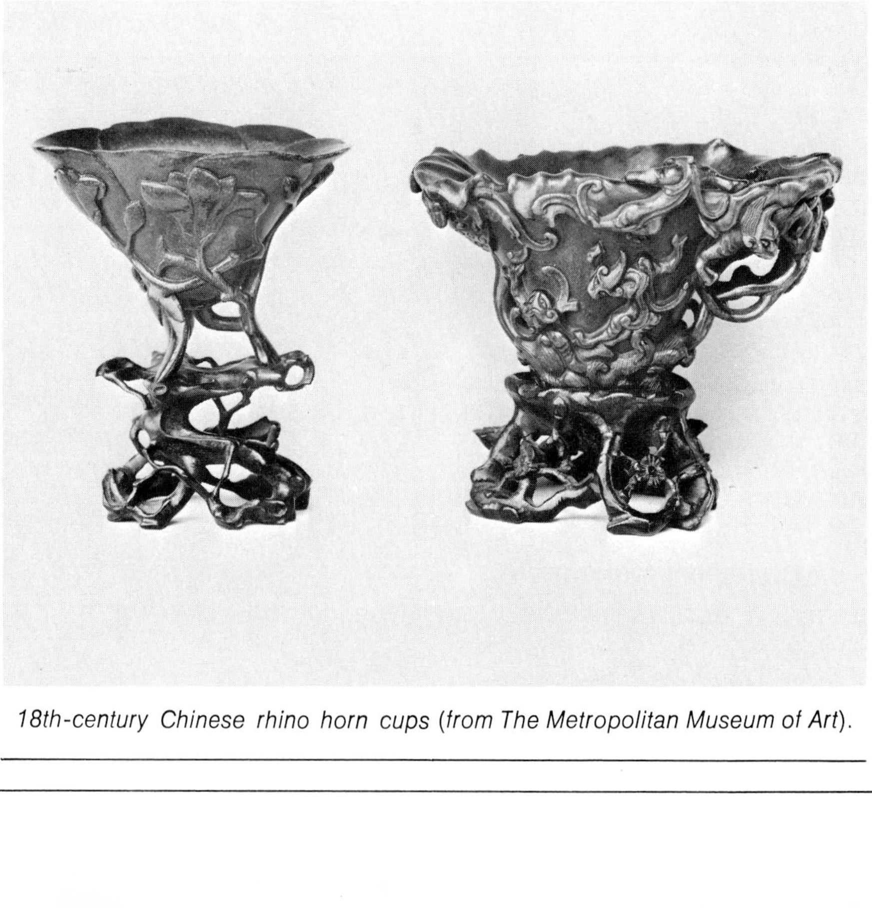

18th-century Chinese rhino horn cups (from The Metropolitan Museum of Art).

The Precious Drink of Tea

According to the modern Chinese scholar Lin Yutang, tea has been a beverage in China since the year 300 A.D. Today, it is the most common and popular drink of the country, where it is consumed before, after and between meals—and always hot—to quench the thirst or simply to pass the time with friends or colleagues. However, unlike the custom promulgated in Western restaurants, the Chinese prefer soup or wine with their meals.

The Chinese have attributed the most surprising qualities to tea. In the eighth century Lu Yu wrote: "Tea tempers the spirits, calms and harmonises the mind; it arouses thought and prevents drowsiness, lightens and refreshes the body, and clears the perceptive faculties." And its popularity reinforces these claims.

There are hundreds of varieties of tea, which can be roughly classified into three groups, with other variations: green teas; black, or fermented, teas (which the Chinese more accurately call "red" from the coppery color of the leaves and brew); and semi-fermented oolong teas. The best teas are green and black. Both are made from the most tender leaves around the bud at the end of a stem. Essentially, green tea leaves are simply dried. But to ferment tea, the leaves are partially dried and rolled until the juice is exposed and oxidized. They are then put on cool tables to wilt and finally fired over charcoal. Green, black or, especially, oolong teas can also be scented with flowers, such as narcissus, rose, jasmine, chrysanthemum, litchi or gardenia, depending on the type of tea used. Or they may be smoked like lapsang-souchong, a black, heavy tea from Hunan which is more popular in the West than it is in China. Some of the specific favorites have poetic and fanciful names. Dragon Well and Cloud Mist, for instance, are some of the most highly prized green teas. And Fukien cliff tea, often called "the iron goddess of mercy," is the most well-known in the oolong family.

Thea sinensis, which produces all this liquid delight, is an evergreen shrub that can tower 30 feet but is kept bushy by pruning. It thrives in a warm, damp climate on high land that is otherwise poor for farming. The higher the land elevation, the more tender are the leaves of the plant. The British took over the southern Chinese name for the beverage, "tay," later altering the pronunciation to the one we know today.

To save fuel, concentrated tea is often made in the mornings and hot water is stored in a family thermos to mix with the concentrate, as needed. But for a special friend or a special occasion some rare and wonderful tasting tea will be freshly made—and served straight. No sugar, milk or lemon is used in tea, with the exception of chrysanthemum flower tea, which the Cantonese sweeten with a piece of rock candy. And don't be shy about making a little noise when you drink; the Chinese habitually inhale a little air as they drink tea to cool it.

Clay Teapot with Strainer A:64

The unglazed, red-brown clay and classic shape of this charming little teapot lend it a look of timelessness. In keeping with its artful form, a bamboo handle arches gracefully over the pot and grasps it through a clay loop on either side. A narrow, unglazed cup, perforated with rows of holes from top to bottom, slips inside the pot to hold and strain out the tea leaves once the tea is brewed. With this design you can easily control the strength of each brew and quickly dispose of the spent leaves. The pot is 4½″ high to the rim and almost 4″ across the top. It holds 3 cups, a perfect size if you are serving tea for two —or simply for yourself. If you prefer, it is available in a smaller and a larger size as well.

Eur-Asian Imports (B-787) $4.00

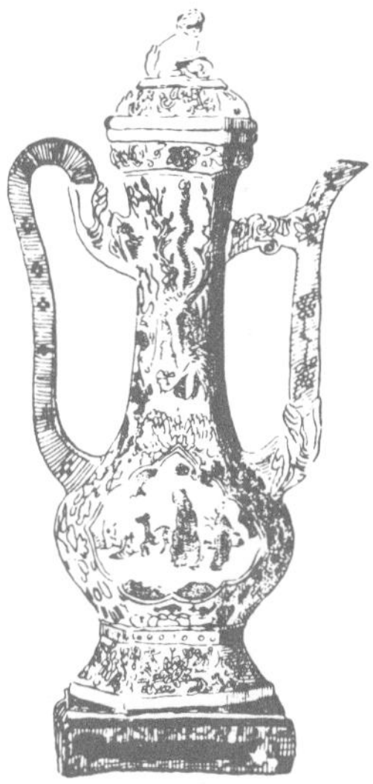

"China tea, with its hundreds of varieties, is a delightful beverage. It not only quenches thirst, including thirst for quarrels, but also cools temper, though it is drunk hot. . . ."

Musings of A Chinese Gourmet *by F. T. Cheng. Hutchinson, 1954.*

Small Earthenware Teapot A:65

When it's tea for two, this little reddish-brown earthenware pot will do quite nicely. It's only 4″ tall, with the lid, and 5″ wide at its fullest; and it holds 1¾ cups. The pot comes from the province of Fukien, where people like their tea very strong, but in small amounts—almost like a cup of espresso. Hence the small size of the pot. We find it irresistible, as much for the forthright loop of the handle and the perfectly corresponding spout as for the appealing water buffalo that reclines on the lid, forming its handle. The Chinese characters on one side describe the cherry blossoms on the other.

Kung's Trading Co., Ltd. $4.50

"The secret of good tea lies in the water, which should be taken from a good spring. . . . When water is new it is raw. Aged water is sweet. . . . If the leaves are tightly curled the flavor will be subdued. . . . When you come to brew the tea, bring the water to the boil over a low fire. Do not boil it too much, or the water will change flavor (the best point at which to stop is when tiny bubbles called 'crab's eyes' appear to stream from the sides of the pot). Drink a cup immediately, then cover the pot. The flavour will change again."

Yuan Mei (1716–1799)

Rice Pattern Teapot A:66

A translucent pattern of rice grains in familiar blue and white porcelain give this tea pot a delicate lacy appearance. The rice pattern effect is achieved by simply making indentations in the clay before it is glazed and fired so that light will penetrate through the depressions. This fairly straight-sided pot has a richly decorated base of dark blue leaves. It stands 6″ high, is 5″ wide and has a capacity of 3 cups—an ideal size for the average family. Interior perforations at the base of the pouring spout keep tea leaves inside the pot—if you stick to the large-leafed China teas. (With smaller-leafed Ceylon and Indian teas you will have to strain the tea again if you are concerned about having leaves in your cup.) Most important, the loveliness of the pot should enhance your total enjoyment of the brew, and that can be quite considerable. To quote Emperor Chien Luing, "You can taste and feel, but not describe, the exquisite state of repose produced by tea, that precious drink which drives away the five causes of sorrow."

Continental Crafts Co., Inc. (CH 425) $8.00

In a discussion of the merits of Chinese tea-brewing methods, Sir Kenelme Digby Kt. (in his book of 1671) advises the English that: "In these parts . . . we let the hot water remain too long soaking upon the Tea, which makes it extract into itself the earthy parts of the herb. The water is to remain upon it, no longer than while you can say the Miserere *Psalm very leisurely. . . . Thus you have only the spiritual parts of the Tea, which is much more active, penetrative and friendly to nature. You may for this regard take a little more of the herb; about one drachm of Tea will serve for a pint of water; which makes three ordinary draughts."*

Rice Pattern Tea Cup and Saucer A:67

In pristine blue and white, this porcelain tea cup and saucer represent an interesting fusion of old and new. The delicate china set, decorated with the traditional pattern of translucent rice grains, has been cast in Western shapes—a large cup with a handle and a matching saucer. This is the result of long contact with tea drinking Westerners, as well as of the enormous popularity of the rice pattern. The broad-bowled tea cup—3½″ across and 2″ deep—sits on a 5½″-wide saucer. If you like a large cup of tea, as many Chinese do, you may find this cup more comfortable than the traditional, small, handleless version. And, of course, with this shape you can just as easily use it for coffee (pardon the word).

Continental Crafts Co., Inc. (CH 408) $4.00

"Tea has a myriad of shapes. If I may speak vulgarly and rashly, tea may shrink and crinkle like a Mongol's boots. Or it may look like the dewlap of a wild ox, some sharp, some curling as the eaves of a house. It can look like a mushroom in whirling flight just as clouds do when they float out from behind a mountain peak. Its leaves can swell and leap as if they

were being lightly tossed on wind-disturbed water. Others will look like clay, soft and malleable, prepared for the hand of the potter and will be as clear and pure as if filtered through wood. Still others will twist and turn like the rivulets carved out by a violent rain on newly tilled fields. Those are the very finest of teas."

Classic of Tea, *translated by Francis Ross Carpenter. Little, Brown & Co., 1974.*

Porcelain Tea Cup A:68

This exceptionally fine ivory-colored porcelain tea cup is decorated with a design of cranes and fish in a subtle shade of blue-gray. Had the artist been Cantonese the crane might have been replaced by the indigenous heron; but, in either case, both birds represent longevity and happiness. The cup is 3″ in diameter, 1¾″ deep, and has a simple border design around its rim in the same soft blue-gray color. When it is full of hot tea, pick up and hold the cup around the raised rim on which it sits to avoid burning your fingers. The small, handleless type of cup is typical of any you might find in Chinese restaurants across America, but it is not the Chinese custom to drink tea throughout the meal, as you might think. Light, palate-cleansing soups are served between courses to quench thirst; tea is drunk at the beginning and end of the meal, without sugar, milk or lemon.

Quong Yuen Shing & Co. **$0.85**

"Tea is also used as part of the presents to be sent to the family of the girl in engagements. It is used because the tea plant would not grow if moved from one place to another. Seeds have to be employed, if one wants to grow tea. This peculiar nature of the tea plant suggests loyalty, oneness, and abidingness—the best symbols of a lasting engagement, preliminary to matrimony. Hence to say that a girl has accepted tea from another means that she is engaged, and to say that she has spilt tea means that she has lost her fiancé. *Hence also a girl drinking tea would in the old days take care not to have it upset, a bad omen on a special occasion."*

Musing of a Chinese Gourmet *by F. T. Cheng. Hutchinson, 1954.*

Insulated Tea Basket A:69

If you're a tea drinker and a picnic lover, you may not want to dine *al fresco* without this unusual tea set. The idea is simple enough: tea for two, to go. A covered teapot and two cups nestle in one of the prettiest baskets we've seen. Closed so that its contents are concealed, the basket looks like an elegant summer handbag of tightly-woven bamboo strips with decorative latch, hinges and a double handle of silvery metal in imaginative shapes. The latch, for example, is in the form of a tiny curved fish. Inside is a Chinese version of a vacuum bottle. Both pot and cups are imbedded in a thick, cushioned layer of insulation that will keep the tea hot for as long as 24 hours if the pot is heated with boiling water before it is filled with tea. The fabric lining is a wondrously colored Chinese cotton print of pink dogwood blossoms, peonies and blue heart-shaped flowers and—if we're not mistaken—exploding fireworks, against a bright red background. In keeping with its fancy container, the 6-cup teapot is gold, except for a graceful white panel on each side. Stalking across one panel is an orange, green and gold dragon, and flying across the other is an orange, green, plum and gold phoenix—symbols of power and long life. The cups match the pot, but with less gold, and, like it, they are white inside. The flat lid fits the pot snugly and can be lifted by slipping your fingers into two depressions made for that purpose. Incongruous in this context is the teapot's handle, made of two lengths of bent wire wrapped in red plastic. With that exception, it's a delight.

Oriental Country Store **$25.00**

An Indian saint traveling in China is often credited with creating the first tea plant. In one version of the legend, described by Lafcadio Hearn in Some Chinese Ghosts (1887), *the saint lapsed into a lustful revery while meditating. Penitent, he severed his eyelids, flung them away and resumed an attitude of profound meditation. When the new day began, he found that his eyes were intact. "In vain he looked for the severed lids that he had flung upon the ground; they had mysteriously van-*

Continued from preceding page

ished. But lo! there where he had cast them two wondrous shrubs were growing with dainty leaflets eyelid-shaped, and snowy buds just opening to the East." Thus, the magical tea plant.

Wine Cup A:70

Few wine cups are as inviting as this diminutive one of porcelain. Inside, the cup is bright white; on the outside, in sharp contrast, a field of dark blue is scattered with bright mauve and yellow flowers with green leaves. Only 2″ across and 1″ deep, the cup holds a mere thimbleful of wine by Western standards. But this is considered a perfectly adequate size for a wine cup in China where people are traditionally moderate in their drinking habits. This attitude toward drinking displays the restraint and concern for balance that permeate Chinese thought and behavior. Wine is never taken alone since intoxication is frowned upon. It is usually drunk only at the beginning of the meal with *dim sum* (steamed dumplings) or some other hors d'oeuvre or cold dishes. The richer and stronger dishes of the rest of the meal are considered likely to alter the taste of both the wine and the food, which, like all tastes in Chinese eating, are meant to be fully appreciated. Banquets are the exception, however; wine usually accompanies every course of these great meals. The most commonly drunk Chinese wine is rice wine, which tastes like mild, dry sherry and is called yellow wine because it is sometimes amber colored. Wine is served warm—not too hot or too cold, since cold drinks are considered bad for one's health. Although it may seem innocuous, and it is, relatively speaking, the wine reacts quickly because it is warmed, and because such a small cupful is sometimes swallowed in one gulp. As the Chinese say, "Kan-pei" (bottoms up).

Quong Yuen Shing & Co. $1.00

Three-Tiered Lunch Box A:71

An example of Chinese ingenuity is this triple-tiered lunch box. Florence Lin, a well-known cooking expert, says that when she was in school, her nurse would bring her one like it at mealtime. However, because the lunch box is made of aluminum, it will not hold heat for long. So unless you have a burner and a pot of hot water to heat the lunch box in, plan on having a cold meal. As the Chinese use it, rice goes in the bottom section, a meat dish in the middle one, and vegetables in the top. Covering the lunch box is a domed lid that becomes a rice bowl when turned upside down. A second inside lid doubles as a plate and a spoon is tucked above it. The handle of the lunch box extends down its sides and, when flipped into place, clamps the sections tightly together. The bottom container is about 3¼″ deep, 4¾″ across and holds a full quart. Those above it are 2½″ deep, and the whole lunch box, fully assembled, is just over a foot high. For those with a large appetite, a four-tiered lunch box can also be obtained.

Oriental Country Store $6.50

The Cooking of Korea

Because Korea is contiguous to northern China and lies just west of Japan (by which it was at one time dominated), it has become commonplace to say that Korean cooking, too, falls between the cuisines of its two more powerful neighbors. There's enough truth in that cliché to make it endure, but also enough difference between the countries to give Korean cooking an individual flavor. Commonly used ingredients include celery cabbage, soy sauce, scallions, sugar, seaweed and dry salted fish. Those that are used by Koreans in notable amounts are sesame seeds and sesame seed oil, garlic, hot red chiles, and a lot of beef. It is true to say that much Korean cooking developed in response to bitterly raw winters.

Take *kim chee,* for example, the ubiquitous fire-hot pickle whose flavor may alienate the foreigner but brings a warm flush to the skin of the Korean. *Kim chee* of some kind is served at every meal, providing in one dish a condiment, a salad and a cooked vegetable. Every November, winter *kim chee* is made in such extensive quantities that Korean businesses advance their workers a month's salary to buy the ingredients: celery cabbage, turnips, garlic, ginger, hot chiles, onions and, perhaps, meat or fish. The fresh pickle is stored in crocks with brine and buried underground so that it will not freeze during the hard winter months.

Soups and stews are popular in Korea, as one would expect in a nation whose winter climate is so relentless. One notable soup, *sinsul-lo,* is prepared at the table in an "angel pot," similar to the Chinese hot pot. Partially cooked foods are arranged in a large bowl with a central chimney which is then set over coals. Hot broth is poured over them at the table where the cooking is completed. Another dish cooked at the table is *pul ko-kee:* strips of thinly-sliced beef are marinated in a mixture of soy sauce, sugar, garlic, scallions and ground roasted sesame seeds and then cooked on a table-top grill similar to the *hibachi.* Chicken, pork or shrimp may also be grilled in this manner. In Korean grill-house restaurants, guests pick up strips of meat with their chopsticks and lay them on racks over the glowing coals. When the meat is seared on both sides, it is dipped in a bowl of soy sauce and eaten with plenty of rice and *kim chee.*

But the most famous food of Korea is part medicine, part tea, part sexual panacea. We mean, of course, the venerable ginseng, a bifurcated root which suggests, by its shape, the human form, and which is reputed to be a cure for every ailment from psoriasis to diabetes. Helpful as these curative powers are, however, ginseng has retained its popularity through the centuries not because it cures rashes or flatulence, but because it is supposed to be a cure for impotence. If you are interested, take a look at our simple earthenware ginseng pot, made for brewing a hot and stimulating ginseng tea.

Clay Bowl A:72

Korean earthenware, unlike that of the Japanese, is designed first for utility and then aesthetics. Take, for example, this dark brown earthenware bowl. It is quite plain, slightly flared toward the top, and has a simple glaze and texture. An all-purpose bowl, it will keep food warm in the oven and can then be brought to the table. Use it for everything from soups to vegetables and rice dishes. Chicken broth with *mandoo* is especially delicious. *Mandoo* are dumplings filled with a mixture of ground beef, ground roasted sesame seeds, soy sauce, garlic, mushrooms, scallions, celery cabbage and bean sprouts. Our Korean bowl is about 7½″ in diameter, 3″ deep and holds 5 cups.

Sam Bok Grocery **$4.50**

Genghis Khan Grill A:73

A legacy of Mongolia that has made its way to Korea is the Genghis Khan or Mongolian fire grill. In Korea, thin slices of steak are marinated in a mixture of toasted, ground sesame seeds, soy sauce, sugar, garlic, scallions and hot red chile. They are then laid on sizzling-hot broilers such as this one. In the East, the broilers get their heat from table-top, charcoal-filled stoves called *hwa ru,* that are similar to *hibachis,* but in your kitchen, believe it or not, they can go right over the burner of your stove. No fat or marinade will drip through the holes or catch fire because a carefully-constructed system of indentations drains liquids into a trough that runs around the circumference of the grill. The broiler is a heavy dome of cast iron, 10″ in diameter, with small handles of the same material protruding from either side. Watch those handles: they are going to get hot! And, if you are cooking indoors, always make sure the room is extremely well ventilated because charcoal releases carbon monoxide.

Bloomingdale's **$7.50**

Ginseng Pot A:74

Ginseng does not serve ordinary dietary needs, but some people may consider it a necessity. This pot was made to brew Korean ginseng root—one of those ancient Oriental cure-alls that has gained a worldwide reputation as an aphrodisiac. Devotees, who believe this mysterious root can cure all ailments from flu to depression, say its greatest virtue is in giving endurance to gentlemen. When unearthed, a well-aged root may actually resemble a human body with head, arms, torso and legs. Thus, the Chinese called it "ginseng" or "manroot." Korea produces one of the two most sought after varieties. An old root of human form may command thousands of dollars, but the more humble variety sells for around $7 to $15 an ounce. This earthenware pot has a full belly, a top that tapers inward and a long 5″ handle. It is 5″ high and 6½″ at its widest. Both the bowl and handle are glazed beige and have a rough texture. If you want to try some ginseng yourself, throw a piece of the root into a ginseng pot full of water, and cover. Then set the pot in a pan of water and slowly simmer for an hour or so. Some say ginseng tastes earthy and wildly bitter, similar to a white radish; but opinion varies. See what you think.

Sam Bok Grocery **$3.95**

The Two French Kitchens

by Jacques Pépin

I come from the Lyons area, from a family of restaurateurs. My mother is a fine cook, who has deliberately kept her repertoire small so that every dish she makes is perfect. That is typical of French *cuisine de famille*, or home cooking, and I would say that most people cook in this simple way, except perhaps when they are having company. Even then, they can buy many of the most complicated dishes. Elaborate food is prepared primarily in wealthy homes that have a kitchen staff, or in restaurants.

Naturally, for the fairly simple fare that we eat at home, it is not necessary to have an elaborate *batterie de cuisine*. In fact with few exceptions, the kitchen in a French home is poorly equipped by American standards. There are few machines, since small appliances are only now coming into fashion; but you would find a few knives, spoons, bowls, a food mill, pots and a reliable though modest stove. Any copper pots would most likely have been inherited from parents or grandparents, and they would be treasured.

Above all, the French housewife is eminently practical and willing to make do by putting a few pieces of equipment to a number of uses. She will own at least one deep, straight-sided pot which she calls a *fait-tout* (does everything) because it does just that. Covered, it is a casserole; uncovered, a sauté pan; it need not be made of tin-lined copper, though it should be of a metal that conducts heat well and is heavy enough to prevent scorching. And, of course, she will have one or two skillets and a few saucepans. Also, she will probably have a good carbon-steel knife, sharpened over and over again on a steel. Whatever she lacks, she will improvise: a wine bottle, for example, makes a suitable rolling pin, and a *fait-tout* can be made into the bottom part of a double boiler. Yet she will not compromise when it comes to ingredients.

Everything made by a French cook at home will contain only the highest quality ingredients. And there are certain things like fresh mayonnaise and fresh produce for which there can be no store-bought, prepared substitutes. But if the French cook can't do better in her kitchen than the professional can at his shop or bakery, she doesn't try. In this she is, again, eminently practical, and also fortunate because she can rely on her local *boulangerie* (bread store), *charcuterie* (cold cut and sausage shop) and *pâtisserie* (pastry shop) for first-rate products. There is no real need for her to bake croissants, a pâté or a baba unless she really wants to. The American woman, on the other hand, lives with different traditions. She can't simply stop around the corner to buy French breads, a superb pâté or a fancy dessert. To have them, she must meet the challenge of making them herself, which she is learning to do very well.

Restaurant kitchens in France, of course, are another matter. When I cook as a professional, I take for granted a great many types of equipment—as well as a *brigade de cuisine* (kitchen team)—which I would not expect to find in my mother's house. In a large restaurant I know that the *garde-manger* (cold food cook) will be at his station, preparing salads and cold sauces. The *pâtissier* (pastry cook) will be at his board, rolling pastry or whipping fillings. The *poissonnier* (fish cook), the *saucier* (sauce cook) and the *rotisseur* (broiler cook)

Churning butter, one of France's notable products.

The journalist George Augustus Sala visited an unusual section of the market, Les Halles: "a double line of stalls heaped high with the most astonishing array of cooked foods. . . . Fish flesh, fowl, vegetables, fruit, pastry, confectionery and cheese are all represented here, ready cooked, but cold, and arranged not on plates or dishes, but on . . . old newspapers. Imagine one pile, consisting of the leg of a partridge, the remnants of an omelette, the tail of a fried sole, two ribs of a jugged hare, a spoonful of haricot beans, a scrap of filet, a cut pear, a handful of salad, a slice of tomato, and a dab of jelly. . . . The pile consti-

tutes a portion . . . there are piles here to suit all pockets. Are your funds at a very low ebb, indeed? On that scrap of the Figaro you will find a hard-boiled egg, the gizard of a fowl, two pickled gherkins, and a macaroon. . . . The fragments which form the 'jewellery' of the Halles Centrales are brought down . . . by the garçons of the great Boulevard restaurants. . . . The purchasers are the Quiet Poor, the people who are too ashamed to beg . . ."

Paris Herself Again *by George Augustus Sala, 1880. From* The Great Travelers *edited by Milton Rugoff. Simon & Schuster, 1960.*

A chef at work.

will be attending to their own jobs. To say nothing of a whole crew of *commis* (kitchen assistants), all the way down to the apprentices at the bottom of the pecking order who peel or chop vegetables, sweep up and take out the garbage. I was 13½ years old when I started, which was typical, at the time, and it took a year to start working at a stove, learning first the simple things like cooking vegetables and consommé. Then, every pan in the kitchen was made of copper.

All of these specialists in a kitchen have their own highly professional equipment that has been developed over the centuries. They have all kinds of knives, truffle cutters, sieves of all shapes, *terrines*, *pâté* molds, every type of copper or other heavy metal pan, cake molds of every description; and many of these things will be of colossal size. Since the American family cook attempts feats of cuisine, which a French housewife can avoid, she is lucky that so much of this specialized equipment has recently been adapted to the smaller stoves of private homes. Now, too, it is made of hardy new materials: *tamis* (sieves) of brass wire rather than horsehair, lighter weight aluminum- or stainless-steel pans rather than copper, where appropriate.

Basically, French cooking stems from home cooking and rests on the perfection of simple skills. At home, the professional chef makes himself an omelet, a chop and a salad dressed with a perfect vinaigrette. Escoffier himself was opposed to excessive complication of cooking. At formal banquets, we admire elaborate composed dishes, but basically all Frenchmen love simple cooking, and it is wrong to think that a dish must be complicated and take forever to prepare to be good. Every course does not demand hours of preparation. To end a meal with fruit and cheese or, at the most, some poached fruit or a caramel custard rather than an elaborate pastry is in excellent taste. Above all, a French meal should be balanced, and prepared and presented with care. Good planning, the right ingredients and a few pieces of excellent equipment are all that is needed for most purposes. But, if you are lucky enough to have a full complement of kitchen equipment, then there is nothing that you cannot do in the world of French cuisine.

When I am giving cooking demonstrations, I have often noticed that people are most interested in watching me chop an onion, whip egg whites or roll out some pastry: the most basic cooking techniques. In this they are quite correct, because the secret of the best cuisine lies in the perfection of the simplest steps rather than in complicated procedures. Once those are understood, all the rest follows.

The Cuisine of France

An author who spent her childhood in the hills above Nice wrote reverently of "a delicious cream of vegetable soup that would have done honor to a private house in the French provinces before the war of 1870." She herself was born in this century, but evidently the halcyon time before the Franco-Prussian war represented to her the moment in time when France reached her gastronomic peak. Perhaps the old days were better; we'll never know. But it is safe to say that at this moment the best food of France, simple or complex, does honor to anyone's palate.

French cooking is based on a regard for quality. Only the finest and the freshest will do. It is better to dine on a length of bread and a piece of honest cheese than to settle for a second-rate *filet de boeuf*

Continued from preceding page

(fillet of beef) napped in *sauce bordelaise* (a red wine sauce). If the meat is worthy of the sauce, fine; but a sauce is meant to enhance a basic ingredient, not to mask it. Fortunately, French cooks—and diners—can depend on the best of basics. The sheer diversity and abundance is staggering—marbled beef from Burgundy, golden cream from Normandy, lobsters and oysters from Brittany's cold Atlantic waters, red mullet from the mild Mediterranean. In a country smaller than Texas there are eleven distinct regional cuisines; you may choose among robust *choucroûte* (sauerkraut) or refined *foie gras* (goose liver) from Alsace, delicate river trout from Touraine, truffled pâté from the Bordeaux region; all very different tastes, all part of French cooking.

Eating habits are changing slowly. Fewer people now come home to a large midday dinner, and lighter meals are more and more the fashion. But demand for the best remains, especially in *la nouvelle cuisine* (new cuisine) that includes *cuisine minceur* (slimming cuisine), exquisite food made with fewer fattening ingredients and frills.

In many ways, Americans are freer in their approach to French cooking than the French themselves. There, fine cuisine is usually dominated by two groups: male professionals and mothers of families. Each approaches food in a different manner; each is traditional and in many ways inflexible.

Both schools turn out superb food, but there is a difference. The master chef Fernand Point said that although he greatly relished his sister-in-law's excellent bourgeois cooking, it was "another thing," a style of cooking that he himself did not do, and in which he would never dream of interfering. Apparently, she had no qualms about serving him the food she fed her family, nor would she ever venture into his realm of *grande cuisine*.

Americans don't feel that restraint. The pioneer spirit, Yankee ingenuity, or sheer bullheadedness tell us that we can do what we set our minds to; if our aspirations reach to the Everests of the classic repertoire, we pitch in and try. Although we may not plant the flag at the very pinnacle, we at least reach some of the higher foothills. Unhampered by strictures of what we should and shouldn't attempt, we often achieve cuisine of delicacy and elegance. What's more, we enjoy cooking it, and our happy friends delight in eating it.

Dining in France as depicted by an artist in 1883.

"Mme Darblay, famous for her beans."

Emma Bovary's introduction to opulence . . . and discontent: "As soon as Emma entered the room, she felt herself enveloped in a gust of warm air which smelled of flowers, fine linen, roast meat, and truffles. The flames of the candles in the sconces rose. . . . The cut-crystal lustres, misted over with a dull sheen of moisture, gave back a dull glow. There were bunches of flowers . . . and on the wide-bordered plates, the napkins, in the form of Bishops' mitres, held small oval rolls in the yawning gap beween their folds. The red claws of lobsters hung over the china rims of dishes. Luscious fruit, set in open baskets, stood piled on beds of moss. The quails were served with all their plumage. The cloud of steam rose to the ceiling."

Madame Bovary *by Gustave Flaubert, translated by Gerard Hopkins. Oxford University Press, 1949.*

Cutting and Mixing Equipment

French cooks who comb the early morning markets, fiercely bargaining with stall-keepers for the freshest, sweetest carrots and the palest, close-grained veal, wouldn't dream of submitting their tender finds to the mercies of inferior kitchen implements. They believe that fine food demands respect at every stage of handling, from preliminary slicing to final presentation.

A housewife in modest circumstances may have few utensils in her kitchen, but they will be the best she can afford, and chosen with an eye not only to utility but to durability. Choosing a new mortar and pestle is a serious business; if possible, they should be as sturdy and as handsome as the set *maman* bequeathed to her oldest daughter. They should serve the housewife well, and she in turn will pass them on to her daughter, as a link with the warm kitchen of her girlhood home. In addition, this housewife would have, at the least, a few fine knives (carefully wiped after each use), a strong sieve or two with different meshes, a food mill, a peppermill, of course, and perhaps a *lardoir* (larding needle). If she lives near Normandy or Bresse, where the finest chickens in the world are raised, she would probably have a *batte* (pounder) for carefully flattening *suprêmes* (chicken breasts) or whole butterflied chickens. She will add to her supply of tools only as the need arises.

The same holds true for the professional chef. He chooses only what he needs, and of the finest quality he can afford to last his working life. In his case, however, a *mandoline*, food processor, truffle cutters and a balloon whip and copper bowl for egg whites will also be obligatory.

Mortar and Pestle B:1

Aïoli (a garlicky mayonnaise) is one of the taste treats of the Provençal kitchen. To make it, garlic is first ground to a paste in a mortar, sometimes with a few bread crumbs to give it body. Then egg yolks are worked in one at a time, and finally olive oil and seasonings are added. The sauce is an essential accompaniment to *bourride* (a hearty fish soup) and is also served with plain, hot or cold boiled fish, or used like mayonnaise with vegetables. This French mortar of white, non-porous porcelain is perfect for mashing small amounts of any food, including garlic, because it will absorb no flavors. The mortar is 2⅝″ deep and 4¾″ in diameter at the inside rim, ample enough to make grinding easy. Both the mortar and pestle are highly glazed except on the exterior bottom of the mortar and the lower half of the pestle where a rougher surface helps to prevent slipping and to grind food. The well-formed spout makes it easy to pour your *aïoli* right into a serving dish; you might even be tempted to carry the graceful mortar right to the table.

Schiller & Asmus, Inc. (P9001-13) **$20.00**

AÏOLI MÉNAGÈRE

Garlic-Flavored Mayonnaise

Aïoli ménagère (home style) is made with the addition of a boiled potato to the classic ingredients, which adds a wonderful texture to the sauce. It can be most successfully achieved if all the ingredients are at room temperature.

4 large cloves garlic (1 ounce)
1 medium-sized baking potato, boiled, peeled and broken with a fork
1 egg yolk
Pinch salt
½ cup olive oil
Lemon juice
Cold water

Crush the garlic to a paste in a mortar and pestle. Add the potato and blend in thoroughly. Blend in the egg yolk and salt, then add the olive oil in a slow stream, all the while beating very rapidly with the pestle, and squeezing in a little lemon juice from time to time. Beat in a little cold water at the end to keep the *aïoli* from separating. If it does separate, beat in another egg yolk.

Serve with *bourride,* boiled salt cod, cold meats or a *provençal* platter comprised of such things as cold vegetables, snails, salt cod, sea snails, shrimp, cold meats and hard boiled eggs.

Yield: approximately 2 cups.

(Courtesy of Robert Renaud, Le Jacques Coeur Restaurant, New York City.)

Paring Knife B:2

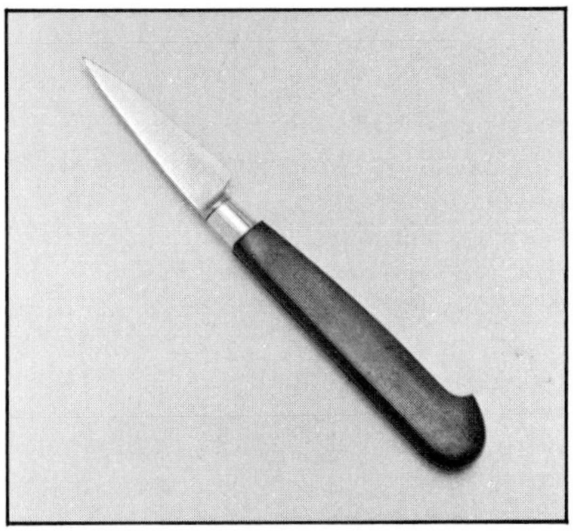

To turn a humdrum tomato into a full-blossomed rose, or the peel of an orange into a scallop-edged cup to garnish a duck *à l'orange* takes practical skill and a very sharp paring knife (*couteau d'office*). This knife

Continued from preceding page

from one of the Sabatier licensees would be admirably suited to any decorative job. The 2″-long, high-carbon steel blade is hard enough to hold the sharpest edge and make quick turns and twists. A straight, well-balanced handle of very hard, tough rubber completely encases the tang. From tip to end of grip the knife measures 6⅝″.

Rowoco Inc. (3102) $3.50

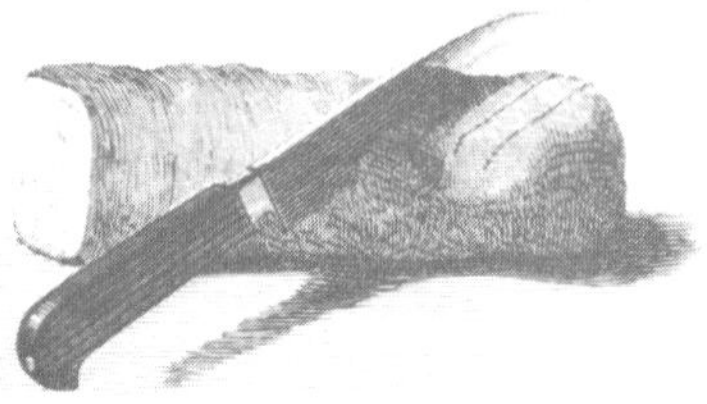

Cutting slits in andouillette *before it is cooked.*

Chef's Knife B:3

Incised on the blade of this chef's knife is a K topped by a crown, the trademark of Sabatier Jeune, perhaps the best of the dozen or more licensees of the Sabatier name. A chef's knife is meant for chopping and must be strong, well-balanced and of top quality to perform cleanly and efficiently. Countless French sauces, soups and meat dishes call for a *mirepoix* (a mixture of finely diced vegetables, such as carrots, onions, leeks and celery); and the need for chopped tomatoes, parsley and shallots in the French kitchen is endless. No knife is better equipped to deal with chopping tasks than this one. Its blade is made of heavy carbon steel that will hold a fine edge. The cutting edge is curved so you can rock the knife up and down to chop without having to lift it completely with each stroke, and the blade is wide at the narrow handle so you can grip the knife comfortably without rapping your fingers on the cutting surface as you work. The thickened portion, or bolster at the back of the blade keeps your hand from riding forward. In addition, a full tang all the way through the handle helps to counter vibrations from the chopping and adds weight to the handle so the knife will balance well. A typical French feature of this knife is its collar, or extension of the blade that caps the rosewood handle. The knife is so handy you might want more than one size: you can choose between this 17⅛″ length with a 12″ blade, or others with blade lengths of 4″, 6″, 8″ and 10″.

B.I.A. Cordon Bleu, Inc. (K968/30) $25.00

Butcher Knife B:4

From Sabatier Jeune comes a stellar butcher's knife for cutting any raw meat. The highly-finished, 12″-long carbon-steel blade would make short work of cutting boneless beef for a *boeuf bourguignonne* (beef stew with red wine) or veal for a *blanquette de veau* (a veal ragoût with an egg-rich white sauce). Because the knife is designed for cutting rather than chopping, it has a half rather than a full tang and the blade is almost flat, except at the tip. The unfinished wood handle is thick and contoured for a sure grip. A shoulder next to the blade acts to cushion the hand and increase leverage when cutting. The knife measures 17″ long overall and is 2⅜″ wide.

E. Dehillerin (568) $10.00

Boning Knife B:5

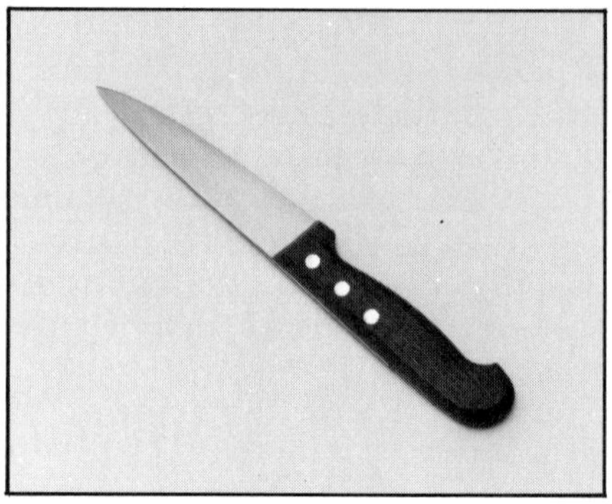

Called a blooding knife by its manufacturer, this knife has an extremely rigid stainless-steel blade and a sharp point for letting blood out of veins. But it is also perfectly suited to boning meats and is preferred by some chefs who find it superior to the more typical, narrow- and curve-bladed, flexible boners. The split-resistant rosewood handle is shaped like that of a standard butcher's knife with a full, contoured grip and protective shoulder next to the blade. Three closely spaced brass rivets secure the partial tang to the handle. The knife is 10½″ long overall, and the blade is 5¼″ long and 1″ wide.

Le Roi de la Coupe (3) $10.00

Fillet of Sole Knife B:6

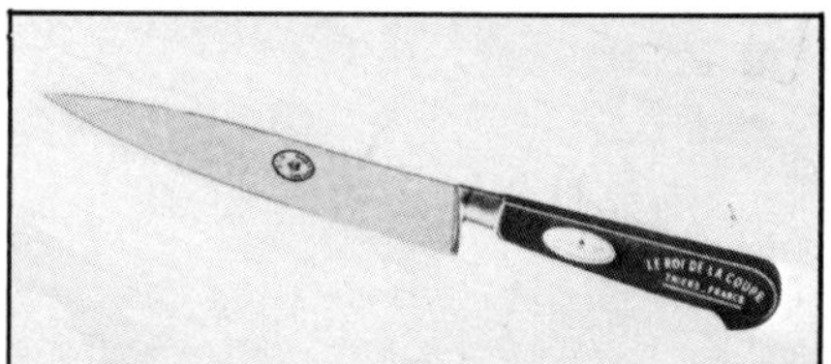

There are at least 40 simple to elegant ways suggested by Escoffier to prepare boned fillet of sole. Most often we buy sole already filleted, but there are other flat fish in the sole family like flounder for which a sharp, thin, flexible blade is valuable. This knife's 6″-long, stainless-steel blade, rigid at its base for firm hand control but tapering to a flexible, sharply-pointed tip for easy maneuvering, is admirably suited to the task. Its sturdy, black plastic handle is dishwasher safe. The knife measures 10¼″ long overall.

Le Roi de la Coupe (22) $10.00

Mandoline B:7

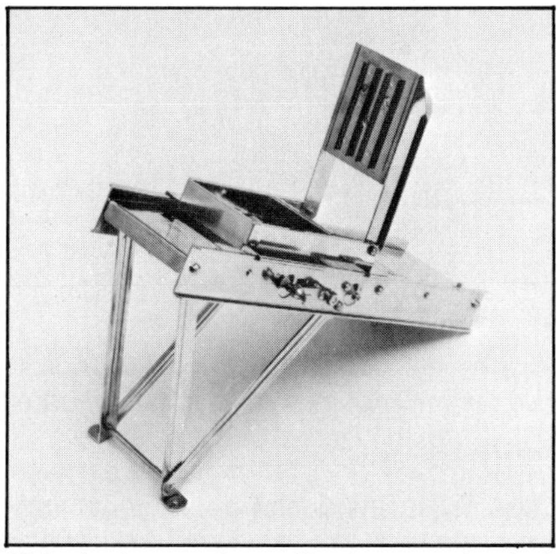

This instrument won't play music, but its myriad uses enable French chefs to compose culinary masterpieces. A standby of the professional kitchen, the mandoline will cut with lightning speed thin potato slices for a perfect *pommes Anna* (a decorative potato cake), rippled slices of beets, thin julienne strips of celery root, or thicker strips of potato for french fries. By using the ripple-edged blade, you can even make the fancy waffled potato slices that are deep-fried and called *pommes gauffrettes.* Simply turn the potato 90° with each cut. The frame of the mandoline is made of nickel-plated steel, and the four cutting blades are of high-carbon steel. To julienne, slice or ripple cut any firm fruit or vegetable, prop the mandoline at an angle on its hinged stand. If you want to fix the implement permanently on your counter, two screw holes are provided at the base of the stand. By adjusting two levers beneath the mandoline, you can control the thickness of the cuts. To protect hands from the sharp blades, food can be placed in a lidded metal carriage that rides back and forth on a track set into the sides of the mandoline. A wooden knob on the lid permits a firm grip on the food below. In addition, the underside of the lid is equipped with two pairs of ridges that hold the food in place as it is moved across the blades. The mandoline is 15½″ long, 4¼″ wide and 10¼″ high with the stand extended. A versatile, first-rate slicer, it matches the food processor as a culinary wonder in its own right.

Charles F. Lamalle
Mandoline (583) $66.00
Guard (583A) $19.00

CELERY ROOT IN RÉMOULADE SAUCE

Céleri-Rave en Rémoulade

1 very large celery root, cleaned and peeled
Lemon juice
2 egg yolks
1 tablespoon Dijon mustard
Salt to taste
Pinch of cayenne pepper
2 cups peanut oil

Using a large knife or mandoline, cut the celery root into fine julienne strips. Immediately toss it with fresh lemon juice to keep it white.

Make a mayonnaise: beat together the egg yolks, mustard, salt and cayenne. Add the oil in a slow stream, whisking constantly and rapidly.

Toss the mayonnaise and celery root together, taste for seasoning, cover and refrigerate until ready to serve.

Yield: 6–8 servings.

(Courtesy of Robert Renaud, Le Jacques Coeur Restaurant, New York City.)

A graceful cucumber.

"Presently, we were aware of an odour gradually coming toward us, something musky, fiery, savoury, mysterious—a hot drousy smell, that lulls the senses, and yet inflames them, the truffles were coming. Yonder they lie, caverned under the full bosom of the red-legged bird. My hand trembled as, after a little pause, I cut the animal in two. G— said I did not give him his share of the truffles; I don't believe I did. . . . The poor little partridge was soon a heap of bones—a very little heap. A trufflesque odour was left in the room, but only an odour."

Memorials of Gourmandising *by William Makepeace Thackeray.*

Truffle Cutters B:8

Though highly esteemed by both the Italians and French for centuries, the truffle has always remained somewhat of a mystery. Until the 19th century, people believed that the wild fungi were created by lightning or out of the spit of witches. Alexander Dumas wrote that "The truffles themselves have been interrogated, and have answered simply: eat us and praise the Lord." The finest black truffles come from Périgord, a small region in southwestern France. They are rough-skinned with a penetrating scent and are scented in the soil among the roots of oak trees by the sensitive noses of pigs or dogs. Because they are so hard to find and their flavor is so distinctive, truffles have always been associated with French *haute cuisine.* Truffle slices are tucked under the breast skin of fowl to

Continued from preceding page

give them an extraordinary flavor while cooking; diced truffles are the keystone of *sauce Périgourdine;* and truffle slices cut into decorative shapes embellish all kinds of cold buffet dishes, aspics, *galantines* (boned fowl stuffed with forcemeat) and pâtés. There are 12 truffle cutters in this set, including a tulip, rosette, clover, fleur-de-lys and heart. Each is made of tinned steel—soldered to a flat backing piece with a smooth finish—and has a sharp cutting edge at the bottom. The cutters are tiny, about ½″ across and 1″ deep. If your truffle supply has run out, the cutters will work just as well on pimentos, black olives, carrots, radishes or even angelica. Simply use your imagination.

Charles F. Lamalle (1286D) $50.00

A fearless truffle-hunter of Périgord.

"Of all the dishes that the ingenuity of man has invented, the truffled turkey or capon is the most delicious. On this point there is no difference of opinion."

Essays *by Dr. Austin Flint from* Books and My Food *by Elisabeth Cary & Annie M. Jones, 1904.*

"A sauté of truffles is a dish whereof the mistress of the house always does the honours herself; in a word, the truffle is the diamond of cookery.

I have sought an inner reason for this preference, for it seemed to me that other substances had as equal claim to the honour; and I found it to be due to a generally accepted notion that truffles are the food of love; and what is more, I am persuaded that nearly all our perfections, predilections, and admirations are born of the same cause, so closely are we held in bondage by the most capricious and tyrannical of the senses."

The Physiology of Taste or Meditations on Transcendental Gastronomy *by Brillat-Savarin. Dover Publications, 1960.*

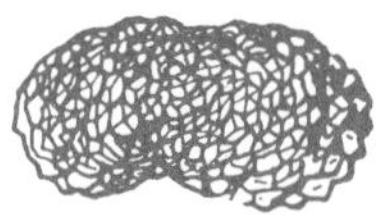

A truffle.

Gelée Cutters B:9

Gelée is a French culinary term for a clear, jellied beef, veal, chicken or fish stock. It is not synonymous with aspic, which is also gelatinous, because aspic may be opaque and made of various substances, though the terms are used interchangeably. In a thick liquid state, *gelée* is used to coat such things as braised beef slices or whole birds and lobsters. For a garnish, it is poured into a large shallow baking dish or flat pan to make an even layer, chilled until firm, and then cut into various decorative shapes known as *croûtons de gelée* that create a jewel-like effect around food. This set of cutters contains twelve shapes, ranging from a diamond and crescent to a star and teardrop. The cutters are fairly large, about 1″ across and 1⅛″ deep. Made of strong, tinned steel, the cutters are backed with flat pieces of metal that give stability to their shapes. For convenient storage, the set fits into its own clear plastic container.

H. Roth & Son $25.00

Meat Pounder B:10

Subjecting *escalopes de veau* (veal scallops) to a brief pounding will leave them meltingly tender and evenly thin. It will do the same to slices of beef if you are making *paupiettes de boeuf* (beef rolled around a forcemeat and barded with bacon slices). Utilitarian and professional, this carbon-steel French *batte* (pounder) makes the job easy. Weighing in at a hefty 2 pounds 6 ounces, one blow of its massive (about 5″-square) head is sufficient to flatten any scallop. Though the center of the *batte* is thick, both sides taper to beveled edges that are sharply honed. Thus, turned on either side, it will also cut through bones. The comfortable handle is 6″ long. To prevent the *batte* from turning into a rusting hulk, it must be carefully dried after each use.

Charles F. Lamalle (1104) $22.00

Poultry Pounder B:11

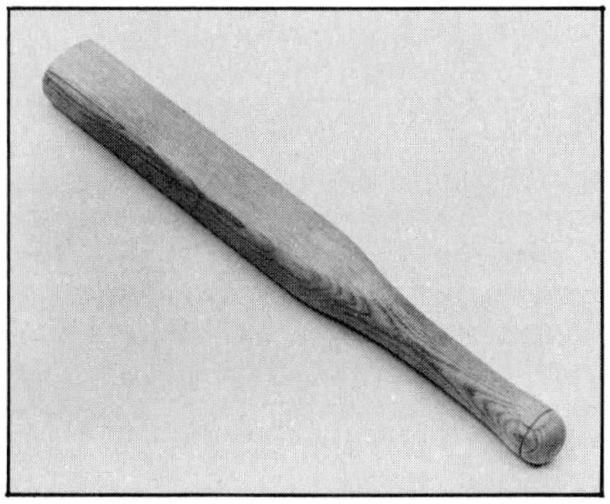

Babe Ruth would not have achieved any home runs with a *batte* (pounder) like this; but Escoffier would have made many hits with it in the culinary field. It is meant to flatten a whole butterflied chicken or boned *suprêmes de volaille* (poultry breasts). When flattened, chicken breasts may be simply sautéed and served with a creamy Madeira sauce, or they may be rolled around herb butter, breaded and deep-fried to make a memorable chicken Kiev. Made of smoothly finished wood, the *batte* has a paddle-shaped head that is 10″ long and 2″ across; the rounded handle is 7¾″ long.

Charles F. Lamalle (5022) $4.50

Duck Press B:12

A duck press is always associated with an unusual French dish known as *canneton rouennais à la presse* (pressed Rouen duckling). Duckling from Rouen is prized by connoisseurs for its flavor, derived from the blood content of its meat and bones. The ducks are killed by smothering so they will lose a minimum amount of blood before being cooked. To make pressed duckling in the Escoffier fashion, the bird is cooked for only 20 minutes, after which the legs are removed. Then the breast is carefully sliced, set in a chafing dish and seasoned. The remaining carcass is chopped up and pressed with a glass of red wine to make the sauce that is finally blessed with a few drops of brandy. Covered with the sauce, the breast is reheated, but not to the boiling point, before it is served. (Escoffier didn't use the wings and legs, but they may be finished with bread crumbs and seasonings in the kitchen and returned to the table.) Obviously, a duck press is a culinary extravagance almost without parallel. If you do have access to smothered birds, be sure to cook them the same day they are killed to avoid any toxins that might develop. If you don't, the press makes wonderful sauce from ordinary ducks. Made of gleaming chromed cast iron and steel, this elaborate duck press is a showpiece that is meant to be used at the table, the way it is in French restaurants. The press is 20¾″ high, 12½″ wide and sits on four curved legs that can be screwed permanently in place, if desired. In the center of the press is a removable, 4″-deep, 5½″-diameter container, lined with a strainer, that sits on a rimmed plate with a spout. After the container is filled with the duck carcass and set in place, the wheel, which is connected to a press, is turned to force the juices out of the meat and bones.

Hammacher Schlemmer/HOAN Products Ltd. (DP1) $385.00

Mushroom-Shaped Pestle B:13

Happily, and logically, the shape of a *champignon* (mushroom) is the best for pressing food through a drum sieve. The wide, almost flat, cap is able to push a substantial amount of food through the mesh of the sieve with each stroke, and its softly-rounded edges can be brought to bear effectively on difficult bits, like a tough piece of carrot or celery. The head is nice and (large 5″ in diameter), and the 5½″-long handle is well contoured for a good grip. Of smoothly-sanded, unfinished hardwood, it would be a pleasure to hold while sieving shrimp butter or puréeing raspberries to crown a dish of sliced strawberries.

Bridge Kitchenware Corp. $5.00

Drum Sieve B:14

Like an embroidery hoop, the *tamis* (drum sieve) is a simple, homey device that is brilliantly effective. It stretches fabric permanently in a frame so that it is easy to use for sifting or sieving ingredients. Originally the mesh in a *tamis* was made of horsehair, but now we have more durable materials like the brass in this example. Impervious to strong flavors, the sieve may be used for any purées where a very fine mesh is required. It is especially recommended for vegetable purées like mashed potatoes; but make sure to push straight down on the potatoes to get the right texture. Our *tamis* is 13¾″ in diameter, and its wooden frame is 4½″ high.

Bridge Kitchenware Corp. $13.95

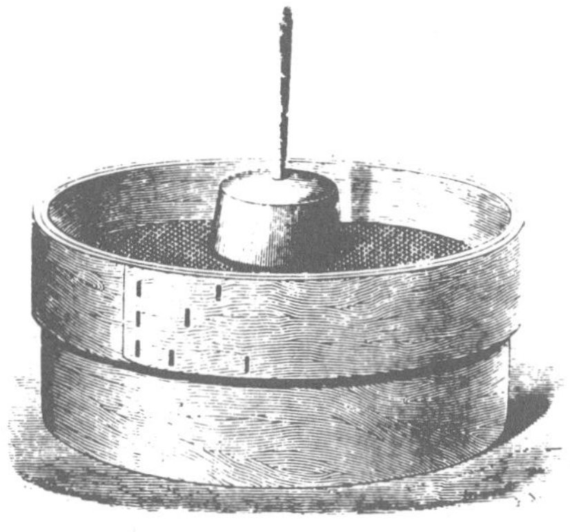

A drum sieve and wide pestle for making a purée.

Bouillon Strainer B:15

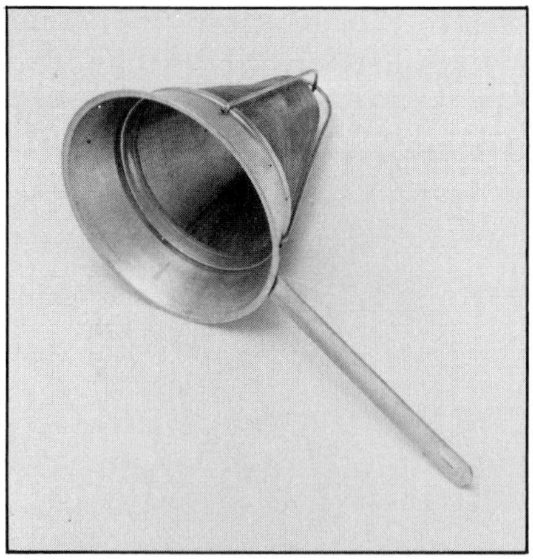

A *chinois* (literally Chinese, but actually a conical sieve) is made for straining or puréeing foods. This one has such a fine mesh of tinned-steel wires that it is best suited for straining a clarified stock or a sauce. The *chinois* is 9½″ deep, and its tinned-steel frame is 8″ in diameter. Two tinned-steel bars are bent around the outside of the sieve and fastened to opposite sides of the frame to protect the mesh. The handle provides good leverage and is perforated with a slot by which the sieve may be hung.

International Edge Tool Co. (1143) $27.50

Chinois B:16

If your pleasure be *purée bretonne* (puréed white beans with a sauce of butter, onions, tomato, garlic and parsley), or a purée of carrots with butter and cream, this *chinois* (conical sieve) is up to the task. Actually it is like an old-fashioned muslin jelly bag translated into metal, in this case, tinned steel. Sturdily constructed, the lengthwise seam is folded tightly and the rim is rolled for a smoothly-finished edge. Closely-spaced perforations are set in wavy longitudinal rows around the sieve, a visually appealing touch, but one that calls for careful cleaning. The sieve is 7½″ deep and 8″ in diameter across the top. Its 7″-long handle of tinned cast iron is riveted close to the rim and has a hole for hanging. A hook at the base of the handle will anchor the sieve on the edge of any bowl deep enough to hold it.

H. Roth & Son $17.95

A conical sieve from the late 19th century.

Food Mill B:17

A food mill is actually a second generation sieve. Like a sieve, it separates skins and seeds from food to make a purée. Unlike a sieve, however, a mill has three interchangeable blades of fine, medium and coarse gauge, making three sieves out of one implement. Best of all, the mill is easier to use than a regular sieve. With the leverage of the handle, puréeing takes little or no effort: a blade at the base of the handle forces food through the perforated disc set into the bottom of the mill. Two arms extending from opposite sides of the mill will hold it steady on any bowl from 7″ to 10″ in diameter. With the fine blade you can sieve a purée of pike to make the smoothest possible *quenelles mousseline de brochet* (poached pike mousse dumplings). The medium blade will make a thick purée of apples for an apple charlotte (a bread-covered apple dessert made in a special mold), and the coarse blade will turn out an even thicker tomato sauce. The mill is made of tinned steel with a plastic handle. It is 3¾″ deep, 9″ in diameter at the top, 5½″ in diameter at the bottom and holds 2 quarts. Sizes of 1- and 3-quart capacity are also available.

Charles F. Lamalle (471A) $12.00

Food Processor B:18

No French export has caused as much of a stir in the culinary world as the revolutionary food processor. This compact machine (9″ by 6½″ at the base and 14½″ high) eliminates hours of slicing, chopping, shredding, mixing and puréeing from the schedule of any cook. It makes many complex recipes easy and certainly eases the problems of entertaining. To grind the veal and pork, and chop the shallots for a pâté, will take several minutes instead of half an hour or more; puréed carrots, chopped onions or parsley, or grated Parmesan will take seconds. The processor will also mix flavored butters, mayonnaise or pastry dough, and grind fish for *quenelles* or a mousse. This marvelous invention is driven by a strong motor with a heat-sensitive, automatic circuit breaker that keeps the engine from overheating. The motor is housed in a metal case. With the processor come an instruction and recipe booklet and eight attachments: a plastic work bowl; a cover (with an oval chimney) that locks on the bowl; an oval pusher that feeds solid foods down the chimney; three stainless-steel blades for chopping, shredding and slicing, respectively; a plastic mixing blade; and a plastic spatula. All the parts, except for the pusher, are dishwasher safe and are made of either stainless steel or shatterproof Lexan plastic. Optional attachments include: a fine shredding disc; a fine, vegetable slicing disc; a superfine, serrated slicing disc; a ripple-cut, fine vegetable slicing disc; a french fry cutter; and a juice extractor. Although the processor seems to do almost everything, it does not beat egg whites or heavy cream well, and it cannot be used for the precision cutting required in garnishes or Chinese cooking. Nonetheless, once you own one, you will wonder how you ever lived without it.

Cuisinarts, Inc. (CFP-5) **$225.00**

FILLET OF SOLE STUFFED WITH SOLE MOUSSE AND SALMON

Ballottine de Sole

3 pounds fillet of sole
3 eggs
Salt
White pepper
1½ cups heavy cream
½ pound salmon fillet
Fish stock

Prepare a *mousseline* of sole. Cut one pound of the fillet of sole into pieces and chop it in a food processor; add the eggs, 1 teaspoon salt and pepper to taste and process until the eggs are incorporated. With the machine running, *quickly* add the heavy cream in a stream. Stop processing as soon as all the cream is incorporated.

Wet and wring out a linen dish towel (approximately 14″ x 20″). Spread this out on a work surface and cover it completely with overlapping layers of wax paper. With the remaining two pounds of sole, form a layer on the paper by just barely overlapping the edges of the fillets. Season with salt and spread the *mousseline* over the entire layer.

Cut the salmon into strips approximately the size of a finger (*aiguillettes*). Place these end to end in a lengthwise strip across the long edge of the rectangle closest to you, several inches in from the edge. Using the towel as a guide, carefully roll the fish into a cylinder, being careful not to roll the wax paper or towel *into* the *ballottine.* Roll the wax paper and towel tightly *around* the fish and securely tie the ends and middle of the roll.

Place the *ballottine* in a large pot, cover with fish stock and cook at the gentlest simmer—the surface of the stock should barely shiver—for 30 minutes. Remove it from the stock. Once the roll is cool enough to handle, untie the ends and roll the paper and towel more tightly around the *ballottine* to make it firmer and more compact. Refrigerate overnight. Serve sliced with a *sauce émeraude* (see recipe below).

Yield: 8–10 servings.

Sauce Émeraude
⅓ cup finely minced parsley
⅓ cup finely minced raw spinach
⅓ cup finely minced watercress
2 cups spicy mayonnaise

Place the minced greens in a linen towel and twist the ends until the juices are extracted. Add to the mayonnaise.

Yield: 2 cups.

(Courtesy of André Soltner, Lutèce Restaurant, New York City.)

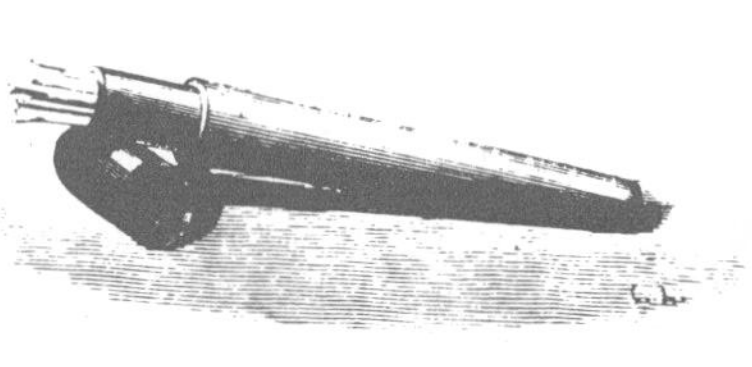

A full case of larding needles.

Peppermill B:19

In French cooking, freshly-ground pepper is essential to almost every dish that precedes dessert. For this reason you are likely to find a peppermill in every kitchen. Preground pepper is inferior because the spice loses its aroma and pungency soon after it is crushed. Peugeot makes a classic beechwood peppermill with a durable mechanism that is virtually fool-proof and really is adjustable. To fill the mill, remove the nut, lift off the top cap and pour in some peppercorns. Replace the top and turn the nut tight for a fine grind, or leave it loose for a coarse grind. Available in natural beechwood or stained a deep walnut color, the peppermill is 3¾″ high. There is a matching salt shaker as well.

HOAN Products Ltd. (707) **$10.00**

Larding Needle B:20

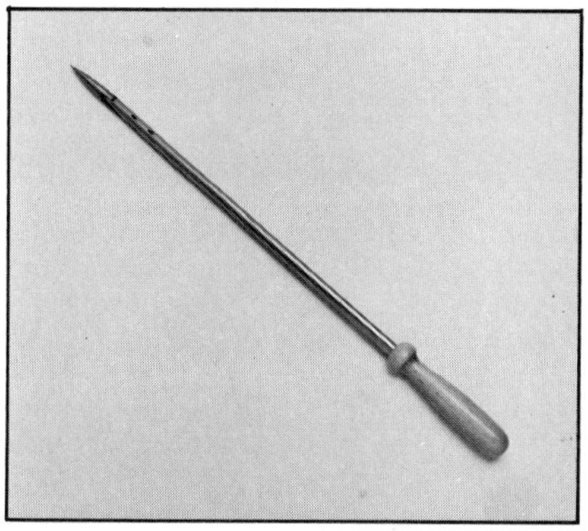

Larding is a method of adding fat to lean meat, such as a bottom round of beef or venison roast, to make it more flavorful and to keep it moist while cooking. To lard a piece of meat with

Continued from preceding page

this needle, catch one end of a strip of fresh pork fatback or blanched salt pork in the serrated edge of the hinge at the tip of the needle (the tip will bend open to expose the teeth). Then straighten the tip of the needle, clamping the fat between the teeth, and lay the strip along the trough on one side of the needle. Shove the needle through the meat in the direction of the grain; this is easier to do than going against the grain and will look prettier later when the meat is carved across the grain as it should be. When the tip of the needle, including the hinged section, emerges on the other side of the meat, remove the wooden handle, detach the strip of fat, or lardoon, from the hinge and fit the handle over the tip of the needle where it will sit snugly. Then pull on the handle to extract the needle, leaving the lardoon in place. It's easier than it sounds, and the strips of fat can be inserted to make an attractive pattern in the meat. Chilling the fat before larding it into the meat also eases the procedure. Overall, the *lardoir* (larding needle) is 20½″ long; the needle itself is 17⅞″ long and is made of stainless steel.

R. H. Forschner Co., Inc. (1400) — $21.60

Balloon Whisk B:21

Air fills balloons, and balloon whisks fill egg whites or heavy cream with air. The full shape of the traditional balloon whisk gathers up a maximum amount of egg whites or cream and quickly turns it to snowy clouds or peaks ready to lighten a soufflé or a chocolate mousse. The flexible tinned-steel wires of this 16″-long whisk are bent into the natural wood handle, and the ends are secured by a collar of wrapped wire. Because the coils of wire catch food, always make sure to clean them carefully. The whisk is also made in 10″, 12″, 14″ and 18″ lengths.

Charles F. Lamalle (1346/B) — $4.30

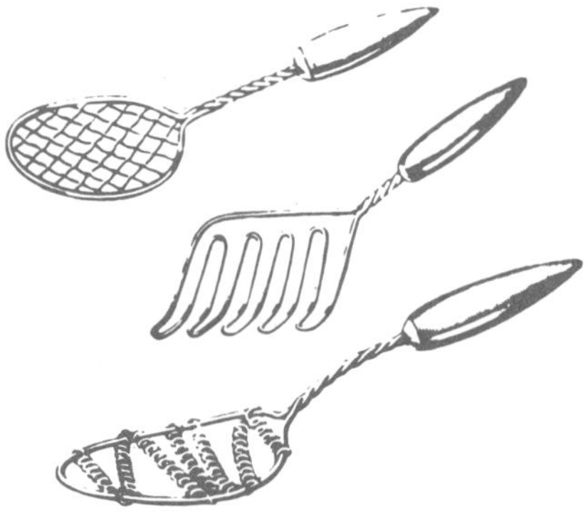

A variety of egg whisks.

SOUFFLÉ AUX FRUITS DE MER

Mixed Seafood Soufflé

Butter and flour for lining mold
½ cup warm, well-seasoned *béchamel* sauce
½ pound raw lobster, puréed (½ pound fillet of sole may be substituted)
3 egg yolks
¼ cup cooked lobster, cut in small dice (*en salpicon*)
¼ cup slightly blanched scallops, cut in small dice
¼ cup cooked shrimp, cut in small dice
¼ cup raw mushrooms, cut in small dice
3–4 egg whites

Preheat oven to 400 F. Butter the inside of one 6-cup or six 1-cup molds and coat with flour, shaking out any excess.

Blend the *béchamel* sauce and the puréed lobster together. Beat in the 3 egg yolks, then stir in the *salpicon* of lobster, scallop, shrimp and mushrooms (they should all be cut in pieces approximately the same size). Correct for seasoning, if necessary.

Beat the egg whites until stiff but not dry and quickly, but gently, fold them into the soufflé base.

Turn the mixture into the mold or molds and cook 20 to 25 minutes for the large mold, or 15 minutes for the small molds. Serve with a *sauce Nantua.*

Yield: 6 servings as appetizer.

(Courtesy of André Soltner, Lutèce Restaurant, New York City.)

Whisk B:22

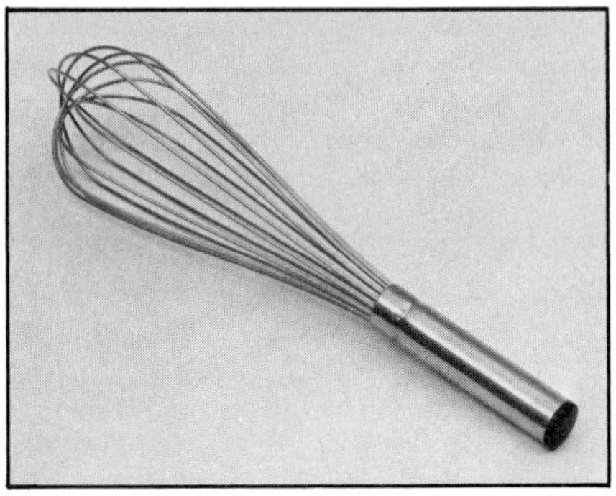

Unlike the thin, flexible wires of a balloon whisk, those of narrower whisks are thick and fairly stiff for beating and blending heavier foods. Not even the thickest béchamel sauce or *panade* (thick paste of flour or other starch used to bind sauces or forcemeats) will phase this whisk. It consists of eight stainless-steel wires looped over and under each other with their ends anchored firmly in a stainless-steel handle. From end to end, the whisk is 12″ long; 8″ and 10″ sizes are also available.

Charles F. Lamalle (1312/3) — $8.00

Copper Bowl B:23

The success of a good soufflé is often due to the airiness of its egg whites. In the great tradition of the French kitchen, a copper bowl and a balloon whisk are synonymous with fluffy egg whites—for very good reasons. The copper is slightly acidic, producing a chemical reaction with the egg whites that helps them hold their volume, and the round bottom of the bowl keeps them falling toward the center. The large whisk lifts most of the whites at each stroke so they build up very quickly. Always make sure that the bowl and beater are immaculately clean and dry before you use them; moisture or grease on either one will diminish the potential volume of the egg whites. French chefs clean their copper bowls with a mixture of salt and vinegar, which, incidentally, is one of the great secrets of keeping all copper pots bright with little effort and expense. There is yet another argument for this bowl: it is the most beautiful one to be had. Made of heavy copper, hammered for added strength, the bowl also has a ring by which it can be hung on your wall for constant admiration. It is 6″ deep, 12″ in diameter and holds 7 quarts; other sizes are 9½″, 10¾″ and 14″ in diameter.

Charles F. Lamalle (290-B) **$60.00**

Cul de Poule Bowl B:24

Rather indelicately named after the bottom of a chicken, this bowl has a flat bottom and flared sides and is smoothly rounded on the inside. It is the typical French mixing bowl, stable and well proportioned for beating egg yolks and sugar, tossing mussels in a *rémoulade* sauce (a mustard-flavored mayonnaise with capers, gherkins, herbs and seasonings) or stirring the ground meats and seasonings together for a pâté. Made of steel with a rolled rim, the bowl is 9″ in diameter at the rim, 4⅝″ deep and holds 4 quarts. It also comes in capacities of 1 and 2½ quarts.

Nordiska **$11.95**

A hare, the subject of many a terrine.

Charcuterie

Ever since their "ancestors, the Gauls" (as the French refer to those fierce Celtic warriors who once ranged from Aix to Lutèce) first celebrated battle victories with haunch of pig, undoubtedly a very tough hind leg of wild boar, pork cookery has held an esteemed place in the national cuisine. And it has made great strides since then.

Charcuterie, defined as "the art of preparing various meats, in particular pork, in order to present them in the most diverse ways," goes back to Roman times. It may have come to France with Caesar when he divided—and licked—the Gauls. At any rate, the art survived. During the Middle Ages, Parisian *charcutiers* (literally, flesh cookers) could vend only cooked meats; not until 1476 did they obtain the right to sell fresh pork; and they had to wait until the 16th century for the privilege of butchering their own pigs.

The art of *charcuterie* is based on thrift. Not stinginess by any means, but rather good management. Every possible part of the porker is used. Blood pudding may sound awful, but we defy you not to be tempted by an aromatic *boudin noir,* surrounded by mashed potatoes. Each region of France has its own *charcuterie,* and its natives, of course, claim their own as superior. Nobody wins and nobody loses in this contest; they are all marvelous. If you are ever in Paris just before Holy Week, go to the *Foire au Jambon*—the Ham Fair—taste the specialties from the provinces, and see for yourself.

Still, everyone has favorites. There used to be a shop on the rue de Seine in Paris, kept by the meanest woman who ever left Brittany. She had a disposition of pure bile, and a fat, smelly, snarling dog. But she also had goose *rillettes* (potted goose) that would sway a dieting angel.

Alas, *charcutiers,* nasty or nice, are rare on these shores. In most cases, we who love pâtés (forcemeat baked in pastry), *terrines* (forcemeat baked in a dish) and *galantines* (boned fowl stuffed with force-

Continued from preceding page

meat and baked) must make them ourselves. However, they are amusing to concoct (especially if you have a food processor) and are always met with glad cries. A *terrine* can be the mainstay of a cocktail party, and a pâté or *galantine* will awe the most sophisticated of formal diners. Both keep well for about ten days in the refrigerator.

Rillettes Pot B:25

A common hors d'oeuvre on menus all over France is a preparation known as *rillettes.* The dish is usually made from diced pork shoulder or neck meat that is cooked with lard until tender, then shredded and recombined with the fat and some salt and pepper. It is poured into small stone or porcelain jars like this one, covered with a thin layer of pork fat and a lid, and then thoroughly chilled. (Potted goose and rabbit are also popular.) Eaten with a crunchy slice of French bread, the rich taste and wonderful texture of *rillettes* is one of the joys of country cooking. Our white pot has slightly-rounded sides and a snugly-fitting domed lid. It holds ¾ cup of *rillettes* and is 3¼″ deep and 3″ in diameter. Ovenproof, it is completely glazed except on the exterior bottom rim and the inner rim on which the lid rests.

Charles F. Lamalle (6011C) $5.00

"Also, truffled galantines of turkey, tongues, hams, rillettes de Tours, pâtés de foie gras, fromage d'Italie *(which has nothing to do with cheese),* saucissons d'Arles et de Lyon, *with and without garlic, cold jellies peppery and salty—everything that French* charcutiers *and their wives can make out of French pigs, or any other animal whatever, beast, bird or fowl (even cats and rats), for the supper."*

Trilby *by George du Maurier, 1895.*

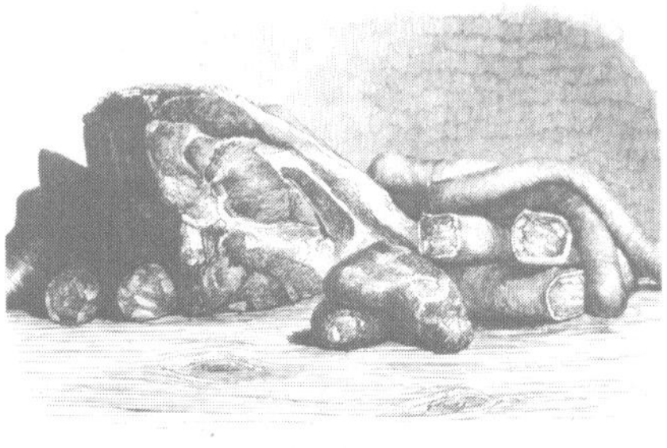

Some pork products.

Porcelain Terrine B:26

The *terrine*—traditionally made of earthenware—takes its name from *terre,* the French word for earth. It is typically an oval-shaped, handleless dish, with a lid that has a hole through which steam can escape. The hole is necessary because the *terrine* is sometimes sealed shut with dough to retain heat and moisture. This technique was particularly helpful when ovens were less controlled than they are today. The mixtures of meat cooked in a *terrine* are also served in it: chilled and sliced. They should always be called *terrines* (like the dish), but are often confused with pâtés that are baked in a crust. A common and delicious *terrine* is made with ground pork and veal, laced with veal strips (marinated in cognac with seasonings), ham strips and, if possible, truffles. The whole is wrapped in strips of fresh fatback to keep it moist. Our *terrine* is made of white porcelain instead of earthenware, but it follows the simple, classic form. It is 7⅝″ long, 5½″ across, 3″ deep and holds 1½ quarts. With the exception of the bottom on the outside and the rim of the lid, the *terrine* is completely glazed. *Terrines* of 1- and 2½-quart sizes are also available.

Schiller & Asmus, Inc. (P4303-15) $18.00

Enameled Cast-Iron Terrine B:27

A narrow rectangular *terrine* bakes more quickly than a wider oval one and provides a loaf that can be evenly sliced. For these reasons, the *terrines* used in restaurants and specialty food shops are nearly always rectangular. The meat mixture baked inside the *terrine* can vary enormously but almost always includes ground pork and veal. During the hunting season, wonderful variations can be made with the addition of pheasant, rabbit or other game. If you aren't in the mood for cooking a full-fledged lunch or dinner, a slice of *terrine* (the contents take the name of the dish) with French bread or toast, a salad and a glass of good French wine make a terrific meal. And it would look most attractive served in this enameled cast-iron dish that comes in marigold-yellow, flame or brown with a creamy beige interior. The rim of the *terrine* is extended at both ends for lifting, and the lid is perforated with a steam hole. With a capacity of 1 quart, the *terrine* is 3¾″ deep, 11″ long and 4¼″ wide. It is also available in a 1½-quart size.

Schiller & Asmus, Inc. (0524-28) $24.95

TERRINE OF SOLE

Terrine de Poisson

This recipe may be done most easily in a food processor, in which case all the ingredients should be divided into two equal portions, since the bowl of the food processor is not large enough to contain them all at once.

2 pounds fillet of sole
3 eggs
1 cup *crème fraîche*
½ bunch chives, chopped
1 shallot, chopped
1 truffle, sliced (optional)
Salt to taste
3 cups heavy cream
2 ounces green peppercorns

Preheat oven to 350 F. Place the fillet of sole in the bowl of a food processor and purée it. (If you do not have a food processor, grind the fish several times and then force it through a food mill or sieve. Next, place it in the bowl of an electric mixer fitted with a whisk.) Add the eggs, *crème fraîche,* chives, shallot, optional truffle and salt. Process or mix until the fish has absorbed all the egg and *crème fraîche.* With the machine still running, quickly add the heavy cream in a stream, being extremely careful not to overprocess. Once the cream has been completely incorporated, add the green peppercorns and process or mix a moment longer, just to distribute them through the purée. If done in a food processor, repeat with the remaining half of the ingredients.

Butter a 1¾- to 2-quart *terrine,* (deep oval or rectangular baking dish), line it with parchment paper and butter that also. Fill the *terrine* with the fish mousse, cover tightly with aluminum foil, place in a *bain-marie* and bake for 20 to 25 minutes, until set. This *terrine* may be served hot with a *sauce Nantua* or cold with a green sauce or mayonnaise.

Yield: 8 servings.

Note: This is a very basic recipe which may be embellished in numerous ways: stir in scallops, shrimp, pieces of lobster or poached salmon, whatever you desire—before turning the mousse into the *terrine.*

(Courtesy of Jean-Jacques Rachou, Le Lavandou Restaurant, New York City.)

Mock Pâté en Croûte Terrine B:28

So artfully conceived is this trompe l'oeil *terrine* that it would grace the table of your fanciest soirée. Disguised in the form of its pastry-covered cousin, a *pâté en croûte* (pâté in a crust), the porcelain *terrine* is glazed to resemble a baked crust, rough in texture and biscuit-brown. The handsome green-blue duck's head that serves as a handle on the lid is meant to indicate that the *terrine* within the creamy white interior of the dish is made with duck, but you may suit yourself. If the duck is not to your taste the *terrine* comes topped with a rabbit, pheasant, partridge or snipe instead. The *terrine* holds 3 cups and is 3″ deep, 9″ long and 4½″ wide. It is also made in 2- and 5-cup sizes.

Schiller & Asmus, Inc. (P431995C) $47.00

A pâté mold.

Galantine Mold B:29

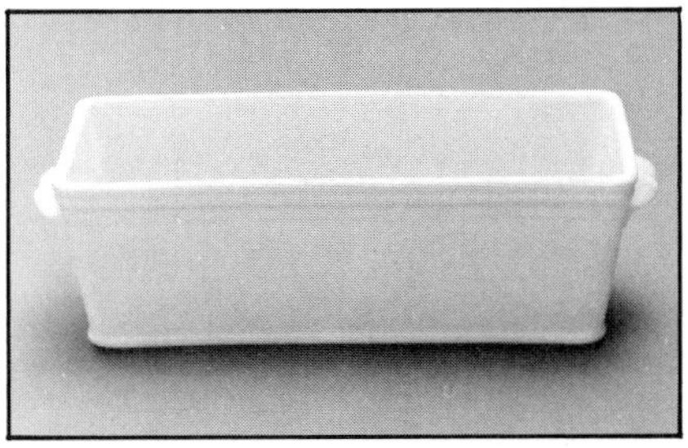

One of the most elaborate ways to prepare a forcemeat of pheasant, duck or chicken is to stuff and poach it in the skin of the bird. Before serving, you then coat it with aspic and decorate it fancifully with cutouts of such things as truffle, tomato skin and a tracery of fine leek-stem strips. That briefly describes a *galantine,* but it leaves out one important step. After the *galantine* is poached, it must be allowed to sit for a day or so to let the flavors marry and the juices drain off. Sometimes it is weighted, which helps make its shape more compact, and sometimes it is put in a rectangular dish like this with a weight on top to mold it in the shape of a loaf. Made of classic, white French porcelain, the dish has slightly-flaring sides and is bordered around the rim and base with thick ridges. At both ends a fluted protrusion beneath the ridges serves as a handle. The dish has a 2½-quart capacity, and it is 11¾″ long, 4½″ wide and 3¾″ deep. It would also make a handsome *terrine* because it is ovenproof; you can use aluminum foil for a cover.

Charles F. Lamalle (A6002) $27.00

Hinged Pâté Mold B:30

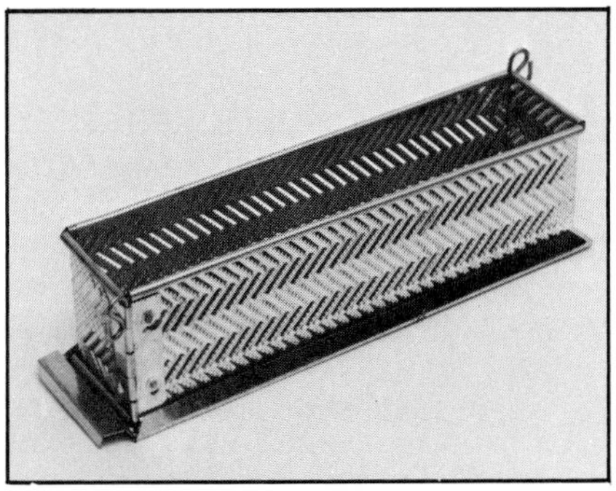

It is said that a pâté saved the life of an enemy Huguenot captured by

Continued from preceding page

Charles IX. The king, after tasting a pâté warmed by the man's fire, pardoned him on the condition that the recipe be surrendered. The story may be apocryphal but the French do value a good pâté. Technically, a pâté (pie) is a mixture of ground meat or fish enclosed in pastry slit on the top with steam holes, baked in an oven and served hot or cold. It requires a baking pan of special construction that will release it without damaging the crust. This three-piece mold is designed to do just that. Simply lift out the two pins at opposite corners of the mold, and then slide the two L-shaped side pieces out of the groove in the bottom piece that holds them. An extension at one end of the bottom hooks up to form a handle, which you can then hold onto while removing the pâté. The mold is solidly built of heavy tinned steel, and its edges are smoothly rolled over thick wire. A lovely herringbone pattern imprinted in the sides of the mold adds strength to the metal and decoration to the pastry. This mold is 12″ long, 2¾″ wide, 3¾″ deep and holds 1½ quarts, but you can also obtain a 14″-long size.

Charles F. Lamalle (8048) **$16.00**

Pâté en Croûte Mold B:31

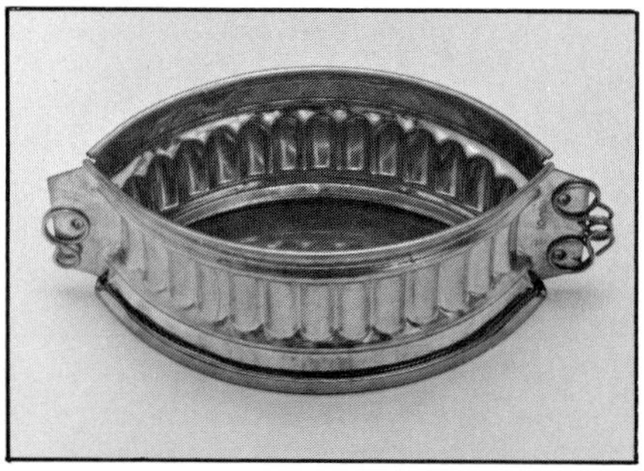

No pâté is more regally turned out than one made in this type of traditional mold. The pâté is usually made of the finest meats, and its pastry casing, fluted on the sides from the mold, is covered with golden pastry leaves or other fancy shapes. When the pâté is sliced, it may reveal a rich mosaic of soft green pistachio nuts; liver; squares of pink ham, white pork fat or veal; and perhaps a whole truffle. To unmold the pâté, release the aluminum clips at the ends of the mold and lift away the two sides; they fit snugly in a groove formed by the upturned edges of the bottom. The tinned-steel mold shown here is 8⅝″ long, 4⅝″ wide and 2⅞″ deep; it is also available in lengths of 7½″ or 9¼″.

Charles F. Lamalle (755A) **$18.00**

An elaborate pâté.

Escargots

The little land gastropod mollusk called a snail (*escargot*) has caused a lot of amusement outside of France. Do people actually *eat* those things? They do, with gusto and garlicky shallot butter. The finest snails thrive in vineyards, which accounts for the fame of those from Burgundy.

The snail's trip from vine to *escargotière* (snail dish) is a lengthy one. First, snails must be starved for a period to throw off any toxin they have eaten that might harm humans; then they are washed, soaked in salt water, rewashed, blanched, deshelled, cleaned, cooked and finally popped back into their thoroughly scrubbed shells with some savory butter, and warmed in the oven. Most snails we eat in this country come ready-prepared in cans, and they are excellent.

Escargot Tongs and Fork B:32

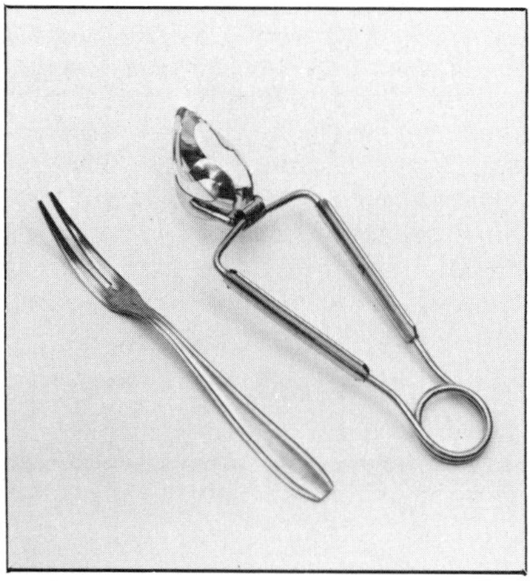

Without the proper equipment, eating snails can be more of a struggle than a pleasure. *Escargots à la bourguignonne* (snails baked or broiled in the shell and swimming in garlicky butter) are hot and buttery, making it difficult to hold a shell securely while plucking out its rich meat. As always, the French have cleverly devised equipment to perfectly suit their needs: snail tongs and fork. A slender stainless-steel wire, bent in the middle and given an extra turn for added tension, forms the handle of these tongs; the clamp section is fashioned in the contoured shape of a snail so that a shell can be held fast inside it. The simple, traditional snail fork has long, sharp, curving tines, which will extract the snail from its shell better than any other utensil. The only ornament on the stainless-steel fork is an incised border at either edge of the gracefully curving handle. The fork is 5⅝″ long overall, with 1½″-long tines; the tongs are 6½″ long.

Charles F. Lamalle
Tongs (1140) **$2.80**
Fork (1148) **$1.20**

"In Burgundy . . . the snails are most beautiful, piled in baskets in the stores, the shells one of the most luminous, gentle browns in the world, like the hair of a Leonardo Virgin. The round holes are filled very full and smooth with the butter, cold now, firm, and a tender green."

The Art of Eating *by M. F. K. Fisher. Vintage Books, 1976.*

ESCARGOTS DE BOURGOGNE

Snails with Garlic-and-Shallot Butter

Snail Butter:
½ pound butter
½ bunch parsley, finely minced
3 large cloves garlic, finely minced
1 medium-sized shallot, finely minced
1 tablespoon bread crumbs
1 walnut, chopped
½ teaspoon salt
Pinch pepper

Court Bouillon:
1–2 cups veal stock
½ cup dry white wine
1 small clove garlic, chopped
¼ small onion, chopped
Bouquet garni (bay leaf, thyme and a few parsley stems tied in a cheesecloth bag)
1″ to 2″ piece celery
½ small carrot, chopped
Salt and pepper to taste

48 snails (2 cans of 24 each)
½ tablespoon cornstarch
Small glass French brandy

To make the snail butter, simply cream the butter with the rest of the ingredients and refrigerate until ready to use.

Place all the ingredients for the *court bouillon* in a saucepan and simmer gently, covered, for 30 minutes. Strain.

Rinse the snails thoroughly under cold running water. Add them to the *court bouillon* and simmer for 20 minutes. Stir the cornstarch into the brandy and add slowly to the simmering snails, mixing with a wooden spoon. Let it boil for a minute or two, until the stock thickens, then allow the snails to cool in the *court bouillon.* (Adding the cornstarch causes the aromatic bouillon to totally "envelope" the snails, heightening their flavor.)

Once the snails have cooled, stuff them into shells or little porcelain snail cups and cover each with a good dollop of the snail butter. Before serving, heat them in a 350–400 F. oven for about 5 minutes, being careful not to allow the butter to burn.

Yield: 8 servings.

(Courtesy of Robert Renaud, Le Jacques Coeur Restaurant, New York City.)

Stainless-Steel Escargot Dish B:33

The most highly esteemed snails are the large white variety (*helix pomatia*) that thrive in vineyards. But so many of these tasty gastropod mollusks are consumed by the French that the snail population of the country has been seriously threatened in the past, and many snails still have to be imported from other parts of Europe and elsewhere. It is easy to understand why they are disappearing so quickly when a serving of 12 is common, as indicated by the number of depressions in this stainless-steel *escargotière* (snail dish). But it's hard to stop eating, once you get started, until the last bit of garlic butter is mopped up with a piece of French bread. The dish is 7″ in diameter, and its rim is extended on opposite sides so it can be lifted from the oven and carried to the table. If your appetite is more moderate, a smaller 6-snail size is available.

Bridge Kitchenware Corp. **$5.95**

Porcelain Escargot Dish B:34

Although preparing snails from scratch is a lengthy process, snails and snail shells are readily available, separately, in gourmet food departments. To remove the canned flavor from snails, simmer them for a few minutes in a little white wine with some butter, shallots and salt; then proceed with your recipe. If you want to serve them with style and restraint (only 6 per person) as an hors d'oeuvre, you might like some dishes like this one of pristine white porcelain. Completely glazed, it is 5½″ in diameter, with a rim that extends on opposite sides to form handles. The dish rests on a second rim around the bottom. Larger dishes are obtainable for servings of 12 snails.

Charles F. Lamalle (1151) **$5.00**

"On a bush . . . snails are beautiful, unless you are the gardener who planted the bush. They are beautiful on plates, too, each one in its little dent, shell full of hot green butter like a magic cup."

The Art of Eating *by M. F. K. Fisher. Vintage Books, 1976.*

Escargot Cup B:35

One of the French words for a cup is *godet;* hence this *godet à escargot* (snail cup). Only 1¾″ in diameter and ⅞″ deep, it is meant for the singular snail and does away with the need for both snail shells and tongs. The dish is one of a set of six. All are a deep dark brown finished with a lustrous glaze, except on the bottoms, which have been left rough to prevent them from sliding on a baking sheet or plate.

Schiller & Asmus, Inc. (P2763-24) **$1.00**

Pots and Pans

The best French home cooking is highly regional in nature. The cuisine of each area depends on a small but excellent repertoire of dishes based on foodstuffs raised locally. Both the regional cuisines and their cooking vessels have developed side by side; in rich sections of the country, people could afford metal, in poorer sections, they made do with what they had.

In the Languedoc, home of the celebrated *cassoulet,* clay is abundant. As that multi-meat bean dish evolved and became famous (it even has its own fan club, *Les Compagnons du Cassoulet*), so did the fine earthenware pots in which it is cooked. Earthenware is usually seasoned, both inside and out; the exterior, and often the interior, are rubbed with garlic. The pot is then filled with water (sometimes an onion, a few herbs and a bit of oil are added) and allowed to heat and simmer slowly in the oven. The garlic rubbings bake into the clay, forming a faintly odiferous, oily glaze that seals the pores and promises fine eating to come.

For general cooking, the most satisfactory—and expensive—pans are of heavy copper (at least ⅛″ thick) lined with tin (to prevent chemical reactions between the copper and acidic or salty foods). A French cook may or may not have one or two of these; if she does, they might well be inherited. Copper is the best and most desirable, for many purposes, because it spreads the heat evenly and well; but it *is* heavy to handle and *does* exact some maintenance to be kept attractive looking. (A mixture of vinegar, salt and elbow grease is the traditional and most economical cleanser.) Also, the pots must be retinned periodically. It's all right to cook in pots with a little of the tin worn away, but it can be dangerous to let food remain in them for any time. Acidic foods, like tomatoes, can produce toxic effects, and salty foods, which cause the copper to corrode, may take on a metallic taste. As an alternative to copper, there are many new pots and pans on the market made of heavy aluminum, or stainless steel, sometimes combined with a thick layer of copper, that are perfectly satisfactory, depending on the way they are used. Heavy aluminum, for instance, is ideal for a stock pot or sauté pan when egg yolks or highly acidic foods are not cooked in it. (Aluminum will discolor some foods and give them a bitter taste.)

The great diversification of pots and pans—one for every possible purpose, it would seem—came with 18th-century professional cooking. In great houses, restaurants and luxury hotels, battalions of chefs, *sous-chefs* (assistant chefs), and their apprentices toiled in vast kitchens, each turning out separate specialties. Gifted practitioners of *grande cuisine* were given the freedom and the means to perfect their art. Such unique and luxurious pieces as the *turbotière;* a pan shaped to the peculiar dimensions of the turbot, were developed as a result of this expansive approach to fine cooking, considered one of the refinements of the gracious life.

". . . I should like to set down one or two simple and almost mystical phrases I heard from the lips of Mme Yvon, a thoroughbred cordon bleu. *One day at her house, after I had eaten a* boeuf à l'ancienne *which completely gratified at least three senses out of the five—for apart from its dark, velvety savor and its half-melting consistency, it shone with an amber-colored, caramel-like sauce, ringed at its circumference with a light shimmer of fat the color of fine gold—I cried:*

"Madame Yvon, it's a masterpiece! What do you put in it?"

"Beef," Madame Yvon replied.

"Heavens, I can tell that . . . But all the same, there must be a mystery, some sort of magic in the way the ingredients are combined . . . . With a marvel like this, it should surely be possible to give it a name? . . ."

"Of course," Mme Yvon replied. "It's a beef casserole."

All it would take to preserve, to rescue and to justify France's pride in her gastronomy would be a few more Mme Yvon's. But she is a rare species in an age that is bent on making silk without silk, gold without gold, pearls without oysters, and Venus without flesh . . ."

Prisons et Paradis *by Colette, from* Earthly Paradise, An Autobiography *by Robert Phelps. Farrar, Straus & Giroux, 1966.*

Clay Poêlon B:36

Traditionally, a *poêlon* is either a squat and homely earthenware pot with a fat handle and a country French accent, or a long-handled metal pan used for cooking sugar. This is the earthenware type, round and brown, with a hollow bulb handle and domed lid; every surface is curved save its flat bottom. Earthenware is good for the long, slow cooking of dried beans, like the special French *flageolets.* Cooked with onions, carrots, garlic, cloves and some herbs, the beans are best served with mutton or lamb. The inside of the *poêlon* is glazed gold, but the bottom has been left unglazed for greater heat absorption. If you use the pot on top of the stove keep the heat low; an asbestos mat is also a good idea. The *poêlon* is 7″ in diameter, 2⅛″ deep and has a 4-cup capacity.

Henry et Fils $10.50

A tranquil scene from the early 19th century.

La bonne soupe.

Cast-Iron Poêlon B:37

Like an *haute couture* version of a peasant dress, this *poêlon* is sleeker, slimmer and more modern in shape than its earthenware relatives. It is available in yellow, green, brown or flame enamel on a cast-iron base; but the bottom of the pot has been left free of enameling for the sake of good heat conduction. The handle of the domed cover is a plastic strip set across a hollow depression. This pot holds 2½ quarts and is 3″ deep and 7″ in diameter at the top, a good size for cooking a vegetable like glazed carrots, or a slow-simmering tomato sauce. The pan is also made in capacities of 1, 1½ and 2 quarts.

Hammacher Schlemmer/Schiller & Asmus, Inc. (C2507-20) $22.95

Copper Saucepan B:38

A high, straight-sided saucepan with a handle is known in France as a *casserole russe* (Russian saucepan). The name remains a mystery, but the advantages of this pan are no secret. Handsomely made of the best heavy-gauge copper, hammered for extra strength and tin lined, the pan will cook food so beautifully and last so long that it deserves to be an heirloom. Copper is still the best conductor of heat, and this pan is particularly suited for creamy soups, vegetables, rice or any other food that will also benefit from the tendency of the straight, 4″-deep sides of the pot to reduce evaporation, and encourage steaming. The long, curved cast-iron handle (lighter and more finely wrought than the average) provides excellent leverage and is perforated for hanging. This pan is 7″ in diameter and holds 2½ quarts. Other sizes include capacities of ¾, 1, 1¾ and 3 quarts.

B. I. A. Cordon Bleu, Inc. (LEC 3301/18) $95.00

BÉARNAISE SAUCE WITH TOMATO

Sauce Choron

Sauce Choron is simply a *béarnaise* sauce to which a little diced tomato is added at the last moment.

2 tablespoons tarragon vinegar
2 tablespoons dry white wine
1 tablespoon chopped shallot
1½ tablespoons chopped fresh tarragon*
1½ tablespoons chopped fresh chervil
Pinch salt
Pinch cracked pepper
3 egg yolks
1 teaspoon water
6 ounces unsalted butter
Lemon juice
1 tablespoon tomato, peeled, seeded, juiced and finely diced

Place the vinegar and wine in a stainless-steel, enameled or tinned saucepan and add the shallot, ½ tablespoon each of the tarragon and chervil, and the salt and pepper. Reduce by two-thirds over high heat and allow to cool to lukewarm, then beat in the egg yolks and water.

Place the pan on the corner of a low flame while beating the sauce constantly with a wire whisk. When the egg yolks begin to thicken, start adding knobs of the butter, whisking one piece in completely before adding the next. Once all the butter has been incorporated, squeeze in several drops of lemon juice and strain the sauce through a sieve or *chinois.* Stir in the remaining tablespoon of tarragon and chervil and the tomato.

Yield: Approximately 1½ cups.

* If fresh tarragon is not available, use tarragon preserved in vinegar.

(Courtesy of André Soltner, Lutèce Restaurant, New York City.)

Slope-Sided Sauté Pan B:39

If you can only indulge in one copper pan, a strong argument can be made for this *sauteuse évasée* (sauté pan with flared sides). It can do most everything: for example, you could sauté chicken in it, and then remove the meat while you make a Madeira-flavored cream sauce with the cooking juices right in the same pan. Copper, the best conductor of heat, will reduce a sauce without scorching (under watchful eyes, of course), and the sloping sides of this pan expose a maximum amount of sauce to the air for a quick reduction. It is also possible for a whisk to reach the whole bottom of the pan, which is not always feasible in a pan with straight sides (and hence, sharp corners). The hefty iron handle stays relatively cool because it conducts heat more slowly than copper. The heavy-gauge copper has been hammered for extra strength on the sides but left smooth on the bottom to allow for maximum contact with the heat on electric and heat-sensor burners. To prevent chemical reactions between the copper and food, the inside of the pan is tin lined. With a 2½-quart capacity, the pan is 3¼″ deep and 8¾″ in diameter across the top. A larger, 10¼″-diameter pan is also available. Lids for both sizes

Continued from preceding page

can be purchased separately.

Charles F. Lamalle (250) **$68.00**

A true bain-marie.

Bain-Marie Pan B:40

A *bain-marie* is a large, fairly shallow pan containing hot water into which a number of tall, slender, covered pans like this one, filled with prepared sauces or other foods, are set to keep food warm before serving. It is the precursor of the steam table, and was in use in Roman times when so many different foods were devoured at the same time that the hot-bath system was used to keep them all warm. The 5½″-deep sides of this pot keep water from spilling into it, and its thick hammered-aluminum body will embrace the most delicate preparations with even warmth. Always make sure, though, that the water in the *bain-marie* never reaches a boil. (A *bain-marie* can be used either on top of the stove or in the oven.) Because this pan is only meant to be lifted in and out of a water-bath, its black-coated, cast-aluminum handle is rather short, and its lid is made of light-gauge copper. It holds 1½ quarts and would actually make a strikingly handsome serving vessel for a creamy mussel soup.

Charles F. Lamalle (59YA) **$16.75**

Tales about the origin of the bain-marie *abound. One legend credits an Italian alchemist, Maria de Cleota, with the invention of the* bagno maria. *In* The Modern Housewife *(1853), the origin of the name is explained by the translation "sea-water bath"* (marie *from the word for sea). The water in the pan was thought to be from the ocean since salty water boils at a higher temperature, making it useful in some experiments. One more legend gives another Mary as the inventor, but the heat-maintaining element in this version of the device was hot sand.*

Double Boiler B:41

This curvaceous double boiler with a white porcelain bodice and sleek copper skirt should win the heart of any sauce, cream or custard cook who wants a pot as exquisite as its contents. Your *crème patissière* (pastry cream) would be a sure success with this team. There are four parts to the double boiler: a tin-lined, slope-sided copper pan with two sturdy brass handles—one long and one short; a non-porous porcelain insert with a removable copper band attached to a brass handle; and a slightly domed copper lid. The copper pan is 6¼″ in diameter at the bottom, 3¾″ deep, holds 2¼ quarts, and can be used by itself with the lid. The porcelain pan holds 1 quart and is 4½″ deep and 5¾″ in diameter; a 1¾-quart size is also available.

Charles F. Lamalle (246A) **$125.00**

Copper Sautoir B:42

Chances are the steak for the *tournedos Rossini* (fillet of beef served with goose liver, truffles and Madeira sauce) you swooned over on your last visit to France were prepared in a pan identical to, but perhaps slightly larger than, this one. A *sautoir* is a heavy, straight-sided, fairly shallow pan with a handle, in which small pieces of meat and vegetables are cooked in butter or fat and shaken so they jump (*sauter*) while they are cooking. Shaking the pan back and forth over the fairly intense heat required for proper sautéing prevents food from sticking to the pan and burning. This tin-lined, heavy-gauge copper *sautoir* is wonderfully suited to its task. Its long cast-iron handle remains cool at all times and provides good leverage for maneuvering the pan, and the copper is hammered all over for added strength. The hammered bottom is a slight disadvantage on flat heat-sensor stoves where a completely flat bottom would provide better heat conduction. This *sautoir* is 2½″ deep, 8″ in diameter and holds 2 quarts. It also comes in 2½- and 3-quart capacities. (Matching hammered copper lids with long iron handles are also available.) A pan like this represents a substantial investment, but how many things do you buy that will last more than a lifetime?

B. I. A. Cordon Bleu, Inc. (LEC 3302/20) **$90.00**

MEDALLIONS OF VEAL IN MADEIRA SAUCE WITH MORELS

Médaillons de Veau aux Morilles

½ saddle of veal, boned and trimmed completely
Salt and pepper
Butter
10 ounces fresh *morilles* or 2½ ounces dried*
1½ ounces Madeira
1½ cups heavy cream

Cut the veal into 10 to 12 ½″-thick *médaillons* (2 per person), and season each lightly with salt and pepper. In a large *sautoir,* brown the *médaillions* in butter, about 1½ to 2 minutes on each side. Add the *morilles,* cover and simmer gently for about 4 minutes.

Remove the *médaillons* to a warm platter and deglaze the pan with the Madeira. Whisk in the heavy cream and continue to simmer until it starts to thicken and becomes velvety in texture. Correct for seasoning and pour over the *médaillons.* Serve with fresh noodles.

Yield: 5–6 servings.

* Dried *morilles* must be soaked overnight, washed 5 or 6 times to remove all the sand and cooked in salted water for approximately 8 minutes before using.

(Courtesy of André Soltner, Lutèce Restaurant, New York City.)

Hammered-Aluminum Sautoir B:43

The French kitchen is undergoing a revolution. Copper pots, as marvelous as they are, are being replaced, for certain uses, by a new generation of metal pots that are both light in weight and good conductors of heat. This heavy-gauge, hammered-aluminum *sautoir* (straight-sided frying pan) is a good example. Aluminum will still discolor acidic foods and impart a bad flavor to very acidic ones, but there are hundreds of uses for which it is perfectly fine. And, of course, it is less expensive than copper. This 10½″-diameter *sautoir* is ideal for sautéing meats, like a good piece of sirloin for a *steak au poivre* (steak with pepper). After the steak is browned and cooked to the degree desired, the pan is deglazed with cognac and some rich brown sauce is added. The sauce is then strained into a smaller pan and some cold butter is swirled into it to give it the velvety texture for which French sauces are so well noted. The pan is 3″ deep and has a long, black cast-aluminum handle riveted to the side. It is also available in diameters of 8″ or 9½″.

Charles F. Lamalle (5924) **$30.00**

Plat à Sauter B:44

This *plat à sauter* is fairly deep (4⅝″) and roomy enough (12½″ in diameter) to sauté all the pieces of a chicken at once, perhaps with some garlic and herbs like thyme, basil and fennel. You can then cover the chicken and leave it to cook. When it is done, remove it, deglaze the pan with wine and make a perfect egg-rich, buttery sauce. It is also an ideal pan for stews like a *navarin à la printanière* (lamb stew with spring vegetables) that calls for both browning on top of the stove and cooking in the oven. The pan is lined with tin, its copper sides are hammered, and even though it may be larger than any single burner, the copper distributes heat well enough to make it completely effective.

Charles F. Lamalle (3291) **$175.00**

Omelet Pan B:45

One restaurant we know of serves only omelets, more than 500 different kinds, which proves that the garnishes for an omelet are only limited by one's imagination. That is one reason why omelets are always so popular. They can be filled with cheese, tomatoes and/or mushrooms, flavored with spices and herbs, dotted with caviar, or garnished with asparagus. And they are good at any time of night or day because they are light, nourishing and easy to prepare. But the success of an omelet is ultimately dependent on the proper pan: it should be heavy, conduct heat well, have shallow sloping sides over which the omelet can be rolled, and a good long handle for gripping and turning the pan. This one answers all those needs very well. It is made of heavy, non-porous, low-grade steel that responds quickly to heat, and its long iron handle is riveted securely to the sloping sides. Before using, the pan must be scrubbed with soap and hot water to remove its protective lacquer coating, and then it must be seasoned. Rub the surface with vegetable oil, heat the pan slowly until it gets very hot. Cool it and wipe off any excess oil. Thereafter spare it from soap cleanings. Simply scrub it with salt and wipe it clean. If you don't use the pan often, it is always best to heat it with oil and rub it with salt each time you use it. This will help prevent the omelet from sticking. The pan is 8″ in diameter, large enough to make an omelet of two or three eggs.

Charles F. Lamalle (492) **$12.75**

If your tastes run to the light and pure, eschew the following:
"Eggs or Quelque chose
Break forty eggs, and beat them together with some salt. Fry them at four times, but on one side. Before you take them out of the pan, make a composition or compound of hard eggs, and sweet herbs minced, some boiled currants, beaten cinnamon, almond-paste, sugar and juice of orange. Strew all over these omelets, roll them up like a wafer, put them in a dish with some white wine, sugar, and juice of lemon; then warm and ice them in an oven, with beaten butter and fine sugar."

The Accomplished Cook *by Robert May. London, 1678.*

OMELETTE MARIANNE

Omelet with Tomato, Cheese
and Herbs

1 teaspoon butter
½ medium-sized tomato, peeled, seeded, pressed and cut into small cubes
3 eggs
Salt and pepper to taste
2 pinches fresh, minced *fines herbes* (parsley, chives, tarragon, chervil)
3 tablespoons grated Gruyère cheese

Place the butter in a well-seasoned, 7″ or 8″ omelet pan over a very high flame. Add the tomato and sauté for about one minute, until it starts to get pale. Beat the eggs with a drop of water and the salt and pepper. Pour into the pan and sprinkle the *fines herbes* on top. Cook for about 1½ minutes, always over very high flame, constantly bringing the edges of the omelet to the middle with a fork. It should still be soft when done. Sprinkle on the cheese, roll the omelet and serve immediately.

Yield: 1 serving.

(Courtesy of Chef Bob Benson, Madame Romaine de Lyon Restaurant, New York City.)

Of the many unbelievable explanations that have been offered with regard to the origin of the word "omelette," *the following is perhaps even less credible than some: "The King of Spain was taking a walk in the country one day. Feeling hungry . . . he went into a peasant's hut and asked the peasant to prepare some food. . . . The man set to work, and with a speed which delighted the hungry King, proceeded to cook some beaten eggs in oil in a pan.* 'Quel homme leste,' *(What an agile man!) [naturally a Spanish King speaks French] exclaimed the King on savouring the dish, which it appears he had never tasted before . . .*

And from that day, say some authors, beaten eggs cooked in a pan have been called omelette *in memory of the* homme leste. . . .

What weakens this story somewhat is the fact that in Spain an omelette *is called* a tortilla. . . ."

Larousse Gastronomique *by Prosper Montagné, edited by Nina Froud and Charlotte Turgeon. Crown Publishers, 1961.*

Crêpe Pan B:46

Crêpes have a chameleon quality. They suit any hour, any course and any taste, and they change color and shape, depending on their use. They can be sliced into fine strips to garnish a consommé for an hors d'oeuvre, rolled around a creamy chicken filling and sauced for an entrée, or folded and bathed in a buttery, orange-flavored Grand Marnier sauce for dessert. Whatever their end, the means for getting them there must include the right pan; one of heavy iron is traditional. This iron crêpe pan (*poêle à crêpes*) makes a perfect 5″-diameter, dessert-sized crêpe. Its sides slope smoothly for ease in turning and shaping the crêpe, and the well-balanced handle, riveted to the side, is slanted up and away from the heat for good protection. Like any iron pan this one should be scrubbed with hot, soapy water and seasoned before use. Then it should be maintained with no-soap cleanings. Larger sizes—to produce 6″-, 6½″- and 8″-diameter crêpes—are also available. If you don't use the pan often, before each use, rub it with oil and heat it. Then wipe it out and rub it with salt before you pour in the batter. This will prevent sticking.

Charles F. Lamalle (489) $5.50

Norman Crêpe Pan B:47

This enormously heavy cast-iron crêpe pan, *galetière normande,* is used to make large, crisp, wonderfully thin Norman pancakes. A recipe pasted to the pan tells you how to make the crêpes as well as a very special dessert known as *galette à la normande.* The *galette* is a stack of warm crêpes layered with sweetened apple purée. Sugar and shredded almonds are sprinkled over the top and the whole thing is then flamed with calvados and served immediately, cut into wedges. You can also create a main course for a luncheon by stacking the crêpes with seafood in a sauce, and cloaking the whole with more of the sauce, *sans* seafood. Sprinkle grated Gruyère over the top and heat it through in the oven. The 10½″-diameter, matte-black enameled pan is almost flat, and has a long handle with a thumb-depression and a hole for hanging.

Schiller & Asmus, Inc. (C2050-4) **$14.95**

Oval Sauté Pan B:48

Multi-purpose pans are always desirable, especially when they are as beautiful as this oval one of tin-lined copper. With its elongated shape, the pan is well-suited for sautéing fish fillets (or veal scallops dipped in flour, egg and fresh bread crumbs) in a generous pool of bubbling butter. When the fish or veal has turned a golden brown, the pan can be carried directly to the table where both the container and its contents will share the limelight. In restaurants, pans like this are often brought into the dining room for finishing an entrée or a dessert by flambéing it with cognac or a liqueur. Although these pyrotechnics are frowned upon by traditionalists and in no way guarantee the quality of food, they are nonetheless spectacular. You should certainly consider this pan for presenting *crêpes Suzette* (crêpes with orange-and-Grand-Marnier butter), flambéed or not. Only 1⅝″ deep, the pan is 11⅞″ long and 7⅞″ across. It is made of medium-gauge copper and has a brass handle with a hole for hanging. Three other sizes are available as well: 10⅜″ by 7″, 13⅞″ by 9″ and 15⅞″ by 10⅛″.

Charles F. Lamalle (272) **$50.00**

Chestnut Pan B:49

If you have ever experienced Paris in the fall, you will never forget the slightly sweet smell of roasting chestnuts that emanates from the carts of countless vendors in the chilly streets. To bring the memory home, use a pan like this 10″-diameter (across the top), perforated steel skillet made especially for roasting those delicately flavored nuts. Cover the bottom of the pan with chestnuts and hold it over a low to moderate flame, shaking it occasionally to keep the nuts from burning. (The handle is 10″ long so you can even reach safely into a fireplace.) When toasted, the nuts are especially delicious accompanied by a glass of milk. Before using, be sure to wash off the protective coating on the pan, and season it with oil.

Charles F. Lamalle (494 B) **$4.50**

DAUBE OF BEEF

Boeuf en Daube

For 6 persons:

3 pounds rump of beef
¼ pound salt pork
4 tablespoons minced parsley
1 garlic clove, minced
Salt
Freshly ground black pepper
4 tablespoons minced shallots
1 bottle dry red wine
1 Bouquet Garni
2 thin sheets of fresh pork fat
4 tablespoons lard
Flour and water paste

Cut the beef into large cubes. Cut the salt pork into lardoons, or short strips, and roll them in a mixture of the minced parsley and garlic. Lard the cubes of beef with these strips and season with salt and pepper.

Put the meat into a bowl (do not use aluminum) with the shallots, the red wine and the *bouquet garni.* Marinate for 2 hours. Line a casserole or a *daube* pot with the sheets of fresh pork fat.

Drain the meat cubes and sauté them in the lard in a skillet. When they are browned on all sides, put them into the casserole lined with the pork fat and add the marinade.

Seal the lid on the casserole hermetically with a flour and water paste. Cook in a preheated 325° F. oven for 4 hours.

Serve from the same casserole.

(From LA CUISINE: SECRETS OF MODERN FRENCH COOKING by Raymond Oliver. Copyright 1969 by Tudor Publishing Company. Reprinted by permission of Tudor Publishing Company.)

Toupin B:50

From the potters of Vallauris on the Côte d'Azur come some of the finest pieces of earthenware to be found in France. Shapes such as this, which might seem pure fancy, echo the historic traditions of the provinces. This narrow-necked, fat-bellied earthenware

Continued from preceding page

pot is called a *toupin* or *daubière.* In the Béarn region of southwestern France, it is used to cook soup (like the thick cabbage and bean soup called *garbure*), stews and beans. Such dishes will cook slowly in the earthenware, while the narrow neck and top opening limit evaporation. The pot is glazed only on the interior and on its ill-fitting green cover. Together, pot and lid are 9″ high; at its chubbiest point, the pot is 8¾″ in diameter. This *toupin* will hold 6 quarts. Traditionally, earthenware pots are seasoned before use with an overall rubbing of garlic, then filled with water and given a long, slow bake in the oven.

Charles F. Lamalle (8040) **$45.00**

Clay Marmite B:51

Marmites are deep pots—usually with straight sides, a lid and two handles—that are exceptionally good for making soups and slow-cooking stews and bean dishes. Although this earthenware *marmite* is large in size it would do very well for a soup called *petite marmite* (named for its container), a classic clear beef consommé garnished with cabbage balls, shreds of chicken, rounds of beef marrow, diced beef, croutons and slender strips of vegetables. Traditionally, the soup was served right in a smaller *marmite* in which it was cooked, and this pot, too, can go right to the table. It would also do beautifully for a savory, slow-cooked *cassoulet* (a white haricot bean stew made with pork, bacon or salt pork and various other meats—such as sausage, duck, goose or lamb, depending on locale). Our generous 5½-quart pot with strap handles, is 9″ in diameter and 4½″ deep. It may be primitive looking, but the pot is from Vallauris where some of the finest clay in France is found. The top and interior of the pot are glazed a rich brown; the exterior is glazed natural earthenware. To season the *marmite,* rub it inside and out with garlic, fill it with water and then bake it for a while in a 300 F. oven.

Charles F. Lamalle (8900) **$45.00**

Round Cocotte B:52

In culinary terms, a *cocotte* is a fairly deep, round or oval pot with short handles and a tightly fitting lid that is usually used for meat, poultry or goose. Whatever its contents, they are generally served right in the pot, or *en cocotte.* This brass-trimmed, smooth copper cocotte can be used on top of the stove or in the oven, but would certainly be an asset on the table as well. Although a little shallow for a whole chicken, it would easily hold two game hens *bonne femme* (cooked with onions, bacon, potatoes and seasonings). This pan holds 3½ quarts and is 4″ deep and 8″ in diameter. It is available in ¾-, 1¾-, 5- and 6¾-quart capacities. If you prefer an oval pan, it comes in capacities of 4½ cups and 2, 3, 4 or 7 quarts.

Charles F. Lamalle (261) **$74.00**

"This Bouillebaisse a noble dish is—
A sort of soup or broth, or brew
Or hotch-potch of all sorts of fishes,
That Greenwich never could outdo:
Green herbs, red peppers, mussels, saffron,
Soles, onions, garlic, roach and dace:
All this you'll eat at Terré's tavern
In that one dish of Bouillebaisse."

By William Makepeace Thackeray, from Books and My Food *by Elisabeth Luther Cary and Annie M. Jones. Rohde & Haskins, 1904.*

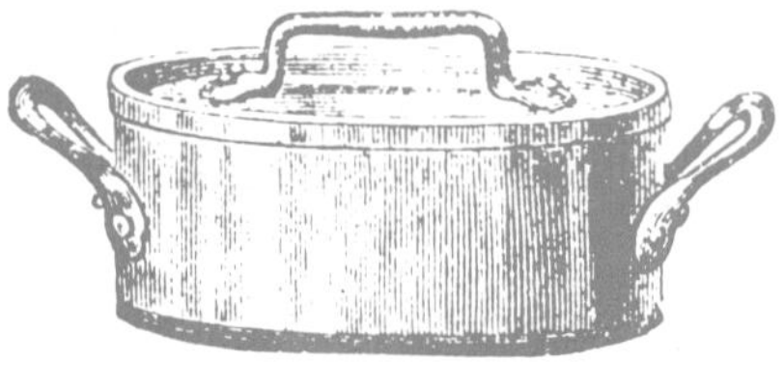

"I was born in the country, in a region where people still treasured recipes, which I have never found in any cooking guide, as they would the secret of a perfume or some miraculous balm. They were passed on by word of mouth alone, on the occasion of some feast accompanied by the sound of bells, the christening of a first-born, or a confirmation. They escaped during lengthy wedding feasts, from lips unlocked by vintage wines: this was how my mother came to receive, in strictest confidence, the secret of how to make a certain chicken 'ball', an ovoid missile sewn into the skin of a boned chicken. How could one reconstitute now the secret of that 'ball', set out on the table, in large, round slices studded with the glittering black eye of the truffle and the brilliant green of the pistachio nut?"

Prisons et paradis *by Colette, from* Earthly Paradise, An Autobiography *by Robert Phelps. Farrar, Straus & Giroux, 1966.*

Oval Cocotte B:53

Pheasant Souvaroff, baked with truffles and *foie gras* in a Madeira sauce, is one of the best things that can happen to the bird—from the point of view of a gourmet. To cook it properly, the pheasant and its sauce are usually placed in a deep *cocotte* (a straight-sided oval or round pot with a lid), and covered. The lid is then sealed, often decoratively, with a flour-and-water dough that helps to concentrate the flavors in the pot and prevent moisture from escaping while the pheasant is finished in the oven. When it is ready, the *cocotte* is carried right to the table where the pastry seal is broken and the beautiful aroma is released from the dish to be completely appreciated by all. Of course, there are dozens of ways of roasting a whole chicken or other kinds of meat *en cocotte* (in a casserole) as well, for which the pastry seal is not necessary. Chicken with tarragon is a favorite. What makes this tin-lined, hammered copper *cocotte* so attractive is not only its exceptional cooking qualities, but the fact that it also makes such a fine serving dish. And it is deep enough (8″) and long enough (11¾″) to hold most any kind of bird except a turkey.

Charles F. Lamalle (259A) **$175.00**

Bassine à Ragoût B:54

A whole chicken, a boneless veal rump or a large bottom round roast would fit comfortably in this generous-sized, copper *bassine.* The chicken might be the proverbial *poule en pot* (chicken in the pot), stuffed with rice, onions, sausage and herbs, simmered in stock and then served with an assortment of vegetables. The veal could be browned in the pot, then simmered with some stock, vegetables and herbs in the oven and served with the pan juices. As for the beef, it would be delicious marinated and then braised in red wine with seasonings for a *boeuf à la mode.* This heavy, hammered, tin-lined pot with brass handles and a lid is excellent for braising large pieces of meat, or for cooking substantial quantities of soup or stew. And it certainly could go to a large dining or buffet table. It is 11″ in diameter, 6″ deep and holds 8 quarts.

Charles F. Lamalle (290H) **$180.00**

CASSOULET

For 4 persons:

1½ pounds shoulder of mutton
3 tablespoons goose fat or lard
½ pound garlic sausages
½ pound scraped fresh pork rind, cut into small pieces
1 pig's hock
3 (or more) cups beef consommé
½ pound dried white beans, soaked overnight in cold water
1 onion, stuck with 1 clove
1 bouquet garni
Salt
Freshly ground black pepper
1 tablespoon tomato paste

Cut the shoulder of mutton into pieces and brown the pieces in the goose fat or the lard in a large casserole. Add the sausages, pork rind and pig's hock. Simmer, covered, for 20 minutes, then add enough hot consommé to not quite cover the meats. Simmer, covered over low heat for 1 hour. Cook the beans with the onion and the *bouquet garni* in boiling salted water until the beans are half tender, about 30 minutes. Then drain them and add them to the meats. Season with a little salt and pepper. Simmer, covered, over low heat for 1 more hour. After 30 minutes, add the tomato paste and check the seasoning. Serve in the same dish, very hot.

(From LA CUISINE: SECRETS OF MODERN FRENCH COOKING by Raymond Oliver. Copyright 1969 by Tudor Publishing Company. Reprinted by permission of Tudor Publishing Company.)

A little less than haute cuisine: *"What a hole they'd made in the* blanquette *. . . a spoon was planted in the thick sauce, a good yellow sauce that trembled like jelly. People fished for pieces of veal . . . and their faces were bent over looking for mushrooms. The huge breads, leaning against the wall behind the guests, seemed to melt. . . . The sauce was a little too salty, four liters were required to drown the blessed* blanquette, *which you swallowed like a cream custard and which made a bonfire in your stomach."*

L'Assommoir *by Emile Zola, 1877. Unpublished translation.*

Oval Doufeu B:55

Before modern stoves came to be, pots were generally designed to be hung or set over a fire or placed directly in the flames. In some cases, of which this is an example, pots for braising were constructed so that the fire could sit on *them.* The depressed area in the lid of the pot was meant to hold hot coals that produced a soft (*doux*), even fire (*feu*) around it, hence the name *doufeu.* Today coals are no longer needed, but the feature is preserved for tradition's sake, and because it now serves another function. If cool water is poured into the depression, it promotes heavy condensation within the pot that will keep moist a braising *daube de boeuf* (casserole of beef braised in wine with vegetables). Replenish the cool water as necessary. This enameled cast-iron *doufeu* is 4″ deep, 12″ long, 9″ across and holds 6 quarts. Made in brown, yellow, green and flame, it can be ordered to suit any decor. A smaller 4½-quart size is also available.

Schiller & Asmus, Inc. (C2582-16) **$59.95**

"NOTE BY A PATRIOTIC GOURMAND

I remark with pride that coquetry and gourmandism, those two great modifications born of extreme sociability in response to our most pressing needs, are both of French origin."

The Physiology of Taste or Meditations on Transcendental Gastronomy *by Brillat-Savarin. Dover Publications, 1960.*

A rotisserie from about 1860 that was capable of roasting more than 100 chickens.

Braising Pot B:56

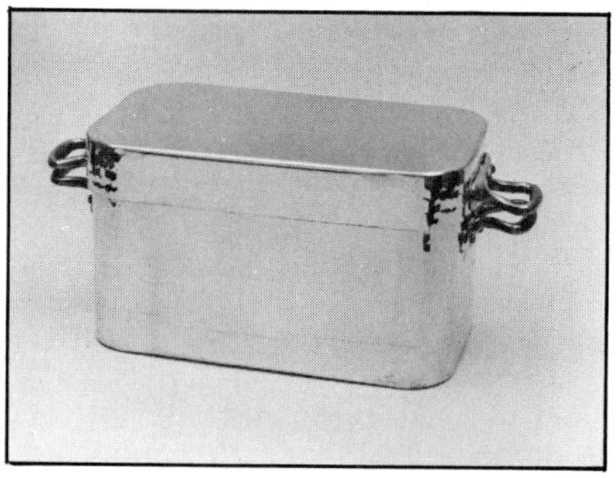

Herculean muscles or a friend are prerequisites for coping with this 20-quart braising pan (*braisière*). But it will hold enough to feed a sizeable group, perhaps a real *pot-au-feu* for 16 people: a large piece of beef and one of pork, a stewing hen, sausages and vegetables—served with broth and one or two creamy sauces. A double *poularde Derby* with two chickens would also be extravagantly sensational in this treasure chest: two chickens stuffed with a mixture of rice, *foie gras* (goose liver), and chopped truffles are placed on a bed of diced vegetables and herbs, braised in veal stock and then served in a Madeira-flavored sauce made with the pan juices. If you simply need a roasting pan, the 2⅛″-deep lid will serve quite nicely. Otherwise, it fits snugly down over the top of the large pan. Both lid and pan have a pair of riveted brass loop handles that overlap each other. This splendid copper coffer is 16″ long, 9″ wide and 8¾″ deep.

Charles F. Lamalle (3292) **$300.00**

Stock Pot B:57

It's no accident that in France stocks are called the *fonds de cuisine* (foundations of cooking): most French dishes benefit from some kind of stock. The most important are of beef, veal, chicken or fish, and they are easy to make because you don't have to watch over them closely. But you do need a special, large, deep pot for a number of reasons: it must hold a lot of bones, meat and vegetables; the surface area must be relatively small for minimum evaporation; it should be deep so the liquid bubbles up well through the ingredients; and the bottom of the pan must be thick enough to prevent heavy ingredients from scorching next to the heat. This heavy-gauge, hammered-aluminum pot not only answers all those needs but is reasonably light as well, a real advantage when it comes to lifting a vessel of this size. (To avoid straining yourself, use a small saucepan as a ladle when emptying the pot.) With a 22-quart capacity, this pot measures 12″ in diameter and is 11½″ deep. The lid is slightly wider, 12½″, and is 2″ deep. Both lid and pot have pairs of matching loop handles that can be held together for lifting.

Charles F. Lamalle (5938) **$90.00**

Small attelets.

Attelets B:58

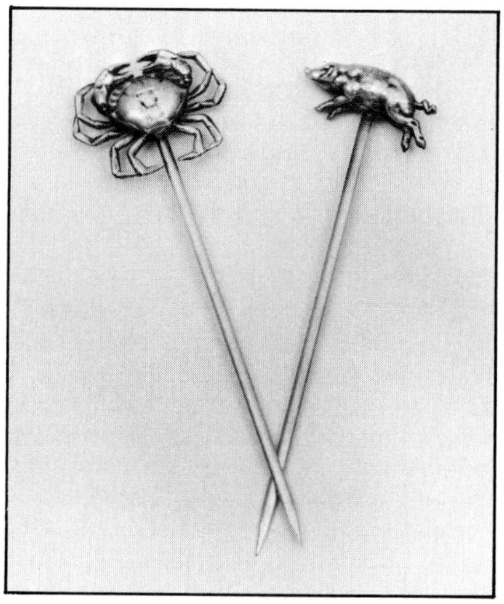

In addition to gracefully shaped vegetables or glistening jewels of *gelée*, formal cold buffet dishes are frequently embellished with ornamental metal skewers called *attelets.* The top of the skewer is always crowned by a figure of some sort like this crab or pig. Then a number of things like a whole truffle, carved lemon, tomato, part of a lettuce head or a specially prepared piece of food are threaded onto the *attelet* to cover the plain metal shaft. A decorative *attelet* adds height and balance to a presentation. For example, a duck in orange-flavored aspic perched in the middle of a large tray may need more height to look comfortable on the tray aesthetically; an *attelet* solves the problem beautifully. These silver-plated *attelets* are 8″ long. A swan, pheasant, ram, peacock and lobster are also obtainable.

Charles F. Lamalle (553A) **$11.00**

STRIPED BASS WITH SORREL SAUCE

Bar à l'Oseille

2 cups white wine
2 cups fish stock
1 cup beef consommé
3–4 shallots, minced
2–3 tablespoons parsley
½ teaspoon black peppercorns
1 onion, chopped
2 cups heavy cream
1 cup *crème fraîche*
2 bunches fresh sorrel, cut *en chiffonade* (very fine julienne strips)
Butter
1 4-pound striped bass, filleted*
White wine and fish stock for poaching

Make a white wine sauce as a base for the sorrel sauce: place the wine, stock, consommé, shallots, parsley, peppercorns and onion in a saucepan, bring to a boil and reduce over high heat until syrupy. Whisk in the heavy cream and *crème fraîche* and continue to reduce until the sauce thickens slightly and is velvety in texture. Set aside.

While the sauce is reducing, gently cook the *chiffonade* of sorrel in a little butter, just until it wilts. Set aside. Poach the striped bass fillets in enough white wine and fish stock to just cover them for approximately 8 to 10 minutes. DO NOT OVERCOOK!

When the fish is cooked, divide the fillets into 6 to 8 equal portions. Combine the sorrel with the white wine sauce and spoon liberally over each portion. Garnish each serving with a fluted mushroom cap, sliced truffles, or whole shrimp, if desired.

Yield: 6 to 8 servings.

* Save the fish bones when you (or your fishmonger) fillet the bass to make the stock.

(Courtesy of Jean-Jacques Rachou, Le Lavandou Restaurant, New York City.)

Fish Poacher B:59

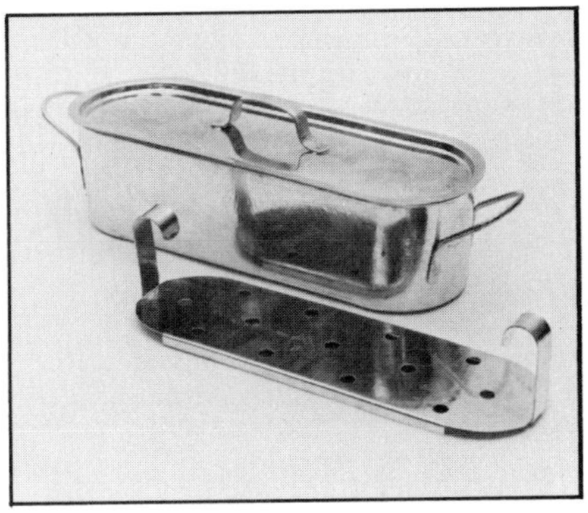

Poaching is probably the most natural way to cook a fish: certainly no other method leaves fish moister or more pure in flavor. In addition, the poaching liquid can be used to make a wonderful sauce to suit the impressive catch. One of the most succulent of all fish is the striped bass, favored by the French for its tender white flesh and subtle, sweet flavor. In the spring it is frequently served with sorrel sauce (*à l'oseille*); the rest of the year a white wine or champagne sauce or a golden hollandaise is its most constant companion. When poaching fish, always make sure the water doesn't boil to overcook it or break it apart; and wrap the fish in a doubled layer of dampened cheesecloth so that you can lift it safely from the poaching rack. A fish for two should just fit the 14″-long rack of this poacher. Overall, the poacher is 16″ long, 5½″ across and 4″ deep. It is made of tinned steel with rolled edges and has two strong, large loop handles. The rack has curved handles for easy lifting. If you need a larger poacher, it comes in lengths of 20″, 24″, 28″ and 36″.

Charles F. Lamalle (460) **$60.00**

"Fish, taken collectively in all its species, is to the philosopher an endless source of meditation and surprise.

The varied forms of these strange creatures, the senses which they lack, and the limited powers of those which they possess, the influence of the peculiar surroundings in which they live and breathe and move, all combine to extend the range of our ideas, and reveal the infinite modifications which may arise from matter, movement, and life.

For myself, I look upon them with a feeling akin to respect, being deeply persuaded that they are the most antediluvian of creatures; for the great cataclysm, which drowned our granduncles eighteen hundred years after the creation of the world, was a time of rejoicing, conquest, and festivity for the fishes."

The Physiology of Taste or Meditations on Transcendental Gastronomy *by Brillat-Savarin. Dover Publications, 1960.*

Turbot Poacher B:60

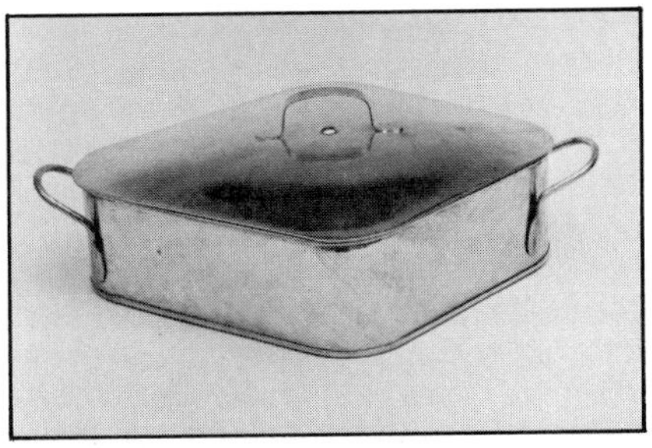

Fish, like people, are geographically defined, so the French have the turbot. A virtually scale-free flatfish, the turbot has been best described as a fish that's been put through a wringer. Proust once described it as a fish that is "all profile." Likened to its relative, the American halibut, the turbot's flesh is so delicate that the French accord it special treatment and have named and reserved for it its own particular utensil: the *turbotière.* Diamond-shaped and made of tinned steel throughout, the *turbotière* measures 18″ by 15¼″ and is 4⅜″ deep. The inside rack has strong looped handles at either end and there is a flat handle atop the tightly-fitted lid.

Debuyer **$100.00**

Gratin, Egg and Soufflé Dishes

Pleasing the eye is as important as pleasing the palate in French cooking. For this reason, many ovenproof porcelain or enameled-iron dishes are designed to go right from stove to table. Numerous vegetable and meat specialties are topped with bread crumbs or cheese and lightly browned under a broiler before they are served; others are simply baked in the upper part of a hot oven until golden brown. Both require shallow, ovenproof dishes that will expose most of their contents to the heat; such are the classic oval gratin dishes and porcelain shells. But other shapes are required for different foods and cooking techniques: a bowl for onion soup; an egg dish, just large enough for two; cups for hot hors d'oeuvre or custard; and last, but far from least, a large, deep, straight-sided dish for the ethereal soufflé.

Porcelain Gratin Dish — B:61

Golden crusted dishes called gratins are usually made in shallow, open, ovenproof containers like this. Food (that may have been partially cooked on top of the stove) is placed in a gratin dish, sprinkled with butter and bread crumbs or grated cheese, and then placed in the upper third of an oven or under a broiler to create a crisp, crusty top. Perhaps the most famous gratin dish is *pommes de terre à la dauphinoise,* the dish we know as scalloped potatoes. Thinly sliced potatoes are mixed with milk, egg, grated Gruyère and seasonings, topped with more sprinkled cheese and baked in a garlic-rubbed dish until golden brown and tender. They make a superb complement to a leg of lamb or beef roast. No container could be more classic than this graceful oval gratin dish of white porcelain adorned simply by two handles formed by the extended rim of the dish and ridged to resemble shells. The dish is 11″ long, 7″ across and 1⅝″ deep. Lengths of 6¾″, 9″ and 15¾″ are available as well.

Schiller & Asmus, Inc. **$7.50**
(P2403-28)

Enameled Cast-Iron Gratin Dish — B:62

One of the advantages of an oval gratin dish is its long shape that is so well suited to cooking fish—fillets of sole *à la parisienne,* for example. The fillets are first baked with butter, shallots and white wine and then masked with a cheese-and-egg sauce made from the pan juices. The top is dotted with butter and sprinkled with cheese and the fish is returned to the oven briefly to heat through. As a finishing touch, it is passed quickly under a broiler until the top browns, and then is taken right to the table. Not only is this dish unbreakable (though the enamel will chip if you are not careful), but it comes in four colors, all with a white interior: flame, green, yellow or chocolate brown. This 11″-long size is 8″ wide, 1¾″ deep and holds 6 cups. Its curving handles, integral to the rim, are fluted. In addition, you may choose from several other lengths: 8″, 9½″, 12½″ or 14½″.

Hammacher Schlemmer/ Schiller & Asmus, Inc. **$16.95**
(C-7013-28)

Porcelain Scallop Shell — B:63

For centuries the scallop shell has been the symbol of St. James, the patron saint of Spain whose shrine is in Santiago de Compostela. Pilgrims to the shrine wore or carried such a shell to proclaim their devotion to him. Thus the shell is known as the pilgrim shell, and in France, it is called a *coquille St. Jacques* (St. James shell). The shell is so beautiful and large that its use as a serving dish has long been appreciated for seafood. A favorite is scallops served in a white wine sauce with mushrooms, topped by a golden crust of melted Gruyère, otherwise known as *coquilles St. Jacques à la parisienne.* A scallop was not responsible for *this* creamy white shell, but what the porcelain version lacks in natural beauty is made up for in stability and size. Porcelain is less fragile than shell, and three small projections on the bottom of this dish keep it from tipping the way a natural shell does. Also, the porcelain dishes are of consistent size and a bit deeper than their natural counterparts. This one is 5¼″ across and 4¾″ long. Two other sizes are: 4″ by 3⅝″ and 4″ by 4″. All are dishwasher safe.

Pillivuyt S.A. **$5.00**
(240312)

COQUILLES SAINT-JACQUES NANTAISE

Scallops on the Shell with Mushrooms and White Wine Sauce

1½ pounds scallops
2 shallots, minced

2–3 parsley stems
1 bay leaf
Salt and pepper to taste
Water
Dry white wine
1 pound mushrooms, sliced
Lemon juice
¼ cup (4 tablespoons) butter
2 tablespoons flour
1 cup heavy cream
2 egg yolks
Pinch cayenne pepper
¾ pound tiny shrimp, cooked
Grated Gruyère cheese

Place the scallops in a saucepan with the shallots, parsley, bay leaf and salt and pepper to taste, and add enough water and wine, in equal proportions, to just cover the scallops. Bring to a boil and remove from the heat.

Meanwhile, cook the mushrooms with a little water, lemon juice, salt, pepper and a tablespoon of butter. Once cooked, reserve the liquid.

When the scallops and mushrooms are done, make a *roux blanc:* cook together, until foamy, 2 tablespoons each of butter and flour, for approximately 1 minute. Add the cooking liquid from the mushrooms and one-half of the liquid in which the scallops cooked. Whisk together and simmer for 10 minutes; then add the heavy cream and simmer 5 to 6 minutes longer, whisking occasionally.

Remove the pan from the fire and add the remaining tablespoon butter, bit by bit, whisking in each addition before adding the next. Whisk in the 2 egg yolks, one at a time. Squeeze in a little lemon juice, add a pinch of cayenne pepper and taste for seasoning.

Strain the sauce through a fine sieve or *chinois* and stir in the scallops, mushrooms and shrimp. Divide between six individual, heatproof serving dishes and sprinkle each with a little grated Gruyère. If the mixture is still hot, simply run the dishes under a hot broiler to brown the top. If cold, bake in a preheated 375–400 F. oven for 10 minutes.

Yield: 6 servings.

(Courtesy Robert Renaud, Le Jacques Coeur Restaurant, New York City.)

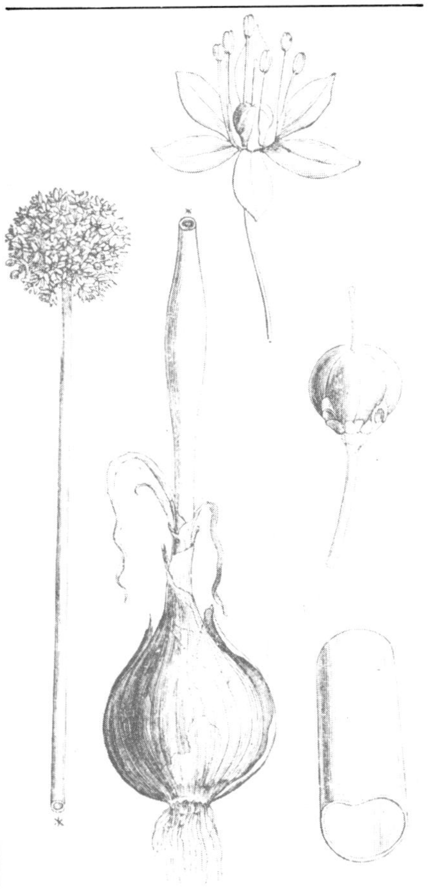

The central character of onion soup with all its particulars.

Onion Soup Bowl B:64

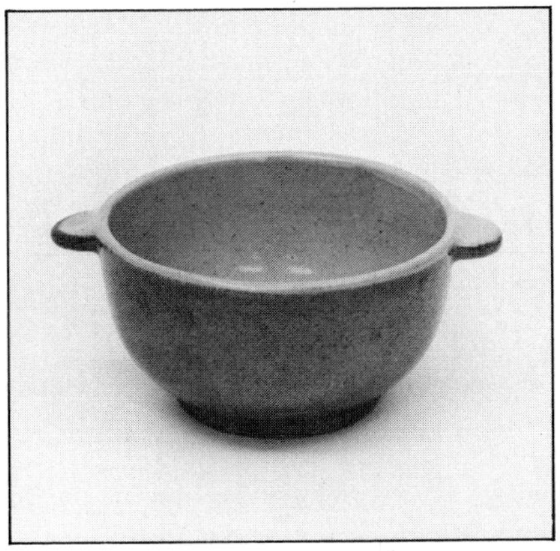

When Les Halles was still located in the heart of Paris, a late-night, post-party tradition was to head for this bustling market for a bowl of onion soup. In numerous little bistros, some dating from the 1550s, couples in ball gowns and dinner jackets could be seen—alongside butchers in bloody aprons—savoring *soupe à l'oignon gratinée* (gratinéed onion soup). Rich onion soup, its deep flavor sealed with a crust of bread and Gruyère cheese gratinéed under a broiler—is still served all over France in crocks such as this. It is a generous round bowl of glazed earthenware that is 5″ in diameter across the top, 2½″ deep and holds 2 cups. Inside, it is gray and the surface is textured, but the outside is a smooth dark brown. Its only adornment are two half-rounds of clay at the rim that serve as handles.

Bridge Kitchenware Corp. **$3.75**

Salamander B:65

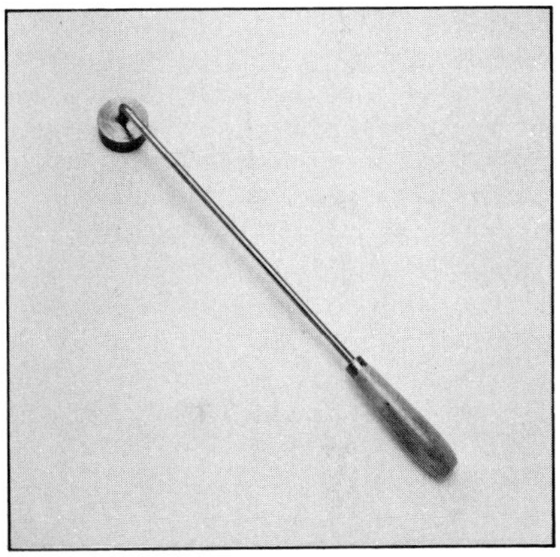

If you want to gratinate a dish with a delicate sauce or other ingredients that might suffer from overheating, a salamander will quickly brown the top without damaging the food. It will also save you from using a broiler, and if you need the oven for something else you won't have to disturb it. Just put the metal end of the salamander (*salamandre*) on your stovetop burner for a few minutes until it becomes red-hot, then pass it over a dish like chicken-filled crêpes bathed in a Mornay (cheese) sauce and you will see it turn golden brown before your eyes. Our 18½″-long salamander has a comfortable wood handle that is held by a brass collar to a heavy steel rod. The other end of the rod curves to hold a 2″-diameter steel disc.

Charles F. Lamalle (459/N) **$7.50**

Shirred Egg Dish B:66

Oeufs sur le plat (eggs in the cooking dish) are made by melting some butter in a heatproof dish or pan, carefully sliding in two eggs and cooking them slowly, covered, on top of the stove or in the oven for several minutes. The whites come out a brilliant white and the yolks are thinly veiled and beautifully smooth; and there is no danger of breaking them because the same dish goes right to the table. A porcelain dish like this with its fluted handles is excellent for cooking in the oven, looks lovely as an individual serving dish and will keep the eggs nice and warm. It will also continue to cook them after it leaves the oven, so calculate that factor into your cooking time. Of course, the eggs may be garnished after they are cooked with any number of things like sausage slices, asparagus spears and/or some kind of sauce. Our pristine white dish is 5″ in diameter.

Schiller & Asmus, Inc. $3.50
(P2303-12)

"Just as . . . [Jorrocks] was taking breath, a garçon entered with some custards and an enormous omelette soufflée *whose puffy brown sides bagged over the tin dish that contained it. 'There's a tart!' cried Mr. Jorrocks. 'Oh my eyes, what a swell! Well, suppose I must have a shy at it.—In for a penny, in for a pound! As we say at the Lord Mayor's feed. Know I shall be sick, but however, here goes. . . ." The first dive of the spoon undeceived him as he heard it sound at the bottom of the dish. 'Oh, lauk, what a go! All puff, by Jove:—a regular humbug—a balloon pudding in short! I won't eat such stuff—give it to Mouncheer there,' rejecting the offer of a piece. 'I like the solids;—will trouble you for some of that cheese, sir. . . ?"*

Jorrocks' Jaunts and Jollies *by Robert Smith Surtees from* Epicure's Companion *by Anne Seranne and John Tebbel. David McKay, 1962.*

Soufflé Dish B:67

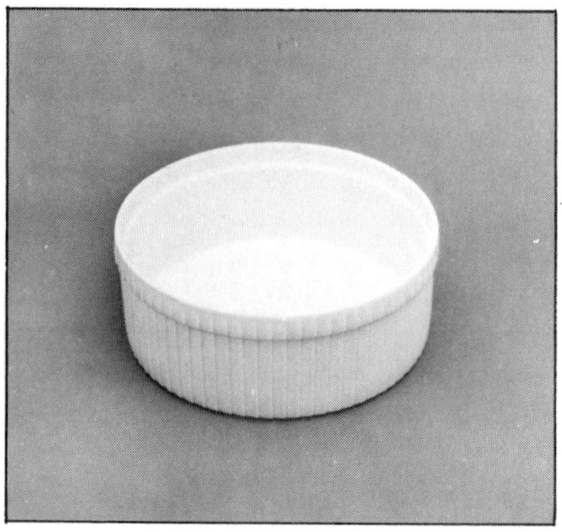

Few French dishes are treated with greater respect than the soufflé, whose airy nature is a culinary triumph. Whether savory or sweet, a soufflé should be as light as a breeze, yet moist and even a bit creamy in the center. One basic expedient is the dish in which it is cooked, typically one of porcelain with straight, deep sides that support the soufflé on its rise to glory. The inside of the dish must be perfectly smooth, but the exterior may be decoratively fashioned like this fluted example. The dish is completely glazed except on the bottom for better heat absorption. It holds 2 quarts and is 8″ in diameter and 3″ deep, a good size for a billowy Grand Marnier soufflé for six. Remember to stop beating the egg whites for a soufflé when they are just thick enough to stand in a peak on the end of a beater; over-beating can make them break down when you are folding them into the soufflé mixture. Other dishes are available in capacities of 1, 1½, 2½ and 3 quarts.

Schiller & Asmus, Inc. $10.50
(P2611-21)

"These dishes, being the last of the Dinner, require the greatest care and taste in executing, as, by the time they come on the table the appetites of those around it are supposed to be satisfied; the eye and the palate require to be pleased in order to sustain the enjoyments of the table; this is the period of dinner when another of the senses may be gratified by the introduction of music (and which is continually practised on the Continent), and all ought to be of a light and inviting character.

Formerly it was the custom never to give a dinner without a soufflé as the last dish, or, professionally speaking, remove. I do not dislike them, but they require the greatest care and nicety, and are rather difficult to perform in our old-fashioned kitchens, but easy in my new stove."

The Modern Housewife or Ménagère *by Alexis Soyer. Simpkin, Marshall, & Co., 1851.*

Ramekin B:68

Ramekins are individual baking dishes, known as *cassolettes* or *cocottes* in French. They can be used to make *oeufs en cocotte* (eggs baked in an individual dish in a water bath) with some cream or a delectable sauce added for variation. Almost any hot, savory ragout or gratin hors d'oeuvre would also do nicely in the dish, as would a portion of *crème caramel* (custard with caramelized sugar) for dessert. The fluted, white porcelain dish is perfectly smooth on the inside and is glazed, except on the bottom. It holds 5 ounces, is 1⅝″ deep and 3¼″ in diameter, and comes in a set of 6.

Schiller & Asmus, Inc. $8.00
(P5404-15)

A pleasure commonly known as oeufs en gelée: *"I became aware that I was eating something particularly delicious, soft-boiled eggs embedded in a layer of meat jelly, seasoned with herbs, and discreetly iced."*

Madame Husson's Rose-King *by Guy de Maupassant, from* Eating and Drinking: An Anthology for Epicures, *edited by Peter Hunt. Ebury Press, 1961.*

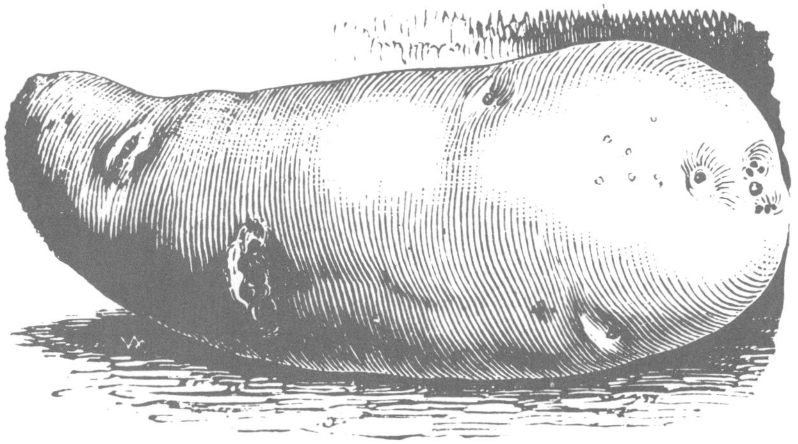

Parmentier's gift to France.

Potatoes

Few of us have ever seen a potato flower, but it was as an ornamental plant that this South American tuber entered France around 1540. Sporadic attempts to cultivate the root as a food were made, but the suspicious population feared it caused leprosy and a host of other nasty diseases. Not until 1787 did the agronomist-pharmacist-economist Parmentier raise the potato consciousness of the French. With shrewd psychological understanding of his fellow man, he reasoned that people who shunned a food freely offered them would clamor for it if it was withheld. He had an acre near Paris planted with potatoes. It was closely guarded by soldiers during the day, but left unsupervised at night. Human nature prevailed, the potatoes disappeared into the cookpots of the curious and a new glory was added to the repertoire of French cuisine. Since Parmentier's success, the peasant drinking his breakfast soup, the shopkeeper eating his steak and *pommes frites* (french fried potatoes), and the master chef turning out *pommes Anna* (a fancy potato cake) and tiny, golden potato nests have been thoroughly satisfied with the potato.

Potato Baller B:69

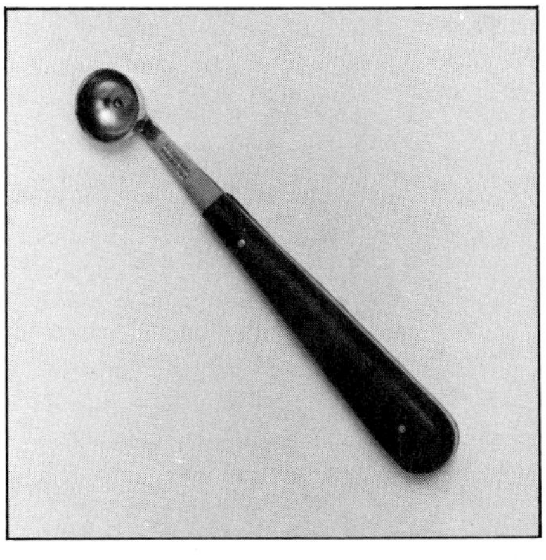

Call it a melon ball cutter if you wish, but this instrument is also used to carve tiny rounds for *pommes noisettes* (tiny potato balls sautéed until golden brown in butter), to accompany meat and fowl dishes. This hemispheric, high-carbon-steel cutter, has sharply honed edges, and is smoothly soldered to a stainless-steel shaft whose full tang is visibly embraced by a resilient rosewood handle. The utensil is 6″ long, and the cutting cup is ⅞″ in diameter. Cook the remaining potato scraps in water and purée them for soup or mashed potatoes.

B. I. A. Cordon Bleu, Inc. (KE 122) $4.70

Column Cutters B:70

Column (*colonne*) cutters are used to cut potatoes or any other firm vegetable into slightly tapered cylinders, or to hollow out vegetables or core fruit. To make *pommes de terre gastronome,* cut long pieces of potato with the 1″-diameter column. Then cut the pieces into ¼″-thick, round slices and sauté them in butter with Madeira, chicken jelly and truffle slices until golden. Squeeze a bit of lemon juice on the potatoes before serving. Or use the cutter to make *pommes de terre à la basquaise:* hollowed out potatoes, filled with a garlic-flavored tomato mixture and baked in butter. The seven columns in this set are 4″ long and range from ⅜″ in diameter to 1¼″ in diameter; all fit a cylindrical tinned-steel case. They, too, are made of tinned steel and the top of each is smoothly rolled; the bottom has a sharp cutting edge.

Bridge Kitchenware Corp. $20.00

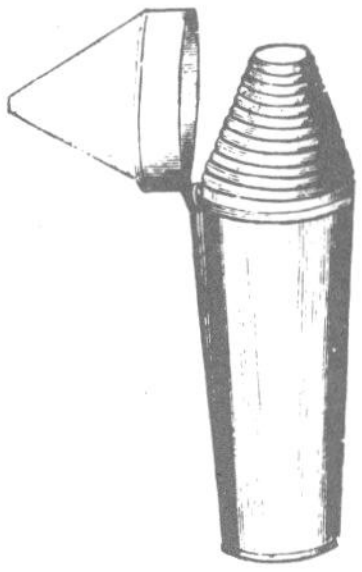

A set of vegetable cutters.

POTATO NESTS

Les Nids en Pommes Paille

Potatoes
Fat for deep-frying
Salt

With the help of a shredder, called a *mandoline* in France, or by hand, cut the potatoes into julienne strips.

Shape the julienne potatoes into a nest with the help of a special double frying basket. Or use 2 strainers, one slightly larger than the other. Plunge them into hot fat heated to 360° F. on a frying thermometer.

Fry in hot fat, without separating or loosening the two strainers.

When the potatoes are beginning to turn golden, remove from the fat and unmold the nest.

Plunge the potato nest back into the hot fat taking care that the potato nest turns golden on all sides. Keep it down in the fat with a slotted spoon.

Drain it on kitchen paper and sprinkle it with salt. Serve very hot.

(From LA CUISINE: SECRETS OF MODERN FRENCH COOKING by Raymond Oliver. Copyright 1969 by Tudor Publishing Company. Reprinted by permission of Tudor Publishing Company.)

Birds' Nest Basket B:71

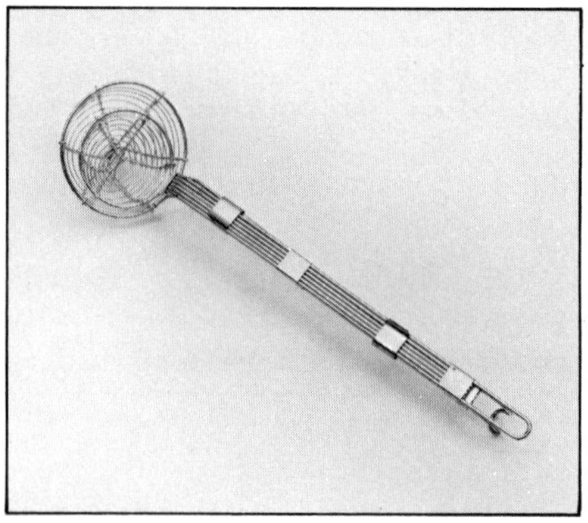

With potato nests you can serve potatoes and impressively garnish a platter at the same time. First, the potatoes have to be cut into the finest possible julienne strips with a mandoline. Next, the strips are pressed into an even layer in the larger of two wire baskets. The smaller basket is then set over the potatoes, both baskets are clamped together and the nest is dipped in hot oil until it turns golden brown. Such nests are really effective filled with *pommes de terre soufflées* (puffed, deep-fried potato slices) or croquettes. This nest of baskets is made of heavy-gauge tinned wire; the larger one is 4″ in diameter and the smaller one is 3″ in diameter. Overall, the implement is 17″ long. Both hook and wire loop at the end of the handle permit hanging.

Charles F. Lamalle (943E) $10.00

Pommes Vapeur Pot B:72

For the kitchen that has everything, here is the fanciest piece of equipment for the simplest recipe: steamed potatoes (*pommes de terre à l'anglaise*). Peeled potatoes, or any other large vegetable for that matter, are steamed royally in this copper bucket. First, pour water into the flattened copper ball that forms the bottom of the bucket. Then insert the tinned-steel grate that fits above it. Add the vegetables, cover and place the steamer on a burner. The bucket holds about 6½ cups and is 6″ deep and 6½″ in diameter; the ball is 5½″ in diameter. Both loop handles on the bucket and the knob on the tight-fitting, domed copper lid are of brass.

Charles F. Lamalle (290R) $120.00

Pommes Anna Pan B:73

No list of outstanding French potato dishes would be complete without *pommes Anna,* a glorified potato cake made in a special pan like this one. To make it, potatoes are first trimmed into even cylinders and then cut into fine round slices that are sautéed lightly in clarified butter. Next, the slices are placed in overlapping concentric rings around the bottom or top of a buttered *pommes Anna* pan, and the sides of the pan are also lined carefully. The buttered pan is then filled, until slightly heaping with layers of potatoes (added more casually, but sprinkled with lots of clarified butter and seasoned). There are several alternatives for cooking the potatoes: they may be cooked on top of the stove, covered; in the oven, uncovered; or started on top of the stove, covered, and finished in the oven, uncovered. Take your choice, but if you use the oven, it should be hot (about 425 F.), so the potatoes will turn golden brown. Always let the *pommes Anna* sit for about five minutes after they are taken from the heat to let them shrink a bit and prevent sticking. Then turn the decorative potato cake onto a platter and serve it at once. Although our tin-lined, hammered-copper pan has a diameter of only 6½″, the top is 1¼″ high and will make enough *pommes Anna* to feed four people; the 2½″-deep bottom should hold enough for 6 to 8 people. (If you use the oven alone to cook the potatoes, either the top or the bottom of the pan can be filled.) The matching pair of handles on top and bottom are made of solid brass.

Charles F. Lamalle (287) $80.00

The interior of a 16th century French kitchen.

Bread, the ubiquitous companion of wine, seems to be missing at this editorial gathering at the Chat Noir.

Bread and Butter

A typical American vision of a Frenchman is that of a small, neat fellow in a black beret bicycling home from the local *boulangerie* (bread store) with a crusty *baguette* tucked under one arm. In reality, the gentleman probably has a slight paunch, wears a homburg or no hat at all, and is stuck in a traffic jam on his way to a bakery across town where the bread is much superior to the stuff in his own neighborhood. Alas, "progress" has hit that holy of holies, the French bakery. The price is still fixed by law so that no one may suffer from lack of bread, and the ingredients must be flour, water, salt and yeast, nothing more; but the charcoal-fired brick ovens are being replaced by electric ones. Few young bakers are now willing to get up in the middle of the night to stoke old-fashioned fires.

A few years ago there was a minor riot when outraged patrons discovered that their bakery—outwardly the usual spic-and-span, white-tiled emporium with curlicued baker's racks and the baker's wife making change at the *caisse* (cash register)—was using *frozen dough!* Only the American newspaper, the Paris *Herald-Tribune*, saw any humor in the situation! *Figaro* and *France-Soir* were thoroughly shocked and disapproving. Bread to the French is no laughing matter. They eat it with every meal, from the morning *croissant* to the heel of the loaf that accompanies the last nugget of cheese at dinner. The schoolchild's favorite afternoon treat is bread and chocolate (*pain au chocolat*), a curious combination to us.

The French would no sooner think of making bread at home than the English would think of making Worcestershire sauce; both operations being the province of professionals. But Americans, with no recourse to a *boulangerie*, willingly attempt French baking, and with good results. They make not only the *baguette* and its thinner sister, the *ficelle*, but fine-textured *pain de mie* and puffy *brioche*. It would be ironic if, some sad day, Americans had to teach their Gallic friends how to bake at home!

Our phrase "to earn one's bread and butter" would be meaningless to a Frenchman. Why put them together? Butter rarely accompanies bread, the exception being the *tartine*, buttered bread eaten as a snack and occasionally at breakfast. When butter does appear on the table, it's for other uses. If you absolutely must have a little butter on your bread, next time you're in France, order radishes; butter always comes with them.

Bread Rising Basket — B:74

This attractive coiled reed basket known as a *banneton* will leave a lasting impression on round, country-style loaves of bread. For the final rising punch the bread dough down, shape it into a ball and place it in the heavily floured basket. When it has doubled in bulk, turn the dough out upside down onto a buttered and floured baking sheet to bake. The beehive impression made by the coils of the basket will usually remain to give the baked loaf a homespun appearance. This *banneton* is 8″ diameter, 2½″ deep and can hold 1½ pounds of bread dough.

Williams-Sonoma — $10.00

Pain de Mie Pan — B:75

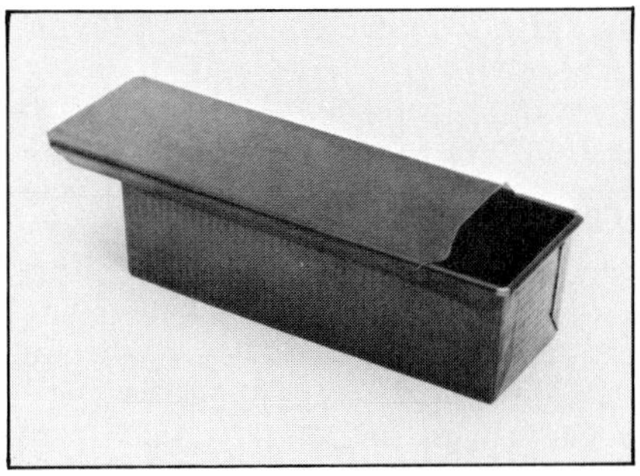

Most French bread is elongated and very crusty; but there are times when an evenly shaped, close-grained bread with little or no crust is a great advantage—in making sandwiches, canapés, or croutons, for instance. With a completely closed, rectangular baking tin, like this one, such a loaf—known as *pain de mie* (soft crumb, as opposed to crust, bread)—can be baked very readily. The lid keeps air from drying the dough and forming a crust on it, and it forces the rising bread to expand into the corners of the box. American bakers call this a Pullman loaf pan, perhaps because it bears some resemblance to a Pullman car. Made of heavy-gauge, black, sheet steel, spot-welded at the corners, the pan is sturdily built to withstand years of use. The lid is removable for easy cleaning, and the top of the pan is rolled around a heavy steel rod for a smooth finish. It is 10″ long, 3¾″ wide and 3″ deep.

H. Roth & Son — $8.95

Black-Steel French Bread Frame — B:76

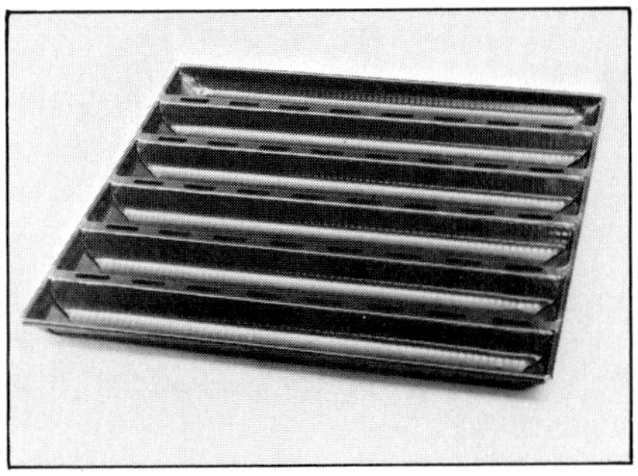

Tucked into a string shopping bag, a

Continued from preceding page

briefcase, school bag, or simply under the arm, the *baguette* (long, thin French bread) is one of the most familiar sights and tastes of France. More than that, it's the daily bread for most Frenchmen. One bite into a crusty, flavorsome loaf will tell you why. Fortunately for the French there are bakeries in every neighborhood and around every corner, but those of us without that benefit must bake our own. To help us is this black-steel pan with troughs for six loaves that give the bread shape while it is rising and baking. It is 17″ square, and each trough is 2¼″ wide. The troughs are divided by flat ridges perforated with holes to let air circulate between the loaves, and the darkened steel will assure an evenly browned crust. (For a good crust, you should also put a pan of water at the bottom of the oven.) To be honest, this pan is a trifle shorter than a *baguette,* so it will fit in your oven.

H. Roth & Son (30-16) $16.95

CLYDE BROOKS' FRENCH BREAD

1 package active dry yeast
1 tablespoon salt
1–2 tablespoons sugar
2½ cups lukewarm water (80–100 F.)
7 cups flour, approximately
1 egg white

In a large bowl dissolve the yeast, salt and sugar in the warm water. Stir in as much flour as you can with ease, then turn the dough onto a well-floured board and knead in as much more flour as is necessary to form a workable dough. Once all the flour has been incorporated, continue to knead for 10 minutes longer, until the dough is smooth and elastic, though still soft. Place in a buttered bowl, turn to coat the top, cover and allow to rise in a warm place until doubled in bulk, approximately 1–1½ hours.

Butter and flour two Paris bread pans (to make four long loaves).

Punch down the dough and turn it onto a floured board. Knead several times, divide into four equal portions* and roll each into a ball. Cover with a towel and allow to rest for 10 minutes before proceeding.

Roll each ball into a cylinder several inches shorter than the bread frames and place in the pans. Beat the egg white with a drop or two of cold water and brush the top of each loaf (this produces a nice, brown, slightly shiny crust). Slash each loaf diagonally 3 or 4 times to a depth of about ¼″–⅜″, using the tip of a very sharp knife or a razor blade. Allow to double in a warm place, about 1½–2 hours.

Preheat oven to 450 F. Bake the loaves for 15 minutes, then turn the oven down to 350 F. and continue baking for 30 minutes longer. Cool on a wire rack.

Yield: Four 18″-long loaves.

* To use a six-loaf French *baguette* frame, simply divide the dough into six equal portions and proceed with the recipe. Cooking time will need to be reduced, however, so start watching the loaves after 30 minutes.

Note: This bread freezes very well. Cut the loaves in half (or leave whole, as you wish) and wrap tightly in aluminum foil. To use, take them from the freezer and put directly into a preheated 350 F. oven and reheat for 20 minutes.

(Courtesy of Clyde Brooks, Paris Bread Pans, Washington, D.C.)

Aluminum French Bread Pans B:77

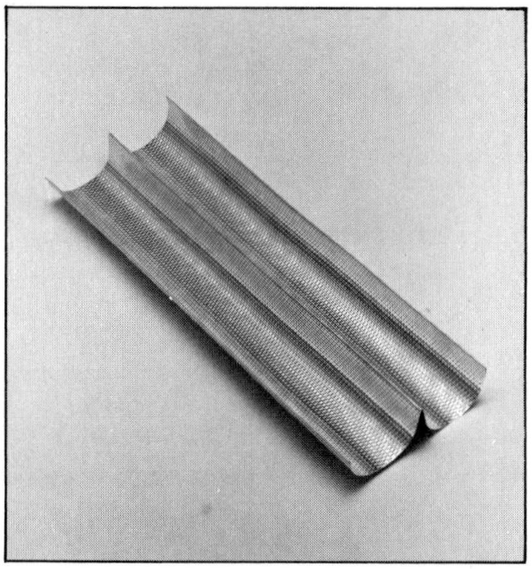

Among the myriad contributions French food has made to the improvement of our gustatory lives, bread is one of the greatest. Although it is difficult to precisely duplicate those long tasty loaves of French bread in the home, you can come reasonably close, especially with unbleached bread flour and the proper equipment. One of the problems faced is obtaining a loaf of the right shape. While the loaves are rising, it is necessary to support them along the sides. To do this, you can either improvise something or obtain a special bread tray like this one made of aluminum, waffled for extra strength. It was designed by a man in Washington, D.C., who fell so much in love with French bread that he had to devise a way to make it in this country. His pans are meant to hold the bread for its final rise and while it bakes. Two pans, each with a pair of 18″-long twin troughs, come in a package. The troughs are 2¾″ wide and 1¾″ deep; and each pan is 5⅝″ wide. An instruction booklet with the manufacturer's own, very detailed recipe for bread accompanies every set of pans.

Paris Bread Pans $7.95

Bread Slasher B:78

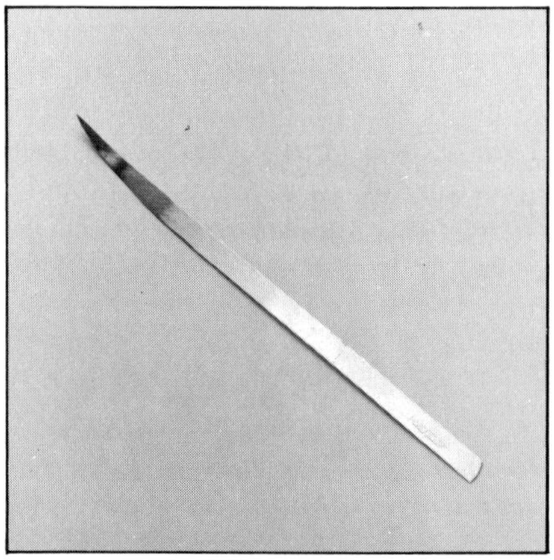

A loaf of French bread is characterized by oblique slashes across its top made with a razor-sharp *lame* (blade). The slits allow the bread to puff open in an attractive pattern as it bakes. To get the proper line, the blade really should be curved, like this 4½″-long one of spring steel, which has been tempered to a fine point. Because the blade is so fine and fragile, it would be best to keep it in an envelope or jar to prevent it from getting lost or damaged—or into the wrong hands.

Bridge Kitchenware Corp. $0.75

Brioche Mold B:79

In French slang, to make a mistake or act foolishly is to *faire une brioche* (to make a *brioche*). The phrase originated long ago when members of the French Opera were fined for playing out of tune. The money collected was spent on *brioches,* which the whole orchestra then shared at a gathering; but all those fined had to wear an emblem representing a *brioche.* There is no mistaking a *brioche* or its form, however. The *brioche* has a very particular shape: fluted sides (as you can see by the mold), but also a round cap that is made by anchoring a small ball of the yeast dough in the center of the *brioche* before it is baked. Thus, it is called a *brioche à tête* (brioche with a head). A *brioche* is golden colored and lightly textured, and makes wonderful eating for breakfast with unsalted butter and homemade jam, especially when it is still a little warm from the oven. For variation, you can add some Gruyère to the dough and serve the *brioche* as luncheon bread. The dough can always be made a day in advance and kept in the refrigerator, if time is short. This tinned-steel mold holds 5 cups and is 8″ in diameter across the top and 3¼″ deep. If you prefer individual *brioches,* 5-ounce molds, 3½″ in diameter, are also available.

Charles F. Lamalle (721) $2.00

BRIOCHE

The ingredients below will make 1 large or about 16 small *brioches.*

5 cups sifted all-purpose flour
1 ounce compressed yeast, or 2 packages active dry yeast
1 tablespoon salt
3 tablespoons sugar
½ cup lukewarm milk
2 whole eggs
6 extra egg yolks
1 cup sweet butter, softened
1 egg, beaten with 1 tablespoon heavy cream

Have all ingredients at room temperature.

Place ¾ cup of the flour in a bowl and make a well in the center. Mix the compressed yeast with ¼ cup of lukewarm water (80° to 90° F.), or use ⅓ cup of warmer water (105° to 115° F.) if using dry yeast, and pour the mixture into the flour well. Stir the flour into the yeast mixture to make a fairly firm dough and knead it into a ball. In French, this is called a *levain,* or sponge. Place the sponge in a bowl and cover it completely with lukewarm water. Set the bowl in a warm place until the sponge expands and rises to the surface of the water. Then remove it. Do not allow it to remain too long or it will disintegrate.

Place the remaining flour on a marble slab or pastry board and make a well in the center. Put in this well the salt, sugar, milk, whole eggs and extra egg yolks and half of the butter. Blend the flour into the other ingredients and then knead in the sponge.

Knead for about 15 minutes in order to get a smooth and elastic dough. Then knead in the remaining butter, which should be of the same consistency as the dough. To do this, flatten out the dough, spread the butter over half of it, and cover with the other half. If the butter breaks out, the dough will become very sticky, but do not add more flour. Simply continue kneading until the dough no longer clings to the board or marble and it is completely smooth and homogenized.

Grease a large bowl with butter and put the dough in it. Cover the bowl with a kitchen towel and keep in a warm place for about 2 hours, or until the dough has doubled in bulk. An oven with only the pilot lighted is excellent, provided the temperature is not above 95° F.

When doubled in bulk, turn the dough out on the marble slab or pastry board and punch it down. Return it to the bowl to rise again in a warm place until doubled in bulk and then punch it down again.

Place the dough in the refrigerator overnight to mellow, punching it down once after the first 2 hours.

To bake a single large *brioche,* pull off a piece of dough about the size of a plum and roll the remaining dough into a ball. Place the ball in a lightly greased round 5- to 6-cup fluted mold. It should fill the mold about two thirds full. Roll the small piece into a ball, punch a small depression in the larger ball with the forefinger, and insert the smaller ball. Place the mold in a warm place until the dough has doubled in bulk and then brush the top with the egg beaten with heavy cream. Bake on the second rack from the bottom of a preheated 400° F. oven for 45 minutes. Remove the *brioche* from the mold immediately.

Small individual *brioches* may be baked in greased 3-inch fluted molds or in muffin tins. They are formed in the same way as a large *brioche,* reserving about one fifth of the dough to form the knobs at the top. If exact uniformity of size is desired, weigh out 2-ounce pieces of dough to form the larger balls. The baking time should be decreased to 15 minutes.

(From LA CUISINE: SECRETS OF MODERN FRENCH COOKING by Raymond Oliver. Copyright 1969 by Tudor Publishing Company. Reprinted by permission of Tudor Publishing Company.)

Brioche Mousseline Mold B:80

Brioche mousseline is the soufflé of the bread world. It is baked with a *brioche* dough, modified to include

Continued from preceding page

more butter for a richer texture. The mold for baking this column-shaped bread is a tinned-steel cylinder, 4½″ in diameter and 5⅝″ deep. Not content to make a bread nearly 6″ high, the French usually fill the 6-cup mold two-thirds full and tie a paper collar about the top so that by the time the bread has finished rising and baking it stands a majestic 8″ to 10″ high. Cut round slices of the *brioche mousseline* to serve at luncheon or tea. Or hollow it out and stuff it with a savory filling of scallops in Mornay (cheese) sauce. Slice and serve it with additional sauce.

Bridge Kitchenware Corp. **$5.75**

Bread Cutter B:81

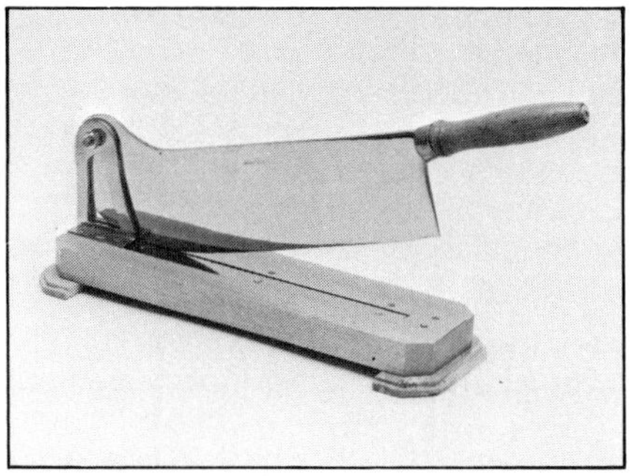

In a restaurant or brasserie where French bread is consumed in large quantities, slices are often lopped off into 2″ lengths with a special bread cutter similar to this one. It works like a paper cutter. Lift the stainless-steel knife by its handle and push it down through the bread and into the steel groove that runs lengthwise along the board. The knife blade, a heavy, slightly curved (14″-by-3½″) rectangle, is a fearsome weapon, fixed, fortunately, to a triangular brass stand that is screwed securely into a wooden base. Overall, the base measures 14″ by 4″, but the knife handle extends another 5½″ beyond it. If you wanted to, you could cut six loaves or more a minute with this cutter.

Charles F. Lamalle (1452) **$48.00**

"The day the supply of melted butter was made for the winter, I myself skimmed off, from the large 20-liter pans, the russet foam that rises on boiling butter while it clarifies. This impurity of the butter was kneaded with flour and salt by my nurse, then put in the oven. . . . Where will I find again the peasant taste, a little bitter, the sandy consistency of such biscuits. Nowhere."

Paysages et portraits *by Colette. Unpublished translation.*

Butter Mold B:82

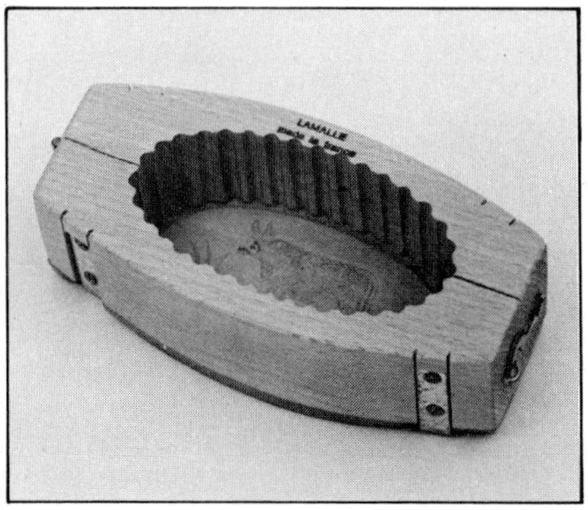

Stamping a design on a block of butter before serving it is not unique to France; but this hinged wooden mold is a typical French design. It comes in three separate parts: a removable oval base plate, carved with a cow eyeing a few tufts of grass, and two side pieces that are hinged together at one end and hooked together at the other. Two sets of aluminum clips on each side of the mold extend downward to hold the base in place. Pack the mold with softened butter, chill it and then unhook the sides to release a block with fluted sides that is 4″ long, 2″ across and 1½″ high.

Charles F. Lamalle (5041) **$16.00**

Butter Chip B:83

A friendly alternative to the communal butter dish is a set of individual *beurriers* (butter servers). This chubby 3″-diameter earthenware butter chip is very appealing. It is a textured sandy brown on the outside and a glazed gray within. Each chip can hold approximately 3 ounces of sweet butter filled to the top and simply smoothed flat. Inexpensive, a set of them adds a nice personal touch to any table.

Charles F. Lamalle (1802) **$2.00**

Butter Dish B:84

French butter is unsalted and absolutely delicious. But it tastes slightly different in various regions of France, so that Frenchmen can argue the merits of each kind, just as they debate the best wines. One reason for its quality and pure taste is that French butter is often washed two or three times in clear cold water before it is sent to market. Another way of keeping a pure taste in butter, and keeping it firm before serving, is to keep it submerged in cold water so it doesn't soften unduly. This glazed earthenware pot—dark brown on the outside, gray on the inside and decorated with three narrow bands of beading—stores butter in its 1¾″-deep cup. While it is being used, the cup perches on a straight-sided container that is 2⅞″ in diameter and 3¼″ deep. Otherwise, the cup is inverted and set into the container that is filled with ice water.

Bridge Kitchenware Corp. **$7.95**

Sweets

We can thank Louis XIV, the king with the gargantuan appetite, for desserts as a daily habit. Before his time, sweets were reserved for *fête* days. But the king had a sweet tooth, and he commanded "quantities of sweet things which always delighted him." Where he led, fashion followed. (That sweet tooth was only figurative—the king had no teeth and lived mainly on soup, hash, eggs, fruit and dessert.)

In the reign of the ill-fated Louis XVI, a new profession arose, that of making *petits fours,* those charming tiny iced cakes. In the rigid catering hierarchy of the time, these practitioners filled a spot "halfway between the *pâtissiers* [pastry bakers] proper and the confectioners."

Today the French still regard pastry as an item belonging to professional purveyors. For an important party a hostess will order a *savarin* (a yeast cake) or *génoise* (sponge cake) from the finest *pâtisserie* (pastry shop) she knows. Far from feeling apologetic at fobbing "store-brought cake" off on her guests, she feels that she is honoring them with the finest she can afford. Fancy baking is not the province of the home cook.

Tarts (or flans), crêpes and custards are another matter. They belong to the *cuisine bourgeoise,* and therefore she feels quite at home with them. What's more, she can trust her oven—apt to be primitive by our standards—to turn out a satisfactory tart.

Americans, except for those in large cities, don't have a first-rate *pâtisserie* at the corner. On the other hand, we do have finely calibrated ovens we can trust, and the enthusiasm to try our hands at creations as dazzling as a towering *croquembouche* (pyramid of caramel-covered cream puffs), a fancy charlotte or a golden *savarin* (a round kirsch-soaked yeast cake).

Madeleine Tin B:85

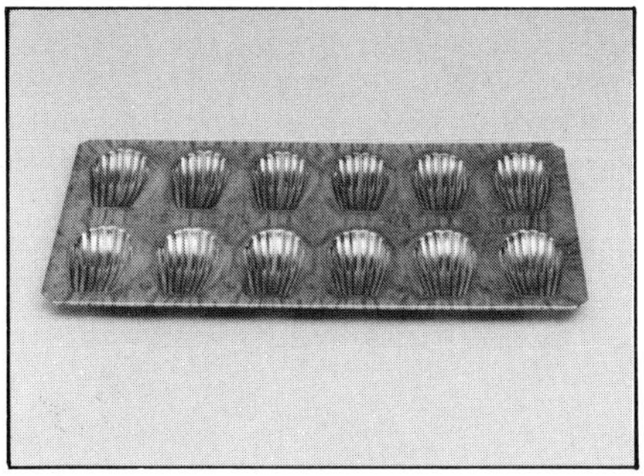

One wintry day Proust's mother sent out for "one of those short, plump little cakes called *petites madeleines,* which looked as though they had been molded in the fluted scallop of a pilgrim's shell." With the *madeleine* she served tea into which Proust dipped the small cake that was to trigger the famous experience he described so memorably. "I raised to my lips a spoonful of the tea in which I had soaked a morsel of the cake. No sooner had the warm liquid, and the crumbs with it, touched my palate than a shudder ran through my whole body. . . . an exquisite pleasure had invaded my senses." Thus, he began to recall the experiences and feelings of his childhood associated with the *madeleine.* Although you might not remember things past when you bite into a moist, spongy *madeleine,* the experience is worth remembering. They are beautiful, golden cakes made simply of sugar, butter, eggs, flour and a touch of lemon or vanilla and then baked in shell-shaped tins like this one. *Madeleines* from the town of Commercy are particularly famous. This 14⅛″ by 7⅜″ pan is stamped from a single sheet of tinned steel with the edges folded over, and holds 12 *madeleines.*

Charles F. Lamalle $5.00
(742/A)

MADELEINES

2 tablespoons butter, softened, to grease molds
2 eggs
¼ cup granulated sugar
½ teaspoon vanilla
½ cup all-purpose flour, sifted
¼ cup unsalted butter, melted and cooled to room temperature

Preheat oven to 375 F. Grease *madeleine* molds with the 2 tablespoons of softened butter.

Place the eggs, sugar and vanilla in the large bowl of an electric mixer. Beat until a thick ribbon drops from the beater when it is lifted from the bowl. The mixture should triple in bulk.

With a rubber spatula fold in the flour, a tablespoon or two at a time. Fold in the melted butter in the same fashion.

Place the mixture in a pastry bag fitted with a large plain tube. Fill the buttered *madeleine* pans two-thirds full and bake the cakes in the preheated oven for 8 to 10 minutes, or until delicately browned.

Remove *madeleines* from the molds to a wire rack to cool.

Yield: about 12.

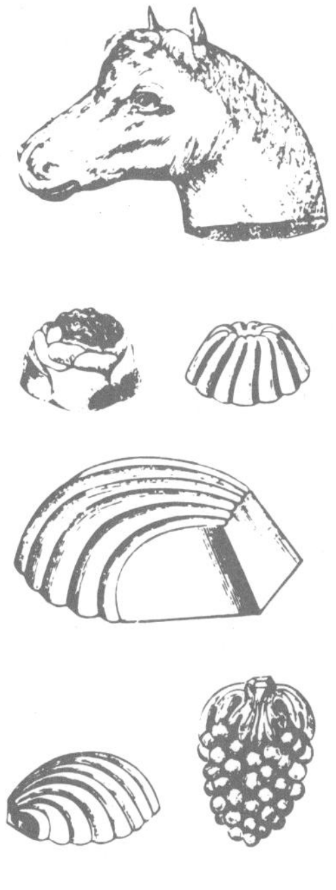

Some curious madeleine *molds from an 1886 catalogue.*

From the late middle ages through the seventeenth century, several kinds of wafers—hosties, gauffres *and* oublies—*were the main bakery products in France. They were often baked in intricate irons like these.*

"The cakes were made of three kinds—Babas, Madeleines, and Savarins—three sous apiece, fourpence-halfpenny the set of three. No nicer cakes are made in France. . . . You must begin with the Madeleine . . . then the Baba; and finish up with the Savarin, which is shaped like a ring, very light, and flavoured with rum. And then you must really leave off."

Trilby *by George du Maurier, 1895.*

Ladyfinger Tin B:86

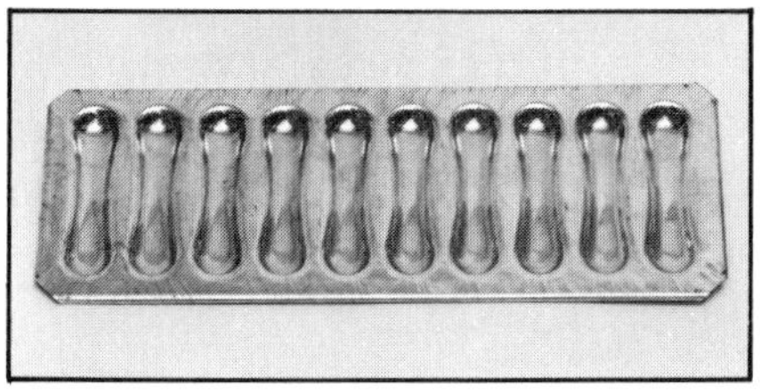

Ladyfingers, or *biscuits à cuillère,* are elegant served with champagne, tea, ice cream or a fruit dessert. They are wonderful sandwiched around some buttercream or a bit of jam. And they are perfect for lining a charlotte (cake- or bread-covered dessert) mold that can be filled with a number of delicious mixtures such as a rich chocolate cream alternated with layers of more ladyfingers and then chilled. Stamped out of a single sheet of tinned steel with rolled edges, this pan is 12½″ long and 4⅞″ wide. It has 10 shallow, 3½″-long depressions into which the ladyfingers are spooned, or piped with a pastry bag.

Charles F. Lamalle (741) **$6.00**

Dents de Loup Tin B:87

Dents de loup are slender, pale yellow cakes, plain in appearance but deadly in appeal: the name, after all, means "wolf's teeth." They are made from a thick batter of eggs, sugar, flour and lemon zest, which is piped into the crevices of a special accordion-pleated pan. It's a simple device, 11¾″ square and 1″ high, the ends neatly rolled around steel wires. Eight zigs of the tinned steel make eight lengths of cookie, which, cut in half, give you 16 wolf's teeth. Dust them with confectioners' sugar and bite into them with your morning coffee.

Williams-Sonoma **$6.95**

GÉNOISE AU CITRON

Lemon Sponge Cake

½ cup (1 stick) unsalted butter
1 teaspoon vanilla
1 tablespoon lemon juice
1 tablespoon grated lemon rind
6 eggs
1 cup granulated sugar
1 cup all-purpose flour

Butter and lightly flour the bottoms of two shallow 8″ cake tins.

Melt the butter over low heat, set aside, and let it stand for a few minutes. Skim off and discard the foam on top. Slowly pour the clear yellow liquid—the clarified butter—into a cup, discarding the sediment remaining in the pan. Stir in the vanilla and lemon.

Blend together in a very large bowl the eggs and ½ cup of the sugar. Place the bowl over a saucepan of barely simmering water and heat the mixture until it is very warm, stirring frequently and thoroughly.

Meanwhile, sift the flour and return to the sifter.

Preheat oven to 350 F.

With an electric beater beat the eggs, now off the heat, for 5 minutes at high speed. Gradually add the remaining ½ cup of sugar, continuing to beat the mixture at high speed for about 10 minutes, until it resembles a soft, glossy meringue.

Sift in about a quarter of the flour and delicately fold it into the eggs. Fold in about a third of the clarified butter, then alternate additions of flour and butter, working quickly and lightly.

Turn the batter gently into the pans. Bake the cakes in the preheated 350 F. oven for about 30 minutes, or until springy in the center when touched lightly. Unmold and cool on a rack.

Génoise Pan B:88

Most popular of all French cakes is the *génoise,* or basic sponge cake. It appears in frosted *petits-fours,* as the liner for molds and is the foundation of almost all fancy French layer cakes. One of the best is a mocha cake made from two 1″-thick cakes, sliced in half or in thirds horizontally and then stacked in alternating layers with mocha buttercream. More buttercream is then spread over the whole thing and may be piped into fancy swirls from a pastry tube. The final touch could be sliced, toasted almonds pressed against the sides of the cake. If you like mocha, it's irresistible. If you don't, change the flavor of the cake, or buttercream, to orange, chocolate, or whatever you like. In addition to this 6¼″-diameter size, the pan comes in diameters graduated at intervals of almost an inch and ranging from 4″ to 12″. All are 1″ deep and made of heavy-gauge tinned steel with a rolled rim.

Mora & Cie. **$1.00**

Baba Mold B:89

In Poland, where it is said to have originated, Ali Baba was the original name

Continued from preceding page

of the baba, a yeast-dough cake. Someone there had set in vogue a variation of the Austrian *Gugelhupf* cake, by sprinkling it with rum and flaming it; and King Stanislas Leczinski, who was enamored of both the dessert and the *Thousand and One Nights,* named it. By the 19th century the cakes made their way to Paris where the name was shortened and the alcohol increased. The cakes were simply immersed in rum-flavored syrup. Traditionally, the cakes are supposed to contain raisins and/or currants, but many recipes omit them. Babas can be made and frozen, if you like, then defrosted and warmed through before they are soaked in syrup. They are especially tasty with the addition of strawberries and whipped cream. The mold in which the rich yeast dough is baked is a slightly-tapered, 2″-deep cylinder of tinned steel with a 2¼″-top diameter, a rolled rim and a flat bottom. Fill it half full of dough, allow the dough to rise and then bake it to golden perfection. These molds are also called *darioles* and as such may be used for all manner of molded vegetables, aspics and desserts. Filled to capacity, the mold holds ½ cup.

Charles F. Lamalle (713T) $1.25

If you're sick of making babas you can use your molds to throw together this fancy timbale *supper, as suggested in* Larousse Gastronomique *(from an old recipe): "Butter a dozen dariole molds and sprinkle in each truffle and pickled tongue, both finely chopped. Prepare 1 pound of chicken forcemeat with cream, finished with a few tablespoons of Soubise purée. Fill the molds with the forcemeat, leaving a hole in the center of each, which should be filled with a* salpicon *of chicken and truffles bound with a Sauce Espagnole made with Madeira. Close the tops of the molds with a layer of raw forcemeat, set them in a pan with hot water to come half way up the molds. Poach for 12–15 minutes. Turn the timbales out on a layer of forcemeat which has been poached on the plate. Spoon over the forcemeat a little Sauce Espagnole which has been cooked with the trimmings and truffle liquor."*

Savarin Mold B:90

The *savarin,* a yeast cake, was born around the mid-18th century from the same dough as the baba. But it was given a distinctive shape, a different flavor and a new name, *brillat-savarin,* in honor of the famous gastronome. The creation was conceived by a Parisian baker named Julien, who omitted raisins from the cake, baked it in a hexagonal mold and soaked it in kirsch—instead of rum-flavored syrup. Between then and now, the name has been shortened and the shape of the *savarin* has changed again to a distinctive, round ring baked in a pan of the same name. Usually a *savarin* is brushed with apricot glaze, then decorated with almonds, glacéed fruits or fresh berries. The center of the cake is filled with whipped cream or pastry cream and/or berries or mixed fruit that have been soaked in kirsch with sugar. This tinned-steel *savarin* mold holds 4 cups and is 8½″ in diameter and 1⅞″ deep with a 3⅞″-diameter center hole. Small, individual molds are also available.

H. Roth & Son $2.98

A savarin with fruit.

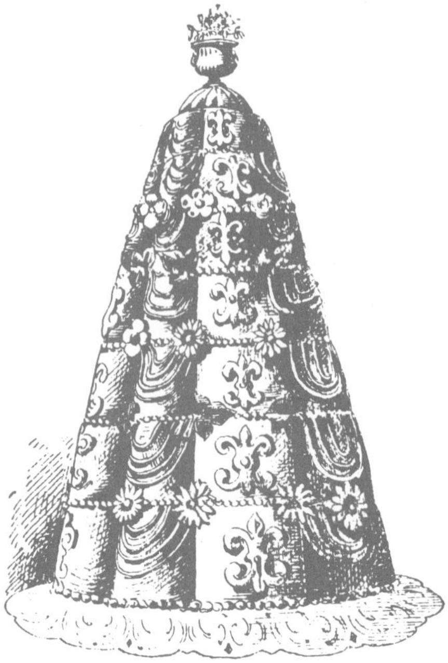

A fancy Breton cake.

Trois Frères Mold B:91

In 19th-century Paris, three brothers by the name of Julien were all celebrated pastry cooks. They invented a special cake called *trois frères* (three brothers, aptly enough), for which a special pan was created. Reminiscent of the Austrian *Gugelhupf* pan but much flatter (only 3½″ deep), this pan also has a pattern of oblique swirls around its sides. The cake traditionally made in the pan is composed of rice flour, sugar, butter, eggs, angelica and a bit of maraschino liqueur and salt. After it is baked, the cake is spread with apricot syrup and sprinkled with almonds and diced angelica. Should that confection fail to transport you, the pan can also be used for a pound cake or *savarin,* a fancy aspic or *bavarois* (a creamy molded dessert made with gelatin). The pan holds 6 cups.

Charles F. Lamalle (801) **$9.00**

Croquembouche Form B:92

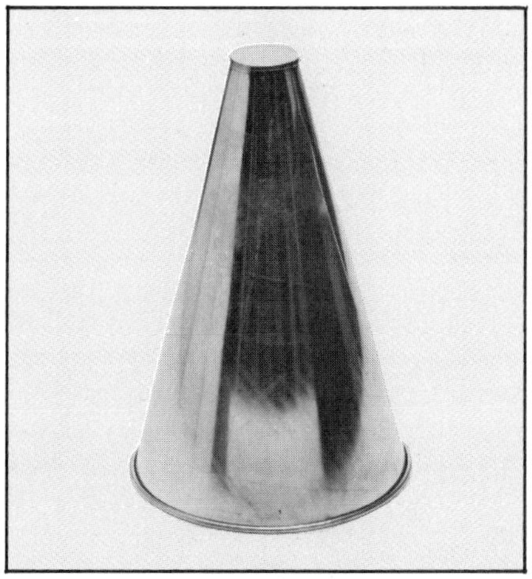

In French, *croquembouche* sounds like what it means: crunch in the mouth. That is what you do to the confection constructed around this 15″-high, tinned-steel form that resembles a party hat. Only for a party, in fact, would you go to the trouble of making a *croquembouche,* traditionally a towering cone of cream puffs dipped in, and then cemented together with, caramelized sugar. The crunch comes from the thin shell of sugar around each cream puff. (Actually a *croquembouche* can be any kind of sweet, a chestnut or a piece of fruit like an orange section or strawberry, that is glazed with hardened sugar.) Before using the mold be sure to butter it, then start building your tower, layer upon layer until you reach the top. When the sugar is completely cool slip the form out and admire your free-standing masterpiece.

Jurgensen's (22-15) **$29.95**

Cyrano de Bergerac, desiring to be alone with his beloved Roxanne in The Bakery of Poets sends off her duenna with the following exchange:

"Have you a good digestion?"

"Wonderful!"

"Good. Here are two sonnets, by Benserade—"

"Euh?"

"Which I fill for you with éclairs."

"Ooo!"

"Do you like cream puffs?"

"Only with whipped cream."

"Here are three . . . six-enbosomed in a poem by Saint-Amant. This ode of Chapelin looks deep enough to hold —a jelly roll. Do you love nature?"

"Mad about it."

"Then go out and eat these in the street. Do not return—"

"Oh, but—"

"Until you have finished them."

Having devoured the pastries, the duenna returns, whereupon Cyrano tells her that she should now go back outside to read the poems.

Cyrano de Bergerac *by Edmond Rostand, translated by Brian Hooker in* Sixteen Famous European Plays. *Modern Library, 1943.*

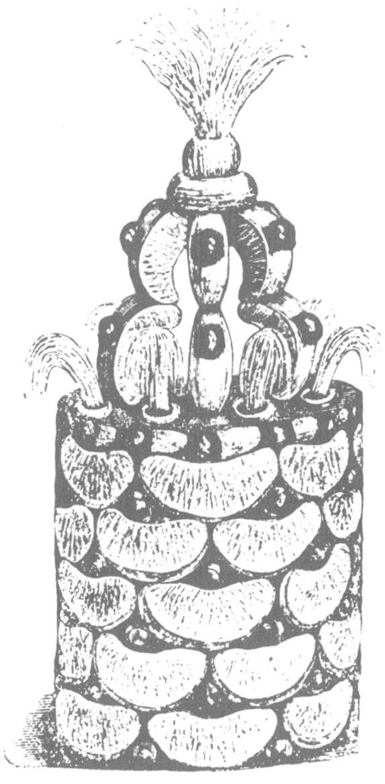

A croquembouche of orange segments.

Sugar Pan B:93

Imagine a *crème caramel* or praline without caramelized sugar. Impossible, right? Here is an unlined, hammered copper pan designed just for caramelizing sugar, or making any sugar syrup, for that matter: the copper conducts heat perfectly, the hollow copper handle riveted to the side is easy to grip, and the pronounced pouring spout eliminates the hazard and mess of dripping hot syrup in the wrong places. Caramel is also used for darkening soups, stews and sauces. But it darkens very quickly; and, if not watched carefully, may easily burn, turning bitter and black, described by Carême as "monkey's blood." Our pan is a perfect hemisphere, 6½″ in diameter at the rim and 3″ deep, with a 6½″-long handle. It holds 3⅓ cups. An 8″-diameter pan is also available. Be sure to confine the use of the pan to sugar, because the unlined copper will react deleteriously with any acids.

Charles F. Lamalle (1422) **$56.00**

Hydrometer B:94

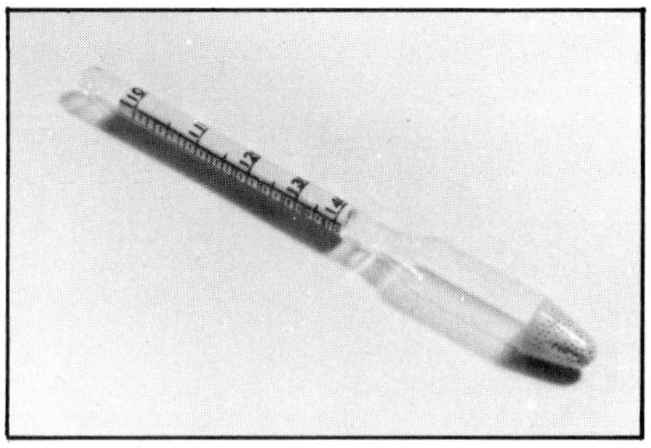

Knowing the ratio of the water to sugar in solution is essential to anyone working with sherbets. Without the

Continued from preceding page

right proportions, a sherbet won't freeze. This hydrometer, or densimeter, measures degrees of density in water-sugar solutions. It consists of a 6¼″-long, sealed glass tube with a 2″-by-⅝″ bulb at the end terminating in a weighted, nippled tip. A scale runs along the side of the opposite end. When the weighted end is allowed to sink into a water-sugar solution, the reading on the scale tells you its density. The further the tube sinks, the less dense the solution. The scale of 1.000 to 1.3199 corresponds to a range of 5 to 35 degrees Baumé (an older measuring system). The hydrometer comes with a protective cylindrical, plastic case, capped at both top and bottom.

Bridge Kitchenware Corp. **$8.95**

Straight Rolling Pin B:95

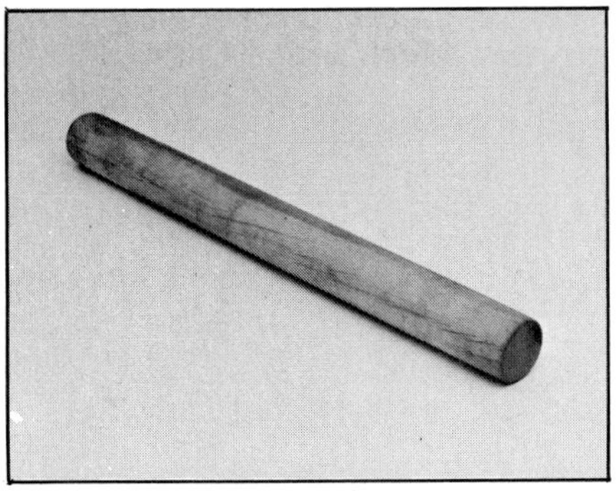

A simple, heavy, beautifully balanced and smoothly rounded rolling pin—without ball bearings—is preferred by many French chefs for small amounts of dough. The reason they like it so much is that such a pin gives them a close feeling of the dough as it is rolled gently beneath the palms, permitting the greatest flexibility of touch to accommodate differences in the texture or thickness of the dough. This pin measures a generous 20″ in length and 2¼″ in diameter, an excellent size for rolling out large sheets of *pâte brisée* (short crust pastry) for a strawberry tart, or puff pastry for a batch of croissants.

Schiller & Asmus, Inc. (J240-3) **$3.50**

Tutové Rolling Pin B:96

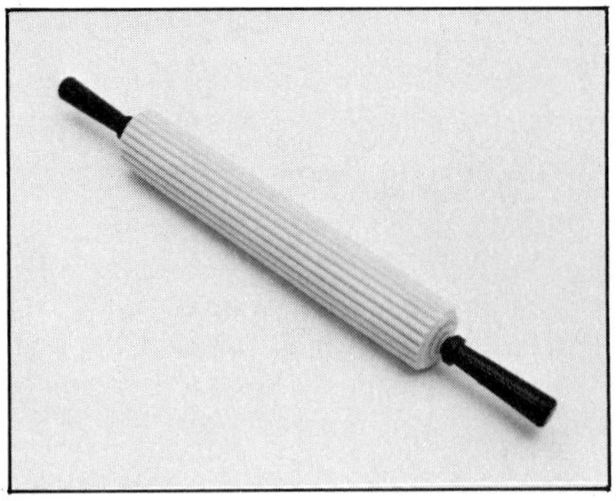

Its manufacturer claims this rolling pin is "magic." And there's truth to the statement. The remarkable, ridged rolling pin distributes butter beautifully through the multiple layers of puff pastry (*pâte feuilletée*), poetically known as "thousand leaf pastry." (Of course, you use a smooth pin for the final rolling.) With the bite imparted by its grooved surface and its considerable weight, the pin can also pound chilled dough into pliancy before the rolling begins. With its 15″-long plastic cylinder fixed to black plastic handles, the pin measures 25″ long overall. It's expensive, but worth it if you can't do without Beef Wellington or Napoleons.

Kitchen Glamor, Inc. (M415) **$39.95**

Croissant Cutter B:97

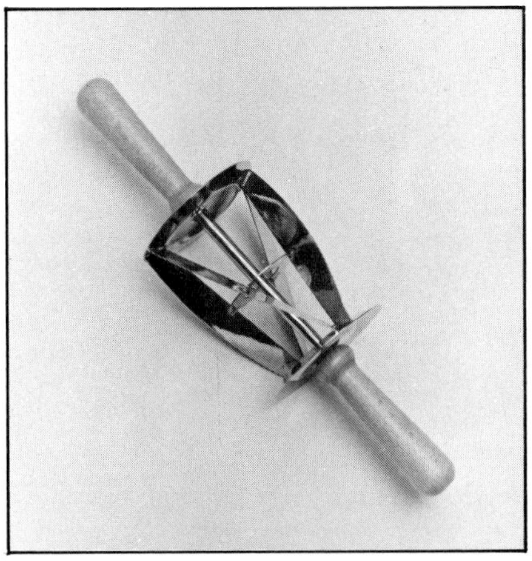

The flaky, crescent-shaped rolls known as croissants, so sacred to the French breakfast, are coveted by foreigners as well. With a large cup of *café au lait* (coffee with hot milk) and some jam, a croissant or two are rich enough to tide one through a morning. This croissant cutter of nickel steel will trim enough croissants out of a sheet of dough to last you for days. With a minimum of waste, it cuts a continuous strip of triangular dough pieces that must then be rolled and curved into the shape of a quarter moon before baking. Some professionals feel the cutter is unnecessary for small amounts of dough, but it is efficient—if croissants whet your appetite. The cutter is 14″ long overall, with wooden handles and a blade that is 5″ long and 3¾″ in diameter.

Charles F. Lamalle (729/F) **$40.00**

Vol-au-Vent Cutter B:98

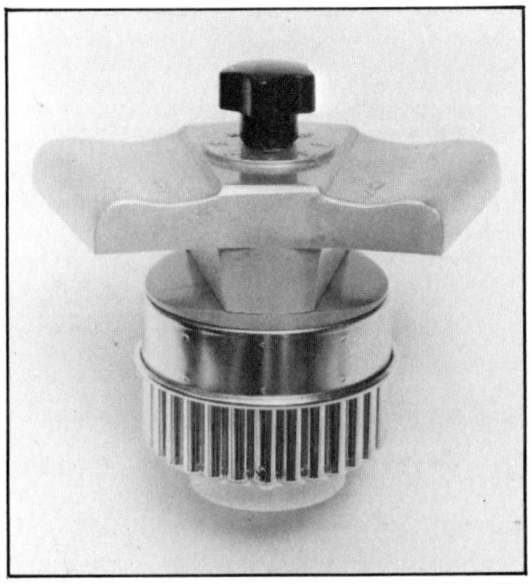

Carême said of vol-au-vents, "This entrée is pretty and good." That was an understatement. Nothing is more appetizing than a golden case of puffed pastry filled with an exquisite dish like sweetbreads *à la financière,* banker's style, in truffle-flavored Madeira sauce with green olives, mushrooms, truffles and veal mousse dumplings. As for almost every special culinary preparation, the French have devised time-saving professional tools especially for shaping vol-au-vents. Normally, a vol-au-vent is made with two pieces of dough: one for the bottom and one for the sides. With this cutter only one piece of dough is necessary. The handle of the implement (attached to a stainless-steel blade about 3″ in diameter) cuts out a scalloped circle while a 2″-diameter nylon plunger in the center presses a well in the middle of the pastry. The well remains during baking, as the sides rise around it, forming a perfect case. Overall the cast-aluminum cutter is 6″ long and 3½″ in diameter at its widest. It comes with four stainless-steel pyramids that are used to prop a rack over the vol-au-vents while they are baking, so the tops will rise evenly.

Cuisinarts, Inc. $60.00

Round and Oval Pastry Cutters B:99

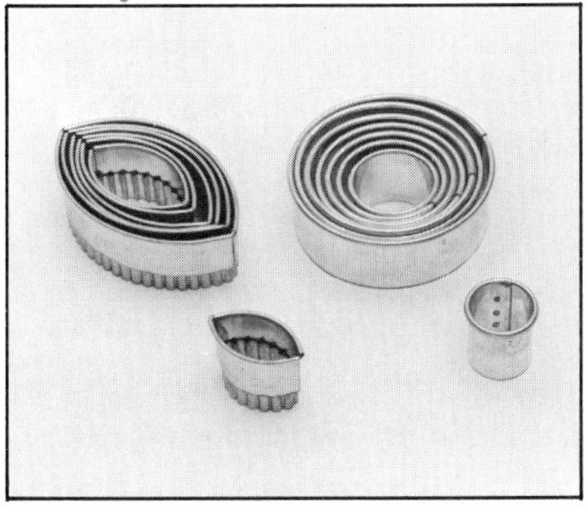

Any dough benefits from being crisply cut; but puff pastry dough is especially sensitive around the edges. A blunt cutter can seal the delicate layers of dough together, preventing them from separating and rising properly while baking. With a set or two of heavy-gauge, tinned-steel cutters like these you can avoid last minute disappointment. You can cut either circles or oblong *barquettes* and then bake them in tartlet tins of the matching shapes, or you can use the cutouts simply to garnish a dish. Tiny golden crescents of puff pastry would be lovely surrounding a platter of sole Dugléré, for example: fillet of sole masked with a creamy, tomato-flavored sauce. You can also use the cutters for short crust pastry, and make tartlets filled with an artichoke purée to serve as a canapé or hors d'oeuvre. The oval set has seven graduated cutters; the round set has eight. The oblong cutters range in size from 2″ by 1″ to 4¾″ by 2⅞″; the circles range in diameter from 1¼″ to 4″. All are 1⅜″ deep with smoothly rolled top edges. Plain oval and fluted round cutters are also available.

Charles F. Lamalle
Round (884L) $11.00
Oval (8920) $45.00

Horn Molds B:100

A *cornet* (horn) may be savory or sweet, and like the cornucopia it resembles it can be filled with a rich variety of tempting foods. Slices of salmon, ham or beef are rolled, placed inside the *cornet* and then filled with a vegetable or egg mixture for a tantalizing hors d'oeuvre. On the sweet side, a long piece of puff pastry can be wrapped in overlapping layers around the outside of the mold and baked on it. The resulting 4″-long pastry horn is then filled with whipped cream or a velvety rich pastry cream. Made of tinned steel, the form has a single lengthwise seam, and the 2½″-diameter top opening is cut at a slant. For pastry purposes you will need more than one; they come in sets of 6.

HOAN Products, Ltd. (9996) $4.00

Barquette Tins B:101

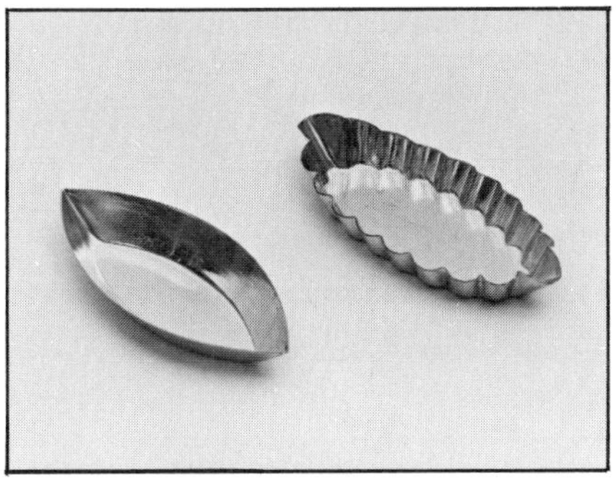

Named after a boat (*barque*), which they resemble, these *barquettes* (little boats) are lined with a short crust pastry, baked blind (empty) and loaded with a sweet or savory filling. They are always appealing. Escoffier called them *frivolités.* Imagine one filled with pieces of lobster in a creamy white wine sauce, or with glazed fresh raspberries. Fluted or plain, these tins are 4″ long, 1⅝″ across and ½″ deep. Lengths ranging from 2¼″ to 5¾″ are also available.

Charles F. Lamalle
Plain (791F) $0.60
Fluted (790) $0.30

RASPBERRY BARQUETTES

Pâte brisée sucrée:
8 ounces unbleached, all-purpose flour (approximately 1⅔ cups)
2 tablespoons sugar
Pinch salt
4 ounces (1 stick) unsalted butter, well-chilled
2½ tablespoons vegetable shortening, well-chilled
1 egg yolk
⅓ cup ice water

Almond cream:
1 egg yolk
3 tablespoons sugar
2 tablespoons unsalted butter
1 ounce pulverized almonds

½ cup currant jelly
½ pint raspberries, washed and well-drained

Pâte brisée sucrée:
For the most consistent results in making a short pastry, it is best to weigh the flour rather than measuring it by volume. If you do not have a scale, however, measure the flour by scooping the measuring cup into the flour and leveling the top with a knife. (Do not shake or knock the cup to pack the flour down.) The amount of ice water necessary to attain the proper consistency—soft and pliable, but not sticky—will vary according to weather conditions. You will find that you need less water in the summer, when humidity adds moisture to the flour. The only other trick to turning out a perfect pastry lies in speed—the faster you combine the ingredients, the more tender and flaky will be your pastry.

Toss the flour, sugar and salt together in a bowl. Cut the butter and shortening into small pieces and add them to the bowl. With your fingertips (if your hands are cool), a pastry blender or two knives, rapidly cut the fat into the flour until the bits of butter are the size of a pea. Beat the egg yolk with ⅓ cup ice water and add it to the flour mixture. Stir with a fork

Continued from preceding page

until all the liquid has been incorporated and all the flour moistened. If the mixture appears too dry, dribble in a little more ice water. Scrape the dough into a ball, place it on a pastry board and quickly rub egg-sized pieces of it away from you with the heel of your hand. This is known as a *fraisage* and serves as a final blending of butter and flour. Scrape the pastry back into a ball, sprinkle it with flour, cover with plastic wrap and refrigerate for at least 2 hours.

Almond cream:
Beat the egg yolk and 1½ tablespoons of the sugar together with a wire whisk until thick and pale yellow. Cream the butter with the remaining sugar, then blend it into the yolk mixture with a rubber spatula. Stir in the almonds and refrigerate until ready to use.

To assemble:
Butter the inside of twelve 4½″ *barquette* tins and the outside of twelve additional tins. (The extra *barquettes* are used to weight the pastry during its first baking.) If you have only 12 *barquette* tins, make the pastry boats in two batches of six each.

Roll the pastry into a ⅛″-thick sheet. Using an oval pastry cutter or the tip of a sharp knife, cut the pastry into 12 ovals approximately 1″ bigger around than the *barquettes.* Press the pastry gently into the tins that are buttered on the inside. Trim the edges and prick the bottom and sides of the pastry with a fork. Press one of the extra tins over each *barquette.* Place the *barquettes* on a baking sheet and refrigerate for at least 30 minutes.

Preheat the oven to 375 F.

Bake the weighted *barquettes* for 5 minutes. Remove the tin liners and prick the pastry again with a fork. Return the *barquettes* to the oven for a minute longer until the pastry begins to set. Remove them from the oven and cool almost completely. Then spread a spoonful of the almond cream over the bottom of each one, leaving enough room for a layer of raspberries. Return to the oven and bake until the pastry is completely cooked and the almond cream is puffed and golden brown, about 10 to 12 minutes. Cool the *barquettes* completely and remove them from the tins.

Place the currant jelly in a small saucepan and boil for several minutes to make a glaze. Brush the almond cream in each *barquette* with the hot glaze, then cover it with a layer of raspberries. Dribble more glaze over the raspberries and chill the *barquettes* thoroughly before serving.

Yield: 12 barquettes.

(*Courtesy of Susan Lipke.*)

Loose-Bottomed Tartlet Pan B:102

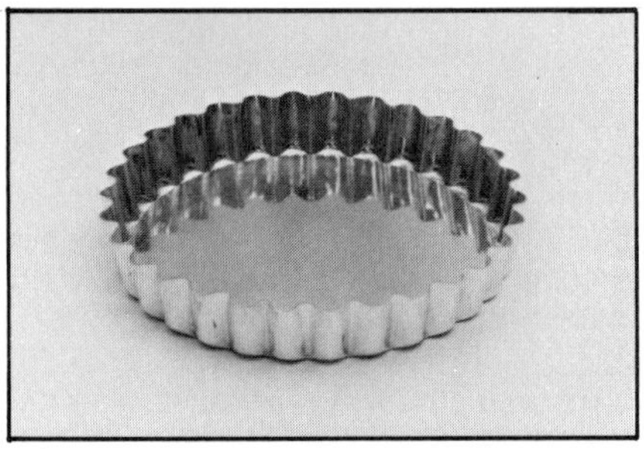

The alternative to a solid tartlet pan is one with a removable bottom. This feature reduces the risk of breaking the crust when you remove it from the tin and also makes the operation a lot easier. Fill the tartlet with mussels in a white sauce flavored with mushrooms, lemon juice and parsley, or make individual spinach quiches for your next dinner party, if you really want to give your guests something to talk about. This heavy-gauge, tinned-steel pan is 4½″ in diameter at the rim and ¾″ deep.

Charles F. Lamalle (761B) **$0.75**

Loose-Bottomed Tart Pan B:103

A French *tarte* or *flan* (the terms are sometimes used interchangeably) is a straight-sided open pie that is filled with a savory or sweet mixture. It can be baked in a one-piece pan, a loose-bottomed pan like this one, or inside a frame set on a baking sheet. For a Brillat-Savarin filling (eggs scrambled with truffles and browned quickly with a little Parmesan cheese), the pastry lining would be ordinary pie dough or a flaky variety. But for a fresh apricot tart with custard, you would probably use a *pâte sucrée* (sweetened pastry). Whenever you make a tart, it is a good idea to place it on a cookie sheet, preheated with the oven, so the pastry will cook evenly. The dull black finish of this steel pan has a culinary edge over light-colored metal because it absorbs heat more readily. Thus the crust of your apricot tart will be golden all over when you lift it easily from the fluted sides of the pan. Simply push up from the bottom after the tart has set for a while. The pan is 9¼″ in diameter and almost 1″ deep. It also comes in diameters of 8″ and 10¼″.

Jurgensen's (22106) **$2.50**

Porcelain Tart or Quiche Dish B:104

Although this glazed, white porcelain dish would make a lovely apple tart, it would also be perfect for bringing that popular Lorraine specialty, a quiche, to the table. The classic quiche is a pastry shell lined with pieces of blanched and lightly fried bacon and filled with a cream-based custard. But that is only one kind of quiche. You can add cheese, tomatoes, spinach, onions, shrimp, crab or lobster, whatever appeals, as long as it belongs in the hors d'oeuvre or main dish category. (Quiches are never served as desserts.) With a salad, a piece of French bread, wine and a dessert, a quiche makes one of the most refreshing meals possible. To ensure a golden crust, the bottom of this dish has been left unglazed for better heat absorption. Graceful flutes parade around the 1½″-deep sides that will hold 5 cups. This dish is 10″ in diameter, but others are available in diameters of 7½″ and 11½″.

Jurgensen's (1-81) $20.00

BACON AND MUSHROOM QUICHE

6–8 ounces bacon strips
4 large mushrooms
1 shallot, minced
2 tablespoons butter
Pinch, plus ½ teaspoon salt
Lemon juice
1½–2 cups heavy cream
3–4 eggs
Nutmeg, freshly ground
Black pepper, freshly ground
1 8″ to 9″ partially-cooked pastry shell
2–3 tablespoons grated Gruyère cheese (optional)

Preheat oven to 375 F.

Fry the bacon until crisp, then drain it on paper toweling and crumble or break it into pieces.

Mince the mushrooms and squeeze them in the corner of a towel to extract all the juices. Sauté the shallot for a minute in one tablespoon butter, then add the minced mushrooms, a sprinkling of salt and a squeeze of fresh lemon juice. Cover and cook over a low flame for a minute or two, then uncover, raise the heat and cook until all the rendered juices have evaporated and the mushrooms begin to sauté in the butter.

Combine 1½ cups heavy cream with 3 eggs, or 2 cups cream with 4 eggs, depending upon the size and depth of your pastry shell. Add ½ teaspoon salt and a few grinds each of pepper and nutmeg. Place the pastry shell on a baking sheet, scatter the bacon and mushrooms over the bottom of the shell and pour in the egg/cream mixture. Sprinkle on a little grated Gruyère, if you like a nicely browned top, and dot with the remaining tablespoon butter. Bake until puffed and golden brown, 25 to 35 minutes.

Yield: 4 servings.

(Courtesy of Susan Lipke.)

Flan Forms B:105

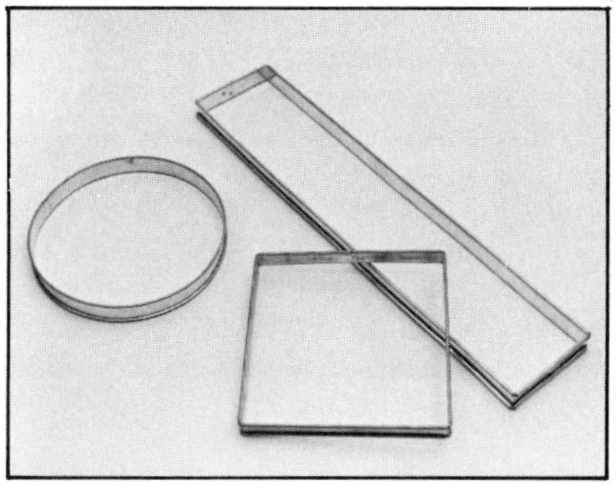

As early as the 6th century the *flan* was documented in Rome. Because it was usually round, the name was probably derived from the word for a metal disk, a *flan.* (The term can be used interchangeably with "tart," but is commonly associated with a custard filling or the well-known custard that is served alone.) Like everything else the *flan* has undergone changes, at least in shape, so that rectangular or square pans are even more common today than round ones. For one thing, it is much easier to cut equal slices out of shapes with square corners; after all, no one likes to be cheated when it comes to a *flan.* To use any one of these forms, simply butter the inside, place it on a buttered baking sheet and proceed with your recipe. Use any filling and pastry you wish. All three forms are made of spot-welded tinned steel with smoothly rolled rims, top and bottom. The ⅝″-deep ring comes in diameters of 3½″, 4″, 6″, 7″, 8″, 8¾″ or 10″; the square is 6½″ across and ¾″ deep; and the rectangle measures 22″ by 4½″ and is 1″ deep.

Charles F. Lamalle
Ring, 8¾″ (735) $1.70
Square (732 D) $2.80
Rectangle (8732) $7.20

Flan Form with Baking Sheet B:106

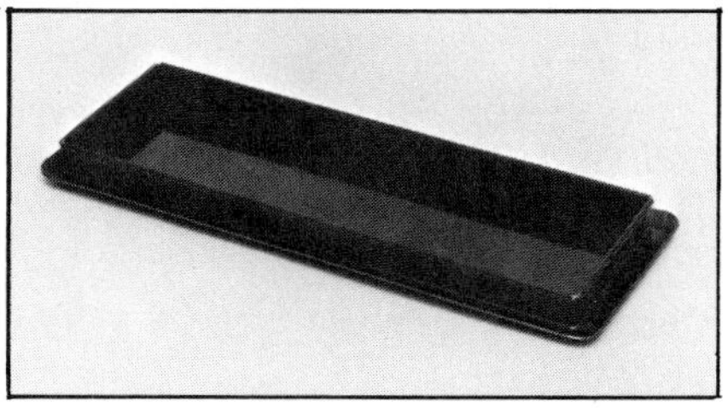

Here is a heavy-gauge *flan,* or tart, form with its own baking sheet that will not demand an entire oven shelf. Both are black for good heat absorption, and the edges of the baking sheet turn up slightly to keep the *flan* from slipping and any juices from dripping out. When using this type of form, be sure to shape the top of the pastry crust inside the rim; otherwise you will damage it when you lift off the form. Both top and bottom edges of the form are smoothly rolled around thick copper wire. It measures 14″ by 4½″ and is 1″ deep—perfect for a fresh plum tart for six. The baking sheet is 15″ by 5⅝″.

Bridge Kitchenware Corp. $7.50

TARTE TATIN

Upside-Down Apple Tart

Butter
Sugar
7–8 large apples (average 8-ounces each), preferably Rome Beauty or McIntosh
10 ounces puff pastry*

Preheat oven to 375 F. Very heavily butter a 12″-round, 2″-deep mold and cover the bottom with a ¼″-thick layer of granulated sugar.

Peel and core the apples and cut them into small wedges. (If you cut thin slices they will disintegrate during cooking.) Sauté the wedges in butter until golden but not soft—*do not overcook.* Turn them into the mold.

Roll the pastry into a sheet and prick it all over with a fork. Place it over the apples and trim the edge a good inch beyond the edge of the mold. This will form a nice border when the tart is cooked and will also keep the syrup from escaping when the tart is turned over.

Bake the *tarte Tatin* for about 45 minutes, or until the pastry is golden brown. Turn onto a fireproof dish or tray in order to keep it hot until it is served.

Yield: 8 servings.

* As it is virtually impossible to make such a small quantity of puff pastry, this is a delicious way to use up any extra pastry left over from another recipe. You might also make enough

Continued from preceding page

pastry for 2 or 3 tarts and freeze the unused portion, since puff pastry freezes very well. A puff pastry made with ½ pound flour, ½ pound butter and ½ cup water will yield enough pastry for two tarts.

(Courtesy of Robert Renaud, Le Jacques Coeur Restaurant, New York City.)

Tarte Tatin Pan B:107

Who were the *demoiselles* (maidens) Tatin whose names are immortalized in the upside-down apple tart that bears their name? It is said they were joint owners of a hotel; but, aside from that, the circumstances of how the dessert originated are shrouded in the mists of history. At first, the tart was baked over charcoal in a heavy, buttered and sugared pan. The sugar caramelized while the tart baked, so that when it was unmolded the top was the color of amber. Most modern recipes call for caramelizing the mold before filling it with apples and topping it with pastry. That is always safe; but with this tin-lined, hammered-copper pan it is not necessary. Simply sprinkle in the sugar, add butter and complete the recipe. It is one of the best of all French desserts, and this 2″-deep, 2½″-quart pan, with its flaring sides, will make a 9½″ tart that is especially beautiful. Pans of 13″ and 14″ diameters are also available.

Charles F. Lamalle (1430) $44.00

"For dinner, we had deliciously fresh fish, mushrooms, taken off the fire before they were reduced to the condition of tasteless rags in which most French people serve them, and a semi-liquid crème au chocolat *to satisfy those who like eating it with spoon as well as those who prefer to drink it straight out of the little white pot."*

The Tender Shoot *by Colette, from* The Stories of Colette *translated by Antonia White. Secker & Warburg, 1958.*

Coeur à la Crème Mold B:108

Coeur à la crème, sweetened fresh white cheese molded in the shape of a heart, is an exception to the French practice of almost always eating cheese with bread. Often served with fresh wild strawberries, *fraises des bois,* it combines both the fruit and cheese courses into the dessert course of a full French meal. The cheese is made from whole milk that is allowed to curdle; then the curds are drained in heart-shaped molds or baskets. Often the cheese is mixed with cream and sprinkled with sugar before draining. This heart of pure white porcelain is pierced across the bottom with tiny holes to allow excess liquid in the sweetened cheese to run off as it chills. Line the container with dampened cheesecloth, fill it with cheese, and set it on a plate in the refrigerator to chill. Raised above the plate on three little feet, the mold will be clear of any liquid that drains out. To serve, unmold and unwrap the heart and accompany it with berries, a colorful fruit sauce or thick, fresh cream. The mold measures 7″ by 6″ and will serve 6. Two smaller versions, 3″ and 2¾″ wide, will make individual hearts.

Charles F. Lamalle (557/B) $13.00

Coeur à la Crème Basket B:109

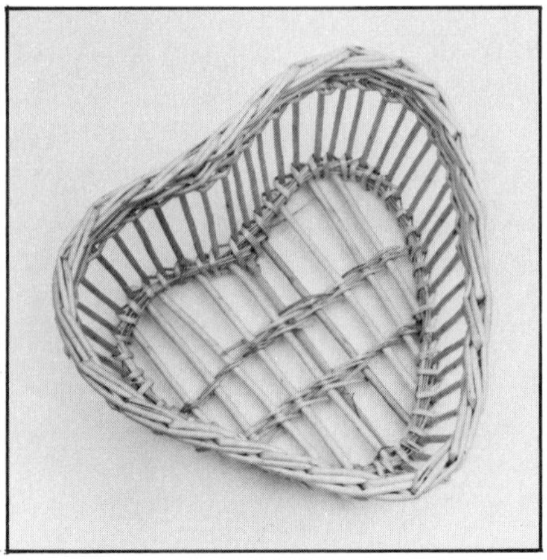

For more than 100 years the French have been enjoying a heart-shaped dessert made of a slightly sweetened, fresh, whole-milk cheese. Often, the curdled milk is drained into a basket, similar to this wicker one, that has first been lined with dampened cheesecloth. When all the excess liquid is gone the cheese is then unmolded and served with berries—usually wild strawberries—or a fruit sauce. Fresh cheeses like this may be kept for a day or two but no longer. This stout basket, gracefully bound and finished, is about 9″ across at the widest point, 3½″ deep and holds about 2 quarts.

H. A. Mack & Co., Inc. $16.50

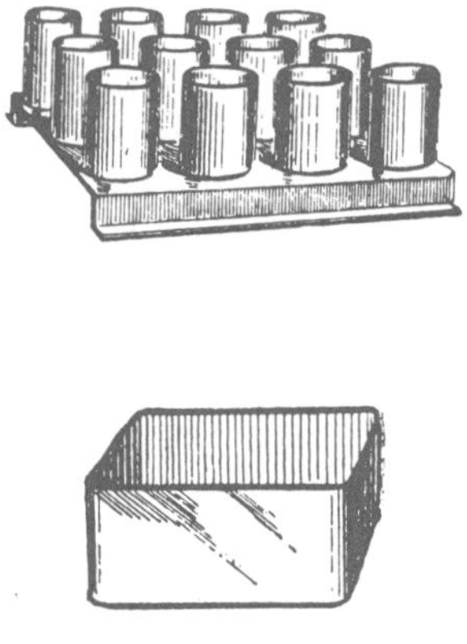

Cheese molds.

Pot à Crème Set B:110

Although chocolate mousse is sometimes served in little pots like these, they are ovenproof and really meant for cooking custards of all flavors in a water bath (*bain-marie*). Served either at room temperature or chilled, a rich custard is one of the easiest and most delicious desserts ever conceived. Graceful little pots like these would make it doubly successful. Blossoms of yellow, rust, mauve and violet with bright green leaves (the *Quatre Saisons* pattern of the manufacturer) accent both the pots and the tray that will carry them to the table. Each pot has a lid that prevents a thick skin from forming on the custard and holds ½ cup. The cups are 2¼″ in diameter and 2¼″ deep, and the tray measures 10″ by 7½″.

Porcelaine de Paris (42260) $120.00

Charlotte Mold B:111

Charlottes run hot or cold, but both are made in the same kind of mold. For a hot charlotte (the original kind), the mold is lined with thin, overlapping slices of buttered bread, then filled with a fruit mixture of some kind (apple, most often), baked and served hot with a fruit sauce or whipped cream. A cold charlotte, or *charlotte russe,* is Carême's invention. It is made by lining the mold with sponge cake (*génoise*) or ladyfingers and filling it with a Bavarian cream. Other creams or a chocolate mousse can also be used, frequently with a few layers of cake or ladyfingers for body and texture. When unmolded, the patterned slices of bread or ladyfingers on the sides, and the flower formation that is most always shaped on the top, make a truly impressive-looking dessert. A real advantage to the cold charlotte is the fact that you can make it a day in advance, a boon for entertaining. The mold can also be used for a soufflé. Charlotte molds come in a range of sizes from 6 ounces to 2 quarts; all have two heart-shaped handles on the sides. This 1-quart size of tin-washed steel is 6″ in diameter and 3½″ deep. A matching tinned lid with a simple strip handle is also available.

Charles F. Lamalle
Mold (729B) $10.50
Lid (729BLID) $4.50

CHARLOTTE AUX POMMES

Apple Charlotte

10 medium-sized apples
¾ cup butter
½ cup sugar
¼ teaspoon ground cinnamon
1 piece of vanilla bean, 6 inches long
4 tablespoons apricot preserves, heated and puréed
12 slices of white bread, crusts removed

Make an apple compote in this way: peel and core the apples, cut them into small pieces, put them in a saucepan with ¼ cup of the butter, and cook them over low heat until they are soft. Stir them frequently to keep them from sticking. Add the sugar, cinnamon and the vanilla bean, halved lengthwise.

Cook slowly for about 15 minutes, until the compote is very thick and reduced. Remove the vanilla bean. Add the apricot-jam purée and mix thoroughly.

Melt the remaining butter and quickly sauté the slices of bread on both sides until golden. Line a 6- to 8-cup charlotte mold with the slices of bread, reserving a few for the top. Spoon the apple compote into the mold and cover the top with the remaining bread slices. Bake the charlotte in a 300° F. oven for 30 minutes. Cool it, chill, and then unmold before serving.

(From LA CUISINE: SECRETS OF MODERN FRENCH COOKING by Raymond Oliver. Copyright 1969 by Tudor Publishing Company. Reprinted by permission of Tudor Publishing Company.)

Square Ice Cream Mold B:112

If you want to add a final flourish to your homemade ice cream, or make storebought ice cream look homemade, this decorative mold is for you. It has the well-balanced design of a truncated pyramid: trim sloping sides with a flat top that is heightened by a raised rosette pattern. Make your ice cream fancier still by filling the domed top with one flavor and the rest with another, say strawberry and vanilla, and serve it with fresh strawberries. Or alternate layers of different flavors, or line it with one flavor and fill it with another. When the mold is filled, cover it with its tightly fitting lid. Made of tinned steel, soldered and spot welded to prevent leaking, the mold is 4¾″ square, 2⅝″ deep and holds 3 cups. It is also available in a 1-quart size.

Charles F. Lamalle (739A) $8.00

The winter garden of the Champeaux Restaurant in 1864.

Coffee with the flower and berry.

Porcelain Filter Pot B:113

Although coffee was brought to Paris in 1644, it was not until a certain Suleiman Aga started offering it to all his visitors in 1669 that the brew really caught on. Mr. Aga, who was an ambassador to the court of Louis XIV, was in the right circles to make a lasting impression. Rather than a passing vogue, coffee became a necessity that the French indulge in from morning till night. This 10″-high, winsome white porcelain filter pot with its curvaceous silhouette would be welcome on any table. The round-bellied pot is topped by a cylindrical filter chamber that is perforated with tiny holes on the bottom, ridged top and bottom for decoration, and embraced by two long, delicately turned handles. A perforated porcelain insert slips on top of the cylinder to distribute the water poured through it evenly over the coffee grounds below. The lid is crowned with an acorn-like knob. Beauty aside, the pot makes superb coffee; but preheat it first with hot water. To keep the coffee warm, you can set the covered pot, minus the filter, on an asbestos mat over low heat. The 5¾″-deep pot holds 6 cups and will double for tea. Pots of 2-, 4- and 8-cup capacities are available as well.

Schiller & Asmus, Inc. $24.00
(P3001-06)

Coffee

The French traditionally begin the day with a large cup—or bowl—of coffee with heated milk. Curiously, it seems old-fashioned to call this drink *café au lait.* Most people ask for a *café crème* (coffee with cream), or if they want it heavy on the milk, they order a *crème renversée* ("reversed" cream). Black coffee is taken after lunch or dinner, usually as *café filtre* (filtered coffee), served in individual drip containers. Another excellent coffee is often produced at home by the drip method, known as *chausette* (sock). And very good it is, too. Freshly ground coffee is placed in a little bag and boiling water is dripped through to a lower heated pot. (Don't be put off by the name; the little bag is often fashioned by an old nylon stocking, but it is always scrupulously clean.) In popular cafés, the gleaming, hissing, espresso machine is making heavy inroads. It's quicker, and many people prefer the pronounced aromatic flavor of *espresso.*

To discuss French coffee without mentioning French cafés would be inexcusable. For well over a hundred years the intellectual and artistic life of Paris has been nurtured by her cafés. (Remember those shivering lads in *La Vie de Bohème*?) The price of a cup of coffee made anyone a member of a kind of club, where he could meet with friends, argue and spark ideas. Some café proprietors still let unknown artists settle bills with a painting, in the hopes that a young dauber will become the next Picasso.

Modern life is too fast and too expensive to let patrons linger through the day, taking up valuable space; but in gentler times, certain literary cafés were proud of the writers who sat there scribbling all afternoon, paying for their tables with only a cup or two of strong black *filtre.* The café called Chez Francis was such a one; there, the playwright Jean Giraudoux wrote *The Madwoman of Chaillot.* (She *did* exist; she lived across the square from the café, under the Alexandre III bridge.) Chez Francis itself became part of Giraudoux's fantasy: some of the action of the play takes place in it.

Other drinks are dispensed at cafés as well—there's tea, which usually manages to be tepid despite the white-hot handle of a metal teapot. The French do not take tea seriously. (To be fair, though, a Montmartre café for years had a helpful sign in the window advertising "the five o'clock tea at any hour.") Soft drinks and hard liquor are sold, as are "sandwichs" and "pain-beurré" (bread with butter) to tide you over until lunch or dinner. Of course, wine is available, too. But a café isn't really the proper place to savor wine. To give it the respect it's due, wine must accompany an honest French meal.

Coffee mill.

Melior Coffee Pot B:114

In this pot (which resembles a glass in a soda-fountain-like metal frame) coffee is infused, or steeped, in boiling water and then filtered. The resulting brew is strong and delicious and requires only one heaping tablespoon instead of two per cup. Here is how it works. Spoon the coffee directly into the heat-proof pot; pour in the appropriate amount of boiling water and put on the lid with the plunger fully raised. Let the coffee steep for 3 to 5 minutes, then push the plunger down; the perforated steel and wire mechanism at the other end has a wire mesh filter under it that forces all the coffee grounds to the bottom of the pot. *Enfin!* The coffee can now be poured from the pot's well-defined spout—all 12 cups, if you've filled the pot. Overall, the pot is 9½″ high and 4½″ in diameter; the frame and lid are made of nickeled steel, and the wide, arching handle is of heat-resistant plastic. All the parts can be dismantled for thorough cleaning. The unit also comes in capacities of 3, 6 and 8 cups.

Charles F. Lamalle (173A) $54.00

Individual Filter Glass B:115

Here is a five-part combination filter

There are coffee pots.... and there are coffee pots. This one of gold was made in 1880.

pot and glass that does away with the coffee cup. At the bottom is a 2⅛″-deep chromed-steel container that resembles a sawed-off mug. In it sits a simple, 4½″-tall, single-serving, heat-resistant glass. Next, there is a chromed-steel, 2½″-tall filter cup, perforated in the bottom, that rests securely atop the glass, nestling into its rim. This cup has a loop handle, decorative ridges that match those on the base and a lid with a flat handle. To make coffee, spoon 2 tablespoons of finely ground French or Italian roast coffee into the cup. Slip the weighted perforated filter disc (now inside the cup) onto the metal shaft in the center of the cup. Pour in enough hot water to fill the cup and cover; refill with water when the cup has drained. Now lift off the filter cup and invert it on the lid, which will prevent coffee from dripping on the table.

Charles F. Lamalle (226) **$12.00**

Corkscrew B:116

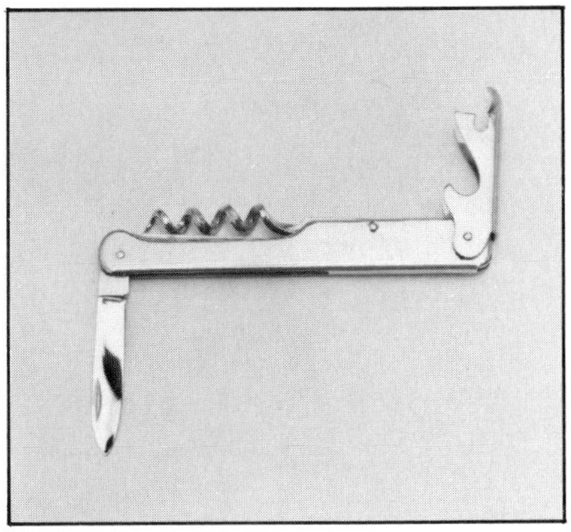

The corkscrew that seems to appear magically out of the pocket of an efficient wine steward or waiter is most probably just like this one. Made of heavy nickel-plated steel, wide enough to be comfortable in the hand and 4½″ long, the corkscrew is even more versatile than you imagined. It opens both corks and caps (large and small), and it even has a short, strong knife blade with which you can remove the covering on corks. It's a great tool for traveling and, of course, for the kitchen.

Edwin Jay Inc. (5221) **$4.00**

Truth is in the grape.

Cork Retriever B:117

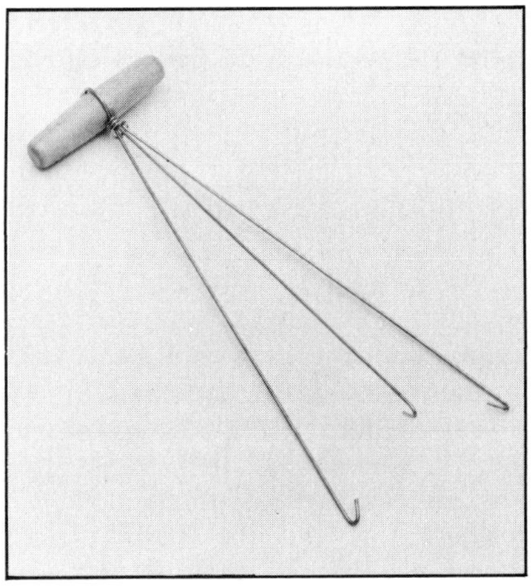

Love of the grape has caused the French to invent this cork retriever. Simple to manipulate, it will fish out any cork left floating atop your Bordeaux or Burgundy. Slip the four, long flexible wires into the bottle, and with their hooked ends grapple the cork. Once caught, it can be held firmly in place by slipping the small, plastic ring down the wires until they are closed tightly enough together to hold the cork securely. Slowly and carefully pull the handle until the cork is removed from the bottle. Together the handle and tinned-steel wires are 10½″ long.

Beard Glaser Wolf Inc. (500) **$2.25**

"At an age when I could still scarcely read, I was spelling out, drop by drop, old light clarets and dazzling Yquems. Champagne appeared in its turn, a murmur of foam, leaping pearls of air providing an accompaniment to birthday and First Communion banquets, complementing the gray truffles from La Puisaye."

Prisons et paradis *by Colette, from* Earthly Paradise, An Autobiography *by Robert Phelps. Farrar, Straus & Giroux, 1966.*

Champagne Pliers B:118

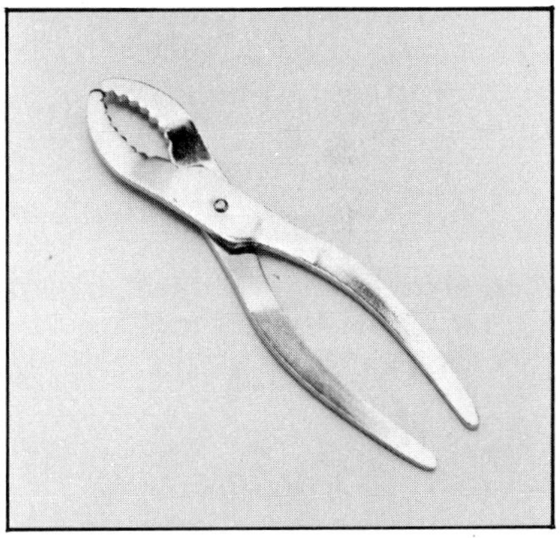

Other countries have wines, but we can thank France for champagne, and one Frenchman in particular, Dom Perignon. At the end of the 17th century, Dom Perignon, the blind cellar master of a Benedictine abbey near Rheims, discovered he could keep the bubbles in champagne by plugging a bottle with a cork and tieing it down. Even more to the man's credit was the way he blended the wines with which he made champagne, an art that is still practiced the way he taught it. Because the process of making champagne is laborious and time-consuming, more so than for most other wines, it is expensive and should not be wasted in the careless opening of a bottle. Hold the bottle at a 45 degree angle and ease the cork out slowly: hold the cork in one hand and twist the bottle with the other. If you need help, these elegant, 6″-long pliers are equal to the task. Of zinc-plated steel they have the look and feel of quality—to match the drink.

Rowoco Inc. (140) **$3.50**

The Flavor of Spain

by Ramón San Martin

The way I became a restaurateur is both logical and amusing. I grew up in a very poor family in Valencia, Spain. We did not starve, but we barely had enough to eat. To this day, I remember my mother making the poor man's dish of garlic soup for supper: garlic, bread, olive oil and water. That's all. Sometimes, if we had one, an egg would be stirred into the hot broth. I also remember going with the other boys to the waterfront where we would catch tiny sardines, stick twigs through them, and cook them over a fire; but we could never get enough to fill up on. Boys in Spain still catch sardines and cook them this way, I think.

When I was a teenager, growing taller and hungrier all the time, I happened to get a job as a busboy in a resort hotel, and a new world opened up for me. Being in the dining room and kitchen meant that I could eat anything that I wanted. That first summer I was rarely seen without a pastry or piece of bread in my hand!

After that, I worked summers as a busboy and winters as a helper or an apprentice in the hotel kitchen. There, I was even closer to the food source. As I worked, I learned the techniques of fine cooking. Eventually I stopped growing and my appetite quieted down, but by then I was already trained as a restaurateur.

Today I have two restaurants: I run a dining room at the Spanish Cultural Center, where the Spanish community of New York comes to eat and relax in an atmosphere that reminds them of home. And I have recently opened my own place, the Café San Martin, where I hope non-Spanish people will discover the pleasures of Spanish food. Unfortunately, there is a common misconception that Spanish cooking is very spicy. That's because it is confused with the cooking of Mexico. Obviously many of the ingredients such as potatoes, tomatoes and beans are the same in Spanish and Latin American cooking because of our historical association, but the traditions of each area are very different. Corn, a staple of South American cooking, for instance, never really took hold in Europe. Spanish cooking is really European in nature. It can be either very subtle or robust in flavoring, depending on the dish. We use a great deal of olive oil, tomatoes, onions, garlic, saffron and almonds. We like to eat eggs, fresh fish and shellfish, and chicken and rabbit when we can get them. As for starches, Spaniards, like most poor people, eat many of them: bread, of course, and also beans, potatoes, or, in the case of my own region, rice.

If I were to introduce you to Spanish cooking, I would have you taste a *cocido madrileño* or a *fabada*. Both are long-cooking dishes of beans or chick-peas, vegetables and meat that are made in earthenware casseroles. I suppose it is possible to make them in metal pots, but no Spaniard would believe it! Or I would make you one of the hundreds of rice dishes that I know; since in Valencia, where I come from, rice is eaten six days a week—on the seventh day, we fasted. No doubt you already know about *paella* (rice baked with a mixture of meats and seafood) and *arroz con pollo* (rice with chicken), but maybe you would like to try *arroz al horno* (rice cooked in a clay pot along with sausages, veal, chicken, olives and chicken broth, and then topped with sliced red tomatoes). To drink, you would have a good

Almonds.

Figs.

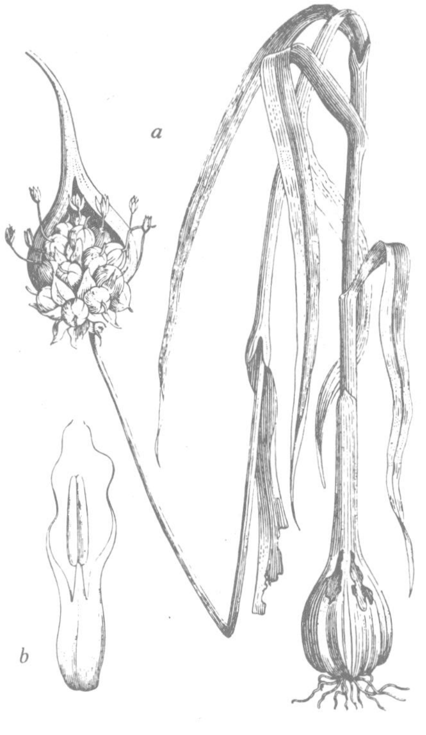

Garlic.

local wine, or some *sangría*, a mixture of wine and fruit juice or sherbet or egg whites. And for dessert you could have the classic flan, of course, a cool custard made of eggs, milk, sugar, cinnamon and caramelized sugar. Or try one of my childhood favorites, *torrijas*, made by dipping stale bread in red wine and then dredging it in egg and flour and frying it. Like so many Spanish dishes, *torrijas* is a poor man's dish, designed to use up the stale bread left over from the day before. But it is really delicious, especially when sprinkled with cinnamon.

All of these dishes are made in modern restaurants, but they originated in the simple kitchens of the home. I remember my mother fixing dinner on a coal stove in some sort of clay pot, either a deep, short-handled *olla* or else a saucepan, called a *cazo*. Even the *cazo* was made of earthenware, but the earthenware worked very well over a hot coal fire. The only metal pot we owned was a *paella* pan.

To keep food cool, we had a *fresquera*, a wooden-framed box with sides made of fine mesh wire that was placed on the windowsill. There, the sausages or cheese would get whatever breezes were stirring while they were protected from insects and birds. In later years, my mother had a refrigerator, or rather an ice box, but to this day there are *fresqueras* in many Spanish villages.

All of our baking had to be done at the local bakery. My mother would put a recipe together in a clay pot, and I would carry the pot to the baker's oven. In my pocket I had the two or three *pesetas* that he charged for allowing us to cook our supper in his oven for half an hour or so. While there, I would also buy a loaf of bread. How well I remember that hungry little boy, carrying home a steaming-hot casserole full of rice and chicken, with a crusty loaf of bread tucked under his arm. Nothing ever tasted as good as those meals. Should you try to cook a proper Spanish meal, you may well experience the same pleasures that have been the greatest influence in my life.

Wooden Mortar and Pestle C:1

A mortar and pestle are essential to authentic Spanish cooking. With them the garlic and herbs that form the basis of so many Spanish sauces are pressed and ground. Since even the most closely-grained hardwoods will absorb some of the strong garlic essence, it is a good idea to reserve one mortar and pestle just for such sauces. This round, squat wooden mortar—4″ across the top, 3½″ tall and 2½″ deep—is unfinished on the inside to provide a good grinding surface. The 6¼″-long pestle, curved to provide a solid grip, has a flat unfinished bottom to match the inside of the mortar. The set would be super for a thick, tangy *ali-oli* sauce: basically a creamy garlic-olive oil combination, sometimes flavored with a bit of lemon juice, that is served (in the mortar in which it is made) with boiled meat or fish. Or make *pollo en pepitoria*, chicken braised in white wine seasoned with a paste of pulverized almonds, hard-cooked egg yolks, garlic and saffron, all crushed and blended in a mortar.

H. A. Mack & Co., Inc. (Z112) **$3.50**

HAKE IN GREEN SAUCE

Merluza en Salsa Verde

1 tablespoon olive oil
½ onion, finely chopped
1 clove garlic, finely minced or crushed to a paste in a mortar
1 teaspoon chopped parsley, finely minced
2 pounds fillet of hake (*merluza*), cut into 12 3″- to 4″-pieces (3 pieces per person)
Flour for dredging
Salt
1 cup fish stock*
2 ounces (¼ cup) white wine
8 clams
8 mussels
4 asparagus tips, blanched
⅓ cup peas, cooked
2 hard-cooked eggs, cut in half
Red pepper flakes

Preheat oven to 250 F.

Make a *sofrito:* heat the olive oil in a large, shallow earthenware baking dish and sauté the onion, garlic and parsley until the onions are softened.

Dredge the hake in flour and season with salt to taste. Add the fish to the dish and brown lightly on each side. Pour in the fish stock and wine and distribute the clams and mussels around the pan. Bake for 10 minutes; add the asparagus tips, peas and hard-cooked eggs for the last 2 minutes. Sprinkle very sparingly with red pepper flakes before serving.

Yield: 4 servings.

* Make your own stock with the hake (or other fish) bones: put a carrot, a stalk of celery and the fish bones in a pot with water to cover; add salt and pepper to taste and simmer for 20–30 minutes. Strain before using.

(Courtesy of Ramón San Martin, Café San Martin, New York City.)

Foreigners have long been dismayed by the Spanish garlic habit: "The day closed as I was wandering about the Duchess's mansion, surprised at the slovenly neglect of the furniture . . . the exhalations of paint, and the still more pestilential exhalation of the gar-

Continued from preceding page

lick-eating women. Universal apathy and indifference to everything seems to pervade the whole Iberian peninsula."

The Travel Diaries of William Beckford of Fonthill. *Kraus Reprint Co., 1972.*

Poplar Pestle C:2

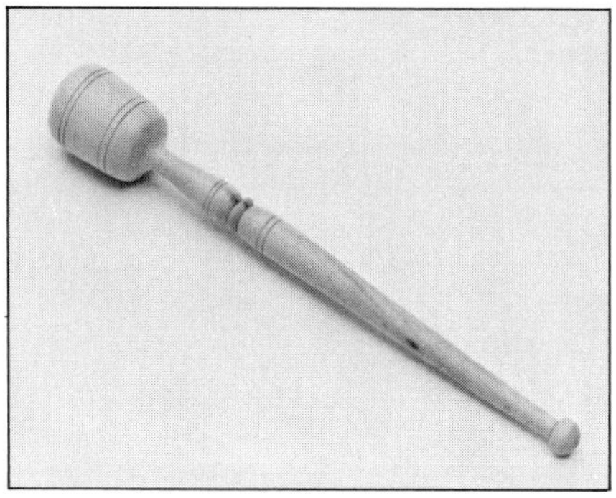

A pestle—meant for crushing, mashing or pressing—does not always come with a mortar; this long-handled tool of poplarwood operates in whatever bowl, sieve or pan you want to crush or press food. It will prove its worth in a variety of Spanish dishes. To make a *potaje de vigilia* (vigil soup) for Good Friday or another fast day, you must drain and squeeze cooked spinach dry in a large sieve. You then add it to a simmering broth containing cod and chick-peas. Or if braised rabbit in wine with chocolate sauce (*conejo a la ampurdanesa*) is what you desire, our pestle comes in handy for mashing together the almonds, pine nuts and grated chocolate for the sauce. It is 12¾″ long.

H. A. Mack & Co., Inc. (Z55) **$1.50**

Strainer Spoon C:3

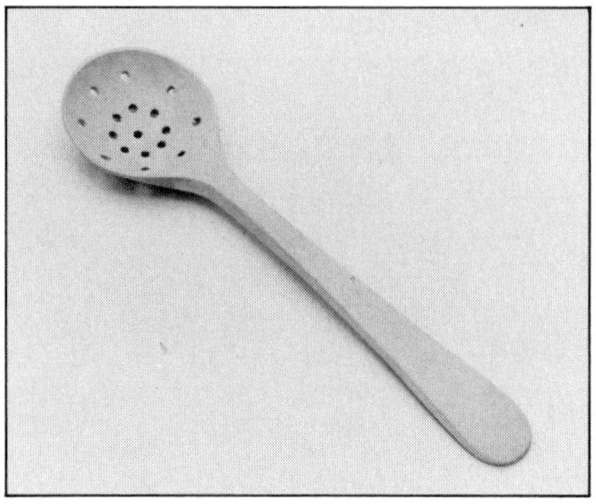

Perforated with two concentric circles of holes, this 12¼″-long, planewood spoon would serve many functions in the Spanish kitchen. It is as useful for scooping olives from a crock as it would be for lifting and draining pieces of food from a pot. A *cocido* or *pote* (dish of boiled meats and vegetables), for example, is frequently served in three courses: first the broth, then the vegetables, and finally the meat. The *cocido* is known in dozens of regional variations and by as many names, all evidently descended from the *olla podrida* (rotten pot) that gave physical sustenance to the hapless idealist, Don Quixote. For an unusual *cocido,* try the Andalusian version, which is seasoned with saffron, paprika and mint.

H. A. Mack & Co., Inc. (Z16) **$3.00**

A bocan, or cocoa-drying house in Granada in the mid-19th century.

Utensil Set C:4

These attractive wooden utensils will add a Spanish touch to your kitchen and ease the preparation of your favorite Spanish dishes. The 10¾″-long, planewood spatula is tapered to slip easily under sizzling *buñuelos*—sweet or savory fritters dripping with honey or seasoned with minced ham, chicken or egg. Both wooden spoons are 12″ long with partly rounded handles; but the bowl of one is round—2½″ in diameter, with a pouring spout; and the other is oblong—2¾″ long for simple mixing and mashing. The poplar soup ladle is 11½″ long with a 2½″-diameter bowl. It will serve half a cup of steaming *sopa de ajo* (garlic soup) or iced *gazpacho* (cold puréed vegetable soup). A hook at the end of the handle provides a means of securing the ladle to the edge of a deep pot.

H. A. Mack & Co., Inc.

Spatula (235)	**$3.25**
Mixing spoon (Z20A)	**$1.25**
Testing spoon (Z45)	**$1.75**
Ladle (Z10M)	**$3.50**

Wooden Grater C:5

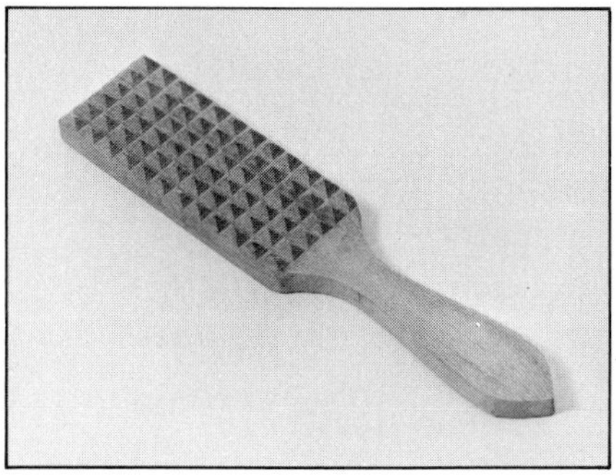

Wood prevails over metal when it comes to hand tools in the Spanish kitchen. Even a grater may be made of wood. This one of beech has six dozen sharp pyramidal teeth on a 4½″-by-1¾″ grating surface. Grasped tightly by its 4″-long handle, the grater will tear into anything rubbed against it. Grate lemon and orange peels with it when making *tortas de aceite* (anise-and-sesame-seed cookies laced with wine, cinnamon, almonds and grated citrus peels).

H. A. Mack & Co., Inc. (Z50) **$3.00**

Fish Scaler C:6

The Atlantic and the Mediterranean, not to mention the mountain streams and lakes of the interior, supply the Spanish with a spectacular variety of fish. Consequently, seafood comprises a large part of their cuisine. Even if you don't do your own fishing, you will find this sturdy fish scaler useful to clean off those last scales your fishmonger missed. Made of stainless steel, it has a 2″-by-1¾″ scaling surface perforated by holes with rough edges that hook onto and pull off the slippery scales. The wire handle is 5″ long. Clean a red snapper, set it on a layer of sliced potatoes in an open casserole and sprinkle it with bread crumbs, garlic, parsley and paprika. Baste it with olive oil, and then bake it in the oven for a Spanish-style fish *al horno* (oven-baked).

H. A. Mack & Co., Inc. **$2.75**

SPANISH PORK SAUSAGE

Chorizo

This a very old, home-style recipe for *chorizo.*

- 1 pound pork loin or shoulder (the meat should be about ¾ lean and ¼ fat)
- 1 teaspoon salt
- ½ teaspoon pepper
- 1 teaspoon paprika
- 1 ounce (2 tablespoons) white wine
- Oregano (optional)
- Pork casing, well-cleaned

Grind all of the ingredients except the casing together. Tie off one end of the casing and then stuff the ground mixture firmly into the other end. Tie off into sausages of whatever length desired and hang in a cool, dry place for at least a month, until dry.
Yield: ½ pound.

(Courtesy of Ramón San Martin, Café San Martin, New York City.)

Sausage Funnel C:7

In *cocidos* (dishes of boiled meats and vegetables), in *huevos a la flamenca* (eggs and peas with sausage in a spicy tomato sauce), or simply alone as a *tapa* (appetizer), *chorizos* (sausages) add spice to Spanish life. To make these spicy, peppery sausages yourself, you will need some casing and a handy metal funnel. This one is made of aluminum and measures 3¾″ in length and 3¼″ across the top. Tie a knot in one end of the casing and pull the other end over the narrow, ¾″ tube; bunch a fair amount of casing over the tube. Then, hold it there with one hand while stuffing the seasoned ground pork in the hopper with the other. When the casing is nearly full, tie it at regular intervals to form individual links and hang them in a cool, dry place to cure for the number of days or weeks your recipe requires. Most *chorizos* are also smoked as part of the curing process. But you needn't wait until the sausages are cured for a taste. Make some extra stuffing and do what the Spanish do at pig-slaughtering time: have your friends and neighbors in for a glass of wine and *la prueba* ("the test" of all the ingredients) that is cooked and then, with long wooden spoons, sampled from a communal pot.

Casa Moneo **$0.75**

Churro Press C:8

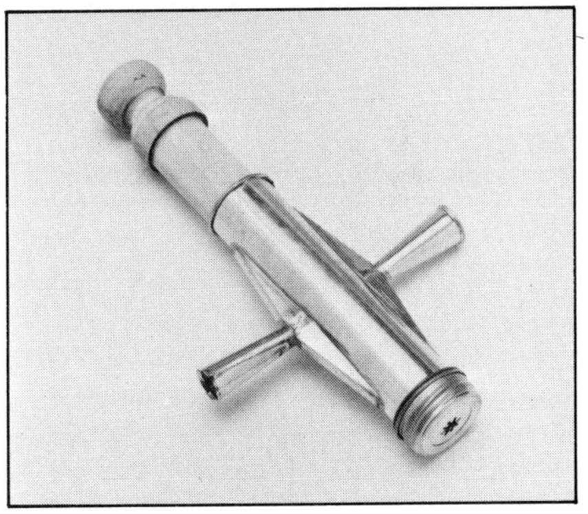

Churros are thin, fluted, loop-shaped crullers that are crisply fried and sold on Spanish street corners at all hours of the day, frequently by women vendors called *churreras.* Armed with a press like this one—only bigger—the vendor fills the tube with a thick flour dough, grasps the handles firmly, and pushes the wooden plunger to squeeze the *churros* out through a star-shaped opening directly into a pot of hot olive oil. When cooked, the golden loops are sprinkled liberally with sugar and sold in batches of five or six tied together with a green reed. They may be carried off to a café and enjoyed with a cup of strong, dark coffee or frothy chocolate. *Churros* are also a mainstay of the Spanish *desayuno* (breakfast) that usually consists of some kind of bread and coffee or chocolate. This *churrera* (*churro* press) is made of tinned steel with a wooden plunger, and has a central tube that is 7″ long and 1⅝″ in diameter. Two larger sizes are available.

Casa Moneo **$3.98**

The olive.

Olive Oil Can C:9

In England the height of redundancy is to carry coals to Newcastle; in Spain the equivalent would be to take olives to La Mancha, for the olive tree thrives in that hot, dry plateau region of central Spain. (*My Fair Lady* notwithstanding, the rain in Spain falls only rarely on the plain.) Here, olives are cured or pressed into the oil that forms the basis of almost every Spanish dish or sauce. In the old days, olive oil was purchased in large, unwieldly pigskins that were hung in the pantry; from them, Spanish cooks would draw off smaller quantities into a handy little dispenser like this one that would stand right next to the stove, ready for constant use. Shaped something like the Tin Woodsman's hat in *The Wizard of Oz,* it has a hinged lid, a gracefully arched handle, and—perhaps its greatest virtue—a long thin spout from which you can pour the oil in a slow, steady stream. It's just the thing for adding oil gradually to a garlic paste to make the classic *ali-oli* sauce that goes so well with grilled meats and fish. The tinned-steel oil can is 6″ tall and will hold 2¼″ cups of oil. You'll find that keeping oil in the can will help keep it rust free.

The Critical Cook/ H. A. Mack & Co., Inc. $8.50

Gazpacho Bowl C:10

Centuries ago, the ingenious Andalusians found the answer to a light, nourishing and thirst-quenching meal for a hot climate. They soaked bread in olive oil and then ground it with some garlic, salt and seeded tomatoes in a mortar. Then they poured the mixture into a clay pot and left it in a cool, shady spot so the flavors could marry for a while. Before being eaten, it was thinned with water and vinegar and garnished with chopped vegetables. This potable salad was called *gazpacho* after the Arabic for "soaked bread." And just as salad is often served in wooden dishes, *gazpacho* is traditionally eaten from a wooden bowl. Made of willow, this smooth, handsomely-carved bowl is 5″ across the top and 2¼″ deep. It will hold 2 cups of the savory cold soup, a refreshing meal or appetizer for those blistering salad days of summer.

H. A. Mack & Co., Inc. (Z52) $4.00

ANDALUSIAN GAZPACHO

Gazpacho Andaluz

2 medium cucumbers, peeled
2 green peppers
3 medium tomatoes, peeled
½ small onion, peeled
1 3″-long chunk Italian-style bread
1 clove garlic
Pinch of cumin
Pinch of paprika
2 tablespoons olive oil
1 tablespoon wine vinegar
1 cup water
1 tablespoon mayonnaise
Salt
Pepper
Croutons

Chop 1 cucumber, 1 green pepper and 2 tomatoes, and place them in a large bowl. Add the chunk of bread, garlic, cumin, paprika, olive oil, wine vinegar and water, toss together, cover and refrigerate for 24 hours. Add the mayonnaise and salt and pepper to taste and blend to a purée in a blender or food processor, or pass through a food mill.

Dice the remaining cucumber, green pepper and tomato and serve as garnish, along with the croutons, in small bowls on the side.
Yield: 4 servings.

(Courtesy of Ramón San Martin, Café San Martin, New York City.)

Theophile Gautier, poet and critic, was not overly impressed with gazpacho: "This gaspacho is worthy of a special description, and we shall here give the recipe, which would have made the hair of the late Brillat-Savarin stand on end. You pour some water into a soup tureen, and to this water you add a dash of vinegar, some cloves of garlic, some onions cut into quarters, some slices of cucumber, a few pieces of pimento, a pinch of salt; then one cuts some bread and sets it to soak in this pleasing mixture, serving it cold. At home, a dog of any breeding would refuse to sully its nose with such a compromising mixture. It is the favourite dish of the Andalusians, and the prettiest women do not shrink from swallowing bowlfuls of this hellbroth of an evening."

From Mediterranean Food *by Elizabeth David. Penguin Books Ltd., 1965.*

Tomatoes—an invaluable import from the New World—are usually part of the ubiquitous sofrito *(basic fried sauce) and* gazpacho *that are some of the glories of Spanish cuisine.*

Gazpacho Spoon C:11

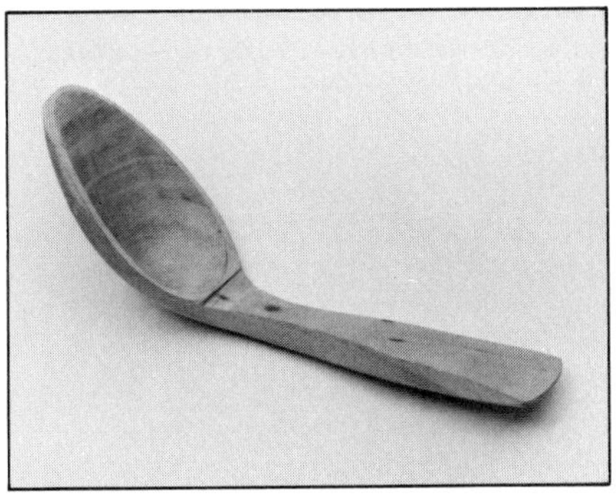

Gazpacho, the famous, Spanish cold vegetable soup, has as many regional variations as *paella.* Essentially a purée of tomatoes, bread, garlic, olive oil and vinegar, it is chilled and garnished with chopped vegetables such as cucumbers, tomatoes, green peppers and onions. In southern Spain, where *gazpacho* originated, it is often eaten with a wooden spoon. Ours comes in smooth, willowwood with a sweeping, 4½″-long handle and a narrow bowl that enables you to sip the soup comfortably from the side. If you consider wooden spoons suitable only for cooking rather than eating utensils, you may find this one convenient for sampling broths, or serving sauces, like the simple vinaigrette the Spanish serve with shellfish and cooked vegetables on hot summer days.

The Critical Cook/ H. A. Mack & Co., Inc. (Z42) $1.50

Ceramic Colander C:12

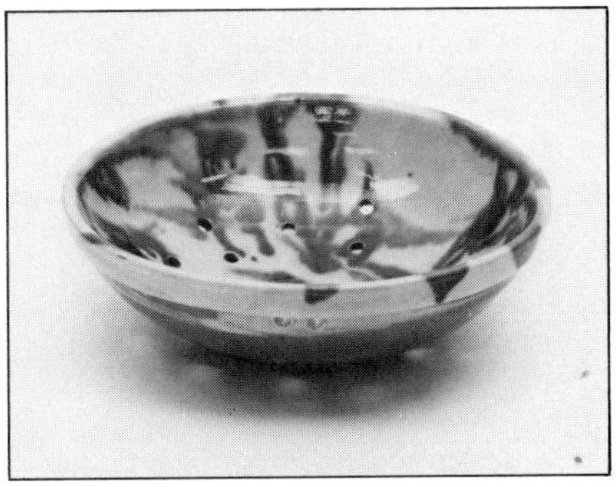

A pretty, pale yellow with streams of green meandering through it, this earthenware colander has several good-sized holes for draining fruits and vegetables after they've been washed. A length of string, or a thong, could be slipped through the two holes just under the rim in order to hang the dish, an attractive Spanish abstract for your kitchen. Glazed inside and out, the colander is 9″ across and 2½″ deep. Use it with a wooden pestle to squeeze cooked spinach dry for *potaje de vigilia* (vigil soup); or perch it atop a pot and steam string beans to serve Spanish-style in a fresh tomato sauce.

La Placetena Distributing $10.00

EGGS FLAMENCO STYLE

Huevos a la Flamenca

Butter
2 eggs
Salt
Pepper
2 slices *chorizo* (Spanish pork sausage)
1 small slice prosciutto (*jamón serrano*)
10–12 green peas, cooked
1 small asparagus tip, blanched
2–3 strips sweet red pepper, blanched until soft
1 teaspoon tomato purée

Preheat oven to 350 F.

Butter a small egg dish well. Break in the eggs and sprinkle with salt and pepper to taste. Arrange the *chorizo,* prosciutto, peas, asparagus tip and red pepper strips around the yolks and place a dollop of tomato purée in one corner. (This is a strikingly colorful dish.)

Bake for 10 minutes, until the egg whites are set.

Yield: 1 serving.

(Courtesy of Ramón San Martin, Café San Martin, New York City.)

Spinach.

Earthenware Egg Dish C:13

Individual dishes like this one are used in Spain to bake eggs, which are often

Continued from preceding page

served as a first course or as a light lunch (*comida*) in the summer. Made of a tawny brown terra-cotta and smoothly glazed, except on the outside bottom, the shallow dish will comfortably hold an individual portion of *huevos a la flamenca* (eggs baked with ham, sausage, sweet red peppers, asparagus, peas and tomatoes). The dish is 4¾″ in diameter on the bottom and its sloping sides arch up to two handles, each imprinted with the design of an ornamental fan.

Casa Moneo **$0.89**

Earthenware Baking Dish C:14

Originally, *tapas* were the "lids" of bread put over wineglasses to keep out flies. But some enterprising barkeeper or restaurateur must have noticed hungry drinkers munching on the crusts and decided to serve other snacks as well. These appetizers, still called *tapas,* have so proliferated in Madrid that one can easily spend the cocktail hour nibbling and sampling and never bother with dinner at all. Small, straight-sided earthenware dishes like this one may be used to cook, store and serve your own array of *tapas* or individual portions of a first course. Made of terra-cotta, 6½″ in diameter and 1¼″ deep, the dish is glazed on the inside, unglazed on the outside and decorated with two small, ear-shaped handles. Typical *tapas* might include shrimp in olive oil with red pepper and parsley, fried green peppers with spicy pork sausage, and small pork meatballs. A larger casserole 12″ in diameter and 2¾″ deep is also available.

Casa Moneo/ La Placeteña Distributing **$4.00**

"Sir Kenelme Digby . . . having resided in Spain some time, is able to give a recipe for the Spanish olla-podrida as it was prepared in the seventeenth century. The medium of a good plain 'Spanish oglia' is, of course, 'a great pot' of water which must be kept gently boiling for five or six hours, and the materials consist of a rump of beef, a loin of mutton, a piece of veal, two chickens, or else three pigeons, a piece of 'enterlarded bacon,' and three or four onions. Each ingredient, beginning with the beef, and ending with the onions, must be thrown into the pot at such a time as will ensure the whole being completely cooked at the same moment. About half an hour before the oglia is done a 'porrender full' of the broth should be taken out, flavoured with pepper, salt, five or six cloves, and a nutmeg, and then poured back again."

Good Cheer: The Romance of Food and Feasting *by F. W. Hackwood. Sturgess & Walton, 1911.*

Round-Bottomed Earthenware Cazuela C:15

Some would say the simplest and finest cooking of the Spanish peninsula is that of the Basque provinces, where gastronomic societies are found in nearly every city and even in some villages. There are twenty-five in San Sebastián alone. The phrase *a la vasca* (in the Basque style) is found on menus throughout Spain and, if an authentic recipe has indeed been followed, it guarantees an excellent dish. A popular fish in this northern region of Spain is hake from the cold waters of the Bay of Biscay. The Basques prepare it in a simple green sauce (*salsa verde*), flavored with garlic and olive oil, that takes its verdant color and fresh flavor from peas and chopped parsley. The fish is prepared and served in an earthenware dish (*cazuela*) that can be used on top of the stove over low heat or in the oven. Ours is 15½″ across the top, 4″ deep and made of coarse terra-cotta. The bottom is rounded and unglazed on the outside to better absorb and hold heat. Four small handles grace the sides of the orange-brown pot; but hold it securely with both hands by the sides and bottom, not by the handles, when you carry your hake *en salsa verde* to the table. Similar *cazuelas* are available in smaller and larger sizes.

Casa Moneo/ La Placeteña Distributing **$20.00**

"In a village of La Mancha the name of which I have no desire to recall, there lived not so long ago one of those gentlemen who always have a lance in the rack, an ancient buckler, a skinny nag, and a greyhound for the chase. A stew with more beef than mutton in it, chopped meat for his evening meal, scraps for a Saturday, lentils on Friday, and a young pigeon as a special delicacy for Sunday, went to account for three-quarters of his income."

Don Quixote *by Miguel de Cervantes Saavedra, translated by Samuel Putnam. Viking Press, 1951.*

Early 18th-century Spanish earthenware dish with tin enameling (from The Metropolitan Museum of Art).

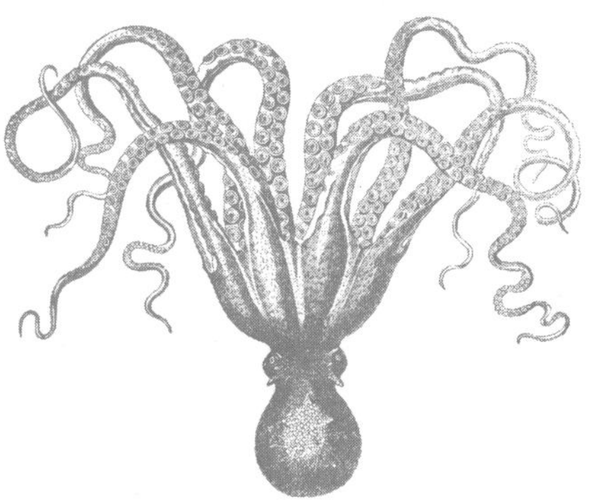

Octopus.

Rectangular Earthenware Baking Dish C:16

Cafés and bars in Madrid pride themselves on the variety and abundance of their *tapas,* cold and hot appetizers, that Madrileños relish while sipping an evening sherry. Grilled mushrooms and *serrano* ham, sautéed kidneys, pickled cauliflower, stewed quail, stuffed green peppers—thirty, forty, even fifty such choices are not unusual, all crowded together on a counter, each in a large earthenware baking dish. You'll find a myriad other uses for this practical, handsome dish. A smooth, clear glaze covers the dark, caramel-colored casserole, except on the outside bottom that has been left unglazed and is ridged slightly to distribute heat and keep the dish from slipping. The dish is 11″ long, 8″ wide and 1¾″ deep. It is capacious enough to bake several trout Navarre style—in a marinade of red wine scented with mint, thyme, rosemary and bay leaf—a dish that like the rosemary in it is for remembrance.

Ceramicas Punter, S.L. $12.00

Earthenware Bean Pot C:17

This earthenware *olla* (pot), a kissing cousin of the Boston baked bean pot, makes us think of *fabada asturiana*—a white bean soup cooked with pork shoulder or ham, bacon and *morcilla* (blood sausage)—that warms body and soul in the damp Asturian highlands. There it is eaten with corn bread to soak up all the delicious pot liquor. But an *olla* needn't be restricted to beans. Glazed entirely on the inside and unglazed below the two tiny handles on the outside, the *olla* would make a good pot for *cocidos* (stews). The Spanish love deprecatory names for these humble dishes: a perfectly lovely stew of shredded beef in a tomato sauce is known as *ropa vieja* (old clothes); and a boiled dinner of cabbage, beans, leeks, tomatoes and several meats is called *olla podrida* (rotten pot). Prepare them in this *olla,* and you too can join the Spanish game of one-downmanship. The pot is 5¼″ deep, 5⅜″ across at the top, and holds 7 cups.

La Placeteña Distributing $8.00

A native of South America that became known as the Spanish bean in French and the Spanish runner bean in English.

Paella

By far the best-known specialty of Spanish cuisine is *paella,* that colorful one-dish meal of meat, seafood, vegetables and saffron rice that may be elaborate or simple to suit your taste, whim, locale or budget. It originated in Valencia on the eastern coast of Spain, a landscape criss-crossed with rice paddies, vegetable farms and orange groves. From neighboring Murcia with its fields of purple crocuses, came the saffron that lends its expensive yellow pungency to the dish. (The dried stigmas of crocus blossoms are the source of saffron.)

Paella is named for the dish in which it is made: the word derives from the Latin *patella,* in Roman times a broad, flat metal or pottery dish used for cooking or serving food. At first, it was a humble repast of snails, eels, green beans and rice cooked in olive oil. Now, it may include such foods as lobster, clams, shrimp, mussels, chicken, duck

Continued from preceding page

and sausages. The recipe varies from region to region, chef to chef and season to season.

Today in Valencia, as elsewhere in Spain, *paella* prepared alfresco is still the best kind. Spanish picnickers carry the ingredients with them and build fires with whatever twigs and fallen branches are at hand, and country restaurants have outdoor kitchens where every *paella* is cooked over its own wood fire. Whatever the regional variations in meat, seafood and vegetables, the custom of eating *paella* right out of the pan with wooden spoons—everyone sharing the common pot—adds to the convivial *ambiente* (ambiance) of the dish.

Classic Iron Paella Pan C:18

The classic Spanish pan for preparing *paella* is broad and shallow with sloping sides and two handles. This one of medium-weight steel is the real thing: 14″ in diameter at the top, 12″ in diameter at the bottom and only 1⅜″ deep. The flat bottom surface is lightly hammered to strengthen it. Because few burners will heat such a large area evenly, most recipes for *paella* in this country suggest baking it in the oven. But why not do what the Spanish do? Cook it outdoors. Most charcoal grills are the right size; just remember, the heat will probably be more intense than that of a wood fire or a hot oven and may cook the rice more quickly. And make sure to remove the moisture-resistant film that protects the pan with a good hot, soapy scrub before using.

Casa Moneo $6.00

VALENCIAN PAELLA

Paella a la Valenciana

1 tablespoon olive oil
8 ounces veal, cubed
8 ounces pork, cubed
1 small chicken (2-2½ pounds), cut in parts
10 ounces *chorizo* (Spanish sausage)
1 cup raw rice
¾ cup tomato purée
4½ cups saffron-flavored chicken broth
8 clams
8 mussels
8 shrimp
2 1-pound, freshly killed lobsters, cut in 4 pieces (optional)
2 ounces string beans, blanched
2 ounces green peas, blanched
1 sweet red pepper, cut in strips
1 lemon, cut into 4 wedges

Preheat oven to 350 F.

Heat the olive oil in a paella pan. Add the veal, pork, chicken and *chorizo* and fry for about 5 minutes, until lightly browned. Stir in the rice and fry for several seconds, until thoroughly coated with oil. Stir in the tomato purée and saffron-flavored chicken broth. Distribute the clams, mussels, shrimp, lobster, string beans and peas over the rice. Place in the oven and cook for 15 minutes, or until the rice is tender. Adding the garnish of sweet red pepper strips and taste for seasoning after 13 minutes. To serve, garnish with a wedge of lemon for each person.
Yield: 4 servings.

* To make your own broth, simmer the bones of one chicken (or an equal quantity) in water to cover (approximately 1½ quarts) with a pinch of saffron threads, a chopped tomato, some green pepper and onions and a prosciutto bone (if available) for 3 to 4 hours, Add salt and pepper to taste, once the broth is reduced to desired strength. Be sure to season well, as the broth provides seasoning for the entire dish.

(Courtesy of Ramón San Martin, Café San Martin, New York City.)

Steel Paella Pan C:19

Deeper than the classic Spanish *paella* pan, this large steel version will come in handy for an especially big *paella* —chock-full of lobster, mussels, clams, and shrimp. Or use it for any dish requiring a sizeable skillet, without a lid —say, eight portions of *merluza marinera* (poached hake fillets with tomato and almond sauce), a Catalonian specialty. The rounded sides of the pan reach up to give it a depth of 2½″, and the top is 15″ in diameter. With its trim lines and matte-gray finish, the pan will elegantly frame the colorful splendor of a festive *paella.*

Atlas Metal Spinning Co. (28PP15) $11.00

Enameled Cast-Iron Paella Pan C:20

For a *paella* pan to complement your dinnerware or dining room decor, pick one of the colorful Copco pans with white enamel inside and red, white, blue, yellow or brown enamel on the outside. With its sweeping modern lines, this pan—which is 16½″ long by 14″ wide and 2½″ deep—has evolved from the simple, classic form into a presentation piece that will set off the bright saffrons, reds and greens of the *paella.* But it isn't just for show. Beneath the pretty enamel exterior lives a practical, heavy iron pan that will distribute and hold heat well. Moreover, the wide bottom is ground flat to fit flush against electric burners for an even, efficient transfer of heat.

Copco, Inc. (114) $45.00

"We ate in pavilions on the sand. Pastries made of cooked and shredded fish and red and green peppers and small nuts like grains of rice. Pastries delicate and flaky and the fish of a richness that was incredible. Prawns fresh from the sea sprinkled with lime juice. They were pink and sweet and there were four bites to a prawn. Of those we ate many. Then we ate paella with fresh sea food, clams in their shells, mussels, crayfish, and small eels. Then we ate even smaller eels alone cooked in oil and as tiny as bean sprouts and curled in all directions and so tender they disappeared in the mouth without chewing."

For Whom The Bell Tolls *by Ernest Hemingway. Scribner's, 1940.*

Individual Flan Mold C:21

Flan is the national dessert of Spain: a light, creamy custard baked in a dish lined with caramelized sugar. It is the perfect finale to a multicourse Spanish meal and may be made in a large baking dish or in individual cups like this one, which is 3″ in diameter and 2″ deep. Appropriately, the dish is a rich caramel color to frame the golden custard inside, and it is glazed inside and out, except on the bottom outside. The outer sides are embellished with ridges, but the inside is completely smooth for easy unmolding. Caramel custard is not the only Spanish flan—it may also be made with chocolate or fruit and flavored with orange juice, cinnamon or rum.

Ceramicas Punter, S.L. $1.25

With typical tolerance, blue-blooded William Beckford of Fonthill describes one of his culinary adventures: "For the first time in my life I tasted the genuine Spanish chocolate, spiced and cinnamoned beyond all endurance. It has put my mouth in a flame, and I do nothing but spit and sputter."

The Travel Diaries of William Beckford of Fonthill. *Kraus Reprint Co., 1972.*

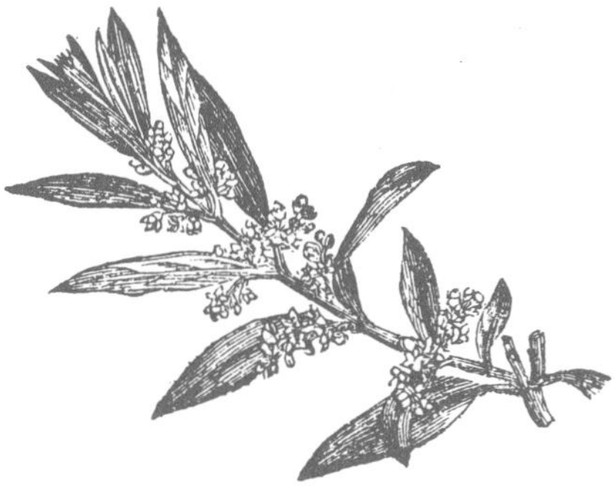

FLAN

½ cup, plus 4 teaspoons sugar
1 pint milk
Peel of 1 orange
Peel of 1 lemon
1 stick cinnamon
2 eggs
Several drops vanilla extract

Preheat oven to 200 F.

Carmelize ½ cup of the sugar in a small saucepan and pour into 1 large (2½ - 3 cup) mold or 4 small (6-8 ounce) molds. Tip and turn the mold or molds to coat the interior with the carmelized sugar.

Bring the milk to a boil with the orange and lemon peel and cinnamon stick. Simmer for 5 minutes, then remove and discard the peel and cinnamon stick.

Beat the eggs together, then beat in the remaining 4 teaspoons sugar and several drops vanilla extract. Add the hot milk and beat together, then strain. Pour into the mold, filling it right to the brim, and place in a baking pan filled with enough cool water to come two-thirds up the sides of the mold.

Bake for 15 minutes, or until set. Chill thoroughly. Unmold before serving.
Yield: 4 servings

(Courtesy of Ramón San Martin, Café San Martin, New York City.)

Chocolate Swizzle C:22

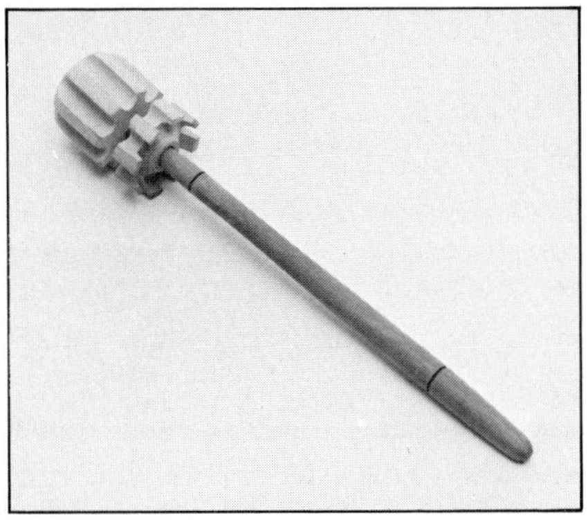

The Spanish, of course, were the first Europeans to discover the cacao bean; that was one of the perks of conquering Mexico. From the Aztecs they learned to make hot chocolate foamy by churning it with a wooden *molinillo* (swizzle) similar to this one. It has a 2″-long stirring head, part of which is a stable, ridged knob, and part a similarly ridged, movable ring. By holding the 10½″-long handle between your palms and rubbing them together, you set the knob and ring twirling at different speeds. In no time at all the melted chocolate and the light cream or milk will be thoroughly mixed and frothy, ready to enjoy with a hot *churro* (Spanish cruller) on a cold winter day.

H. A. Mack & Co., Inc. (Z51) $1.50

Sangría Spoon C:23

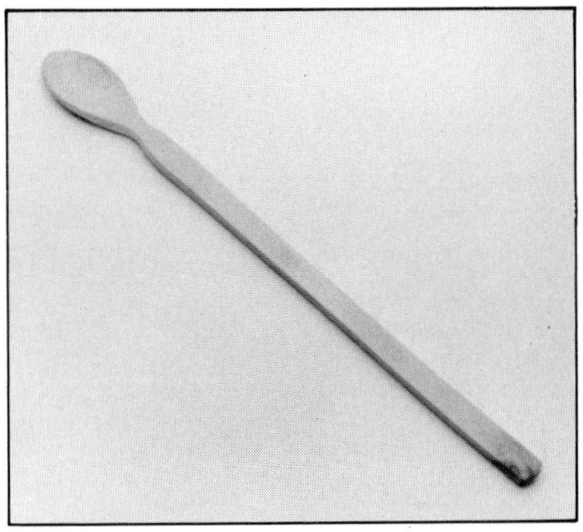

Nothing beats the heat like a glass or two of cool, refreshing *sangría.* When the mercury threatens to shatter the thermometer, this 11¾″-long, beechwood spoon will blend the red wine, brandy, ice-cold club soda, sugar and fruit slices to make the famous Span-

Continued from preceding page

ish beverage. Serve it with a midday salad like *ensalada sevillana* (crisp escarole and green olives tossed with a tarragon dressing), or with an evening's *paella* on the patio. As they say in Valencia, to grow rice takes lots of water, to cook rice takes lots of water, but to wash it down takes lots of wine.

H. A. Mack & Co., Inc. (Z47) **$1.00**

Sangría Pitcher C:24

No Spanish cupboard would be complete without a *sangría* pitcher. Our ceramic *jarro,* with its full skirts and high waist, stands proudly at attention, handle arched by its side and pinched spout ready to hold back ice while releasing the cooling drink. The 7″-tall pitcher is made of reddish-brown, glazed earthenware. It is 5″ in diameter across the bottom and holds 3 pints. From the rustic kitchen to the flamenco nightclub, you will find pitchers like it filled with *sangría* to quench thirsts on hot summer days and nights. To make it, cut lemon, orange and apple slices and put them in a pitcher of red wine. Add sugar and a generous splash of brandy, stir and chill. Before serving, stir in some chilled club soda and add ice. But a note of caution: earthenware glazes are destroyed by acidic juices. So as tempting as it seems, don't use the *jarro* to keep a constant supply of *sangría* in the refrigerator.

Ceramicas Punter, S.L. **$8.00**

16th-century Spanish pottery water bottle (*from The Metropolitan Museum of Art*).

The aristocratic sybarite, William Beckford, was charmed and repulsed by his visit to Portugal in the late 18th century. Here, in Colares, he describes one of the more appealing landscapes: "Droves of cows and goats milking; ovens out of which huge cakes of savoury bread had just been taken; ranges of beehives, and long pillared sheds, entirely tapestried with purple and yellow muscadine grapes, half candied, which were hung up to dry."

The Travel Diaries of William Beckford of Fonthill. *Kraus Reprint Co., 1972.*

The Flavor of Portugal

by Maria Odete Laia

During the winter, my family lived in a modern apartment in Lisbon, but in the summer we went to a country house in Beira Baixa, the province where my father was born. The house was made of gray stone, which made it beautifully cool throughout the hot summer months. Like so many Portuguese kitchens, ours was tiled, and it had a fireplace in which nearly all the cooking was done. There was no other source of heat in the room, so if we wanted to cook stews or soups, or rice pudding, or fried eggs, it had to be done in that fireplace. It was there that the maid prepared the *cozido à portuguêsa* (the Portuguese boiled dinner) or the *caldo verde* (kale, potato and garlic soup) that warmed us on cool summer evenings.

In the morning she would start a wood fire in the bottom of the fireplace. Then, if she wanted to make a stew for supper, she would hang a large, three-legged iron kettle from chains suspended from a hood inside the top of the fireplace. These kettles came in all sizes, from the small ones in which she made vegetables for lunch to the largest, in which she would put together a hearty *açorda* made of bread soaked in broth, and poached eggs. If she was going to prepare grilled sardines or fried eggs, then she would remove the pot and its chains from the fireplace and would, instead, cover the wood fire with a sort of long-legged tripod or trivet that had a grill-like top. On this trivet she could put a frying pan or a saucepan, and make dishes like the rich *bolinhos,* codfish cakes fried in garlic-flavored oil.

Most of our pots were made of iron; in our province there was little of the lovely earthenware than can be found in other parts of Portugal. Perhaps you have seen the amusing earthenware pots that look like nesting chickens, or the earth-colored casseroles that are made locally all over Portugal. They are among our most popular exports, along with our beautiful painted tiles. In our province, however, we used metal pots made of black iron. But we did have an amusing casserole, a hinged, clam-shaped copper casserole called a *cataplana* in which we made a clam, tomato and sausage stew.

Outside the kitchen door sat a huge brick oven that was shaped like a beehive. That oven was fired up only one day a week, and on that day the cook made all the loaves of wheat and rye bread for the week. She also cooked the sweet cakes, like the *pãodeló,* that the Portuguese love so much, and any roasts that were needed. For the following day or two, we would feast on roasted chicken, leg of lamb, sweet almond cakes and fresh bread. The rest of the week, we would eat fish, eggs or sausage.

Our kitchen was so simple that it had no running water and no refrigerator. The cook drew water from fountains that stood within the walls of our property, and food apt to spoil was kept in a cool basement. The plain earth floor of the basement remained cold year round. Meat, especially sausages, could be kept there for some time; deeply-smoked hams and sausages hung from the ceiling. Other sausages were stored in big clay pots and submerged in olive oil that prevented mold from growing on the meat.

That kitchen must have caused lots of work for the cook, but we children had a wonderful time there. On baking day she would give us small pieces from the huge mass of yeast dough she had made, and we would form them into rolls. Just before they went into the oven, we stuck a piece of sausage or bacon into each one. Believe me, we were very careful to keep an eye on those rolls, to make sure we would get our very own back from the oven. I can still taste those delicious, crusty envelopes of bread folded around a spicy *chouriço* (Portuguese sausage).

If you come to Portugal—and I hope you will—you'll find that the cooking is very special and very delicious. It is less oily than Spanish cooking; I like to think that it is more like the French cuisine because we use many sauces, lots of cream and butter, and many fresh herbs, including coriander and mint, which make our food distinctive. But, of course, it is an Iberian style of cooking after all, and you will partake of many dishes made with sweet peppers, onions and tomatoes, with good black olives and spicy sausage, and what we immodestly like to think is the world's best shellfish.

Willowwood Mortar and Pestle C:25

In the fifteenth and sixteenth centuries, Portuguese explorers were leaders in the search for new trade routes to the spices of India. Every schoolchild reads about Bartholomeu Dias' discovery of the Cape of Good Hope, Vasco da Gama's sea voyage to India and Fernão de Magalhaes' passage through the strait that is named Magellan after him. Influenced by the exotic cuisines of Portuguese colonies in Brazil, Africa, India and China, Portuguese cooking includes hot chiles, paprika, fresh coriander, and favored Indian spices, such as cumin, cinnamon and nutmeg. To prepare these herbs and spices, a mortar and pestle are indispensable. The pale, satin-sleek willowwood of this set is not only beautiful to see and touch, but solid enough to do some serious crushing and grinding. The mortar, which sits firmly on a flat bottom, is 3¼″ in diameter and 2″ deep. The pestle, with its flat grinding surface and rounded knob for holding, is 4¼″ long. With this set you can crush the hot, dried red chiles for an authentic *amêijoas na cataplana,* steamed clams prepared in a *cataplana* (a clam-shaped metal casserole) or mash garlic, salt and fresh coriander for a *sopa à alentejana* (garlic flavored soup with fresh coriander, poached eggs and pieces of fried toast).

Newark Hardware & Paint Co., Inc. **$1.69**

While visiting Portugal in 1787, William Beckford dined at the Cork Convent and described it thus: "We had

Continued from preceding page

a greasy repast and abundance of high-flavoured cabbage stewed in the essence of ham and partridge, four sucking pigs, as many larded turkeys, and two pyramids of rice, as yellow as saffron could tinge them. . . . Our dessert both in point of fruit and sweetmeats was truly luxurious. Pomona herself need not have been ashamed of carrying in her lap such peaches and nectarines as rolled by dozens about the table."

The Journal of William Beckford in Portugal and Spain 1787–1788, *edited by Boyd Alexander. Rupert Hart-Davis, 1954.*

Pine Mortar and Pestle C:26

The wavy grain of Portuguese pine ripples through this mortar and pestle, making the set particularly attractive. Use it to pulverize blanched almonds for a rich Portuguese custard made of egg yolks and almonds and served with a sugar syrup flavored with lemon peel and cinnamon: *fatias da China.* A small bowl—3½" in diameter and 2½" deep—perches securely atop the strong pedestal base of the 5"-high mortar. The accompanying pestle is 6" long and feels pleasantly smooth.

H. A. Mack & Co., Inc. $3.50 (P34M)

Slotted Pine Spoon C:27

Portuguese pine, a handsome wood with a dark, wavy grain, was used to carve this 12"-long wooden spoon with two slots in its 3"-long oval bowl. Sturdily fashioned, it would be perfect for lifting poached eggs out of their cooking water and slipping them onto *bolinhos de bacalhau* (codfish cakes flavored with parsley, onion and garlic), or for transferring the chicken, ham, sausages and vegetables from their cooking broth to a serving platter for a *cozido à portuguêsa* (a Portuguese boiled dinner).

H. A. Mack & Co., Inc. $1.25 (P54K)

CODFISH CAKES

Bolinhos de Bacalhau

1 pound boneless salt cod*, boiled and ground
4 to 5 medium-sized potatoes, peeled, boiled and mashed
Pepper to taste
1 teaspoon fresh parsley, finely chopped
1 small onion, finely chopped
1 clove garlic, very finely chopped
3 eggs, separated

Mix the salt cod and the mashed potatoes. Stir in the pepper, parsley, the chopped onion, garlic and the 3 egg yolks. Beat the egg whites until stiff and blend them into the codfish mixture. With 2 tablespoons shape the codfish mixture into small, round cakes and deep fry the cakes until dark gold. Serve them with tomato rice and a green salad.

* The Portuguese use salted, dried codfish that must be soaked for about 12 hours, with several changes of water, before it is cooked.

(Courtesy of Maria Odete Laia, New York City.)

Wooden Utensil Set C:28

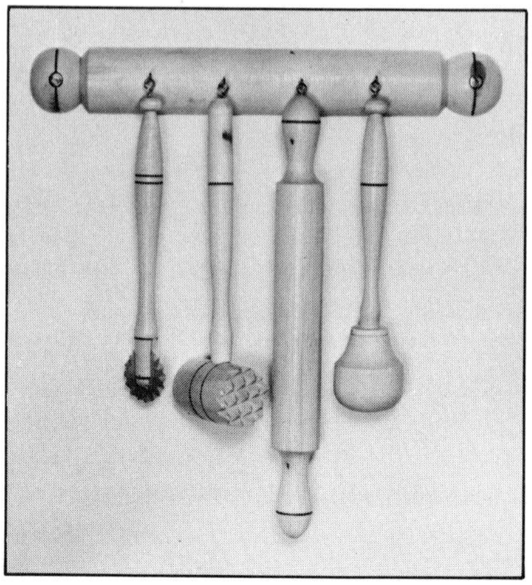

No tableau of the Portuguese kitchen would be complete without a set of wooden utensils. This one is picturesque and combines both pastry and stovetop cooking tools. A meat tenderizer and a potato or bean masher hang side by side with a rolling pin and dough crimper. All four implements are made of a smooth, blond wood with a gray, whorled grain, and each can be conveniently hung by a screw eye in the handle from a matching, 16"-long rack. Use the meat tenderizer on a beef steak for *befes* café style, with a sauce of browned butter, flour, brandy, salt and pepper. The masher will purée the beans for a *creme de favas* (bean soup) and the rolling pin will flatten the dough for *queijadas de Évora,* sweet cheese tarts with a touch of cinnamon. With the dough crimper, cut small *rissois* (deep-fried shrimp, whiting or codfish turnovers) that are served as an appetizer.

Newark Hardware & Paint Co., Inc. $5.98

For centuries the finest food (and sometimes the only food) has been available solely within the embrace of the mother-church. The monastery at Alcobaça was no exception, as described in William Beckford's travel diary: "The three prelates led the way to, I verily believe, the most distinguished temple of gluttony in all Europe . . . Through the center of the immense and nobly-groined hall, not less than sixty feet in diameter, ran a brisk rivulet of the clearest water, flowing through pierced wooden reservoirs, containing every sort of the finest riverfish. On one side, loads of game and venison were heaped up; on the other, vegetables and fruit in endless variety. Beyond a long line of stoves extended a row of ovens, and close to them hillocks of wheaten flour whiter than snow, rocks of sugar, jars of the purest oil, and pastry in vast abundance, which a numerous tribe of lay brothers and their attendants were rolling out and puffing up into an hundred different shapes, singing all the while as blithely as larks in a corn-field."

The Travel Diaries of William Beckford of Fonthill. *Kraus Reprint Co., 1972.*

Pine Spoons, Ladle and Spatula C:29

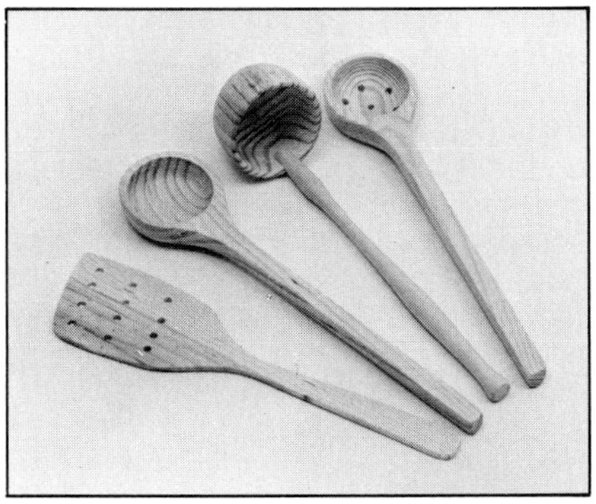

These four tools of satin-smooth Portuguese pine are both good-looking and functional. The spoon and spoon-strainer are the same design, except for a series of holes that pierce the strainer. Both are 13″ long with shallow, 2½″-diameter bowls; they lie completely level, since the bowls have flat bottoms, and the sleek handles are rounded for comfortable gripping. The soup ladle consists of two sections: a wide, deep bowl—1¾″ deep and 3″ in diameter—and a 10″-long handle that grasps the edge of the bowl tightly. The flat, 12″-long spatula, with its generous 3″-wide-by-4½″-long surface and dozen small holes for draining off liquid, can be used for both deep-frying and sautéing. Use it to turn *scas* (liver, marinated in wine with garlic and bay leaf and served with a sauce of the marinade, chopped bacon and parsley). The four utensils make a practical quartet for stovetop cooking.

H. A. Mack & Co., Inc.
Spoon (P76T) $2.25
Straining spoon (P71T) $2.50
Ladle (P80T) $3.00
Spatula (P32T) $1.75

Earthenware Steamer/Colander C:30

This beguiling, simple dish of glazed terra-cotta with a pie-crimp rim is 2½″ deep, 10″ in diameter and perforated across its flat bottom. Set over a pan of boiling water, it becomes a steamer for vegetables or fish, the unglazed bottom helping to distribute heat quickly between the holes where the steam pours through. Perched on an empty bowl, it becomes a strainer, just the thing to drain *bacalhau* (dried salt cod) after soaking it to remove the salt, and before preparing it in one of the 1001 ways the Portuguese have devised for their favorite fish.

The Complacent Cook $2.00

Earthenware Baking Dish C:31

Portuguese recipes often call for slow simmering in earthenware dishes. This rugged clay dish will fill the bill for making scores of Portuguese specialties, either on top of the stove or in the oven, and can then be carried piping hot to the table. Like much peasant pottery, the dish has a rough, grainy texture. A natural terra-cotta color, it is glazed on the inside and unglazed on the outside, the better to absorb heat. The dish is 3″ deep and 8¾″ in diameter, just right for a side dish of baked rice or a *caldo verde* (kale and potato soup usually enriched with slices of garlic-flavored pork sausage). *Caldo verde* is to Portugal what onion soup is to France—virtually the national dish. A smaller dish (2″ deep and 6″ in diameter) and a larger one (3½″ deep and 10½″ in diameter) are also available.

Newark Hardware & Paint Co., Inc. $4.98

Earthenware Casserole C:32

With its 4″-high straight sides, arched handles and slightly domed lid, this earthenware casserole is somewhat reminiscent of a turret. A sturdy, solid pot useful for any cuisine, it is glazed reddish-brown on the outside and gray on the inside; the outside bottom is unglazed. The lid, which is speckled with a slightly different brown, remains unglazed underneath and sits securely on the inner rim of the casserole. You will find this pot ideal for all those Portuguese *estufados* (stews) whether a hot, spicy *caldeirada* (seafood stew), or a *dobrada* (tripe stew with chickpeas, tomatoes and garlic-flavored sausage). The casserole measures 7″ in diameter and holds 5 cups.

The Pottery Barn $6.75

KALE SOUP

Caldo Verde

6 cups water
¼ cup olive oil
4 potatoes, peeled and quartered
1 small onion
1 bunch kale, finely shredded (or substitute 1 medium-sized head green cabbage)
Salt to taste
1 or 2 *chouriços* (Portuguese pork sausages), sliced

Bring the water to a boil with the olive oil. Add the potatoes and onion, and cook for about 25 to 30 minutes, until soft. Mash the potatoes and onion together and return them to the cooking water. Add salt to taste. Add the kale to the pot and cook 15 to 20 minutes more. Add the sausage slices and cook until they are heated through.

Serve the soup with a slice of sausage in each bowl and a slice of corn bread on the side.

(Courtesy of Maria Odete Laia, New York City.)

Decorated Earthenware Casserole C:33

Charmingly festooned with typical Portuguese designs painted in white on a dark terra-cotta background, this casserole comes from a market in Lisbon. Fully glazed inside and out, the pot is 3½″ deep and 8″ in diameter, and will hold 3 quarts. Cure it by rubbing the inside with garlic, filling it with water and leaving it over a low flame for several hours. That will strengthen the pot for years of oven or top-of-the-stove cooking. Then use it to give a festive air to a Portuguese stew or to one of the Alentejo garlic soups known as *açordas,* which are made of a garlic-flavored broth poured over bread and sometimes garnished with poached eggs. Be careful to keep the flame low if you are cooking on a burner; an asbestos pad under the pot is also a good idea to prevent cracking.

Newark Hardware & Paint Co., Inc. $5.98

"The Portuguese had need have the stomach of ostriches to digest the loads of greasy victuals with which they cram themselves. Their vegetables, their rice, their poultry are all stewed in the essence of ham and so strongly seasoned with pepper and spices that a spoonful of pease or a quarter of an onion is sufficient to set one's mouth in a flame. With such a diet and the continual swallowing of sweetmeats, I am not surprised at their complaining continually of headaches and vapors."

The Journal of William Beckford in Portugal and Spain, 1787–1788. *Introduction and notes by Boyd Alexander. Rupert Hart-Davis, 1954.*

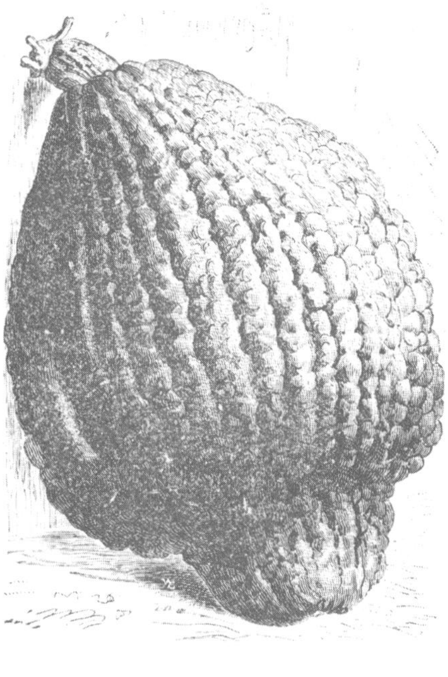

A South American native that traveled to Portugal—squash.

Frango Na Pucara Pot C:34

This pot announces *frango na púcara,* and the saucy chicken's head on top dares you to guess what that means. If you think it promises a chicken in every pot, you're not far wrong. *Frango* means chicken and *púcara* is a deep earthenware pot with a lid. The Portuguese specialty traditionally cooked in the pot is a chicken stewed with ham, onions, garlic, bay leaf and tomatoes in a mixture of port and dry white wine seasoned with sharp mustard. This fanciful handmade pot of fully glazed terra-cotta draped and dotted with white designs is 5″ deep, 5″ in diameter at the top and will hold 2 quarts. It may be cheating, but we'd be tempted to use it for other chicken dishes, too; it would make a delightful tureen for a Portuguese *canja,* a simple chicken soup flavored with lemon and fresh mint.

Newark Hardware & Paint Co., Inc. $4.98

When Infanta D. Maria de Portugal was married in 1565 she took with her this recipe for boiled and stewed chicken: "Take a hen and poach it with parsley, coriander, mint, and onion. Then season it with vinegar and after the seasoning and simmering, pour the broth into a púcara, and put the hen to boil in another one, adding half a dozen eggs to the pot. In this same broth put four egg yolks and beat them to make a yellow sauce. Then arrange the chicken on slices of bread; when this has been done, place the hard-boiled eggs around the hen, pour the yellow sauce made with the other eggs on top and sprinkle with ground cinnamon."

O "Livro de Cozinha" da Infanta D. Maria de Portugal, *edited by G. Manuppella and S. D. Arnaut, unpublished translation by D. Childress. Coimbres: University Press, 1967.*

CHICKEN IN A POT

Frango na Púcara

¼ pound sliced prosciutto
12 small onions
4 tomatoes, peeled, seeded and diced
3 cloves garlic
¼ pound butter
2 scant tablespoons mustard
1 small glass port wine or sherry
1 small glass white wine
1 whole, medium chicken, rubbed with salt and pepper

Place the prosciutto at the bottom of the *púcara* (deep clay pot with a lid), and add all the other ingredients in order. Cover the *púcara,* place it in the oven, and let the chicken cook at low heat, shaking the pot with a vertical, up-and-down motion a few times. When the chicken seems tender, reremove the cover, turn the heat a bit higher and let it cook a little longer until it turns golden on the top. Serve with rice or potatoes.

(Courtesy of Maria Odete Laia, New York City.)

The raison d'être of the Portuguese dish known as frango na púcara *(chicken in a pot).*

Terra-Cotta Chicken Pot C:35

Made of unglazed terra-cotta, this 7″-deep pot is expressly designed for cooking chicken. Plump at the bottom, the pot narrows to a small, 3¾″-diameter opening at the top and holds 2½ quarts. The smooth, curved sides, decorated only with two horizontal parallel lines incised near the base, and a small ear-shaped handle, give the pot a classic simplicity. Use it to make a spicy dish of chicken cooked with sausages and *piri-piri* (olive oil seasoned with chopped, hot red peppers), a sauce the Portuguese adopted from their African colonies. The distributors caution us never to use soap on the pot, but only to rinse it in hot water.

Bloomingdale's $12.00

With characteristic noblesse-oblige, the English nobleman, William Beckford of Fonthill, describes eating in Lisbon in the late nineteenth century: "We had . . . among other good things, a certain preparation of rice and chicken, which suited me exactly, and no wonder, for this excellent mess had been just tossed up by Donna Isabel de Castro with her own illustrious hands, in a nice little kitchen adjoining the queen's apartment, in which all the utensils are of solid silver."

The Travel Diaries of William Beckford of Fonthill. *Kraus Reprint Co., 1972.*

Sausage Cooker C:36

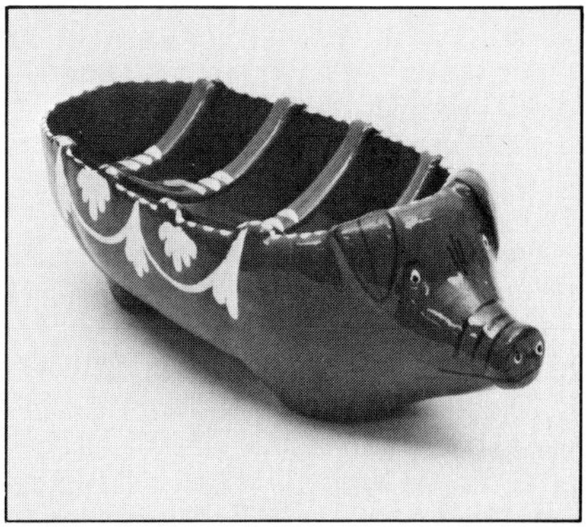

Though he resembles a pastry chef's fanciful creation of gingerbread and sugar icing, this irresistible, 11″-long porker is actually a terra-cotta sausage cooker. It is handmade, fully glazed and amusingly shaped to suggest its function. Garlicky pork sausages—*chouriços,* or the more finely textured *linguiças*—are placed across the four earthenware strips. Then, several jiggers of *aguardiente* (burning water), or brandy, are poured into the pig's belly and flamed. In a few minutes, the pungent sausages will be sizzling and crisp, a delectable hors d'oeuvre or snack to eat with bread and a strong, dry red wine while listening to the mournful, nostalgic Portuguese folk songs called *fados.*

Newark Hardware & Paint Co., Inc. $9.98

Copper Cataplana C:37

From the southern province of Algarve comes the *cataplana,* a large, heavy, metal pan inspired, perhaps, by the humble clam. It has the curved shape of that close-mouthed mollusk—only its two halves are perfectly round—and the top and bottom are hinged together. This beautiful *cataplana,* made

Continued from preceding page

of hammered copper lined with tin, has copper nail heads, hinge and handles, and two clamps on the sides to anchor the top securely to the bottom. The pan is 9″ across and each half is 3″ deep; the lower half will hold 6 cups. Although the *cataplana* is used for the stovetop cooking of quite a number of Portuguese dishes, and brings out the fullest flavor of whatever it cooks—from fish to lamb or pork—we especially like the idea of using it of *amêijoas na cataplana,* a casserole of clams with *chouriço* sausages, *presunto* ham, tomatoes, onions, hot peppers, garlic and wine. Imagine the effect of throwing open your handsome copper bivalve to a cloud of steam redolent of herbs and shellfish and a splendid array of open clams.

Bloomingdale's $45.00

CLAMS IN A CATAPLANA

Amêijoas na Cataplana

3 onions, cut into thin rounds
3 tablespoons olive oil
1 teaspoon paprika
1 teaspoon crushed, hot red pepper
1 medium *chouriço* (Portuguese pork sausage), chopped
3 tablespoons of chopped prosciutto or ham
2 tomatoes, peeled and seeded
1 bay leaf
1 teaspoon fresh, chopped parsley
1 clove garlic, finely chopped
½ glass white table wine
3 to 3½ dozen medium clams

In the *cataplana,* sauté the onion in the oil until it is translucent. Add the paprika, red pepper, *chouriço* and prosciutto and mix. Then add the tomatoes, bay leaf, parsley, garlic and wine. Cook for a little while to reduce the liquid by one-third. Arrange the clams in the pan, cover tightly and reduce the heat. Cook for 8 to 10 minutes, until the clams open. Discard any clams that did not open. Serve the clams, complete with shells, in soup plates, and spoon the sauce over them.

(*Courtesy of Maria Odete Laia, New York City.*)

Clams form the basis of a celebrated dish, amêijoas na cataplana, *cooked in a* cataplana *or pan that resembles the tasty bivalve.*

Cast-Iron Cauldron C:38

Not a stage prop around which to dance singing "Double, double toil and trouble," this cast-iron pot is a functional kettle, used in Portugal to cook rice and stews over an open fire. Its balloon-shaped belly rests on three tapered legs, but for cooking it would be suspended over the fire by its 4″-high handle. Only 8¾″ high and 4⅝″ across the top, this *panela de ferro* will nevertheless hold 8 cups. Larger sizes, up to 16″ in diameter, are also available. With a chain for raising and lowering the *panela* to adjust the heat, you can use it for fireplace or outdoor cooking—its solid, heavy construction is clearly meant for such dishes as a hearty peasant *estufado* (stew).

Newark Hardware & Paint Co., Inc. (6) $9.00

Fish Mold C:39

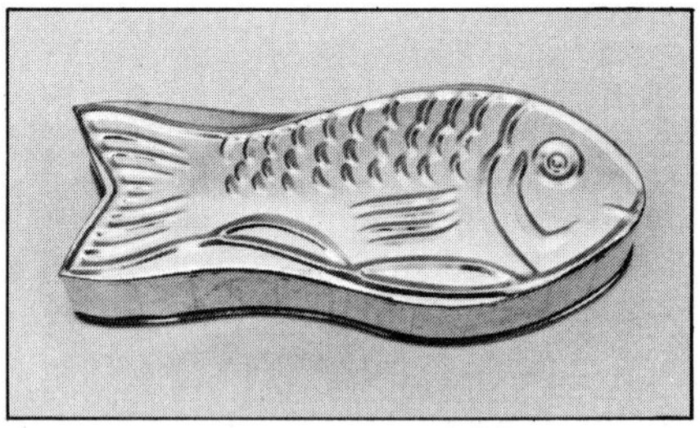

The Portuguese are great lovers of seafood; this whimsical mold, however, is not necessarily intended for a cold fish aspic. In Portugal it may shape a special thick chocolate dessert studded with pieces of biscuit. When unmolded, the fins, scales, eye and smiling mouth of the chocolate fish are outlined with sugar icing. You will also want to use the mold for gelatin desserts or salads, aspics or a fanciful cake. The tinned-steel mold has straight sides and rolled edges. It is 10½″ long, 4″ wide (at the widest point), 2¼″ deep and holds 4½ cups.

Bloomingdale's $6.00

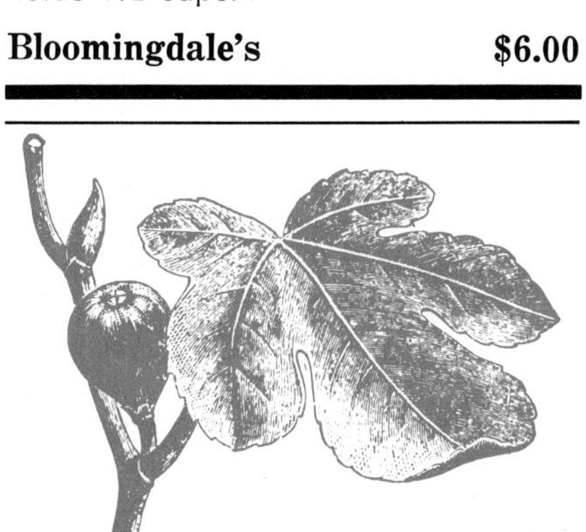

Figs.

Triple-Tiered Lunch Box C:40

This lunch box of three stacked pots will hold three separate dishes, all of which can be reheated, if desired. One pot may hold soup, the next stew or fried fish, and on top a piece of cake or fruit for dessert. Each 6″-diameter aluminum pot fits snugly into the next, and a tall, flat cover fits over the top one. Working almost as steamers, the upper units can be heated when the bottom one is placed on a stove, or each pot can be warmed individually. Portuguese schools provide facilities for children to warm their lunches; and outside large factories, men gather around small fires to heat theirs. All three pots are held together by a U-shaped aluminum band, which fits through the handles of the three pans. A clasp under the wooden handle at the top of the aluminum band presses tightly against the cover and swings open so that the sections can be removed. The entire lunch box is 10½″ high. A smaller, two-pot model is also available.

Casa Moneo **$5.00**

"There are an extraordinary number of street-cries in Mexico, which begin at dawn and continue till night . . . the grease man . . . [calls], *'Mantequilla! lard! lard! at one real and half! 'Salt beef! good salt beef!' ('Cecina buena!') interrupts the butcher in a hoarse voice . . . Behind stands the Indian with his tempting baskets of fruit, of which he calls out all the names. . . .*

A sharp note of interrogation is heard, indicating something that is hot, and must be snapped up quickly before it cools. 'Gorditas de horna caliente?' 'Little fat cakes from the oven, hot?' This is in a female key, sharp and shrill. . . .

Then comes the dulce-men, the sellers of sweetmeats, of meringues . . . and of all sorts of candy. . . .

Towards evening rises the cry of 'Tortillas de cuajada?' 'Curd cakes?' or, 'Do you take nuts?' succeeded by the night-cry of 'Chestnuts, hot and roasted!' and by the affectionate vendors of ducks: 'Ducks, oh my soul, hot ducks!' 'Maize-cakes,' etc., etc. As the night wears away the voices die off, to resume the next morning in fresh vigour."

Life in Mexico, 1839–1842 *by Frances Calderón de la Barca.*

The Flavor of Mexico

by Elia Padilla

Before my family moved to Acapulco, we lived in the small town of Chilapa. I love small town life in Mexico; it is there, I think, that you will find the true life of the country.

When I lived in Chilapa, life was much simpler than in Acapulco. Our kitchen was a cool room made of clay and bricks; our stove was just like a big chest of bricks with some holes cut in the top. My mother would put wood down into the holes and then, when the fire was going strong, she would put a clay pot over the hole. We had no metal implements at all. Instead, we had many clay pots and wooden spoons. Even our tortillas were fried on an earthenware griddle! I think of that sometimes when Americans say that they can't put pottery dishes over a flame.

Mexican pottery is very famous, beautiful and varied. In Guerrero, the pottery was a beautiful reddish-brown color; but in Oaxaca, where the clay was different, the pots were almost black. Some were plain and some were decorated, but they were all very inexpensive. That was lucky, since they tended to break easily.

What we lacked in modern appliances in our country kitchens, we made up for in beauty. In most houses, an array of brick-red earthenware pots, interesting wooden spoons and baskets was hung on the wall behind the stove. In my house we had something even prettier. Someone had pounded nails into the wall in a pattern of arc upon arc that resembled a series of concentric rainbows. On these nails we hung a full set of dishes, so that the wall was totally covered with a pleasing design in beautiful earthenware.

Mexican food, of course, is not very much like what you in this country call Mexican food: the border food of Texas and Mexico. When I invite people to my home in New York, where I am now living, I make Mexican food for them, although I have a little trouble finding the ingredients. For example, I love green sauce, a special kind of sauce made of Mexican green tomatoes, chiles and fresh coriander. It is possible to buy the coriander in an Italian or Spanish market, but I have to go out of my way to get the canned Mexican green tomatoes and canned green chiles; or I persuade someone to bring them to me from Mexico. The sauce is usually made in a mortar at home, but I find that a blender works very well. I am also able to buy ready-made tortillas, but they are not as good as those that are bought, ready-made, in Mexico; and they are nothing at all like homemade tortillas.

Continued from preceding page

Life for a woman in the small towns of Mexico is a constant round of tortilla-making. She buys corn and sets it to soak overnight in a solution of slaked lime and water. The lime eats away at the skin of the kernels so that the next morning the outer layer of the kernels comes off and can be washed away. Then, if it is a very primitive village, the woman will grind the corn herself on a stone slab with a stone rolling pin. If she lives in a more modern village that has electricity, she can take her corn to a special place, where it will be ground for her into a fine meal. She then makes a dough out of the corn meal and water, pulls off small pieces of dough, and pats and slaps each one into a perfect, round, thin shape. I can't do this at all, so if I am making my own tortillas at home, I will use a press. At home in Acapulco, my mother simply goes to a store and buys ready-made tortillas by the pound. Finally, the tortillas are cooked on an ungreased griddle. In our house, as I said, the griddle was made of clay, but there are now many places in Mexico where it would be made of metal.

Tortillas are only the beginning. When a tortilla is filled with meat, sauce and perhaps some cheese and eaten with the fingers it is called a taco; when the tortilla is rolled around a filling and covered with warm sauce it is called an enchilada; and when a tortilla is fried flat until it is crisp and then covered with various combinations of foods, it is called a *tostada.* In one way or another, tortillas are eaten at almost every meal in Mexico. And beans (*frijoles*) are important, too. With corn and beans to eat, most Mexicans feel that they have had an adequate meal, especially if some tomatoes, garlic and spicy chiles are added. The poor people and farmers get by quite well with just those foods, and squashes. But of course our cooking is more varied than that. Mexican food can mean anything from a *tamal* (a plain or filled corn-dough cake wrapped and steamed in a corn husk), to an earthenware dish full of *puerco en adobo* (pork cooked with onions and garlic and served with a savory red chile sauce flavored with cinnamon, cloves, cumin, garlic, salt and pepper).

If you have experienced the best Mexican food, you will understand why I sometimes get the urge for black beans, for a spoonful of green sauce to clear my head, for freshly-cooked tortillas or a cup of foamy chocolate. Then I go searching through the markets to make a feast for myself. That's almost—but not quite—as good as a trip back to Mexico.

Lava Stone Mortar and Pestle C:41

The traditional Mexican mortar and pestle shown here look for all the world like pre-Colombian artifacts, and, indeed, are still known by their ancient names: *molcajete* and *tejolote.* Made of porous, dark gray volcanic stone, these time-honored kitchen tools are still preferred by authentic Mexican cooks for blending and grinding together their indispensable sauce ingredients—chiles, herbs, garlic, onions, nuts and seeds—which would lose much of their texture if puréed in a blender. New *molcajetes* and *tejolotes,* unless fashioned from superior quality black basalt, a rarity today, are potentially gritty, and must be cured before they are used. First, scour the surfaces with a stiff brush and plenty of water; then grind a handful of raw rice into the stone. Wash the tools again, then repeat the operation at least two or three times. At first the rice picks up the stone's gray color, but eventually one batch will remain white. The three-legged *molcajete* stands 4″ high, and its shallow bowl is 6″ in diameter. The stubby, triangular-shaped *tejolote* is 3½″ long and 2″ across at the base.

Casa Moneo $7.00

AVOCADO DIP

Guacamole

About 1¾ to 2 cups

The word *guacamole* comes from the Nahuatl words *ahuacatl* (avocado) and *molli* (a mixture, or concoction). In Mexico it is often eaten at the beginning of the meal with warm tortillas—and that is how one can really savor it—or with *tacos* and sour cream, rice, or *chicharrón.*

A *molcajete* or mortar and pestle
¼ small onion, finely chopped
1 or 2 *chiles serranos*
2 springs fresh coriander
¼ teaspoon salt, or to taste
1 very large or 2 medium avocados
1 large tomato (½ pound)
¼ small onion, finely chopped
2 sprigs fresh coriander, finely chopped

Grind the onion, chilies, coriander, and salt together to a smooth paste.

Cut the avocado in half. Remove the seed and scoop out the flesh. Mash the flesh roughly with the chili paste in the *molcajete.*

Skin, seed and chop the tomato and add it, with the chopped onion and coriander, to the *guacamole.* Mix well and serve immediately.

This is such a beautiful concoction, pale green flecked with the red of the tomato pieces and the darker green of the coriander, and a delight aesthetically if served in a *molcajete,* where it rightfully belongs. It is so delicate it is best eaten the moment it is made. There are many suggestions about keeping it—leaving the pit in, adding a little lime juice, not adding the salt until last, putting it into an airtight container. They all help a little, but in no time at all that delicate green has aged.

There are many variations—making it with *tomates verdes,* or leaving out the tomato altogether, mashing the avocado with just a little chili and salt and a suspicion of lime juice. Practically anything goes, but within certain limits, which does not include the unnecessary additions that I see in most pedestrian cookbooks.

(From THE CUISINES OF MEXICO by Diana Kennedy. Copyright 1972 by Diana Kennedy. Reprinted by permission of Harper & Row, Publishers, Inc.)

A few chile peppers from Mexico's vast repertoire.

"The Indians use a kind of corn which they call 'Mamaix' (maize), which is of the size of a pea, yellow and red: and when they wish to eat it, they take a stone, hollowed like a mortar, and another, round in the shape of a pestle: and after the said corn has been steeped for an hour, they grind and reduce it to a flour in the said stone: then they knead and bake it in this manner. They take a plate of iron, or of stone, which they heat on the fire: and when quite hot, they take their paste, and spread it upon the plate rather thin, like tart-paste; and having thus cooked it they eat it while hot, for it is good for nothing, cold or kept."

A Voyage to the West Indies and Mexico in the Years 1599–1602 *by Samuel Champlain, translated by Alice Wilmere, edited by Norman Shaw. Burt Franklin, New York, n.d.*

Lava Stone Corn Grinder — C:42

A large, rectangular lava stone slab, called a *metate,* and its companion stone roller, known as a *mano* or *metlapil,* are still the oldest and by far the most primitive tools used in Mexico. They grind corn, mash softened corn kernels into dough for tortillas, and purée the ingredients for sauces. As if time had stopped since the days of the ancient Indian civilizations, women can still be seen kneeling before their *metates* in country villages, pressing and scrubbing the roller back and forth across the sloping surface of the stone, just as their ancestors did centuries ago. Our *metate* measures 14¾″ by 10½″ and stands 7″ high on three sturdy, triangular legs; the accompanying *mano* is 20¼″ long. Clearly designed for durability, these rough-hewn implements have a pleasant, earthy quality to them, and the heavy, coarse volcanic stone provides a most effective grinding surface. Before using the tools, be sure to cure them: first scrub them with a stiff brush under running water, then grind three or four batches of rice, alternating with more rinsings, until the ground rice stays white.

Casa Moneo — $19.95

Mexican women grinding corn and making tortillas.

Gourd Spoon C:43

Some agricultural scientists believe that squash and pumpkin were the first crops cultivated in ancient Mexico. And if any one natural material from this culture were to be singled out for its numerous re-incarnations, surely these vegetables and their dried version, the common gourd, would head the list. In Mexico, the seeds are eaten like peanuts, the flowers garnish soups, the meat is used in stews and the hard shells—the gourds— function as ordinary drinking mugs and simple utensils. The 6½″-long, 3″-wide ladle shown here is a gourd that has been carefully split in half, emptied of seeds and scraped of all pulp, then dried hard. A true vestige of resourceful, primitive eras, this ladle should please any "back-to-nature" cook or hostess.

Mexican Folk Art Annex Inc. **$0.95**

Perforated Earthenware Spoon C:44

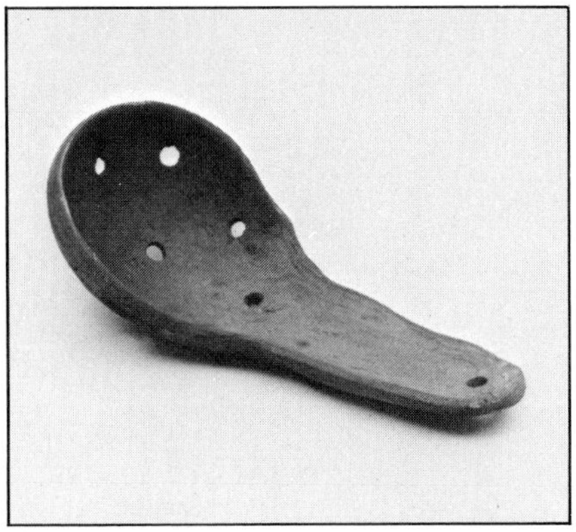

This simply-fashioned brown pottery spoon, hanging from the conveniently-located hole in its handle, would enhance the natural beauty of any country kitchen. It is, however, also useful for lifting herbs, vegetables or meat from sauces and broths. The 4″-wide, 1½″-deep bowl is punctuated by several more holes, and the entire tool measures 8½″ long from stem to stern. The rim is decorated with streaks of terra-cotta colored paint.

Mexican Folk Art Annex Inc. **$5.75**

Gourd Strainer/ Sieve C:45

In all probability, this charming, lightweight gourd strainer is originally a native of the Yucatán or the desert regions of southern Mexico. It is made from a nearly perfect oval-shaped gourd whose top quarter has been lopped off to form a 4″-wide opening. The 5½″-deep interior has been completely emptied of all traces of pulp and seeds, and the outside is divided into two sections: smooth, skinless, blond gourd, below; and olive-colored, dried rind, above. Three wavy, zig-zag lines are carved into the upper section, and the bottom is pierced with small random holes to form the strainer. Ecologically-minded cooks or collectors of genuine folkloric kitchen utensils would surely admire this strainer. It won't tarnish or rust, and serves nicely for draining small amounts of vegetables.

Mexican Folk Art Annex Inc. **$6.75**

Tin Whisk C:46

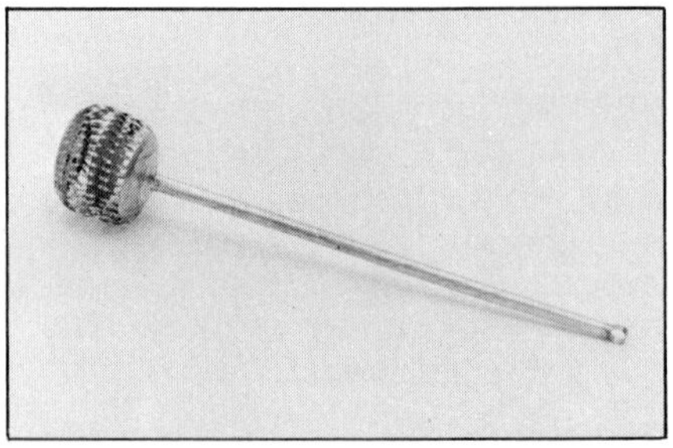

Here is a novel and useful whisk for all sorts of light egg batters, such as *huevos revueltos a la mexicana* (scrambled eggs with cream in a hot pepper sauce). Or beat together milk, sugar, egg yolks and brandy (then thicken and flavor it with ground almonds and cinnamon) for a Mexican eggnog called *rompope;* not just a holiday drink in Mexico, it is a treat served in small liqueur glasses to late afternoon visitors at any time of year. Made of strips of twisted tinned steel emanating from a central disc (2″ in diameter) that are soldered to similar discs at the top and bottom, this ingenious Mexican beater would be a charming addition to any kitchen. Attached to the beater is a 9½″-long, hollow tin handle with a loop at the end by which to hang it.

Mexican Folk Art Annex Inc. **$2.50**

Bean Masher C:47

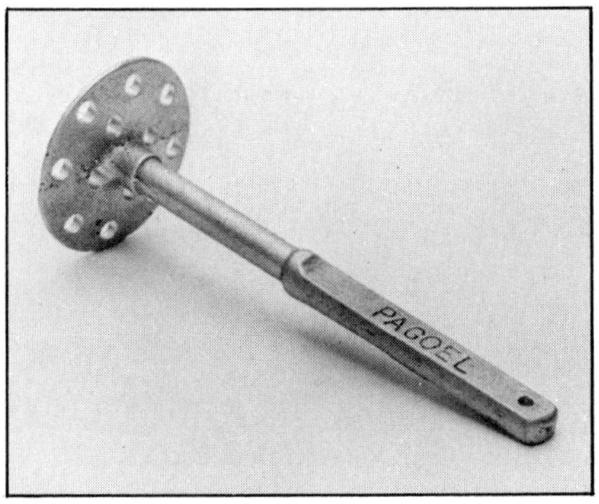

A durable implement designed expressly for mashing the protein-rich beans, so important to the Mexican diet, is this heavy-duty cast-aluminum bean masher. It is 9¼″ long and has a flat, round base that measures 3¼″ in diameter. The base is perforated with a number of holes through which the beans emerge as they are mashed, thus increasing a little the efficiency of the procedure.

HOAN Products, Ltd. **$4.00**
(182)

Meat Tenderizer and Chopper C:48

Made of cast aluminum, this sturdy meat pounder might well be found in any traditional kitchen in Mexico, where cooks are inordinately fond of opening up and flattening out cuts of meat prior to pickling, breading or smothering them in fiery chile sauces. Because meat South of the Border is not always of the very best quality, the raised studs on the head of the pounder serve as a tenderizing device to break down tough fibers while the meat is being pounded. One can easily imagine this tool in constant use during the process of making *cecina,* a dried beef staple of the arid northern cattle country. Our pounder is 9¼″ long overall, and its head measures 2¼″ by 2″, including a small, dull-edged blade used for chopping through bones.

HOAN Products, Ltd. **$4.00**
(181)

Tortillas

We feel honor bound to tell you that the machine age has reached Mexico. Except in remote places that don't have electricity, nearly everyone eats tortillas fresh off the assembly line. In small villages, this may involve lines of women entering the local *tortillería,* or tortilla factory, with baskets of shelled corn on their heads. The grain is weighed before it goes into a hopper; then it is shaped and pressed into individual patties that are fully cooked as they are passed along on a conveyer belt over jets of flame. The *señora* carefully collects the proper weight in finished tortillas—all untouched by human hands—from the pile at the end of the production line. In the cities, of course, ready-to-go tortillas are available at convenient take-out *tortillerías.*

Metal Tortilla Press C:49

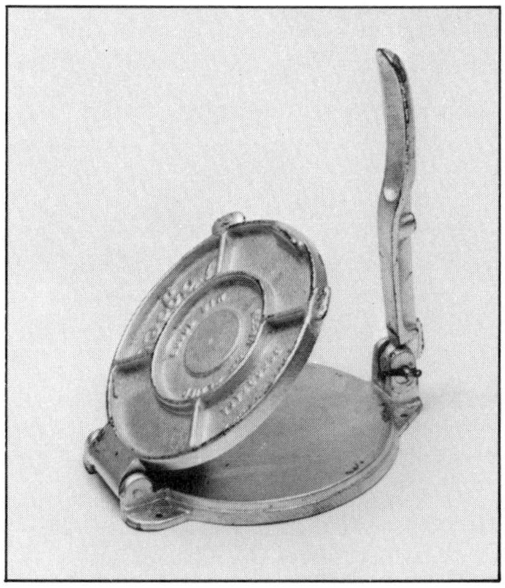

For centuries the sound of gentle hand-clapping was heard throughout Mexico as women everywhere ritually prepared each meal's tortillas from scratch. Sadly, the ancient and difficult art of *torteando*—slapping a small ball of corn dough into the translucent flatness of a tortilla—is rapidly dying out. Nearly everyone in Mexican cities buys ready-made tortillas these days. But for those of us who live far from a tortilla factory or prefer to make our own, a simple, heavy-duty tortilla press like this one is essential. It consists of two round, flat, aluminum-painted cast-iron plates (6½″ in diameter) with a hinge at one end and an 8¾″-long handle at the other end. To use the press, lay a double thickness of 8″-square plastic wrap—a sandwich bag is ideal—on the bottom plate, then place a walnut-sized ball of special corn dough on it. Cover with another double layer of plastic wrap, close the press, and push the handle down firmly. Open the press and lift off the top section of plastic. You should have a flat, round tortilla ready for the griddle.

HOAN Products, Ltd. **$9.00**
(255)

TORTILLAS

16 small tortillas about 5 inches across

1 or 2 thick griddles or frying pans
1⅓ cups cold water (approximately)
2 cups Quaker *masa harina* or 1½ pounds prepared *masa*

Set the pans (it is quicker to work with two) over a medium flame and let them heat up thoroughly; the dough should just sizzle faintly as it touches the pan. Lightly grease the pans before you start making the tortillas.

Add the water all at once to the flour and mix quickly and lightly. Don't compress the dough into hard pieces. Set the dough aside for about 20 minutes, then try it for consistency by making a tortilla.

A tortilla press
2 sandwich-sized polyethylene bags

Open up the tortilla press. Place one of the polyethylene bags on the bottom plate. Take a piece of the tortilla dough and roll it into a ball about 1½ inches across. Flatten the ball slightly and set it onto the bag, a little more toward the hinge than the handle of the press, then place the second bag, flat and smooth, onto the dough. Close the press and push the handle down hard. Open it up and peel off the top bag. Lift the second bag with the flattened tortilla on it, and place, dough side down, on your hand, right or left, more on the fingers than the palm. Peel the bag from the dough—don't attempt to peel the dough from the bag—and lay the tortilla carefully onto the hot griddle. Don't slam it down, or you will get air bubbles in the dough.

Pause at this stage and consider the dough. If the tortilla is rather thick, with a grainy edge, then the dough is too dry. Work a little more water into it. Be careful not to add too much water, or the dough will become unmanageable

Continued from preceding page

—it will be impossible to peel the bag off, leaving the dough in one piece—or even if it isn't quite as bad as that, your tortillas will be sodden and won't rise nicely.

If the griddles are at the right heat, the tortilla should take no more than 2 minutes to cook.

Assuming that the dough is now the right consistency, press out the next tortilla and place it on the griddle. When it has just begun to dry out around the edges (don't wait for the dough to dry out completely and curl up, or your tortilla will be tough), flip it over and cook for a slightly longer time on the second side, or until it just begins to color. Flip it back onto the first side and finish cooking through. If the dough is right and the heat of the pans is right, the tortilla should puff up invitingly. (This is the "face" of the tortilla, and this is the side the filling goes on when you are making *tacos* or *enchiladas*.) Remove it from the griddle and keep warm in a thick napkin. As each tortilla is cooked, stack one on top of the other in the napkin and cover. In this way they will retain their heat and flexibility.

As you work, the dough may dry out a little, and you may have to add a little more water.

The first few batches may be rather trying (they were to me the first time I made them in New York after living in Mexico, where for many years I had a patient little person in the kitchen patting them out fresh for every meal), but you will soon get the knack of it. Besides, it is the sort of thing the whole family can become involved in.

You can make tortillas about 2 hours ahead of time. Wrap the package of tortillas in foil and reheat in a 275 degree oven before serving.

(From THE TORTILLA BOOK by Diana Kennedy. Copyright 1975 by Diana Kennedy. Reprinted by permission of Harper & Row, Publishers, Inc.)

"Novices, as a rule, find the warm damp, flabby tortilla insipid and unpalatable, but the veterans are as fond of them as the Indians themselves."

A Peep at Mexico *by John Lewis Geiger, 1874.*

Wooden Tortilla Press — C:50

Obviously hand-crafted, this splendid, rough-hewn wooden tortilla press is a sturdy device that works on exactly the same principle as a more modern metal tortilla press. The tortillas are pressed between two 9″-by-10″, 1″-thick pieces of wood that are hinged together at one end. Overall, the implement is 6″ high, and stands on two wooden slats that function as legs. The ingenious craftsman who fashioned it re-used the scalloped half-ovals cut from the slats to decorate the sides. A 13½″-long handle is attached to the bottom of the press by two iron strips that are long enough to give the handle leverage when it is clamped down over the top. Whenever the top is lifted to insert balls of *masa* (dough), or to remove a flattened tortilla, a 4″-long wooden strip below the hinge holds the top of the press vertical. Though less compact and popular than its metal counterpart, this old-fashioned tortilla press would certainly win a personality contest hands down.

El Mercado — $18.00

". . . when one has overcome the dislike of having his food prepared in this way, the tortillas are not so bad after all. They are tasteless but satisfying, and, when accompanied by frijoles, fattening."

Through the Land of the Aztecs *by "A Gringo," 1883.*

Tortilla Basket — C:51

It is easy to imagine the pleasure of discovering a delightful basket just like this one among the myriad offered at a basketweaver's stand in a typical, riotously colorful and bustling Mexican market. Our little basket, even though it is not a traditional *chiquihuite* (square, woven tortilla basket), is still a perfect size and shape to hold a batch of cloth-wrapped tortillas hot off the *comal* (griddle). Made of stylishly patterned interlaced reeds, the basket is 3″ deep, and measures 7″ in diameter. Remember to re-fold the cloth and replace the lid each time the basket is opened to keep the tortillas warm and soft.

Exposición Nacional de Artes Populares — $1.00

Earthenware Griddle — C:52

Made of splendid, unglazed earthenware, this *comal* (griddle) is a lovely example of the type that has been used by the Indians of Mexico since time immemorial for cooking tortillas. This 16″ disc is shaped into a slight curve that rises 1½″ from the bottom to the outer edge, and is capable of holding several tortillas at a time. It must be noted, however, that the *comal* has to be cured to seal its pores before it is used, and the best way to do this is the traditional Mexican way. Make a thick paste of unslaked lime and water, and slather the substance over the entire surface. Place the *comal* over charcoal or gas heat—never on an electric burner—until the coating bakes dry and burns away without blackening. Scrub with plenty of hot water, then start planning your next fiesta! If you are using the griddle over charcoal, be sure to place it right on the coals, not on a grill, because you want quick heat for tortillas.

The Critical Cook/ Primitive Artisan **$8.00**

Single Cast-Iron Griddle C:53

This round *comal*—griddle to you—made of heavy cast iron, holds only one 6″ tortilla at a time; but it takes up little space on the stove, and can be easily stored when not in use. It resembles our familiar American pancake griddle, and measures 9″ in diameter with a ½″-thick rim and a 4″-long handle. You'll be able to make sure each tortilla browns delicately without burning by working with just one at a time; but because the cooking process takes only 2 minutes or so, a batch can be finished in a jiffy. Try pressing the center of the tortilla with your fingers after you have flipped it over, and just before you think it is finished, to make sure it has inflated a bit. Mexicans call this process "tickling," and it indicates that the tortilla is done. As for all cast-iron implements, be sure to dry this one thoroughly after washing to prevent rust. The manufacturer suggests seasoning the pan before its first use by placing the empty griddle over low heat for 10 minutes, then scrubbing it well with detergent and a stiff brush. Dry it, and apply a light coating of cooking oil to protect against moisture and prepare the surface for cooking.

HOAN Products, Ltd. (142) **$8.00**

Steel Griddle with Wooden Handle C:54

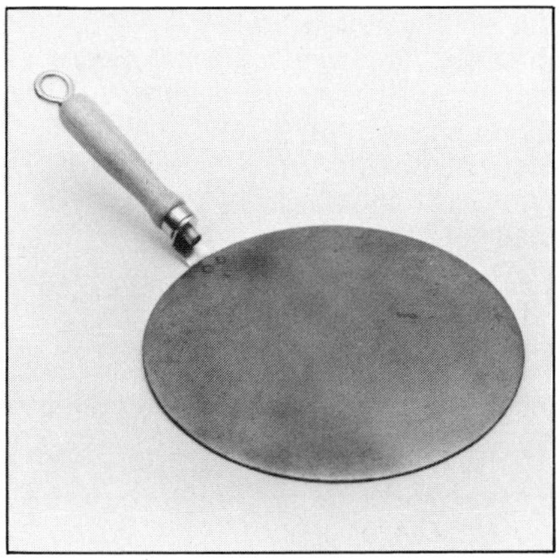

We heartily recommend this handsome, round *comal* (griddle) made of heavy, 12-gauge steel, mainly because its flat surface is very responsive to heat, and thus excellent for the rapid cooking of tortillas. The *comal* measures 11″ in diameter, and is equipped with a smooth, 7″-long wooden handle attached to a metal bar, which is spot-welded to the griddle. A metal ring at the tip of the handle is a boon for cooks who like to hang their favorite utensils. Be sure that the griddle is dried thoroughly after washing, and take care not to burn the handle when the implement is in use. It can be used on both gas and electric stoves.

Atlas Metal Spinning Co. (30TP11) **$7.50**

ENCHILADAS OF THE PLAZA

Enchiladas De Plaza

6 servings

As dusk falls, the archways around the cathedral square in Morelia begin to fill up with benches, tables, and improvised stoves for the brisk supper trade of *enchiladas de plaza.*

Have ready:
12 freshly made tortillas
½ pound farmer cheese, crumbled and lightly salted
1 medium onion, finely chopped
A large serving dish, warmed
A 3-pound chicken, poached and cut into serving pieces
Strips of canned *chiles jalapeños en escabeche*

The garnish:
A saucepan
½ pound red bliss or waxy new potatoes (3 small ones), unpeeled
½ pound carrots (3 medium)
Boiling water to cover
1 teaspoon salt
2 tablespoons red wine vinegar
A colander

Wash the potatoes well and cut them into quarters; scrape the carrots and cut them into smaller pieces (so they will cook in the same time as the potatoes). Cover the potatoes and carrots with boiling water, add the salt, and cook them for 10 minutes only.

Add the vinegar to the vegetable water. Let the carrots and potatoes cool off in the water and become slightly acidy. Drain, peel the potatoes and cut them, with the carrots, into small cubes. Set aside.

The sauce:
A griddle or comal
2 *chiles anchos*
2 *chiles guajillos*
A small bowl
Hot water to cover
A blender
2 cloves garlic, peeled and roughly chopped
¼ medium onion, roughly chopped
¼ teaspoon salt
1 cup water

Heat the griddle and toast the chilies lightly, turning them constantly so that they do not burn. Slit them open and remove the seeds and veins.

Cover the chilies with the hot water and leave them to soak for 20 minutes, then transfer with a slotted spoon to the blender jar. Add the rest of the in-

Continued from preceding page

gredients and blend to a smooth sauce.

The enchiladas:
A frying pan
6 tablespoons lard
The tortillas
The sauce
Water, if necessary
The farmer cheese
The chopped onion
The serving dish
The chicken
The cubed vegetables
The remaining sauce
The chili strips

Melt the lard, and when it is hot, but not smoking, dip each tortilla into the sauce, which should just lightly cover it—if the sauce is too thick dilute it with a little water—and fry it quickly on both sides.

Remove from the frying pan and put about 1 good tablespoon of the cheese and ½ tablespoon of the onion across each tortilla. Roll them up loosely and set them side by side on the serving dish. Keep warm.

In the same fat, fry the pieces of chicken until they are golden brown. Arrange them around the *enchiladas.*

In the same fat, fry the vegetable cubes and scatter them over the *enchiladas.*

In the same fat, cook the remaining sauce for a few moments and pour it over the *enchiladas.* Garnish with the chili strips and serve immediately.

Double Cast-Iron Griddle C:55

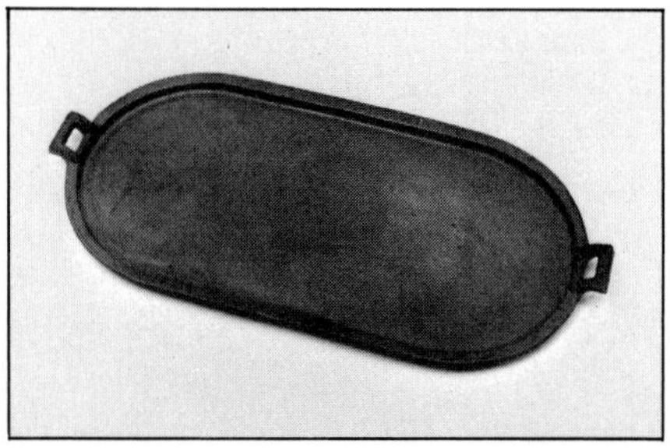

A double *comal* (griddle) is capable of holding two regular-sized, or even four small, tortillas at once. This heavy, cast-iron griddle—18½″ long and 9½″ wide—is equipped with a rectangular handle at either end. Unfortunately, the handles heat up when the pan does, so don't grab them with your bare hands. The *comal* is just long enough to be placed over two burners on most stoves, but would work even better over a charcoal or wood fire, as it would be used on a *finca* (ranch) in the Mexican countryside. Although it is a time-saver when making a large batch of tortillas, the griddle does take a while to heat up. Before using for the first time, it should be seasoned. Set the empty pan over low heat for 10 minutes, then wash it with detergent and scrub it with a firm brush. Dry it thoroughly—always—and coat the surface with a light film of cooking oil. Do not use the *comal* for frying meats, because the scouring required after such use would make the surface unsuitable for preparing tortillas afterward.

Casa Moneo $12.98

Wire Grill C:56

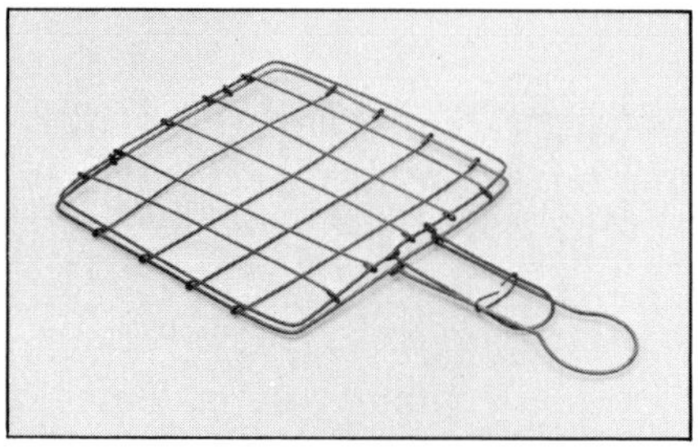

At any picnic or cookout, a meal of meat or fish can be quickly prepared over charcoal or an open fire using a simple hand-crafted Mexican wire grill like this one. The two 9″-square sides of the grill form a grid: the wires of one side cross the wires of the other at right angles. The grill is hinged together at one end by twisted wires and has a double handle, opposite, equipped with a thin wire loop that holds it closed while in use. Although this device is a bit light, our rustic little grill would do well propped over a fire for cooking a nice snapper *en tikinxik* (marinated and then grilled with a paste of toasted oregano, paprika, garlic, salt, pepper and orange juice).

El Mercado $2.00

Cast-Iron Grill C:57

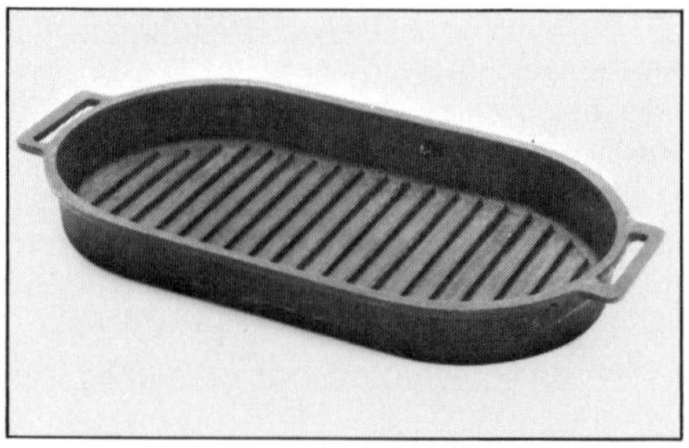

Mexican cuisine is by no means limited to the familiar tortillas, *frijoles* (beans) and chile sauces. Grilled meats are also popular, often flavored with oranges in coastal regions. This heavy, large, 17½″-long, 9¾″-wide grill can be used outdoors over a fire or indoors on the stove where it just covers two burners. (It will maintain a steady heat if both burners are equally adjusted.) The grill is 2″ deep and has a series of ¼″-high ridges on the bottom to keep the meat slightly above the fat. The ridges also leave grill marks, lending a pleasing, charcoal-broiled appearance to the cooked meat's surface. A rectangular handle is located at either end of the pan for lifting the grill on and off the heat source. The instructions that come with the grill recommend tempering it before use. First, set the empty pan over low heat for 10 minutes, then scrub it with a brush and detergent. Dry thoroughly, and apply a light film of cooking oil to prevent rust.

Casa Moneo $16.95

Small Baking/Serving Dish C:58

Any of those fiery sauces that are as common on Mexican tables as salt and pepper are in this country would be handsomely set off against the creamy beige sides of this lovely baking or serving dish. Azure flowers, lacy ferns and simple stripes embellish the outside of the dish, and a small handle reaches straight out from its side. A light red *salsa mexicana*—made of finely chopped tomatoes, onion, coriander and those deceptive little green mountain chiles that bring tears to the eyes of the unwary—is especially delicious. But small as it is—only 6¾″ in diameter and 1½″ deep—the dish is also for baking and was left unglazed on the bottom to absorb heat. It is a good size for individual portions of *huevos en rabo de mestiza* (eggs baked in a chile-tomato sauce and topped with cream cheese). A smaller and several larger sizes are available: 5½″, 8″, 9½″ and 11″ in diameter. The potter has thoughtfully provided a hole in the handle by which to hang the dish, since no one would want to hide such a lovely *cazuela* (earthenware cooking dish) in the cupboard.

Pan American Phoenix $3.50

Oval Greenware Baking Dish C:59

From Oaxaca comes this striking earthenware dish, glazed a rich, dark green. Crimped edges around the oval rim, two loop handles and a graceful flower with leaves etched on the inside bottom add decorative touches. Not a large dish—10″ long, 6¾″ wide and 1¾″ deep—it may be used in the oven for any recipe requiring a small casserole. Chicken breasts in *mole verde* (green sauce) would be quite lovely. The sauce is made with Mexican green tomatoes, fresh coriander, pumpkin seeds, nuts and chiles and may have other greens blended in—lettuce, parsley, string beans, zucchini, or avocado.

Pan American Phoenix $6.50

Mexican women making bread.

The Zacatecas market was described by an Englishman in the 1820's: "The quantity of chile disposed of was really prodigious; waggons laden with it drawn each by six oxen, were arriving hourly from Aguas Calientes, yet their contents rapidly disappeared, piles of capsicum sufficient to excoriate the palates of half London vanishing in the course of a few minutes."

Ward's Mexico, *vol II:* Personal Narrative. *London, n.d.*

Oval Terra-Cotta Baking Dish C:60

Vegetables, small stuffed fish or bananas with cinnamon and brown sugar would bake beautifully in this oval *cazuela* (earthenware cooking dish) of terra-cotta. Glazed inside and out, except for the outside of the bottom, it is adorned only with little white dots painted on a dark brown band along the rim. It is 12″ long, 7″ wide and 1½″ deep and is available in both smaller and larger sizes: 11″, 13″ and 14½″ long. You would also find the dish useful at a party for serving refried beans, *guacamole* (an avocado dip), a side dish of Mexican rice or the thin noodles called *fideos.*

Pan American Phoenix $6.50

"'Enchiladas; a greasy tortilla sandwich containing chilies and a number of uninviting looking compounds and other nasty messes, are sold everywhere, filling the air with a pungent, nauseous smell."

Through the Land of the Aztecs *by "A Gringo," 1883.*

Rectangular Terra-Cotta Baking Dish C:61

Simple, glazed terra-cotta baking dishes will be called into service again and again for preparing and serving Mexican food. This large rectangular one is 14″ long, 11½″ wide, 2½″ deep, and the bottom is unglazed on the outside. It's the one to reach for when making enchiladas (rolled, stuffed tortillas in a spicy sauce), or red snapper *a la veracruzana* (baked with tomatoes, olives, onions and *jalapeño* peppers). Or, try a festive tamale pie: chicken, olives, raisins and almonds in a hot tomato sauce baked in a lining of tamale dough and topped with grated cheese. *Buen provecho!* Or happy eating, as gringos would say.

Pan American Phoenix $10.50

"Women brought [Moctezuma] maize-cakes. When he began his meal they placed in front of him a sort of wooden screen, richly decorated in gold, so that no one should see him eat . . . [His] food was served on Cholula ware, some red and some black. While he was dining, the guards in the adjoining rooms did not dare to speak or make a noise above a whisper. His servants brought him some of every kind of fruit that grew in the country, but he ate very little of it."

The Conquest of New Spain *by Bernal Díaz, translated with an introduction by J. M. Cohen. Penguin Books, Ltd., 1963.*

19th-century Mexican majolica ware (from the Metropolitan Museum of Art).

Earthenware Bean Pot C:62

An earthenware *olla* (deep pot) like this one is depicted in one of the invaluable codices or manuscripts commissioned by the ruling Spanish viceroys after the conquest of the Aztec empire. These documents, illustrated by native Indian artists and lettered by Spanish priests, were designed to record the habits of the so-called "savages" for the King of Spain. Today, a pot similar to ours, which stands 8″ high and holds 7 quarts, is still an ever-present feature in the traditional Mexican kitchen. This lightweight utensil is ideal for the slow simmering required for Mexican bean dishes—sometimes flavored with sprigs of pungent *epazote,* a uniquely Mexican herb, and a bit of onion. The *olla* can go right to the table from the kitchen. But before using an earthenware pot, it should be seasoned. Fill it with water and add a whole head of garlic, which acts as a curative agent and a disinfectant. Heat the contents—using a protective device over the burner, if you have an electric stove—until the water evaporates. Wash out the *olla,* and cook up another garlic "broth." Then it will be ready for preparing *frijoles* (beans): the most common way is to simply add a little onion and lard, and when the beans are done, some salt. Before eating, you can add a good creamy cheese that will melt and string, or a piquant touch of chile.

Mexican Folk Art Annex Inc. $20.00

BEANS COOKED IN A POT

Frijoles de Olla

10 servings

Frijoles de olla are traditionally served, beans and broth together, in small earthenware bowls, after the main course and before the dessert. They are often just scooped up with a tortilla, although for the uninitiated this is a rather noisy and messy business, so it is permissible to compromise and use a spoon. Sometimes small pieces of good cream cheese, which melt and string invitingly, are dropped into the hot broth. Or you may add a little piquancy, a little *chile serrano* or *jalapeño en escabeche.* They are much better a day or so after being cooked.

1 pound beans—black turtle, pink, or pinto
An earthenware bean pot
10 cups water (see note)
¼ onion, roughly sliced
2 tablespoons lard
1 tablespoon salt, or to taste
2 large sprigs *epazote* (only if black beans are used)

Rinse the beans and run them through your hands to make sure that there are no small stones or bits of earth among them.

Put the beans into the pot and cover them with the cold water. Add the onion and lard and bring to a boil.

As soon as the beans come to a boil, lower the flame and let them barely simmer, covered, for about 2 hours for black beans and 1½ hours for the other varieties, or until they are just tender but not soft. Do not stir during this time.

Add the salt and *epazote,* if you are using it, and simmer for another 30 minutes. Set aside, preferably until the next day. There should be plenty of soupy liquid.

Note:
10 cups water should be enough for the black beans, but more like 12 to 14 cups will be needed for the pinto or pink beans, since these seem to absorb more. Of course much will depend on such considerations as the size of the pot, what it is made of, and how tightly fitting the lid is, so it is difficult to be exact.

(From THE CUISINES OF MEXICO by Diana Kennedy. Copyright 1972 by Diana Kennedy. Reprinted by permission of Harper & Row, Publishers, Inc.)

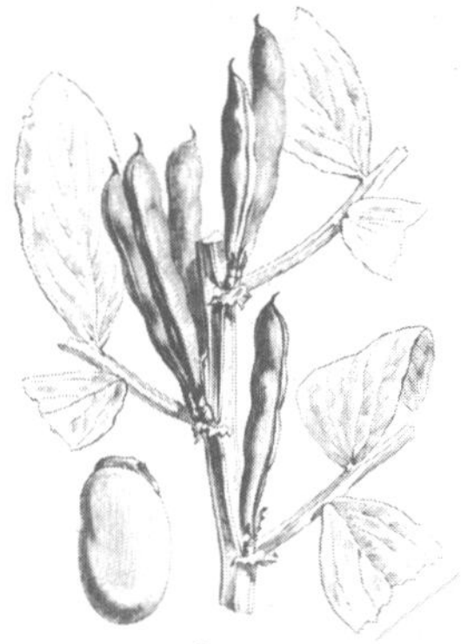

Beans.

Earthenware Casserole C:63

With its 4″-high straight sides, arched handles and slightly domed lid, this earthenware casserole is somewhat reminiscent of a turret. A sturdy, solid pot useful for any cuisine, it is glazed reddish-brown on the outside and gray on the inside; the outside bottom is unglazed. The lid, which is speckled with a slightly different brown, remains unglazed underneath and sits securely on the inner rim of the casserole. You will find this pot ideal for all those Portuguese *estufados* (stews) whether a hot, spicy *caldeirada* (seafood stew), or a *dobrada* (tripe stew with chick-peas, tomatoes and garlic-flavored sausage). The casserole measures 7″ in diameter and holds 5 cups.

The Pottery Barn $6.75

Spatterware Pot C:64

The bright blue of this spatterware pot reminds us of the glorious Acapulco sky at midday or the beautiful cloak worn by the Virgin of Guadalupe. Made of a lightweight steel clad in white-speckled blue enamel, the bucket-shaped pot—8″ in diameter and 5½″ deep—has a steel loop for a handle and a slightly domed lid that rests on its rolled edges. If you have a small rack to put inside, it would make a good pot for steaming tamales (corn-flour pastries stuffed with meat and hot chiles, or filled with cinnamon, sugar, nuts and raisins, and then wrapped in corn husks or banana leaves to cook). Or take advantage of its ample capacity to make a gallon of *caldo de pollo* (chicken broth), the basis of a wide range of delicious Mexican soups such as tortilla soup with chiles, cheese and fried tortilla strips.

La Cuisinière $9.50

Earthenware Brazier C:65

During the opulent reign of Moctezuma II, the last Indian monarch prior to the Spanish conquest, even the lowliest peasant household had a rudimentary charcoal *brasero* (brazier), for warming foods and dispelling the chill mountain air of the Mexican highlands. The temples of the emperor himself featured huge ritualistic braziers, reportedly as tall as an Aztec warrior. At the sovereign's magnificent court, it was not unusual for some 1000 dishes to be offered at a single meal, many of which were at the ready for his tasting on individual earthenware braziers, more elegant, perhaps, but much like ours. Such delicacies as turkey spiced with elaborate chile sauces, fish with plum sauce, dried duck, or even honey-flavored tamales, were among the everyday fare prepared to serve the lord's whim. Simple *braseros* can still be found in use if one ventures into remote Mexican villages. Our squat clay *brasero* is painted a rusty matte red on the outside with a band of red on the upper rim. The inside is the natural color of the original clay. The brazier is 5½″ high, and measures 11″ across, providing enough room over the fire to place a good-sized, round casserole, pot or serving dish on the three horn-like projections at its sides. Heat is provided by placing a bed of hot coals in the perforated 2″-deep, 8½″-diameter depression in the center, which has been reinforced under the rim by a metal strip. The base of the *brazier* features a cut-out window that allows air to fan the fire and makes emptying the ashes easy.

Mexican Folk Art Annex Inc. $20.00

Maguey Scouring Pad C:66

The majestic *magueys* (plants with long, thick pointed leaves, that flourish in central and southeastern Mexico) are not just ornamental. The *aguamiel* (honey-water) drawn off from the center of the plant, just before the tall flower-bearing stem emerges, may be made into honey, sugar, *pulque* (a milky-white drink of the fermented sap with a fierce wallop), yeast or vinegar. The roots provide a starchy vegetable, the thorns make needles, and the leaves may be made into paper; but most often they are used to obtain strong yellow fibers to twist into rope or other valuable goods. Our scouring pad is a completely flat, 5″-diameter mass of *maguey* fibers, machine-stitched around the edge and across the center with red and blue thread. More abrasive than a sponge, and gentler than a metal scouring pad or cloth, this natural fiber pad will scrub Mexican pottery dishes effectively without damaging their delicate glazes. If food sticks to a *cazuela* or *olla*, let it soak a while, and then wipe it clean with this dandy little pad.

Pan American Phoenix $0.50

Collapsible Wire Basket C:67

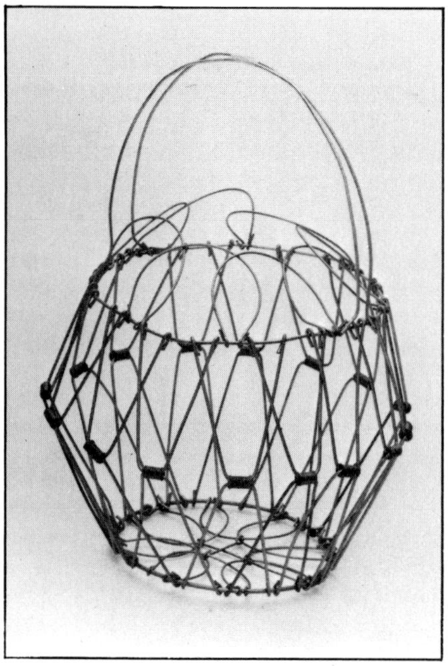

Fruits are an indispensable part of nearly every Mexican's diet, and nothing could be more refreshing after a heavy, three-hour-long, multicourse *comida* on a sultry afternoon. Markets everywhere are piled high with a wildly colorful array and in countless Mexican kitchens, an expandable wire basket like this one can be found heaped with a freshly-washed selection of delectable produce. The wire loops of the basket collapse into a pronged, flat star shape for convenient storage, and expand to form a container 11″ in diameter and 8½″ high. The top has a large 7″-wide opening with a fold-over loop trap to keep your mangoes and oranges, lemons and limes safely inside. Two long wire handles are provided so that you can hang the basket or carry it right to the table.

The Critical Cook/Tracy Dawson Imports Inc. (300) $6.00

COUNTRY EGGS

Huevos Rancheros

1 serving

These fried eggs are served on tortillas and covered with a *picante* tomato sauce.

Have ready:
½ cup Salsa Ranchera, warmed
An individual warmed serving dish

A small frying pan
2 tablespoons peanut or safflower oil
2 small tortillas
Paper toweling
2 eggs

Heat the oil and fry the tortillas lightly on both sides, as you would for *enchiladas*—they must not become crisp. Drain them on the toweling and place them on the warmed dish.

In the same oil, fry the eggs, then place them on the tortillas.

Cover the eggs with warmed sauce and serve immediately.

This makes an attractive breakfast or brunch dish served in a shallow *poêle* as I have often had it in a Mexican home: the tortilla is cut to fit the dish. The sauce is sprinkled with grated Cheddar cheese and the dish put briefly under the broiler until the cheese melts. For a change, you could garnish with strips of *chile poblano* or canned, peeled green chili and a little crumbled cream cheese.

(From THE CUISINES OF MEXICO by Diana Kennedy. Copyright 1972 by Diana Kennedy. Reprinted by permission of Harper & Row, Publishers, Inc.)

COUNTRY SAUCE

Salsa Ranchera

1 serving (about ½ cup)

A blender
1 tomato (about ½ pound), broiled
1 or 2 *chiles serranos*, toasted
½ clove garlic, peeled

Blend the tomato, chilies and garlic together to a fairly smooth sauce. Do not overblend.

A small frying pan
1 tablespoon peanut or safflower oil
A thick slice of onion, finely chopped
⅛ teaspoon salt, or to taste

Heat the oil and cook the onion, without browning, until it is soft. Add the blended ingredients and salt and cook the sauce over a brisk flame for about 5 minutes, until it reduces and thickens a little.

This sauce is most commonly used for huevos rancheros, but it also makes a very good base sauce for a shredded meat filling for tacos. You can always make it ahead of time, as it keeps very well and freezes quite satisfactorily.

(From THE CUISINES OF MEXICO by Diana Kennedy. Copyright 1972 by Diana Kennedy. Reprinted by permission of Harper & Row, Publishers, Inc.)

Chicken-Shaped Wire Basket C:68

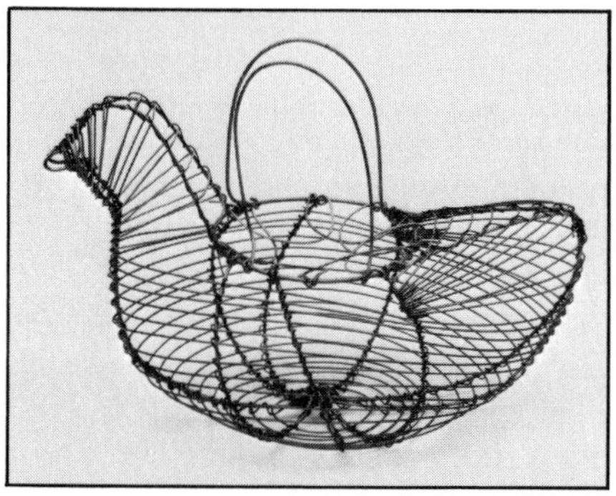

Domestic hens came to the New World with the Spanish *conquistadores*. Their ever-resourceful Indian cooks added the zap of native chiles and the wealth of their varied corn cuisine to produce uniquely Mexican egg dishes that became a perennial staple of the classic *almuerzo* (midmorning brunch). Anyone who has tasted *huevos rancheros* (eggs served on tortillas and covered with a spicy tomato sauce) at that hour knows what an eye-opener they can be —especially after too much *tequila* the night before! Like most Europeans, Mexicans believe that eggs should always be fresh, never refrigerated; and they keep their supply at room temperature, often in wire baskets. We think this decorative wire chicken, a *pollo para huevos* (chicken for eggs), is a charming storage idea. The chicken measures 11½″ from beak to tail, stands 7″ high and has two long wire handles for carrying. A trap of overlapping wire loops across the 4″-wide top opening keeps the contents from tumbling out. If you prefer refrigerated eggs, you could use this *pollito* (little chicken) for onions or fruits.

Tracy Dawson Imports Inc. (319) $7.00

Cat-Shaped Cookie Cutter C:69

Primitive *galletitas* (cookies) made of a corn-based dough, flavored with honey, were known to the Aztecs; but the Spanish horticulturists that accompanied Cortés and his warriors imported wheat and sugar to Mexico. Those essential ingredients, without which no North American children's party fare could be prepared, have over the years become essential to Mexican fiestas as well. How delighted a child of either culture would be to receive an edible *gatito* (little cat) shaped like this languid feline. The tinned-steel cookie cutter shown here is 4½″ long and 3¼″ wide with ½″-deep, thin strips of tin bent to form the outline of the body and the eyes.

Tracy Dawson Imports Inc. (610) $2.50

Multiple Cookie Cutter C:70

This ingenious, compact, tinned-steel cookie cutter is designed to punch out a dozen cookies in one fell swoop. Twelve small cutters—a square, circle, diamond, heart, star and fish, among other shapes—are comfortably ensconced within a 1½″-high ring that measures 5¾″ in diameter. The top has a smooth safety rim, but the bottom cutting edge is sharp enough to cut out a dozen perfectly-shaped cookies in a flash. Tin rusts easily, so always dry the cutter thoroughly, and keep it coated with a tasteless cooking oil when not in use.

El Mercado $2.00

Pig-Shaped Cake Mold C:71

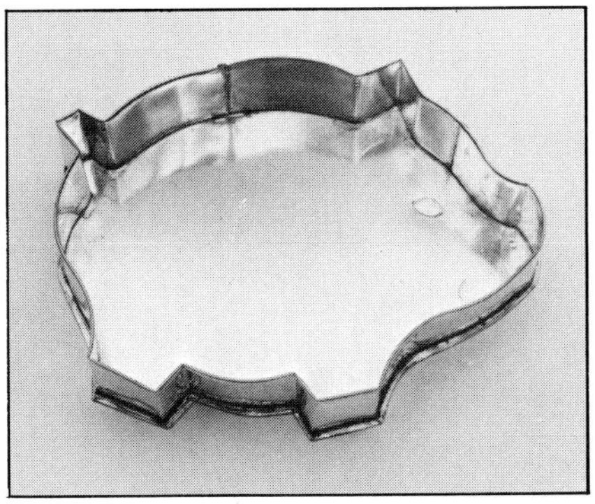

Pigs were another novelty brought to Mexico by the Spaniards, and pork-based dishes rapidly became essential to *mestizo* (Indian-Spanish) cuisine. Therefore, this pig-shaped pan, unlike so many other Mexican cooking implements, would seem genuinely exotic to a pre-Colombian cook. Our friendly piglet, made of rather light-gauge tinned steel, measures 10″ from snout to tail, 7¼″ from underbelly to back and holds 6 cups. Of somewhat primitive construction, the pan is not terribly sturdy; but it is perfectly adequate for baking a *panque* (pound cake) or a *pastel de mocha* (mocha cake). The flat bottom is soldered to 1¾″-deep sides, and the top edge is smoothly folded over. As for all tin objects, rust is a problem; so we suggest popping piggy into a warm oven for a few minutes after washing, then rubbing him lightly with a tasteless cooking oil.

Tracy Dawson Imports Inc. (588) $8.00

Dessert Mold C:72

This delicate-looking, round tinned-steel mold is so enchanting we hate to think of it as merely a pan that stays in the kitchen once the meal is served. Of course it would make a lovely unmolded almond pudding served with a custard sauce, but it would also make a handsome serving dish for *guacamole.* The straight upper sides of the mold are decorated with a hand-tooled progression of dots and arcs in different patterns, but the lower sides that slope toward the flat, 2¾″-wide base are perfectly plain. The vessel measures 5½″ across the top, is 3″ deep and holds 4 cups. It should be cared for like any other tin object, with extra careful drying and protection from rust with a light coating of tasteless cooking oil.

Fred Leighton Imports Ltd. (23-291) $2.00

Chocolate Swizzle C:73

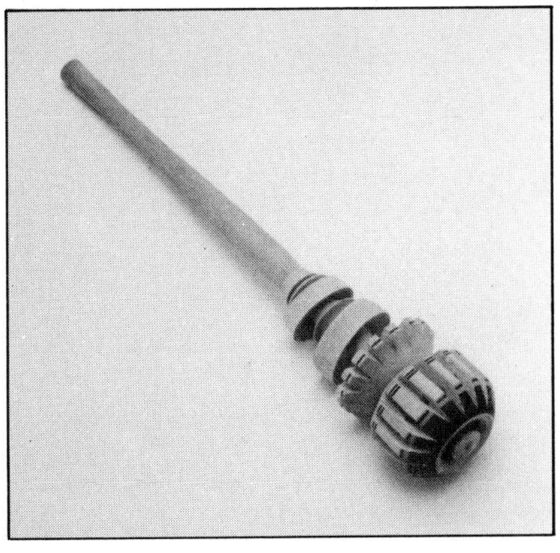

Forbidden to women and reserved for men of superior rank, chocolate was

Continued from preceding page

the royal drink of Mexico. According to eyewitness reports, some 2000 jugs of frothy chocolate, sweetened with wild honey and often flavored with vanilla or *achiote* (annato, a red seed used as a coloring agent), appeared daily at the Aztec court. Moctezuma himself sipped his favorite beverage from solid gold cups. Modern Mexico is still a land of chocolate lovers, and they customarily use delightfully carved wooden beaters called *molinillos* (little mills) to whip up their foamy delicacy. *Molinillos* look more like exotic musical instruments than hardworking utensils, and ours is no exception. Decorated with simple geometric designs, this typical beater is 12½″ long, and has three sliding rings that do the work. Mexican *chocolate* (spelled the same as the English word), if you can find it, differs from ours in that it is presweetened, lighter in body, pleasantly textured and often flavored with cinnamon, cloves and ground almonds. Drinking-chocolate should be prepared in small batches in an *olla,* or earthenware pot. If you'd like to try the real thing, crumble the chocolate into boiling water—1½ ounces per cup—stir until it melts, then boil slowly for five minutes. Insert the *molinillo,* and rapidly whirl the stick between your palms until the chocolate is frothy. It's much more fun than a blender, and a *molinillo* is a delightful kitchen accessory to have on display.

Mexican Folk Art Annex Inc. — $2.50

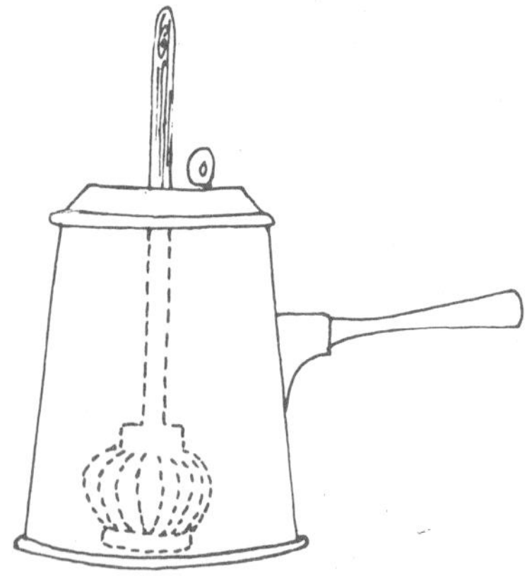

An American version of a chocolate swizzle from the 19th century.

Bernal Díaz, soldier and chronicler of Hernán Cortés, observed hot chocolate for the first time as follows: "Sometimes they brought [Moctezuma] *in cups of pure gold a drink made from the cocoa-plant, which they said he took before visiting his wives. We did not take much notice of this at the time, though I saw them bring in a good fifty large jugs of this chocolate, all frothed up, of which he drank a little."*

The Conquest of New Spain *by Bernal Díaz, translated by J. M. Cohen. Penguin Books, Ltd., 1963.*

Metal Ice Shaver — C:74

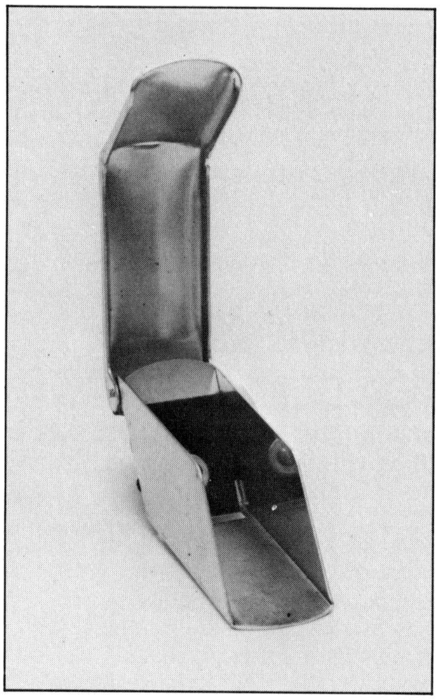

Legend has it that Moctezuma was so fond of chilled fruit drinks that he dispatched runners to the snow-capped peak of Popocatepetl (the looming, ever-visible volcano), to fetch ice for his daily pick-me-up. Apocryphal or not, the taste for fruited ice is a strong one south of the border. In Mexico City's diverting playground, Chapultepec Park, and all over the city, a special treat sold by vendors is a *nieves* (snow)—a cup of shaved ice drenched with one of a variety of sweetened fruit extracts. An ice shaver similar to the ones they use is available for preparing your own *nieves* at home. Our aluminum ice shaver is 6″ long and about 2″ wide. It is equipped with a blade that can be adjusted to regulate the thickness of the shavings by loosening a screw-type nut inside. Provided you have access to ice blocks, or the time and space to freeze solid hunks yourself, shave some ice into your guests' punch glasses at your next cocktail party, add some fruit syrup and call it an "Aztec Legacy." Or, pour some maple syrup over shavings to make individual *nieves* for the children at a special birthday party. It's an easy way to lend an original *latino* flair to either occasion!

Maprosa S.A. — $1.30

Lime Squeezer — C:75

In Mexico, the correct proportions of fresh lime juice and tequila are as critical to the perfect Margarita as the right amount of vermouth and gin or vodka is to the quintessential martini. A lightweight lime press like this one, made of non-corroding cast aluminum, quickly provides that special zest needed for the Margarita. Two hinged, 2″-diameter domed sections fit into each other, and between them goes ½ a lime, cut-side down. As you squeeze the 4″-long handles together, the top presses down on the fruit, forcing juice through the perforated bottom. Because most American limes are somewhat larger than the native Mexican varieties, you might have to squeeze smaller pieces. For a traditional Mexican Margarita, rub the rim of a cocktail glass with a slice of lime or a bit of peel, then dip the moistened edge in coarse salt. In a cocktail shaker, combine an ounce of freshly pressed lime juice with 1½ ounces of tequila and ½ ounce of Triple Sec, then add ice and shake well. Strain the mixture into the prepared glass. *Salud, amigos!* (To your health, friends).

HOAN Products, Ltd. (170) **$2.50**

Orange Squeezer C:76

Called an *exprimidero para naranjas,* this popular type of orange squeezer can be used to make fresh orange juice for all sorts of Mexican specialties, from the festive *pato en jugo de naranja* (duck cooked in orange juice) to the ever popular *sangría* (fresh fruit and wine punch adopted from the Spanish). The bottom half of the squeezer consists of a concave strainer that cups the press on the top half. These 4″-diameter sections are hinged at one end and each has a 6″-long handle at the opposite end; the handles interlock when the press is closed to give the tightest squeeze possible. This handy tool is made of rustproof cast aluminum, but should still be thoroughly dried after use. You might also try a *sangrita:* Seville orange juice and tequila combined with grenadine and an eye-opening pinch of powdered chile.

El Mercado **$2.50**

Sweet orange.

Glass Pitcher C:77

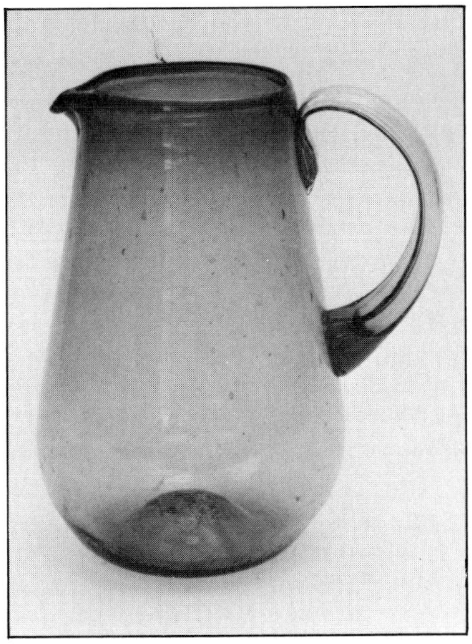

On sunny days near Chapultepec Park in Mexico City, and in parks, markets and squares all over Mexico, vendors set up stands with a colorful array of *aguas frescas* (fresh waters) in large glass barrels to tempt thirsty passers-by. The barrels are filled with cooling *limonada* (lemonade), *tamarindo* (tamarind juice), or *jamaica* (a slightly tart, refreshing infusion of Jamaica flowers—*hibiscus sabdariffa,* often labeled "sorrel" in Mexican and West Indian markets in the U.S.). A large, hand-blown pitcher from Mexico like this one would be perfect for serving and storing your own *jamaica.* Made of pale gray-green recycled glass, rimmed with amber at the top, and full of tiny bubbles, the 9″-tall pitcher with its large, well-placed handle, will hold 3 quarts—or 2 quarts and lots of ice—for those sultry days when quantities of a cold beverage are in great demand.

Pan American Phoenix **$10.00**

Four-Tiered Lunch Box C:78

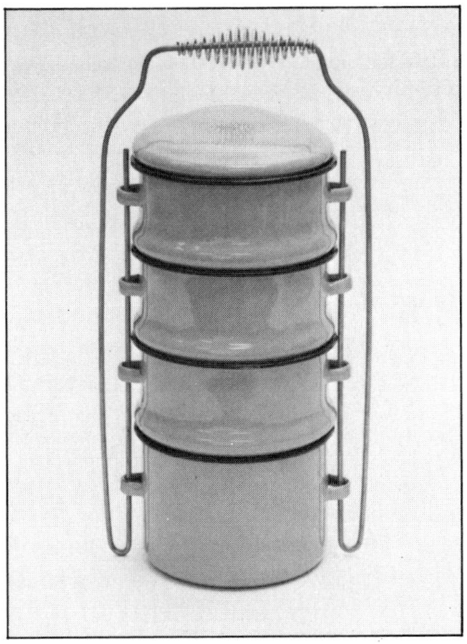

This tiered lunch box from Mexico permits you to reheat food, if you want it good and hot. The top three food containers, which bulge slightly just above their bases, are 2½″ deep, 5″ in diameter, and sit on a 3¼″-deep bottom pan, designed to hold water for steaming. Made of light blue enameled steel, the black-rimmed pots fit neatly, one atop the other, to form a tidy 11″ stack; and all four pans have a pair of ear-like handles on the sides. The assembled structure is held together by a continuous piece of sturdy wire that loops through the handles on both sides of the pots to keep them from slipping about. Around the wire, at the top, is a second piece of wire, coiled to form a comfortable grip for carrying the lunch box. In Mexico, lunch would typically consist of *frijoles* (beans), *arroz* (rice) and tortillas, but you could vary the menu to suit your own needs or taste and be sure that, regardless of its contents, your lunch box would be a conversation piece.

El Mercado **$12.50**

The Flavor of Peru

by Elena Pastor

Basically, there are three types of cooking in Peru: one is derived from the Spanish influence, predominant along the coast; the second comes from the jungle areas, noted for exotic meats and fruits; and the third is from the mountainous highlands.

In the coastal area, where I come from, the people speak Spanish and think of themselves as very European and up-to-date. The kitchen in my own house in Lima is probably not very different from your own; I would bet that it has the same sort of appliances, and more or less the same pots and pans. Unfortunately, I am not very familiar with the jungle and its people, though I know they eat strange things like boa constrictor, which is supposed to taste like chicken, and they have wonderful kinds of unusual fruit.

It is in the Andean highlands, the area that we call the sierra, that you meet the true Peruvian people and food. Two languages are spoken there, Kuechua and Imara, both related to the ancient Incan tongue. Life is hard in the highlands; it is very cold and because the air is thin it is arduous to move. The poorest people can't get through the day without chewing on coca leaves, which give them strength and take their minds off the hardships of their lives. There is never enough food to go round, so what there is must provide as many calories as possible.

The Indians cook over open fires in a kind of unglazed earthenware that we call *ollas de barro* (earthenware pots). It is inexpensive and extremely handsome. In Lima we like to use these pots for planters or for holding fruit, but we don't usually cook with them. The unglazed earthenware imparts a distinctive flavor to food that the people of the highlands find very agreeable.

Let me tell you about the *pachamanca* that originated in the Incan highlands. We have it in Lima, too, but there it is only a city imitation of the real thing. First, a big hole is dug in the ground. Then, large stones are gathered and carefully cleaned, and used to build a hollow mound in the hole. The stone construction is filled with fuel: in Lima we use coals, but I am sure that in the highlands they use wood. A fire is started and burns until the stones themselves become red hot. Then someone removes the embers and ashes and fills the stone cave with food, such as lamb and pork, tamales, potatoes and corn. (We have 200 kinds of potato in Peru, where they originated, so you can see that great variety is possible in a *pachamanca*.)

Next, the stones are covered with leaves and, finally, with earth. Several hours go by. Everyone gets hungrier and hungrier, but nobody is allowed to open up the sealed chamber until the special *pachamanca* cooks say when. They make holes down between the stones into which they stick long tubes to draw out bits of food. At last, when the cooks declare that everything is ready, the meal is unburied. You can't imagine the wonderful smell that emerges when the first stones are rolled away, and what a good time everybody has eating the food.

Most Peruvian cooking is related to that of the rest of South America. In the coastal areas, for example, we eat a lot of fish. We believe that *ceviche* originated there. This well-known specialty is made by marinating raw fish in lime juice until it "cooks," or turns white. Now, you can get *ceviche* all over coastal South America. We

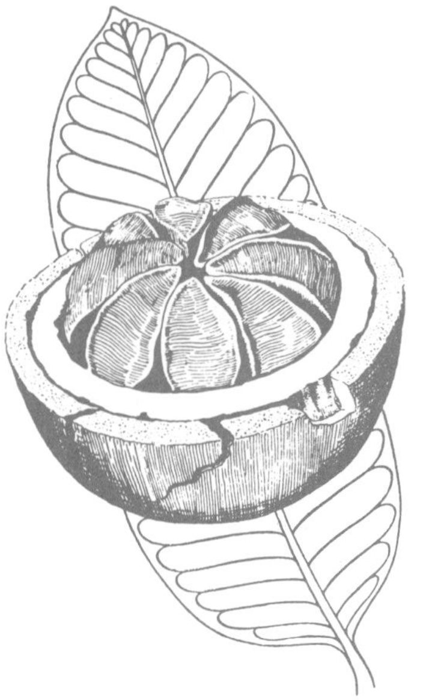

The segmented flower shaped in the center of this round fruit is made up of Brazil-nuts (really the seeds of the fruit). Grown in towering trees all over South America, the rich, creamy nuts must first be subjected to a complicated shelling and dehydrating process before they are shipped abroad for world-wide consumption.

The Swiss naturalist and diplomat, Johan Jakob von Tschudi, scornfully described a not-so-new vice, noshing, in his Travels in Peru *(1838–1842):* "Gourmanderie *is one of the evil habits of the female inhabitants of Lima. Between meals they are continually eating sweetmeats and a variety of things. At one moment they order* tamal *(a preparation of finely bruised maize mixed with morsels of pork and rolled in maize leaves) served up, next* omitas *(sweet cakes made of maize and raisins), then* pan de chancay *(a sweet sort of bread) and biscuits, then* masamorita morada *(a syrup made from the pulp of a fruit), or* frijoles coladas *(preserved peas with syrup), &c.; and yet dinner is partaken with as hearty an appetite as though none of these interludes had been introduced. Can it be a matter of surprise that the good ladies are constantly complaining of indigestion and* mal de estomago?"

The Great Travelers, *Vol. II, edited by Milton Rugoff. Simon & Schuster, 1960.*

also have tamales, similar to those in Mexico. They are made of corn dough filled with pieces of meat, cheese or olives and wrapped in banana leaves or corn husks to cook. In Peru we have no flat corn breads like the tortilla, but in nearby Colombia, *arepas* (a type of unleavened flat corn bread) are eaten with every meal.

Another food that you find in Peru as well as in the rest of South America, is the *yuca* plant, a long tuber (sweet cassava) that is cooked in all the ways that the potato is, even grated and boiled into a form of porridge. A thin solution of *yuca* even makes a good starch for clothes!

Now that I live in New York, I am glad that there is some similarity among the different cuisines of South America. If I want to have a spicy *escabeche* of fish or chicken, I can sometimes find it in a number of South American restaurants, or I can make it myself and pretend that I am at home.

Metal Grain Mill C:79

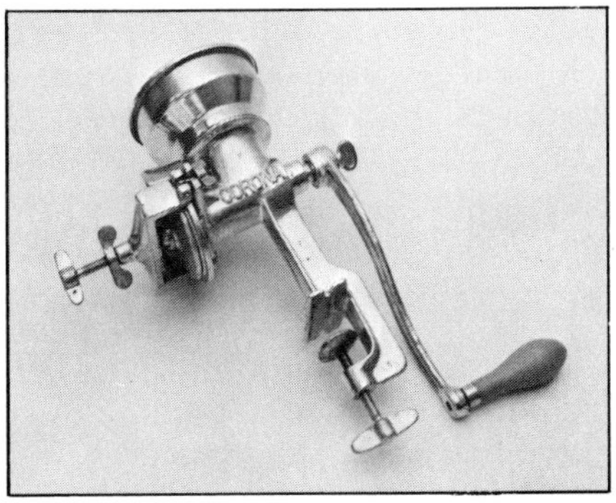

In South America, where no self-respecting cook would buy pre-packaged cornmeal or tinned coffee, a grain mill like the one shown here from Colombia is a standard piece of kitchen equipment—when, that is, it has not been supplanted by a speedier electric model. Although the device resembles a conventional meat grinder, it is used to pulverize pre-softened corn kernels into dough for *arepas*, flat breads that are daily fare in Colombia. Corn dough is also used for those delectable meat turnovers called *empanadas*. Fresh coffee beans can be ground in the mill, too, for the never-ending procession of *cafecitos* (small cups of coffee) that most Latins consume daily. This heavy, zinc-plated, cast-iron implement consists of: a sturdy 7¾″-high body with a firm C-clamp at its base to hold the mill securely to your work surface, a long handle, and the grinding mechanism. The grinder has a 2½″-high hopper that holds a small quantity of beans or kernels, and a 2½″-long extension that accommodates about 3 cups. A semicircular guard hood, much like the shield over lawn-mower blades, snaps over the top of the grinding apparatus to direct the food into a waiting receptacle. The working principle is simplicity itself: after the hopper is loaded, the handle turns a thick worm that forces the corn or coffee between two grooved grinding discs. The discs are held together by an adjustable brace that controls the degree of fineness or coarseness desired. Although the 23-piece mill appears to be an intricate piece of machinery, it is fairly easy to assemble; a simple diagram of the various parts (identified in Spanish) accompanies the implement. All the components come apart easily for cleaning and for snug storage in a compact, rectangular box.

Casa Moneo $18.00

FLAT COLOMBIAN CORN BREAD

Arepas

Makes 4 to 6

2 cups dried white corn kernels (sold prepackaged in Spanish markets)

Cook the corn in enough water to cover it by about 2 inches. Add additional boiling water, as necessary. When the corn is tender to the touch, drain off any excess water and grind the kernels finely in a grain mill. Work the dough with your hands for about 5 minutes, until it is very soft and smooth. Break off pieces of dough, about the size of a large walnut, and pat each one into a disc about ⅛″ thick, like a tortilla. You may find this easier to do, if you first wet your hands with warm water because the dough can be sticky.

Preheat a wire grill and then put one or more *arepas* on it, depending on its size. Cook the *arepas* directly over a burner until they are light gold on both sides. Serve at once with butter.

Note: You may blend some *queso blanco* (white cheese, substitute farmer cheese) to the dough, if you like. Or serve the *arepas* with cheese on the side. Hot chocolate is also a traditional accompaniment.

(*Courtesy of Blanca Velasquez, New York City.*)

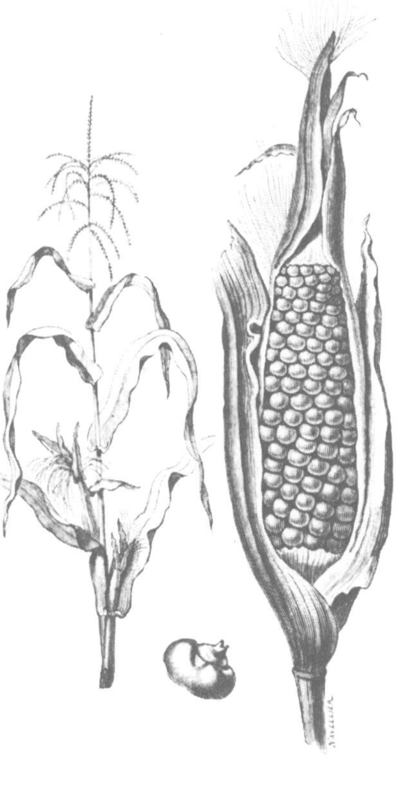

A stalk, ear and grain of corn.

"There is another fruit called 'Plante,' [plantain] of which the trees may be twenty or twenty-five feet high, which has a leaf so large, that a man might cover himself with it. There grows a root from the said tree on which are a quantity of the 'plantes,' each of which is as thick as the arm, and a foot and a half long, of a yellow and green colour, of very good taste, and so wholesome,

Continued from preceding page

that a man can eat as much as he likes, without its doing any harm."

A Voyage to the West Indies and Mexico in the Years 1599–1602 *by Samuel Champlain, translated by Alice Wilmere, edited by Norton Shaw. Burt Franklin, n.d.*

Plantain Press — C:80

In Cuba, Puerto Rico and other Caribbean islands, as well as in all tropical regions of Latin America, *platanos* (plantains), those large relatives of the banana, are widely used in almost every type of dish. Slender, deep-fried chips (*tostones*) nearly always accompany cocktails; and plantain slices appear in soups and stews, as vegetables and in desserts that are frequently laced with rum. Used both unripe and green, or mature and dark brown, this indispensable staple is always cooked; when hard and immature, it is often pounded first. This *tostonera* (plantain press) smacks of *tourismo,* but it was designed for the purpose of flattening plantain slices before frying. It consists of an 8″-long, paddle-shaped top section, hinged to a 4¾″-by-3½″ bottom piece. In the center of the bottom is a ¼″-deep, 3″ circle into which the plantain slice fits. The top folds firmly down over the plantain-filled depression to form a patty. A cowhide loop at the paddle is provided for hanging the device. The top bears a simple blue, yellow and green flower design, and, unfortunately, in bold letters the word "TOSTONERA." We show the press largely as a curiosity, since most self-respecting Caribbean or South American cooks follow the traditional method of flattening *platano* slices with the heel of a hand.

Casa Moneo — **$0.98**

Cassava: Both Sweet and Bitter

Two varieties of cassava or manioc, a starchy root vegetable, are eaten as staples in South America; one is sweet, the other is bitter and poisonous, at least until it undergoes special detoxification.

Sweet cassava (*Manihot dulcis*) is called *yuca* in Spanish-speaking lands, and usually *aipím* or *macaxeira* in Brazil. The very poor eat it as a tasteless, but filling, starchy vegetable, peeled and boiled or fried like potatoes. The most prevalent variety by far, however, is bitter cassava, known all over the South American continent as *mandioca* and botanically as *Manihot esculenta.* Once the lethal hydrocyanic acid in the roots is removed, the cassava is consumed in great quantities by jungle people and sophisticated jet-setters alike. To North Americans this strange crop is best known as the source of tapioca or Brazilian arrowroot. The huge tubers—some weighing as much as 20 pounds—were originally found growing wild in the jungle by aboriginal Indians centuries before the Portuguese, Spaniards and other Europeans arrived on their continent. One assumes that by painful trial and error, they learned to grate and squeeze out much of the poison, then heat the pulp by toasting, boiling or baking to make the substance safely edible. Thus, bitter cassava, baked into bread, prepared as a vegetable or sprinkled as meal over other food, became their principal staple besides indigenous fruits, fish and wild game.

Although bitter cassava meal is now manufactured by machines, for the most part, rudimentary graters, squeezers and sieves are still used in primitive areas. More urbanized Latin Americans collect these artifacts as treasures of their rapidly disappearing heritage.

Cassava Grater — C:81

Bitter cassava is a staple food in many areas of South America, but it requires detoxification before it can be eaten. To begin the process, some type of grater is a necessity. This one from tropical Colombia is made according to centuries-old Tukano Indian tradition by a native craftsman. From a rough piece of wood, a carver shapes a slightly bowed paddle-like base—this one measures 17½″ long and 7½″ across at its widest part, with a gently curved 7¾″-long handle. Next the board is soaked in water to soften it, so that tiny, pointed stone chips can be inserted into the board—below the handle—to form a rough grating surface. When the wood dries, and the stones are set, the top surface of the device is coated with raw rubber. Finally, the edges and the handle are painted with primitive rust-colored brush designs and black and rust-colored cross-hatchings. As proof of its authenticity, the untreated underside still shows the gouges of the carver's tools. Peeled cassava root is grated against the stones and put into a basket-like sieve to filter out some of the dangerous juice. The pulpy residue must then be squeezed and heated to make it safe for eating. Because grating a lethal, 20-pound nasty-looking root may not exactly be your idea of good, clean fun, our *rallador para mandioca* would nonetheless be a curious and fascinating addition to your display of ethnic cooking artifacts from other times, other places.

Sermoneta **$24.00**

Cassava Sieve/ Sifter C:82

This delicate, handwoven sieve/sifter from the Colombian tropics is made of fine palm-leaf fibers. In primitive areas, baskets like this one are used for various tasks. A basket may strain out the first escaping poisonous juices from the grated pulp of bitter cassava; but it also functions as a sifter for the poison-free end product, called manioc meal, or as a winnower to separate foreign matter, such as pebbles, from dry kidney beans and rice, those other dietary staples of Latin America. Extremely soft and pliable to the touch, this 5″-high *cedazo y cernador* measures 19″ in diameter and is encircled at the rim with a pair of reinforced bent reeds, bound with braided fiber. Be careful, however, to use it only to hold lightweight items: the slender fibers are rather flimsy.

Sermoneta **$24.00**

Visiting the Tupi-Kawahib, an Amazonian tribe, Claude Lévi-Strauss found each home equipped with more or less the same "basics": "hammocks made of cotton thread; a few earthenware pots and a basin in which maize or manioc pulp could be dried over the fire; some calabashes; a few wooden pestles and mortars; some manioc-scrapers made of thorn-inlaid wood; some wickerwork sieves; . . . When night fell the chief ceremoniously brought us . . . a ragout of giant beans and peppers. Hot as these were to the palate, they were a delight after six months among the Nambikwara, who know nothing of either salt or pepper and whose palates are so delicate that all food has to be drenched in water, and thus effectively cooled, before they can begin to eat. The native salt came in a little calabash; it was a brownish liquid so bitter that the chief, who contented himself with watching us eat, insisted on tasting it in our presence to reassure us that it was not a poison . . ."

Tristes Tropiques *by Claude Lévi-Strauss, translated by John & Doreen Weightman. Atheneum, 1970.*

Cassava Squeezer C:83

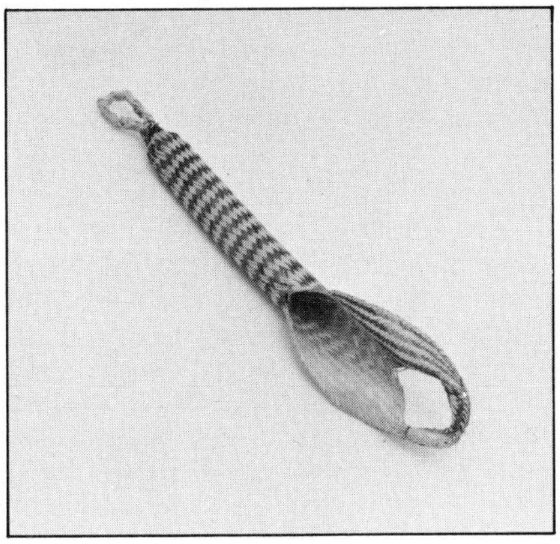

Curious, oddly beautiful, and vaguely resembling a large-stemmed straw flower, this basket is actually a supremely functional device called a cassava squeezer. Such baskets are still employed by natives throughout the torrid forests of the Amazon basin to extract the lethal acid present in the roots of bitter cassava. We vividly recall seeing bare-breasted Arawak Indian and Black Djuka maidens, preparing the omni-present cassava for the communal village meal, stuffing the grated pulp into the body of an identical basket, then hanging it by the large top loop and tying a heavy rock to the bottom loop. This opposing action helps force out a major part of the poison from the cassava. After this, the native women shape the residue into large, flat cakes that are dried on the tops of palm-thatched huts, prior to the baking or roasting process that finally renders the cassava edible. The classic Tukano Indian manioc squeezer from Colombia, with its interwoven pattern of blond and caramel-colored palm fronds, is an unusual example of indigenous basketry. The basket is 12″ long and 2″ in diameter.

Sermoneta **$7.95**

Manioc, or cassava, a major staple in South America.

Gourd Bowl C:84

A good-sized gourd with a very round bottom has been cut, dried and tooled to make this delightful bowl. Inside, it is beige with a smooth but unfinished surface; outside, it is covered with a jungle of tan, curvilinear leaves and flowers in a raised pattern. Of generous dimensions, it measures about 9″ in diameter and is 5″ deep. On the north coast of Colombia where the bowl was made, it would be used for fruit juice or soups, like a *sopa de coco* (coconut milk soup with egg yolks and crushed almonds). But we think its light weight and round bottom make it too tippy to entrust to anything liquid. Lightweight finger food—bread, for instance, or the airy Colombian orange puffs called *hojuelas de naranja* (flour, butter and orange juice fritters deep-fried and sprinkled with powdered sugar) would be far safer.

La Tienda $15.00

Large Wooden Trough C:85

Although this wooden trough might be mistaken for a genuine aboriginal artifact, it is actually a product of the Colombian government-sponsored program called *Artesanias de Colombia.* A carefully controlled operation, it sponsors the manufacture of authentic handcrafts, following the styles and traditions handed down over generations from both Indian and Spanish heritage. The trough is called a *batea* and is fashioned of very crudely carved blond wood; its rough-hewn surface still shows clearly the marks of the woodcutter's tools. A large receptacle—17½″ by 12″ and 3½″ deep—it is used for mixing dough and would also be ideal for holding fruits or bread at a large gathering.

Sermoneta $12.00

Black Earthenware Bowl C:86

Made of black, Colombian La Chamba pottery, this small and utterly charming bowl is more or less round, but its slightly irregular shape shows the hallmark of non-factory-made authenticity. To keep the contents from spilling, the bowl is molded with a relatively flat bottom, and comes equipped with two small volcano-shaped handles, decorated with simple grooves. The container will hold about 2 cups of liquid, and measures 5½″ in diameter and 2¼″ deep—just about the right dimensions for a generous serving of an irresistible *ajiaco Bogotano* (a creamy Colombian soup of chicken, potatoes and corn, topped with capers and sliced avocado), or a hearty stew such as a *sancocho,* made with beef, pork, *yuca,* plantains, potatoes, corn, cabbage and fresh coriander.

Sermoneta $4.50

Antonio Pigafetta, Magellan's secretary, wrote the only known first-hand account of the celebrated voyage around the world. Here he describes a stop made in Brazil for the purpose of replenishing the ship's miserably depleted larder: "Here we laid in a good stock of fowls, potatoes, a kind of fruit which resembles the cone of a pine tree, but which is very sweet and of an exquisite flavor, sweet reeds, the flesh of the anta, which resembles that of a cow, etc. We made excellent bargains here: for a hook or a knife we purchased five or six fowls; a comb brought us two geese; and a small looking glass, or a pair of scissors, as much fish as would serve ten people. The inhabitants, for a little bell or a ribbon gave a basket of potatoes, which is the name they give to roots somewhat resembling our turnips and which are nearly like chestnuts in taste. Our playing cards were an equally advantageous object of barter; for a king of spades I obtained half a dozen fowls, and the hawker even deemed his bargain an excellent one. . . ."

The Great Travelers, *Vol. I, edited by Milton Rugoff. Simon & Schuster, 1960.*

COLOMBIAN SOUP

Sancocho

Serves 7 to 8

3 pounds pork chops
3 pounds beef round, cut into thick slices
4 ears of corn, each cut into 3 rounds
3 *yuca* peeled, each cut into 3 lengthwise strips (*yuca* is available frozen in Latin American markets)
2 pounds boiling potatoes, each potato cut in half
2 pounds *arracacha,* each cut into 2 or 3 large pieces
3 green plantains, each cut into 3 lengthwise strips
3 ripe plantains, each cut into 3 lengthwise strips
1 cabbage cut into large pieces
4 onions, cut in half lengthwise and then sliced
3 sprigs fresh coriander
1 bay leaf
Paprika to taste
Salt to taste
Pepper to taste

Put the meats and corn in a deep pot with enough water to cover them by 2 inches. Cook over medium heat until the meat is half done. Add the remaining ingredients and cook until they are all tender. Serve in deep dishes accompanied by *arepas* and avocado salad.

(*Courtesy of Blanca Velasquez, New York City.*)

Large Earthenware Cooking Dish C:87

Earthenware dishes are basic cooking utensils everywhere in Latin America. This one, made in Raquira, Colombia, of a coarsely textured terra-cotta, has a broad, rounded bottom that sits nicely on a charcoal brazier and is used for frying, especially pork. It is painted a pale orange with a few bold stripes and splashes of red and has been left unglazed; the oil used in frying seals off the porous inner surface of the pan. It will hold 3 quarts, and is 10″ across the top and 3⅜″ deep. A short 4″-long handle and a small ear-shaped handle opposite provide support and leverage for pouring off excess fat through the handy spout just under the rim.

La Tienda **$20.00**

Black Earthenware Casseorle C:88

Colombian blackware pottery, made in the little town of La Chamba, is at once sturdy and elegant, as evidenced by this large, glazed clay casserole. A deep vessel, like this one, could easily be used for slow oven-simmering of a robust Colombian soup like *sopa de cebollitas* (a pearly onion broth with meat, tiny pickled white onions, tapioca and *achiote,* a red seed used for coloring. This classic pot is 11″ in diameter, 5½″ deep, holds 6 quarts and comes equipped with a snug-fitting high-domed lid. The top edge of the pot protrudes at two sides to form solid, flat handles with simple, grooved decorations, somewhat reminiscent of Art Nouveau motifs. This truly handsome piece of pottery also makes an inexpensive, yet beautiful serving dish. Try the popular *frijoles antioqueños* (red beans cooked with pork, plantains and various seasonings).

Sermoneta **$16.50**

OLD-FASHIONED BEANS

Frijoles Antioqueños

1 pound red kidney beans
2 pig's feet
2 green plantains, coarsely chopped
Salt
1 teaspoon paprika
1 tablespoon vegetable oil
7 scallions, finely chopped
2 large tomatoes, peeled and finely chopped

Soak the beans for 2 to 5 hours in a large pot. Wash them and cull out any bad ones. Place the beans in a pot, cover with cold water and set over medium heat. Partially cover the pot. When the water begins to boil, add the pig's feet; turn the heat down and cook, partially covered, until the meat and beans are almost done. About 10 minutes before the beans are ready, add the plantains, salt and paprika.

In a small skillet, sauté the scallions lightly in the oil. Add the tomatoes and cook for a few minutes; then add the mixture to the beans, and bring the beans to a boil. Serve with rice, *arepas,* avocado and grilled meat.

(*Courtesy of Blanca Velasquez, New York City.*)

Threshing the hard way, or "The Old-Fashioned Process in Chili (sic)."

"At Rosario Oéste [an Amazonian town with one thousand inhabitants], dishes for 'state occasions' are divided down the middle: half of each chicken is served roasted and hot, the other half cold, with a sauce piquante. Half of each fish is fried, and the other half boiled. The meal is rounded off with a cachaça, an alcoholic drink made from sugar cane. . . ."

Tristes Tropiques *by Claude Lévi-Strauss, translated by John & Doreen Weightman. Atheneum, 1970.*

Serving Basket C:89

Baskets, like earthenware pots, are typical of South American countries. As varied in shape, texture, size and function as the regions from which they come, they reflect ancient artistic traditions. This intricate woven Colombian basket—called a *balay* in the Tukano Indian dialect—bears a classic linear fret motif, not dissimilar to the work of our Southwestern Indian tribes. Made of contrasting blond, black and tan palm-leaf strips, the basket is reinforced below the rim, both inside and out, with bent reeds. The 12″-wide, dish-shaped container forms a shallow bowl, approximately 1¾″ deep, and comes equipped with a string loop for convenient hanging. A harmonious blend of straw texture, color and traditional design, the native tribesmen use a *balay* for serving cassava cakes. It would, however, be perfect for holding a batch of the delightful, puffy, orange-flavored sugar cookies known as *hojuelas de naranja* (little orange leaves).

Sermoneta **$14.50**

"I would spend hour upon hour at the baker's, while he was preparing bolachas *by the sackful.* (Bolachas *are loaves made with unleavened flour that has been thickened with fat; they are as hard as stone, but the oven gives them a marrowy quality, and when they have been shaken into small pieces on the road and impregnated with the sweat of the oxen they finish up as a form of food for which it is difficult to find a name: and as rancid, certainly, as the dried meat from the butcher.*)

Tristes Tropiques *by Claude Lévi-Strauss, translated by John & Doreen Weightman. Atheneum, 1970.*

Wire Grill C:90

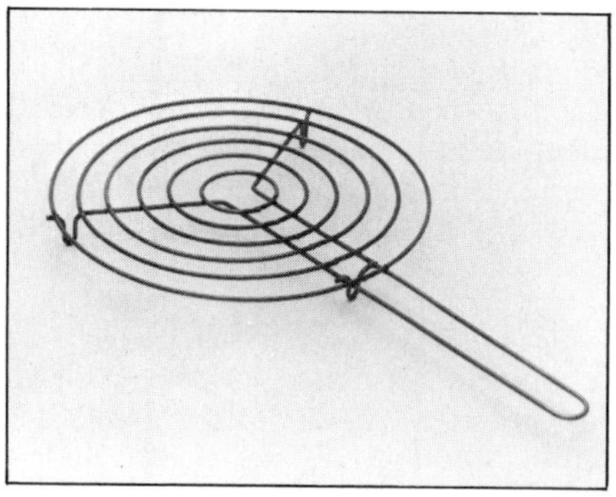

A *parrilla* (grill) is an essential item in a Colombian or Venezuelan kitchen, where it is in constant use for cooking the beloved *arepas,* flat breads made simply of cooked ground corn mixed with water and sometimes a bit of salt. This small, but sturdy, grill is comprised of six concentric wire circles. It measures 9½″ in diameter and has a 6½″-long looped wire handle that extends onto the grill itself to act as a support. The implement resembles a trivet, with three small legs welded to the grill itself for greater strength. Traditionally, the grill was set over a charcoal fire; but today, in urban areas, it fits conveniently over the electric stove burner most commonly used in these countries. To some, the unadorned *arepa* is a tasteless, leaden mass somewhat resembling an English muffin, only thinner. *Arepas* are briefly toasted on a lightly greased grill like this one, and, though the result is not a gourmet's dream—barely cooked inside, and not even crusty outside—they are still eaten avidly by almost everyone, especially the poor. Sometimes a fresh white cheese (*queso blanco*) is added to the dough. In any case, the day always begins with *arepas,* which are often accompanied by sliced beef, eggs and mugs of foamy hot chocolate.

Casa Rivera **$1.50**

Brass Chocolate Pitcher C:91

In the damp, chilly Andean mountain regions, a warming batch of frothy hot chocolate might well be served in a pitcher like the one shown here from Colombia. Made of brass, this pitcher stands 7″ deep, and measures 4″ in diameter, with a cast-iron handle. To make hot chocolate in the Colombian manner, first boil some water in the pitcher, add *panela* (unrefined brown sugar), then melt large chunks of either semi-sweet or unsweetened chocolate in the water. Boil the mixture, and froth it vigorously with a swizzle. Tradition dictates that the chocolate should be brought to the boil and frothed seven times before it is ready to serve, but few people take the trouble to do it more than two or three times. Chocolate is a breakfast favorite, particularly for children, and until recently, the drink was served in similar copper pots, in lieu of tea, at the afternoon break in the intellectual and social cafés of Bogotá.

La Tienda **$30.00**

Peruvian pottery vessel with a stirrup spout (from The Metropolitan Museum of Art).

The evergreen cacao tree that bears the seed-rich pod pictured here, is cultivated in both Central and South America. The melon-shaped pod grows on a tiny stem close to the trunk and often reaches a length of twelve inches. The interior beans, responsible for the production of cocoa, chocolate and cocoa butter, were once used as currency in Mexico.

Wooden Chocolate Swizzle — C:92

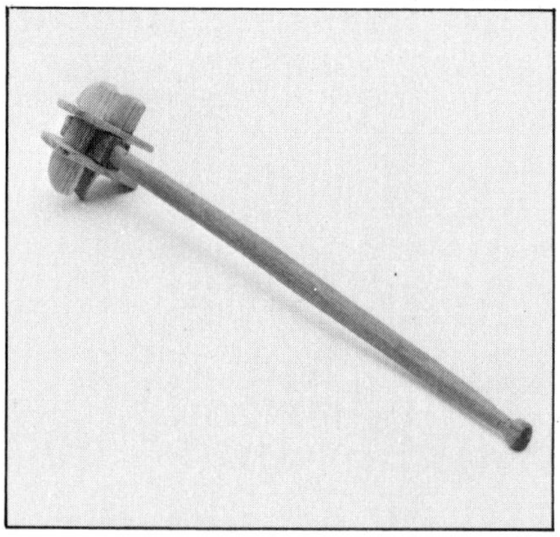

To make hot chocolate foamy, some go to the extreme of adding beaten egg white; but all you really need is a *molinillo,* a wooden swizzle with a long handle that you rub between the palms of your hands. The motion is quick and easy, more effective and less tiring than cranking a rotary beater or whipping with a whisk. This Colombian *molinillo* is made of four pieces of notched wood that resemble the parts of wooden puzzles called *rompecabezas* ("head-breakers") in Spanish. They are arranged around, and nailed to, the squared-off end of a 15″-long handle. This length permits you to prepare the chocolate in a tall *jarro* (pot) and still have plenty of handle by which to spin the *molinillo.* The principle is identical to that of our mechanical milkshake machines, and the result is also the same: a light, frothy beverage that is difficult to resist.

La Tienda — $5.00

Chocolate has been a great stimulator of the imagination, as well as the libido, for a long time. In one of her letters, the Marquise de Sévigné (1626–1696) describes another in a long list of chocolate-wrought miracles: "The marquise de Coëtlogon took too much chocolate, being pregnant last year, that she was brought to bed of a little boy who was as black as the devil."

An Irreverent and Thoroughly Incomplete Social History of Almost Everything *by Frank Muir. Stein & Day, 1976.*

Mate Gourd — C:93

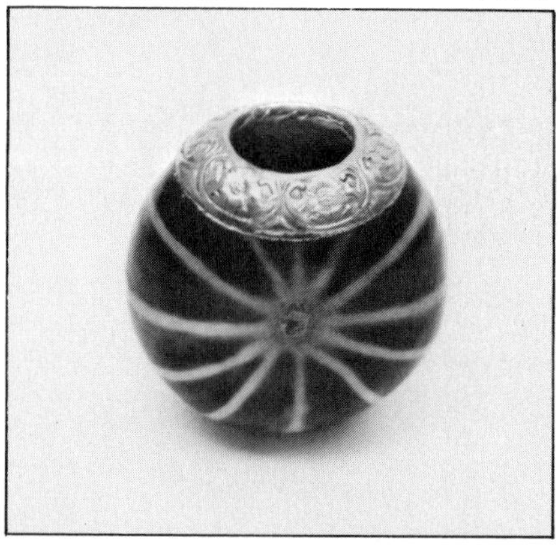

If any beverage rivals coffee in Latin America it is *yerba mate,* a tea-like brew made from the dried leaves of a shrub of the *Ilex,* or holly, genus. Since ancient times, long before the arrival of the white man, South American Indians have made a drink from these plants, which grow wild along the banks of the Paraguay River. Today, millions of Argentines, Uruguayans, Chileans, Brazilians and, of course, Paraguayans, of every ethnic background and every walk of life, quaff the caffeine-loaded potion daily and constantly. *Mate,* as it is commonly called, is made by pouring about 2 teaspoons of the crushed leaves—the *yerba*—into a special fist-sized gourd cup—the *mate.* The gourd is filled with hot, not boiling, water, and is allowed to steep for a bit, after which the infusion is slowly sipped through a special metal or wooden straw-like tube called a *bombilla.* The elegant, 3″-high Uruguayan *mate* cup shown here is a classic example of these traditionally hand-decorated utensils. The hollowed-out and dried gourd has a 1″-wide opening at one end with a silvery metal rim, embossed with delicate curlicues and gold-tinted flowers. Inside, the gourd still bears rough traces of the dried pulp; outside, the seashell-like, tortoise-colored vegetable is adorned with natural blond markings resembling spokes. Because the gourd does not have a flat bottom, it is designed to be kept cupped in the palm of the hand, and custom dictates that the gourd be passed from person to person as long as the supply lasts, a ritualistic practice not unlike smoking an Indian peace pipe.

Casa Moneo — $3.98

Bombilla — C:94

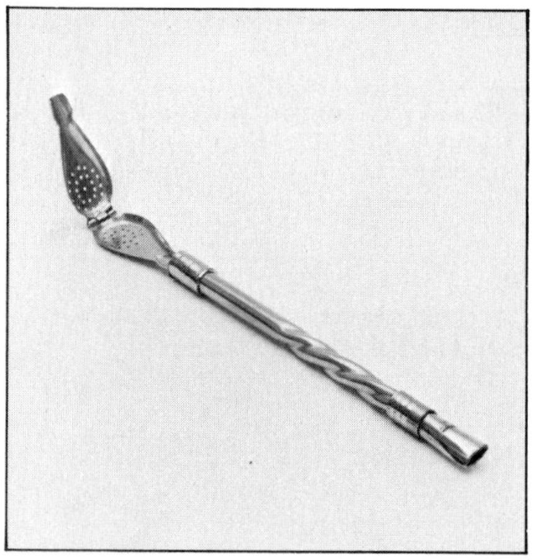

This tubular device, called a *bombilla,* is an integral element in the uniquely South American rite of drinking *yerba mate* (South American holly tea), passionately consumed at all hours, and by nearly everyone in the southern part of the continent. These straw-like implements, employed to suck out the beverage from the gourd in which it is brewed, are often fashioned entirely of silver; but occasionally, like the Bolivian *bombilla,* the implements for daily use are made of metal alloys. This classic, 8″-long *bombilla*'s hollow stem is charmingly twisted at the top for a decorative, braided effect. And as always, the "straw" comes equipped with a flat, spoon-shaped strainer, perforated with tiny holes, at the bottom end. An oval-shaped, copper-covered mouth-piece is provided at the top end. The strainer, which can be opened for cleaning, sits at the bottom of the *mate* gourd and keeps the crushed leaves from being sipped up the tube. Aficionados collect *bombilla* and *mate* gourd sets, particularly antique ones that are sometimes embellished with pure gold. *Mate* etiquette dictates that the gourd is passed around from hand to hand as each member of the crowd takes a sip from the *bombilla,* a custom that indicates the conviviality and good will of the *latinos.*

Casa Moneo $5.98

Cloth Coffee Filter C:95

Coffee, whatever its intimate associations with South America, originated in Africa. It made its way to Europe via the Middle East, and finally to the New World in the early 1700s, thanks to a Frenchman who is said to have brought the first seedling to Martinique. Today, coffee has become a major industry, as well as an indispensable element of Latin American society, and is consumed in such quantities by the masses and the elite alike, that caffeine-conscious health mavens would be truly alarmed. Pleasure-loving Latins are unconcerned, and casually imbibe dozens of sugar-laced cups of the strong, heavy infusion as a matter of course nearly every day of their lives. South Americans think that our coffee is second only to dishwater. They use a special drip process, and carefully selected and roasted beans, to make their thick, dark beverage. One of the essential, and traditional, secrets is a conical filter bag—called a *coador* in Brazil or *colador* in other Hispanic lands—like the one shown here. This typically Brazilian coffee filter consists of an 8″-long, 4″-wide flannel drip bag, suspended from a 4″-wide round steel frame, attached to a black-painted wooden handle. Before using the *coador* for the first time, rinse it, and after each use wash it well with hot water and soap. To prepare a perfect cup of South American coffee, first select the appropriate beans—high roast, dark brown ones from Santos, or a fragrant blend from the mountainous, but tropical slopes of Colombia. Then either grind the beans in a coffee mill or pound them in a wooden mortar until they have the consistency of fine powder. Suspend the sock-like filter bag over a container, and add at least 1 tablespoon of pulverized coffee per serving. For each portion, measure out ¾ cup of cold water, then heat it to a point just before the boil. Pour the hot water into the strainer, very, very slowly so that none of the essential oils are lost, and serve the flavorful concoction in the typical, milky-white demitasse cups used all over South America.

H. Roth & Son $1.98

Small Coffee Cup and Saucer C:96

"I have measured out my life with coffeespoons . . . ," Prufrock lamented in T. S. Eliot's poem. In most of Latin America, the same refrain—without the angst—could be echoed by millions of people, rich and poor, young and old, were they to count the myriad cups of coffee habitually downed. Particularly in Brazil, Colombia and Cuba, countless, coffee-crazed *latinos* live their lives surrounded by a never-ending procession of little porcelain cups (called *cafezinhos* in Portuguese, or *cafecitos* in Spanish) like this classic example from Brazil. The sturdy little cup comes equipped with a solid handle for easy holding, and measures only 2¾″ in diameter and 1½″ deep. But dedicated coffee drinkers make up for its diminutive size; they think nothing of downing some 20 or more servings a day of the heavy, dark liquid called *café prêto* (in Rio or São Paulo) or *café tinto* (from the Spanish word for ink) in Bogotá. In Brazil, where coffee drinking is a passion, metal trays laden with these small, rounded cups, sugar bowls filled with special, moist coffee sugar, and steaming pots of freshly-brewed coffee appear everywhere, from beauty parlors and factories to board rooms.

Bloomingdale's $1.50

Coffee.

Two Indian Kitchens

by Madhur Jaffrey

When I was a child growing up in a large, rambling house owned by my grandfather in Delhi, our kitchen was not attached to the main building. It formed part of an annex that was separated from the living quarters by a brick courtyard. This annex was reserved for the various activities that went with the preparation, serving, eating and storing of foods. The rooms here were spacious, the kitchen having, among other things, windows with a view of the Jumna River, access to a fresh-water well, and three fixed stoves plus several portable ones. One stove was the wood-burning, black-iron kind. The second, and most frequently used stove, was made of bricks plastered over with clay. It had ten burners. (We were, after all, a joint family of over forty people!) The third stove, also made of bricks and clay, was designed especially for charcoal grilling and for cooking with extra-large pots. If my father went hunting and wished a wild boar's leg cooked whole, this is where it would be done.

Along one length of the kitchen were open shelves holding pots, pans and other utensils. The pots were generally made of brass—heavy brass on the outside and tin on the inside. Once a month all pots were retinned by an itinerant tinner (*qalayi-wallah*), who came to the house with his hand-operated bellows, charcoal and coils of tin, and then settled down for the day under the shade of a tree. He would dig a small pit, place the lips of his bellows at the bottom of it, and then pile on hot charcoal. Next, he would invert one pot at a time over the fire, heat it (the bellows working furiously), rub the inside with the end of the tin coil, spread the tin around with cotton wool, and finish by immersing the pot in cold water to "set" the tin.

Besides the pots, those kitchen shelves also contained iron *karhais* (round-bottomed frying pans) in varying sizes; pock-marked, practically unliftable grinding stones; mortars and pestles made of brass, iron and stone; sets of *chakla* and *belan,* the former a round pastry board with three tiny legs and the latter a wooden rolling pin that matched it in color and detail; various sizes of cast-iron *tavas* (slightly convex griddles); *chimtas* (tongs), for stirring coals and lifting hot *chapatis* (flat breads); *paraats,* large, round brass platters with sides two to three inches high, used for kneading dough; beige-glazed bowls for making fresh yoghurt and for storing fresh mint chutney; *mutkas,* rounded terra-cotta pots for making water pickles; *surahis,* large, intricately patterned, terra-cotta jars for storing and cooling water; skewers about a third-of-an-inch thick for making ground-meat *seekh-kababs; kalchis,* round slotted spoons used for lifting fried foods and tiny dumplings; dippers; ladles; graters; slicers; sieves; knives; and cleavers.

Near the main stove sat a rectangular spice box. It was made of wood and contained about twenty compartments, all covered by a single lid. Large quantities of whole spices were kept in the storeroom adjacent to the kitchen; but, daily, small quantities of the same spices, both whole and freshly ground, were put into the spice box for immediate consumption.

The storeroom was lined on three sides with shelves. One side had nothing but rows of large, glazed crocks containing my grandmother's pickles and chutneys. The other shelves had tightly lidded jars of whole

Cinnamon.

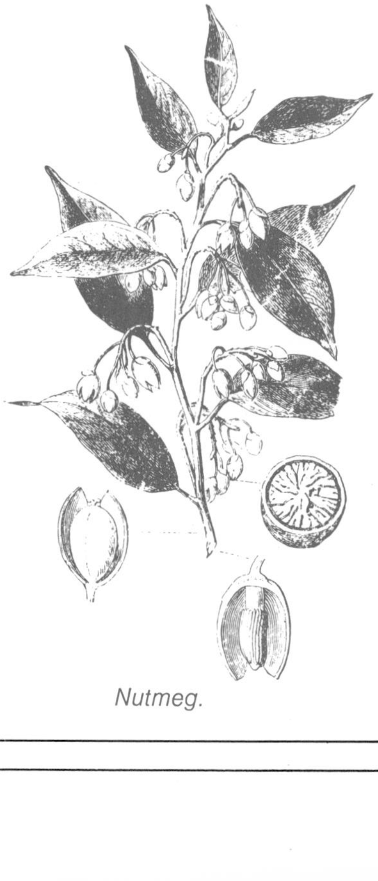

Nutmeg.

Black pepper.

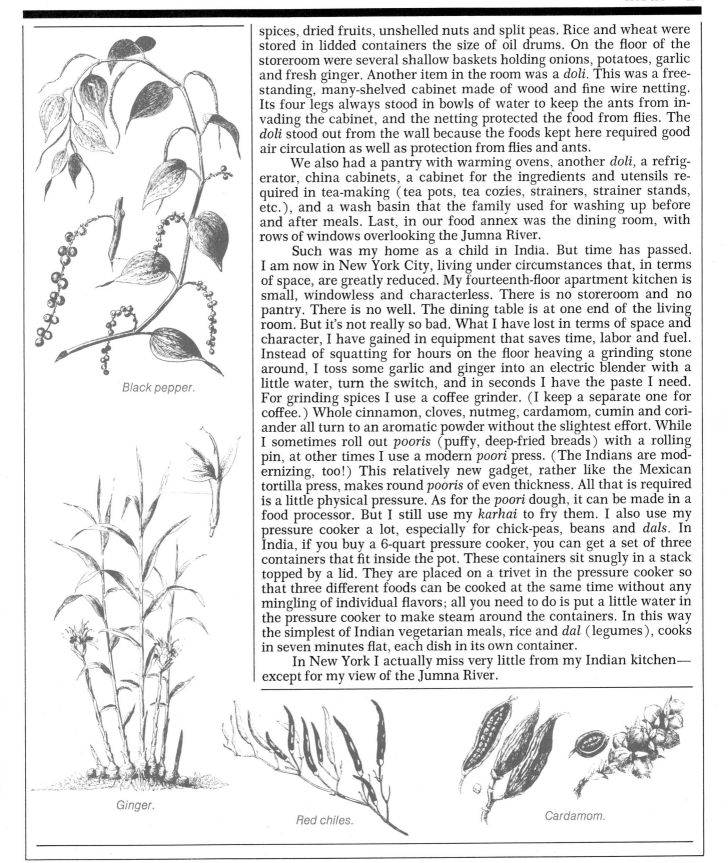

spices, dried fruits, unshelled nuts and split peas. Rice and wheat were stored in lidded containers the size of oil drums. On the floor of the storeroom were several shallow baskets holding onions, potatoes, garlic and fresh ginger. Another item in the room was a *doli.* This was a free-standing, many-shelved cabinet made of wood and fine wire netting. Its four legs always stood in bowls of water to keep the ants from invading the cabinet, and the netting protected the food from flies. The *doli* stood out from the wall because the foods kept here required good air circulation as well as protection from flies and ants.

We also had a pantry with warming ovens, another *doli,* a refrigerator, china cabinets, a cabinet for the ingredients and utensils required in tea-making (tea pots, tea cozies, strainers, strainer stands, etc.), and a wash basin that the family used for washing up before and after meals. Last, in our food annex was the dining room, with rows of windows overlooking the Jumna River.

Such was my home as a child in India. But time has passed. I am now in New York City, living under circumstances that, in terms of space, are greatly reduced. My fourteenth-floor apartment kitchen is small, windowless and characterless. There is no storeroom and no pantry. There is no well. The dining table is at one end of the living room. But it's not really so bad. What I have lost in terms of space and character, I have gained in equipment that saves time, labor and fuel. Instead of squatting for hours on the floor heaving a grinding stone around, I toss some garlic and ginger into an electric blender with a little water, turn the switch, and in seconds I have the paste I need. For grinding spices I use a coffee grinder. (I keep a separate one for coffee.) Whole cinnamon, cloves, nutmeg, cardamom, cumin and coriander all turn to an aromatic powder without the slightest effort. While I sometimes roll out *pooris* (puffy, deep-fried breads) with a rolling pin, at other times I use a modern *poori* press. (The Indians are modernizing, too!) This relatively new gadget, rather like the Mexican tortilla press, makes round *pooris* of even thickness. All that is required is a little physical pressure. As for the *poori* dough, it can be made in a food processor. But I still use my *karhai* to fry them. I also use my pressure cooker a lot, especially for chick-peas, beans and *dals.* In India, if you buy a 6-quart pressure cooker, you can get a set of three containers that fit inside the pot. These containers sit snugly in a stack topped by a lid. They are placed on a trivet in the pressure cooker so that three different foods can be cooked at the same time without any mingling of individual flavors; all you need to do is put a little water in the pressure cooker to make steam around the containers. In this way the simplest of Indian vegetarian meals, rice and *dal* (legumes), cooks in seven minutes flat, each dish in its own container.

In New York I actually miss very little from my Indian kitchen—except for my view of the Jumna River.

Ginger.

Red chiles.

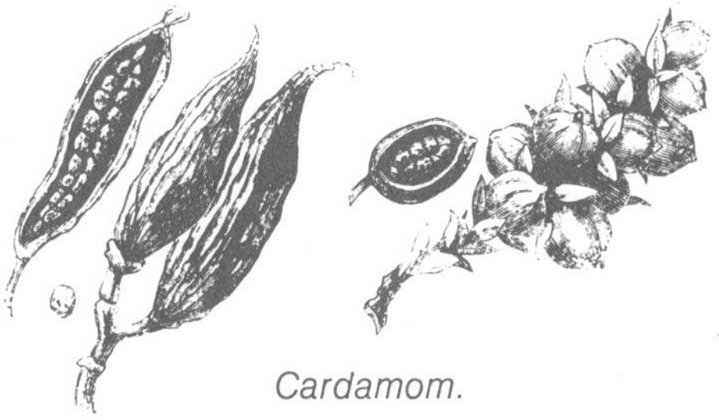

Cardamom.

The Cuisine of India

Indians will tell you they have no national cuisine, since the food varies greatly from district to district; but that is rather like hearing the members of a red-haired, blue-eyed family tell you that they don't look alike *at all*. They see only the differences between themselves, while the outsider sees the similarities. For a country that contains such startling multiplicity—Hindus, Christians, Moslems, vegetarians, meat-eaters—there is, nonetheless, a readily perceived common culture. And although it is true that northern Indians, influenced by Moslem invaders, generally eat meat and breads, cook with *ghee* (clarified butter) and drink tea, while southern Indians are vegetarian rice-eaters who cook with oils and drink coffee, even those generalizations break down when you examine specific families; and you are left with the flavor not of their differences, but of their similarities.

The great unifying factor in Indian cooking is its use of spices. Western cooking takes its character from the quality of the raw ingredients; the seasonings are incidental to the basic content of the dish. In India, on the other hand, the essence and character of a dish derives primarily from the particular blend of spices (*masala*) in which the shrimp, vegetables or lentils are cooked. In that land, where famine is not uncommon, over two million acres of precious farmland are devoted to the production of spices. Pragmatic westerners would plant wheat instead; that the Indians do not, gives us some idea of the status of spices in their cuisine.

But by "spice," we don't mean curry—that imprecise, portmanteau word which tries to describe both mixture of flavors and a whole method of cooking. No one can determine the origin of the word: it may come from *kari*, a Tamil word for "sauce," or else from *karhi*, a northern Indian dish, or perhaps from the small green *kari* leaf, used as a seasoning. Whatever its origin, it received its stamp of legitimacy from the British, after which it spread to the rest of the world.

If there is no such thing as curry, then what is curry powder? There's no pretending that those depressing tins full of commercial blends of common Indian spices—mixtures that include cumin, turmeric, peppers, coriander and fenugreek—don't exist, becoming stale and flavorless on the kitchen shelf. Curry powder is used all over the world, but it is not used in India. And that is logical. Putting the same combination of spices in every dish would make everything taste the same. It would be as though we packaged a mix that contained a certain proportion of salt, pepper and garlic, and then used it on everything we cooked. Easy and safe, but boring; especially if you have access to an incredible range of spices as the Indians do, and are as inventive as they are.

It's just like their clothing. Westerners feel well-dressed when everyone is wearing the same thing: a glance around the grill of a New York restaurant last week showed that every woman was wearing dark, wintry colors. It's simply a matter of style. But Indians like to combine orange and pink and green, setting off one pattern against the other for visual excitement, and then adding a fistful of jewelry at the end. Again, a matter of style. One is no better than the other, but a people who like to dress with fiery color combinations wouldn't dream of using the same blend of spices on everything they cooked.

The spices of India are as varied—and nearly as abundant—as its people. Each prepared dish requires its own *masala* that is ground or

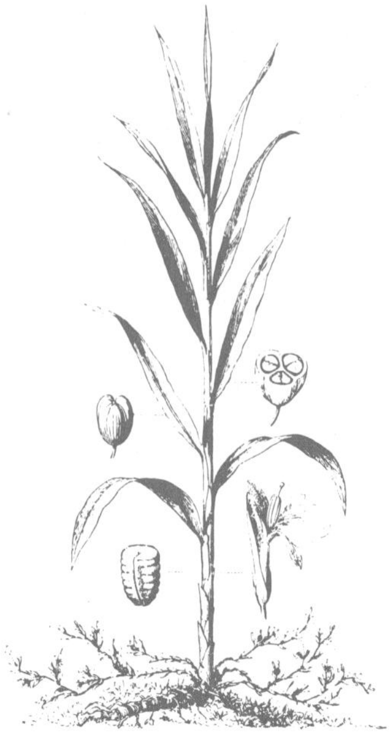

Cardamom.

GARAM MASALA

This is a mixture of several "hot" spices, generally prepared ahead of time in small quantities and used as needed to flavor meats and vegetables. It can be bought in specialty stores, but has a fresher taste if you grind it yourself. To make about a cupful, you will need:

25 cardamom pods (use seeds only)
½ cup whole black peppercorns
⅓ cup whole cumin seeds
¼ cup whole coriander seeds
3 sticks of cinnamon, each about 3 inches long
4–6 whole cloves

Combine all ingredients and grind very fine, using an electric blender or a coffee grinder. (If you want to make your *garam masala* less hot, decrease the amount of black peppercorns and increase the cumin proportionately.) Store in a tightly covered container, away from sunlight and dampness. If carefully stored, this *garam masala* can be kept for a couple of months.

(From AN INVITATION TO INDIAN COOKING, by Madhur Jaffrey. Copyright 1973 by Madhur Jaffrey. Reprinted by permission of Alfred A. Knopf, New York.)

pounded fresh when the cook begins to make the dish. In the north of India, *masalas* are usually dry mixtures of ground or crushed spices; while in the south, they are wet from being mixed with water, lime juice or coconut milk. Sometimes you will hear a *masala* called by the name of its dominant flavor: thus, a cumin *masala* or a ginger *masala*.

The technique of combining spices is the great secret of Indian cooking. You can't always add spice to a pot all at once. Suppose you are cooking a dish of cauliflower or lentils. You not only have to know *what* spices to use, but whether the spices are to be used whole or pulverized, when to add each one to the pot, and how long each one should be cooked. Cumin can be roasted much more quickly than cardamom, for example. Indian recipes are full of directions that say such things as "cook until the red peppers darken" and "fry until the mustard seeds pop." And no matter what spices are used, they must not overpower a dish. Clearly, this is an area of technique that is totally new to the American cook.

What should you do? First buy a very good Indian cookbook. Then follow the directions in it precisely, and try not to substitute one spice for another. Most of the spices common in Indian food are available right in your supermarket if you live in a fairly cosmopolitan area, and by mail order if you don't. The purist will tell you that they are bound to be stale from sitting on the supermarket spice rack. He may be right by Indian standards; but we, unaccustomed to such delights, are not likely to detect the loss of full pungency. Just make sure, when possible, to buy spices whole and grind them yourself. Some *masalas* can then be stored for several months in an airtight container kept in a dark, cool and dry place. Once you make a true *masala*, you are likely to find that the heady aroma of freshly ground spices will make you a lifelong convert to Indian cooking.

Mortar and Pestle D:1

Nothing is more important in Indian cooking than freshly ground spices, and the traditional implements for grinding them are a mortar and pestle. In some areas of the country, an upright mortar such as this one is the favored style; in other regions a flat stone tablet and oblong grinding stone are preferred; and often both types are found in the same kitchen. Whatever the shape, a mortar and pestle are so personal and important to an Indian woman that she often takes them with her, as some of her prized possessions, when she is married. This gleaming mortar is worthy of any dowry. Made of a heavy brass alloy incised with decorative lines, the mortar stands 3″ high and is 2¼″ deep. The 6″-long, blunt-ended pestle fits it snugly and is heavy enough to easily crush the *masala,* or spice mixture, for any dish. A 4″-high, 3″-deep mortar and a 7½″-long pestle are also available.

Spice & Sweet Mahal $10.50

Try using your mortar and pestle on a few exotic mixtures. If the following recipe is appealing, remember to wash off the onion before preparing less powerful concoctions.

"The ancient writers affirm that if a man grinds the grain and root of the trapa beipinosa, kasurika, jasmin and liquorice, and an onion, mixes the composition with milk, sugar and ghee, then, after boiling the mixture, drinks it, he will be able to enjoy innumerable women without fatigue or a diminution of his powers."

Classical Hindu Erotology (Kama Sutra of Vatsyayana) *The Olympia Press, 1958.*

"Do you put cayenne into your cream-tarts in India, sir?"

From Vanity Fair *by W. M. Thackeray.*

Cayenne pepper, a plant of the nightshade family (genus Capsicum) *is responsible for the heat of a Vindaloo curry. According to legend, it is best to sow the pepper seeds while in a red-hot rage, or to have a red-headed person do the job for you.*

Spice Box D:2

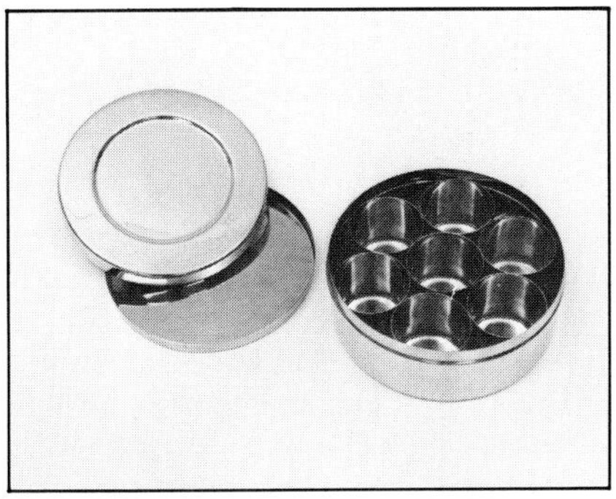

This straightforward, shiny spice box, a *masala dabba,* contradicts everything we might once have expected of Indian design. It could just as easily have been made in Denmark with its pure-and-simple, less-is-more, functional look. But stainless steel is now the popular material for utensils in India. The small circular spice box is 6½″ in diameter and 2¼″ deep. Inside, it snugly holds seven small cups, each 2″ in diameter. To seal the box, a disc of stainless steel with a lip is first placed over the cups, and then a good tight lid is placed over the box. Sealed off from the air in this manner and kept in a cool, dry place, ground spices will stay reasonably pungent for weeks. We think that this is a good way for the American cook to keep under one roof many of the special spices

Continued from preceding page

needed for Indian cooking, such as turmeric, coriander, cumin, fennel, cardamom, mustard seed and fenugreek.

Spice & Sweet Mahal $10.50

Spice box.

MOGLAI CHICKEN CURRY

3 cloves garlic, crushed
½ teaspoon grated fresh ginger or ¼ teaspoon ground ginger
3-pound fryer, disjointed, and skinned
3 tablespoons shortening or vegetable oil
2 onions, chopped
1 cup yogurt
¼ teaspoon ground cloves
6 peppercorns, crushed
¼ teaspoon ground cinnamon
½ teaspoon ground turmeric
1 tablespoon ground coriander
1 teaspoon ground cumin
½ teaspoon crushed red pepper flakes, or 1 teaspoon paprika
1 cup boiling water
Salt to taste
3 tablespoons parsley

Combine garlic and ginger, and rub the mixture into the chicken pieces which have been pricked all over with a fork. Set aside for 1 hour.

Heat 2 tablespoons of the shortening or vegetable oil, add onions, and fry until light brown. Add yogurt, cloves, peppercorns, and cinnamon. Stir, and simmer on low heat for 5 minutes. Add chicken, mixing well to coat each piece, and cook for 5 minutes more. Remove from heat and set aside.

Combine turmeric, coriander, cumin, and crushed red pepper flakes or paprika with enough water to make a paste. Heat the remaining 1 tablespoon shortening or oil in a large pan, and fry the spice paste for 3 to 4 minutes, sprinkling with water occasionally to prevent burning.

Add the chicken-yogurt mixture, boiling water, and salt to taste. Cover, and cook on low heat until chicken is tender (about 20 minutes). Remove the chicken and gravy to a serving dish, sprinkle with parsley, and serve with rice.

Serves 4.

(From THE ART OF INDIAN COOKING, by Monica Dutt. Copyright 1972 by Bantam Books, Inc. Reprinted by permission of Bantam Books, Inc., New York.)

Betel Nut Slicer D:3

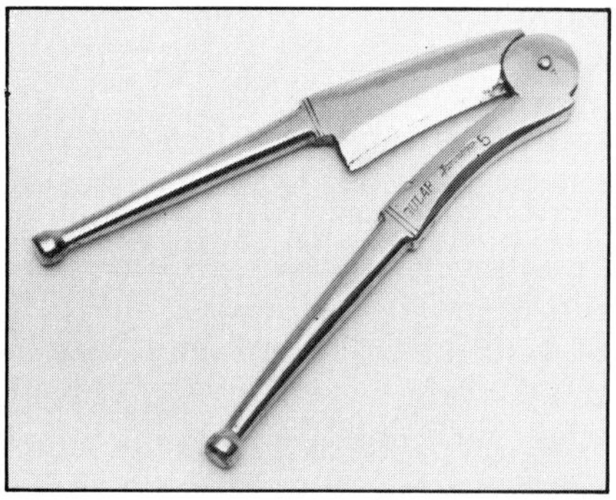

Betel nuts are hard and brown and woody. If you chewed one, your lips and teeth would turn dark red (remember Bloody Mary?), but your mouth would be refreshed with a cool, clean taste. In India, betel nuts are one of the common ingredients in *paan,* a widely popular after-dinner or between-meal chew made of a betel leaf wrapped around a mixture of exotic ingredients. One well-known combination includes sliced betel nuts, a paste of lime and water, coconut and cardamom. Both in India and here you can buy the nuts already sliced, but if you should find yourself confronted with a whole betel nut, a slicer like this one is ideal. It is made of two gently-curved pieces of nickel-plated steel tapered into handles at one end and joined by a pin at the other. Near the pin, the lower part of the cutter has a blunt, slightly notched surface to hold the nut, while the upper part is shaped into a curved 2″-long blade that slices down through the nut when the handles are pressed together.

Foods of India $2.25

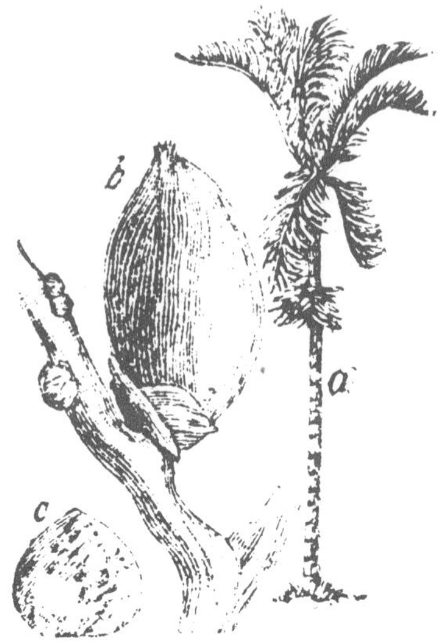

Betel nut.

Having used your betel-nut cutter, you might enclose the bits of nut in a betel leaf (paan) *with appropriate flavorings and serve it at the proper moment. The following is merely a guide as to what might be considered a "proper moment." Correct usage varies.*

"At the end . . . (lovers should) *part and modestly, without looking at each other, go separately to their toilet. Afterwards, they should sit together and enjoy their feeling of well-being. They should share a 'paan' and the citizen should annoint with some pure extract of sandalwood or other such perfume the body of his beloved. He should put his left arm around her and make her drink water out of a cup which he holds in his right hand. They should eat delicately flavored sweetmeats and drink cool and refreshing juices, soup, gruel, meat extract, sherbets, mango juice, or lime juice mixed with some essence that is popular in the land and is known to be sweet, agreeable and pure. The lovers can also sit on the terrace of the mansion and converse softly in the clear bright moonlight."*

Classical Hindu Erotology (Kama Sutra of Vatsyayana) *The Olympia Press, 1958.*

Vegetable or Fruit Slicer D:4

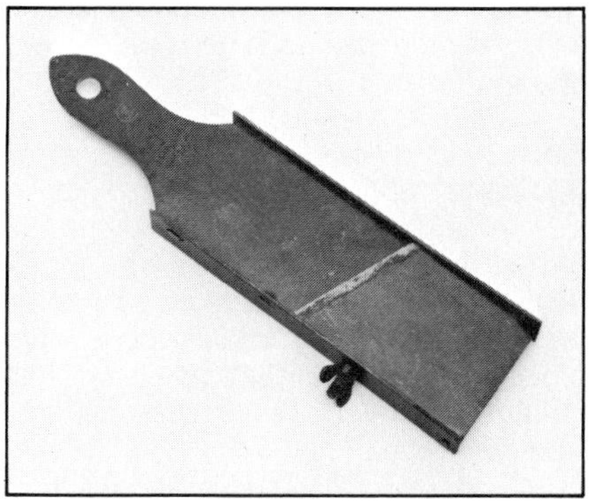

Here is one of those universal devices, an ideally designed implement that turns up in similar form in many parts of the world. This slicer is perhaps an adaptation of its western counterpart, but that does not detract from its utility. Made of steel with a protective rust-proof coating, the foot-long slicer is sturdy enough to quickly cut squashes, plantains, or any other firm vegetables or fruits. The cutting surface is made of two sections of 3″-wide steel, joined along the sides by ¾″-wide steel strips. The longest section is stationary and has a handle with a hole by which the implement may be hung on a wall. The second section slightly overlaps the first with a sharp cutting edge, and, when the nut on one side is loosened, it can be adjusted up or down to vary the thickness of slices. Simply pass any food to be sliced back and forth rapidly over the blade.

Kalpana **$3.00**

Vegetable Grater D:5

Surely this grater resembles one you already have in your kitchen, except for its legs. Because Indian women work while sitting or squatting on the floor, many implements in the Indian kitchen are made to stand off the ground. But there is no reason why this implement will not perform just as well on a counter. After use, if shelf space is a problem as it often is in India, the grater may be hung by its loop on a wall. Well-made, in shiny stainless steel, the grater has raised tubular projections all over the top, and it is easy to clean. It measures less than 6″ long and is 4″ wide and 2¼″ high. A larger version—7″ long, 5¼″ wide and 2″ high—is also available.

Spice & Sweet Mahal **$3.95**

Oval Stainless Grater D:6

In India, graters are made to stand parallel to the ground or floor where women do all their food preparation. Before use, a grater is customarily placed on a *thali* (tray) to catch the cut food and its juices. Extremely well-made, of sturdy stainless steel, this oval grater is 10″ long, 7½″ wide and stands 1″ high. It is shaped like a gratin dish that has been carefully perforated with holes of two different sizes: large ones for coarse grating and small ones with raised, rough edges for fine grating. All the cutting edges are sharp, particularly those around the small holes, which are a real hazard for nails and knuckles. The outside edges of the grater are smoothly and tightly rolled, and a loop has been welded to one end so the utensil can be hung on a wall. This grater also comes in a slightly smaller size, only 8″ long by 6″ wide.

Spice & Sweet Mahal **$6.50**

According to the Kama Sutra of Vatsyayana *an ancient Indian sex manual, more or less, a woman worth any consideration whatsoever should be versed in sixty-four arts, among which we find: "Tattooing; the art of cooking; the preparation of sherbets, fruit juices and alcoholic drinks with the appropriate essences and colouring; the art of bed-making and arranging carpets and cushions in the most comfortable way; how to play musical water bowls; the drainage and storage of water in aqueducts, cisterns and reservoirs; the solution of riddles, puzzles, conundrums and enigmatic questions; the study of phrases difficult to pronounce; chemistry and mineralology; gardening —the art of curing illness with herbs and plants, and a detailed knowledge of how to grow and tend these herbs; the art of teaching parrots how to talk; the art of disguising or changing the appearance of people; the science of war, arms and armies." And that's just for starters.*

Brass Turtle Grater D:7

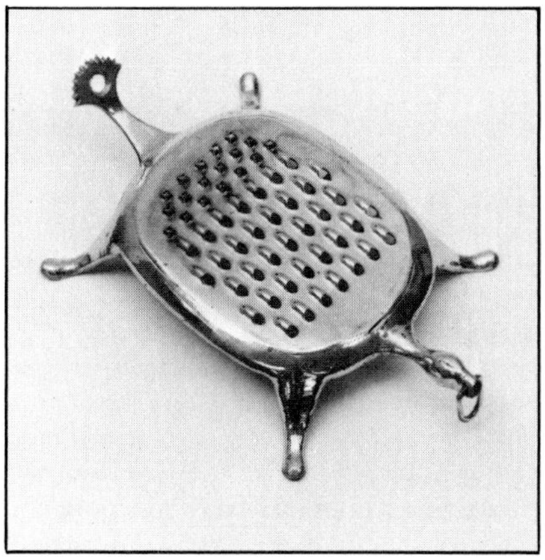

Functionally, this grater may not be as practical as any you've ever seen, but it is certainly the most charming. Someone, in a flight of fancy, decided to make it in the shape of a turtle. Actually, turtle-shaped graters are traditional in India. The most elegant one we've seen was an antique of heavy brass with sharpened, raised ridges protruding in a pattern all over the turtle's back. This version of lighter-weight brass has a flat back, and the turtle's mouth holds a loop by which the grater can be hung. The turtle's amusing, albeit zoologically inaccurate, tail is outlined with sharp projections that are used for grating coconut. Unfortunately, the tail is too small to be really effective for a large amount of

Continued from preceding page

coconut. The cutting surface, 7″ by 5½″, is divided into two different grating areas. The largest is perforated with a raised cutting edge to one side of each hole. Behind it is a smaller area broken by closely-spaced, faceted projections for finer work. From head to tail this snappy turtle measures 11″ long, and it stands 1¼″ high.

India Nepal **$15.00**

Rotating Coconut Grater D:8

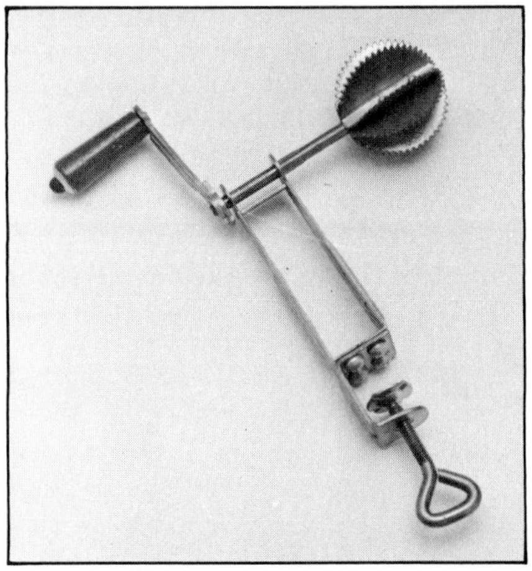

Coconut is eaten primarily in the south and along the west coast of India. And, as might be expected, the Indians have cleverly devised more than one way to grate its delectable meat. This rotating grater is one of them. It's a tin-plated device that is easily clamped onto the edge of a counter or table. Two metal rods extend upward, 4″ from the clamp, to support a strong metal bar with a wooden handle at one end, and a round, jagged head—shaped something like the interior membranes of an orange—at the other. A substantial amount of coconut can be grated fairly quickly by holding a large piece of the meat (in its shell) against the rough edges of the grater and moving the coconut about while turning the handle. If you have not discovered an easy way to open a coconut, try this method adeptly demonstrated to us by an Indian friend. You may first puncture the eyes of the coconut and drain out the liquid, if you like. Or simply catch the liquid in a dish when you crack open the coconut. Just make sure to always taste it. If the liquid is rancid the quality of the coconut meat is suspect. To crack the shell, take a heavy, sharp implement such as the claw end of a hammer and tap the coconut around its equator. Since this is its weakest point, the coconut should split easily apart.

Spice & Sweet Mahal **$1.99**

Coconut palm.

FRESH COCONUT CHUTNEY

1 cup fairly well-packed, grated fresh coconut
½ cup fairly well-packed, chopped Chinese parsley (coriander greens or cilantro)
1–2 fresh hot green chilies (use as desired)
A piece of fresh ginger, about ½-inch cube, peeled and chopped
1 clove garlic, peeled and chopped
6 tablespoons plain yogurt
½ teaspoon salt
1 teaspoon lemon juice
1 tablespoon vegetable oil
⅛ teaspoon *urad dal* (the hulled, split variety) grains
¼ teaspoon whole black mustard seeds

Put the coconut, parsley, green chilies, ginger, and garlic, along with 5 tablespoons of water, into the container of an electric blender. Blend at high speed until you have a smooth paste, stopping occasionally to push down the ingredients.

Pour contents of blender into a bowl. Add yogurt, salt, and lemon juice. Mix well.

In a 4–6-inch skillet, heat the oil. When very hot, put in the *dal* grains and mustard seeds. As soon as the *dal* darkens and the mustard seeds pop, pour contents of skillet into bowl with chutney. Mix well. Cover and chill until ready for use.

To serve: This South Indian chutney goes well with vegetable *pakoris.* It is also very good as a relish with most meals.

(From AN INVITATION TO INDIAN COOKING, by Madhur Jaffrey. Copyright 1973 by Madhur Jaffrey. Reprinted by permission of Alfred A. Knopf, New York.)

Pastry Cutter D:9

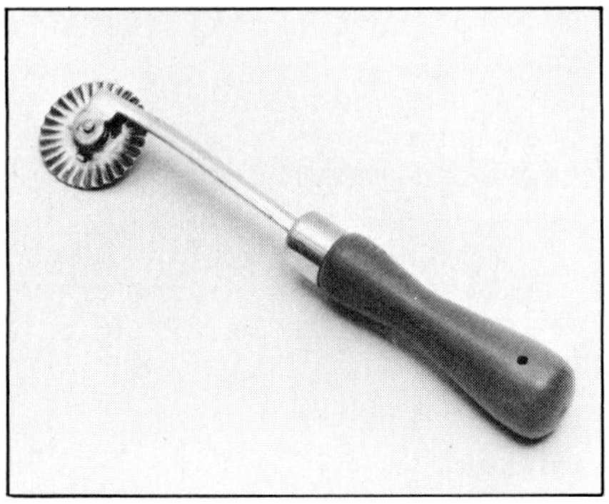

Here is a circular cutter that looks as if it were intended for cutting ravioli, and most likely it is an adaptation of a western utensil. The cutter is worked in the same fashion as a ravioli cutter, by grasping the handle and pulling or pushing the wheel across rolled-out dough. Indians use it for making sweet- or savory-filled turnovers. The cutter is 7″ long and has a tomato-red wooden handle and a fluted wheel that is 1¼″ in diameter.

Kalpana **$2.00**

Among the diversions appropriate for a man of breeding in Ancient India, we find the following: "Spending the night playing dice; Walking in the moonlight;

Mughal, early 17th century. "Women Eating on a Balcony" (from The Metropolitan Museum of Art).

Continued from preceding page

Celebrating a spring festival; Picking mango buds and fruit; Eating lotus seeds and soft kernel of corn; Holding picnics in the forests when the trees are dressed in their tender new green foliage."

Classical Hindu Erotology (Kama Sutra of Vatsyayana). *The Olympia Press, 1958.*

Rolling Pastry Cutter D:10

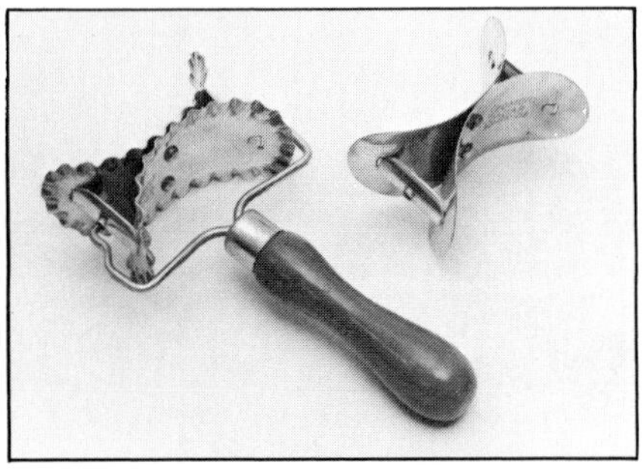

Made in India, but not precisely Indian in heritage, is this rolling pastry cutter with interchangeable blades. It's a familiar device: we find one like it in Italy, where it is used for cutting *agnolotti,* filled, half-moon-shaped pasta. The wooden handle, painted stop-sign red, has two aluminum bars extending out from it. Prongs on the end of the bars hold an ingenious cutter made of two thin metal ovals bent into half moons and fastened together back to back. When run over a piece of dough, the smooth-edged blades cut out a series of perfect 3″ circles. An alternate set of blades makes 3″ circles with fluted edges. Overall, the cutter is 6″ long and is reasonably well-made. In India it might be used to make stuffed savory turnovers or half-moon pastries like *karanjias* that are filled with coconut and sugar.

Kalpana $2.50

The Pervasive Snack

Indians, like Americans, are great eaters of snacks. Hundreds of varieties of these quickly-devoured foods—in all shapes and sizes—are sold in the streets, bazaars and coffee and tea houses all over the country. Many of them are so appetizing and nutritious that a person could easily survive on them, plus one full meal a day. And many Indians do just that, especially during festivals.

Most Indian snack foods are made with vegetables and are wonderfully spiced and deep-fried. True, chick-peas or puffed rice, simply roasted, make tasty tidbits. And steamed *idli* or *dhokla,* lentil-and-rice-flour cakes, eaten with chutneys or vegetable mixtures are great favorites. But deep-fried delectables are far and away the most popular. One of these is *saive,* golden noodle-like curls, made of a chick-pea flour dough, flavored with one or more spices—perhaps anise—that is passed through a special press into a hot oil. Another is *boondi,* tiny dumplings pushed through a perforated spoon into the deep-frying pan. Yet another type of dough puff, *panipuri,* is filled with tamarind water.

No snack is more in demand than *pakoras,* pieces of vegetable, such as eggplant, potato or cauliflower, dipped in spicy chick-pea-flour batter and then fried. They are sold everywhere. So are *samosas,* triangle-shaped pastries with a savory vegetable or meat filling, that are eaten with a chutney or dipped into yoghurt flavored with fresh coriander.

With such nourishing snacks it's no wonder a meal or two might be skipped without detriment to one's health!

Brass Noodle Press D:11

At first glance, this lovely brass object appears to be an exotic grinder or mill of some kind. Actually, it's an Indian noodle press. Indian spiced noodles, or *saive,* are deep-fried and eaten as snacks, usually around 11:00 in the morning or at mid-afternoon. *Saive* made of chick-pea-flour dough are the most popular of all, and they may be flavored with a single spice like anise or caraway seeds, or with a mixture of spices. Once cooked, *saive* can be stored in an air-tight container for up to a month. This *saive*-maker has six parts: a central cylinder, open at both ends; four interchangeable discs—perforated with small holes, medium holes, thin slots and a large, single star—that fit on the bottom of the cylinder; and a flat disc-shaped press attached to a spiral shaft with a top and handle that drives the dough downward inside the cylinder. The unit is 6″ high and 2¾″ in diameter. To make *saive,* drop the disc of your choice into the cylinder, place some dough on top of it and attach the press. Turn the handle while rotating the press slowly over a pan of hot oil. In just a few minutes the golden, curled noodles will be ready to serve.

Spice & Sweet Mahal $6.99

FRITTERS

Pakora

1 cup chick-pea flour
1/8 teaspoon baking powder
Chili powder to taste
1/2 teaspoon ground coriander
1/4 teaspoon ground turmeric
Salt to taste
Vegetable shortening for deep frying
1 small cauliflower, separated in flowerets
1 small eggplant, sliced thin
8 spinach leaves

Place chick-pea flour and baking powder in mixing bowl. Add enough water to make a thick batter. Beat well. Add chili powder, coriander, turmeric, and salt. Beat well. Heat vegetable shortening for deep frying in large skillet. Dip vegetables in batter. Deep-fry golden brown and crisp. Serve immediately. *Yield* 4 to 6 servings.

(*From THE ART OF INDIA'S COOKERY, by William I. Kaufman & Saraswathi Lakshmanan. Reprinted by permission of Doubleday & Company, Inc., New York.*)

Aluminum Noodle Press D:12

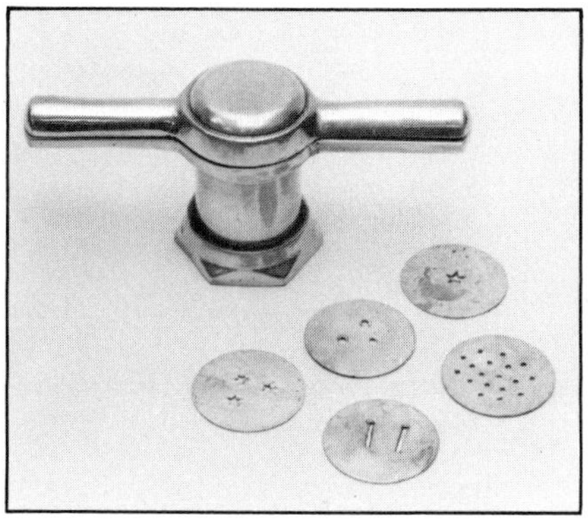

With its simple propeller-like lines, this cast-aluminum *saive*-maker looks, and is, efficient. It is made of two parts. The lower one is a hollow trunk with two half-rounded, 3″-long arms on the top, and a hexagonal base into which one of five perforated discs is set. The upper half of the implement is a 3″-tall solid cylinder, also topped by two half-rounded arms. To make *saive,* or spicy noodles, the dough is placed on top of one of the discs in the base of the implement, and the solid cylinder or press is then inserted into it. By aligning the arms of the *saive*-maker and squeezing them together the dough is forced through the disc and into hot oil. The patterns of the discs are rather crudely cut but they are typical of most *saive*-makers: stars, large holes, small holes, slots and a single star. Aluminum construction makes this implement light and easy to handle as well as to clean.

Annapurna $4.80

CURRIED MEAT TURNOVERS

Samosas

2 tablespoons instant minced onion
2 tablespoons water
2 tablespoons vegetable shortening
1/4 teaspoon garlic powder
1/4 teaspoon ground cinnamon
1/4 teaspoon ground ginger
1/4 teaspoon cayenne
2 teaspoons ground coriander
1/4 cup chopped fresh tomato
1 1/2 cups finely ground lamb or beef
1 1/4 teaspoons salt
1/4 cup water
2 teaspoons fresh lemon juice
Pastry
Egg white, beaten slightly
Vegetable shortening

Soften onion in the 2 tablespoons water. Sauté in shortening. Add spices and stir and cook 1 minute. Add tomato, beef or lamb, and salt. Stir and cook 2 to 3 minutes. Add water and lemon juice and cook until all liquid is absorbed. Turn out onto a plate to cool. Roll pastry very thin on a lightly floured board. Cut into circles with a 2 1/2-inch cooky cutter. Brush edges lightly with slightly beaten egg white. Place a rounded 1/2 teaspoon of the mixture in center of each. Fold over the dough and crimp edges with a fork, being sure they are well sealed. Fry in hot deep vegetable shortening (360° to 375°) until golden brown. Drain on absorbent paper. Serve. *Yield* about 60 turnovers.

PASTRY

2 cups sifted all-purpose flour
1 teaspoon salt
1/4 cup vegetable shortening
7 tablespoons yogurt

Sift flour with salt. Melt vegetable shortening and add to flour. Mix well. Stir in yogurt gradually, working it with hands about 5 minutes. Knead until satiny and smooth. If desired, use your own pastry recipe and bake the puffs in a preheated hot oven (400°) 12 to 15 minutes. *Yield* Pastry for 60 turnovers.

(*From THE ART OF INDIA'S COOKERY, by William I. Kaufman & Saraswathi Lakshmanan. Copyright 1964 by William I. Kaufman and Saraswathi Lakshmanan. Reprinted by permission of Doubleday & Company, Inc., New York.*)

Cinnamon.

"Cinnamon is about the oldest known spice in the world, and comes from the bark of a species of laurel. In America and on the continent of Europe it is often confounded with cassia, which goes by the name of Chinese cinnamon. The true cinnamon is the cinnamon of Ceylon; but it also comes from Madras, Bombay and Java, though of inferior quality. When the Dutch held possession of Ceylon, they were known at times to burn the cinnamon, in order to limit the supply and to keep up the price. But the supply is limited in any case, for though the bark grows again on the cinnamon trees, it takes three years to do so; and a crop which comes but once in three years cannot be considered abundant."

Kettner's Book of the Table. *E. S. Dallas, 1877.*

"Chota Haziree," or Little Breakfast, in India. From a photograph by A. Williamson.

The Basic Breads of India

In southern India, an individual may eat as much as two-thirds of a pound of rice a day; but in northern India few meals are complete without bread. Even when rice is served in the north, bread is always included in greater quantity.

Although Indian breads are varied, they share some basic characteristics. Most of them are unleavened, made with whole wheat flour, and, when first rolled out, are thin, flat and circular in shape—like the Mexican tortilla. Any similarity with the tortilla ends there.

Most common of all are *chapatis,* flat breads made without shortening, baked on a concave griddle (*tava*), and then puffed up over an open flame. *Pooris,* made of a similar whole wheat dough, have the added richness of a little clarified butter or oil and are deep-fried until they puff into golden rounds. Another bread with some shortening added is a *paratha.* This sometimes triangular bread is cooked on a griddle and is traditionally served with yoghurt or a dish of yoghurt mixed with vegetables.

The most famous leavened breads are *naan.* The long, teardrop-shaped *naan* loaves are made with refined flour flavored with yoghurt and black onion seeds. Each loaf is slapped against the inside of a vertical clay oven (*tandoor*) to bake, where it takes on a distinctive flavor from the open fire at the bottom of the oven and the skewered meats cooking beside it. Although made with yeast, *naan* are actually very flat, about ¾″ thick, so they are toothsomely crusty.

The only disadvantage in making these breads is that they are best eaten right from the pan. In India, one of the women in a household is often obliged to cook the bread while other members of her family eat. The true liberators from this onerous task are aluminum foil and the oven, which make the cooking of Indian breads a complete pleasure for every member of the family.

Flour Sifter D:13

Sifting is a multi-purpose activity. It is done in order to aerate flour, to prepare it for accurate measuring, and also to remove impurities or refine it. In India, where whole wheat flour predominates, it is this second, straining function that is paramount. Whole wheat flour is coarser than our white flour and occasionally has husks in it, so Indian cooks will often sift flour two or three times to make it as powdery as possible. This *chalni,* or strainer, of lightweight aluminum has three interchangeable plastic meshes of different gauges and colors, ranging from pink, the coarsest; to blue, medium; and white, the finest. With two meshes in place, the cook can achieve a good double sifting of flour in one procedure, shaking the strainer back and forth and tapping the sides to force it through. Also, the sifter may be used to wash any dried legumes, such as lentils, which are a mainstay of Indian cooking. The sifter is well made, easy to clean and comfortable in the hand. This one is a little over 7″ in diameter and 2″ high, but a larger one, 9″ in diameter, is available, too.

Spice & Sweet Mahal $1.75

Kneading Tray D:14

This deep tray looks like a giant's pie

plate, but, in fact, it is a *paraat* that is used in the preparation of Indian bread dough. When working, the Indian cook sits on the floor with the *paraat* placed in front of her. In it she kneads a mixture of fine whole wheat flour and water to make unleavened bread dough. Kneading is done with fists clenched so most of the work is done with the knuckles. After 10 or 15 minutes the dough is covered with a damp cloth and left to rest until it is patted, rolled, or pressed into shape for cooking. Our handsome *paraat,* made of heavy-gauge plated steel, is a whopping 15¾″ in diameter and 2½″ deep. Its large size makes work easier. Besides, Indians—especially poor ones—eat a lot of bread. It is nothing for an Indian peasant to eat 10 or 12 *chapatis* (flat wheat breads) at a meal. Of course, the rest of the meal would be proportionately diminished.

Kalpana **$22.40**

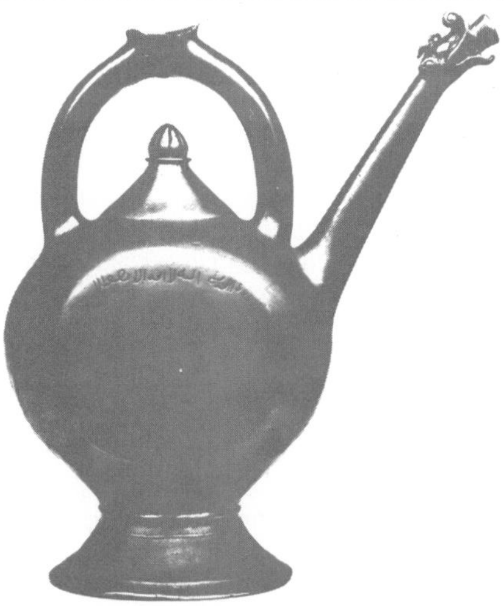

Brass Indian Water Pot (from The Metropolitan Museum of Art).

CHAPATI

Serves 4

This simple bread requires only whole wheat flour and water. It needs to be rolled out very evenly on a floured surface. Indians keep a quantity of plain whole wheat flour on the side and keep dusting the *chapati* with it as they roll. Next, the *chapati* needs to be cooked on a hot griddle. Give the griddle time to heat before you put the first *chapati* on. When both sides of the *chapati* are roasted, it is taken off the griddle and placed on an open fire. This makes it puff up with hot air. A *chimta* or some flat unserrated tongs are essential for the making of the bread. Note: Some whole wheat flour is very coarse. Many Indians prefer to mix it half and half with all-purpose white flour.

1 cup whole wheat (not coarse, stone-ground) flour for dough
About ½ cup finely ground whole wheat flour to keep on the side for dusting

Place the flour in a bowl. Slowly add up to ½ cup water and mix until all the flour adheres and you can knead it. (You will probably need a little less than the ½ cup water.) Now knead it for 7 to 8 minutes. Roll into a ball. Cover with a damp cloth and leave for ½ to 3 hours. (If you wish to leave it longer, cover it with a plastic wrap and refrigerate. It will easily stay 24 hours.)

Dampen hands and knead the dough again. Put the *tava* or cast-iron griddle or skillet on a *medium* flame to heat. Knead dough while the griddle is heating. Divide the dough into 8 balls. Keep balls covered with damp cloth. Flour the rolling surface and keep some dry flour on the side for dusting. Take out one ball. Flatten it. Dip it in the dry flour. Now roll it out evenly into a *chapati* about 5 inches in diameter. You can get it even bigger and thinner if you like. It will stick to the surface as you roll it unless you keep dipping it in the dry flour. Always keep your surface well floured.

The *tava* or griddle should be smoking hot by now. Place the uncooked *chapati* on it. Within half a minute or so bubbles will start rising. Now turn the *chapati* over with the *chimta* or tongs. Let the other side cook for half a minute. Both sides should have light brown spots on them. Lift off *chapati* with the tongs and lay it directly over the medium flame of another burner. (You could use the same burner, but you would have to lift off the *tava* or griddle every time. As a matter of fact, this *is* what most Indians do!) Keep it there a few seconds. It will puff up immediately. Now turn it over and keep the other side over the flame for a few seconds.

Either serve hot immediately, or butter on one side very lightly and place *chapati* on a large sheet of aluminum foil. Fold over the aluminum foil and shut edges firmly. Do all *chapatis* this way. They will stay warm for 20 to 30 minutes if well covered in the foil and kept in a warm place.

To serve: *Chapatis* are eaten with nearly all Indian main dishes.

(From AN INVITATION TO INDIAN COOKING, by Madhur Jaffrey. Copyright 1973 by Madhur Jaffrey. Reprinted by permission of Alfred A. Knopf, New York.)

Rolling Pin D:15

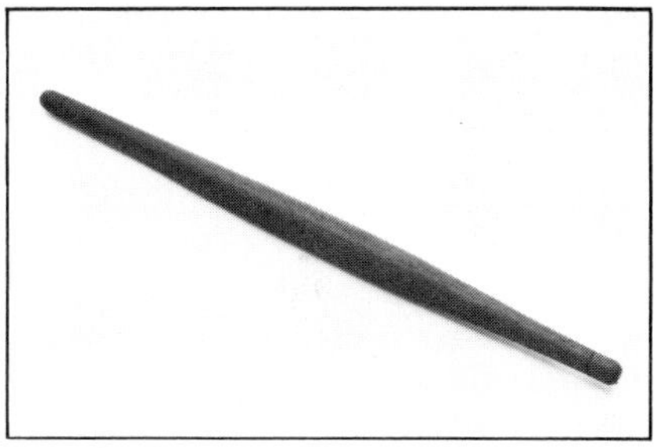

This type of Indian rolling pin, or *belna,* may not be much different from one you own already, except that its size conforms to the typically small Indian rolling board. The narrow, tapered pin is about ⅞″ thick in the center and 15″ long. It is made of heavy, dark, reddish-brown wood and is perfectly suitable for apple pie dough as well as for small *pooris,* deep-fried Indian whole wheat breads that puff when they cook. Many Indian women are so expert at the art of rolling out their flat breads that they can make perfect circles in seconds. We are told that while they roll the pin they also rotate it in a way that speeds their work and makes the dough uniform in thickness and shape.

Spice & Sweet Mahal **$0.65**

Large Rolling Pin D:16

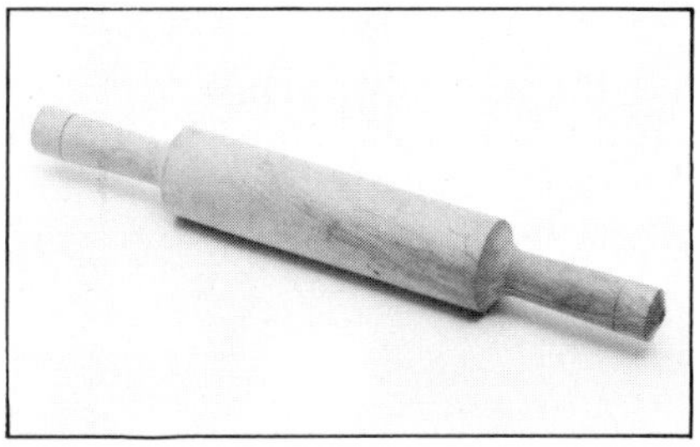

A good rolling pin should be smooth, cleanly designed and well-balanced

Continued from preceding page

like this one. Then half your work has been done before you start to cook. If there is a flaw on the surface or in the balance, your *chapatis* (tortilla-like wheat breads) will be lumpy, or you will have difficulty making them perfect. This implement is made of pale, hardwood in a predictable shape. It looks like an American rolling pin until you notice that it has no ball bearings. The working surface of the pin is 9″ long—short by western standards, but adequate for rolling *chapatis*—and the overall length is about 17″ so that it can be easily grasped beyond the edges of a small Indian rolling board. The rolling pin handles so beautifully, with its voluptuously smooth surface that we feel it is worth far more than its modest price.

Foods of India $1.99

Upon visiting an Indian city in 1537, a Portuguese chronicler, Domingo Paes wrote:

This is the best provided city in the world, it is stocked with provisions such as rice, wheat, grains, Indian-corn, and a certain amount of barley and beans and moong (lentils), pulse, horsegram (channah), and many other seeds which grow in this country and are the food of the people, and there is a large store of this and very cheap. . . . There is much poultry; they give three fowls in the city for a coin worth a vintem, outside the city they give five fowls for a vintem.

In the country there are many partridges . . . as also quails and hares, and all kinds of wild fowl, and other birds which live in the lakes and which look like geese. All these birds and game animals they sell alive and they are very cheap for they give six or eight partridges for a vintem, and of hares they give two and sometimes one. Of other birds they give more than you count, for even of the large ones they give so many that you would hardly pay attention to the little ones they give you, such as doves and pigeons and common birds of the country. . . . The sheep they kill every day are countless, one could not count them, for in every street there are men who will sell you mutton so clean and so fat that it looks like pork; and you also have pigs in some streets of butchers' houses so white and clean that you could never see better in any country; a pig is worth four or five fanams. Then you see the many loads of limes which come in each day, such as those of Povos [near Lisbon] are of no account, and also loads of sweet and sour oranges, and wild brinjals (aubergine) and other garden stuff in such abundance as to stupefy one.

Rolling Board D:17

The legs on this *chakla,* or rolling board, remind us that an Indian cook works sitting on the floor of the kitchen. In an Indian home, many women might sit cross-legged on little square mats, in a large, sunny room or courtyard, gossiping, while they knead and roll out flat wheat breads for the next meal. There might even be three generations of a family working together, shaping perfect circles of dough with the quick action of their rolling pins. This rolling board is made of a thick circle of wood that is 9½″ in diameter; the top surface is smooth and unpainted, but the edges and the squat legs are painted a gay, glossy yellow.

Spice & Sweet Mahal $2.65

Chapati Press D:18

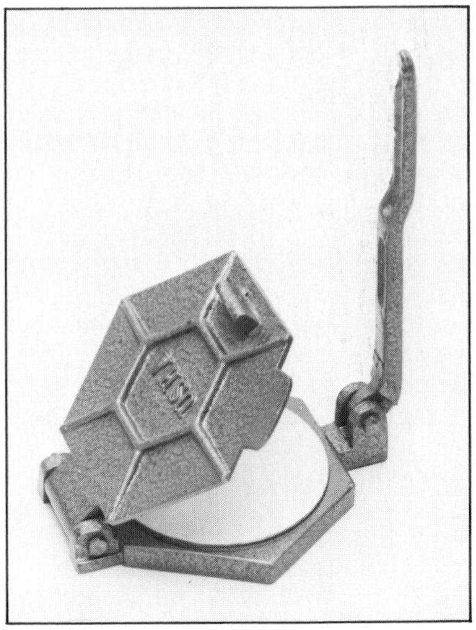

It is not easy to roll thin, evenly shaped *chapatis* or *pooris* out of damp and sticky whole wheat dough. As a matter of fact, if you don't have an Indian grandmother or mother to emulate, a press like this may well be the best means of making proper Indian breads. Even in India, many urban families have taken to using presses for their bread-making. The device strongly resembles the tortilla press, familiar to many westerners, and it works on the same principle. A ball of dough, placed in the center of the press, is quickly and smoothly flattened into a perfect circle when the press is closed over it. This press is made of two hexagonal pieces of enameled cast aluminum that are joined by a large, barrel-shaped hinge. Circles of pale blue plastic, 5″ in diameter, are fastened to the inner surfaces of the press to prevent dough from sticking. With an implement like this in your kitchen you should have no hesitation about making a variety of Indian breads.

Foods of India $8.99

YOGURT WITH TINY DUMPLINGS

Serves 6–8

The only yogurt relish served at all our family wedding banquets was this one. Tiny little droplets of a chickpea flour paste are dropped into deep fat and fried. They are then softened in warm water. Finally they are combined with yogurt and spices, freshly roasted cumin being perhaps the most important ingredient used. You can make this relish as hot as you like. When I make it in America, I put in just a touch of cayenne pepper. But at those wedding banquets in India, it was a cool scorcher!

In India the dumplings are made by pushing the batter through the holes of a slotted spoon into the hot oil. The Indian slotted spoons have round holes about 1/8 inch wide. If you can find a spoon like that, use it. If you have a colander with holes this size, it could work as well.

FOR THE DUMPLINGS
4 heaping tablespoons chickpea flour
1/4 teaspoon baking powder
1/4 teaspoon salt
1/4 teaspoon ground cumin seeds
Vegetable oil for deep frying, enough to have 1 inch in the skillet

FOR THE YOGURT
24 ounces (3 containers) plain yogurt
1 1/2 teaspoons salt
1/8–1/4 teaspoon freshly ground black pepper
1 teaspoon freshly roasted, ground cumin seeds
1/8–1/4 teaspoon cayenne pepper (optional)
1/8 teaspoon paprika

Place the chickpea flour and the baking powder in a bowl. Add a little water at a time (about 1/3 cup altogether) and mix to a thick, smooth paste, stiff enough to stand in tiny peaks. Use a wooden spoon or your fingers to do this. Add 1/4 teaspoon salt and 1/4 teaspoon cumin and mix well. Set aside.

In an 8–10-inch skillet, heat the vegetable oil over medium heat. Get your slotted spoon or colander, whichever you are going to use. When the oil is hot, place a tablespoon of batter on the slotted spoon or the colander and push it through with the back of a clean wooden spoon. Little droplets will fall into the oil. They should cook slowly—turning crisp, but staying a golden yellow; they should not turn brown. This will take about 5 minutes. Adjust flame if necessary. As each batch gets done, remove it with a slotted spoon and dump it in a bowl filled with warm water. Continue until all the paste is used up. Let dumplings soak in water for 30 minutes.

Now get the yogurt ready. In a bowl, mix the yogurt well. Then add the salt, black pepper, roasted cumin, and cayenne, reserving a pinch of the cumin for garnishing later. Cover and refrigerate the yogurt until almost ready to serve.

Just before serving, take out the dumplings, a handful at a time. Lay your other palm over them and gently squeeze out excess water. Do not break them. Put them in serving bowl. Pour yogurt over them and mix well.

Garnish by sprinkling paprika and the pinch of roasted cumin over the top.

To serve: This yogurt dish goes very well with nearly all lamb and pork dishes.

(From AN INVITATION TO INDIAN COOKING, by Madhur Jaffrey. Copyright 1973 by Madhur Jaffrey. Reprinted by permission of Alfred A. Knopf, New York.)

Small Perforated Spoon D:19

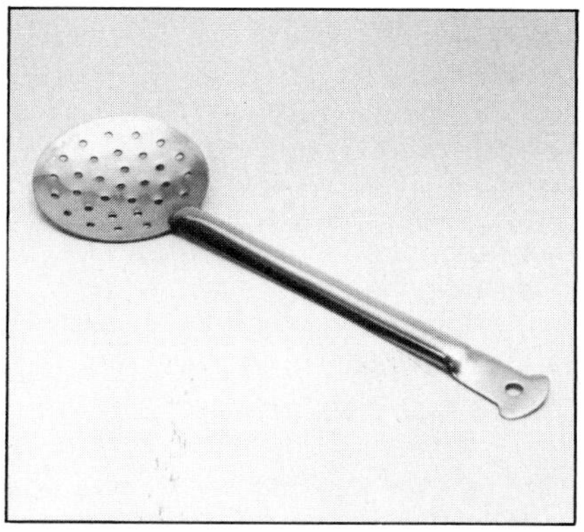

This shiny paddle, a *tambakhash,* is the equivalent of a western skimmer or slotted spoon, and it is particularly useful for deep-frying. When *pooris* (fried, whole wheat breads) are cooking away briskly in a pan of boiling oil, it is this implement that the cook uses to push them down and turn them over so that the dough will be thoroughly cooked. Within a minute or two, the bread puffs evenly and turns golden in color. Then it is lifted out of the pan with this spoon, so the excess fat can drain back into the pan through its holes. The 10″-long *tambakhash* is well made of shining stainless steel, and it has a hole in the handle so it may be hung out of the way.

Spice & Sweet Mahal $1.65

Skimmer D:20

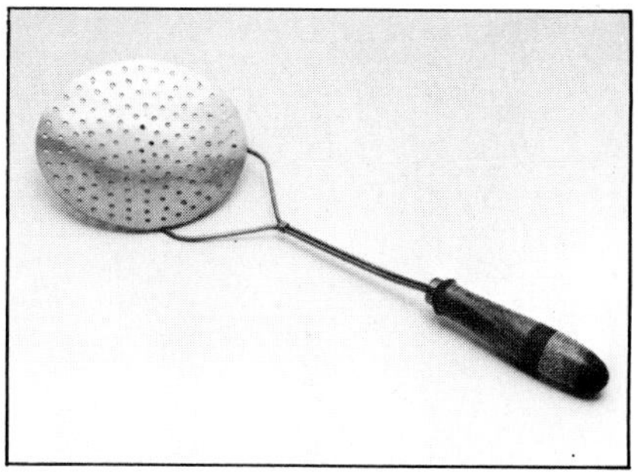

This elegant skimmer is large enough to fish a number of *pakoras* (deep-fried vegetable savories) or *samosas* (deep-fried pastries with meat or vegetable fillings) out of hot oil. It is also large enough, about 7″ in diameter, to set across the top of your *karhai* (deep-frying pan) to make small *boondi* (dumplings). One kind of *boondi* is made of a chick-pea-flour paste flavored with cumin. The paste is forced through small holes, usually those of a perforated spoon or strainer, into hot oil to make tiny dumplings that are then served with cumin-and-pepper-flavored yoghurt. Of course, this strainer is also the perfect utensil to use for removing the cooked *boondi* from the pan. It is almost two feet long, a safe distance to be from hot oil, and made of sturdy, stainless steel with a painted wood handle.

Spice & Sweet Mahal $4.55

Ladle D:21

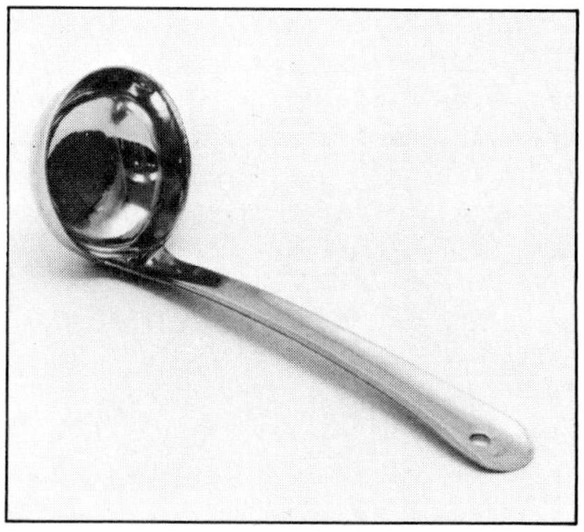

Here is a ladle that is perfect for serving *dals,* cooked legume mixtures that are

Continued from preceding page

eaten with bread or rice daily throughout India. A *dal* is literally a legume, but it might just as well mean "life" to millions of Indians. When you realize that more than 80 per cent of India's population is vegetarian, and that legumes—lentils, chick-peas, kidney beans and split peas, among others—provide their main source of protein, you will understand why *dals* play such an important part in their cuisine. Indians grow more than 40 varieties of *dal* that are used to make almost every type of dish from breads and main courses to snacks and desserts. *Dals* may be ground into flour, or cooked along with other vegetables and spices, or, in the richest and poorest home alike, simmered slowly in plain water with spices. The *dal* mixture served with rice or bread can be very thick or as thin as soup. Our small stainless-steel ladle, ideal for dishing out *dals,* is a fraction under 8″ long and its bowl is 2½″ across. The handle is pierced with a hole so the ladle may be hung on a wall.

Spice & Sweet Mahal $2.75

The lentil, a leguminous plant of considerable venerability, appears in many soups and purées (dal(s)) *which are a mainstay in the Indian household. Or they may be combined with rice and fermented for the steamed* idli *or the pan-baked* dosa. *An estimated sixty vegetables are used in the preparation of Indian meals. So well-loved are they that a Hindu proverb declares: "Rice is good, but lentils are my life."*

Lentil.

"Rice Boiled in the Indian Fashion

Wash it well in cold water two or three times, then put it loose into a saucepan with a large quantity of boiling water: boil it very fast for twenty minutes. Strain through a colander, until all the water is gone, then lightly shake the rice into a hot dish, let it dry for a few minutes before the fire, and serve.
N.B. Many English cooks, after straining the rice, replace it in the saucepan, and either cover it with the lid or a cloth, like potatoes, and set it on the hob to dry; but the method which I give, from Indian experience, will be found the best, as it makes the rice 'rocky,' which is the great point of 'native' cookery. 'Sticky rice, beat wife,' is a well known Hindustanee maxim."

The Dinner Question: or, How to dine well and economically *by Tabitha Tickletooth. Charles Selby, 1860.*

COCONUT RICE

(*Narial Chawal*)

2 cups grated fresh coconut or *unsweetened* flaked coconut
3¾ cups boiling water
2 tablespoons clarified butter or shortening
1 onion, chopped
½ teaspoon ground cinnamon
¼ teaspoon ground cloves
¼ teaspoon ground cardamom
¼ teaspoon turmeric
2 cups long-grain rice
½ teaspoon salt

First, make coconut milk. Put the grated fresh coconut or *unsweetened* flaked coconut in a bowl. Add the boiling water, and let stand for 30 minutes. Strain through cheesecloth, squeezing all liquid from coconut. If necessary add enough water or coconut liquid to make 3¾ cups coconut milk. Set aside.

Heat the clarified butter or shortening in a deep heat-proof casserole, and fry the onion, cinnamon, cloves, cardamom, and turmeric for 5 minutes, sprinkling with a little water to prevent burning. Add rice, coconut milk, and salt. Bring to a boil, lower heat, cover tightly, and cook until rice is tender and most liquid is absorbed. Place, tightly covered, in a slow (300°) oven for 10 minutes to dry out.

Serves 6 to 8.

(From THE ART OF INDIAN COOKING, by Monica Dutt. Copyright 1972 by Bantam Books, Inc. Reprinted by permission of Bantam Books, Inc. New York.)

Rice Spoon D:22

A pretty implement for serving rice, one-third spoon, one-third spatula and one-third anthropomorphic hand. It is made out of shiny stainless steel in the form of a palm; there is no reason for this save art, but that alone makes it interesting. The palm is 2½″ wide and the spoon is 8″ long overall and rather flat in shape, just right for sliding under a mound of rice and carrying it to a serving tray.

Spice & Sweet Mahal $1.65

"To make Pullow, the Meat is first Boiled to Rags, and the Broth or Liquor being strained, it is left to drain, while they Boil the Rice in the same; which being tender, and the aqueous parts evaporating, the Juice and Gravy incorporates with the Rice, which is Boiled almost dry; then they put in the Meat again with Spice, and at last as much Butter as is necessary, so that it becomes not too Greesy or Offensive, either to the Sight or Taste; and it is then Boiled enough when it is fit to be made into Gobbets, not slabby, but each Corn of Rice is swelled and filled, not burst into Pulp."

A New Account of East India and Persia. Being Nine Years' Travels, 1672–1681 *by John Fryer.*

Before he could propose, a rich young man, smitten by an exquisite but impoverished girl, put her to the test of preparing a complete meal with two pounds of unthreshed rice. She quickly won his heart by demonstrating a wealth of culinary ingenuity. After threshing the rice gently, "the girl placed the rice grains in the shallow mortar of kakuba wood with a flat, wide bottom, and began pounding them with a long, heavy, iron-tipped, smooth bodied pestle of khadira wood that was slightly hollowed in the middle to form a grip. She tired her arms in a charming play of raising and dropping, picking up and picking out single grains, which she then cleaned of chaff and awn in a winnowing basket, washed repeatedly in water, and after a small offering to the fireplace, dropped in boiling water, five parts water to one part rice.

"As the grains softened and began to jump, and swelled to the size of a bud, she lowered the fire, and holding the lid on the pot, poured out the scum. Then she plunged her ladle into the rice, turned the grains with the ladle, and having satisfied herself that they were evenly boiled, turned the pot upside down on its lid, to let the rice steam (dum). She poured water over the firesticks which had not burned up entirely, and when the flame had died down and the heat was gone, she sent this charcoal to the dealers. 'Buy with the coin you receive as much of vegetables, ghee, curds, oil, myrobalan and tamarind as you can get.'

"When this had been done she added two or three kinds of spices, and once the rice broth had been transferred to another bowl, placed on wet sand, she cooled it with gentle strokes of a palm-leaf fan, added salt and scented it with fragrant smoke. . . . Two bowls . . . were placed on a light, green banana-tree leaf from her own garden—a quarter of one leaf was used—and she set the rice broth before him. He drank it and feeling happy and content after his journey let a sweet lassitude pervade his body. Then she served him two spoonsful of rice kedgeree and added a serving of butter, soup and condiment. Finally she served him the remaining boiled rice with yoghourt mixed with mace, cardamoms and cinnamon, and fragrant cool buttermilk and fermented rice gruel." (An old Indian folk tale.)

Indian XVIII century, Muhammad Salim, "Bahram Gur in the Camphor-Colored Palace" (from The Metropolitan Museum of Art).

From Stoves to Pans

Before the pot there was fire. In short, in order to talk about pots, we must first talk about stoves. It is impossible to understand Indian cookware without knowing how it is used.

The common Indian stove (*chula*) is, basically, a metal pail. That's all. It may be larger than your basic floor-mopping pail; it may have a grate set halfway down for coals to rest on, and an air hole in the base into which fuel is fed and out of which ashes are carried; and

Continued from preceding page

it may even be lined with heat-conserving unglazed terra-cotta. But when all is said and done, it's a pail. That means it is portable; meant to be filled with coals or cakes of cow dung, lit out in the yard and then carried into the kitchen by its metal handle. Rich households and commercial kitchens may have complicated *chulas* built of brick with many holes cut in the top, but the heating principle is the same.

In either case, the essential fact is that there is no heat surface as such, but only an opening above the burning coals. That means there is no benefit to be gained from having flat-bottomed pans. And, indeed, you will see that the basic *karhai* (deep-frying pan), *tava* (bread griddle) and *degchi* (sauce pan) display a most sensuous variety of curved bottoms. It also means that earthenware pots would quickly shatter on the direct exposure to the heat, so that almost all Indian cookware is made of brass, aluminum, stainless steel or iron. If you should come upon a clay pot in an Indian shop, it is probably made of half-baked clay and intended for the aging of pickles rather than for slow oven cooking as it would be in the West.

There is, in fact, very little Indian ovenware per se, a natural outgrowth of the fact that ovens are uncommon. Some households possess earthen platforms that they cover with warm ashes. To bake, pans filled with food are set in the ashes, and then covered with coals or more warm ashes. Clay ovens called *tandoors* are to be found in exceptional homes, restaurant yards or, communally-owned, in villages. These ovens are large clay jugs that are most often sunk into the ground out of doors; great skewers with chicken or lamb are stuck into them, where the reflecting heat of the coals at the bottom of the oven sears and rapidly cooks the meat. A marvelous bread, called *naan,* is made by slapping pieces of dough against the inner walls of the *tandoor.* But *tandoori* cooking is very special; it is used only by meat-eaters; and it is, besides, a form of cooking that seems to have generated no cookware of its own outside of the mighty skewers whose tips rest in the red-hot coals on the bottom of the oven, and whose tops lean against the inner surface of its sides.

Iron Deep-Frying Pan D:23

In India, a deep, round-bottomed pan called a *karhai* is used for deep-frying. The shape of the pan is determined by the burners of traditional Indian stoves: open holes over the fire and into which the pan fits. The lower the pan sinks into the hole, the closer it is to the heat, which explains why the *karhai* is so deep and wide at the top. This *karhai* is stable enough to sit on some gas burners—test before using it—but it should not be used on an electric range without a collar to support it. *Karhais* can be made in iron, like this one, cast iron, stainless steel, aluminum or brass, and all have the typical high-looped handles. The advantage of deep-frying in a wide-rimmed, round-bottomed pan is that it requires less oil than a flat pan to fry limited amounts of food. This *karhai* is the family size—10″ in diameter and 3¼″ deep—just right for making fried Indian breads or the countless variety of savory or sweet snacks that are such a delightful part of the Indian repertoire.

Spice & Sweet Mahal $4.00

Stainless-Steel Deep-Frying Pan D:24

Similar both in form and function to the wok of China, the *karhai* is more steeply curved than the Chinese pan and provides a perfect well for frying. Three cups of oil will create a generous 2″- to 3″-deep pool in the bottom of this *karhai.* The pan, made of medium-weight stainless steel, measures little more than 10″ in diameter and is 3¾″ deep. The shape of its tall, circular handles is characteristic of all *karhais. Pooris,* a popular Indian, unleavened, whole wheat bread are deep-fried. So are *pakoris,* a favorite Indian snack. *Pakoris* are prepared by dipping pieces of a vegetable such as eggplant, spinach leaves or potato into a spiced chick-pea-flour batter and frying them until delectably golden. Your guests will applaud.

Spice & Sweet Mahal $8.55

POTATO BALLS

Batata Bondas

4 cooked potatoes
1 tablespoon vegetable oil
¼ teaspoon mustard seed
1 onion, chopped
1 fresh or canned green chili pepper, chopped, seeds removed
¼ teaspoon salt
2 tablespoons raisins
2 tablespoons chopped parsley
1 cup chick-pea or lentil flour*
A pinch of salt
¼ teaspoon turmeric
Water
Vegetable oil for deep frying

Break potatoes into small bits. Heat 1 tablespoon vegetable oil, and fry the mustard seed until they crackle. Add the onion, and green chili pepper, and sauté until onion is soft. Add potatoes, salt, raisins, and parsley. Mix well, form into walnut-size balls, and set aside.

Mix the chick-pea or lentil flour, salt, and turmeric with enough water to make a medium-thick batter. Dip each potato ball in the batter until well-coated.

Heat the vegetable oil (365°), and deep fry the *bondas* a few at a time until light brown. Drain on paper towels, and serve hot or cold.

Yield: 20–25 small bondas.

* ½ cup flour and ½ cup cornstarch may be substituted for 1 cup of chick-pea or lentil flour in this recipe.

(From THE ART OF INDIAN COOKING, by Monica Dutt. Copyright 1972 by Bantam Books, Inc. Reprinted by permission of Bantam Books, Inc., New York.)

Griddle D:25

When we showed this *tava,* or griddle, to one of our experts, she smiled. "Ah, yes," she sighed, "a *tava.*" Why that pleased recognition? Because on a *tava* one cooks *chapatis,* and *chapatis* are the daily bread of India. The bread is made of a whole wheat flour and water dough that is rolled out into small, flat circles. And this is the griddle that cooks *chapatis* perfectly, a 9½″ concave disc of heavy, blackened iron that has a rough geometric design incised on its baking surface and a shiny loop so it can be hung on the wall. Before a meal, the *tava* is laid on an open-fire stove. When it is smoking hot, the *chapatis* are placed on the *tava* one by one. The cook, alert to prevent scorching, keeps moving the bread around constantly until it is lightly browned on one side; she then grasps it with smooth-edged tongs and cooks it on the other side. Finally, she holds the *chapati* with the tongs over a flame for a few seconds until it puffs up, and then serves it immediately. If you turn the *tava* over and cook on the convex side with the same dough you can make what is known as "other-side-of-the-*tava* bread." One of our Indian informants swears that it tastes absolutely different from *chapatis.* Our *tava* is also available 12″ in diameter.

Spice & Sweet Mahal $2.75

Griddle Tongs D:26

Heat will pass through a handleless Indian griddle, or *tava,* directly to your fingers unless you find adequate means for holding it. Most potholders are not heavy enough for full protection and would soil quickly. The best solution is what the Indian cook uses, a set of tongs like these. They are made of two lengths of stainless-steel rod held together with a pin at the fulcrum. The tool is 10″ long, with flat surfaces at one end for grasping the griddle, and long, straight handles at the other. The spread of the handles provides leverage that enables you to lift the griddle with one hand.

Kalpana $3.50

Griddle with Handle D:27

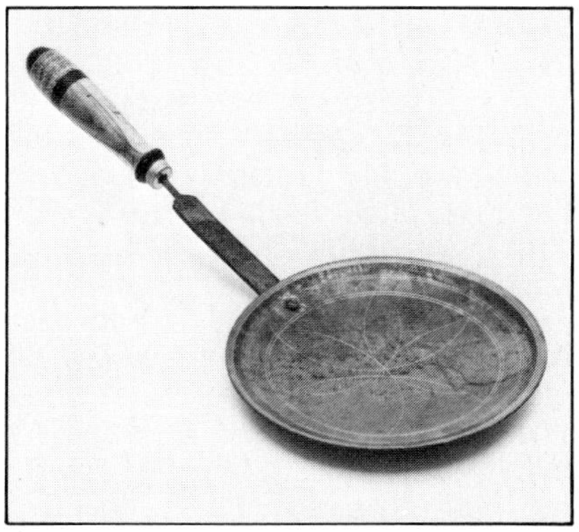

This variant on the *chapati* griddle (*tava*) is available with a handle for use in the western kitchen. It is less common and more citified than the simple *tava,* but it is easier to use near the hot burners of a western stove. A pointed iron bar extends from one side of the 8½″ griddle, and fits into a detachable wooden handle; the two together extend 11″ in all. Unfortunately, we have to warn you about the poor design of the iron spoke that slips too easily out of its wooden sheath.

Spice & Sweet Mahal $2.75

Sandwich Grill D:28

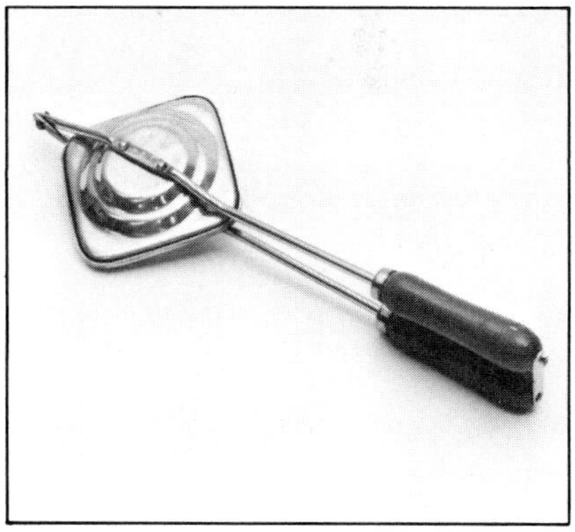

Here's an old friend; we use one like it in this country when we want to make grilled-cheese or ham-and-cheese sandwiches over a gas burner. In India you would use it over an open fire; but the principle, if not the recipe, is the same. Two slices of western bread are spread with *ghee* (clarified butter) and filled with a mixture of vegetables and spices or meat, perhaps combined with onions and cinnamon, then grilled and eaten as a snack at tea. The sandwich is placed within the two parts of the

Continued from preceding page

press; the handles are closed, and it is all cooked over an open fire. Then bliss: hot, crisp, buttery, spicy, all at once! The working part of the grill consists of two 3¾″ squares of aluminum that have been molded with depressions in the center for the filling. These are attached to two lengths of steel, that are hinged together at one end, then bent around the holders and set into red-painted wooden handles at the other end. The grill is 14″ long. The handles are fastened together with an aluminum hook and nail to hold the sandwich together so that none of the savory filling will be lost.

Kalpana **$3.00**

Chapati Box D:29

Indian bread is usually cooked to order. At mealtime, there must be someone in the kitchen cooking *pooris* or *chapatis* while the family devours them hungrily. But suppose the cook gains on the eaters. Or suppose a modern Indian woman wants to make her *chapatis* and then eat with the family. That is the time this covered dish is used. It is a *chapati* box, a 3″-deep, round dish, 8″ in diameter, with a snugly-fitting domed lid. In go the *chapatis* and on goes the lid, and the heat is trapped within. The box and its contents may be kept warm in the oven. It is made of heavy stainless steel, and the cover fits so tightly that you can lift the whole box by the knob on its cover. This container provides a perfect way to make your *chapatis* and eat them, too.

Kalpana **$16.25**

Stainless-Steel Steamer D:30

We are calling this a steamer, but that is only one of its many uses. It's a flat, circular dish made out of stainless steel that is 9″ in diameter and 2″ deep, and is perforated with holes across the bottom. The cook may use it as a colander or strainer to wash lentils or dried peas. Or it could serve as a sieve through which tiny dumplings (*boondi*) are pressed into a pan of boiling oil. Propped on a saucepan or in a *karhai,* it would make a good steamer for reheating rice or cooking delicious *dhoklas,* savory cakes filled with spices and vegetables and, sometimes, a bit of yoghurt. This slick, modern implement is far easier to use and clean than the old-fashioned bamboo steamer it replaces.

Spice & Sweet Mahal **$5.25**

Dhokla Steamer D:31

Dhokla are diamond-shaped cakes that are eaten at breakfast and as snacks throughout the day in western India, especially around Bombay. Unlike sweet brioches or Danish pastries, *dhokla* are savory. They are made of lentil and rice flours, yoghurt, coconut and spices. The dough is mixed in the evening and set aside to ferment lightly overnight; the next morning it is patted flat and cooked on a steamer tray over boiling water. When ready, the cake is cut into pieces and served with a green chutney made of hot, green chilies, fresh coriander leaves, onion, grated coconut and tamarind water. If the cook is lucky enough to have a *dhokla* steamer like this one, she can place spoonfuls of dough in its diamond-shaped indentations. The three-tiered steamer is meant to be ankle-deep in simmering water in a large saucepan so that the steam can rise through the holes on each level and cook the tasty cakes. It looks something like a little pagoda made of aluminum, with three identical round trays, about 7½″ in diameter, that fit on a central post. Each tray holds four *dhoklas* and is perforated with many tiny holes for passage of the steam.

Spice & Sweet Mahal **$5.25**

Idli Steamer D:32

One of the great treats of southern Indian cooking is the *idli.* To make *idli,* ground rice and lentils are mixed with water to form a thick dough that is left to ferment and rise overnight. The next morning, the dough is formed into small cakes and cooked in a special steamer with trays that have circular indentations, 3″ in diameter, into which the *idlis* are placed. This steamer has three trays that together hold 12 *idlis.* It is 5″ high and 8″ across and will fit into most any medium-sized saucepan. The steamer is made of aluminum, and has a black plastic knob on the top so that it may be lifted from the pot when the *idlis* are fully cooked. Tender, spongy and slightly sour, *idlis* are served hot for breakfast and are also a great favorite in south Indian coffee houses. They are usually accompanied with some kind of chutney—coconut chutney is especially delicious—and a *sambar* (a lentil purée that can be flavored in many different ways with spices and other vegetables).

Spice & Sweet Mahal **$5.25**

"Tapp's Sauce

Take of green sliced mangoes, salt, sugar and raisin each eight ounces; red chillis and garlic each four ounces; green ginger six ounces; vinegar three bottles, lime-juice one pint, Pound of several ingredients well; then add the vinegar and lime juice; stop the vessel close, and expose it to the sun a whole month, stirring or shaking it well daily; then strain it through a cloth, bottle and cork it tight.
Obs.—The residue makes an excellent chutney" (which one could certainly enjoy had not one's head been blown off by the sauce alone).

Indian Domestic Economy, *anonymous. Madras, 1850.*

IDLIS

⅔ cup urid dhal*
1 cup Cream of Rice
Pinch of salt

Soak the urid dhal in cold water for 12 hours or overnight. Drain and purée with a little water in an electric blender.

Place the Cream of Rice in a bowl or saucepan and rinse under cold running water. Drain in a fine-mesh sieve, leaving it in the sieve for about five minutes, until almost completely dry.

Combine the urid dhal purée, the Cream of Rice and a pinch of salt, beating thoroughly. The batter should be quite thick. Set aside in a warm place to ferment for 8 hours.

Grease a 12-cup miffin tin or idli steamer and divide the batter evenly between the cups. If using a muffin tin, place it on a rack over boiling water in a large Dutch oven or roaster. If you use an idli steamer, place it in an inch of boiling water in a casserole or large, deep saucepan. In either case, cover tightly and steam until the idli are cooked through, about 15 minutes.

Serve hot with coconut chutney.

* Urid dhal is available in Indian specialty shops. Lentils may be substituted if urid dhal is unavailable, and should be treated in the same manner.

Krishna Karanth and Vijay Bhatia, Madras Woodlands Restaurant, New York City.

Puttu Steamer D:33

Undoubtedly you are wondering what *puttu* are. They are breakfast cakes made of rice flour and water mixed with freshly grated coconut. The dough is steamed in a cylindrical mold, traditionally a piece of hollow bamboo. When cooked the cylinder of dough is cut into individual cakes that are served hot with bananas or palm treacle. In Sri Lanka (Ceylon), where this mold was made, *pittu,* as they call it, are eaten with fresh coconut milk or served as a perfect foil for hot *sambars* (lentil purées with vegetables and spices) and curries. This modern, lightweight aluminum *puttu*-maker consists of a deep, perforated steamer—6″ deep and about 8″ across—that will fit over the edge of a pan. A rack with five 4¾″-high cylindrical molds with removable, perforated discs on the bottom, fits snugly into the steamer, and a center post with a handle permits the rack to be lifted as a unit. The next time you want something deliciously different, try *puttu.*

Kalustyan **$15.00**

In Sri Lanka (Ceylon) two staple foods, coconut and rice, are combined in a ritual which is meant to appease the goddess Pattini, who, when sufficiently angered, imperils the rice crop. Village men form two lines opposite each other and toss coconuts back and forth, trying to break the hurtling missiles with coconuts held in their hands. They do this until one breaks, repeating the performance daily for a time relative to the danger their crop is in. A feast concludes the ceremony.

Serving and Etiquette

The whole manner of Indian service is different from ours. There are no courses, and no bowls of food are passed around or used communally. Instead, each diner is usually served his own *thali,* a round, metal tray. In the center of the tray, or near it, there will be a mound of rice or some flat wheat breads. Around the side, in small matching bowls, will be the different dishes of the meal, including a sweet dish. Each person can then choose to combine the foods he likes. In this way, no food passes from one person to another or from one *thali* to another, a practice that is considered unhygienic, even between husband and wife. Certain Hindus even refuse to eat from *thalis.* They serve their food on banana leaves or other leaves sewn together, which they believe are cleaner than reused trays.

As for eating, the only proper way is with the fingers of the right hand, generally the first two fingers and the thumb. The left hand is considered unclean and therefore unsuitable to eat from, although you can pick up a tumbler of water with it. A further refinement is made in picking up food. Northern Indians are careful not to soil more than the tips of their fingers and look down on southerners who sometimes reach palm-deep into their food. But the right hand, no matter how it is used, is somehow felt to be more sanitary than our method of reusing cutlery, even though it is washed before being passed on to another person.

The technique of handling food is as follows. In rice-eating areas, the diner will roll up a small ball of rice, mix it with some food from one of the bowls on the *thali,* and neatly pop the whole thing into his mouth. If bread is the staple, he will tear off a bit of bread and deftly scoop up some other food inside it.

Lastly, if you really want to follow all the proper customs relating to Indian food, make sure to wash both your hands and mouth before, as well as after, a meal.

Serving Tray — D:34

A *thali* is a round serving tray. It may be as large as a table and used as one, or as small as a plate and used for that purpose. In India, the various dishes that make up a meal are arranged on a *thali* for each individual. In some areas, and for special occasions, large banana leaves are traditional replacements for the *thali.* The center of the tray is reserved for a mound of rice or some *chapatis.* Around the sides are placed small bowls (*katoris*) filled with various wet, dry, hot or sweet dishes and the chutneys, pickles and *raita* (a yoghurt and vegetable combination) that may accompany them. Three bowls of food are considered the minimum to serve: one for yoghurt, one for a *dal* (legume dish), and one for another vegetable. In the territory of Marharashtra, the arrangement and appearance of food on the *thali* is extremely important. A Marharashtrian hostess may be complimented for creating a particularly original left side of the *thali,* the side on which she is free to express her ingenuity in developing the foods to accent a meal. Very fine *thalis* are made of decorated brass or silver. Ours is a simple but attractive disc of shiny stainless steel, the most popular type found in India these days. It is 9½″ in diameter, a good size for serving an individual meal.

Spice & Sweet Mahal — $6.00

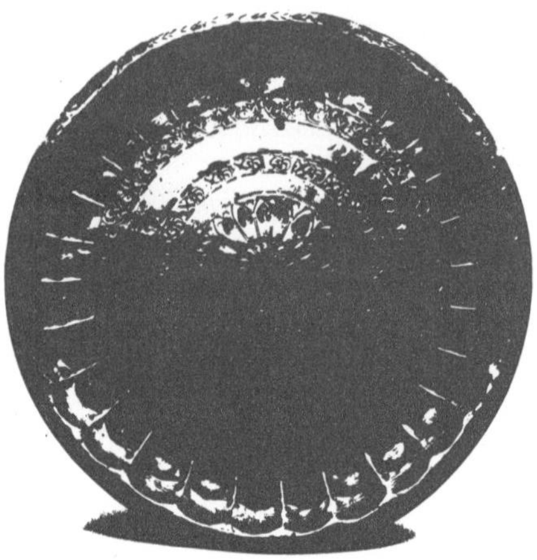

19th century Indian Brass Tray (from The Metropolitan Museum of Art).

KASHMIR LAMB CURRY

(Kashmiri Rogan Josh)

3 tablespoons shortening or vegetable oil
2 pounds lean stewing lamb, cut up
1 cup yogurt
½ teaspoon grated fresh ginger, or ¼ teaspoon ground ginger
½ teaspoon crushed red pepper flakes
1 teaspoon paprika
2 tablespoons tomato paste
¼ teaspoon ground cloves
¼ teaspoon ground cinnamon
2 cardamom seeds, crushed
2 teaspoons aniseed, crushed
¼ teaspoon saffron or turmeric
Salt to taste
2 cups boiling water

Heat the shortening or vegetable oil, and brown the meat. Add the yogurt, and simmer until quite dry. Remove any excess fat.

Add the rest of the ingredients, except the boiling water. Stir well to coat the meat. Add the boiling water and simmer on low heat until meat is tender. Serve with rice.

Serves 4.

(From THE ART OF INDIAN COOKING, by Monica Dutt. Copyright 1972 by Bantam Books, Inc. Reprinted by permission of Bantam Books, Inc., New York.)

"It is usual for natives in some parts of India, however wealthy they may be, to have their food served on leaves for plates. But those whose habits we have the best opportunities of observing, eat their meat from unglazed earthen plates. By some castes, in accordance with their peculiar notion in regard to cleanliness, these plates must not be used more than once. After serving a single turn, they are thrown away, but, being very cheap, they are easily replaced. Certain classes, such as the Bengal sepoy, and many of our domestic servants, eat their curry and rice from a brass pan. They have also a small brass vessel for holding their drinking water."

The Domestic Life, Character and Customs of the Natives of India *by James Kerr. London, 1865.*

Serving Bowl D:35

A meal served in India is presented in a number of identical *katoris,* more or less like this one, assembled on a *thali,* one for each person. *Katoris* come in sets and are filled with all the prepared dishes and relishes that make up the meal. One might hold a chicken dish;

Sherbet making, Jahdingin Album, India, 17th century. Berlin State Library.

Continued from preceding page

another, a spicy vegetable; a third, a cool and creamy mixture of yoghurt and vegetables. There may be as few as three *katoris* or as many as eight or more. On ceremonial occasions, such as weddings, both *thalis* and *katoris* may disappear, replaced by banana leaves and tiny, disposable earthenware bowls. (The leaves are ultimately disposed of as cattle feed.) We show you a typical stainless-steel *katori* that is 1¼″ high and 2¾″ in diameter. *Katoris* are also marvelously useful for serving relishes at non-Indian meals and for steaming custards.

Spice & Sweet Mahal **$1.25**

Carême, the nineteenth century French chef, was inordinately fond of pièces montées, *such as this one, which depicts his sugar-paste version of an Indian pavilion. From* Le Patissier Royal Parisien *by M. A. Carême, Second volume, 1828.*

Red chiles.

CUCUMBER RAITA

1 small cucumber
1 2-inch slice fresh ginger
1 hot green chili pepper
1 cup plain, natural yogurt
½ teaspoon salt
1 tablespoon vegetable oil
½ teaspoon urid dhal*
¼ teaspoon mustard seeds
1 whole, dried red chili pepper, crushed
Black pepper
Fresh coriander leaves

Peel and grate the cucumber, removing the seeds if they are too large and bitter. Grate the ginger and green chili pepper. Stir up the yogurt with a spoon, then stir in the cucumber, ginger, green pepper and salt.

Heat the oil in a small frying pan and add the urid dhal, mustard seeds and the crushed red chili pepper. Cook over high heat, swirling the pan, until the ingredients are golden brown and begin to sizzle and crackle in the oil. The *sound* is more important than the color in determining when the ingredients have cooked long enough. Drain the oil from the pan and stir the ingredients into the yogurt mixture. Add freshly grated black pepper to taste and sprinkle with fresh coriander leaves.

* Urid dhal is available in Indian specialty shops.

Krishna Karanth and Vijay Bhatia, Madras Woodlands Restaurant, New York City.

Tumbler D:36

Cool on a hot day, warm on a cold day, the stainless-steel tumbler is becoming the most common form of drinking vessel in India, where it is found in the homes of rich and poor people alike. Indian children hold two hands around its middle when they sip their frothy hot milk; women wrap it in the folds of their saris when it is filled with scalding tea; and everywhere, at every meal for water, or for a refreshing drink of whipped yoghurt or fruit juice during the day, Indians drink in a similar tumbler. It is smooth and elegant, with a slightly dull finish. It is also extremely washable, obviously nonbreakable, and it comes in a variety of sizes. This one is 4¼″ high and 3″ in diameter and holds 12 ounces. Our supplier also has a 5″-tall version.

Spice & Sweet Mahal **$1.65**

Tea Strainer D:37

Since the English introduced Indians to their own native tea soon after the turn of the century, tea has become the beverage par excellence in India. Although it is more popular in the north than in the south, where coffee is grown and preferred, tea is available everywhere. And it is usually served frothy, with hot milk and sugar already added. The froth comes from deftly pouring the tea back and forth between tumblers before serving it, a custom that applies equally to plain hot milk and to coffee (also served with hot milk). You may presume, from western habit, that tea should accompany an Indian meal. Wrong! Water alone is the accepted beverage to drink with a meal. Tea is served after eating. It may also be the first thing you drink upon waking in the morning, and, following the English custom, it may be cause for the high point of the afternoon. Regardless of when it is made, the best method of making tea is as follows: preheat a pot, toss in some loose tea, pour in water that has just come to the boil, cover and let the tea steep for a few minutes, then pour it through a strainer. This stainless-steel one will do very nicely. The strainer cup is 3⅛″ across and has a 4½″-long bent-wire handle on one side and bent-wire loop on the other side to catch the side of a cup. Next time you make tea, try these Indian variations: add a *masala* of cardamom and cloves, or a little fennel seed. You'll like it!

Spice & Sweet Mahal **$2.30**

Lunch Box D:38

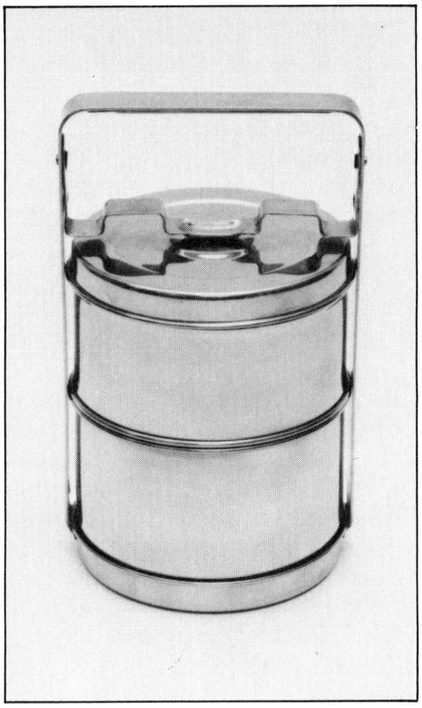

This is a *tiffin* carrier, a lunch box, made of a framework of stainless steel into which are fitted two covered steel boxes, each 3″ tall. When the boxes are in place, a serpentine side bar is pressed down, clamping them all together and holding them firmly so that they can be carried by the handle formed by the top arch of the framework. In India, most *tiffin* carriers contain four compartments, one each for the *chapati* or rice, *dal* (legume dish), vegetables and pickles or relishes that make up the traditional midday meal. Poorer workers hang them over the handlebars of their bicycles as they pedal off to work in the morning; the middle classes make use of squads of delivery boys who gather freshly-cooked luncheons from suburban homes and deliver them, by some miracle of organization, to the proper central-city offices; and the rich, of course, are brought their lunches by their house servants in *tiffin* carriers which may well be enclosed in thermal containers. A four-layer box is also available.

Annapurna **$14.25**

A branch of tea in flower from Le Boire et Le Manger *by Armand Dubarry, 1884. Darjeeling, Assam and Ceylon teas are among the memorable black teas of the world.*

Small Lunch Box D:39

This lunch box is minute by western standards. But it is adequate for the millions of office workers and school children who carry one just like it in India. A typical lunch that it would hold might consist of two *parathas* (whole wheat flat breads) either stuffed with a spicy vegetable or accompanied by a spicy vegetable or meat dish, and some pickle. The lunch box is made of lightweight aluminum and is somewhat larger than a sandwich—5¼″ long, 4″ wide and 1¼″ deep. At either end is a bead-trimmed, aluminum handle that turns up to clamp the lid loosely into place; for security, a string or rubber-band is advisable. The lunch box is nicely made and its rounded edges make it easy to tuck into the smallest places.

Annapurna **$1.99**

Italy's Beautiful Utensils

by Edward Giobbi

What I, as an artist, find most interesting about Italian kitchen equipment is the quality of the craftsmanship, the perfect mating of shape and material to function, and the beauty of the objects themselves. Most basic Italian cooking utensils are the same as those in other countries of the Western world; but there are exceptions, some of which are essential to the success of certain Italian dishes. More important, though, are the pride and skill of Italian craftsmanship apparent in many kitchen objects, which are often as beautiful as they are practical.

Take the instrument used to make *maccheroni alla chitarra*. *Chitarra* means "guitar," and there are several similarities between this object and its namesake. Essentially, the *chitarra* is a rectangular frame made of sturdy wood, not unlike an artist's canvas stretcher, with pegs stuck into one end; thin piano wires run from nails on the opposite end across the length of the frame to the pegs. The pegs are used to tighten up the wires when they become slack, just as the pegs at the end of the fingerboard of a guitar are used to tighten up and tune the strings. A thin, rectangular sheet of rolled-out pasta dough is placed over the wires. With a wooden rolling pin the dough is pressed through the wires, which cut the dough as it is forced between them. The wires cut the pasta into thin, thin strands, like spaghetti. If the strips are then placed crosswise on the *chitarra* and pressed through the wires with the rolling pin a second time, tiny pillows of pasta to be floated in soup are the result. *Maccheroni alla chitarra* is a specialty of the region of Abruzzi, and wonderful handcrafted *chitarre* made locally can be found in the marketplaces of Abruzzi and the Marches. They are simple and beautiful and cost very little. I have seen more expensive, fancy models in the large city stores, but I prefer these rustic ones for the spirit of the countryside they convey.

One item that serves a variety of purposes in my kitchen is a meat pounder; the one I use is made of brass and is such a lovely object that I think of it as a piece of sculpture. It has a good hand grip and is of a perfect weight. I use it to pound veal or crush black pepper, garlic, and hot pepper pods, among other things.

Italians make wonderful things out of straw, cane and wood. The straw objects are usually fashioned by local farmers from leftover materials, and then sold in open-air straw markets. Fish steamers, pasta strainers, fruit baskets and other such objects are lovely, well made, quite inexpensive, and exhibited in a great range of colors, shapes and sizes. Then there are the wooden objects: pasta forks, spoons, mortars and pestles, rolling pins—including the very long ones for pasta—and an endless assortment of useful kitchen tools.

Terra-cotta ware has always been used a great deal in Italian cooking, and the selection is still excellent, from completely glazed to semiglazed and unglazed pots and casseroles of all shapes and sizes—also at very reasonable prices. Italian marble is known throughout the world as an excellent material for architectural and sculptural purposes; in its home territory, however, it is used just as frequently for functional objects. Marble mortar and pestles, of every size, are used for grinding coarse salt, crushing pepper or making *pesto* or mayon-

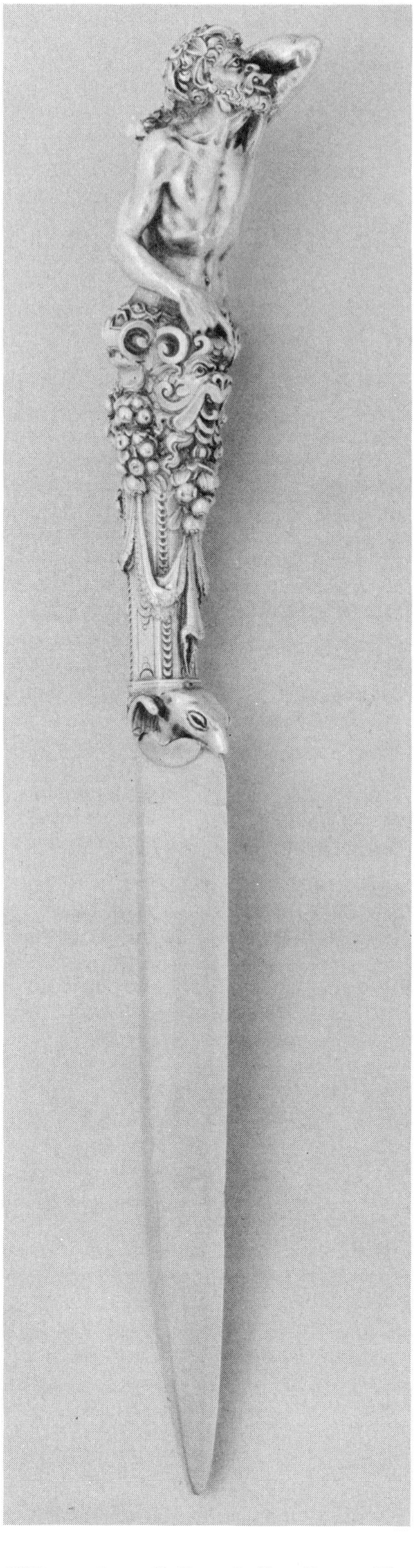

18th-century Italian knife (from The Metropolitan Museum of Art)

18th-century Italian spoon (from The Metropolitan Museum of Art)

naise. Marble cheese servers and other serving accessories such as lazy Susans are also quite beautiful and useful, although somewhat heavier than similar objects made of wood or basketry. And then there are ingenious items, such as sausage stuffers, juice presses and a variety of gadgets for producing the different forms of pasta and dessert pastries for which Italians are so well known.

Pots and pans are generally the same in Italy as those used for most European cooking, although I have noticed that Italian manufacturers prefer stainless-steel pots to aluminum. As a result, Italy produces a greater variety of high-quality stainless-steel pots than any other nation. I might add that Italians would never hesitate to spend a considerable sum of money on a good saucepot—absolutely essential for an Italian kitchen—since quality is recognized and appreciated. Despite the profusion of stainless steel, however, copper pots of excellent quality are still used and, for a reasonable price, a local artisan will make one to order.

I have always found it difficult to locate certain types of pots and pans in smaller sizes. The correct size and weight of a pot will influence the result of a dish to a large degree. For boiling pasta, a generously large pot and a large colander are both necessary. But for baking *lasagne*, the pan size must be just right, or the results will be all wrong. It was frustrating for me to bake *lasagne* for six in a pan that was too large for the amount I wanted to cook. The ideal size for a pan to hold six to eight portions is about 12 inches long by nine inches wide and about two to three inches deep. I finally found the perfect size in Italy. The problem with baking *lasagne* is that the pan should be just deep enough, and those available in America are usually too large and the metal is too thin. But in Italy I purchased excellent pans made of heavy aluminum and stainless steel in sizes impossible to find here.

The Italians have since time immemorial used a marvelous, semi-automatic rotisserie that is practically unknown in America, called a *girarrosto*—which translates as "turn roast." You wind it up like a clock and place it in front of a fireplace (or on an outdoor grill). The spitted meat cooks as it turns in front of the flame. Once the clockwork is wound up, the spit will turn for about 45 minutes. Just before it stops a little bell rings to remind the cook to rewind it. A rectangular pan with short legs and a long handle is placed underneath the *girarrosto* to catch the meat drippings. This pan is called *la ghiotta*, "the greedy one." Embers are placed under it, and vegetables (potatoes, onions, cauliflower, etc.) are put in it to cook in the drippings. They taste so good that one tends to overeat—hence *la ghiotta*. Although I believe it is basically of Florentine origin (at least my Florentine friends seem to think so), the simpler metal *girarrosti* are available throughout Italy. However, I was fortunate enough to find an antique one, as well as several antique *ghiotte* to use with it. They are beautiful to look at even when not in use.

All of these are things to search out when you travel abroad. Search the marketplaces for straw or wood, the hardware stores for stainless-steel items you cannot find at home. Look for the terra-cotta wares and the more sophisticated ceramics as well: Italians do lovely, colorful things with baked and glazed clay. Here at home you may be able to find some of these things in the combination hardware-grocery stores in the Little Italy sections of some cities, brought back lovingly and enthusiastically by the proprietors for their transplanted countrymen's enjoyment and appreciation.

The Cuisine of Italy

There used to be a popular song that claimed that every American had two hometowns, his own and Paris—a romantic thought, we think, in spite of being a little out of date. But wherever he lives, it is unquestionably true that every American has two cuisines—his own and Italian.

By "his own" we mean an amalgam of ancestral traditions and modern American grub—hamburgers one night, and Hungarian goulash, or chow mein the next. We're willing to bet that on the third night he'll have spaghetti, veal parmigiana or pizza. We're so used to it that we never stop to think that we're eating foreign food. In fact, in a very real way, our cooking is deeply rooted in the Italian kitchen. For, at the time the Romans were spreading the Latin tongue and culture (by force albeit) throughout Europe, they already had a highly developed cuisine. As a result, they left a deep culinary impression on the rest of Europe and, therefore, America.

Native Italian cooking is regional and diverse (a fact poorly represented in this country), depending for its character on local traditions and produce. There are twenty different culinary regions in Italy, corresponding roughly to the twenty independent states that existed until recently on the peninsula. Beyond the specialties of each region, however, there is a national tradition that makes use of foods such as pasta, cheese, vegetables, seafood, wine and coffee. It makes use of these foods in accordance with two general styles: that of the North and that of the South.

Northern cooking is elegant and voluptuous, rich with truffles, fine cheese, and wines, and more European and less Mediterranean than that of the South. Butter, cream, cheese, meat, game and mushrooms are relied on heavily. As we might expect, Northern cooking is related to the cuisines of neighboring Switzerland and France, even boasting a fondue-like dish composed of melted cheese and toast, the *fonduta.* This style of cooking is born of a region with fertile fields and thriving industries.

Southern Italy, on the other hand, is poor, dry and infertile, a land inhabited by a proud people whose lives are governed by a code of behavior that is all but Oriental in its stringency and reliance on the past. The food of the area is simple and hearty and practically vegetarian, making great use of bread and pasta, wild mushrooms and herbs, and shellfish. This is the cuisine of pizza, mozzarella and hearty tomato-dependent sauces; it is the Italian cooking with which we are most familiar in this country.

These two opposing traditions influence all the foods in Italy, even staples such as pasta and bread. The bread of southern Italy is unparalleled in quality. Made of mixed grains, it is slow-rising and has a crisp crust. Northern bread, which is not required for filling empty stomachs, is more refined and delicate. It was the Piemontesi who invented the pencil-thin breadsticks called *grissini.*

Pasta exemplifies even more the difference between the two regions. Northern noodles are flat and opulently yellow from the enrichment of egg yolks, while Southern machine-made pastas are tubular and very white, made from only white flour and water. It is in the South that we find the greatest variety of pasta types and the most inventive sauces to serve with them.

After the pasta—generally a light, appetite-whetting course—the

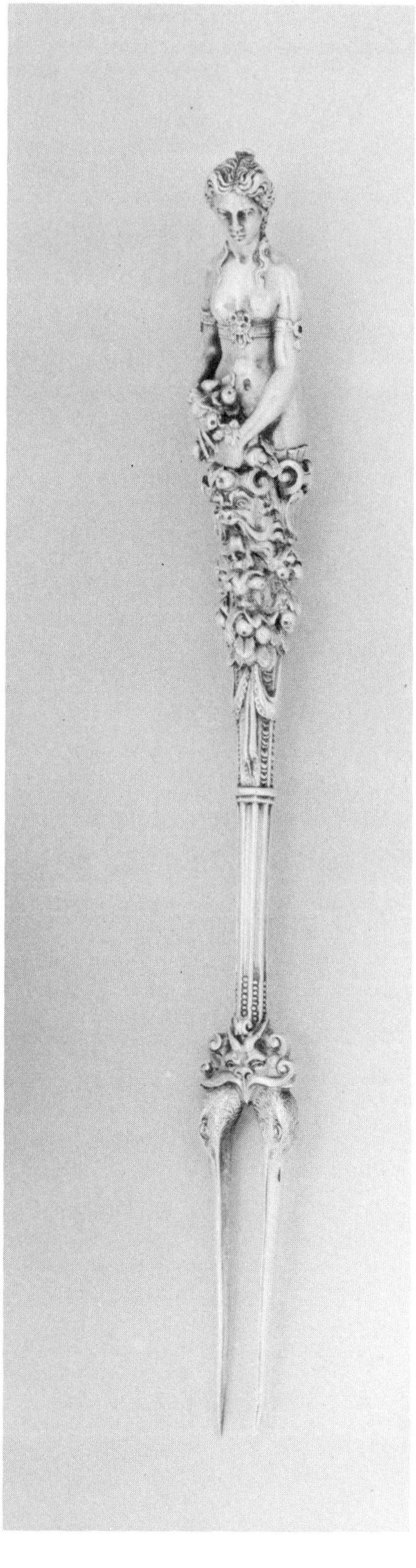

18th-century Italian fork (from The Metropolitan Museum of Art)

rest of the meal depends upon the produce and traditions of each area. Southerners are too poor to eat much meat, and the meat of the North—the famous Tuscan beef and veal—is too expensive to be eaten in large quantities. There is a great deal of seafood, however, as we would expect in a country that is almost all seacoast. And there is widespread use of chicken and game by those who can afford them. There are always fresh vegetables and salads on an Italian menu—olives, tomatoes and parsley in the South: beans, rice, beautiful tiny artichokes, broccoli or broad beans in the North. Northern cheeses are the various and justly famous products of a rich dairy country, beginning with the ubiquitous Parmesan and including Gorgonzola, Bel Paese, and Fontina. Southern mozzarella and ricotta have become famous throughout the world. Northern wines are the equals of all but the greatest wines of France; Southern wines are harsh and direct.

And, because so many southern Italians emigrated to America, it is the cooking of the poor South, and not that of the rich and sophisticated North, that we in this country have adopted as our own.

Wood Mortar and Pestle E:1

Our classic, everyday Italian mortar and pestle are perfect for crushing rosemary, sage, juniper berries and other herbs and spices in order to release their pungent essences. The 3″-high sides of the mortar's 1½-cup bowl keep the spices nicely contained with little chance of their flying out. With its pedestal base, the mortar is 5⅞″ high; its diameter at its mouth is 3″. The natural blond wood of the mortar is varnished on the outside, but left unfinished on the inside. The 7½″-long wooden pestle has a varnished handle with an egg-shaped ball of unfinished wood at its working end. The unfinished wood on both grinding surfaces enhances friction. Because the wood is unfinished, and therefore absorbent, some cooks may want to reserve this for dry herbs and spices, using a separate mortar of non-absorbent material (like marble) for fresh, pungent ingredients like basil or garlic.

H. Roth & Son / Berarducci Brothers (H2) $4.50

Marble Mortar E:2

Genoans claim that their pungent, mouth-watering *pesto* (garlic, basil and cheese sauce) can be made nowhere but in a good marble mortar. The classic one we show here could make a *pesto* that would knock the socks off even the most critical of *genovesi*. And small wonder, since it belongs to James Beard. It is not likely that you will find a duplicate of this splendid mortar in this country. However, one just like it can be shipped to you (via a French distributor) by boat. The ultra-elegant mortar, when it arrives, will measure 6¼″ in height, and 11″ in diameter at its widest. Its 5″-deep bowl holds almost two quarts, but it is equally effective for pulverizing and blending much smaller quantities, since its interior curves sharply like the pointed end of an egg. There are four semi-circular ears for carrying the heavyweight mortar should you ever be tempted to heft it.

Jules Gaillard et Fils (141) $150.00

Mortadella, *the much appreciated Bolognese sausage, was already a favorite delicacy in the fourteenth century. Its name is thought to have evolved from the heavy mortar* (mortaio della carne di maiale *or "mortar for pig flesh") which was used to crush the ingredients for its production.*

PESTO

The original way to make pesto is with a mortar and pestle. The solids and the olive oil are added slowly as the pesto is worked. The result is a looser pesto with a rougher texture.

- 5 cups fresh basil leaves, washed, drained, and tightly packed
- ¼ cup chopped parsley, Italian if possible
- ¾ cup olive oil
- 2 tablespoons finely minced garlic
- ½ cup pignoli nuts
- 1 teaspoon salt
- ½ cup pecorino or Parmesan cheese (I prefer pecorino)

Add all the ingredients to the container of an electric blender and blend, stirring down with a rubber spatula as necessary, until a smooth paste forms. Unless the pesto is to be used immediately, spoon it into a Mason jar or plastic container and cover with about ¾ inch of olive oil. Cover tightly and store in the refrigerator or in a cool place.

It may be kept indefinitely and used at any time, spooned directly from the jar onto pasta or into a sauce. Use about ½ cup pesto or less, diluted with about 2 tablespoons of warm water, for each pound of freshly

Continued from preceding page

cooked pasta. Toss quickly and serve immediately on hot plates. Yield: 2 cups of pesto.

(From ITALIAN FAMILY COOKING, by Edward Giobbi, illustrated by Cham, Lisa and Gena Giobbi. Copyright 1971 by Edward Giobbi. Reprinted by permission of Random House, Inc.)

Basil.

Basil, pesto's fragrant principle, plays conflicting roles in the legends and myths of the Mediterranean. Sacred and evil, it is the symbol of lovers in Italy, but often the emblem of hate in Greece. In both countries cursing is a necessary part of basil-planting, for it ensures a good crop. In some parts of Italy the plant is said to generate scorpions, while in other parts it is eaten to cure their sting; in still other regions, it is thought that sniffing basil will breed scorpions in the brain. Superstition also has it that basil, if consumed regularly, will double the size of the male member. If your goals are more spiritual, the useful herb has been recommended as being beneficial for the head and in maintaining good cheer.

Mezzaluna E:3

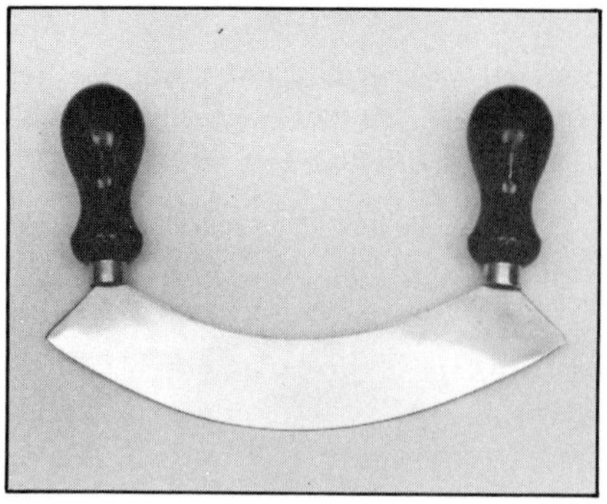

In Italy they call it a *mezzaluna,* or half-moon, and it is simply a knife by another name and shape. Use it to mince and chop by grabbing both of its painted wood handles, and rocking the blade back and forth over the parsley or other minceables. In order to master the rhythm of the *mezzaluna,* you may be forced to practice by making a different Italian dish every night—beginning with *peperoni imbottiti* (baked stuffed peppers), which calls for the fine chopping of garlic, anchovies, capers, olives and parsley. The *mezzaluna*'s 10⅜″-long, 1⅞″-wide, gracefully curved stainless-steel blade is bound to the knobs by nickeled-steel collars.

HOAN Products Ltd. (304) $5.00

Chestnut Knife E:4

Castagne (chestnuts) hold an exalted position in Italian cuisine: they are boiled as a side dish, sieved for soup, stuffed inside poultry, candied, braised with red wine and sugar, puréed and served with whipped cream, and ground into flour for sweet cakes. They even have a knife all their own. This 5″-long mini-knife prepares the chestnuts for any of its culinary destinies. First, use the concavely curved side of the knife to score the outer covering on the rounded side of the chestnut. Place the chestnuts in boiling water, the oven or a dry cooker to loosen the shell. Then, use the point of the knife to help peel away the loosened covering. The chestnut knife's 1″-long, stainless-steel blade is anchored firmly in its 3⅞″ wood handle by two brass rivets.

Rowoco Inc. (40) $1.75

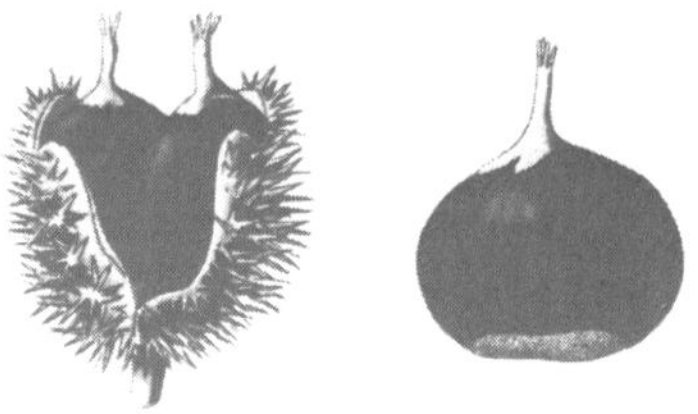

POLLO CON CASTAGNE

Chicken with Chestnuts

A 3-pound fryer, cut in pieces
3 tablespoons olive oil
Salt and freshly ground black pepper
1 onion chopped
1 clove garlic, chopped
1 cup sliced fresh mushrooms
¾ cup dry Marsala, imported if possible
1 tablespoon rosemary
1 teaspoon thyme
12 fresh chestnuts
2 tablespoons butter

Sauté chicken in olive oil, turning the pieces often. Add salt and pepper to taste. When chicken is brown, add onions, garlic and mushrooms. Cook until onion wilts, then add Marsala, rosemary and thyme. Cover, lower heat and simmer for 5 minutes.

While chicken is cooking, split each chestnut and boil in water to cover for 5 minutes. Remove shells, cut chestnuts in half and add to chicken. Stir in butter and simmer gently for 15 minutes. Serves 4 to 6.

(From ITALIAN FAMILY COOKING, by Edward Giobbi, illustrated by Cham, Lisa and Gena Giobbi. Copyright 1971 by Edward Giobbi. Reprinted by permission of Random House, Inc.)

Truffle Slicer E:5

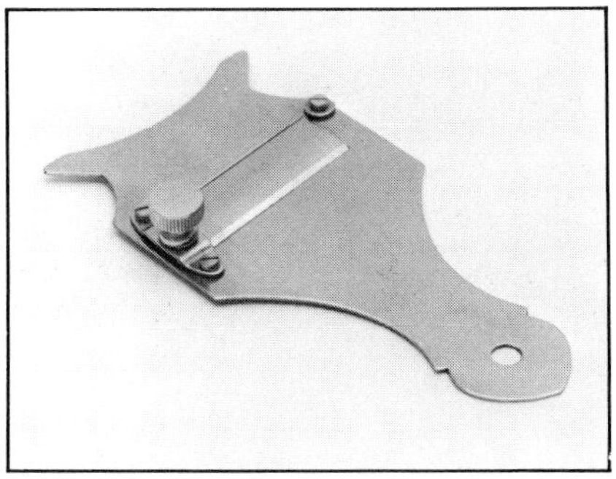

Late at night (best to do this when the competition can't see you), in northern Italy, in the dead of winter, take one well-trained hound and let him sniff at the roots of trees (oaks, chestnuts and poplars, if possible). It sounds like a fraternity initiation, but it's actually an extremely serious gastronomic search for the white Piedmont truffle—a very special, very coveted gourmet fungus. If you should chance to come up with a white truffle, you will want to use it sparingly, shaving off delicate aromatic curls of it with this Italian truffle cutter. Use the truffle slices to flavor sauces, meat and poultry dishes, *polenta,* or a melted cheese dish called *fonduta.* Made of solid stainless steel, this flat, 6½″-long cutter has a removable and adjustable 2″-wide stainless-steel blade.

Rowoco Inc. (133) $5.00

Zucchini Corer E:6

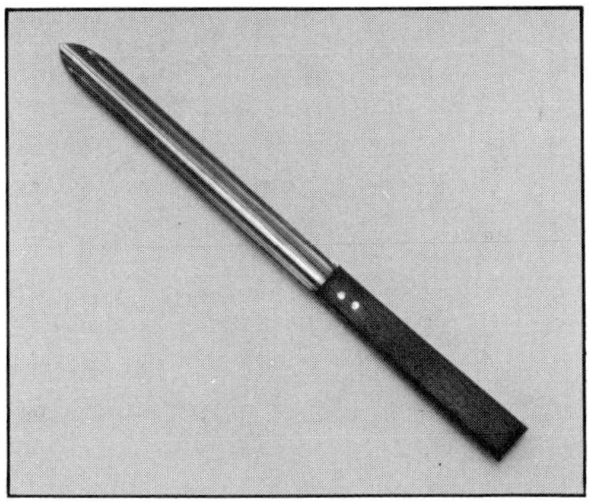

Zucchini ripieni (stuffed zucchini) can be most properly and deftly executed with this wonderful, long, skinny corer. Its trough-shaped stainless-steel blade neatly hollows out the squash's innards to make room for savory meat or cheese fillings. It would, of course, be equally useful for preparing all those delicious Middle Eastern stuffed squash dishes, or, for that matter, for coring apples or pears. The 6¼″ blade of this well made corer is secured firmly into a 4⅛″ rosewood handle by two brass rivets.

Rowoco Inc. (81) $2.00

Egg Beater E:7

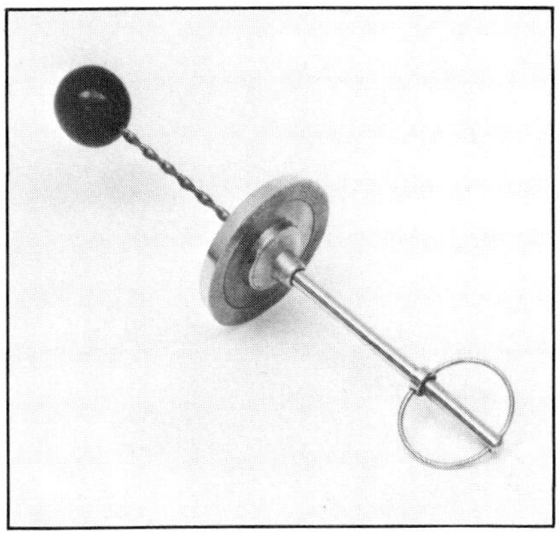

This small, 10″-long egg beater, built on the same principle as a child's mechanical spinning top, is as clever a gadget as we've seen. By pushing down on the black wooden handle, the tool's corkscrew mechanism transforms a simple wire circle into an industrious beater. Beating a couple of eggs for an omelet takes no time at all. An aluminum splash plate 3″ in diameter prevents the eggs (or whatever else you might be beating) from splattering you and your kitchen.

E. Rossi and Co. $2.98

Garlic Press E:8

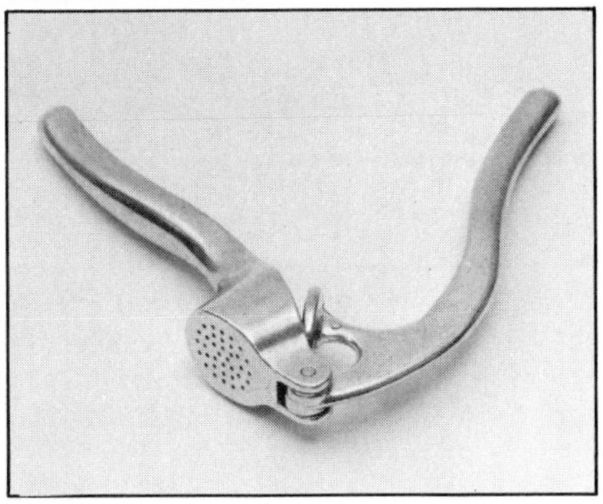

Every kitchen that has a can of tomatoes or a box of spaghetti needs a garlic press as well. One pungent clove of garlic is placed, peel and all, in the perforated chamber of the press. Then the cook squeezes together the two gently-curved handles, forcing down a plunger, which pushes the garlic and juices through tiny holes and leaves the discarded peel behind. This Italian-made garlic press is made of lightweight aluminum. Six inches long when the arms are folded together, it opens out on a connecting hinge to twice that size, one arm containing the perforated space for the garlic, and the other side an oval plunger that fits into the space to do its job.

International Edge Tool Co. (330) $2.65

Garlic.

Wood and Metal Sieve E:9

This Italian *tamis* is only one member in a family whose range of sizes and meshes should accommodate all the sifting and sieving chores presented

Continued from preceding page

them. Our 12″-diameter, 4½″-high sieve has a stainless-steel mesh stretched taut between the two concentric rings of the unfinished wooden frame. Its older brother is 15″ in diameter and 5½″ high with a coarse mesh. Its younger brother has a very fine mesh—set in a 7″-diameter, 3″-high frame—which could be used to finish chestnut purée for a *Monte Bianco.* All sizes also come with the more traditional horsehair mesh.

Oscar Zucchi (1151) $18.00

Tomatoes were formerly known as love apples, which many historians believe to be an etymological slip. The mixup occurred in this way: when tomatoes were first imported into Italy from North Africa, they were called apples of the Moors. Arriving in France, the words "Moro" (Moor) and "amour" (love) were confused and the confusion was passed on into English.

Spremipomodoro E:10

If you've grown too many tomato plants in your suburban garden; if your aunt and uncle have brought you more tomatoes from their garden than you can use before they go bad; or if you have an urge to beat commercial tomato sauce canners at their own game, then our *spremipomodoro* is for you. This stainless-steel contraption turns uncooked *pomodori* into delicious tomato purée in a matter of minutes. To use it, clamp it to your work surface with its C-clamp; insert the removable crank handle, place the tomatoes in the funnel-shaped part on top, turn the handle and presto!, tomato purée slides down the chute and into an awaiting bowl. A metal drum inside the funnel top presses the tomatoes through a perforated screen while ejecting seeds and skin via a small chute on the opposite side of the funnel top. The machine stands 10¼″ high; its funnel is 6½″ square at its mouth and 4″ deep. A yellow plastic strip around the 4⅜″-square base —to match the 3¾″-long yellow handle—serves as a cushion. The entire apparatus comes apart for easy cleaning.

HOAN Products Ltd. (292) $20.00

An ancient illustration of the tomato

William Alcott, the dourest of cookbook writers, greets the tomato (in The Young Housekeeper, *1838) with his customary enthusiasm: "Of the tomato or love apple, I know very little. It is chiefly employed as a sauce or condiment. No one, it is believed, regards it as very nutritious; and it belongs, like the mushroom and the potatoes, to a family of plants, some of the individuals of which are extremely poisonous. Some persons are even injured, more or less, by the acid of the tomato. Dr. Dunglison says it is wholesome and valuable; but a very slight acquaintance leads me to a different opinion."*

Tomatoes were long thought to possess evil and/or aphrodisiac properties. With some extraordinary syntactical hairpin turns, a mid-eighteenth century horticulturist writes warily of the "love apple":

"The Italians and Spaniards eat theses apples as we do cucumbers with pepper, oil, and salt, and some eat them in sauces, etc., and in Soups they are now much used in England, especcially the second Sort which is preferred to all the other. This fruit gives an agreable Acid to the Soup; though there are some persons who think them wholesome from their great Moisture and Coldness not and that the nourishment they afford must be bad."

from "Gardener to the Worshipful Company of Apothecaries at their Botanick Garden in Chelsea," in The Gardener's Dictionary *by Phillip Miller, 1752.*

Veal Pounder E:11

Stunning is perhaps too appropriate and graphic an adjective to apply to this professional, heavyweight veal pounder. No *scaloppina* of veal would dare to argue with this all-business, nickel-steel-plated iron instrument. It is 12¾″ overall, and weighs a solid 2½ pounds. The circular head that comes in contact with the veal (or other meat) is 4¼″ in diameter. The handle rises at a slight angle from the head so that the pounder will make contact with the meat before your knuckles do with the work surface. With a veal pounder like this, your *scaloppine al Marsala* (sautéed scallops of veal with dry Marsala) will sing.

Rowoco Inc. (132) $17.00

SALTIMBOCCA ALLA RUGANTINO

Saltimbocca *literally means "jump in the mouth" and when you've tasted these delicious veal and Prosciutto scallops, that's what you'll want them to do. The dish is named for Rugantino, a popular Roman folk hero who loved good food.*

2 pounds boneless veal (from leg), cut in thin slices
½ cup flour (approximately)
½ cup vegetable oil (approximately)
6 thin slices Prosciutto (approximately)
½ teaspoon dried sage
2 teaspoons finely chopped parsley
Freshly ground black pepper and salt
½ cup (1 stick) butter
⅔ cup Marsala or sweet sherry wine
2 packages (10 ounces each) frozen leaf spinach, defrosted (or 2 pounds fresh spinach)
2 hard-cooked eggs, peeled and sliced into rounds

Place veal slices between two pieces of waxed paper and pound into thin scallops, using a mallet or the flat side of a cleaver. Lightly dust the veal scallops with flour. Heat ½ the oil in a large skillet. Place as many veal scallops in the pan as it will hold without crowding. Cook until very lightly golden on one side, turn and cook second side until golden. Remove from pan and drain on absorbent paper. Repeat with remaining scallops, adding more oil as needed. Cut prosciutto slices in half, or to approximate the size of the veal scallops. Sprinkle each veal slice with sage, parsley and 2 turns of the pepper mill.

Lay a half-slice of prosciutto on each veal slice.

Wipe the skillet clean or use another large skillet and melt ¼ cup (half a stick) butter over medium-low heat. Sprinkle with a pinch of salt and 2 turns of the pepper mill. Place all the veal slices in the pan, prosciutto side up, and cook slowly for 6 minutes. Add the wine to the pan and cook for 10 minutes more.

Meanwhile heat the defrosted frozen spinach in a skillet with the remaining ¼ cup butter. (If fresh spinach is used, wash very well in cold running water. Cook in a covered pan in just the water that clings to the leaves after washing. Cook about 5 minutes, or until just tender. Drain, stir in the butter.) On a large platter, make a bed of the hot spinach.

Arrange the veal on top. Place a slice of egg on each scallop. Spoon the pan juices over all.

(From ITALIAN INTERNATIONAL DINNER PARTY. Copyright 1974 by Burton Richard Wolf.)

Ham Rack E:12

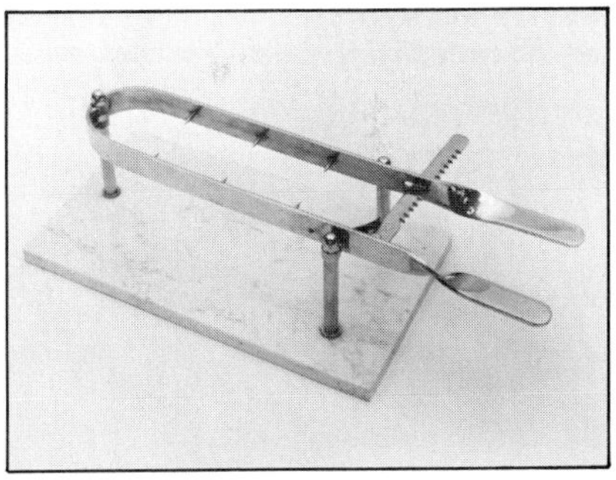

Consider the elegant prospect of having an entire, sweet and delicate *prosciutto di Parma,* and then needing an authentic Italian ham rack to hold it while you carve its paper-thin slices. The polished white marble and gleaming stainless steel of this rack should meet the challenge admirably—although it will certainly work as well for less ambitious hams. The elongated horseshoe-shaped rack grips the ham with three pairs of prongs, while a flexible knife makes a neat job of slicing. A notched crossbar can be set to adjust the space within the horseshoe so that hams of any size or shape can be accommodated. The marble base, 17½″ long by 9¾″ wide and ¾″ high,

Continued from preceding page

is very heavy, and needs no clamping to stay in place on table or sideboard. The steel grip stands about 7″ high on three sturdy legs.

HOAN Products Ltd. (HC1) **$200.00**

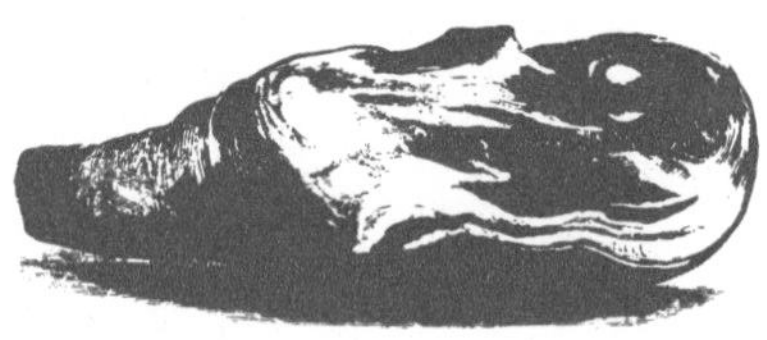

In the sixteenth century the salted and air-dried ham of Parma, prosciutto, *was served in a very different fashion from the finely sliced appetizer with which we are now familiar: it was kept whole, braised in wine and served with capers, grapes and sugar. This style of service is detailed in the menu from a banquet served on the fifteenth of October, 1570, in which fifty other dishes were also served, including* prosciutto *in more usual guises.*

Tritacarne Three E:13

The *meraviglioso* Bialetti Tritacarne Three does almost everything to prepare a hearty Italian meal except pour the Chianti and pinch the cook. Looking somewhat like a lunar landing module, this multi-function food processor will grind meat, pulp tomatoes and grate cheese. Each of the three major components (grinder, pulper and slicer/shredder/grater) attaches to a 9¼″-long, 4″-wide and 6¾″-high white plastic base that houses a 115-watt, fan-cooled motor. The meat grinder attachment comes with coarse and fine tempered-steel cutting heads, plates and a sharp knife blade. The pulper attachment has a plastic hopper and food pusher, and a tinned-steel pulping cone. (One cautionary note: the internal sieve in the pulper tends to heat up from friction when in use, so this pulper is best suited to foods that won't be harmed by heat.) Finally, the slicer/shredder/grater comes with three stainless-steel drums, one for each of the abovementioned chores. The plastic parts are all dishwasher safe.

Gary Valenti (V-200) **$68.00**

Sausage Funnel E:14

A bit fat in the nozzle, this heavy-gauge, polished-aluminum funnel is for stuffing those marvelous, irresistible, sweet or hot and anise-flavored Italian sausages (or any other kind for that matter). It is 3¾″ from top to bottom, and will hold about ½ cup of ground meat and spices at a time. The diameter of the funnel opening is 3½″, while that of the nozzle is ¾″. We recommend it as a useful aid if sausage-making is a sometime thing in your kitchen. It also serves to funnel anything that might get stuck in the narrower nozzle of a normal funnel.

Berarducci Brothers (D-61) **$1.00**

Sausage Stuffer E:15

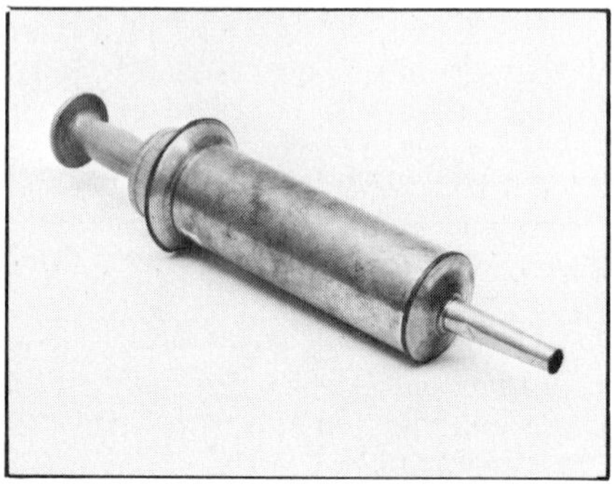

If you are serious about making fresh sausages, like the delicate northern Italian *cotechini* (pork rind, shoulder, cheek and neck meat, salt, pepper, nutmeg and cloves), then this equally serious sausage stuffer is a must. Sturdily made of tinned steel with folded and soldered seams, it has a large wood plunger for forcing the sausage mixture into casings. It is quite long, 15¾″ (20″ with the handle), with a diameter at the top opening of 4½″; the nozzle has a ¾″ opening. Fill the funnel with up to 6 cups of the ground meat and spice mixture, slip a casing over the nozzle and hold it tightly with one hand while you push with firm, even pressure on the plunger. When the casing is filled, twist it around to finish off the completed sausage and release a few more inches (in the case of *cotechini,* at least 8″) for the next sausage.

Macy's **$29.95**

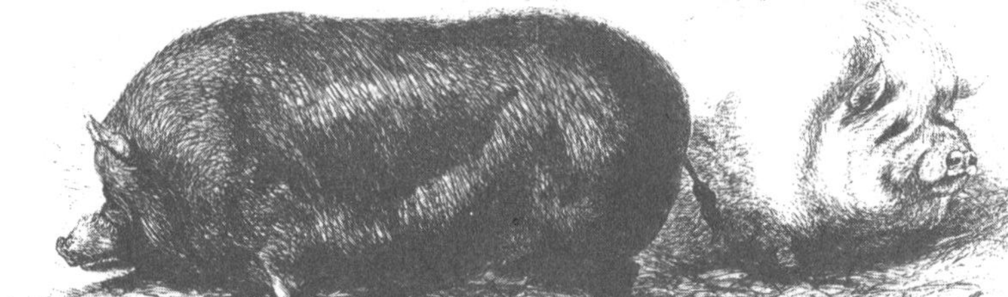

SIENA SAUSAGES

2 pounds pork butt, ground only once
1 large clove of garlic, crushed
1 ounce of salt
A pinch of hot pepper flakes
About 5 black peppercorns
Casing

1. Add garlic, salt, hot pepper flakes and peppercorns to meat and mix through thoroughly with a wooden spoon.

2. Soak casing in a small bowl of lukewarm water for 10 minutes, then remove from the water and dry with paper towels.

3. Attach casing and insert meat as directed in the description of the sausage machine or the funnel.

4. When the casing is full, tie a long string to one end. Now, 3 inches from the end where it is tied, draw the long string around, pass it through and knot it tight. Every three inches, tie the long string around in the same manner, in this way making a long series of sausage links.

5. Let the sausages hang in a cool room with lots of fresh air. About the third day, they should turn a reddish color. Allow them to hang for another 3 or 4 days; the salt will cure the meat in this period. After six or seven days they may be used or refrigerated.

(courtesy Giuliano Bugialli, author of THE FINE ART OF ITALIAN COOKING)

"Macaroni" had many meanings during the late 17th and 18th centuries, but most generally the word referred to an arrogant, dandified person full of affectations and devoid of character. The following description of a macaroni is from the Oxford Magazine of 1770 (quoted in Portrait of Pasta *by Anna Del Conte, 1976): "There is indeed a kind of animal, neither male nor female, a thing of the neuter gender, lately started up amongst us. It is called a Macaroni, It talks without meaning, It smiles without pleasantry, it eats without appetite, it rides without exercise, it wenches without passion."*

A Roman banquet

Cheese Knife E:16

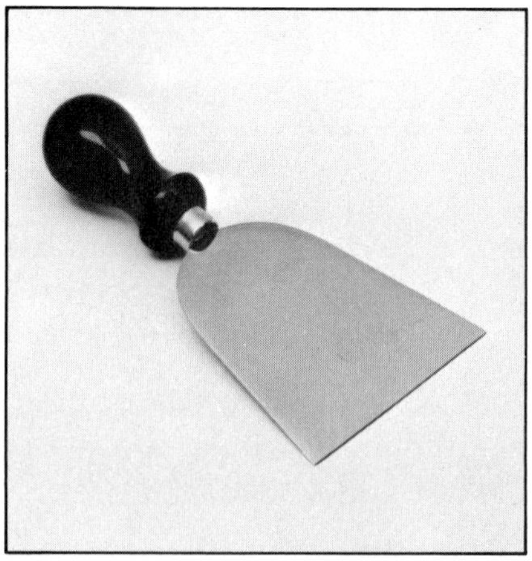

This firm and broad-bladed cheese knife reminds us of a contemporary Italian design for a putty knife. Although its cutting edge is not sharp, it need not be to cut wedges of Bel Paese, provolone, or mozzarella (the water-buffalo-milk variety, please). The shiny stainless-steel blade, 4⅛″ at its widest by 4¾″ long, is secured to its 3½″-long black wooden handle by a metal collar.

Bridge Kitchenware Corp. (132) **$7.00**

Cheese Gouger E:17

To approach the unapproachably hard *parmigiano reggiano* or *pecorino romano* cheeses, use the sharp edges of this gouger to carve out enough cheese for a grater. The 5″-long stainless-steel blade is secured through a metal collar into a 4¼″-long painted wooden handle. The blade—2¼″ wide at the broadest point in its pear shape—is extraordinarily rigid and thick, sharpened only halfway up from the point. And it will not break!

Bridge Kitchenware Corp. **$7.50**

Cheese Grater with Bowl E:18

Freshly grated cheeses, like *parmigiano* and *romano* are essential ingredients in the Italian cuisine. This stainless-steel cheese grater fits into its own flat-bottomed bowl. The bowl is 7¾″ in diameter (as is the grater), 2½″ deep, and holds 6 cups of grated cheese without overflowing. The grater has a raised lip to catch any errant bits of cheese, and air holes around its perimeter allow you to see how much cheese has been grated. The bowl and grater come apart for easy cleaning.

Edwin Jay Inc. (68934) **$7.00**

Deluxe Cheese Grater E:19

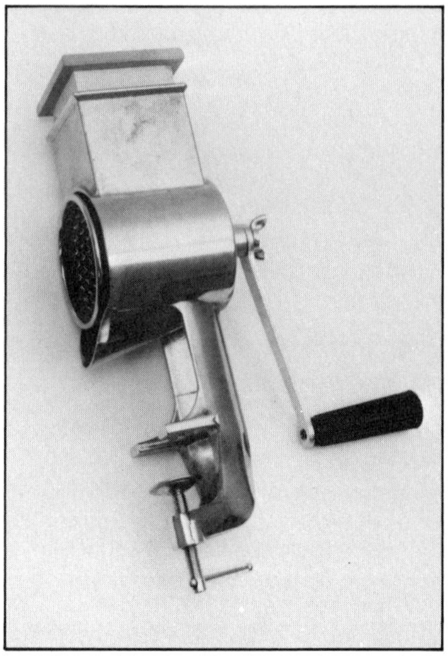

This, we are advised, is the Ferrari of cheese graters. Although we're not sure how it would fare in the Grand Prix, it makes short work of hard Italian grating cheeses. Our 11″-long grater has a cast-aluminum frame and stainless-steel grating drum, and it attaches to a table or countertop by means of its own built-in C-clamp. The box-like hopper is 2½″ by 2¾″, and

2⅝″ deep—big enough to hold a good-sized chunk of cheese. The pusher is a rectangular wooden block with a concave bottom that follows the curve of the grating cylinder. The crank handle, with a black, ridged, hard-plastic grip, attaches by means of a nut-and-bolt mechanism to the grating drum. Below the grater, the aluminum housing curves down into a trough into which the grated cheese falls. Place a small dish or bowl beneath it to catch the cheese as it falls out.

Berarducci Brothers (C-5) **$19.95**

Electric Cheese Grater E:20

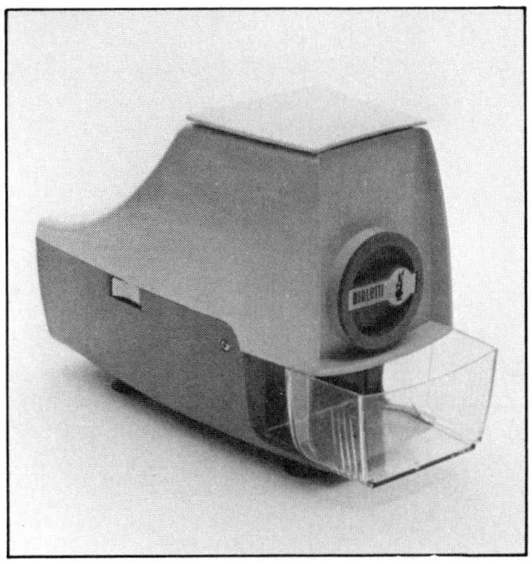

To prepare *sbira genovese* (beef broth fortified with wine, bread and tomatoes), *linguine con pesto,* and *cima alla genovese* (stuffed rolled veal, Genoa style) for eight people, you will need four full cups of grated Parmesan—a task made considerably easier by this electric cheese grater. Place the cheese in the square opening at the top of the machine and use the plastic plunger to force it against the sharp-toothed tinned-steel cutting drum. The grated cheese falls into a clear plastic cup that tucks into its compartment in the base and can be removed for pouring and easy cleaning. The plastic outer casing of the grater is white with orange trim and measures 9″ long by 4″ wide by 6½″ high. The cheese catcher holds 1 cup.

Gary Valenti (V-196) **$39.95**

Oil Can E:21

An oil can is a handy thing to have nearby when cooking Italian style: to add a quick dash of oil to the pasta pot to keep the *linguine* from sticking, or to liberally lubricate a pizza—both dough and topping—before baking. The size (8½″ tall) and capacity (about 5 cups) of this oil can make it easy to dispense small quantities of oil. The 7″-long thin spout is ideal both for controling the quantity of oil poured and for directing its flow. Of tinned steel with a brass lid, it has a roomy, open handle for easy grasping.

Kalian Products Corp. (OT42) **$10.00**

Olives evoke the cuisine of the entire Mediterranean area. Most historians agree that Egyptians, in the 3rd millennium B.C. were the first to cultivate them. In Italy olive branches were used to ward off lightning, witches and wizards. The trees were believed to become more fruitful if tended by innocent children. If a man were unfaithful to his wife, the crop perished. Athenian wealth was often measured in olive trees, for only the rich would afford a crop that took about forty years to show a profit. Athenian brides, like the Roman conquerors, wore crowns of olive leaves.

sixteenth-century olive oil manufacture

Pasta

Pasta is to Italy what rice is to China and corn is to Latin America. And Italians are fiercely proud of their claim to the copyright on this staple. Pasta historians at Italy's Museum of Spaghetti History now contest the long-standing belief that the Chinese gave spaghetti (*lo mein*) to Marco Polo. Archival evidence has the Romans eating ravioli in 1284, nine years *before* Signor Polo got back home.

Pasta thrived in Italy for 500 years before it was introduced in the New World in 1786 by Thomas Jefferson, who discovered spaghetti—along with ice cream, French wines and other delicacies—during his stay in Europe as Minister to France. He ordered from Italy a die for making spaghetti so that he could have his cooks duplicate the dish. It was not until 1848, however, that spaghetti was produced commercially in the United States. And not until the beginning of the present century, when a large wave of immigrants arrived here from southern Italy, did it become popular.

But spaghetti is only one of more than a thousand different forms of pasta. *Pasta* is a generic term used to refer to a multitude of products made from a flour-and-water dough that is kneaded, rolled

Continued from preceding page

out, cut and/or shaped, and allowed to dry in the air before it is cooked. The word *macaroni,* sometimes used in place of the word pasta, properly refers to hollow or pierced forms of this food. The different names and shapes the Italians give to pasta tell us something about the enthusiasm with which they regard this food. There are: peppercorns (*acini di pepe*), fat little lambs (*agnolotti*), large reeds (*cannelloni*), angel's hair (*capelli d'angelo*), clown's hats (*capelli di pagliaccio*), cocks combs (*creste di gallo*), little thimbles (*ditalini*), butterflies (*farfalle*), small tongues (*linguine*), little worms (*vermicelli*), small muffs (*manicotti*), seashells (*maruzze*), hazelnuts (*nocciole*), sparrow's eyes (*occhi di passeri*), little stars (*stelline*), snails (*lumache*), clam shells (*vongole*) and bridegrooms (*ziti*) —to name only a few.

In Italy, modest portions of pasta dishes are usually served as a first course to whet the appetite. Eaten this way, they add nutritional balance to a meal without adding an excessive number of calories. Styles of pasta differ from northern and southern Italy. In the North, the dough is the traditional homemade *pasta fresca,* enriched with eggs and cut into flat, ribbon-like shapes. The pasta of the South is the eggless, commercial *pasta secca,* often made in hollow shapes. Either way, they may be eaten in soup as *pasta in brodo;* as *pasta asciutta,* which is boiled, drained and served with a sauce; or as *pasta in forno* which is oven-baked, stuffed or layered, as in *lasagne* and *manicotti.* And there are sauces that range from simple butter or olive oil with freshly grated cheese, to elaborate combinations of ingredients.

The *cognoscenti* agree that there is no comparison between authentic, fresh, homemade pasta and the supermarket variety. To really savor pasta you must either make it yourself or, at the very least, buy a fine Italian *pasta secca.*

Rolling Pin for Pasta E:22

Certamente, this is one of the longest rolling pins we've ever seen. Twenty-four inches from one end to the other, this 2″-thick, smooth, solid hardwood pin is perfectly suited to rolling out enormous sheets of *pasta fresca* to be cut and formed into any of dozens of fresh pastas—from delicate *spaghettini* to plump, meat-filled *agnolotti.* Aspiring Italian pastry chefs will also find this heavy, well-balanced pin splendid for rolling out dough for *cannoli* (crisp pastry tubes filled with ricotta, candied fruit and chocolate) or *crostate* (sweet pastry tarts). After use the pin should be wiped clean with a damp cloth.

Cross Imports Inc. (676) $6.00

Pasta Knife E:23

For those who roll their pasta dough by hand, a knife with a very sharp and perfectly straight edge is necessary for cutting folded layers of dough into strips for *fettuccine, fettucce* or other widths. The blade of a traditional slicing knife is not straight enough, and a Chinese cleaver, which might work, is not long enough. This 11″-long, wide-bladed 2″ knife is the answer. Its nearly rectangular stainless-steel blade has a full tang secured in the dark-stained rosewood handle by three brass rivets.

Rowoco Inc. (1201) $14.00

Pastry/Pasta Jagger E:24

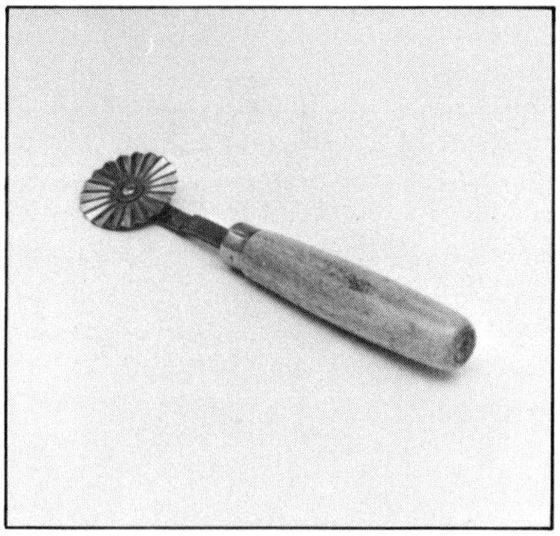

A venerable member of the pasta or pastry cook's *batteria di cucina,* this fluted-wheel pastry jagger is used to make the familiar "pinked" edges on *ravioli* or *farfalle* (butterfly-shaped pasta), or to spruce up the lattice strips on the top of a *crostata di ricotta* (cheese tart). The jagger's 1½″-diameter stainless-steel wheel is held firmly in a nickel-steel frame set into a polished wood handle, and is of top quality.

August Thomsen Corp. (1397) $1.75

A particularly far-fetched Bolognese legend explains the appearance of tagliatelle (*from* tagliare, *to cut*) *in this way: a nobleman's cook was so enchanted by the long, yellow locks of an elegant guest that he created a dish for her. The blond damsel, Lucrezia Borgia by name, came to be known for a few dishes of her own, which some might say have had even more of an impact on history than these slender, ivory noodles.*

Double Dough Cutter E:25

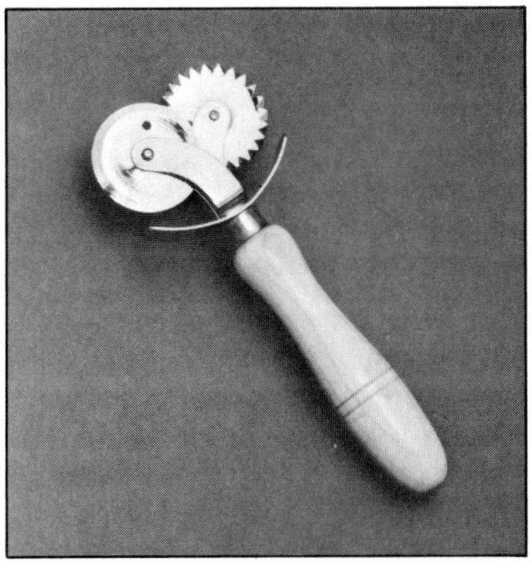

This professional-quality tool gives you two pastry/pasta wheels at once: one plain and the other a jagger, both mounted on a sturdy, 4″-long wooden handle. A curved, metal hand guard prevents the cook's fingers from making contact with either of the sharp, stainless-steel cutting wheels. Use the jagged wheel to cut broad noodle strips for ruffle-edged *lasagne*; or flip the cutter over and use the plain wheel to cut long, straight-edged strips for *cenci* (sweet pastry strips tied into knots and deep fried). This implement is not only well made, but is also possibly the only pastry wheel you will ever need to buy.

Rowoco Inc. (139) $2.25

Chitarra E:26

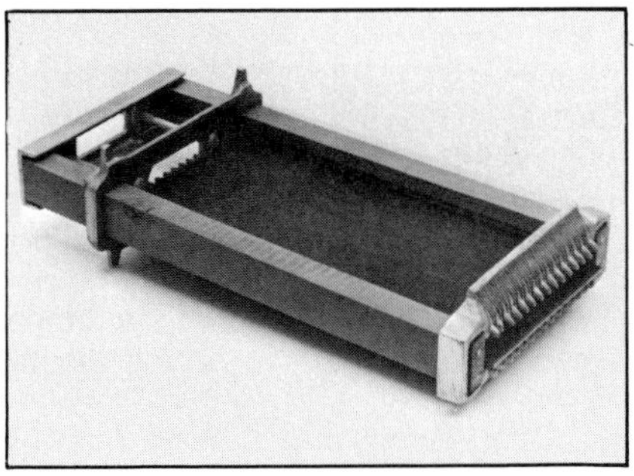

A modern version of an old, provincial device, this rectangular cast-aluminum and wooden frame strung with steel wires—called a *chitarra,* or guitar, for its resemblance to that instrument—is still used to make spaghetti. A thin sheet of rolled-out pasta dough is placed across the *chitarra* wires and then gently pressed through with your hand or a rolling pin. The spaghetti thus formed will fall neatly onto a sliding masonite tray beneath. This *chitarra,* unlike some of the old, hand-fashioned ones, is strung on both sides, with wires 1/16″ apart on one side and 1/8″ apart on the other, to produce two different widths of noodles. The frame is 20″ long, 8½″ wide and 4½″ high, with the wires attached to aluminum terminals at each end. Should the wires slacken, they can be tightened by turning the thick aluminum nuts on one end of the frame.

Berarducci Brothers (A-17) $29.95

Pasta Machines

Making fresh pasta involves four separate procedures: mixing, kneading, rolling and cutting the dough. With skill, a light touch, and an Italian grandmother, you can become adept at all four; with a pasta machine you can become a whiz at the mixing and let the machine do the rest. Purists sneer, claiming that machine-made pasta has a slippery surface to which sauces won't cling properly. We sneer back, maintaining that homemade pasta of any sort is a world apart from the packaged variety.

All pasta machines work in the same way. In the machine, the kneading and rolling are reduced to a single procedure as a ball of dough is fed over and over again through the smooth, mangle-like rollers of the machine. You cut off a lump of dough the size of a large lemon, and feed it through the smooth rollers, which are set as far apart as they can go. When you have done this a few times, folding the dough after each passage, then you set the rollers a notch closer together and begin to thin out the dough. Now, instead of folding it, you pass the elongating oval shape through over and over again, moving the rollers closer together every few times, until they are as close as they can get. After anywhere from eight to twelve trips through the machine—the number varying according to how much you have kneaded the dough beforehand—it will be a long strip of well-kneaded pasta dough, about 1/16″ thick, shiny and stretchy.

If you are making a stuffed pasta such as ravioli or *cappelletti,* you can go ahead now to cut and stuff it while it is flexible. If you are

Continued from preceding page

making noodles, however, you should allow the thin sheets of dough to dry on a dish towel for around 15 minutes. Then move to the cutting blades of the pasta machine. Set them for the type of noodle you choose to make, flour the dough, and feed it through the blades. In one side goes a bland and boring sheet of dough; out the other side comes *tagliatelle* or *fettuccine*. After a few minutes of proper awe and admiration, bestir yourself to throw the noodles into a pot of boiling water. But be careful not to overcook them! Noodles as fresh as these will be cooked almost as soon as the water in the pot returns to the boil.

Atlas Pasta Machine E:27

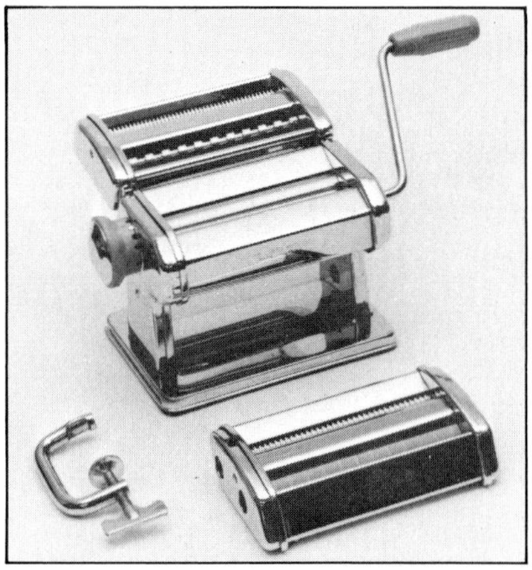

A long rolling pin and a straight sharp knife are the basic tools for making pasta by hand. But it is admittedly hard to knead and roll stiff pasta dough without working up a *sudore* (sweat). This *macchina per pasta* will make the chore considerably easier. It is a sturdy, well-made machine with a 7½″ by 5¼″ chromed-steel base and nickel-steel kneading and cutting rollers. The cutting head that comes with the machine has two sets of rollers, one that will cut *fettuccine,* and the other, somewhat narrower noodles, like *tagliolini.* An optional cutting head attachment makes even finer noodles —*capelli d'angelo,* or angel's hair— and has a wavy-edged form for *lasagne.* The machine stands 5¼″ high, comes with a detachable handle and has a C-clamp that secures it to the work surface.

Gary Valenti
Pasta Machine (V-190) $35.00
Attachment (V-193) $18.00

Altea Pasta Machine E:28

This top-quality pasta machine has three sets of steel rollers, 6″ long, housed in a 6½″-high chromed-steel case. One pair of rollers, smooth and with an adjustable space between them, performs the kneading and rolling operations. The other two are cutting rollers, one fine and the other for broad noodles. The machine clamps to a work table and has a detachable hand crank that is moved to the appropriate set of rollers as required. To increase this pasta machine's versatility, five additional cutting rollers that clip on to make noodles of other widths (1.5, 4, 8, 12, and 50 mm.) are also available.

Berarducci Brothers (160) $49.95

FETTUCCINE CAPRICCIOSE

"Whimsical" Egg Noodles

To enjoy these delicate egg noodles as you would in Rome, cook them *al dente*—still firm to the teeth. Do not overcook. Have all the other ingredients at hand, ready to mix with the fettuccine as soon as they're cooked. Tortellini are also delicious prepared this way.

4 thin slices prosciutto
½ cup peas—fresh, frozen or canned
4 quarts water
1 tablespoon salt
1 pound green fettuccine, imported if possible
½ cup (1 stick) butter
¾ cup heavy cream
Freshly ground black pepper
⅔ cup freshly grated Parmesan cheese (serve additional grated cheese at the table)

Ahead of time, cut prosciutto into 2-inch lengths across the grain and then into ¼-inch strips with the grain. If you're using fresh peas, shell and cook in boiling, salted water 3 minutes, and drain; if frozen, defrost; if canned, drain.

Bring water and salt to a boil. Add fettuccine and cook exactly seven minutes; drain. Melt the butter in a large skillet over low heat.

Add drained fettuccine and toss thoroughly with butter, using a large fork so you can lift, turn, and stir. Add the cream and prosciutto, and continue to mix well for two minutes. Add peas, pepper to taste, and finally cheese. Blend thoroughly. Fettuccine must have a rich, creamy look.

Serve at once in shallow soup plates. Pass the pepper and additional grated cheese at the table.

(From ITALIAN INTERNATIONAL DINNER PARTY. Copyright 1974 by Burton Richard Wolf.)

"Of Italian dishes none is better known than macaroni. It first attracted the notice of English travellers in the eighteenth century, and the young bloods of that day, on their return from the grand tour borrowed its name for their most fashionable club. This set of travelled fops, as vicious as they were exclusive, called themselves the macaronis and introduced the dish. . . ."

Good Cheer: The Romance of Food and Feasting *by F. W. Hackwood. New York, 1911*

Macaroni vendor, 1834

Macaroni Makers at Naples

Electric Pasta Machine E:29

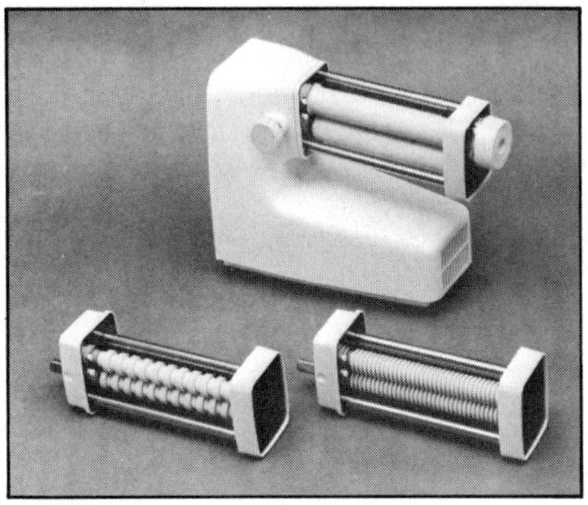

There's no doubt on the part of anyone whose taste buds have been consulted that *pasta fresca* is infinitely superior to the factory-made, store-bought variety—even the best Italian brands. If you've always wanted to take advantage of this fact but felt put off by the preparation time involved, an electric pasta machine may be just what you need to make your *pappardelle* (broad noodles), *tortelloni* (small, stuffed pasta), or *vermicelli* lighter and fresher. The electric motor is housed in a white plastic L-shaped base (9″ long, 8″ high, 4″ wide); a series of suction cups keeps the base from "walking" when the motor is operating. The machine comes with three nylon roller attachments: smooth, adjustable rollers for kneading; and broad- and narrow-noodle cutting rollers. Our experts testify that the machine's nylon rollers produce a noodle with a less slick surface—with more "grab" to it—that will absorb sauce better than pasta made on a machine with metal rollers. In addition, because the rollers are not enclosed, as on most manual pasta machines, they are much easier to clean. Best of all, for those who have little time to spend in the kitchen, a batch of fresh pasta can be whipped up—with the aid of a food processor—in as few as 15 minutes.

Gary Valenti (V-195) **$129.95**

Fusilli Pin E:30

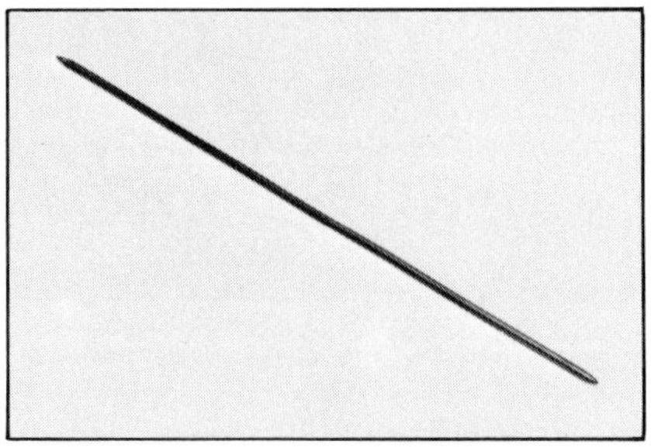

It looks like a double-pointed knitting needle and one might very well ask, what's it doing in the kitchen? This simple, handy gadget of heavy-gauge steel, 12″ long and about $\frac{3}{16}$″ in diameter, is for shaping the curly noodles known as *fusilli.* To make *fusilli,* take a long, thin strip of fresh pasta and wrap it around this pin like the stripes on an old-fashioned barber pole. Then push it down and off and you have one *fusilli* as twisty as Shirley Temple's long-gone curls. After it dries, *fusilli* can be used for most *pasta asciutta* (pasta served with sauces) recipes, like *pasta alle vongole in bianco* (with white clam sauce) or *pasta al pesto* (with basil, garlic and cheese sauce).

E. Rossi and Co. **$0.98**

Pasta Stamps E:31

Here we have three versions of a cookie-cutter device for shaping and cutting filled pastas like ravioli, *agnolotti* (round ravioli) or *cappelletti* ("little hats"). One of the stamps forms a 2¾″ square, another a 2½″-diameter circle, and the third a smaller, 2″-diameter circle. Unlike a regular cookie cutter, the edges of a pasta stamp have tightly zigzagged edges that cut and seal the pasta package firmly. The business end is of solidly constructed, gleaming, chromed brass, attached to a lacquered, natural-wood knob, which is easy to grasp and use. The heights are in proportion to the size of the base, the large round stamp standing 3½″ high, the small round one 3″ high, and the square one 3½″ high.

Berarducci Brothers

Large circle (A-26)	**$1.95**
Small circle (A-28)	**$1.75**
Square (A-25)	**$1.95**

"If you're bored with lonely dinners at home, Toranius, come starve yourself at my table. You won't have to do without appetizers, if that's what you're accustomed to: I've plenty of coarse Cappodocian lettuce, and strong green onions, and chunks of tuna fish, garnished with egg-slices. Next we'll have green broccoli, freshly picked from my cool garden and served on black earthenware plates—so hot you'll scorch your fingers eating it—and sausages wrapped in batter as white as snow, and yellow beans, and red bacon. And if you favor a dessert to top things off with, you can have your choice of raisins, and pears that are said to come from Syria, and chestnuts grown by the clever Neapolitans and toasted on a slow fire. You'll add distinction to the wine by drinking it. And after that, if Bacchus, as he usually does, stirs up a second appetite, choice olives recently harvested from Picenian trees will relieve it—and roast lupins and chick-peas."

a verse from Epigrams from Martial *(V, lxxviii, Rome, first century A.D.), translated by Barriss Mills. Purdue University Studies, 1969*

Rolling Pasta Cutter E:32

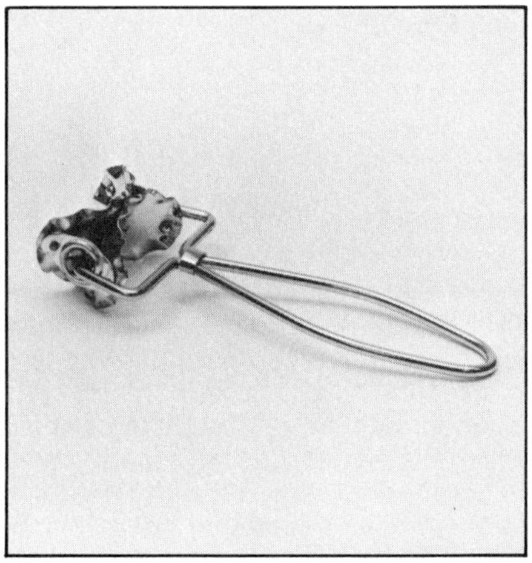

We are showing you an unusual device for making filled pasta forms like *agnolotti* or *tortellini.* Our cutter is rolled over a single sheet of pasta dough to produce an endless chain of scalloped-edged circles. A dab of filling is put in the center of each circle, and the edges are moistened with water and sealed together. Cutter and handle are 6″ long, the handle is made of a rigid stainless-steel wire which is bent so that its ends fit into the sides of the cutter fashioned out of lightweight steel. It looks as though it creates ovals, but roll it over pasta dough—or cooky dough, for that matter—and you can watch it create an infinite sequence of circles.

E. Rossi and Co. $1.98

Plump tortellini *are pasta rings filled with a choice or combination of turkey,* prosciutto, *sweetbreads, eggs and many other delicious mixtures. A nineteenth century journalist wrote of them:* "Tortellini *is more essential than sun for a Saturday and love for a woman." Probably as stunningly accurate as this declaration are the legends explaining the origin of the dish. In one version, a cook, impassioned by the sight of his employer's wife asleep in the nude, created the circular dumpling to represent her ravishing navel. Another explanation equally fanciful, one might assume, is that a Bolognese chef spent a good deal of his time at the window watching a glorious young woman dress and undress across the courtyard. One day, upon perceiving his gaze, she pulled down the shade—but not all the way down; he was still able to see her hopelessly unobtainable bellybutton, which he immortalized in* tortellini *form.*

Cappelletti Cutter E:33

To make *cappelletti,* cut pliable pasta dough into 1½″ squares, and then put a dab of filling on each. Fold each square diagonally, seal the edges, and then mold the triangular pocket around the top of your forefinger. The result will look like a miniature babushka—or whatever the Italian equivalent is—and, thus, a *cappelletto,* or "little hat." Here is the cutter to use for *cappelletti*: 3″ of nicely-turned light wood handle from which a stainless-steel holder extends, opening into two arms. Between these arms are the cutters: two wheels connected by an inch-wide stainless-steel, double-edged blade, the whole attached to the holder by two brass rivets which allow them to turn easily. The tool is 6″ long: serviceable, attractive and easy to clean.

Cross Imports Inc. (113) $2.00

Ravioli Maker E:34

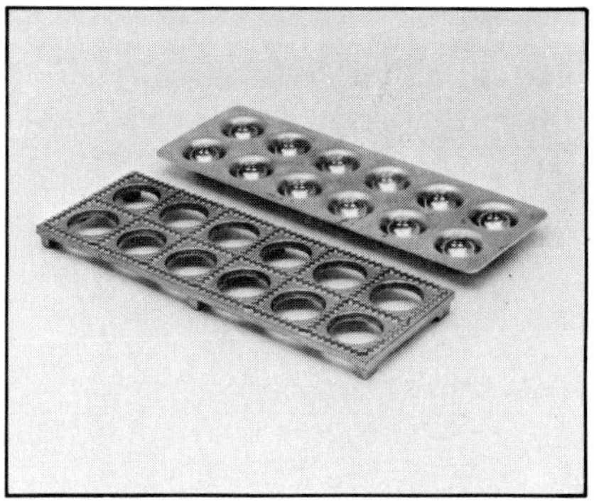

Ravioli were invented by some thrifty cook who was looking for a way to make use of the quarter-cup of chicken, the end of cheese, and the few limp leaves of spinach that were not eaten at lunch. But by now it has evolved into one of the most sophisticated forms of pasta. Many devices exist to produce ravioli in quantity. Here we show a good quality one that will make your ravioli look uniform and professional. It consists of two rectangular cast-aluminum plates: one looks something like an egg carton with a series of round depressions in it; the other has a raised zigzag pattern that forms squares, each with a circular cut-out in the center. To use it, cut a sheet of pasta dough into two rectangles, each slightly larger than the ravioli maker plates. Sprinkle both plates with flour and tap out the excess. Place one dough rectangle over the zigzag plate and gently press the egg-carton plate into it to stretch the dough and form a pocket in each cut-out. Remove the egg-carton plate, fill the pockets with your favorite ravioli stuffing, then, using a small pastry brush

Continued from preceding page

dipped in water, moisten the dough along the zigzag lines before topping it with the other dough rectangle. Work a rolling pin over the dough until all the ravioli are cut and sealed tightly. Release by turning the zigzag plate upside down. This ravioli maker is available in two sizes: one that will make twelve 2″ ravioli (shown here) and another that will make ten 2½″ ravioli.

Vitantonio Mfg. Co. (512) **$9.75**

Ravioli Rolling Pin E:35

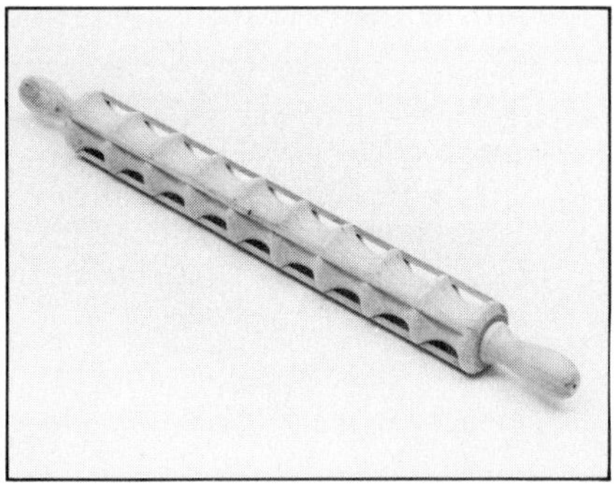

Any search for Italian cooking equipment is likely to turn up this ridged hardwood ravioli rolling pin. The pin's rolling surface is a cylinder 16¼″ long and 2″ in diameter, with nine shallow, rounded grooves about ½″ deep carved out of it. Running the length of the pin are four flat ridges, that divide the grooves into 36 individual squares. To make ravioli with this device, you will also need a plain rolling pin and a pasta jagger: use the regular rolling pin to roll out the pasta; then, once the ravioli filling is in place, this segmented pin is used to press the two pasta sheets together, marking out the individual ravioli; finally, a jagger is used to cut the ravioli apart.

HOAN Products Ltd. (295) **$6.00**

"According to Mr. Tom Murray, a writer on culinary matters, the word Macaroni had a most interesting origin. He says: A wealthy Palermitan noble owned a cook with an inventive genius. One day, in a rapture of culinary composition, this artist cook devised the farinaceous tubes which all love so well, and the succulent accessories of rich white sauce with grated parmesan.

Having filled a large china bowl with this delicious compound, he set it before his lord—a gourmet of the first water—and stood by, in deferential attitude, to watch the effect of his experiment.

The first mouthful elicited the ejaculation 'Cari!', idiomatically equivalent to 'Excellent' in English. After swallowing a second modicum he exclaimed, 'Ma cari!' or 'Excellent, indeed!'

Presently, as the flavour of the toothsome dish grew upon him, his enthusiasm increased, and he cried out in a voice tremulous with joyful emotion, 'Ma, caroni! Ma, caroni' or 'Indeed, most supremely, sublimely and superlatively excellent!'

And, in paying this enthusiastic tribute to the merits of his cook's discovery, he unwittingly bestowed a name upon that admirable preparation that has stuck to it ever since."

Good Cheer: The Romance of Food and Feasting *by F. W. Hackwood. New York, 1911*

Ravioli Machine E:36

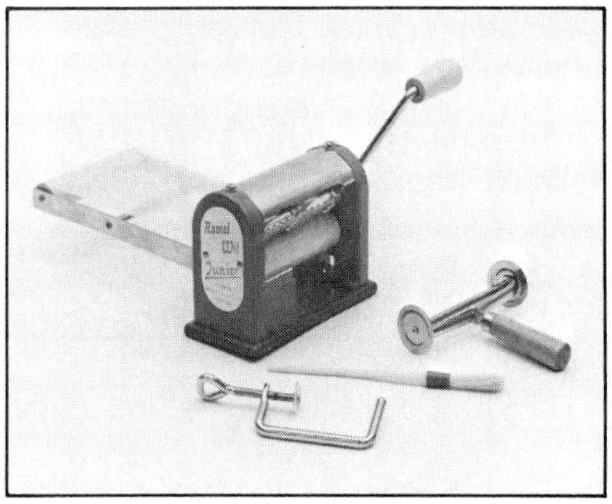

This is an attractive, tough little machine that actually makes ravioli with some efficiency. We are especially fond of it because it comes with an instruction booklet that is a classic of malapropisms: one that you know was written by a clerk equipped with a single semester of English lessons and a rather large dictionary. We could quote it, but that would spoil the fun for you. We do assure you that you will be able to understand how the machine works in spite of the jumbled vocabulary and, once you have understood, to discover that it works well. Picture a 4½″-tall device shaped something like a laundry mangle, the bottom roller smooth, the top roller containing zigzag ravioli-shaped cutting edges. You place a double layer of pasta dough—with the ravioli fillings between the two sheets—on a polyethylene conveyor belt, which feeds the dough into the machine. As the handle is cranked, the dough is pulled into the zigzag cutters, which perforate the dough sandwich, so that what comes out the other side are perfect squares of ravioli. It's made of plastic-coated wood, and chromed steel. It comes with a clamp that secures it to the work surface and a detachable handle, and is easy to assemble, use and disassemble. But, buy it quickly before someone rewrites the instruction booklet.

Rowoco Inc. (154) **$35.00**

Cavatelli Maker E:37

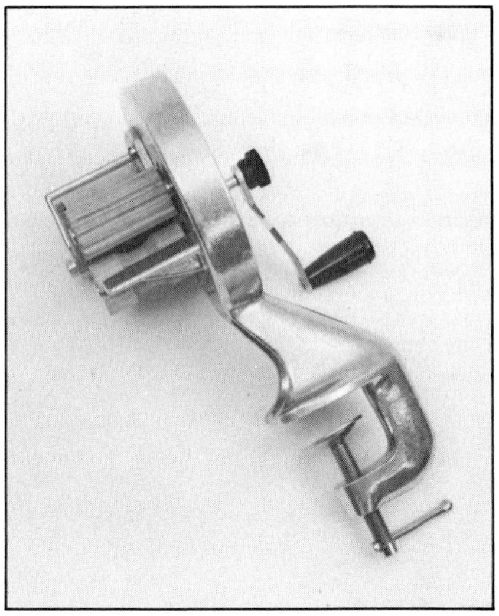

This device is for those who are mad for *cavatelli,* a short, curled noodle whose shell-like shape captures lots of good, rich sauce. To make *cavatelli* with this *cavatelliatore,* feed pasta dough—very, very stiff and ⅜″ thick —one strip at a time into the machine, working it slowly and steadily with one hand while with the other you turn the wooden handle that operates two wooden rollers. The rollers send the dough past a drum with two tiny blades. The blades cut the pasta into even-sized bits and at the same time press them against the cutting drum housing which is etched with deep ridges, leaving the *cavatelli* with a seashell-like pattern. After the cutting drum cuts and patterns the *cavatelli,* it forces them out an opening on the other side. The *cavatelli* maker is made of cast aluminum, stands 9½″ high and has its own C-clamp extension.

Berarducci Brothers (A-16) $15.95

Gnocchi Paddle E:38

Not quite pasta, *gnocchi* are dumplings made from a variety of starches. One region of Italy will cook corn-meal *gnocchi;* another makes potato *gnocchi;* and in another you will be served *gnocchi* made from pure semolina. The dough is rolled out and chilled and cut into small circles, or it is fashioned by hand into long tubes that are sliced into inch-long pieces, and cooked in broth, in water, or in a baking dish, layered with melted butter and grated Parmesan cheese. This 8″-long, 4½″-wide beechwood paddle will help you to make *gnocchi.* Once the stiff *gnocchi* dough has been rolled into long tubes like so many childhood clay "snakes," they are laid across this ridged wooden paddle, and the pleats in the paddle serve as a guide for the knife or roller which cuts the tubes into small pieces. Then the pieces are rolled along the grooves in the paddle, creating small ridges on the surface of the *gnocchi.* The grooves serve to both add visual interest and trap pools of sauce, making each forkful of *gnocchi* tastier.

H. A. Mack & Co., Inc. $1.50

GNOCCHI DI PATATE

Potato Dumplings

4 large Idaho potatoes, or other dry, mealy potato
1 teaspoon salt
1 large egg, beaten
2½ cups flour
2 cups meat sauce
1 cup grated cheese (half Parmesan and half pecorino)

Cook the potatoes with their skins on in boiling salted water until tender. Drain and when cool enough to handle, peel and work potatoes through a ricer or food mill. Spread the mashed potatoes on a flat surface and let cool to room temperature.

Meanwhile, bring 4 quarts of salted water to a boil. Add salt and the beaten egg to the potatoes. Sprinkle 2 cups of the flour over the potatoes and knead the mixture as for bread. When smooth and doughlike, set aside.

Lightly sprinkle a flat surface with flour from the remaining half cup. Cut a piece of "dough" from the potato mixture about the size of a 3-inch ball. Roll it on the board with your hands into a tubular roll about ½ inch thick. Then cut the roll into 1-inch lengths. Continue this process until all the mixture is used.

Drop the gnocchi into the boiling water and simmer about 5 minutes. Drain in a colander and immediately place the gnocchi on a hot serving dish. Add the meat sauce and cheese and mix gently with a wooden spoon. (Also excellent served with butter and cheese.) Serve immediately to 6.

(From ITALIAN FAMILY COOKING, by Edward Giobbi, illustrated by Cham, Lisa and Gena Giobbi. Copyright 1971 by Edward Giobbi. Reprinted by permission of Random House, Inc.)

Neapolitan Pasta Stand

Cooking Pasta

Now that your pasta is made, you have to cook it. *Pasta fresca* takes much less boiling time than *pasta secca;* freshly made *pasta verde* takes shorter still. To cook pasta well, you must use five to seven quarts of water per pound of pasta to keep starch from building up and making the pasta gluey. Add salt to the water as it comes to a boil—not before—and then add the pasta (all at the same time so it cooks evenly), pushing it down gently until it is all submerged. Stir it,

Continued from preceding page

again gently, with a wooden fork to keep the pasta separate. (Some American cooks add a tablespoon of olive oil to the boiling water to prevent sticking.)

To test the doneness of pasta, the best, and only, way is to fish out a piece and bite into it. For pasta *al dente*—the way true pasta lovers insist it should be—cook it only long enough so the hard kernel has disappeared, but the dough still offers resistance to the teeth. Drain it as soon as it's done to keep it from overcooking. However, remember that well after you remove the pasta from the water, it will continue to cook some; so try to catch the pasta when it is truly *al dente* and not just a bit beyond.

Spaghetti Pot with Colanders E:39

Is there anyone who has never tried to carefully pour steaming spaghetti and boiling water out of a pot and into a colander, only to have the spaghetti move a little faster and with more force than the colander was ready for? This special spaghetti pot with two built-in colanders is a very simple and handy answer to some of those slippery problems. The 8-quart aluminum pot comes with a lid, a short upper colander and a full-sized colander. The larger colander is a cylinder—with large perforations on sides and bottom—that fits exactly into the pot. To drain your pasta, simply lift the perforated liner by its ear handles and out it comes, leaving all the cooking water behind—which, if the pasta has been cooked properly, should be from five to seven quarts for each pound of pasta. The upper colander is short, only 3⅜″ high with a bail handle, sloping sides, a flat bottom and small perforations on its bottom and sides. This upper colander can be used for any small pastas that would escape through the holes in the larger colander. This large (10⅜″-diameter, 6½″-deep) pot can also be adapted for steam-cooking. Two adjustable vents in the lid are opened to allow steam to escape while the pasta cooks, but can be closed completely when a tight seal is needed.

Leyse Aluminum Co. (2588) $18.50

Pasta Strainer E:40

This lovely stainless-steel strainer is ideal for scooping *farfalle* (butterfly-shaped pasta), or other compact pasta shapes, from a large pot of boiling water—although the perforations are a bit too large for very thin shapes such as *pastine* or *acini di pepe* (literally "pepper-corns," very small pasta for soup). The bowl of the strainer is 8½″ long, 6½″ wide and 3″ deep, just about the right size for scooping up healthy-sized servings. A metal handle is welded to one side of the bowl and is covered by a sandwich of black plastic that will not conduct the heat of the cooking water. A hook on the side opposite the handle allows you to suspend the strainer over a pot or bowl when you are draining something—other than pasta—whose cooking liquid is to be reserved.

Berarducci Brothers (A-45) $8.95

"Sparghetti is a peculiar form of macaroni. Ordinary macaroni is made in the form of long tubes, and when macaroni pudding is served in schools, it is often irreverently nicknamed by the boys gas-pipes. Sparghetti is not a tube, but simply macaroni made in the shape of ordinary wax-tapers, which it resembles very much in appearance. In Italy, it is often customary to commence dinner with a dish of sparghetti, and should the dinner consist as well of soup, fish, entrée, salad, and sweet, the sparghetti would be served before the soup. . . . This is very cheap, very satisfying, and very nourishing; and it is to be regretted that this popular dish is not more often used by those who are not vegetarians, who would profit both in pocket and in health were they to lessen their butcher's bill by at any rate commencing dinner, like the Italians, with a dish of sparghetti."

Cassell's Vegetarian Cookery *by A. B. Payne, B.A. 1891*

Spaghetti Fork E:41

This long beechwood spaghetti fork is meant for those moments when the spaghetti has just been lowered into the pot of rapidly bubbling water, and you want to get down in there and give it a stir so that the pasta will not stick together. Metal would break the brittle strands of spaghetti: not so this 13½″ length of wood with its three flared prongs.

Charles F. Lamalle $4.00

Tomato.

Spaghetti Rake E:42

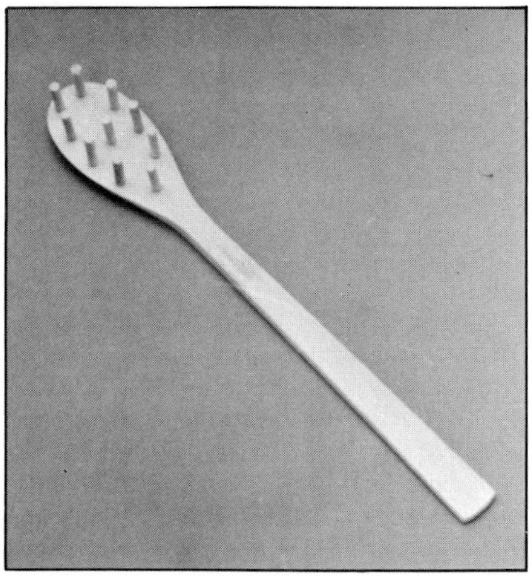

To remove pasta from its cooking water you can simply up-end the potful into a colander. But if you have struggled with huge, heavy pots of boiling pasta water, or if you believe —as some cooks do—that pasta gets cold and sticky during the time required for dumping it into a colander, there's another way: a pasta rake. Our sample is of unfinished beechwood, 13″ long, and looks something like a sparsely bristled hairbrush. You simply dip it into the potful of strands, give it a twirl, and up you come with a bank of *linguine* or spaghetti, ready to drain for an instant and then be deposited in a warmed bowl for saucing and serving.

H. A. Mack & Co., Inc. $1.15

Pasta Tongs E:43

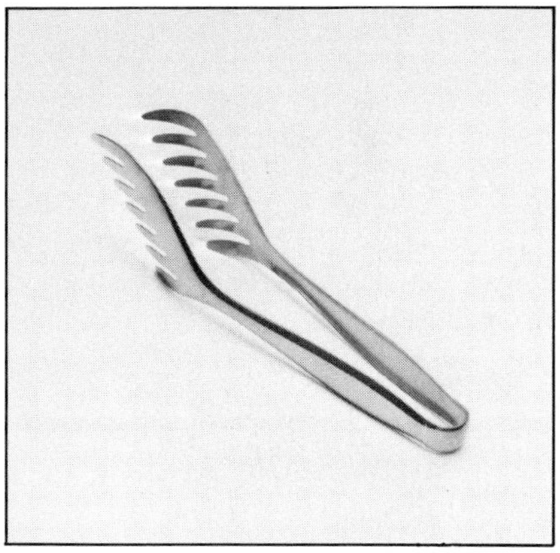

In action, this stainless-steel gadget looks like a pair of seven-clawed fists coming together. Only 9¼″ from its U-shaped top to the tip of the farthest "claw," its length is inadequate for plunging into a pot of spaghetti, although it is ideal for snaring a single strand to test for doneness. It is best used once the pasta has been heaped in a warm serving bowl, both for tossing it with butter and cheese, and for serving. It does both jobs more easily and neatly than the conventional serving spoon and fork.

Edwin Jay Inc. (39306) $3.75

SALSA AL FILETTO

1–2 tablespoons minced onion
2 tablespoons olive oil
2 tablespoons butter
2 slices prosciutto, cut in julienne strips
1 cup consomme
3 tablespoons dry white wine or vermouth
1 clove garlic, peeled
1 leaf fresh basil
2 large tomatoes (or 6–8 plum tomatoes), peeled, seeded, juiced and chopped very fine

Sauté the onion in the olive oil until browned. Add everything but the tomatoes and reduce over high heat until the liquid is almost completely evaporated—it will be very thick and syrupy.

Drain the chopped tomatoes well and add to the pan. Reduce over high heat until the rendered tomato juices begin to thicken, then lower heat and continue to simmer until sauce is thick and smooth about 15–20 minutes altogether.

Remove and discard the clove of garlic. Add cooked fettucine (or your favorite pasta) and toss together. Serve with freshly grated parmesan cheese.
Yield: 2–4 servings

(Courtesy The Bank Restaurant, New York City)

Earthenware Lasagne Pan E:44

Does anyone need to ask what *lasagne* is? Is there some deprived person who has never tasted that inspired layering of pasta, *ragù bolognese* (meat sauce), ricotta and mozzarella cheeses? Or its relative, green *lasagne* layered with *ragù bolognese* and bechamel sauces, with mushrooms, ham and Parmesan cheese? Wouldn't it be nice to have a pan like this one to make it in? This slickly-glazed, dark brown earthenware pan (with an unglazed bottom) was made deep enough to hold a number of repetitions on the basic layers. It is 13¾″ long, 7½″ wide, 2¼″ deep and has an 8-cup capacity. Ear type handles run nearly the full width of the pan, so that they can be comfortably grasped at the moment when the bubbling *lasagne* is borne triumphantly from the oven.

Macy's $14.00

Italian food is usually considered to be fairly simple and straightforward. This has not always been so, as one may judge from the following recipe for game pie published in The Italian Banquet *of Epulario (1516, translated into English 1598):*

"To Make Pies that the Birds May be Alive in Them, and Flie Out When It is Cut Up.

Make the coffin of a great pie or pasty, in the bottome thereof make a hole as big as your fist, or bigger if you will. Let the sides of the coffin bee somewhat higher than ordinary pies, which done put it full of flower and bake it, and being baked, open the hole in the bottome and take out the flower. Then having a pie of the bigness of the hole in the bottome of the coffin aforesaid, you shal put it into the coffin, withall put into the said coffin round about the aforesaid pie as many small live birds as the empty coffin will hold, besides the pie aforesaid. And this is to be then at such time as you send the pie to the table, and set before the guests: where uncovering or cutting up the lid of the great pie, all the birds will flie out, which is to delight and pleasure shew to the company. And because they shall not be altoghether mocked, you shall cut open the small pie, and in this sort you may make many others, the like you may do with a tart."

quoted in The Delectable Past *by Esther Aresty. Simon & Schuster, 1964*

Enameled Cast-Iron Lasagne Pan — E:45

This enameled cast-iron *lasagne* pan—with its pristine white interior and a choice of brown, blue, yellow, red or white exteriors—is attractive enough to go straight from the oven to the table. Although we have chosen it for its *lasagne*-pan qualities, we venture to say that *polenta pasticciata* (baked *polenta* with cream sauce and mushrooms) baked in it would taste superb, as would *cannelloni* (stuffed pasta tubes), or even *triglie alla calabrese* (baked red mullet with black olives and capers). The pan's cast-iron core deals efficiently with oven heat, while the double-fired porcelain-enamel coating does not discolor. With a depth of 2″, this 8¾″-wide by 14″-long rectangular vessel has a capacity of 3 quarts—enough *lasagne* or other baked pasta to satisfy the heartiest of appetites.

Copco, Inc. (111) — $36.00

ED GIOBBI'S LASAGNE

Serves 8–10

MEAT SAUCE
1 pound sweet Italian sausages
1 pound ground chuck
Salt
Freshly ground black pepper
½ pound mushrooms, sliced or chopped
1 teaspoon chopped garlic
6 cups fresh marinara sauce

WHITE SAUCE—BESCIAMELLA
3 tablespoons butter
3 tablespoons flour
1 cup milk
1¼ cups heavy cream
Salt and pepper to taste
¼ teaspoon nutmeg

PASTA AND ASSEMBLY INGREDIENTS
1-pound package lasagne (imported, if possible), green or white, preferably green
½ pound mozzarella cheese, cut in small cubes
½ cup freshly grated parmigiano
6 tablespoons melted butter

Cook the sausages in a 10-inch glass-ceramic skillet over medium heat until brown all over. Remove sausages and set aside. Pour off and discard almost all of the sausage fat; add to the skillet the beef, salt and pepper; cook, breaking up the lumps of meat with the side of a large kitchen spoon. Add the mushrooms and garlic. Stirring frequently, cook until the meat loses its red color. Then, stirring occasionally, continue to cook until meat starts to brown.

While the meat mixture cooks, skin the sausages and slice them thin. When beef begins to brown, add sausage slices and the marinara sauce. Lightly mix all ingredients together. Partially cover skillet with a lid, pulled up on one side to allow steam to escape. Simmer sauce about 45 minutes, stirring occasionally. Set aside.

Preheat oven to 375 F. Meanwhile, cook the lasagne in a big pot of salted boiling water until it is *al dente.* (If lasagne is homemade, it will take 5 minutes or so; if packaged, about 10.) Carefully drain off half of the water from the pot, and set pot under cold running water until cool enough to remove each lasagne by hand. Lay lasagne on paper towels (do not let pieces overlap or they will stick together), then blot each one on top with more paper towels.

To make Besciamella: In a saucepan, over low heat, melt the 3 tablespoons of butter and, using a wire whisk, stir in flour until blended. Gradually, stir in the milk with the whisk and keep stirring until thickened. Stir in the cream, and season with salt, pepper and nutmeg. (This white sauce should not sit long or it will become too thick.)

Assemble the dish: Spoon a layer of the meat sauce into an open, 13-inch-long ovenproof roaster; cover the entire surface of the bottom. Over the meat sauce, spoon 3–4 tablespoons of the white sauce; lengthwise on top of the sauces, arrange a layer of lasagne strips. Over the lasagne, spread a thin layer of meat sauce, a few tablespoons of white sauce, and a layer of mozzarella cubes. Sprinkle with a little of the parmigiano. Trickle 2 tablespoons of melted butter over the surface.

Begin again with lasagne, and construct each layer as just described, ending with meat sauce, white sauce, mozzarella, parmigiano and melted butter. Bake about 45 minutes, or until piping hot and bubbling throughout.

(From THE GREAT COOKS COOKBOOK, by The Good Cooking School, Inc. Copyright 1974 by The Good Cooking School, Inc. Reprinted by permission of Ferguson/Doubleday)

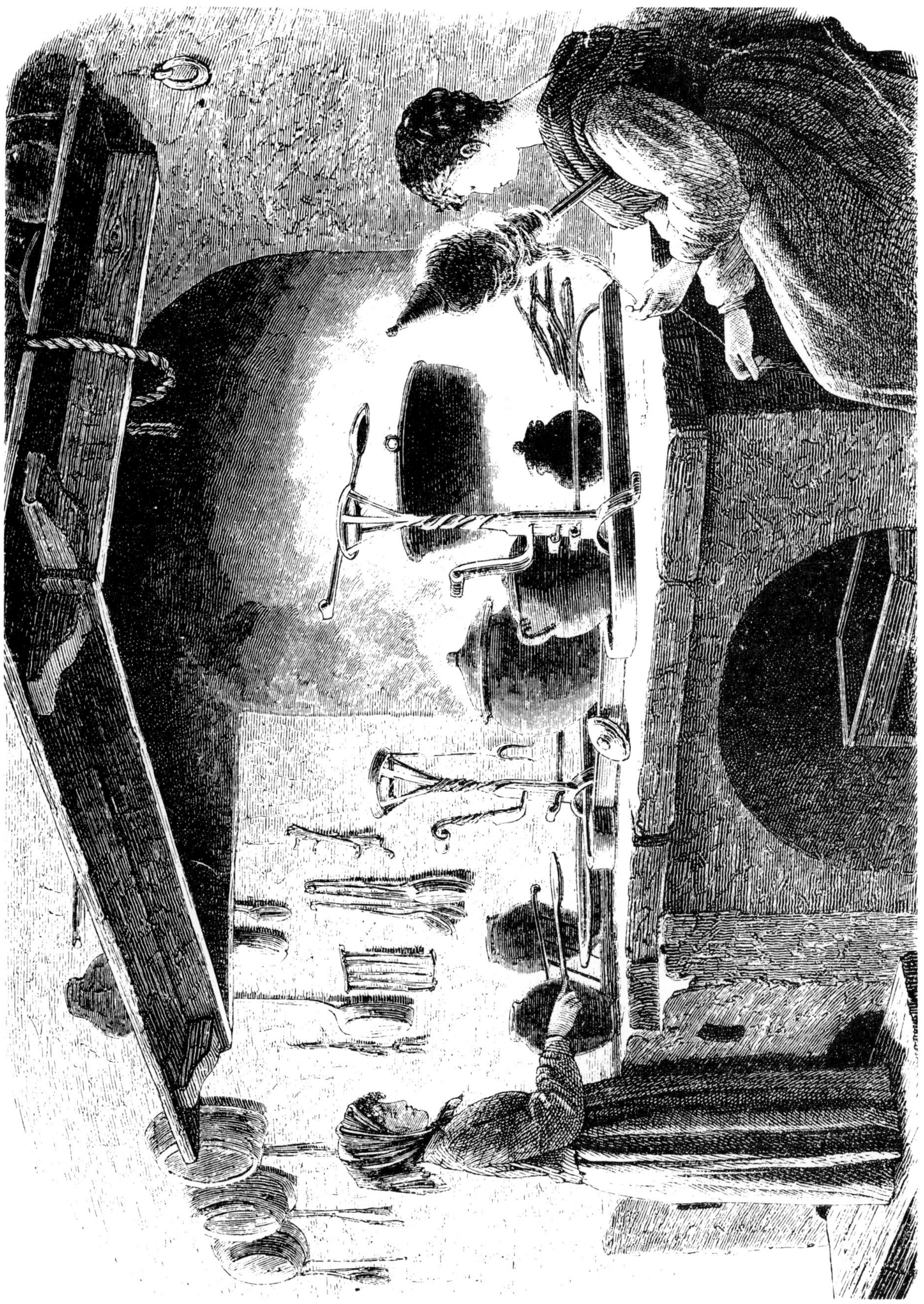

An Italian Kitchen

Pizza Pan E:46

For a crisp crust, bubbling sauce and melted cheese, pizza must be baked quickly in an intensely hot oven. This pan made of aluminum (an excellent heat conductor) is, therefore, ideally suited. It is available in two diameters, 12″ or 14″, so you can choose according to the size of your appetite.

HOAN Products Ltd.
12″ (612-12) $3.00
14″ (614-14) $3.50

Pizza Peel E:47

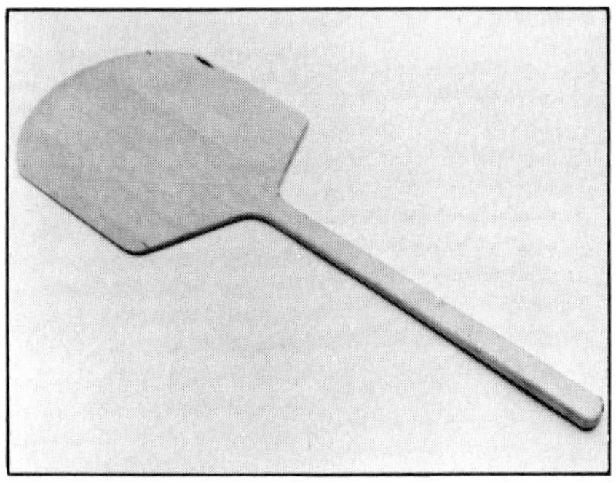

A peel is a paddle, a long-handled shovel with which the professional baker carries a pizza (*sans* pan) to the oven and then removes it when it's done. Although the average household does not have a pizza oven—and therefore no need for a pizza peel—the hot, even baking surface of a baker's oven can be simulated by placing fire brick tiles over the metal rack in a standard oven. The pizza crust baked directly on the fire bricks will have the crunch of authenticity, but will have to be transported to and from the oven by a peel. Ours is 36″ long, but you can also get a shorter one. The spade-end is 15″ long and 14″ across—also available a few inches narrower or wider. Check the width of your oven before you buy one. Made of good looking, bleached wood, it's the sort of thing you might just want to hang on the wall of your kitchen even if you don't plan on going into the take-out pizza business.

International Edge Tool Co. (5116) $12.00

Pizza Cutter E:48

You have seen the baker in the local pizzeria zipping his way through a pie with a gadget like this in a matter of seconds. This professional quality pizza cutter has a round, 2¾″-diameter, stainless-steel cutting wheel with a hollow-ground edge. The removable blade revolves freely in a nut-and-bolt arrangement that attaches it to the handle. The 4⅛″-long handle is made of cast aluminum and is curved to fit comfortably in the hand; and a finger-guard shields the cook from the cutter's sharp edge. The balance and weight of this cutter make it easy to slice through pizza crust quickly and with little effort.

Russell Harrington Cutlery, Inc. (S3A) $4.95

Grill E:49

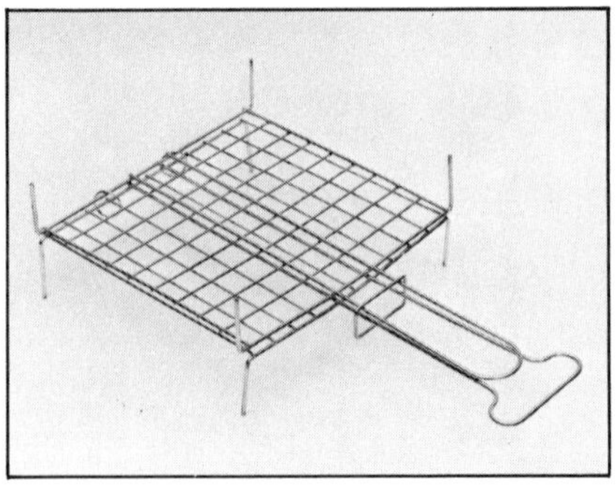

Tuscans insist that to make a proper *fiorentina* (broiled Florentine steak), you need a T-bone steak from a beef raised in the Chiana valley. Texans could probably challenge the Tuscans; but in either case, to broil the steak in the Florentine manner, you will need a grill like this one. It consists of two 9¾″-square wide-mesh grids of rigid tinned-steel wire; both grids have four 2″ wire legs, one at each corner. The grids are hinged together loosely on one side by two wire rings that allow the grill to open wide enough to hold a ¾″-thick steak. Wire handles extend beyond the grids by 8″ and have a rectangular loop that keeps them together when the steak is in place. To make a *fiorentina,* place it between the grids; close them and slide the rectangular handle loop over both handles. Then hold the grill over the fire in your fireplace, or rest it on its legs over the coals in your barbecue pit. When one side is done, turn the entire apparatus over to cook the other side. Salt the just broiled side. Once the steak is done (it should be rare), wet each side with a small amount of olive oil, and serve.

E. Rossi and Co. $2.98

Earthenware

The traditional earthenware pots and pans of a provincial Italian kitchen are not always easy to find in this country, but the search will prove worth the effort. Earthenware has very specific qualities and characteristics that are essential to Italian cuisine's saucing and simmering, and that are not duplicated by any other cookware material. To make earthenware, clay is fired at temperatures too low for it to become vitrified, or glassified, as are stonewares and porcelain; this leaves the surface of earthenware fairly porous. As a result, once earthenware has absorbed heat—which it does slowly but thoroughly—it will retain the temperature for a very long time. Correctly used over low to moderate heat, the contents of these pots will keep simmering steadily, making them perfect for cooking sauces.

A bare, unglazed earthenware surface absorbs and transmits heat more efficiently than a glazed surface, and so most pots have unglazed bottoms and sometimes completely unglazed exteriors. The interiors, on the other hand, are usually glazed to seal the clay and prevent the absorption of food juices and flavors. (Glaze is actually a kind of glass, applied as a thick liquid to once-fired ceramics; a second firing fuses the raw ingredients to the clay body and forms the glaze.)

The typical Italian earthenwares, whether baking dishes or saucepots, have unglazed bottoms, and dark, glossy brown exteriors. The interior glazes are usually clear to allow the lighter color of the natural clay to show through—providing a rich and appetizing counterpoint to the dark tomato-red of the sauces and stews cooked in them.

All of these pots must be cured before they are used for the first time. Methods for curing will vary with the composition of the earthenware clay body, and very likely with customs, as well. One Italian manufacturer suggests the following method: 1) soak the entire pot in cold water to cover for 24 hours; 2) wipe dry and air dry, bottoms up, for 24 hours; then 3) rub all unglazed surfaces with a cut clove of garlic. (Although it sounds old-wives-taleish, we have an Italian chef friend who swears by the garlic method.) Another manufacturer recommends soaking the entire pot in very hot water for at least ½ hour before using for the first time, then towel and air-dry bottoms up.

As substantial and hearty as earthenware looks, it can be quite fragile if not treated properly. For instance, flameproof or not, earthenware should never be subjected to drastic changes in temperature: for stovetop use, start the pot over a low flame, increasing to moderate if necessary, always bearing in mind that it is specifically suited to slow cooking over low heat. In addition, never place a refrigerator-cold earthenware pot directly on a hot burner or in a hot oven; extremely cautious cooks often start their earthenware casseroles in a cold oven.

Small Saucepan E:50

This small earthenware saucepan, with its dark brown glazed exterior and clear glazed interior, is handsome enough to go directly from stove to table. The saucepan has a 3″-long handle attached halfway down one side and an unglazed underside for better heat absorption. With an inner diameter of 7″ and standing 2½″ high, this saucepan has a capacity of just 1 quart—enough for two to four servings of *piselli al prosciutto* (braised peas with *prosciutto*) or *peperonata* (braised sweet peppers with tomatoes and onions). Its size also makes this saucepan perfect for reheating small portions of sauces prepared in quantity. The manufacturer recommends that it be given a 24-hour cold-water soak and garlic-rub treatment before using.

Forzano Italian Imports, Inc. **$4.98**

Sauce source supremo

MARINARA SAUCE

6–8 cups

½ cup olive oil
4 cups coarsely chopped onions
2 small carrots, peeled and cut into rounds (about 1 cup)
3 cloves garlic, finely minced
8 cups canned Italian plum tomatoes with their liquid (about 2½ 28-ounce cans)
Salt and freshly ground black pepper
1 tablespoon finely minced Italian parsley
¼ pound butter
1½ teaspoons dried orégano
2 tablespoons chopped fresh basil, or 2 teaspoons dried basil

In a 10-inch glass-ceramic skillet, heat the oil; add the onions, carrots, and garlic. Cook, stirring until vegetables turn golden brown.

Meanwhile, strain the tomatoes through a sieve into a bowl and push the pulp through with a wooden spoon. Discard the seeds.

Add the puréed tomatoes to the vegetables in the skillet; season to taste with salt and pepper. Partially cover the skillet and simmer for 15 minutes.

Set a sieve (conical, chinois type, if possible) into a bowl; pour the sauce into it, and press with a wooden spoon to push the solids through. Pour sauce back into the skillet; add the butter and herbs. Partly cover the skillet, and simmer 30 minutes more, stirring occasionally. This is best freshly made,

Continued from preceding page

but it can be stored, tightly covered, in the refrigerator for 2 days.

(From THE GREAT COOKS COOKBOOK, by The Good Cooking School, Inc. Copyright 1974 by The Good Cooking School, Inc. Reprinted by permission of Ferguson/Doubleday)

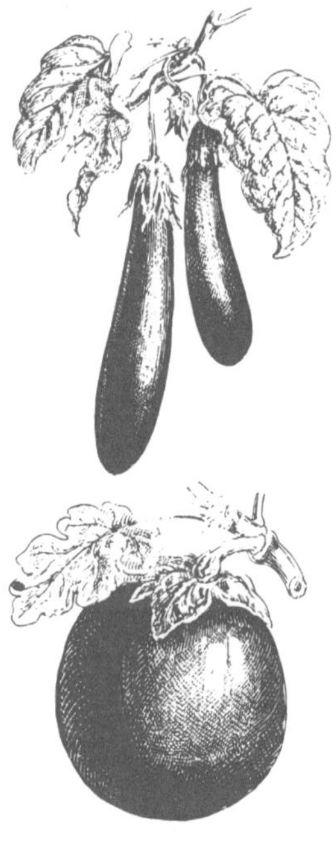

Eggplant.

Double-Handled Casserole E:51

This is a generous casserole, made for feeding a family. Fill it with *peperonata,* a dish made of peppers, tomatoes and onions; then make a series of depressions in the *peperonata* with the back of a spoon and drop an egg into each one. Bake it in the oven until the eggs are set; it will make as many portions as you have eggs. The pan itself is made of earthenware, 13″ in diameter and 3¾″ deep, with a capacity of 6 quarts. It is glazed dark brown on the outside, clear on the inside, and is unglazed on the bottom. It can be used over a flame—carefully—as well as in the oven. The saucepan handle on one side and the loop handle on the other indicate the same double function.

The Pottery Barn $14.95

Covered Casserole E:52

The curviness of this earthenware casserole makes it look a bit like a bean pot to us, although with a capacity of 6 cups it holds less than most of its American look-alikes. But there is no doubting its provenance: its unglazed bottom, dark brown glazed exterior, and clear-glazed terra cotta interior are characteristic of Italian earthenware. So to promote harmony in international culinary relations, use this casserole to make an Italian bean dish called *salsicce con lenticchie* (sausages with lentils). And if you have the good fortune to eat your lentils on New Year's—or so Italian folklore goes—you will be rich all the coming year. Our casserole is 4″ high, 5¾″ in inside diameter, has two ear handles and a knobbed lid. This manufacturer's wares should be soaked in hot water for half an hour and air-dried thoroughly before using.

Hammacher Schlemmer (54/74) $10.00

PENNE CON POMIDORI VERDI ALLA PARMIGIANA

Penne with Green Tomatoes and Parmesan Cheese

Serves 6–8

2 small fresh eggs
Salt and freshly ground pepper
2 pounds green tomatoes (medium to large), cut into ½-inch slices
Flour
Vegetable oil
½ recipe marinara sauce
Grated parmigiano
1 pound penne or rigatoni (imported if possible)

Beat eggs; add salt and pepper. One side at a time, dip tomato slices into beaten egg; and then lightly into flour; set aside.

Pour vegetable oil about ¾-inch deep into a medium-size skillet. Heat oil, and check for correct temperature by flicking a few specks of flour into it. Oil should boil violently when flour goes in. With a slotted spoon, place tomato slices into the hot oil a few at a time. Be careful; this spatters. Brown slightly on both sides, remove and place between paper towels to drain. Repeat process until all tomato slices are used.

Put ¼ of the marinara sauce in the bottom of a deep, ovenproof glass casserole. Place a layer of tomato slices on the sauce, then pour a little sauce on the tomatoes and sprinkle with grated parmigiano. Repeat process until all tomato slices are used. Pour sauce over top layer of tomatoes and sprinkle with parmigiano. Preheat oven to 350 F. and bake, covered, for 20 minutes. If there is too much liquid, remove cover so some can cook away.

Cook pasta in rapidly boiling salted water until *al dente.* Drain. Heat remaining marinara sauce and put into a serving bowl. Toss pasta in the sauce, add freshly ground black pepper and grated parmigiano. Serve sauced pasta and casserole of baked tomato slices separately, but spoon onto the same plate to complement each other.

(From THE GREAT COOKS COOKBOOK, by The Good Cooking School, Inc. Copyright 1974 by the Good Cooking School, Inc. Reprinted by permission of Ferguson/Doubleday)

Tomato Casserole E:53

To give its components the time to contribute their flavors to the whole, a sauce should be slowly simmered. The heat retention qualities of an earthenware casserole like this make it the traditional choice of an Italian cook for a *ragù* (meat sauce) or other *salse* (sauces). Our casserole comes with a lid so you can cover, partially cover, or uncover the sauce as it simmers, to control the amount of liquid evaporating. With the dark brown glaze on the outside and a clear glaze on the inside, it is handsome enough to be carried to the table by its two handles. The bottom is unglazed for better heat absorption. You can make about 6 cups of sauce in this 8″-diameter, 3⅛″-high casserole; a larger size is available with an 11″-diameter and 4½″-tall sides.

Hammacher Schlemmer (24/76) $10.00

Tall Casserole E:54

The most striking feature of this elegant, straight-sided casserole is the way it is proportioned, with its 7″ inner diameter matched by its 7″ height. A tall casserole it is indeed, of typically Italian brown-glazed earthenware with an unglazed bottom. With a capacity of 4 quarts we unhesitatingly recommend it for the slow simmering of *salsa di pomodoro* (tomato sauce) or a Tuscan fish soup (*cacciucco*) that calls for plum tomatoes, red wine, seasoning, vegetables and an impressive array of marine life, including lobster and squid. If your sauce or soup needs covering, you can top this pot with a dinner plate as the Italians do.

Forzano Italian Imports, Inc. $7.98

OSSO BUCO

Veal Shanks

6 pieces veal shank, about 3 inches thick
Flour
3 tablespoons olive oil
2 whole garlic cloves
1 medium onion, finely chopped
½ cup chopped carrot
1 tablespoon basil
Salt and freshly ground black pepper
1 cup dry white wine
2 cups tomatoes, strained
2 tablespoons butter

Preheat oven to 400° F.

Dredge veal wtih flour. Heat olive oil in a wide skillet. Add veal and cook, uncovered, over medium heat. Turn shanks when they begin to brown. Add garlic, and continue to simmer until brown on all sides. Add onion, carrot, basil, and salt and pepper to taste. When onion wilts, add wine, cover and lower heat. Simmer for 7 to 10 minutes, stirring often. Add tomatoes and butter. Cover again, and continue simmering for a few minutes longer.

Place skillet in oven and cook ½ hour. Then, lower heat to 350° F and bake for 30 minutes. Meanwhile, prepare gremolada.

GREMOLADA
2 tablespoons chopped parsley, Italian if possible
1 clove garlic, chopped
1 teaspoon fresh or ½ teaspoon dried sage
1 lemon rind, grated

Mix together all ingredients and scatter over veal shanks. Return to oven and cook 10 more minutes.

(From ITALIAN FAMILY COOKING, by Edward Giobbi, illustrated by Cham, Lisa and Gena Giobbi. Copyright 1971 by Edward Giobbi. Reprinted by permission of Random House, Inc.)

Tall Covered Casserole E:55

A wonderfully capacious pot made of brown-glazed earthenware, this casserole begins its work over a burner and finishes it in the enveloping heat of the oven. *Osso buco,* for example, is started when the cook softens chopped onions, carrots, celery and garlic in

Continued from preceding page

melted butter and oil. Meanwhile, he flours and browns pieces of veal shank in a metal skillet, and then adds them to the melting vegetables. All goes into the oven in a bath of red wine and tomatoes, there to cook slowly until the bits of meat all but fall off the bone. And this is the perfect pot in which to make it: efficient in the oven, beautiful in the presentation. This large size holds 9 quarts of food, with a 9½″-diameter top, and a height fully 10½″ when the cover is in place. The gently bowed sides taper to the top, with two ear handles sitting vertically near the lid. The cover fits neatly onto the pot, and the bottom is unglazed so that it will better absorb heat when it is used over a flame. There are 3½- and 6-quart versions available in addition to this largest one.

The Pottery Barn $17.50

Potato Cooker E:56

This funny-looking, unglazed terracotta pot is a potato cooker, and can also be used for cooking chestnuts. Called a diable, it was traditionally used for cooking over a charcoal fire, but it can be used in modern kitchens over a low gas flame or electric heat if you remember to mediate the direct heat by means of a protective asbestos mat, a Flame-Tamer or other similar device. This squat, bulbous pot is just a shade over 6″ tall, with a large clay cylinder-shaped handle protruding from its side. Its slightly domed lid can easily be lifted by the knob in its center. This pot is specifically intended for dry cooking, and can of course be used in the oven as well as on top of the stove. To cook potatoes in the diable, scrub and dry medium potatoes (leaving the skins on), and heap into the pot. On top of the stove, shake the pot several times; potatoes will cook in about 35 minutes. In a moderate oven it will take about an hour and a quarter. For chestnuts: score the shell with a sharp knife, put them into the pot and bake in a moderate oven for an hour and a half. The manufacturer of the diable suggests eating them just as they are, with a dribble of butter and salt; but we would shell them in order to prepare a *Monte Bianco* (purée of chestnuts with whipped cream). Never wash this pot; rinse quickly with warm water when you first buy it, and dry it thoroughly. Then never dampen it again.

Bloomingdale's $12.50

PASTA CON VONGOLE AL BRANDY

Pasta with clams and brandy

Serves 6

6 tablespoons olive oil
1 cup chopped green pepper
2 tablespoons finely chopped parsley (Italian if possible)
2 cloves garlic finely chopped
1 cup tomatoes (preferably fresh), put through a food mill
1 tablespoon finely chopped fresh basil or 1 teaspoon dried basil
1 teaspoon dried orégano
1 teaspoon dried mint—or 1 tablespoon fresh chopped mint
Salt and hot pepper flakes or freshly ground black pepper
1½ dozen small fresh clams, in shell, scrubbed
1 pound short, tubular pasta, such as penne, rigatoni, etc.
1 pound fresh shrimp, shelled, deveined and cut into ½-inch pieces
¼ cup brandy (or bourbon)
3 tablespoons butter

Put olive oil, green pepper, parsley, garlic, tomatoes, basil, orégano, mint, salt and hot pepper to taste in a medium-size saucepan. Cover and cook gently for 20 minutes. Add clams; recover; raise heat and cook until clams open. As soon as clams open, remove them from the sauce. Continue cooking the sauce, covered, for 5 minutes over moderate heat. Preheat oven to 450 F.

Remove the clams from shells; discard shells and cut each clam into 2 or 3 pieces; using scissors may be the easiest way.

Bring 4 quarts of salted water to a boil. Add pasta and stir with a wooden spoon. As soon as water comes back to a boil, drain pasta. Put drained pasta in 4-quart ovenproof glass casserole or baking dish approximately 3″ high by 10″ in diameter. Add sauce, clams, shrimp, brandy or bourbon and butter; mix. Cover tightly and place in oven. Bake, stirring often, until pasta is tender but firm to the bite, *al dente.* About 15 minutes.

NOTE: Sauce may be made a day ahead of time; refrigerated and gently reheated before using.

(From ITALIAN FAMILY COOKING, by Edward Giobbi, illustrated by Cham, Lisa and Gena Giobbi. Copyright 1971 by Edward Giobbi. Reprinted by permission of Random House, Inc.)

Earthenware Baking Dish E:57

Our favorite way of preparing *gnocchi* is to lay them in a shallow baking dish, dribble them with melted butter, and then to sprinkle over them some of the freshly-grated Parmesan cheese that was used in their preparation. A quarter of an hour in the oven makes them bubbling, browned and saturated with Parmesan-flavored butter. Not bad for a cold night. Next time we prepare it, we will do it in this slickly-glazed oval baking dish, dark brown all over, with an unglazed bottom and a delicately-incised scallop pattern on each end. We have chosen a large size—13″ long, 9″ wide and 2″ deep—even though it comes in two smaller versions (10″ long and 8″ long).

Macy's **$15.00**

Copper Baking Pan E:58

A tin-lined pan of hammered copper like this one is an elegant container for eggplant parmigiana, or *polpette alla pizzaiola* (beef patties with anchovies and mozzarella). From a 9¾″ diameter across the top, the sides slope inward to a 7½″-diameter bottom. Two large brass ears are riveted to the outside under the rim. The pan is 2″ deep and has a capacity of 2 quarts. It is ideal for any occasion on which you need a flameproof baking dish—but at oven temperatures under 425° F. only, or the tin lining may melt. We would feel secure in recommending not only the container but the contents as well if you use this pan for *triglie alla calabrese,* in which a blend of butter, olive oil, oregano and pepper are heated together on top of the stove before several small (one pound) whole fish are rolled in the mixture and placed in the oven to bake.

Hammacher Schlemmer (329-24) **$17.95**

Casseruola Bassa E:59

This beautiful *casseruola bassa,* or brazier, is what modern Italian cooks are using to simmer their *ragù* (meat sauce) and other sauces for pasta. The heavyweight stainless steel has an aluminum plate on the bottom for even heat distribution so that your *osso buco* (braised veal shanks) will cook evenly and not burn. Note the larger-than-usual size of the stainless-steel handles, welded onto the *casseruola* in a position that makes it easy to lift even when it is filled to its 4½-quart capacity. The satin finish of the body is punctuated by the mirror-finished banding of the thick rim for an aesthetic quality that makes this brazier welcome at the table. The bottom of this brazier measures 9½″ across and is only 3½″ deep. It is also available in capacities of 7, 10½, 15, 20½ and 28 quarts. A matching lid can be ordered separately.

Alluminio Paderno/The Professional Kitchen **$75.00 (1109-24)**

SALSA PER POLENTA

Sauce for Polenta

This sauce was usually made on my grandfather's farm with very ripe fresh tomatoes.

¼ cup salt pork or pancetta, chopped with a heated knife
½ pound fresh Italian sausage
1 medium onion, chopped
10 ounces dried mushrooms or ½ cup sliced fresh mushrooms
2½ cups tomatoes, strained
1 teaspoon basil
Salt and freshly ground black pepper
Polenta
Grated Parmesan or pecorino cheese

Heat salt pork. As it dissolves, add sausage and brown, uncovered, over moderate heat. Turn occasionally. When sausage is brown, remove salt pork and discard. Add onion and cook until wilted. Set aside and keep warm.

In the meantime, if dried mushrooms are used, soak in warm water for 15 minutes. In a separate pot, cook tomatoes for several minutes. Slice sausage into ¼-inch pieces and add with fat to tomatoes. Add mushrooms, basil, salt and pepper to taste and simmer, partially covered, over low heat for about 45 minutes.

Pour cooked polenta, ½ inch thick, on each heated plate. Pour sauce, including mushrooms and sausage, over each plate of polenta. Serve with a generous amount of grated Parmesan or pecorino cheese. Serves 6.

NOTE: To make polenta, boil 1 quart water with 2 teaspoons salt. Add 1 cup finely ground yellow corn meal and stir constantly, cooking over medium flame for about 20 minutes.

(From ITALIAN FAMILY COOKING, by Edward Giobbi, illustrated by Cham, Lisa and Gena Giobbi. Copyright 1971 by Edward Giobbi. Reprinted by permission of Random House, Inc.)

Hammered Copper Polenta Pot E:60

A staple food of the northern Alpine regions of Italy, *polenta* is made of yellow cornmeal and is similar to that American southern standard, cornmeal mush. It is eaten as a first course, second course, side dish, bread and dessert. But this does no justice to a food which, like pasta, has the ability to nourish the body when eaten by itself, or to amplify and make even more delicious a number of sauces that are served with it. Traditionally *polenta* is made in an unlined copper pot, called a *paiolo,* that is narrower at the bottom than at the top. The one we show you here is made of hammered copper and looks something like a very large thimble. As it cooks, *polenta* becomes very thick, with bubbles rising sluggishly through it until they pop suddenly to the surface. The shape of this pot facilitates heat distribution through the mixture, and also facilitates stirring, which should be done every few

Continued from preceding page

minutes so that the *polenta* cooks evenly. The pot has a 9″-long brass handle riveted to its side and a small earlike handle on the opposite side to make it easier to lift. This 7-quart size seems quite generous, but the same pot also comes in 12-, 9- and 5-quart sizes for large families of *polenta* mavens, and 3- and 1½-quart sizes for more modest establishments. Because the pot is unlined, it should be used only for *polenta* and never acidic or highly salted foods. In addition, unless you plan to put this *polenta* pot to constant use (which would keep its inside corrosion free), be sure it is thoroughly cleaned before using.

Berarducci Brothers (J-19) **$31.00**

Polenta Knife E:61

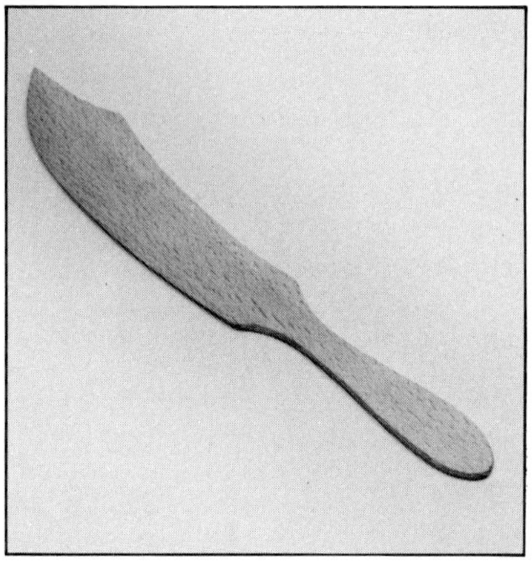

The sole function of this nicely shaped little wooden knife is to cut *polenta* after it has been poured onto a beechwood board. Properly cooked *polenta* has the consistency of congealed cereal, and if you were to cut it with a metal knife it would stick not only to the knife but to itself. The wooden knife is thicker and therefore makes a wider and more precise cut. Traditionally, *polenta* is cut with a taut piece of thread, string or wire, but this 10¾″ knife carved from a single piece of beechwood may be reassuring to those whose experience with this unusual and excellent dish is limited.

H. A. Mack & Co., Inc. (H70) **$1.25**

15th-century Italian Maiolica dish (from The Metropolitan Museum of Art)

Dolci Italiani

The customary way to end a meal in Italy is with fruit and cheese. But Italians—especially southern Italians—have a highly developed sweet tooth, and their *dolci* (sweets) are wondrous and varied. Marvelous ice creams (*gelati*) and ices (*granite*) are layered with cakes, nuts, cream or other delights in molds to make each mouthful a surprise. Or, like the sinful *granita di caffè* (strong, sweetened espresso frozen to a crystalline mush), are eaten plain with whipped cream and wild abandon. And then there are the sweet, crunchy, creamy, chocolaty, fruity Italian pastries. There is *cassata alla siciliana,* a many-layered confection of fruit, chocolate, ricotta cheese and liqueur that must stand for at least a day to weld the flavors into a truly unforgettable cake. There is *crostata di ricotta,* a light and fruity cheesecake; and the improbably named *zuppa inglese,* which is neither soup nor English, although it does bear a vague resemblance to English trifle. There is *panettone,* which is either a fruited coffee cake or a yeast-leavened fruitcake, depending on your point of view. And all manner of small, sweet, crisp things like *cenci* (bow ties of dough, deep fried and sugared), *amaretti* (hard almond-flavored macaroons), and *strufoli* (honey-coated balls of lemon- or orange-flavored dough).

Most Italian sweets do not require special equipment in order to make them—only motivation, an accurate recipe and time. But some *dolci* should be made in, or with, utensils designed for their creation. *Zabaglione* (syllabub), for instance, is best made in its traditional copper pot. In addition, life for the serious *dolce* cook can be made easier with special forms for *cannoli* (deep-fried tubes of pastry with a creamy ricotta filling); *pizzelle* irons to make those sweet, crisp cookies; a mold for forming *spumone* (a rich, frozen mousse); and a heavy-duty púréeing device for *Monte Bianco* (chestnut purée topped with whipped cream).

Pizzelle Iron E:62

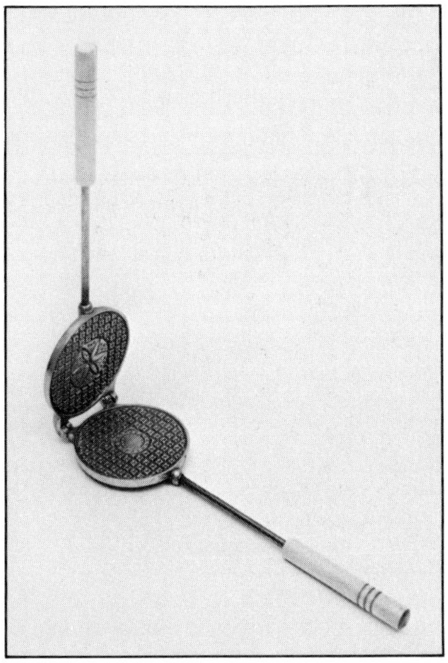

Pizzelle are thin, crisp, sweet, waffle-like Italian cookies that—like their Scandinavian *krumkake* cousins—are rolled into cylinders while still hot. One long-ago Christmas our Italian neighbors brought over some of these marvelous wafer-like goodies filled with the pressings left from making wine, and the taste still lingers. Served this way, *pizzelle* are a traditional holiday treat; but among other customary fillings is one made with chick peas, which we are told is equally delicious. So are these crisp cookies eaten plain. A hand-held *pizzelle* iron like this one will produce a traditional result when used over a modern stove burner. This iron consists of two 5½″-diameter, cast-aluminum grids hinged together. Two 11¾″-long handles end in lightly varnished natural wood grips. *Pizzelle* irons and their many patterns—including this typical waffle grid and rosette combinations—are also used to make similar wafer cookies called *cialde.*

Berarducci Brothers $8.95
(F-9)

Electric Pizzelle Maker E:63

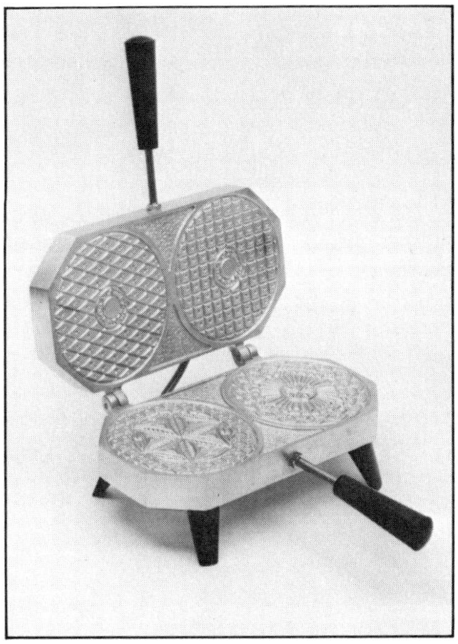

This electric *pizzelle* maker is a foolproof way to make those sweet Italian wafer-like cookies. The twin cast-aluminum grids stamp out two different, intricate *pizzelle* patterns. With one pouring, the iron turns the thin *pizzelle* batter (flavored with vanilla, lemon, chocolate or the characteristic anise) into two crisp and embossed wafers, each 5″ in diameter. An automatic pilot light tells you when the *pizzelle* are *finite.*

Berarducci Brothers $29.95
(E-1)

LEMON-FLAVORED PIZZELLE

12 eggs
3 cups sugar
1½ cups oil (vegetable, peanut or olive)
6 tablespoons fresh lemon juice
Grated rinds of four large lemons
4 cups flour
½ teaspoon baking powder

Beat the eggs until lemony in color. Add the sugar gradually and beat well to incorporate each addition. Add the oil, lemon juice and lemon rind and beat until smooth. Add the flour gradually, again beating until well blended.

Chill the batter for from two (minimum) to eight hours, or for as long as several days, to enrich its flavor.

When ready to make *pizzelle,* grease both grids of a heated *pizzelle* iron and spoon batter into the center of the bottom grid. Close the iron and cook *pizzelle* until golden brown on both sides. It will take several test runs to know how much batter to use and how long to cook the *pizzelle.*

Yield: four dozen

An ancient kitchen in Pompeii

Cannoli Forms E:64

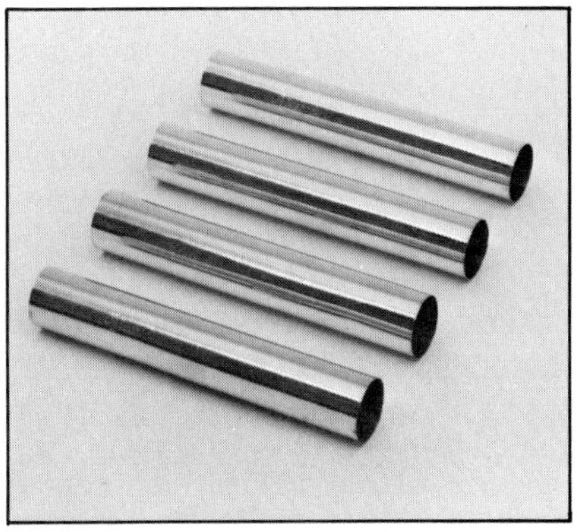

When we see *cannoli,* we are reminded of long afternoons spent talking about the meaning of life over *espresso* and these delicious fried tubes of pastry filled with sweetened ricotta. To make these Sicilian sweets yourself is not too intricate a task, but you will need this inexpensive set of four tinned-steel forms for shaping and frying the pastry

Continued from preceding page

tubes. Solidly constructed, each tube is 5⅝″ long, ⅞″ in diameter, with a double-folded seam running its length. These are identical to the forms used in every *pasticceria.*

August Thomsen Corp. (660) **$2.55**

Zabaglione Pot E:65

A warm velvety custard froth made from beaten egg yolks, sugar and Marsala, *zabaglione* is considered a great restorative in the Piedmont region where it originated. Whether or not it actually can restore one's health, it most certainly restores one's spirits as a delicious and satisfying way to end a meal. You can produce *zabaglione* over the kitchen stove; but to give it the dramatic presentation it deserves, *zabaglione* should be prepared at the table. This round-bottomed copper pot, 6½″ in diameter and 3½″ deep, is the classic utensil to use. To make *zabaglione,* grasp the long brass handle, hold the pot over a low flame (an alcohol burner is perfect) and whisk away until the egg yolks thicken and hold a soft peak. This pot, with its 6-cup capacity, will make enough *zabaglione* to satisfy 6 appetites.

Charles F. Lamalle (1422Z) **$40.00**

ZABAGLIONE

Egg and Wine Custard

If strawberries are not available, substitute sliced fresh, frozen, or canned peaches, pitted fresh or canned apricot halves, or sliced bananas. Be sure to drain frozen or canned fruit very well.

1 pint fresh strawberries, washed and stemmed
8 egg yolks
½ cup sugar
⅔ cup Marsala or sweet sherry wine

Divide strawberries among six stemmed wine glasses.

Put egg yolks, sugar and wine into a round-bottomed copper pot or glass double-boiler top of at least 2-quart capacity, as egg yolks almost triple in volume. Sprinkle with a little cold water.

Place the copper or glass pot over a pan of simmering water and beat mixture rapidly with a wire whisk until it becomes a thick, creamy custard.

Immediately pour over the strawberries in the wine glasses, dividing evenly, and serve at once.

(From ITALIAN INTERNATIONAL DINNER PARTY. Copyright 1974 by Burton Richard Wolf.)

Neapolitan Ice Cream

"Mix with one pint of water the yolks of 14 eggs and two glasses of Maraschino, add sugar to taste, place the whole in a pan, put it on a slow fire and keep it whisked all the time. When almost to the boil lift it off the fire and keep it well whisked until it foams, then pour it in a Neapolitan ice box; place the box in a tub surrounded with small pieces of ice, well mixed with salt, for four or five hours or till required. When wanted, dip the box into tepped (sic) water for a second, take off the cover and it will slip out. Part of this block of ice may be scooped out and filled with cream custard ice if preferred."

from a late 19th-century book called The Confectioners' Handbook and Practical Guide to the Art of Sugar Boiling

Spumone Mold E:66

Spumone—which should go by the name frozen mousse instead of its more plebeian monniker, "ice cream" —is usually formed in a bowler-like mold like this. To make this southern Italian *dolce,* a custard-base made light by whipped cream or egg whites is mixed with almonds, fruit (preserved or fresh) and sometimes anise, and then poured into this mold and frozen. Unmold your creation by wrapping a hot towel around the mold for a few seconds, before inverting over a serving dish. This 3¾″-diameter mold holds 1¾ cups, or three to four ultra-rich servings. An individual, 5-ounce capacity mold is also available.

Oscar Zucchi (1109) **$3.00**

"Macrows

Take and make a thynne foyle of dowh (a thin paste), and kerve (cut) it in pieces, and cast hem on boillyng water, and seeth it wele. Take chese, and grate it, and butter, cast bynethen, and above as losyns (lozenges), and serve forth."

This recipe from The Forme of Cury *(1390) is reprinted and annotated (as above) in* Antiquitates Culinariae or

Curious Tracts Relating to the Culinary Affairs of the Old English *by Reverend Richard Warner (1791)*

Monte Bianco Maker E:67

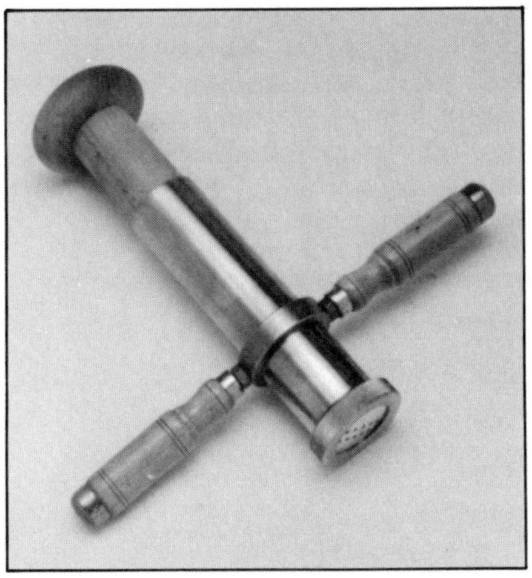

This is an esoteric device for turning out divine swirls of chestnut purée for the fabulous dessert that the Italians call *Monte Bianco,* and the French know as *Mont Blanc.* Topped with whipped cream to form a replica of the snow-capped Alpine peak, this dessert comes as close as we can imagine to offering a foretaste of heaven. This is a substantial item, with a cylindrical body of stainless steel. Two long varnished handles of natural wood are perpendicular to the body, and an unfinished wooden plunger pushes the sweetened chocolate-and-rum-enriched chestnut purée through perforated discs. There are three tinned-steel discs, each with a different number of perforations, to control the amount of purée expressed. This device is a professional-quality tool, superbly fashioned. The body is 9½″ long and 2¼″ in diameter; the handles are each 6½″ long, and the plunger is 10″ long. The bottom screws off to allow for changing of discs, and to make cleaning easier. The *Monte Bianco* maker, however, will not be much help to the solitary cook; operating it requires the services of two people, one to hold the handles and move the device about until the desired form heaps up on the platter beneath, while the other works the plunger.

Oscar Zucchi (355) $60.00

MONTE BIANCO

1½ pounds chestnuts
Milk
½–¾ cup sugar
¼ teaspoon salt
2 teaspoons vanilla
1 cup heavy cream, whipped and lightly sweetened

Score the chestnuts, drawing an X across the rounded side of the shell. Cover with cold water, bring to a boil and simmer for 10 minutes.

Drain and shell the chestnuts while they are still warm, being certain to remove the inner brown skin. Place chestnuts in the top of a double boiler, add milk to cover and simmer gently until they are tender but not mushy, about 30–45 minutes. Add more milk if necessary, to keep them from drying out.

Drain the chestnuts of any remaining milk and purée them in a blender or through a food mill. Add the sugar, salt and vanilla and heat gently until the sugar melts.

Force the purée through a food ricer with large holes or a *Monte Bianco* syringe, letting it fall in light vermicelli swirls on a plate. Move the ricer or syringe in ever tighter circles to form a mountainesque mound of purée.

Top the mound with whipped cream, letting it flow down the sides like snow atop *Monte Bianco.*

Chestnut.

Chestnuts, the subtle raison d'être *of* Monte Bianco *(and its soul-sisters* Mont Blanc aux Marrons *and Peking Dust) carry good luck with them in many folktales. In Germany they cure backaches if carried in a back pocket. In Tuscany they are the sacred food for St. Simon's day; in Piedmont they commemorate All Saints' Eve, keeping away the souls of the dead if left out on a table.*

Caffè

The word *espresso* means fast, and *can* refer to an express train. But mostly it is used to mean coffee: the dark-roasted, deeply flavored coffee beans themselves, as well as the method of brewing them. To make *espresso,* water is forced under pressure through a container of tightly packed coffee grounds. The water comes in contact with the coffee only long enough (thus the term *espresso*) to extract from it a rich, undiluted coffee essence—leaving behind the less pleasant chemicals. The coffee grounds are replaced after making two cups—at the most—to insure the freshness of the *espresso.*

The Italians use the thick syrupy *espresso* as the basis for all their coffee drinks, from the true, unadulterated *espresso* (or the eye-opening *doppio,* a double portion of *espresso*) to *caffellatte,* a gentle, morning cup of coffee made of one part *espresso* to three parts hot milk. (The popular compromise between the two is *cappuccino,* which is one part *espresso* to two parts foamed milk.) How you take your *espresso* in Italy will depend on where you come from (Northern Italians, for instance, live in rich dairying territory and can afford to drink more milk with their coffee), or how long you plan to stay awake.

Throughout the day, Italians drop into their neighborhood coffee bars to have a cup of *espresso*—plain, with a twist of lemon peel (making it an *espresso romano*), flavored with anisette or almond extract, or as *cappuccino.* The coffee bar and its strong brew are a way

Continued from preceding page

of life in Italy—a focal point of neighborhood society and usually a hotbed of local political debate.

At home, coffee is usually made in a drip pot like *la napoletana.* Steam machines to make *espresso* are most often found in the coffee bars; and since there is always a coffee bar just around the next corner, there is little demand for a machine in the home as well. In this country, since there is no equivalent of the Italian coffee bar, one of the *espresso* machines we show you might be just the thing to help you turn your dining room into one. Whether or not you invite the neighborhood to join you there in political debate, we guarantee you will savor the brew.

Coffee Mill E:68

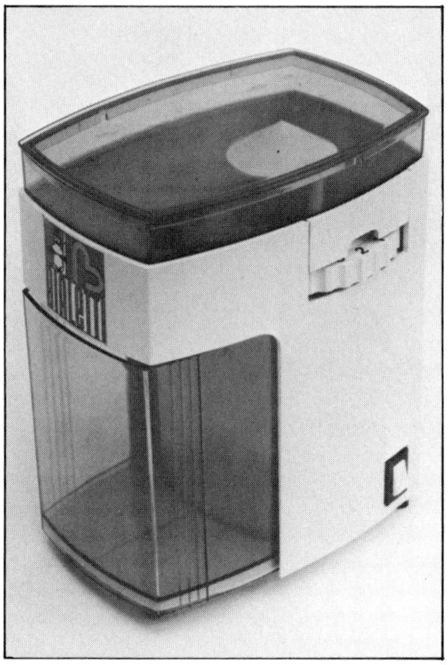

For a fresher cup of *caffellatte,* coffee beans should be ground just before brewing. Bialetti offers an electric mill that will not only provide the service aforementioned, but will also let you pre-select the grind you need. A dial is marked with numbers from one to eight, from coarse to very fine. To add the beans, lift off the plastic top; then flick the switch and the beans are funneled down into the grinding mechanism below. A little white plastic "coolie cap" helps to keep the beans on the right path. They emerge from a chute, custom-ground, into an easily removable, covered, plastic container that holds up to 1¾ cups. The rest of the machine—which stands 7½″ high, and uses only 4″ by 6″ of counter space—is white, easy-to-clean plastic. Little rubber feet cushion vibration quite satisfactorily, but not sound.

Gary Valenti (V-148) $12.00

Neapolitan Filter Pot E:69

This three-part coffee pot produces a rather strong *café filtre.* Known as *la napoletana* (whether it was invented in Naples or not, nobody knows), it consists of twin cylinders of polished aluminum, plus a third, smaller cylinder that fits inside and does the work. The outer cylinders, both 3¾″ in diameter, have identical handles of heatproof black plastic. One has a spout and the other has a collar. These cylinders are set one above the other, open-end to open-end, enclosing the filtering cylinder, which has the coffee. Place cold water in the collared cylinder, slip the coffee-filtering cylinder into it, spoon in the coffee (preferably very fine or filter grind), and screw on its perforated lid. Place the spouted cylinder over the whole thing (with the spout pointing *down*), fitting it securely over the collar, and set the coffee pot on the heat. As soon as steam issues from the tiny hole in the side of the bottom cylinder, grasp both handles and invert the entire *napoletana.* This will cause the hot water to filter downward through the coffee into the pot that has the spout. If you opt to remove the superstructure before serving time, cover the pot with its separate knobbed lid.

Edwin Jay Inc. (67407) $6.00

Individual Espresso Pot E:70

If you can't have the biggest *espresso* machine on the block—the *fin-de-siècle* giant ablaze with chrome and brass tubes and handles—then why not have the smallest? It works on the same principle as the pride of your neighborhood coffee house, forcing boiling water under pressure through a small amount of tightly-packed coffee. This aluminum pot is really tiny, measuring 5½″ only if you include its plastic handle. Put water into the bottom section. When it comes to a boil over a flame, the water will shoot up through a funnel, passing rapidly over a trapful of coffee grounds and thence to a miniature rococo tube, from which it sprays down into the cup that you have put beneath it. Get it?

E. Rossi and Co. $4.98

If you prefer your pasta hand-made, perhaps you'll enjoy grinding your own coffee, too.

La Moka E:71

This friendly-looking, octagonal *la moka,* brews a serious *tazza di espresso.* The cast-aluminum pot comes in three pieces: the bottom, water container; the spouted, handled top where the *espresso* ends up; and a waistband coffee basket between the two. To use *la moka,* fill the bottom container with water and the basket with the finely ground dark-roast coffee; screw the top and bottom together and place the whole apparatus over medium heat. As the water boils, and pressure builds, the water is forced up through the grounds and arrives in the top chamber as deep, rich coffee. Not only does *la moka* make a good cup of coffee, but its friendly looks are matched by an equally friendly price. Our pot holds 9 *espresso*-sized cups, but is also available in 3-, 6- and 14-cup sizes.

HOAN Products Ltd. (309) $15.00

Euro Espresso Pot E:72

This is the slick modern version—all done up in shining stainless steel—of a traditional *espresso* maker. The old pot was aluminum and hexagonal; the new one is as tubular as a snake, as severely functional as the purest of Scandinavian implements. Both old and new work, however, on the same three-layered principle. Water is put into the bottom of the pot, and coffee grounds into the middle layer. There is even a tamper to help you compress the grounds to the proper density. Over the burner, the water heats until it builds up steam, at which point it shoots up through the coffee grounds into the top. It works quickly, and you have to be nearby and alert, ready to turn off the burner as soon as you hear the telltale swoosh that means that the water is shooting upwards. It is available in 3-cup, 6-cup (shown here) and 12-cup models: and that's *espresso* cups, not measuring cups, remember.

Bloomingdale's/The Professional Kitchen $25.00

Vesuviana Espresso Maker E:73

The Vesuviana *espresso* maker has the turn-of-the-century look of old Italian coffee houses, with its dull cast-aluminum finish, its circular handle atop the container, and its long-handled basket for coffee grounds. The volcanic principle on which the Vesuviana operates is somewhat more venerable than 19th century, however. To make *espresso* in the Vesuviana, pour water into the gently-curved, bottle-shaped water container, and screw its cover tightly into place. When the finely ground coffee has been locked into place, too, you begin to heat the water over a burner; soon enough pressure will build up to force the water up, across the bridge, and down through the grounds, where it drips into an attractive coffee pot which waits underneath. There are three sizes, accommodating 3, 6 (shown here) and 9 *espresso*-sized cups of coffee. The machine also comes in a model that heats electrically.

Bloomingdale's/Gary Valenti (V-23) $32.50

Cappuccino, *the simple but splendid combination of deep-flavored* espresso, *and steam-frothed milk was named for its color, which is thought to resemble that of the robes of the Capuchin monks.*

CALGIONETTI

This pastry has a provincial honesty that is a delight. It is a Christmas specialty from the Marches and was always my favorite. My mother made calgionetti only during the Christmas holidays and they were made two different ways. The first was with grape concentrate (set aside when we made wine in the fall), mixed with bits of chocolate and almonds. The other way was with chick peas (ceci beans) and honey.

FILLING
¾ cup shelled almonds
1½ cups canned or dried chickpeas, soaked overnight and cooked until tender
2 tablespoons grated orange rind
¼ teaspoon cinnamon
4 tablespoons honey

DOUGH
3 cups flour
½ cup dry white wine
½ cup water
½ cup olive oil
Pinch of salt

Put almonds in boiling water. Boil for about 1 minute or less, drain and remove brown skins. Place on tray and put in 400° F oven, mixing occasionally. Remove when brown, cool and finely chop. Set aside.

Drain chick peas and put through mill or sieve. Add almonds, orange rind, cinnamon, and honey. Mix well and set aside.

Make a well in the flour. Put other ingredients in well. With a fork gradually work in flour until mixture thickens. Then continue mixing with hands. Knead dough until well blended. Roll into a ball, then cut in half and make 2 balls. Flour a board, roll out one ball with rolling pin to a circle about 1/16 inch thick. About 2 inches from the top of the circle put 1 teaspoon of filling every 2 inches across the width. Roll 2-inch strip over top. Seal bottom edge. With sharp knife or pastry wheel, cut out individual calgionetti in half circles as you would ravioli. Seal edges with a fork and set aside. Repeat process until all of the circle is used. Then roll out other half of dough and repeat process.

In a skillet put about 1 inch of corn oil or peanut oil. When oil is very hot add 5 or 6 calgionetti, one at a time, and deep-fry until they are golden brown on both sides. Remove from oil, blot with paper towels and repeat process. Sprinkle sugar over calgionetti when finished. Yield: About 60 calgionetti.

(From ITALIAN FAMILY COOKING, by Edward Giobbi, illustrated by Cham, Lisa and Gena Giobbi. Copyright 1971 by Edward Giobbi. Reprinted by permission of Random House, Inc.)

Atomic Espresso Maker E:74

Atomic, indeed. We don't doubt it. This marvelous, gleaming *espresso-cappuccino* maker appears to have all the knobs and tubes it might take to split the atom. Or, at any rate, to make an excellent cup of *espresso.* You won't need a degree in particle physics to operate this pot, but a modicum of mechanical ability will help. To make coffee, unscrew the black knob in the back of the gooseneck section (water container) and pour in water. Grasp the long black handle, twist and pull the coffee container out; fill it with coffee and return it to its place. Then, place the coffee-catching pitcher under the coffee container, and put the whole thing on the stove. When it starts bouncing around it means that the water has been turned to steam and is being forced through the coffee to become *espresso.* A round knob directly below the coffee container and above the pitcher turns the flow of coffee on and off. Another round knob (on the gooseneck) opens and closes the skinny spout connected to it to allow steam to escape and froth up milk to make *cappuccino.* The entire apparatus is made of cast aluminum and has plastic knobs. Our 9″-high model makes 6 to 9 *espresso*-sized cups.

Berarducci Brothers (B-31) $79.95

Europiccola Espresso Machine E:75

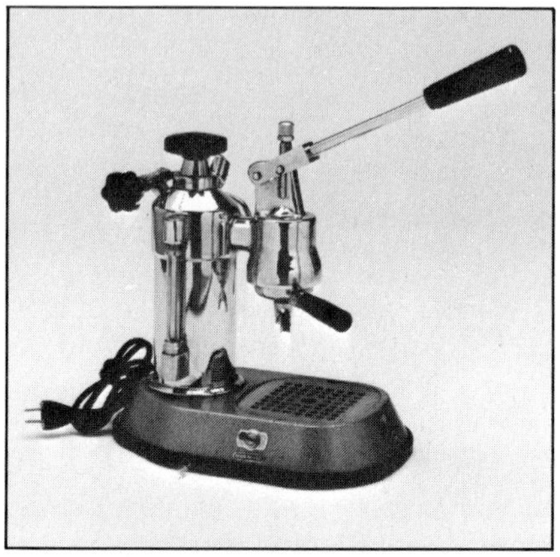

It seems *espresso* machines don't come without a certain, obligatory number of levers, cylinders, knobs and spouts. This comparatively giant-sized version consists essentially of a chrome-plated bronze cylindrical boiler rising from a heavy stove-enameled steel base fitted with a grid-topped well to catch the drips. A rubber pad underneath provides cushioned protection for your countertop or buffet server. Black heat-resistant plastic knobs and handles are attached so you can work all the parts. Despite its seeming complexity, this machine isn't difficult to operate. Put two and a half measuring cups of water, enough for 6 to 8 diminutive *espresso* cups of coffee, into the boiler. Put the coffee, ground almost to a powder, into the small metal filter cup beneath the black handled lever, and plug in the machine. Push the switch to *massimo* and wait for the steam to rise. Sixty seconds after the water boils, move the switch to *minimo.* Hold your *espresso* cup or cups (two can be filled at a time) over the grid in the base and raise and lower the large lever to release finished *espresso.* The steam to foam milk for *cappuccino* or heat other drinks pours from a narrow nozzle operated separately by turning a black plastic knob. Although the cylinder holds enough for up to 8 *espresso*-sized cups, you will have to refill the filter cup with coffee after every two cups are produced. We would find this miniscule quantity a nuisance if the filter cup weren't so easy to detach and attach. This arrangement certainly does insure the freshest cup of *espresso* you can get. This is not an enormous machine, and it will occupy an area of about 8″ by 11½″ on your sideboard, standing 11¾″ high. It comes with a coffee plunger, one 1-cup and one 2-cup filter, and a coffee measure.

Ramsey Imports **$250.00**

Cremina Espresso Maker E:76

It's expensive; but no more so than your Cuisinart or your KitchenAid, and like everything else, it's a matter of making choices. One can easily imagine that there are people—bachelors, countesses, very *thin* people—who would get more use out of a super coffee-maker like this one than any other cooking aid. The Cremina is a scaled-down version of the beautiful baroque device in the coffee house on the corner. It works differently from the household versions because the pressure is exerted not by steam but by pulling down on a lever. This forces water through the small coffee trap. Remember that even in the biggest commercial machines, it is common to replace the coffee after making two cups at the most; one cup is even better. The nice thing about this stainless-steel machine with its brass interior, its bakelite knobs and handles, is that, like the professional boys, it heats and froths up milk as well, and then shoots it down into a cup, producing *cappuccino* or *caffellatte.* Or even *moka,* a fabulous beverage made of one part *espresso,* one part chocolate and one part hot and frothy milk. This 13″-high model holds 18 *espresso* cups of water.

Zabar's **$200.00**

Sama Electric Espresso Machine E:77

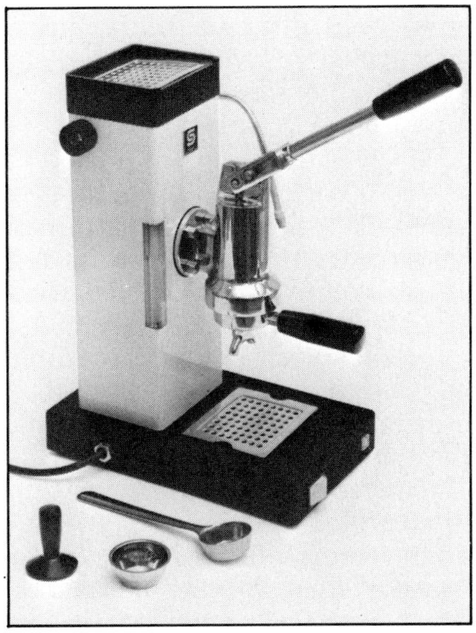

This may be the least futuristic and the most efficient of the home *espresso* machines. A vertical enameled-steel tower, 14½″ high, sits on a black metal base and encloses a superbly constructed brass boiler that will heat 12 *espresso*-sized cups of water. Two handles protrude from the chromium-plated brass cylinder mounted on the front. One holds the container for the ground coffee; depressing the other handle forces the water through the coffee. One or two cups can be dispensed at a time. There is a steam valve for heating milk for *cappuccino* and a window with a colored indicator to indicate the water level. The grid on the bottom catches the drips while the one on top of the tower will heat the cups.

Eli Barry Co., Inc. **$300.00**

Coffee entered Europe through the ports of Venice. In 1585 the Venetian ambassador to Turkey spoke to the senate about 'the habit of the Turks of drinking a black water as hot as you can bear it, taken from seeds called cavee, [*which*] *they say . . . has the power of keeping men awake." An Italian, Propio del Coltelle (called Procope) was responsible for opening the first coffee house in Paris in 1670, one which still stands today, bearing his name.*

Espresso Cup E:78

No matter what the size or the method of the *espresso*-maker you have chosen, it all comes down to this little cup. It looks just like the cups in which your coffee is served in Italy: straight-sided, practical, with a squared-off handle and a good sturdy saucer. Made of heavy china, it has a coffee-colored dark brown glaze on the outside and on the top of the saucer, a clear glaze on its other surfaces. It holds three ounces of dark, aromatic coffee, served, perhaps, with a twist of lemon floating on the top to make an *espresso romano.* It also comes in all white, with a clear glaze.

Bloomingdale's **$2.50**

The Cuisine of Japan

Japan is a country in which land, art and food express a common world-vision. As a small country, with little arable land and relatively limited natural resources, Japan has always made a virtue of simplicity. Only two sprigs of pussy willow and a single chrysanthemum stand in a vase; the furniture of a house is rolled up and stored in a closet; the flight of a seagull is expressed by three sweeps of the painter's brush. And none of these expressions is considered lacking in any way. Rather, the Japanese are inclined to see the simplicity and purity of their style as superior to the excesses of western taste. No Versailles here, and no *choucroute garnie*. Food is served in small portions, and the diner is expected to eat everything on his plate. At one time, he was even expected to hide his fruit pits and stems in the sleeves of his kimono rather than leave them on his plate! Even today, Japanese meals are planned so that there will be no leftovers, a rule that is aesthetic as well as economic. This sparseness, simplicity and cleanliness is described by a single word in Japan, *sappari.*

This elegance of simplicity also brings a separateness to Japanese cuisine: thin slices of rosy tunafish on a flat ceramic rectangle, kept company only by a tiny pyramid of horseradish paste; clear clam broth with a single mushroom and a single slice of lime in a pristine black bowl; plum-red cabbage pickles alone in the center of a porcelain square. Even when several elements are combined—as in *sukiyaki*—each of the ingredients is complementary but discrete. In Japanese cooking, no one thing should ever be allowed to overpower a dish. Strongly flavored foods like horseradish or scallions are often served as garnishes, to be added to the dish only after it's cooked, and at the diner's discretion.

Basic to the simple beauty of Japanese cooking—and life—is a reverence for nature and natural harmony. When they are not moon-viewing, or waiting for the sound of a lotus blossom opening, or watching fireflies, the Japanese look for perfect harmony of the seasons with the food they eat. (In fact, restaurants, as well as many households, in Japan have a set of serving dishes for each season, so that winter meals need never be served on dishes decorated with summery daffodils.) Instead of preserving foods so they can be eaten all year round, the Japanese eat foods fresh and as they come into season. In November, rice is newly harvested and all Japanese wait hungrily for this annual prize. As winter moves in, hot, steaming casseroles like *mizutaki* (chicken and vegetables simmered in a broth) or *shabu shabu* (a beef version of *mizutaki*) are cooked at the table. In early February, incredibly large, juicy strawberries arrive; then, all summer long, refreshing cold noodle dishes are served with pungent dipping sauces; and in early fall, hordes of Japanese go in search of a large, meaty mushroom called *matsutake.*

All year long, the cuisine is dominated by fish, shellfish, vegetables and rice—with a little help from poultry and the aristocratic, beer-fattened Kobe beeves—and a handful of distinctive flavorings: rice vinegar, sesame seeds (ground, in a paste, or as an oil), *sake, mirin* (sweet *sake*), *wasabi* (hot, green horseradish), *daikon* (sharp-tasting radish), *katsuobushi* (dried bonito) and seaweed. Not to mention the prolific, prominent, proteinaceous soybean, which makes itself indispensable in many forms: as *miso,* a fermented paste; as *tofu,* bean curd; and as *shoyu,* soy sauce.

Practically, Japanese cooking should be fairly accessible to the American cook. The special foodstuffs are well represented in this country (especially on the West Coast), as are most of the utensils. To begin stocking a Japanese kitchen, you will need a mortar and pestle, knives, cooking chopsticks, a grater, pans for frying and steaming, and a rice cooker. Then, when you begin to shop for serving pieces on which to present your perfectly executed *sashimi* or *tempura*, remember to look for certain qualities: for simplicity, for a reflection of nature, and for the degree to which each piece can heighten your awareness of the meal's beauty.

Earthenware Mortar and Wooden Pestle F:1

At first glance, this looks like an ordinary Japanese bowl, the dulled, light-brown area inside the bowl beautifully framed in a rich brown glaze. Looking more closely at the inner circle, you can see sharp ridges furrowed in an arrangement of wedge-shaped patterns. This is a *suribachi*, the unique earthenware mortar in which the Japanese mash cakes of *tofu* (soybean curd), grind sesame seeds or work *miso* (fermented soybean paste) into a smooth consistency. It is 6″ across the top and 2¼″ deep. The mortar's rolling-pin-shaped pestle, or *surikogi*, is a 9½″ cylinder of unfinished wood, rounded off at the mashing end, and with a hole in the other end for hanging. You might be wary of pressing down as hard with it as you would in a bowl of brass or marble, but the baked-clay mortar is surprisingly substantial. Both mortar and pestle come in a range of sizes: the *suribachi* in 7¼″, 8¾″, 9½″ and 10¾″ diameters; and the *surikogi* 12″ and 7″ long.

N.Y. Mutual Trading, Inc.
Suribachi (mortar) $2.00
Surikogi (pestle) $1.25

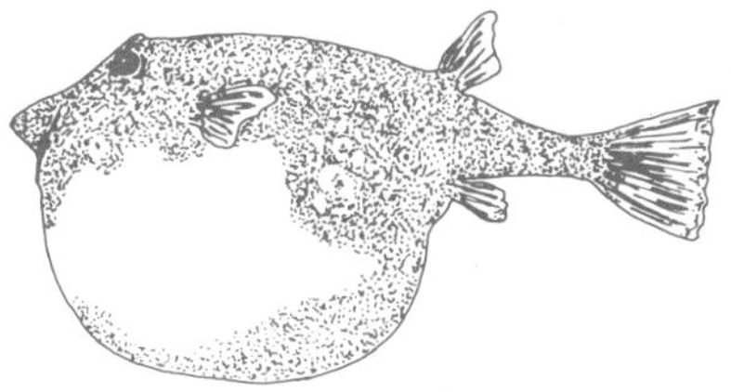

Fugu *(globefish or puffer fish) is one of the more dramatic components used in* sashimi *in Japan. Long considered a powerful aphrodisiac, it has graced many a midnight banquet. Yet it also possesses a lethal toxin in its liver and ovaries, which are tricky to remove. A practical test (and subsequently a license) are required in order to serve this potentially deadly speciality.*

Basic Knife Set F:2

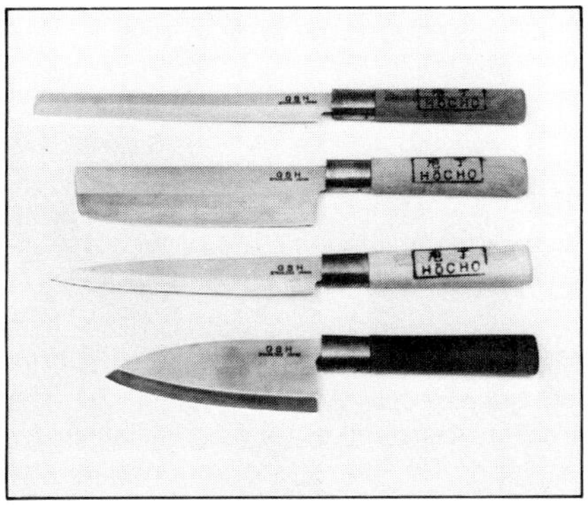

The sharp beauties in this knife set are brought to you by the same factories that produce *samurai* swords. And the Japanese chef's pride in and reliance upon a sharp blade nearly matches that of the *samurai*. The knife, or *hocho*, is absolutely indispensable to both the preparation and presentation of all Japanese foods—from the thinly sliced *sashimi* (raw fish), to the artistically carved and sculpted vegetables that give aesthetic balance to any Japanese dish. Nowadays, although many Japanese chefs in New York and Tokyo are turning to straight-edged knives with triangular blades of molybdenum steel, knives very similar to these have been used in Japan for thousands of years. They have an honest, functional appearance, and would be practical in any household (especially for seafood).

This classic four-*hocho* set includes (bottom to top) a boning knife, a *sashimi* knife, a vegetable slicer and a fish-slicing knife. The blades, made of iron in the past, are now made of stainless steel. They are ground along only one side, which allows Japanese chefs to achieve perfectly controlled, straight slicing. The cutting edge is very sharp indeed, and requires only occasional whetting; the cook must, however, exercise some caution to prevent such finely-ground edges from chipping. The handles are 5¼″-long, unfinished solid magnolia wood, each with the word *hocho* burned into it. The handle is bound, where it meets the blade, by a ¼″-deep brass collar; a single brass pin passes through the collar to rivet the partial tang in the handle. The *hocho* that looks like a foreshortened chef's knife, is called a *deba* and is a boning knife for filleting fish. The curved triangle of the blade, 5¼″ long and 1¾″ wide, slips easily along the bones while the sharp edge separates the skin of the fish from its flesh. The *sashimi* knife, or *yanagi*, is a little like an attenuated chef's knife. The 7″ blade is perfect for the precise, diagonal slicing of raw fish for *sashimi*, as well as for slicing vegetables. The *usuba hocho* is a slim piece of stainless steel, used for preparing the ubiquitous shredded vegetables so characteristic of Japanese cooking. While the boning knife is ground on one side only, this mini-cleaver is ground on both sides. The blade is 6¾″ long and 1½″ wide, with a slightly curving but essentially squared-off tip. The fourth knife in the set is still another knife for slicing fish, but we bet you've never seen one quite like it. This *tako-biki* has a thin, straight-edged, 8″ blade ground half its width on one side, and with a squared-off tip. Use the *tako-biki* to transform fresh tunafish or salmon into paper-thin slices for *sashimi*.

Cardinal China Co. (1318) $15.00

MAGURO NO SASHIMI

Sliced Raw Tuna

2½ ounces fresh tuna fillet
2 teaspoons *wasabi* (green horseradish powder)
2 teaspoons soy sauce
¼ cup thinly sliced *daikon* (white radish)

Cut the fish, which should be a deep rose color, into ¼-inch-thick slices. Professional chefs slice the fish on a slight diagonal halfway through the slice, then reverse the angle of the knife for the rest of the slice.

Arrange the fish on a medium-sized platter. Mix the horseradish with water to make a smooth stiff paste and place beside the tuna slices. Pour the soy sauce into a small bowl. Using chopsticks place a little bit of horseradish on a slice of tuna, fold the fish over, then dip it in soy sauce and eat. Dip the radish in soy sauce and eat, alternating with the tuna. Serves 4.

(From THE COMPLETE BOOK OF JAPANESE COOKING, by Elisabeth Lambert Ortiz with Mitsuko Endo. Copyright 1976 by Elisabeth Lambert Ortiz. Reprinted by permission of M. Evans and Company, Inc., New York.)

Fish Boning Knife F:3

It looks like a miniature chef's knife, but the curve of the triangular blade is pure Japanese. The 6½″-long, stainless-steel blade, 2″ wide near its base, is ground on one side only to permit absolute control of the cutting edge. In Japan, the flat side of the knife is usually held against the knuckles of the opposite hand, which is used to steady the food. (That makes our knife ideal for left-handers!) Although this sturdy *deba hocho,* or boning knife, can be used for many purposes in a western kitchen, it is prized in Japan for the ease with which the blade slips under the flesh and along the bones of a fish. The handle is of smooth, unfinished wood, which meets the blade in a shiny brass collar. The razor-sharp blade won't pit or rust, but it may chip . . . so don't use it to cut through any bones tougher than those of a fish.

The Japan Mart, Inc. $8.25

Coarse and Fine Whetstones F:4

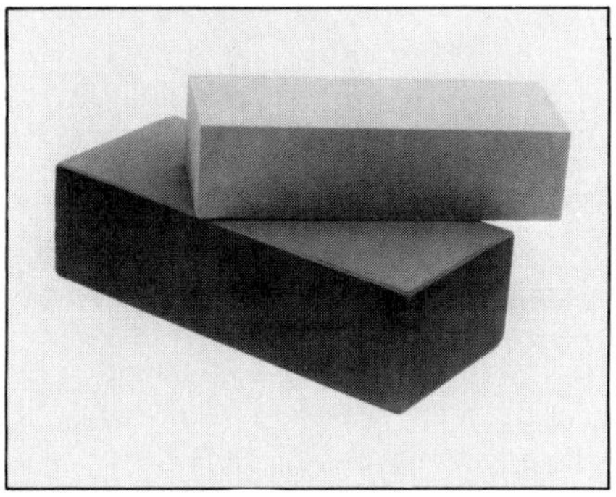

Ideally, knives should be sharpened—on a whetstone or steel—every time they are used. The constant impact of steel against the firm surface of a chopping block will inevitably dull the finest edge—and do it more quickly than you would imagine. Again ideally, the knife should be sharpened first on a coarse stone, then finished with a few strokes on a fine grit. Our handsome pair of whetstones, sold separately, will do the job admirably. The smaller stone, which looks like a slab of gray-green potter's clay, has the coarse grit; it is 8″ long, 3″ wide and 2″ high. The larger stone, with the fine grit, is grayish-red in color and 9½″ long, 4″ wide and 2¾″ high. And they are heavy! Therefore, as useful as they are, it would be practical to keep them in the open rather than inaccessible in a drawer. Like most Japanese cooking utensils, these whetstones have an honest, forthright design that makes them perfectly suitable for display.

N.Y. Mutual Trading, Inc.
Fine $25.00
Coarse $15.00

Tuna, the shining star of sushi *and* sashimi

Although of French origin (Gluttony *by Eugene Sue, 1899), the following description could well be the preamble to a spectacular* sashimi *feast: "Fringed with long seaweeds of a light green colour, were fish of the most diminutive size and exquisite flavour: sardines gleaming like silver, others of ultramarine blue, others still of bright red, and dainty grill fish with backs as white as snow and rose-coloured bellies."*

Fish Scaler F:5

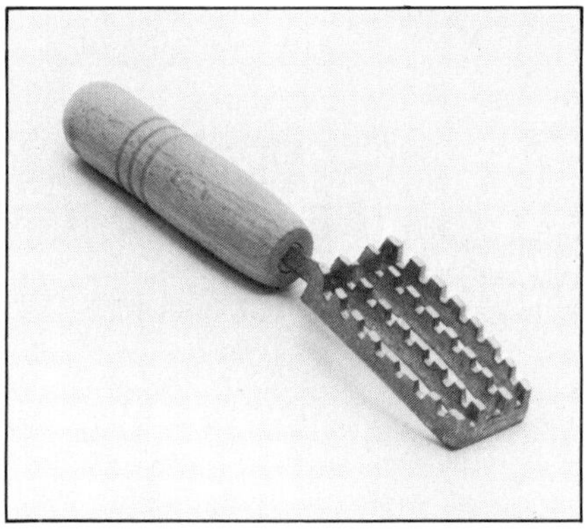

The predominance of fish—especially raw—in Japanese cooking accounts for all the kitchen utensils on hand for its preparation. Here is a terrific-looking tool that will help you scale the Japanese culinary heights in no time at all. This fish scaler, called a *urokofuki,* is 7¼″ overall; its no-nonsense scraping edge consists of four slightly arched brass strips, with deep, sharp notches cut into them. The 4″ wooden handle slopes upward at a slight angle to facilitate work. Any non-*sashimi*-oriented fisherman will also appreciate this handsome tool; for even if he doesn't eat his catch, how can he give it away uncleaned?

Main St. Foods $2.95

Fish Tweezers F:6

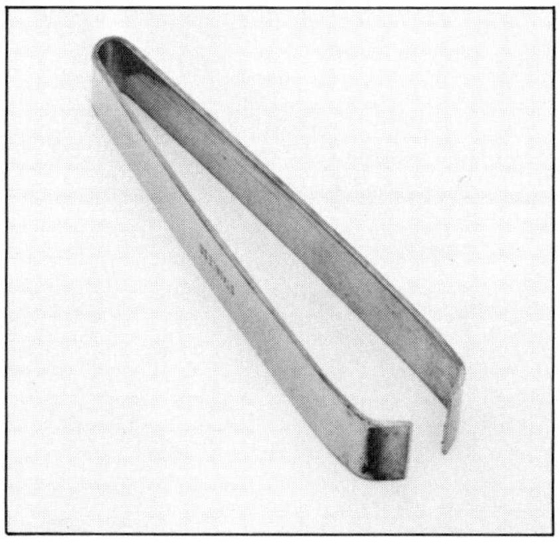

No, Japanese fish don't have eyebrows—but they *do* have bones. Leave it to the fastidious Japanese to come up with a small, handy, inexpensive gadget to pluck the fine bones from mackerel fillets before marinating them in *sake, shoyu* (soy sauce) and *dashi* (soup stock) for *yuanzuke* (broiled, marinated mackerel). No matter how long your fingernails are, nor how firm your determination, only these tweezers will easily and quickly rid fish of bones, insuring the safety of you and your guests (just think, no more cautious hunting for the elusive villain as you chew). Our 4″-long throat-saver is made of stainless steel. It curves in at the top and has a ½″, straight, very sharp edge to grasp the offending bones.

N.Y. Mutual Trading, Inc. $1.75

Wooden Chopping Board F:7

Dicing, slicing, chopping and cubing of meats and vegetables are intrinsic steps in aesthetics-oriented Japanese cooking. Thus, a chopping block, along with a knife, is a fundamental necessity in the Japanese kitchen. If you don't have a large butcher block—or even if you do—a convenient portable slab like this one allows you to prepare ingredients on any table. The meticulous Japanese use one side for fish, the other side for vegetables and meat. It is narrower than most chopping blocks, only 8½″ across, 17½″ long and 1¼″ thick. Lovely verticals of natural cedar-wood grain run through the board, which is pierced at the top with a hole for hanging. A good weight, our board won't jump even under the most strenuous chopping, and its added length is perfect for filleting fish or slicing *daikon* (a long, white radish).

N.Y. Mutual Trading, Inc. $7.79

Tofu Knife F:8

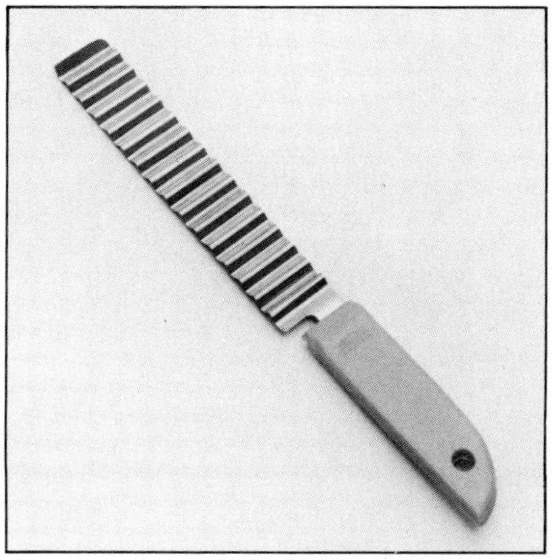

That all knives are not flat blades is made abundantly clear by this wavy-edged *tofu* knife. *Tofu* (soybean curd) is that somewhat bland, custardlike staple that holds a position of great respect in Japan: the Japanese eat *tofu* boiled, broiled, sautéed, deep-fried, scrambled and as a garnish. It doesn't take a sharp or heavy blade to cut *tofu,* but the appearance-conscious Japanese find decorative designs more fun than straight edges. They like the undulating waves created by the unusual blunt edge of our *tofu* knife and even use it to cut gelatin. Its fluted, steel blade, 5⅜″ long and 1″ wide, is set into a plastic handle. Although you can live without it, our *tofu* knife is so inexpensive, you might treat yourself to this frippery the next time you serve *tofu-dengaku* (broiled *tofu*).

Katagiri and Co., Inc. $1.69

DENGAKU TOFU

Grilled Soybean Curd with Miso Dressing

The appearance of skewered "tofu" decorated with white and/or green "miso," may remind Americans of an ice-cream popsicle. There, of course, the resemblance ends, although "dengaku tofu" is treated as a sweet course by the Japanese. The green-colored "miso" is made, in Japan, with ground "sansho" leaves, which are not available in the United States. Spinach makes an admirable substitute, with packaged "sansho" powder added for flavor.

To serve 4

2 cakes fresh *tofu* (soybean curd), cut into 8 pieces each ¾ inch wide by 3 inches long
¼ pound fresh spinach leaves, stripped from their stems
4 ounces (½ cup) *shiro miso* (white soybean paste)
Kona sansho (Japanese pepper)

Prepare ahead: 1. Preheat the broiler to its highest point. Place the pieces of *tofu* side by side in a flameproof baking dish just large enough to hold them in one snug layer. Add enough cold water to come halfway up the sides of the *tofu,* then slide the dish under the broiler, as close to the heat as possible. Sear the *tofu* for a few seconds, then turn the pieces with a spatula and sear the other side. The *tofu* will be speckled but not evenly browned. Remove the pan from the broiler and set aside.

2. In a 1½- to 2-quart saucepan, bring 2 cups of water to a boil. Add the spinach leaves and boil uncovered for about 2 minutes. Then drain in a sieve and run cold water over the spinach to cool it quickly and set its color. Squeeze the spinach firmly to rid it of all its moisture and chop it fine.

In a *suribachi* (serrated mixing bowl) or with a mortar and pestle, pound or mash the spinach to a paste. Then with the back of a large spoon, rub it through a fine sieve into a mixing bowl.

3. Stir half of the *shiro miso* and a few sprinkles of *kona sansho* into the spinach, continuing to stir until the *miso* paste has turned a delicate green.

Continued from preceding page

4. Place the remaining *shiro miso* in a small bowl and mix until smooth.

To cook and serve: Over moderate heat, bring the pan of seared *tofu* (with the water still in the pan) almost to the boil. Remove from the heat and spoon the green *miso* dressing into a pastry bag equipped with a No. 47 ribbon tip. Squeeze the *miso* along the top of 4 pieces of *tofu,* covering the top of each piece. (Lacking a pastry bag, spread a thin film of *miso* on each piece of *tofu* with a spatula, and run the prongs of a fork down the *miso* to create serrated lines.) Cover the remaining *tofu* with the plain *miso.*

Insert two 4- to 6-inch bamboo skewers or small lobster forks halfway through the length of each piece of *tofu.* Return the *tofu* to the water in the baking dish and sear under the broiler for a few seconds. Serve at room temperature, as the sweet course in a Japanese meal.

(*From FOODS OF THE WORLD,* The Cooking of Japan, *TIME-LIFE BOOKS, New York. Copyright 1969 by Time Inc.*)

Vegetable Cutters F:9

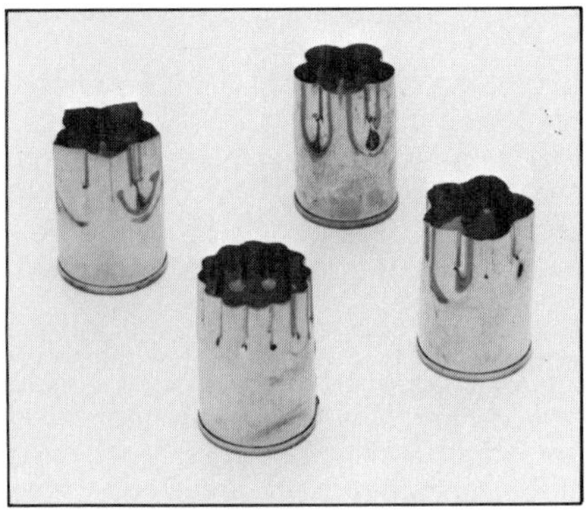

If you have longed to emulate the Japanese chef's gift for making carrot cherry blossoms or cucumber chrysanthemums, vegetable cutters like these are a shortcut to artistry. This set of cutters—called *yasaino nuki-gata*—consists of four, 2″-high, 1¼″-diameter, stainless-steel tubes in traditional Japanese shapes: chrysanthemum, autumn leaf, cherry blossom and plum blossom. The cutters' shaped bottom edges are sharp, but their top rims are safely rolled. The Japanese use cutters like these to dress up *tofu* (bean curd) and gelatin desserts as well as vegetables.

Katagiri and Co., Inc. $2.69

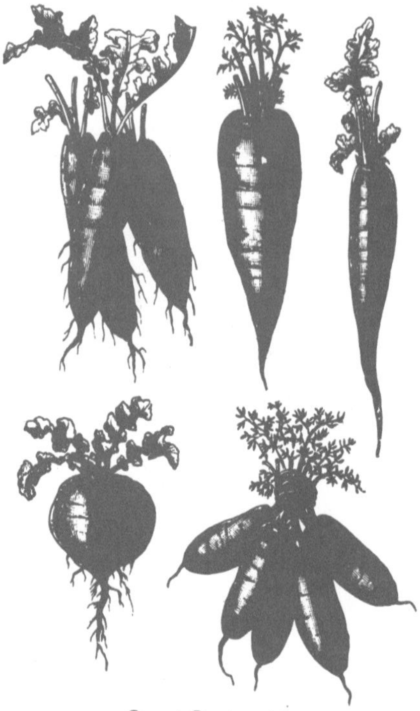

Great Grate-ables.

Wooden Shredder F:10

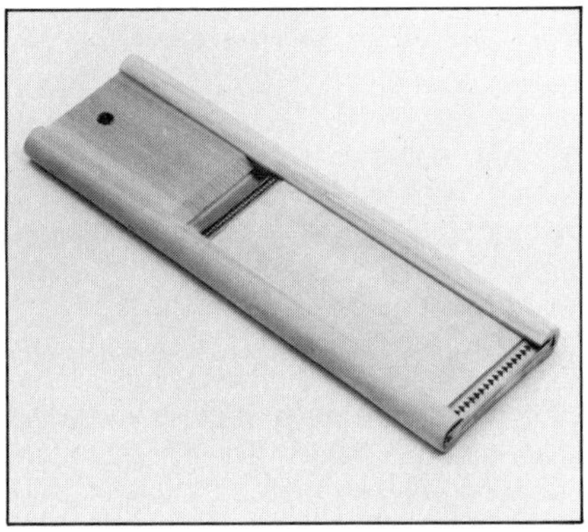

This wooden shredder is a basic Japanese kitchen tool used to grate roots—ginger, horseradish, carrots, sharp-tasting *daikon* (white radish)—or water chestnuts. The sides of the thin, flat board are grooved dowels into whose tracks slides a piece of wood with sharp, shredding teeth at either end. One set of teeth is for coarse shredding, the other for fine. A tinned-steel cutting blade is attached to the main body of the board and remains stationary. To use the shredder, the board must be held at an angle. Our board is 3⅜″ wide and 10¾″ long.

Rafu Bussan $3.00

Porcelain Grater F:11

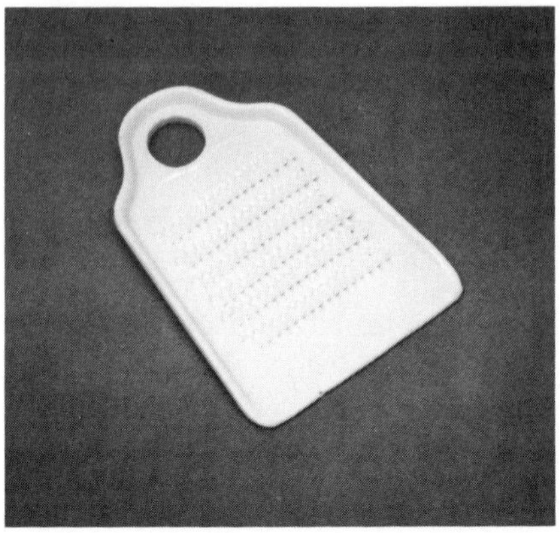

This fragile-looking porcelain *objet* is actually a hard-working grater, 5½″ long and 3½″ at the widest end, with six furrows of coarse, draculian teeth. Handy for the numerous grating tasks called for in Japanese cooking, this grater has the added advantage of being forever rust-free. However, it will probably last longer in a household free of dogs, cats and small children; for drop this and your grater is much the lesser.

H. A. Mack and Co., Inc. $3.00

"Buddhism has left its impress here, as on everything in Japan. To Buddhism was due the abandonment of a meat diet, now over a thousand years ago. The permission to eat fish, though that too entailed the taking of life, which is contrary to strict Buddhist tenets, seems to have been a concession to human frailty. Pious frauds, moreover, came to the rescue. One may even now see the term 'mountain whale' (yama-kujira) *written up over certain eating-houses, which means that venison is there for sale. The logical process is this: A whale is a fish. Fish may be eaten. Therefore, if you call venison 'mountain whale,' you may eat venison."*

Things Japanese: Being Notes on Various Subjects Connected with Japan *by Basil Hall Chamberlain. London, 1902*

Aluminum Grater with Catch Pan F:12

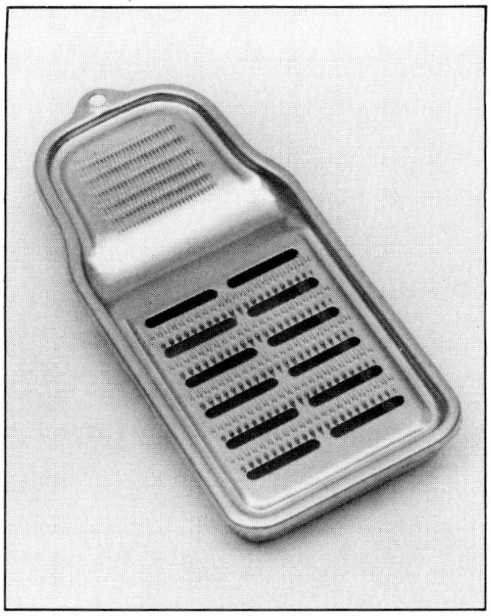

This gold-colored, anodized-aluminum grater comes with its own shallow catch pan. Its work surface is divided into two areas, one with coarse teeth, the other with fine teeth. The rows of coarse teeth alternate direction (half point toward the top of the grater, half toward the bottom) so that vegetables can be grated with a back and forth motion. The grated radish (*daikon*) or other root vegetable falls through the holes near the teeth and into the catch pan below. The fine teeth—for grating ginger or *wasabi* (Japanese horseradish)—have a small depression in front of them to catch the grated vegetables. The rolled sides of the grating plate keep it firmly snapped to the catch pan while in use, and the unit comes apart for cleaning. It is a convenient 7½″ by 3¾″, small enough to stuff in a drawer; but it can also be hung by the hole at one end.

Main St. Foods $1.79

Grater with Pan and Spoon F:13

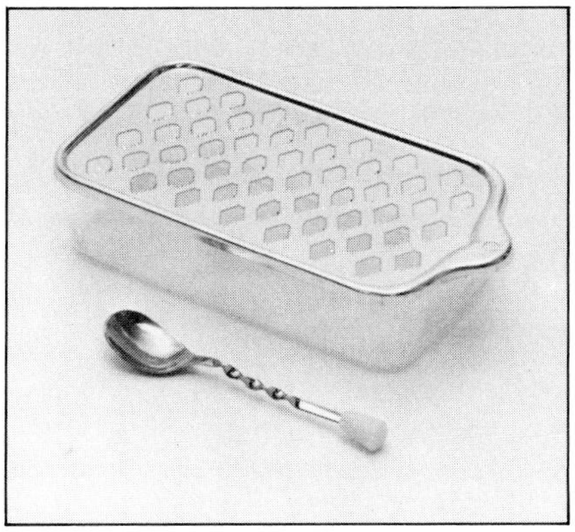

Covered with large, diamond-shaped holes with sharp serrated edges, this aluminum grater fits over a plastic catch pan. The grater is 6½″ long and 3¾″ wide and the catch pan 1½″ deep. The handy 4½″-long, stainless-steel spoon that comes with the grater would be perfect for parceling out individual servings of grated *wasabi* (yellowish-green, hot Japanese horseradish) to accompany *sashimi.*

C. H. Food Market $1.39

Shredding/Slicing Machine F:14

The Italians may have their pasta machines and the French their vegetable mills, but leave it to the Japanese to figure out a way to slice, shred and curl vegetables in spaghetti-thin spirals. Place any cylindrical vegetable or root on the turning disc of this clever machine, push it against the cutting blade, crank the handle and your vegetable is metamorphosed: potatoes come out as rice-noodle shreds, cucumbers make crêpe-paper spirals, radishes form mountains of fine threads. The shredding/slicing ma-

"A Japanese Breakfast"

Continued from preceding page

chine is made of lightweight plastic and steel, and rests on a plastic base 10¾″ long, 4½″ wide and 1″ high. The crank and turning disc are mounted on a sliding platform that moves the vegetables toward the cutting blades. There are four interchangeable steel blades that fit into the stationary 5½″-high, 3⅞″-wide blade holder at one end of the base: a straight-edged blade for plain slicing and three comb-like blades with fine, medium and coarse teeth for various grades of shredding. This moderately priced miracle slicer makes it easier to live up to the aesthetic standards of the Japanese kitchen. The unusually straightforward directions that come with this gadget are still marked with the characteristic inscrutability of Japanese translated into English. In the middle of a sequence of slicing instructions we find a photograph of a bridge whose caption reads, "Look at the charming curve of the bridge. This is the Kintai Bridge, which is the most famous in Japan. From this fantastic area, we present you this slicer."

C. H. Food Market $8.75

Wooden Sieve F:15

Infinitely more attractive than the average western sieve, the silky, pliant, unfinished wood of our Japanese *uragoshi* is wrapped into an 11¾″ circle and sewn together with peeled bark. This circle is attached to a slightly wider (12¼″) base, similarly wrapped and sewn; the sieve itself is 5½″ deep. A fine horsehair mesh, caught firmly between the two circles, prevents seeds, bones, skins and stems from passing through. The sieve is used in Japan primarily to purée fish or *miso*, the ubiquitous soybean paste. It is light but sturdy, and would be as valuable on display in a country kitchen as it would be useful in puréeing tomatoes for a sauce.

N.Y. Mutual Trading, Inc. $38.00

ZARU SOBA

Buckwheat Noodles on Bamboo Plates

3 tablespoons *mirin*
5 tablespoons soy sauce
1 tablespoon sugar
4-inch square *kombu* (kelp)
½ cup flaked *katsuobushi* (dried bonito)
1 scallion, trimmed, using white and green parts
10 ounces *soba* (buckwheat noodles)
1 tablespoon *wasabi* (green horseradish powder)
2 sheets *nori* (dried laver seaweed)

In a small saucepan bring the *mirin* to a boil over low heat. Add 1¼ cups cold water, the soy sauce and sugar. Clean the kelp with a damp cloth, cut into a ½-inch fringe and add to the sauce with the bonito. Cook, uncovered, over low heat until the mixture is about to boil. Lift out and discard the kelp. Simmer the mixture gently for 5 minutes longer, then strain through a double thickness of cheesecloth into a bowl. Put the bowl of sauce into a larger bowl of cold water to chill it quickly. It should be a little cooler than room temperature so add a few ice cubes to the water if necessary. Pour the sauce into 4 soup bowls.

Finely chop the scallion and divide among 4 tiny bowls. Put one at each place setting with a soup bowl.

Cook the noodles . . . and chill in cold water. Drain and divide among 4 *zaru* (bamboo plates).

Mix the horseradish to a paste with a little water and place a small mound of it on each plate beside the noodles.

Toast the sheets of seaweed for a few seconds over a gas flame or electric burner then crumble in a piece of cheesecloth, or with the fingers, and sprinkle over the noodles.

To eat the noodles add the horseradish to the chilled sauce. This is very hot, so the amount of horseradish used is a matter of taste. Add the scallions to the sauce. Dip the noodles into the sauce before eating. This is a summer dish, wonderfully refreshing on a hot day.
Serves 4.

(From THE COMPLETE BOOK OF JAPANESE COOKING, by Elisabeth Lambert Ortiz with Mitsuko Endo. Copyright 1976 by Elisabeth Lambert Ortiz. Reprinted by permission of M. Evans and Company, Inc., New York.)

Set of Bamboo Strainers F:16

These round baskets of woven bamboo are *zaru*—strainers that can also be used as serving plates for some foods. They are slightly curved, and are 8½″, 9¾″ and 10⅞″ in diameter respectively. Use them for draining and then serving *zarusoba*, a refreshing summer meal of buckwheat noodles garnished with scallions and served with sharp horseradish paste (*wasabi*) and dipping sauce.

N.Y. Mutual Trading, Inc. $14.00

"Setsubun *is the name of the movable feast occurring sometimes late in January, sometimes early in February, on the eve of the first day of spring, Old Calendar. Beans are scattered about the house on the evening of this day in order to scare away demons, and of these beans each person present eats one more than the number of the years of his age."*

Things Japanese: Being Notes on Various Subjects Connected With Japan *by Basil Hall Chamberlain. London, 1902*

"Young lady playing the samisen while her lover is being served refreshments by a girl attendant" by Nishikawa Sukenobu (1671–1751) (from The Metropolitan Museum of Art)

Bamboo Cooking Chopsticks F:17

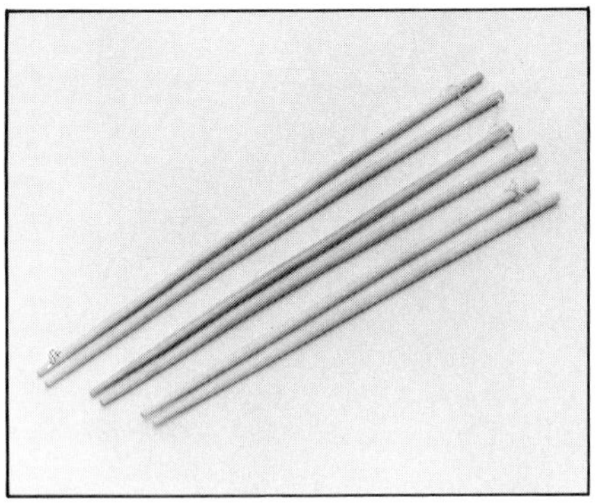

Chopsticks for cooking and serving should usually be longer than those used for eating. This package contains three pairs of smooth, natural-bamboo chopsticks, each a different length. You can choose whichever of the 10½″, 11¾″ or 12¾″ tapering cylinders is more convenient for a particular job. Each pair is tied together through tiny holes, so that you can always put your hand on a set. Cooking chopsticks have a versatility surprising to those of us who rely on a battery of specialized tools. Use them, for instance, for cooking and serving *sukiyaki*, stirring *sunomono* (vinegared vegetables or fish) or dipping ingredients in batter for *tempura*. But practice before you use chopsticks for cooking, so you can remove the fried shrimp when it's golden brown, and not drop it back in the pot for cremation! It's a good idea to wash and dry the chopsticks thoroughly after each use, and replace them from time to time, as they do absorb flavors. But unlike metal, lacquer or plastic, bamboo chopsticks won't burn your hands, chip or melt.

N.Y. Mutual Trading, Inc. $1.25

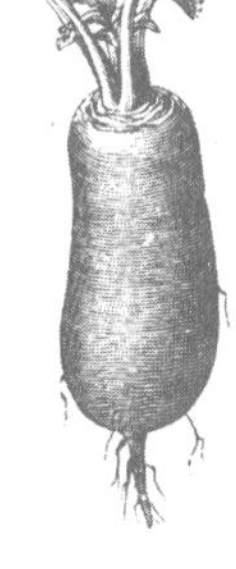

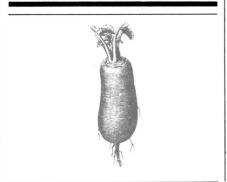

Stainless-Steel Cooking Chopsticks F:18

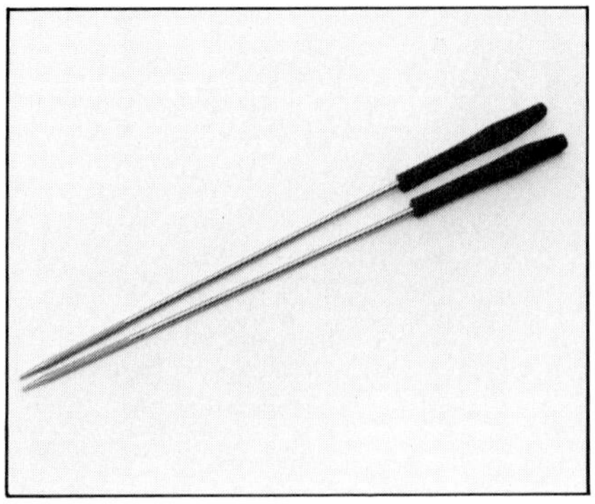

These modern cooking chopsticks of stainless steel were designed especially for frying delectable batter-coated *tempura* tidbits. The tiny ridges near the tips are meant to grasp slippery morsels of shrimp, or vegetables, and the black plastic handles are heat-proof. The 13½″-long chopsticks have holes in their handles so a length of string or chain can be used to hang them up as a pair.

Rafu Bussan $1.50

Mesh Skimmer F:19

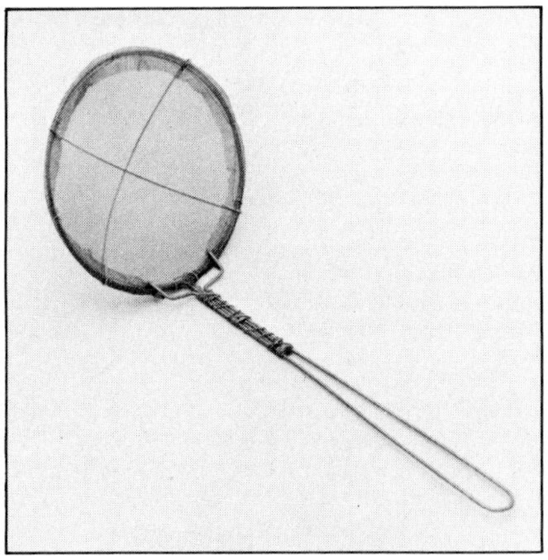

Our round, brass mesh skimmer, attached to a graceful wire loop handle, can be hung up right alongside the stove—which is where you'll want this handy gadget if you do any deep-fat frying. After each batch of delicate shrimp *tempura* or *agedashi* (deep-fried bean curd) has been removed from the oil, simply slide the curved circle of superfine mesh through the fat, scooping up any particles of fried batter or food. Then proceed with the next batch, secure in the knowledge that the oil is as immaculate as when you began frying, and there will be no danger of a burnt, acrid taste to subsequent batches. Be sure and use the skimmer after you've completed your frying, so you can store and re-use the not-inexpensive oil. Other sizes are available (4″ and 7″), but we find our 6″ skimmer perfect for *tempura* pans.

N.Y. Mutual Trading, Inc. $1.75

Bean Paste Ladle F:20

This odd-looking item may not be beautiful, but it *is* functional. It's sole purpose is to break up the somewhat gummy-textured *miso* (paste made from fermented cooked soybeans). The Japanese, who yearly consume 49 pounds of *miso* per capita, use it as a seasoning, in marinades, and, most importantly, as the basis of *miso-shiru*—a rich, opaque soup that can be served at all meals, including breakfast. Of gold-toned anodized aluminum, this forked ladle has a 3¾″-diameter bowl and an 8½″-long handle.

Katagiri and Co., Inc. $1.98

"Snow grains! Hail grains!—In your kitchen dumplings are boiling; beans are too boiling; the huntsman is returning; the baby is squalling; the ladle is missing!—Oh what a flurry and worry!"

a child's song from A Japanese Miscellany *by Lafcadio Hearn. Little, Brown & Co., 1901*

A Paean to the Omnipurpose, Omnipresent, Omnipotent Soybean:

"One—*for ground peas—*
the peas made into flour;
Two—*for trampled peas*
the peas which were crushed;
Three—*the peas made into* miso-
sauce—fermented peas;
Four—*the selected peas—*
the beautiful peas;
Five—*for parched peas—*
the belly-cut peas;
Six—*for peas given to us—*
the peas which we gained;
Seven—*for growing peas—*
the peas in the pod;
Eight—*the peas given away—*
the peas that are lost;
Nine—*the peas which we paid for—*
the money-bought peas;
and Ten—*for the peas that we took—*
the stolen peas!"

a song of Japanese children quoted in A Japanese Miscellany *by Lafcadio Hearn. Little, Brown & Co., 1901*

The miraculous Oriental life-sustainer, the soy plant.

Slotted Bean Curd Servers F:21

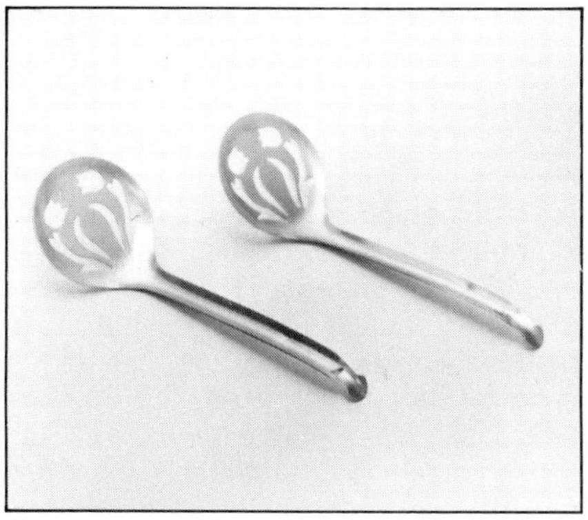

Once cooked, *tofu* is exceptionally delicate and easily broken, so that it must be lifted very carefully. To do the job, you need special, slotted *tofu* servers like these. They come as a set of two 6¾″-long, anodized-aluminum spoons, whose flat, spatula-like bowls have tulip-shaped cut-outs. To serve *sumashi wan* (clear soup with *tofu* and shrimp), arrange a shrimp, a cube of *tofu* and a thin curl of lemon peel in the bottom of each soup bowl; then pour in the hot broth.

Katagiri and Co., Inc. $0.98

Scrubbing Brush F:22

This handy scrubbing brush, of natural, light-brown vegetable fiber, has a tightly closed oval shape that fits comfortably in your hand. Its stiff bristles soften when wet, yet somehow manage to retain enough firmness to make short work of scrubbing a *nabe* (pot), or cutting board. The brush can also be used for cleaning *daikon,* potatoes and other tuberous or root vegetables. Four and a half inches long by 3″ wide and 2″ thick, the brush is held together by braided wire, pulled across the middle and covered with a twisted length of the fiber for eye appeal. The wire security belt terminates in a loop at one end. Hang the brush up near the sink to keep it handy, and let it dry overnight after use. We noted one drawback, though: when used to clean a rice cooker, individual grains of rice tended to get caught between the bristles, and it took a bit or rinsing and intricate finger work to pry them out.

Main St. Foods $0.99

Rice

From the poorest hut to the imperial palace, a bowl of steamed rice is an intrinsic part of every Japanese meal. More than merely a food staple, *gohan*, the Japanese word for rice, literally means "honored food" or "meal." (The word for breakfast, *asagohan*, means "morning meal;" lunch is *hirugohan*, "noon meal," and dinner, *bangohan*, means "evening meal.") In the past, rice was a measure of wealth: great feudal lords were ranked according to the number of rice fields they owned, and the ruthless *samurai* warriors were paid in sacks of rice. Even today, every Japanese looks forward to the November harvest; for everyone knows that moist new rice is the best-tasting grain imaginable, so highly esteemed that it has a special name, *shinmai*, and is always served pure and natural, without sauces or flavored broth.

Japanese rice, unlike American or Chinese varieties, is short-grained. It should be somewhat sticky when served, as is Chinese rice; if left to stand a while after cooking it will be of chopstick-manageable consistency. But, unlike the western habit of cooking or eating rice with other ingredients, so that it will absorb flavors, the Japanese most often serve it just plain steamed, in small individual bowls. It is eaten by itself, as a palate cleaner between different taste sensations, and at the end of a meal. It is also used in other ways: fermented it becomes *sake* (rice wine); rice-wine vinegar is used to flavor rice for *sushi*, thus rice on rice. Thriftly, nothing is wasted: the stalks of the plants are woven into baskets, *tatami* (floor mats), rain hats, rain boots and packaging.

Inari – The Rice Bearer.

Electric Rice Cooker F:23

In the past, rice was cooked in a heavy, covered pot called a *kama*, heated on a *hibachi* and carefully watched. Nowadays, most Japanese cooks carefully measure out rice and water, put them into an electric rice cooker like this one, flick the switch and forget about it. Here's how it works: rice and water are measured into a rustproof aluminum insert, which is lowered into the body of the cooker where it rests on the heating plate at the bottom; the lid is put on and the switch flicked to "cook." Twenty minutes later a bell (described in the manufacturer's instructions as a "merry ting") goes off to signal that the rice is done. Then, the rice cooker automatically switches to "warm" to keep the rice at the correct temperature until it is served. The "warm" level can also be used to reheat leftover rice. To convert the cooker to a steamer—for custard, vegetables, steamed meats and poultry—the manufacturer supplies a perforated steaming plate that fits inside the cooker insert. This rice cooker is 9″ high and 8″ across; the cooker insert is 4″ deep and holds 5½ cups of cooked rice. The exterior of the cooker is enameled steel (available in white, avocado, flame or harvest gold), and has black plastic handles, knob and control panel. It comes with a measuring cup as well as the steaming plate, and is also available in two larger sizes—8⅓ cups and 10 cups.

Hitachi Sales Corp. (RD4051) $34.95

Rice Paddle F:24

An indispensable tool in the Japanese kitchen is a bamboo *shamoji*, or rice paddle. The *shamoji* is used to serve rice into individual bowls; but it is never used for stirring rice, since rice is never stirred. Or, it can be used to mix cooked rice with a piquant dressing—rice vinegar, sugar, salt and *mirin* (sweet *sake*)—to transform it into *sushi*. To keep rice from sticking, dip the paddle in cold water before using it and the rice will slide off easily. The paddle is a flat, silky-smooth piece of bamboo, with its characteristic light color and thin-lined grain. It has a shallow spoon-shaped profile; but the wide part is only slightly curved, not at all like the bowl of a spoon. The "bowl" part is 2¾″ across at its widest, and accounts for 4″ of the 9¾″ overall length. A slightly smaller *shamoji*, 7″ long, is also available.

Main St. Foods $0.89

"Rice, Japanese Style—Put half a pound of well washed rice into a double kettle, with one pint of milk or water, one heaping teaspoonful of salt, and a quarter of a medium sized nutmeg grated, boil it until tender, about forty minutes; if it seems very dry add a little more liquid, taking care not to have it sloppy when it is cooked. When milk is used it may be served with milk and sugar as a breakfast or tea dish; when water takes the place of milk, the addition of an ounce of butter, and half a saltspoonful of pepper makes a nice dinner dish of it." [*Almost authentic, if you forget the milk, salt, nutmeg, sugar, butter, pepper and cooking method.*]

Twenty Five Cent Dinners for Families of Six *by Juliet Cornson. New York, 1878*

Covered Rice Server and Paddle F:25

This contemporary plastic interpretation of an *ohitsu*, the classic Japanese container for serving rice, is dark brown, decorated only with fine gold lines. It is 7½″ round and 4″ deep, and holds 4 cups of rice—enough for 3 to 5 Japanese-sized portions. The accompanying black paddle, or *shamoji*, is 7½″ long, with a 2″-wide bowl. To act as an insulator and keep the rice warm, the *ohitsu* has a removable plastic liner. Both bowl and liner have a small indentation for the spoon. The cover is recessed in the middle, with a typically-Japanese knoblike handle in the center.

Katagiri and Co., Inc. $12.00

Individual Rice Bowl F:26

No matter how many dishes are served, no Japanese feels that he has had a complete meal without his bowl of rice. At most meals, a classic rice bowl such as this—the sides fanning out from a small round base—is placed before each person at the beginning of the meal. Ours comes in a delicate spring pattern of peonies and lacy foliage, with orange, moss green, lavender and gold against a pearl white background, and two blue stripes circling the base. It is 4⅝″ across the top and 2½″ high; filled, it will hold one cup. Although an American-sized portion invariably fills a dish, the Japanese serve only a moderate amount of rice at one time so that the aesthetic balance of the delicate porcelain is not overwhelmed.

Bloomingdale's (51/3) $1.60

"Japanese rice is the best in Asia . . . Every one lives on it who can afford to do so; but as a rule the peasantry cannot. Wheat, barley and especially millet, are the real staples throughout the rural districts, rice being treated as a luxury to be brought out only on high days and holidays, or to be resorted to in case of sickness. We once heard a beldame in a country village remark to another with a grave shake of the head: 'What! Do you mean to say that it has come to having to give her rice?'—the unexpressed inference being that the patient's case must be alarming indeed, if the family had thought it necessary to resort to so expensive a dainty."

Things Japanese: Being Notes on Various Subjects Connected with Japan *by Basil Hall Chamberlain, 1902*

"—Oh Lady Moon,
Come down from over the Temple of Kwannon,
And help yourself to some boiled rice!
—Rice? no: I do not like rice.
But if you have ammochi,* *let me have three!"*
* ammochi *or* mochi *are sweet rice cakes*

A Japanese Miscellany *by Lafcadio Hearn. Little, Brown & Co., 1901*

Tubular Rice Mold F:27

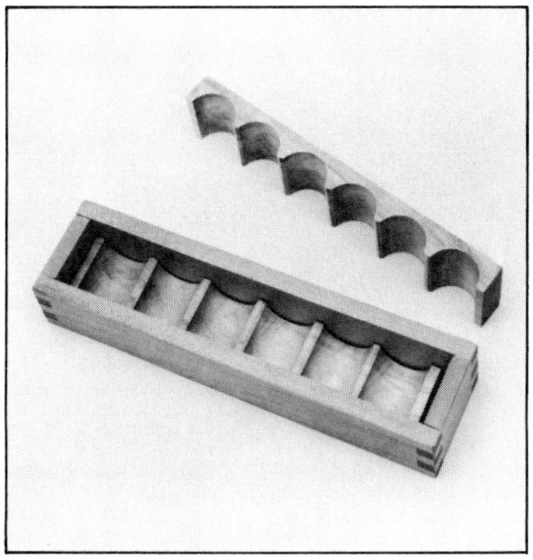

Not the child's puzzle it appears to be, this wooden box is actually a rice mold, used for packing cooked rice into compact cylinders for picnics and snacks. The mold consists of three sections: a rectangular wooden frame almost 9″ long, 2¼″ wide and 1½″ deep; and two matching wooden strips each scalloped with six half cylinders—which, when put together, form six whole cylinders. To mold the rice, wet both of the half-cylinder strips with lightly salted water (to keep the rice from sticking), place one strip into the frame, pack the frame with rice, press the second strip in place and press. Then, unmold the rice and voilà, six short columns about 1″ wide and 1⅜″ tall.

Main St. Foods $2.49

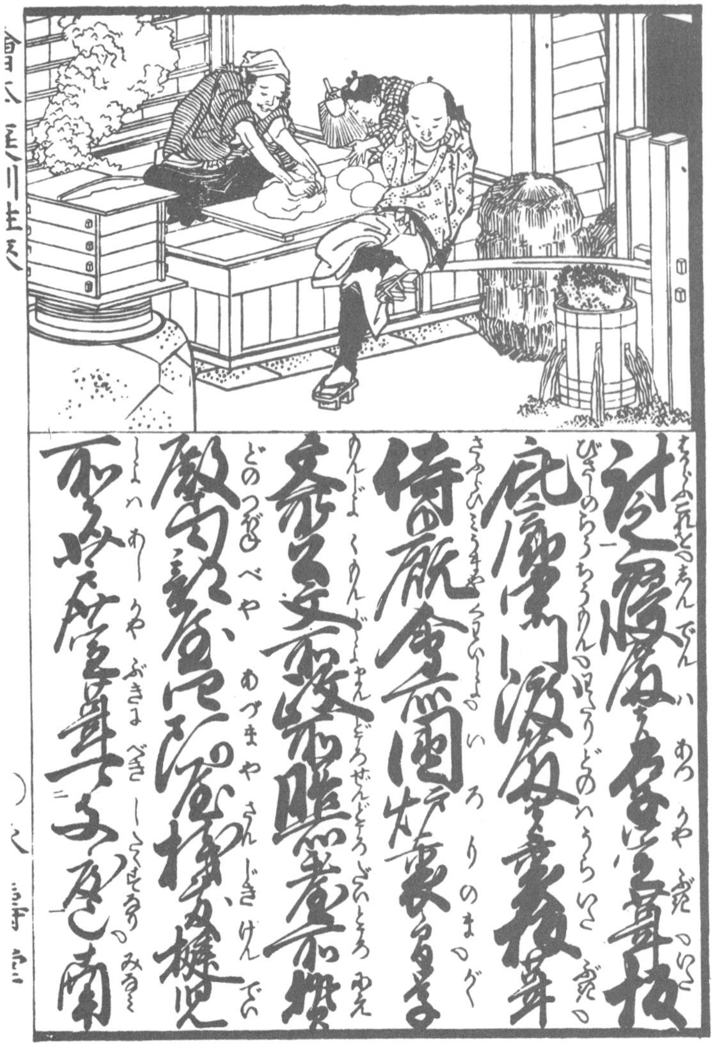

Illustration by Hokusai for a book entitled Household Precepts Illustrated *(1828)*

Sushi

One of the great delights of Japanese cuisine is *sushi,* vinegared rice dishes molded into different forms and garnished with any number of ingredients, from raw fish or vegetables to omelet strips or seaweed. Little *sushi* cakes are nibbled with drinks, taken on picnics, eaten as a first course or a full luncheon, or munched as snacks during the day. And judging from the scores of *sushi* snack bars opening up throughout the United States, Americans have quickly become addicted. The *sushi* rice itself is simply rice steamed with *kombu* (kelp) and mixed with a vinegar dressing that also includes sugar, salt and *mirin* (sweet *sake*). Now you must decide whether to roll the *sushi* rice and vegetables in seaweed to make *makizushi* rounds; pat it into oblong "sandwiches" to be topped with raw or cooked fish, for *nigirizushi;* or combine the *sushi* rice with vegetables and seafood for a piquant *mazezushi* salad.

Sushi Fan — F:28

This dainty paper fan—an *uchiwa*—is not destined to screen the blushes of modest maidens but to fan the fire of charcoal and to cool the "fire" of hot *sushi* rice. Briquets in a *hibachi* can be maddeningly slow to burn white-hot, and a fan is certainly safer and more convenient to use than charcoal igniter. The *uchiwa* would be just as convenient to use while waiting—impatiently, if you are a *sushi* fan—for the vinegared rice to cool before forming or molding it. You might even use it to cool *your* fire, if you are slaving over the proverbial hot stove on a hot day. The 9½″-wide *uchiwa* is made of two sheets of paper held taut by bamboo spokes emanating from a 4¼″-long, bamboo handle. The tranquil painted scene is designed, we assume, to restore a sense of balance and aesthetics to the harried *sushi* cook.

K. Tanaka and Co. — $0.89

SUSHI

Rice in Vinegar Dressing

To make about 6 cups

Vinegar Dressing
- ¼ cup rice vinegar, or substitute 3 tablespoons mild white vinegar
- 3½ tablespoons sugar
- 2½ teaspoons salt
- 1½ tablespoons *mirin* (sweet *sake*), or substitute 1 tablespoon pale dry sherry
- ½ teaspoon MSG
- 2 cups Japanese or unconverted white rice, washed thoroughly in cold running water and drained
- A 2-inch square of *kombu* (dried kelp), cut with a heavy knife from a

sheet of packaged *kombu* and washed under cold running water

Dressing: Combine the rice vinegar, sugar, salt and *mirin* in a 1- to 1½-quart enameled or stainless-steel saucepan. Bring to a boil uncovered and stir in the MSG. Cool to room temperature.

Note: This dressing can be made in large quantities and stored unrefrigerated in a tightly covered jar for as long as 1 year.

Rice: Combine 2½ cups of cold water and the rice in a 1½- to 2-quart stainless-steel or enameled saucepan and let the rice soak for 30 minutes. Then add the square of *kombu* and bring to a boil over high heat. Cover the pan, reduce the heat to moderate, and cook for about 10 minutes, or until the rice has absorbed all of the water. Reduce the heat to its lowest point and simmer another 5 minutes. Let the rice rest off the heat for an additional 5 minutes before removing the cover and discarding the *kombu*.

Transfer the hot rice to a large nonmetallic platter or tray—made of wood, enamel, ceramic, glass or plastic. Immediately pour on the vinegar dressing and mix thoroughly with a fork. The rice is ready to use when it has cooled to room temperature. Or it may be covered and left at room temperature for as long as 5 hours before serving.

(*From FOODS OF THE WORLD,* The Cooking of Japan, *TIME-LIFE BOOKS, New York. Copyright 1969 by Time Inc.*)

Sushi Press F:29

Made of pale blond, unfinished wood with beautifully mortised joints, this elegant oblong box appears at first glance far more suitable for storing jewelry than for mundane kitchen chores. But—unsurprisingly, when one reckons with the Japanese for purity of design—its form and function are beautifully matched. The 8½″-long, 5″-wide box, called an *oshiwaku,* has a removable top and bottom. It is used to press *sushi* rice and its garnishes of fish, omelet strips or vegetables into a firm cake that can then be sliced into individual servings. The vinegared rice is spread over the bottom of the box (the interior area is 5¾″ long by 2″ wide), topped with the garnish of choice, and pressed down with the inset top. When the top and the frame are removed, the rice cake remains sitting on the base. You can be certain that the meticulous Japanese designed the box so that everything comes apart for cleaning—even the three-piece base on which the frame rests! Unless it is washed—by hand, please—in vinegared water after each use, the rice will stick when it is used again.

N.Y. Mutual Trading, Inc. $21.00

Wooden Cut-Out Sushi Mold F:30

Although the most popular form of *sushi* are *nigirizushi* (vinegared-rice oblongs topped with fish), more fanciful creations can be formed with this *sushi* mold. The mold consists of a wooden block 8¼″ long, 2¾″ wide and 1″ deep, with three cut-out designs in the shape of a fan, a plum blossom and *mitsuba* (a trefoil-shaped plant used as a garnish in soups). The missing shapes that match the cut-outs are held together by a 7¼″-long bar of wood, and are used to press the packed rice out of the mold. Such whimsical forms make eating rice fun for children (the Japanese are notoriously indulgent parents) as well as for adults.

Main St. Foods $2.49

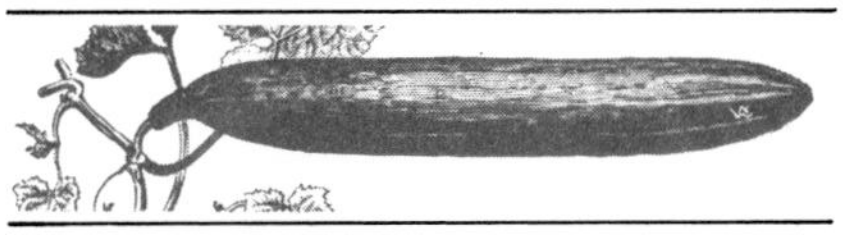

Makizushi Mat F:31

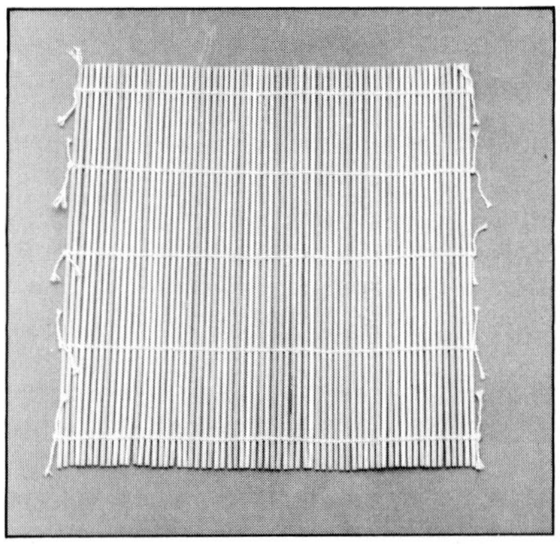

Uniquely Japanese are the delicacies called *makizushi,* in which vinegar-seasoned rice is spread over a thin sheet of seaweed called *nori* and then rolled around a center of raw fish or crisp vegetables. This gadget, which resembles a small bamboo roll-up window shade, is known as a *sudare,* and is helpful in rolling up the whole assembly. It is used in the same way as a linen towel or napkin is used to roll up a jelly roll. (And you can perfectly well roll *makizushi* with a damp linen napkin.) But this 9½″-square bamboo mat is the authentic way to do it, and it works very well. The round slats are held together by five rows of twisted string, knotted together with short ends left hanging at opposite sides of the mat. After rolling, be sure to leave the *makizushi* resting in the *sudare* for five minutes until it "sets." Then unroll, and cut the *nori*-wrapped cylinder into 1″ lengths. Serve as an hors d'oeuvre or as a first course, preferably on round bamboo or lacquer trays, arranged attractively for all to admire the contrasting concentric circles formed by the ingredients.

N.Y. Mutual Trading, Inc. $0.75

Sushi Brush F:32

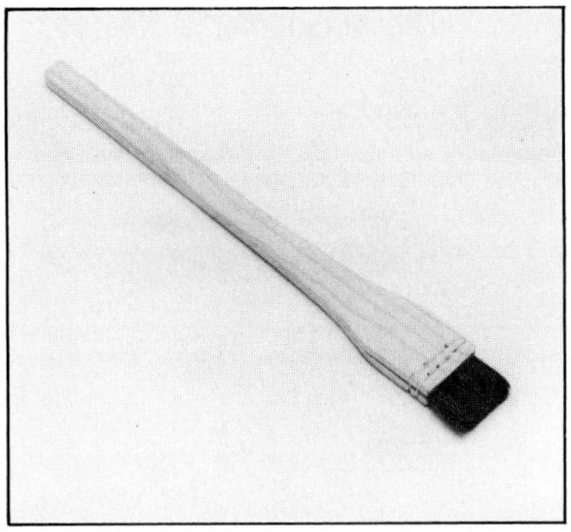

Although this lightweight, graceful brush, called a *hake,* is meant specifically for spreading a sweet soy-and-*mirin* (sweet *sake)* sauce on some types of *sushi* (in particular, those morsels of vinegared rice topped with cooked octopus, eel or the Japanese fish called squill), no one would know if you used it to brush melted butter on fish fillets. The short (3/4″) bristles are exceedingly soft; the distributor claims they come from a *tanuki,* which translates as either raccoon-dog or badger. Whatever the fur, the brush is a delight to use. The tapering, cedar-wood handle is 8″ long.

N.Y. Mutual Trading, Inc. $2.25

HIRAME NO NIGIRI-ZUSHI

Sole with Vinegared Rice

Wasabi (green horseradish powder)
1/4 pound fillet of sole
Vinegared rice (see recipe for *Sushi*)
Soy sauce

Mix a little green horseradish powder, about 1/2 teaspoon, with water to make a smooth paste.

Cut the fish into 8 diagonal slices. Wet the hands. Take a slice of fish and put a dab of horseradish on top of it, then top with about a tablespoon of vinegared rice, making it into an oblong patty. Continue with the remaining slices of fish. Arrange on a plate and serve with a little soy sauce poured into a small saucer. Eat with chopsticks or by hand, dipping in the soy sauce as liked. Serves 1 as a main course, 4 as an appetizer.

In Japan a variety of fish would be served, including tuna, striped bass, red snapper, cuttlefish, octopus, clams, sea urchins, salmon caviar, abalone, shrimp, scallops, etc.

(From THE COMPLETE BOOK OF JAPANESE COOKING, by Elisabeth Lambert Ortiz with Mitsuko Endo. Copyright 1976 by Elisabeth Lambert Ortiz. Reprinted by permission of M. Evans and Company, Inc., New York.)

Sushi Server F:33

Once *sushi* (vinegared rice) has been pressed in a mold, rolled up in seaweed, or patted into shape, it is served on a round, shallow lacquer tray called a *sushioke* or *bandai.* The deep tones of the tray are designed to contrast with the white rice so that the fanciful shapes and colorful ingredients are clearly defined. These days authentic lacquerware—which is extremely expensive—has given way to plastic imitations. But the shiny, smoothness of plastic is much like a lacquered surface; and, in many cases, the reproductions are so effective in mimicking the traditional color and shape of lacquerware, that it is often difficult to recognize the copy. This plastic *sushi* server comes in dramatic black with matte, rust-orange stripes and a rust-orange interior. It is 1 1/2″ deep and 8″ in diameter.

Katagiri and Co., Inc. $2.98

Sushi Serving Tray F:34

Colorful, oblong mounds of *sushi* topped with fish, or wound in black *nori* (seaweed), are often served on this traditionally shaped tray. The design is a miniature of the low, individual Japanese table with legs. It also looks like the Japanese wooden clog called a *geta.* The tray is made of extremely heavyweight plastic (which along with its sturdy design makes it virtually untippable). It measures 9″ long, 5 1/4″ wide and 1 3/4″ high, and has a wood-grain veneer top and a black base.

N.Y. Mutual Trading, Inc. $6.50

A Rather Unusual Japanese Recipe

"To Make a Pearl
1 healthy spat
1 mature oyster
1 bead
1 wire cage
ligatures
scrubbing brushes, etc.
unnameable wound-stringent provided by Japanese government
1 diving girl

Introduce the spat, which should be at least 1/75 of an inch long, to the smooth surface of the cage. Submerge him in quiet clean water, where the cage will protect him from starfish, and frequent inspections and scrubbings will keep his rapidly growing shell free from boring-worms and such pests.

In three years prepare him for the major operation of putting the bead on his mantle (epithelium). Once the bead is in place, draw the mantle over it and ligature the tissues to form a wee sac. Put the sac into the second oyster, remove the ligature, treat the wound with the unnameable astringent, and after the oyster has been caged, put him into the sea.

Supervise things closely for seven years, with the help of your diving-girl. Any time after that you may open your oyster, and you have about one chance in twenty of owning a marketable pearl, and a smaller but equally exciting chance of having cooked up something really valuable."

from "Consider the Oyster," included in the collection, The Art of Eating *by M. F. K. Fisher. Vintage Books; A Division of Random House, 1976*

In this eighteenth century sketch by Hokusai, rice and rice cakes are being prepared for the New Year. On this day, glutinous rice—pounded and formed into sweet cakes representing the male sun and female moon—was offered in home shrines all over the country.

Hibachi F:35

The traditional Japanese *hibachi* was often a tubby earthenware brazier with a round opening on top in which a casserole or pan was set; it was used to heat everything from water, to oil for *tempura.* However, we *amerikajin* (Americans) have taken this square, flat-topped version of the *hibachi* to our bosoms for its excellent service as a barbecue grill. To make the most traditional Japanese use of this *hibachi,* hamburgers and hot dogs should be temporarily foresaken for a go at *yakimono* (literally, broiled things). To make salmon *teri-yaki,* skewer pieces of fresh salmon, baste with a marinade made of soy sauce (*shoyu*), sugar and sweet *sake* (*mirin*), and broil. This *hibachi* is a 10″-square, black, cast-iron container with handles at either side, and short legs. A black-iron grate fits in the bottom to hold charcoal, and a sliding vent near the bottom adjusts to control the amount of oxygen reaching the coals. A ridged rack on one side of the *hibachi* lets you raise or lower the square grill. A double *hibachi* measuring 10″ by 17″ is also available.

Krischer Metal Products Co., Inc. (1010) $6.00

CHICKEN LIVERS ON SKEWERS WITH SCALLION & MUSHROOMS

Yaki-tori

½ pound chicken livers
1 bunch scallions
¼ pound fresh mushrooms, medium
⅓ cup soy sauce
⅓ cup rice wine or dry sherry
1 tablespoon sugar
Bamboo skewers

Cut the scallions into 1-inch lengths. Cut the mushrooms in half.

Affix one length of scallion, one chicken liver, and half a mushroom on each skewer. Combine the soy sauce, rice wine, and sugar. Dip the skewers in this mixture, then grill them over a charcoal fire, turning once or twice, for about 4 minutes. Brush with additional sauce while cooking.

Serve as an appetizer.

(From JAPANESE CUISINE, by John D. Keys. Copyright 1976 by Charles E. Tuttle Company. Reprinted by permission of Charles E. Tuttle Company, Japan.)

Small Hibachi F:36

Although the table-top charcoal broiler known as a *hibachi* is best used out-of-doors—or at least, if indoors, standing in a fireplace or by a window—this pint-size grill is meant for the buffet or cocktail table. It is firmly attached to a round wooden stand and is only 5″ in diameter, with room for three or four charcoal briquets. The grill swings away to give you access to the bottom. The *hibachi* comes with small skewers, which can be fit into the ten holes around the base of the stand. Guests can then grill their own *gyuniku no negimaki* (*teri-yaki*-glazed steak-and-scallion rolls); or *yakitori* (chunks of marinated chicken alternated with strips of scallion and chicken livers). It's charming, and it works! But, find a way for the smoke to leave the room before your guests do.

Town Food Service (TH-5) $2.75

"It has been noted as a curious fact by Professor A. Henry that the Chinese, Japanese, and Koreans, who number one-third of the human race, abstain from the use of milk, cheese and butter, to which abstention he says, it is probable they owe the absence of zymotic disease among them. He notices also that they are a grave people, who never unbend in laughter, whereas the Thibetans, who indulge largely in milk, cheese and butter, are a merry, mirth-loving people."

Good Cheer: The Romance of Food and Feasting *by F. W. Hackwood. New York, 1911*

Hibachi Skewers F:37

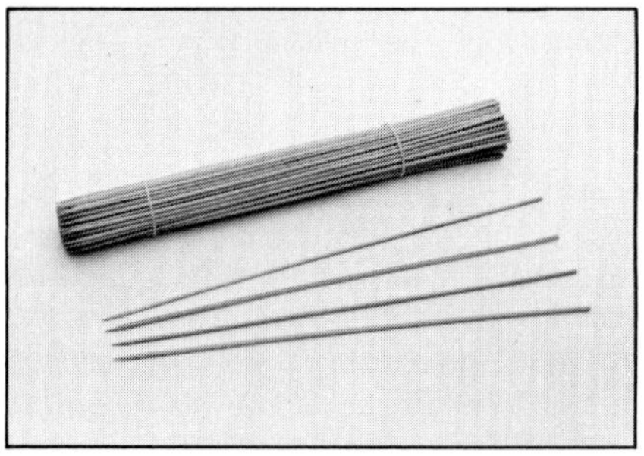

These thin sticks of bamboo, pointed at one end, are the skewers, or *yoji*, to use with your *hibachi*. They come 100 to a package, and are simple, rough, unfinished, and disposable. *Yoji* are available in various sizes—6″, 8″, 10″ and the 12″ ones shown here. The size to be used will vary with the size of the *hibachi*. Use them for toasting, broiling, roasting, barbecuing (says the package label); they are perfect for all *teri-yaki* (literally, "shiny broiled") and related grilled dishes. (The *teri-yaki* shine is produced by basting with a soy sauce marinade several times during the cooking process.) It would be crossing cultures, but there's no reason, except lack of authenticity, not to use these disposable skewers for *shish kebab* as well. Incidentally, our scrutable Japanese chef friend warns us to cover the whole skewer with food, or it may burn.

N.Y. Mutual Trading, Inc. $1.20

We might safely conclude from the following comments (in Things Japanese *by Basil Hall Chamberlain, 1902) that the delicacy of Japanese cuisine was not wholly appreciated by some hearty, foreign (English) appetites: "Japanese dishes fail to satisfy European cravings . . . If Dr. Johnson had ever partaken of such a dinner, he would surely have described the result as a feeling of satiety without satisfaction, and of repletion without sustenance. The food is clean, admirably free of grease, often pretty to look at. But try to live on it—no!"*

Wire Barbecue Grill F:38

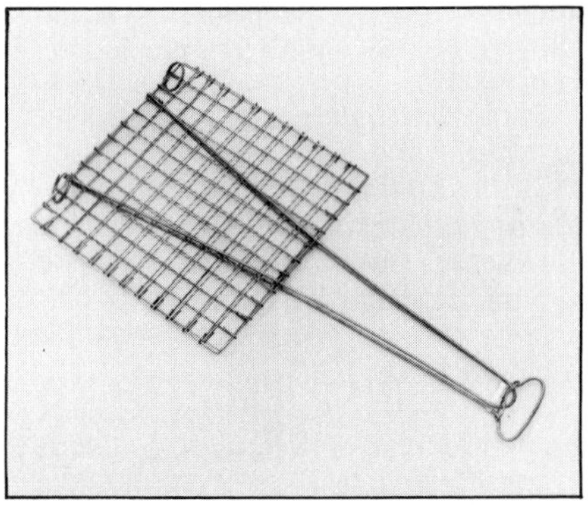

Charcoal grilling is as popular in Japan as in America—and a double *hibachi*, properly vented through a window or up a chimney, makes indoor barbecues as convenient as the outdoor, summer variety. Added to this convenience is a highly efficient wire grill. Simply place the food to be grilled—marinated salmon steaks or skewered shrimp—between the grill's two wire grids. Two large rings hinge the 9″-square frames together and also allow them to adjust for different thicknesses. The long (9″) wire handles let you keep your distance from the fire; and a wire loop slides over both handles to keep the two grids firmly closed.

N.Y. Mutual Trading, Inc. $2.59

"Three girls having tea" attributed to Nishikawa Sukenobu (1671–1751) (from The Metropolitan Museum of Art)

Stovetop Fish Grill F:39

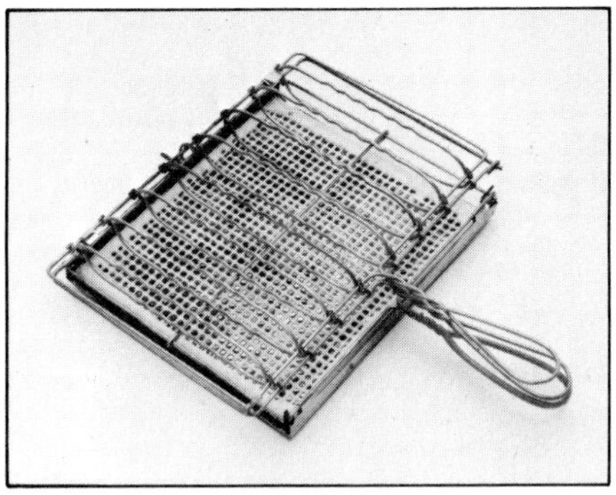

The Japanese are fond of grilled fish, and pride themselves on cooking food evenly; since food is an aesthetic experience, each part of the fish, from its glossy surface to its flaky middle, must look equally appealing. One way to maintain even cooking is by constantly turning the fish from one side to another. The *sakanayaki* (broiled fish) grill is the Japanese indoor answer to outdoor barbecues. This miraculous device is a stovetop grill that sits directly on a gas or electric burner. A once-fired ceramic heating element, 7″ long and 6¼″ wide, sits atop a slotted metal pan that is designed to evenly conduct and disperse heat to the ceramic element. Once the element is hot, its mesh pattern creates an extremely even heat source. A second unit—a rectangular wire cage, 9″ long by 5¾″ wide—is loosely hinged to the heating section by a wire loop at the back. Thus, without disturbing the fish inside, you can flip the grill to broil the other side. Use it to prepare *shioyaki,* a remarkably moist salt-broiled fish; or *yuanzuke,* mackerel fillets marinated in *sake*-and-soy-flavored broth.

N.Y. Mutual Trading, Inc. $3.19

Rectangular Omelet Pan F:40

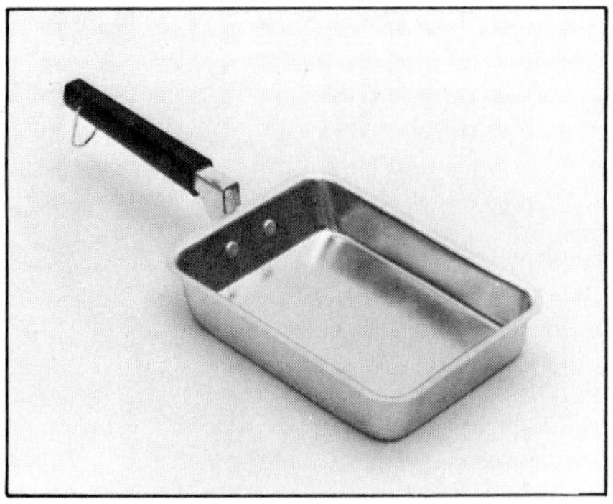

This rectangular frying pan is the traditional shape for the Japanese omelet, *tamago dashimaki.* Unlike our scrambled eggs or the French folded *omelette,* the Japanese omelet is a flaky, rolled egg dish cooked by folding successive layers of beaten egg mixed with *dashi* (soup stock) and soy sauce, one around the other. To make this egg package, pour just enough of the batter into an oiled *tamago-yaki nabe* (omelet pan), so that it coats the bottom of the pan lightly. Then, using chopsticks or a wooden spatula, roll up the set eggs and slide the roll to one end of the pan. Next add a touch more oil, pour in more egg batter, and roll the set eggs once again toward the end, enveloping the first roll. Repeat the process, sometimes enfolding a sheet of *nori* (dried seaweed) in each egg layer before it is rolled, to produce a spiraling black filling. Such a neat rolled omelet can only be made properly in this special rectangular pan. Traditionally, the *tamago-yaki nabe* was of cast iron with a long wooden handle; but the old-style pan has given way to this easy-care, lightweight aluminum one. It is 6½″ long, 4¾″ wide and 1¼″ deep, with a 4¼″ black, heat-resistant plastic handle, which is held in place by a two-pronged aluminum brace.

Katagiri and Co., Inc. $6.95

DASHI-MAKI TAMAGO

Rolled Omelette with Soup Stock

6 eggs
Dashi (soup stock)
Salt
½ teaspoon *usukuchi shōyu* (light soy sauce)
2 teaspoon *mirin*
2 dashes msg
Vegetable oil
½ cup grated *daikon* (white radish), lightly squeezed
4 teaspoons soy sauce

Break the eggs into a bowl and stir with chopsticks until well blended but not foamy. Measure the eggs. Add ¼ the amount of cold soup stock to the eggs, then add salt to taste, light soy sauce, *mirin* and msg and stir to mix.

Heat a *tamago-yaki nabe* or omelette pan and pour in just enough oil to film the surface. Pour in ⅓ of the egg mixture, tilt the pan so that the egg covers the whole surface and cook over moderate heat until the egg is set. Using chopsticks, or a spatula, roll up the omelette to the end of the pan. Add more oil and another ⅓ of the egg mixture, tilting the pan as before so that the egg runs down to the cooked omelette. When the second omelette is set, roll it towards the handle of the pan, incorporating the first omelette. Repeat with the remaining egg, rolling the 3 omelettes towards the end of the pan.

Carefully lift the omelette roll out of the pan and place it on a *sudare* (bamboo mat) or a kitchen cloth and roll up very gently. Weight with a plate until it is cold, then cut into 12 slices. Serve 3 slices per person on small platters. Garnish with a mound of white radish with the soy sauce poured over it. Serves 4.

Variation: For *Tamago Yaki* (Rolled Omelette) break 6 eggs into a bowl and stir with chopsticks until well blended but not foamy. Add 6 tablespoons freshly cooked peas, 2 tablespoons *sake,* 2 teaspoons sugar and ½ teaspoon salt to the eggs and stir to mix. Make into an omelette following the instructions above. The omelette can accompany a main dish at a meal or be served as an appetizer. It is a special favorite for picnics. It can be made, if preferred, without the peas.

(From THE COMPLETE BOOK OF JAPANESE COOKING, by Elisabeth Lambert Ortiz with Mitsuko Endo. Copyright 1976 by Elisabeth Lambert Ortiz. Reprinted by permission of M. Evans and Company, Inc., New York.)

Tempura

Tempura, undoubtedly the best-known Japanese food, is only one in the *agemono* (fried things) class of cooking. Although shrimp is perhaps the most well-known ingredient, others that are traditionally batter-coated and deep-fried include small eggplant slices, snow peas, rounds of sweet potatoes, slices of fish fillet, small asparagus stalks, strips of carrot and blanched string beans. The success of *tempura*—which is never fat-saturated, soggy or heavy—depends on the batter and your deep-fat frying technique. As to the batter, it consists of an egg yolk, flour and ice-cold water. The ice water insures the formation of crust as soon as the battered food hits the hot oil; ideally the batter is so thin that the faint color of the coated food can be seen through it, and the taste is delicate and airy. Fry the *tempura* fritters in a *tempura* pan, using a light vegetable oil like peanut or safflower, flavored with a small amount of sesame oil. Fry until the *tempura* are just golden, and serve as quickly as possible after cooking. It is essential to keep the oil clean during the frying, using a mesh skimmer to remove food particles.

Tempura Cooker and Accessories F:41

Tempura is any food (but especially shrimp and vegetables) coated in a thin batter and deep-fried, Japanese-style: crisp, delicate and never greasy. Ironically, this dish, which we think of as typically Japanese, is an adaptation of the deep-frying that Portuguese missionaries introduced to Japan long ago. The name comes from the missionaries' requests for fried shrimp on meatless Ember Days, which they called *Quattuor Tempora* because they came four times a year. This *tempura* cooker is a round, fairly shallow pan of heavy-gauge steel, 12″ across. A handy chromed-steel draining rack, shaped almost like a half-moon, hooks over the pan's rim to provide a shelf on which just-fried food can sit to drain off any excess cooking oil. There are two handles on the cooker, which comes with a pair of 13″ cooking chopsticks.

Taylor & Ng (10180) $11.00

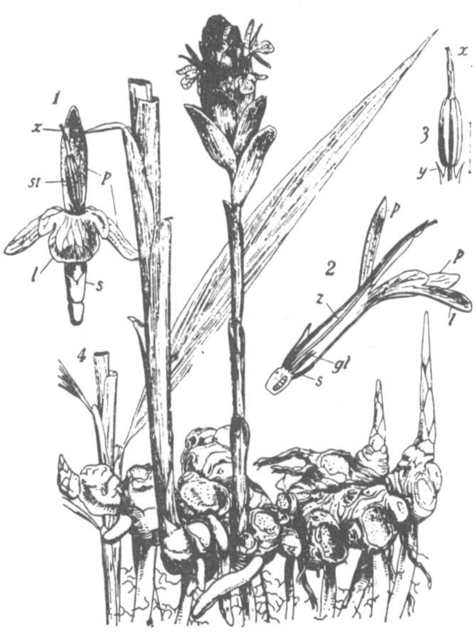

Ginger.

TEMPURA

Batter-Fried Shrimp and Vegetables

8 large shrimp
12 large green beans
2-inch slice from top of a large carrot
1 small potato
2-inch square *nori* (dried laver seaweed)
2-inch slice *daikon* (white radish), about ⅓ cup
Grated fresh ginger root, optional
1 egg
1 cup cake flour *or* all-purpose flour
Vegetable oil
¼ cup *mirin*
¼ cup soy sauce
¼ cup flaked *katsuobushi* (dried bonito)
2 or 3 dashes msg

Peel and devein the shrimp leaving the last segment of shell and the tail on. Make a small, shallow slit on the inside of the shrimp at the head end to prevent its curling when it is fried. Straighten the shrimp by bending the tail back slightly, taking care not to break it. Cut off the point of the tail of the shrimp as it has some water in it which makes the shrimp splutter in the hot oil.

Trim the beans and cut into 2 or 3 diagonal slices. Scrape the carrot and cut into thin lengthwise strips. Peel the potato and cut into ⅛-inch lengthwise slices. Cut the seaweed into four 1-inch squares. Divide these ingredients into groups of 4 and cook each portion separately.

Peel the radish and grate it. Squeeze it out lightly, then place in mounds on 4 tiny individual dishes. Grate the ginger if it is to be used; place next to the grated radish on the individual dishes.

Break the egg into measuring cup and stir with chopsticks until it is well blended but not foamy. Add enough water to increase the liquid to ⅔ cup. Stir to mix and pour into a bowl. Sift the flour, and add to the egg mixture, stirring lightly.

Heat 2 or 3 inches oil in a *tempura* pan or a saucepan to between 345°F. and 350°F. on a frying thermometer, or until bubbles form on wooden chopsticks stirred in the oil. Another test of temperature is to drop a small piece of batter into the oil. If it rises immediately to the surface, the heat is right.

Dip the shrimp in the batter. Make little bundles of the beans and carrot and dip in the batter. Dip the potato slices in the batter. Coat one side only of the seaweed in the batter. Fry the ingredients until golden, turning once, about 2 minutes, being careful not to overcrowd the pan. Drain on the rack

Continued from preceding page

of the *tempura* pan or on a paper towel on a *zaru* (bamboo plate) or on paper towels. Continue until all the ingredients are cooked.

In a small saucepan bring the *mirin* to a boil. Add ¾ cup water, the soy sauce and the bonito flakes. Bring back to a boil, strain and add 2 or 3 dashes msg. Pour into 4 small bowls. This is *tentsuya* sauce.

Arrange the *tempura* on 4 plates. The effect is very pretty with the black seaweed, white potato, pink shrimp, orange carrot and green beans. To eat place a little of the grated ginger on top of the radish, if liked. Add the radish to the sauce and mix. Using chopsticks, dip each piece of *tempura* into the sauce. Serves 4.

Squid or cuttlefish, any white fish, sweet potato, green bell peppers, eggplant, scallions or celery, cut into bite-sized pieces, may be used for *tempura.*

(From THE COMPLETE BOOK OF JAPANESE COOKING, by Elisabeth Lambert Ortiz with Mitsuko Endo. Copyright 1976 by Elisabeth Lambert Ortiz. Reprinted by permission of M. Evans and Company, Inc., New York.)

Stainless-Steel Tempura Set F:42

This handsome stainless-steel *tempura* pan is well-suited for deep-fat frying: it is sturdy, well-balanced and is equipped with a draining rack that hooks over the pan's rim. The black plastic-covered handles are heat resistant, as are the ends of the accompanying 12½″ stainless-steel cooking chopsticks. The 11″-round, 2½″-deep pan holds a generous three quarts, and has a copperclad bottom for even heat distribution. The small pouring lip on the rim of the pan is handy for pouring off the frying oil into a storage container.

Eur-Asian Imports (M201/N) $19.00

Oil Storage/Strainer Can F:43

Anyone who has ever done significant amounts of deep-fat frying knows the difficulties of saving the cooking fat to use again. In Japan, where frying *tempura* can be a daily activity, an oil strainer/storage can is an essential household gadget. This one looks like an aluminum coffee pot, complete with pouring spout; but inside, specially designed metal filters clean used cooking oil for storing. To strain the oil, use a combination of three filters: first insert the ruffled, funnel-shaped, metal filter, then a disposable paper filter and, finally, the shallower metal filter pierced by concentrically arranged holes. Then pour the oil from the *tempura* pan into the pot and the filters will catch any stray batter or bits of food. The lid, fitted to cover the whole top, including the spout, protects the oil while it is stored. A plastic handle makes pouring the oil back into the pan easy. The 5½″-tall pot comes with six paper filters and holds approximately one litre of oil. We think it's a wonderful invention to have around for *tempura* or *pommes frites.*

Katagiri and Co., Inc. $17.98

Square Steamer F:44

Have you ever seen a *mushiki* quite like this one? Probably not—unless you have been to Japan and know how indispensable a steamer is to the production of *mushimono,* or steamed things. The leading *mushimono* star is the wonderful individual egg custard dish called *chawan-mushi.* To steam *chawan-mushi* in this three-part aluminum steamer, fill the bottom section with boiling water, set the middle steamer section on top, place five custard cups with lids inside, cover and steam for about 15 minutes. Anything you might cook in a non-Japanese steamer can certainly be cooked in this, but might we suggest you try something with the preposterously long name of *hikiniku dango no mochigome-mushi*—which is minced-chicken dumplings rolled in rice, steamed and served with a garlic-flavored dipping sauce. The steamer is

9½″ square and 9½″ tall overall: the bottom water pan is 3½″ deep; and the steamer is 4″ deep, with an additional 2″ added to its capacity by the high, flat-topped lid. Both water and steamer sections have two black plastic handles riveted to their sides for easy lifting; the steamer top has a single black plastic handle.

Takashimaya, Inc. $39.50

Custard Loaf Pan F:45

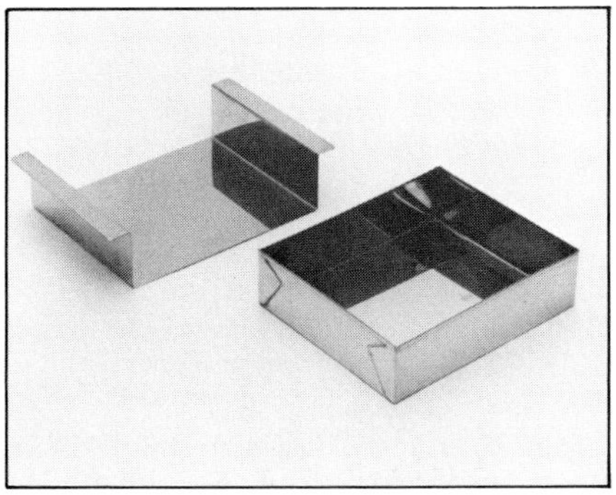

This rather western-looking, lightweight and flexible stainless-steel loaf pan (called a *nagashikan*) with a lift-out tray is actually meant for a very Japanese dish: *tamago dofu.* Eggs, seasoned and blended with *dashi* (soup stock), are poured into the pan, which holds nearly a quart of liquid. The pan is then placed in a steamer or in a water bath in the oven. Once the custard is steamed, the tray may be lifted out by means of the handles that overhang the 7″-long, 5¾″-wide and 1¾″-deep loaf pan. The custard is then cut into individual portions and slid off the tray. It is served with dipping sauce as a light lunch dish or part of a multi-course meal, and you can probably think of a million ways in which to vary the seasonings, or add ingredients like gingko nuts or small pieces of shrimp.

N.Y. Mutual Trading, Inc. $13.50

STEAMED DUMPLINGS OF MINCED CHICKEN ROLLED IN RICE, WITH GARLIC-FLAVORED SOY SAUCE

Hikiniku-dango no mochigome-mushi

2 cups minced chicken
1 cup rice, uncooked
¼ cup minced onion
½ cup finely chopped mushrooms
2 tablespoons sugar
3 tablespoons cornstarch
1 garlic clove
Soy sauce

Soak the rice overnight; drain.

Combine the minced chicken with the onion and mushrooms. Add the sugar, cornstarch, and 3 tablespoons soy sauce. Mix well and form into small balls about 1 inch in diameter. Roll the meatballs in the rice until they are coated completely; press gently to make the rice adhere. Steam the dumplings for about 20 minutes.

Serve the dumplings with a sauce prepared by adding the finely minced garlic to ½ cup soy sauce.

(From JAPANESE CUISINE, by John D. Keys. Copyright 1976 by Charles E. Tuttle Company. Reprinted by permission of Charles E. Tuttle Company, Japan.)

Porcelain Custard Cup F:46

And now for *chawan-mushi,* that marvelous Japanese custard made of eggs, broth and tiny pieces of chicken, fish, shrimp or mushrooms. Unlike western custard—the Spanish *flan* or the French *crème caramel*—it is not a dessert dish but a main course, one of the *mushimono,* or steamed dishes. To make *chawan-mushi,* combine eggs with *dashi*—a soup stock made from kelp (*kombu*) and flaked dried bonito (*katsuobushi*)—a dash of soy sauce, sweet rice wine (*mirin*) and selected diced ingredients. Our delicate white porcelain cup—really just a teacup, called a *chawan,* with a lid to keep the surface of the custard smooth—sits on a small, unglazed circular foot, and is 2½″ deep, 3¼″ in diameter, and holds ⅔ of a cup. The blue floral designs that cover the cup and its lid represent the four seasons: a panel of plum blossoms signifies spring; spikes of the bamboo plant, winter; the ubiquitous chrysanthemum, fall; and graceful iris, summer.

N.Y. Mutual Trading, Inc. $2.50

CHAWAN-MUSHI

Steamed Egg Custard

4 *shiitake* (dried Japanese mushrooms)
Sugar
¼ pound boned and skinned chicken breast
½ teaspoon *sake*
1¼ teaspoons *usukuchi shōyu* (light soy sauce)
4 large leaves spinach *or mitsuba* (trefoil) if available
Boiling water
4 medium-sized raw shrimp
8 canned ginkgo nuts
4 slices *kamaboko* (fish sausage), ¼ inch thick
3 eggs, about ⅔ cup
2⅔ cups *dashi* (soup stock)
Salt
4 small pieces lime peel

Soak the mushrooms in warm water with a pinch of sugar for 30 minutes, drain, remove tough stems and squeeze out.

Cut the chicken breast into diagonal slices about 1½ by ½ inch. Put into a small bowl and mix with the *sake* and ½ teaspoon of the light soy sauce.

Drop the spinach leaves into boiling water for 1 minute, drain, rinse in cold water and squeeze lightly.

Peel and devein the shrimp, leaving the tails on.

Place the chicken, ginkgo nuts, mushrooms, shrimp, spinach and fish sausage, divided equally, in four 8-ounce custard cups or bowls.

Stir the eggs thoroughly with chopsticks but do not beat as they must not be foamy. Stir in the soup stock, a little salt, and the remaining ¾

Continued from preceding page

teaspoon light soy sauce. Strain and divide among the custard cups. If there are any bubbles on the surface, break them with chopsticks as they will otherwise pit the surface of the finished custard. Garnish with the lime peel, cover with lids or with aluminum foil and arrange in a steamer over boiling water. Partially cover the steamer and cook the custards over moderate heat for 15 to 20 minutes, or until set. The custard, unlike other dishes where only chopsticks are used, is eaten with a spoon and chopsticks. Serves 4.

(From THE COMPLETE BOOK OF JAPANESE COOKING, by Elisabeth Lambert Ortiz with Mitsuko Endo. Copyright 1976 by Elisabeth Lambert Ortiz. Reprinted by permission of M. Evans and Company, Inc., New York.)

Black-Iron Sukiyaki-Nabe F:47

Thin slices of meat (usually beef, but also chicken or pork), various vegetables, and noodles and bean curd, simmered together in a *sake-shoyu* broth, usually at the table over a heat source—that is a brief description of *sukiyaki*. But it cannot begin to convey the succulence of this best known of the *nabemono* (one-pot dishes). The proof is in the tasting—and the cooking is in this heavy, matte black-enameled, cast-iron pan or *nabe*, which sits on three little feet. It has a broad downward-sloping lip covered with a faint raised design and to which two rings are attached. It is 8″ in diameter, 2¼″ deep, and it will hold 5½ cups of meat, vegetables and sauce. Use it at the table, over a *hibachi*, or any table-top heat source.

Pampered Kitchens $13.50

Sukiyaki-Nabe with Handle F:48

This heavy, well-made cast-iron pan, or *nabe*, is a modern interpretation of the classic *sukiyaki-nabe*. Originally *sukiyaki*, like all foods called *nabemono* (one-pot dishes), was prepared at the table, over a heat source. The removable 5¼″ plated cast-iron handle hooks firmly onto one edge of the pan and makes it quite convenient to use directly on the stove as well. Unlike the more traditional round-bottomed *sukiyaki-nabes*, our modern version has a flat (9″-diameter) bottom with straight (1½″) sides and a 6-cup capacity. The untranslated Japanese instructions included with this pan surely warn the new *nabe* owner to season it before using.

N.Y. Mutual Trading, Inc. $15.00

The word sukiyaki*—pronounced SKI-YAKI, without the "U"—comes from words meaning "plow-blade"* (suki) *and "broil"* (yaki). *It is said that centuries ago meat was so scarce that the peasants were forbidden to eat it; therefore, when any small game was caught, it was butchered and cooked on the spot, literally broiled on the blade of a plow. Over the centuries the preferred method of cooking changed, and so, technically,* sukiyaki *is misnamed. But no matter; it is definitely delicious.*

SUKIYAKI

Beef and Vegetables Simmered in Soy Sauce and Sake

To serve 4

1 pound boneless lean beef, preferably tenderloin or sirloin
An 8-ounce can *shirataki* (long noodle-like threads), drained
1 whole canned *takenoko* (bamboo shoot)
A 2-inch-long strip of beef fat, folded into a square packet
6 scallions, including 3 inches of the stem, cut into 1½-inch pieces
1 medium-sized yellow onion, peeled and sliced ½ inch thick
4 to 6 small white mushrooms, cut into ¼-inch-thick slices
2 cakes *tofu* (soybean curd), fresh, canned or instant, cut into 1-inch cubes
2 ounces Chinese chrysanthemum leaves, watercress or Chinese cabbage

SAUCE
¼ to ¾ cup Japanese all-purpose soy sauce
3 to 6 tablespoons sugar
¼ to ¾ cup *sake* (rice wine)

Prepare ahead: 1. Place the beef in your freezer for about 30 minutes, or only long enough to stiffen it slightly for easier slicing. Then, with a heavy, sharp knife, cut the beef against the grain into slices ⅛ inch thick, and cut the slices in half crosswise.

2. Bring 1 cup of water to a boil and drop in the *shirataki;* return to the boil. Drain and cut the noodles into thirds.

3. Scrape the bamboo shoot at the base, cut it in half lengthwise, and slice it thin crosswise. Run cold running water over the slices and drain.

4. Arrange the meat, *shirataki* and vegetables attractively in separate rows on a larger platter.

To cook and serve: If you are using an electric skillet, preheat to 425°. If not, substitute a 10- to 12-inch skillet set over a table burner and preheat for several minutes.

Hold the folded strip of fat with chopsticks or tongs and rub it over the bottom of the hot skillet. Add 6 to 8 slices of meat to the skillet, pour in ¼ cup of soy sauce, and sprinkle the meat with 3 tablespoons of sugar. Cook for a minute, stir, and turn the meat over. Push the meat to one side of the skillet. Add about ⅓ of the scallions, onion, mushrooms, *tofu, shirataki,* greens and bamboo shoot in more or less equal amounts, sprinkle them with ¼ cup *sake* and cook for an additional 4 to 5 minutes.

With chopsticks or long-handled forks (such as fondue forks), transfer the contents of the pan to individual plates and serve. Continue cooking the remaining *sukiyaki* batch by batch as described above, checking the temperature of the pan from time to time. If it seems too hot and the food begins to stick or burn, lower the heat or cool the pan more quickly by adding a drop or two of cold water to the sauce.

(From FOODS OF THE WORLD, The Cooking of Japan, *TIME-LIFE BOOKS, New York. Copyright 1969 by Time, Inc.)*

Covered Nabe with Spoon F:49

Nabe means "pot," and *nabemono* (literally, "pot things") are one-pot dishes cooked at the table. This enameled cast-iron pot (called a *tetsu-nabe*) is 8¼″ in diameter and 3¼″ deep, with a 2-quart capacity—perfect for a freeform *yosenabe* (a Japanese-style chowder with just a little bit of everything: pork, chicken, shrimps, oysters, white-meat fish, eggs, cabbage, mushrooms, chrysanthemum leaves, gingko nuts and more, simmered in a fish broth). The *nabe* comes with a dark-grained wooden lid, which fits down inside the pot and is only used to keep food warm after cooking, since most *nabemono* dishes simmer uncovered. It also has a 7¾″-long ladle, with a roughly chiseled dark wood handle and a smooth, lighter wood bowl. A handle arches over the dark brown, baked enamel interior of the pot, the rounded bottom of which sits on three stubby feet. The manufacturer recommends boiling water in the pot before using it the first time, and warns that it cannot be placed directly on an electric range. Use it at the table over a *hibachi,* or other table-top heat source.

Takashimaya, Inc. $19.99

Cast-Iron Casserole F:50

A charming—and practical—casserole for two, this matte-black enameled, cast-iron *nabe* with reddish-brown interior is only 6″ wide and 1¾″ deep. It holds a little more than 1½ cups for a hearty solitary meal, or two smaller portions, of *yudofu* (bean curd in broth) for a nourishing lunch. The casserole has ridged earlike handles, and the lid, for no particular culinary reason (except to imitate their earthenware-casserole cousins called *donabes*), has a steam-hole in its top.

N.Y. Mutual Trading, Inc. $15.00

Glazed Earthenware Casserole F:51

This elegant, flameproof earthenware pot, called a *donabe,* is used for guests and family alike, to make one-pot dishes called *nabemono.* Each ingredient is carefully prepared ahead of time and set aside, beautifully arranged until ready for use. Then the *donabe* is set over a tabletop heater or *hibachi* and, depending on the dish—which might be the classic *shabu shabu* (beef, vegetables and bean curd), or a *tarachiri nabe* (codfish stew) or *kaki no mizutaki* (oysters with Chinese cabbage)—the stock, fish, shellfish or meat is added, followed by vegetables and garnishes. Our *donabe* is beautifully glazed in speckled gray and decorated with broad, dark brown brush strokes. It is 12½″ in diameter, 4½″ deep and holds 4 quarts. Like all traditional Japanese casseroles, the glaze only goes halfway down to the bottom, both inside and out—the better to retain heat. The domed cover, which is pierced with a tiny steam-hole, rests securely on an unglazed rim inside the *donabe.* Two ear handles are fused to the sides, while the lid comes with the classic raised ring, allowing it to sit upside down as a serving platter beside the casserole once the dish is uncovered. If the *donabe* is used over a stove burner instead of the traditional *hibachi,* remember to soak it first, then start it off over low heat and raise it gradually to moderate heat.

Pampered Kitchens $50.00

KAKI NO MIZUTAKI

Oysters with Chinese Cabbage

2 dozen shucked oysters
1 pound *hakusai* (Chinese cabbage)
12 medium-sized fresh mushrooms
4-inch square *kombu* (kelp)
Soy sauce
½ cup grated *daikon* (white radish)
1 lemon cut into 4 wedges
2 small scallions, trimmed using white and green parts
Shichimi-tōgarashi (seven-flavor spice)

Rinse the oysters in cold salted water and drain. Pull the leaves from the cabbage and wash and drain them. Stack the leaves and cut into 1-inch crosswise slices. If they are very large, cut them in half lengthwise, then slice. Trim the mushroom stems. Arrange the oysters, cabbage and mushrooms on a large platter.

Clean the seaweed (kelp) with a damp cloth and cut into a ½-inch fringe. Put into the bottom of a large fireproof *donabe* (earthenware casse-

Continued from preceding page

role) and put on a table heater, or use an electric skillet. Pour 4 cups water into the casserole, about half filling it. Start it off on low heat so as not to crack the earthenware. Raise the heat to moderate and bring to a boil, removing the seaweed just before the water boils.

Have the soy sauce in a small jug. Lightly squeeze the moisture out of the radish and put it into a small bowl. Put the lemon wedges into a small bowl or on a plate. Finely chop the scallions and put into a bowl. Put a bowl with chopsticks at each place setting. Group the garnishes together with the seven-flavor spice round the casserole in the center of the table.

Add the cabbage and mushrooms to the casserole and simmer until the cabbage is tender, 10 to 15 minutes. Add the oysters, a few at a time, and cook just long enough to plump them, about 1 minute. To eat take the garnishes as liked and put into the small bowl at the place setting. Use as a dipping sauce for the contents of the casserole, taking more garnishes as needed. Serves 4.

(From THE COMPLETE BOOK OF JAPANESE COOKING, by Elisabeth Lambert Ortiz with Mitsuko Endo. Copyright 1976 by Elisabeth Lambert Ortiz. Reprinted by permission of M. Evans and Company, Inc., New York.)

Donabe F:52

This modest earthenware *donabe*, used to prepare Japanese one-pot dishes at the table, is roughly-glazed in a speckled-mustard color on the outside, with a matte green glaze inside. The bottom half remains unglazed and the domed cover—complete with a small steam escape-hole, and a raised ring that serves as a handle and as a base that supports the lid when it is set upside down on the table—sits on an unglazed rim. Knuckle-like side handles add a jaunty note to an otherwise sober casserole. However, like all earthenware they should be heated slowly and cooked over low-to-moderate heat to prevent cracking. Our flameproof *donabe* holds 2 quarts and is 9⅝″ in overall, outside diameter. Forever impressed with Japanese meticulousness, we can't help mentioning the elaborate packaging—no *donabe* from this manufacturer would arrive in pieces.

Katagiri and Co., Inc. $16.50

Sesame Seed Toaster F:53

Unlike many other national herbs and spices, sesame seeds add texture as well as distinctive flavor and aroma to Japanese dishes. Sesame seeds (*goma*), which come in both black (*kuro goma*) and white (*shiro goma*) varieties, are toasted and then sprinkled on rice, vegetables, pork, chicken or beef. Or they are ground into a fine powder or paste, and then used. However they are prepared, sesame seeds are almost always toasted before use. This specialized task calls for a specialized tool like our small tinned-steel toaster. It is a 4¼″-diameter, 1″-deep circular pan with a mesh screen cover that is hinged on the side of the pan away from the 6½″-long plastic handle. Dry roast the seeds (no oil) in the pan until they begin to jump (whence our trusty lid). Then, if you are preparing *goma joyu-ae,* a soy-and-sesame-seed dressing for string beans, grind the seeds in a *suribachi* before adding them to the *sake,* sugar and soy sauce. The manufacturer also suggests that the toaster can be used to dry roast soybeans, or even tea leaves, for a unique, smoky taste.

K. Tanaka and Co. $1.55

Pickle Maker F:54

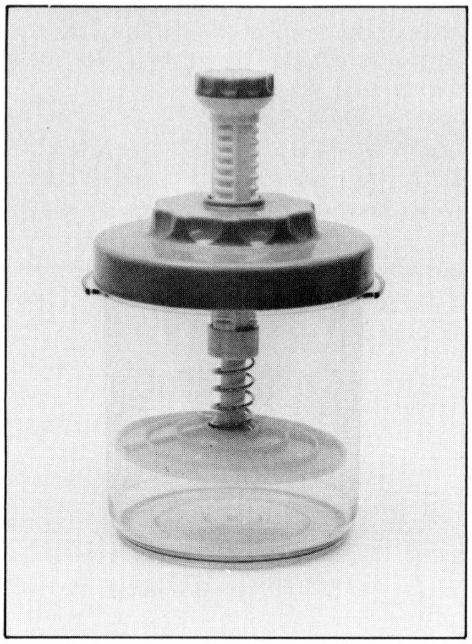

In some old-fashioned parts of Japan, the test of a new bride is still how well she makes *tsukemono,* or pickles. Sharp tasting pickles are eaten as a contrast to plain, unflavored rice at every meal, and are thought to aid in digestion. To make pickles, various vegetables, fruits and roots—including small plums, Chinese cabbage, fiddlehead ferns and ginger root—are pickled under pressure in salt- or vinegar-based brines. Traditionally, *tsukemono* were made by sprinkling the pickle candidates with salt, placing them in a wooden tub or stone crock, and then covering them with a wooden lid called a *otoshibuta* that was weighted down with a 15- or 20-pound rock. After several days of this constant pressure, the pickles were ready to eat. Today, the time-conscious cook—or anxious new bride—can use this modern, plastic *tsukemono-ki* (pickle maker). A plunger, with a 6″-diameter plastic disc at its working end, screws down into the 7″-high, 3-quart-capacity cannister to apply pickling pressure to the vegetables. This handy tool cuts down considerably on pickle preparation time: most vegetables are pickled in one to three hours—although edible chrysanthemum blossoms, we are told, take two months (but then, wouldn't pickled chrysanthemums be worth waiting for?). This pressure device disassembles easily for cleaning, and the plunger's stainless-steel spring resists the onslaught of acidic brines.

Takashimaya, Inc. $10.00

"The person called Mr. Pickled-Plum [umeboshi] is wrinkled all over from feet to face, wrinkled all over! Sour on that side! Sour on this side!—Sour, sour, sour!"

Japanese children's song quoted in A Japanese Miscellany *by Lafcadio Hearn. Little, Brown & Co., 1901*

Bamboo Chopsticks F:55

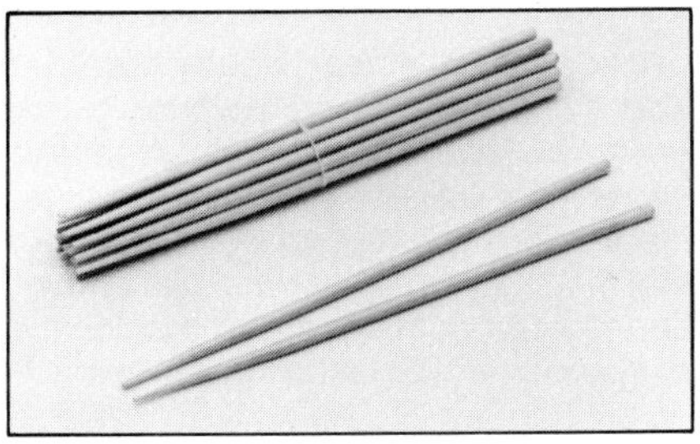

Japanese chopsticks (*hashi*) taper to a point and are often round for their entire length—unlike the straighter, blunt-ended, square-topped Chinese variety. This package contains ten pair of 9″-long bamboo chopsticks for everyday family use. The bright red dots on their non-eating ends may help remind you that you must always reverse your *hashi* before helping yourself to food from a communal serving dish.

Japanese Foodland $0.89

Fancy Eating Chopsticks F:56

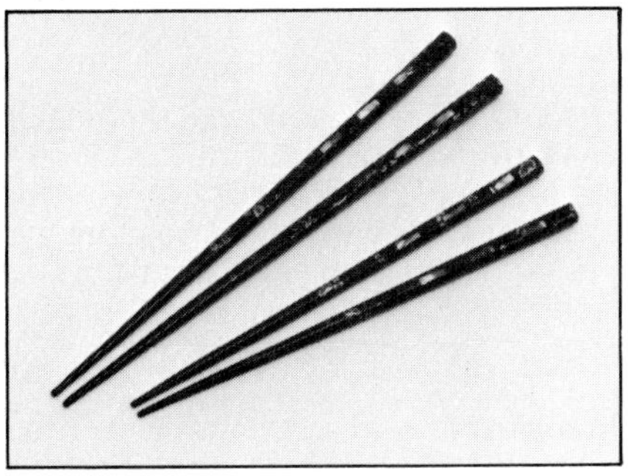

Despite a growing use of plastics and disposables, there is still room for time-honored materials and customs. Often given as gifts, these rust-and-gold-spattered, black-lacquered bamboo chopsticks are inlaid with oblong pieces of abalone. The custom in Japan is to give these two different-sized pair—8¾″ and 7¾″—as a set, to husband and wife, father and son or mother and daughter.

Eur-Asian Imports (UHS-1) $2.00

Ploughing and Planting Rice.

Children's Chopsticks F:57

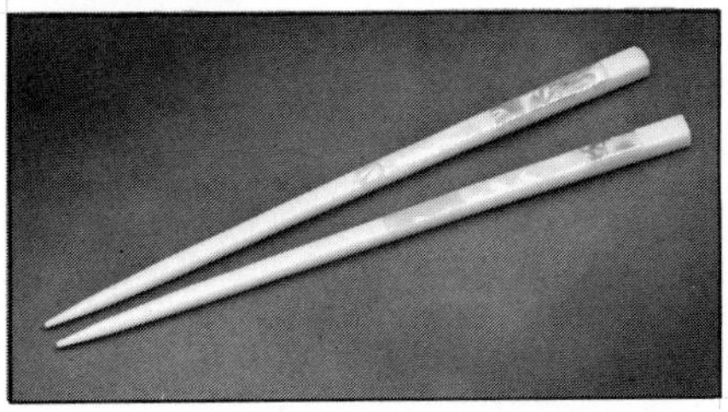

There you are in the restaurant, awkwardly sliding a few recalcitrant slices of beef *teri-yaki* from one side of your plate to the other, hoping to maneuver them into your mouth. And across the room, a child of three deftly wields her chopsticks with the aplomb of the initiated. Of course, you can comfort yourself with the thought that child-sized chopsticks *do* make it easier for the toddler. Children in Japan generally begin using chopsticks at two or three years of age. They start out with mini-chopsticks such as these, 6½″-long, plastic imitations of ivory, gaily decorated with white, gold and green insets. It's curious that although westerners sometimes have difficulty with plastic chopsticks—finding that they slide off the food too easily—Japanese children don't seem to be concerned. And they can even speak the language!

Katagiri and Co., Inc. $0.79

Throwaway Chopsticks F:58

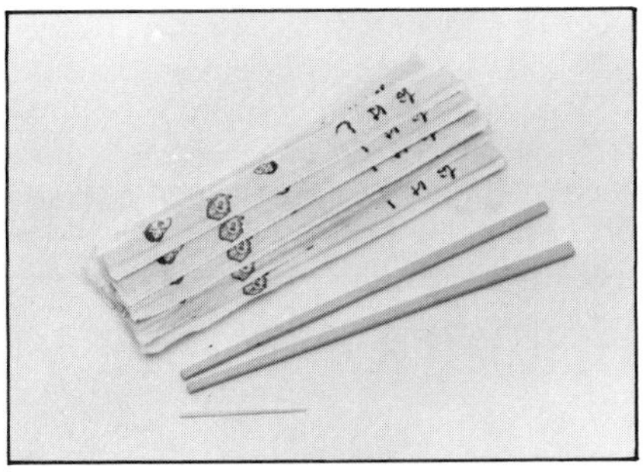

Here is a no-nonsense package of 40 pair of *waribashi*, breakaway wooden chopsitcks, each 8″ pair in its own sanitary wrapping together with a bonus toothpick. Using these at home, you may feel as if you were in a restaurant, as this is how most Japanese restaurateurs proffer chopsticks to their guests. However, *waribashi* are also used by many Japanese hostesses at formal dinner parties, as well as picnics and buffets.

N.Y. Mutual Trading, Inc. $1.29

Chopstick Rest F:59

In some circles in Japan, it is just as gauche to leave your chopsticks leaning against a dish as it is in the West to leave a soup spoon inside a bowl. And so the Japanese use delicate little chopstick rests (in a variety of traditional shapes), which are placed on the table in front of each diner. This one is pure white porcelain, decorated with blue circles representing the shields of historically prominent Japanese families. Its gentle curve resembles the top of a *torii*, the gate to a Shinto shrine. It is 3″ long, nearly 1″ wide and ½″ high at its highest.

N.Y. Mutual Trading, Inc. $0.60

"Sleep little one: happily sleep: On your next birthday I will give you red rice cooked with fish.
—Shall I then feed you with the honorable chopsticks of your father?
—The honorable chopsticks of your father smell of fish.
—Shall I then feed you with the honorable chopsticks of your mother?
—Mother's honorable chopsticks smell of milk.
—Then I shall feed you with the honorable chopsticks of your elder sister.
—Sleep! Pleasantly go to sleep!"

quoted in A Japanese Miscellany *by Lafcadio Hearn. Little, Brown & Co., 1901*

Japanese Serving Pieces

Because more than 50 percent of the Japanese eating experience is appreciating the way the food looks, the Japanese chef often spends more time harmoniously arranging the components of a meal than he does cooking them. In fact, for meals prepared at the table, like *sukiyaki,* the ingredients are even carefully arranged *before* they are cooked. Thus, a significant portion of the Japanese *batterie de cuisine,* if we may, are serving dishes. The shapes, colors and textures of the serving pieces—as well as the arrangements of the food in or on them—is equal to, and occasionally surpasses, the importance of the food itself.

Covered Soup Bowl F:60

Soup is an honored, versatile part of the Japanese cuisine. The critical element in every traditional breakfast is *miso shiru,* fermented bean paste soup, also served at the beginning or end of a meal. Most dinners are preceded by one of the great repertoire of clear soups, which achieve their variety through the hundreds of eye-and-mouth pleasing garnishes. The traditional lacquered soup bowl has been superceded by attractive plastic imitations such as this. Rust with black interior (also available in black with a rust interior), these rich shiny colors are perfect foils for the pale gold broth and vivid garnishes. The 1½-cup-capacity bowl is 4½″ in diameter and 1⅞″ deep. The lid, which serves to keep the soup hot, has a round handle and fits snugly inside the bowl. Incidentally, soup spoons are unheard of. One first eats the solids with chopsticks, then drinks the liquid from the bowl.

Taylor & Ng (11661) $6.00

Domburi F:61

The *domburi* is a large bowl used to serve noodle- or rice-based lunch and snack dishes that have taken the name of their container and are also called *domburi.* Our elegant porcelain *domburi* is decorated with a colorful blend of green, blue, red and gold against a white background. It has a 2-cup capacity and is 4½″ high. Use it—without its lid, to be traditional—to serve the cooling summer noodle dish *hiyamugi:* wheat-flour noodles mixed with shrimp, spinach leaves, mushrooms and omelet squares, chilled and served with a lime-flavored dipping sauce. Or use the *domburi,* with its lid on, in the thrifty, Japanese-housewife fashion: top a portion of rice with reheated leftovers (cooked fish, meat or vegetables) moistened with a dipping sauce.

Burdines (51-85) $7.50

MISOSHIRU

Clear Soup with Soybean Paste

"Miso" soups—clear soups flavored with white and/or red soybean paste—are sweeter than other Japanese soups and usually are served toward the end of a formal Japanese meal. All are made in precisely the same way, and may be garnished with a selection of appropriate garnishes listed below.

To make 6 cups of each type

AKA MISO (summer *miso* soup)
6 cups *ichiban dashi*
½ cup *aka miso* (red soybean paste)
MSG

SHIRO MISO (winter *miso* soup)
6 cups *ichiban dashi*
1 cup *shiro miso* (white soybean paste)
MSG

AWASE MISO (combination *miso* soup)
6 cups *ichiban dashi*
½ cup *shiro miso* (white soybean paste)
½ cup *aka miso* (red soybean paste)
MSG

Prepare ahead: Place the 6 cups of *dashi* in a 2-quart saucepan and set a sieve over the pan. With the back of a large spoon, rub the *miso* (*aka, shiro* or a combination of the two) through the sieve, moistening it from time to time with some of the *dashi* to help force it through more easily.

To cook and serve: Bring the soup to a simmer over moderate heat. Then remove from the heat and stir in a small pinch of MSG.

Pour the soup into bowls, add a garnish and serve at once. If the soup seems to be separating, stir to recombine it.

(From FOODS OF THE WORLD, The Cooking of Japan, *TIME-LIFE BOOKS, New York. Copyright 1969 by Time Inc.*)

Sweet Bean Paste Bowl F:62

The Japanese demand total harmony between food and the dish it is served in; so this small, chunky, red bowl is designed for a pasty sweet called *oshiruko,* made of red beans and sugar. Wine red on the outside and black on the inside, our little cup dramatically echoes and frames the bean paste it is meant to hold. It is of plastic made to look like lacquer with chisel marks on it. This round bowl, 3¾″ diameter at the top, is 2½″ deep and holds about 1¼ cups of liquid.

Katagiri and Co., Inc. $2.50

A Japanese Lullaby

"Sleep, sleep, sleep, little one! While my baby sleeps I will wash some red beans and clean some rice—then adding some fish to the red rice, I will serve it up to this best of little babies."

The distinctive Japanese diet is carried over into lullabies: sweets are no part of the child-vocabulary, even in dreamland.

quoted in A Japanese Miscellany *by Lafcadio Hearn. Little, Brown & Co., 1901*

Individual Serving Bowl F:63

Stylized blue chrysanthemum leaves, a symbol of the fall season, decorate the white outside and inside of this charming all-purpose porcelain bowl, which holds 1½ cups and is 2¼″ high with a top diameter of 5¼″. It can be filled —but never to the brim—with neat slices of *sashimi,* or the tantalizing side dishes known as *aemono* (mixed things) and *sunomono* (vinegared things). The popular *suzuko mizore-ae* (red caviar dressed with grated white radish and lemon juice) would be elegant and colorful in our bowl.

Bloomingdale's (51/61) $3.00

Round Serving Plate F:64

Before the vegetables and meats for such *nabemono* as *sukiyaki* are cooked at the table, they are first presented, elaborately positioned, on an elegant serving platter. The design of this 12″-diameter, porcelain plate is dominated by daffodils, the traditional symbols of spring. Encircling the flowers are multicolored geometric designs, flowers and the royal phoenix, symbol of the empress. So, you can arrange your sliced beef, bamboo shoots, sliced mushrooms, Chinese cabbage, scallions and cubed *tofu* on our plate and be sure that they will be keeping elegant company.

Burdines (98/66) $25.00

Square Serving Plate F:65

This square serving plate comes from the Japanese province of Mashiko, whose clay dishes are as famous in Japan as Royal Doulton is in England. Its glaze reproduces a special antique patina effect, and is intended to look like much-handled old wood. The dark brown glaze has slashes of tan that form stalks of bamboo—the traditional symbol of winter—and the whole is overlaid with speckles of blue. The slightly raised edges of the 8¾″-square plate are designed to hold skewers of *yakimono* (broiled things). In keeping with Japanese aesthetics, lay skewers of grilled abalone horizontally across the dish to form a grid with the more-or-less vertical sweep of bamboo in the design. And in the right-hand corner, place a small mound of grated *daikon.*

Takashimaya, Inc. (59/111W) $14.00

Eating Noodles

GYUNIKU NO NEGIMAKI

Scallion-stuffed Beef Rolls

¾ pound beef: London broil, top round, or similar cut
2 tablespoons soy sauce
1 tablespoon *mirin*
1 teaspoon finely grated fresh ginger root
3 scallions, trimmed, using white and green parts
Flour
Vegetable oil
½ lemon, cut into 4 wedges

Cut the beef into pieces about 5-by-3-by-⅛-inch thick. This is easier to do if the beef has been partially frozen. Place the beef slices in a dish. Combine the soy sauce, *mirin* and ginger and pour over the beef, mixing well. Marinate for 30 minutes.

Cut the scallions into pieces as long as the beef is wide. Divide the scallions so that there will be some white and some green to stuff each roll.

Lift the beef slices out of the marinade and lay the scallions on the beef and roll up. Dab a little flour on the end of each beef strip to hold the rolls together. Coat the rolls with flour, shaking to remove the excess.

Heat 2 to 3 inches oil in a *tempura* pan or a saucepan to about 340°F. on a frying thermometer, or until bubbles form on wooden chopsticks stirred in the oil. Fry the rolls, a few at a time, for about 2 minutes, turning once or twice. Drain on the rack of the *tempura* pan or on paper towels. Garnish with the lemon wedges and squeeze the lemon over the beef rolls. Serve hot and as freshly cooked as possible. Serves 4.

(From THE COMPLETE BOOK OF JAPANESE COOKING, by Elisabeth Lambert Ortiz with Mitsuko Endo. Copyright 1976 by Elisabeth Lambert Ortiz. Reprinted by permission of M. Evans and Company, Inc., New York.)

Woven Bamboo Tray F:66

This handsome woven bamboo tray, 9½″ long and 6¾″ wide, would be perfect for passing a selection of *zensai,* or Japanese hors d'oeuvre, such as *kamo sakamushi* (*sake*-steamed duck) or *hamaguri shigure-ni* (sweet-cooked clams). It would also be appropriate to use as a plate for *tempura,* with the protection of a paper napkin between food and tray. The shape of the tray, with its raised ends, is held by brass wires that run along the sides. Strips of bamboo are lashed to the sides and ends, and two narrow strips of bamboo on the tray's underside raise it slightly off the ground.

Katagiri and Co., Inc. $3.95

Plastic Zaru and Case F:67

This plastic "bamboo" tray is a modern version of the bamboo *zaru,* a curved basket tray that both strains and then serves buckwheat noodles and its garnishes. Purists might be dismayed by the ersatz nature of the tray, but would have to admit that plastic wears better than bamboo, and cleans grease-free. The imitation-lacquer carrying case is black with gold speckles, 12″ in diameter, 2¼″ high and sits on three legs. The *zaru* in its carrying case could be used much like a lunchbox. We are told it is popular in Japan for serving cold noodles like *hiyashi somen* (wheat noodles with shrimp and a dipping sauce).

Katagiri and Co., Inc. $11.50

"Most Japanese towns of any size now boast what is called a seiyo-ryori, *which, being interpreted, means a foreign restaurant. Unfortunately, third-rate Anglo-Saxon influence has had the*

upper hand here, with the result that the central idea of the Japano-European cuisine takes consistency in slabs of tough beefsteak anointed with mustard and spurious Worcestershire sauce. This culminating point is reached after several courses—one of watery soup, another of fish fried in rancid butter, a third of chickens' drumsticks stewed also in rancid butter; and the feast not unfrequently terminates by what a local cookery book, unhappily disfigured by numerous misprints, terms a 'sweat omelette.' "

Things Japanese: Being Notes on Various Subjects Connected with Japan *by Basil Hall Chamberlain. London, 1902*

Four Seasons Condiment Plates F:68

At the end of a traditional Japanese meal, pickled vegetables are served with rice to cleanse and refresh the palate; but today, in many Japanese homes and restaurants, these *tsukemono* also appear as appetizers at the beginning of the meal. Whether served at the beginning, middle or end of a meal, pickles are essential, and are served on their own special little square plates. Each 4⅝″-square porcelain dish in this modern set bears a different design—one for each of the four seasons—on a gray-blue, cracked-glaze background. A sparrow on a camelia branch designates summer; a quail among chrysanthemums, fall; a pair of sparrows riding bamboo shoots mark winter; and a finch enveloped by cherry blossoms, spring.

Gimbels (52/4) $4.00

Set of Three Condiment Dishes F:69

These three small ceramic bowls look very contemporary with their opaque glazes, but they are truly an ancient, traditional style for serving—and storing—such *tsukemono* as *umeboshi* (pickled plums) or pickled eggplant. Each 3″-diameter, 1¼″-deep bowl has the same round cup shape with a slightly domed lid, and holds about ½ cup. While the insides are all white, each of the outsides is decorated differently. One comes with reddish-brown sunflowers and green birds on a cream background; another, also in cream, has a swirl motif; and the last bowl is a waxy-looking blue glaze with layers of cream showing through for a brick-like effect. The lids of all three rest securely on unglazed lips, and each is decorated with a little bamboo reed tie.

Takashimaya, Inc. $11.99

Tempura Sauce Bowl F:70

Once the golden, batter-coated *tempura* has been taken from the pan, it is eaten immediately, while it's still hot. But like almost all other *agemono* (fried things), each small *tempura* fritter is first dipped in one of a variety of special sauces. *Ten tsuyu*—made from *mirin* (sweet *sake*), soy sauce, flaked *katsuobushi* (dried bonito) and *dashi* (soup stock)—is the standard accompaniment. But whatever the sauce, it is served in little dishes like this. Slightly boat-shaped, the dipper handle at the end enables you to lift the bowl toward your mouth while maneuvering the food with chopsticks in your other hand. Our 4½″-diameter porcelain bowl is decorated with blue magnolias and holds ⅔ of a cup of liquid.

Takashimaya, Inc. (51/81) $1.60

18th-century Japanese cake dish. (from The Metropolitan Museum of Art)

18th century Japanese wine pot (from The Metropolitan Museum of Art)

SOBA TSUYU

Mirin-and-Soy Dipping Sauce for Tempura and Noodles

To make 1½ cups

¼ cup *mirin* (sweet *sake*), or 3 tablespoons pale dry sherry
¼ cup Japanese all-purpose soy sauce
1 cup *niban dashi*
2 tablespoons preflaked *katsuobushi* (dried bonito)
Salt
MSG

TEN TSUYU
¼ cup *usukuchi* soy sauce, or substitute 3 tablespoons Japanese all-purpose soy sauce
¼ cup *mirin* (sweet *sake*), or 3 tablespoons pale dry sherry
1 cup *niban dashi*
⅛ teaspoon salt
MSG
¼ cup preflaked *katsuobushi* (dried bonito)

GARNISH
3 tablespoons finely grated *daikon* (Japanese white radish), or substitute 3 tablespoons peeled, grated icicle radish or white turnip
1 tablespoon scraped, grated fresh ginger root

To cook: Heat the *mirin* in a 1-quart saucepan over moderate heat until lukewarm. Turn off the heat, ignite the *mirin* with a match, and shake the pan gently back and forth until the flame dies out. Add soy sauce, *niban dashi, katsuobushi,* a pinch of salt, and sprinkle lightly with MSG. Bring to a boil over high heat, then strain the sauce through a fine sieve set over a small bowl. Cool to room temperature and taste for seasoning (adding a little salt if necessary).

(From FOODS OF THE WORLD, The Cooking of Japan, *TIME-LIFE BOOKS, New York. Copyright 1969 by Time Inc.)*

Soy Sauce Bottle F:71

This charming little *shoyu sashi* (soy sauce holder) looks like a mini teapot. In Japan, soy sauce is a seasoning, like salt, whose quantity is dictated by individual tastes; and each diner should have the option of adding a drop here or there at will. Our porcelain soy sauce bottle is decorated with a blue fishnet design and comes with a 2½″-diameter saucer to catch the *shoyu* that doesn't quite make it to your *sake cha-zuke* (salmon braised in *sake* and served with sesame and green tea sauce). It has small depressions on either side to make it easier to pick up; it stands 3″ tall with the saucer, and holds about ⅔ of a cup of soy sauce.

A.C. Gifts New York, Inc. $3.77

SWEET GLAZED YAM ROLLED IN TOASTED SESAME SEEDS

Yama-imo no ame-daki

1 pound yams
¼ cup sugar
2 tablespoons soy sauce
2 tablespoons sesame seed, black, toasted
Vegetable oil

Pare the yams and cut them into small, angular pieces. Fry them in 1 inch of vegetable oil until they are lightly browned; drain.

Pour off the oil from the pan. Add to the pan the sugar, soy sauce, and 2 tablespoons water. Cook and stir until the mixture is quite viscous, then add the fried yam. Over high heat, toss the yam to coat it evenly with the syrup. When the moisture is gone from the pan, sprinkle the yam with the sesame seed, toss well, then spread out on an oiled plate to cool.

Serve as a dessert.

(From JAPANESE CUISINE, by John D. Keys. Copyright 1976 by Charles E. Tuttle Company. Reprinted by permission of Charles E. Tuttle Company, Japan.)

Three Tiered Container F:72

The Japanese, unlike westerners, are not terribly concerned with sweets; and many things we might call a dessert, would more properly be categorized in Japan as a snack. These varied nibbles are served with tea or munched during the day between meals—and they might be housed in a convenient, three-tiered porcelain container like the one shown here. Each of the three sections holds about a cup; but you wouldn't put liquid inside. Instead, place slices of thick, pasty, super-sweet bean-paste jelly (*mizoyokan*) in the top; *ohagi* (balls of sweet rice mixed with sweet bean paste and sugar) in the middle; and cherry blossom cut-outs of glazed yam rolled in sesame seeds (*Yamaimo no amedaki*) in the bottom. Each straight-sided section measures 4½″ across and 1½″ deep. The bottom section rests on a completely flat base, and an almost flat lid fits down into the top bowl, resting on a sunken lip.

Burdines (98/62) $13.00

". . . three geishas trooped in in full regalia, knelt in turn at the head of the table, and bowed first to our host and then to us. Then they sat down between us and set to pouring egg-cup-sized bowls of hot sake *for us in a never-ending succession. I say 'never-ending' because, as soon as you put your little bowl down, it has to be filled again. Short of throwing the bowl out of the window, there is no way of halting this chain delivery until the flagon is empty or you fall over."*

from "Tokyo" essay in Thrilling Cities *by Ian Fleming. New American Library, 1964*

Porcelain Sake Set F:73

Sake, the national Japanese wine, is made from fermented rice. Traditionally it is served lukewarm either at the beginning of a meal with appetizers, or, for special party dinners, throughout the various courses. There is great variety in the styles of *sake* sets, but the classic model invariably includes a ½-pint bottle called a *tokkuri* and small handleless cups called *sakazuki*. This porcelain set comes with two *tokkuri* and five *sakazuki*. The uneven number of cups reflects Japanese custom, which considers even numbers bad luck. Ironically, most sets for the western market are now packaged with four cups—a number the Japanese avoid because it is homophonous with their word for death. The flasks in this set stand 5″ high, are 2″ across at the bottom, and have a small 1″ opening at the top. Each 2″-diameter, shallow, bowl-shaped cup sits on a ¾″-high foot.

Takashimaya, Inc. $18.00

Wooden Sake Set F:74

This unusual *sake* set includes a rectangular flask 4¾″ high and 2″ square, and two square cups only 1½″ high. They are all made of 300-year-old cypress, whose unique fragrance blends with the *sake* for a special flavor. The rustic elegance of this set is a modern interpretation of an ancient Japanese custom: peasants, unable to afford ceramic *sake* sets, drank their *sake* out of wooden measuring cups (often putting a pinch of salt on the cup's flat rim to add a kick to the refreshing rice wine). The manufacturers warn, however, that this modern set should *not* be used for warmed *sake*. It should be used instead to serve *toso*, a cold, spiced *sake* traditionally served on New Year's Day.

Katagiri and Co., Inc. $8.50

19th century Japanese tea pot (from The Metropolitan Museum of Art)

Porcelain Tea Set F:75

Since tea drinking is such an important part of daily life, it is not surprising that the Japanese feel their tea pots and cups must blend harmoniously with each other and with the place in which they are used. It is not unusual for a family to own four or more tea sets, one for each season, each hand-painted with symbolic designs. This porcelain tea pot and six handleless cups are decorated in a delicate spring pattern of flowering magnolias. A bamboo handle reinforced with wire arches over the lid. The pot sits on a narrow unglazed base and holds 1 quart; the cups hold 4 ounces each.

Abraham & Straus (56/26) $17.00

18th century Japanese tea pot (from The Metropolitan Museum of Art)

"Strangely enough humanity has so far met in the tea-cup. It is the only Asiatic ceremonial which commands universal esteem. The white man has scoffed at our religion and our morals, but has accepted the brown beverage without hesitation. The afternoon tea is now an important function in Western society. In the delicate clatter of trays and saucers, in the soft rustle of feminine hospitality, in the common catechism about cream and sugar, we know that the Worship of Tea is established beyond question. The philosophic resignation of the guest to the fate awaiting him in the dubious decoction proclaims that in this single instance the Oriental Spirit reigns supreme."

The Book of Tea *by Okakura Kakuzo (1906). Charles E. Tuttle Company, 1956*

Cast-Iron Tea Pot **F:76**

This cast-iron tea pot is a practical utensil for everyday use. It can be used to boil the water—3 cups of it—and then an aluminum strainer is fit inside to hold the tea leaves while they steep. The pot's belly is covered with a hobnail bas-relief, and its inside with a smooth enamel. A large curved iron handle circles above, and the pot rests on a flat bottom. It is one of our favorite accessories for cozy breakfasts and winter afternoon teas.

Albert Kessler (PX150E) $17.00

Japanese Tea Gardens

The Tea Ceremony

The drinking of tea in Japan can be as much an aesthetic as a culinary experience. The traditional tea ceremony, or *cha-no-yu,* is a social ritual rooted in Zen Buddhism, with rules laid down by the great tea masters of the 15th and 16th centuries. Baldly, it is merely the brewing and drinking of tea in the company of friends, while contemplating objects of beauty. One is not allowed to discuss politics or business! The heart of the experience is the profound Japanese concern for harmony with nature and self.

The ritual itself is carefully choreographed: once the guests have arrived in the special tea ceremony room, hut or corner of a room, the host or hostess—a trained "tea master"—brings in the utensils and arranges them in an artistic pattern around the *furo* (brazier) and *okama* (tea kettle). The bamboo tea spoon and tea caddy are, of course, already immaculate; but the host ceremoniously wipes them with a silk napkin called a *fukusa.* A bamboo dipper, *hishaku,* is used to transfer a small amount of hot water from the iron kettle to the tea bowl, which is then wiped with a *chakin,* a small oblong cloth of pure linen. The public washing of these objects does honor to the guests, and the stylized movements help the tea master to focus his thoughts on the ceremony ahead. Using the bamboo tea spoon, the tea master gently transfers a few measures of a brilliant, green, powdered tea from the caddy to the tea bowl. After the last scoop, the tea master lightly taps the spoon against the bowl's rim to shake off any specks of tea. This tapping is recognized as a call to contemplate the ritual. The tea master lowers the bamboo dipper into the tea kettle, rotates it gracefully as it sinks into the water, and tips out the water over the center of the tea bowl. The final step in the tea's preparation is to whip it into a glorious jade frost with a bamboo whisk. The tea bowl is then placed on another silk napkin, and the first guest picks up both. Before and during the slow sips of tea, the guest notes and appreciates the tea's froth and color as well as taste and aroma. The ritual is then repeated, and the tea bowl is passed from person to person. Formal tea ceremonies can last as many as four hours and are preceded by a special *kaiseki ryori,* or tea ceremony meal; the more abridged informal service might last just under an hour. The emphasis is on simplicity of form: while the tea ceremony utensils—and the bowls, trays and serving plates for the *kaiseki ryori*—are the finest the host can provide, they are never ostentatious; for the Zen principles of simplicity, serenity, withdrawal and contemplation prevail. And indeed, our western friends who have participated in the tea ceremony, speak nostalgically of the serene, timeless quality of the experience.

Black Tea Ceremony Bowl F:77

This is a 20th century model of a classic *chawan,* the bowl used in the Japanese tea ceremony. The form and glaze of this bowl were copied from Chinese wares over 700 years ago by potters in the town of Seto, where today the bowl is made in exactly the same way. This bowl, which comes in a brown so dark that the manufacturer calls it black, has occasional striations of a lighter brown. It is 5″ across and 3¼″ deep and will hold 3 cups—but it would not, of course, ever be filled to capacity. It comes beautifully packaged in a light wood box, marked with the potter's seal and tied with an *obi*-bow ribbon. It would make a unique gift of art—if you could bear to part with it.

Block China Corp. (144) $25.00

"English as she is spoke and wrote in Japan forms quite an enticing study. It meets one on landing, in such signboard inscriptions as:
'Manufacture. By Cake & A. Piece. Of. Bread [*on a baker's cart*]*'*
'Fuji Beer. The efficacy of this Beer is to give the health and especially the strength for stomach. The flovour is so sweet and simple that no injure for much drink [*on a beer label*]*'*
'Fulish. Ruttr. Criam. Milk. [i.e., *Fresh butter, cream, milk*]*'*
'Japan Insted of Coffee [i.e., *a Japanese substitute for coffee*]. *More men is not got dropsg of the legs who us this coffee, which is contain nourish.' "*

Things Japanese: Being Notes on Various Subjects Connected With Japan *by Basil Hall Chamberlain. London, 1902*

White Tea Ceremony Bowl F:78

This *chawan* is a contemporary version of the traditional tea ceremony bowl. Its Shino glaze is typical of the 16th century Monoyama (Peach Mountain) Period, when Japan's aesthetics were led back from the ornate imported Chinese wares to the deceptively simple peasant pottery. The thick white glaze appears almost transparent where it runs thin. This piece shows the exciting *hi-iro* (fire color) effect: a reddishness bleeds through the glaze because of the iron in the clay. The naturalistic "flaws" in the glaze are highly prized, imparting a look of antiquity. The 5″-diameter, 2⅞″-deep bowl comes beautifully packaged, as befits such a work of art.

Block China Corp. (145) $25.00

Tea Caddy F:79

The tea caddy, which holds powdered green tea leaves, is one of the most important pieces in the ritualized tea ceremony. Ours is 4½″ high and has an unusual "spear sheath" shape and a Shinsha glaze. This glaze is characterized by "blood red" coloring, and was adapted from a 15th century Chinese glaze originally used for porcelain. Like most of our tea ceremony pieces, it is packaged in an elegant wooden box.

Block China Corp. (105) $15.00

"Girl performing the tea ceremony" 20th century watercolor on silk by Suizan Miki (from The Metropolitan Museum of Art)

"Those who cannot feel the littleness of great things in themselves are apt to overlook the greatness of little things in others. The average Westerner, in his sleek complacency, will see in the tea ceremony but another instance of the thousand and one oddities which constitute the quaintness and childishness of the East to him."

The Book of Tea *by Okakura Kakuzo (1906). Charles E. Tuttle Company, 1956*

19th century Japanese water pot (from The Metropolitan Museum of Art)

Tea Ceremony Spoon F:80

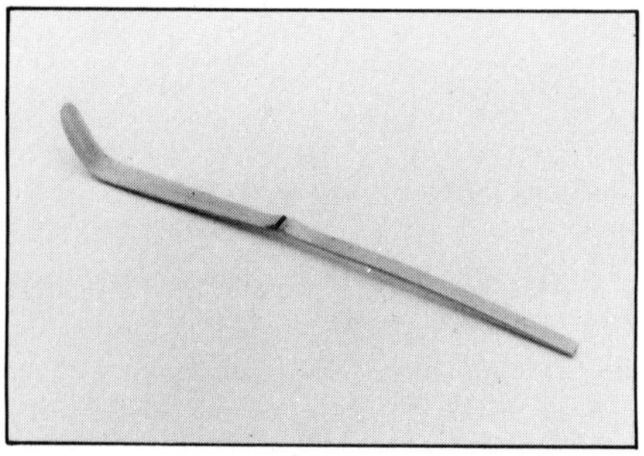

Unlike the other tea ceremony utensils, which are either antiques passed from one generation to another, or are expensively made only by those exceptional craftsmen who have been dubbed "Living National Treasures" by the Japanese government, the *chashaku,* or tea ceremony spoon, is replaced each time the ceremony is performed. It is a slender strip of bamboo that curves up at the end to make a tiny, flat bowl. The tea master dips the spoon into the tea caddy and transfers a small amount of the powdered green tea to the tea bowl. Our bamboo spoon, a small but essential part of the aesthetically-oriented ritual, is 7¼″ long.

Katagiri and Co., Inc. $2.75

Tea Ceremony Whisk F:81

It takes more than 50 steps to turn a single piece of bamboo into this graceful tea ceremony whisk, or *chasen.* It is made entirely by hand—shaped into a handle at one end, and at the other, carved to form small tines. The whisk is used—in an almost choreographed fashion—by the tea master to whip a small amount of the powdered green tea and hot water into an emerald-green froth. The *chasen* is 4¼″ long overall, with 2¼″ of that devoted to the whisk part.

Katagiri and Co., Inc. $10.00

"Tea is a work of art and needs a master hand to bring out its noblest qualities. We have good and bad tea as we have good and bad paintings—generally the latter. There is no single recipe for making the perfect tea, as there are no rules for producing a Titian or a Sesson. Each preparation of the leaves has its individuality, its special affinity with water and heat, its hereditary memories to recall, its own method of telling a story."

The Book of Tea *by Okakura Kakuzo (1906). Charles E. Tuttle Company, 1956*

The Tea Plant (thea viridis)

Side Dish F:82

The bowls and serving dishes for the formal tea ceremony meal are chosen with as much care and concern for their color, shape and texture as the tea ceremony utensils and the food itself. The graceful shape and polished, glasslike luster of this 6″-long, 4½″-wide side dish—whose name, *mukozuke,* literally means "pushed to one side"—goes back four centuries, to the famous tea master Furuta Oribe. It is executed in rich contrasting colors, generally deep greens or (like ours) brown on a sandy tan background. The dish is meant to hold—actually, display—a portion of the formal *kaiseki ryori,* the meal preceding the tea ceremony. Such a dish might hold slices of a delicately-flavored broiled fish or duck.

Block China Corp. (102) $20.00

Tea Ceremony Tokkuri F:83

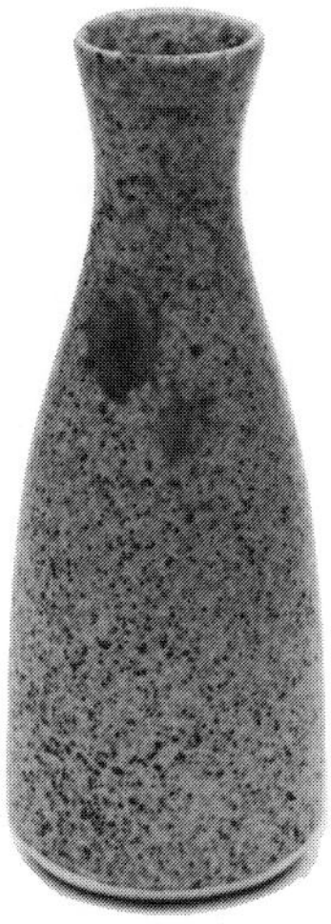

Sake is customarily served at the end of the ritualized tea ceremony meal (*kaiseki ryori*), but it can also be served throughout. Our graceful, tawny-glazed, stoneware *tokurri* (*sake* server) holds 10 ounces within its 7¼″-high curve—enough for one serving each for the usual three to five guests at a tea ceremony, although generally each guest would have his own.

Block China Corp. (146) $15.00

Lunch Box F:84

In Japan, box suppers and lunches are quite elaborate affairs (often prepared by caterers) that involve an assortment of different foods. Thus picnic and lunch boxes come with multiple compartments. This curious half-moon box (called a *hangetsu*) is the kind of individual lunch box (or *bento*) you might get for a special picnic, or during the *entr'acte* at the *kabuki* (if you order ahead of time). Ours has four sections: three triangular partitions that are part of a removable tray, and the fourth, a larger, lopsided, pie-like slice. Traditionally, the *hangetsu* was a lacquered box; ours is a plastic look-alike with a red-speckled black exterior, and a solid black interior. *Hangetsu* would come in particularly handy for working hosts or hostesses, who with these could prepare a cold dinner-party meal in advance, arrange the *sushi,* pickles, *sashimi* and cold meats inside, then relax and act like a guest. This almost-circular box is 9″ in diameter and 2¼″ high when covered.

Japanese Foodland $8.95

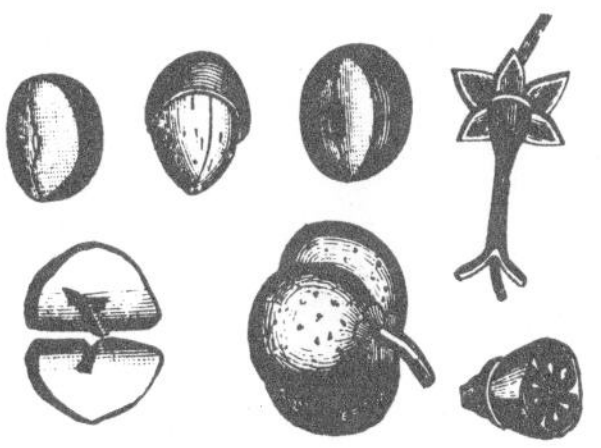

Seed Pods of Tea Plant

Three-Tiered Picnic Box F:85

For an especially elaborate picnic, or for the New Year's celebration, a lidded, multi-tiered box like this is needed. At New Year's—the most important Japanese holiday—special celebration dishes called *juzume* are prepared in advance (since stores close for several days) and served at room temperature in *jubako* (nested boxes). A typical *jubako* might contain half-moon-shaped slices of fish cake (*hinode-kamaboko*) on the first level, snowflake lotus roots in *mirin* (*seppen renkon*) on the next, and finally the special New Year's dishes *kuromame* (black beans) and *gomame* (glazed dried sardines) in the last. Our box consists of three 7½″-square interfitting trays in imitation lacquer (plastic). The box's rust-orange exterior is decorated with gold *bonsai* branches and three flying cranes—the symbol of the emperor. The interior is solid black—the better to set off the beauty of the food.

Takashimaya, Inc. $16.00

BRAISED SALMON OVER RICE WITH TOASTED SESAME GREEN TEA SAUCE

Sake cha-zukė

1 small can salmon
2 tablespoons rice wine or dry sherry
2 tablespoons soy sauce
3 tablespoons sesame seed
Hot cooked rice
Green tea

Prepare green tea in a teapot. Parch the sesame seed in a dry frying pan, until they begin to jump. Chop them fine in a nut chopper.

Remove any skin or bone from the canned salmon. Combine with the wine and soy sauce in a small pan, cover, and place over low heat. Braise the salmon until the liquid is nearly evaporated.

Heap the hot cooked rice into large individual bowls, filling them half full. Arrange the braised salmon over rice, then sprinkle with the parched sesame seed. Pour about ½ cup green tea over the salmon, cover the bowls with their lids, and allow to stand for 2 minutes before serving.

(From JAPANESE CUISINE, by John D. Keys. Copyright 1976 by Charles E. Tuttle Company. Reprinted by permission of Charles E. Tuttle Company, Japan.)

Middle Eastern Utensils

by Paula Wolfert

On all my recipe research trips through the Middle East I've always been struck by the simplicity of kitchens—the small number and primitive quality of the traditional utensils that are used. In fact it's been my experience in this part of the world that the more elaborate and delicious the feast, the more modest and simple the kitchen where it was produced is likely to be. No Cuisinart there, nor blenders, nor thermostatically controlled ovens and stoves; nothing electrical, and only rarely something that has moving parts. Rather, the most simple implements do the required jobs: a few pots and pans, glazed and unglazed earthenware cooking and serving dishes, always a mortar and pestle to grind the spices, and a simple machine to grind coffee beans, too. There are a few special utensils for special dishes such as a *couscousière* (a two-part steamer for making a North African grain dish called *couscous*), and, almost inevitably, a small charcoal brazier. Community ovens are used for the bigger baking jobs.

In this part of the world, you see, labor is still relatively cheap. When I convert a recipe to a book intended for American readers, I figure out ways of executing it with labor-saving devices, an important point to us, but something barely understood even now in the Middle East.

There is another reason, too, that time-saving kitchen equipment

Ah! For the good old days when craftsmanship was really appreciated!

"The Moors have singular ideas of feminine perfection: The gracefulness of figure and motion and a countenance enlivened by expression are by no means essential points in their standard: with them, corpulence and beauty appear to be terms nearly synonymous. A woman of even moderate pretensions must be one who cannot walk without a slave under each arm to support her, and a perfect beauty is a load for a camel. In consequence of this prevalent taste for unwieldiness of bulk, the Moorish ladies take great pains to acquire it early in life; and for this purpose, many of the young girls are compelled by their mothers to devour a great quantity of kouskous and drink a large bowl of camels' milk every morning. It is of no importance whether the girl has an appetite or not; the kouskous and milk must be swallowed, and obedience is frequently enforced by blows."

Travels in the Interior Districts of Africa *by Mungo Park (1795–97).*

has not developed. Cooking is not regarded as a profession in the Middle East. It is a job, surely; and when a cook (almost always a woman) is really good, she is regarded as a great treasure, and her temperament and whims are deemed worthy of support. But there are no centers of gastronomic instruction in these countries, no Cordon Bleu, no professional cadre of chefs, nor are there gourmet cooks who invent dishes or seek new ways of making them with greater ease. It's only foreigners like me who come and try to codify these cuisines, to write out precise recipes for dishes whose secrets have been handed down from mother to daughter for centuries. As a result, the equipment is always traditional, and the women who cook in these countries see no reason why this should be changed. To the great black women chefs who work in the palaces of Marrakech, the only way to make *couscous* or *bisteeya* (a huge, flaky-pastry pigeon pie) is to prepare everything by hand. I've even thought that to them, perhaps, this process makes part of the value of a dish: every semolina pellet of *couscous* must be hand rolled, hour after hour; every pastry leaf for a *bisteeya* must be made, one leaf at a time, often consuming an entire afternoon.

Serving dishes are something else. Here you will find elaborate and beautiful things, nearly always handmade, sometimes very inexpensive in the local markets; but they can become transformed into high-priced decorator items by the time they're imported—unbroken—to the United States. Greek *meze* (appetizer course) dishes, painted pottery, North African *tajine slaouis* (beautiful glazed earthenware serving dishes with high conical tops), Yugoslavian pickling jars, Syrian water-pipes and incense-burners, plus wonderfully designed platters, and all sorts of beautiful implements for the roasting, grinding, making and serving of coffee. There are lovely teapots, too, in all these countries, and glasses and cookie cutters, and skewers for *kebab*—a dish served throughout the region, although the spicing and/or marinating of the meat varies greatly from place to place. In Istanbul you can buy elegant brass-plated skewers that can turn a *shish kebab* dinner into a feast out of the Arabian Nights.

A friend who is a great authority on food once told me that he always visits a hardware store and cooking equipment store as soon as he arrives in a country; between the two, he says, one can understand a nation's culture. Ever since I heard that I've been taking his advice, buying and collecting cooking equipment through the years. Now I have a great quantity of beautiful and inexpensive bread and sifting baskets, serving pitchers, and also cooking utensils made for special native use.

In Morocco, for example, a native cook will often make her own *warka* (thin pastry) leaves for her *bisteeya* (something I specifically do not recommend for American cooks). For this purpose, I discovered, the Moroccans make a special pan, which, when I first saw it, struck me as very odd. It seemed to be an apprentice pan maker's mistake, since inside it was plated with copper, and outside with tin! However, as I learned more about Moroccan cooking, the logic of this pan became very clear: it was made to set upside down over charcoal, so that the tinned bottom became the top, where the *warka* leaves were cooked. Another time I bought a really odd looking uneven earthenware dome in Meknes. This sculptural unglazed device is called a *gdra dil trid,* on which the dough for *trid* (a savory, flaky-pastried chicken pie, alleged to have been the Prophet's favorite food) is stretched.

Continued from preceding page

One thing I heartily recommend are the wonderful brass mortar and pestle sets you find all over this part of the world. They're well-made and will last forever; and they make a good investment, too, since they can be used to grind spices for Indian, Indonesian, Mexican and other spice-oriented cuisines.

There's another marvelous mortar and pestle device that's traditional for pounding the meat for Lebanese *kibbi* (pounded lamb and *bulgur* wheat). It consists of a great hollowed-out square of stone in which the meat is placed, then mashed with a wide wooden pestle. However, in and around Beirut, one finds this method used less and less, supplanted in this most modern of Middle Eastern cities by a Western-style "*kibbi* blender."

Another type of goods I particularly like and recommend are the many forms of wicker baskets used for storing and serving bread. Bread is terribly important in this part of the world, where it is not only "the staff of life," but is often endowed with mystical and religious significance. For this reason it is lovingly offered in baskets that are beautiful objects in their own right.

Unquestionably, if you're interested in food, when you visit Greece, Turkey, Israel, Egypt or Morocco, one of the things you'll want to do is visit the markets where food is sold. Near them, inevitably, you'll find utensil and dish stores, and as you prowl in them, many beautiful, simple things will catch your eye. Superb glazed and unglazed earthenware pots and painted dishes will stand out against the cheaply made aluminum pots and pans, as will fine wicker baskets and special implements for grinding coffee and exotic spices. Don't hesitate to snap these items up. Usually they're inexpensive, and well worth bringing home.

Dining in Ancient Persia.

The Cuisine of the Middle East

Calling for a definition of the Middle East is a chancy business these days—unless the expert you consult is a cook. Any definition of the area is bound to be arbitrary, but a good claim can be made that those countries ringing the eastern end of the Mediterranean Sea have a cousinship of cuisine that binds them in a cultural unity transcending politics and religion. For our purposes, the Middle East embraces Greece and Turkey, the Arab States, the North African lands of the Maghreb—Morocco, Algeria, Tunisia—Israel and modern Persia. In all these countries the principal meat is lamb, the chief carbohydrate wheat. (Iran is an exception; here rice is the preferred starch.) This is not to say that the cuisine of Greece is the same as that of Iran, nor

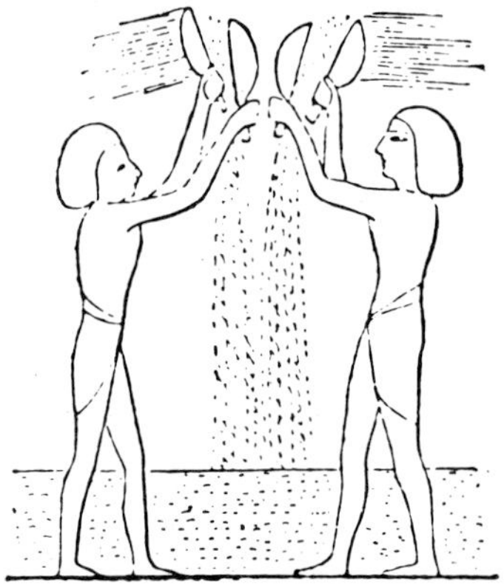

Melons

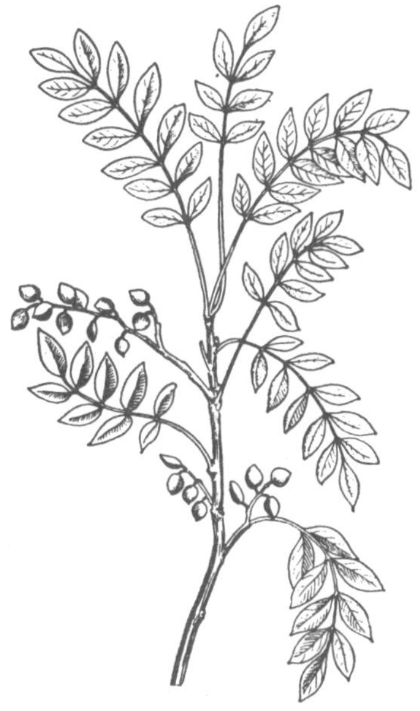

Pistachios—along with pomegranates and rose water—set the scene for an Arabian night.

that of Turkey the same as Morocco. There are national and sectional variations, and even village and family traditions. Each variant developed out of local resources and in response to local events. Yet there are so many basic similarities throughout the region—in methods of preparation and relationships of ingredients—that it is possible to speak of a Middle Eastern cuisine.

This part of the world has irreverently been dubbed the Eggplant Empire, and with justification. And try to imagine Middle Eastern cooking without the sharp, sweet scent of lemon, of eye-wateringly hot peppers, garlic, cucumber and creamy, curd-thick yoghurt! Oranges, dates, figs—quinces, melons and pomegranates—peaches, apricots and nuts of all kinds are to be found in their seasons. And of course, the ubiquitous olive and its oil.

Middle Easterners are hearty eaters. Except in Europeanized and cosmopolitan circles, leanness is not admired. A pretty woman is a plump woman. (*"Megalosite,"* the Greeks say in admiration, "You've gained weight.") Ah, if only that standard of beauty applied in America! Bread and rice are consumed in quantities that dumbfound the Westerner. But in a part of the world where meat is often scarce, expensive and served only for special occasions, that is understandable.

From Fez to Teheran, meals are likely to begin with a profusion of hors d'oeuvre. The name of this course, like the dishes served, is apt to vary from country to country; it is called *meze* in Greece, *mezze* in Turkey and *mazza* in the Arab States. Savory pastries stuffed with spinach or lamb, tiny mint-flavored meatballs, minute fried fish, yoghurt stiff with cucumber and garlic—tidbit succeeds tidbit, adding up to a gargantuan blow-out by our standards, but just an appetite-whetter to a Turk or Syrian.

The women of the Middle East probably invented what we call the casserole. Not because a large, one-pot meal is quickly prepared—time in the kitchen is never begrudged—but because fuel is scarce. City dwellers have recently acquired stoves, but most villagers still cook over portable one-burner stoves, or take a pan of food down to the communal bakery oven to cook after the bread is baked. Legumes such as lentils and beans are frequently the substances of these dishes. Morocco's chicken *kdra* is fleshed out with chick-peas and tender baby turnips and elevated to culinary heights by the addition of ginger and saffron. *Dizi,* which could be called Iran's national stew, consists of lamb, chick-peas again, plus tomatoes, onions and a touch of turmeric, and sometimes dried fava beans. In both ragouts, chicken or lamb is more flavoring agent than main ingredient.

In the Middle East three great religions sprang to life—Judaism, Christianity and Islam. And despite the wars and quarrels among the differing adherents of these faiths, it would be well for all to remember that they share a deep body of tradition. The three monotheisms were wrought in a land where food was hard to come by, life was harsh and sharing could mean the difference between existence and death by thirst or hunger. Hospitality is pleasing to the God of both Old and New Testaments, and the Koran specifically outlines the duties of the Faithful, and of their guests. Hospitality is both duty and honor. Mohammed's followers entertain warmly and joyously. A host does not ask his guests if they would like food or drink; he provides it automatically and as copiously as he can, pressing guests over and over to eat and drink. Courtesy demands that the guest first refuse, then reluctantly accept. Naturally both sides know the rules of this social rite, and play it out with gusto. "My *lokum* (a sticky, powdered candy)

Continued from preceding page

is not fit for dogs!" bewails the host. "No, no," cries the guest. "Never have I eaten finer!" The candy is, of course, very good, and the guest may indeed have had superior *lokum*. What does it matter? Ritual has been satisfied.

Christians of the Middle East are equally welcoming. Among Greeks, a glass of cool water is first offered. Greeks have a reverence for water that surely dates to ancient times. Country people are as proud of their well or spring water as Frenchmen might be of their vineyards. "Isn't it good?" they ask. "The most delicious you have ever tasted?" Then, no matter what the hour, food comes forth, even if it be only a few olives. Nor is offering food always just a charitable act of kindness: for example, to deny a pregnant woman *any food she demands* is to risk marking her child, and thereby standing guilty and responsible for the rest of one's life. Superstition? Perhaps, but even among the educated, expectant mothers are never denied such a whim.

An attitude shared by most Middle Easterners is an aversion to pork. "The flesh of swine" is forbidden to Jew and Muslim, and even Christians rarely eat it. Anyway, the pigs, like the cattle, tend to be scrawny and tough. Lamb fares much better on the area's sparse pasturage, and the chickens seem content to scratch for a living. They are served up in endless variations—with lemons, apricots, celery, *couscous*, rice, chick-peas.

In traditional Middle Eastern households, the kitchen is the lively, noisy nerve center of the family. Women of several generations live under the same roof, working together while children run underfoot and little girls watch their elders deftly shaping the meat pies called *sfeeha*, or preparing the leaf-thin wafers, *malsouqua*. This is the way the art is handed down, from mother to daughter, aunt to niece. The best cooks, as everywhere, are highly appreciated. Cookbooks? The idea is puzzling, unreal. You learn by watching, then by performing for a chorus of teachers.

No one can point with certainty to the originators of the dishes or methods that we associate with Middle Eastern cooking. For thousands of years conquering armies and peaceful merchants swept back and forth across the area, carrying ways of preparation, like spices and melon seeds, from place to place. Greeks invading Persia, Romans occupying the Holy Land—both groups must have tasted new foods and remembered them, while introducing their subject peoples to fare from their own homes.

Next came desert Arabs—followers of Mohammed—with the limited cuisine of poor nomads. But in the wars following the Prophet's death in 632, his armies began their conquest of much of the world. Rich Byzantium, Persia, North Africa, Iberia and Sicily all fell. But some luxuries remained, and the puritanical Muslims, in their turn, succumbed to the fruit-and-honey laden delights of gentler climates.

If the Middle East can be said to have a Mother Cuisine, it is Turkish. The Ottoman Empire, after all, lasted—with periods of great splendor—from 1299 to 1918. At times it dominated southwestern Asia, northeastern Africa and southern Europe. Greece had 400 years of Turkish rule and parts of the Balkans endured it even longer. Bitterness and enmity still remain as the heritage of the departed occupiers. Paradoxically, so does the love of *shish kebab, baklava* and yoghurt. Whatever Middle Easterners disagree about today, it most definitely is not food.

Greek Liter Measure G:1

This Greek liter measure is a homely, unpretentious object still to be found in village taverns. It is a cylindrical, flat-bottomed tinned-steel can with a rolled rim and soldered seams—shaped somewhat like a tankard. Its handle is a tapered band soldered to its side. This measure will hold a liter of wine, water, broth or any other liquid you might use for cooking. At the present time, it is useful for Greek, Middle Eastern and European recipes, and it will become increasingly so as we change to the metric system. Unfortunately, it is not calibrated to indicate deciliters.

Greek Island Ltd. $4.50

"The whole Mediterranean, the sculpture, the palms, the gold beads, the bearded heroes, the wine, the ideas, the ships, the moonlight, the winged gorgons, the bronze men, the philosophers—all of it seems to rise in the sour, pungent taste of these black olives between the teeth. A taste older than meat, older than wine. A taste as old as cold water."

Prospero's Cell and Reflections on a Marine Venus *by Lawrence Durrell. E. P. Dutton, 1960.*

Olive Jar G:2

The olive has occupied a position of prominence in Greek life—both economic and culinary—for nearly five millennia. How fitting, then, that this charming terra-cotta olive jar should look as though Athena herself had ordered it made for us. Although it should, out of respect for its place of origin, hold olives from Crete, you may be somewhat more tempted to lay in a store of Greece's best olives, *kalamata* or *amphissa.* The 8½″-tall, 2½-quart jar is glazed a deep, rich terra-cotta color inside, and is left unglazed outside. Four classic-looking ear handles ring the jar just below its neck.

Greek Island Ltd. $8.50

A complaint that has not changed over the years: "Good olive oil is not over abundant. . . . About 1000 years ago (A.D. 817) it was so scarce in Europe that the council of Aix la Chapelle authorised the priests to manufacture anointing oil from bacon. Imagine divine right shed over kings in the essential oil of swine; and image how, as the Hindoo now dies happy with the tail of a cow in his hand, the good Christian of those days went shining to heaven in the extreme unction dropped from a flitch of bacon. We are driven to no such straits in these days . . . but still it is not easy to get the oil of Lucca good, and it is much adulterated with inferior kinds."

Kettner's Book of the Table, *1877.*

IMAM BAYILDI

Eggplant stuffed with aromatics

There should be no merriment about the name of this dish: "The Imam swooned" seems appropriate, since the dish is as colorful to behold and as rich to taste as a vegetable dish can be.

To Serve 5
2½ pounds eggplants (about 5 five-inch or 3 long ones)
Salt
3 medium onions, peeled and sliced into thin rings
½ cup water
4 to 5 tablespoons olive oil
5 peeled, sliced fresh tomatoes or 8 canned plum tomatoes, sliced
½ cup chopped fresh parsley
3 to 4 cloves garlic, peeled and sliced lengthwise
Freshly ground pepper
Pinch of granulated sugar
Fresh parsley for garnish

Wash the eggplants, cut off the stem end if using large ones and cut in half lengthwise. With the tip of a sharp knife, make at least 3 lengthwise slashes on the cut sides of the eggplants, being careful not to pierce the skin on the opposite side. Sprinkle with salt and let stand for 30 minutes. Rinse with cold water, dry, and invert to drain.

Meanwhile, put the onions in a small pan with the ½ cup water and simmer a few minutes. Drain and discard the water or save for soup.

In a medium frying pan, heat 2 tablespoons of the oil and sauté the onions until soft, then put approximately a third of them in the bottom of a buttered casserole large enough to accommodate all the eggplants. Set 4 to 5 tomato slices over the onions in the casserole and add the rest of the tomatoes to the onions remaining in the frying pan. Sauté onions and tomatoes for 10 minutes, then stir in all but 2 tablespoons of the parsley and remove from the heat. Set the eggplants into the casserole, tuck a slice of garlic into each eggplant slash, and stuff the slashes with the filling, allowing some to cover the top of the eggplant. Season lightly with salt, pepper, and a pinch of sugar, then dribble the remaining oil and chopped parsley over the eggplants. Cover the casserole with a lid or aluminum foil and bake in a moderate oven (350 degrees) for 30 to 40 minutes, until fork-tender, removing the cover during the last 10 minutes to allow the sauce to thicken. Garnish with parsley and serve warm.

Note: This is excellent as a first course of a subsequently light meal topped with fresh fruit and Turkish coffee.

If you wish you may leave the eggplants whole, slash one side and remove some of the pulp with a small spoon. This pulp is then sautéed with the filling and stuffed into the eggplant, a very attractive method for the smaller eggplants. As you might suspect, both variations may also be prepared on top of the stove.

(From THE FOOD OF GREECE, by Vilma Liacouras Chantiles. Copyright 1975 by Vilma Liacouras Chantiles. Reprinted by permission of Atheneum)

Greek Oil Can G:3

From Greece comes this tinned-steel oil can, which holds about 4½ cups inside its tapered body. This thin, 7″-long spout, almost as long as the can itself, is so well designed it is virtually drip-proof—a blessing to the cook who must drizzle oil into such dishes as *imam bayildi* (braised eggplant with tomatoes and onions). Legend says that the *imam*—or priest—fainted

Continued from preceding page

when he discovered the amount of oil his wife had used! The cover is hinged to the can and a half-moon-shaped overflow guard beneath the lid prevents the oil from splashing and spilling when the can is tipped for pouring. Plan to keep the oil can always full of oil, since it is not very easy to clean.

Greek Island Ltd. $11.50

Spices

For many centuries, Middle Easterners have been the spice merchants of the world, routing their precious merchandise from the Far East to Europe and the West. They are experts on the subject, knowledgeable about a vast array of seasonings, some of them unique, like *mahlab*—an extract of black-cherry kernels—and virtually unknown in the West.

Almost every country of the Middle East has its favorite mixture of spices. These can be bought in the *attarine,* or spice markets. Generally people roast spice seeds themselves, crushing and blending them with pestles in heavy mortars to release freshness, strength and aroma at the last moment before use.

The spices of the Middle East—cinnamon, ginger, turmeric, cumin and allspice—are combined gently and subtly to give meat, poultry, fish and rice dishes a distinctive flavor. Rose water and orange water—the first distilled from the pink damask rose, the latter from the blossoms of the bitter orange tree—are used to flavor puddings, sweet dough and a rich array of fruited confections.

Iranian Spice Jar G:4

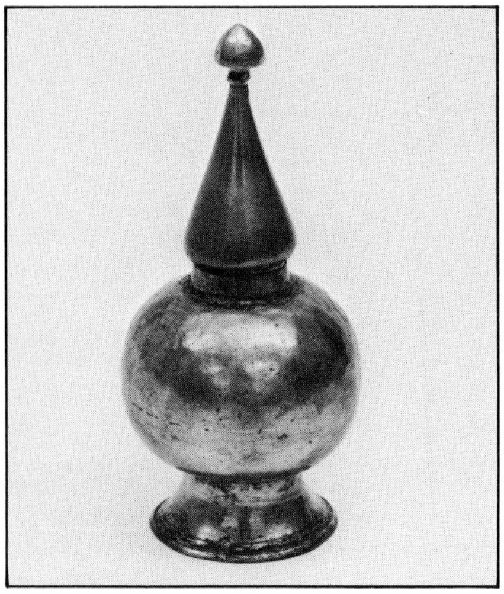

This engaging spice holder comes from Iran. It's made of tin-washed copper, and stands 6¾″ high. The care with which it was made reflects a tradition in which spices are a symbol of a good, luxurious life filled with sensuous delights. Iranians, like all Middle Easterners, are lavish in the use of herbs and spices. For centuries Middle Eastern traders controlled the routes by which precious spices were transported from the Orient to Europe. Many became fabulously rich from the trade; but rich or poor, all acquired a love of highly-flavored foods. All of which is to say that not only spices, but their containers, are given serious consideration. Our exotic 1½-cup pot should hold an exotic ingredient, such as *sumak,* (also called the herb of Hebron). It's a lemony, woodsy wild berry that sparks *chelo kebab,* the marinated lamb and rice dish so popular that many Teheran restaurants serve nothing else.

Pampered Kitchens $16.50

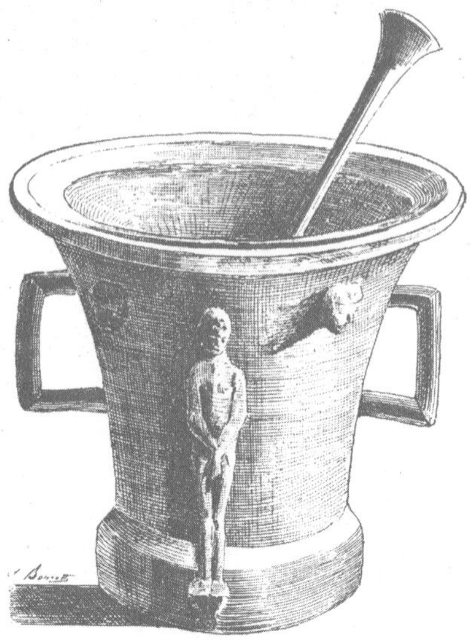

16th-century bronze mortar and pestle.

Greek Wooden Mortar and Pestle G:5

The scent of herbs and spices evokes the very soul of Greece. Wafts of wild marjoram from the hillsides of Hymettus aswarm with honey bees, the perfume of grilling cumin at a *souvlaki* stand, and everywhere the smell of roasting coffee. Or the mouth-watering smell of cinnamon bark being crushed in a wooden mortar and pestle like this for a *kota kapama,* meltingly marvelous chicken in tomato sauce. This wooden mortar is 5½″ deep and has a flat bottom; the 10¾″ wooden pestle has a squared-off bottom to conform perfectly to the mortar's shape. The crushing end of the pestle and the interior of the mortar are deliberately left unfinished to offer the best "tooth" to the grinding surface, but the mortar's exterior and the pestle handle are handsomely smoothed to show off the grain of the wood. One caution is in order: never grind onions or garlic in a wooden mortar. The juices penetrate and linger, ghostlike, to add unwelcome flavors to subsequent dishes.

Ethnikon Gift Shop **$11.00**

KOTA KAPAMA

Spicy Chicken Braised with Cinnamon and Cloves

A superb dish for family or guests. I have seen Greek cooks slip a few hot red pepper seeds into the pot, but *kapama* is delectable without them. Another meat, especially lamb, may be used as a substitute for the poultry.

To Serve 5
1 frying or roasting chicken (2½ pounds), cut into serving pieces
Juice of 1 lemon
4 to 5 teaspoons sweet butter and vegetable oil, mixed
½ cup dry white wine (optional)
1½ pounds fresh or canned tomatoes, peeled, chopped, and drained
1 tablespoon tomato paste diluted in ¼ cup water
1 large stick cinnamon
3 whole cloves
Salt and freshly ground pepper
Fresh parsley or watercress for garnish

Arrange the chicken parts in a glass or earthenware bowl and rub all over with lemon juice. Allow to stand while heating the butter and oil in a heavy braising pot. Slip the chicken into the fat and cook over medium heat, turning with tongs to avoid pricking the flesh; sauté until light chestnut in color. Heat the wine in a small pan, pour over the chicken, shake the pan, and continue cooking over low heat. Stir in the tomatoes and tomato paste, slip the cinnamon and cloves in among the pieces, and cover. Simmer over the lowest possible heat for 1½ hours, or until the chicken is tender and the sauce thick. Or, transfer to a medium slow oven (325 degrees) to complete the cooking. Season with salt and pepper. Serve warm over cooked grain or mashed potatoes with green raw or cooked vegetables and chilled wine. Garnish with parsley or watercress.

(From THE FOOD OF GREECE, by Vilma Liacouras Chantiles. Copyright 1975 by Vilma Liacouras Chantiles. Reprinted by permission of Atheneum)

Syrian Apricotwood Mortar and Pestle G:6

Squat, rustic and useful. These characteristics describe a sturdy little mortar made of unfinished apricotwood —that hard, orange-brown wood with a beautiful grain from which the Syrians make so many kitchen utensils. The short, rounded shape of the mortar (it is only 2⅜″ deep with a diameter of 4″, and stands about 3″ high on its turned base) gives it stability under pressure. Its rounded sides curve in slightly at the rim to form a small protective collar that will prevent ground spices from flying out. The matching pestle is 7⅛″ long and has a hefty working end, 2″ in diameter, that makes contact with a substantial portion of the mortar's bottom.

Sahadi Importing Co., Inc./Continental Crafts Co. (S120) **$4.00**

"I sent Ismail for 'mast' or curds [yogurt]; the village headman came back with him, carrying them in a blue bowl, not too cordially: I was a Christian; he would not share my meal. But his two wives by and by adventured their less important souls with a little chicken, while the men smoked, and I lay in the grass and wished I knew the names of all the birds."

The Valleys of Assassins *by Freya Stark. John Murray, Ltd., 1930.*

Syrian Brass Mortar and Pestle G:7

There is garlic to be mashed, sesame seeds to be ground, mint leaves to be ever-so-lightly bruised, and cardamom seeds to be crushed. A Middle Eastern cook would not get very far without the services of a sturdy mortar and pestle like this one from Syria. The 4¾″-high brass mortar has a solid pedestal foot to give it weight; the 3″-deep bowl will hold a healthy quantity of crushables. The 6¾″-long pestle is well balanced and fits the mortar's bowl nicely.

Continental Crafts Co. (S131) **$20.00**

Some tribes have rather unique methods of carving, as "Lawrence of Arabia" observed: "As the meat pile wore down (nobody really cared about rice: flesh was the luxury) one of the chief Howeitat eating with us would draw his dagger, silver hilted, set with turquoise, a signed masterpiece of Mohammed Ibn Zari, of Jauf, and would cut criss-cross from the larger bones long diamonds of meat easily torn up between the fingers; for it was necessarily boiled very tender, since all had to be disposed of with the right hand, which alone was honourable."

The Seven Pillars of Wisdom *by T. E. Lawrence. Doubleday & Co., 1935.*

Egyptian Brass Mortar and Pestle G:8

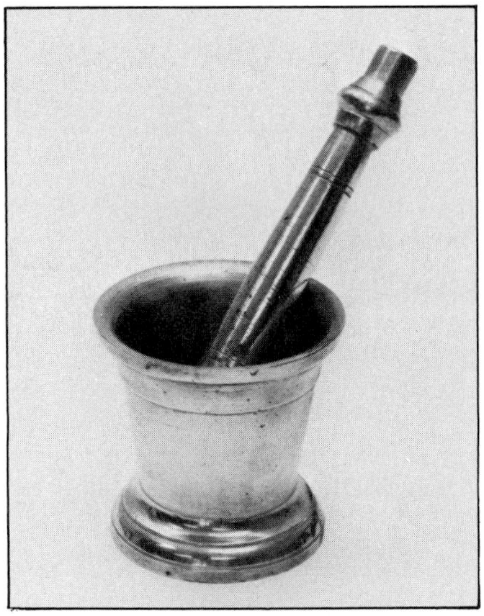

In Egypt a lathe-turned brass mortar and pestle might be used to grind cumin and coriander to season wild quail before grilling, or to crush the peanuts sprinkled on sweetened *couscous* (cooked semolina pellets), a favorite dessert. This 3″-high mortar has an exceptionally heavy base, so that it doesn't "walk" when in use. The grinding surface is about 1½″ wide, rough-textured and flat. The pestle, 6″ long, has a flattened end to crush any spice or nut thrown against it. It is decorated with several lathe-turned bands, and is capped with a little knob.

Beirut Grocers, Inc. $12.00

Iranian Stone Mortar and Pestle G:9

Infatuation would best describe how we feel about this diminutive stone mortar from Iran. The satiny-smooth mortar carved of native basalt is nice to touch and charming to look at. It is just a shade over 2″ high and only 1⅜″ deep. Its matching pestle, 3¾″ long, is rounded at the business end to facilitate crushing. The other end tapers to a small knob. This tiny twosome was obviously never meant to deal with large quantities; but for crushing the few threads of fiendishly expensive saffron that flavor the rice and lamb dish called *tah chin,* it would be perfect.

Iranian National Handicrafts $2.00

Kibbi Pounder G:10

Both Syria and Lebanon claim *kibbi* as the national dish. It also turns up in Iraq as *kubba,* and in Jordan as *kobba.* It can be fried, grilled, baked, stuffed or even eaten raw. No matter what its final form may take, *kibbi* begins with a base of lamb beaten to a paste, to which soaked *bulgur* wheat is added. Further pounding incorporates the meat and wheat. *Kibbi* can now be achieved by more modern methods like the food processor, but the old-fashioned three-pound basher shown here is quite efficient—and as a tension-reliever it has it all over an electric grinder! The mallet is carved from a foot-long chunk of apricotwood; the pounding surface has a 4¼″ diameter. Traditionally, it is used with a large marble mortar. In the not too distant past the sound of women pounding *kibbi* with club-like pestles like this one could be heard from early in the morning until well into the afternoon, all over Syria; the pounding of the *kibbi* and its shaping were part of the daily rhythm of many women's lives. As more modern, labor-saving devices for making the lamb-and-wheat paste come into use, we look back with admiration at the strength and patience of the cooks of the past.

Sahadi Importing Co., Inc. $5.50

Syrian Sausage Stuffer G:11

Although the Middle East is overwhelmingly Muslim, there are small Christian communities in most countries of that area; and some, as in Greece and Armenia, are mostly Christian. Muslims are forbidden pork and wine, but Christians are not. A delicious, spicy pork and wine sausage, called *loukanika* by the Greeks, is eaten in these communities in stews and omelets. A Syrian version called *mah'anet* is made of lamb (and occasionally pork). Ground meat, salt, pepper and coriander are first marinated for a day with dry wine. Before stuffing the casings, the cook then fries a small patty to see if the seasoning is exactly to her taste. In Syria a very narrow tin sausage stuffer like this one is used to fill the lamb or pork casings. This funnel-shaped sausage stuffer has a section of the rim cut away in a U shape. The seams of the stuffer are soldered together and the rim is rolled so that there are no raw edges to cut yourself on. The nozzle is exceedingly narrow which means that any sausage stuffing used with it must be very finely ground and not very dense.

Malko Importing Corp. **$2.75**

Squash Corer G:12

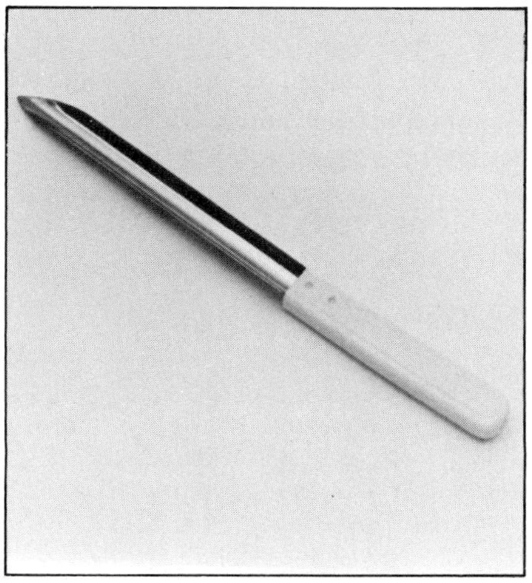

For the stuffed eggplant and squash dishes so much a part of Middle Eastern fare, this inexpensive corer can save endless time and trouble. The narrow blade is curved like a trough along its length. With very little practice, anyone can deftly hollow out vegetables without breaking through their shells. Use it for *koosa minshee*—zucchini stuffed with rice and ground lamb, simmered in a mint-spiked tomato sauce. The 5¾″-long, stainless-steel blade is secured by two small rivets in a 3½″-long, beige plastic handle.

Bridge Kitchenware Corp. **$2.00**

Leaf from manuscript of Dioscorides; recipe for medicine and a doctor preparing it. Mesopotamian, 1222–1223 (from The Metropolitan Museum of Art). It translates as: "The making of a drink (shirab) *for catarrhs, coughs, swelling of the belly, and loosening of the stomach. Take myrrh ¼* uqiyya, *roots of susan ⅛* uqiyya, *white pepper ¼ and (. . .) ⅛* uqiyya. *Pound them together, tie in a rag, put into 3 qusts of good wine, and let stand 3 days. Then strain and put into a clean vessel. Drink after supper."*

Threshing wheat in Egypt.

Citrus Reamer G:13

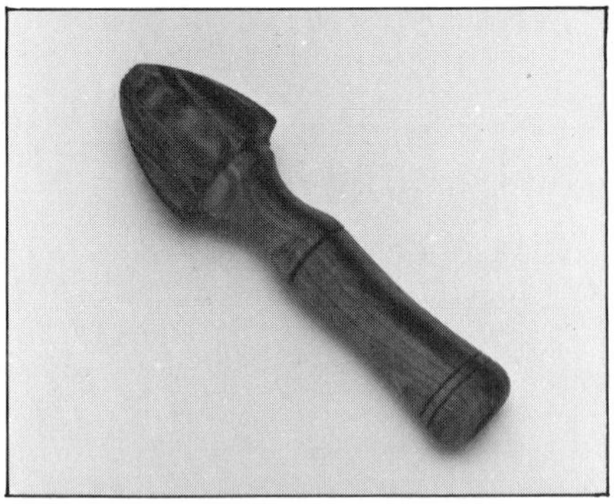

This dome-shaped citrus reamer carved out of a single piece of hard apricotwood is just the implement to use to extract lemon juice to flavor marinated grilled chicken, carp roe salad (*taramosalata*), or lemony-chicken soup (*avgolemono*). The sharp, long rachets are carved to resemble the petals of a flower. To use, press the reamer into half a lemon, and, holding onto the handle, twist it against the lemon's interior, letting the juices drip into a bowl. It does a surprisingly effective job of scraping pulp to extract every bit of juice from a lemon, and we see no reason why it couldn't be used on oranges and limes as well. The comfortable handle is about 4″ long with a hole in the end by which it can be hung.

Continental Crafts Co. (S129) $2.50

TARAMOSALATA

2 large potatoes (about 1 pound), peeled
¼ to ½ cup *tarama* (salted carp roe)
¼ cup grated onion
¼ cup lemon juice
1 cup olive oil (preferably Greek oil)
Kalamata or other Greek olives for garnish

Boil the potatoes and force them through a ricer.

Beat the *tarama* into the poatoes, spoonful by spoonful, tasting as you add; *tarama* varies in intensity and saltiness.

Beat in the onion, lemon juice, and as much of the olive oil as you like; I like a very oily *taramosalata*. Refrigerate for several hours or overnight.

Return the *taramosalata* to near-room temperature before serving; cold deadens the flavors. Mound the *taramosalata* on a serving plate and make a small well in the center; fill it with olive oil.

Surround the *taramosalata* with olives and serve with crusty bread as a *meze*, or appetizer.

(*Courtesy of Lyn Stallworth*)

"The usual Drink is Sherbet, made of Water, Juice of Lemons, and Ambergreece, which they drink out of long, thin Wooden Spoons, wherewith they lade it out of their Bowls.

Sherbets are made of almost all Tart pleasing fruits as the Juice of Pomegranets, Lemmons, Citrons, Oranges, Prunella's, which are to be bought in the Markets. Thus, by Diet, as well as Air, they procure not only a firmness of Constitution, but Properness and Tallness of Body, for none excell them either for Beauty or Stature."

A New Account of East India and Persia. Being Nine Years' Travels, 1672–1681 *by John Fryer.*

Felafel Shaping Set G:14

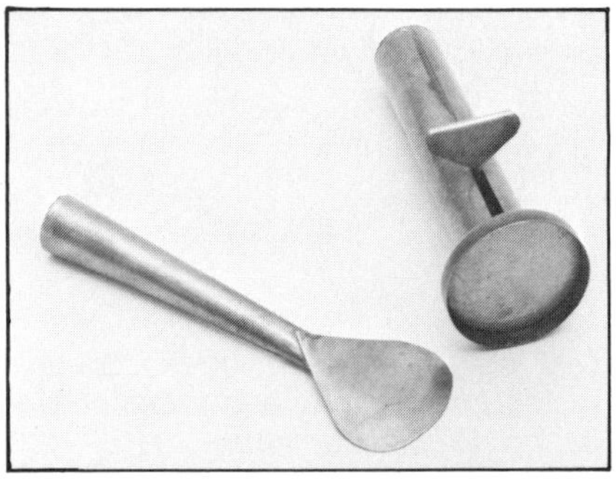

Felafel (or *ta'amia* as it is called in Egypt) are fried patties of ground beans, garlic, onions and spices. *Ta'amia* patties are made with fava beans (*ful nabed*); but in Israel, where *felafel* is sold by street vendors, chick-peas replace the *ful nabed.* For centuries *felafel* has been shaped between the palms with a few brisk and efficient pats. But the old way evidently was not good enough for the anonymous Syrian who invented this *felafel* shaper, the Middle Eastern equivalent of the hamburger press. It consists of a brass spatula and a circular mold—2″ in diameter and ¼″ deep—at the end of a brass cylinder. To shape *felafel,* use the spatula to spread a dollop of paste inside the mold, then press down on the plunger lodged inside the cylinder. A *felafel* patty the shape of a mini-hamburger is thus formed and is ready to cook.

Karnig Tashjian $12.00

Iranian Skimmer G:15

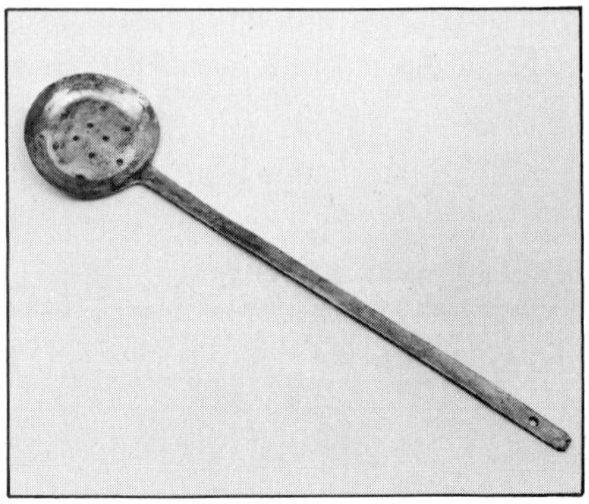

Skimmers like this one were designed for use in households where large pots simmered over wood or charcoal fires. If you cook chick-peas or fava beans for *felafel* (fried, spicy ground bean patties), the flat, 4⅜″-diameter bowl of this hand-hammered, tin-washed copper skimmer will handily remove the bean skins that rise to the surface of the pot. Because its size (20″ long) may make it somewhat awkward to store in a drawer, the skimmer should really be hung by the hole in its handle and displayed as an *objet d'art* as well as a practical device.

Pampered Kitchens $17.00

Iranian Ladle G:16

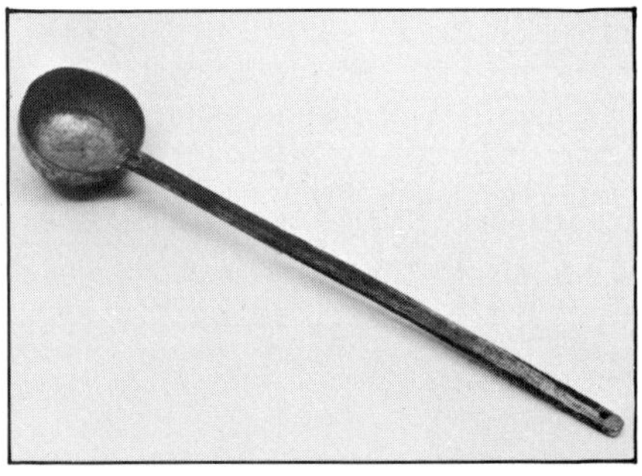

Tin-washed, hammered-copper ladles like this one from Iran are survivors from the days of extended—very extended—households, when to feed thirty mouths was all in the day's work. With a deep bowl (3½″ in diameter, 1½″ deep) soldered to a 15″-long handle, the ladle is just the ticket for serving a savory *koresh* of chicken and sour cherries over rice to a horde of hungry guests.

Pampered Kitchens **$20.00**

Iranian Server G:17

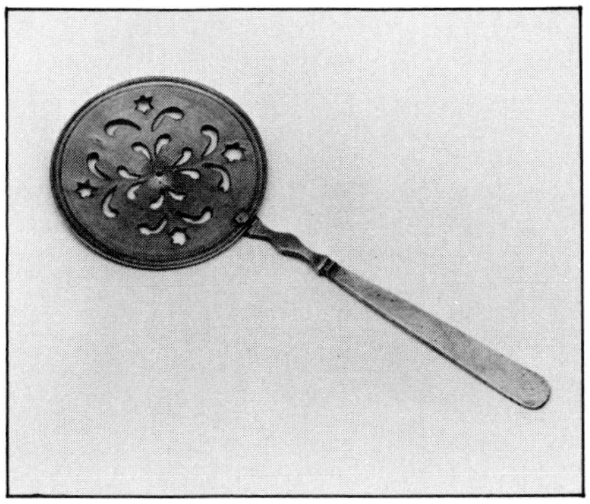

Iranians consume rice in quantites that would stagger a Westerner: many recipes call for 2½ pounds of rice to serve four. Iran's rice is excellent, and the long-grain variety grown around the Caspian Sea is superb. There are literally dozens upon dozens of ways that Iranians prepare and serve this grain. But whatever the dish, they all begin by boiling the rice, draining it and turning it into a heavy, covered pan. It is then either baked in a moderate oven, or steamed gently, in butter, on top of the stove over a low flame. Sometimes it is cooked for as long as three-quarters of an hour in order to produce a crunchy brown crust, called *tah dig,* on the bottom of the pot. The Iranians consider the quality of *tah dig* as a standard by which to judge a cook's skill. The largest piece of crisp *tah dig* is a choice morsel, offered first to guests. Appropriately enough, it is often presented on a beautiful, pierced, flat serving spoon. This round brass server is 4½″ in diameter and is riveted to a 6½″-long brass handle.

Pampered Kitchens **$15.00**

One of the legends describing the origin of rice, mainstay of Persian cuisine, is given in the chronicles of a seventeenth century English traveller: "On a time, Mahomet *being earnest in his prayers was accidentally conveighed to Paradize, where being very earnest in beholding its rare varieties, at length hee cast his eyes upon the glorious Throne of the Almighty; and (perceiving the Lord to turne about) fearing he should bee severely whipt for such presumption, blushes for shame, and sweats with terror; but loth to have it seene, wipes off his brow the pretious sweat with his first finger, and threw it out of Paradize: it was not lost, for forthwith dividing it selfe into . . . drops, all of them became miraculous creatures: the first drop became a fragrant Rose . . . the second, a grain of Ryce, (a holy graine)."*

Some Yeares Travels into Africa and Asia the Great: Especially Describing the Famous Empires of Persia and Industant, 1638.

Greek Spoon G:18

A handsome wooden spoon, 14½″ long, makes a fitting serving piece for such rustic Greek offerings as *taramosalata* (a dip of carp roe, oil, lemon and bread) or *tzatziki* (thick yoghurt flavored with parsley, cucumber and tongue-numbing amounts of minced garlic). These two dishes often appear as part of the panoply of *meze,* little appetizers always eaten when drinks are served before a meal. The heavily carved spoon is made of lightweight wood, and is not meant for kitchen use. The tip of the handle ends in a beak-shaped hook for easy hanging.

Greek Island Ltd. **$12.00**

Moroccan Soup Spoon G:19

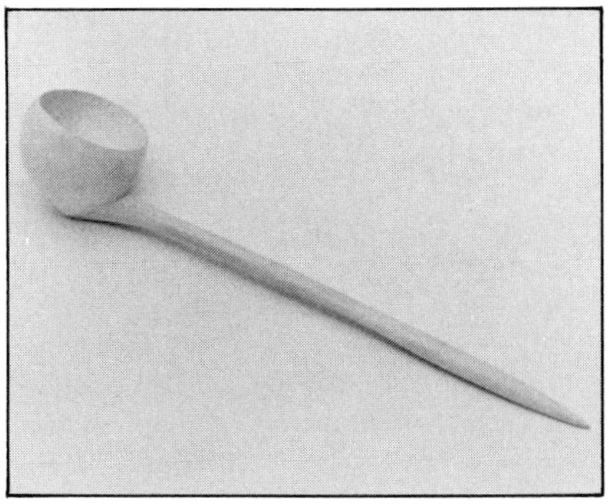

This hand-carved soup spoon is shaped like an old-fashioned clay pipe. It is made of hard, close-grained, pale yellow lemonwood, and comes from Morocco. The bowl holds about 2 tablespoons in its hollowed, rounded interior. The 8″-long handle tapers to a point. Although the spoon is lightweight and balances nicely in the hand, it might take a bit of practice before soup eaters could manage it without spills. But as a small ladle, it's a dandy.

The Store at Sugarbush Village/H. A. Mack and Co., Inc. (M3) **$1.80**

TZATZIKI

Yoghurt, Cucumber, Garlic Dip

2 cups plain yoghurt (16 oz.)
1 cucumber
Salt
1 to 3 garlic cloves
Pepper
Parsley

Spoon the yoghurt into a fine-meshed sieve and set it over a bowl. (If the yoghurt is very thin and runny, line the sieve with a double layer of rinsed cheesecloth.) As water drips through the sieve, the yoghurt becomes stiffened. In Greece this is called *sakoula,* "little sack" yoghurt, and can be bought at the local *galaktopoleon,* or dairy store, or is delivered by the yoghurt vendor to his customers along his daily route. Drain the yoghurt for a few hours or overnight in the refrigerator; if the yoghurt seems too stiff, beat a little of the liquid back into it.

Grate a large peeled cucumber and

Continued from preceding page

salt it heavily. Let it drain in another sieve or colander for an hour or two; toss the shreds from time to time. The salt causes the cucumber to give up a great deal of juice; squeeze out as much additional juice as you can with your hands. Add it to the *sakoula* and mix well.

Finely mince a few garlic cloves, or force them through a press. I use at least three cloves, but not everyone shares my enthusiasm for the pungent little buds.

Stir the cucumber shreds, garlic and a few generous grindings of black pepper into the mixture along with a tablespoon of minced parsley.

Cover the bowl with plastic wrap and let it sit in the refrigerator for at least two hours to "marry" the flavors. Return it to near-room temperature before serving and add salt if needed.

Tzatziki can be eaten at once, but as it sits the garlic calms down considerably. Serve *tzatziki* with chunks of crusty bread as a dip, or use it as a sauce with grilled swordfish.

Note: If you like, substitute minced chives or scallions for the garlic.

(*Courtesy of Lyn Stallworth*)

Hummus Dish G:20

Shaped like an open flower, this handsome earthenware bowl is a server for *hummus bi tahina* (a garlicky, cold chick-pea purée). *Hummus* appears by itself, or as one of the dishes of the *mazza,* the traditional array of appetizers that is served to guests before dinner in Arab homes and restaurants. The open, almost flat shape of the dish makes it easy to scoop up the delicious purée with *khoubz araby* (what we call *pita* or pocket bread). The inside of the bowl is covered with a caramel-colored glaze streaked with yellow, and the outside is unglazed earthenware. The bowl rests on a small shaped foot and holds 1¼ cups of *hummus.*

Sahadi Importing Co., Inc. $3.00

HUMMUS

Cold Chick-pea and Garlic Purée

2 cups dried chick-peas
½ cup *tahina*
½ cup olive oil
¾ cup lemon juice
6 cloves of garlic
Salt
Paprika

Cover the chick-peas with water and leave to soak for at least 12 hours.

In the same water, cook the chick-peas until tender (1–1½ hours), adding water if necessary. When the chick-peas are done, drain off the cooking water and reserve.

Place the *tahina,* ¼ cup of the oil, the lemon juice and the garlic in a blender or food processor. Blend well. Add the chick-peas slowly, blending after each addition. When the purée begins to get stiff, start to add the reserved cooking water a little at a time to maintain a smooth consistency—about that of sour cream—which may take as much as ¾ cup of the water. Add salt to taste and blend again. Chill.

Put the *hummus* in a shallow bowl and smooth the surface with the back of a spoon. Make one large, or several small, depressions in the center of the *hummus* and pour in the remaining ¼ cup of olive oil (this is optional for those who haven't yet developed the Middle Eastern taste for olive oil). Sprinkle liberally with paprika.

Serve with *pita* bread.

Shish Kebab

Sis (pronounced shish) means sword or skewer in Turkish, and *kebab* means roasted meat. Claudia Roden, author of the excellent *A Book of Middle Eastern Food* writes that *shish kebab* "is said by the Turks to have been created during the splendid conquering era of the Ottoman Empire, when Turkish soldiers, forced to camp out in tents for months on end, discovered the pleasure of eating meat grilled out of doors on open fires of charcoal or dry wood."

Though *shish kebab* is probably Turkey's most famous dish, meat grilled on skewers is eaten all over the Middle East. There are many versions and elaborations of this dish. In one, the meat is first marinated in a mixture of oil, lemon and spices, or spices blended with yoghurt. For another *kebab,* vegetables—bell peppers, onions, tomatoes—alternate with skewered meat chunks. The vegetables bathe in the meat drippings and, in turn, flavor the meat. Frequently, herbs are thrown on the cooking fire to perfume the food.

Cubed meat is by no means the only thing that is cooked on skewers over an open fire. Swordfish, ground meatballs called *köfte,* shellfish, chicken, liver, heart, and—yes—intestines are also cooked this way. All these dishes are expensive in the countries of their origin and, in most households, are served only on special occasions.

Syrian Skewer G:21

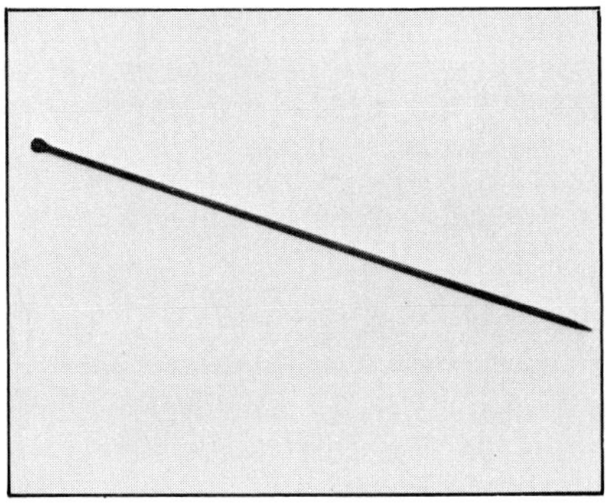

We don't know if this long, slim, six-sided skewer used for broiling *shish kebab* was actually made in a village blacksmith shop, but it certainly looks as if it were. Skewers like this one, made in Syria, are the most commonly used ones in cooking *köfte* (ground mutton), *tuhal* (lamb medallions stuffed with pine nuts and hot peppers) and other *kebabs* in the Arab world. The unpolished carbon-steel shaft is not particularly elegant, but it is functional, transmitting heat to the interior of the meat and thereby helping the *kebabs* cook more quickly. This skewer is 20¼″ long and ¼″ wide. It is pointed at one end to spear the meat and flat at the other. Needless to say, caution should be exercised with a heated skewer.

Oriental Pastry & Grocery Co. $0.45

Iranian kebab vendor.

Turkish Skewers G:22

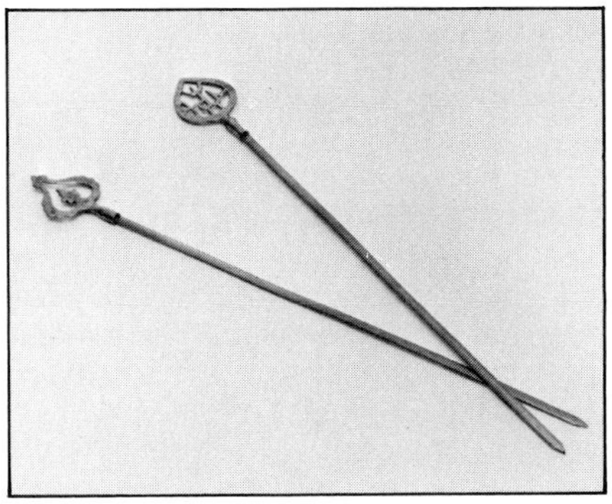

These two sword-like stainless-steel skewers, with pierced brass handles in the shape of traditional Middle Eastern finials, were made in Turkey. Nonetheless, they seem perfect for cooking and serving *chelo kebab,* the pride of the Iranian kitchen, and the most elegant *kebab* of all. *Chelo kebab* is made of cubes of marinated lamb or chicken that are spitted, broiled and served on *chelo,* which is steamed rice with sweet butter: Raw egg yolks, each presented in a half egg shell, are tipped from the shell onto the rice at table and mixed into it, often with a spoonful of the herb called *sumak.* These skewers are 13⅝″ long and are sold separately.

Pampered Kitchens $3.00

"There was a man, a householder, who had a very sneering, dirty, and rapacious wife. Whatever food he brought home, his wife would consume it, and the man was forced to keep silence.

One day that family man brought home, for a guest, some meat which he had procured with infinite pains. His wife ate it up with a kabáb *and wine. . . .*

The man said to her, 'Where is the meat? The guest has arrived: one must set nice food before a guest.'

'This cat has eaten the meat,' she replied: 'hey, go and buy some more. . . !'

He said to the servant, 'O, Aybak, fetch the balance: I will weigh the cat.'

He weighed her. The cat was half a mann. *Then the man said, 'O deceitful wife, the meat was half a* mann *and one* sitír *over; the cat is just half a* mann, *my lady, If this is the cat, then where is the meat? Or if this is the meat, where is the cat? Search for her.' "*

A Persian moral tale from the Mathnawi *of Rumi, 1207–73, translated by Reynold A. Nicholson (1868–1945).*

Greek Skewers G:23

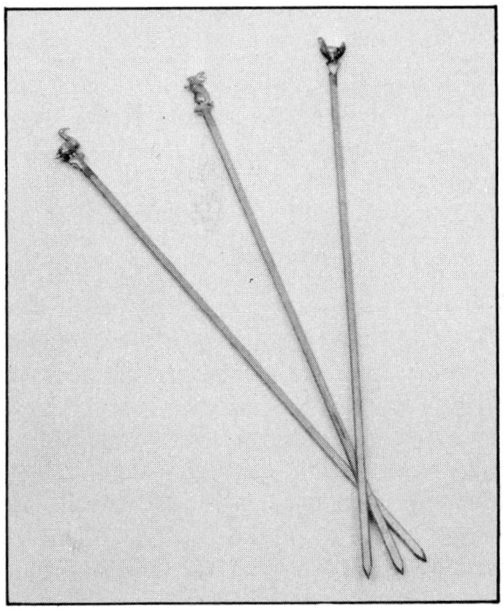

Greeks love grilled food, from lambs roasted whole at Easter, turned for hours on the *souvla* (spit), to tiny chunks of pork or fish quickly cooked by a street vendor. Because wood, and therefore charcoal, is scarce, owing to centuries of overgrazing by rapacious goats, people in the countryside grill over crushed olive pits. The crushed pits retain just enough oil to ignite and smoulder. It takes patience and time to light olive pit fires, but country people have plenty of both. Charcoal is easier, and just as effective for turning out *xifias souvlakia*—swordfish grilled with peppers and tomatoes—especially if you present this Macedonian treat on 12½″-long stainless-steel skewers, each topped with a different animal fashioned in brass. In addition to our tiny barnyard menagerie of chicken, hare and duck; goose, rooster and hen shapes are also available. The skewers are sold separately.

Greek Island Ltd. $1.25

Shish Kebab Broiler G:24

Both ingenious and efficient is this device for broiling *shish kebab* over the flame of a gas stove. At first glance, it looks like an aluminum tube pan plugged with a sink strainer. Look again, and you'll see that the interior rim is only ¾″ high, and a 4¼″-wide perforated disc perches over the center hole on a copper wire fitted to the interior rim. To use the *sha-weh,* pour a little water into the bottom of the pan to keep dripping fat from sputtering. Balance skewers of *shish kebab* across the 10″-wide pan, and light the flame. Heated air rising from the burner causes the perforated disc to spin like a pinwheel, deflecting heat evenly to the meat. To broil steak, simply place a grill over the *sha-weh.*

Oriental Pastry & Grocery Co. $3.90

SHISH KEBAB

5–6 cloves of garlic
Salt
6–8 scallions
Freshly ground black pepper
1 teaspoon ground cumin
1 teaspoon tarragon
2 lbs. lamb, cut into ¾″ cubes
¼ cup olive oil
1 green pepper, quartered
1 sweet red pepper, quartered
1 tomato, cut into 8 wedges
1 small zucchini, sliced into ¼″ to ½″ rounds

Mash the garlic and salt together into a smooth paste. Mince the scallions, very fine, and mix into the garlic paste, adding the other seasonings.

Mix thoroughly the meat, paste and olive oil in a large bowl, being sure that the meat is fully and evenly coated. Cover and refrigerate overnight.

As the meat and vegetables will be done at different times, place them on separate skewers. Alternate the peppers, tomato and zucchini slices on one set of skewers; on the lamb skewers, be sure to leave space between the cubes of meat so they will cook on all sides. Start the meat a few minutes before the vegetables. Place the skewers about 4 inches from the heat source (charcoal or gas flame) and turn every few minutes. With cubes this size, the meat will cook in less than ten minutes and should be done through when the outside is sizzling.

Serve on the skewers over rice.

(Courtesy of Garden of Delights Restaurant, New York City)

Turkish Sac G:25

Sac (pronounced sash) is the Turkish name for this slightly convex iron disc. It is used with the hollow side down over an open fire to bake a very thin, tortilla-like bread called *yufka.* Traditionally, two women work together to make *yufka.* One rolls out the dough into very thin, round pieces while the other puts it on the hot *sac* to bake. She leaves it draped over the disc until it bubbles and blisters, and then turns it over to bake the other side. In this manner they make 50 or 60 of these thin pieces of bread at a time. Once it is baked, the *yufka* is stored, then dampened and reheated when it is needed. *Yufka* is used to scoop food from the communal dish at meals and is eaten cold by people working in the fields or tending their flocks. Often it is used instead of *filo* (paper-thin dough) to wrap *börek,* savory little packages filled with cheese or seasoned meat and fried to a crisp in hot oil. This *sac* is 11″ in diameter and has a ring riveted near the rim by which it can be hung when it is not in use. Place it directly over a flame or electric burner.

K. Kalustyan $1.70

"A dish eaten all over North Africa, from the Red Sea to the Atlantic is Kuscoussoo; and it is prepared to-day as it was in the primitive centuries of long ago. It consists of wheaten flour, dusted on to drops of water and mixed lightly and quickly by the hands of a woman. The mass of moistened particles growing gradually larger, the art of the operator being to cause it to granulate, and to prevent it from clotting. Each grain is only the size of a pinhead, and when enough has been formed, it is put into a conical basket of palmetto leaves, which is placed over an earthen pot containing boiling water and cooked by the steam. The poor eat it alone, the wealthier class with meat."

Good Cheer: The Romance of Food and Feasting *by F. W. Hackwood. Sturgess & Walton, 1911.*

Couscousière G:26

A very special kind of steamer shaped somewhat like an hourglass is called a *couscousière.* It is used in North Africa to prepare a traditional grain dish called *couscous. Couscous* is cooked semolina pasta pellets usually topped with a meat and vegetable stew; it is served as a Sabbath lunch, or on special occasions. The word *couscous* can refer to the complete dish or to the grain alone. The *couscousière*'s two compartments cook both the *couscous* and its stew. When the stew in the pot below is almost done, the grain is put to steam in the upper basket. The lower part of the *couscousière* is called a *gdra.* The upper perforated colander, called a *kskas,* fits quite snugly into the bottom pot. The *kskas,* unlike baskets in other steamers, is perforated only on the bottom and sits high over the *gdra* so that the cooking liquid from the stew will not touch it. Because the *couscous* must cook in the vapors that rise from the stew, as little steam as possible should be allowed to escape before it can reach the grain. We recommend twisting a dampened and floured length of cheesecloth around the *couscousière* at the joint between the top and bottom pots to make a perfect steamtight seal. Though many *couscousières* come with lids, these should not be used when cooking *couscous.* In a closed pot the steam would only condense on the lid and drip back onto the grain, making it soggy and dense—a mortal offense in the eyes of any self-respecting aficionado, since the mark of a good *couscous* is its lightness, and much preparation time is spent fussing with the grains to keep them separate and fluffy. At one end of the North African scale are the simple, unglazed earthenware *couscousières* of the Berbers, while the prosperous merchants of Fez steam their meals in tin-lined copper ones. The *couscousière* we show here comes from France. It is aluminum, with loop-shaped, chrome-plated handles riveted to both the bottom and the top sections. It is 10½″ in diameter and stands 14″ high. The *gdra* of this *couscousière* holds 11 quarts, but since the stew should not touch the bottom of the *kskas,* its actual capacity is somewhat smaller. The *couscousière* comes with a lid which, as we mentioned, is unnecessary for making *couscous,* but it would come in handy if you use the *couscousière* for steaming rice, and perhaps a companion stew to go with it. We heartily encourage exploration of the contemporary potential of this traditional and highly specialized pot.

Charles F. Lamalle (59/2 D) **$40.00**

STEAMED LAMB

Baha

If you really love the taste of lamb you will love this dish. It's a pity that we Americans know so little about steaming meats; just as steamed vegetables keep their original flavors, so do steamed chickens and lamb.

If you don't have a steamer, use a *couscousière* or a colander with a tight-fitting lid that fits snugly over a kettle.

Some people think that steamed lamb looks unattractive (though no one denies that it is incredibly good). If you feel this way you may brown the meat quickly in butter or oil at the end, or roast it at high heat until it browns.

Steamed food should be eaten the moment it is ready, when it is at its peak: if left too long, it will dry out.

INGREDIENTS
5 to 5½ pounds shoulder and part of the rib section of young spring lamb
Pinch pulverized saffron
Sweet butter, softened
1½ teaspoons coarse salt
½ teaspoon freshly ground black pepper
1 bunch fresh parsley sprigs
4 to 5 whole baby onions (optional)
Vegetable oil (optional)

EQUIPMENT
Paring knife
Steamer, or *cousousière,* or colander over a kettle
Cheesecloth
Tight-fitting lid

Working time: 5 minutes
Steaming time: 2 hours
Serves: 8 (as part of a Moroccan dinner)

1. Trim the lamb of excess fat: the thin fell can be left on. Blend the saffron with ¼ cup butter, salt, and pepper. Rub into the lamb flesh.

2. Bring plenty of water to a boil in the bottom of a steamer, kettle, or *couscousière* (to borrow a trick from Diana Kennedy, author of *The Cuisines of Mexico,* toss in a penny—when the penny stops clicking you need more water). Dampen a piece of cheesecloth and twist into a strip the length of the circumference of the kettle's rim. Use this strip to fasten the perforated top so that it fits snugly on top. Check all sides for effective sealing: steam should rise only through the holes. Make a bed of parsley over the holes and rest the shoulder of lamb on it. Surround with the onions, if used, and cover with a double layer of cheesecloth and then, tightly, with a lid. *Do not lift the lid during the first 1¾ hours of steaming.* Be very careful, and stand back when lifting the lid. If the lamb is tender and falling off the bone it is ready; if not, continue steaming 15 to 30 minutes longer.

3. If desired, brown in oil and butter or rub again with butter and brown in a very hot oven (highest setting). Serve with bowls of ground cumin and salt, to be used as a dip.

(From COUSCOUS AND OTHER GOOD FOOD FROM MOROCCO, by Paula Wolfert. Copyright 1973 by Paula Wolfert. Reprinted by permission of Harper & Row)

Couscous Serving Dish G:27

This platter is no production-line item. It is an individual work from the Moroccan town of Safi, known for fine pottery. The craftsman who fashioned and then decorated the piece thought enough of it to sign his name on the underside. It is meant to hold the national dish, *couscous,* and measures 14½″ in diameter. The wide rim slopes to a shallow bowl, deep enough to hold the fluffy grains topped by a somewhat liquid *tajine* (stew), but flat enough to allow diners easy access to the food, eaten daintily with the right hand. Two holes pierce the pedestal foot so that a string can be inserted and the plate hung against a wall, out of harm's way when not in use. The

Continued from preceding page

underglaze is creamy white, and the platter is decorated in black and burnt orange in an adaptation of a traditional Moroccan design.

Morocco Designs, Inc. **$40.00**

Couscous Spoon G:28

From Morocco comes an orangewood spoon with the loving touch of a craftsman. It was carved from a single piece of wood and appears to be a copy in a humble material of an elegant silver spoon. The tearshaped bowl is carved so that the point rises above the handle, and it measures 10½″ overall. It was intended by its creator as a spoon to serve *couscous*.

The Store at Sugarbush Village/H. A. Mack and Co., Inc. (M6) **$1.50**

Syrian Cooking Pot G:29

This aluminum cooking pot from Syria has the domed lid so characteristic of Middle Eastern cookware. It is a fine pot for cooking rice in the Syrian manner: turn the washed grains in clarified butter until it becomes milky, then cook the rice in rich chicken broth. The pot's lid nestles securely into the flared rim, and steam condensing on its sloping surface runs easily back down into the pot. Without its lid, it stands 5½″ high. The straight-sided pot is 7″ in diameter, and holds 3 quarts.

Oriental Pastry & Grocery Co. **$7.90**

"Kazem soon produced a saucepan—our only tureen—half full of nearly boiling soup. Chicken and rice came next, and Kazem to my surprise, declared that he had cutlets of mutton 'quite ready', and an omelet 'to follow'. He had accomplished all this, including potatoes, with nothing but three big stones for his fireplace."

Through Persia by Caravan *by Arthur Arnold. Harper & Row, 1877.*

Syrian Copper Frying Pan G:30

Rough but tough is this frying pan from Syria, made of hammered copper lined with tin. The pan is 8″ in diameter and 2″ deep. The long handle is fashioned from two pieces of heavy iron and is securely riveted to the body. The handle's length—it is 9¼″ long—makes this an ideal pan to use over an open fire; you will cook only the food, not your hand as well—which is sometimes the problem with short-handled pans. For picnic fare or a camping breakfast, try *chakchouka*—a peasant omelet of eggs, tomatoes, green pepper and onions.

Continental Crafts Co. (S111) **$14.00**

Greek Skillet with Embossed Fish G:31

A tin-lined copper skillet embossed with fish and hammered flowers is so pretty most of us would be content to hang it on the wall by its brass handle and leave it there so that everyone could admire it. That is mainly what happens in modern Greek homes, but this was not always the case. Until very recently, few people in Greece or other countries of the Middle East had ovens in their homes. They used communal bread ovens for long, slow-baking dishes and made all sorts of pancakes, cakes and other quickly-cooked confections in pans on top of the fire. One of our experts tells us that when "baking" this way, the side of the cake or confection that is nearest the fire turns a lovely reddish brown color and the cake is flipped over so that this side is upright when served. Cakes or pancakes made in this 8¼″-wide skillet would bear the imprint of fish and flowers on their tops, and would most likely be bathed in honey syrup before serving.

Pampered Kitchens **$37.50**

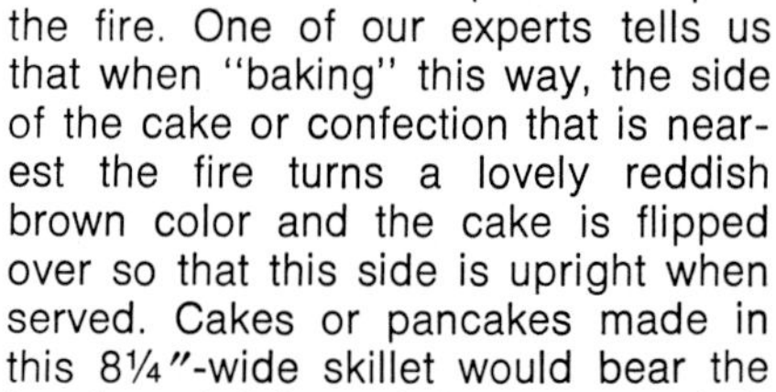

Fifth-century B.C. Iranian rhyton (from The Metropolitan Museum of Art).

Syrian Copper Pan G:32

This tin-lined, hammered-copper pan with two large, brass loop handles riveted to its sides is handsome enough and large enough (it has a 4-quart capacity) to go from stove to table when company comes to call. In Syria, where it was made, pans like this one are used to prepare and serve *labou immos,* lamb braised with yoghurt and mint. In Syria, the shallow (2½″-deep) straight-sided pan comes with its own lid; here it is sold without one, but finding a lid to fit should not be difficult.

Continental Crafts Co. (S104) $25.00

Eggah Dish G:33

This handsome, 10″-wide, tin-lined copper pan with seven round depressions is a highly specialized piece of equipment designed expressly for making and serving a Middle Eastern dish called *eggah* (pronounced "edge-uh"). Known as *coucou* in Iran, where it plays an important role in the cuisine, the dish consists of various vegetable and meat mixtures, bound together by eggs. It is either baked in a covered pan or allowed to set over a low flame. The result is more cake or thick pancake than omelet. It can be served warm or at room temperature, and is ideal picnic fare. While *eggah* is usually made in a flat-bottomed pan, then cut into wedges like a pie, Syrian cooks often prefer to make individual servings. One cook we know uses a cupcake tin, which is adequate but hardly decorative. This pan is the ideal compromise. The pan has loop handles of brass riveted to the outside just below the rim.

Continental Crafts Co. (S107) $14.00

ZUCCHINI EGGAH

½ pound zucchini
6 eggs
1 teaspoon salt
½ teaspoon black pepper
¼ cup chopped scallions
1 teaspoon oregano
3 teaspoons dried mint leaves
Olive oil

Wash and shred the zucchini. In a separate bowl beat together the eggs, salt, pepper, scallions, oregano and mint. Add the zucchini. Place a teaspoonful of the olive oil into each compartment of the *eggah* dish and heat over a medium flame. Drop a tablespoonful of the egg mixture into each compartment. When browned on the bottom, turn with a spoon and brown on the other side. When done, drain on paper towels. Serve with a salad or rice.

Greek Earthenware Beanpot G:34

"When Greeks are abroad, they get together, eat *fassolia,* think of home, and cry. We have a gorgeous time." *Fassolia* are beans, and the speaker is our friend Drossoula. She is Athenian, and an excellent cook. And we know she would proudly serve beans in pots like this one: humble earthenware serenely translated into the sure and spare de-

Continued from preceding page

sign that is the Greek potters' heritage. The pot, just 5″ high, bellies up gracefully to the arched handles, bearing the swift indentation of the potter's thumb. It holds about 4½ cups. The dark brown glaze is incised with a zigzag design around the widest part, and the snug-fitting lid is slightly domed. Remember that earthenware can easily crack if temperature changes are too abrupt; don't move it from refrigerator to hot oven. Also, never store acidic foods—those containing tomatoes or lemon—in earthenware containers: the traces of lead in the glaze, however faint, must be respected. But if earthenware is used just for cooking, there's no need for concern. Greek pottery—and Greeks—have been around for millennia!

Greek Island Ltd. $7.50

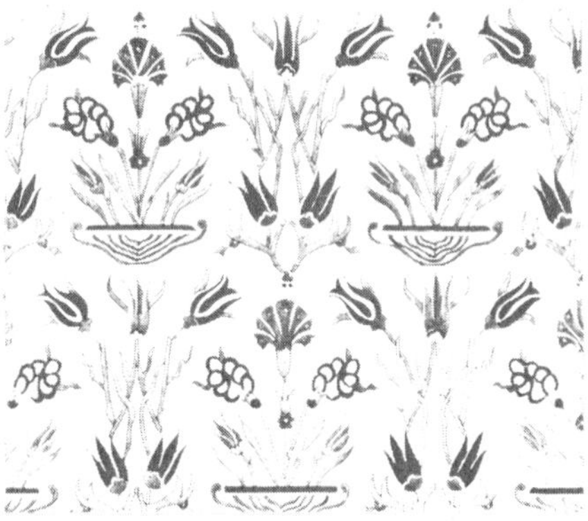

17th-century Turkish wall painting.

19th-century Turkish wall decoration.

Tajines

In Morocco, Tunisia and Algeria a *tajine* is a savory stew of fish, meat or poultry. The variety is endless—a *tajine* can be a subtle red snapper ragout, an assertive mélange of mutton and quince, or a perfumed blend of chicken with preserved lemons.

A *tajine* is slowly simmered in a *tajine slaoui*, a round, shallow, flat-bottomed earthenware dish with a high conical lid. (*Slaoui* is a form of the word Salé, the Moroccan city in which the domed pot supposedly originated.) The lid fits snugly into a lip in the dish so that steam and flavor cannot escape during cooking.

When the *tajine* is set before diners, the cover is removed with a dramatic flourish. Everyone dips into the pot, using only the first three fingers of the right hand.

Tajine Slaoui G:35

Tajine is most often translated as "stew," but that homely word is a masterpiece of understatement for the imaginative combinations of ingredients that go into this North African slow-cooked meat-and-vegetable mélange. This covered stoneware casserole is a *tajine slaoui,* in which the *tajine* traditionally is both cooked and served. Its lower section is a round, shallow baking pan, 11″ in diameter and 1¾″ deep, with a black glaze on the interior and the ½″-thick rim that caps the sloping sides. The exterior of its flat bottom is left unglazed. The most notable feature of the *tajine slaoui* is its outsized—almost 6″-high—conical lid that widens out at the top to form a handy knob. The lid is glazed a deep black on the inside, and sits well down in the lower section to retain heat. On the lid's outside, the glaze is an earthy meld of greens, browns and beige. The baking pan will hold 4 cups, but effectively quite a bit more if its contents are piled high under the conical lid. In Morocco the *tajine slaoui* (or any other pot for that matter) is usually placed directly over the charcoal in a brazier. (For baking, if surround heat is needed, a layer of charcoal is placed over and around the pot.) Native *tajines* are usually made of fragile earthenware; however our domestic *tajine*—made in this country by young American potter, Todd Piker—is a sturdy, functional stoneware. Use it over a low flame on an asbestos pad, or in a moderate oven.

Cornwall Bridge Pottery $30.00

LAMB TAGINE WITH FRIED EGGPLANT

Brania

I adore this dish, especially the tiny nuggets that are the peeled stems of small eggplants, and that taste like mushrooms when they are cooked in a *tagine.* Note that this dish is for people who don't mind fried foods.

INGREDIENTS

For the lamb and sauce:

3 pounds rib or shoulder of lamb, cut into 1½-inch chunks
½ cup chopped parsley
5 cloves garlic, peeled and chopped
1¼ cups grated onion
¼ cup salad oil, or less
1 rounded teaspoon paprika
¼ teaspoon ground cumin
¼ teaspoon freshly ground black pepper
Pinch of pulverized saffron
Salt to taste
2 to 3 tablespoons lemon juice

For the eggplant garnish:
4 pounds small eggplants
Salt
Vegetable oil for frying
4 cloves garlic, peeled and chopped
2 teaspoons sweet paprika
¼ teaspoon ground cumin
⅓ cup lemon juice

EQUIPMENT
Paring knife
5½-quart casserole with cover
Colander
Paper towels
Skillet
Spatula
Potato masher
Large serving dish

Working time: 1 hour
Cooking time: 2½ hours
Serves: 6

1. Trim the lamb of excess fat. Place in the casserole with all the ingredients for the sauce except the lemon juice. Cover with 4 cups water and bring to a boil. Reduce the heat and simmer, covered, 1½ to 2 hours, or until the meat is very tender—that is, falling off the bones—and the sauce has reduced to a thick gravy. Add water, if necessary, during the cooking time. Add the lemon juice and taste for seasoning.

2. Meanwhile, cut off the stems of the small eggplants. Peel the stems and throw these little "nuggets" into the casserole as soon as possible, to cook with the meat. Peel the eggplants in alternating strips lengthwise. Cut into ¼-inch-thick slices, sprinkle heavily with salt, and let drain in a colander 30 minutes to draw off bitterness. Rinse the slices well and pat dry with paper towels.

3. Heat the oil in the skillet and fry the eggplant slices in batches until they are well browned and crisp on both sides. Drain, reserving the oil.

4. Mash the fried eggplant with the garlic, spices, and salt to taste. Reheat the reserved oil and fry the mashed eggplant until crisp and "firm" (about 20 minutes), turning the puree over and over in the oil so that all the water evaporates, and only the oil is left to fry the eggplant, which will become very thick and rich in texture. Drain again and fold in the lemon juice.

5. Arrange the lamb and sauce in the serving dish. Spread the eggplant over the meat and serve hot or warm.

(From COUSCOUS AND OTHER GOOD FOOD FROM MOROCCO, by Paula Wolfert. Copyright 1973 by Paula Wolfert. Reprinted by permission of Harper & Row)

Decorated Tajine G:36

This spectacular *tajine* is a serving piece only: its fragile network of glazed design should not be exposed to direct heat. It is a one-of-a-kind work from the Moroccan town of Safi, known for its fine pottery. The artisan who made it and decorated it proudly signed his name on the underside of the bowl. The low bowl—2½″ deep, 7½″ in diameter—has a stepped lid inside its broad rim for the conical lid to rest on. Three bands of exuberant geometric designs circle the lid: cross-hatched black lines on creamy white. Topping the lid is a small circular knob that serves as a handle. Moroccans would prepare *el labm el m'gali*—a *tajine* of lamb with olives and lemons—in a plain and sturdy *tajine slaoui*, then transfer it to this showpiece for presentation.

Bloomingdale's $36.00

"Si Kassem never had to call twice . . . She ran with her skirt in great folds. . . . Each time she brought a new offering: a straw pagoda, tented with velvet and braided with gold, sheltering round loaves of pure wheat flavored with aniseed; covered dishes of red clay with a conical lid pierced by a smoking chimney, or perhaps some ewers. . . . Ceaselessly Azil fetched and carried the red bowls. . . . new peas in a pot decorated with orange trees, . . . small turnips, marrows and carrots appeared under swelling yellow enamel, with whole eggs broken over the dish a quarter of an hour before serving. . . ."

"Morocco" in Places *by Colette. Bobbs-Merrill, 1971.*

Apricotwood Rolling Pin G:37

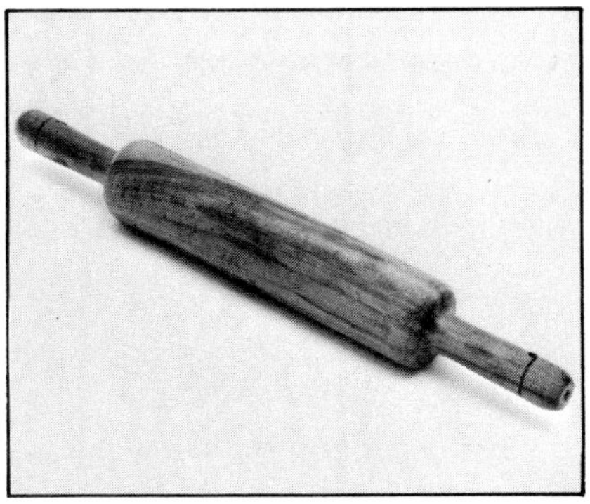

This short rolling pin, turned out of a single block of apricotwood, is used in Syria to make such meat pies as *sfeeha* (spiced ground lamb in yeast dough). *Sfeeha* is served alone or as one of the dishes of the *mazza* (appetizer course). The rolling pin is 2″ in diameter and 15¼″ long; the rolling surface is 9″ long. A hole in the end of one handle allows the pin to be hung up when not in use.

Oriental Pastry & Grocery Co. $2.90

Baking Tray G:38

If you are serious about Middle Eastern cooking, this sturdy baking tray could qualify as a necessity. It is made of aluminum, distributes heat evenly and is about 14″ in diameter. The size is important if you are working with recipes, designed for this type of baking pan. It is about 2″ high, flares slightly,

Continued from preceding page

and has a rolled rim. The pan is perfect for both sweet and savory concoctions, such as baked *kibbi* (a lamb and *bulgur* wheat dish), the Greek (or, if you prefer, Turkish) dessert called *baklava,* or a Syrian *halawa* cake, flavored with cinnamon and almonds.

Oriental Pastry & Grocery Co. **$3.25**

Lebanese Tube Pan G:39

A Lebanese tube pan for making sponge cakes? Yes indeed, and a good one at that. It is made of aluminum and is 9″ in diameter, 2″ deep and has a 3″-diameter hole in the center. The bottom is flat, the sides slightly flared and the rims safely rolled. In Lebanon, as in all countries of the Middle East, hospitality is a duty, an honor and a pleasure, and is almost always interpreted as plying your guests with food—sweet food in particular. Cakes, cookies, sweetmeats, fruit, nuts and coffee, the greater the variety brought forth, the better. Among the cakes are ones like our sponge cakes, some of which are made with apricot-flavored nectar, with oranges or nuts, and served un-iced and doused in syrup.

Kalamata Food Imports, Inc. **$2.95**

MA'AMOUL

Nut-Filled Cookies

FILLING
1 cup ground walnuts
1 tablespoon sugar
1 teaspoon cinnamon
1 egg white, stiffly beaten

DOUGH
¼ cup milk
¾ cup sugar
¾ cup melted butter, cooled
1 egg, well beaten
3½ to 3¾ cups sifted all-purpose flour (approximately)
¼ teaspoon baking soda

Confectioners' sugar

Combine all the ingredients for the filling in a small bowl and mix well. Set aside.

Prepare the dough by combining the milk and sugar in a small sauce pan. Cook over low heat until sugar is completely dissolved, stirring frequently. Remove from the heat and cool. Place the melted butter and egg in a large bowl and blend together. Add the milk mixture and mix well. Gradually blend in the flour and soda to make a soft dough.

Prepare each cookie as follows: Take a small portion of dough and form into a ball about 1 inch in diameter. Indent with your forefinger, pressing gently to make a hollow. Place about 1 teaspoon of the filling in the hollow, bring the edges together, and seal. Gently flatten the ball with the palms of your hands or form into small egg shape. Place on a baking sheet. Bake the cookies in a preheated 325° oven about 20 minutes or until very lightly browned. Remove from the oven and cool slightly on racks. Sift the confectioners' sugar generously over the tops and cool.

Makes about 4 dozen

(From THE CUISINE OF ARMENIA, by Sonia Uvezian. Copyright 1974 by Sonia Uvezian. Reprinted by permission of Harper & Row)

Apricotwood Tartlet Molds G:40

These spoon-shaped devices made of orange-brown apricotwood are molds for forming the date- or nut-filled tartlets called *ma'amoul,* baked in Syria and elsewhere in the Middle East to celebrate special occasions. A simple design of concentric circles and ridges is carved into the bowl of each mold to leave its mark on what will become the tops of the filled pastries. One of the two molds shown here will shape a tartlet with a somewhat conical top, 2⅜″ in diameter and about 1¼″ thick; the other forms a flatter and slightly broader pastry 2⅝″ in diameter and ½″ thick. The molds are sold separately and are also available in many other patterns. Including their handles, they are, respectively, 9″ and 8⅛″ long. The pastry shell for these filled tartlets is made from an orange-flower- or rose-water-flavored dough; the fillings are sweetened chopped date or nut mixtures. The pattern identifies the filling: one cook we know uses the mold on the left for a pistachio mixture, the one at right for chopped walnuts. After preparing the dough, dust the mold with flour and place a walnut-sized piece of dough in it. Press the dough into the mold with your fingers so that it covers the design and forms a hollow shell ¼″ thick. Spoon some of the filling—the amount will depend on the depth of the mold—into the shell and distribute it evenly, filling the mold to within ¼″ of the top. Cover the whole with another flattened piece of dough, joining it to the edges of the shell. Invert the mold over a baking sheet and tap it to release the tartlet; then bake. When cold, sprinkle with confectioners' sugar. How you eat these confections depends on your fancy. As for us, at first we'll refuse them so as to display our good manners. Then, if we are urged enough, we may try one, and then maybe another, and then. . . .

Sahadi Importing Co., Inc./Continental Crafts Co. (S121) **$2.50**

Moroccan Teapot G:41

Tea was brought to Morocco from the Far East in the 1880s by British traders, and that perhaps explains the shape of this teapot. It is the so-called "Manchester" shape with arching spout, pear-shaped body and high-domed lid hinged to the rim of the pot. The top knob is cleverly insulated by a ring of plastic (traditionally bone). A large, loop-shaped handle is attached to the back of the pot and has two decorative discs of insulating plastic. We are told that teapots of this shape are available in different metals in Morocco; the one we show is made of nickel. Moroccan tea is made from green tea (preferrably the type known as Gunpowder) and is excessively sweet and flavored with fresh spearmint or, in season, with fresh orange blossoms. It is poured out of the pot from great heights into small, ornamental glasses held between thumb and forefinger. Tea is drunk before meals, after meals, and whenever a visitor knocks at the door.

Morocco Designs, Inc. **$15.00**

Date Trees

Sugar Axe G:42

Until recently, granulated and cubed sugar were rarely seen in the Middle East. In the old days, to break loaves of sugar up into smaller pieces for use, cooks placed them on a board under a cloth and smashed them with a sugar axe, or whatever else was handy. This ornate, iron-bladed, brass sugar axe from Iran is heavy and sharp enough to smash even the hardest sugar loaf. The tiny pieces are then held between the teeth and used to sweeten tea as it is sipped from the glass. Its 4½″-broad blade is set into an intricately molded, 10″-long brass handle decorated with stylized birds and hammered designs set with colored stones. It is handsome enough to appear at any table as a super-star conversation piece.

Pampered Kitchens **$85.00**

Tea Glass and Saucer G:43

Turkey may be a land of zealous coffee drinkers, but tea is given great respect as well. Like coffee, it is a social lubricant. Without one beverage or the other no business is conducted, no visit complete. Tea is usually heavily sugared to suit the Turkish sweet tooth. Like the Russians, Turks use the samovar and drink their tea from glasses. This tea glass is globular at the bottom, nipped in at the waist, and flared at the rim. It is hand-decorated with gold birds, leaves and curling tendrils. Its saucer is deep, with a rosette pressed into the center. To drink tea as the Turks do without burning the fingers, hold the glass on the rim, between thumb and forefinger.

Karnig Tashjian **$3.00**

"I view the tea-drinking as a destroyer of health, an enfeebler of the frame, an engenderer of effeminacy and laziness, a debaucher of youth and a maker of misery for old age."

The Vice of Tea-Drinking *by William Cobbett (1762–1835).*

Coffee

The preparation and service of coffee is surrounded by tradition and ceremony in the lands of the Eastern Mediterranean. Middle Easterners, many of whom are forbidden alcoholic beverages by their religion, endow coffee with the same potent properties Westerners attribute to wine or cocktails.

In the Middle East it is coffee, not the martini, that eases social interchange. Coffee is served on all special occasions and whenever a distinguished visitor comes to call. Business transactions and bargaining cannot—absolutely cannot—proceed without the accompaniment of numerous tiny cups of coffee. Serious conversation does not begin until coffee has been served. Men in Greece, Egypt, Syria and other countries of the Middle East spend hours in cafés sipping cup after cup while they talk, argue, tell stories and play backgammon.

The brew usually begins with freshly roasted and freshly ground coffee beans. Mocha beans from Yemen are preferred, but other varieties are also used. The Bedouin pulverize their coffee in a mortar with a metal pestle; elsewhere, a grinder is used.

There are basically two ways of brewing coffee in the Middle East: Turkish and Arabic. Turkish coffee is made by stirring together water, coffee ground to a powder, and sugar to the drinker's taste. The coffee is prepared in a *jezve*, a small pot with a long handle, and served in small cups whose shapes vary from country to country. When the mixture begins to boil, it is whisked off the fire for a second or two and then returned briefly once or twice more to build up a foamy head which is first poured into each cup in equal amounts, to be followed by the rest of the contents of the pot. The dregs soon settle to the bottom of the cup, and the thick, rich coffee is ready to be drunk. Only a few demitasse cups of coffee are made at a time so that each drinker will have a maximum amount of foam; a fresh pot is brewed for second helpings.

Arabic coffee—made with powder-fine grounds, sugar and water—is brought to a boil only once. In some households it is poured into a second pot for serving, leaving the sediment behind in the first pot. In the second pot, the coffee is spiced with cardamom seeds or cloves. Occasionally spices are added while the coffee is still on the fire, and it is then served directly from the pot in which it was made.

Coffee Roaster G:44

Some clever fellow in Syria improvised this coffee roaster from sheet metal, a few strips of iron, a little iron wire and a piece of wood. We love it because it is ingenious, simple and straightforward, and it does what it is supposed to do: roast green coffee beans. A rod runs through the roaster, one end attached to the wooden handle and the other extending out the far side. The iron ring that suspends the roaster has two built-up notched supports to hold the cannister. The wooden handle rotates the contraption so that the beans roast evenly without scorching. To use, first slide open the little door cut in the side of the canister, fill halfway with green coffee beans, then slide the door closed. Set the ring over a fire (no reason not to try it over a gas burner as well) and crank the handle. There is a caution, however: jagged edges can cut, and the wobbly construction makes it easy to burn oneself.

Oriental Pastry & Grocery Co. **$4.90**

"After the meal Turkish coffee was served. Young Mala held a narrow, high brass container with a long protruding handle they called a jezbeh *over the flames of the fire. As the water boiled she added sugar, and after letting it boil a little longer, she put in high-heaped spoonfuls of powder-fine coffee. She let this mixture boil up three or four times in rapid succession, taking away the container from the flames just before its contents would spill over. It was a powerful brew. . . ."*

The Gypsies *by Jan Yoors. London, George Allen and Unwin Ltd., 1967.*

Turkish coffee-seller at Constantinople.

Coffee plant and beans.

Turkish Coffee Grinder G:45

It looks like a particularly treasured peppermill, and it operates on the same principle. Its elegance can be explained by the fact that it is made to grind coffee, the Middle Eastern beverage served to distinguished visitors and on special occasions. This 7½″-tall brass mill has incised abstract decoration (Muslim law forbids representations of living things) and is made up of four different parts. To grind coffee, remove the handle and little domed lid, put the beans in the upper section, and replace the dome and handle. As you grind, powdery fine coffee drops into the bottom section. A screw at the base of the upper section can be turned to control the fineness of the grind.

Paprikás Weiss (621) $39.95

Turkish Coffee Pot G:46

The English word "coffee" is derived from the Turkish *kahve,* which seems appropriate enough since it was the Ottomans who first introduced this beverage to Europe in the 16th century. Abetted by historical vicissitudes, both the Turkish pot for making *kahve* and its name, *jezve,* have spread well beyond the boundaries of Turkey to the lands encircling the Mediterranean and nearby waters. It is also called *imbrik* in Turkish, *briki* in Greek, and *brico* in Italy (where the little vessel is never employed for making coffee). This *jezve* of tin-lined brass, which holds two demitasse cups, was made in Lebanon; but its twin could come from almost anywhere in the region. The bottom of the pot is 2¾″ in diameter, and perfectly flat. The sides slope inward to form a narrow neck that flares out into a collar with a tiny pouring spout. The pot's 5⅝″-long brass handle is riveted to one side and extends up at an angle; at the handle's end is a hole for hanging. To make the thick, sweet and foaming brew, powder-fine grounds are heated in the pot with water and a generous helping of sugar. The coffee is brought to a foaming boil—intensified by the pot's narrow neck—three times, and then served in demitasse cups with the prized foam on top. The grounds settle to the bottom if the coffee is well made, and are never consumed. The cups may be inverted to let the grounds run down into the saucer, where they form a pattern that foretells the future. One adept at "coffee-fortune telling" is eagerly welcomed into any group, sophisticated cityites or simple country folk alike. This *jezve* is also available in 3-, 5- and 6-demitasse-cup sizes.

H. Roth & Son (45-8) $8.95

Egyptian Coffee Pot G:47

This plump and pleasing little pot is an Egyptian *tanaka. Tanakas* come in a number of sizes: this one will yield two demitasse cups of rich "Turkish" coffee. It also insures a goodly dollop of the froth—called *wesh*—to each portion. The tin-lined brass *tanaka* rests on a broad, 3½″ base. The body narrows above the bulbous lower portion, helping to prevent bubbling-up spillovers. (The coffee must boil and rise three times.) A tiny pouring spout is pinched into the rim. The brass handle is 5½″ long, riveted to the pot, and pierced for hanging. Egyptians, like other Middle Easterners, take this kind of coffee in varying degrees of sweetness according to individual

Continued from preceding page

choice. Exceptions are happy occasions like weddings when extra sugar is added, or sorrowful ones like funerals, when mourners drink their coffee bitter.

Karnig Tashjian $6.25

Greek Copper Coffee Pot G:48

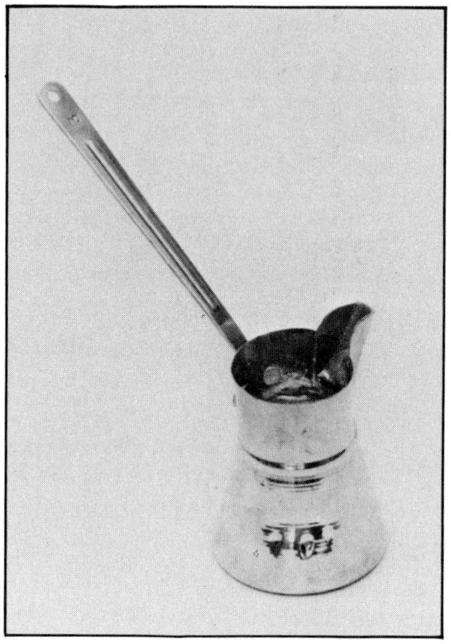

Kafe turkiki in Greece means Turkish coffee. As we have noted, all along the Eastern Mediterranean and in the Near East, the preparation, the time, place and the way coffee is served is very ritualized. In Greek homes, guests are served an incredibly sweet and sticky *gliki* (sweet) on a dessert plate accompanied by a glass of ice water. *Kafe* either accompanies or immediately follows the sweet. At busy, fashionable coffee houses in Athens, people sit for hours talking over a demitasse of coffee and a glass of ice water. Ice water always accompanies *kafe*. To help the grounds settle, many Greeks dip three fingers into the water and flick the water rapidly into the *kafe* —it works almost every time. Traditional *kafeneia* (coffee houses) are male domains—places where men meet to talk, argue, play cards or a version of backgammon called *tavli* and, of course, to drink coffee. The Greeks call their coffee pots *briki*. This *briki* is made of copper lined with tin. Its perfectly plain, 5½″-long brass handle is riveted to the pot with aluminum rivets. The wide rim that rises from the pot's narrow neck is molded into a wide, rather flat spout for ease in pouring the dark brown coffee with its precious froth into tiny cups.

Panellinion Gifts $7.50

Greek Coffee Pot with Braided Handle G:49

This pretty *briki*, only 3″ high, is made of hammered copper lined with tin, and has a handle of twisted brass strands that form a loop on the end for hanging. By its 5½″-long handle, remove the *briki* from the heat as soon as the coffee boils up. But, if you want a lot of froth (which Greeks consider the best part of the coffee), replace it on the burner to repeat the process once or twice more before pouring the coffee from the *briki's* tiny lip into two demitasse cups.

Greek Island Ltd. $8.50

There are always extremists: "I am fully convinced that coffee is the chief cause of the blood-poverty prevailing among the female sex. What will it lead to, if the evil is not checked in time? Many young mothers told me in tears how infirm and miserable they were and how, in consequence of their inability to perform their domestic duties, they were forsaken or despised by their husbands. Although too much coffee-drinking was not always the cause of the misery, yet it was so very often, and in all cases the distress was invariably connected with an extravagant and irrational way of clothing."

Thus Shalt Thou Live *by Sebastian Kneipp, 1897.*

Bedouin Coffee Pot G:50

To the Arab, coffee is the prime mover of wit, the fuel of philosophy. And Bedouin coffee is a heady, aromatic brew that actually tastes as good as it smells. Nomads, of necessity, have few material possessions; but pride of place is given to coffee-making equipment. The preparation, serving and drinking of coffee is a serious business. Green coffee beans are roasted to a velvety chocolate brown, cooled in a special container, then pulverized in a mortar. Coffee and water are boiled briefly; the grounds are allowed to settle, and the finished brew—sometimes spiced with cardamom—is poured into a gleaming serving pot, like the one shown here. The handmade brass pot is lined with tin, and has an insulating handle-cover of woven simulated-leather strips. Rows of stamped designs encircle the body and lid. The pot is 10″ high and holds five cups. The 5″-long spout has a cover that can be lifted by a little knob to give the server more control in pouring.

Continental Crafts Co. (S138) **$25.00**

Coffee Service G:51

An ornate Lebanese coffee service bears witness to the respected role coffee plays in the social life of the Middle East. The 7″-high brass pot is a server; the coffee would be made in another and, doubtless, plainer pot. On the tip of the beaked spout a tiny fish does a backflip, and a small bird perches atop the hinged, domed lid. The round, hollow handle is riveted to the side, at right angles to the spout. The 2″-high, slightly flared brass cup holders are incised with a dotted zig-zag design, and rest on a small, round pedestal. The six cups, which fit in the holders, were made in China expressly for export to the Middle East. They are 12-sided, with rounded bottoms and a flared rim decorated with a gold band. Little blue and orange flowers are strewn on the sides of the china cups. The tray on which the set is to be carried is made of brass and is 11½″ in diameter with a raised, flared rim. The center of the tray is incised with a round, many-petalled flower enclosed by several bands of leaves and flowers. Traditionally, the service is placed on a pedestal table.

Tripoli Restaurant **$25.00**

TURKISH COFFEE

Serves 4

Turkish coffee is a process, a ritual, a ceremony . . . Roasting, grinding, brewing, and serving are all equally important steps. If you must use pre-ground coffee (and sacrifice 50% of the flavor), do so, but know that you are not making "real" Turkish coffee.

4 tablespoons coffee, freshly ground
1 cup water
2 tablespoons sugar
Pinch of cardamom

Stir together all of the ingredients in the *jezve.* Place over medium heat to boil. As it begins to boil, a brown, crusty foam will begin to form and rise up the sides of the pot. Just before it boils over, remove from the flame and let settle. Repeat this process twice more, until the foam stands up well when taken off the heat. Pour immediately into four demitasse cups. Be sure that each cup gets its fair share of foam (coffee without foam in a Turkish household is an insult to the guest). Let the grounds settle for a moment before drinking. When the coffee has been drunk, a thick paste of grounds will remain. This should be poured out into the saucer and read like tea leaves.

Greek Cup and Saucer G:52

Well-designed, stark-white cups and saucers like these are standard *kafeneon* (coffee house) equipment throughout Greece and her islands. In the cities, white-jacketed waiters scurry from the coffee house at the foot of each office building, delivering fresh coffee to the workers above throughout business hours. Coffee is a serious and individual business, and the idea of a communal office pot would astonish and offend a Greek. Though the cups may be alike, the brew that fills them certainly is not. Everyone knows *exactly* how he likes his coffee, and righteously blisters the ear of a waiter who passes the wrong cup. *Metrios vrastos*—medium sweet and strong—vies with *glykos vrastos*—unbelievably sweet and strong—as the most popular choices; but there are infinite and exquisite variations between these two. *Sketos*—no sugar—is taken by eccentrics and sufferers from stomachache. Chip-resistant and sturdy, this ceramic demitasse cup is 2″ high and has a solid, pinched, ear-shaped handle. The saucer is about 4″ in diameter.

Greek Island Ltd. **$2.25**

Greek Wine Liter G:53

Retsina, like many other wines, costs less if you buy more. And those who've acquired a taste for the white *retsina* or pink *kokinelli*—with the faintest undertaste of turpentine—usually want to buy more. Greek wine is traditionally sold not by the liter but by the kilo, in large, straw-covered bottles called *dramagianni,* a name possibly derived from the English demijohn. *Dramagianni* are awkward to heft at table, so the wine is usually decanted into carafes. This molded glass wine liter is typical of modest Greek establishments. It has a pleasing shape, is easy to handle, and is only 12″ high. It is also available in ¼-liter and ½-liter sizes.

Greek Island Ltd. **$4.50**

African Cooking Equipment

Here we show you several pieces of equipment from different parts of Africa for preparing, washing, storing, carrying and serving food. Many of these objects are ingeniously devised out of natural materials to do a particular job, and they have a simple, straightforward honesty about them that speaks of the way of life of the people who made them. Some go beyond this to achieve a special kind of beauty. All of them are still used in Africa, and are available in this country.

What is not available are specialized cooking utensils from Africa; perhaps because the Africans themselves are using more and more imported pots, pans, knives, spoons and other equipment. Inexpensive pots and enameled dishes from China, Poland and Japan are readily available in markets in all but the most inaccessible places on the African continent and can be found in the cooking huts of even the smallest villages. More expensive equipment from Western Europe and the United States is available in the major cities.

Possibly, too, the demand for authentic African cooking utensils is not yet such as to make their importation economically feasible. With increased American travel in Africa, however, and the interest in our African heritage stirred by Alex Haley's *Roots*, we predict that one day we will be able to find among the gourmet cookware in this country West African grinding stones, wooden paddles for mixing and shaping *foofoo* (cassava or yam paste from West Africa), and covered clay griddles for making Ethiopian *injera* bread.

Zaire Mortar and Pestle G:54

When we think of African mortars and pestles, we usually think of the large ones carved out of tree trunks that are used for a variety of food processing chores. Perhaps slightly better suited to the average American kitchen is this small, goblet-shaped mortar and pestle from Zaire, both pieces made of oak and stained a dark brown. The mortar sits on a round pedestal and is 8″ tall and about 3¼″ in diameter. Its cone-shaped interior is 4″ deep, and its rounded bottom is smooth, but not finely finished. The 8″-long pestle is a tapered cylinder with rounded ends. You'll want to use this mortar for crushing and grinding dried red peppers and black pepper with herbs and spices to make pungent African stews.

Pampered Kitchens $20.00

The West African staple dish, yam paste (foofoo) *was observed to be made as follows: "Yams are boiled . . . on a fire, and peeled either before or after boiling. They are then pounded in a large wooden mortar. As they are pounded they become stiffer and tougher . . . When they have been pounded to the desired degree of stiffness, they are moulded into a large doughy loaf . . . Yam loaf and other vegetable loaves are always eaten with one of the stews and anyone who eats a vegetable loaf alone or with any food other than stew may be ridiculed, saying 'He is eating yam without sauce.' Yam loaf is one of the most important foods in life; it is served on an imported china plate or in a covered black dish of local manufacture. . . ."*

"Yoruba Cooking" by William R. Bascom in Journal of the International African Institute. *Oxford University Press, 1951.*

Ethiopian Chopping Bowl G:55

To prepare an Ethiopian *yataklete kilkil,* you will need to cut carrots, string beans, onions, green pepper, hot chiles, garlic and ginger. What better way than in this clever wooden cutting bowl from Ethiopia? It is a rather ordinary, flat-bottomed, dark brown bowl with slightly flared sides, except for one thing: a curved ridge runs across the center of the bowl. Like the sides of the bowl, it is 2¾″ high, but it is a good 1½″ thicker. This wooden ridge is a cutting surface. Put the vegetables to be chopped on the ridge, and as you cut, the pieces will collect neatly in the bowl. The outside of this practical contrivance is carved with an attractive design of lines and triangles.

Pampered Kitchens $50.00

African earthenware.

Upper Volta Basket Sieve G:56

The people of West Africa might use a basket like this one to wash and drain sorrel and carrot tops for leaf soup, or to purée well-cooked yams for yam soup. The basket's deep bowl is 10″ in diameter and 6″ deep, and is made of grass stalks woven in a graceful spiral pattern and lashed to a thin wooden rim.

Craft Caravan, Inc. **$5.00**

YAM SOUP

A deliciously thick and yellow soup.

2 tablespoons peanut or other vegetable oil
1 large onion or a bunch of small green onions
3 small hot chili peppers or ¼ to ½ teaspoon red pepper, to taste
2 medium tomatoes, peeled
1 pound yams or sweet potatoes
2½ cups beef stock
1 teaspoon salt, or to taste
Chopped parsley

Heat the oil in a pan. Peel and chop the onion. Cook the onion in the oil until soft. Grind or chop finely the peppers and tomatoes. Add to the softened onion. (If ground red pepper is used, add with the salt later.) Peel and cube the yams or sweet potatoes and add them to the mixture. Add the beef stock and salt. Bring the ingredients to a boil, then lower the heat and cook very slowly until the potatoes are soft, 20 to 30 minutes. Press the mixture through a sieve or puree in a blender. Return soup to the pan and heat through before serving. Sprinkle with chopped parsley.

3 to 4 Servings

(From A WEST AFRICAN COOK BOOK, by Ellen Gibson Wilson. Copyright 1971 by Ellen Gibson Wilson. Reprinted by permission of M. Evans & Co.)

Ethiopian Sieve G:57

In Ethiopia, where it was made, this basket would be used as a sieve for washing fruits, vegetables, beans or grains. It would be just the thing for preparing the lentils for *yemiser selatta*—an Ethiopian lentil salad with shallots and hot, green chiles. The 2″-high, slightly flared sides are made of coiled wild grasses or grain stalks; the flat bottom of the sieve, 11½″ in diameter, is of loosely woven grasses.

Craft Caravan, Inc. **$5.00**

Ethiopian Winnowing Basket G:58

From Gambele in southwestern Ethiopia comes this trough-like basket with short stubby handles at each end. It is used for separating the chaff from such grains as wheat, barley or millet. The trick is to toss a basketful of dried, unhulled grain up into the air on a breezy day, let the wind carry off the light, unwanted chaff, and catch the heavier grain neatly back in the basket. The grain may then be ground into flour for bread; or, if it's barley, it may be roasted and mixed with spiced butter oil into a thick paste called *chiko.* Tightly woven of rushes on a reed framework and striped with light and dark brown against a tan background, the long, deep basket (18½″ tip to tip, 7½″ across and 3½″ deep) would make an attractive bread basket for chunks of Ethiopian honey bread or spice bread.

Tribal Arts Gallery (1170) **$15.00**

With unusual asperity Mrs. Beeton describes a variety of millet which thrives in the Middle East and Africa: "It grows in sandy soils that will not do for the cultivation of many other kinds of grain, and forms the chief sustenance in the arid districts of Arabia, Syria, Nubia, and parts of India. It is not cultivated in England, being principally confined to the East. The nations who make use of it grind it, in the primitive manner, between two stones, and make it into a diet which cannot be properly called bread, but rather a kind of soft thin cake half-baked. When we take into account that the Arabians are fond of lizards and locusts as articles of food, their cuisine, altogether, is scarcely a tempting one."

The Book of Household Management
by Mrs. Isabella Beeton, 1861.

Injera and Wat

The national dish of Ethiopia is a stew called *wat,* which is usually served over *injera,* a thin, tortilla-like bread. *Wat* comes in various forms: it may use meat, chicken, fish, lentils or chick-peas. What all these forms share is a hot, spicy sauce made with red and black peppers, onions and garlic, and a shelfful of spices: cinnamon, cloves, nutmeg, turmeric, ginger, cardamom, fenugreek, coriander and cumin. *Injera* is a round, flat bread made from a fermented batter of finely ground teff, the finest grain in the millet family. Cooked quickly on a ceramic griddle with a domed lid, the bread has a smooth, browned underside, and a pitted surface ready to soak up the fiery juices of the *wat.*

In Ethiopia, *wat* is served from a circular basket table that has been lined with layers of *injera*—the bread providing linen, plate and food. The diners eat the *wat* with their fingers, using pieces of the bread as scoops. It is considered especially polite to seek out a choice morsel, wrap it in *injera,* and pop it into your table companion's mouth. *Tej,* a honey wine, accompanies the food, and the feast comes to a close with a rich, highly-concentrated, unsweetened black coffee.

Ethiopian Injera Basket-Table G:59

In Ethiopia, the *injera mesob* serves a double purpose: it is both a table and a serving dish. It consists of three parts: a large basket with sloping sides that is turned bowl side down to form the base of the table, a smaller basket that sits on the first one and functions as a serving platter, and a dome-shaped lid that fits snugly into the platter to keep the food warm. Ethiopians spread the serving part of the basket-table with a layer of folded *injera* and then pour over the bread a peppery stew called *wat.* They eat the hot stew with their fingers by wrapping it in pieces of the bread—the bread serving both as vehicle for the meat and as a buffer to the fiery spices of the sauce. The *injera* basket shown here is a smaller version, although the larger, table-high ones are also available. The bowl-shaped platter is about 7″ in diameter and 3″ deep, the base 10″ in diameter and 4¾″ high. Woven in bright shades of rose, green, yellow and dark purple in a traditional diamond pattern, it would be an attractive centerpiece, perfect for table-top serving.

Craft Caravan, Inc. $12.00

Ethiopian Food Basket G:60

This is the niftiest lunch box we have ever seen. It is called an *al gil gil.* From the outside it looks like a maroon leather canteen with tan leather thongs for tying its two halves closed and for carrying it over the shoulder or around the neck. Untie the leather thongs and open the *al gil gil,* and inside are two pretty, almost identical baskets of coiled straw, one the dish, the other the lid. Ethiopians use these leather-covered baskets for carrying their *injera*—a thin round bread—and their dried, cured meat while tending their crops or driving their livestock in search of water. The *al gil gil* is 11″ in diameter.

Craft Caravan, Inc. $20.00

Niger Spoon G:61

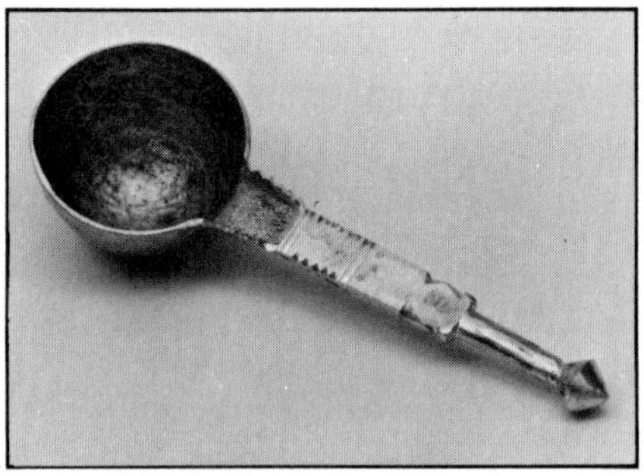

The wide, deep bowl of this shiny aluminum spoon from Niger will scoop up healthy portions of West African specialties like Ibo pepper soup (fish, hot chiles and tomatoes), *gari foto* (a blend of cassava meal, eggs, tomatoes and onions) or chicken and peanut stew. The spoon's 5¼″-long handle is incised with traditional African geometric designs, and the bowl is 2½″ in diameter and 1½″ deep.

Knobkerry $4.00

PEPPER SOUP

It baffles me why this relatively simple, tasty and much-eaten dish, with no more pepper than some others, is known as Pepper Soup in Sierra Leone, but it is. It is made without any fat, and when very peppery, it is sometimes given people with head colds. These directions came from Miss Isatu Mustapha, the chef at the Africana Restaurant in Freetown.

1 pound stewing beef
3 to 4 hot green chili peppers, or more to taste

1 medium onion
2 medium tomatoes
4 to 6 tablespoons tomato paste
A few sprigs of fresh thyme or ½ teaspoon dried
½ teaspoon black pepper
1 teaspoon salt

Cut the beef into bite-sized cubes and put into a pan with just enough water to cover. Bring to a boil, skim, lower the heat and cook gently for about 20 minutes, covered. Remove seeds from peppers and grind with the peeled onion, using the fine blade. Add to the meat. Peel and slice the tomatoes and add. Add the tomato paste, thyme, pepper and salt, and stir to blend. Cover and cook for about 45 minutes or until the meat is very tender. Eat with boiled rice.

4 Servings

Note: An Ibo Pepper Soup (in Nigeria) calls for fresh fish instead of the meat. In this dish the peppers and onion are ground together first and cooked five minutes in boiling water before the fish and some fresh, sliced okra are added. The mixture cooks a further 20 minutes.

Another Sierra Leonean used three-quarters of a pound of fresh fish or a large fish head in her Pepper Soup and added three Irish (white) potatoes, thickly sliced.

(From A WEST AFRICAN COOK BOOK, by Ellen Gibson Wilson. Copyright 1971 by Ellen Gibson Wilson. Reprinted by permission of M. Evans & Co.)

Ethiopian Scoop G:62

This magnificent carved wooden scoop from Ethiopia means business. With its large, deep bowl (4½″ by 5½″ across the top and 2⅝″ deep) and long, 11″ handle, which sensibly emerges halfway down the bowl to provide the best balance, it could be used to ladle a chicken *wat* (stew) over *injera* bread, to fill drinking cups with generous portions of honey wine or *talla* (beer), or simply to scoop rice or grain from a bin.

Pampered Kitchens $26.00

SIK SIK WAT

Beef Stewed in Red-Pepper Sauce

To serve 6 to 8

2 cups finely chopped onions
⅓ cup *niter kebbeh*
2 teaspoons finely chopped garlic
1 teaspoon scraped, finely chopped fresh ginger root
¼ teaspoon fenugreek seeds, pulverized with a mortar and pestle or in a bowl with the back of a spoon
⅛ teaspoon ground cloves
⅛ teaspoon ground allspice
⅛ teaspoon ground nutmeg, preferably freshly grated
¼ cup paprika
2 tablespoons *berberé*
⅔ cup dry red wine
½ cup water
1 large firm ripe tomato, coarsely chopped and puréed through a food mill or rubbed through a sieve with a spoon
2 teaspoons salt
3 pounds lean boneless beef, preferably chuck, trimmed of excess fat and cut into 1-inch cubes
Freshly ground black pepper

In a heavy 4- to 5-quart enameled casserole, cook the onions over moderate heat for 5 to 6 minutes, until they are soft and dry. Slide the casserole back and forth over the heat and stir the onions constantly to prevent them from burning; if necessary, reduce the heat or remove the casserole from the stove occasionally to let it cool for a few moments before returning it to the heat.

Stir in the *niter kebbeh* and, when it begins to splutter, add the garlic, ginger, fenugreek, cloves, allspice and nutmeg, stirring well after each addition. Add the paprika and *berberé,* and stir over low heat for 2 to 3 minutes. Stir in the wine, water, puréed tomato and salt, and bring the liquid to a boil. Add the beef cubes and turn them about with a spoon until they are evenly coated with the sauce. Then reduce the heat to low. Cover the pan partially and simmer the beef for about 1½ hours, or until it shows no resistance when pierced with the point of a small, sharp knife. Sprinkle the *wat* with a few grindings of pepper and taste for seasoning.

To serve, transfer the entire contents of the casserole to a deep heated platter or bowl. *Sik sik wat* is traditionally accompanied by *injera* or spice bread, but may also be eaten with Arab-style flat bread or hot boiled rice. *Yegomen kitfo* and/or plain yoghurt may be served with the *wat* from separate bowls.

(From FOODS OF THE WORLD, African Cooking, TIME-LIFE BOOKS, New York. Copyright 1969 by Time Inc.)

Ethiopian Horn Spoon G:63

What could be nicer for serving Ethiopian *yataklete kilkil*—fresh vegetables with garlic and ginger—than a large spoon carved out of a cow's horn? This one, with its 8″-long, gracefully curved handle and shallow bowl (4″ long by 2⅝″ wide), is a translucent silvery gray; but unlike mass-produced, modern-material utensils, each horn spoon has a distinct personality. The sizes vary (most are between 11″ and 13″ long), and the colors range from opalescent whites, yellows and greens, to an opaque burnt umber.

Craft Caravan, Inc. $10.00

Kenyan Drinking Horn G:64

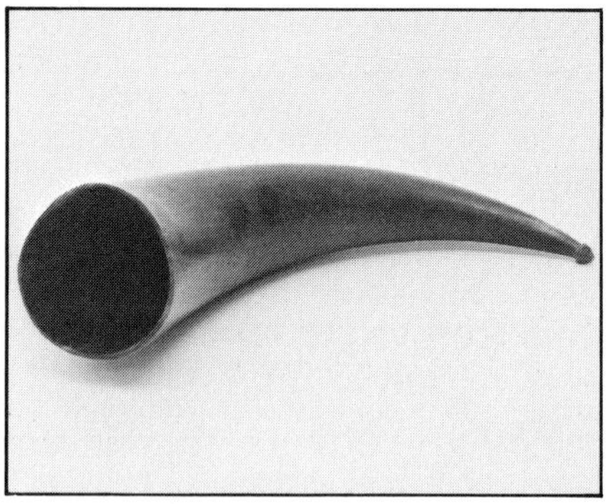

Classic in its simplicity, this dark brown, opaque drinking horn from Kenya is embellished only by the small pyramidal carved knob at the tip. Although it can hold over a quart of ale, you probably won't want to fill it that full unless you have a rack to set it in —a wine basket would do nicely. It is about 15″ long overall and is carved from a single piece of horn.

Craft Caravan, Inc. $20.00

Ethiopian Horn Cup G:65

Cut from a large cow's horn, this handsome, translucent, 4½″-tall drinking cup holds a full sixteen ounces of Ethiopian *tej*—a honey wine like the fabled hydromel of the ancient Greeks or the mead of the early English. By cutting the narrow end of the horn into sections and inserting these sections into one another, the Ethiopian craftsman provides a neat, tight-fitting bottom to the cup. A more conventional, European-style goblet with foot and stem is also available, but we prefer this one because it has the traditional shape.

Craft Caravan, Inc. $16.00

Ethiopian Wooden Bowl G:66

Used not for cooking but for eating, this roughly carved wooden bowl is from the Harar region of Ethiopia. The bowl has been stained dark brown on the outside, and is a mottled gold-brown on the inside. It is large enough—9″ across the top and 3″ deep—to serve such typical side dishes as buttermilk curds and collard greens. Or, if you are an aficionado of hot, spicy foods, you could use it to hold the fierce *berberé* dip, a volcanic paste of red pepper, spices and herbs, reputed to be fiery enough to cook the raw meat served with it.

Craft Caravan, Inc. $18.00

Rwanda Tray Plate G:67

Made of reed and bamboo, this elegant yet sturdy basket from Rwanda is double woven, with an inner surface of fine reeds in a black and white diamond pattern and an outer surface of split bamboo. Both layers are lashed to a wooden frame 14½″ in diameter. A small loop on the rim provides a means of hanging it, since you will, of course, want it to grace your kitchen or dining room wall when you are not using it as a tray or platter to serve fruit or bread.

Craft Caravan, Inc. $12.00

Upper Volta Gourd Container G:68

Calabash gourds of all sizes abound in Africa. Hollowed out, dried, cut and trimmed in various ways, they provide Africans with their simplest domestic utensils. This charming calabash container from Upper Volta was made by cutting the top quarter off a dried gourd. Strips of bamboo were then neatly lashed with a natural brown fiber, one to the top and one to the bottom of the gourd, thus forming a neck on the upper part that slips tightly into the collar of the lower part. Voilà: a useful pot for storing your cassava meal or ground baobab seeds. The stem of the gourd is left as a handle, and the whole is left its natural pale-pumpkin hue, which over the years will ripen to a deep amber. This one is about 8½″ tall, but 6″ and 12″ sizes are also available; our first thought on seeing them together was what a delightful set of cannisters they would make.

Craft Caravan, Inc. $6.00

FOOFOO

Raw cassava roots are peeled, washed and soaked in water for two days to soften. Then they are grated or pounded in a mortar. The pulp is put into a sack and pressed under heavy weight, to eliminate water, for another two days. Next the cassava is re-pounded to a fine flour, mixed with water and strained. The liquid is allowed to settle overnight until a white sediment collects in the bottom of the vessel. The water is poured off and this white flour is either formed into balls and dried for future use (this is the way it is often sold in the markets) or it is cooked at once.

To cook, the flour or sediment is mixed with enough water to form a thick paste. This is put into an iron pot over the fire and cooked slowly, stirring all the time with a flat wooden paddle or spoon. This is "pulling" or "turning" the foofoo. Gradually the foofoo becomes smooth and translucent and it begins to leave the sides of the pot. Additional water may be sprinkled on with the fingers to keep the texture right. The skilled cook can shape the loaf as it cooks in the pot with swift slaps of her paddle and wetted hand, turning and shaping it until the smooth mass is ready to transfer to the serving dish. The cooking process may take about 30 minutes. It takes, however, in addition, muscle and a skill which only comes with experience.

MAKE-DO FOOFOO

Mrs. Josephine Akwei, a Ghanaian in the United States, helpfully introduced me to this substitute foofo prepared by expatriate Africans and their American imitators.

½ cup instant potatoes, Idaho-type
½ cup potato starch
2 cups water

Measure instant potatoes and starch into a mixing bowl and blend, preferably with your hand, until all the starch lumps are gone. Add the water gradually, mixing carefully into a smooth consistency. Pour the mixture into a heavy pan over low heat. Have ready a small bowl of water nearby. Cook the foofoo, stirring constantly, scraping it from the sides and bottom, turning and pulling as it cooks. A flat wooden paddle or shallow spoon works well. Dip the stirrer into water frequently as the mixture thickens. This keeps the foofoo from sticking to the spoon. Sprinkle drops of water in the bottom of the pan if the mixture seems likely to scorch. Gradually the foofoo becomes an elastic mass which will leave the sides of the pan. After about 15 minutes, it should be ready. Rinse a plate in cold water and turn out the foofoo on it. With wet hands, quickly shape and smooth it into a long or round loaf. Serve with a stew which includes green leaves.

4 to 6 Servings

Note: It is permissible to add ½ to 1 teaspoon of salt, but most West Africans eat it unseasoned.

(From A WEST AFRICAN COOK BOOK, by Ellen Gibson Wilson. Copyright 1971 by Ellen Gibson Wilson. Reprinted by permission of M. Evans & Co.)

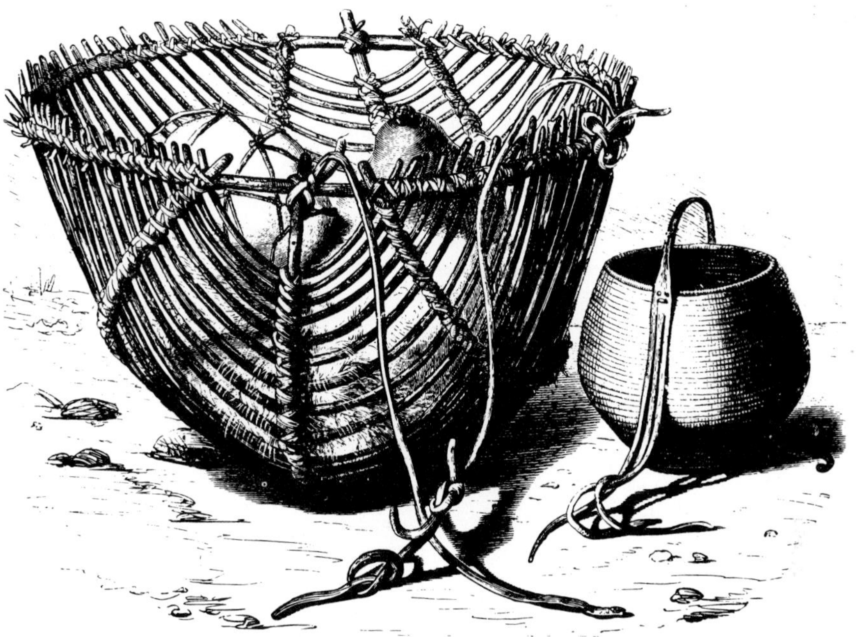

African Baskets and Water Gourds.

Gourd bottle.

Mali Gourd Bowl and Spoon G:69

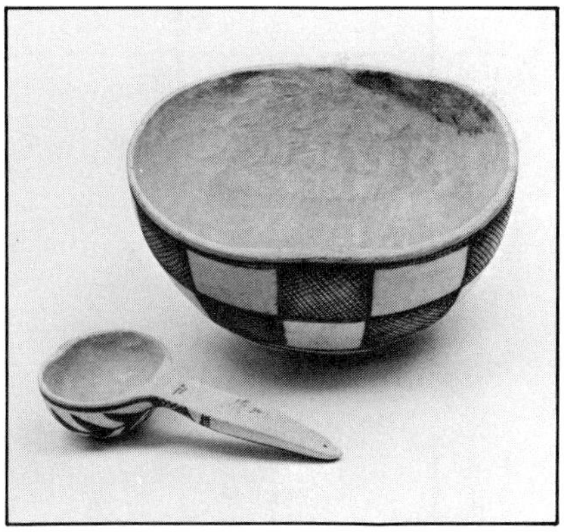

This large gourd bowl—13½″ across the top and 6¼″ deep—could be used for mashing cooked yams or bananas or cassava into a paste known as *foofoo*. Or you might use it with its matching 10½″-long serving spoon to serve the finished *foofoo* balls or Jollof rice, a West African specialty made with marinated meat or chicken, peppers, onions, tomatoes and rice. A globe-trotting friend of ours tells us of having seen peanut soup served at a train station in Upper Volta from a bowl just like this one. The bowl and spoon have been left their natural color—which will darken with use and age—and are

Continued from preceding page

burnt with traditional designs: a checkerboard pattern, coiled snakes and leaves on the bowl, and on the spoon a lizard flicking its tongue.

Craft Caravan, Inc.
Bowl **$16.00**
Spoon **$ 2.00**

Gourd vessel enclosed in wicker.

Kenyan Wakamba Gourd G:70

Rancid butter—usually made from goat's milk—is a common ingredient in nomadic cooking. But that's not all it's used for: it is a wood and leather polish, a skin cream, a hair ointment, you name it. Small wonder, then, that we find such a large and ornamental receptacle for it. This gourd, which is about a foot tall and two feet around at its widest point, could easily hold four pounds of butter. Whoever made it etched a simple geometrical design all over the surface and carved a wooden stopper. Wherever the gourd cracked or split—owing no doubt to the weight of the butter—it has been carefully darned with a fiber, the ends entwined and plaited, and the patch sealed with pitch. The inside has also been lined with pitch, but the brownish-orange outside has been burnished to a high gloss. How? Why, with the rancid butter, of course.

Craft Caravan, Inc. **$30.00**

Among the curious African beliefs associated with milk and its production are the following: If milk is boiled, the cattle will die (Masai and Bahima); milk vessels should be washed with cow's urine instead of water—as water is thought to give an odd odor to the container (Masai); sexual activity is forbidden while the cattle are grazing in the pasture (Akamba and Aikikuyu); milk must not be drunk while in mourning (Dinka and Banyoto).

Milk Jug G:71

Carved on simple, classic lines, this wooden milk jug from Ethiopia or Somalia looks like the sort of container that has been used for generations to carry and store milk. It is 10¼″ tall and is a good-looking, rustic piece of work. Although it comes with a strap for carrying it, and thongs that tie across the top of the jug to keep its stopper tightly closed, we expect you will enjoy it more as a decoration than as a container to keep milk in.

Craft Caravan, Inc. **$30.00**

African tribes observe different rites with regard to the combining of the concepts of milk and blood. Among the Zulus, for example, a man with an open wound may not milk a cow until he has been purified. In some tribes a menstruating woman may not look at the cattle, or is merely allowed the milk from an old cow. Among the Hottentots, however, a girl reaching puberty touches all the milking vessels to bring good luck, and the Herero consecrate all their milk to a woman newly delivered of a child.

Turkana Blood and Milk Carrier G:72

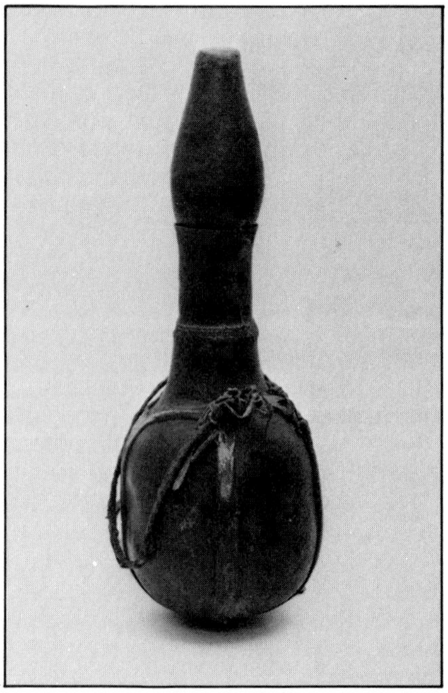

The nomads and herdsmen of East Africa have created many different types of vessels to carry their diet of blood and milk as they follow their sheep, goats and cattle from pasture to pasture. This large Turkana container —it stands about 13″ tall without the stopper—has been carved out of wood and lined with pitch to make it waterproof. A 3½″-wide band of leather, sewn to the wood, forms a neck, and leather straps, knotted and braided for extra strength, provide a handle. A special feature is the stopper—a 6½″ carved piece of wood, hollowed out to form a drinking cup.

Craft Caravan, Inc. **$40.00**

One of the more valuable members of the gourd family, the loofah—or dishcloth gourd—has fibrous innards that when dried provide a durable scrub brush.

This curious wooden contrivance makes a special kind of rice vermicelli popular among Kenyans of East Indian and Arab descent. It works on the same principle as a potato ricer or garlic press: cooked rice is put into a hole in the center and a solid wood cylinder is pushed against the rice with the upper arm, forcing the rice through a perforated metal plate in long thin noodles.

Masai Blood and Milk Carrier G:73

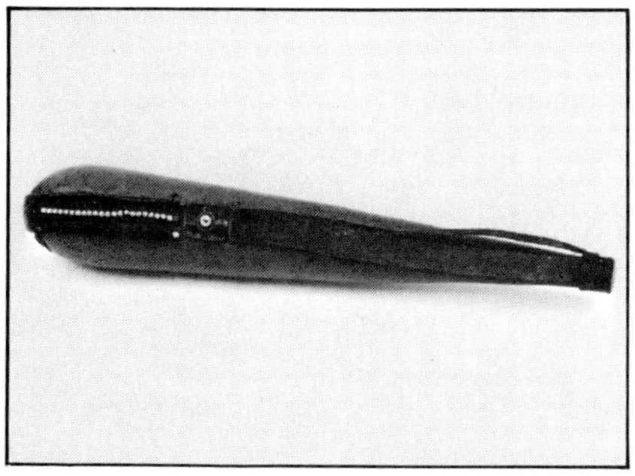

The tall, handsome Masai of Kenya, and other related East African herdsmen, subsist mainly on milk and blood drawn from living cows. As they tend their cattle, they carry this drink with them in long gourd containers that look like sleek, ornamental shillelaghs. Each is made of an elongated, dried gourd —this one is 25″ long—with the narrow stem end cut off. Leather straps are stretched around the bulb-shaped base and up the length of the gourd to end in a small leather cap. Colorful beadwork adorning the strap gives each carrier its individual stamp. It is light and can be slung over the shoulder: a simple and convenient way to carry liquid food.

Craft Caravan, Inc. $30.00

Kenyan Honey Pot G:74

Honey, whether from wild or domesticated bees, has long been the principal sweetener available to East Africans. It is still customary in rural areas to sweeten coffee by putting a dab of honey under the tongue and then letting it melt into a mouthful of hot coffee before swallowing. And honey is also used in cooking. Laurens van der Post writes in *African Cooking* of a Kenyan feast of *kudu* (antelope) steaks served with wild gooseberries in a sauce of butter, banana gin, cream and wild honey. This honey carrier is precisely what Kenyans use to gather and store that pungent wild honey. Made of a single sheet of thin bark rounded into an oval shape and lashed together with strips of leather, the two-foot-tall pot has a bottom and a lid of cowhide with remnants of the original fur. The lid fits snugly over the rim of the pot to keep out flies and other insects. A rope handle runs up the sides of the pot through the leather lashings so that it can be carried from hive to hive.

Craft Caravan, Inc. $70.00

Somali Grain Bag G:75

Creative artistry often reaches down to even the smallest items of daily life in Africa—as we can see in this handsome grain bag from Somaliland. Woven out of a hemp-like fiber, in a black and tan checked and striped pattern, it is used by Somali women to carry their millet, sorghum or corn home from the market. The bag is almost a foot wide at the bottom but narrows to 5″ across the top, leaving an opening just wide enough to pour from, yet narrow enough to keep the valuable grain from spilling out. It has a woven handle and a long, decorative fringe.

Craft Caravan, Inc. $16.00

Burundi Food Carrier G:76

Burundi natives carry these baskets (without their picturesque conical lids) two at a time, coolie-style, suspended from a wooden bar by straps of braided fiber made from the bark of the baobab tree. The thick, tightly-woven baskets would usually be made watertight with pitch and mud. Our sample, however, comes without lining or straps. The neat weaving of the natural-colored straw, adorned only by a simple stairstep design in purple, and its amusing shape, make it an attractive object that could be used to store spare kitchen equipment or to hide a large bag of potatoes or onions. The "hat" fits tightly over the basket edge. The sizes vary: this one is two feet tall with its lid, although the basket is only 10″ deep. A much smaller version, more intricately wrought of a whiter fiber with a black design, is also available.

Craft Caravan, Inc. $40.00

A Country Kitchen in Hungary

by Paul Kovi

I had the most beautiful childhood one could imagine, growing up in a traditional Hungarian family. Three generations of us lived together in the country with my grandfather as the head of the family. I was lucky because I was chosen to manage the family's affairs and, eventually, to succeed my grandfather's role of leadership. Instead of being sent off to school, I was brought up at home, where I was kept very close to my mother and my grandfather, a marvelous man, a strong powerful figure and a great storyteller.

These days, it seems remarkable that we were so self-reliant. We produced everything that we needed; I think that the only things we ever bought were sugar, flour and salt. We slaughtered our own pigs and calves and raised our own poultry. We hunted for boar, pheasant and partridge and fished for pike, trout and carp. From our pigs, we made lard, which is the staple cooking fat of Hungary. We grew fruit and berries from which we made jam and desserts, and we made wine from our three acres of grapes. From the cows' milk we made our own butter. And every week a man who worked in the household would bake two huge ten-pound loaves of bread made out of a mixture of rye and wheat flours. One loaf was oval and one was round. The oval loaf was always cut first because the person who made the first cut would have the coveted piece with the most crust. In the summer, we made a bread that was leavened with hops instead of yeast, a small high loaf that had a dark black-brown crust. Nothing has ever been more wonderful than that bread, which was very fluffy with large holes in the crumb. I was allowed to assist the baker in putting the bread in and taking it out of the oven.

I loved to fish, too; and when I was very young I became skillful at cleaning and filleting the catch. Four times a year, we killed one of our own pigs for meat. It was my job to hold on to the animal's tail so that it wouldn't get away. At the time, I was maybe five years old, and the pigs weighed something over 400 pounds apiece. They were as big as a dining table. But I would hold on tightly and believe that my assistance was necessary. Later, as a reward for my hard work, my grandfather would give me the first taste of the roasted meat.

Then, as is the case with most country houses today, all of our family life was conducted in the kitchen. It was huge—20 feet by 20 feet—and it contained wooden tables and chairs, commodes and cupboards that had been hand-carved by my grandfather and the men who worked on the farm. Most of the food preparation took place on these tables. Later on, the family would eat on them. There was a fireplace in the corner of the room, and two stoves. A brick stove was used in the winter, because it gave off heat that helped to heat the room; an iron stove was used in the summer.

We also had a summer kitchen. It was a room enclosed on only two sides, with the other two sides open to the gardens. Just outside the summer kitchen was a table set beneath the trees. In the warmest months, when it was too hot to cook inside the house, the family would move out to the summer kitchen. That was one of the many beauties of our lives.

There was, of course, no refrigerator in our kitchen. We did not know of such things, nor did we have any use for one. Other methods

For well over a thousand years, shepherds in Hungary have prepared their soup-stew, gulyás, *in a heavy iron pot called a* bogrács. *Early versions of the dish were made from meat that had been cooked with onions and then sun-dried. When a meal was needed, the leathery flesh was revived with water and a simmer in the* bogrács.

"There was a lavish variety of food. The long tables were heavily laden with all kinds of meat: beef and pork barbecued at the spit, the first flavored with rosemary and liberally sprinkled with cayenne peppercorns, the other flavored with just a hint of aniseed; roast goose seasoned with sage, thyme and marjoram and stuffed with currants and apples; an abundance of fried chicken. There were large bowls of lettuce and tomatoes and side dishes of cucumbers, some in yogurt and others in brine with a sprinkling of dill. There were numerous dishes of beans, some vibrant red from the paprika seasoning, cold white beans with vinegar, mashed chick peas with sesame oil, green beans with sour cream and lentils. There were plates of potato salad with chives and parsley, and plates of Bryndza cheese. There was an overflow of small containers of horseradish, of black olives, and of cold baked eggplant mixed with chopped raw onion, jokingly called the 'poor man's caviar.' And there were collapsing sacks of freshly baked bread, and meat balls richly spiced with nutmeg and deep-fried onion rings. . . ."

The Gypsies *by Jan Yoors. George, Allen & Unwin, 1967.*

Fashionable folk snacking in a Viennese coffeehouse at the turn of the century.

of preservation were available, from the smoking and salting of meats, to the canning of fruit and berries with sugar. Every summer a huge kettle was set up outside over a wooden fire. In it would go plums that were cooked for a whole day and half a night. When they had boiled down to the proper consistency, the *lekvar*, or plum jam, would be stored in jars. Later, when my mother needed it for making pastries or spreading on bread, she would open a jar.

We did have a kind of ice house though, a small cellar buried in the earth, in which we would keep the winter's ice for some months. But it really wasn't used much. The food that needed to be kept cool was stored in a small room on the north side of the house. Since that room had only one little window and a northern exposure, its temperature was always cool. It was there that we kept our butter, cheese and eggs.

The pots that we cooked in were made of heavy iron or enameled steel, and, as I remember, we had a different pot for every use you can imagine. I've already mentioned the big kettle for making *lekvar;* well, there was also a huge, shallow, wooden trough where a pig was placed after it was slaughtered. There were frying pans and kettles and saucepans of all sizes. And it's hard to imagine the incredible assortment of knives we had because, of course, they were needed for all the butchering as well as cooking chores.

It was a good life, punctuated by seasonal events like the killing of the pigs. Each of the four days a year it happened was filled with great work and celebration. It began with the arrival of the master butcher the night before to check and see that everything had been properly prepared, and it ended with a feast that lasted well into the night. All the aunts and uncles and cousins would gorge themselves on sausage and wine and goulash and, naturally, wine and *slivovitz* (plum pit brandy). Then, late at night, the gypsies would arrive to serenade the sleepy family. I always sat by my grandfather's side, that marvelous man, and I would fall asleep listening to his tall stories and the music of the gypsies.

The Cuisine of Middle and Eastern Europe

Whipped cream and chocolate cake; dumplings, roast duck and sweet red cabbage; sausages, noodles and crisply fried veal—Middle European food makes us smile with pleasure at the thought of it. It is the antithesis of the *cuisine minceur,* but oh, how the corners of our lips turn upward when we think of tender pancakes wrapped around apricot jam, and how we sigh with pleasure at the sight of caraway-studded goulash and noodles.

In all of the countries of Middle Europe—Austria, Czechoslovakia, Germany, Hungary, Poland, Western Russia, and Switzerland—people like to eat and to eat heartily. The average Central European is twenty percent heavier than his American counterpart because he frequently eats five meals a day (including two or three substantial sweets). In Vienna in the Gay Nineties, for example, rich people began the day with a *Frühstück* (breakfast) of rolls, jam, hot milk, coffee and perhaps a boiled egg. Midmorning found the men, especially, at a *Gabelfrühstück,* a more substantial meal of sausages or

Continued from preceding page

goulash requiring a fork (*Gabel*). At about 1 p.m., a five-course *Mittagessen* would be consumed by both sexes. Tea, coffee, canapés and *Torten* sustained the women, and often the men as well, through the gossip and intrigues of the 5 p.m. *Jause*. Then, after the opera, they would finally dine again.

Though the pace of modern life has cut down on such extravagance, many people in Central Europe are still apt to have some hot food at the midmorning break and a rich pastry in the afternoon, in addition to three meals—morning, noon and night. Also, a favorite form of entertaining is to serve a rich dessert or two with coffee in the evening.

Although the countries we are looking at do not form a political, geographical, or linguistic unit today, in many ways they do form a culinary unit. It is determined in part by such physical links as the great Danube River, which runs from the Black Forest to the Black Sea, and in part from a shared history.

In the early Middle Ages, Central Europe was invaded by waves of barbarians from the East—the Visigoths, Huns, Mongols, Slavs, Franks, Magyars and others—many of whom remained and settled there. During the Crusades, a principal land route to the Holy Land lay through Middle Europe, and returning Crusaders brought Eastern spices to Western cuisines. Perhaps the strongest link was the Austro-Hungarian Empire, which began in the thirteenth century and lasted until the twentieth century. At one time or another it included some part of all of the countries (except Russia) that we are discussing.

Marriage alliances of medieval monarchs with Byzantine princesses and Italian noblewomen also brought Turkish and Italian influences. Strudel dough, for example, that quintessentially Central European pastry, was inspired by the Turks, who introduced the *filo* or *phyllo* dough of the Middle East to the area. Hungarians call it *rétes* and claim it as their own. In any event, the dough was originally lighter and more delicate in Hungary than in the other countries, because of the high gluten content of the native wheat. The dish that is called *Nockerl* in Austria, *nockedli* in Hungary, and *noki* in Czechoslovakia, originated in Italy, where it is known as *gnocchi*.

Other linguistic evidence also reveals the culinary homogeneity of Central Europe and the historical basis for many shared dishes. Pancakes were popular in what is now Rumania when they were discovered by Roman legionnaires, who called the flat, round cakes *placentae* and spread their popularity throughout the Roman Empire. They became the *Palatschinken* of Austria, *palacsinta* of Hungary, *palacinky* of Czechoslovakia, the *blinchiki* and *bliny* of Russia and (although given an unrelated name) the *Pfannkuchen* of Germany.

Still other similarities in cuisine may be due to a similar climate, crops and flocks: all of these countries share a love of noodles, dumplings, pancakes, pastries and breads made from wheat and rye. All value the winter nourishment provided by cabbage and potatoes. They pickle vegetables, fruits and meats in wine or cider vinegars for winter consumption and preserve meats by air-curing, smoking and making sausages. They produce beer, cider and wine from abundant grains and fruits, and gather honey from wild and domesticated bees. And milk products abound: yoghurt, cheeses, sour cream, heavy sweet cream and butter are basic elements in the Middle European diet.

Yet, in spite of all these similarities, the individual Middle Euro-

"No nation abandons itself more completely to banqueting and entertaining than the German. It is accounted a sin to turn any man away from your door. The host welcomes his guest with the best meal that his means allow. When supplies run out, the host takes on a fresh rôle; he directs and escorts his guest to a new hostelry. The two go on, uninvited, to the nearest house. It makes no difference; they are welcomed just as warmly. No distinction is ever made between acquaintance and stranger as far as the right to hospitality is concerned."

Germania *by Tacitus, translated by H. Mattingly, from* Tacitus on Britain and Germany. *The Penguin Classics, 1960.*

In a scene typical of the 16th century, village farmers enjoy a festive meal alfresco seated around long tables.

pean cuisines have quite distinct regional personalities. Certain foods are inseparably linked with particular nations: Germany with sausages, beer and potatoes; Switzerland with cheese; Russia with caviar, vodka and tea; Poland and Czechoslovakia with hams and sausages; Hungary with paprika, cabbage, noodles and goulash; and Austria with pastries. It's no wonder eating is such a favored pastime in the lands of *Mitteleuropa*.

Fine Cutting Equipment

Slicing, shredding, chopping, grating and grinding can be the bane of any cook. Fortunately, many specialized tools have been devised for the cutting chores of the Middle European cuisine. There are cheese knives, asparagus peelers, horseradish graters, plum pitters and poppyseed mills. The names alone evoke visions of a Middle European feast. The common implements also include knives, graters and grinders appropriate for other kitchens, because fine cutting tools have long been a hallmark of Middle European industry.

Already in medieval times, the Ruhr valley in western Germany was a major manufacturing center for cutlery. The valley contained rich deposits of iron and coal and was close to the markets of Köln on that busy commercial artery, the Rhine. By the fourteenth century the skilled craftsmen of Solingen were famous throughout Europe for their knives, and it was common for both men and women to carry one. A Solingen knife at one's waist was like the Gucci handbag of the day.

To this longstanding tradition of excellence, modern invention has added blades of high-carbon stainless steel—that keep their sharp edges well but will not stain, pit or rust—and handles of plastic-impregnated wood for extra strength. Modern commerce has also brought Brazilian rosewood to Europe. This good looking hardwood is particularly suitable for knife handles because its multi-directional grain resists cracking and splitting, and its rather tacky surface keeps a knife from slipping in your hand. With these superior tools, any cutting task becomes a pleasure rather than a nuisance.

Large Chef's Knife H:1

This monster chef's knife with its 3″-wide, 13″-long, stainless-steel blade is an excellent example of German craftsmanship. A heavy knife, it will perform almost all of your cutting tasks, whether cubing meat for goulash, slicing cabbage or potatoes, mincing pickles or onions, or carving a saddle of venison. (But resist the temptation to use it as a cleaver!) Just follow the instructions incised on the blade: the tip end is marked "zum schneiden"—for cutting—the section closer to the handle "zum spatten"—for chopping. The 6″-long rosewood handle is curved for easy gripping and tightly riveted to the full tang. All in all, a handsome and practical tool.

R. H. Forschner Co., Inc. (946) **$34.00**

Paring Knife H:2

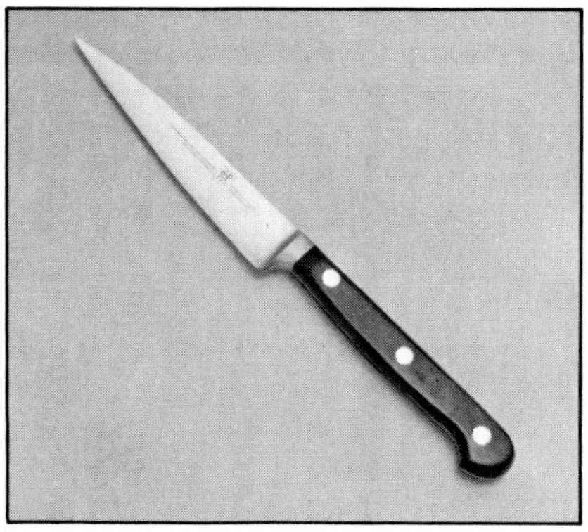

Here is a first-rate paring knife from Henckels with a 4″-long Friodur blade. Friodur is the trade name for a high-carbon stainless steel that will not stain, or rust; yet, because of its high carbon content, will retain an excellent degree of sharpness. With its full tang, tightly riveted to a 4″-long, plastic-impregnated Durawood handle, the knife is strong enough to pare apples and potatoes quickly and its sharp point is ideal for scooping out any stubborn potato eyes. A popular combination of apples and potatoes served with liver and roasts is *Himmel und Erde* (heaven and earth)—potatoes and apples topped with onion rings and bacon.

J. A. Henckels Twinworks, Inc. (31060-4) **$13.50**

Utility Slicer H:3

Roasted and braised meats of all kinds —veal, beef, mutton, ham, pork, veni-

Continued from preceding page

son—are Sunday fare in Middle Europe. A heavy-duty slicer like this Wüsthof knife from Germany is essential for cutting quickly through these bulky meats. The no-stain, high-carbon stainless-steel blade has a fine, 10″-long cutting edge and a sharp tip that is useful for cutting around bones. The full tang, secured by three rivets to the black, plastic-impregnated wooden handle, gives weight to the handle end for good balance. You'll especially appreciate the rigid blade and weighted handle when dealing with large, heavy roasts or with a ham.

S. I. Moss Co., Inc. (183) **$23.50**

Round-Tipped Slicer H:4

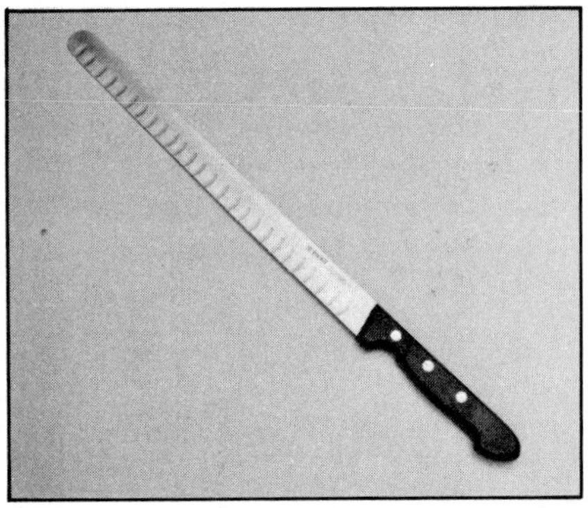

Known as a "ham slicer," this type of knife is useful for cutting large, thin slices of any roast meat whether hot or cold. With its 12″-long Friodur blade (a non-staining steel with a high carbon content to hold sharpness), this Henckels slicer will reach easily across a large ham or roast of venison; its round tip will prevent any unintentional gashes in the slices. The narrow blade is secured to a 5¼″-long wooden handle by three nickel-silver rivets. At staggered points along both sides of the thin, flexible blade, hollow, oval indentations have been ground to decrease friction at the slicing edge. Use the knife to carve even slices of even the most delicate cooked meats, such as *Kalbsrolle,* a braised veal roll with a sausage stuffing.

J. A. Henckels Twinworks, Inc. (32751-315) **$25.00**

ROAST HONEY-CURED HAM IN PORT WINE SAUCE

1 (5-to 6-pound) pre-cooked smoked ham
1½ cups water
1½ cups Port wine
1 tablespoon butter
1 onion, peeled and thinly sliced
1 medium tomato, peeled, seeded, chopped
1 whole clove, crushed
1 bay leaf
Butter
1 tablespoon flour
½ cup honey (or corn syrup)
½ cup orange juice
1 cup brown sugar

Preheat the oven to 350° F. Separate the rind from the ham, using a small sharp knife; put the rind into a medium-size saucepan. Trim the ham of all but ¼″ layer of fat. Pour 1½ cups of water over the rind, bring to a boil over a high heat, then reduce the heat to low, and simmer, uncovered, for 20 minutes. Strain the liquid through a sieve into a bowl and discard the rind.

Pour 1¼ cups of the rind stock into a shallow roasting pan just large enough to hold the ham comfortably. Add half the wine, butter, onion, tomato, clove, and bay leaf. Place the ham, fat side up, in the pan and bake, uncovered, in the center of the oven for 1 hour. Baste the ham thoroughly every 20 minutes with the juices. The ham is done when it can easily be pierced with a fork. Place ham in a heated dish.

Strain and discard all the fat from the juices in the pan and stir in the rest of the wine. Bring to a boil over high heat for a minute or two. Make a paste of butter and flour in a small bowl and stir it bit by bit into the pan. Cook over low heat, stir constantly. Strain and taste for seasoning. Mix honey with orange juice, and pat over the meat. Pat 1 cup of brown sugar on the meat, and cook for about 5 minutes until brown.

To serve, carve ham into ¼-inch slices and arrange attractively on a large heated dish. Moisten the slices with a few spoonfuls of wine sauce. (*Serves 4 to 6.*)

(From LÜCHOW'S GERMAN FESTIVAL COOKBOOK by Gene and Fran Schoor. Reprinted by permission of Doubleday & Company, Inc.)

Ham Boning Knife H:5

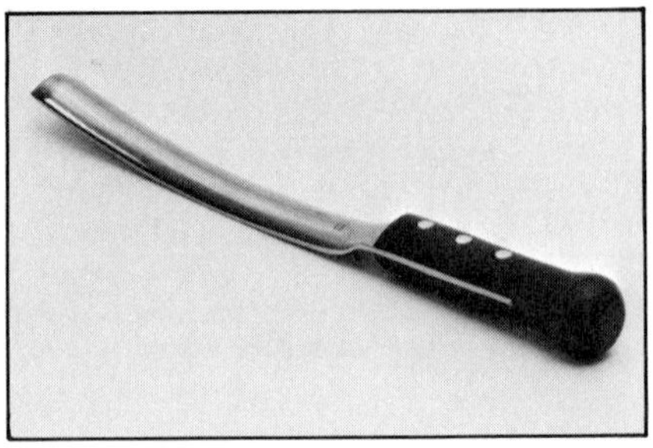

A highly specialized tool for boning hams and other cuts of meat with a large center bone, this knife reflects the practicality for which Central Europeans are famed. The 8½″-long stainless-steel blade is curved to fit around a bone so its razor sharp cutting edge, 1¼″ wide at the end of the knife, will scrape as much meat as possible off the bone. The tang, which extends two-thirds of the way up the wooden handle, is held by three nickel-silver rivets; and the cylindrical handle partly balances the long, heavy blade. A sturdy, handsome implement, this boning knife will certainly fulfill its singular purpose: to pick a bone clean.

R. H. Forschner Co., Inc. (S171) **$20.00**

Tripe Knife H:6

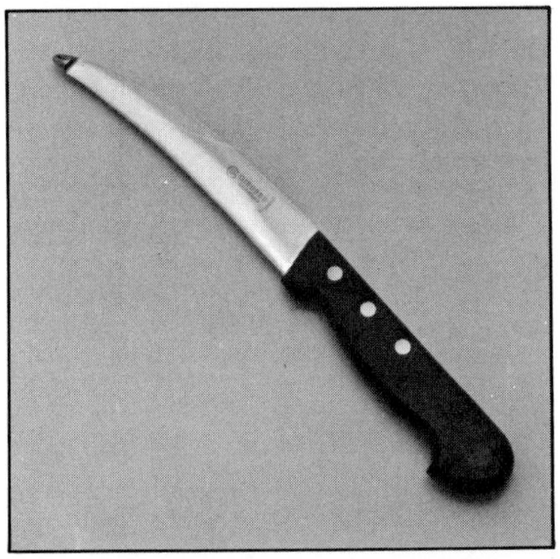

At a quick glance, this specialized tool resembles in a curious way the snout of an anteater. The cutting edge is on the concave side of the blade; and the tip, instead of being thin and sharp, is a thick, blunt cone of shiny stainless steel. This is a tripe knife. Tripe comes from the animal in thick pads covered with a layer of fat. As you scrape the fat away by pulling the knife toward you across the top of the fat pad, the blunted tip prevents the blade from cutting into the delicate membranes beneath. This knife, with a 6¼″-long, 1″-wide blade and a 5¼″-long plastic handle (secured with three nickel-silver rivets), will do the job nicely for all Middle European tripe dishes, whether Polish style with vegetables, or German style in a peppery innard stew. Or try a more unusual Hungarian dish that joins boiled tripe cut into julienne strips with an elegant sauce of egg yolks and lemon juice.

Johannes Giesser (Messer) KG (3420R) **$15.00**

The English, too, delight in tripe—and other pleasures of the flesh: "After with great pleasure lying a great while talking and sporting in bed with my wife (for we have been for some years now, and at present more and more, a very happy couple, blessed be God), I got up and to my office. So home and dined there with my wife upon a most excellent dish of tripes of my own directing, covered with mustard, as I have heretofore seen them done at my Lord Crew's, of which I made a very great meal."

Passages from the Diary of Samuel Pepys, *edited by Richard Le Gallienne. The Modern Library, Random House, n.d.*

Lard Knife H:7

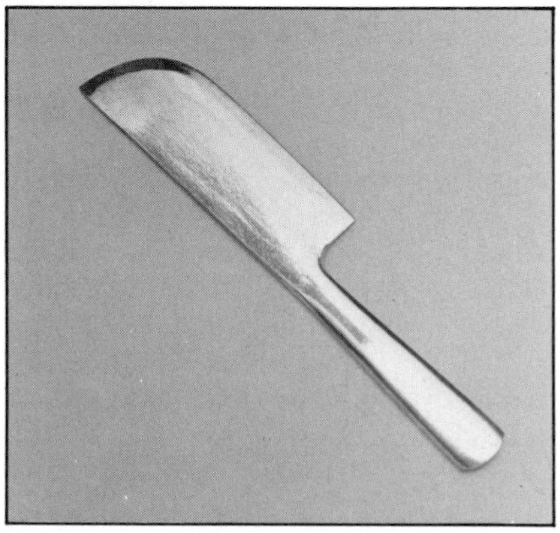

One of the characteristics of Middle European cuisine is the use of lard in preference to butter or oil for sautéing many meats and vegetables. This 10″ knife, a solid piece of cast aluminum, has a slightly rounded handle, and a 1¾″-wide flat blade that is perfectly designed to cut or spread lard. With its smooth finish, the knife has no joints or cracks where fat can lodge and turn rancid, and it is easy to clean. But there's no need to wash it often, since it can live right in the fat pot in your refrigerator, ready to use every time you start the onions for goulash, or sauerkraut, or a smoked pork loin.

S. Ostrowsky, Inc. (4296) **$4.00**

Milking pail.

Single-Handled Cheese Knife H:8

This cheese knife, solidly constructed of stainless steel and rosewood, has an 8½″-long and 1½″-wide blade that is stepped down from the handle for added leverage in cutting through firm cheeses like the Swiss Emmentaler, Appenzeller and Gruyère. Its single handle allows you to cut into a wheel of cheese from one side only and to slice out a wedge without cutting across the entire cheese. Why not use it to cut wedges of *Brätkase* (broiling cheese) to melt on a stick over the fire after a day's skiing?

Swissmart Inc. (713) **$21.50**

Double-Handled Cheese Knife H:9

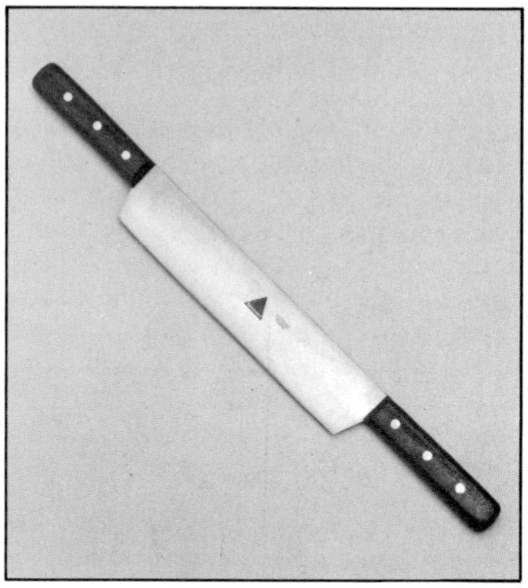

With this double-handled knife you can bring all your weight to bear on a large chunk of firm cheese that would normally give you and other knives a hard time. The use of both hands helps to distribute all your force evenly with no risk to your fingers from the sharp blade. The cutter, with a 9½″-long and 2″-wide stainless-steel blade riveted to two rosewood handles, means business. Use it to cut wedges of Emmentaler and Gruyère to make a communally satisfying cheese fondue. Accompanied by white wine, this creamy Swiss meal will warm the cockles of your heart on the coldest, dreariest winter days.

Swissmart Inc. (711) **$30.00**

Guillotine Cheese Knife H:10

To overpower the firmest of Swiss cheeses, try this sturdy guillotine slicer. Since the rosewood handle is above

Continued from preceding page

the blade, you can apply pressure right where you need it: directly above the sharp, stainless-steel cutting edge. The blade, which is almost square—5⅞″ by 5½″—is wide enough to slice through the thickest wheel of Emmentaler or Gruyère cheese. The handle, 3¼″ by 5⅞″, is riveted to tangs extending from the two sides of the blade, and it is large enough to accommodate both hands. You might also find the knife useful for chopping sliced cheese into smaller bits for melting or for a *Zwiebelwähe*—a popular Swiss onion and cheese tart.

Swissmart Inc. (712) $30.00

Cheese Wire H:11

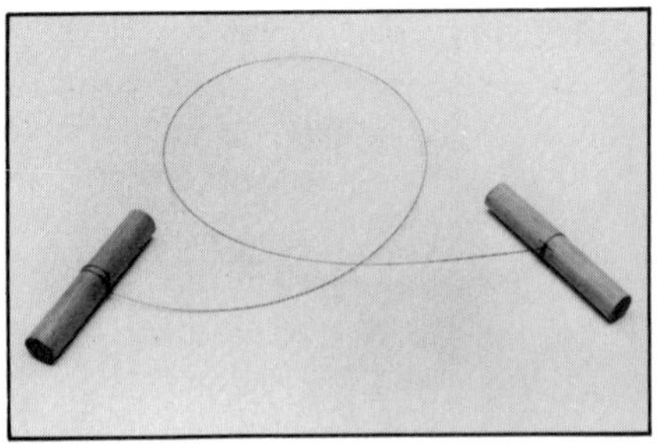

Piano wire not only makes fine music, but fine cheese cutters as well. This cheese cutter consists of 39″ of piano wire attached firmly to two hardwood handles. It is intended for cutting through the large, firm wheels of cheese turned out by the Swiss. To cut through a wheel of cheese, make incisions on the top, on opposite sides of the cheese, where you want to divide it. Slip the wire under the cheese and into the incisions to give you some purchase. Pull the ends of the wire in opposite directions across the top of the cheese, and the wire should cut it neatly. If you want to shorten the cutting edge for a smaller piece of cheese, wind the wire around the handles and then, with your hands on either side of the cheese, push the wire down and through it. The wire is an efficient way to cope with a large piece of cheese, such as reducing a whole wheel of Appenzeller into wedges to serve at a big party.

International Edge Tool Co. (115) $2.25

A cheese factory in Gruyère in the late nineteenth century.

VEAL CUTLET WITH HAM AND CHEESE

Kalbsschnitzel Cordon Bleu

According to the Germans, it was a German chef in Dürkheim, the Palatinate wine center, who invented this extravagantly delicious method of preparing Schnitzel, with both ham and cheese sealed inside thin slices of veal. That he gave the dish a French name is not surprising; don't we frequently do the same thing?

8 individual veal cutlets
Salt and pepper
4 slices Swiss or Gruyère cheese
4 thin slices ham
1 egg, beaten
4 tablespoons flour
½ cup fine dry bread or cracker crumbs
3 tablespoons butter
1 tablespoon oil

Pound veal with mallet or the bottom of a plate to flatten, working in salt and pepper sprinkled from shakers; trim edges. Place 1 slice cheese and 1 slice ham over half the cutlets, so that neither cheese nor ham overlaps edges. Brush edges with beaten egg, top each with another cutlet, pound edges to seal. Roll each in flour, then dip in egg, then in crumbs. Sauté in mixture of butter and oil until well browned. Transfer to casserole or roasting pan, place in oven preheated to 375° F., complete in oven, baking for 20 to 35 minutes. (*Serves 4*).

(From LÜCHOW'S GERMAN FESTIVAL COOKBOOK by Gene and Fran Schoor. Copyright 1976 by Gene Schoor. Reprinted by permission of Doubleday & Company, Inc.)

Poultry Shears H:12

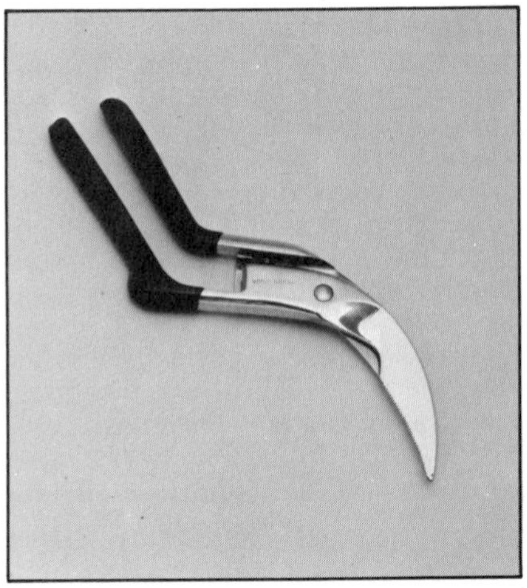

These highly curved shears are marvelously constructed for the difficult job of disjointing a large goose or a rabbit. Only 10¼″ long overall, the shears have blades of chromed steel joined by a visible spring of twisted wire (far easier to clean than the more common exposed springs of flattened, coiled steel). One blade has a serrated edge to help cut through skin and meat, and it is arched in one area to grip a bone. The black handles are plastic coated. Practical and strong, these shears will come in handy, whether serving roast goose with sauerkraut and apple stuffing, or cutting up a rabbit in the kitchen for *Hasenpfeffer*.

Norbert Stryer (5013) $20.00

PAPRIKA CHICKEN

Paprikás csirke

4 servings

2 medium-sized onions, peeled and minced
2 tablespoons lard
1 plump chicken, about 3 pounds, disjointed, washed, and dried
1 large ripe tomato, peeled and cut into pieces
1 heaping tablespoon "Noble Rose" paprika
1 teaspoon salt
1 green pepper sliced
2 tablespoons sour cream
1 tablespoon flour
2 tablespoons heavy cream

1. Use a 4- or 5-quart heavy casserole with a tight-fitting lid. Cook the onions in the lard, covered, over low heat for about 5 minutes. They should become almost pasty, but definitely not browned.
2. Add chicken and tomato and cook, covered, for 10 minutes.
3. Stir in paprika. Add ½ cup water and the salt. Cook, covered, over very low heat for 30 minutes. In the beginning, the small amount of water will create a steam-cooking action. Toward the end of the 30-minute period, take off lid and let the liquid evaporate. Finally let the chicken cook in its own juices and fat, taking care that it does not burn. (If the chicken is tough, you may have to add a few more tablespoons of water.)
4. Remove chicken pieces. Mix the sour cream, flour and 1 teaspoon cold water, and stir in with the sauce till it is very smooth and of an even color. Add green pepper, replace chicken parts, adjust salt. Put lid back on casserole and over very low heat cook until done.
5. Just before serving whip in the heavy cream. Serve with egg dumplings.

Note: The combination of sour cream and heavy cream is the almost forgotten, but ideal way to prepare this dish. Today, more often than not, the heavy cream is omitted. In Hungary, the lily is gilded by spreading several tablespoons of additional sour cream on top of the chicken in the serving platter.

(From THE CUISINE OF HUNGARY by George Lang. Copyright 1971 by George Lang. Reprinted by permission of Atheneum.)

Egg Scissors H:13

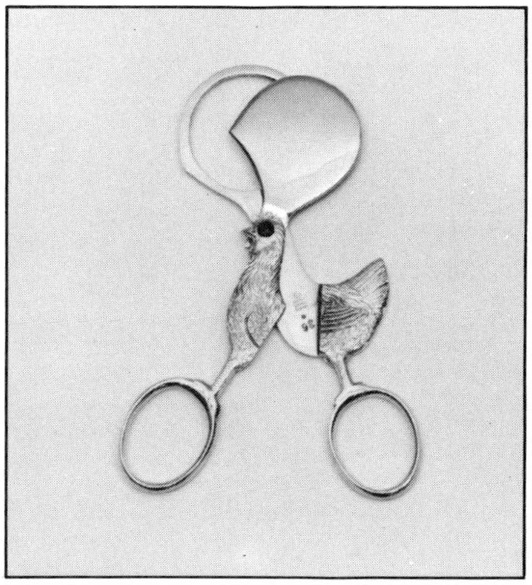

Most German breakfasts consist of a hearty array of breads, served with butter and jam and often accompanied by soft-boiled eggs served with egg-cups. People have different methods for opening an egg: the timid tap around the top with a knife handle until they break off enough little pieces to slip in a spoon; the bold slice off the narrow tip in one swift sweep of the blade. We recommend this elegant compromise. Instead of messing around with bits of shell, or taking the risk of splattering egg yolk around the table, use a pair of 5½″-long scissors of steel like these. Work the circular, serrated loop of one "blade" around the egg until its teeth catch in the shell, then close the scissors so the disc-shaped blade cleanly decapitates the egg. With its handsome golden cockerel astride the oval finger holes, this pair of scissors is certainly worth crowing about.

Milton Gumpert (1582) $12.95

"ASPARAGUS.—The ancients called all the sprouts of young vegetables asparagus, whence the name, which is now limited to a particular species, embracing artichoke, alisander, asparagus, cardoon, rampion, and sea-kale. They are originally mostly wild sea-coast plants; and, in this state, asparagus may still be found on the northern as well as southern shores of Britain. It is often vulgarly called, in London, sparrowgrass; and, in its cultivated form, hardly bears any resemblance to the original plant. Immense quantities of it are raised for the London market . . . but it belongs rather to the classes of luxurious rather than necessary food. It is light and easily digested, but is not very nutritious."

Beeton's Book of Household Management *by Isabella Beeton, 1861.*

Asparagus Peeler H:14

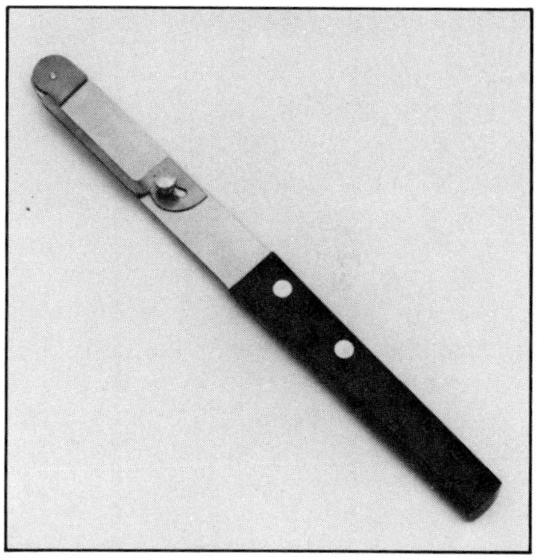

Asparagus tops the social scale of vegetables in Germany and heralds the beginning of spring. White, thick and tender, it is often a course or a meal unto itself. Drenched in melted butter, with or without bread crumbs, it is traditionally eaten with the fingers—forks in this case being considered very non-U. Hollandaise sauce is also a favored topping and ham is a frequent partner as well. To remove the tough outer layer of the stalk so that stalks and tips cook in the same length of time, asparagus should be peeled; but a paring knife is apt to remove too much. Instead, use this small (8½″-long) asparagus peeler, with which you can control the depth of each cut. Attached by a screw to the razor-sharp stainless-steel blade (4¾″ long and ¾″ wide) is a 3″-long adjustable guard. By loosening the screw and pushing the guard forward, you can get an extremely thin peel; move it back for a thicker one. This handy tool will also peel the tough skin from broccoli stalks.

Williams-Sonoma (1537F) $11.00

Plum Pitter H:15

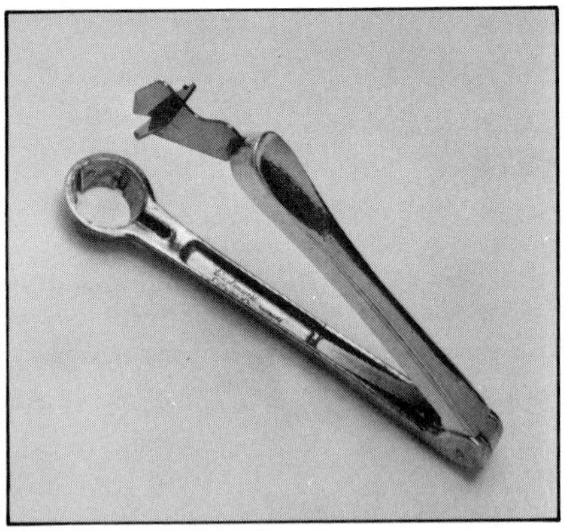

Plums are used in *Zwetschgenknödel,* those luscious dumplings made with little blue plums stuffed with cubes of sugar and then encased in pastry. They are also used to make fruit soup, that heady mixture of fruit, white wine and cinnamon; and in the many plum tarts and cakes found everywhere in *Mitteleuropa.* But in order to make any of these dishes, you will first have to pit the plums. Try this simple 6½″-long device from West Germany: a pair of cast-aluminum pincers with tension supplied by a simple spring. One end has an open cup for holding a small plum; the other has crossed stainless-steel blades that push into the ring, pitting and quartering the fruit at the same time. It is sturdy, inexpensive, and very simple to operate and clean. Who could resist such a logical invention?

Creative House (S1958) $4.50

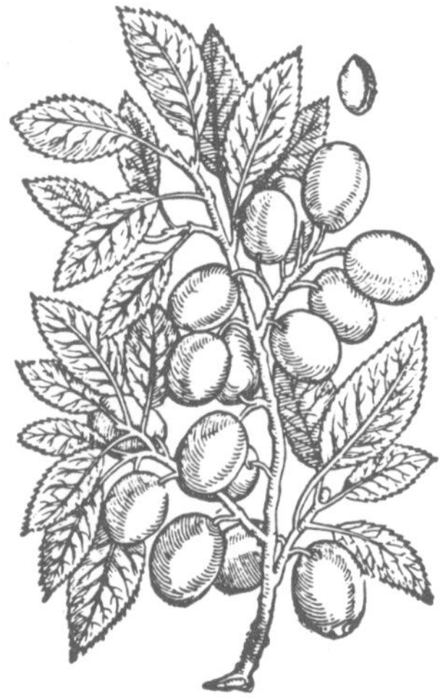

Pickle Slicer H:16

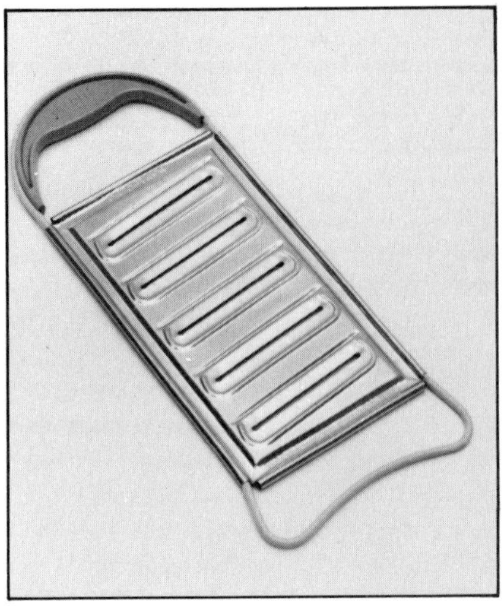

This handy, stainless-steel pickle slicer is designed to give you five pickle slices in one quick sweep of a gherkin. It is 11″ long with a rubber-coated base to prevent slipping, and has a 4″-wide plastic handle. Use the pickle slices as a garnish, or chop the slices to make *Bauernschweinekotelette,* pork chops cooked with sausage, potatoes, tomatoes, caraway seeds and pickle. Dishes with pickles are frequent antidotes for a *Katzenjammer* (hangover).

Kalkus, Inc. (963) $3.25

Rotating Horseradish Grater H:17

Freshly grated horseradish root mixed with whipped cream, sour cream, apples, vinegar, or grated lemon rind, and always with a little sugar and salt, is an essential accompaniment to many of the meat, poultry and fish dishes served in Middle Europe. There are some tricks for peeling onions and not crying, but, for very sensitive people there is no way to grate horseradish without tears unless you have an enclosed grater. This simple glass jar, 4½″ high and 3½″ in diameter, is fitted with a circular, tinned-steel grater and a red plastic cover with a 1½″ hole and cap in the center. First soak horseradish in cold water for about 24 hours to tenderize it and remove some of the bitter taste. Then peel it. Remove the cap from the top of the grater, place the root in the hole and rotate the top over the grater. When you have the desired amount of horseradish, sprinkle the pungent root with lemon juice to keep it from blackening. Replace the cap, and you can then store the horseradish in the jar. The top and the grater are held together by a screw and can be easily taken apart for cleaning.

H. Roth & Son (10-7) $7.95

Flat Horseradish Grater H:18

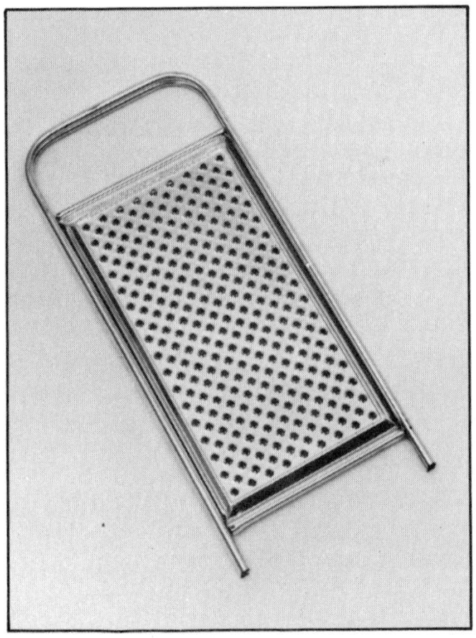

This tinned-steel grater, measuring 10″ by 4¼″, with small, rough holes set closely together, is made expressly for grating horseradish. It could be used for any root, but because it is difficult to wash, and horseradish is particularly pungent and aromatic, it might be best to keep the grater for only one purpose. Use it to grate horseradish for *Roter Rübenkren,* a beet and apple salad with caraway seeds and fresh horseradish, or for a whipped cream sauce that will add zest to poached fish fillets or boiled tongue.

H. Roth & Son (15-1) $1.20

HORSERADISH SAUCE

3 tablespoons butter
3 tablespoons flour
1 cup hot milk
½ cup beef stock
¼ teaspoon grated nutmeg
1 tablespoon white vinegar
½ teaspoon salt
¼ teaspoon white pepper
½ cup freshly grated horseradish

Melt butter; stir flour smoothly into it. Add hot milk and stock; stir and cook until well blended. Add nutmeg, vinegar, salt, and pepper; mix well. Stir continually until smooth and thickened. Strain through sieve; beat horseradish in just before serving. Makes about 1¾ cups; serves 8 to 10.

(From LÜCHOW'S GERMAN COOKBOOK by Jan Mitchell. Copyright 1952 by Leonard Jan Mitchell. Reprinted by permission of Doubleday & Company, Inc.)

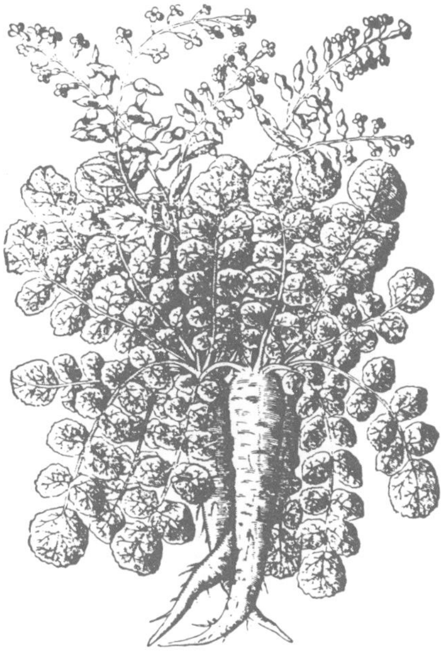

Horseradish in full (and poisonous) plumage.

"Take fasting, some pieces of this beneficent and despised root, and the most inveterate poisons will be changed for you into inoffensive drinks.

Would you have the power to handle and play with those dangerous reptiles whose active venom causes a speedy and sure death? Wash your hands in the juice of horse-radish.

Do you seek an efficacious remedy for the numerous evils which besiege us unceasingly? Take horse-radish—nothing but horse-radish."

The Pantropheon by Alexis Soyer. Semkin, Marshall & Co., 1853.

All-Purpose Grater H:19

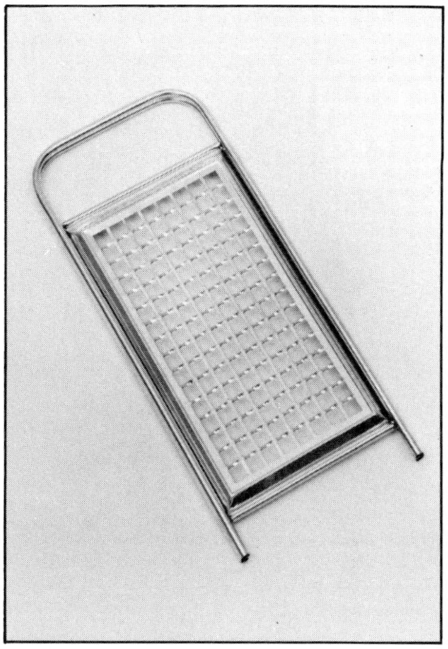

Effective is an apt word for this simple-looking checkerboard grater that will make shreds of cabbage, cucumbers and other firm vegetables. Just the thing for making red cabbage with apples or coleslaw. The grater's horizontal bars are scored to create a ruffled cutting surface with ¼″-wide openings. The thickness of the slices is determined by the pressure of your hand. A large handle at one end assures a steady grip, and the generous 6½″-by-3¼″ tinned-steel cutting surface makes for quick work. Overall, the grater is 10″ long.

H. Roth & Son (15-4) $1.20

Fine-Toothed Grater H:20

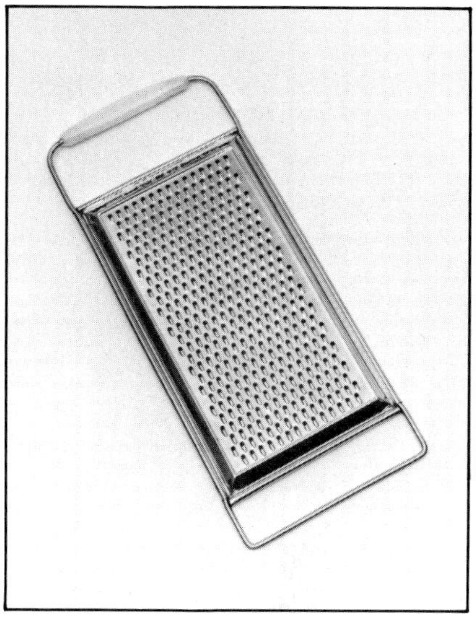

A grater like this one of stainless steel with closely set teeth is excellent for finely grating fruits and vegetables. Perfect for adding that bit of lemon or orange peel called for in so many cake and cookie recipes, it is also useful for grating onions for *Kartoffelpuffer* (potato pancakes). Its coarse surface is hard to clean, but a good, stiff brush will help. The handle is made of lemon-yellow plastic, and the grater measures 10½″ by 4¼″.

H. Roth & Son (15-2) $2.49

Pea Masher H:21

Dried yellow peas, cooked and pressed through a sieve with carrots, celery, leeks, chopped onions and marjoram and topped with crumbled bacon

Continued from preceding page

or onion rings provide a hearty vegetable. Cooked with sausages the purée becomes a one-dish meal, perfect for a Saturday lunch in many Central European homes, the sort of meal that you need to restoke the fire between a morning and an afternoon of raking leaves on a cold autumn day, hiking in the Alps, or schussing the slopes of your favorite mountain. A smashing wooden pea masher like this one will make the puréeing a cinch. With a good grip on its 9½″-long handle, press down and roll the masher by describing a circle with your hand. The broad, smoothly sanded head, 4½″ in diameter and 1″ deep, will force peas and other vegetables quickly through a drum sieve, the curved edges of the head widening the masher's sphere of influence as it moves. Not just for peas, this tall wooden mushroom will extract the cooking juices from vegetables for sauces and for soups, such as the Polish *barszcz,* a clear beet soup.

Scandicrafts, Inc. (W-140) **$2.25**

GERMAN PEA SOUP WITH SLICED SAUSAGES

Echte Deutsche Erbsensuppe mit Wursteinlage

1 pound whole yellow peas
1 quart water
½ pound fat salt pork or smoked ham bone
1 onion, peeled and diced
½ cup chopped celery
¼ cup chopped parsley
½ teaspoon thyme or rosemary
1 bay leaf
2 cups milk (approximately)
1 pound frankfurters (approximately) sliced
Salt, pepper to taste

Wash peas, soak in water overnight. Bring the water to a boil. Add peas, cover, remove from the heat, and let stand for 1 hour. Add the fat salt pork or ham bone, onion, celery, parsley, thyme, bay leaf; simmer until the peas are soft (1 to 2 hours).

Remove the ham bone or salt pork; rub the soup through a sieve or crush peas with a blending fork. Dilute as you like with milk. Add the frankfurters, and heat. Season to taste with salt and pepper. (Serves 4 to 6.)

Marcel of Lüchow's suggests a few crisp croutons and a few green fresh peas in each cup would make a most attractive garnish.

(From LÜCHOW's GERMAN FESTIVAL COOKBOOK by Gene and Fran Schoor. Copyright 1976 by Gene Schoor. Reprinted by permission of Doubleday & Company, Inc.)

Chestnut and Potato Ricer H:22

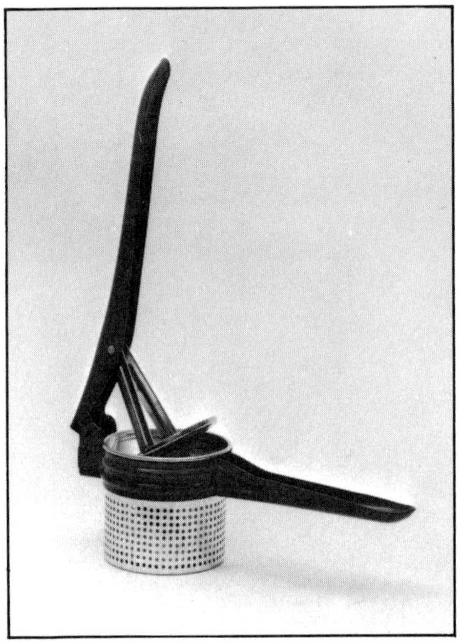

Chestnuts are a cherished delicacy in Central Europe; potatoes a humble staple. Either may be puréed perfectly with this 11″-long, tinned-steel ricer with enameled handles and a basket 3½″ in diameter and 3″ deep. To use it, put boiled chestnuts or potatoes into the basket and bring the upper handle down so that the plunger attached to it forces the purée out through the small perforations in the bottom and sides of the basket. Use the potato purée to make *Kartoffelklosse* (potato dumplings), delicious for soaking up the spicy gravy of a *Sauerbraten,* or dumplings filled with prunebutter for dessert. Puréed chestnuts are used in Hungary for a thick cream of chestnut soup with veal. Or, for a rich, chocolate-coated chestnut torte: mixed with butter, sugar, egg, rum and melted chocolate, the chestnut purée becomes a superb filling for the three-layered cake.

Paprikás Weiss **$4.98**

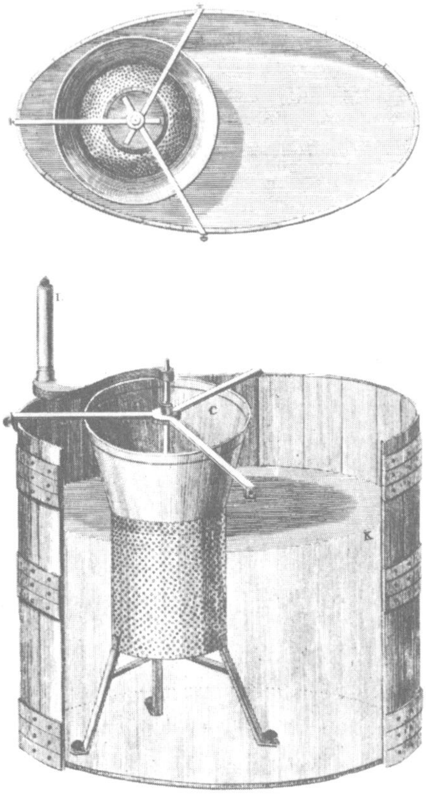

Potato mill.

Nutmeg Grinder H:23

No, *not* another pepper mill! Into this beautifully finished, 4½″-high, beechwood grinder you can slip a whole nutmeg to keep in the kitchen or even on the table, along with salt and pepper, for the discriminating palate. To open, turn the bottom cap clockwise and lift it off. Place the nutmeg on the three-pronged unit in the center, pull the handle slightly away from the grinder to properly lodge the nutmeg, and replace the cap. Freshly ground nutmeg is lovely in sauces and on soups, vegetables, meats and desserts. Let your taste be your guide. In the 19th century, it was customary among Hungarian peasants to sleep with a whole nutmeg under the pillow to conjure up dreams of one's sweetheart.

H. Roth & Son (37-5) **$6.95**

A Czech chaplain at the battlefront comments on a proper sauce: "Take sauces, for example. Now an intelligent man when he's making onion sauce, will take all kinds of vegetables and steam them in butter, then he'll add nutmeg, pepper, more nutmeg, a little clove, ginger, and so on."

The Good Soldier Schweik *by Jaroslav Hasek, translated by Paul Selver. Signet Classics, New American Library, 1963.*

Poppyseed Mill H:24

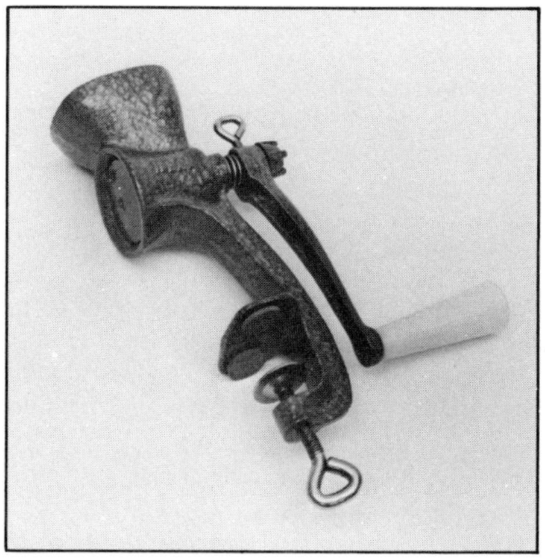

The tiny, grayish-blue seeds of the opium poppy (*papaver somniferum*) have no narcotic properties, for opium is only found in the flower bud before the seeds form; but their nut-like aroma and taste are delightful. Known to the Egyptians earlier than 1500 B.C., poppyseeds have also been used in parts of Middle Europe since prehistoric times. They are often scattered on breads, rolls and cakes, or ground into a paste, which combined with raisins and grated apple or apricot jam, makes a wonderful filling for strudel. A mill is essential for grinding the seeds into paste. This one, made in Czechoslovakia, is of cast iron, enameled in a pleasing light brown. It is fairly small and well-proportioned, 9″ high and 7″ wide, with a 1½″-deep hopper. The clamp includes two tightly-fitting rubber discs that protect the table or countertop to which the mill is secured. A coil spring in the handle provides tension and makes it possible to adjust the degree of coarseness. All the parts are removable for cleaning and are simple to reassemble. In order to keep poppyseeds from turning rancid, they should be refrigerated and then ground only as needed.

H. Roth & Son (10-5) **$12.95**

"A very large Bratwurst"—to say the least.

Sausages At Any Hour

Throughout Middle Europe the pause that refreshes is frequently sausage. Nowhere is this truer than in Germany. German laborers and skiers relish *Weisswürste* in the predawn hours on their way to work or play. A slice of *Leberwurst* is apt to accompany bread and a boiled egg for breakfast, and *Knackwurst* with mustard and a crust of bread makes a typical midmorning snack. The popular Saturday lunch of lentil soup is almost always enriched with *Würstchen* (little sausages). And at night an array of *Cervelet, Mettwurst* and *Teewurst* often comprises the major part of the evening meal (*Abendbrot*). At midnight, a snack of *Bratwurst* with a hard roll might well top off an evening's beer drinking. And should you still have a craving for *Wurst* after all the shops are closed, convenient sidewalk automats will supply you with a pair of *Landjaegerwurst* at the drop of a coin.

This passion for sausages is only slightly less intense elsewhere in Middle Europe. In Czechoslovakia, stopping off for a couple of *párky* at midmorning or late afternoon is as common as taking a coffeebreak here. In Vienna, it's *Würstel* (known everywhere else as wieners) that one snacks on at all hours. And if in Germany there are more than 300 different kinds of *Wurst*, in Poland there are more than 70 kinds of *kielbasa*.

Pork is the favored meat for sausages in Central Europe, although beef and veal are also used. The infinite variety is achieved by using all the animal's parts in different combinations, with different spices and different smoking or cooking techniques. Hungarian *kolbase* is, of course, seasoned with paprika; and many Polish *kielbasa* gain their distinctive flavor from being smoked over juniperwood.

The technique of making sausages is a method of preserving

Continued from preceding page

meat that the Middle Europeans probably learned from the Romans, and it is easy. Ground or minced meat mixed with spices is stuffed into a casing made of the intestines of sheep, hogs, or cattle, or into a strong cloth bag. The casing or bag is tied in several places, and the sausages are then smoked or cooked. Natural casings hold the juices in while the meat is being cooked and add their own flavor to the finished product.

With a meat grinder, a sausage stuffer and some casing, you can go whole hog and concoct your own *Bratwurst* and *Leberwurst*.

Meat Grinder H:25

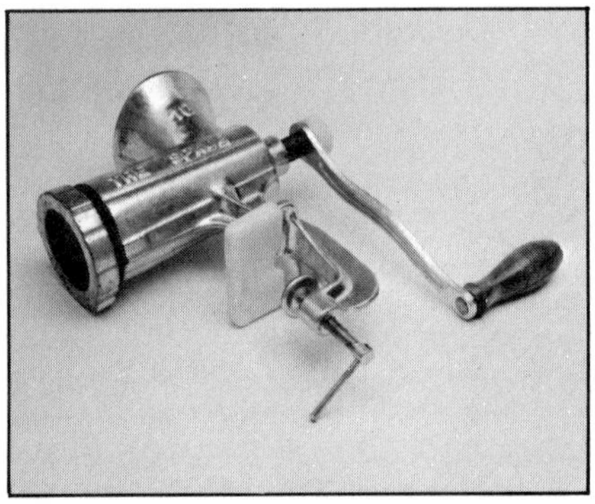

All business, this heavy-duty, meat grinder from Czechoslovakia makes no concessions to modern concepts of style. To resist rust and corrosion, the cast-iron body and handle, 7″ wide and 12″ high overall, are double-dipped in zinc, and the steel attachments are zinc plated or chromed. So that it can handle large chunks of meat, the cutting plate and the cutting edges of the rotary worm are of self-sharpening hard steel. Although the grinder has many parts, it is not difficult to assemble and use. Put the worm through the base of the grinder, secure the handle with a bolt at one end of the worm, and at the other fit the four-sided steel knife, its sharpened edges facing out. Then fit the steel chopping plate over the end of the blade and screw on the zinc-plated ring to hold it in place. (Additional cutting plates are available separately.) Such optional attachments as a nut grater, a cookie press or a fruit press can be substituted for the cutting blade and the plate and used to prepare nuts and fruit for a *Linzertorte* or for other pastries. The fruit press has a fine mesh that yields only pulp—no seeds or skin—making it effective even for berries. But you will be most grateful for this machine's efficiency at grinding meat for your own homemade sausages or the very finest beefsteak Tartar in town.

H. Roth & Son Grinder (11-1) **$21.95**
Each extra plate (11-2) **$14.50**

Small Sausage Stuffer H:26

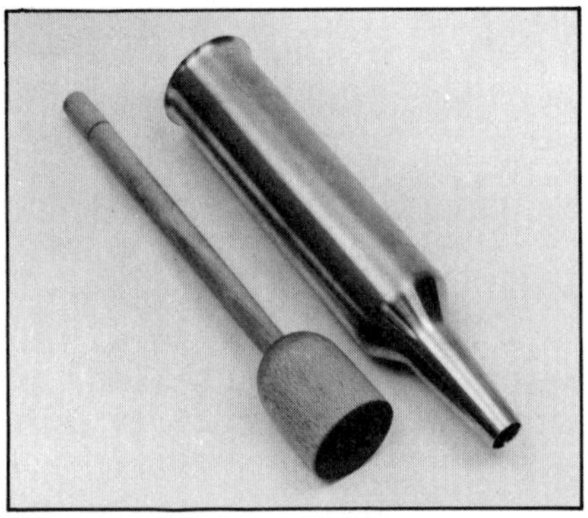

This small, light and reasonably-priced sausage stuffer has a 12½″-long tube of aluminum and a long wooden stick with a bell-shaped knob, 2″ in diameter, for a plunger. With it, you can make your own string of frankfurters wrapped in real animal casing. Or be more adventurous: discover the glories of *Bauernwurst, Mettwurst and Truffel Leberwurst*—or invent our own recipes. Sausages are simple to make, and if you have a home smoker, you can try smoked varieties, too.

Paprikás Weiss (454-13½″) **$12.98**

A Czech soldier on the battlefield reminisces about the fall butchering of pigs that was a high point of the year at home. "It's slaughtering time there now," said Baloun in tones of yearning. "Which do you like best, saveloys or liver sausage? Just you tell me, and I'll write home this very evening. I should reckon my pig weighs round about three hundred pounds. He's got a head like a bulldog, and that's the best kind. Pigs like that never let you down. That's a good breed, if you like. They can stand plenty of wear and tear. I bet the fat on that animal's a good eight inches thick. When I was at home I used to make the liver sausage myself and I always had such a rare old feed of it that I was fit to bust. The pig I had last year weighed over three hundred pounds.

"Ah, that was a pig for you," he continued rapidly gripping Schweik's hand as they reached the parting of the ways. "I brought him up on nothing but potatoes and I used to watch him growing visibly, as you might almost say. I put the ham into brine, and I tell you, a nice slice taken from the brine and fried with potato dumplings, soaked in pork dripping and some greens on top of it, that's a fair treat. And after a good blowout of that sort, you wash it down with a nice glass or two of beer. But the war's put a stop to all that."

The Good Soldier Schweik *by Jaroslav Hasek, translated by Paul Selver. Signet Classics, New American Library, 1963.*

BRATWURST

¾ pound fresh veal
1½ pounds pork loin
2 teaspoons pepper
¾ teaspoon grated nutmeg
½ teaspoon mace
Pork casings
Milk

Combine all ingredients; except casings and milk; put through grinder three times. Mix with about ½ cup water; fill pork casings. Cover Bratwurst with hot water. Bring to a boil and remove from the heat immediately. Let stand in the hot water for a few minutes until firm. Drain; dip Bratwurst in milk. Place in broiler and cook until golden brown under low to moderate heat (*Serves 4 to 6.*)

(From LÜCHOW'S GERMAN FESTIVAL COOKBOOK by Gene and Fran Schoor. Copyright 1976 by Gene Schoor. Reprinted by permission of Doubleday & Company, Inc.)

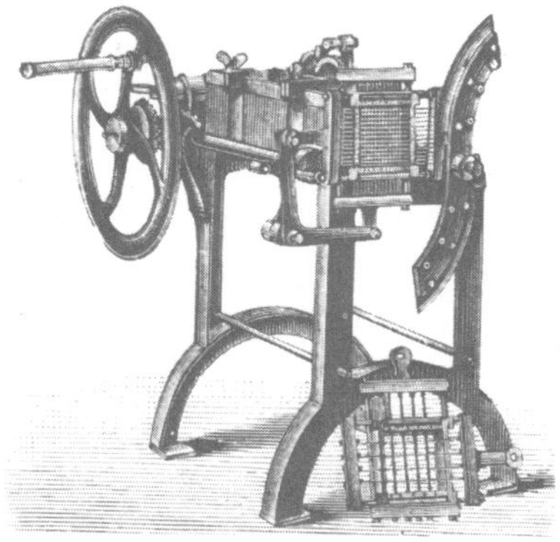

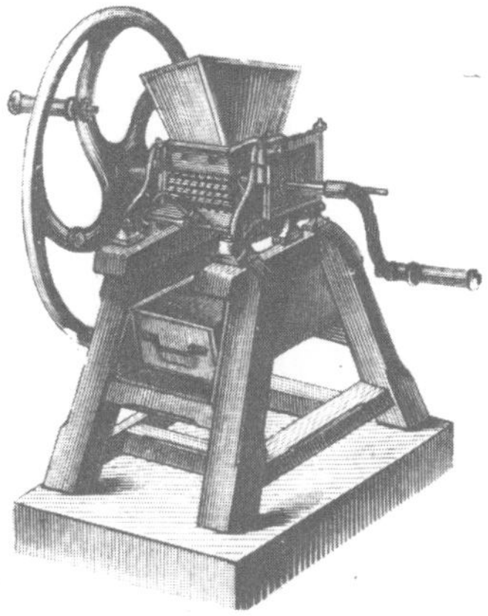

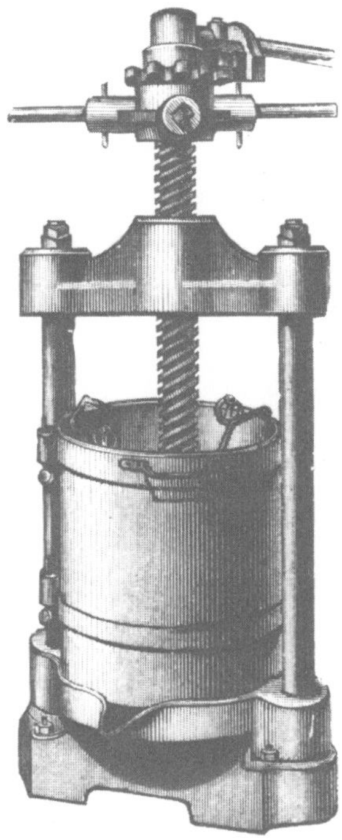

Various meat grinders from Germany and Austria.

Large Sausage Stuffer H:27

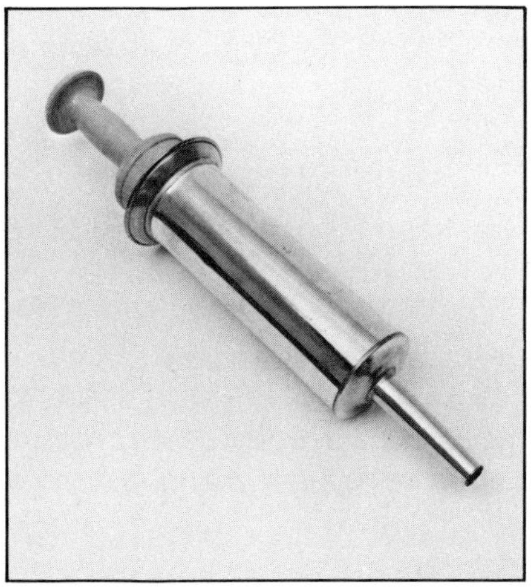

You can make links and links of sausages—all kinds—with this tinned-steel and wood sausage stuffer. Essentially, it is a 9¾″-long, 3⅛″-wide funnel with a flared top (4½″ in diameter) leading into a 4″-long, straight tube with a bottom opening about the size of a penny. The solid beechwood plunger (3″ in diameter) looks like a fat rolling pin with a large knob handle. To use it, slip a quantity of sausage casing over the straight tube at the bottom part of the funnel and tie the free end into a knot. Put the ground meat seasoned with fresh herbs and pepper into the funnel and press the mixture down with the wooden plunger. When the casing fills to the desired shape—don't fill it too tightly—twist and tie it with string (as you would a balloon). You can buy casing in Hungarian or German butcher shops; be sure to wash it thoroughly but gently in cold water to remove the salt or brine in which it was preserved. As one expert points out, making sausages at home is no more difficult than making meatloaf or hamburgers; why not give it a try.

Paprikás Weiss (454-20″) $29.98

Sausage-Tying Knife and Pricker H:28

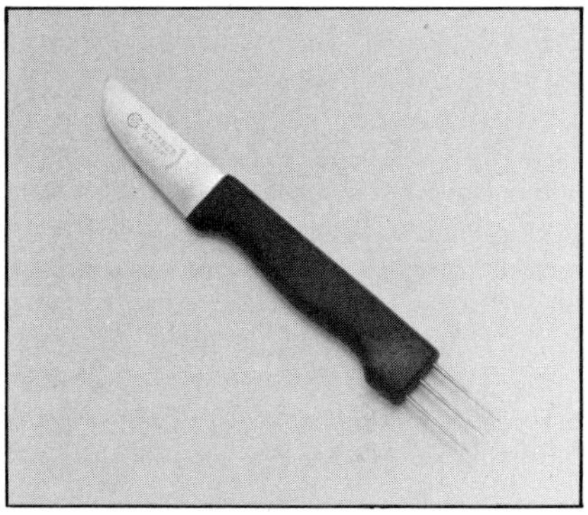

After you have pushed sausage meat into a casing, you will need to twist and tie it into separate links. This handy, 8½″-long tool will help considerably. At one end is a sharp, stainless-steel blade to cut off the string. At the other end are three needle-sharp prongs, protected by a black rubber cover. Every so often, too much meat will be bunched together in one part of the casing, making it difficult to tie. Use the prongs to prick holes in the casing through which you can squeeze out small amounts of meat until the casing is loose enough to tie. You'll also find this knife useful at a later stage to cut off individual sausages and to prick them so they will release fat as they cook.

R. H. Forschner Co., Inc. (1106B) $5.50

The Realm of Cabbage

"The time has come, the walrus said, to talk of many things; of shoes —of ships—and ceiling wax—of cabbages and kings." The association of cabbages with kings is a natural one in Middle Europe where cabbage reigns with the potato over all other vegetables. Rich in vitamins A and C, cabbage has long sustained Central Europeans through the cold, snowy continental winters.

The Romans valued cabbage, too—especially as a cure for a hangover—and probably imported the vegetable to Middle Europe. Modern names for cabbage—Hungarian, *kaposzta;* Russian, *kapusta;* German *Kohl*—derive from the Latin words for "head" (*caput*) and

Continued from preceding page

"stalk" (*caulis*, which is what the Romans called cabbage).

It was the Mongol and Tartar invaders, however, in the thirteenth century, who taught the Russians, Austrians and Hungarians how to preserve cabbage in salt brine to produce sauerkraut. Pickling halves the vitamin content of cabbage but it saves more vitamins than would be left in a head of cabbage that is simply stored in a cool cellar over the winter.

A comprehensive cookbook of fresh and sour cabbage dishes from *Mitteleuropa* would be staggering. One Hungarian authority has counted more than 800 recipes for Hungarian potted cabbage alone. With the equipment we show you here—graters, a corer, a sauerkraut crock, tongs and a fork—you can tackle any cabbage recipe and serve it up in style.

Large Cabbage Cutter H:29

Serious coleslaw and sauerkraut lovers might do well to invest in this enormous cabbage shredder. Made of light, natural wood, it has a 7⅛″-long cutting blade of sharp carbon steel, which lies diagonally across the large wooden board (20¾″ long and 7⅞″ wide). A wooden box, 7¾″ by 6″ by 2¼″, runs back and forth on tracks that are raised along either side of the board. To use it, cut a cabbage in half or quarters and fit a piece into the box; hold the palm of your hand on top of the cabbage and rub it back and forth over the cutting edge. Strictly specialized for big vegetables like cabbage and lettuce, this cutter is marvelously efficient. In no time at all, you could shred enough cabbage to make a barrel of sauerkraut, and then, when the season's right, you could treat a chalet-full of hungry skiers to a Tyrolean *Bauernschmaus:* pork in various guises with sauerkraut and bacon dumplings.

Schiller & Asmus, Inc. (K1347) $30.00

Cabbage and Squash Cutter H:30

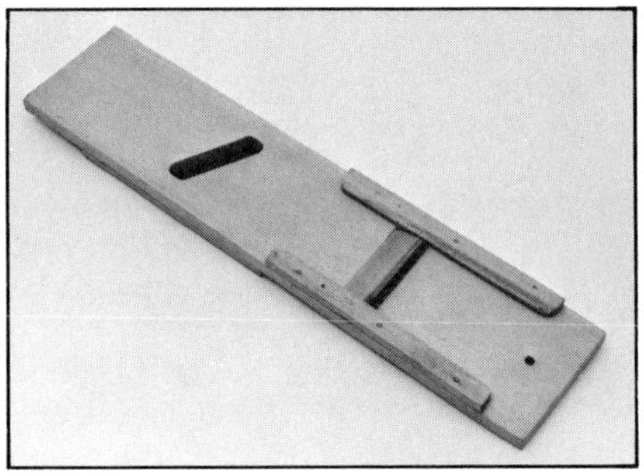

This combination cutter, measuring 18½″ long and 4″ wide, shreds cabbage on one side and slices squash into julienne strips on the other. Essentially, it is a wooden board with two stainless-steel blades: the cabbage side has a simple, straight cutting edge, and the squash side has a slotted blade with eight partitions, ¼″ apart. The cutter has a hole by which it can be hung, and wooden strips along the sides of each cutting edge provide maximum knuckle protection. It is easy to clean, durable and versatile. You can use it to prepare a variety of *crudités* (coleslaw, cucumbers or carrots), to slice potatoes or onions, or to cut summer squash into julienne strips for *tejfeles tökkáposzta,* a special, lightly-cooked Hungarian slaw with onion, dill, sour cream and a bit of sugar.

H. Roth & Son $9.95

Cabbage Grater H:31

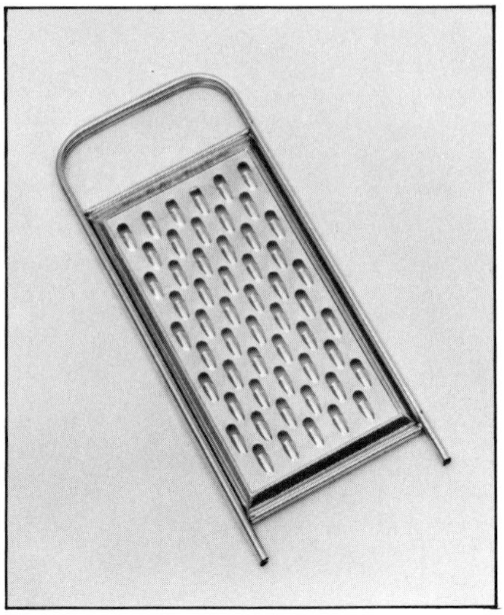

Along with wood-framed shredders, a large variety of all-metal graters with different sized cutting edges are used in the Middle European kitchen. This one of tinned steel, 10″ long by 4¼″ wide, has ½″-long oblong holes set fairly close together with a raised cutting edge at one end of each hole. With it, carrots and cucumbers as well as cabbage can be sliced into large shreds. Or use it to grate raw potatoes to add to sauerkraut or to make *Kartoffelpuffer*—crisp, golden potato pancakes, served with applesauce or lingonberry preserves.

H. Roth & Son (15-5) $1.20

Cabbage Corer H:32

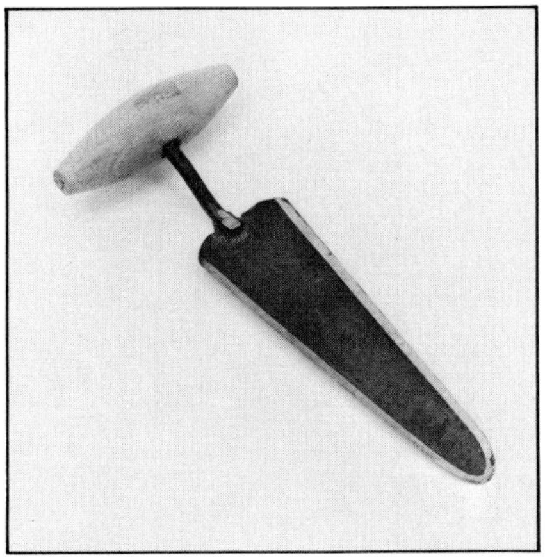

Cabbage lovers will welcome this tool for getting to the core of a cabbage. The sturdy, 6½″-long steel spade, with its sharp, curved cutting edges, is firmly attached to a 3¾″ wooden handle, and is menacing enough to deal with even the most recalcitrant core. No where could it be used to better advantage than in the Central European kitchen where you will find a multitude of stuffed cabbage recipes. One basic Hungarian recipe calls for stuffing cooked cabbage with a combination of ground pork and beef, rice, onion and sour cream lightly spiced with paprika. The cabbage rolls are then cooked and served in a casserole with sauerkraut and smoked pork butt, and finally topped with sour cream.

H. Roth & Son (35-4) $9.95

APPLE CABBAGE GÜL BABA

Gül baba almás káposztája

6 to 8 servings

2½ pounds red cabbage
Salt
1 small onion, minced
2 tablespoons butter
1 tablespoon sugar
1 cup chicken broth
2 pounds sour apples
2 tablespoons flour
1 tablespoon lemon juice

1. Slice or cut cabbage to a fine slaw. Mix with 1 tablespoon salt, cover, and let stand for 2 to 3 hours.
2. Squeeze cabbage well, a little at a time, and set it aside.
3. Wilt the onion in butter for about 10 minutes. Add sugar and brown carefully so as not to burn it.
4. Mix in the cabbage and pour in ½ cup of the chicken broth. Cover and cook over low heat for 30 minutes.
5. Meantime peel the apples and cut into fine pieces. Add to the cabbage. Cook until both apples and cabbage are properly done.
6. Mix flour with remaining ½ cup chicken broth; make sure that the mixture is not lumpy. Add lemon juice and pour into cabbage.
7. Simmer cabbage for another 5 minutes. Adjust salt, sugar and lemon juice to your sweet-and-sour liking.

Note: Gül Baba was a rare phenomenon: a beloved member of the occupying Turkish forces in the sixteenth century, who established rose gardens and fruit orchards in Hungary. This dish is a tribute to him: it was created in the 1920's for one of the dinners given in connection with the International Hoteliers and Restaurateurs Convention.

(From THE CUISINE OF HUNGARY by George Lang. Copyright 1971 by George Lang. Reprinted by permission of Atheneum.)

Cabbage Tongs H:33

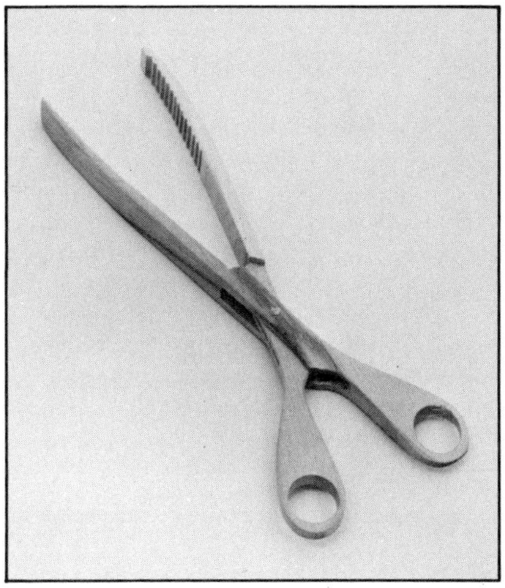

Central Europeans eat a lot of cabbage. They eat it steamed, stuffed, sweet-and-soured, or sauced (white, brown or with wine); they eat it with meat, with dumplings, with potatoes, with raisins, with sausages or in dozens of other combinations. They pickle it in brine to make sauerkraut and then add apples, caraway seeds or noodles. They even wrap sauerkraut in strudel dough. For most of these dishes, the cabbage must be shredded; and when shredded and cooked it is somewhat difficult to handle. These tongs of unfinished wood from Germany are the answer. They look something like scissors, but have "blades" that curve outward and meet only at the ends, working more like pliers or forceps to grip the shredded cabbage between ridged jaws. The parts are held together by a wooden pin. This pair is 11¼″ long; a smaller 7½″ size is also available.

H. Roth & Son (42-5) $3.85

"The cabbage was adored by the Egyptians, who raised altars to it. Afterwards, they made this strange God the first dish in their repasts. The Greeks and Romans ascribed to it the happy quality of preserving from drunkeness; and Erasistratus looked upon it as a sovereign remedy against paralysis."

Good Cheer: The Romance of Food and Feasting *by F. W. Hackwood. Sturgess & Walton, 1911.*

Sauerkraut Fork H:34

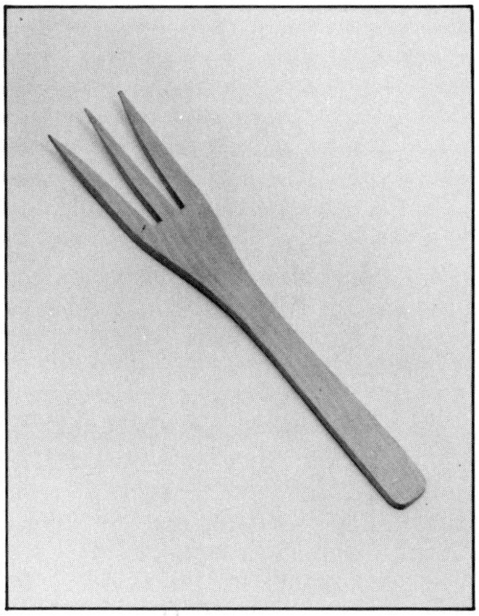

Give a lift to your sauerkraut with this specially designed, 11½″-long sauerkraut fork. The tines are spaced just the right distance apart to pick up sauerkraut, and the relatively short, broad handle makes the fork easy to use. It is made of light, beechwood. As one of our experts explained, wooden utensils are popular in Europe because wood is cheap and plentiful, and it does not scratch cooking pots or react unfavorably with acidic foods the way some metal implements are apt to. We like it for its simple good looks. Why not use it to serve pineapple sauerkraut, a tangy side dish for smoked pork?

Paprikás Weiss (3616) $1.98

"Sauerkraut . . . of which [the Germans] are so immoderately fond, is merely fermented cabbage. To prepare this, close-headed white cabbages are cut in shreds, and placed in . . . a cask; this is strewed with salt, unground pepper, and a small quantity of salad oil; a man with clean wooden shoes then gets into the cask,

Continued from preceding page

and treads the whole together till it is well mixed and compact. Another layer is then added, which is again trod down, and so on until the cask is ensubjected to heavy pressure, and allowed to ferment; when the fermentation has subsided, the barrels in which it is prepared are closed up, and it is preserved for use. The preparing of sauerkraut is considered of so much importance as to form a separate profession, which is principally engrossed by the Tyrolese . . . October and November are the busy months for the work, and huge white pyramids of cabbage are seen crowding the markets; while in every court and yard into which an accidental peep is obtained, all is bustle and activity in the concocting of this national food, and the baskets piled with shredded cabbage resemble mountains of green-tinged froth or syllabub.' "

A History of the Vegetable Kingdom: Embracing the Physiology, Classification, and Culture of Plants, With Their Various Uses to Man and the Lower Animals: and Their Application in the Arts, Manufactures, and Domestic Economy *by William Rhind. Glasgow, c. 1842.*

Cabbage.

"Armed with a plate, that moment came
Into the cellar goes the dame,
To take a portion from the pot,
Where she her Sauer-Kraut has got,
A dish which warmed with proper care,
Was to the widow very dear."

Max and Moritz: A Story in Seven Tricks *by Wilhelm Busch. Braun & Schneider, 1961.*

SAUERKRAUT WITH CARAWAY SEEDS

Kümmelkartoffeln

2 pounds fresh sauerkraut
2 or 3 apples, peeled and sliced
1 large onion, peeled and sliced
2 tablespoons butter
½ teaspoon caraway seeds
1 teaspoon sugar
1 raw potato, peeled and grated
2 cups white wine (or water)
½ teaspoon salt

Rinse sauerkraut with warm water, drain well. Sauté the apples and onion in butter until soft. Add the caraway seeds, sugar, and rinsed kraut. Simmer, covered, for 30 minutes. Add potato, wine or water, and salt. Continue cooking until sauerkraut is tender. *(Serves 6.)*

(From LÜCHOW'S GERMAN FESTIVAL COOKBOOK by Gene and Fran Schoor. Copyright 1976 by Gene Schoor. Reprinted by permission of Doubleday & Company, Inc.)

Sauerkraut Crock H:35

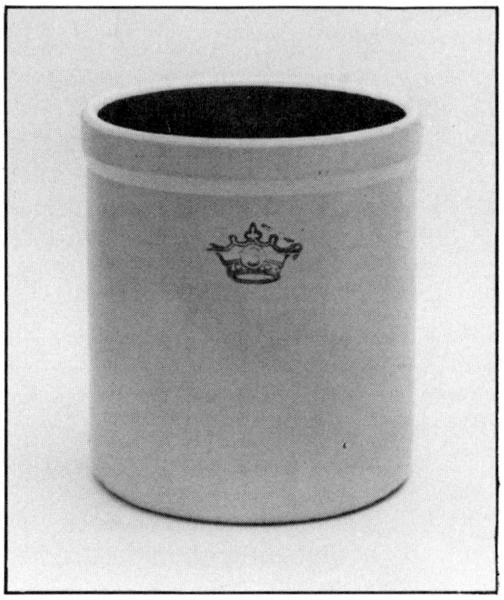

Sauerkraut aficionados will want to ferment cabbage themselves, the old-fashioned way, in this handsome, glazed, beige crock with its rich brown interior and soft blue crown decoration. Twelve quarts of finely-shredded white cabbage can be layered in the crock with salt (2 teaspoons for each pound of cabbage). As the layers are built up they should be pounded down with a wooden mallet, and finally covered with a clean cloth and some heavy rocks or other weights. During the fermentation process, the crock should be stored at 60 F. and the brine that rises above the cloth removed every few days. In a month you will have a generous supply of sauerkraut, ready to be spiced as you wish—with juniper berries, peppercorns, bay leaves, caraway seeds or allspice—and steamed with your favorite sausages or pork.

H. Roth & Son $9.98

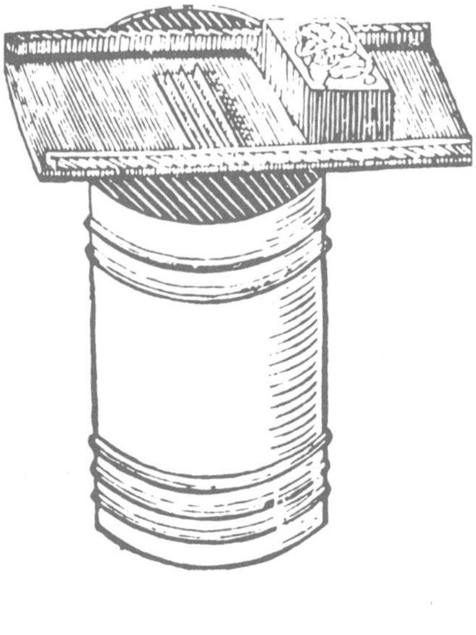

Pennsylvania Dutch Grout-Huvvel, *or cabbage plane.*

Dumplings, Noodles and Potatoes

Much of the Middle European heft comes from a diet rich in dumplings, noodles and potatoes. These tasty starch-laden foods embellish soups, soak up the rich gravies of stewed and braised meats, or drip with butter alongside roasts. They may also be tossed with vegetables, or provide a robust dessert with fruit, pot cheese or sour cream.

The word "dumpling"—often used as a term of endearment—evokes soft, round, tender, pinchable bodies, which are common enough in Middle Europe. Dumplings are said to have journeyed to Europe from China in the caravans of Marco Polo, and since medieval times they have been a staple of the peasant diet. Dumplings come in all shapes and sizes. Made with or without yeast, of flour, bread, semolina or potatoes, they may be flavored with such things as parsley, nutmeg or bacon, and filled with meat, pot cheese or fruit. Then they may be steamed, poached, baked or fried.

Noodles came to Central Europe from Italy, also during the Middle Ages. Made from flour, water and perhaps an egg or two, noodle dough is rolled out and cut by hand or with a noodle machine. The noodles are then cooked in soups or boiled in water and served as a side dish or as part of a main course. Noodles, like dumplings, are also found in a number of desserts, especially in Hungary. A classic is *Palffy metélt:* freshly made noodles cooked in milk, then baked with raisins, apples, nuts and lemon and covered with a meringue.

Potatoes, however, are the backbone of Middle European cuisine. Steamed, boiled, roasted, mashed, made into dumplings, fritters, salad or soup, mixed with apples and onions or sauerkraut, baked into strudel (yes, the Hungarians do this), potatoes are the *sine qua non* of a Central European menu. Yet they are relative newcomers to that part of the world. Although brought from America to Europe by Columbus and other early explorers, the potato did not become popular in Central Europe until the eighteenth century, when hungry peasants finally overcame their fear of this newfangled food.

We show you a *Spaetzle* board and various *Spaetzle* machines for those popular tiny dumplings. For noodles there is a rolling pin and board, a noodle press and a noodle machine. And for potatoes, a special fork and slicer that will make you the swiftest potato cook in town.

Noodle Rolling Pin H:36

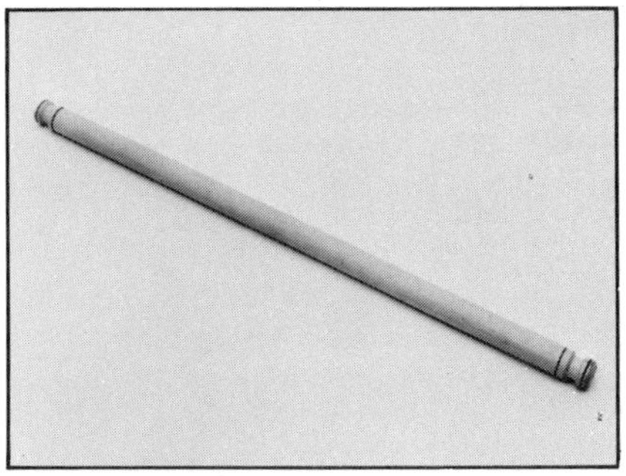

This rolling pin may not appear to carry much weight, but don't let it fool you. It does a good job. Made from a solid piece of unfinished wood, 27¾″ long, it is light and easy to manipulate when grasped by its turned ends. One Hungarian cook we know uses a pin like this for all the Hungarian noodle dishes she prepares, including large quantities of dough she needs for *laskatészta leveshe* (vermicelli noodles) for soup. She also uses it to start strudel pastry. So don't let the name of any utensil confine its use; experiment.

H. Roth & Son $4.50

PÁLFFY NOODLES

Pálffy metélt

6 to 8 servings

1 cup flour
5 eggs
Salt
1 quart milk
2-inch piece of vanilla bean
6 tablespoons sweet butter
¼ pound raisins
Rind of ½ lemon
½ cup sugar
5 sour apples, peeled, halved and cored
¼ cup bread crumbs
Butter for greasing pan
¼ cup ground walnuts
1 tablespoon lemon juice

1. Knead a dough from the flour, 2 eggs and a pinch of salt. If eggs are large, you may have to add a little additional flour.
2. Stretch the dough into a thin sheet and let it rest for 15 minutes. Cut it into strips about ¼ inch wide, like egg noodles.
3. Bring to a boil the milk, vanilla bean, a pinch of salt and 1 tablespoon butter. Reduce heat and put in the egg noodles. Cook until the noodles absorb all the liquid, stirring often. This should take 10 to 12 minutes.
4. Mix in the raisins, remaining butter, the lemon rind, ¼ cup of the sugar and the yolks of remaining 3 eggs. Mix well. Preheat oven to 375° F.
5. In a separate pot cook the cored and peeled apple halves in 1 cup water and 2 tablespoons sugar until they are half cooked. Remove apples and pat them dry.
6. Sprinkle the bread crumbs in a well-buttered baking-serving casserole of porcelain or heatproof glass.
7. Put three quarters of the noodle mixture in the casserole and pat down evenly. Place the half-cooked apples with cavities upwards in 2 even rows. Fill cavities with ground walnuts. Cover with remaining noodle mixture.
8. Bake the noodles in the preheated oven for 20 minutes.
9. Meantime, whip the egg whites with the last 2 tablespoons sugar and the lemon juice to make a meringue.
10. Pour the meringue on the partly baked noodle casserole and bake for 15 minutes longer, till the meringue is golden brown.

Note: As a shortcut you may use ½ pound packaged egg noodles.

This Hungarian classic is the *à la financière* of noodle dishes. In the past only financiers or aristocrats like Count Pálffy could afford it.

It might interest music lovers to know that this same Count Pálffy introduced the six-year-old prodigy Mozart

Continued from preceding page

to the Court and the music world of Vienna.

(*From THE CUISINE OF HUNGARY by George Lang. Copyright 1971 by George Lang. Reprinted by permission of Atheneum.*)

Noodle Rolling Board H:37

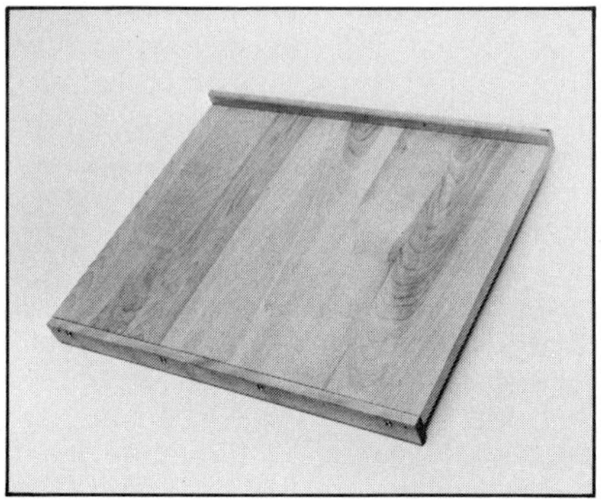

Here is a particularly practical board for rolling and cutting out noodles, or the dough for savory *pirozhki* (Russian meat pies), or the dough for sweet *Ischler Tortchen* (jam tarts with almonds and cinnamon). Made of smooth, unfinished hardwood, it differs from other rolling boards in having two wooden bars attached to the long sides, one projecting 3/4″ above the upper surface, the other projecting 3/4″ below the lower surface. To use it, place the board so that the bar that projects downward overlaps the edge of the table nearest you; as you roll out the dough, this bar will keep the board from shifting position. The other bar, projecting upward at the far end of the board, will act as a stop for the dough. This board is 16″ by 22″ and 3/4″ thick; it also comes in three larger sizes: 24″ by 18″, 27″ by 18″ and 30″ by 20″. Although it isn't a chopping block, we see no reason why you couldn't use one side of it for chopping and reserve the other for rolling out dough. In a kitchen where counter space is at a premium, this board would be especially appreciated for converting any table into a functional preparation area.

H. Roth & Son (44-3) $21.95

Noodle Press H:38

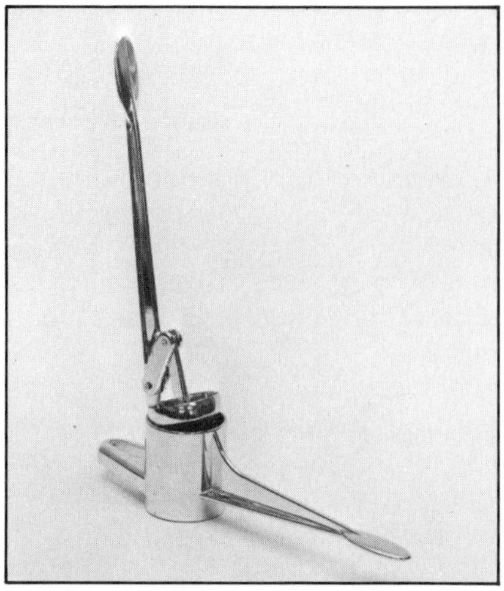

From Swabia in southwestern Germany comes this cast-aluminum gadget for making noodles out of *Spaetzle* (tiny dumpling) dough. Measuring 16″ long, with a 3″-diameter, 3½″-deep container, this noodle maker works on the pressure principle: the hinged upper handle with its attached circular press forces dough through the perforations in the bottom of the container. Since the holes are less than ⅛″ in diameter, the noodles produced are very thin. To make short noodles, rest the dough-filled press two to three inches above the boiling water and squeeze the handles together; for longer noodles hold it about 5 inches above the water. The press works best if rinsed with cold water before filling or refilling. For easier cleaning, rinse it immediately after

Making noodles.

use, too. Cooked potatoes, vegetables and fruits could also be puréed with this press. Or you could sieve cottage cheese for those mouthwatering *Topfenknödel*—cheese dumplings swimming in hot jam.

H. Roth & Son (14-3) $16.98

Noodle Machine H:39

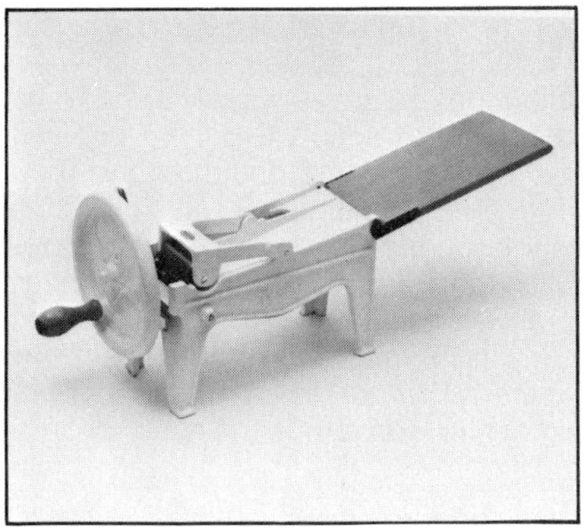

A collector's item for kitchenware buffs and noodle makers, this highly specialized device appears to be from another age. It fashions but one kind of noodle, a short, vermicelli soup noodle popular in Central Europe. Made of cast iron and painted white, the machine has a wooden board that slopes down toward double rollers and a cutting wheel. The iron section is 10½″ long and 7¾″ high, and the board measures 9″ by 4½″. To make noodles, first roll and cut a long strip of dough to the 2″ width of the rollers. Lay the dough over the board and feed one end into the rollers; the upper roller is hinged so you can lift it to catch the end of the dough. The wheel is geared to turn the rollers—one of smooth steel, the other of deep and sharply grooved wood to cut the noodle strips. Rigged with three equidistant razor-sharp blades, the wheel will cut perfect 2″-long noodles. After use, the board folds over the machine for storage. Just beware of the wheel; it has no safety brake and the blades are merciless if your fingers should get in their way. But they do turn out lovely short noodles that make a delicious garnish for a wholesome chicken soup.

Paprikás Weiss (450) $59.95

Illustration from a 1587 German cookbook.

Snail Paddle H:40

No, it isn't a tool for poking reluctant escargots into their shells, but a device for making small, ridged coils of noodle dough (called snails) for soup. The paddle is small (4¾″ by 3⅜″) and made of unfinished wood with a narrowly-grooved surface and a handle. With it comes a 6¾″-long conical stick that tapers to a point and fits into a hole next to the handle for storage. To use it, place about a spoonful of egg-and-flour dough on the paddle. Hold it by the handle over simmering water, and use your other hand to work the dough into a thin layer with the narrowest end of the rolling stick. Then pick the dough up by curling it around the stick (like twisting spaghetti around a fork) and slide it off the end of the stick into the simmering water. An expert can do this very rapidly. To make snails for storage, drop them one by one onto a clean, floured cloth instead of letting them fall into water, and let them dry. In *The Cuisine of Hungary* George Lang writes: "In the villages during winter months it is a social event when cooks get together to make these snail noodles, which will last throughout the year." You'll find them an appealing and tasty garnish for a hearty Hungarian chicken or bean soup.

H. Roth & Son (42-1) $3.98

Dumpling Board H:41

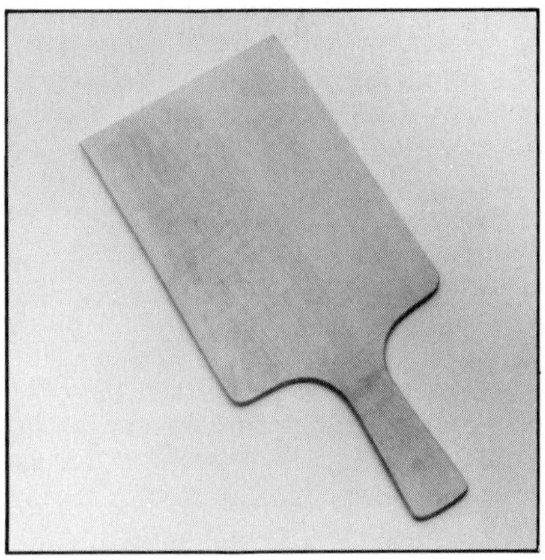

Made of light, unfinished wood, 5½″ by 7½″ with a 4″ handle, this board

Continued from preceding page

features a sloped front edge, which makes it a handy aid for cooking the tiny German dumplings known as *Spaetzle*. Wet the board and hold it at a slight angle over a pot of boiling broth while you cut off little bits of the thick egg dough with a knife, or a *Spaetzle* scraper. The pieces will easily slide off the slanted front edge of the board. Such little dumplings may be added to stews or soups. Or toss cooked *Spaetzle* in butter and bread crumbs, and serve them with a salad, and you'll have a full meal in the style of southwestern Germany.

H. Roth & Son (43-10) $2.65

Spaetzle Scraper H:42

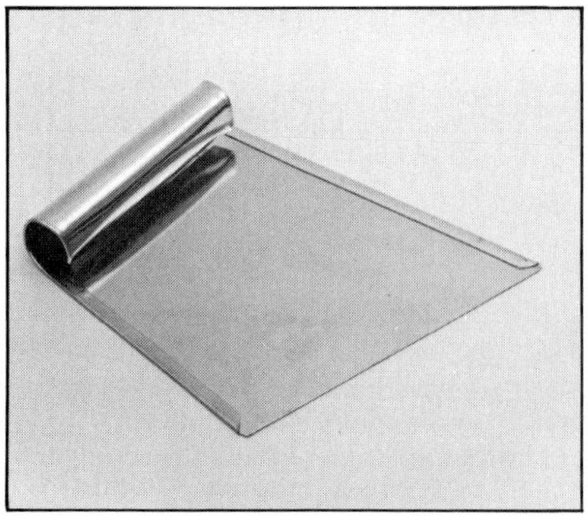

A sleek metal gadget like this is a great help in cutting egg-rich dough into *Spaetzle* (tiny dumplings) and scraping them off a board into the cooking pot. Made of sturdy tinned steel, it is simply a tapered four-sided sheet, curled at one end to form a 3½″-long handle, and left flat at the other to provide a 4½″-long cutting edge. The blade is not sharp; but like a cookie cutter, it is just right for cutting through dough. The side edges of the scraper—one 5″ long, the other 4″ long—have been folded over for a smooth finish. With this scraper, a small dumpling cutting board, and a bit of practice, you can turn out a batch of tasty little *Spaetzle* in no time at all. What's more, you can vary the size of the *Spaetzle* according to whim —tiny rice-like bits for soup, or somewhat chunkier dumplings to make a side dish for *Sauerbraten.*

H. A. Mack & Co., Inc. $1.50

LITTLE DUMPLINGS

Spaetzle

1 teaspoon salt
½ cup water or milk
1 egg, well-beaten
1½ cups flour

Add the salt and water or milk to the egg and blend together. Add the flour slowly, beating well, until a smooth batter is formed.

Bring a large pan of water to a rapid boil, and add some salt. Fill a *Spaetzle* machine with the dough and set it over the pan, making sure the water in the pan does not reach the machine. Force the dough through the holes. When the water reaches a boil again, the *Spaetzle* should rise to the surface and be cooked through. Drain them in a colander and pour tepid, slightly salted water over them.

Turn the *Spaetzle* onto a hot platter, and garnish with fried onions; cracker crumbs, combined with sugar and cinnamon; bread crumbs browned in butter; grated cheese; seasoned cottage cheese; or chopped walnuts. Or mix the *Spaetzle* with scrambled eggs.

Note: You may also let the *Spaetzle* dry for a few hours and then toss them in hot fat.

(Courtesy of H. Roth & Son, New York City.)

German Spaetzle Maker H:43

Spaetzle, or "little sparrows," are tiny dumplings that often take the place of potatoes in southwestern Germany and elsewhere in Central Europe. Traditionally, the stiff, golden egg dough was pinched into small pieces by hand and dropped into boiling water or soup. Now, a special utensil like this one that hooks securely onto the edge of a pot, enables you to make *Spaetzle* of uniform size in a jiffy. Made of sturdy tinned steel, it has a 2″-deep bowl that is 7″ in diameter and perforated with ¼″ holes. The implement is held on one side by means of a 7″-long plastic-and-wire handle; a wooden handle on top turns the cutting blade. It comes apart for easy cleaning. To make *Spaetzle,* hook the device over a pot of boiling water or broth, place some dough in the bowl, and turn the handle slowly; the blade will force the dough through the holes and into the pot. Cook the dumplings, one batch at a time, for 5 to 8 minutes, stirring to keep them from sticking together. Then drain them in a sieve or colander. Serve them as an accompaniment to a rich stew thickened with sour cream, or with *Sauerbraten* and gravy, or with venison. If you haven't prepared gravy, top the *Spaetzle* with bread crumbs toasted in butter or simply drench them in melted butter.

Vitantonio Mfg. Co. (259) $10.95

Small German Spaetzle Maker H:44

Although it resembles a food mill, this is a dumpling maker of tinned steel and wood that can be completely disassembled for cleaning. The crank turns a disc that forces the dough through the mill and cuts off the tiny *Spaetzle* dumplings in one simple movement. Because the holes are very small, the *Spaetzle* will be as fine as rice—the Austrians call these tiny dumplings *Krumpli* and use them in soup. Make a liver dumpling dough, and with this device you can enhance a beef bouillon with a delicious *Leberreis* (liver-rice). The *Spaetzle* maker comes with a thick masonite board (13″ by 5″ with a 4″-diameter hole in the center) to hold the dumpling maker in place over a cooking pot. The efficient utensil is 11¼″ long with its handle and 6½″ high with its crank; the tapered 2¾″-deep bowl is 4¾″ in diameter at the top and 3½″ in diameter at the base.

Paprikás Weiss (432) $11.98

Austrian Spaetzle Maker H:45

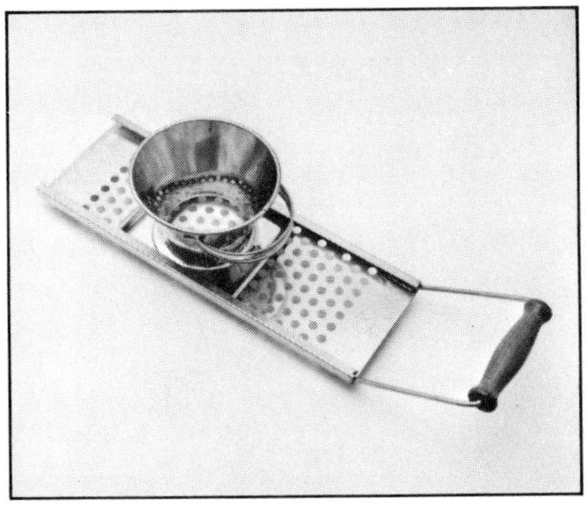

This *Spaetzle* maker, used in Austria, is of tinned steel with a handle of shellacked wood. It has two parts: a perforated tray—13″ long and 4½″ wide—and a hopper—4½″ in diameter and 3½″ deep—that can be separated for easy cleaning. To make *Spaetzle,* rest the tray across a pot of boiling water so the hook on its bottom catches the side of the pot. Put some dough in the hopper, press it lightly and slide the hopper across the tray. Press and slide again. Avoid the temptation to cook too many of the tiny dumplings at once; they must not touch each other while cooking. Serve them in soup, add them to lentils or cabbage, or make them a buttery side dish for roast pork.

H. Roth & Son (14-1) $8.95

One Czech soldier reacting to Italian pasta: "You know, in my part of the country we make small dumplings with raw potatoes, we boil 'em, soak 'em in egg yolk, stick plenty of bits of crust over 'em, and then fry 'em on bacon."

He pronounced the last word with mysterious solemnity.

"And they're just fine with sauerkraut," he added in melancholy tones. "I got no use for macaroni."

The Good Soldier Schweik *by Jaroslav Hasek, translated by Paul Selver. Signet Classics, New American Library, 1963.*

Dumpling Ladle H:46

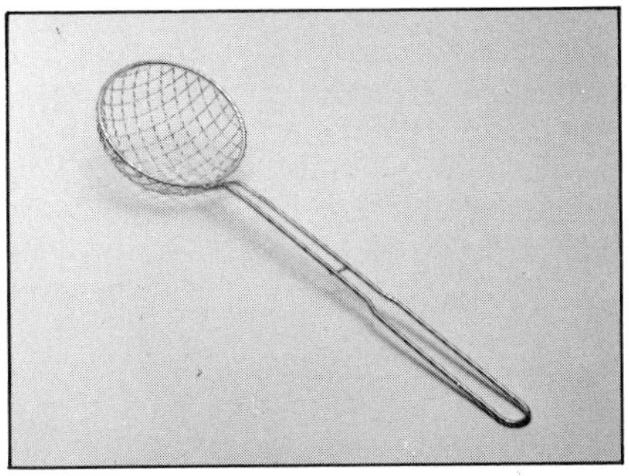

If you make dumplings, you will certainly need a tool to remove them from their simmering broth or water. This skimmer, known as a dumpling ladle in Germany (where it originates) is perfect for the job. Made of tinned steel, the ladle measures 16″ long overall and has a bowl 4⅛″ in diameter and 1⅞″ deep. The wide-set wires in the bowl allow the poaching liquid to run off easily, and the foot-long handle enables you to reach down into the deepest pot safely. The bowl is set at an angle to facilitate lifting even large pieces of food. Simple and sturdy, this versatile ladle would be useful to doughnut fans as well as dumpling lovers; it makes an excellent implement for turning and fishing from hot oil those delectable, jelly-filled doughnuts the Viennese call *Faschingskrapfen.*

Christian Oos KG (21311) $4.00

Strainer/Colander H:47

This red ball of fire from Poland will add color to your kitchen and a charm-

A German kitchen from a 1587 cookbook.

Continued from preceding page

ing, pot-bellied shape to your peg board. The colander is made of enameled steel. It is 8″ in diameter, 4½″ deep and has a rolled rim with a black, loop handle in front and an 8″-long handle at the back with a hole for hanging. Clusters of small holes perforate its sides and bottom, providing easy separation of fluids and solids. The long handle makes this colander particularly safe for draining hot foods such as noodles. Its round shape fits nicely over a mixing bowl or saucepan, and the enamel coating is acid as well as chip resistant.

Macy's **$4.50**

Potato Slicer H:48

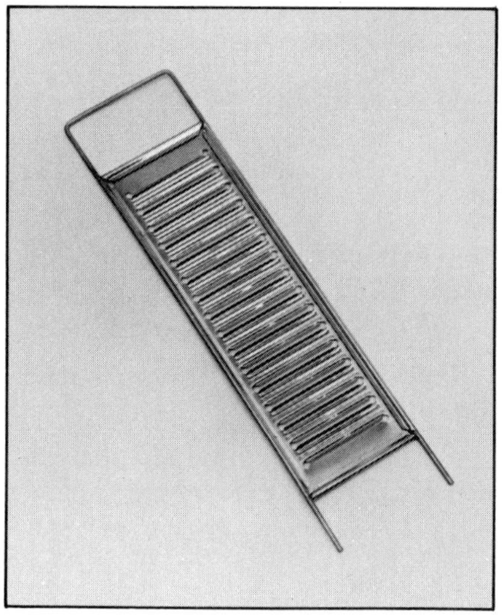

In 1744, Frederick the Great had free potato seeds distributed for planting throughout his kingdom. In spite of initial resistance from the peasants, who feared the strange tubers were poisonous, the potato soon caught on and spread rapidly across Middle Europe. A real find for making many Central European potato recipes is this 16″-by-4″, stainless-steel slicer. It has 16 raised cutting edges on its 12″-long surface, thus making it possible to produce 16 raw or cooked potato slices at a single stroke. For best results, select large potatoes of uniform size, and do not overcook them before slicing; the potatoes should be just tender when pierced with a small sharp knife. May we suggest some simple *Bratkartoffeln* (home fries) or *Kartoffelsalat mit Speck* (hot potato salad with bacon).

H. Roth & Son **$4.98**

HOT POTATO SALAD

11 medium-sized new potatoes
7 slices bacon, chopped
1 tablespoon flour
¼ teaspoon dry mustard
½ cup sugar
7 tablespoons vinegar
1 cup chopped celery*
⅓ cup chopped green pepper*
½ cup chopped onion
½ tablespoon salt
⅛ teaspoon pepper
2 tablespoons chopped parsley

Steam the potatoes in their jackets until easily pierced with the tip of a sharp knife.

While the potatoes are cooking, sauté the bacon. Drain and reserve ⅓ cup of the bacon fat. Just before the potatoes have finished cooking, reheat the bacon fat and stir in the flour. Add the dry mustard, sugar and vinegar and cook for a few minutes. Add the celery, green pepper and onion and cook several minutes longer.

Peel and slice the potatoes while hot. Add the salt, pepper and all but 2 tablespoons of the cooked bacon and mix together gently. Pour the hot bacon fat over the potatoes and again mix gently.

Correct the seasoning and sprinkle the reserved 2 tablespoons of bacon and the parsley over the salad.

Yield: 6-8 servings.

*Although celery and green pepper are not traditional ingredients in a hot German potato salad, they make a delicious variation.

Courtesy of Grace Anderson, Oak Park, Illinois.

Unlikely as it may seem from the array of German dishes in which it is featured, the potato was adopted late in that country's culinary history. In the mid-eighteenth century (nearly two hundred years after the potato's European début) Frederick the Great "encouraged" systematic cultivation of the "earth-apple." It was grown, but not as a staple crop, by distributing seed-potatoes and keeping a force of soldiers in the fields to ensure the planting. Happily, the results of the forced adoption have been inspired. The potato appears in German meals from potato soup through potato dumplings with plum sauce for dessert.

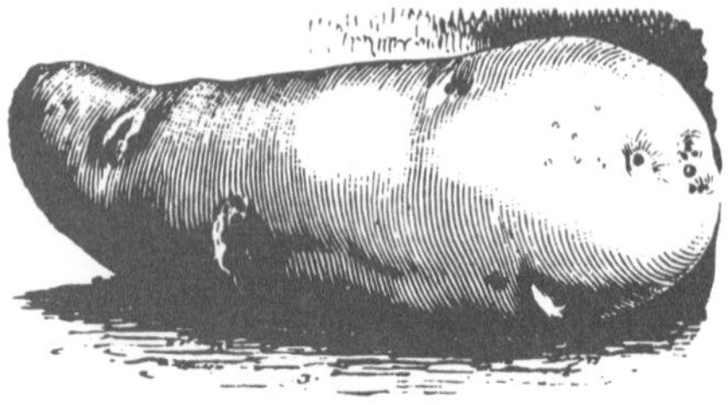

A tidy potato.

Potato Fork H:49

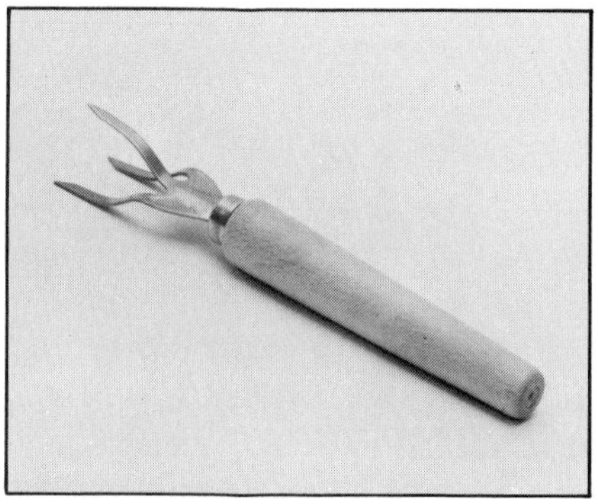

This little gadget from Austria is a real find: it's a three-pronged fork to hold hot boiled potatoes while you peel off their skins. The 3¾″ handle is just long enough for a good grip, and the prongs are cleverly twisted so that the potato won't slip off. No more burnt fingers or precarious balancing of heavy potatoes on the end of a long cooking fork! And think how much quicker you'll be at making all those wonderful potato dishes essential to Middle European cooking—potato dumplings (whether plain ones to serve with braised veal shanks or sweet ones filled with jam to have as dessert), hot potato salad to accompany *Bratwurst* or *kielbasa,* or simply mashed potatoes with lots of butter and sweet cream whipped in.

The Store at Sugarbush Village/Kalkus, Inc. (140) **$1.75**

Casseroles, Pots and Pans

The casseroles of Middle Europe tend to be made of sturdy, ovenproof porcelain in clean, modern designs. Roasters, Dutch ovens, large frying pans and tall soup pots are made of heavy cast iron, enameled iron, cast aluminum or stainless steel. Most of these thoroughly functional items are rarely imported to this country, perhaps because of their bulk and weight and because our own old-fashioned "spiders" and other heavy professional cookware are already available. In all probability, your kitchen already has most of the equipment suitable for the braising, stewing and roasting of Central European cuisine. But we show you three lovely pieces of crockery—two for cooking and one for making sauerkraut—several good vegetable steamers, skewers for German *Rouladen,* two attractive baking dishes, a handsome kettle for Hungarian goulash and a unique storage container called a fat pot to hold the indispensable lard for Central European cooking.

Tinned-Steel Vegetable Steamer H:50

Any vegetable can be steamed in this colander/steamer of tinned steel. It sits neatly on three 2″-long feet and measures 6¼″ in diameter at the top and is 5½″ deep. Sturdy and well-made, it has two loop handles for easy lifting and well-spaced perforations on the bottom and sides. Simply place the colander full of vegetables in any pot big enough to hold it (bigger than 7½″ deep and 9½″ in diameter), cover tightly and steam. Your vegetables, whether asparagus or cauliflower, brussel sprouts or beets, string beans or potatoes, will be tender, tasty and nutritious (few nutrients will be lost into the simmering water). They may be served with butter and bread crumbs, puréed with cream and butter or mixed with sour cream and paprika or dill.

Paprikás Weiss **$9.98**

Tinned-Steel Steamer Pot H:51

The Germans and Austrians, like most Europeans, think of fresh asparagus as a welcome delicacy and look forward to spring when the first tender stalks are harvested. The German asparagus are thick and white; the Austrian thin and green. This Austrian steamer is excellent for cooking the long, elegant vegetable. But you'll also find it useful for leeks, corn and other vegetables. Made of tinned steel, the straight-sided pot is 7⅝″ tall and just about as wide. It has a slightly domed cover with a loop handle on top and a ¾″-deep lip, which fits snugly into the top of the steamer. The steamer-tray unit, also made of tinned steel, is half an inch narrower than the pot and has dime-sized holes in its surface for proper steam circulation; a handle in the center of the tray makes it easy to lift from the pot. All seams and joints are folded and soldered for extra strength.

Paprikás Weiss **$19.98**

Enameled-Steel Steamer Pot H:52

A tomato-red steamer imported from Poland might be just the thing for the cheerful cook and carefree hostess. You can serve in one part of this unit and save yourself the trouble of having to wash another pot. Made of enameled steel, the bottom pot measures 6¼″ in diameter and is 4⅝″ deep. It has two black, ear-shaped handles on opposite sides near its black, rolled rim. The steamer section, slightly shorter and narrower than the pot, has small holes across the bottom and a black, ear-shaped handle on either side. The whole unit is equipped with a tight-fitting domed cover. When the vegetables are tender, simply lift out the top unit, pour any remaining water out of the bottom pot and transfer the vegetables to it. It's a perfect vehicle for making and serving *Spargelbohnen,* those delectable wax beans that are revered in Germany and served like asparagus *à la polonaise,* with butter and bread crumbs.

Macy's **$12.00**

Small Gratin Dish H:53

The lustrous glaze and fine proportions of this Polish earthenware gratin dish caught our fancy. It is a dark green hue with two gold horizontal stripes bordering faint rust-colored zig-zags between them. Inside, it is a rich terra-cotta color. Small in size—5⅞″ in diameter and 1½″ deep—with two solid ear-shaped handles, it can be used to serve an appetizer or individual helpings of vegetables, boiled and sprinkled with cheese, and then set under a broiler for a few minutes.

Cepelia Corp (2354) $4.00

Large Baking Dish H:54

Practicality and beauty are joined in this large oval baking dish from Germany, for it will go directly from oven to table. The elegant white porcelain will set off the food while holding it warm for second helpings, and the hard, non-porous glaze will wipe clean after a soaking in detergent. A generous 21¾″ long, 10⅞″ wide, and 2¼″ deep, the dish will easily bake a large fish or whole fowl. Try a Hungarian baked carp, *ponty fűszermártással,* made with onions, tomatoes, peppers, paprika and sour cream—or roast a goose for a traditional German St. Martin's Day on November 11. For a really authentic *Martinstag,* send the children out to beg for pennies. Instead of shouting "Trick or treat!" German children sing a ditty that translated goes: "Here lives a rich man, who can give us a lot. Long may he live! Much may he give!" The dish is also available in lengths of 10½″, 12″, 14¼″ and 16½″.

H. E. Lauffer Co., Inc. (OV-5) $49.00

ROAST GOOSE WITH APPLE STUFFING

During the entire year that Debbie Reynolds starred in the Broadway musical "Irene," she visited Lüchow's at least once a week. Lovely Debbie invariably would order Roast Goose and upon finishing the meal would pick up a musical instrument and parade through the restaurant with the Oompah Band to the delight of the midnight diners.

1 (8- to 10-pound) goose, dressed
Salt
Freshly ground pepper
Apple Stuffing (recipe below)
3 apples, peeled, cored, and chopped
1 celery leaf
½ sliced onion
3 sprigs parsley
1 cup red wine
1 cup consommé
1 cup water
Giblets from goose
1 stalk, celery with leaves, cut up
1 carrot, cut up
1 onion, cut in half
6 peppercorns
1 teaspoon salt
1 bay leaf
1 clove
1 tablespoon flour
¼ pound butter

Have the goose cleaned and drawn, the wings, neck, head, and feet chopped off. Wash goose inside and out; dry well; drain. Cover with cold water and let soak 15 minutes. Drain; pat dry. Season with salt and pepper inside and out. Stuff the goose with the Apple Stuffing, apples, celery leaf, onion, and parsley. Close the opening with a metal skewer and place on a rack in a shallow roasting pan. Bake at 400° F. for 1 hour. Turn the goose and continue to roast for another hour. While the goose is roasting, put the red wine, consommé, water, giblets, celery, carrot, onion, peppercorns, salt, bay leaf, and clove in a pot and bring slowly to a boil. Reduce the heat and let simmer for about 45 minutes. Strain and reserve.

After the goose has roasted for 2 hours, remove it from the oven, and pour off all the fat. (This fat is wonderful for making home-fried potatoes.)

Reduce the oven temperature to 350° F. and roast the goose for another 1½ to 2 hours, basting every 15 minutes with the reserved stock. Remove the goose from oven and put on a preheated serving platter.

Thicken gravy with the flour, butter, and wine mixture, and serve in a gravy boat. Before serving the goose, remove the skewer, parsley, onion, and celery leaf. (*Serves 6.*)

Apple Stuffing:
8 cooking apples, peeled, cored, and chopped (coarsely)
1½ cup currants
1 cup fine breadcrumbs
Pinch of cinnamon
2 eggs, beaten

Mix the apples, currants, breadcrumbs, cinnamon, beaten eggs, and stuff into the goose.

(From LÜCHOW'S GERMAN FESTIVAL COOKBOOK by Gene and Fran Schoor. Copyright 1976 by Gene Schoor. Reprinted by permission of Doubleday & Company, Inc.)

Rouladen Needles H:55

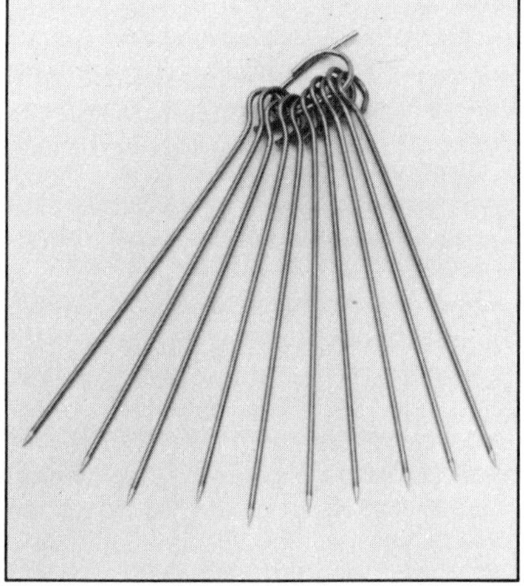

These ten small, 4″-long, stainless-steel needles are a big improvement over toothpicks for skewering *Rinderrouladen* or *Kalbsrouladen,* German dishes familiar to Americans as beefrolls or "veal birds." Slices of beef or veal from the round or leg are cut into rectangular pieces, spread with a variety of things and then rolled, secured and braised in water, stock—plain or with wine—and perhaps some vegetables for flavoring. The broth is then thickened with flour or sour cream to make a rich gravy. One recipe calls for spreading meat strips with Düsseldorf-style mustard, chopped onions, half a pickle, and a strip of bacon. Inserted horizontally like a hairpin, each steel skewer will hold a roll while it is browned and braised. Serve the *Rouladen* with dumplings and red cabbage. *Guten Appetit!*

Kalkus, Inc. (827) $1.25

Römertopf H:56

Invented to simulate the primitive method of cooking in wet clay, the Römertopf is made of totally unglazed earthenware. It has a rough, porous texture and is more or less oval in shape, with a top and bottom of the same size that fit tightly together. Before each use, the pot must be soaked in cold water until, like a clay flower pot, it becomes wet all the way through. This method of cooking produces tenderly braised meat, poultry or vegetables, using no fats and little additional liquid, so that the nutrients and the flavor remain in the food. The inside of the bottom is ridged to prevent food from sticking and to enhance the circulation of steam. We show you a 3-quart Römertopf, large enough to hold a family-sized roasting chicken for a juicy *Huhn im Topf,* or a four- to six-pound rolled roast. It is also available in a three-to-four-pound or an eight-to-twelve-pound capacity. All sizes have the same raised decoration over sides of the top that is the insignia of the Römertopf.

H. Roth & Son/Reco International Corp. (109) $15.00

Schlemmertopf H:57

Here is a gracefully shaped earthenware pot with a close-fitting top that simulates the primitive method of cooking in wet clay. To do this, both the pot and its lid must be soaked until wet through before each use. Once filled and covered the pot is then put into a cold oven and the temperature is turned to a high setting. The advantages to this type of cooking are that it requires a minimal amount of liquid, it saves nutrients in the food, and it leaves meat and vegetables tender and very tasty. The *Schlemmertopf* darkens with use but that does not impair its cooking ability. The entire pot is unglazed to let it "breathe," with the exception of the inside bottom which is glazed for easy cleaning. With a 3-quart capacity, the pot measures 13″ by 9¼″ by 3¼″; the lid is approximately the same size, but somewhat shallower. A large roasting chicken or a five-pound rolled roast would fit nicely in the *Schlemmertopf.* Other dishes are suggested in the lengthy recipe booklet that comes with the pot. In case you were wondering, the raised decorations on the outside of the lid are called sgraffiti.

Reston Lloyd, Ltd. (832) $20.00

Hungarian Kettle H:58

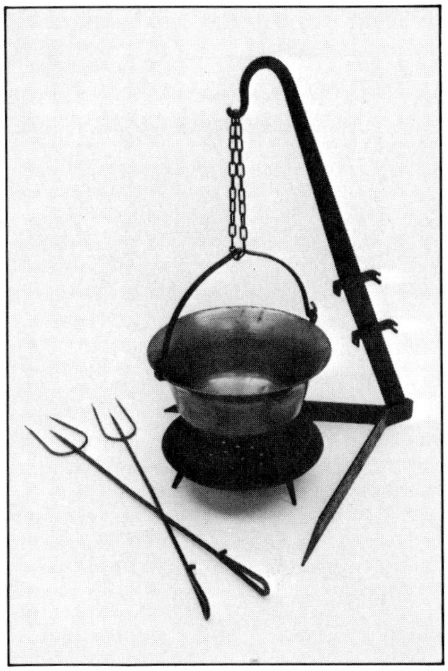

The *bogrács,* or large cast-iron kettle, was the basic cooking vessel of the nomad Hungarians, and was hung behind their saddles even when they went on marauding expeditions. Cubed meat and cut-up onions were slowly cooked in the *bogrács* until no liquid was left, and then spread out to dry completely in the sun. Thus dried, the beef could be carried on long journeys and reconstituted as needed by stewing with water. With a lot of water it made a soup, with a little, a stew—one a thin, the other a thick type of *gulyás* (goulash). Our *bogrács* is a 4-quart cauldron of steel with a wrought-iron handle. It comes with its own *szolgafa,* or holding stick. In this case, the holding stick is actually a stand consisting of a hook at the end of a vertical post attached to a V-shaped base. There is also a grill—a wok-shaped basin on three legs topped with a grate—and two long-handled, three-pronged cooking forks. The kettle is suspended from the hook by means of a large-linked chain. In its original Hungarian version, *gulyás* was made only with meat, lard and/or bacon, chopped onion and caraway seeds; later, paprika joined the list of basic ingredients. Now, the stew may be varied with the addition of garlic, tomatoes, potatoes and green or hot peppers; but flour, other spices or garnitures and wine are absolutely forbidden. No matter which

Continued from preceding page

variation you choose, this *bogrács* will give your goulash an air of authenticity.

H. Roth & Son (8-10) **$29.95**

KETTLE GULYÁS

Bográcsgulyás

8 servings

2 medium-sized onions
2 tablespoons lard
2½ pounds beef chuck or round, cut to ¾-inch cubes
½ pound beef heart (optional), cut to ¾-inch cubes
1 garlic clove
Pinch of caraway seeds
Salt
2 tablespoons "Noble Rose" paprika
1 medium-sized ripe tomato
2 green frying or Italian peppers
1 pound potatoes
Little Dumplings

1. Peel onions and chop into coarse pieces. Melt lard in a heavy 6- to 8-quart Dutch oven. Sauté onions in lard. Heat should be low in order not to brown the onions.
2. When onions become glossy, add beef and beef heart. Stir so that during this part of the process, which should last for about 10 minutes, the meat will be sautéed with the onions.
3. Meanwhile, chop and crush the garlic with the caraway seeds and a little salt; use the flat side of a heavy knife.
4. Take kettle from heat. Stir in paprika and the garlic mixture. Stir rapidly with a wooden spoon. Immediately after paprika is absorbed, add 2½ quarts *warm* water. (Cold water toughens meat if you add it while the meat is frying.)
5. Replace covered kettle over low heat and cook for about 1 hour.
6. While the braising is going on, peel the tomato, then cut into 1-inch pieces. Core green peppers and slice into rings. Peel potatoes and cut into ¾-inch dice.
7. After meat has been braised for about 1 hour (the time depends on the cut of the meat), add the cut-up tomato and green peppers and enough water to give a soup consistency. Add a little salt. Simmer slowly for another 30 minutes.
8. Add potatoes, and cook the *gulyás* till done. Adjust salt. Add hot cherry pepper pods if you want to make the stew spicy hot.
9. Cook the dumplings in the stew.
10. Serve the *gulyás* steaming hot in large extra-deep bowls. The meat should be tender, but not falling apart.

Note: The meat can be an inexpensive cut. It is a waste of money to use steak or tenderloin. The more different cuts you use, the better tasting the stew will be.

The paprika *must* be Hungarian "Noble Rose." Spanish paprika and other types are only coloring agents.

(From THE CUISINE OF HUNGARY by George Lang. Copyright 1971 by George Lang. Reprinted by permission of Atheneum.)

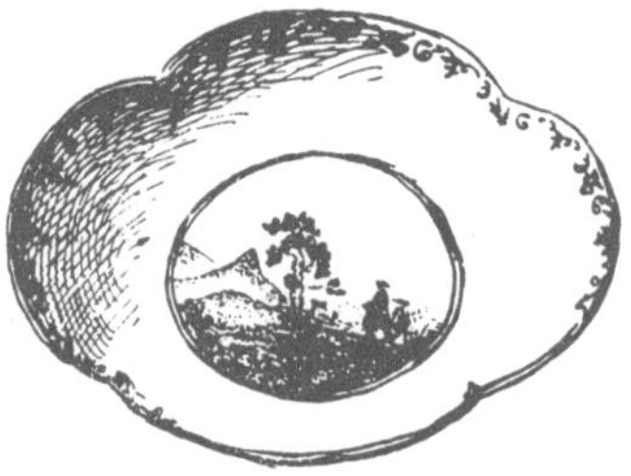

LITTLE PINCHED DUMPLINGS

Csipetke

about 8 servings

½ cup flour
1 egg
Salt
Flour

1. Make a hard dough by kneading the flour and egg for about 5 minutes. Let the dough rest for 15 minutes.
2. Cut the dough into 6 pieces and roll each to finger thickness. You will get about a 6-inch length from each.
3. Bring 4 quarts water with 1 tablespoon salt to a boil. Sprinkle a little flour on the dough and pinch off little pieces. Drop them into the boiling water. Use thumb and index fingers to pinch off the pieces.
4. Boil the dumplings till they come to the surface, then sample one to make sure it's cooked through.

Note: You may drop the *csipetke* directly into goulash soup, bean soup, or any other soup you use it for.

Joseph Wechsberg once said that the real experts can tell not only if the cook was left-handed, but can even identify by the shape of the dumpling the person who pinched off the *csipetke.*

(From THE CUISINE OF HUNGARY by George Lang. Copyright 1971 by George Lang. Reprinted by permission of Atheneum.)

Fat Pot **H:59**

These days, when so many people spend time trying to lose fat, this pot seems anachronistic. But not to Central Europeans who save pork and bacon drippings for sautéing meat and vegetables for many of their dishes. For their cooking, the white, urn-shaped pot of enameled steel is a practical item. It is 6″ in diameter and 6″ deep and has two loop-shaped handles. The slightly domed cover has a black plastic knob in the center and 6 small holes that permit the fat to "breathe." Americans are apt to save drippings in an empty coffee can, stick the can in the refrigerator, and after a couple of months throw it out; but in Europe everything is saved and *used!* Sometimes the rendered fat is spread on coarse bread and sprinkled with salt, providing a nourishing snack. It is even used in some pastries—the flakiest strudel dough, an Austrian pastry chef told us, is made with lard.

Paprikás Weiss **$4.98**

Fondue and Raclette

The fondue cuisine of Switzerland, which has become popular the world over, calls for special equipment in a category all its own. Pots, forks, plates, grills and burners have been developed for both cheese and beef fondues.

Fondue means "melted." Whether in fact the glories of melted cheese were discovered accidentally by a cold shepherd who warmed his humble repast over a wood fire is moot. We need only rejoice that someone once thought of mixing wine and cheese over a fire and dunking his bread into it. Almost as important was the idea of sharing a pot of fondue with others, to create a congenial atmosphere that is one of the main pleasures of the dish—it will soften the heart of even the most resolute grouch.

Fondue is not the only melted cheese dish in the Swiss cuisine. Slices of *Brätkase* (roasting cheese) may be simply warmed on a stick or in a pan over a fire and then eaten with boiled potatoes and pickles. A similar and even more popular dish is *raclette* from the French word *"racler,"* which means to scrape. For this specialty, a half wheel of cheese—one of four or five particular varieties—is exposed to an open fire or grill. The melted cheese on the surface of the wheel is then scraped onto a plate and served with boiled potatoes, sour gherkins and, often, pickled onions.

The meat fondues, *fondue bourguignonne* and *fondue orientale* are not really fondues at all, since the meat is not melted but cooked in oil or bouillon. They are probably called fondues because they retain the fun of sharing one pot.

The best vessels for cooking cheese fondue are made of ceramic or heavy metal coated with enamel. The pots should be wide and shallow so that several forks may be dipped and twirled in the cheese at the same time. Meat fondue pots, on the other hand, should be made of heavy-weight cast iron or steel, enameled on the inside. Aluminum is too light for deep frying and pottery pots are too shallow and liable to crack. Ideally, *fondue bourguignonne* should be cooked in a deep pot that is narrow at the top to prevent spattering and wide across the bottom for good stability. Burners must be stable and easy to ignite, regulate and put out; meat fondue forks must have insulated handles.

Cheese Fondue Pot H:60

This fondue pot (*caquelon*) of enameled steel, with its wide, relatively shallow shape, is ideal for cheese fondue. It has a 1½-quart capacity, is 7⅛″ in diameter, and its handle is solidly attached and easy to hold. A one-quart size is also available. The pot comes in two dramatic color combinations: yellow inside and black outside, or black inside and yellow outside. Use it for a main course of *fondue Gruyère*—Gruyère cheese, wine and garlic. To make perfect, creamy cheese fondues, the cheese must be well-aged and the wine must have the proper acidity. If the cheese and wine should separate, you can save it by mixing 1 tablespoon of cornstarch with 1 teaspoon of lemon juice in warmed white wine and whisking it into the fondue.

Swissmart, Inc. (224) $13.00

BASIC RECIPE FOR SWITZERLAND CHEESE FONDUE

The following recipe will serve four persons for dinner or 12 to 20 as a snack. Allow 15 minutes for preparation and an additional 15 minutes for cooking.

1 clove garlic
1½ cups dry white Swiss wine
1 tablespoon lemon juice
1 pound shredded Switzerland Swiss Cheese
3 tablespoons flour
pepper, nutmeg to taste
2 loaves Italian or French bread

Preparation
Grate, shred or dice (if using presliced cheese) 1 pound Switzerland Swiss Cheese. (You can do this in advance and keep cheese refrigerated in a tightly closed plastic bag.) Dredge cheese with flour.

Serving and eating
Adjust flame of burner so fondue continues bubbling lightly.

Serve each guest a handful of bread cubes from bread plate or bread basket.

Spear prongs of fork through bread, crustless part first, securing prongs in crust.

Dunk and stir (!) well to bottom of pot.

Remove fork and twist over pot to remove surplus fondue on bread. Eat.

When the fondue is eaten, a crust called *la religieuse* (the religious one) will have formed on bottom of pot. Lift crust with wooden spoon or fork and distribute evenly among diners. It is a delicacy!

Cut bread into 1″ cubes. Each cube should have crust on one side. (If prepared in advance, keep in closed plastic bag.)

Cooking
Rub inside of pot with cut garlic clove. Discard garlic.

Place pot on stove. Pour 1½ cups of wine into pot.

Heat over medium flame until wine is warm but not boiling.

Add lemon juice.

Add cheese by handfuls, stirring constantly with wooden spoon until cheese is melted and cheese-wine mixture has the appearance of a light creamy sauce.

Continued from preceding page

Add pepper and nutmeg to taste.
Let boil once.
Remove pot and put on lighted burner on top of table.

(*From LA FONDUE by Heinz P. Hofer. Reprinted by permission of the Switzerland Cheese Association, Inc.*)

"Brillat Savarin's Fondue.
(*An excellent recipe*)

Ingredients: Eggs, cheese, pepper and salt. Mode.—*Take the same number of eggs as there are guests; weigh the eggs in the shell, allow a third of their weight in Gruyère cheese, and a piece of butter one-sixth of the weight of the cheese. Break the eggs into a basin, beat them well; add the cheese, which should be grated, and the butter, which should be broken into small pieces. Stir these ingredients together with a wooden spoon; put the mixture into a lined saucepan, place it over the fire, and stir until the substance is thick and soft. Put in a little salt, according to the age of the cheese, and a good sprinkling of pepper, and serve the fondue on a very hot silver or metal plate. Do not allow the fondue to remain on the fire after the mixture is set, as, if it boils, it will be entirely spoiled. Brillat Savarin recommends that some choice Burgundy should be handed round with this dish. We have given this recipe exactly as he recommends it to be made; but we have tried it with good Chesire cheese, and found it answer remarkably well."*

Beeton's Book of Household Management *by Isabella Beeton, 1861.*

Cheese Fondue Forks H:61

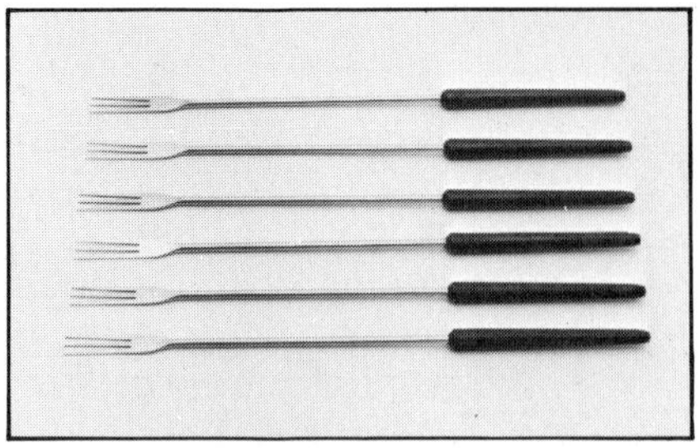

Three-pronged forks are the traditional forks for cheese fondue; for all we know, they date back to the famous fondue Brillat-Savarin introduced to Boston in 1795, after which the dish immediately became the rage. Made of stainless steel with black nylon handles, these 11″-long forks come in a set of six. The three flat prongs will hold crusty bread securely, although no one minds if a piece drops off into the bubbling cheese: according to Swiss custom, whoever loses his chunk of bread must kiss one of his fellow dunkers. Half the fun is seeing who kisses whom. Of course, fondue need not be accompanied by bread alone: flavor your fondue with pear brandy and dip slices of fresh, firm pears along with the bread; or make a tomato and cheese fondue and dunk cubes of ham and whole mushrooms in it.

Spring Brothers Co., Inc. (9031) **$21.00**

"After the oysters, which proved admirably fresh, came grilled kidneys, a jar of truffled foie gras, *and then came the* fondue.

The ingredients were at hand in a chafing-dish, which was placed on the table over a spirits-of-wine burner. I officiated on the field of battle, and none of my movements escaped the notice of my cousins.

They surrendered wholly to the charms of the dish, and besought me to give them the recipe. . . ."

The Physiology of Taste, or Meditations of Transcendental Gastronomy *by Brillat-Savarin. Dover Publications, 1960.*

Cheese Fondue Set H:62

An evening gathered around a fondue pot dipping crusty bread into hot melted cheese is more than just a meal, it's an experience of warmth and sharing that satisfies body and soul. The cheerful mustard yellow ceramic pot of this set adds to the festive ambiance of a fondue. Measuring 8¾″ in diameter and 3″ deep, with a heavy, hollow 4¼″-long handle, it holds a generous two quarts. The pot sits on a wrought-iron stand that measures 11″ by 7¾″; the stand holds a square, black-enameled sheet-metal platform with a hole in the center for the alcohol burner. Made of copper, with an aluminum flame regulator, the burner can be lifted out for easy filling and igniting and has a copper lid for snuffing the flame. The set comes complete with six two-pronged fondue forks, 11″ long, with black, plastic, heat-resistant handles, each marked at the base with a different color. All you need to add is some denatured alcohol for the burner, a dry, white Swiss wine such as Neuchatel, a little lemon juice, grated Swiss cheese, some flour, a bit of nutmeg, crusty bread, six small glasses for kirsch—and five friends!

Spring Brothers Co., Inc. (170-4) **$52.00**

Interior of a cheese factory in Switzerland at the end of the 19th century.

Fondue Bourguignonne Pot H:63

A cheese fondue pot is not suitable for *fondue bourguignonne:* its wide, shallow shape is not safe for boiling oil, and a ceramic pot might crack when exposed to the higher flame needed for frying the cubes of beef. Instead, use a heavy, enameled-steel pot shaped like this one. Metallic gray on the outside and a shiny black on the inside, this pot is bottom-heavy for maximum stability and narrow at the top to prevent the oil from spilling or spattering out. (A piece of raw potato dropped into the hot oil just before serving will also help cut down on spattering.) The sturdy wooden handle is well insulated from the heat of the pot and securely attached to it. The pot comes with a matching lid topped by a wooden knob and is also available in yellow or green. It holds 3 cups. For a seaside variation on *fondue bourguignonne,* try shrimp, scallops or pieces of lobster tails, and serve them with drawn butter and tartar sauce.

Swissmart, Inc. (413) **$16.50**

Fondue Bourguignonne Forks H:64

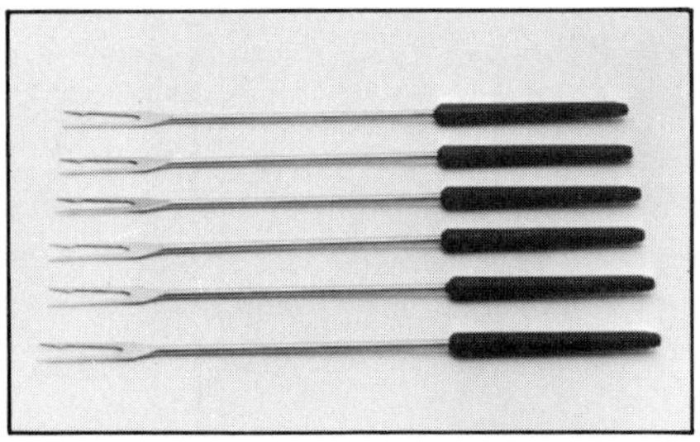

These two-pronged, stainless-steel *fondue bourguignonne* forks have black nylon handles to protect your hand from the hot metal of the pot and its scalding contents of oil or bouillon. The two flat prongs are sharply pointed for piercing meat and are widest at the tips, like spears, to discourage the chunks from dropping off while cooking. Each of the six 11″-long forks in the set is marked in a different color at the base of the handle so that each person will remember which fork in the communal pot is his. Although some purists might blanch, these forks will do just as well for dipping bread in cheese fondue, or, if you have to appease a sweet tooth, for dunking strawberries and bite-sized macaroons into a velvety mass of melted chocolate lightly laced with brandy or kirsch.

Spring Brothers Co., Inc. (9037) **$12.00**

Fondue Bourguignonne Plate H:65

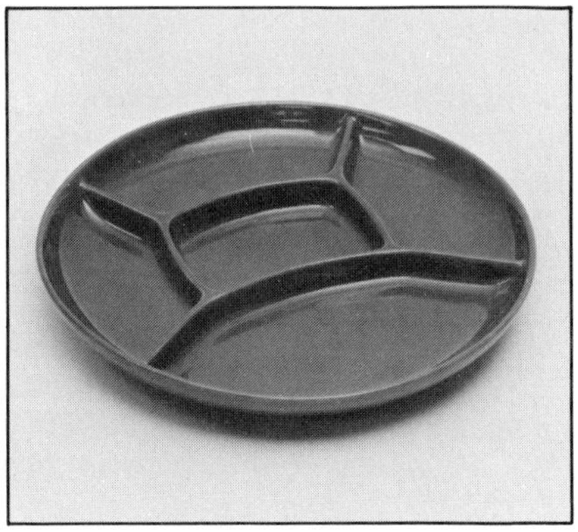

Once you've cooked a tender chunk of beef in the hot oil of a *fondue bourguignonne* pot, you will need to transfer it from the hot cooking fork to a dinner fork. This round, 8¾″-diameter plate, glazed a dark apple-green (also available in red or yellow) will hold not only the meat, but all those delectable sauces that go with it. The plate is divided into five compartments to keep the sauces discreetly apart so that you can savor their contrasting flavors. You might have a rich béarnaise, a sharp mustard cream, a tangy tomato sauce, and one of hot, spicy curry.

Swissmart, Inc. (451) **$3.50**

Stainless-Steel Fondue Bourguignonne Set H:66

This 7½-cup *fondue bourguignonne* set is handsome and practical. In addition to the traditional method of frying beef, it could lead you into all kinds of fondue experimentation. Try frying grated Swiss cheese balls (held together with beaten egg whites) seasoned with shallots and rolled in bread crumbs. The pot, the burner and a tray to catch drippings are all made of easy-to-clean stainless steel; the heat-resistant handle is of black plastic; the wrought-iron stand is rustproof. This pot has a 7″-wide bottom for good stability and the tapered sides you need in a deep-frying pot. The narrow, 5″-diameter top holds in splattering oil. Additional protection is provided by an aluminum spatter shield with a scalloped opening for inserting the forks. The 4″-high, three-legged stand is sturdy and graceful; and the alcohol burner has a flame regulator and a cap for extinguishing the flame. The 9″-diameter tray underneath it all will protect tabletop and cloth.

Spring Brothers Co., Inc. (175-6) **$47.50**

FONDUE BOURGUIGNONNE

In a metal fondue pot, heat 2 cups cooking oil till hot. (Test with a cube of bread; if it browns in 1 minute, the oil is the right temperature). Place pot of hot oil on burner at the center of the table in reach of all diners.

Provide each person with about ½ pound of lean, tender beef (filet or top sirloin) cut into ¾″ cubes, a variety of sauces, and 2 forks (a fondue fork, which gets very hot, and a fork to eat with). Diners spear a beef cube, dunk it into the hot oil to cook, then change forks, dip in sauce and eat. Serve with green salad, Rösti (Swiss-style browned potatoes) and red wine.

(From LA FONDUE by Heinz P. Hofer. Reprinted by permission of the Switzerland Cheese Association, Inc.)

Copper Fondue Bourguignonne Set H:67

What nicer way for you to share an evening with friends than to let everyone be his own cook by dipping succulent chunks of steak into a pot of sizzling oil? This beautiful *fondue bourguignonne* set provides all the equipment you need for a fondue feast for four. For the sake of expediency, it is best to limit one pot to four people. More than four pieces of meat will lower the temperature of the oil too far for efficient cooking. The 3¾-pint pot is of shining copper lined with stainless steel, a bimetal construction used to great purpose: the copper conducts heat peerlessly, and the stainless steel can neither melt off (as tin might from the intense heat needed for frying) nor react with the food. Protection from spattering oil is obtained by the tapered sides of the pot—it is 7″ in diameter at the bottom and 5″ in diameter at the top. An aluminum spatter shield with a scalloped center hole for inserting the forks offers further safety. A rustproof, wrought-iron stand with three curved legs, 4″ high, supports the pot above an alcohol burner, also made of copper lined with stainless steel. A flame regulator controls the amount of oxygen reaching the flame, and a separate cap covers the burner to extinguish the flame when the feast is over. A copper tray, 9¼″ in diameter, protects the tabletop and catches any drips. The set comes with a tube of copper cleaner to keep it shiny bright. When that runs out, you can resort to an old-fashioned remedy: a good solution of vinegar and salt.

Spring Brothers Co., Inc. (100-7) $59.50

Alcohol Burner H:68

A special pot is not absolutely essential for a feast of bubbling cheese fondue: most flameproof ceramic or enameled saucepans will do. But you will need a burner to keep the cheese soft and creamy while everyone eats. This small, lightweight burner has a base and grill of a matte-black enameled steel. The base is 7″ in diameter and 3⅝″ high, large enough to accommodate a two-quart saucepan and low enough to provide good stability. The stainless-steel burner unit burns wood alcohol and may be lifted out for easy filling and igniting. It comes with a flame regulator to adjust the amount of heat given off and a cover to extinguish the flame when it's time to scrape off *la religieuse*—the crust of cheese that forms in the bottom of the pot—and divide it as a last treat to be shared by all.

Swissmart, Inc. (247) $20.00

Raclette Stove H:69

Raclette is a dish made by placing half a wheel of *raclette* cheese before a wood fire—or on an electric *raclette* grill like this one—and scraping off layers of cheese as it softens. A popular meal after skiing or hiking, *raclette* is served on hot plates with boiled potatoes, small, sour gherkins and, often, pickled onions. Besides *raclette,* several Swiss cheeses—Gomser, Bagnes and Belalp—have the right firmness, creaminess and mild taste for an authentic *raclette.* This electric *raclette* stove is made primarily of enameled steel with a 19″-by-13″ base. It has an infrared cooking reflector set at a 45° angle from the base, adjustable clamps to hold the cheese in place, and a platform for plates. The reflector may be shifted from side to side; when the cut surface of the cheese has been melted to just the right point, the reflector can be shifted to warm the plates while the softened cheese is scraped off onto them, then moved back to melt more cheese. For a *raclette* treat without the fuss of building a fire, this neat, easy-to-clean stove is the thing to have.

Swissmart, Inc. (914) $275.00

Breads: Light and Dark

From earliest times, the bread in Middle Europe was made from the wheat, rye and barley that thrive in its soil and climate. Every region, every town developed its own particular breads. Thus, more than two hundred different kinds of bread are now produced in West Germany

Continued from preceding page

alone. A single bakery in Vienna turns out twenty-three kinds of breads and rolls, and a Ukranian shop in Kiev offers thirty varieties. The differences among breads depend on their shapes, ingredients and the toppings that are used—caraway seeds, coarse salt, linseeds, almonds, poppyseeds or oatmeal.

White bread, traditionally a status symbol, is often made into small breakfast rolls, the *Kaisersemmeln* (Kaiser rolls) of Austria or *Brötchen* (little rolls) of Germany. These are also likely to accompany lunches and hot sausages later in the day. Larger white loaves are used for open-faced sandwiches and provide the crusty bread for *fondue*. Elegant rolls and bread sticks topped with poppyseeds, caraway seeds and coarse salt are served with dinners. Sweetened white breads, such as the hard bagel-like *bublyky*, are popular in the Ukraine.

Dark breads, made from rye or a mixture of rye and wheat flours, are baked in large, round loaves, dusted with oatmeal and eaten with cheese, ham or sausages; they also consort well with sauerkraut and other robust peasant dishes. Unleavened cracked wheat flour makes *Knäckebrot* to spread with liverwurst or soft cheeses. And the simplest, coarsest breads, like the German *Vollkornbrot* and Russian black bread made from whole, cracked or rough-ground kernels of rye and wheat, are now as popular for their nutritional value among the affluent as they are among the peasants.

Pig-Shaped Breakfast Board H:70

Animals always have a winning way. Just so, with this amusing bread board from Hungary in the shape of a perky pig. Made of light, natural wood and available in 11″-by-5″ or 12″-by-6″ sizes, the board is ¼″ thick and has a hole in its tail for hanging. It is meant for an individual serving of bread or a roll, so each person at the table may have his own board. Although commonly used at breakfast when bread, butter, jam and coffee with milk are enthusiastically consumed, this board can be used at any meal. It also makes a particularly appropriate hors d'oeuvre tray when stacked with thin slices of Westphalian ham.

H. Roth & Son (43-12) $3.95

Breakfast Board H:71

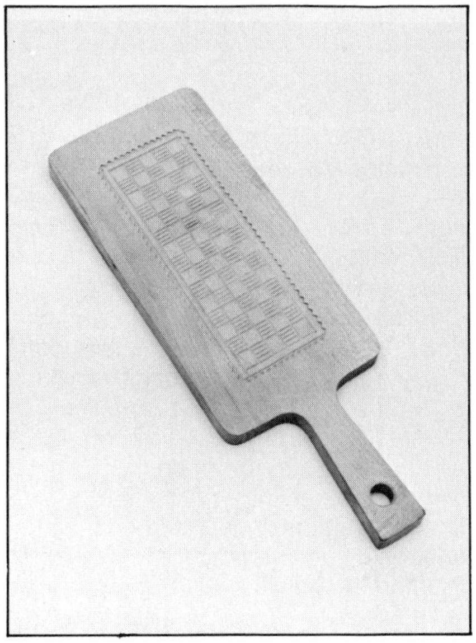

Here is a breakfast board from Poland. Made of hardwood with a smooth top and a carved checkerboard design on the back, it is rectangular in shape—11⅞″ long with the handle, and 4¼″ wide. The handle has a large hole through it for hanging. A good ½″ thick, the board is small and sturdy and could add a decorative touch to your peg board when not being used to serve crusty chunks of thick brown bread.

Cepelia Corp. (6408) $5.50

POTATO BREAD WITH CARAWAY SEEDS

Köménymagos krumplis kenyér

1 loaf

3 medium-sized potatoes
1 envelope of dry granular yeast or 1 cake of compressed fresh yeast
2 pounds bread flour (see Note)
1½ tablespoons salt
½ tablespoon caraway seeds

1. Boil potatoes in their skins. Peel them, and mash through a sieve or potato ricer while warm. You should have 1 cup mashed potatoes. Let cool.
2. Place yeast in ½ cup warm (not hot) water, and mix well with 3 tablespoons flour in a 4-quart bowl. Let the starter rise for 30 minutes.
3. Add 2 cups lukewarm water, the salt and the caraway seeds. Add the rest of the flour and the mashed potatoes.
4. Knead the dough until it separates from hands and sides of the pot. This will take from 10 to 12 minutes.
5. Let the dough rise until it doubles in bulk. Depending on the temperature, the nature of the flour and the yeast, it will take anywhere from 1 to 2 hours.
6. Preheat oven to 400° F. Place the dough on a floured board and rework it for a few minutes. Shape it into a loaf, and let it rise for about 30 minutes.
7. Dip a brush into water and brush it on the center of bread. Then make an incision in the loaf. Bake it in the preheated oven for 45 minutes, or until it is done.

Note: You may be able to purchase bread flour from a local baker. For this recipe, try to get some. At least use *unbleached* all-purpose flour. Bread flour is made from hard wheat with high protein content. All-purpose flour is a blend of hard and soft wheats; while it is satisfactory for most home uses, it will give different results from bread flour.

It is most difficult to get the texture of Hungarian homemade bread using the home oven, but following this procedure you will come very close to the type of bread that is eaten in Hungarian homes.

As a child I had two standing jobs; one was cutting little labels and writing our name on them so my mother could stick one on each of the two huge loaves baked every week. The other was delivering the loaves in their basket to the "Nyuli-Bakery." I guess I wasn't trusted with the taking-home part.

(From THE CUISINE OF HUNGARY by George Lang. Copyright 1971 by George Lang. Reprinted by permission of Atheneum.)

Butter Mold H:72

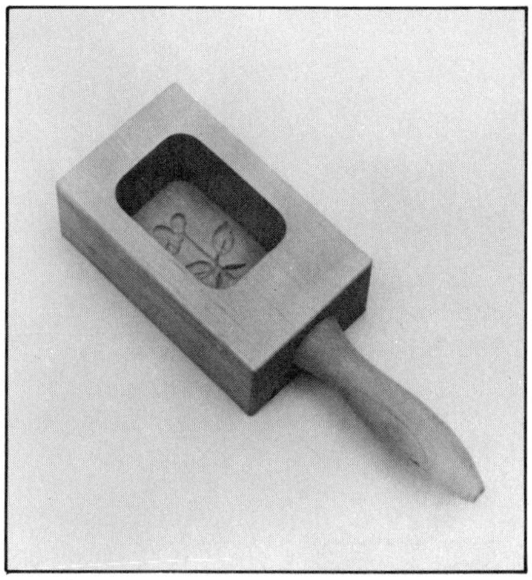

What could be better than fresh butter to go with a good piece of nutritious homemade bread? Nowadays, few people make their own butter, but they can still add a personal stamp to it by means of a hand-carved wooden mold. To use the mold, dip it in water, let it stand a minute, then press slightly softened butter into the hole in its center. Remove the butter by loosening the edges with a thin knife, turning the mold over, and smacking it down firmly. The block of butter should come out easily with the raised flower design clearly embossed on the top. This block holds five ounces of butter and measures 3″ by 5″. The handle is 4¼″ long. In the center is a 1½″-deep rectangular hole with the simple, attractive flower carving at the bottom.

H. Roth & Son (41-9) $12.75

Of the virtues of butter, the grim Dr. Alcott is doubtful: "A little fresh butter, spread on stale bread, and the latter well masticated, cannot be very hurtful. It gives a relish to the bread, which is favorable to its digestion. . . . this is the only instance in which I deem butter at all admissable."

The Young Housekeeper, or Thoughts on Food and Cooking *by Dr. Alcott.*

Two-Piece Butter Mold H:73

If you think you wouldn't melt at the sight of an engagingly plump chicken made out of butter, look carefully at this Polish butter mold. It is irresistibly crafted. Made of smooth hardwood, the mold separates into two 1″-thick blocks, both of which are carved on the inside with the design of a chicken, complete with feathers. One block has two pegs on the inside that fit into holes on the other block, to hold them firmly together. Before filling the mold, put it in the freezer for an hour. Then fill both halves of the mold generously and quickly with softened butter, join them, and scrape off the excess butter that will be extruded through the oval hole at the bottom of the mold and the two notches at one side. Return the mold to the freezer. To unmold the butter, rap the mold firmly on a counter, then pry the halves apart with a knife. The mold will hold about five ounces of butter. Of course, not many of your guests will want to be the first to cut into this charming chicken.

Cepelia Corp. (6379) $10.50

Honey Dispenser H:74

This delightful honey dispenser from Germany, with its attractive honeycomb design, is cleverly planned to minimize waste and sticky mess. Lift the glass dispenser out of its holder, press the lever in the chrome-plated top, and a rod inside the jar lifts a plastic stopper to let honey stream out the bottom. The flow of the honey is controlled by your finger on the lever. The glass cup that holds the dispenser will catch any last little drips. What could be nicer for storing and serving those glorious Middle European heather, thyme or linden honeys? The dispenser is 5½″ tall and holds one cup of honey.

Scandicrafts, Inc. (G9060) $16.00

Vienna Roll Stamp H:75

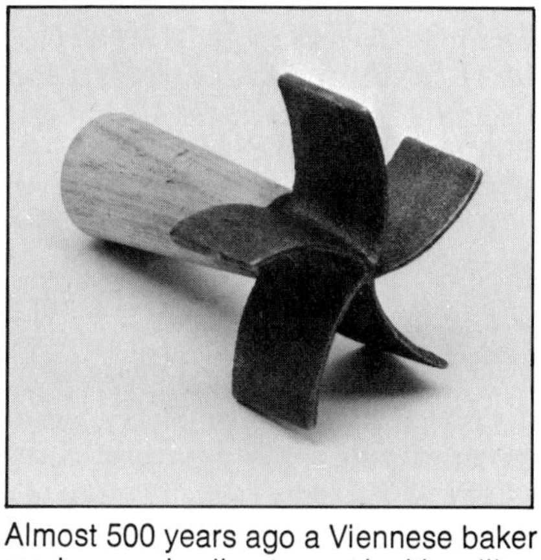

Almost 500 years ago a Viennese baker made round rolls stamped with a likeness of Emperor Frederick V for distribution to children. In the modern

Continued from preceding page

republic of Austria, these soft, round, airy rolls are no longer marked with the Emperor's picture, but they are still called Emperor's rolls (*Kaisersemmeln*). Today, they are impressed with a pinwheel-like stamp that makes it easy to break the rolls into sections. This cast-aluminum stamp with a detachable wooden handle will make the traditional swirled design on your rolls. Roll the bread dough into fist-sized balls and, just before baking, press the stamp almost all the way through the dough. Each of the arms is an inch long, and the stamp measures 4″ in overall length.

Maid of Scandinavia Co. (45845) **$5.95**

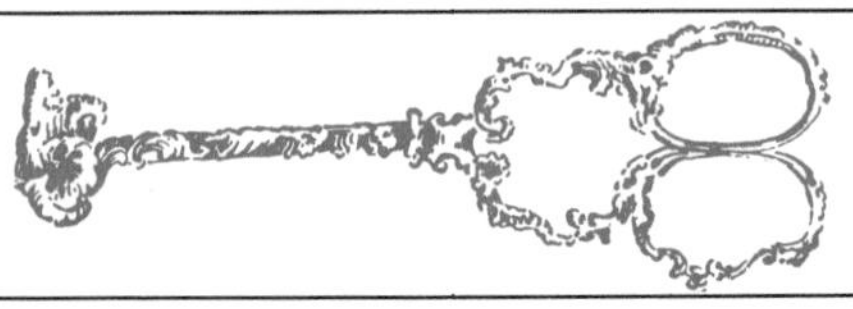

The Consummate Coffee Break

In Middle Europe, from Switzerland to Estonia, the afternoon coffee break is more than just a hastily downed cup of instant; it is a leisurely meal of rich, dark-roasted coffee, served with generous gobs of whipped cream, and a splendid pastry, usually served with still more gobs of sweetened whipped cream. On weekends and festive occasions, it is a ritual to be shared with friends and family. The hot coffee and sweet food stimulate conversation that can last for hours and create a glow of warmth and well-being. One is more apt to be invited to a German or Austrian home for *Kaffee* than for any other food, since that is when a hostess can show off her baking skills without the fuss of preparing a whole meal.

But the *Kaffeetisch* ("coffee table" in Germany) or *Jause* (as it is called in Austria) is not only enjoyed at home. Countless pastry shops or *Konditoreien* in Germany, Austria and Switzerland serve coffee, cakes and pastry. You will find one in almost every town. In summer you may be served in a garden or orchard, in winter in an elegant room overlooking an old square. Even on weekdays, the coffeehouses do a brisk afternoon business, as patrons come in to relax over a sweet and perhaps glance through the newspapers.

The most famous coffeehouses—such as Demel's in Vienna, the Café Glockenspiel in Munich and Sprüngli's in Zurich—date back to more leisurely days, and display an incredible assortment of tempting delights in resplendent Old World surroundings. And in the grand old hotels in Central European spas, strolling musicians or a string quartet may serenade you while you feast on pastry and cream.

The richest pastries to choose from are, perhaps, the *Torten:* round, relatively flat cakes made with little or no flour but full of ground nuts and eggs, glazed with jam, chocolate, or caramelized sugar and decorated with whipped cream. Less outrageously rich are the coffee cakes, such as a *Gugelhupf, Bundtkuchen* or *Sandtorte,* flavored with vanilla and lemon or rum, and often enriched with raisins or currants and nuts and sprinkled with powdered sugar. There is always a fruit tart (*Obsttorte*) and a light, flaky strudel as well as a selection of other cream-filled pastries and cookies.

With the baking tins and molds we show you here, you can re-create your own Old World *Jause* and imagine yourself carried back to the carefree Vienna of the Gay Nineties.

Mixing Bowl H:76

A *Waitling* is a big, heavy Austrian mixing bowl. Despite its large size and fairly substantial weight, the bowl's round, sloping shape and big, well-placed handles make it simple to hold in the crook of your arm. Hold it waist high encircled by one arm, and with your other arm mix the batter with a wooden spoon. Better yet, sit down and hold the *Waitling* in your lap. Or do what the Austrians do when it's time to make a batch of *Buchteln* (yeast buns filled with jam): because the thick yeast dough must be worked with a wooden spoon for half an hour, the Austrian cook recruits the children of the household. One sits holding the *Waitling* by its handles, while another works the dough with a wooden spoon until he gets tired; then the next team takes over. It's easy to get help when the reward is a warm, sugar-sprinkled, jam-filled, golden brown *Buchtel.* This *Waitling* is made of tinned steel and measures 13½″ in diameter and 5¾″ deep. If you prefer, the bowl is also available in brown enameled steel with an oyster white interior.

Paprikás Weiss **$15.98**

Wooden Spoon H:77

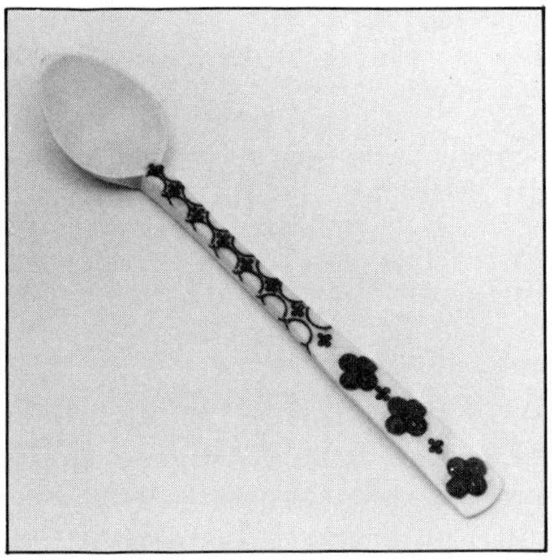

This simple spoon of unfinished wood

is both decorative and functional. It is 14¾″ long and has a large oval-shaped bowl. The long handle is graced by dark-brown, wood-burned swirls and arcs, fashioned into stylized flowers. The spoon is a lovely implement for kitchen tasks or for serving.

Cepelia Corp. (6180) **$2.50**

Pastry Jagger H:78

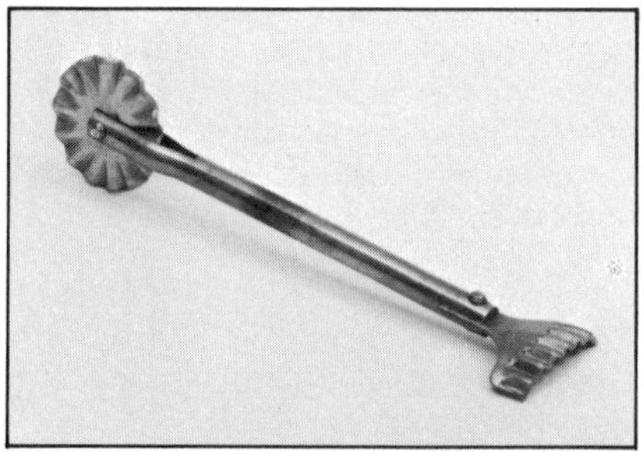

A pastry jagger is simply a pastry wheel that cuts with a saw-toothed edge through rolled-out dough. This handsome jagger made of sturdy brass has a crimper at the other end of its 3¼″ long handle; both the turning wheel of the jagger and the stationary, slightly curved crimper are attached by brass rivets to the handle. One end will crimp the rim of a pastry shell for a Swiss *Apfelwähe* (an apple tart with an apricot-glazed custard topping), or seal the edges of Russian *varenyky* (savory or dessert dumplings filled with sauerkraut, cheese or cherries). The other end will give lacy edges to cookies, to noodles, or to the lattice pastry top of a *Linzertorte* (almond torte filled with raspberry jam).

Maid of Scandinavia Co. (47074) **$2.10**

Swizzle Blender H:79

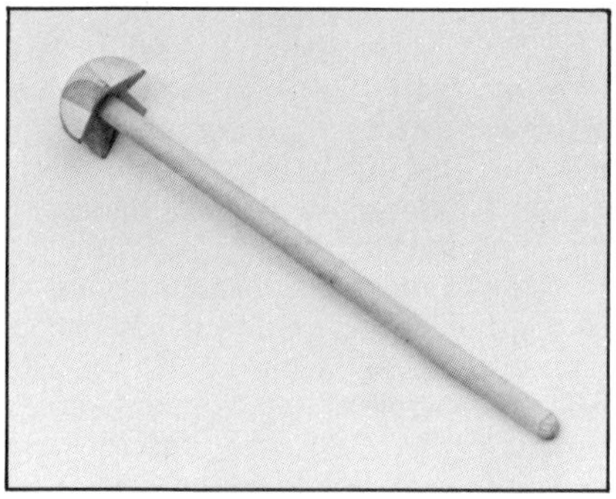

This swizzle stick is not for mixing a drink, but for beating batter. Just a simple 10″-long wooden stick with a 5-sided, smooth-domed swizzle, it is ideal for blending the egg and milk mixtures for *Pfannkuchen* or *Kaiserschmarrn* (German and Austrian pancakes). Hold the stick between your palms and rub them back and forth; the swizzle will twirl the egg into the milk in a jiffy and leave the batter light and foamy. Add rum-soaked raisins to your pancake batter and you'll have a dessert fit for a king—or, in fact, for a kaiser.

Paprikás Weiss (5211) **$1.59**

Goose Feather Pastry Brush H:80

Viennese pastries such as *Tasherl* (jam pockets) or *Aprikosenblätter* (apricot leaves) call for a light coating of egg white before baking. The best pastry brush for doing this is one made of goose feathers, since it will pick up only a small amount of liquid and leave the lightest of glazes on your pastry. This 7″-long brush is made of eight goose feathers, their quills braided and lashed together to form a handle.

H. Roth & Son (32-9) **$0.79**

Rolling Pin H:81

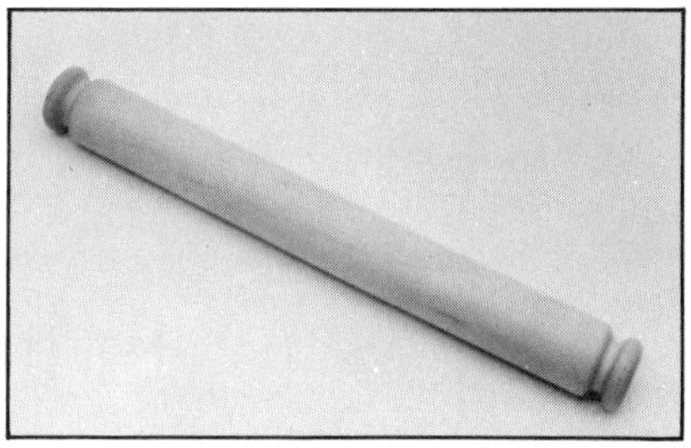

Made from a single piece of unfinished, satiny wood, this plump German rolling pin is rounded and smoothed near the ends to form knob handles. Sturdy and well-balanced, it would be perfect for rolling out large quantities of pastry—a big batch of *Springerle* cookies, say, or the dough for a scrumptious poppyseed strudel. The rolling pin is 17¾″ long and 2″ in diameter.

H. Roth & Son **$3.95**

Rosette Cookie Cutters H:82

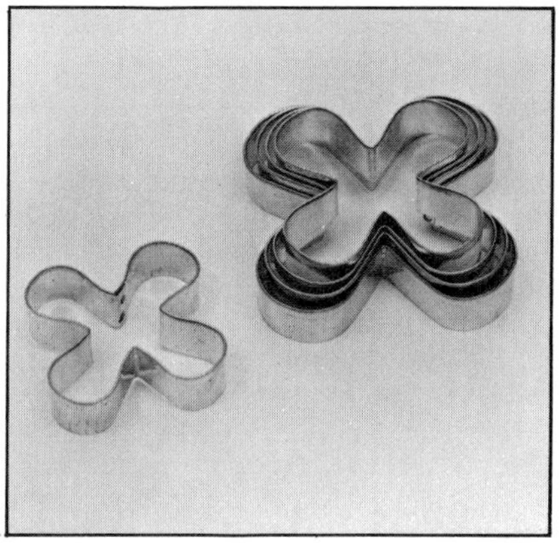

Some of the loveliest cookies are Hungarian *Rózsa Fank* (rose fritters). To make them, several rosettes, graduated in size, are first cut from a thinly-rolled, egg-rich cookie dough flavored with rum. Then, the center of each rosette, except for the smallest top one, is brushed with egg white and the rosettes are superimposed one on the other, and gently pressed together in the middle. Usually, only three layers of dough are necessary, but you may try all five sizes at once, if you like. Next, the cookies are dropped into hot oil, which makes their petals curl up softly like roses, and they are fried until golden. Before serving, the roses are dusted with confectioners' sugar and their centers are filled with raspberry jam. The largest of these cutters is 4¾″ across, the smallest 3½″; each one is an inch deep. They are made of tinned steel with neatly spot-welded seams, and have a folded rim on one edge and a knife-sharp blade on the other. A recipe is included with the set.

Maid of Scandinavia Co. (A1815) **$3.20**

Gingerbread Cookie Cutter H:83

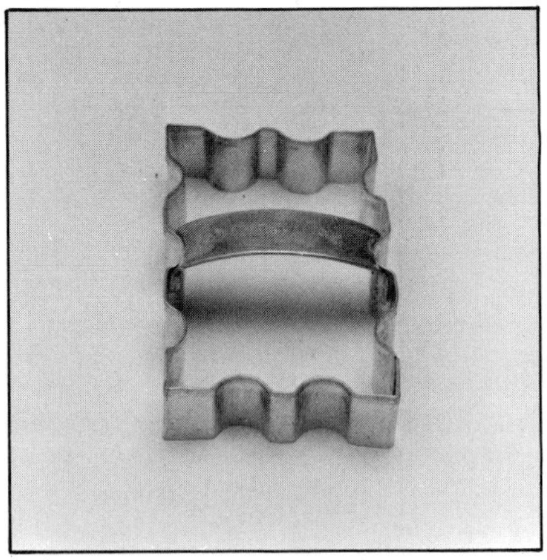

Gingerbread or *Lebkuchen*—also called *Honigkuchen* (honey cake)—is made with eggs, flour, honey, almonds, candied lemon and orange peel, ground cinnamon and cloves. Honey cakes of some kind were eaten in Egypt as early as 1500 B.C., and it was possibly the Romans who introduced the sweets to Switzerland and southern Germany. But the most famous *Lebkuchen* have always come from Nürnberg, which is located near the beekeeping areas of the Bavarian forests and was an important center of trade in medieval times. Glazed with sugar icing or plain, gingerbread is a delectable holiday treat. This rectangular cutter of tinned steel cuts gingerbread into a traditional shape for Christmas eating. An arched handle with smoothly rolled edges makes the cutter easy to use; the half-circles bitten off along the sides of the cutter will give the large cookies a lacy touch. A generous 3⅝″ long and 2¼″ wide, the cutter is deep enough (¾″) for thickly-rolled gingerbread dough.

H. Roth & Son (19-47) $0.69

NÜRNBERGER HONEY SPICE CAKES

Nürnberger Lebkuchen

About 30 cookies

3 eggs
¾ cup sugar
1 pound honey
½ cup grated unblanched almonds or filberts

Viennese gingerbread cakes.

"Who is knocking on my little house."

½ cup mixed citron and candied orange peel, chopped
1 teaspoon cinnamon
½ teaspoon powdered cloves
1 cup strong black coffee or milk
4½ cups flour
1½ teaspoons baking powder
Egg white icing or hard chocolate icing or Lebkuchen glaze, below

Beat eggs with sugar until mixture is thick and pale yellow. Add honey, nutmeat, candied fruit and spices, then coffee or milk (the first makes a darker, richer cookie; the other makes a pale golden one with a mild flavor) and mix well. Sift flour with baking powder and gradually stir into batter. Blend thoroughly. Grease and flour a baking sheet or jelly-roll pan and spread out dough, to about ½″ thickness. Bake in preheated 400° oven about 12 minutes, or until golden brown. If you are using egg white icing or Lebkuchen glaze, brush on cookies immediately. If you use chocolate icing, spread on cold cookies. When cold, cut into rectangular cookies.

Lebkuchen Glaze:
Mix ⅓ cup confectioners' sugar with 1½ tablespoons cornstarch. Sprinkle with ½ teaspoon almond extract and a little rum or lemon juice. Mix in hot water, a tablespoonful at a time, until you have a thick, smooth paste. Spread on warm cookies. If mixture cools and thickens as you work with it, stir in more hot water.

(From THE GERMAN COOKBOOK by Mimi Sheraton. Copyright 1965 by Mimi Sheraton. Reprinted by permission of Random House, Inc.)

"A sweet fragrance greeted him; it reminded him of home, it was the smell of the parlor in his mother's house at Christmas time. With trembling hand he lit his lamp; and there lay a mighty parcel on the table. When he opened it, out fell the familiar ginger cakes. On some of them were the initial letters of his name written in sprinkles of sugar; no one but Elisabeth could have done that."

Immensee *by Theodor Storm, from* Great German Short Novels and Stories. *Modern Library, 1952.*

Santa Claus Cookie Cutter H:84

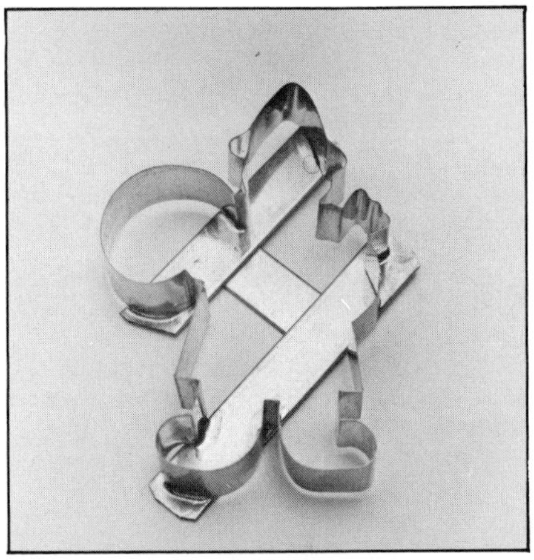

What more delightful shape for a Christmas cookie than the silhouette of that generous, jolly old man, whose visit little children dream about? This tinned-steel cutter will turn out 5½″-tall Santas, each with a peaked cap and a nicely bulging bag of gifts. Heavily tin-plated for extra strength, the 1″-deep cutter also has a sturdy handle soldered in several places so that the detailed design will not be pulled out of shape, even after years of use. Frosted with sugar icing, gingerbread or sugar-cookie Santas will make festive homemade decorations for your Christmas tree. Poke a hole in the cap before baking and when the cookie is cool, pull a piece of colored yarn through it to make a loop for hanging. Make some extras just for eating, though, or the tree will not stay decorated very long.

Handcraft from Europe (951) $12.75

A Swiss Christmas cookie called a Tirggel.

Small Springerle Board H:85

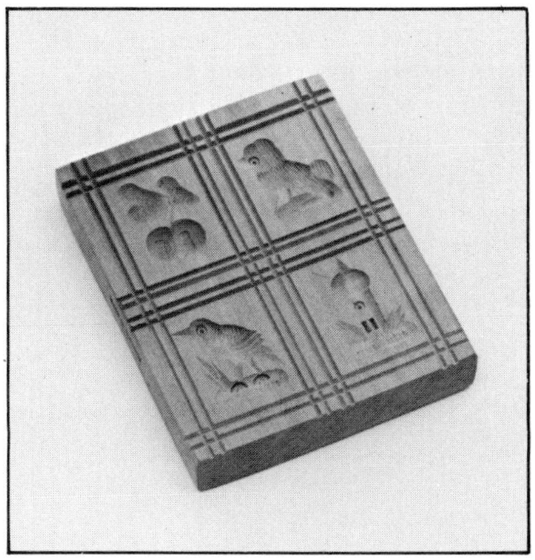

Springerle are among the most beautiful cookies in the world, and they are an old tradition in both Germany and Switzerland. In Switzerland, they are known as *Anisbrötli* or *Ainsli* because of their distinctive anise flavor. The stiff dough is made with eggs, sugar and flour and flavored with anise and lemon. To use the board, first dust it with flour. Then press it firmly but evenly down onto a $\frac{1}{4}$″- to $\frac{1}{2}$″-thick sheet of rolled-out cookie dough. Gently lift the board off, and then cut the dough into rectangles or squares, each with an embossed figure in the center. All of the incisions in this *Springerle* board are sharp and clear, and the cuts slope outward toward the top to permit free release of the dough. The designs—a dog, a bird, a church tower and cherries—are charming and separated by double, incised lines that frame them. Air-dry the cookies for 24 hours and then bake them for only about 15 minutes until they are the palest gold color, never brown. The rock-hard cookies keep a long time and soften after a few weeks in a cookie jar. *Springerle* are usually baked about a month before Christmas. The board is made of ash and measures $4\frac{1}{4}$″ by $3\frac{1}{2}$″ by $\frac{1}{2}$″; a larger board with six images is also available.

H. Roth & Son (41-1) $4.95

A Swiss Tirggel *cookie of molded gingerbread from the 1800s.*

Springerle Woodsman Board H:86

The bearded man striding across this *Springerle* mold is perhaps a woodsman bringing home a Christmas tree. His rucksack is full, a hatchet and horn hang from his belt and a jaunty feather pokes out from his hat. This handsome fellow would not only contribute to the festivities of *Weihnachten* (Christmas), but would add year-round embellishment to any kitchen. You can even keep him company with a Snow White, Puss in Boots and a Goose Girl, which are also available separately. All four molds are the same size—$7\frac{7}{8}$″ by $4\frac{1}{4}$″ by $\frac{1}{2}$″—and all are made of ash.

H. Roth & Son (40-13) $17.95

Springerle Rolling Pin H:87

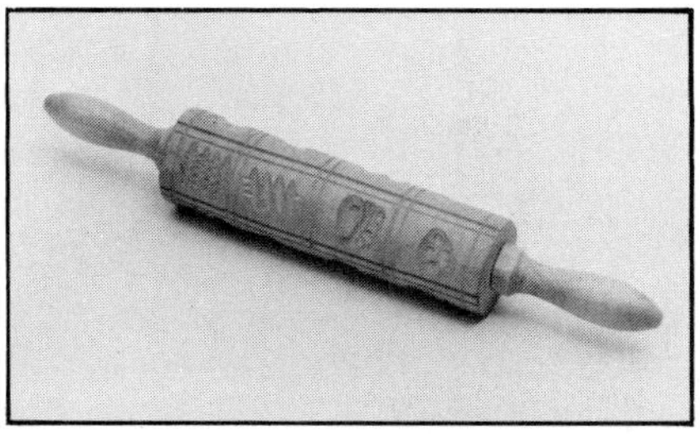

Nothing proclaims Christmas more delightfully than *Springerle,* pale, cream-colored cookies embossed with familiar images and flavored with lemon and anise. Leave your *Springerle* decoration to a maplewood rolling pin like this $15\frac{3}{4}$″-long model with sturdy, finished handles. The rolling surface alone is $8\frac{1}{8}$″ long and has 16 designs that include birds, flowers and fruits. It is sometimes helpful to chill the pin for several hours in the refrigerator before rolling the dough, to prevent it from sticking. Cut along the ridges between the cookies with a large, sharp knife to separate them neatly. If you haven't already thought of it, *Springerle* make irresistible ornaments on Christmas trees and packages.

H. A. Mack & Co., Inc. $5.00

Germanic tribes in pre-Christian times celebrated the winter solstice by sacrificing animals. Later, shaped dough took the place of the live creatures and, eventually, they were represented by stamped cookies. The Springerle *(little horse, in a German dialect) was one of the amiable beasts favored for a cookie motif. Hence, some surmise, the name.*

A scene from Alsace.

Springerle Cookie Roller H:88

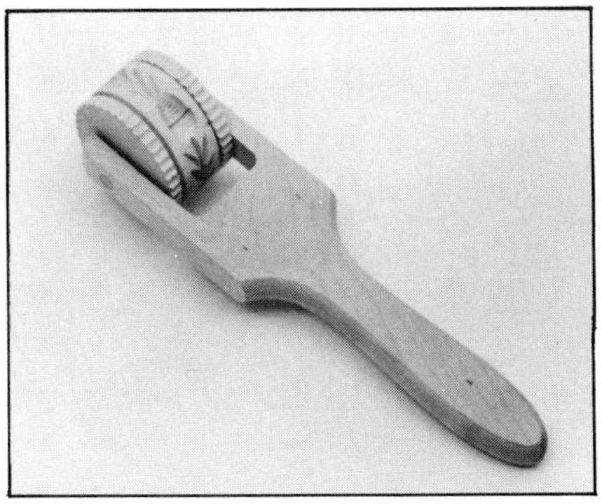

With this diminutive cookie roller, you or your offspring can make pineapple-figured *Springerle* for Christmas. Three pineapples are carved into the wooden wheel, which is 1½″ wide and 2¼″ across. Turning the wheel with the 9½″-long, unfinished wooden handle is child's play—and what nicer way to get assistance for the pastry chef?

H. Roth & Son (41-12) $6.95

SPRINGERLE

About 75 cookies

4 eggs
2½ cups fine, quick-dissolving granulated sugar
grated rind of 1 lemon
5½ cups flour
about ¾ cup anise seeds, for pan

Beat eggs with sugar 30 minutes by hand, or 10 minutes in an electric mixer. Mixture must be almost white, and thick enough to ribbon. Add lemon rind. Sieve flour into mixture gradually, stirring well between additions. Dough should be thick enough to knead. Add more flour if necessary. Knead dough on floured board until shiny. With a floured rolling pin, roll out dough to ¼″ to ½″ thickness. Flour a Springerle board or rolling pin, and press or roll design on dough. Cut squares apart. Grease a baking sheet and sprinkle liberally with anise seeds. Place cookies on baking sheet and let dry uncovered, at room temperature, 24 hours. Bake in preheated 250° oven until pale golden but not brown, 15 to 20 minutes.

(From THE GERMAN COOKBOOK by Mimi Sheraton. Copyright 1965 by Mimi Sheraton. Reprinted by permission of Random House, Inc.)

Obsttorte Pan H:89

The Germans are fanatics about the health-giving properties of fruit, but they also have a weakness for *Kuchen* (cakes). *Obsttorte* (fruit torte) provides the happy solution for someone torn between eating healthy food and indulging his sweet tooth, and *Obsttorten* of all kinds are understandably popular in most areas of Central Europe. The depressed center area of the baked cake is spread with fresh fruit according to the season. In the fall, a flurry of canning ensures that *Obsttorten* will still grace the winter *Kaffèetisch* (coffee table). Often a variety of fruits is used: bananas, pears, cherries and peaches may be arranged in colorful patterns. The fruit may be glazed with gelatin and the torte is often served with generous mounds of whipped cream. This form for making *Obsttorten* is stamped out of a single sheet of metal. The waffled bottom gives the metal added strength and the fluted sides provide a decorative finish to the rich cake-like pastry that will hold the fruit. The pan is 10″ in diameter and 1¼″ deep—large enough to hold a quart of batter. It is also available in 9″ and 11″ diameters.

HOAN Products Ltd. (1866) $2.25

Three-In-One Springform Pan H:90

Central European cookbooks often contain more dessert and pastry recipes than anything else. Many of these recipes are for *Torten*—those fabulously rich, round cakes often made with little, if any, flour and no baking powder at all. Because they break easily, these delicate cakes are difficult to remove from ordinary cake pans. The solution? A springform pan. A clamp on the side of the form releases it from the cake so that the cake can be easily lifted from the bottom of the pan. This pan of tinned steel does triple duty: the 2½″-deep side band has a groove at the bottom into which

A Nürnberg kitchen from a toy catalogue of 1836.

Continued from preceding page

three differently shaped, interchangeable bottoms will fit. One has a fluted central tube ringed by deep, rounded depressions for a rich pound-cake-like *Sandtorte.* Another is tubeless, but the bottom is molded with a pattern of fluted swirls to beautify the top of an elegant torte that you would serve without icing—a *Mandeltorte* (almond torte), say, decorated with almonds and sprinkled with powdered sugar. The third bottom is flat and waffled with tiny circular depressions to strengthen it, so it will support the heaviest batter. Use it for a creamy white cheesecake or a cake topped with apples and a rum custard. This pan is 10″ in diameter and will hold three quarts; a 9″ diameter size is also available.

HOAN Products Ltd. (1877) **$5.00**

MARIA DENHOF'S WET CHOCOLATE CAKE

Feuchte Schokolade Torte

As in many *Torten* this one has a nut rather than a flour base. It is a great party cake because it should be made a number of hours or a day before serving so the chocolate icing can soak into it. The *Torte* is also very easy to make.

Torte:
6 ounces semi-sweet chocolate, cut into bits
8 eggs, separated
3 ounces grated almonds
⅔ cup sugar
juice of half a lemon and its grated rind

Icing:
6 ounces semi-sweet chocolate, cut into bits
⅔ stick butter
2 tablespoons water

Preheat the oven to 375 F. Melt six ounces of the semi-sweet chocolate bits in a double boiler. Beat the egg yolks and add the almonds and sugar. Add the lemon juice and peel, and then the melted chocolate, stirring constantly. Beat the egg whites until stiff and fold them into the batter. Butter a 9½″ springform pan and pour in the batter. Bake for 35 minutes. Test the center with a toothpick and remove the cake from the oven when it is done. (*Torten* remain relatively flat.) Let the cake cool.

Melt the rest of the chocolate in a double boiler. Add the butter and water and stir until the icing is smooth. Put the cooled *Torte* on a sheet of wax paper on a large board and pour the icing over it. Leave the *Torte* on the wax paper overnight to let the icing really soak in. Transfer it to a serving plate. As an optional treat, serve the *Torte* with a bowl of whipped cream.

(Courtesy of Maria Denhof, New York City.)

Sandkuchen Pan H:91

A *Sandkuchen* is made in a mold shaped like this one with fluted sides, a center tube and thumbprint-like depressions around the bottom. The cake, which is really heavier than a torte, resembles a pound cake. But it has a slightly grainy texture because it is traditionally made with cornstarch rather than flour, hence the name *Sandkuchen* or *Sandtorte.* For variation, the cake may be flavored with lemon peel, cinnamon, cloves, cardamom and rum. *Sandkuchen* will keep for weeks covered in the refrigerator, and gets better the longer you keep it —an ideal cake to have on hand for unexpected guests. Made of heavy-gauge tinned steel, 8″ in diameter and 3″ deep, the mold has a 1-quart capacity. It is also available in an 11″, 3-quart size.

H. Roth & Son (32-8) **$3.98**

Bundtkuchen Pan H:92

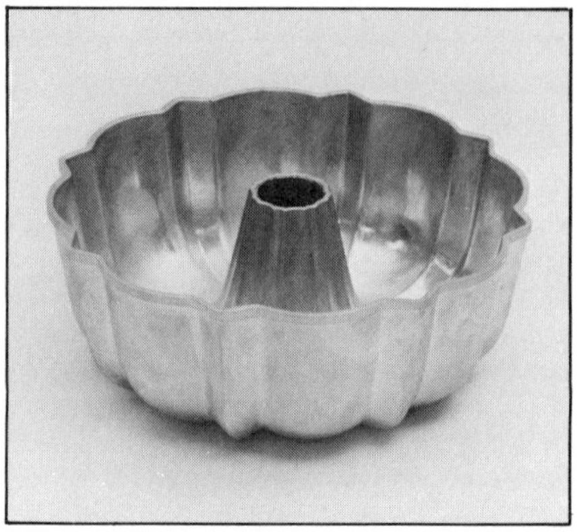

Made of cast aluminum, and therefore seamless, this large, elegantly-shaped cake pan has the broad fluting and wide center tube you need for making traditional *Bundtkuchen. Bundtkuchen* resembles our traditional pound cake. Either dusted with confectioners' sugar or spread with a chocolate icing, *Bundtkuchen* makes a decorative and delicious treat for a *Kaffeeklatsch* (coffee get-together) or birthday party. This pan is 10″ in diameter and 3½″ deep, with a 3-quart capacity.

Northland Aluminum Products, Inc. (50100) **$7.50**

Rehrücken Pan H:93

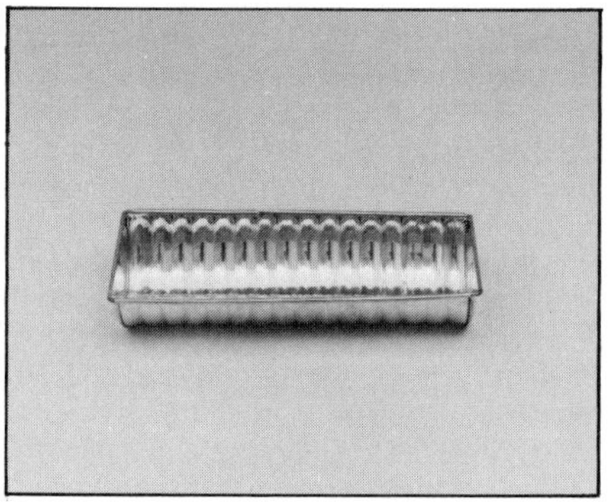

Rehrücken is the German term for saddle of venison, but this mold has nothing to do with preparing game. It is a special tin for an Austrian chocolate cake shaped to resemble a deer's back, with a flat 1″-wide backbone running the length of the cake and sixteen curved ribs that make it easy to slice the cake into uniform portions. The egg-rich cake, made with grated almonds instead of flour, is glazed with dark chocolate and studded with almonds to complete the picture of a venison saddle larded with strips of salt pork. Made of tinned steel, the mold is 10½″ long, 4½″ wide and 2½″ deep; it will hold a quart of batter.

H. Roth & Son (31-12) $3.95

Christstollen Pan H:94

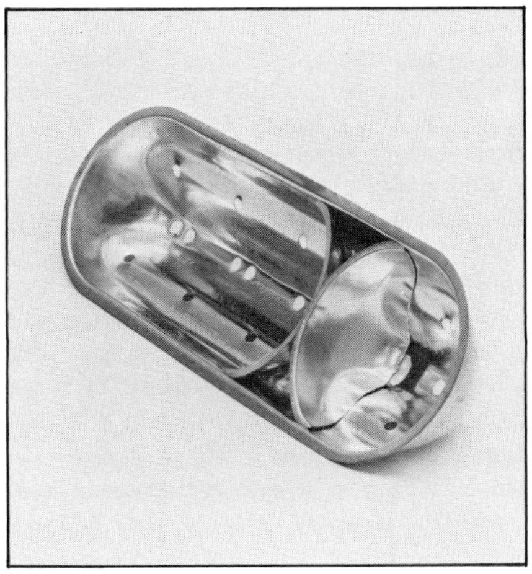

Stollen is a delicious sugar-dusted yeast cake richly filled with almonds as well as raisins, currants and candied fruits that have been steeped in rum. It is a traditional part of every German Christmas. The *Stollen* is usually folded into loaves whose tops are higher than their sides, which are slightly ridged. The dough may also be baked under this tin-plated mold, which will give the cake its traditional shape, but will make a softer crust. The mold, 15″ long and 5″ wide at the bottom, has a flat lip around the edge that rests on the baking sheet. An attachment may be screwed into the mold to divide the dough into two loaves of equal or unequal size, as you prefer. Divide the dough accordingly and form it with your hands into an oblong shape that fills the mold a little less than half way. Place a baking sheet over the inverted mold and quickly turn the mold and baking sheet over together. Then leave the dough in place to rise again before baking. Dredged in powdered sugar, this simple, fruit-filled cake is lovely with morning or afternoon coffee, and it improves with age.

Maid of Scandinavia Co. (79650) $15.75

Tinned-Steel Kugelhopf Pan H:95

A German *Kugelhopf,* Austrian *Gugelhupf* or Hungarian *Kuglof* is an elegant, fluted coffee cake dusted with powdered sugar. It is usually prepared with a yeast or a sponge-cake dough enriched with dark raisins and almonds and flavored with vanilla and rum, and sometimes a hint of citron or orange peel. To achieve its characteristic swirled fluting, you must bake the cake in a special pan. This one, made in West Germany of smoothly-seamed, heavy-gauge tinned steel, is excellent. As in all *Kugelhopf* pans, the center tube extends above the sides—in this case ½″—so that, when inverted, the tube provides a base on which the pan can rest while the cake cools. This pan is 8½″ in diameter and 3½″ deep and holds 2¼ quarts, approximately one pound of cake. It is also available in diameters of 6½″ and 9½″. If the traditional *Kugelhopf* hasn't tempted you, try a marbled version or a chocolate sponge.

HOAN Products Ltd. (1814/8) $5.50

KUGLOF

Yield: 2 large or 3 small *kuglofs*

2 ounces fresh yeast
⅓ pound sugar
2½ cups milk
3 eggs
Vanilla extract
2 pounds all-purpose flour, approximately
4 teaspoons salt
3½ sticks unsalted butter
Cinnamon
Sugar
Raisins

Cream the yeast and sugar together in a mixer. With the machine running, add the milk in a stream; the eggs, one at a time; and vanilla extract to taste. If you have a machine with a dough hook, sprinkle in enough flour to form a soft dough. Add the salt, once all the flour has been incorporated. Knead until the dough is smooth and elastic and leaves the sides of the bowl and the dough hook clean. (If you do not have an electric mixer with a dough-hook attachment, combine the ingredients in a bowl in the same order and knead by hand.) Turn onto a table, cover with a clean towel and allow to rest for 30 minutes.

Soften the butter in the mixer (or knead by hand), until somewhat malleable but still quite cold. Pinch off bits of the butter and roll it into the dough, folding and turning as necessary. (The butter will remain in lumps in the dough.) When all the butter has been incorporated, roll the dough once more. Cover and place in the refrigerator to rest for 30 minutes. Roll the dough again, folding and turning, until it is almost completely homogeneous. Only tiny flecks of butter should remain visible.

Divide the dough into two or three equal parts and roll each into a rectangle. Sprinkle each rectangle of dough with cinnamon, sugar and raisins to taste and roll into a log. Twist the cylinders of dough around the tube of two large, or three small, buttered *kuglof* pans, and pinch the ends together. Allow to rise in a warm place until doubled in bulk, approximately 1 hour.

Preheat the oven to 375 F.

Bake the *kuglofs* for 45 minutes to an hour, depending on the size of the pans. Remove the cakes from their pans almost immediately and cool them on a wire rack.

Note: You may sprinkle powdered sugar over the cake before serving. And slivered almonds may be added to the cake, if you like. For another variation, a sprinkling of cocoa powder and sugar may be substituted for the cinnamon, sugar and raisin filling. Leftover *kuglof* is excellent toasted and buttered.

(Courtesy of Mrs. Herbst's Homemade Strudels and Pastries, New York City.)

Glass Kugelhopf Form H:96

Unlike the thick, heavy glass we usually think of as ovenproof, this *Kugelhopf* mold of Jena glass is light and graceful. One imagines using it for a gelatin dessert with layers of fruit or for an elegant Bavarian cream. But it is intended for the tall, sugar-dusted coffee cake called *Kugelhopf* in Germany and *Gugelhupf* in Austria. With its handsome, swirled fluting and narrow center tube (which is high enough above the edge of the mold to let air circulate under the inverted cake while it cools), this 2-quart mold is suited not only for the raisin-and-almond-filled *Kugelhopf,* but also other heavy batters, such as those of nut cakes and pound cakes. The tube allows heat to reach the center of the batter and provides a cavity that can be filled with fruit or whipped cream when the cake is unmolded. The mold is 9½″ in diameter, 3½″ deep and holds 2 quarts. It is also available in a 1½-quart capacity.

Schott-Zwiesel Glass Inc. (3057) $20.00

Bismarck Tube H:97

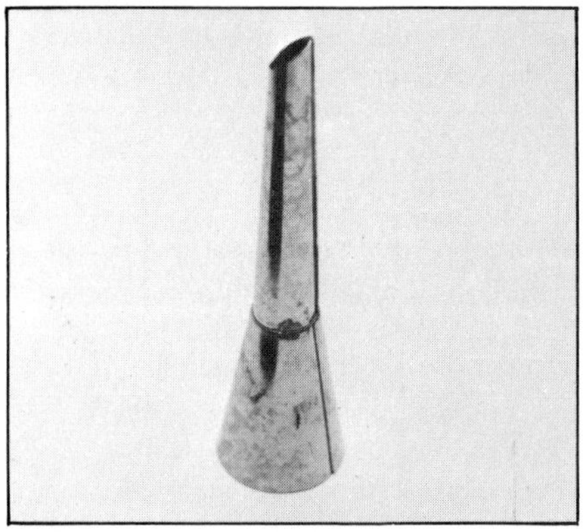

"Bismarck" is the name given by Germans long ago to jelly doughnuts, in honor of that favorite Prussian statesman. They are also known more commonly as *Berliner Pfannkuchen.* Made of nickel-silver, the tube is 2⅝″ long and ⅝″ in diameter at the widest end. With its slanted opening—measuring only 3⁄16″ diameter at the small end—it is designed to make the narrowest possible hole in the surface of a cooked doughnut. After frying the yeast-raised doughnuts and allowing them to cool, fit a pastry bag on the tube and fill it with thinned jam or jelly. Inject the jam into the centers of the doughnuts, dust the doughnuts with powdered or granulated sugar and watch them disappear.

August Thomsen Corp. (230) $1.10

Indianer Tin H:98

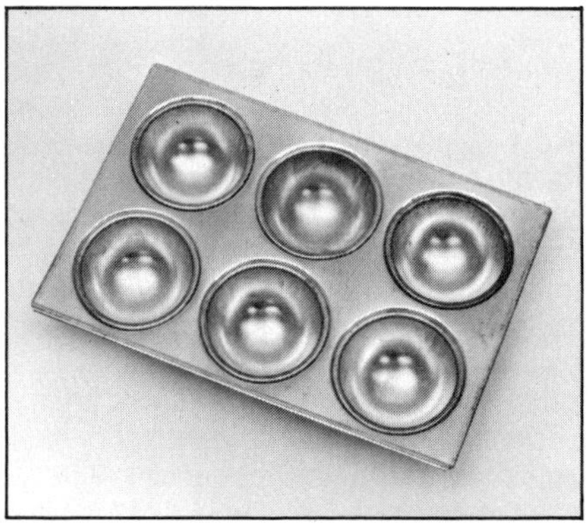

This baking tin, 9⅜″ long and 6¼″ wide, with its six seamless hemispheres about 2¼″ wide and 1¼″ deep, is for baking *Indianer*—a popular pastry created in Vienna, purportedly by a Hungarian. A light dough of eggs, flour, cornstarch, sugar and vanilla is baked into puffy balls that are then hollowed out, filled with sweetened whipped cream and glazed with chocolate. Of the many legends concerning the origins of *Indianer,* our favorite is the one about the Viennese baker's wife who became entranced with an Indian tightrope walker. When her husband objected, she threw a handful of dough at him; the baker ducked and the dough landed in a pot of hot fat. The frugal baker's wife fished it out, filled it with cream, coated it with chocolate and named it after the handsome *Indianer.* Not that we really believe the story; after all, *Indianer* are baked, not fried.

Paprikás Weiss $1.75

Indiáner, *the chocolate-glazed, whipped cream-filled cupcakes of Hungarian origin, have a curious* raison d'être, *according to George Lang in* The Cuisine of Hungary. *A Hungarian count, dabbling in the production of plays in fashionable early nineteenth century Vienna, found that the audience attending a play at his theater was less than responsive. He decided to liven up the action by adding an Indian juggler to the program, but this didn't seem to fire up the crowd either. The showman count then went a step further: he had his Hungarian pastry chef dream up a confection to be passed out at intermission. He hoped it would remind the spectators of the exotic juggler. Thus the* Indiáner *was born. We know that the pastry, at least, was a big hit.*

Schillerlocken Form H:99

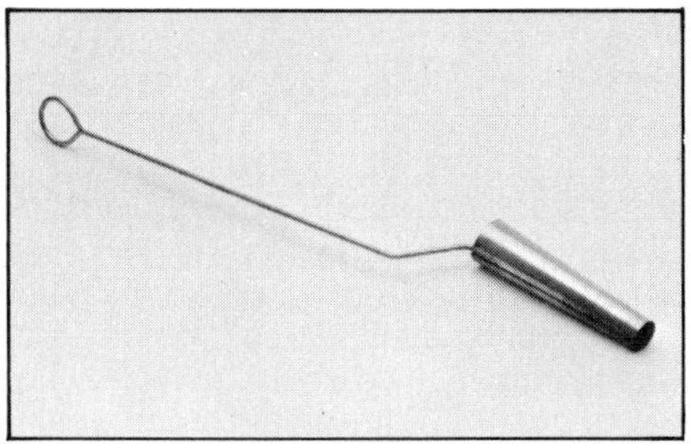

Schillerlocken are pastries named after the long curls of the famous German dramatist and poet, Friedrich Schiller. Pastry dough is cut into strips and wrapped around the form, each layer slightly overlapping the previous one. The form with the dough on it is then dipped into hot oil, the long handle keeping the cook at a safe distance. The "locks" may also be baked; for this method, similar forms are available in 5½″ and 7¼″ lengths without the handle. After baking or frying, the tubes are filled with sweetened whipped cream and consumed with afternoon coffee. This 5¼″-long, tapered, tinned-steel tube is 1¼″ in diameter at the top and ¾″ in diameter at the bottom, and is welded to a 14″-long handle.

H. Roth & Son (33-6) $2.75

Tarkedly Pan H:100

This handsome pan is especially designed for making *tarkedly*, a Hungarian pastry made with a yeast batter. The steel pan is enameled in a reddish-brown color on the outside and is white on the inside. Four round indentations, each almost 3″ in diameter and ¾″ deep, hold the spherical cakes while they are cooking. The cakes are browned on both sides in butter and then served with apricot jam, a tart plum jam or a plum compote.

Paprikás Weiss $12.98

Palatschinken Pan H:101

Made in Austria of steel enameled in two tones—a rich brown outside and a light, speckled gray inside—this pan is used to make *palatschinken, palaccinta* or *palacinky* (Austrian, Hungarian or Czechoslovakian pancakes). It is lighter in weight than the traditional crêpe pan, and its handle is longer, making it easy to swirl batter around the bottom of the pan for the thinnest of pancakes. The pan's smooth, rounded bottom also makes it very easy to roll up an omelet. As with French crêpes, the list of pancake fillings is endless. One we like is a Hungarian version: crayfish purée with mushrooms, paprika and cream. The pan is 9″ in diameter and 1⅜″ deep.

Paprikás Weiss $12.98

PALACINKY

Yields 10 to 12 pancakes

1 cup milk
2 eggs
2½ teaspoons sugar
Pinch of salt
1 cup flour
3 tablespoons butter
Jam or preserves
Confectioners' sugar

Mix the milk, eggs, sugar and salt thoroughly together in a large bowl. Add the flour slowly, stirring continuously. (This process can also be done in a blender at low speed.) Set a medium-sized skillet over low heat and add a teaspoon of butter. Pour a small amount of the pancake batter into the pan and tilt it around until the bottom is completely covered with a thin layer of batter. Cook for 2 to 3 minutes, or until golden; turn and cook the other side.

To serve, spread each pancake with jam, roll it up and lightly sprinkle the top with confectioners' sugar.

(Courtesy of Ruc restaurant, New York City.)

"If you want a good pudding, to teach you I'm willing,
Take twopennyworth of eggs, when twelve for a shilling,
And of the same fruit that Eve once had chosen,
Well pared and well chopped at least half a dozen;
Six ounces of bread (let your maid eat the crust);
The crumbs must be grated as small as the dust;
Six ounces of currants from the stones you must sort,
Lest they break out your teeth and spoil all the sport;
Six ounces of sugar won't make it too sweet,
Some salt and some nutmeg will make it complete.
Three hours let it boil, without hurry or flutter,
And then serve it up—without sugar or butter."

A Pudding Recipe *by Sidney Smith (1771–1845).*

Tin Pudding Mold H:102

Any one of the many varieties of steamed chocolate pudding so popular in Germany should emerge looking as elegant as it tastes from this classic pudding steamer. The heavy-gauge, 1-quart container of tinned steel has a deep bucket shape with fluted sides; it produces a tall pudding with a domed ring shape on top. The lid fits over two protrusions on the upper edge of the mold and is then twisted tightly into place to prevent water from seeping into the pudding while it steams. The lid also has a well-attached handle. Don't forget to butter the mold and to sprinkle it with sugar before using. And never fill the mold more than ⅔ full; the pudding must have room to expand. Serve a hot, dark chocolate pudding enriched with toasted almonds, and accompany it with lots of whipped cream.

Bridge Kitchenware Corp. $18.00

"Life's a pudding full of plums;
Care's a canker that benumbs.
Wherefore waste our elocution
On impossible solution?
Life's a pleasant institution;
Let us take it as it comes."

The Gondoliers *by William S. Gilbert.*

Ceramic Mold H:103

Pleasing to the eye, this compact white, glazed ceramic mold is the one you would reach for when making any one of the numerous gelatin desserts so popular in Germany and Austria. A simple raised flower design decorates the top of the mold, and the sides and top edges are fluted. Use it to make an attractive *Weingelee*—layers of fresh fruit in a gelatin made with dry white wine and flavored with lemon and rum. The mold is 2″ deep, 6½″ in diameter at the top, 5″ in diameter at the bottom and holds 3 cups.

Bridge Kitchenware Corp. **$5.00**

Paskha Mold H:104

Paskha means Easter in Russian, and no Russian Easter meal is complete without a finale of a *paskha* cake. This famous Easter cake is made of pot cheese, sugar, heavy cream, eggs, almonds and candied fruit, and it is usually decorated with the Cyrillic letters X B, which proclaim the Easter message *Christos Voskres,* Christ is risen. This wooden 8-cup mold, in the traditional form of a truncated pyramid, is made of notched plywood, held together by thick rubber bands. To use the mold, line it with cheesecloth and pour in the thick batter; weight the lid and let the *paskha* sit in a dish, refrigerated, for 8 hours or overnight. Any liquid left in the cheese will drain off through the four perforations in the bottom of the mold. When it is firm, remove the form and cheesecloth from the *paskha.* Then ornament the cake with almonds and candied fruit. *Paskha* is traditionally served with *kulich,* a rich yeast cake, studded with candied fruit and nuts, that is baked in a tall cylindrical mold. Both desserts are carried with other Easter foods to church to be blessed at the midnight Easter service. After church, which may last until 4 a.m. with the Easter mass, the feast begins and continues for several days. The *kulich* is sliced into rounds and spread with the creamy *paskha.* But *paskha* is also delicious with simple pound cake and you may be tempted to use this mold more often than once a year. The mold is 6½″ deep, 3″ square at the top and 6″ square at the bottom.

H. Roth & Son **$12.95**

RUSSIAN TEA ROOM PASKHA

To make 3 pounds

1¼ lb. farmer cheese
8 oz. granulated sugar
8 oz. unsalted butter, softened
1 egg yolk
2 oz. glazed fruit, diced
2 oz. yellow raisins
1 teaspoon vanilla extract, approximately
1 teaspoon orange extract, approximately

Mix the above ingredients together for 20 minutes. Add vanilla and orange extract to taste. Line a *paskha* mold with cheesecloth.

Pour the *paskha* mixture into the mold. Cover the mold, weight the top and put it on a dish to catch the excess liquid that will drain out of the bottom. Refrigerate for 2 to 3 hours, until the liquid is completely drained.

To serve, remove the mold and cheesecloth from the *paskha* and place the cake on a serving plate. Cut a slice for each person.

(Courtesy of The Russian Tea Room, New York City.)

Chocolate Fondue Set H:105

For the ultimate in sybaritic desserts, try a chocolate fondue. The main thing to remember in making it is that chocolate burns easily. The spirit burners and metal pans of many fondue sets are too hot for this delicate process. An enamel-lined metal pot with a heavy bottom or a double boiler will do, but the best pots are earthenware. This set, especially designed for chocolate fondue, includes an earthenware bowl, a three-legged wrought-iron stand (4½″ high) and a copper or stainless-steel candle holder. The attractive bowl, with a brown geometric design around the rim, comes in mustard yellow and holds 2 cups. The recipe is simple: nine ounces of milk chocolate, ½ cup of cream, and 2 tablespoons of brandy, rum, or liqueur. For a non-alcoholic version, add a tablespoon of instant coffee or ¼ teaspoon each of ground cinnamon and cloves. For a darker version, make half the chocolate bittersweet. What you dunk in this irresistible concoction is up to you: small cream puffs, chunks of angel food or pound cake, ladyfingers, tangerine slices, strawberries, pineapple, roasted chestnuts—whatever appeals to your sweet tooth.

Spring Brothers Co., Inc. (356-6) **$22.00**

"The fare of the Russian peasantry is sufficiently coarse, but it is an error to suppose it mainly consists of rye bread, cucumbers, caviare, and train oil. Certain national dishes of Russia are regularly served in their best hotels. A good Russian dinner is preceded by a variety of 'snacks' placed on a tray either on the sideboard of the dining room or on a table in the drawing-room where the guests are received. These relishes may include fresh caviare, raw herrings, smoked salmon, sun-dried sturgeon, raw smoked goose, radishes, cheese, sliced sausages, cod-sounds, raw ham, bread, and butter. With these appear tiny liqueur glasses of kümmel, kirschwasser, maraschino, anisette and vodka . . ."

Good Cheer: The Romance of Food and Feasting *by F. W. Hackwood. Sturgess & Walton, 1911.*

Berry Bag — H:106

Berries of all kinds abound in Central Europe: blackberries, gooseberries, raspberries, red and black currants, strawberries and lingonberries are eaten fresh and cooked, baked into pastries or preserved in jams and jellies. They are also squeezed into juice and served with sugar and soda water on a hot summer day. A simple and ingenious way to make berry juice is to use the berry bag pictured here. Made of coarse, unbleached muslin, the bag measures 17½" by 11", has a drawstring at the top and a strong, wooden ring 3½" wide and 1½" in diameter. Put the berries in the bag, draw it closed and slide the ring down over the top of the bag to force the liquid out the bottom. This clever device has the added feature of being easy to clean: just wash the cloth bag thoroughly and hang it up to dry. Why not take advantage of the summer berry crop and fill the bag to press enough juice for a batch of homemade jelly you'll enjoy all winter long?

H. Roth & Son — $1.98

Rumtopf — H:107

A *Rumtopf,* or rum pot, is a large, heavy stoneware crock made for preserving fruit with rum or, as the Germans say, for storing summer in a pot. This glazed crock has a gay, raised fruit design in the natural gray color of the clay that contrasts with the bright blue color of the pot's sides. Empty, the crock weighs a hefty 12 pounds, and it will hold two gallons of luscious, rum-soaked fruit. The recipe is painted on the back of the jar in German, but no complicated instructions are necessary. The idea is a simple one: beginning with the first strawberries in late May or early June, fruit is added to the crock in layers as it comes into season. Only apples, black currants, bilberries and blackberries cannot be used. Each type of fruit is washed, drained and dried, then tossed with half a pound of sugar for every pound of fruit and left in a bowl to stand an hour. The sweetened fruit is then put into the crock, and enough rum is poured over it to cover it by half an inch. The first pound of fruit will need about a fifth of rum; the next will need only half that. Store the crock in a cool place, tightly covered, and check it occasionally to see if it needs more rum: the level should always be half an inch above the fruit. Each layer takes six weeks to mature to the eating stage, but your patience will pay off. For Thanksgiving, you can stir up a bit of *Rumtopf,* mix it with whipped cream and serve it chilled with raspberry juice. And all winter long you can enjoy it as a compote, over ice cream, or in fabulous desserts, and recall the warmth and leisure of sunny summer days. The crock is 7¾" in diameter and 11" high, without the lid; the lid adds 3" to the height of the crock.

Kitchen Glamor, Inc. (1105) — $43.95

A somewhat romanticized view of a nineteenth-century peasant's home in Russia.

"The Russians drink enormous quantities of very strong, fine tea. A recent war report gives the following account of its use in the army.

'The Russian soldiers are said to live and fight almost wholly upon tea. The Cossacks often carry it about in the shape of bricks, or rather tiles, which before hardening, are soaked in sheep's blood and boiled in milk, with the addition of flour, butter and salt, so as to constitute a kind of soup. The passion of the Russian for this beverage is simply astonishing. In the depth of winter he will empty twenty cups in succession, at nearly boiling point, until he perspires at every pore, and then . . . rush out, roll in the snow, get up and go on to the next similar place of entertainment. . . . With every group or circle of tents travels the invariable tea kettle . . . and it would be in vain to think of computing how many times each soldier's pannikin is filled upon a halt. It is his first idea. . . .' "

Twenty-Five Cent Dinners for Families of Six, *by Juliet Corson, 1878.*

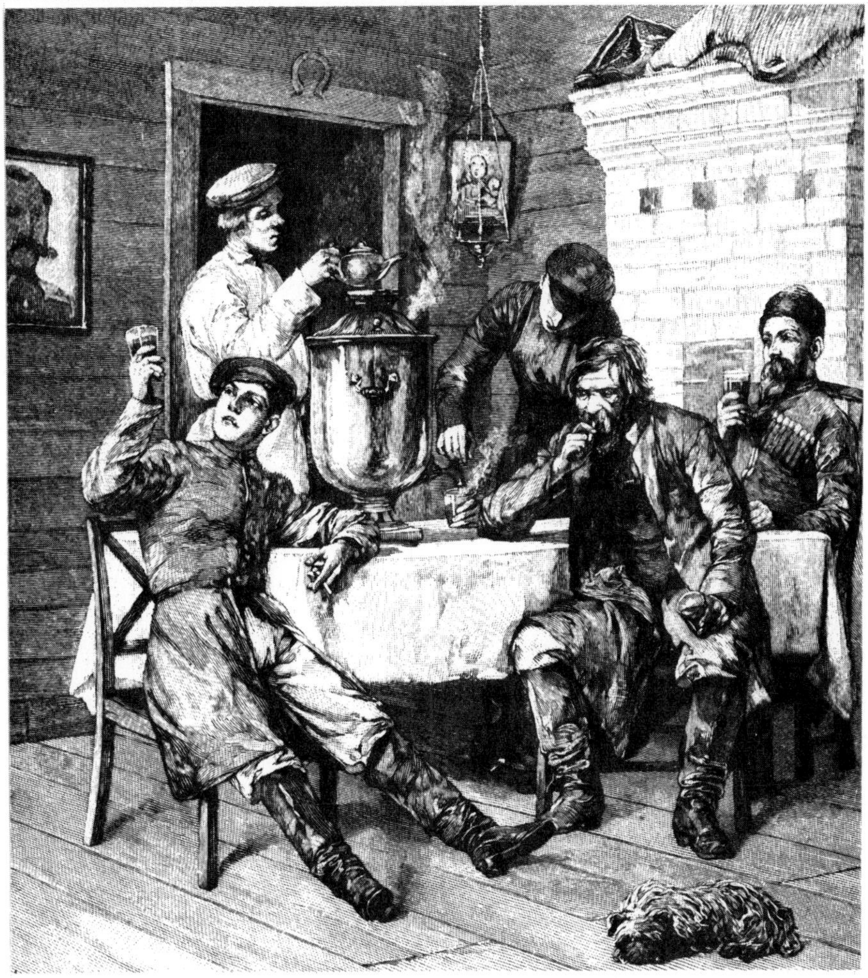

Around the samovar.

Samovar H:108

Tea was introduced to Russia by the Mongols. That "Golden Horde" conquered all of southern Russia and held northern Russia in pawn for more than two centuries until driven forth by Ivan the Terrible. With them came the samovar, an ornate brass urn for preparing and serving tea. Ever since, tea and the samovar have been an integral part of Russian life; from early morning to late evening, at every meal and between meals, Russians gather around a samovar for a cup or glass of hot tea. There is even a verb in Russian meaning "to pass time in drinking tea." This handsome samovar, although made in Italy, has the authentic Russian shape and decoration. Two feet tall and 11½" in diameter, it is made of heavy brass decorated with cutout designs at the top and on the pedestal. The base has two large brass handles with wooden grips by which the whole samovar may be lifted. The upper part may be removed by two smaller handles so that the urn can be filled with cold water—it will easily hold three gallons. Burning charcoal is then put into a vertical metal tube in the center of the urn. When the water boils, a strong essence of tea is brewed in a china teapot; the pot is then placed atop the reassembled urn. Cutout designs on the teapot holder permit steam and hot air to escape while enveloping the teapot in warmth. A hole with a sliding top just above the boiling water allows more steam to escape if necessary and lets you check the level of the water. To serve the tea, pour a bit of the strong essence from the china teapot into a cup and dilute it with boiling water drawn from the elegant spigot with its elaborately curved brass handle.

Hammacher Schlemmer **$300.00**

Beer and Wine

In the first century, Tacitus commented that the Germanic tribes were so addicted to a drink of fermented barley or grain that the Romans could put away their arms and conquer them simply by providing them with an unlimited supply of it. Beer is still the most popular alcoholic drink in Central Europe, notably in Germany where some two billion gallons are consumed each year—four million quarts at the *Oktoberfest* alone. It is brewed in a variety of ways with different types of yeast to produce a wide range of colors, flavors and alcoholic content. *Pilsener* beers that originated in Pilsen, Czechoslovakia, exemplify the light variety; and the dark *Bock* beer of Germany, which appears at Eastertime, is a brew of stronger flavor. The sweetness and alcoholic content depend mainly on the length and the temperature of the fermentation process.

Wine drinking is also a popular, long standing custom in Middle Europe. The Romans planted vineyards on the steep hillsides of the narrow, sinuous Mosel Valley and along the Danube around a settlement called Vindobona—which became modern Vienna. Legend has it that, some centuries later, Charlemagne, looking out across the Rhine from the Imperial palace at Ingelheim, noticed that the snow melted soonest on a sunny bluff on the north bank of the river. There he planted the vines that were to become the famous vineyards of Schloss Johannisberg. Soon grapes were cultivated all along the short stretch of the river between Mainz and Bingen known as the Rheingau, where the finest Rhine wines are made today. Through the Middle Ages vines were cultivated and wine was made by assiduous monks; viticulture spread with Christianity across Europe. Other areas of Central Europe also produce famous wines: to the west, we find Switzerland's lightly sparkling white wines from the shores of Lake Neuchatel; to the east, is Hungary's legendary Tokay, a wine of such a dark golden color that it was believed to contain real gold. The Swiss alchemist Paracelsus was actually prompted to visit Hungary in hopes of discovering how gold could be grown.

Beer Stein H:109

The various types of Central European beer are served in different ways: bitter Czechoslovakian *Pilsener* in tall, footed goblets of thin glass; the delicate *Berliner Weisse* in large, broad chalices. But the two main types of beer, the light and the dark—*Helles* and *Dunkles*—whether bottled or on tap, go into thick, heavy beer mugs of barrel-shaped pressed glass or of clear-glazed earthenware, like this one. Made of a sandy-colored clay, this hefty stein weighs 20 ounces by itself and will hold some 17 ounces more of beer—0.5 liter to be precise; the measure is stamped near the rim. The handle is large enough so that you can grip all that weight comfortably. A colorful decal on the front advertises the *Dinckelacker* label, but of course you'll use it for your favorite brew. And if you like it ice-cold, chill the mug in the freezer and its thick sides will keep the beer frosty to the last drop.

Bremen House, Inc. $4.95

Vinometer H:110

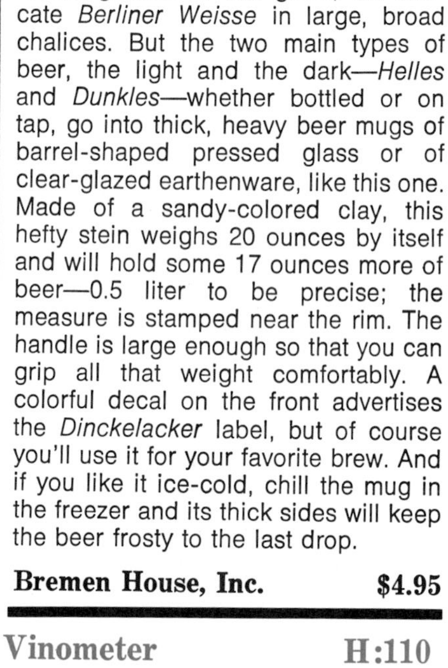

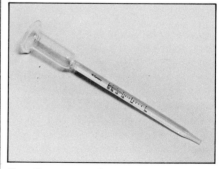

For the enterprising individual who

makes his own wine, this remarkable little glass tube will prove invaluable. It measures the alcohol content of wine to let you know whether sugar must be added. Increasing the sugar raises the alcohol level and improves the wine's stability. Testing the wine could not be simpler: hold the vinometer over a bowl or cup and pour some fermenting wine into the wide end. When it starts running out the narrow opening at the other end, then invert the vinometer. The wine will retreat part way through the tube again and stop: the calibrations on the tube opposite the level of wine will clearly indicate the alcohol content of the wine from 0 to 25 percent, a range wide enough to include dessert wines. The vinometer is 5″ long and measures ¾″ across the widest end.

Berarducci Brothers (N-9) **$3.95**

Middle European Wine Glass H:111

A *Roemer,* often misleadingly translated as "rummer," is a wineglass with a long history, for it is probably named after the Romans who brought viticulture and glassmaking north of the Alps. It was they who manufactured the attractive Rhenish glassware that was sent all over the Roman Empire and beyond—fragments of it have been found as far away as northern Scotland. Glassmaking survived in Central Europe throughout the Middle Ages, usually as a green or yellowish glass called *Waldglas* (forest glass) because it was made from potash obtained by burning forest vegetation. Large, elegantly decorated medieval beakers were the ancestors of the modern *Roemer,* which keeps the characteristic chalice shape and wide, hollow stem. This *Roemer* is available in 2-, 5¼- and 9¾-ounce sizes. The pressed-glass stem, resembling a widening stack of glass rings, comes in vine-leaf green and in amber, the colors of medieval European glass. The stem is solid, leaving no hollow to clean. The wide-mouthed, unadorned cup is of clear, thin blown glass. Made originally in the Rhineland for Rhine wine, *Roemer* are also used elsewhere in Middle Europe and are appropriate for all light, German-style white wines: from the dry Swiss wines of the Valais, to the pale Mosels; from the fragrant Austrian Traminers, to the fresh, mild Johannisberger wines of California and New York.

Bremen House, Inc./ Schott-Zwiesel Glass Inc. (2213-2) **$2.50**

Austrian Wine Dispenser H:112

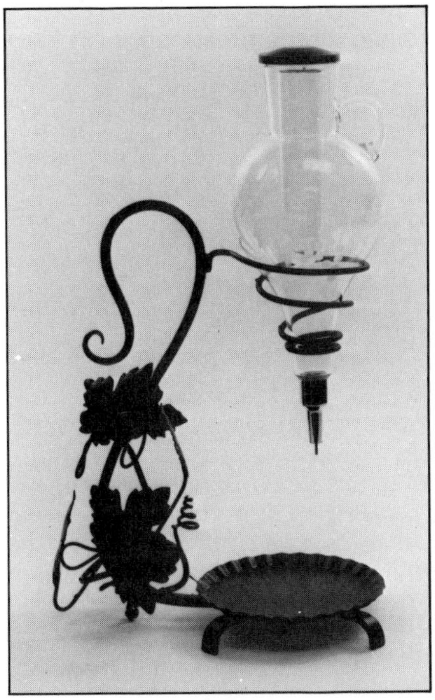

Austrian vintners hang out a fir branch, a bundle of straw, or green boughs to announce that the new wine, or *heurige,* is ready. Made mostly of Riesling, Sylvaner and Traminer grapes (grown in lower Austria around Vienna and along the Danube in a region called the Wachau), the light, fruity white wines are drunk young—a custom that like their advertisement goes back to the Middle Ages. Each vintner is allowed to sell the wine in his own cellar or even in his garden and the grape arbors themselves. On fine spring and summer afternoons and evenings, especially in the wine villages of Grinzing, Sievering and Nussdorf—now suburbs of Vienna—friends meet to enjoy the new wine: have a cold supper of smoked meats, cheese, bread, hard-boiled eggs and radishes; and sing to the accompaniment of a zither or a guitar. Fanciful wine dispensers like this one originated in the *Heurigen* (places where new wine is sold); today they are used at restaurants and inns throughout Austria, even for bottled wines. An arabesque of grape leaves and tendrils of black wrought iron hold the glass container, which is itself frosted with leaves and bunches of grapes. The graceful fount has its practical features, too. Everyone can fill his wineglass easily by pressing it against the valve at the bottom of the glass container; below, a wrought-iron tray will hold the wineglass to catch any last drips. And to keep the wine cool, a plastic inset at the top with a black plastic lid, may be filled with cracked ice. The dispenser is 18½″ high, overall, and will hold a full bottle of fresh, spicy *Gumpoldskirchener* or a light, heady *Dürnsteiner.* Or make your own *heurige* to serve in this charming Austrian way.

Bremen House, Inc. **$29.95**

"Glances coy give sign
She will soon be thine!
Wine-cup seizing,
Thirst appeasing,
Quickly let it pass
From hand to hand!
Hail victorious,
Tokay glorious,
May heaven bless our native land! Ha!"

Die Fledermaus *by Johann Straus, libretto by C. Hoffner and Richard Genée, translated by Alfred Kalisen. Joseph Weinberger, Ltd., n.d.*

A Scandinavian Kitchen

by Eric Friberg

You ask me to describe to you the differences between American and Swedish kitchens; to tell you the truth, there is very little difference. After all, Swedish design is the most modern and streamlined in the world, and many of the finest utensils in America either come from Scandinavia or copy a Scandinavian design. Of course when I was a boy, kitchens were much more old-fashioned than they are now. I grew up in the country, and we had a big coal-and-wood-burning stove, and a refrigerator—or rather a very large and cool cellar that we used like a refrigerator. There was a long wooden table where the preparation was done, and most of the pans that I remember from that time were made of heavy, black cast iron, like the *plätt* pans and *krumkake* pans that you show in your book. But I would guess that this would be a pretty accurate description of a country kitchen in America at that time, isn't it so?

Today, of course, there are all sorts of beautiful pots and pans and spoons and spatulas made in Sweden. You find them mainly in the home, where they are used to do *husmanskost*, as we say, or home-cooking. But my career has been in commercial kitchens, and there is absolutely no difference between a restaurant kitchen in Scandinavia and in the United States. In both places they use the same large aluminum pots, the same steel knives and long-handled mixing spoons.

I started out in kitchens when I became an apprentice in a Swedish restaurant at the age of 15. I worked my way up through all its departments, learning how to rinse the salt herrings and flavor them with sweet and sour brines, how to mix the capers and beets and onions into chopped meat for *biff à la Lindström,* how to weight down a *gravlax* and how to roll out fancy cakes and flat breads. When I came to the United States it was first as a waiter, and later as the manager of the Gripsholm restaurant. In recent years I have had a double business of my own, running a Scandinavian food shop in Westchester

BIFF À LA LINDSTRÖM

1½ pounds ground beef
½ medium onion, cut in ¼″ dice
1–2 small cooked beets, cut in ¼″ dice
1 sour pickle, cut in ¼″ dice, or 2 tablespoons capers, chopped
1½ teaspoons salt
Freshly ground black pepper
2–4 tablespoons clarified butter (or butter and oil)
4 eggs, fried
Capers

Combine the ground beef with the diced onion, beets and pickle or capers. Add salt and freshly ground black pepper to taste and form into four large, fat patties.

Sauté the patties in clarified butter or a combination of one-half butter, one-half vegetable oil until nicely browned on each side.

Top each patty with a fried egg and sprinkle with capers.

Yield: 4 servings.

(Courtesy Joseph (Seppi) Renggli, Executive Chef, The Four Seasons Restaurant, New York City)

"The Sisters and the young maids bore them as seemly and ate as nicely as though they had been sitting at the finest feast [they are in a convent]. There was abundance of the best food and drink, but all helped themselves modestly, and dipped but the very tips

of their fingers into the dishes; no one spilled the broth either upon the cloths or upon their garments and all cut up the meat so small that they did not soil their mouths and ate with so much care that not a sound was to be heard. Kristin . . . fancied they were all looking at her, so when she had to eat a fat piece of breast of mutton, and was holding it by the bone with two fingers, while cutting morsels off with her right hand, and taking care to handle the knife lightly and neatly—suddenly the whole slipped from her fingers; her slice of bread and the meat flew on to the cloth and the knife fell clattering on the stone flags."

Kristin Lavransdatter *by Sigrid Undset*
Alfred A. Knopf, 1923.

Wooden Mortar and Pestle I:1

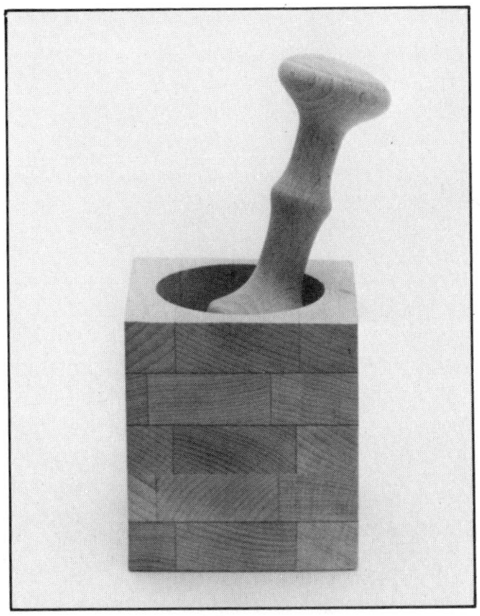

Scandinavian crafts are justifiably famous for combining simplicity with sophistication; thus, this Danish mortar and pestle of bleached wood. Use it to crush cardamom the next time you make what the Danes call Vienna bread, and we call Danish pastry. The mortar is a cube of sandwiched-together beechwood, with 3¼″-square sides and a 3⅛″-deep well-shaped hole in its center. The pestle is 6½″ long, carved with a cylindrical pounding end that fits perfectly into the mortar's narrow well.

Nordiska **$4.95**

County, New York, and also doing catering for parties. In the catering business, I do all sorts of cooking, but most of all I like to do a Swedish Smörgåsbord, with its ample variety of meat and fish dishes, both hot and cold, and its many different kinds of bread and cheese and salad. Some of the herring I serve in old wooden crocks that look like buckets, and I import a special Swedish rye bread that is shaped like a doughnut and is served on a plate that has a central pole going through the holes in the stack of breads.

This is different from the simple, hearty *husmanskost,* and is a more complicated style of cooking than, for example, the traditional Thursday night meal of pea soup and pancakes. But it is very good and very typical of Scandinavian food, nonetheless. Sometimes I fear that this special local kind of cooking will soon disappear. A friend of mine recently went back to Sweden, and he told me that there are now pizzerias in Stockholm. He also told me that there is a great vogue for McDonald's hamburgers; and that the young king, giving a night-long party at the castle, served hamburgers for a midnight snack. When the Swedish king serves hamburgers instead of *biff à la Lindström,* then you know that eating habits will soon be the same all over the world.

The Cuisine of Scandinavia

Two tables dominate the cuisine of Scandinavia: the *smörgåsbord* (*koldt bord* in Denmark) and the coffee table. The long *smörgåsbord* laden with fish and meat is a national celebration, a feast whose sequence of courses is laid out according to centuries of tradition. First the herrings: fried, pickled, smoked, mixed in cream and in spiced vinegar. Then more fish: eel or salmon, smoked, fried or poached and mixed with mayonnaise, with a few crisp slices of sweetened cucumber for contrast. Next: cold meats and salads, with emphasis on ham and roast beef and tongue, liver pâté, together with sweet pickles and onions. And finally the hot dishes: assortments of meatballs, varied omelets, casseroles and croquettes. We go back again and again to the table, putting bits of food on ever-renewed clean plates which become, to our surprise, heaped high after we have made only a few selections. Finally, we collapse on a banquette, able to force down only a few pancakes, a spoonful of lingonberries, a cup of coffee.

But there is another table that stands four-square in the middle of the Scandinavian cuisine. Instead of beer or aquavit, the beverage is coffee: hot and strong, and taken at any hour of the dark winter day or well into the sunfilled summer night. And with the coffee there is served a *smörgåsbord* of cakes, a selection of faintly spiced, delicately sweetened cookies, waffles and yeast cakes. Etiquette demands that

Continued from preceding page

your hostess always have a fresh cake to serve you; etiquette also demands that you do not insult her by taking only one. In a part of the world that is famous for its butter and cream, where eggs are given identifying numbers so that they may be eaten when they are fresh as possible, it is not surprising that the baking should be of the highest quality. At ten in the morning or at four in the afternoon, the *konditorier* or coffee houses of Sweden will be filled with people partaking of these delicate sweets, along with huge cups of sweet and creamy coffee. Which means that at seven that morning and at one that afternoon, housewives and bakers have been hard at work. We will show you a few of the remarkably varied tools they use in the pursuit of their craft.

Marble Mortar and Pestle I:2

A heavy-weight marble mortar and pestle from Sweden, the outside surface polished to a voluptuous smoothness, the inside left rough for efficient grinding. Each mortar and pestle set comes in subtly different colors, but their principal tones are ivory and green. The mortar comes in three sizes, 4″, 4½″ and 5″ in diameter; we show you the middle one, which is 2¾″ deep and has a silky-smooth column of a pestle that is 5¾″ long.

La Cuisinière $32.50

Traveling in Lapland, Paul Du Chaillu wrote in The Land of the Midnight Sun *(1882): "There was not the slightest appearance of shyness in these people; we were welcomed at once; the coffee-kettle was put over the fire; coffee, already roasted, was ground, boiled, and clarified with a piece of dry fish-skin, and served to me in a queer-shaped little silver cup, which I admired very much; it was a family heirloom, said to be about a hundred years old."*

Pestle/Masher I:3

A disarmingly simple example of Scandinavian design: a sturdy pestle and masher carved out of beechwood, to be used for crushing peppercorns and cloves and, just as likely, for mashing potatoes and turnips in a wooden bowl. The handle is slender and smooth, and is glued firmly to the working end, a stubby cylindrical shape made flat toward the handle and gently rounded at the other end. The whole is 10¼″ long.

Nordiska/Scandicrafts, Inc. (W136A/32) $1.29

"Oh the potato is a lordly fruit . . . A man may lack corn to make bread, but give him potatoes and he will not starve. Roast them in the embers and there is supper; boil them in water and there's a breakfast ready . . . Potatoes can be served with what you please; a dish of milk, a herring, is enough. The rich eat them with butter, poor folk manage with a pinch of salt . . . Poor despised potato—a blessed thing."

Growth of the Soil *by Knut Hamsun. Alfred A. Knopf, 1921.*

Potato Masher I:4

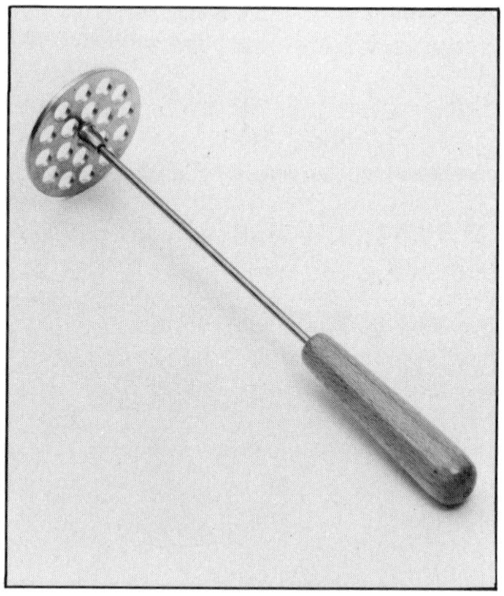

Scandinavian winters are long. The potato is a vegetable that survives the long northern winters. Therefore, potatoes are a staple item in the Scandinavian diet: new potatoes steamed in butter, older potatoes carved so that they will fan out under the drippings of a roast. And, inevitably, mashed potatoes, boiled and then combined with melted butter and hot milk and crushed into a mass that is cheering to the soul and productive of the calories with which to combat the cold, dark days. This potato masher is made of aluminum and wood. At one end there is a shiny, cigar-shaped length of polished wood; into this is fitted a metal rod. The rod, in turn, is attached to a flat perforated plate. The handle is a foot long, the masher 3⅛″ in diameter, and you use it in the simplest way imaginable, thumping and pounding on the boiled potatoes in your saucepan or bowl until they are transformed to a fluffy steaming mass.

Nordiska $4.95

Scandinavian Meat

Unfortunately, much of the meat available in Scandinavia is expensive and tough. Cattle in the more northerly countries have to scramble over rough, rocky terrain, and as a result are poor and sinewy. Local cooks (except in Denmark whose rolling countryside has been kind to cattle) have had to devise ways to make meat more palatable.

First, and most obvious, there are many stews—dishes whose long, gentle cooking serves to break down the tough fibers of the animal's muscle. One of the best of these is the famous "seaman's beef," in which meat, potatoes and onions are layered in a casserole and then left to cook for hours.

But the tough muscle fibers are also broken down by mechanical means, both by grinding and by pounding. Meatballs made of ground beef are popular all over Scandinavia: *frikadeller* in Denmark, *vorsmack* in Finland, and *biff à la Lindström* in Sweden. And, finally, it is possible to tenderize meat by pounding it. *Rulader*—the Swedish form of roulades—are thin strips of beef that have been pounded with the bumpy end of a hammer-like tool. They are then rolled up around a stuffing—typically bacon, pickles and onions—and are slowly braised in a sauce.

Wooden Meat Pounder — I:5

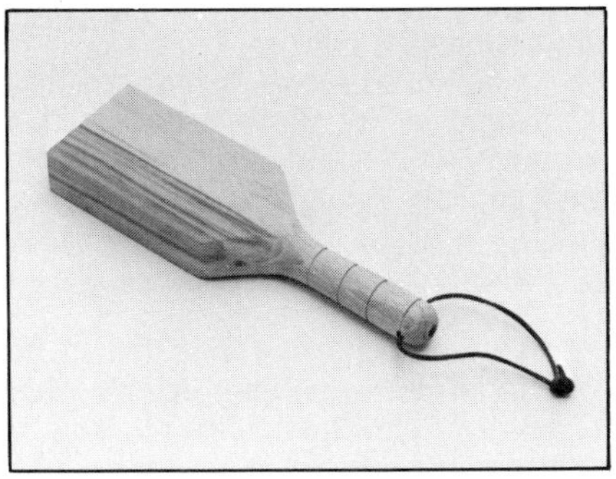

There are a number of ways of breaking down the tough connective tissues in meat, ranging from the application of papaya juice to brute force. And so we offer this simple, but hefty, Danish meat pounder. It is 11″ long and a good 1¼″ thick, giving it the weight and power needed to prepare *okseroulader* (slices of beef steak pounded thin, rolled around fat back, pickle, onion and carrot and cooked in a spicy tomato gravy). This is a good example of the simplicity and sophistication of Scandinavian design: a traditional kitchen tool made up of a collection of attractive curves and planes in smooth beechwood. The handle is nicely turned and incised with four decorative rings, while the working end (6½″ by 3⅜″) is a simple paddle grown fat. A hole through the handle permits the insertion of a strip of leather or string for hanging.

Nordiska — $3.45

BEEF ROULADES

2¼ pounds (12 3-ounce slices) top round of beef, trimmed
Salt
Freshly ground black pepper
⅓ cup mild mustard, approximately
4 sour gherkins or 8–10 tiny cornichons, cut into strips
2 tablespoons butter
2 tablespoons oil
Beef stock

Preheat oven to 350 F.

Pound the slices of meat between two pieces of wax paper until quite thin. Season with salt and pepper and spread about 1½ teaspoons of mustard over each slice. Place several strips of gherkin or cornichon on each slice of meat and roll up. Secure with a toothpick or kitchen twine.

Brown the rolls over medium-high heat in the butter and oil. Pour off the fat and add enough beef stock to cover the rolls. Bring to a boil, cover and place in the oven. (If you do not have a large, covered frying pan or sauteuse, place the browned rolls in a casserole or deep, covered baking dish and deglaze the frying pan with ½ cup of the beef stock. Add this to the casserole or dish with enough additional stock to cover the rolls, and proceed with the recipe.) Cook for 45 minutes to an hour, or until meat is tender.

If stock does not reduce sufficiently during cooking, remove the roulades and reduce stock rapidly over high heat. Remove strings or toothpicks from the beef rolls and serve each with a spoonful or two of sauce.
Yield: 6 servings.

(Courtesy Eric Friberg, Westchester, New York)

Metal Meat Pounder/Cleaver — I:6

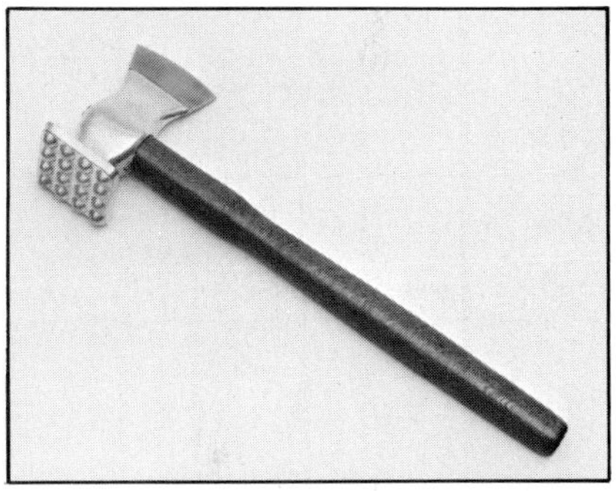

One side breaks up bones; the other pounds and softens the tendons of meat. This lethal looking weapon is part of the armament not of a Comanche chief, but of a Scandinavian housewife. Many traditional Scandinavian meat sources, like reindeer and elk, are tougher than most cuts of meat and need the special attention of a meat pounder. To prepare Norwegian venison goulash, for example, the meat is pounded thin, cut into bite-sized pieces and *then* stewed for 2½ hours to make it chewable. This tool has a stained beechwood handle, 9¼″ long, that fits into a cast-aluminum head. One side of the head is a flat plate bristling with sixteen tenderizers, while the other side holds an axe-shaped, stainless-steel blade. It is 10½″ long and well balanced, with its considerable weight concentrated in the metal head in order to add the power of gravity to the cook's swing.

H. & E. Trading Co. (1901) — $10.00

Pounding Board and Mallet I:7

You may not be planning to cook Arctic Circle reindeer steak on a regular basis, but even veal from a reliable butcher has been known to be tough. Here is a tenderizing set that is cheaper than buying expensive meat, and less traumatic than changing butchers. The board is of beechwood, 9″ by 7″ and a good 2″ thick. A shallow trough runs around the inside edge of the board for catching the meat juices. Holes at one end permit the attachment of a rope for hanging and the insertion of the mallet. When it is removed, the mallet proves to be a long handle attached to a 2¼″ cubical block of wood that is knobbed on two of its surfaces.

Seabon $14.95

SWEDISH MEATBALLS

1 medium onion
¼ cup water (approximately)
2 eggs, lightly beaten
1 teaspoon salt
Freshly ground black pepper
2 cups fresh bread crumbs (approximately)
¼ pound ground pork
¼ pound ground veal
½ pound ground beef
Butter
Oil

Place the onion and water in a blender and blend until finely chopped, but not puréed. Scrape mixture into a large bowl and add the eggs and salt and pepper to taste. Stir in just enough bread crumbs to give the mixture the consistency of a loose porridge. Add the ground meats and combine thoroughly.

Using a small ice cream scoop, form into tiny balls approximately 1″ in diameter. (This can be done even more quickly by taking up a mound of the ground mixture in one hand and scooping the balls from the hand rather than the bowl.)

Fry about a dozen of the meatballs at a time in hot oil or a combination of butter and oil, until nicely browned and cooked through, about 8–10 minutes.

Yield: 6–8 servings.

NOTE: Meatballs may be fried in hot oil just to sear, and then frozen. When ready to use, complete cooking in butter.

(Courtesy Eric Friberg, Westchester, New York)

Participating in a midsummer festival in Sweden, Hans Christian Andersen observed: "The first impression of the whole was striking, but only the first—there was too much disturbance. The screaming of the children, and the noise of persons walking were heard above the singing, and besides that, there was an unsupportable smell of garlic; almost all the congregation had small bunches of garlic with them, of which they ate as they sat. I could not bear it and went out in the church yard."

Pictures of Travel, *1871.*

Fish

Seafood is the chicken of Scandinavia, the source of animal protein that is most abundant, cheap and reliable in quality. The icy-cold northern waters have given birth to a centuries-long tradition of catching and preparing fish.

In Scandinavia, fish are either bought alive or else preserved so harshly that it seems they have never been alive. Fish markets look like pet shops, with their cement tanks from which the shopper can select his own catch while it is still swimming. So fresh will this cod or mackerel be that it has no odor at all; and it is a credit to Scandinavian cooks that they usually prepare such a fish in the manner it deserves: poached or grilled as simply as possible, and served with a spoonful of sauce on the side.

But Scandinavians are also famous for their methods of preserving fish. To this day, cod is dried according to a technique that is more than 1000 years old. It is beheaded and then cleaned and strung up on wooden racks that stand outside in the cool Arctic air. Ten weeks later, it is mummified, with all water evaporated so that no mold will grow in it, it is claimed, for as long as 20 years. Dried cod was famous all over the medieval world, where it went to sea in Viking boats, providing a reliable source of protein to her sailors. Soaked in a lye solution, it is the famous *lutefisk* of the Scandinavian cuisine.

Other forms of preservation are used on Scandinavian seafood as well. The unreliable herring catch—abundant one year and scarce the next—created and then frustrated a taste for these little fish. It was discovered that if herring were salted, they would keep for a time. Later they could be pickled, increasing their palatability and their lifespan.

On the one side, then, we have fish at its freshest: trout pulled from a stream in Finland; salmon not cooked at all but merely cured with sugar, salt and dill; pots of crayfish eaten on a beach in the midnight sun. And on the other hand there is a whole cuisine that arose from the need to preserve seafood: the infinite varieties of herring, cod and eel that are displayed on the *smörgåsbord* table.

Fish Scaler I:8

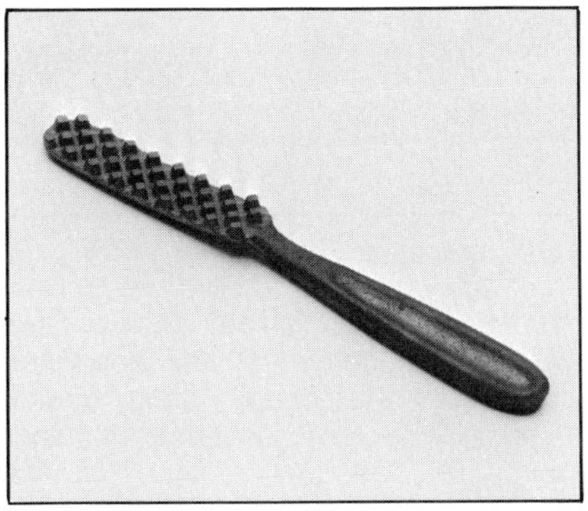

Scandinavia is drenched in water—washed with rivers, lapped by seas—and so, not surprisingly, its most abundant crop is fish, brilliantly fresh. In some Scandinavian fish markets you can buy your dinner alive, catching it by its tail and popping it into your marketing basket, so that it arrives in your kitchen as fresh as though you had pulled it yourself from a mountain stream. Because of this, Scandinavian kitchens often contain tools that look as though they belonged in a carpenter's box rather than a kitchen drawer, tools that help the cook deal with a whole fish, such as this rough and simple cast-iron scaler. The working end of the scaler is 3½″ long and ¾″ wide; its slightly concave surface is covered with sharp diamond-shaped protrusions. Angled up from the scaler end is a heavy 3¾″-long handle. For all its rough appearance, it is perfectly comfortable in the hand. Grasp the handle in your palm and then scrape the sharp knobs across the scales, washing the fish under cold water as you do so.

Nordiska $2.45

Filleting Knife I:9

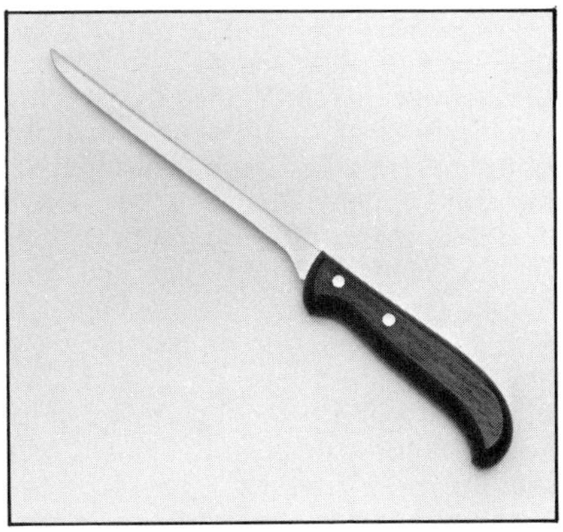

This flexible blade with its lethal edge is designed to separate the tender fillets of a fish from its backbone and skin. A Norwegian cook will then use the head, bones and filleting scraps to make the stock in which she will poach *fiskeboller* (a Norwegian version of *quenelles*). This is a good-quality knife with a 5″ rosewood handle shaped to fit comfortably in the palm. Its slender 7″ blade is attached to the handle with two shining brass rivets.

H. & E. Trading Co. (735R) $7.50

FISKEBOLLER

Norwegian Fish Balls

2 pounds cod or haddock fillet
1½ teaspoons salt
¼ teaspoon white pepper
Pinch nutmeg
2 egg whites, well-chilled
4 teaspoons cornstarch
1¼ cups milk or light cream
1¼ cups heavy cream
2 quarts fish stock
3 tablespoons butter
4 tablespoons flour
1½ cups boiling milk
Salt
Pepper
Grated horseradish

Cut the fish fillets into pieces and grind several times or purée in a blender or food processor. Scrape into the bowl of an electric mixer and beat in the seasonings and chilled egg whites at low speed. Sprinkle on the cornstarch and beat just long enough to incorporate it.

Increase speed and, with the machine running, add enough milk and heavy cream in a thin stream to form a very smooth but still workable mixture—it has to have enough body to take, and hold, a shape.

Bring the fish stock just to a simmer in a deep frying pan or other wide-mouthed pan. Using two teaspoons, form the purée into balls, dipping the spoons into the stock after forming each ball. Poach at a very gentle simmer until the balls rise and turn over easily when tapped with the back of a spoon—about 5–8 minutes. Remove with a slotted spoon and drain on paper towels, then place in a large, buttered gratin dish.

Preheat oven to 350 F.

Rapidly reduce 3 cups of the fish stock by half. Melt the butter in a saucepan and stir in the flour. Cook over low flame, stirring constantly, for 2 minutes. Remove from heat and whisk in the boiling stock and milk and

Continued from preceding page

salt and white pepper to taste. Return to heat and boil over medium-high heat for a minute. If the sauce is too thick, thin it out with a little light cream, whisking in a tablespoon at a time. Stir in freshly grated horseradish to taste.

Pour the sauce over the fish balls and place in the middle of the oven until piping hot, 15–20 minutes.

Yield: 6–8 servings.

Norwegian Fish Poacher — I:10

Four-fifths of Norway's population live within a dozen miles of the water. They can easily reach out to trap quantities of beautifully fresh fish: trout and salmon from the rivers; cod, herring, mackerel, halibut and haddock from the sea. With fish so available, and so sweetly fresh, the Norwegians don't have or need many ways of preparing it. They cook it simply, then add a mustard, horseradish or egg sauce. And one of the simplest ways to prepare fresh fish so that it retains its purity is to poach it. Our 15¾″-long, oval fish poacher, is a generous 9½″ wide and 5½″ deep, and will hold a 15″-long fish on its perforated rack. The poacher is of virgin aluminum, with cast-aluminum handles. The perforated aluminum rack has hook handles for lifting the fish intact out of its poaching liquid. A larger-sized poacher, 19¾″ long, 10″ wide and 5⅞″ deep, is also available.

Nor-Pro, Inc. (HO116) — $64.00

"The Laplanders who are employed in catching salmon, live upon that fish split and dried. Dried fish is eaten by them without any preparatory cooking; but before they put it into their mouth, they dip each piece in train oil. Fish with this kind of sauce is given to children at the breast; and to prepare it for their tender mouths, the mother first puts it in her own, and masticates it before she presents it to the infant: thus they are accustomed to the luxury of train oil from birth, for such every Lap lad esteems it, and considers its flavour far superior to that of butter. . . .

They roast their fish as well as their flesh, and are fond of cod fish fresh caught. The liver of this and other fish, bruised and mixed with cranberries is considered a savory dish; and this . . . is eaten without bread."

Travels Through Sweden, Finland and Lapland To The North Cape *by Joseph Acerbi. London, 1802.*

Henry's Fish Smoker — I:11

Curing-and-smoking is a rather special form of preserving that gives a distinctive, and sometimes overwhelming, flavor to food. But once it was one of the only ways to keep fish and meat through the long Scandinavian winter. To follow the pre-refrigerator traditions of Scandinavian cooking, use this handy, portable Swedish smokehouse. Fish that are going to be smoked must first be cleaned and dried and then rubbed with salt and left to cure for several hours (or up to 24 hours in a refrigerator). Then the fish are placed on a rack inside the smoke box over a layer of Henry's "smoking chips" (chips of alderwood, juniper or cherrywood will also do nicely). A small cooking alcohol container slides under the smoke box, which is raised off the ground by an aluminum stand that also acts as a wind shield. An aluminum pan catches drippings from the fish and protects the wood chips. The manufacturer's instructions advise that when the dorsal fin can easily be pulled off, the fish is done. They also recommend adding rosemary or juniper needles to the "smoking chips" to vary the flavor of the fish. Henry's smokehouse comes with seven pieces: an 11″-long, black, enameled-steel smoke box (also available in aluminum); an aluminum catch pan; a stainless-steel rack; an aluminum sliding cover for the box; an aluminum wind shield/stand; a plated-steel fuel container; and a chromed-steel cleaner-scraper.

Jurgensen's
Smoker (56-1) — $25.00
Smoke Chips (56-2) — $1.50

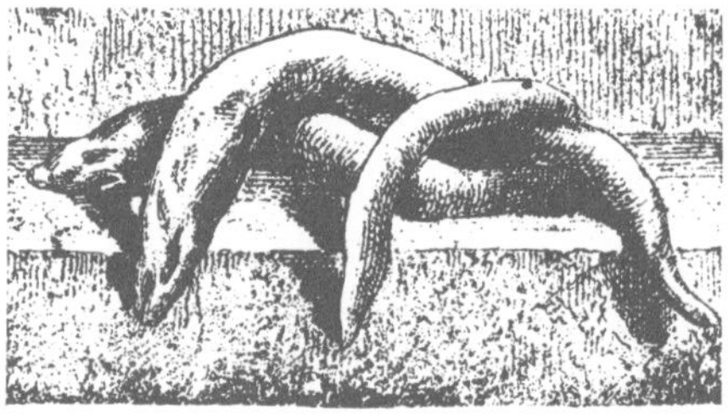

*Eels are a great favorite in all the Scandinavian countries: they appear smoked, baked, jellied, poached, in pies and in soups. Of the "common eel," the ever-chatty Mrs. Beeton (*Beeton's Book of Household Management*, 1861) has this to say: "This fish is known frequently to quit its native element, and to set off on a wandering expedition in the night, or just about the close of day, over the meadows, in search of snails and other prey. It also, sometimes, betakes itself to isolated ponds, apparently for no other pleasure than that which may be supposed to be found in a change of habitation. This, of course, accounts for eels being found in waters which were never suspected to contain them. This rambling disposition in the eel has been long known to naturalists, and, from the following lines, it seems to have been known to the ancients: 'Thus the mail'd tortoise, and the wandering eel,/Oft to the neighbouring beach will silent steal.' "*

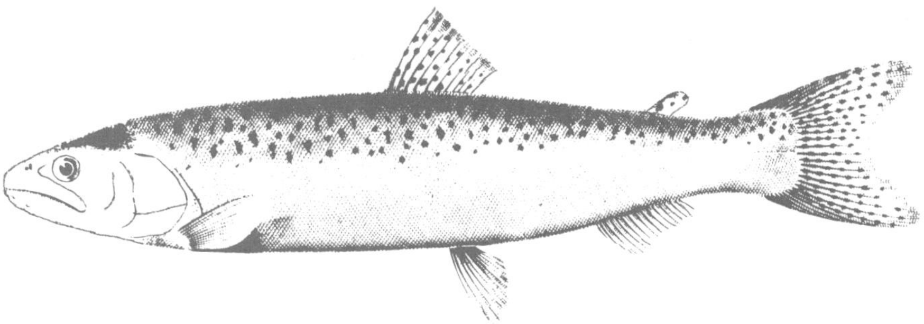

Salmon Knife I:12

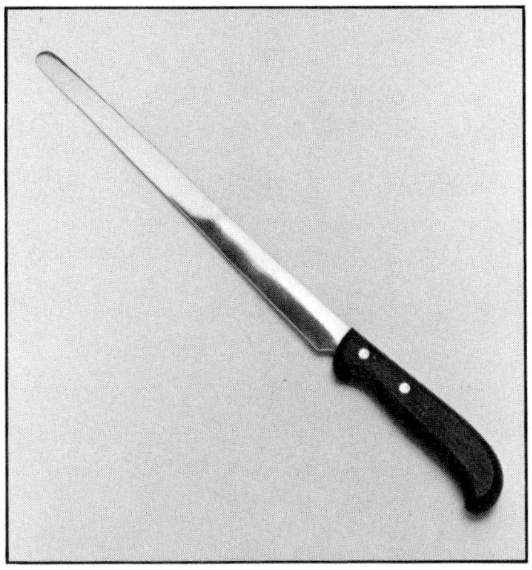

Smoked salmon is often served on the groaning *smörgåsbord* table, decorated with feathery dill, dabs of sharp, freshly grated horseradish and mounds of—are you ready?—whipped cream. The long, narrow and flexible blade of this Swedish knife will carve a thick slab of smoked salmon into tender, paper-thin slices. It would also be the perfect tool with which to slice salmon in another, even more traditional Scandinavian guise: *gravlax,* that piquant specialty in which an uncooked center cut of salmon is cured by dredging it with coarse salt, sugar, peppercorns and a huge bouquet of fresh dill, then sliding it into the refrigerator for several days of cool marination. In either case, the knife should be drawn across the grain of the salmon, cutting on a diagonal to, and away from, the skin. The salmon knife's dishwasher-proof, rosewood handle is attached to a gleaming 10″-long, stainless-steel blade by two brass rivets; the handle is slightly curved to fit your grip. As the blade is long and narrow with a rounded tip, it resembles a ham slicer; but it is more flexible.

H. & E. Trading Co. $12.00
(738R)

GRAVLAX

1 10–12 pound salmon, cleaned and filleted, but with skin left on (the fillets should weigh about 3 pounds each)
1 large bunch fresh dill
1 pound sugar
½ pound salt
¼ pound white peppercorns, crushed

Place one side of salmon, skin-side down, in a large, deep stainless-steel, glass or enameled pan. Spread the dill sprigs over the entire surface of the fish. Combine the sugar, salt and white peppercorns and spread evenly over the dill branches. Cover with the remaining side of salmon, skin-side up.

Cover the dish with plastic wrap, place a weight on top (canned goods work nicely) and place in refrigerator to marinate. Turn after 12 hours, always replacing weights. Marinate at least 24 hours altogether (by this time, the salmon should be swimming in brine), turning every 12 hours, although 2 to 3 days is even better. Do not remove the *gravlax* from the marinade until you are ready to serve it.

To serve, remove the salmon from the brine, scrape off the dill and pat dry. Cut into very thin diagonal slices, as for slicing smoked salmon, and serve with mustard sauce (see below).

MUSTARD SAUCE
¾ cup mild mustard
¼ cup sugar
1 tablespoon wine vinegar
Salt
Freshly ground pepper
3 tablespoons oil
Fresh dill, chopped

Combine the mustard, sugar, vinegar and salt and pepper to taste with a wire whisk. Add the oil in a thin stream, beating constantly. Sprinkle with fresh dill just before serving.

Yield: 1 cup (enough for 6–8 servings *gravlax*).

(Courtesy Eric Friberg, Westchester, New York)

Sardine Fork I:13

Here is a fork only 5″ long that is made of juniperwood. The flattened shape and the wide end with its four tines allow you to lift whole small sardines and herrings without breaking them. To us, this seems the very quintessence of Scandinavian design, with its simple shape and purity of material. We think that it looks like a miniature gardening fork, something to be used by trolls in the light of the midnight sun.

Harriet Chapman, Inc. $3.00
(K-803)

"As the guest, I was invited to help myself first [*but*] *I was at a loss how to begin: the meal was eaten standing. . . . I kept up a conversation with the host, but observed the proceedings warily all the time, in order to know what to do next; knives and forks were used in common. I began with bread, butter and reindeer meat, which were good; and seeing that everyone was enjoying the graflax, I resolved to try it; but the slice was hardly in my mouth before I wished I had not made the experiment. It was too late; I had to*

Continued from preceding page

eat it; there was no possibility of escape. My stomach was ready to give way. . . ."

The Land of the Midnight Sun *by Paul Du Chaillu. 1882.*

Ham Slicer I:14

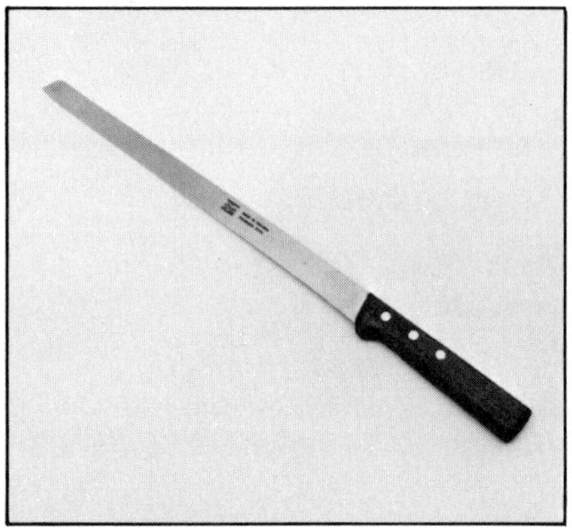

The Christmas ham has the place of honor in Sweden and Finland; Norway makes a wonderful cured-and-smoked ham called *spekeskinke;* and Denmark's favorite edible beast is the pig. A knife for slicing ham may be one of the most used knives in the Scandinavian kitchen. Use it to slice a Finnish Christmas ham (after breaking it out of its rye-bread envelope), or to thinly slice a piece of Danish ham that's been marinated in white wine and baked. Our ham slicer has a 12″-long, razor-edged blade, and is perfectly balanced in the hand. It has a well-shaped walnut handle into which the blunt-ended, stainless-steel blade has been inserted. The blade ends in a half tang that is secured in the handle by three brass rivets.

American Cutlery & Hardware Co., Inc. (3307/12) $9.00

"She laid a cloth on the board and set on it a lighted candle; then brought forth butter, cheese, a bear-ham and a high pile of thin slices of fine bread. She fetched ale and mead up from the cellar below the room and then poured out the porridge into a dish of fine wood."

Kristin Lavransdatter *by Sigrid Undset. Alfred A. Knopf, 1923.*

Swedish Ham Pin I:15

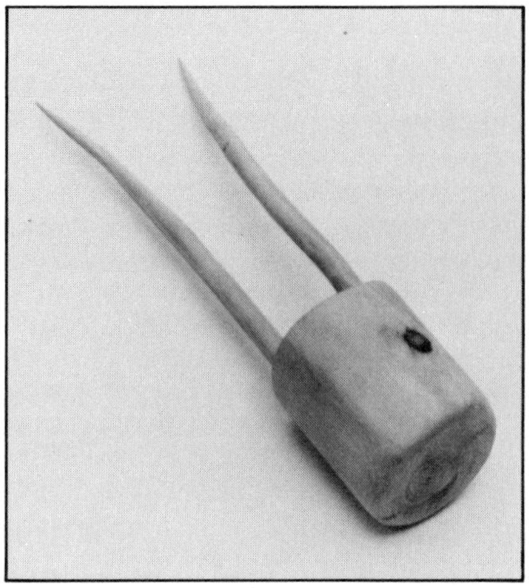

For many Swedes, the elaborate Christmas Eve buffet means ham—boiled, then baked in a crust of mustardy breadcrumbs rich with sugar and egg. Surely on such an occasion—the most lavish holiday feast of the year—the host would appreciate the aid of a ham pin to steady the moist ham as he carved. This curious, graceful (but sturdy) pin was carved from a juniper branch. The two long, narrow, slightly twisted and curved prongs are pushed into the ham, leaving the handle (2″ long and 1¾″ in diameter) with which to hold the ham firmly in place. This pin is 7½″ long overall, but sizes and shapes vary as each pin is hand carved.

Harriet Chapman, Inc. (OB-11) $6.00

Wire Whisk I:16

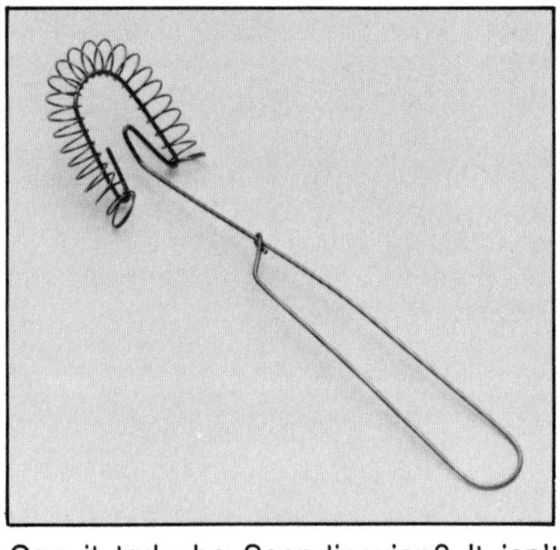

Can it truly be Scandinavian? It isn't wood, and it isn't very pretty. But it works. Heavy cream, lumpy gravy and sauces cannot resist the efforts of this industrious wire whisk. For example, to make a Swedish cold vanilla sauce (for apple cake), an egg-yolk-and-cream mixture is poured into a saucepan where it is combined briskly with sugar and cornstarch; the sauce is then heated and whisked constantly until it is smooth and thick. Because of its flat, horseshoe shape, and the angle at which it sits to its handle, this whisk can scour the bottom and the corners of the saucepan to keep the cornstarch from lumping. The whisk consists of a length of steel wire bent into a looped handle at one end and a horseshoe at the other. A thinner stainless-steel wire is coiled around the horseshoe end to make the whisk. The whisk is 10″ long.

Nor-Pro, Inc. (SVE138) $0.95

Wooden Whisk I:17

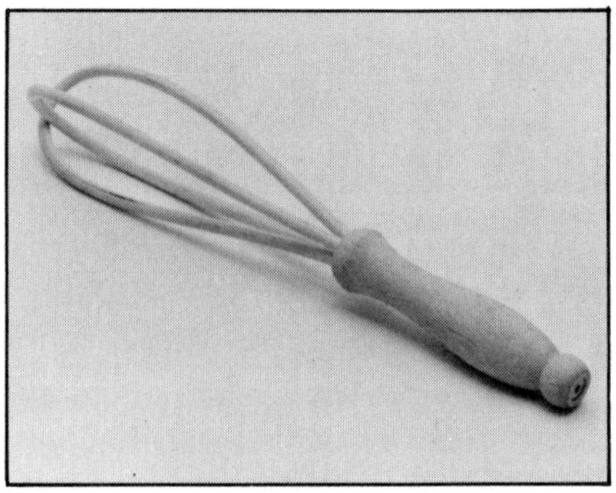

The oldest Scandinavian whisks were bunches of twigs tied together. This Danish whisk is made of traditional materials, but resembles its more modern counterpart, the French, bent-wire whisk. Take advantage of this bentwood utensil to whisk any of the Scandinavian fruit desserts—like Finnish whortleberry pudding, or Danish rhubarb pudding. This whisk is made with a carved, hollow, natural-wood handle into which have been fitted lengths of slender, peeled branches. The whole thing is 10″ long. Since it is fairly lightweight, it may be better suited as a kitchen decoration than to any heavy-duty whisking needs.

Nordiska $0.98

"She had bidden . . . the cook pour buttermilk into the water the fresh fish were boiled in. If only . . . [the priest] *would not deem it a breach of the fast. Sira Eirik had said 'twas no breach, for*

buttermilk is not milk food, and besides, the fish broth is thrown away."

Kristin Lavransdatter *by Sigrid Undset. Alfred A. Knopf, 1923.*

Dough Mixer I:18

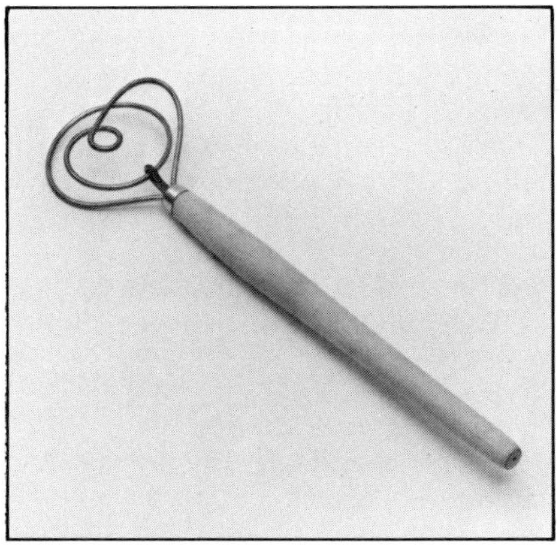

It's always a pleasure to see a beautiful tool—and one that works, too. This dough mixer is made of natural wood and tinned-steel wire. The wood is lovingly turned into a long cigar-shaped form. Capping one end of the handle is a metal collar, and from that collar grows a fantasy of heavy bent wire, an Art Nouveau vine of rigid twisted metal. It is a formidable piece of equipment, 14″ long overall, used for mixing bread doughs like the fragrant Swedish *limpa,* or Finnish rye.

Nordiska/H. A. Mack & Co., Inc. $3.50

Danish Mixing Bowl I:19

To keep up with the mixing demands of a Scandinavian kitchen, especially in Denmark where baking is so prominent, a collection of sturdy, beater-resistant bowls is essential. This heavy, unbreakable, dishwasher-safe Melamine bowl should do the trick. The size shown here will hold 3 quarts of Danish rum pudding, but is also available in 1½-, 2-, 2½- and 4-quart sizes. The bottom of the bowl has a removable rubber grip ring that keeps the bowl in place as you beat; and the top edge has a handle extension on one side, and a pour spout on the other. Its range of bright, modern colors—purple, avocado, orange, sunflower and red—make it hard to hide this bowl away in a kitchen cabinet.

Copco, Inc. (2506) $10.00

Enameled-Steel Mixing Bowl I:20

Whipped cream—on top of Danish cold buttermilk soup, on Norwegian rhubarb compote, for *fyllda strutar* (Swedish pastry cones filled with whipped cream and lingonberries), with fried herring, on waffles, in *mansikkalumi* (Finnish whipped strawberry dessert), everywhere. Since both bowl and beaters should be chilled before whipping cream, and because neither plastic nor ceramics will retain cold, this Finnish enameled-steel bowl is a perfect choice for Scandinavian whipped cream mavens. Filled to its 3-quart capacity with whipped cream—or the food of your choice—this sleekly-designed, rich-brown Arabia bowl will complement any table. The bowl can also be used directly over a flame, although its handleless sides make it awkward to pick up once it's hot.

Arabia, Inc. (4821) $16.00

Stirring Spoon I:21

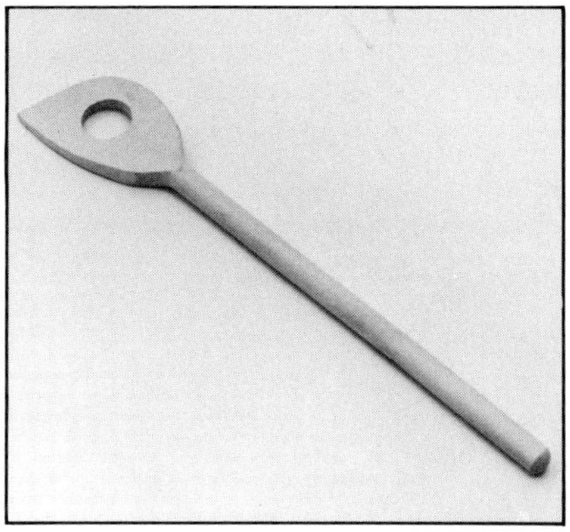

We are calling this attractive piece of design in birchwood a spoon by default, because it certainly isn't a knife or a fork. It would probably be more precise to say that it is a stirrer and let it go at that. Essentially it is a long straight rod that ends in a tapering paddle. The paddle has an elongated point at one corner and a hole in its center. That point pokes into the corners of pots, hunting out the unmixed sauce that often hides there; the hole sets up a counter-motion to the clockwise direction of the stirrer. The entire implement is a 12¼″ piece of sculpture in wood.

Scandicrafts, Inc. (1065A-32) $0.90

Wooden Strainer/ Spoon I:22

Although it looks like the medieval progenitor of the slotted spoon, the large, 4¾″-diameter, shallow bowl of this wooden strainer is handy for lifting large numbers of *melboller* (Danish cardamom-flavored dumplings for meat or fruit soups) out of boiling water, or Norwegian fish dumplings (*fiskeboller*) out of their stock. The

Continued from preceding page

shallow, curved, perforated bowl is inserted into the split end of a gracefully carved, 5¾″-long handle, and joined to it by two small, wooden pegs.

Seabon **$3.95**

MELBOLLER

Dumplings

1½ tbsp. butter
4 tbsp. flour
1⅔ cup (4 dl.) milk
2 egg yolks
2 tbsp. grated cheese
A dash of grated cardamon or a drop of almond flavoring

(Makes 4 servings)

Melt butter over low heat and blend in flour. Add milk, stirring constantly until sauce has thickened. Remove from heat. Beat together egg yolks and 1–2 tbsp. milk, add a little of the sauce to this mixture and blend well. Return this mixture to the rest of the sauce and cook over low heat, stirring vigorously until sauce is hot, thick and well blended. Stir in cheese and cardamon or almond flavoring. Let cool.

Bring 4–6 cups (1–1½ l.) of salted water to a rapid boil. Reduce heat. Gently drop dumplings the size of a quarter to the hot water and simmer for 4–5 minutes. Remove, drain and serve in the broth. The seasoning—cardamon or almond—together with beef broth is unusual and interesting. Exactly the same dumplings, minus cheese, are used in sweet dessert soups—another Scandinavian speciality.

(From SCANDINAVIAN COOKING. *Copyright 1976 by Wezäta Forlag. Reprinted by permission of Wezäta Forlag.)*

"The ale is good . . . but methinks a jade has cooked our porridge for us today: 'While the cook cuddles, the porridge burns,' says the byword; and this porridge is singed."

Kristin Lavransdatter *by Sigrid Undset. Alfred A. Knopf, 1923.*

Egg Lift I:23

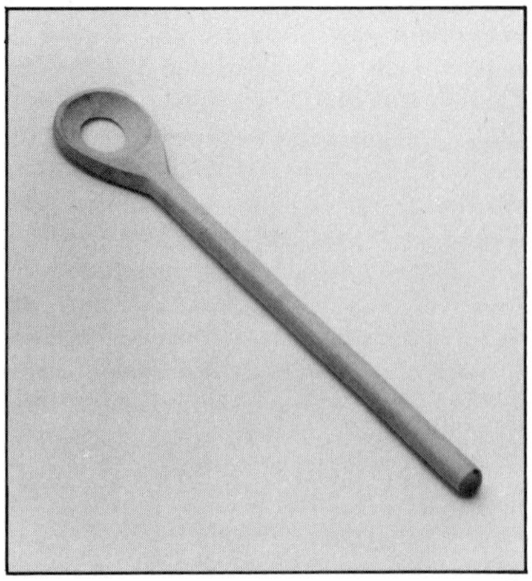

No, this charming wooden spoon will never carry soup from pot to bowl. Nor would it be much use as a tasting spoon. It is, in fact, an egg lift. Use it to rescue soft- or hard-boiled eggs from boiling water. The excess water will drain back into the saucepan through the spoon's generous hole and you will be left with a dry egg by the time you reach your egg cup. The spoon's bowl and its hole will also serve to steady the egg as you carry it. Our 12¼″-long, birchwood egg lift has a 2″-wide flat-bottomed bowl with a 1″-diameter hole in its center.

Scandicrafts, Inc. (W919) **$1.00**

Wooden Fork I:24

Here is a homely wooden fork whose fat tines are cut at an angle to help them get into the corners of pots when you stir stews or thick soups. The cook may also want to use this instead of a spoon when trying to capture long, slithery vegetables like *rødkaal* (sweet and sour red cabbage). The birchwood fork is 13½″ long and has a slender, turned handle.

Scandicrafts, Inc. (W13) **$1.00**

KARELIAN STEW

3 pounds beef (round or chuck), cut into 2″–3″ cubes
Flour for dredging
2 tablespoons butter or oil
1½ pounds salt pork, sliced
Salt
1 bay leaf
4–5 whole allspice, plus a few pinches freshly ground
Water

Preheat oven to 350 F.

Dredge the beef in the flour and sauté in butter or oil in a casserole or deep sauteuse until browned all over. Pour the fat from the pan and add the salt pork, a little salt (don't forget that the salt pork will provide most of the salt), bay leaf and the whole and freshly ground allspice. Add cold water to cover (about 4–5 cups) and bring to a boil. Cover, place in preheated oven and cook until beef is tender and easily pierced with a fork or the tip of a sharp knife, about 2–3 hours.

Yield: 6 servings.

(Courtesy Maija-Leena Aho-Frayer, Nyborg & Nelson, New York City)

Butter Paddles I:25

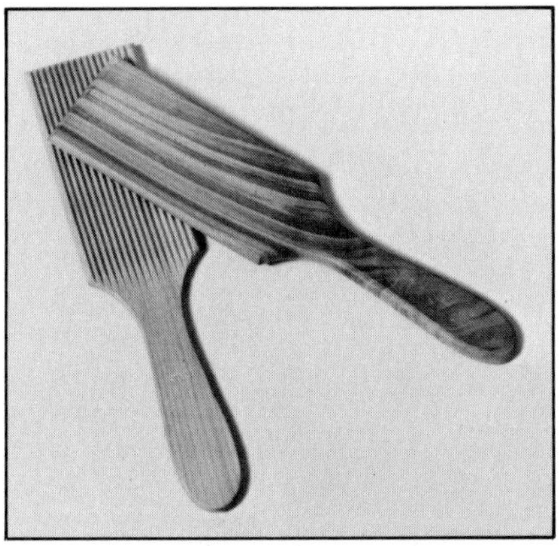

Danish butter is the mortar that holds its cuisine together. What would Danish pastry be without it? What could replace the thickly spread, buttery foundations for open-faced sandwiches?

Here is a pair of birchwood (a material that doesn't absorb grease) butter paddles. One side of each is covered with narrow ridges. Place a small lump of cold butter on top of one paddle and, holding a paddle in each hand, rub together in a circular motion (the same way you form meatballs between the water-dampened palms of your hands). The result will be a butter-ball, decoratively ridged. The paddles are 2″ wide and just under 9″ long; they are carved from unbleached and untreated wood which will become even more beautiful as the fat from the butter enriches its surface.

Nor-Pro, Inc. (EH9500) **$2.00**

Butter Mold I:26

In Scandinavia, bread is nothing unless it is accompanied by butter. The word *smörgåsbord* means bread-and-butter table; and *smørrebrød* (the Danish open-faced sandwich buffet) means buttered bread. So, naturally, on a Scandinavian table there will be not only the loaf of dark bread, but also plenty of butter, either served in a large cheese-like slab, or else in prettily shaped pats made in a butter mold like this one. It looks like a child's toy, is 5½″ high overall, and consists of a hollow cup with a hole at the bottom, through which there has been inserted a wooden plunger with a ball on its end. Attached to the end of the rod inside the cup is a small wooden disc incised with circles. Draw the disc to the bottom of the cup by pulling back on the ball, fill the interior space with softened butter, and then one shove on the plunger and a knob of butter—printed with circles—comes flying out. All of which took a lot longer to describe than it does to do.

Nordiska **$0.98**

Mrs. Beeton, in her Book of House-Hold Management *provides some charming alternative methods for creating buttery whimsies: Tie a strong cloth by two of the corners to an iron hook in the wall; make a knot with the other two ends, so that a stick might pass through. Put the butter into the cloth; twist it tightly over a dish, into which the butter will fall through the knot, so forming small and pretty little strings. The butter may then be garnished with parsley, if to serve with a cheese course; or it may be sent to table plain for breakfast, in an ornamental dish. Squirted butter for garnishing hams, salads, eggs, &c., is made by forming a piece of stiff paper in the shape of a cornet, and squeezing the butter in fine strings from the hole at the bottom. Scooped butter is made by dipping a teaspoon or scooper in warm water and then scooping the butter quickly and thin. In warm weather, it would not be necessary to heat the spoon."*

Engagement Utensil Set I:27

This set of birchwood kitchen utensils is a traditional Scandinavian engagement gift, perfectly suited to any new bride or householder. The set consists of five spoons of varying lengths (from 8¾″ to 11¾″): a tasting spoon, two stirring spoons (one with a pointed end), and two serving spoons—one with a large, 3″-diameter bowl, and the other with a blunt, shovel end. The two butter paddles are rectangular and ridged, and are used to roll dabs of butter into balls. The birch-twig whisk is a traditional Scandinavian tool for smoothing gravies and sauces or whip-

Extracting the mainstays of Danish cuisine—milk, buttermilk, cream and butter.

Continued from preceding page

ping egg whites. All eight utensils come tied together with a colorful ribbon that laces through holes in their ends.

Scandicrafts, Inc. (W2007) **$10.00**

Melamine Utensils I:28

The shapes are familiar; only the material has been changed to vary tradition. The look of these utensils will not astonish any student of Scandinavian design, since they are so clearly the descendants of earlier wooden utensils. There is a stirring spoon that resembles a needle with a gigantic eye. Then there is a slotted spoon and a spatula with one corner pulled into a point that can fit into the awkward corners of a pan. The news is that all three are made of tough Melamine, a material that is durable and sufficiently resistant to heat to go equally calmly into your dishwasher and into a pan full of sizzling potatoes. They are, respectively, 13″, 12″ and 11″ long, and come in a dazzling assortment of colors: red, yellow, green, blue, orange, white and brown.

Copco, Inc.
Stirring Spoon (2519) **$1.50**
Slotted Spoon (2532) **$1.90**
Spatula (2531) **$1.90**

"Dinner in Sweden is invariably preceded by a smörgås, *a series of strange dishes eaten as a relish.*

I was led to a little table, called a smörgåsbord, *around which we all clustered, and upon which I saw a display of smoked reindeer. . . . ; fresh, raw sliced salmon called* graflax *. . . ; caviare; raw, salted Norwegian herring, exceeding fat . . . ;* sillsallat, *made of pickled herring, small pieces of boiled meat, potatoes, eggs, red beets and raw onions; smoked goose-breast; . . . soft brown and white bread . . ;* knäckebrod, *a sort of flat, hard, bread made of coarse rye flour, and flavored with anise-seed . . . ;* gammal ost, *the strongest old cheese one can taste . . . [and] three crystal decanters, containing different kinds of* bränvin *(spirits)."*

The Land of The Midnight Sun *by Paul Du Chaillu, 1882.*

Juniperwood Spreader I:29

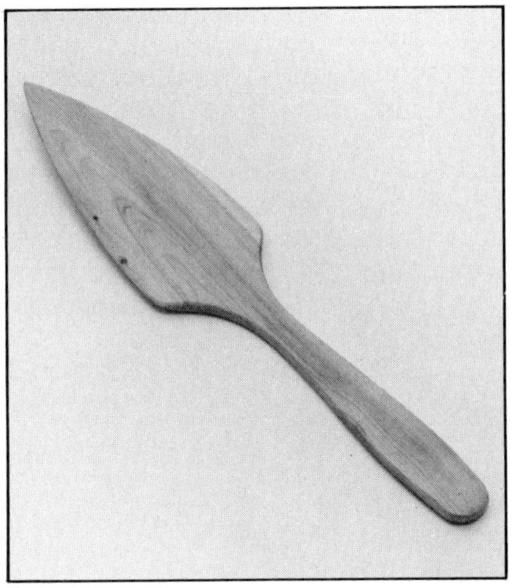

Corned beef and heroes are all very well, and peanut butter and grilled cheese have a certain simple charm, but if you want to talk sandwiches—really *sandwiches*—then you have to talk about Denmark. There the *smørrebrød*—literally, "buttered bread"—has been raised to a work of art, and to a whole meal. *Smørrebrød* is the name of the meal and of the countless varieties of individual open-face sandwiches as well. They begin with thin slices of sour rye bread spread thickly with celestial Danish butter—and to butter that bread you need a 8″ spreader like this one, carved flint-thin from a piece of unfinished juniperwood. Use it to build on the buttered bread, smoothing out a layer of liver paste, mounding a portion of curry salad, piling high scores of tiny, sweet Danish shrimp. All of these are combined with an eye for design as well as concern for flavor and texture. *Smørrebrød* is the infinitely superior ancestor of a million disappointing cocktail canapés, and is traditionally accompanied by beer or aquavit—or both!

H. A. Mack & Co., Inc. (S4) **$4.00**

A Swedish repast.

Sandwich Spatula I:30

This sandwich spreader has perhaps more versatility than visual grace. It is 8⅝″ long, and consists of a stainless-steel blade attached by two rivets to a rosewood handle. The rounded blade is serrated on one edge and smooth on the other, so that you can spread a filling like liver paste or herb butter onto bread with the smooth side, then cut the sandwich into four dainty triangles with the other. You can use the serrated edge as well to slice tomatoes, or to decorate the sandwich spreads by drawing the knife's ridges across them. This is a nice example of Swedish knife-making, lightweight and comfortable in the hand.

H. & E. Trading Co. (714R) **$6.00**

An open-faced sandwich feature at both smørrebrød *and* smörgåsbord.

Cheese Knife I:31

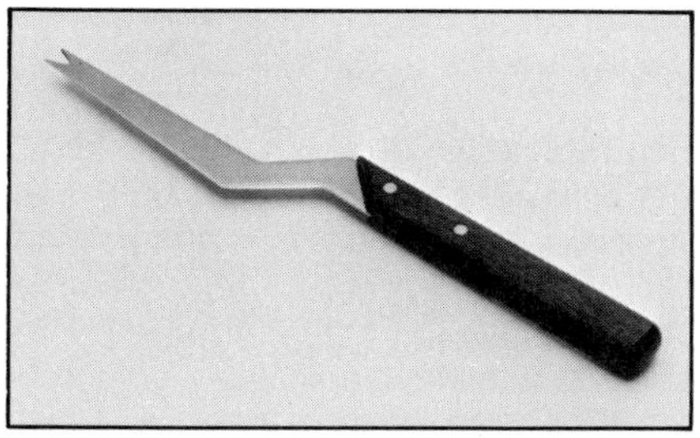

The generous wedges of tangy Danish blue cheese, rust-colored bricks of earthy goat cheese from Norway, and mild yellow Swedish cheeses form an impressive Scandinavian cheese board. And this intelligently designed Swedish cheese knife makes it easy to sample the selection. The knife is 9¼″ overall; the 5⅛″ stainless-steel blade ends with two prongs, used to stab the wedge of cheese and transfer it to your plate (or, if you are more hungry than elegant, your mouth). The rosewood handle is secured with two brass rivets, and the angle at which the blade meets the handle insures that you can cut a straight, even slice no matter how thick or awkwardly shaped the cheese.

H. & E. Trading Co. (734R) **$6.00**

Cheese Plane I:32

If you want a neat, uniform slice of cheese, then you have to cut it; and this device provides one of the most practical ways for the home consumer to do so. It is a familiar tool, one that is made by any number of manufacturers; and we are showing you an especially sturdy one made in Sweden out of stainless steel and wood. It has the familiar club-shaped blade with a sharp-edge slit set at an angle to the rest of the blade. When the slit is pulled over the surface of a wedge of Havarti or Jarlsberg, it produces a slice of cheese whose thickness varies according to the pressure of your hand. This cheese plane is 8¾″ overall, and its blade is 3″ at its widest, with a 2⅛″-wide slit.

H. & E. Trading Co. (CP1000) **$4.00**

Bread Board I:33

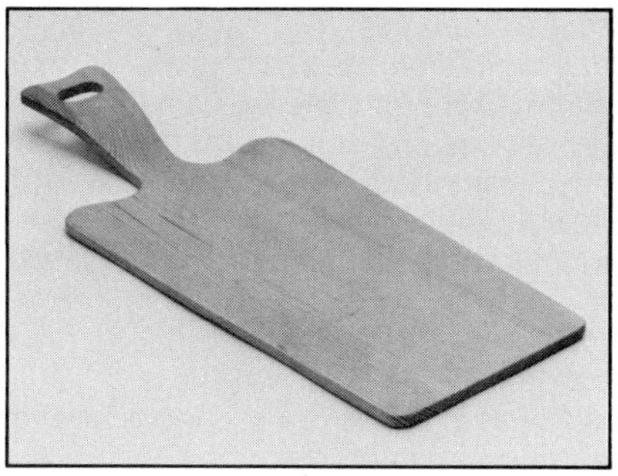

In Scandinavia, the bread is dark and tangy, flecked with seeds and shaped into wheels or biscuits or compact little bricks. So alien is white bread that it is called "French bread" in many Northern countries. The heavy, nutty loaf that is an essential part of the diet is brought to the table at every meal, meant to be sliced there and eaten with lots of butter. This board is meant for just that purpose. It is made of a quarter-inch thickness of pine and shaped like a fanciful hornbook, with the handle lifted at a gentle angle from the plane of the paddle. It is 16½″ long overall and has an oblong hole in the handle so that it may be dusted off and hung on the wall after every meal. When it is not in use as a breadboard, it may well see service as a presentation piece on the *smörgåsbord* table, bearing a careful arrangement of overlapping pieces of sausage, cheese or pâté.

Seabon **$4.95**

Canapé Cutters I:34

These are small cutters which would be used in France for aspic, in Amer-

Continued from preceding page

ica for canapés; but in Scandinavia they would be used to cut decorative shapes in ham, pimento or mushroom for the final embellishment of an open-faced sandwich. They are made of tinned steel and come six to a box, each set containing cutters in the shape of a heart, a circle, a diamond, a square, a crescent and a paisley-like teardrop. Each tiny device is 1″ tall; each has a rolled rim on one side and a cutting edge on the other.

Nordiska **$1.29**

PARIS SANDWICH

1 1/4 pounds very lean ground beef or steak (as for a steak tartare)
1/4 cup minced onion
2 tablespoons capers, chopped
1 1/2 tablespoons minced parsley
3–4 anchovies, chopped
1 tablespoon Dijon mustard
2 eggs
Salt
Freshly ground black pepper
8 slices white bread
Clarified butter
8 eggs, fried in egg rings
Paprika

Combine the ground beef with the onion, capers, parsley, anchovies, mustard, eggs and salt and pepper to taste. Spread a thin layer of the seasoned meat on each of the slices of bread. Using the edge of a spreader or the back of a knife, make a diamond pattern of crossed diagonal lines in the surface of the meat. Trim the crusts from the bread.

Place enough clarified butter to form an 1/8″ layer in a large frying pan and heat over a fairly high flame until quite hot. Add 4 of the sandwiches, bread-side down, and fry until lightly browned, about 30 seconds. Turn and cook 30–45 seconds longer.

Repeat with the remaining 4 sandwiches. Arrange sandwiches on plates or a platter and top each with a fried egg sprinkled with a little paprika. Serve immediately.
Yield: 8 servings as appetizer, 4 servings as main course.

(*Courtesy Joseph (Seppi) Renggli, Executive Chef, The Four Seasons Restaurant, New York City*)

Egg Rings I:35

In the construction of a Scandinavian open-faced sandwich, it is nice to have at hand some beautifully-shaped fried eggs. These neat circles of white and gold sit well on top of a sandwich of dark bread, butter and blue cheese, or temper with their blandness thin slices of peppery ham. And although anyone can fry an egg, no one can fry a perfectly round egg without the assistance of these egg rings. Just butter your frying pan, place the three rings in it, and break an egg into each of them. Each one is a 3 1/2″ circle formed from a steel band 1/2″ wide. At the place where the seam is welded, a triangular handle rises from the side, and at the apex of the triangle there is a red plastic circle which remains cool to the touch even when the ring is in the pan and the pan is on the fire. The handles make it easy to remove the rings when the eggs are cooked.

Edwin Jay, Inc. (33332) **$2.50**

Egg Cup I:36

What does a Dane eat for breakfast, Danish pastry? No, he probably eats a three-minute egg and a slice of dark bread spread with butter. The lucky fellow. And all the luckier if the egg comes to his table in a beautiful Royal Copenhagen porcelain egg cup like this one, 2 1/4″ high, and an ample 2″ across the top, wide enough to hold an egg from a healthy Danish hen. The finish of the egg cup is exquisite, a delicate white, scalloped ever-so-lightly all over and then decorated with an ornate blue tracery.

Royal Copenhagen Porcelain (I-542) **$11.00**

Potato Brush I:37

Potatoes are among the last vegetables to come into our kitchens *au naturel:* crusted with earth. Before carving them into the glorious roasted fan called *hasselback potatis,* or cutting them into triangular wedges for *brynt potatis i ugn,* they must be scoured; and this no-nonsense potato brush is the tool with which to accomplish the task. The 1″-long nylon bristles—colored and shaped to look like natural fibers, but much tougher than the original—are rooted firmly in a natural wood holder with the word *Potatisborste* (potato brush) burned into it. The brush is 5″ long and 1 1/2″ wide.

Scandicrafts, Inc. (W204KS/2) **$1.50**

Traveling in Sweden, Hans Christian Andersen wrote: "I had ordered something to eat and drink, but I got nothing. They ran up and they ran down; there was a hissing sound of roasting by the hearth; the girls chattered, the men drank 'sup' [schnaps]; strangers came, were shown to their rooms and got both roast and boiled. Several hours had passed, when I made a forcible appeal to the girl, and she answered phlegmatically: 'Why sir, you sit there and write without stopping, so you cannot have time to eat.' "

Pictures of Travel, *1871.*

Visp **I:38**

Like the traditional Swedish whisk, this brush, called a visp, is made of birch twigs. *Unlike* that whisk, the visp is used to clean pots, not prepare food. The visp's twig bristles—bound tightly to the 4¼″-long wooden handle with a layer of cord—are made of birch because it will not absorb grease. Altogether a down-to-earth tool made of honest, down-to-earth materials.

Scandicrafts, Inc. $2.00 (W2015)

"Have you not heard of the old wife who sat and wept for that she had only a small bite of swine's flesh to give her seven little ones for Christmas cheer? Pat at the moment, Saint Olav came riding by and he stretched out his hand over the meat and prayed that God might give the poor little ravens their fill. But when the woman saw a whole pig's carcase lying upon the board, she wept that she had not pots and platters enow!"

Kristin Lavransdatter *by Sigrid Undset. Alfred A. Knopf, 1923.*

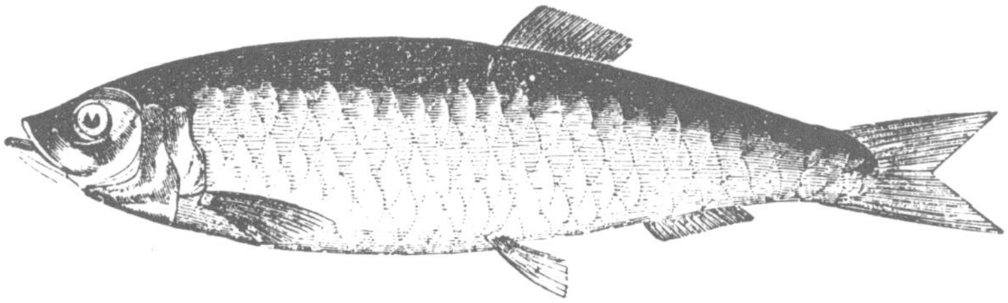

Herring, star of the smörgåsbord.

Preserving

Long, long ago, in the chilly dawn of prehistory, Scandinavians learned how to preserve the bounty of their early harvest so that it could sustain the community through the long nights of winter. They dried fish in the thin Arctic sunlight, buried meat in the snow, and poured brine over vegetables, turning them into pickles that were a source of vitamin C in the winter months. The short growing season; the long, cold winter; the unreliability of the herring catch; the extreme isolation of many farming communities; all of these facts made it essential that Northern man learn to preserve what food he had.

Now that is all changed. We can preserve food for a long time, what with scientific canning and deep-freezing and chemical additives that retard the growth of the bacteria that make food spoil. Strawberries and oranges can be flown into Oslo in January, so that preservation is not nearly so important as it used to be. But we have become accustomed to the flavors that come from the older methods of preservation, and would miss them if they were discarded. Who would do without the tang of mold in a Danish Blue cheese, the salt taste of pickled herrings, the heavy syrup of jam, the bite of fermented barley in a chilled glass of aquavit? All of these familiar tastes result from traditional methods of preservation.

In a sense, all cooking is a kind of preservation, in that it kills the bacteria in food. A fish left uncooked begins to smell after a day, but a broiled fish lasts three days; a smoked fish, three months; a pickled and canned fish, three years. Methods of preservation are really ways of retarding the growth of the bacteria that produce putrefaction.

The method that we call pickling is really a double-barreled form of preservation; the salt creates an environment that limits the growth of certain harmful micro-organisms in food, while the vinegar and sugar encourage desirable fermentation. Used alone, pickling produces a pleasant change in texture and flavor, and serves as a middling-effective means of preservation that is able to stabilize food for a few months: enough to keep it through the worst of the Scandinavian winter. But when it is combined, as it is nowadays, with canning—that is, sterilizing—then it results in herrings and cucumbers and cauliflower that will keep for years.

If you are tempted to underestimate the place of preserving in Scandinavian cooking, think of the traditional Swedish Thursday night dinner: yellow split pea soup, pancakes and lingonberries. The peas will have been dried; the slice of pork that is served in the bottom of each bowl of soup will have been salted at the time of slaughtering and

Continued from preceding page

the lingonberries will have been preserved when they were gathered. Add to that a glass of aquavit—made of fermented barley or potatoes—with a beer chaser—made from fermented malt and hops—and you will see how very important the process of preservation is in the Scandinavian diet even today.

Herring Jar I:39

This open, straight-sided jar is used for making *glasmästarsill,* or glassblower's herring, a layered concoction of salted herring, horseradish, carrots and onions. The fish and vegetables are laid carefully into the jar, and then a pickling liquid is poured over them. After a few days refrigeration, the herring is ready to be served as an appetizer. Of course it could be made in a stoneware crock; but then you'd miss the mosaic of colors visible through the glass. Or it could go into a pickling jar; but then you couldn't get your hand down into it to arrange the fish. Better off in this 3¾-quart glass herring jar, 7¾" high and 5¾" in diameter. Serve it with dark bread, sweet butter and a cordial glass of aquavit.

Seabon $8.95

GLASMÄSTARSILL

Pickled Herring

The classic marinated herring, a must on every Scandinavian *smörgåsbord* and Christmas table.

4 fillets of salt herring
1 piece horseradish, about 1" (2.5 cm) long
1 carrot
2 red onions
2 bay leaves
2 tsp. allspice
2 tsp. mustard seeds
2 small pieces dried ginger or 1 tsp. ground ginger

MARINADE:
¾ cup (2 dl) pickling vinegar
⅔ cup (½ dl) water
1 cup (2½ dl) sugar

Soak herring over night. Wash, drain and cut into 1" (2–3 cm) pieces. Boil water, vinegar and sugar for marinade and cool. Peel horseradish, carrot, and onions and cut into thin slices. Layer herring with onions, carrots, horseradish and spices in a tall, wide-mouthed jar or crock. Cover the fish with marinade. Marinate in refrigerator for 1 day. Fresh horseradish may be hard to find. A tablespoon of ready-made grated horseradish can be sprinkled between the herring layers instead.

(From SCANDINAVIAN COOKING. Copyright 1976 by Wezäta Forlag. Reprinted by permission of Wezäta Forlag.)

Pickle Fork I:40

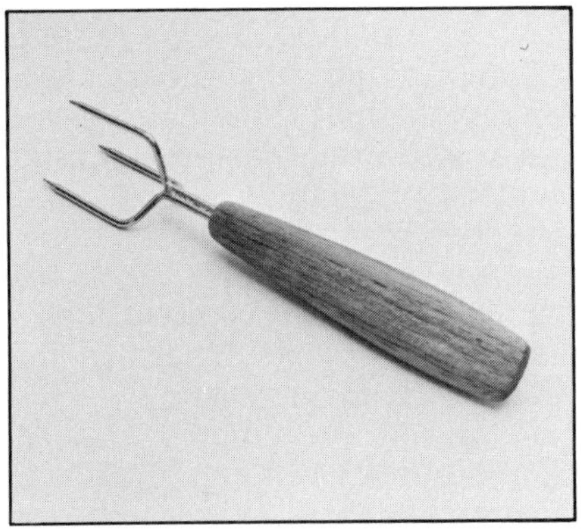

Pickles are just summer's cucumbers eaten the following February. But in Norway they are packed into jars with oak leaves or black currant leaves and then drenched in a lightly sweetened brine so that they turn into an entirely new eating experience. This little fork was made for getting the pickles out of a jar; it is formed like a trident, with three tinned-steel prongs extending out of a wooden handle. Only 5" overall, it is attractive and light in weight, and looks handsome sitting on the table next to a jar of pickles.

Nyborg & Nelson, Inc. $1.00

Preserving Jar I:41

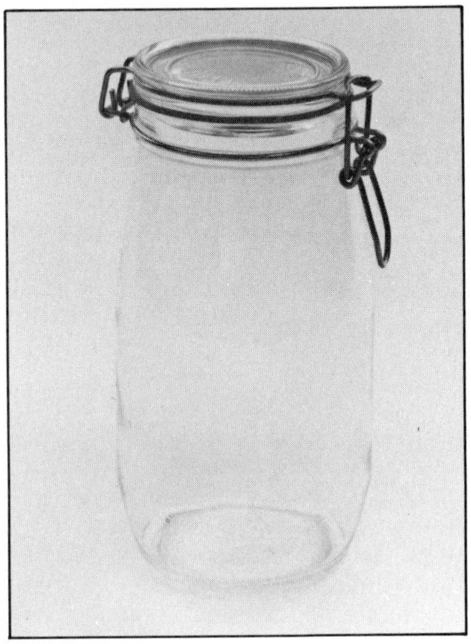

In Scandinavia, people go into the forests every summer to gather berries, which, preserved as whole fruit or as jams, may provide them with their only source of vitamin C through the long winter. Berries thrive in the Arctic climate: raspberries and strawberries, tannic lingonberries and tart cranberries and, most northern of all, the yellow Arctic cloudberry. Most are cooked with a little sugar and then sealed into glass jars like this wire-bail type of preserving jar. Not restricted to fruit preserves, of course, the jar is equally suited to holding any of the myriad Scandinavian pickled vegetables and seafood. The jar's lid and base are held together with a latch of twisted wire; a separate rubber ring is laid between the two to form a perfect seal. These flat-topped jars come from France in sizes ranging from ½ liter to 3 liters. Here we show the 1½-liter (about 1½-

quart) size.

Wheaton Glass (11340) $1.80

Red currant.

Canning Funnel I:42

Pickling and preserving always seem to involve a certain amount of putting large things into small jars. One is forever pouring brines that are lumpy with peppercorns and oak leaves into narrow-necked pickling jars, or else draining huge quantities of stewed raspberries or currants into tiny jam jars. All of this would be considerably more difficult and messy than it is if it weren't for funnels like this one. It's made of lightweight aluminum, and is 5¾″ wide at the top with an ample 2″ opening at the neck, ready to fit into any pickle or jelly jar and see to it that all of the messy stuff goes right where it belongs.

Nor-Pro, Inc. (HO-033) $3.75

Finnish Juice Extractor I:43

During the long, dark Finnish winter, the berries that grew wild in the summer are valued as a rich source of vitamins as well as for their flavor. We know about the esteemed place of lingonberries in the Scandinavian diet; but there are, in addition, vines, bushes and bogs producing raspberries, blueberries, cranberries, honeyberries, loganberries, gooseberries and more. What is not eaten fresh is preserved by being turned into liqueurs, jam and fruit juice. We show you a fine Rube Goldberg contraption that has been used in Finland for generations for the extraction of juice from fresh berries and fruits. The extracting of concentrated juice by steam retains vitamins, minerals, flavors and colors of fruit. The 14½″-high, aluminum extractor comes with five working parts. On the bottom there is a shallow water kettle (4″ deep and 12″ in diameter). Above that sits a larger 11-liter (11½-quart) kettle with a spigot; a rubber draining tube with a metal clamp fits over the spigot. Into this large kettle there is fitted a capacious steamer basket. And over it all sits a lid. Now, how does it work? Water is brought to boil in the lower water kettle; clean fruit (and sugar, if you are making a sweetened juice) is placed in the steamer basket; then, when it is all assembled over a burner, the heat from the steam produced in the water kettle goes to work softening the fruit. In an hour or so, juice begins dripping down from the steamer basket into the juice kettle. Then, when you are ready to bottle, open the draining tube by loosening its metal clamp, and out comes the juice. It is marvelous to own if you are fond of the strong, fresh flavor of unadulterated fruit juices. The extractor can also be used in the preparation of jelly, syrup, wine and vegetable juices. The comprehensive booklet enclosed with the steam-cooker also suggests using it to steam vegetables, fish, corned beef, poultry and puddings. Sets of rubber bottle caps, which fit soda, wine or liquor bottles, are available to seal your unique collection of raspberry juice, pear juice cocktail or spiced apple punch. A smaller, 7-liter (7⅓-quart) version is also available.

Osmo Heila Imports $44.90

Cleanliness being a subjective state, a spoon is washed, Lapland-style: "It was not clean, reindeer milk having dried upon it, and I was much amused at the way the girl washed it. As there was no water at hand, she passed her little red tongue over it several times until it was quite clean and smooth; and then, as if it had been a matter of course, filled it with milk from a bowl, stirred up the coffee, and handed me the cup. I did not altogether admire this way of cleaning spoons. Happily, her teeth were exquisitely white, and her lips as red as a cherry; and, although I have seen many Laplanders since, I think she was the prettiest one I ever met."

The Land of the Midnight Sun *by Paul Du Chaillu, 1882.*

The Small Warm

One end of the *smörgåsbord* table is always given over to a hot buffet. When you have tempted your appetite with salty herrings, teased it with fish, indulged it with cold meat and salad, then it is time to go back a fourth time to sample the composed dishes that are the center of the meal. The Swedes see no gluttony in this: this section of the *smörgåsbord* is called *smovarmt*, "the small warm;" and if you take only a little bit, a taste from each casserole, then you have an outside chance of surviving the meal. Of what is the "small warm" composed? It is made up of tureens of potatoes with anchovies and cream, of fluffy omelets, fried chicken croquettes in tomato sauce, onion leaves stuffed with ground meat and tiny, delicately-flavored meatballs. And more.

To keep up with the demands of the *smovarmt*, much of Scandinavian design has been concentrated on oven-to-table ware: sleekly handsome casseroles with clean lines and intense colors to make the already appetizing *smovarmt* dishes all the more so.

Glass Frying Pan I:44

A Danish egg cake is something like a quiche without a crust, a custard of eggs, milk and flour, sprinkled with chives and decorated with bacon. It is cooked over a burner, made in and served from a skillet: so why not make it in *this* skillet, a surprisingly sturdy frivolity made out of heat-resistant glass. It has a short, broad handle and sides that are rippled all around like those of a soufflé dish. Like Pyrex pans, it is ovenproof; but that's the easy way. The real show comes when it is used over a burner (along with an asbestos pad). And then right to the table, bearing a golden creamy *flaeskeaeggekage.* This 9″-diameter, 2½″-deep skillet has a 2-quart capacity. It's quite delicate looking; but of course its appeal lies precisely in this unexpectedly fragile look.

Fisher Bruce & Co. (S160) $42.50

Cast-Iron Frying Pan I:45

In Scandinavia, where modern designers have created so much beautiful cookware in enameled steel and earthenware, the preferred material is still black cast iron. It was iron that was used traditionally for Scandinavian pots and pans, and it is still iron that is used when traditional dishes are prepared. For example, use it to make *pytt i panna,* a traditional hash made of diced meat, onions and potatoes. Browned in a searing hot frying pan, it is turned out onto a plate, and topped with fried eggs. Cast iron provides just the right material for browning the hash, and the bakelite handle helps the cook to flip it out with the proper flair. The pan is 8¾″ in diameter, but is also available 7″ and 10¼″ in diameter.

Nyborg & Nelson, Inc./ Nor-Pro, Inc. (J10-8¾″) $20.00

PYTT I PANNA

4 large potatoes, peeled, cut into ¼″ dice and blanched
2–3 tablespoons butter (or a combination of butter and vegetable oil)
½–¾ pound roast veal, cut into ¼″ dice
½–¾ pound roast pork, cut into ¼″ dice
1 medium onion, chopped
Salt
Freshly ground black pepper
Worcestershire sauce
4 eggs, fried

Fry the potatoes in the butter (or butter and oil) until nicely browned, then add the veal, pork, onion and salt and pepper to taste. Cook over medium-high heat until all the ingredients are browned, then reduce heat and slide or flip all the hash ingredients to one side of the pan, forming a curved mound the shape of a rolled omelet.

While the hash continues to brown slowly, prepare the eggs, using egg rings if available. After 5–10 minutes, the hash should form a beautiful, solid crust on the bottom. Before turning it onto a plate, sprinkle a little Worcestershire on each side of the "mound" and tip and turn the pan so that the sizzling sauce runs into the hash. Immediately turn the hash (in one piece) onto a serving plate, so that the crusty brown surface is on top. Top with the four fried eggs.
Yield: 4 servings.

(Courtesy Joseph (Seppi) Renggli, Executive Chef, The Four Seasons Restaurant, New York City)

Finnish Enameled-Steel Saucepan I:46

In some cooking pans, the surface is of paramount importance: look at this

1½-quart pan made of steel covered with clean white enamel. No possibility here for the metal to interact badly with the contents of the pan, as it might well do if it were made of aluminum. That means that you can use this saucepan to heat the acidic cranberry juice for a whipped berry pudding, that you can reach for it when you cook the vinegar and sugar brine for a glassblower's herring, secure that the mixture will neither damage the interior of the pot nor be damaged by it. The 6¼″-diameter, 4¼″-deep saucepan has straight sides, a wooden cylinder for a handle, and a well-fitting lid. There are six tiny holes in the lid that provide both ventilation and a means for straining off liquid. It comes in a rich brown and brilliant yellow as well as the white that we show you here; with all colors, the bottom of the pot is enameled black for better heat conduction.

Arabia, Inc. (9316) $28.50

Earthenware Dish I:47

Whoever arranges the *smörgåsbord* table will require many dishes like this one, a flat, attractive bowl in which to arrange herrings or beet salads or potatoes. This is a round dish 10½″ in diameter and only 2″ deep, and in spite of its shallowness it will easily hold 6½ cups of lobster salad or *biff à la Lindström.* A slick glaze covers it completely, including the bottom. It is meant to go into the oven, and then can move directly to the table.

Arabia, Inc. (LM 3) $8.50

". . . The Old Laplanders were busied in cooking their supper, which consisted of various fish cut into pieces and boiled in a pot, together with some dried fat of the rein-deer and a little meal: the whole formed a curious mess when the pot was still on the fire, all the Laplanders sat around it, each with a spoon in his hand, for the purpose of tasting when the soup was ready: when sufficiently boiled, they began to partake of the mess out of the same pot altogether. When anyone had taken as much as satisfied him, he fell asleep, and when he awoke he immediately began to eat again while the others slept; then these would awake and again eat, while the former elapsed into his slumber; and thus they alternatively ate and slept till they were satisfied with the one and incapable of taking more of the other. . . ."

Travels Through Sweden, Finland and Lapland To The North Cape *by Joseph Acerbi. London, 1802.*

Finnish Stainless-Steel Casserole I:48

In Scandinavia, they cook new potatoes with salt, pepper and a kitchen-spoonful of butter in a high-sided casserole with a tightly sealed lid. The potatoes cook over the lowest possible flame, receiving an occasional shake and jostle from the passing cook, until they are tender and ready to be sprinkled with snipped dill. For such a perfect and simple dish you need a pan like this one from Finland, which has the tightest sealing lid in town. It is made of medium-weight stainless steel with an aluminum bottom and has matching stainless-steel handles, top and bottom. It is available in sizes holding from 1½ to 5 quarts; ours is 7″ in diameter and holds 3 quarts.

OPA Oy (TS 202) $22.95

Danish Enameled Cast-Iron Casserole I:49

A familiar face, we think: the durable porcelain-enameled, cast-iron pot manufactured by Copco. These casseroles come in Crayola colors, in blue, yellow, red, white and brown. Specially ground flat bottoms make these pots efficient on electric burners as well as gas. And its tightly-fitting cover can be used separately to good advantage as a gratin pan. We can't imagine anything sturdier or more wholesome for the hearty combinations of herring and potatoes and bits of meat that brighten a family dinner in the dark Scandinavian winter. The one we are showing is 8¼″ in diameter and 4″ deep, with a 2½-quart capacity. But similar ones are available in sizes ranging from 1½ to 7 quarts.

Copco, Inc. (D2) $40.00

Norwegian Cast-Iron Casserole I:50

This 3-quart, cast-iron casserole blends beautifully with the dark, brooding, earthy colors of much of Scandinavian cookware. Its design is simple and functional. Use it in the oven to make *får i kål* (Norwegian lamb and cabbage casserole). Or use it on top of the stove to make Thursday-night Swedish pea soup, or a fragrant Bergen fish soup. The casserole is 9″ in diameter and 3″

Continued from preceding page

deep, and has two flat, earlike handles that match those on the lid. It has a flat ground bottom, for meeting an electric burner head-on.

Nor-Pro, Inc. (J-3) $22.00

Finnish Ceramic Casserole I:51

Summer in Scandinavia is brief and poignant: imagine sitting outside in the evening sunlight, eating *kesäkeitto*—a Finnish soup made of summer vegetables that have been briefly stewed in butter and cream. Your hostess may serve it in just such a simple and sleek, dark-glazed pot as this one, made in Finland of a ceramic especially formulated to survive exposure to gas, to eletric burners and even to the open fire. The bottom is flat to better transmit heat from any source. A flat rim extending out from the bowl-shaped pot serves both as a handle to the casserole and as a base on which the domed cover rests. The lid's handle is a raised circle. The pot is 8¾″ in diameter and 2⅝″ deep, and has a capacity of 1⅓ quarts.

Arabia, Inc. (KB2) $20.00

FINNISH VEAL STEW WITH DILL

3 pounds veal, cut into 1½″ cubes
2 teaspoons salt
1 teaspoon white pepper
2 tablespoons chopped fresh dill
1 bay leaf
Water
¼ cup flour
¼ cup butter
2 tablespoons Swedish vinegar or ¼ cup dry red wine
Fresh dill sprigs for garnish

Place the veal in a heavy, covered casserole with the salt, pepper, chopped dill and bay leaf and add cold water to cover (about 3 cups). Bring to a boil, reduce heat, cover and simmer until meat is tender and easily pierced with a fork or sharp knife, about 1½–2 hours.

Work the flour and butter into a paste. Remove a little of the stock from the casserole and combine it into the paste, blending until totally smooth and free of lumps. Add this, a bit at a time, to the casserole, stirring to thoroughly incorporate each addition before adding more.

When all the flour paste has been incorporated, add the Swedish vinegar (if this is unavailable, substitute the red wine rather than another kind of vinegar) and continue to simmer, stirring constantly, until the stock thickens, about 3–5 minutes. Garnish with fresh dill sprigs.

Yield: 6 servings.

(Courtesy Maija-Leena Aho-Frayer, Nyborg & Nelson, New York City)

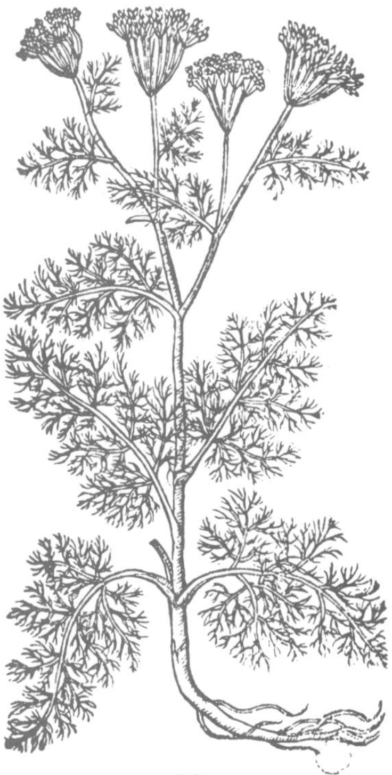

Dill

Swedish Earthenware Casserole I:52

Imagine this glossy, earthenware casserole filled to the brim with yellow pea soup (*ärter med fläsk*)—the traditional Thursday-night meal in Sweden—the rich, hearty, porridge-like contents contrasted against a smooth, maroon-brown glaze. The straight-sided flameproof casserole will hold up to 2½ quarts—enough pea soup for a small family. It has ribbon-shaped handles, a mushroom-like knob on the top, and a lid that fits neatly within the upper rim of the pot. All surfaces are glazed, save the bottom and a thin strip around the bottom of the lid. The pot is 8½″ in diameter and 3″ deep.

Seabon $22.95

SWEDISH YELLOW PEA SOUP

1½ cups dried yellow Swedish peas
2 quarts cold water
1 pound lean salt pork (lightly salted) or ham (use whichever you have available in the refrigerator)
1 bay leaf
1 onion, peeled
Pepper to taste
Thyme tied in a cheesecloth bag

Wash the peas, place in a large saucepan or a casserole, add the cold water and soak for 24 hours.

Bring the peas to a boil in the same water in which they soaked and remove any skins that float to the surface. Reduce heat and add the salt pork or ham, bay leaf, onion and pepper to taste. Cover and simmer until both peas and pork are tender, about 1–1½ hours, adding the bag of thyme for the last 10 minutes of simmering. Remove and discard the onion and the bag of thyme. Remove and slice the salt pork or ham and serve in the soup or separately, with mustard.

Yield: 4–6 servings.

(Courtesy Eric Friberg, Westchester, New York)

Large Aluminum Stew Pan I:53

This large, 8½-quart stew pan is the perfect vehicle for the Scandinavian celebration of the crayfish that begins in late summer when both fresh- and salt-water varieties are caught. To hold a proper crayfish feast, the fresh shellfish should be steeped in water seasoned with dill sprigs and crowns (the yellow flower tops of the dill plant) and ground coarse salt. The Finns often throw in some sugar, vinegar and beer. The crayfish are then boiled in the same concoction and eaten with nothing but butter, toast, aquavit and beer. If you eat crayfish in the Finnish style, each shellfish must be accompanied by a swig of alcohol. Good luck. Of course, the 11″-diameter, 5½″-deep, heavy aluminum pot performs all other kitchen chores suited to its size—like large-family-sized amounts of Swedish Thursday-night pea soup, or its Danish equivalent. Small households might prefer this sturdy pan in a smaller (5.4 liter) size. And its popularity in farm kitchens is testified to by the other sizes in which it is available: 13, 18, 25 and 30 liters. And last, and certainly not least, an awesome, 50-liter restaurant-sized pot. You'd better have a restaurant staff to lift it! All sizes have handles on both pot and tightly fitting cover, and a thick, flat-ground bottom for maximum heat use on electric burners.

Nor-Pro, Inc. (HO615) $69.00

Pancakes and Waffles

Neither bread nor cake, neither breakfast nor dessert, in Scandinavia there is a class of food that falls among all of these categories. They are the many pancakes and waffles that are cooked in special pans on top of the stove, and that are meant to be eaten as soon as they are cooked, fresh from their sizzling-hot pans. In a world where baking is taken seriously—where no housewife can hold her head up if she does not have two cakes and a choice of cookies to offer you for afternoon coffee—these snacks are a kind of game: easy to make and simple to cook.

They are made in iron pans, and have hard-to-pronounce names: *fløtevafler, aebleskiver, plättar.* One can find beautiful old pans in Scandinavian antique stores, irons that impress fantastic designs on the cakes baked inside them. Or you can get other, more modern versions in many gourmet cookware sections of American department stories. These cakes are so good, so nutritious, and so easy to make that they deserve to be more popular than they are in this country.

Swedish Plätt Pan I:54

Plättar are small Swedish pancakes, customarily served with lingonberries or fruit preserves as dessert. This heavy, cast-iron griddle (called a *plättlagg*) has circular depressions, each 3″ in diameter and ¼″ deep, allowing seven pancakes—one hearty serving—to cook at a time. Heat the ungreased pan over a medium-high flame. When the pan is hot, drop a tablespoon of batter into each depression. When the edges begin to brown, after about two minutes, turn the pancakes with a narrow spatula and cook another two minutes to brown the other side. The griddle is 9¼″ in diameter and has a 5″-long handle.

Paprikás Weiss/ $11.50
Eva Housewares, Inc.
(200474)

Danish Aebleskive Pan I:55

Each of the Scandinavian countries has its favorite iron-baked batter specialty. From Denmark comes this *aebleskive* pan, which cooks seven puffy little *aebleskiver* at a time. *Aebleskive* is a favorite national dish that is prepared on special occasions and served with hot, spiced red wine during the long winter months. These apple pancakes are either made of a batter containing bits of apple or they are served with applesauce. The cast-iron pan is 12″ long overall and 8″ in diameter. Each *aebleskive* cooks in a small, bowl-shaped depression 2¼″ in diameter and 1″ deep.

Paprikás Weiss/ $10.00
Eva Housewares, Inc.
(200480)

Apple

AEBLESKIVER

Danish Doughnuts

3½ cups flour
4 eggs
¼ cup sugar
3 cups milk
¼ cup butter
2 oz. yeast
A little crushed cardamom
Grated rind of 1 lemon
½ teaspoon salt

(Serves 8 persons)

In Denmark we call our doughnuts "Apple Slices," possibly because we think the best way to eat them is to slice them open and fill them with apple jam. To make them you require a special frying pan with 6 to 8 round indentations.

Cream yolks and sugar until white. In another bowl, mix flour and milk. Add in the creamed yolks and sugar, thereafter melted butter, grated lemon rind, cardamom and salt. Finally add in the yeast, previously dissolved in a little warm milk. Mix the lot well and fold in the stiffly beaten egg whites. Set aside to rise for about 1 hour. Pour the batter into a jug. Put a little butter in each indentation and then pour in a little of the batter.

They form into semi-spherical "shells," browned underneath, whereupon you turn them upside down with a knitting needle and brown on the other side, so that they close into hollow balls. Serve hot with sugar and jam to taste.

(From DANISH HOME BAKING, edited by Karen Berg, compiled by Kaj Viktor and Kirsten Hansen. Copyright 1957 by Høst & Søns Forlag. Reprinted by permission of Dover Publications, Inc.)

Norwegian Waffle Iron I:56

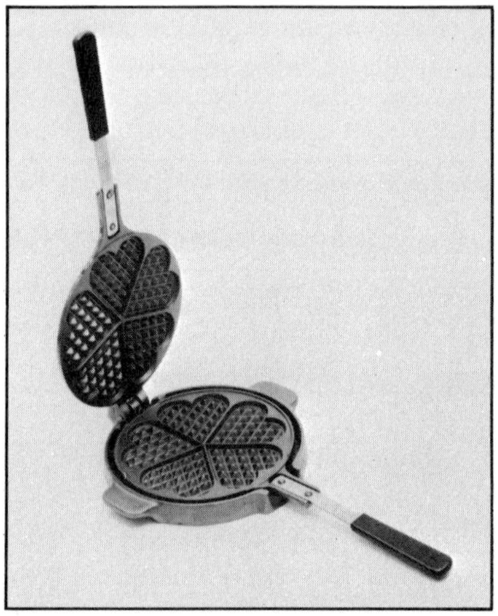

They are tender in design and texture, the crisp heart-shaped waffles that are eaten with cold lingonberries and fresh butter in Norway. This is the traditional equipment for making *fløtevafler.* You place the stand over a burner on top of the stove and rest the iron on it. Heat the iron until a drop of cold water on its surface sizzles, then pour ⅓ cup of ginger-flavored sour-cream batter into the center. Close the top, cook for five minutes, and then swivel the iron around to cook the waffle on the other side. This cast-iron pan is 7¾″ in diameter and contains five heart-shaped sections. A long bakelite handle contributes to its 17¼″ overall length. The cast-iron base has a socket at one side on which the ball hinge of the iron revolves when it is turned over. The accompanying base is 8½″ in diameter.

Eva Housewares, Inc. (200472) **$22.50**

Raspberry.

Electric Waffle Iron I:57

If the crowd around your breakfast table is so fond of Norwegian sour-cream waffles (*fløtevafler*) bathed in sweet butter and glistening with lingonberries, that it calls for encore after encore, you might want to cook them at the table itself rather than dash back and forth to the stove. And so without further ado, we present our chromed-steel electric *vaffeljern,* or waffle iron. The overall length of the iron is a compact 10″; it is 7½″ in diameter, and has two black plastic handles, three black plastic legs, and a black plastic handle on top. The electricity is supplied by a 36″-long detachable cord. Inside are two 7″-diameter surfaces of cast-iron waffle grooves in the traditional multi-heart shape. Both sides cook at once, of course, so the endless batches of waffles you'll be making won't take long at all.

Nor-Pro, Inc. (RR-11) $55.00

Norwegian Krumkake Iron I:58

Thin, sweet, golden cones filled with fruit, whipped cream or ice cream, *krumkaker* are traditional Norwegian Christmas cookies. To imprint *krumkaker* with their typical seasonal or floral patterns, use this cast-iron *krumkake* iron. The iron itself has two patterned plates hinged together; a ball joint at the hinge rests in the socket of a ring that holds the iron over a stove burner. To make the cookies, both sides of the iron are heated until sprinkled water sizzles on it. A teaspoon or so of the sweet—sometimes flavored with cardamom—batter is placed in the center of the iron. The top is lowered and the two sides squeezed together. Bake for a few minutes on both sides, remove the *krumkake* with a spatula. Then let it dry flat as a pancake or, as is more traditional, roll it into a cone. The cone can then be filled with a flavored cream, or stored in an air-tight container for future consumption. The *krumkake* iron is 6″ in diameter and the ring it sits in is 7″ in diameter with two rectangular extensions that act as handles. The two 6½″-long handles are covered for half their length with heat-resistant bakelite.

Eva Housewares, Inc. (200478) $19.00

"The little fair-haired boy slid down under the table and came up by the wall bench beside Simon's knee. 'May I look at that strange sheath you have there in your belt?' . . . It was the great silver mounted sheath to hold a spoon and two knives he had caught sight of . . . He put down the piece of bacon he was holding on the lap of Simon's festal doublet . . . , drew the knife from the sheath and looked closely at it. Then he took the knife Simon was eating with and the spoon and put them all in their places, so that he could see how it looked when all the things were in the sheath. He was exceeding grave and exceeding greasy."

Kristin Lavransdatter *by Sigrid Undset. Alfred A. Knopf, 1923.*

Electric Krumkake Iron I:59

The cornucopia-shaped cookies called *krumkaker* can be easily made in this electric iron. It is a heavy, well-made, compact appliance of chromed steel. The inside cast-iron *krumkake* plates have incised floral designs and produce 5¾″-diameter cookies. To make *krumkaker,* you need only drop a teaspoon of the egg, sugar, butter and flour batter inside; close the iron firmly and bake for a few minutes before removing the pliable cookie and rolling it into a cone. The iron has two heat-resistant bakelite handles, a plastic knob on top, three plastic legs, and comes with a 36″-long detachable cord.

Nor-Pro, Inc. (RR-111) $55.00

Krumkake Roller I:60

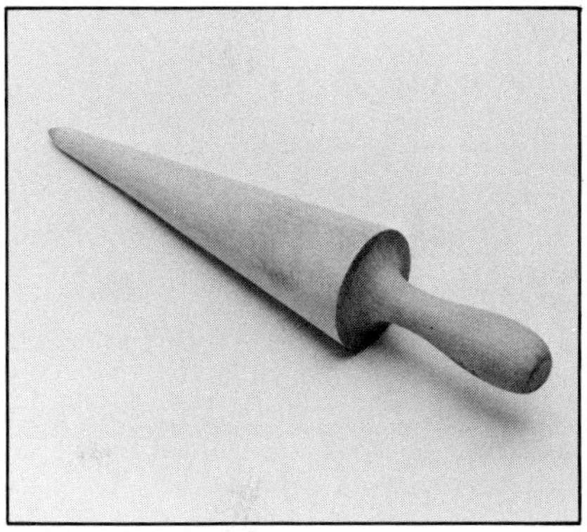

When the finished *krumkake* (thin, sweet Norwegian cookie) comes out of the *krumkake* iron, it will be a fragrant disc, brown at the edges and imprinted with whatever design was carved into the face of the iron. Then quickly, before it has time to cool, it should be rolled around a *krumkake* roller such as this one. Within a few minutes it will have cooled and hardened into a cone-shaped cookie, and it may be eaten just as it is, or filled with a generous spoonful of whipped cream. This 8″-long roller is made of pale unfinished wood, with a softly-curved handle and an end shaped like an elongated Christmas tree. Although it was designed for rolling Norwegian *krumkaker,* its shape is perfect for forming a similar confection called *fyllda strutar,* sweet Swedish pancake cookies rolled into a cone and filled with whipped cream and lingonberries.

Scandicrafts, Inc. (W27) $1.35

Norwegian Goro Iron I:61

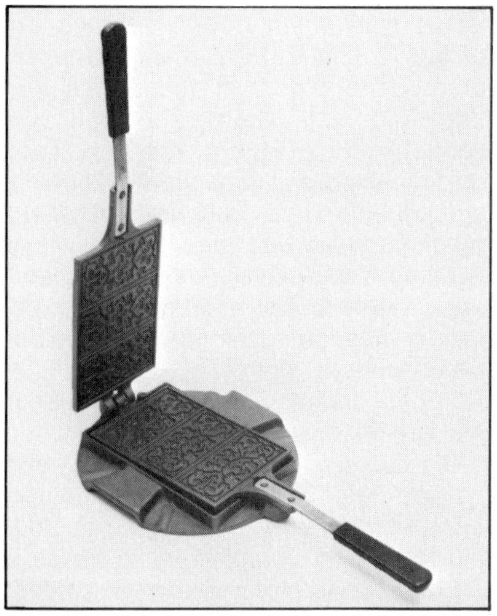

A *goro* is a unique Norwegian cookie made from a butter dough containing brandy and whipped cream. It is rolled out to fit into and bake in this iron, which consists of two 4⅝″-by-7″, cast-iron rectangular plates. They are hinged together at one end, and have 8″-long handles on the opposite end. Each handle has a 4½″-long finger-fitting ridged grip of heatproof bakelite. Each plate is subdivided on the inside into three smaller rectangles with stylized floral designs that will be transferred to the finished cookies when the dough is compressed between the plates. The iron rests in its niche in a circular cast-iron stand, which sits over a burner on top of the stove. The hinge fits into a socket in the stand. Roll out the dough and cut it into rectangles the size of the *goro* iron plate. Some Norwegians cut a paper pattern as a guide; but most, after years of experience, do this by eye. Lift the dough carefully and place it in the open, preheated but ungreased iron. Close the iron and bake until the cookie is golden around the edges; turn the iron in its stand (the ball end of the hinge will turn smoothly in the socket) and continue baking until done. Turn out and cut into individual *goros*.

Eva Housewares, Inc. (200476) **$16.95**

Rosette Iron Set I:62

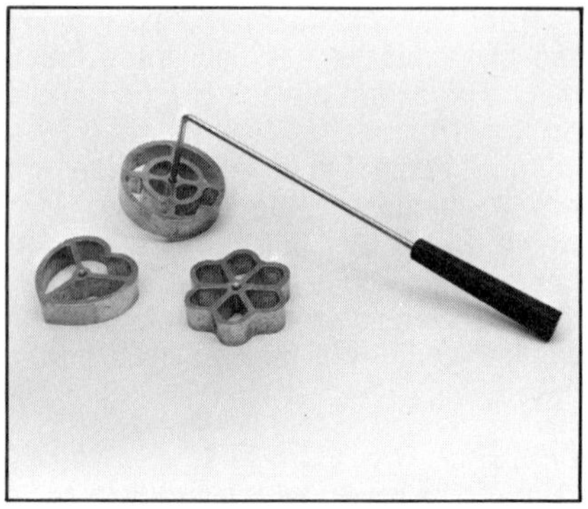

Rosettes are lacy, fried, Swedish pastries made from a light lemon-flavored batter. They can be formed and cooked with the devices in the set shown here, or those in a slightly larger version also available from this manufacturer. Each set consists of an L-shaped, tinned-steel wand with a threaded end, onto which fits any one of three forms. In this set, the wand is 11½″ long, and has a wooden handle. Each of the forms is of cast aluminum, about 3″ in diameter and ¾″ deep. (In the larger set, the forms are a full 4″ across and 1¼″ deep.) To make rosettes put 3″ of vegetable oil in a deep fryer and heat to 375 F. Attach the rosette form of your choice to the threaded end of the handle, and immerse it in oil for a moment. Lift it out, shake off the excess, drain it on a paper towel, and dip it into the batter, which will adhere to the oil-coated metal. Back into the oil again for a quick frying (2 to 3 minutes) until a crisp and delicately brown pastry has been made. Loosen the finished rosette with the tines of a fork, and repeat the dipping procedure until the batter is used up. Change forms for variety as you go, but remember the forms are red-hot! Only one of them can properly be called a rosette; another is a heart, and the third is a sectioned circle. Rosette-making is not as complicated as it sounds, and the boxes that hold the two sets have recipes. The pastries are quickly formed and, when cooled and dusted with confectioners' sugar, they are as quickly eaten.

Berarducci Brothers
Small (M-22) **$10.00**
Large (M-23) **$15.00**

Swedish Rosette Iron I:63

The delicate, fried Swedish cookies known as rosettes are, naturally enough, usually made in the form of rosettes. But this unusual rosette-iron set has two forms—neither a rose. Instead, a bold Lautrec-like butterfly or strong six-pointed star, each made of cast aluminum and each about 2½″ in size, is screwed onto the threaded end of an L-shaped tinned-steel wand. The form is dipped into hot oil, then batter, then oil again, and the finished pastry is even prettier and just as flaky-delicious as those in more traditional shapes.

Nyborg & Nelson, Inc. $2.95

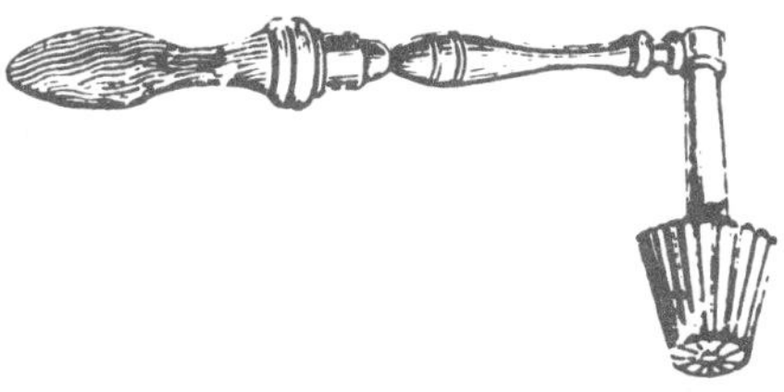

A "Bouche Iron"—from a catalogue of 1886—which resembles the rosette more than a little. Also called a patty iron, dariole mold or timbale iron.

Baking

It would not be wrong to consider Scandinavian baking—all baking, for that matter—as a form of preservation. What better way to insure that the freshly-picked grains of September will be edible come March than to grind them and bake them into bread? How better to slow the process of mortality when it comes to eggs or newly-churned butter than to bake them into cookies? In Finland, wheel-like loaves of sour rye bread are made in the fall, and are then strung on poles and kept in a cool room in readiness for late-winter appetites. And the Scandinavian fondness for crisp breads is explained by the fact that these retain their freshness better than egg-rich loaves like brioche. In Scandinavia, baking has been elevated, through necessity, to a high art.

Knobbed Rolling Pin I:64

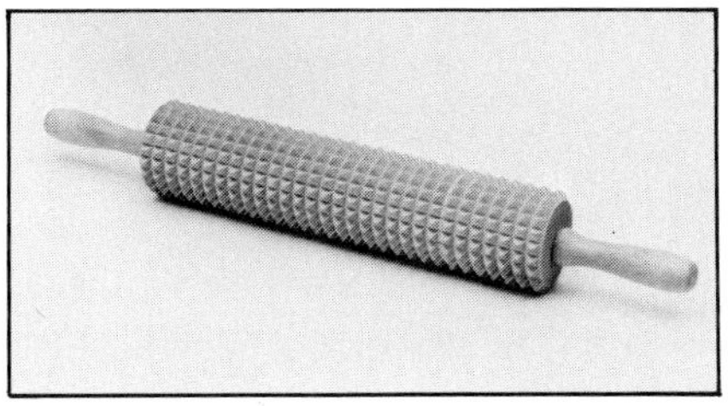

What looks surely to be a Viking instrument of death is actually a flatbread rolling pin. This 19″-long natural wood pin will leave the characteristic holes in rounds of crisp rye-flour flatbread. It can also be used to make *franska vafler* (French waffles), which are two oval-shaped wafers sandwiched around a butter cream filling. To make them, cut rolled out pastry dough into 3″ rounds; then take this rolling pin and roll in one direction only. The result is an oval of dough on which the pyramid knobs of the pin have been translated into indentations. Bake, then fill.

Nordiska $3.50

A Danish cookbook of 1637 gives the following procedure for making bread: "If you wish to have beautiful white bread, sprinkle water over your rye when it is fine and dry, and thereafter, first ascertaining that your feet be clean, trample it well in a bathtub, after which it may be ground. . . . When about to prepare your dough, examine well your flour, your water, your kneading-trough, your hands and nails, that all these be clean and decent in order that no hairs, threads or suchlike find their way into the dough. Be sure you add some leaven, for bread baked with leaven is always more healthy than the sweet kind, especially for the common man here in this country."

quoted in Take A Silver Dish *by Bodil Jensen. Høst & Søns Forlag, 1962.*

Flatbread Rolling Pin I:65

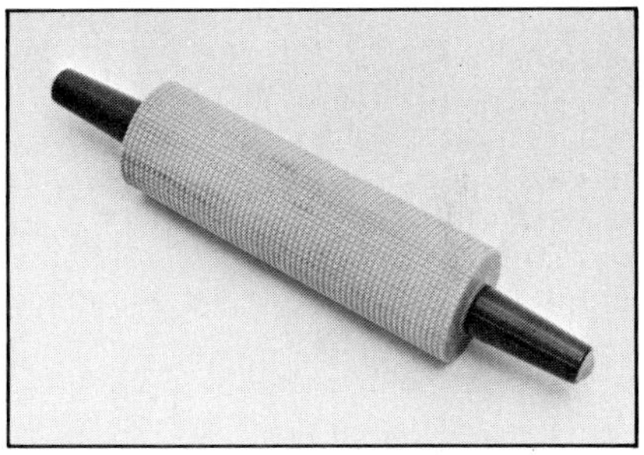

The surface of this flatbread rolling pin, double-cut to form small squares, leaves an interesting texture on cookies, pastries, or its traditional partner, flatbread. This parchment-thin crisp bread is made from mashed potatoes, salt, barley flour and water; the yellowish dough is rolled out into a huge, seemingly fragile circle, baked on the floor of an oven, then brushed off and hung on a rack to dry. Fresh, the bread tastes like a sour cloth napkin; dry, it is light, crisp and a perfect foil for the sweet tang of goat cheese or the concentrated flavor of *fenalår* (Norwegian dried, salted, smoked mutton). The tool to accompish this feat is this beautifully-balanced heavy, hard, sugar maple pin with revolving handles. Its rolling surface is 10″ long; the handles are each 3¼″ long and the diameter is 3″. To clean the pin, use a stiff bristle brush—no water.

Maid of Scandinavia Co. (12505) $5.85

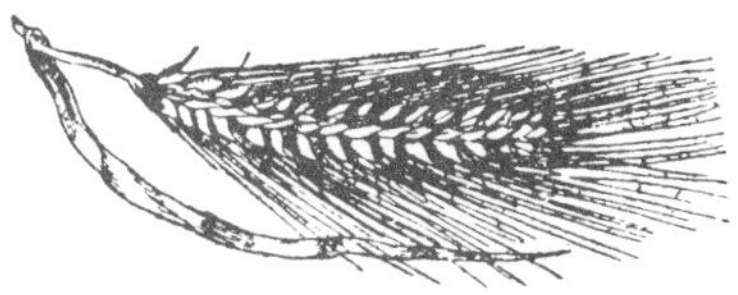

Lefse Rolling Pin I:66

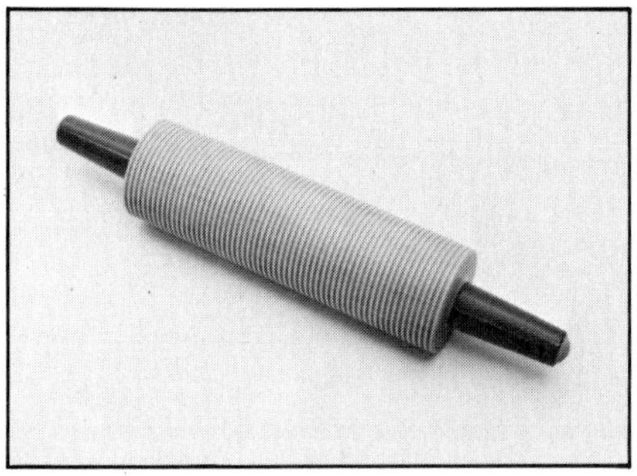

This heavy, free-rolling sugar-maple pin is deeply ridged for rolling out *lefser,* thin saucer-shaped breads made of potatoes, cooked on an ungreased griddle and generally eaten buttered, sugared and folded up like a handkerchief. The die-cut ridges offer interesting options in design for cookies as well as *lefser:* roll your dough one way for a ridged effect, roll it across at right angles for squares, or on the diagonal twice for a diamond pattern. The rolling surface is 10″ long, and the handles are painted red. The pin should always be kept dry and cleaned only with a stiff-bristle brush.

Scandicrafts, Inc. $5.50
(WRC1)

Lefse Turning Stick I:67

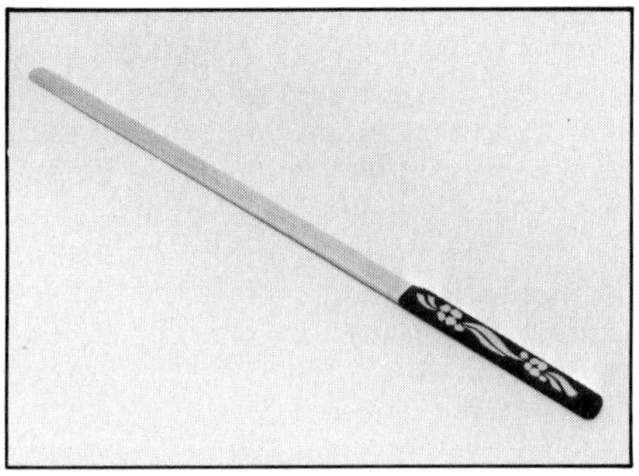

Lefser are quickbreads somewhere in the overlapping area of scone, potato bread and pancake: they are made from a dough of mashed potatoes and rye flour, which is rolled out into pie-sized circles. The discs of dough are put on an ungreased griddle, where they are flipped constantly with a *lefse* turner: surely one of the most arcane pieces of equipment we offer, but one whose proper mastery assures that the finished *lefser* will be sufficiently crisp. So here is a *lefse* turner, an unmarked yardstick 24″ long, thin enough at its turning end to slip deftly under the cooking *lefser.* A thicker, blue-painted handle at the other end is decorated with yellow flowers. There is a hole in the handle for hanging and—what can we say?—if you're going to make *lefser,* then you had better have a *lefse* turner.

Maid of Scandinavia Co. $1.50
(99635)

POTATO LEFSE

3 medium potatoes
2–3 cups water
¼ cup cream
½ teaspoon salt
1½ tablespoons butter
1–1½ cups flour, approximately

Boil the potatoes in the water until tender but not mushy. Drain and mash or put through a food mill. Beat in the cream, salt and butter while potatoes are still hot. Blend in enough flour to form a smooth, soft, but workable dough and allow to cool.

Divide the dough into balls and roll out (with a ridged *lefse* rolling pin, if available) into very thin, round sheets. Bake the *lefse* on a hot, ungreased griddle, turning frequently with a long spatula or *lefse* turning stick, until cooked through.

Lefse may be eaten immediately—buttered and folded into quarters while still warm and soft, or it may be cooled until quite crisp and stored in tins.

Pastry Jagger I:68

This small pastry jagger is a well-made, useful gadget for cutting out as well as marking dough. The ridged stainless-steel blade is perfect for making decorative lattice strips for succulent Finnish meat or giant blueberry pies, or for cutting out new shapes to augment the myriad circles, stars and twists of the Scandinavian cookie jar. The jagger's overall length is 6½″, with a 3½″-long stained beechwood handle. The cutting wheel is 1⅜″ in diameter.

Nor-Pro, Inc. $2.00
(SVE 3115)

Krokane Form I:69

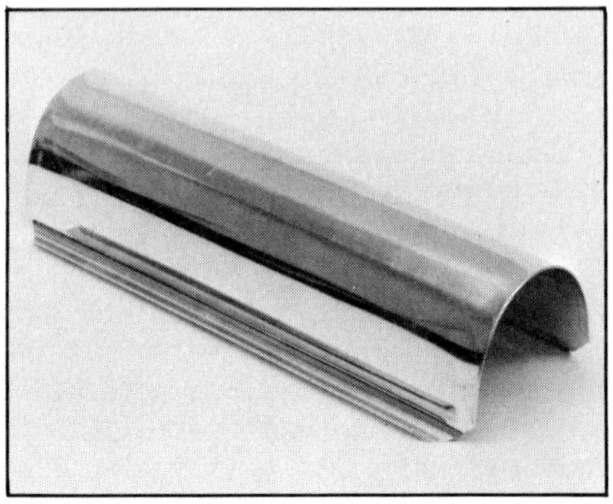

Pastries may be formed by molding as well as cutting, and plenty of Scandinavian cookies are shaped by draping them over a rolling pin or broom-handle when they are taken, still warm and pliable, from the oven. This *krokane* form, a kind of tunnel-like pastry sheet, eliminates a step and allows you to bake the curve right into the cookies. The dough is cut into inch-wide strips with a pastry jagger, and the strips are then laid on the tinned-steel form and baked. Shaped like half of a 3½″-diameter tube, the form is 12¾″ long. The form comes with several recipes for *krokaner.*

Maid of Scandinavia Co. $2.15
(63592)

KROKANER

2 cups (7 ounces) sifted all-purpose flour
¼ cup sugar
1 teaspoon baking powder
Pinch salt
¾ cup (1½ sticks) cold butter, cut into ½″ bits
1 egg
3 tablespoons cold milk
1 teaspoon almond extract
1 cup confectioners' sugar
2 tablespoons water (approximately)
Colored sugar

Combine the flour, sugar, baking

powder and salt and stir together to distribute the ingredients evenly. Cut in the butter until the mixture is mealy in texture, as you would for making a pastry dough.

Beat the egg, milk and almond extract together and add to the flour/butter combination. Rapidly mix together with a fork, blending just enough to incorporate all the flour—be careful not to overwork. Form into a ball, sprinkle with a little flour, wrap in plastic and refrigerate until well chilled, about 2 hours.

Preheat oven to 350 F.

Roll dough into a large rectangle on a floured pastry cloth or between two pieces of wax paper, to a thickness of ⅛″. Use as little flour as possible in rolling for best results—too much flour produces a tough cookie.

Using a pastry jagger or a sharp knife, cut the sheet of dough into strips approximately 1″ wide and 6″ long. Place the strips over a *krokaner* form and bake until lightly browned, about 8 minutes. Remove from form and allow to cool on a rack.

Combine the confectioners' sugar and water to form a thin icing, and frost the *krokaner* once they have cooled. Sprinkle with the colored sugar before the icing hardens.

Yield: approximately 3 dozen.

Muffin Tins I:70

A set of four aluminum cups that look like blunted thimbles is perfect for the Swedish specialty *appelformar,* or apple muffins. "Muffin" is perhaps misleading: the little pastries made in these forms are delicate shells of dough, thinly rolled and pressed into the cups, then filled with chopped apples and apricot preserves, topped with slivered almonds, and sealed with a circle of dough. Four apple muffins are never enough! You will certainly want more than one set. Each 1¼″-deep cup is pressed out of a single piece of medium-weight aluminum, and has rolled edges. The cups rest on a flat, stable, 1⅝″-diameter bottom; the sides gently flare to 2⅛″ in diameter across the top.

Scandicrafts, Inc. (A221P) $1.50

Heart-Shaped Tartlet Molds I:71

A large and generous heart: here are three heart-shaped tartlet molds fashioned of a medium-weight aluminum with reasonably rigid shapes. Press pastry into one of these molds and then run a rolling pin over the top to cut off the excess. If you fill the pastry shells with cream and cherries, or with chocolate mousse or almond paste, they will unmold easily, and each one provides a decent-sized dessert serving. They are 3″ across at their widest point.

Scandicrafts, Inc. (A180P) $1.40

Swedish Sandbakkelse Set I:72

Thirty-six miniature *sandbakkelse* (almond-flavored sandtarts) tins from Sweden, made into different shapes: small and large circles, short and long oblongs, diamonds and hearts. To make *sandbakkelser,* press small balls of almond tart dough into the molds, making it quite thin on the bottom and sides. Place all the molds on a cookie sheet and place in the oven. When the tart shells are cool, fill them with any sweet custard. The molds are all deeply scalloped, all about ¾″ deep, all made of a lightweight tinned steel that will heat up in no time at all to rapidly cook the miniature bits of dough within. They come boxed with their own recipe for almond tarts.

Scandicrafts, Inc. (B212) $3.00

Norwegian Kransekake Forms I:73

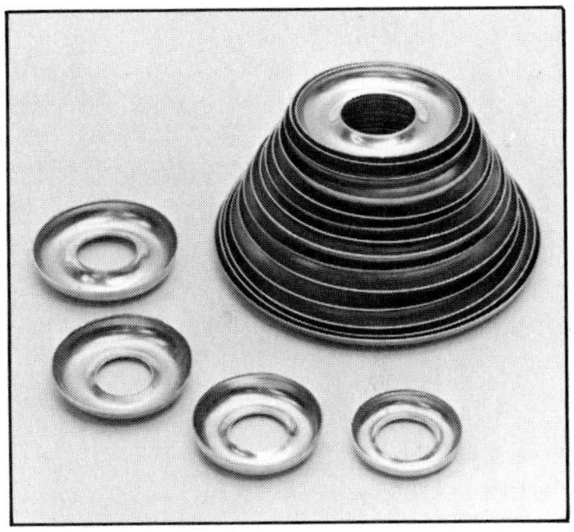

The pride of Norwegian and Danish weddings and other festivities is the *kransekake* ("wreath cake"), 16 and more rings high. Although Scandinavians most frequently buy this towering —sometimes 2½ feet tall—confection in bakeries, it is merely (if we can use such a word to describe this treat) concentric rings of almond pastry, with zig-zag pipings of white sugar icing all around. Our set's 18 aluminum rings range in diameter from the top-of-the-tower 2½″, to the 8″ base. You'll surely be the only kid on the block with *this* birthday cake!

Nor-Pro, Inc. (HO-050) $25.00

"There was a knocking at my door; it was the grandmother . . . with a whole plate full of spice-nuts [gingerbread cookies]. 'I bake the best in

Continued from preceding page

Dalecarlia . . . but they are of the old fashion . . . You cut out so well sir, [Andersen had previously exhibited his découpage skill, cutting out paper minarets for a child of the house] should you not be able to cut me out some new fashions?'

And I sat the whole of Midsummer Night, and clipped fashions for spice-nuts. Nutcrackers with knight's boots; windmills . . . and ballet-dancers that pointed with one leg toward the seven stars. Grandmother got them, but she turned the ballet-dancers up and down; the legs went too high for her; she thought they had one leg and three arms."

Pictures of Travel *by Hans Christian Andersen, 1871.*

Round Cookie Cutters I:74

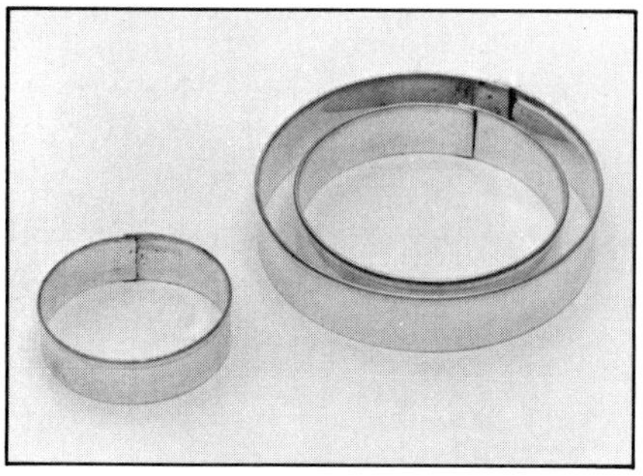

Here are three round cutters in graduated sizes: 4″, 3″ and 2″ in diameter. Round cookie cutters play an active role throughout Scandinavia, and a rather unusual one in Denmark: many Danish cakes are baked first and *then* cut to size with a cutter. For example, to make party cakes called *romtoppe,* small rounds are cut out of a large sheet of thin, crisp cooked cake (like the French *génoise*) and topped with rum-flavored butter cream and then white icing. Each of our cutters is made from a sturdy three-quarter-inch tinned-steel band with a rolled top rim, a sharp blade opposite, and roughly soldered seams. They are exceptionally rigid in construction—unusual in cutters that do not have a cross-bar —and come with a recipe for ginger cookies.

Nordiska $2.00

Heart-Shaped Cookie Cutters I:75

Here are three heart-shaped cookie cutters in graduated sizes to make a vaguely sweet, old-fashioned Scandinavian cookie called *mormors hjerter,* or grandmother's hearts. The cookie dough—somewhat like a sweetened pie dough—is rolled out, cut into heart shapes, placed on a cookie sheet and sprinkled with cinnamon. Both the title of the cookie and its recipe lead us to believe that this is what the original Scandinavian grandmother did with pie dough scraps to keep her grandchildren quiet. The cutters are made of strips of rigid tinned steel that have been roughly soldered at the seams. One edge is folded over, while the other is left sharp for cutting. They vary in size from 4″, measured from auricle to ventricle, down to 2″.

Nordiska $2.00

Swedish Horse Cookie Cutter I:76

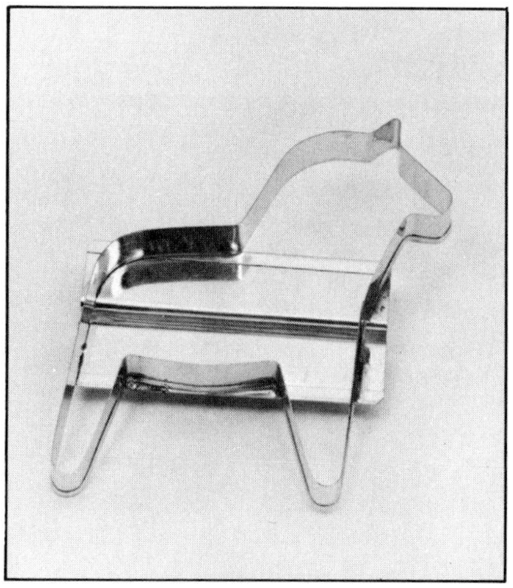

This large tinned-steel cutter for gingerbread Christmas cookies is shaped like the Dala horse, a toy figure carved in olden days on the farm to amuse children. Wooden ones are still to be found—in fact, the Dala horse has become almost a national figure. This cutter has an easy-to-grip 5⅛″ bar across the top, and forms a cookie 6¾″ by 4½″. After baking, ice the cookie in orange and white or other bright colors to duplicate the harness and saddle of the horse.

Maid of Scandinavia Co. $2.45
(98590)

Swedish Fattigmann Cutter I:77

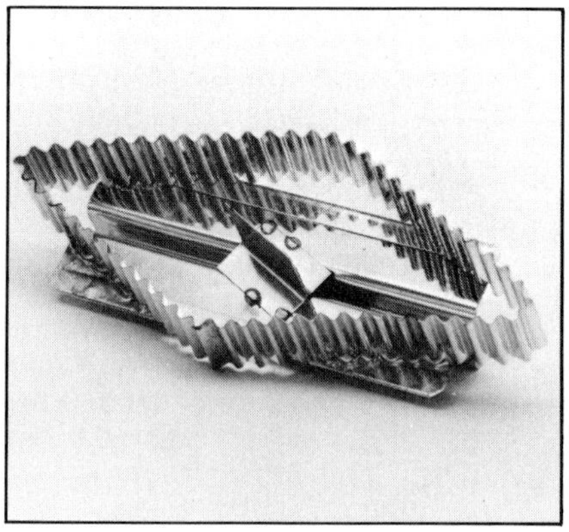

Like our own "poor boy" sandwiches, the Swedish *fattigmann,* or "poor man," biscuit gives a lie to its name with its opulent ingredients: perhaps we are meant to infer that this is what a poor boy dreams about eating. It is a fried cookie made of eggs, cream, flour and cardamom; the dough is rolled out, cut, twisted into shape and fried. Our cutter is a long, fluted-edged diamond with a 1″-long straight-edged blade in the middle. The cutter cuts out the basic diamond pastry shape at the same time the small blade cuts a slit in the middle of the pastry. One end of the diamond is pulled through the slit, forming a pretty bow-knot. Then into the deep-frying kettle it goes, until it is crisply brown and ready to be sprinkled with powdered sugar. The cutter comes both 5″ (shown here) and 6″ in length, and it has an easily-grasped, bent, tinned-steel handle that runs the length of the device.

Maid of Scandinavia Co. $1.15
(71641)

Cookie Press I:78

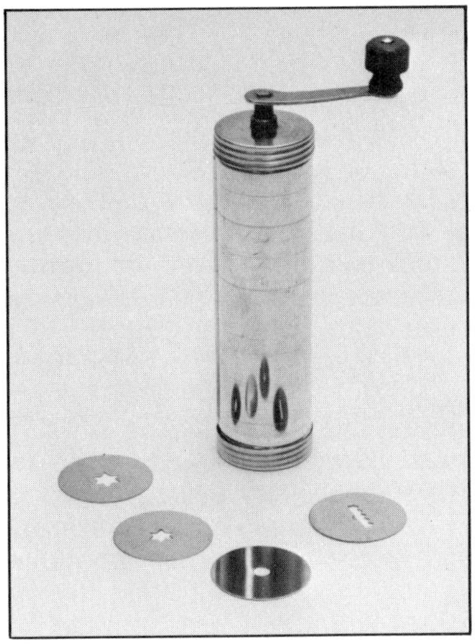

Here is a Swedish device for making fanciful, festive shapes out of plain old cookie dough. It is made of an elongated tinned-steel cylinder. At one end there are four interchangeable discs with cut-out tinned-steel shapes—two stars, a circle and a ridged bar—and a threaded cap to hold the discs in place. At the other end there is another threaded cap through which a heavy, threaded steel rod fits. On one end of the rod (inside the machine) is a flat, disc-shaped press; on the other end, a crank handle. Turn the handle, and the press moves down the cylinder, forcing dough out through the hole in the other end and onto a baking sheet. The cylinder is just under 7″ long and just under 2″ in diameter. The handle is about 3″ long and ends in a slickly-painted red wooden knob.

Nyborg & Nelson/ H. A. Mack & Co., Inc. $5.00

"The mother . . . said: 'With less than eighteen reindeer we shall never win through.' 'Think you we shall need so many?' said her daughter absently. 'Aye, for we must have game to serve up with the pork each day,' answered Ragnfrid. 'And of wild fowl and hare we shall scarce have more than will serve for the table in the upper hall. Remember 'twill be well on toward two hundred people we shall have on the place—counting serving folk and children and the poor that have to be fed.

And even should you and Erlend set forth on the fifth day, some of the guests I trow, will stay out the week at least.' "

Wedding preparation in fourteenth-century Scandinavia from Kristin Lavransdatter *by Sigrid Undset. Alfred A. Knopf, 1923.*

Cookie Machine I:79

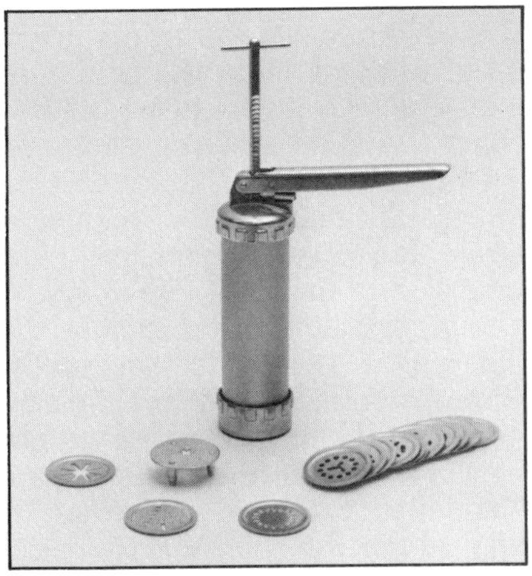

Here is a modern version of the crank-operated cookie press, a golden aluminum cylinder with aluminum caps top and bottom. There are 22 aluminum discs with differently-shaped patterns cut out of them; the discs fit into the bottom end of the cylinder, while a jack-like mechanism works at the other end. Inside the cylinder there is a press that forces dough out through the holes in the discs at the insistent pressure of the jack at the other end. There is a device that allows you to control the amount of dough in each squeeze of the machine and, thus, the size of the finished cookie. The cylinder is 6½″ long and the jack handle 6″ long. An informative booklet comes with the machine, suggesting recipes and designs for cookies, and recommending that you use it not only for cookies but also for making decorative designs in mashed potatoes and whipped cream, shaping meatballs, filling pastries and creating butter curls.

Nor-Pro, Inc. (SAW71) $13.95

Aquavit Glass I:80

So that no one need ever drink alone, the Scandinavians have invented the custom of skoaling: a raised thimbleful of icy aquavit, a courteous nod of the head between two friends, and the aquavit is drained in one practiced gulp. Then another glass is drained, just as steadily. That is the basic pattern, one that grows both steadier and more hilarious as the evening wears on. This is the classic shape for an aquavit glass: a lovely flute 5″ tall, made here of crystal, its

Continued from preceding page

stem displaying a pattern of intertwined strands. But remember: no Dane, no Swede, no Norwegian would think of owning only one aquavit glass. Cordiality demands that there always be two partaking of the "water of life."

Holmegaard of Copenhagen, Inc. (311-16-06) **$6.50**

Klukflaske I:81

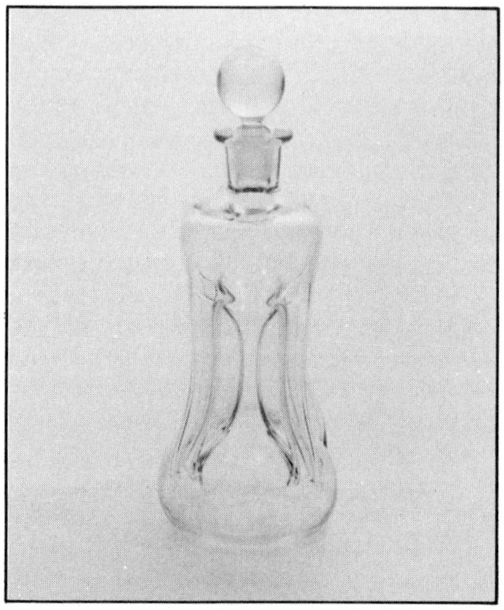

If you want to add a convivial sound to the skoaling ceremony, pour the aquavit from this *klukflaske.* But first you have to learn to say it correctly: *kloog,* with a dropped voice, a lowered chin, and an onomatopoetic "glug" in the back of your throat. Tip the bottle and pour out the liquor; then, when you return it to an upright position, you will be rewarded with a cordial "glug, glug" from the air trapped in the bottle. The flask is an attractive shape, made of five separate sluiceways that are joined at the top and bottom of the bottle. There is a spherical stopper that fits into the neck. It comes in five sizes ranging from a miniature 1/16 liter (2 ounces) up to ¾ liter (25 ounces); we show you the half-liter size (approximately ½ quart), which stands 10¾″ high and has a base that is 4″ in diameter. It comes in clear glass or in delicate shades of gray, blue or green.

Holmegaard of Copenhagen, Inc. **$21.00**

An English Kitchen

by Rona Deme

I have lived in the same New York City neighborhood for thirty years now, but I was born on my Granny's dairy farm in Cheshire, England, and my style of cooking will always be based on what I learned on that farm. It was a simple kind of cooking, using our own fresh produce, cream, eggs and butter. We took so many things for granted then: it never occurred to me that there were families who didn't have freshly-churned butter on the table every day, with the imprint of a cow on every pat; that there were children who didn't eat cheese made from the milk of their very own cows.

We children used to make spending money by gathering cowslips in season so that Grandpa could make cowslip wine. Although we counted ourselves fortunate to receive sixpence for a huge bunch of cowslips, we were never allowed to taste the wine. In other seasons we hunted out huge wild mushrooms—horse mushrooms, we called them—for Granny to use in making mushroom ketchup. Or else we gathered walnuts to be made into pickled walnuts. Every summer we would peddle miles over the hills on our bicycles to gather windberries for pies; and at jamming time we picked huge quantities of plums from the damsom trees and gave them to our mother, who would boil them into jam in a big heavy pot that sat over the kitchen coal fire.

There has never in my life been anything to equal the smells that used to come from that kitchen. The kitchen was the center of the household. And the heart of the kitchen was the old, black-iron coal stove, with its steel edges that were polished until they shone like silver. In its middle there was the coal or coke fire, with a grate that opened in the front for stoking. We children used to sit in front of the grate, holding crumpets up to toast on the end of long brass forks. On one side of the fire there was an oven with a heavy iron door, and on the other side was the heater that produced hot water for the whole household. Across the top of the stove there was a rack for airing clothes; on many a winter morning I would hang my stockings there to warm them up before I pulled them on.

The rest of the kitchen was simplicity itself. There was a big, old-fashioned mahogany table on which all of the cooking and a lot of the rest of the family activity used to take place. My mother did her ironing at one end of the table while I did my homework on the other end. When baking she would put down a clean white cloth, flour it, and use it for rolling out pastry. A slate pastry slab stood out in the pantry, but it was often uncomfortably cold in that unheated room, which was the nearest thing we had to a refrigerator. We didn't have a proper refrigerator at all, just this cold room with stone floors and oak shelves that held plates of cheese, and crocks full of perishable items like mincemeat, and barrels of apples, and a big white enamel can with a lid in which we stored bread. I remember a special bread called "oven-bottom bread" that was baked on the bottom of the oven until it was quite dark and then was packed away in the can for a week; the tradition was that it tasted better the second week after it was made.

I suppose that we were very poor, but I didn't know it at the time. How could we be poor when we had all that we wanted of farm eggs, of fresh milk and butter and cheese, and good brown loaves of bread? How could we feel poor when we spread golden syrup on our bread or went off to school with pork pies in our pockets? My mother cooked all of this good food using only the simplest tools.

Sometimes these days, when I am beating up lemon curd or cream with my electric mixer, I think back and remember my mother beating whipped cream with only a fork. Or, when I see my son Peter forming pie shells in a gigantic machine (made in Scotland just for that purpose), I remember how we used to shape a pastry shell in the old days by pressing it around the bottom of a two-pound glass jar. My mother used to roll out pastry with a glass bottle filled with water to weigh it down; now I realize how the cold water must have helped her when she handled fragile pie crusts. Of course, we had plenty of old skillets and saucepans made mostly of heavy enamelware, and some rather deep cake tins that we never washed, but rather wiped before and after each use with a bit of greased paper. And we had heavy crockery pudding basins in different sizes.

Since that time a lot has happened to me. I married an American GI and came to live with him in this country. For many years I worked with him in a butcher shop where I made, if you please, Hungarian hams and sausages according to the traditions of his family. All that time the old recipes that I had learned on the farm were within me, waiting for the right moment to emerge.

A few years ago I opened a shop called "The Country Host" where I sold a bit of cheese and some tins of tea. Then one day I decided to make some raisin scones. They were gone in an hour, and my customers asked me to make more; that was the beginning of a new career for me. I kept adding more and more of the old foods to the stock of the store, making simple English dishes according to the old farm methods. Now I have a staff of six, and sometimes we cater rather grand parties, but we still follow the simple recipes I learned in my childhood.

We take a great deal of pride in our shop, using brown farm eggs and sweet butter for baking, making our own English "banger" sausages, and steak-and-kidney pies and traditional wedding cakes of fruitcake covered with marzipan and Royal icing. If you could see my kitchen in the back of the shop you would be surprised, however, because it isn't a professional kitchen at all, just a small room designed by my sons with huge bins of flour and sugar and lots of wooden cabinets. I have a long wooden table where I do all the cooking, just as my mother did on her old table. I have an ordinary household stove that is, however, a far cry from her coal fire. My granny wouldn't know what to say about my mixers and freezers and the sausage-stuffing machine; but I know that she would feel perfectly comfortable with the food that comes from the kitchen. She would see that it is the same honest country food that I learned to make in her house. If the edge of a crust or the shape of a loaf isn't perfect, then all the better: it shows that they weren't machine-made. I take pride in the fact that when an apple pie comes from my oven, it has my own thumbprints around the edges.

A GUIDE FOR EATING IN ENGLAND: *"Hints for Etiquette; or Dining Out Made Easy*

As caterers for the public taste, we can conscientiously recommend this book to all diners-out who are perfectly unacquainted with the usages of society. However, we may regret that our author has confined himself to warning rather than advice, we are bound in justice to say that nothing here stated will be found to contradict the habits of the best circles. The following examples exhibit a depth of penetration and a fullness of experience rarely met with:

1. *In proceeding to the dining-room, the gentleman gives one arm to the lady he escorts—it is unusual to offer both.*
2. *The practice of taking soup with the next gentleman but one is now wisely discontinued; but the custom of asking your host his opinion of the weather immediately on the removal of the first course still prevails.*
3. *To use a fork with your soup, intimating at the same time to your hostess that you are reserving the spoon for the beefsteaks, is a practice wholly exploded.*
4. *On meat being placed before you, there is no possible objection to your eating it, if so disposed; still, in all such delicate cases, be guided entirely by the conduct of those around you.*
5. *It is always allowable to ask for artichoke jelly with your boiled venison; however there are houses where this is not supplied.*
6. *The method of helping roast turkey with two carving-forks is practicable, but deficient in grace.*
7. *We do not recommend the practice of eating cheese with a knife and fork in one hand, and a spoon and wine-glass in the other; there is a kind of awkwardness in the action which no amount of practice can entirely dispel.*
8. *As a general rule, do not kick the shins of the opposite gentlemen under the table, if personally unacquainted with him; your pleasantry is liable to be misunderstood —a circumstance at all times unpleasant.*
9. *Proposing the health of a boy in*

Continued from preceding page

buttons immediately on the removal of the cloth is a custom springing from regard to his tender years, rather than from a strict adherence to the rules of etiquette."

Lewis Carroll 1849.

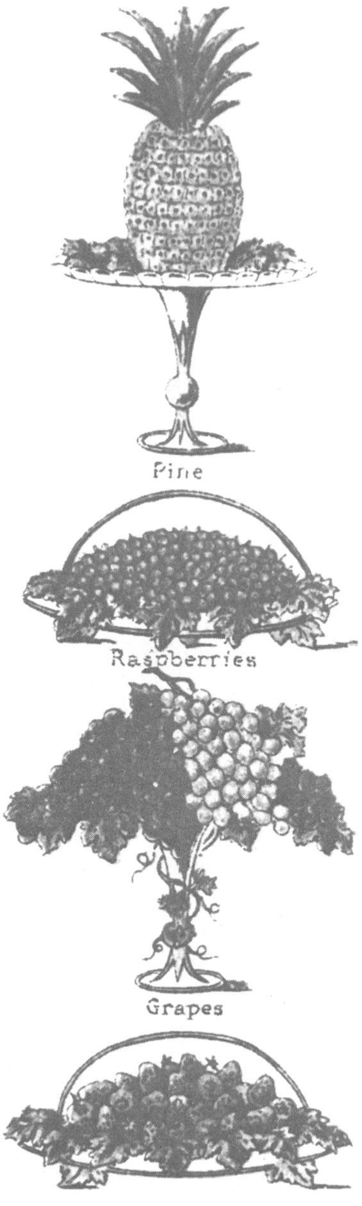

Dessert possibilities, according to the 1909 edition of Beeton's Book of Household Management.

The Cuisine of the British Isles

Still in the northern reaches of Europe, we move westward across the Channel. An English innkeeper, incensed because his hotel had been given a low rating in the *Guide Michelin,* leaned over our table and protested: "What do the French know about our kind of cooking, anyway? They don't understand vegetables. And there's not a Frenchman alive who knows anything about sweets."

Heresy, perhaps, but worth considering. We agree that it isn't fair to judge English cooking as though it were, somehow, French cooking *manqué*. The English kitchen has traditions and character of its own, and at its best it can be superb. There is no scarcity of good things to eat in Britain. We remember with pleasure the inn where we were served seven different vegetables along with our veal chop, every one garden-fresh, each crisper than the next, all delectably cooked to a point which can only be described as *al dente*. And we remember the scones and oatcakes for tea in a small town in Scotland; Wensleydale and Lancashire cheeses, often served with butter and sweet biscuits; gooseberry jam and tart marmalade at breakfast; meat pies in the pocket on an afternoon's walk in the Lake District.

Yet no one would deny that something went wrong somewhere; that there is, in England, a greater disparity between good eating and the common diet than there is anywhere else in the world. Not in calories, mind you, or in nutrition, but in taste. In America we are justifiably sensitive to the horrors we have performed on our superb natural ingredients: the difference between a hamburger broiled over hot coals, served on a toasted English muffin and its fast-food facsimile; the gulf between a Maine lobster served with sweet melted butter and a commercial fried fish-stick sandwich. Yet despite our passion for culinary self-abasement, we will have to admit that even commercial American food is better than the worst English food.

What's it all about? Why is the common commercial diet in England so bad in a country that is, after all, just a generation or two away from the fragrant Edwardian kitchen of Mrs. Bridges? There were the wars, of course, and socialism: but France had the wars, and Sweden has socialism, without suffering similarly devastating effects on their cooking. It probably stems from two factors, both indigenous to English society. The first is the destruction of the agricultural tradition that took place with industrialization. Peasant food is wonderful in Spain, in Norway and, God knows, in France. But in England there is no longer a distinct peasant style of cooking: some time in the 19th century it became a factory-worker's cooking. Industrialization came to Great Britain so long before it came to the rest of the world, that agriculture-based cooking has largely disappeared.

The second thing we should know about the quality of English cooking is that there is a wide gap between publically available cooking and home cooking. Just as there is no comparison between the public face of an English gentlemen and his behavior when he is with his friends, so is there a similar lack of continuity between public and private food. In English homes—and especially in country homes—you can still be served some of the great dishes of Elizabethan and Edwardian cookery.

Don't be fooled by their French names, by the way: they are English inventions called by French names for swank. *Crème brulée* was supposedly invented in Edwardian England as "burnt cream" and then given a French baptism for the sake of elegance. Fools, on the other hand, are desserts made of purëed berries and heavy cream or custard or both. Although the casual etymologist would guess that their name stemmed from their silliness and inconsequence, it comes, in fact, from "fouler" the French verb that means "to crush." Still and all, it is English in origin.

It is in Scotland that the French influence on cooking is strongest. There you find a soup called La Reine after guess-which-queen, and cakes called petticoat tails, by common agreement a linguistic distortion of *petits gâteaux* or "little cakes." Scots food is probably some of the best in the British Isles (although this would probably be hotly disputed by non-Scotsmen), not because of the French influence, but because of the sensitive use of native produce: salmon fresh-caught from a cold stream, smoked haddock, bitter-lemon marmalade, shortbread and scones; and, of course, all the possible variations on oatmeal, from the simple bowl of porridge through bannocks and oatcakes—and finally, that heavenly beverage, *atholl brose,* half dessert and half tipple, made of oatmeal, cream, honey and good Scotch whisky.

Irish food is simpler, more solid, less elegant; its virtues are easily grasped and loved. While the Irish diet depends heavily on potatoes (which, by the way, are not indigenous, but were imported from Peru in the 17th century) in the form of potato cakes and potato scones and that blissful blend of mashed potatoes and green onions known as *champ,* it sings with many other country flavors. In Ireland you eat steaming lamb stew, pots of cabbage and bacon, and soda bread, made in the fireplace in a covered iron pot and then served hot and crisp-crusted with melting sweet butter.

Finally, there is England, where the best cooking is of ancient tradition, and full of regional specialties. Game is abundant, and so are the famous legs of mutton—roasted, with mint sauce; or boiled, with caper sauce—and roast sirloins of beef. But on simpler menus there are shepherd's pie, made with ground beef and mashed potatoes, pease pudding and dumplings, the Cockney accompaniment to boiled beef, and such simple pleasures as devilled beef bones and Cornish pasties. Returned Colonials nostalgically eat their kedgeree at breakfast, mulligatawny soup and curry at dinner, while the working classes enjoy that original carry-out food—the first food born of the Industrial Revolution—every time they buy twisted newspaper cones full of crisply fried fish and chips.

There is certainly no lack of good things to eat in Britain, but it is the beverages that truly lift one's spirits. The British are great wine-drinkers, and there are few good restaurants in England or Scotland where you will not see a bottle of wine on every table. Sherry is more English than Spanish, despite its country of origin. And what of the *vins du pays:* ale and stout, Irish and Scotch whiskies and delicately-flavored gins? Or the true *vin du pays,* the cup of tea, strong and laced with milk and sugar, or milder, China tea, with a slice of lemon?

Only someone who has lived in a country where winter twilight comes early can appreciate the extraordinary solace that teatime affords to the English. It is four o'clock and getting dark. The wind is howling outside; a fine drizzle is beginning. But within, all is *luxe, calme* and *volupté,* the fire in the hearth reflecting off the teapot and the sound of the kettle indicating that another pot is about to be brewed. On the table are scones and walnut cake, toast and jam. Tea provides a moment of cheer and calories at the time of day when they are most needed on that dark and wind-blown island.

Mortar and Pestle I:82

This very traditional English mortar and pestle uses a technique for processing food that is centuries old. And the simple design is as beautiful as it is functional. They are perfect for crushing any herbs or spices you might need; juniper berries to cook with game, or coriander seeds for one of the curry sauces the English have adopted as their own. The mortar is 5¾″ across the top with a generous lip for pouring and is made of a creamy beige unglazed stoneware. Its rough surface is more effective for grinding than either the marble or the glazed china of which mortars are sometimes made. The 8″-long pestle's sturdy, rounded grinding end is made of the same stoneware, and has an elegantly tapered 5¼″-long, wooden handle. The bottom of the mortar is incised with with the word "Acid-proof," which leads us to believe that this was designed for laboratory use and will most certainly withstand the rigors of the average kitchen.

Bloomingdale's/ H. A. Mack & Co., Inc. (3) $15.00

Scottish oatcakes, called bannocks, were like pancakes, and like them, they came in many forms; they were usually "fired on a girdle (griddle)", but were sometimes rebaked or toasted on a fire. There were bannocks carried by midwives called "cryin' bannocks," "teethin' bannocks" served for children cutting teeth, and salted bannocks to be eaten by maidens on Halloween who wished to have visions of their future husbands. All of which leads

Continued from preceding page

one to believe that they were none too tender.

Scottish Spurtle I:83

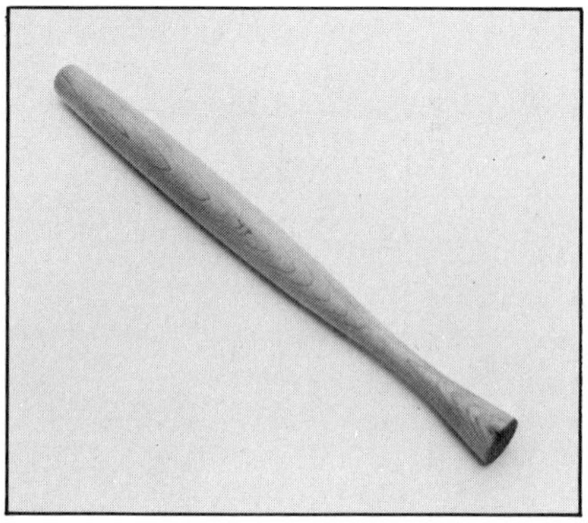

Not a baseball bat, but a traditional Scottish stirring utensil. Originally it was a "porridge stick" in the days when oatmeal was cooked overnight in huge black pots that hung inside the fireplace. This was before oatmeal became the processed variety we use today and it needed endless stirring during the long hours of cooking to insure that there would be no lumps. Often a father or son would carve the end of the family spurtle into some traditional emblem like the Scottish thistle. Though the spurtle is ideal for making oatmeal you can also use it to stir anything you like from soup and mashed potatoes to grits and custard. Our spurtle is 12½" long with a flared handle, about an inch wide at its broadest, and was made in Vermont by a transplanted Scotsman.

The Store at Sugarbush Village $2.00

"Scottish oatcakes are traditionally baked with implements devised expressly for their manufacture: the spurtle, *used to stir the porridge mixture; the* bannock stick, *a rolling pin that makes a criss-cross pattern on one side; the* spathe, *a heart-shaped iron instrument with a long handle which is used to transfer the oatcakes from the board to the griddle; the* banna-rack, *on which the cakes are toasted."*

The Scots Kitchen *by F. Marian McNeil. Mayflower Books, England 1974.*

Ceramic Graduated Jug I:84

The English love to use this type of traditional, blue and white striped Cornishware graduated jug in their kitchens. Since it measures amounts based on the Imperial pint, which is a quarter larger than an American pint (20 ounces instead of 16), it is not much help for measuring, unless you are using an English cookbook. But its 2½-cup capacity is perfect for a breakfast milk or cream pitcher or for holding pancake batter ready to pour onto the griddle.

Boston Warehouse Co. (01-41) $11.00

Stoneware Mixing Bowl I:85

This is the perfect mixing bowl. It is shaped like a laboratory evaporating dish, a low bowl with a pouring spout, and it's glazed in the blue and creamy white that is everybody's dream of an English kitchen. The ample 9" width gives plenty of room for an enthusiastic mixing spoon, and when the batter is all done, there's the spout to assist you in pouring the batter into a pan. Only 3¾" deep, it has, nonetheless, a 3½-quart capacity.

Bloomingdale's $12.00

Glazed Ceramic Gripstand Bowl I:86

This splendid mixing bowl has not changed its design within living memory, and no English kitchen worth the name would be found without one. The inside is a creamy ivory, and the outside a rich buff color with a geometric design in relief and a flattened area on one side. This flat area is the patented "gripstand," which allows the bowl to rest steadily on its side when it is held at an angle for beating. The wide mouth in relation to the height of the bowl makes it ideal for bread making, creaming and beating. It also has two lip handles, good to focus pouring and for butter-fingers to cling to. These bowls from T. G. Green have such a period charm that they would be fun to collect as well as practical to use. We show here the 11"-diameter, 4¼-quart size, but they range both downward and upward from 2 to 12½ quarts.

Boston Warehouse Co. (06-111) $8.50

Ceramic Egg Separator I:87

The magic simplicity and charming design of this little utensil are most appealing. You should not be without one if you love to make meringues and hate getting the sticky egg white all over your fingers. The shallow, round, buff-glazed bowl is 4″ wide and 1½″ deep, with a slot half-way down the cup that lets the egg white dribble through and keeps the egg yolk nestled in the flat bottom. Why risk making a mess when this pleasing little separator can do the job so simply?

Boston Warehouse Co. (10-214) **$3.00**

How much simpler it would be with an egg coddler . . . "To make clean thy shell of an egg with thy fingers is a ridiculous thing that men laugh at; and to do it putting thy tongue into it, is yet more ridiculous. It is done more properly with thy knife."

The Civilitie of Childehode, *with the discipline and institucion of Children distributed in small and compendious Chapiters, and translated oute of French into Englysh, by Thomas Paynell. 1560.*

Egg-marketing in Ireland.

Egg Cup **I:88**

An English egg cup for English eggs. It's a little small for American super-jumbos, but it's quite adequate for mere large eggs, and quite the thing for a brown English egg, fresh from the farm. The cup is clear-glazed stoneware with a bucolic design brushed on in light blue. It has an engaging carelessness in the finish which would comfort and cheer the grumpiest breakfaster; it sits 2¾″ high, and its top opening is less than 2″ across.

La Cuisinière **$3.50**

Egg Coddler **I:89**

To coddle an egg, in case you were wondering, is to break it into this charming little cup with some cream, seasonings and perhaps some fresh herbs if you have any, then put on the

Continued from preceding page

top tightly and simmer the cup in boiling water until the contents are done to your taste. The old name for a coddler is a pipkin. Our clear-glazed stoneware pipkin is the color of clotted cream and is very easy on an early morning eye. It is almost always used at breakfast, although a devotee might demand to have his eggs coddled for high tea. Our one-egg coddler stands 3¾″ high. A flat cover with a small loop handle in the center screws onto the cup. Many decorative and expensive coddlers are made by the famous English china manufacturers in strong bone china, but for this simple breakfast procedure we would stick with this pretty country coddler.

La Cuisinière **$5.50**

Butter Churn I:90

The best of British cooking depends on farm-fresh eggs and sweet country butter made from the milk of local cows. You can try making butter at home with this churn. It is a 14″-tall, 4-quart glass jar with bulging sides and a tinned-steel screw-on top. A crank on the side of the top fits into a bright blue-painted metal egg, which holds the churn's gear mechanism. From the gear housing, an aluminum rod descends into the jar, where it is attached to beechwood paddles. Turn the crank to activate the gear mechanism and make the paddles go round and round. The configuration of the jar's sides serves to channel the cream back into the paddles. Very clear instructions accompany the churn, telling you about the preparation of the cream, the churning, washing and setting of the butter. Is it worth the fuss? That depends on how enamored you are of the taste of fresh butter (we are mad for it). And, given the relatively moderate cost of the churn, we think that it would provide a super activity for a family with preschool children; it would help to teach them that butter doesn't emerge from the cow in neatly wrapped sticks.

Garden Way Assoc. (337) **$39.95**

Butter Mold I:91

A lot of the butter eaten in England now comes from Denmark, but the homemade product is well worth sampling—especially in Ireland or wherever there is a herd of Jersey cows nearby. The milk from these cows produces the richest and best dairy product in the world. Here is a charming, carved wooden butter mold for making decorative pats of butter for the tea or dinner table. It looks like a child's toy, having a 3″-long handle that fits into a hollow cup and slides back and forth in the cup. Draw the wooden plunger all the way back into the cup and fill the space that is left with soft butter. Then dip the mold into iced water until the butter is firm, and push it out. Voilà! You have a pat of butter 1½″ thick embossed with a strawberry design on the top.

La Cuisinière **$10.00**

Thistle Butter Print I:92

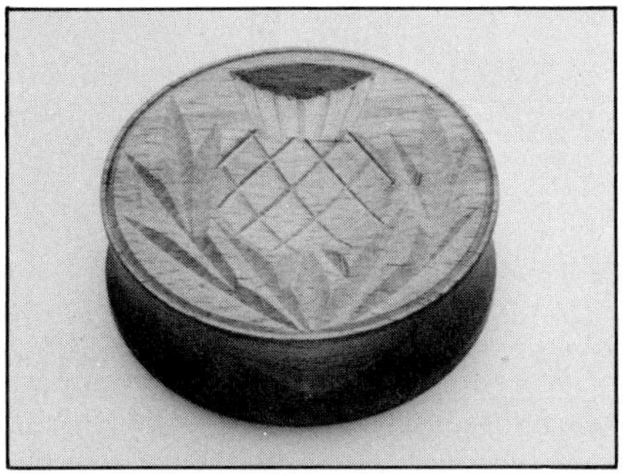

If culinary purism or ambition has led you to churn your own butter, you will no doubt want to carry the operation to its traditional conclusion by imprinting the butter with the design on a wooden butter print. Dip the mold in iced water and then press it onto small dishes of slightly softened butter to decorate them with the traditional Scottish thistle that is deeply etched on the molding side. The satin-smooth hardwood mold is 3¾″ in diameter and 1¼″ thick.

G. Rushbrooke (Smithfield) Ltd. (176) **$5.00**

Butter stamp.

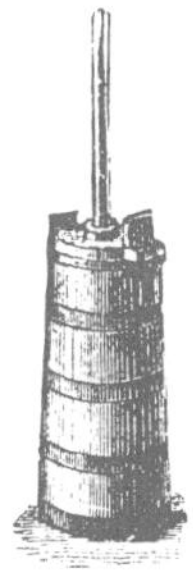

Cheese Board I:93

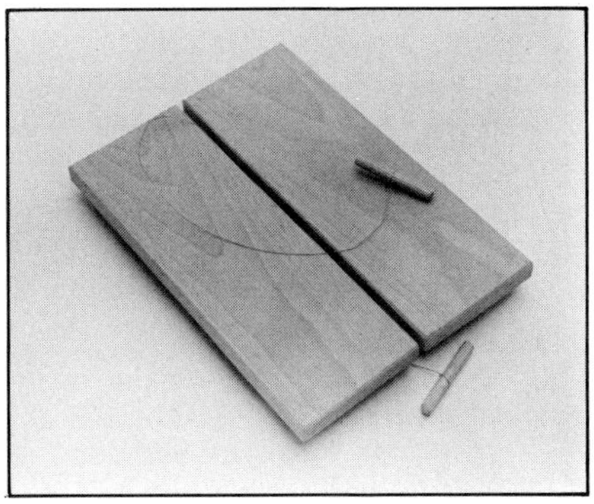

In old grocers' shops in England, you will still find cheese cutting boards like this one used to cut slices from the huge red and white, Cheshires and Wensleydales, Leicesters and Stiltons that line the marble slabs. If you need to serve cheese to a number of people and have a large chunk to deal with, this cutting board would be a great asset. The principle is simple. It is made of two pieces of 14″-long by 10″-wide natural beechwood that do not quite meet in the center, held together by cross pieces at the back. A 29″-long wire with two short dowels at either end is attached to the board on one side. To cut the cheese, the wire is pulled taut and drawn down and through it, and into the slot between the board's two halves. This makes an easier and more even cut with these crumbly cheeses than you could get with a knife. For those dishes like Welsh rarebit, cauliflower cheese or the Welsh favorite, Glamorgan sausages (fried cheese sausages), that call for a lot of grated cheese, you can use the cutting board to cut large cheeses into manageable slices for grating.

G. Rushbrooke (Smithfield) Ltd. (152) **$8.00**

Covered Stoneware Casserole 1:94

Pot ovens being a thing of the past—we couldn't even find one to show you—why not use this brown-glazed earthenware covered pot for all the simple country stews that are the backbone of English cooking. Basic stew cooking is based on the premise that the least expensive cuts of meat, usually on the bone, are the most delicious when cooked at a low temperature for a long time. Put the meat in the oven in the early morning with onions, carrots, or whatever the recipe requires, and simmer all day long while the juices and flavors blend and develop into wonderful dishes like Irish stew, oxtail stew or Lancashire hot pot. Our good looking casserole stands 3½″ high, is 7½″ wide, and holds 2 quarts. A flared rim in a darker mustard brown holds the lid, which has a stubby knob in the center, and a small hole to let the steam escape (this allows the liquid to evaporate and the sauce to thicken). It is also available in a 2¾-quart size.

Boston Warehouse Co. (11-277) **$12.00**

LANCASHIRE HOT POT

10 potatoes, peeled and sliced
4 large onions, sliced
6 fat lamb chops, trimmed
Salt
Freshly ground black pepper
12 oysters (optional)
1–2 carrots, cut into 2″ pieces (optional)
Water

Preheat oven to 350 F.

Spread one-half of the potato slices over the bottom of a deep baking dish

Continued from preceding page

or casserole and cover with one-half of the onion slices. Arrange the six lamb chops in one layer on top and cover with a layer each of the remaining potatoes and onions.* Season each layer with a sprinkling of salt and pepper before adding the next. Top with the oysters and carrots, if desired, and add enough water to just cover all of the ingredients.

Cover tightly, place in preheated oven and cook for 2–2½ hours, removing cover for the last 30 minutes.

Yield: 6 servings.

* If you do not have a sufficiently wide dish, you may use a narrower, deeper pot and make three layers of potatoes and onions and two layers of chops.

(Courtesy Rona Deme, The Country Host, New York City)

Brown Irish Casserole I:95

Since this trim, covered stoneware casserole comes from Ireland, you should think seriously about using it to cook an Irish stew, the taste and smell of which can be compared with nothing else. Traditionally the stew was made with mutton, which was tenderized by the long cooking process. But you will probably prefer to use lamb since it is more available and has a more delicate texture and taste. The slick dark-brown glazed casserole has straight sides and a domed cover with a mushroom-shaped knob in the center. The inside is the color of creamy oatmeal. It is 7½″ in diameter, 2½″ deep and holds 1½ quarts.

The Irish Pavilion $18.50

Dutch Pot I:96

This brown-glazed stoneware casserole is known as a Dutch Pot in England. Its shape is reminiscent of a bean pot, and it would be a perfectly proper vessel in which to bake beans, since the narrow neck and lid combine effectively to discourage evaporation, and the stoneware holds oven heat well. In the British Isles, however, this pot is used for Irish stew, potted pork, oxtail stew, or any similar oven-cooked, sauce-and-meat dishes. Tubby and shiny and wholesome-looking, it is 6″ deep and will hold 2 quarts. There is a line of decorative beading around the girth and on the rim, and two short handles protrude from the sides. It is also available in 1-cup, 1-quart, 1½-quart, 3-quart and 4-quart sizes.

Denby Ltd., Inc. (104) $9.95

Oval Stoneware Terrine I:97

The rough country look of this simple, heavy oval terrine is immensely appealing and decorative. Rich, dark stews of pheasant or venison spiked with Madeira, a jugged hare or a game soup would be splendid in this casserole. So different from the elegant French porcelain terrines. Vive la différence! Of course, you can always use it for the regular pâtés of meat or game, or for coarser country terrines. The dish is 8½″ long, 5¾″ wide and 2¾″ deep yielding a capacity of one quart. The exterior is glazed a dark brown and the inside a creamy beige. The edges of the lid and the surface it rests on are left unglazed to prevent slipping.

Denby Ltd., Inc. (115) $7.50

Rectangular Terrine I:98

A terrine is, by definition, a dish made of earthenware, since the French *terre*, in English, means earth. But it also refers to the food that is served from the earthenware dish, a mixture of ground chopped meat similar to a pâté. Terrines are popular on both sides of the English channel: this one could not be more English in its sturdy yeomanlike design and its high glaze in brown and tan. It is 7″ long and 4″ wide, with suggestions of handles protruding from either end, and it has a 1¼-quart capacity. In it you could make a pork pie, or else the satirically-named Devonshire squab pie that contains no squab at all but rather an interesting combination of lamb, apple and spices.

La Cuisinière/Boston Warehouse Co. (25-202) $18.00

Rectangular Baking Dish I:99

Infinitely useful for dishes hot and cold,

this rectangular baking dish with flared sides and thickened rims has a slick mustard glaze with a darker mustard-colored rim. It could become one of the most useful dishes in your kitchen since it has endless uses in the oven and on the table. As a baker it would be ideal for cooking fish, cauliflower cheese, toad-in-the-hole (sausages in Yorkshire pudding batter) or kedgeree (curried smoked haddock with rice and hard boiled egg)—all of which are lunch or supper dishes. But it is also perfect for some of the most delicious English desserts: apple brown betty, apple crumble and bread and butter pudding. It is 12″ long, 10″ wide and holds 2½ quarts.

Boston Warehouse Co. (11-325) $19.00

TOAD-IN-THE-HOLE

1 pound pork sausage
1 tablespoon fat or drippings (if necessary)
Yorkshire pudding batter (see recipe below)

Preheat oven to 450 F.

Place the sausage in an ovenproof baking dish and bake in preheated oven for 10 minutes. If sausages do not render much fat, add the tablespoon of fat or drippings and return the dish to the oven until the fat is sizzling hot.

Beat the Yorkshire pudding batter for a moment and pour over the sausages. Return the dish to the oven and bake until the batter has set and is nicely browned, about 30 minutes.

Yield: 4 good servings.

YORKSHIRE PUDDING BATTER
1 cup all-purpose flour
Pinch salt
2 eggs
1 cup milk
2 teaspoons butter, melted

Sift the flour and salt together into a bowl. Add the eggs and beat well. Gradually add just enough milk to make a stiff, smooth batter. Allow the batter to stand for a few minutes, then beat in the rest of the milk and the butter. This batter can stand in the refrigerator for some time before using.

(Courtesy Rona Deme, The Country Host, New York City)

Oval Sole Dish I:100

This simple, rustic sole dish of beige stoneware goes over a flame, under a fire, or into the enveloping heat of the oven—and thence to the table. The inside is slickly glazed, while the natural unglazed bottom allows it to absorb heat and holds it steady over a low burner. Use it for baked sole (Dover to be authentic, if you can get it) with lemon butter, or creamed sole with mushrooms. It is also useful for preparing the foods with cheese sauce that the English make for lunch or tea: macaroni or cauliflower or hard-boiled eggs, for example. Topped with cheese, they are then put under a broiler's fire. The dish is a bit over a foot long, is 8½″ wide and 1¾″ deep, and has a 1¾″-quart capacity.

Denby Ltd., Inc. (158) $7.95

Turtle Baker I:101

Originally, as its name suggests, this stoneware turtle baker was used to bake turtle. Although the instructions for preparing the turtle which you find in an early edition of Mrs. Beeton's famous cookbook are best forgotten by the squeamish, the dish was always considered a special delicacy. The chunks of turtle meat were cooked in the blood of the animal with a variety of sweet herbs, onion and a liberal tot of Madeira. Because of its size—4½″ deep, with a 5″-diameter base flaring to an 8″-wide mouth, and 2-quart capacity—and its ceramic composition, the turtle baker would also be useful out of the oven to make salt pork, spiced beef, pickled herring or a rich mincemeat.

The Complacent Cook/ Denby Ltd., Inc. (151) $6.00

Souse Pot I:102

Soused means pickled and pickled means drunk: but in cooking soused just means pickled, as in brine, and this is a souse pot. (Once upon a time the sousing liquid was made not only of spices and vinegar but also of wine and ale so the connection with intoxication was not accidental.) If you look in old English recipe books like Mrs. Beeton's under 'souse,' you will find revolting instructions for pickling a pig's ears, cheeks, snout and trotters; but today you are more likely to be served a soused herring or mackerel. This splendid souse pot is flat-bottomed, straight-sided, glazed in two shades of mustard and has a flared rim, two arcs of handles and a domed cover that sits snugly in the rim. It is 6½″ deep and 6″ in diameter, with a 2-quart capacity.

Boston Warehouse Co. (11-78) $12.50

"A Royal Picnic"

Of Puddings and Pies

It should be simple, this business of pies and puddings. But like so many matters in the world of food, we find that we know what we mean only when we try to define it precisely.

Pudding. Yes, pudding of course. Well, to an American that means a creamy custard. But to an Englishman it means a steamed dish, or the final course of his meal, or the popover-like dough that cooks beneath the Sunday roast, or a sweet dish, such as Marmalade Pudding, or a savory dish that resembles a pie gone wrong, with its crust steamed rather than baked, or a cake-like dish, such as Plum Pudding. The Irish, always ready to call a spade a spade, have something like a Plum Pudding that they simply call a Boiled Fruit Cake.

But then there is pie, which is certainly easier to define. There are sweet pies and savory pies. The sweet pies are different from ours, because they are baked with no bottom crust, and contain a lot of unthickened fruit juice. And there are savory pies, made with crusts that are either baked or—honestly—boiled. Some pies have upper crusts made of mashed potatoes. Others, such as pasties, are free-standing oval envelopes of pastry that are filled with meat and potatoes and meant to fit into a workingman's pocket.

Not a simple matter, this business of pies and puddings.

Oval Pie Dish — I:103

English pies—sweet and savory—are traditionally baked in a dish like this. And there is a staggering range of pies from which to choose—from steak and kidney with its mushrooms and onions, to the beloved blackberry and apple served with a dollop of Devonshire cream or a steaming hot pool of yellow custard sauce. Fish pies like salmon pie usually have a mashed potato topping that is browned under the broiler. Some fish pies, like eel pie, however, traditionally have pastry crusts. And the crusts vary too! (If you are trying to judge an English pie by its cover, remember that meat pies are often decorated with pastry leaves and flowers that have been brushed with egg and milk and baked a shiny golden brown.) Our pie dish is 8″ long and 2⅜″ high. It's glazed all over in a dark oatmeal color and looks as wholesome and homely as the food cooked in it. The sides of the dish flare slightly and become thicker towards the top. The dish is also available in 5½″ and 6½″ sizes.

Jane Products, Inc. (592) — **$3.50**

STEAK AND KIDNEY PIE

1 large beef kidney
½ cup oil
½ cup lemon juice
2 tablespoons vinegar
1–2 tablespoons minced onion
Freshly ground black pepper
4 ounces (1 stick) butter
2 medium onions, chopped
4 pounds beef sirloin, cut into 2″ cubes
Flour for dredging
Bouquet garni (cheesecoth bag containing bay leaf, thyme, and several sprigs parsley
2 tablespoons salt

Water
1½ pounds carrots, cut into 2″ pieces
1 dozen large mushrooms, cleaned
½ cup flour mixed with ¾ cups water to form a paste
3 tablespoons Worcestershire sauce
1 lard crust (see recipe below)
1 egg yolk beaten with a few drops of water

Cut the kidney into cubes and remove the suet. Place in a bowl with the oil, lemon juice, vinegar, minced onion and pepper and marinate for an hour.

Melt the butter in a very large, heavy saucepan and sauté the onion lightly. Dredge the sirloin cubes in flour and add to the saucepan. Toss and mix until the meat is "sticky all over"—until all the flour has been coated with butter.

Add the kidney with its marinade, the *bouquet garni,* salt and enough cold water to cover the ingredients by 2″. Simmer for an hour. Add the carrots and mushrooms and simmer 45 minutes longer, or until the meat is tender. Stir in the flour/water paste a little at a time, to thicken the gravy. After all the paste has been added, simmer about 5 minutes longer, then add Worcestershire sauce and remove from heat. Let cool.

Preheat oven to 350 F.

Turn the filling into one large, deep family-sized pie dish or 4 smaller dishes. Roll out the lard crust to a thickness of ¼″ and lay it over the filling. Trim and crimp the edges. Using the crust trimmings, make pastry leaves and arrange them around the circumference of the pie, which should first be brushed with the egg yolk. Brush the leaves with the egg also. Cut one or several steam vents in the pastry.

Place the pie in a preheated oven and bake for 1 hour to 1 hour and 10 minutes, until the crust is nice and brown and the filling piping hot.

Yield: 6–8 servings.

LARD CRUST
2 cups all-purpose flour
1 teaspoon salt
4 ounces (½ cup) lard, cold
2 ounces (½ stick) cold butter
¼–⅓ cup ice water

Toss the flour and salt together in a bowl. Cut in the lard and butter until the mixture is mealy, but do not overwork. Add the smaller quantity of water and rapidly stir with a fork until all the flour is moistened. Add more water if the mixture is too dry, but be careful not to make it sticky. Gather into a ball and knead once or twice to combine all the ingredients. Refrigerate until ready to use.

(Courtesy Rona Deme, The Country Host, New York City)

Individual Pie Dish I:104

The small white ceramic dish we show here is famous as the individual pie dish found in butchers' shops and pie shops all over Victorian England and long before. The fillings can be as varied today as they were then: veal and ham, steak and kidney, chicken and leek, game and eel. The dish is also excellent for serving hors d'oeuvre such as kipper paste or potted shrimp, made with the tiny shrimp that the English prize for their flavor. The pie dish comes 7″ (shown here), 8″ and 10″ long. The larger dishes can be used to bake any pie you choose for a main course.

Boston Warehouse Co. (05-126) $3.50

Large Pie Dish I:105

This is the larger version of the individual pie dish that is used for single servings of savory pies from the butcher; this one could undoubtedly feed a family—or a classroom (it holds two quarts). It is 11¾″ long, 9″ wide and 3″ deep; in it one could make an apple pie for a big party or a mammoth steak and kidney pie for a picnic. Servings would not, of course, be neatly triangular; but then, English sweet pies are commonly made with lots of juice and no thickeners, and thus are served in large spoonfuls anyway.

La Cuisinière $9.95

"Wery good thing is weal pie, when you know the lady as made it, and is quite sure it an't kittens."

Pickwick Papers *by Charles Dickens.*

Deep Pie Dish I:106

English dessert pies have a juicier filling than their American counterparts—lots of juice and no thickeners—and so it is impossible to cut a slice of one with a knife: you must have a spoon to serve and eat it. A spoonful of gooseberry pie and then some heavy Devonshire cream or hot custard sauce makes a satisfying end to any meal. This 3-cup pie dish is 7″ across the top and 2″ deep, with sides that flare slightly so that pastry can be fitted easily against them. There is a lip around the rim on which the two layers of pastry can meet and be pinched together. It is made of a medium-weight tinned steel that is heavy enough to hold a bubbling meat pie as well as a dessert pie.

George Wilkinson (Burnley) Ltd. (S10) $1.50

Pie Bird I:107

We show you one, not four-and-twenty, blackbirds, to bake in a pie. He looks as though he is singing, but he's really providing a vent so that steam doesn't accumulate beneath the pie crust and make it soggy. This charming little fellow is of black shiny-glazed ceramic, and stands 4″ tall. Set him on the bottom of a pie pan, put in the filling and lay the top crust (with a hole cut out for the bird) over him. His beak should protrude through the unbaked top crust, making it unnecessary for you to slash any other vents in the top of the pie.

Boston Warehouse Co. (05-161) **$3.50**

Yorkshire Pudding Pan I:108

In the respectable chill of the 19th century, no proper British household would do without its roast beef on Sunday; and under the roast there was sure to be a pan that collected the meat juices and drippings. In it a Yorkshire pudding puffed high, magnificently flavored, but also a trifle soggy. We propose, instead, this pan for making individual Yorkshire puddings. Put a spoonful of drippings from the roast in each of its four 1″-deep cups, get it piping hot and then pour in the batter. The result will be individual puddings with a fine beef flavor and a texture that is as crisp and light as popovers. This 9¼″-square tray yields four round, golden puddings, each one with a base that is 4″ wide.

H. Roth & Son **$2.98**

SUMMER PUDDING

- 2–3 cups raspberries, in season, or 1 large can raspberries in syrup (or other fruit)
- 4–5 large, thin slices white bread, approximately, or an equal quantity of sponge cake slices
- Whipped cream

If you are using fresh raspberries (or other fruit), simmer them with a little sugar until tender and strain, reserving liquid. If canned berries are to be used, drain and reserve syrup.

Remove the bread crusts and line the bottom and sides of a 1-pint pudding basin with the slices, cutting them to fit. Fill the basin with the drained fruit and top with another slice of bread. Cover with a sheet of wax or parchment paper, weight and refrigerate overnight.

When ready to serve, turn pudding onto a dish and decorate with the whipped cream. Pass the reserved syrup as a sauce.

Yield: 4–6 servings.

(Courtesy Rona Deme, The Country Host, New York City)

Pudding Basin I:109

Pudding is a purely English weakness, a taste that is inexplicable to foreigners, who tend to feel about puddings the way they do when a friend marries some dull man. Why *him?* Why *pudding?* Be that as it may, pudding is made in a pudding basin. This is the classic: a deep bowl of white stoneware that tapers to a flat and narrow base. Pudding basins come in many sizes (the one shown here holds 3 quarts), but always with this distinctive shape. Notice the indentation under the inch-wide rim, where you are meant to tie a muslin cover in place before you put the pudding in to steam. What goes in a pudding basin? Steak and kidney pudding, with its chunks of meat, and onions and its gravy, all steamed in a soft white suet crust; Christmas plum pudding; ginger pudding with golden syrup; marmalade pudding with orange sauce; chocolate pudding with custard sauce. And, of course, summer pudding: a berry-rich, bread-lined pudding that is left overnight to soak up the fruit juices and coalesce into a dense confection that is cut into wedges and served cold with dollops of Devonshire cream. Mention pudding and you will bring tears to the eyes of an English expatriate. Show him this simple pudding basin and the tears may well flow past his stiff upper lip.

Boston Warehouse Co. (05-123) **$6.50**

PLUM PUDDING

3 cups day-old bread crumbs
½ cup brown sugar
¾ teaspoon cinnamon
½ teaspoon salt
½ teaspoon nutmeg
⅓ teaspoon cloves
⅛ teaspoon mace
1 cup milk, scalded
1 cup raisins
½ cup sultanas
½ cup currants
½ cup figs, chopped
½ cup dates, chopped
¼ cup candied citron, chopped
¼ cup candied orange peel, chopped
¼ pound suet, ground
¼ cup red wine
4 eggs, well-beaten

In a large bowl combine the bread crumbs, brown sugar and seasonings with the scalded milk and allow to cool.

Combine the rest of the ingredients in another bowl and mix well. Turn into the cooled bread crumb mixture and mix until all the ingredients are thoroughly combined.

Divide between 5 or 6 well-buttered, 2-cup pudding basins and cover each first with a sheet of heavily-buttered wax paper, then aluminum foil, and secure with rubber bands around the rim.

Place the pudding basins on a rack in a large, deep pan and add enough hot water to reach half-way up the sides of the molds. Bring the water to a boil, lower heat and cover. Steam the puddings for 2½ hours. Allow to cool and store in a cool place—puddings will keep indefinitely. To reheat, steam for 1 hour. When ready to serve, douse with brandy and flame, if desired, and pass a bowl of custard or hard sauce or cream.

Yield: 5–6 puddings.

(Courtesy Rona Deme, The Country Host, New York City)

"A Haggis, Sir?"

"(1) A plum-pudding, that is not really solid, is mere porridge;
(2) Every plum-pudding, served at my table, has been boiled in a cloth;
(3) A plum-pudding that is mere porridge is indistinguishable from soup;
(4) No plum-puddings are really solid, except what are served at my table.

Univ. 'plum-puddings'; a = boiled in cloth; b = distinguishable from soup; c = mere porridge; d = really solid; e = served at my table.

(Answer: No plum-pudding, that has not been boiled in a cloth, can be distinguished from soup.)"

Symbolic Logic *by Lewis Carroll. 1895.*

The Meal Called Tea

In Britain, tea is not only a drink, but also a meal. It is, in fact, several meals; and one way in which class differences are defined in that far-from-classless society is according to what people eat at tea and what time of day they eat it. If it's eggs and meat pies and herring, then the meal is called "high tea" or "meat tea" and it is eaten when father comes home from the fields or the factory (at 5:30 or 6 o'clock), much like an American supper. But if it's watercress sandwiches and thin slices of bread and butter and walnut cake, then it is simply afternoon tea, taken at around four o'clock to help tide one over until it is time for a fashionably late supper.

When you are invited to have a cup of afternoon tea you will be offered, in addition, something sweet for the good of your soul. Biscuits, maybe, or a seedcake; a slice of brown bread toasted and spread with jam, or scones and honey; walnut cakes and layer cakes and shortbread and tarts. What you eat will depend to some extent where you are, but at its best, English baking is superb, relying as it does on fresh dairy products and an imaginative use of fruits and spices. (A famous American cook schooled in the French kitchen, but acquainted with all the great cuisines, has admitted to us that he finds

Continued from preceding page

British baking the best by far.)

Then there are "cream teas," with strawberry jam and the rich, yellow, clotted cream of Cornwall; and "tea breaks," when mugs of sweetened reddish brew are served up at office and shop; and there are painfully silent and genteel teas in the lunch rooms of London department stores. But no matter how it is made, it is the best prix-fixe meal other than breakfast to be had in Britain, served at every wayside restaurant at tables set with chubby brown teapots, large bowls of sugar and pitchers of milk, and tiered trays laden with sandwiches, plain cakes and scones.

Toast Rack I:110

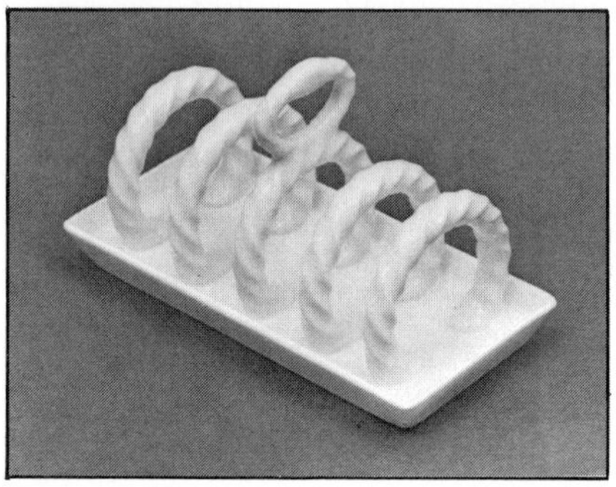

Anyone who thinks that the Americans and the English are one people because they speak the same language should concern himself with the matter of toast. To us, hedonism consists of hot buttered toast. But the English, either by choice or habit, seem to eat it cold. And to ensure that they are never disappointed, the toast is served in racks designed to expose both sides of the bread to the chill of the English dining room, and at the same time keep the slices separate, hard and firm. But what the English don't know about toast, they *do* know about toast racks; and this one is a lovely thing, made of shiny, white-glazed stoneware. Five twisted rings stand upright on a 5″ by 2½″ base with a flared rim; a loop on the center ring serves as a handle. A charming addition to your breakfast tray or table, or at other times when you might prefer cold toast —with pâté, for example.

La Cuisinière $12.50

"I can see my parents' breakfast table yet: the many and varied dishes, hot and cold, the dark and light jellies (black currant and white currant—what has become of white currant jelly?—one never sees it now): then such potato scones, barley scones, and scones that were just 'scones' and nothing else, each kind nicely wrapped up in its snowy napkin, with the little peak that lifted and fell back, falling lower and lower as the pile was diminished; the brown eggs that everyone prefers to white—and why?—the butter, sweet, old yellow butter framed in watercress."

Recollections of a Scottish Novelist *by Mrs. L. B. Walford, 1910.*

Marmalade Pot I:111

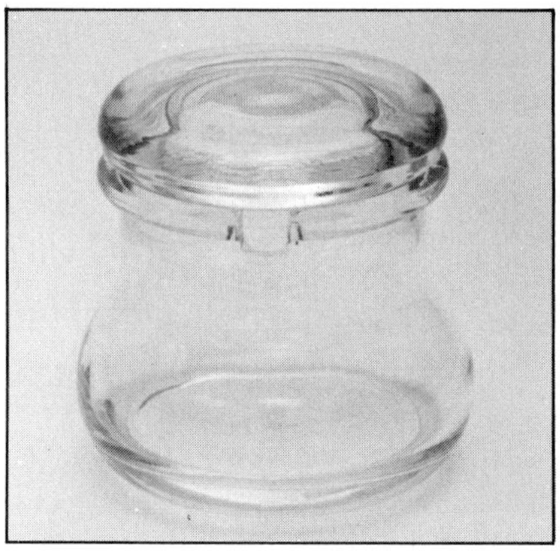

Jam is served in china or earthenware, but marmalade should always, always be served in clear glass. Even in the gloom of an English morning, there will be a stray ray of sunlight to shine through the golden preserves and bring cheer to the breakfast table. Marmalade pots are made in crystal and cut glass or in modern designs like this simple glass pot. It is shaped like a chunky hourglass, 4″ high and 4″ wide, with a flat rim that has been cut out to leave room for a spoon and a wide flat-topped stopper over all.

G. Rushbrooke (Smithfield) Ltd. (MP6) $6.00

Honey Jar I:112

Winnie the Pooh liked honey, as we all know; but so do Englishmen of a less ursine nature. They are served honey at breakfast, where it is the alternative to marmalade for spreading on cold toast; they are served honey with country teas, where it is spooned on scones and muffins in place of gooseberry jam. Here is a sweetly domestic Cornishware honey jar, straight-sided and sturdy, a small bit taken out of its top so that the honeyspoon may rest there. It's 3″ deep, 3″ across the top, holds 1 cup of honey and is made of a thick stoneware that is glazed in blue and white stripes.

La Cuisinière/Boston Warehouse Co. (01-51) $8.95

Buns as a test for youthfulness, as seen by Oliver Wendell Holmes in The Professor At The Breakfast Table *(1883); "In order to know whether a human being is young or old, offer it food of different kinds at short intervals. If young, it will eat anything at any hours of the day or night. If old, it observes stated periods, and you might as well attempt to regulate the time of high water to suit a fishing-party as to change these periods. The crucial experiment is this. Offer a bulky and boggy bun to the suspected individual just ten minutes before dinner. If this is eagerly accepted and devoured, the fact of youth is established. If the subject of the question starts back and expresses surprise and incredulity, as if you could not possibly be in earnest, the fact of maturity is no less clear."*

A Five O'Clock Tea.

Crumpet Rings I:113

English crumpets (or their larger cousin called pikelets) look rather like a thin version of what in America is known as an English muffin. Crumpets, however, are spongier and full of holes. The happy result in that when a crumpet is buttered, the butter soaks right into the tiny holes and down your chin when you take the first mouthful. Gilding the lily means adding honey or jam or Lyle's golden syrup, but many think that crumpets are best all alone. They are cooked in rings in a skillet, each ring 1″ deep and 4″ wide: spoon in the batter, and it will spread out to fill the ring, making a tidy disc. Although they are available in sets of six, you really need twelve to make the procedure worthwhile.

Maid of Scandinavia Co. $2.15 (31690)

Bun/Scone Tin I:114

Traditionally buns in England were made on a greased baking sheet or pan close enough to each other that when they came out of the oven they were loosely joined at the sides but could be easily separated by pulling apart. Scones are baked in the oven, but can also be cooked on a "girdle," or griddle. Both buns and scones, however, can be baked in a tin such as this with equal success. To test the tin, try any of the famous English yeast buns such as Chelsea buns, or (at Easter) spicy Hot Cross buns—not to mention currant buns, iced buns and jelly buns. This sturdy tinned-steel tray is 12″ by 9″ with rolled edges and 12 round, flat-bottomed cups 5/8″ deep.

HOAN Products Ltd. $4.00 (1013)

CURRANT SCONES

2 cups all-purpose flour, sifted after measuring
1/3 cup sugar
1 tablespoon baking powder
3/4 teaspoon salt
2 ounces (1/2 stick) butter
3/4 cup currants
3 eggs
1/4 cup milk
1 egg yolk and a little sugar for glazing

Preheat oven to 350 F.

Toss the dry ingredients together in a bowl. Rapidly cut in the butter with a pastry blender or the fingertips, until the mixture is mealy in texture. Add the currants and mix to coat thoroughly with flour. Scoop up handfuls and allow to dribble through the fingers back into the bowl—this will aerate, and thus lighten, the dough.

Make a well in the center and add the eggs and milk. Stir just enough to combine all the ingredients—the dough will be quite lumpy.

Turn onto a floured board and pat into a rectangle about 1/2″ thick. Brush with egg yolk and sprinkle with a very little bit of sugar. Using a sharp knife, cut into diamond shapes. Transfer to a baking sheet and bake for 25 minutes, or until puffed and golden brown.

Serve with lots of butter and jam and whipped cream sprinkled with a little grated lemon peel. Scones freeze well—reheat in aluminum foil for 15 minutes in a 200 F. oven.

Yield: approximately 16 scones.

(Courtesy Rona Deme, The Country Host, New York City)

A Frenchman traveling in England in 1810 was mildly shocked at some of the customs, such as the one described here: "Towards the end of dinner, and before the ladies retire, bowls of colored glass full of water are placed before each person. All (women as well as men) stoop over it, sucking up some of the water, and returning it, and, with a spitting and washing sort of noise, quite charming—the operation frequently assisted by a finger elegantly thrust into the mouth! This done, and the hands dipped also, the napkins. and sometime the tablecloths, are used to wipe hand and mouth."

Journal of a Tour and Residence in Great Britain during 1810 and 1811 *by Louis Simond, 1815.*

Scalloped Cake Tin I:115

Make scallop-shaped tea cakes in this tinned-steel pan that holds twelve molds in a rectangular frame. Each shell holds one fluid ounce of batter: traditionally a rich cupcake batter, which is varied with the addition of currants, candied fruits, lemon or orange zest. The 2 3/4″-diameter, 3/4″-deep molds were made separately and then joined securely to the tray, making a strong and inflexible whole.

HOAN Products Ltd. $4.00 (1015)

Small Cake Tin I:116

This well-made, tinned-steel tray makes

a dozen small cakes for the tea table. Start with a heavy sponge batter and vary it: Queen's cakes have currants; Brunswick cakes have cloves, cinnamon and nutmeg; and butterfly cakes have jam and cream and decorations that look like butterfly wings on top. The tray is 12″ by 9″, and holds twelve cups, each one 1½″ deep and 2⅜″ in diameter.

HOAN Products Ltd. (1256) **$4.50**

Sandwich Cake Tin I:117

This high-quality cake tin is a plain round form 7½″ in diameter and 1″ deep. It is made of lightweight tinned steel with slightly flared sides and rolled edges. In it is made what we call a layer cake, and what in England is known as a sandwich cake; the assumption being that it is a sort of icing sandwich—two slices of cake with frosting between them. Victoria sandwich, for example, is made with two plain sponge cakes mortared with a filling of jam and cream and sprinkled all over with confectioners' sugar.

George Wilkinson (Burnley) Ltd. (S13) **$1.50**

Cake Tin with Removable Bottom I:118

A cake tin with a removable bottom is especially useful when you are not convinced that the cake you are baking will tumble out of the tin as easily as it should. Then what a pleasure it is to be able to release the ring that holds the sides together and lift out the cake on its tinned-steel base. It is capable of handling a substantial and heavy cake like a Christmas fruit cake, and is the traditional size for a Dundee cake. The pan is 3½″ deep and 7″ in diameter. It is made in two pieces: a disc-shaped bottom and a ring into which the bottom fits neatly.

George Wilkinson (Burnley) Ltd. (C1) **$4.50**

Small Tartlet Pan I:119

English tarts are shortcrust pastry cases filled with wonderful things: gooseberry jam, lemon curd or almond paste. Alice would have eaten jam tarts had the Knave of Hearts not

A pastry maker of some renown.

Continued from preceding page

stolen them, and good little children eat them at tea every afternoon. They are made in pans like this shiny tinned-steel tray, 12″ by 9″, which holds twelve shallow, 2⅜″-diameter cups with rounded bottoms. The edges are neatly rolled and the whole tray sturdily made.

HOAN Products Ltd. (1000) **$4.00**

Tartlet Pan I:120

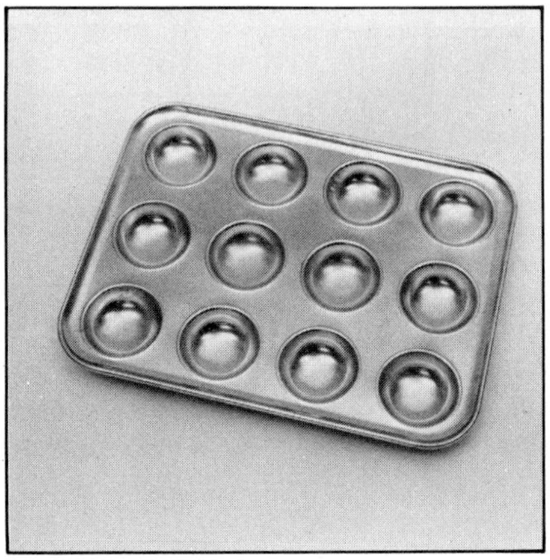

A sensible way to cook many small tarts at once: twelve shallow (⅞″ deep) cups with rounded bottoms have been set into a medium-weight tinned-steel tray 14″ by 10½″. The tray is raised around the edges and the rim has been neatly rolled back. Tartlets are pastry cases filled with jam or lemon curd or custard: Balmoral tartlet, for example, which was named after one of the Queen's Scottish homes, is made with candied citrus peel and glacéed cherries.

H. Roth & Son **$3.50**

LEMON CURD TARTLETS

Grated rind and juice of 3 lemons
3 eggs
2–3 cups sugar (use smaller quantity for a tart lemon curd, larger quantity for a sweet curd)
4 tablespoons butter
1 recipe short pastry

LEMON CURD
Place the lemon peel and juice in the top of a double boiler.
Beat the eggs and sugar together until thick and lemon coloured and add to the lemon rind and juice.
Turn flame under double boiler to medium. Stir lemon mixture often and start adding butter a little at a time. Wait until one piece is melted before adding the next. Continue cooking and stirring until the curd is thick and creamy, about 1 hour. Pour into glass jars, cover and keep in refrigerator until ready to use.
Yield: 1 pint, enough for about 50 tartlets.

TO ASSEMBLE TARTLETS
Make enough short pastry for a one-crust pie or tart. Cut into 2 dozen 3½″ circles, press into shallow tartlet tins and crimp edges. Prick all over with a fork and bake until golden brown and fully-cooked. Cool the tartlet shells and fill with a spoonful of lemon curd, using about 1 cup lemon curd altogether.
Yield: 2 dozen tartlets.

(Courtesy Rona Deme, The Country Host, New York City)

Pastry Cutters I:121

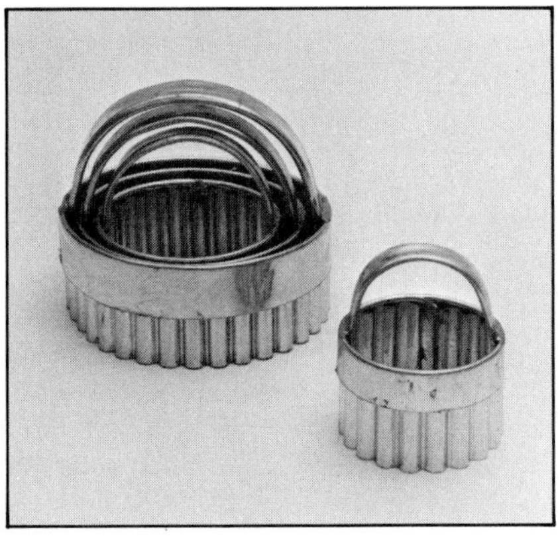

To cut rounds out of tart or biscuit dough, or to make a small Cornish pasty (a rich pastry pocket filled with a meat-and-vegetable mixture), use one of the fluted circles in this set of four tinned-steel cutters. The bottom edges of the cutters are sharp, the top edges protected by rolled-edge collars. Looped handles are soldered to each collar, and the cutters themselves are a good 1½″ deep. The cutters' sizes are 2″, 2¼″, 3″ and 3¼″ in diameter.

H. A. Mack & Co., Inc. (E63) **$5.00**

SHREWSBURY BISCUITS

3½ cups flour, sifted after measuring
1 teaspoon baking powder
½ teaspoon salt
12 ounces (3 sticks) butter
1½ cups sugar
Grated rind and juice of 1 lemon
2 eggs
1 cup currants
1 egg yolk for glaze, lightly beaten
Sugar

Preheat oven to 350 F.
Sift together the flour, baking powder and salt. Set aside.
Cream the butter and sugar together until light and fluffy. Beat in the lemon rind and juice, then the eggs, one at a time. Blend in the flour mixture and stir in the currants. Dough will be fairly stiff.
Divide in half and roll one half into a sheet ⅛″ thick. Cut into rounds with a fluted 2½″–3″ round cookie cutter. Repeat with the remaining dough or cover with a sprinkling of flour and plastic wrap and refrigerate until ready to use—it keeps quite well.
Place biscuits on an ungreased cookie sheet, brush with egg yolk and sprinkle with a little sugar. Bake for 20–25 minutes, until a nice brown color.
Yield: about 5 dozen biscuits.

(Courtesy Rona Deme, The Country Host, New York City)

Pastry Brush I:122

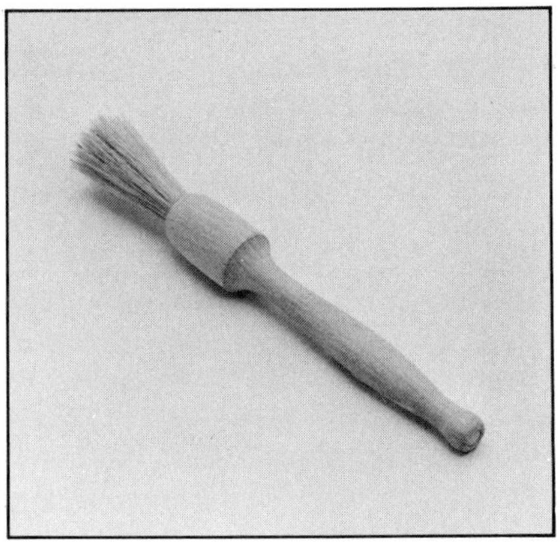

Hot Cross buns get a wash of egg-and-cream, meat pies a glaze of egg-and-milk; and dozens of baking sheets and tins need buttering. In all cases you will find this friendly, comfortable pastry brush with a full head of natural bristles the ideal instrument. The 2″-long bristles are firmly secured in a 6″-long, turned hardwood handle. The wood is smooth and pleasant to the touch, and is the color of that ultimate English nursery food, golden syrup, a heavenly mixture of the flavors of honey and molasses.

H. A. Mack & Co., Inc. $2.25

HOT CROSS BUNS

3 cups all-purpose flour
1 teaspoon allspice
Pinch salt
½ ounce fresh yeast
¼ cup sugar
¾ cup tepid milk
2 tablespoons (¼ stick) butter
4 ounces dried fruit (currants, raisins, etc.)
2 ounces candied peel
2 tablespoons confectioners' sugar mixed with 1 tablespoon water for glaze

Sift the flour, allspice and salt together.

Cream the yeast with 1 teaspoon of the sugar and add the tepid milk and a sprinkling of the flour mixture. Put in a warm place to ferment.

Rub the butter into the flour until the mixture is mealy in texture. Add the remaining sugar, the dried fruit and the candied peel and toss together. When the yeast is ready—it will be foamy and will have doubled in volume—work it into the flour and knead thoroughly, until smooth and elastic. Place in a buttered bowl, turn to butter top, cover and put in a warm place to rise until doubled in volume, approximately 1 hour.

Preheat oven to 475 F.

When the dough has risen, form it into 2½–3 dozen round buns and cut a cross on each one with the back of a knife.

Place on a buttered baking sheet to "prove" for 15 minutes (to prove means second rising). Bake for 10 minutes in the top of the oven.

If the buns are to be eaten straight away, glaze with the sugar/water mixture immediately. If they are to be eaten later, place in the oven to reheat and then glaze.

Yield: 30–36 buns.

(Courtesy Rona Deme, The Country Host, New York City)

Terra-Cotta Bread Baker I:123

The shape of this unglazed terra-cotta bowl is specifically designed to produce a loaf of bread in the shape of a giant popover. The sides of the loaf flare out following the shape of the baker and the top is a semi-circular dome that curves up out of the top. In England, such a loaf would most likely be made of white flour and have a crisp golden crust. After the dough is kneaded it may be placed in the baker to rise, and then, of course, baked in it. The bread baker will make a loaf 6″ in diameter.

David Mellor $8.00

Shod Loaf Tin I:124

The strong, efficient look of this loaf tin should inspire confidence in the shyest of bakers. It's an ideal pan for home bread baking, from white and whole-meal loaves, to the delicious fruit and malt breads that the English love: nut and raisin bread, cherry bread or Christmas bread full of dried fruits and spices. The tinned-steel pan is 4½″ wide, 7¼″ long, 3½″ deep and has a 2-pound capacity. The top edges are rolled, and the bottom is fitted with a second, insulating layer, or shoe (hence the name shod loaf tin), that helps prevent the bottom of the bread from scorching. The sturdiness of the tin is increased by its V-shaped corner reinforcements.

George Wilkinson (Burnley) Ltd. (C7) $2.75

Ceramic Shortbread Mold I:125

We call it shortbread because it is made with shortening: large amounts of the very best butter. The dough for this classic Scottish cookie contains no eggs, and is therefore crumbly, flaky and hard to handle. It is patted—gently—into a mold such as this one and is pricked all over with a fork to prevent blistering. It is then baked in a slow oven until it is dried through. This white ceramic mold is 1½″ high, 3″ in diameter, and is perfectly ovenproof. When the shortbread has baked for about 30 minutes at 300 degrees, the cook inverts the mold over a tea towel. Out will fall a disc of shortbread, hot and delicious, with the Scottish thistle impressed on its top, and the traditional fluting on its edge.

La Cuisinière $5.95

SHORTBREAD

3 ounces (¾ stick) butter
¼ cup sugar
¾ cup all-purpose flour
¼ cup corn or rice flour

Preheat oven to 300 F.

Cream the butter and one-half of the sugar until light and fluffy. Beat in the flour, corn flour and the last of the sugar. Knead well and press into an ungreased 8″ round cake tin or di-

Continued from preceding page

vide between two well-floured, 6″ wooden shortbread molds. If using a tin, crimp the edges and print a design into the top of the dough. This is not necessary with the wooden molds, as they will leave a lovely thistle imprint on the top of each shortbread—just be certain to flour the molds well.

Bake for 40 minutes in preheated oven and cool in tin or mold. If you wish to cut the shortbread into wedges, do so while it is still hot.

Yield: one 8″ or two 6″ shortbreads.

(Courtesy Rona Deme, The Country Host, New York City)

Wooden Shortbread Mold I:126

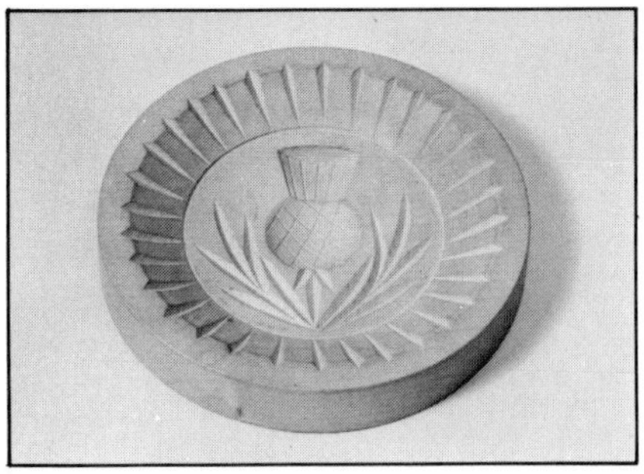

Shortbread is eaten all year round in Scotland and especially on Christmas and New Year's. Although it's good in any shape, one of shortbread's traditional forms is a circle with a ridged edge. To make ridges, which folklorically represent the sun's rays, you can either pinch the edges of the dough, or bake the pattern into the shortbread by using a mold like this. First, press and pat the sticky dough into the mold, working quickly so as not to melt the butter in it with the heat of your hands. Then run a rolling pin over the top to even it off, put it in a slow oven to bake, and finally invert the king-sized cookie over a tea towel or a cooling rack. This unfinished hardwood mold is a little under 7″ in diameter; the pattern is ½″ deep. On one side is impressed the traditional Scottish thistle emblem surrounded by rays of the sun. The flat side of the mold carries the legend "Hand Carved in Braemar; J. & L. Crichton."

H. A. Mack & Co., Inc. $12.00

"The most common name in France for a custard is English cream; and it was so called almost universally until Carême put a stop to it. He was indignant that England should get the credit of the custard; and now it is known by his followers simply as crème au bain-marie. *Carême, however, who refused petulantly to give the name of Crème Anglaise to the custard, put a little bit of isinglass into it and then insisted it should be called Crème Française! A bit of stiffening makes all the difference between French and English."*

Kettner's Book of the Table, *1877.*

Ceramic Dessert Mold I:127

The lovely sculptural lines of this white ceramic mold make it a thing of beauty in itself. It is most often used to make the multicolored gelatin desserts that you see at every children's party in England. Or to make the vanilla, chocolate or even butterscotch *blanc mange,* that British nursery staple. It has a 4-cup capacity and stands 5½″ high with deep swirl patterns twisted into the sides.

Macy's $14.00

Stoneware Custard Cup I:128

This pretty little custard cup is made of ovenproof ceramic. Put it in a bath of boiling water in a hot oven while the custard within it sets; then place it under the broiler so as to caramelize the sugar on top of a burnt cream. (Burnt cream, of course, is the English version of *crème brulée.* The change of name in no way changes the taste of that creamy custard topped with brittle cooked sugar.) The cup is glazed a warm caramel color with a darker rim of the same tint. It is 2¾″ deep, almost 3″ wide and holds eight ounces of custard, rice pudding or bread and butter pudding.

Boston Warehouse Co. (11-292) $2.25

Custard Cup I:129

Plain custards made of only eggs, milk and sugar have always provided a nourishing dessert for nurseries and a comforting meal for invalids. This shallow, rustic-looking stoneware cup (made in Ireland) would be perfect for making such a simple dessert, as well as fruit fools, rice puddings and other such treats. The cup is only 3½″ wide and 1¼″ deep and holds ¾ cup. It has a short, stubby handle protruding from the rim. The attractively glazed outer surface, all dark brown and tan, makes a nice contrast with the creamy white interior or its custard-yellow contents.

The Irish Pavilion $3.00

BUTTERFLY CAKES

½ cup all-purpose flour
½ cup corn flour
1 teaspoon baking powder
Pinch salt
4 eggs, separated
½ cup sugar
¼ cup raspberry jam (approximately)
½–¾ cups whipped cream (approximately)

Preheat oven to 400 F.

Sift together the flours, baking powder and salt.

Beat the egg whites until stiff and "peaky." Gradually beat in the sugar, until thick and smooth. Beat in the egg yolks. Carefully fold in the dry ingredients.

Divide batter between the smallest cake pans you can find—the pans should be either well-buttered or lined with bon-bon papers. Bake in preheated oven until golden brown, about 10 minutes. Allow to cool.

Cut a small cone-shape out of the top of each cake. Put a small amount of jam in the bottom of each hole and top with a dollop of whipped cream. Place the cone-shaped cutout back on top of the cream and dust with a little confectioners' sugar.

Yield: about 2 dozen small cakes.

(Courtesy Rona Deme, The Country Host, New York City)

A Cup of Tea

There is a formula and a ritual to tea-making. While it is not so formalized nor so fraught with symbolism as the Japanese tea ceremony, any variance from the drill will cause the unknowing foreigner to lose points with the English, points which he can ill afford to risk. And even more important, he will end up with an inferior cup of tea.

First, he must bring cold water to the boil in a kettle. When the water is boiling, he pours a bit into the teapot, swirls it around, and dumps it out; now he has warmed the pot. Then he spoons tea into the pot, using one spoonful for each person and another for the pot. (That is the golden rule, but you will find it wise to make the extra teaspoon a scant one or the brew may be so black that it will be undrinkable.) He then takes the pot to the kettle—never the other way around—and pours the boiling water over the leaves. He lets it stand for a few minutes—one early book told its readers to brew tea as long as it takes to say the *Miserere*—gives it a stir, and pours. And that is

Continued from preceding page

the drill, as sacred as cricket and Christmas pudding and cold toast for breakfast.

Tea Infuser I:130

If you are making a single cup of tea and don't want to go through the whole drill with a pot; or if everyone else is having Jasmine and you want Earl Grey; or if you are secretly convinced that tea bags are filled with powdered industrial waste; then what you need is a tea-infuser. This one is a 6″-long, chromed-brass, spoon-shaped device with a hinged lid. You open it by pressing down on one end with your thumb. The spoon end is perforated so that water can reach the tea. All you have to do is fill it with your chosen leaves, snap the lid closed, and let the infuser steep in your cup until the tea reaches the desired strength.

Milton Gumpert (138) $3.00

Miniature Teapot Infuser I:131

This is English equipment at its most charming and inventive: a tiny little teapot, only 1¼″ high. It is made of chromed steel and has perforations all over its sides. There is a 4″-long chain attached to the removable cover. The tea leaves go inside, the cover clamps onto the pot, and then you simply rest it in a cup and cover it with boiling water. And when the tea is made, there is a tiny little saucer, also made of chromed steel, that will catch the excess tea water when you're through. This device has the fascination of all miniature things, and it is well-made, inexpensive, and quite as useful as the traditional spoon-infuser.

Alfred E. Knobler & Co., Inc. (26V3) $2.59

Tea Strainer I:132

Unless you are trained in tealeaf reading or brew your tea with tea bags, you will probably want to strain the tea before it hits your cup. This chromed-steel strainer, with a fine wire mesh bowl, will do the job handily. An openwork design is stamped out of the handle and the short cup-rest that protrudes from the opposite side of the bowl. Six inches in all, it is a pretty thing; and although it is not quite so practical as a strainer with a saucer, there is nothing to prevent you from providing yourself with a small dish to catch the drips.

Gillies 1840 $3.29

"No nation has so large a stock of benevolence of heart as the Scotch. Their temper stands anything but an attack on their climate. They would have you even believe they can ripen fruit; and to be candid, I must own in remarkably warm summers, I have tasted peaches that made excellent pickles. . . ."

Sydney Smith quoted in The Scots Kitchen *by F. Marian McNeil, Mayflower Books, 1974.*

Irish Tea Strainer and Holder I:133

This tea strainer has, most sensibly, its own holder to take care of the tea leaves and their drippings. The 6″-long chromed-steel strainer is decorated with an openwork design (like that on a porringer) at the end of the handle and on the cup-rest that protrudes from the bowl. Lay the cup-rest on the rim of a teacup, pour the tea through the fine mesh strainer, and the leaves will be trapped inside it. This is the point at which you usually wonder what to do with the soggy things. Not to worry: you have at hand a porcelain holder, just the right size to hold the strainer. It is glazed all over with a progression of blue, green and mustard tints.

The Irish Pavilion $8.50

"Our great nurse Miss Nightingale remarks that 'a great deal too much against tea is said by wise people, and a great deal too much of tea is given to the sick by foolish people. When you see the natural and almost universal craving in English sick for their tea, you cannot but feel that Nature knows what she is about. But a little tea or coffee restores them quite as much as a great deal; and a great deal of tea, and especially of coffee, impairs the little power of digestion they have. Yet a nurse, because she sees how one or two cups of tea or coffee restore her patient, thinks that three or four cups will do twice as much. This is not the case at all; it is, however, certain that there is nothing yet discovered which is a substitute to the English patient for his cup of tea; he can take it when he can take nothing else, and he often can't take anything else, if he has it not.' "

Beeton's Book of Household Management *by Mrs. Isabella Beeton, 1861.*

LIPTON'S TEAS
BY SPECIAL APPOINTMENT
TO HER MAJESTY THE QUEEN
DIRECT FROM THE GARDENS
DAMBATENNE ESTATES CEYLON.
LIPTON TEA PLANTER CEYLON
ONE OF LIPTON'S TEA-GARDENS CEYLON
LIPTON
Finest the World can produce
1/7 Per Pound.
Rich, Pure & Fragrant
1/- & 1/4d Per Pound
LARGEST SALE IN THE WORLD
APPRECIATED EVERYWHERE
For their Delicious Flavour
FROM SUNNY CEYLON.
CHIEF OFFICES:- CITY ROAD, LONDON.
Branches and Agencies throughout the World.

Aluminum Tea Kettle I:134

It all begins in the kettle, that ritual that is designed to produce a perfect cup of tea. Here is a kettle made of sturdy aluminum in the classic shape. The spout arches gracefully, and the handle, covered with black plastic, is rigidly secured to the kettle with two rivets at each side. On the lid there is a heat-proof black plastic knob and a triangular vent that acts as a safety valve: if wisps of steam are allowed to escape during the boiling process, the cook is less likely to be scalded when the lid is lifted. The manufacturer recommends that you scald this kettle before you use it; after that, simply rinse it in hot water and dry it thoroughly. It will bring up to 4 quarts of water to the boil. Then you bring the pot to the kettle and carry on with the rest of the ritual.

Bloomingdale's $18.00

DUNDEE CAKE

2 cups all-purpose flour
1½ teaspoons baking powder
1 teaspoon ground allspice
1 pound mixed dried fruits, such as raisins, currants, sultanas, dates, figs, etc.
2 ounces glacéed cherries, floured
2 ounces candied lemon and orange peel
2 ounces chopped almonds
6 ounces (1½ sticks) butter
¾ cup sugar
3 eggs
1 tablespoon treacle (molasses)
2 tablespoons milk
¼ cup rum or brandy (optional)
2 ounces split almonds for decoration
1 egg white for glaze, lightly beaten

Preheat oven to 325 F. Butter and flour a 7″ round, 3″ deep cake tin. Set aside.

Sift together the flour, baking powder and allspice.

Combine the dried fruits, glacéed cherries, candied peel and chopped almonds in a large bowl and mix together well.

Cream the butter and sugar together until light and fluffy. Beat in the eggs, one at a time, then stir in the flour. Add the molasses and enough milk to make a batter of "slow dropping consistency."

Add the fruit mixture and stir together until all the ingredients are well-coated with batter and evenly distributed. For special occasions, stir in the optional rum or brandy.

Turn into the buttered and floured tin and decorate the circumference of the cake with the split almonds. Brush with egg white to glaze and to make the almonds stick to the cake.

Bake in preheated oven for 2–2½ hours, until a toothpick or cake tester inserted in the center of the cake comes out clean. Cool in tin.

If cake has been made with rum or brandy it can be aged for 4–5 weeks. Douse once a week with several spoonfuls of the liquor and keep refrigerated or in a cool place.

Yield: one 7-inch cake.

(Courtesy Rona Deme, The Country Host, New York City)

Copper Tea Kettle I:135

In the case of a tea kettle, the choice of copper is more aesthetic than practical; but wouldn't this shiny kettle look lovely sitting all day long on the back of your stove? It is hand-made in the English Midlands of copper with a tin lining, and has a wooden handle that protects the cook's hand from the hot metal. The twist of coiled copper wire that is threaded through the bottom of the pot becomes white-hot within minutes, and helps conduct heat rapidly to the water inside. Finally, there is an almost invisible whistling mechanism that has been built into the spout to alert the cook of the very moment when the water begins to boil. Part of the mystique of tea-making is that it should be made with freshly-boiled water. Twice—or over-boiled—water will have lost its oxygen in the boiling and give the tea a flat taste. The kettle holds 2¾ quarts and is for use on a gas stove. A flat-bottomed model for electric stoves is also available.

Zabar's $29.95

Brown Betty Teapot I:136

Here's a little teapot, short and stout. It's round and homely and dignified all at once, and it is absolutely ubiquitous in English kitchens (and tearooms). Because of its shiny brown glaze, it has been given the pet name of Brown Betty. In profile, the shape is balanced with a curving spout on one side and a graceful handle on the other; it sits on its broad base with a substantial and dignified look. The lid has a round button knob and a deep rim so that it will stay firmly seated while Mother pours out the last drop of tea. This pot holds 6 cups, but its relatives are available in 3-, 4- and 7-cup sizes.

Boston Warehouse Co. (76-06) $7.00

Tea Spout Brush I:137

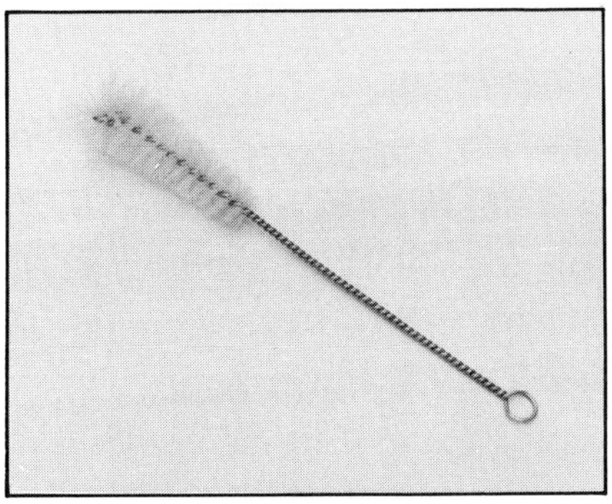

Simple and inexpensive, this tiny brush serves a real function. Stick it down into the spout of your teapot and scrub away like crazy, and you will remove all the nasty tea stains that have collected there since the pot was first used. Then you have the secret satisfaction of knowing that you have the cleanest teapot spout in town. All done with six inches of feather-light aluminum wire, twisted from the loop at one end to the ivory-colored bristles at the other.

John Palmer, Ltd. (M831) $0.75

Tea Cozy I:138

The steeping of tea, during which it takes on its flavor and body, is much helped when the teapot is warmly covered with a nice, thick tea cozy. Of course, it may be decidedly non-U, but no proper English housewife would be without one, and usually she has several for different sizes of pots. This red, plaid quilted cozy is—to make a pun—the *coziest* we could find. It is 11½″ long by 7½″ wide and should fit nicely over a Brown Betty teapot. It has a square pocket on one side holding a tiny Scottish hat that covers the handle of the teapot and protects the pourer's hand. The cozy also bears the legend "Frae Scotland," which is splendid or not, depending on which side of the border you come from.

Scottish Products, Inc. $6.50

Tea Caddy I:139

In the course of processing, tea leaves are sometimes fermented, and then dried: after that, they need to be protected from air and light in order to retain their pungency of flavor and aroma. If you have ever tasted old, tired tea, you will understand why these precautions are desirable, and why we should all keep our tea in metal tea caddies. Far from looking functional, these boxes have traditionally been things of beauty. They are often, as you might expect, rather Oriental in their look, and are covered with designs that we associate with Chinese lacquer objects. Here is a metal caddy 4½″ tall and 4″ in diameter. It is enameled over steel, with a tightly fitting cover and choice of many decorative designs. And it makes good sense, by the way, to store your tea bags in a caddy as well. Even the English do it!

Macy's $2.00

ECCLES CAKES

8 ounces puff pastry
2 ounces (½ stick) butter
¼ cup sugar
2 ounces sultanas
2 ounces currants
2 ounces candied peel
Grated rind and juice of 1 lemon
Good pinch allspice
Milk
Sugar

Preheat oven to 400 F.

Roll the puff pastry to the thickness of a penny. Using a sharp-edged cutter, cut into approximately twelve 4″ rounds.

Cream the butter and sugar together, then work in all the remaining ingredients, except the milk and sugar for glazing the crust. Place a spoonful of the mixture on one-half of each of the pastry circles, fold and press the edges together firmly.

Using a rolling pin and the fingers, carefully roll and stretch the semicircle back as close as possible into a circle shape.

Make several slits on the top of each cake, brush with milk and sprinkle with a bit of sugar. Place on a baking sheet and bake in the center of the oven for 25 minutes, or until golden brown.

Yield: about 12 cakes.

(Courtesy Rona Deme, The Country Host, New York City)

Tea Caddy Spoon I:140

This is the British equivalent of the little plastic measuring cup that comes in your can of coffee. It is a tea-caddy spoon, intended for scooping loose tea out of the container and into the pot. And it's a lot nicer than that little

Continued from preceding page

plastic device: pretty, and natural and made with a shallow circular bowl and a handle that together looks like a thistle. It is small—less than 3″ long—and dark and very Scottish, made to help you count out the required teaspoon of tea for each cup and the extra one for the pot.

H. A. Mack & Co., Inc. $2.75

Irish Coffee Cup I:141

Irish coffee is one part dessert, one part highball, and one part good strong cup of coffee. When you add a half-inch layer of whipped heavy cream to the top of it, you have an irresistible beverage. Here is a charming white and green cup of Galway bone china that stands 4″ deep and 2½″ wide, and is decorated with a scattering of tiny green shamrocks and gold rings around the top and the base. To gild the lily, it has an elegant handle shaped like an Irish harp.

The Irish Pavilion $7.00

"A Merry 17th-Century Dutch Kitchen."

The Cooking of Holland

Holland has a bourgeois cuisine—by which we mean both rich and respectable—but a simple and wholesome one. In Holland one eats cheese and beer, potatoes and pea soup, cabbage and onions and herrings and black bread. The Dutch breakfast consists of black bread, butter and a good wedge of Gouda or Edam cheese. Dutch cuisine shares much with its Scandinavian neighbors, including a deep respect for seafood and baking. It has also borrowed much from its colonial contacts with Indonesia. In Holland it is decreed that you eat potatoes mashed with cabbage for dinner six nights a week; and on the seventh you can have fiery curries and sambals and *satés*. Who could object to that?

Poffertjes Pan I:142

What french fries are to the American teenager, pancakes are to the Dutch. They eat them all the time: little ones like these *poffertjes* (pronounced POFF-er-chiz) only 1¾″ in diameter, or others, big as pizzas, spread with molasses or dusted with powdered sugar. This is a *poffertjes* pan, a 9¼″ circle of cast iron containing 19 shallow circular indentations. Season it first with oil, and then place it right on a stovetop burner. The two square-shaped handles make it easy to lift in spite of its weight, but you might have trouble once these become as hot as the pan. Drop a spoonful of *poffertjes* batter in each hollow. When the edges of the *poffertjes* appear brown, turn each one with a fork so that the other side can cook. Then off to a plate, to a nugget of melting butter and a good sprinkle of powdered sugar. The pan comes in a set that also has a sample of *poffertjes* mix, a brush for oiling the pan, a container for powdered sugar, a pot-holder, and a squeeze-bottle for the batter; none of these accessories, however, is essential to making *poffertjes.*

H. Roth & Son **$19.95**

POFFERTJES

1 package yeast
1½ cups lukewarm milk
2 eggs
1 cup buckwheat flour
1 cup all-purpose flour
½ teaspoon salt
2 teaspoons brown sugar
Butter, margarine or vegetable oil

In a small bowl, dissolve the yeast in the milk with one teaspoon of the brown sugar. In a large bowl, beat the eggs until lemon in color. Add the yeast and milk mixture. Then add the flour slowly, beating well after each addition. Then add the salt and the rest of the sugar. Let the batter stand for one hour, or until its surface is bubbly. (The batter may also be refrigerated for use the next day, but not until it has rested at room temperature for an hour.)

Place the pan on the largest burner of your gas or electric range. Grease the cups with oil, melted butter or margarine. When the pan is evenly heated, fill the cups with batter, beginning with the outside ring. When the *poffertjes* have browned on one side, quickly flip them over by snagging them with a fork. When the second side has browned, remove them from the pan and serve them with butter and powdered sugar. Or, for a very special touch, sprinkle them quickly with a liqueur like Grand Marnier.

A Dutch kitchen.

Speculaas Board I:143

The approach to the winter solstice is marked in Northern Europe by a crescendo of cookie baking. Dusk falls earlier every day, finding kitchens warmed by the heat of the oven and the smell of spices for Christmas cookies. One of the most popular is the Dutch *speculaas,* made from a spice dough and decorated with animals and quaint figures in honor of Saint Nicolaas. The dough is rolled out to a ¼″ thickness and then a carved wooden board is pressed on top of it. When the board is removed, there is a figure left behind in bas relief. Then the dough is cut into rectangles, each one bearing a single figure. This mold, 6½″ by 3¾″ in size, will make four cookies decorated with an owl, a squirrel, a bird and an unidentifiable furry creature.

H. Roth & Son (41-1) **$9.95**

Rotterdam Roller I:144

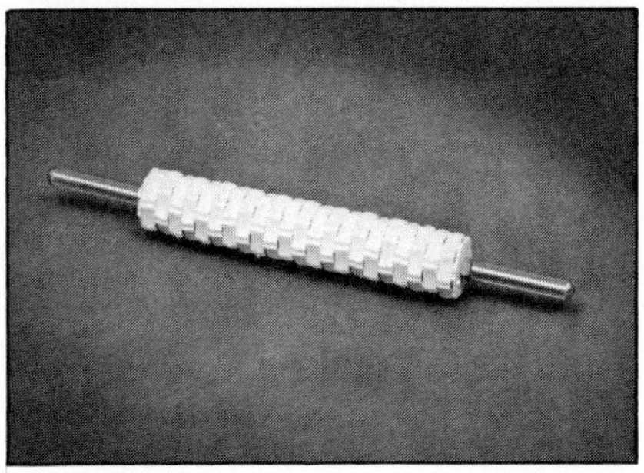

This rolling pin serves a cosmetic, rather than a necessary, function. You don't use it for rolling out dough, but for decorating cakes and cookies: imprinting basketweave designs on sheets of marzipan, on the top of iced cakes or on stiff cookie doughs before they are baked. That's why the pin is made of lightweight plastic instead of weighted wood; that's why the cylinder is a short 8″ long rather than a standard 12″.

Maid of Scandinavia Co. (59706) **$5.50**

Southeast Asian Cooking Equipment

Much of the real Southeast Asian cooking equipment is not sold in stores; it grows on trees. Palm leaves and banana leaves are important cooking and serving utensils: they act as wrappers for steamed or baked food and as plates, or even bowls. The omnipresent, all-important coconut, after giving up its precious meat, then acts as a measuring device, a cooking container and a server. Joints of bamboo stalks are used to hold custard, or anything else that must be cooked in small cuplike containers. And thin splits of bamboo hold skewered meats and vegetables over a charcoal fire.

Beyond these natural, unmanufactured utensils, the Southeast Asian kitchen has little else: one, or several, mortars and pestles for pungent, usually hot, spice pastes; a wok (also called a *kuali* or *wadjan* in Indonesia); a brazier and several simple earthenware casseroles to go with it; a barbecue grill (this is as close as Southeast Asians get to an oven); a cleaver and several knives. Add to those basics several baskets, and tools for dealing with coconut meat, and you're prepared for nearly every dish to come your way. There are, of course, a number of more specialized tools; and we show you several that cannot be easily replaced by utensils in the average Western kitchen.

The Cuisine of Thailand

The story is told that when King Chulalongkorn of Siam intended to spend the night with one of his thirty-two wives, he would first send along a messenger to warn her kitchen staff of his coming so that the king would be as pleased with the meal as he hoped to be with the other pleasures of the evening. This is just possibly an apocryphal story, but it is an appropriate one, nonetheless, because it suggests the care taken in preparing the food of that country.

Although the cuisine of Thailand is superficially similar to the others of Southeast Asia, relying as it does on rice, coconut and vegetables, it has, nonetheless, its own character, which grew from its own history and culture. Most books will tell you that Thai cooking is an amalgam of Chinese and Indian styles; that is quite true, but it doesn't say enough. It doesn't say that in Thailand there is no line drawn between the differing ingredients and techniques. Most meals will include curries reminiscent of India, Chinese-style soups and Indonesian-like relishes called *nam priks;* but each dish will be uniquely and undeniably Thai. The consolidation of the cuisine is understandable when we remember that, unlike so many nations of the region, Siam has had a relatively stable history, never being subjected to European rule and only for short periods having been dominated by other Asian countries. The Thais have managed to integrate an Indian religion, a Chinese-like language and a touch of Western technology into a highly cosmopolitan culture, whose many years of peace and autonomy and whose highly conservative court life encouraged the development of a sophisticated cuisine.

The elegance of Thai cuisine is not only gustatory, but visual as well. Pineapples are cut into spiralling shapes, yams are carved to

"THE COCOA-NUT. This is the fruit of one of the palms, than which it is questionable if there is any other species of tree marking, in itself, so abundantly the goodness of Providence, in making provision for the wants of man . . . To the natives . . . its bark supplies the materials for erecting their dwellings; its leaves, the means of roofing them; and the leaf stalks, a kind of gauze for covering their windows, or protecting the baby in the cradle. It is also made into lanterns, masks to screen the face from the heat of the sun, baskets, wicker-work, and even a kind of paper for writing on. . . . Oars are supplied by the leaves; drinking-cups, spoons, and other domestic utensils by the shells of the nuts; milk by its juice, of which, also, a kind of honey and sugar are prepared. When fermented, it furnishes the means of intoxication. . . ."

Beeton's Book of Household Management *by Isabella Beeton. Facsimile edition, Farrar, Straus and Giroux, 1969.*

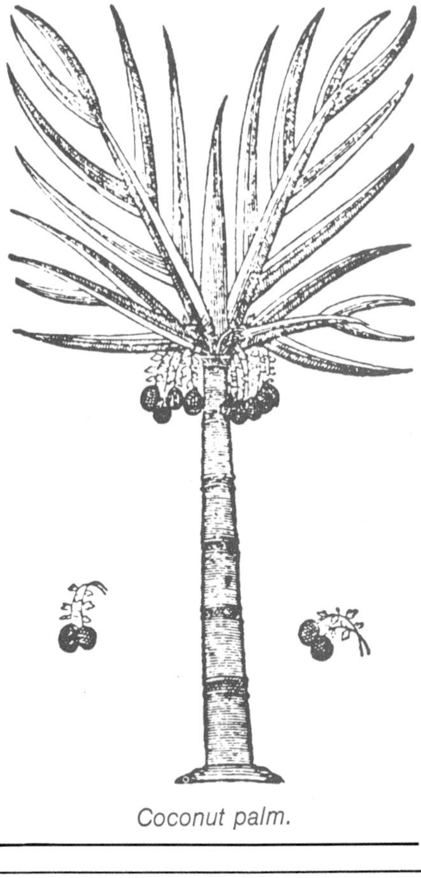

Coconut palm.

resemble roses, scallions become miniature palm trees, and chiles look like little red squid. Everywhere there is an abundance of color. Not only do the different colors of a curry indicate the spices and chiles that were used to make it—and, therefore, its relative pungency—but every finished platter is given a colorful and decorative garnish before it is brought to the table.

So we have a cuisine that is courtly, cosmopolitan and colorful; it is also a cuisine that is often cooked and eaten out of doors and, more than likely, on the water. Many Thais live on barges or in houses standing on stilts that wade knee-deep in the water, because theirs is a country ribboned throughout with rivers and canals. Any barge that goes by may be a residence, a store, or even a restaurant. All day long peddlers in sampans hawk fresh tropical fruits, steaming noodles, fried rice in banana leaves, curries, coffee, ice cream and cakes; for as Krub Chandruang says of his compatriots in his book *My Boyhood in Siam:* "Whatever we are and whatever we are doing, we like first and best to eat."

Everywhere, you can see men and women fanning the flames in their open charcoal stoves, grinding spices in a mortar or wielding cleavers on a hardwood board; and young girls carving radishes and cucumbers to resemble bouquets of flowers. In the kitchen, there is always the scent of fresh coriander, chiles and fish paste, for these three ingredients typify Thai cuisine. A paste called *kapi,* made of dried fish or shrimp, and a fish sauce called *nam pla* underlie the various curry dishes and hot sauces of Thailand; they are the salt and basic seasoning. Fresh hot chiles provide the kick in *nam prik* and the fire in Siamese curries, while fresh coriander, lemon grass, sweet basil and other aromatic leaves supply soothing antidotes to the fiery peppers—fragrant balms for singed palates.

Even more important is rice, the truly universal Thai food that provides a foil for all their spicy dishes. Two-thirds of the people of Thailand earn their living by rice farming; when a Siamese wants to say that he is hungry, he uses an idiom which actually means "I want rice;" and when he wants to refer to food in general, he calls it *khao,* the word for rice.

The equipment we show you includes mortars for grinding chiles and spices, utensils for preparing coconut milk—the basic cooking liquid of Southeast Asia—mesh dippers for cooking meats and noodles, hot pots for serving soups, a clutch of molds and presses for savory pastries and sweet desserts, and two types of food carriers. Other items necessary for Siamese cookery may be found elsewhere in the book: a rice cooker (the Thais often buy theirs from Japan) and a Chinese-style metal wok.

From the diary of a nineteenth-century English diplomat comes this description of dinner in a Siamese court: "Dined with the Prince Krom Hluang Wongsa. An excellent dinner: the soup highly spiced; birds' nests, shark-fins, and sea-slugs were excellent. There was roasted pig, game, delicious fruits, the most remarkable of which was the durian, prepared with cocoa-nut milk, which even the impugners of the durian (I am not one) declared unexceptionally excellent. We had music during the dinner from a band of Siamese, who occupied one of the corners of the large hall. The music was interchanged with songs, and a sort of recitative accompaniment. A Siamese dinner, consisting of nearly one hundred small dishes, was laid on the floor, and, not being touched, was sent to me in the evening."

The Kingdom and People of Siam *by Sir John Bowring. Oxford University Press, 1969.*

Earthenware Mortar and Wooden Pestle J:1

Thai food, like Thai fabric, is beautiful and blazingly intense. But instead of scarlet and gold silk, its elements are crimson chiles and golden turmeric, which must be crushed and combined with other spices in a mortar like this: a big, heavy, slope-sided bowl of gray-brown earthenware. The mortar's thick walls rise 5½″ above a fat pedestal and flare out to an opening 4½″ in diameter; the coarse earthenware is lightly glazed, but still provides a good grinding surface. It comes with a smooth, 8″-long, club-shaped hardwood pestle with a black-striped grain.

Overseas Marketing Corp. **$2.50**

KANG KIEW WARN

Green Curry Paste

INGREDIENTS:
- 10 fresh green chilies
- 2 tablespoons chopped lemon grass or lemon peel
- 1 teaspoon chopped coriander root
- 1 tablespoon chopped red onion (shallot)
- 1 tablespoon chopped garlic
- 1 teaspoon chopped kha
- 1 teaspoon pounded coriander seeds
- 1 teaspoon pounded caraway seeds
- 7 white pepper corns
- 1 teaspoon salt
- 1 teaspoon kapi (shrimp paste)

Continued from preceding page

METHOD:
Stir-fry all ingredients except kapi in saucepan. Then put all ingredients into a mortar and pound until a smooth paste.

Note: You may use a blender, adding a little water to ease grinding.

(From COOKING THAI FOOD IN AMERICAN KITCHENS by Malulee Pinsuvana. Copyright 1976 by Adul Pinsuvana.)

Teakwood Mortar and Pestle J:2

Although it sometimes seems as though the Danes invented teak, it *is*, after all, a tropical tree; and hillsides in Southeast Asia are dark with enormous teak forests. This pleasantly tub-like mortar and its matching pestle, are an example of Thai teakwood craftsmanship. Use them to make one of the fiery Thai curry pastes like *kang kiew warn,* a mixture of hot green chiles, lemon grass, coriander root and seeds, shallots, garlic, *kha* (Thai ginger), caraway seeds, white peppercorns and *kapi* (shrimp paste). Or, if you prefer not to leave the indelible mark of wet ingredients like garlic in the mortar, pound only dry ingredients in it, and use a stone mortar for pungent projects. The mortar's straight (thin but sturdy) sides rise 4″ to hold 1½ cups. The pestle is 6″ long.

Oriental Country Store $5.50

Brass Grater J:3

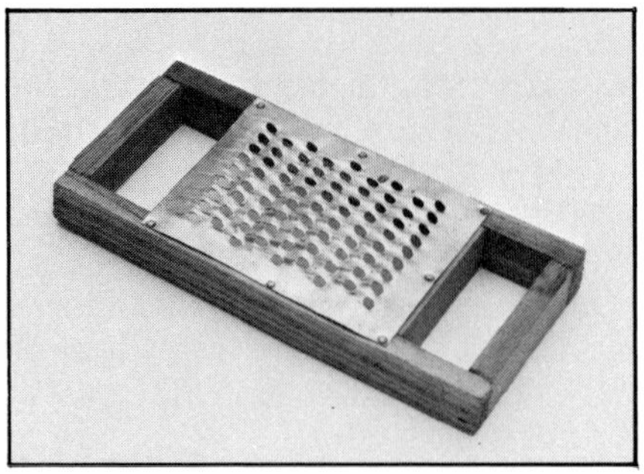

A shiny brass rectangle nailed to an orange wood frame, this grater has a simple elegance all its own. It's a practical tool as well, whose rust-proof grating surface is formed by a number of large, sharp-edged holes each raised on one side. The holes are a good size for shredding fruits and vegetables for Thai salads. Toss together matchsticks of papaya and green mangoes, or try a combination of carrots, cabbage, water chestnuts and celery. For the dressing: lemon juice, fish sauce, brown sugar and garlic—with a few minced chiles for added zest. The grating surface is 3″ by 4″, and the frame extends 1½″ beyond it on each side, so the grater can be rested over a bowl or catch pan.

Siam Grocery $1.50

Brass Coconut Scraper J:4

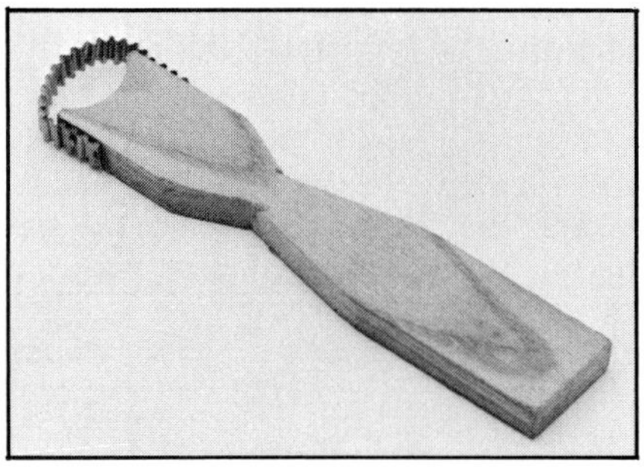

The traditional Thai cook is almost daily faced with the problem of getting at the meat in a coconut in order to make coconut milk, an indispensable ingredient in the Thai cuisine. Instead of prying the meat out of the shell, and then grating the pieces into shreds, the cook simply scrapes the meat out with an implement like this one, made of a wooden handle attached to a metal cutting surface. The 6¾″-long handle has a length of corrugated brass held to its end by four metal nails. Split the coconut and hold half in one hand; with the opposite hand, run the brass cutter over the inside of the coconut, and out will come curls of coconut meat. Toast them briefly in a hot oven to make a snack you'll find hard to stop nibbling on.

J. P. Market $0.65

Iron Coconut Scraper J:5

To make coconut milk, the Thais scrape the meat directly out of a split coconut into a strainer basket atop a larger bowl. They then add some water and squeeze the scrapings dry by hand. This 3¾″-long iron tool by itself doesn't look up to the task. But used properly, it becomes an efficient weapon for quickly reducing coconut to tiny shreds. The scraper is meant to be mounted—by means of screws through the three holes in the handle—on the end of a small rectangular stool. Then sitting astride the stool and holding the coconut in both hands, the cook can press down, aided by body weight and gravity, and scrape the nut against the jagged edge. A basket is usually set directly underneath the scraper to catch the shreds of coconut.

Siam Grocery $1.00

More on the wondrous coconut: "Of the white of these nuts . . . they make porrage, and dress meate withall, strayning and pressing out the milke, wherin with [many] other mixtures they seethe their rice, & to bee short, they never dress any rice, which they cal Carrijl, & is the sauce to their meate thereunto, but they put some of their Cocus milk into it; els the Cocus is but little eaten, for there it is not esteemed of, but serveth for meate for the slaves, and poore people. They likewise break the Cocus . . . and taking off the shell they drie the fruit or white meate that is within it. . . . Of this white substance they make Oyle, which they stampe in cesterns like Olives, and it maketh verie good oyle, as well to eat as to burne, which is likewise very medicinable."

The Voyage of John Huyghen van Linschoten to The East Indies *from the Old English translation of 1598. Lenox Hill Pub. & Dist. Co. (Burt Franklin), 1970.*

Coconut Strainer J:6

To the limited extent that we use coconut in the West, it appears in the form of sweet white shreds and is usually sold as a cake decoration or ingredient. But in Southeast Asia, the primary use of coconut is to make coconut milk, a cooking liquid used in sauces, soups and pastries. To make coconut milk, the meat of the nut must first be grated or shredded. It is then soaked in water, put in a closely woven basket strainer like this one, and squeezed handful by handful until the meat is all wrung dry. The liquid runs through the interstices of the mesh. The strainer—which may also be used to wash rice or drain noodles or vegetables—is an extremely attractive, tightly woven bamboo basket, lashed to a framework of sturdy reed. The strainer has two long ear-shaped handles that will rest on the edges of a larger bowl. It is 8″ in diameter and, like many seemingly fragile articles of basketry, is a lot tougher than it looks.

Siam Grocery $2.50

Beeswax Ladle J:7

Water dippers in Thailand are often made of half a coconut shell attached to a handle of bamboo; but this one, which has the same practical design, is a reed basket coated with beeswax to make it impermeable. The 11″-long stalk of bamboo reaches all the way across the 2¾″-wide cup to provide sturdy support. Use it to add water (it holds ⅔ cup) to coconut meat to make the all-important Thai ingredient, coconut milk. Or ladle a hot, garlicky, gingery peanut sauce over individual servings of chicken and spinach.

The Complacent Cook $3.50

Shell Spoon J:8

Thailand, like the rest of Southeast Asia (except Vietnam and Singapore), lies outside chopstick territory; for the Chinese never conquered the Thais. And having abandoned (for the most part) the old custom of eating with their fingers, Thais today use Western-style forks and spoons. This lovely 5½″-long, nacreous shell spoon would be used not to eat with but to serve fluffy, white mounds of rice. For an ironic contrast to its cool good looks, use it to serve a fiery *kaeng keao wan,* the hottest of the Thai curries. Or one of the spicy *nam priks* made with dried shrimp, fish sauce, garlic, chiles, sugar and lime juice—to accompany raw, boiled and batter-fried vegetables and smoked fish.

Sam Siam Corp. $4.99

"A Siamese makes a very good Meal with a pound of Rice a day, which amounts not to more than a Farthing; and with a little dry or salt Fish, which costs no more. . . . Their sauces are plain, a little water with some Spices, Garlic, Chibols, or some sweet Herb, as Baulm. They do very much esteem a liquid Sauce, like Mustard, which is only Cray Fish corrupted, because they are ill salted; they call it Capi. They gave Mr. Ceberet some Pots thereof which had no bad smell."

A New Historical Relation of the Kingdom of Siam *by Laloubere. Trans. by "A.P. Gen. R.S.S." London, 1693.*

Clay Casserole J:9

This rough clay casserole with its stubby handle and loosely-fitting cover is used in Thailand to serve hot soups. It is a lovely, unglazed oatmeal color, reminiscent of Chinese casseroles. Only the inside of the pot, the portion that will be in contact with the food, is glazed (dark brown). Straight sides flare out from a flat base, and a slightly domed lid with vestigial ribbon handles rests about an inch down inside the rim. The inside diameter is 7½″, and the capacity is 5 cups: that's a lot of hot and lemony chicken soup or clear broth scattered with squid and vegetables. Since earthenware absorbs and holds heat well, the soup, which in Thailand is served with the other

Continued from preceding page

dishes instead of before them, will stay hot throughout the meal. With an earthenware brazier under it, this tureen could also be used as a hot pot for simmering meats and vegetables at the table.

Lord & Taylor **$7.50**

Hot Pot J:10

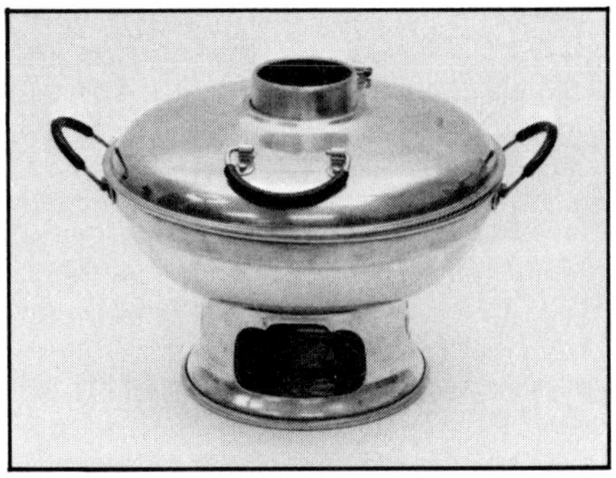

A typical Siamese dinner comprises rice and several other dishes, but these are not served in courses; instead, everything is brought to the table at once. A good idea, for when the hot Thai curries set your palate on fire, you can reach for one of their mild, lemon-flavored soups to extinguish the fire. This shiny aluminum hot pot, nicknamed a Chinese steamboat, will keep that soothing soup warm throughout the meal. Into the hollow pedestal of the tureen go glowing coals; the scalloped opening draws in air to feed the fire, and a central chimney carries the hot air up past the soup. The brazier is carried to the table by a pair of handles coated with black plastic to protect the fingers; a similar pair of handles lifts the cover off the doughnut-shaped tureen to reveal 5½ cups of steaming *tom yam kung,* a tasty shrimp soup flavored with lemon grass, basil and coriander leaves.

Siam Grocery **$15.00**

DOM YAM KUNG

Sour Shrimp Soup

The "sour" soups are typically Thai. They usually contain lemon grass and *makrut* (Kaffir lime) leaves, both of which contribute the tart flavor but are hard to come by in this country. You find bits of red chili floating on top of the *dom yam* too, and the combination makes the unsuspecting eater cry and cough. These recipes are tame. Go easy on the lemon juice and cayenne. Then add as much as you can stand and you will have approximately the genuine article.

1 pound shrimp, shelled and deveined
4½ cups stock
1 clove garlic, crushed
½ teaspoon ground coriander
2 bay leaves
2 lemon slices
1 teaspoon soy sauce
2 tablespoons lemon juice (or to taste)
dash of cayenne
salt to taste
m.s.g.
chopped scallion greens

Combine all the ingredients except the shrimp. Bring to a boil and simmer for 15 minutes. Add the cleaned shrimp and cook 10 minutes longer or until the shrimp are done. Serve garnished with finely chopped scallion greens.

(From SIAMESE COOKERY by Marie M. Wilson. Copyright 1965 by the Charles E. Tuttle Company, Inc. Reprinted by permission of Charles E. Tuttle Company, Inc.)

Hot Pot Strainer J:11

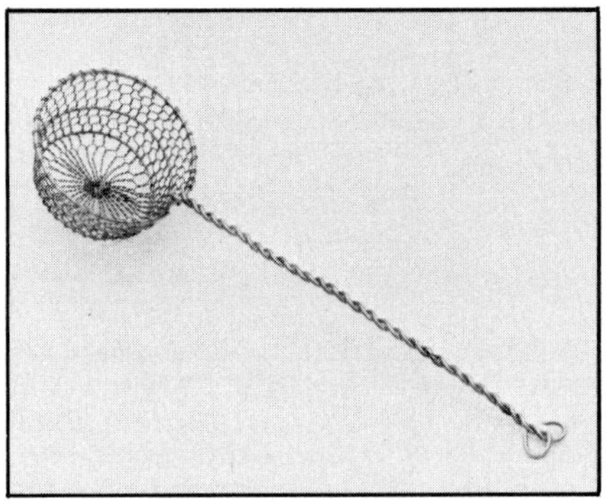

A lacy basket of brass wire, intricately twisted and woven, this attractive strainer has two convenient loops at the end of the 7¼″-long handle by which to hang it. With its wide, shallow cup, 2½″ across the top and 1¼″ deep, it could be used as a skimmer to retrieve food from hot oil, like fluted pastry cups to be filled with spicy chicken, or pastry cockles for snacks. But its real function is to hold meats and vegetables while they cook in steaming broth, a habit borrowed by the Thais from their influential neighbors in China. A clear soup flavored with lemon grass and coriander is served in a hot pot (a metal tureen with a pedestal full of burning charcoal) or an earthenware casserole perched on a charcoal brazier. Chicken, beef or seafood cut into bite-sized chunks is put in the basket and poached in the lemon broth, then dipped in a spicy sauce before it is eaten.

Siam Grocery **$1.00**

Noodle Cooker J:12

Fresh Siamese rice-flour noodles (*kuai tiaw*) need to be cooked only briefly. A noodle cooker like this one, with its long handle, yanks the noodles out the instant they are done. The noodles are placed in the strainer's sturdy brass wire basket, which is 3½″ across and 3½″ deep, and will hold 1½ cups. The basket is securely stapled to the 15½″-long bamboo handle.

Siam Grocery **$3.50**

Egg Noodle Maker J:13

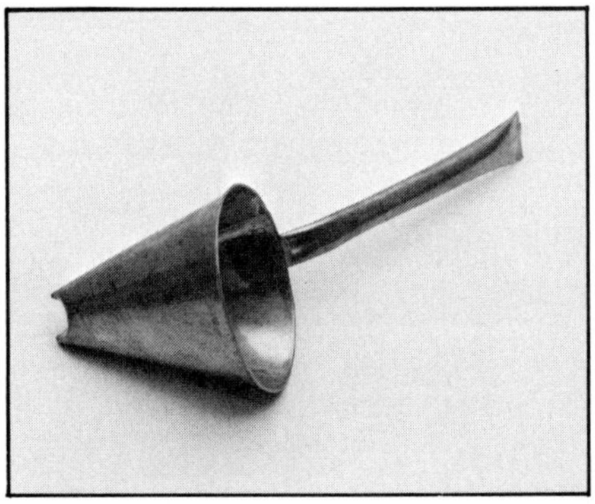

Imagine a wok full of boiling oil; then

imagine dribbling well-beaten and seasoned egg yolks into the hot oil, so that the eggs cook immediately, forming a nest of noodle-like strands. Combine the nest with a savory mixture of shrimp, onions, pork, rice-stick noodles and bean sprouts and it becomes a *mee krob,* a main dish. Or fill the pan with a flower-scented sugar syrup, and strain egg yolks into the boiling syrup for a crinkly dessert called *foi thong.* The tool that makes both concoctions easier to produce is this brass cone with two short prongs at the end, each tip cut off at the bottom to leave a small hole. The cone is filled with the egg mixture—two fingers over the holes to act as temporary plugs—and then moved rapidly over the wok of oil or hot syrup, letting gravity do most of the work. The 3¼″-deep cone holds ½ cup (but not for long), and is attached to a 5¼″, tubular handle.

Siam Grocery **$3.00**

FOI THONG

Sweet Golden Silk Threads

INGREDIENTS:
12 eggs (yolks only and 1 teaspoon thin white)
2 cups *nam chuam* syrup (see below)
4–5 fine point paper cones

METHOD:
Separate eggs. Make sure to put egg white into one bowl and yolks into another. Put remaining egg white that you can scrape out with your finger from the shells, into a third bowl. Only 1 teaspoon of this thin egg white is needed. It is essential for the successful appearance of the *"foi thong."*

Strain the yolk and the thin egg white through a fine sieve. (The rest of the egg white can be used for another dish.)

In a saucepan heat the *nam chuam* syrup over medium low heat. Pour about ¼ cup of the strained egg yolks into a fine point paper cone with your finger over the hole. Remove your finger, releasing the egg yolks in a regular stream into the boiling syrup, moving your hand very rapidly round and round the pan so that you get very fine but unbroken lines of the yellow. The egg strings cook very quickly so remove them almost at once with chopsticks or a slotted spoon. Add a little boiling water each time before repeating this process. (If the syrup is thick the *foi thong* will be crinkly.)

Nam Chuam (Sugar Syrup)

INGREDIENTS:
3 cups sugar
1 cup water
Jasmine flowers or rose petals

METHOD:
In a large pot, dissolve sugar and water; boil for 15 minutes or until the syrup is formed. If necessary, strain through cheesecloth. Cool. Float in jasmine flowers or rose petals.

(From COOKING THAI FOOD IN AMERICAN KITCHENS by Malulee Pinsuvana. Copyright 1976 by Adul Pinsuvana.)

Double Mold J:14

Doubling as a creature from Siamese mythology, no doubt, this curious brass device is a mold for various sweet and savory Thai snacks. There are two brass cups, one with fine and the other with large flutes, each one measuring about 1½″ across. They are attached by 3″-long wires to a yellow-painted wooden handle. To make a savory snack called *miang kai krathong krorp* (which takes longer to say than eat), hold the molds in hot peanut oil until they are heated through, and then dip them in a wheat-and-rice-flour and coconut milk batter. Quickly return them to the oil, and each little cup, now fried, will drift away from its mold. Once they are fished out, they are filled with spicy mixtures of chicken, peanuts and garlic and served as snacks. If the molds are completely immersed in the batter (thus filling the insides of the cups), four shells can be made at the same time. However, the technique takes some mastering, and it may be best to start by only coating the outside of the molds and making two shells at a time. The molds are also used for *thong yib:* a Siamese sweet made of beaten egg yolks dropped by the teaspoon into boiling sugar syrup and then shaped into flowers by pressing the dough around the molds before it cools.

Siam Grocery **$3.00**

"They [the Thais] have neither Nuts, nor Olives, nor any eating Oil, save that which they extract from the Fruit of the Coco; *which, tho always a little bitter, yet is good, when it is fresh drawn: but it presently becomes very strong insomuch that it is not eatable by such as are not accustomed to eat bad Oil. . . ."*

A New Historical Relation of the Kingdom of Siam *by Laloubere. Trans. by "A.P. Gen. R.S.S." London, 1693.*

Wooden Klongkrang Board J:15

Not a butter paddle nor a cookie press, this wooden tool is both a rolling board and a mold to make small shell-shaped snacks called *klongkrang*. Carved out of one piece of wood, the press is 7½″ long, one end providing a handle, the other scored with deep ridges against which spoonfuls of dough are pressed and curled into shells. These are boiled in coconut milk for a sweet cookie, or fried in peanut oil and made spicy with fish sauce and pepper—crisp morsels

Continued from preceding page

for noshing with a glass of rice beer. Serve them alone as an hors d'oeuvre before a Siamese feast, or with bite-sized portions of a popular dish mysteriously called *ma hoh* ("galloping horses")—chunks of sour pineapple with a sweet and spicy topping of ground pork.

Siam Grocery **$1.00**

Aluminum Klongkrang Board J:16

For snacks to nibble on at a picnic or on a journey, the Thais like to prepare *klongkrang,* savory or sweet cakes that will keep fresh for several days. Easy to eat but not that simple to make, they require a deft thumb to shape them on a ridged surface like this one so that they curl up into small cockle shells (second or third cousins to Italian *cavatelli* or the snail soup noodles of Hungary). Holding the handle in one hand and resting the other end of the board at a slant on the table, rub the wheat-or-rice-flour dough against the aluminum ridges with your thumb in a swift downward stroke, rolling it out and shaping it in one sweep of the hand. The shells are then deep-fried and seasoned with fish sauce and pepper, or boiled in sweetened coconut milk and sprinkled with roasted mung beans. Made of aluminum, this *klongkrang* press is 2″ wide and 4″ long; the edges are wrapped around the strong steel rod that forms the 4″-long handle.

Siam Grocery **$1.25**

The cuisine of Laos and Siam as viewed in brief by a nineteenth-century English diplomat: "Kine, pigs, and poultry are plentiful: on the other hand, there are few fish, and those very small, and almost no vegetables: so much so, that during Lent and on the Fridays and Saturdays, we had nothing to eat but eggs, with the leaves of a very bitter kind of radish: there was every day the same repetition without any change. The pigs and fowls are reserved for rich persons. Money also is so scarce, that few families could allow themselves the use of flesh. They commonly live on rice, without any other seasoning than a kind of very strong red pepper—to which the mouth of a European can scarcely accustom itself—or little fishes, which they pound and cause to rot previously: I never could prevail upon myself to eat them."

The Kingdom and People of Siam *by Sir John Bowring. Oxford University Press, 1969.*

Lachong Press J:17

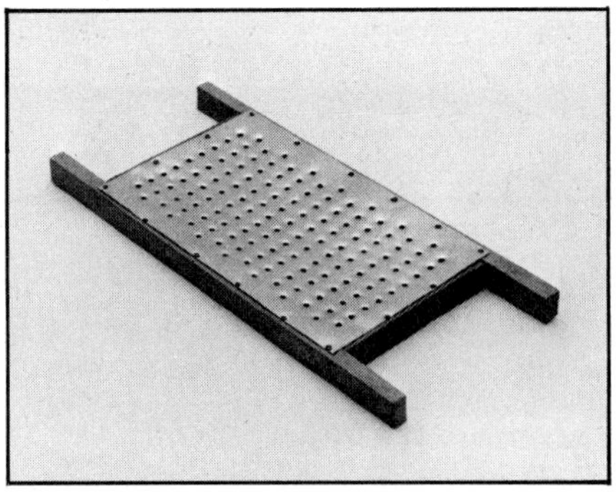

Cassava is one of the great gifts of the New World to the Old. Migrating first to Africa and later to the Far East, probably in Portuguese ships, cassava is now cultivated in all tropical climes. From this starchy tuber the Thais produce tapioca to use in soups, sauces and desserts, such as *lachong,* a sweet-meat in the form of inch-long noodles. This *lachong* press is a simple, rustic implement made of a piece of aluminum—10″ long and 6½″ wide and pierced with small holes—nailed to an orangey wooden frame 15″ long. To make *lachong,* the press is propped across a bowl of ice water, small amounts of cooked tapioca dough are spread on it and pressed through with the flat of the palm. Drained and chilled, the sweet noodles are eaten with a syrup of coconut milk and palm sugar.

Siam Grocery **$3.50**

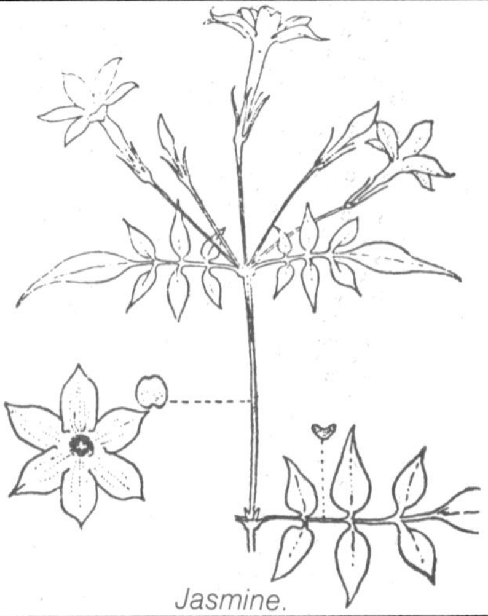

Jasmine.

Salim Press J:18

A cooked paste of mung bean flour, coconut milk and sugar is put into this handsome brass can and then forced out through the small holes in its bottom with the flatheaded plunger to make *salim,* a Thai dessert. The 4½″-tall can will hold three cups of dough, not much of which will escape the insistence of the snugly fitting 3⅞″-diameter plunger. Small, round handles on either side of the press give you something to steady the can with as you force the long, thin noodles out. Collect the *salim* in a bowl of ice water, then drain and serve them chilled, topped with a sweet jasmine syrup. Jasmine syrup? It's simply sugar and water boiled to a syrup to which jasmine flowers are added after it cools. No jasmine? Then use rose petals or other aromatic flowers for that special fragrance of a Thai dessert.

Siam Grocery **$6.00**

Sticky Rice Lunch Box J:19

Glutinous or "sticky" rice is a special type of rice with none of the amylose starch that makes other rice dry and fluffy; instead, it cooks into a gummy mass that becomes sticky as glue if it's cooked too long. Unlike the drier rice common in this country, however, sticky rice does not turn hard and unappetizing when it is cold—and it will stay fresh for many days after it is cooked. Thus, rice prepared in the morning may be put into one of the tiers of a *pinto* (lunch box), or into a covered basket with a shoulder strap like this one, and enjoyed later in the day for lunch. The bamboo basket is woven in a neat herringbone pattern; small loops provide a means of closing it and keep the twisted rope strap in place. Twelve inches long, 3¾″ wide and 5¾″ deep, it will hold a lot of sticky rice (or four peanut butter and jelly sandwiches).

Sam Siam Corp. $8.99

"He gave us a little cold rice, mixed with . . . wild potatoes. . . . This rice was pressed into a kind of rush basket, of which the opening was just large enough to admit the hand. My domestic and I seated ourselves on each side, and by turns we plunged our hands into this strange ragout. *It was so unpalatable, that it was necessary to drink at each mouthful in order to make it go down."*

The Kingdom and People of Siam *by Sir John Bowring. Oxford University Press, 1969.*

A rice mill in Siam.

Five-Tiered Lunch Box J:20

Easily the most ornate lunch box we've seen, this five-tiered affair is a wedding cake next to the commonplace boxy breadloaves schoolchildren and workers use in this country. On the outside, this lustrous anodized aluminum *pinto* (lunch box) is covered with a typically elaborate *chiengmai* relief pattern. On the inside, its five tiers can hold an equally elaborate repast: rice, three main dishes and a dessert. Each of the five lightweight dishes is 6½″ in diameter. The large (3″-deep) bottom dish holds the rice, while the shallow top dish, which has three smaller dishes inside (each 2½″ across and ½″ deep) carries the dessert—three servings of coconut custard or fruit in a sweet syrup. The three intermediate dishes (2½″ deep) might carry *kai kwam* (fried eggs stuffed with crab, prawns and pork), *kai yang* (grilled chicken rubbed with a prodigious quantity of garlic, black pepper and fresh coriander) and beef curry with peanuts and green apples. As the dishes are stacked, they are threaded over two metal bars that continue on to become the *pinto's* carrying handle. The dishes are held firmly in place by a pressure bar attached to the handle.

Siam Grocery $22.00

The Cuisine of Indonesia

No piece of real estate in the world has ever been so heavily invested with romance as the island group which we now call, prosaically, Indonesia. Its names ring in our memories—Java, Sumatra, Borneo, Bali—bringing visions of temple dancers, terraced mountainsides seen through the green mist, and Dietrich singing her heart out in some rain-drenched outpost below the equator. Indonesia is a nation made up of hundreds of islands that stretch, scythe-like, in a crescent extending from the Malayan archipelago on the northwest to Australia on the southeast. Like Poland and Palestine, Indonesia was swept over repeatedly by invading armies, so that its original culture has long since been blurred by the influence of the invaders. The Chinese have been there since 200 B.C., and the Indians since 400 A.D.; the Arabs held a monopoly on trade with Indonesia for many years, leaving their religion behind in exchange; and the Portuguese and the Dutch each fought to gain control of the islands.

Why did they bother? What gem was worth the price of all that effort and bloodshed? Why, these are the Spice Islands, the place where nutmeg, mace and cloves, white and black pepper, and cinnamon are grown, enticing traders and conquerers from all over the world. When the Dutch had control of Indonesia, they also held a monopoly of the world's spice trade; they limited the cultivation and the sale of spices, just as South Africa does of diamonds, and they

NASI KEBULI

2 cups rice
3/4 teaspoon cumin seed
1 teaspoon coriander
1/4 small red or yellow onion
2 cloves garlic
1/2″-thick slice *galangal*
1 small stick cinnamon
2 cloves
1/8 teaspoon mace or nutmeg
1 young chicken, cut into serving pieces
2 cups coconut milk
3 tablespoons oil
1/2 cucumber, sliced
Fresh basil leaves
Onion flakes

Wash the rice well and soak in cold water for about one hour. Drain and set aside.

Grind the cumin, coriander, onion and garlic into a smooth paste. Place this paste in a muslin bag. Add to the bag the *galangal,* cinnamon, cloves and nutmeg or mace, and tie it tightly.

Bring the chicken pieces and spice bag to a boil in the coconut milk and cook until the chicken is tender. Remove the chicken from its broth and set aside. Reserve the broth.

In a saucepan, fry the soaked rice with the oil, stirring occasionally until the rice is a yellow-brownish color; then pour the chicken broth in. Allow to bubble and boil until the liquid has evaporated. Transfer the rice to the rack of a steamer and steam until dry (about 25 minutes).

Fry the chicken pieces in oil until golden on both sides.

Place the rice on a serving dish. Garnish with sliced cucumber and fried chicken.

Sprinkle with fresh basil leaves and onion flakes.

Yield: 5 servings

(Courtesy of Hank Harjodimulyo)

Stone Mortar and Pestle J:21

For any Indonesian dish that calls for spices, the first instruction to the cook will invariably be to grind the ingredients to a paste. The rough surface of this flat, stone mortar and pestle set will make short work of the spice mixture for a *nasi kebuli* (spiced rice and chicken) in which ginger, cumin, coriander, lemon peel, garlic, onions, lemon grass and salt are mashed together. The 7½″-diameter mortar has a shallow depression instead of a bowl. And instead of the ordinary club-shaped pestle, which is grasped in the fist and then pounded down on the spices, this 5″-long pipe-shaped pestle is held by the stem and then rubbed over the surface of the mortar. It provides a more controlled action, which is good for grinding pastes; but it is less efficient for dealing with hard, dry spices than a high-walled mortar.

Beng-Solo Trading Corp. $17.00

prescribed the death penalty for anyone who dared to possess or sell those precious commodities. How strange it seems to us now, this mania which the West had for spices during the late Middle Ages and the Renaissance.

Whatever the results of this succession of masters were to the islands economically and politically, the influence on the cuisine was very positive. In Indonesia there is a marvelously varied style of cooking, with stir-fried vegetables, fire-hot curries and grilled kebabs (*satés*) existing side by side; while the most splendid reminder of the centuries of Dutch domination is the *rijsttafel*, a form of table service based on the colonial household with its staff of many houseboys.

At the heart of Indonesian cooking, however, are three foods, all indigenous: spices, coconut and rice. Paradoxically, the Indonesians are not great users of the very seasonings whose abundance caused the islands to be valued by so many invaders, preferring chiles, ginger and garlic to the gentler tastes of mace, nutmeg and cinnamon. And the cloves once so eagerly sought by Western traders, now spice Indonesian cigarettes, not their food.

The leaning toward chiles and the fiery nature of Indonesian food is probably best displayed in *sambal*, peppery cold relishes related to Indian chutneys, which are made of lime juice, onions, garlic and chile with the addition of other vegetables and herbs. There is an enormous variety of *sambal*, but the Westerner is advised to approach them cautiously, since they are always very, very hot. What he may not realize when he is confronted with an Indonesian dish so full of chiles that it brings tears to his eyes, is that it was meant to be served as a part of a meal that includes the tempering blandness of coconut milk and mountains of plain white rice.

No other ingredient is as basic to Indonesian cooking as the coconut, especially in the form of coconut milk. Oddly enough, the coconut palm may not be indigenous to the area. Although it thrives in the plentiful sunshine of the 70″ annual rainfall of Southeast Asia, it is also found in the Caribbean, and may actually have originated there. Most historians believe that it spread so wide and so far because ripe coconuts fell into the shallow waters near their trees, and then were borne out to sea and from island to island by ocean currents, like an army of edible Kon-Tikis.

As for rice, no visitor to Indonesia could fail to recognize its importance after seeing mile after mile of mountainous terrain carved into terraces devoted to the growth of this crop. Rice is the staple food of Indonesia, counteracting the fiery quality of the spices, holding together the wetter dishes so that the mixtures can be rolled up into neat little balls and eaten with the hands, and providing bulk in an unfortunately sparse diet.

"The nutmeg is a native of the Moluccas, and after possession of these islands by the Dutch, was, like the clove, jealously made an object of strict monopoly. Actuated by this narrow-minded policy, the Dutch endeavoured to extirpate the nutmeg-tree from the islands except Banda; but it is said that the wood-pigeon has often been the unintentional means of thwarting this monopolizing spirit, by conveying and dropping the fruit beyond these limits: thus disseminated, the plant has been always more widely diffused than the clove."

A History of the Vegetable Kingdom *by William Rhind, c. 1842.*

Spice Box J:22

For thousands of years the Molucca Islands were the only source of cloves, nutmeg and mace, while Sumatra and Java had cornered the market on black pepper. Wars were waged over these commodities until a clever Frenchman smuggled spice plants out of the Dutch colonies in Southeast Asia in the eighteenth century and squelched all the furor. Indonesia today still produces most of the world's nutmeg and mace; these and other spices are stored in Indonesian kitchens in small bamboo boxes like this one, which is 6″ long, 2¾″ wide and 1½″ deep. Interior walls divide the box into five discrete chambers. The bamboo is double woven so that no small grains will sift their way through the sides or bottom, and a top fits neatly over them all. An Indonesian cook might use it for dried *salam* leaves (Indonesian bay leaves), a nutmeg or two, coriander seeds, cumin and a few sticks of cinnamon.

Beng-Solo Trading Corp. $2.00

"The Nutmegge tree is like a Peare tree or a Peach tree, but that they are less, and it hath round leaves. These trees growe in the Iland of Banda, not farre from Maluco, and also in the Ilandes of Iavas & Sunda. . . . The fruite is altogether like great round Peaches, the inward part whereof is the Nutmegge. This hath about it a hard shell like wood, wherein the Nut lyeth loose: and this wooden shel or huske is covered over with Nutmeg flower, which is called Mace, and over it is the fruite, which without is like the fruite of a Peach. . . . When the Nuttes begin to be ripe, then they swell, and the first shell or huske bursteth in peeces, and the Nutmegge flowers doe continue redde, as . . . Scarlet, which is a verie faire sight to behold . . . if the trees bee ful of fruite. Sometimes also the Mace breaketh, which is the cause that the Nutmegges come altogether without the Mace, and when the Nutmegge drieth, then the Mace falleth off, and the red changeth into Orenge colour, as you see by the Mace that is brought hether."

The Voyage of John Huyghen van Linschoten to the East Indies *from the Old English translation of 1598. Lenox Hill Pub. & Dist. Co. (Burt Franklin), 1970.*

Chopping Board/ Meat Tenderizer J:23

Indonesian recipes often call for small morsels of meats and vegetables; and Indonesian beef, being extremely lean, is tough. A chopping board and a meat tenderizer are consequently necessary in Indonesian kitchens. This combination tool is intended to satisfy both needs. A simple wooden rectangle 4″ by 8″, it is divided into two parts: half is a smooth chopping square, the other half is carved into dozens of small pyramids whose function it is to break down the fibers of the meat. Use the board to make *lapis daging:* first tenderize a flank steak or a similar cut of meat, then cut it diagonally into thin slices. Coat the meat with a mixture of chopped tomato, onion and garlic, nutmeg, pepper, cinnamon, lemon juice, *sambal ulek* (hot chile paste) and *kecap* (soy sauce). Fry, and thicken the juices with grated coconut and flour.

Beng-Solo Trading Corp. $2.00

Wooden Coconut Grater J:24

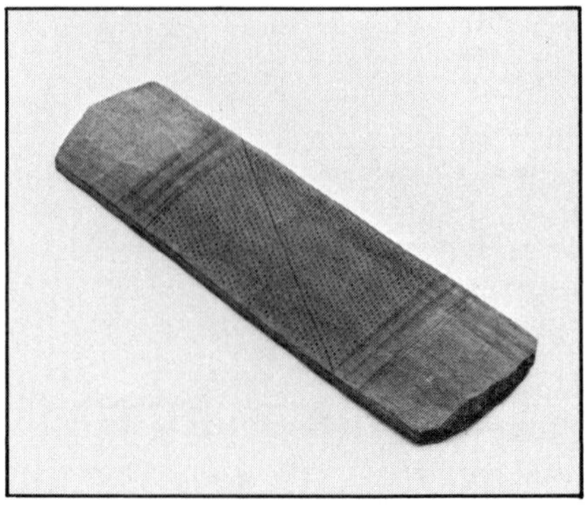

If you really want to make coconut milk the Indonesian way, you'll need this large wooden grater, 13½″ long and 4″ wide, with a hundred-odd nail points sticking a mere hair's breadth above the surface. By gripping the long paddle between your knees and slanting it down into a wooden bowl, you can get the right leverage to reduce a sizeable chunk of coconut to the tiniest of shreds in a jiffy. But beware shredded knuckles and nails: this tool is more dangerous than it looks.

Oriental Country Store $2.95

Coconut Milk Strainer J:25

To make coconut milk the Indonesian way, you must first grate coconut meat into tiny shreds. Then, the meat must be soaked in a small amount of warm water before being placed in a closely woven strainer like this. The coconut shreds are then squeezed tightly in your fist and the resulting liquid is collected in a bowl set under the strainer. The first pressing makes coconut cream: a thick milk often used in making sweets like steamed coconut custard or added in the last stage of cooking to certain dishes like *opor ajam,* chicken with almonds and tamarind. Soak the same coconut shreds in more warm water and squeeze it all again for a thinner coconut milk that will boil without curdling and is used to make *sajur* (a souplike dish) and boiled meat dishes. Or combine the two liquids for an all-purpose milk. This coconut milk strainer is 7⅝″ square, and is framed by 1½″-wide bamboo slats.

Beng-Solo Trading Corp. $5.00

"Co'cas, or Coco . . . The tree grows generally straight without any branches, . . . It bears on the top twelve leaves nearly ten feet long, and half a foot broad, which the inhabitants use to cover their housess &c.

From this tree the Indians extract a liquor which they call suri, of a grateful taste, and when drank in quantity, intoxicates. They also prepare from it a vinegar and a species of sugar, called jagra [in reality from the jaggery, not coconut palm].

The tree bears fruit twice a year, and those sometimes twice as big as a man's head. While the nuts are new, and the bark tender, they yield half a pint of a clear, cooling water; which in a little time becomes first a white, soft pulp, and at length condenses, and assumes the taste of the nut."

A New and Universal Dictionary of Arts and Sciences. *London, 1756.*

Sieve J:26

This pretty bamboo basket, 12″ in diameter and only 4″ high, would make a splendid serving platter lined with large leaves and piled high with yellow turmeric rice or a sunburst of skewered *satés* (Indonesian kebabs). But its principal use in Indonesia is as a sieve, to drain vegetables, noodles or fried foods. Or, lined with cheesecloth so that the small shreds of coconut do not slip through the open weave, it is used to strain coconut milk. The small, square openings suggest still another use for this versatile basket; they're the right size for making *cendol,* a dessert made with *sago* (a flour made of pounded palm pith) or mung bean flour. The batter is pressed through the holes into a bowl of ice water. The one-inch squiggles that result are eaten with coconut syrup (palm sugar dissolved in coconut milk and flavored with cinnamon and pandanus leaf).

H. Roth & Son $4.98

CENDOL

"Tears" Pudding in Brown Sugar Syrup

1 cup rice flour (or ½ cup *sago,* if available)
2 cups coconut milk
A few drops of food coloring

Mix the rice flour (or *sago*) with ⅓ cup of the coconut milk until smooth. In a saucepan, heat the rest of the coconut milk with some food coloring. When it is lukewarm, add the rice flour mixture, stirring well. Bring to a boil and simmer for a few minutes until it is thickened, then remove the pan from the heat.

Fill a large bowl with ice water. Place a strainer with ¼″ holes (a special sieve from Indonesia called a *saringan cendol* is perfect) 3″ above the ice water. Pour the hot mixture into the sieve, and with the back of the spoon, press the mixture gently against the holes. The mixture will drip into the water below, forming tear-shaped drops. Repeat this process until the mixture is used up. Drain the water and set aside.

BROWN SUGAR SYRUP:
½ jar sweet *langka*
1 cup brown sugar
¾ cup water

Slice the sweet *langka* into ¼″ strips. Combine sugar, water and sweet *langka* strips in a large saucepan. Bring to a boil over low heat and stir constantly until the sugar is completely dissolved. Cool the syrup.

1 cup thick coconut milk
A pinch of salt

Bring the coconut milk and salt to a boil. Stir well and remove from heat. Let it stand until cool.

TO SERVE:
Spoon 5 tablespoons *cendol* into sundae glasses. Top with 3 tablespoons syrup. Fill the rest of the glass with 2 ice cubes and the thick coconut milk.

Yield: 5 servings

(*Courtesy of Hank Harjodimulyo*)

The manufacture of sago.

Bamboo Tray J:27

In central Java where it was made, this shallow basket is used to winnow rice. But it may be put to any number of uses, most appropriately as a serving tray for Indonesian food. A 16″ circle of woven bamboo stretched in a 1⅞″-deep ring of bent bamboo, like linen in

Continued from preceding page

an embroidery hoop, it will make a lovely platter for a spectacular *nasi kuning lengkap* ("yellow rice complete"), a sacred mountain of yellow rice surrounded by assorted side dishes, such as grilled spiced chicken, coconut patties, pickled vegetables, tamarind shrimp and crisply-fried peanut wafers.

Beng-Solo Trading Corp. $4.00

Colander/Strainer J:28

Many Indonesian kitchen utensils do double-duty, including this woven bamboo colander. A large 10″-diameter basket, whose squared-off bottom is supported by a 3″-high bamboo base, would probably make its way to the table bearing 6 cups of fluffy white *nasi* (cooked rice). Before it reached the table filled with rice, however, it was no doubt used to wash the rice (frowned on by some, but necessary if the rice is very starchy). The colander's square base makes it both free-standing and sturdy, and its capacity is suitable to washing larger things like beans, broccoli and tomatoes for a *sajur lodeh* (vegetables in coconut sauce) to go with the rice.

H. Roth & Son $5.95

"RICE, oryza. This grain which is so much in esteem in the eastern countries, that it is the principal corn they use, grows to be three or four feet high with leaves broader than those of wheat, bearing spikes much divided and composed of oblong flattish grains, having each a beard or awn, two or three inches long, forked at the top, and frequently coloured at bottom. They are of a white colour, composed of a brown husk or skin. Rice is sown in Italy, Turkey and the East Indies: and we have as large and good from Carolina, as from any part of the world. It is more used for food than physic, being a wholsome strengthening grain, restringent and good for those who have a slipperiness in their bowels, or are inclinable to a flux or looseness."

A New and Universal Dictionary of Arts and Sciences. *London, 1756.*

Rice Steamer J:29

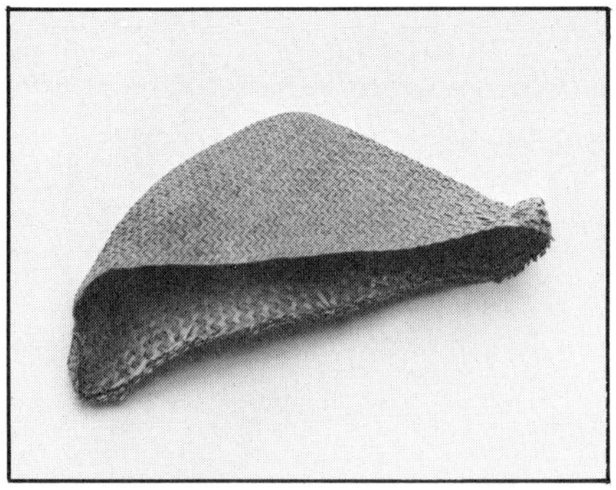

Dewi Sri is the rice goddess of ancient Indonesia. She lived with other deities on a sacred mountain, and they were all honored and propitiated with offerings of food. Today most Indonesians are Muslim, but their reverence for rice is still evident. Javanese rice farmers eschew efficient, modern harvesting implements in favor of small knives sacred to Dewi Sri. And on Muslim holidays and other special occasions, a cone-shaped sacred mountain of rice called a *tumpeng* is prepared, the whiteness of the rice representing purity, the reds, yellows and blacks of the garnishes representing anger, greed and violence: the whole therefore symbolizing the mastery of reason over passion. A special all-white *tumpeng* is placed next to a newborn Javanese child to inspire him to a virtuous life. The same cone shape is used for *nasi kuning,* a yellow rice signifying happiness, appropriate for weddings and other festive events. The characteristic shape of a *tumpeng* or *nasi kuning* is achieved by steaming the rice in a conical mold like this large *kukusan* from Sumatra, which is made of woven bamboo. Measuring four feet around the top, it could make an enormous meal, but smaller amounts of rice may also be prepared in it. The Indonesians use a two-step process: first the rice is parboiled, then it is steamed in the bamboo cone, which fits neatly into the cone-shaped neck of a special pot, or rests on the metal tray of a tall steamer.

Beng-Solo Trading Corp. $2.00

To avoid awakening the wrath of the rice spirit, Indonesians use a knife with a hidden blade when harvesting the grain.

Sifting from the husks, and grinding the rice in Sumatra.

Wooden Rice Spoon J:30

An amusing, wide spatula with a fantastic creature—all nose and headdress and no chin—carved into the handle, this utensil is for scooping up servings of cooked rice. Its size is an indication of the importance of rice on the Indonesian table—it is a full foot long. The almost flat bowl will hold a generous portion of plain rice, boiled briefly and then steamed without salt or any other condiment; for rice is always mixed with spicy food to balance the pungency with a starchy blandness. Our server is roughly carved, and the odd head seems quite accidental until you take the spoon in hand and discover that the receding chin is precisely the most comfortable place to rest your forefinger, and that the teased pompadour fits perfectly into your palm.

H. Roth & Son **$3.98**

Kuali J:31

Called a *kuali* or *wadjan* in Indonesia, this large, round, bowl-shaped frying pan is the principal cooking pot in Indonesian kitchens; we know it already by its Cantonese name, wok. Ideal for stir-frying, it is also right for simmering curries or other sauces; for browning meats, onions and spices to which broth or coconut milk will be added; for steaming vegetables or rice (a rack and lid must be added); and for deep frying. Its only limitation—as far as American kitchens are concerned—is that it cannot be used efficiently on an electric range; over gas (a metal ring may be needed to hold it steady) or over the charcoal or kerosene burners used in Indonesia, the thin steel heats quickly and the curved shape distributes the heat evenly. The gray and white enamel of this wok has the added advantage of being easy to clean. Fourteen inches in diameter and 4½″ deep, it is a good size both for large and small amounts of food.

Beng-Solo Trading Corp. **$14.00**

An eighteenth-century artist's view of Javanese fauna.

A late sixteenth-century description of the "iland of Iava [Java] reveals that it was a land of plenty: "This Iland aboundeth with Rice, and all manner of victuals, [as oxen,] kyne, hogges, sheepe, and hennes, [etc. also] Onyons, Garlicke, Indian nuttes, [and] with al [kind of] Spices, as cloves, Nutmegges, and mace, which they carry unto Malacca . . . there is much Pepper, and it is better then that of India or Malabar, wherof there is so great quantitie, that they could lade yearlie from thence 4 or 5 thousand kin-tales Portingale waight. . . ."*

** 100 pounds*

The Voyage of John Huyghen van Linschoten to The East Indies *from the Old English translation of 1598. Lenox Hill Pub. & Dist. Co. (Burt Franklin), 1970.*

Coconut and Bamboo Spoon J:32

Stir-frying, that quick, efficient method of cooking small pieces of meat and vegetables to just the right crispy texture, is a cooking technique basic to Indonesian cuisine. The process usually begins with onions, chiles and

Continued from preceding page

shrimp paste and concludes with a little coconut milk to provide a sauce. It is performed in a *kuali,* or wok, with this long-handled, shallow-bowled spoon, an appealingly primitive tool made of a round section of coconut shell, 3¾″ in diameter, securely lashed to a 13″-long bamboo stick. An Indonesian would also use it to stir-fry leftover rice for a *nasi goreng* breakfast, a fried rice that is eaten with fried eggs, sliced tomatoes and cucumbers—a dish that has become so popular it is now often embellished with sliced steak, shrimp, cabbage and bean sprouts and served at lunch or dinner.

H. Roth & Son **$0.95**

Bamboo Scoop J:33

No, it isn't a fan, though it would do in a pinch. This tool, made of a 17½″-long piece of bamboo split a third of the way down into ten ribs through which narrower strips of bamboo are interwoven, does in Indonesian cooking what a wire skimmer does in the West: scoops fried foods out of sizzling oil. The bamboo woof is loose enough to allow the excess coconut or peanut oil to run back into the wok as the food is lifted to a serving platter. Eight inches across the broad end, it resembles a giant webbed hand: its wide reach and gently curved shape can dredge up lots of small croquettes or meatballs at a time, and the handle is long enough for good balance and safe distance from the hot fat. In Indonesia it scoops up *pergedel kentang* (potato croquettes) and *rempah* (meat and coconut patties); but evenings during the month of Ramadan when, after their dawn to sunset fast, Indonesian Muslims like to indulge in sweets, it's more apt to fish out crisp fritters made with bananas or stuffed dates.

Beng-Solo Trading Corp. **$1.50**

Coconut Shell Skimmer J:34

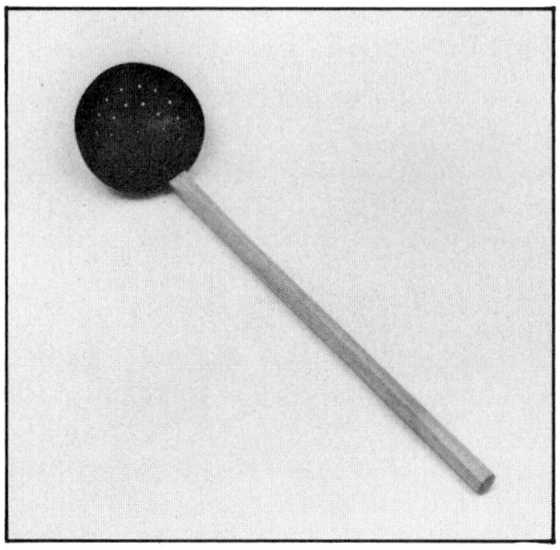

Small holes perforate the polished coconut shell bowl of this attractive skimmer. The smooth, shallow bowl, 3¼″ in diameter, is a thin brown disc; the wooden handle, 11½″ long, is secured to it by two small copper nails. The style, although not the manufacture, is Indonesian. It would come in handy to lift out of hot oil those croquettes and fritters that probably came to Indonesia with the Dutch, but which the Indonesians have adapted to the Southeast Asian palate. Corn fritters (*pergedel djagung*) and shrimp, scallion and carrot cakes (*bahwan*), for example, are spiced with coriander and cumin, sometimes with a few sliced chiles thrown in.

Sermoneta **$5.00**

Coconut Shell Ladle J:35

Coconut shell spoons are basic cooking and serving utensils in Indonesia as elsewhere in Southeast Asia, where coconut palms thrive. They range from a shallow stirring tool to a deep water dipper made from three-quarters of the whole coconut shell. Here, half the shell of a small coconut has been highly polished to a smooth, dappled brown and tan, and converted into a soup ladle that will hold ⅓ cup. The 9″-long wooden handle curves gracefully away from the bowl and is securely attached to it by two small copper nails. Although it was made in Sri Lanka, it resembles authentic Indonesian ladles and will be perfect for serving *soto*—a chunky meat-broth dish that in Indonesia makes a light meal or substantial snack, the way pizza does in this country—or a *sajur,* a side dish of vegetables in a thin coconut milk stock.

Sermoneta **$6.00**

SOTO MADURA

Chicken and Bean Thread Soup

BROTH:
1 young chicken, about 2 lbs.
6 cups water
½″-thick slice ginger
3 macadamia nuts
½ red or yellow onion
2 cloves garlic
½ teaspoon turmeric
⅜ teaspoon white pepper
Salt
½ stalk lemon grass
1 tablespoon soy sauce

Place the chicken (whole or cut up)

in a large pot with the water. Boil the chicken until tender. Grind and mash the ginger, nuts, onion, garlic, turmeric and pepper into a smooth paste. Mix the paste into the boiling chicken water. Add the lemon grass and salt to taste. Remove the chicken from the broth; discard the lemon grass. Add the soy sauce to the broth and set aside. Then bone the chicken and shred the meat into small pieces. Set the chicken aside.

1 pkg. of bean threads, soaked in hot water for 15 minutes, then refreshed in cold running water, drained and set aside
¼ lb. bean sprouts, dipped into hot water until they are just half cooked, drained and set aside
1 tablespoon onion flakes
1 tablespoon chopped celery leaves
2 boiled potatoes, peeled and sliced
½ pkg. broken fish chips or potato chips
1 lemon, cut into 8 wedges
3 hard-boiled eggs, sliced

TO SERVE:
Arrange all the ingredients (including the reserved chicken shreds) on a serving tray and garnish with sliced eggs and lemon wedges. Each person helps himself to a little bit of everything on the tray and puts it in his soup dish. Then ladle the chicken broth over the garnishes. A bowl of white rice is always an accompaniment to this dish.

Yield: 6 to 7 servings

(Courtesy of Hank Harjodimulyo)

A sixteenth-century chronicler wrote of "the Ilandes of Maluco": "These Ilands have no other spice than cloves, but in so great abundance, that as it appeareth, by them the whole world is filled therewith. In this Iland are found firie hilles, they are very dry and burnt land, they have nothing els but victuals of flesh and fish, but for Rice, Corne, Onyons, Garlicke, and such like [and all other necessaries, some are brought from Portingale, and some from other places thereabout, which they take and barter for cloves]. *The bread which they have there of their owne* [baking] *is of wood or rootes, like the men of Brasillia . . ."*

The Voyage of John Huyghen van Linschoten to the East Indies *from the Old English translation of 1598. Lenox Hill Publ. & Dist. Co.* (*Burt Franklin*), *1970.*

A gadogado ingredient.

Coconut Shell Spoon J:36

To serve the bright array of carrots, green beans, tomatoes, cabbage, bean sprouts, spinach and hard-boiled eggs of a *gado gado,* this polished coconut shell spoon will lend the right exotic touch, even though it is not Indonesian but Sri Lankan. With its oval bowl, 3½″ long, and wooden handle, 8¾″ long, attached by two small copper nails, it is the right size, too, for this well-known Indonesian salad. What is so special about this mixed vegetable salad? The dressing: a spicy peanut sauce made with ground roasted peanuts, chiles, vinegar and sugar. Garnished with crunchy *krupuk* (crisp shrimp wafers), fried onion flakes and slices of beef braised in soy sauce, it can become the main attraction of an Indonesian meal.

Sermoneta $5.00

Betel Nut Container J:37

The betel or areca palm is native to tropical Asia, and its dried nuts—wrapped in fresh betel leaves with some slaked lime, mixed with a tannin extract called *catechu* to reduce its harshness—have provided countless generations of Southeast Asians with a good chew, a habit probably already well established before it was noted by Herodotus in ancient times. Its dedicated users say that it helps digestion and prevents infection; it also blackens and loosens the teeth, a circumstance that long made black false teeth fashionable at the court of Bangkok. To store the ingredients and paraphernalia for this habit, now popular chiefly among older people, Indonesians use a small box of woven bamboo divided into separate compartments. The compartments hold: the betel nuts, the betel leaves, the lime, the *catechu,* tobacco and spices (which are often chewed with the betel), some grease for chapping caused by the lime, and often a small brass implement for grinding the various items together. We include a betel box here because we have a weakness for kokoshka dolls, Egyptian burial customs and Chinese boxes. This container—which looks for all the world like a magician's traveling case—consists of a roughly woven box divided into two levels. Into the bottom level fits another box with a shallow tray and two smaller, concealed drawers. When the inner boxes are assembled, they fit into a more finely woven outer box with a lid. The whole measures 7½″ by 4½″ by 4½″.

Knobkerry $25.00

The Cuisine of the Philippines

The Philippines lie midway between Indonesia and Japan geographically, and midway between East and West gastronomically and culturally. To a foundation of Southeast Asian culture, years of Spanish domination added Christianity, cheese and dresses with butterfly sleeves, while further years of American influence have added technology, American slang and Coca-Cola.

In cooking, this means that Philippine food is an amalgam of Asian techniques and tastes—woks and fish pastes—brought to bear upon some unexpectedly Western ingredients, such as sausages, olive oil and steak. It also means that this is a cooking style that is not uncongenial to Western tastes: a cuisine whose spices do not include large numbers of unbearably hot chiles, and whose fish pastes do not remind one so clearly of the fermenting process that wrought them.

It is only by reading the reports of the first explorers to reach the islands in the 16th century that we can guess at what Philippine food would be without its Western accretions. They were greeted by natives who offered the sailors rice that had been cooked in leaves, salt-dried fish and patties of glutinous rice moistened with coconut milk: all dishes that are enjoyed in the Philippines to this day. But outside influences were already at work. The Chinese had introduced noodles, egg rolls and the wok; and from Indochina came a taste, moderated but defined, for spices and chiles.

It was the four hundred years of Spanish domination, however, that made the greatest impact on the native cuisine; so that today, one will also be served spicy sausage, *paellas* and stews similar to those made in Spain. And although the use of the wok is widespread in these islands, it is used for sautéing, rather than for stir-frying; and the sautéing is more than likely done in lard or olive oil, two decidedly non-native cooking oils. Cheese-making was also introduced by the Spaniards: the only native cheese of the Pacific is produced in the Philippines, and is made from the milk of the water buffalo. And every afternoon in Luzon, Filipinos partake of the *merienda*, a meal of afternoon tea and sweets—a habit adopted, fully-formed, from the Spaniards.

What does it amount to when we sit down to eat a Philippine meal? There will be many composed dishes, stews, seafoods and fritters. The predominant tastes will be *sour*—from the use of vinegar and tamarind and other sour fruits—and *salty*—from various fermented fish products. And although there will be many different spices, they will be used with a light touch, so that tender Western stomachs need not be afraid. Fish soups, tangy with the bite of tamarind; *lumpia* (egg rolls stuffed with chicken pork and hearts of palm,

KARI-KARI

Oxtail Stew with Green Beans and Eggplant

To serve 6

5- to 5½-pounds oxtail, cut into 3-inch lengths
1 tablespoon salt
3 tablespoons vegetable oil
2 tablespoons annatto oil
1 large onion, peeled and cut crosswise into paper-thin slices
2 teaspoons finely chopped garlic
4 quarts water
½ cup uncooked long- or medium-grain white rice
¼ cup salted skinned peanuts
1 pound fresh green string beans, washed and trimmed
A 1- to 1½-pound eggplant, washed, stemmed and cut lengthwise into 8 wedges

GARNISH (optional)
1 tablespoon thinly sliced scallions
1 tablespoon finely chopped celery leaves

Wipe the pieces of oxtail with a dampened towel, then sprinkle them with the salt. In a heavy 8- to 10-quart casserole, heat the vegetable oil over moderate heat until a light haze forms above it. Brown 5 to 6 pieces of oxtail at a time, turning them frequently with tongs and regulating the heat so that they color richly and evenly without burning. As they brown, transfer the pieces to a plate.

Pour off all the fat remaining in the casserole and in its place add the annatto oil. Drop in the onion and garlic and, stirring frequently to scrape in any brown particles that cling to the bottom and sides of the casserole, cook over moderate heat for 8 to 10 minutes until the onion is soft and a delicate golden color.

Return the pieces of oxtail and the liquid accumulated around them to the casserole and add 2½ quarts of the water. Bring to a boil over high heat, reduce the heat to low, and simmer partially covered for about 2½ hours, or until the meat can easily be pulled away from the bone with a small fork.

Meanwhile, place the rice in a small, heavy skillet or saucepan (preferably one with a non-stick cooking surface). Frequently sliding the pan gently back and forth over the burner, toast the and served with sweetened soy sauce or minced garlic); hearty *adobos* (stews made from vinegar-soaked beef); *pucheros* (stews, thick with sausage, tripe and sweet potatoes); and *lechon* (roast suckling pig). All of these will be served with rice and spicy relishes, and will be followed by a dessert made from shaved ice and coconut milk. This is the sort of spicy, filling and altogether satisfying food that comes from Philippine kitchens.

rice over low heat for 20 or 30 minutes, or until the grains are golden brown. Pour the rice into the jar of an electric blender and blend at high speed until the rice is reduced to a flourlike powder. Pour it into a bowl. Pulverize the peanuts in the blender, then rub them through a fine sieve with the back of a spoon. Set the rice powder and peanuts aside. (To pulverize the rice and peanuts by hand, pound them as finely as possible with a mortar and pestle and force them through a medium meshed sieve with the back of a spoon.)

When the oxtail has cooked its allotted time, add the remaining 1½ quarts of water, the rice powder and pulverized peanuts. Mix well, then add the green beans and eggplant and turn them about in the stew with a large spoon. Bring to a boil over high heat and cook briskly, uncovered, stirring occasionally, for 10 to 15 minutes, or until the vegetables are tender but still intact.

Taste for seasoning and serve directly from the casserole or from a deep, heated bowl. If you like, garnish the top with scallions and celery leaves. *Kari-kari* may be accompanied by *patis.*

(From FOODS OF THE WORLD, Pacific and Southeast Asian Cooking, *Time-Life Books, New York. Copyright 1970 by Time Inc.)*

Marble Mortar and Pestle J:38

A beautiful gray-white marble was used to sculpt this elegant mortar and pestle, with its highly polished and smooth outer surface. But the inside of the shallow (2¼″-deep) bowl and the almost flat head of the pestle have been left rough to provide a good grinding surface for herbs and spices. The pair are also extremely heavy, an added advantage for serious work. They will quickly and efficiently reduce uncooked rice and peanuts to a fine powder to thicken and flavor *kari-kari,* a popular Philippine stew made with oxtail, green beans and eggplant. The mortar sits only 4½″ high on its small pedestal, but is 6″ wide across the top. The hefty, tapered pestle is 7″ long and 2″ wide at the grinding end.

H. A. Mack & Co., Inc. $20.00

Coconut Scraper J:39

A rough but extremely effective tool, this Philippine coconut scraper has been fashioned out of a 10″ length of iron bar. One end has been flattened and notched with sharp teeth intended for scraping coconut meat out of its shell. The other end is a mini-crowbar for prying the split and drained coconut shell apart. A hole midway between the two ends is provided to secure the tool to the end of a work table or bench.

Oriental Country Store $1.20

"Of the Palme trees, whereon the Indian Nuts called Cocus doe grow . . . The tree waxeth very high and straight, . . . They have no great rootes, so that a man would thinke it were impossible for them to have any fast hold within the earth, and yet they stand so fast and grow so high, that it maketh men feare to see men clime uppon them [least they should fall downe]."

The Voyage of John Huyghen van Linschoten to the East Indies *from the Old English translation of 1598. Lenox Hill Pub. & Dist. Co. 1970.*

Durian.

Melon Baller/ Shredder J:40

Salads and desserts of luscious tropical fruits provide cool, refreshing relief during heat waves. Hot weather comes and we think right away of an ambrosia of papaya, pineapple, mango and banana tossed with shredded coconut. In the Philippines the choice of fruits would be much grander: brown-sugary sweet *chico,* sticky grapelike *lanzones,* acidy pink and green *macopa,* apple-shaped *mangosteens,* sour *guayabano,* thistle-skinned *rambutans,* pine-flavored jackfruit, smelly *durian* (like Limburger, definitely an acquired taste), and sweet, dry *pomelo* would all clamor for your at-

Continued from preceding page

tention. This baller and shredder would be kept busy trying out different combinations. A simple brass tool, 6¼″ long, it has a hemisphere 1″ in diameter at one end and a fan of six small rings at the other, both soldered to a hollow tube. Scoop out spheres with one; scrape out shreds with the other. Use it for *atsara*, a salad of cucumbers and bitter melon (a small, green, tapered melon also called balsam pear), a sour but refreshing combination with vinegar, onions and salt.

H. A. Mack & Co., Inc. **$2.75**

Ice Scraper J:41

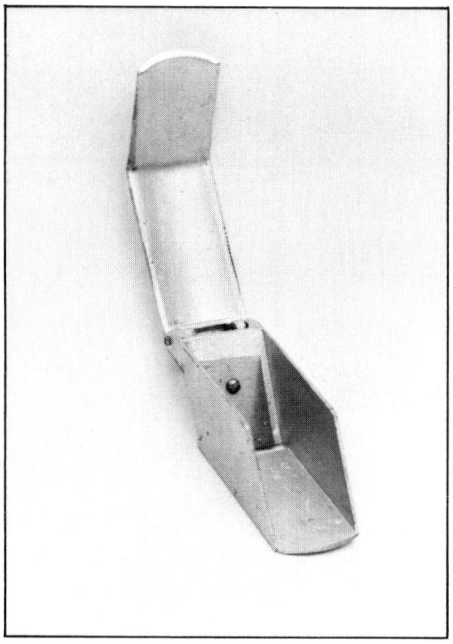

This is neither a carpenter's plane (although it works like one), nor a child's toy (although it looks like one), but an aluminum ice shaver. A parallelepiped (great word!) 6″ long and 2″ high and wide, it has a slit cut in the bottom through which an adjustable razor edge protrudes. Rub the bottom over the surface of a block of ice, and it shaves off slivers that collect in the box. Then lift the lid and scoop it out. What then? Why, you make *halo-halo* ("mix-mix"), of course. Pour coconut milk over the ice and then mix in crisp grains of fried rice, mung beans, pineapple jelly, or bits of corn. Spoon this tropical ice cream sundae into a glass and serve it for dessert.

Filipinas International, Ltd. **$3.50**

Scoop/Sieve J:42

Hold this handwoven sieve in your hand and you will find that you begin to make scooping motions without ever intending to, so suited is the design to the function. It was fashioned from the forked branch of a tree, its limbs softened and bent to form the rim of a woven bamboo basket. Use it for scooping rice from a pot. Or, since the wide spaces between the bamboo slats that form the warp allow liquids to drain off between them, use it for lifting one of the many Philippine fried dishes from its bath of bubbling oil: *ukoy* (shrimp, sweet potato and squash cakes), or *lumpia* (chicken, pork and vegetable egg rolls), or *rellenong alimango* (stuffed crab), or tasty sweet-potato chips. The scoop's handle is 6½″ long and holds a basket approximately 5″ in diameter and 2¾″ deep.

H. A. Mack & Co., Inc. **$1.25**

According to van Linschoten, a sixteenth century chronicler, tamarind—the sour fruit used extensively in Philippine cuisine—derived its name in the following circuitous fashion: it is called by "the Arabians, Tamarindii, because Tamaras in Arabia are the same that with us we call Dates, and because they know not what to liken Tamarinio unto, better then unto Dates, therfore they call it Tamarindi, yt. is, Tamaras or Dates or India, whereupon the Portingales cal it also Tamarinio." Further explaining the curious fruit (and confusing the curious reader), van Linschoten writes: "The nature of this tree is to be wondered at, for that the Tamarinio, that is to say, the long . . . huske wherin it is, in the night time shrinketh it self up under the leaves, to cover it from the cold of the night, and in the day time it uncovereth it self again all naked and outright, as I have often seene and behold it: when it is caryed abroad or sold, it is out of the shelles or huskes, and being put together they make balles thereof, as bigge as a mans fist, but it is clammie and sticketh together. It is not very pleasant to looke on, nor yet to handle, but verie good cheap. . . ."

The Voyage of John Huyghen van Linschoten to the East Indies *from the Old English translation of 1598. Lenox Hill Publ. & Dist. Co. (Burt Franklin), 1970.*

Bamboo Noodle Strainer J:43

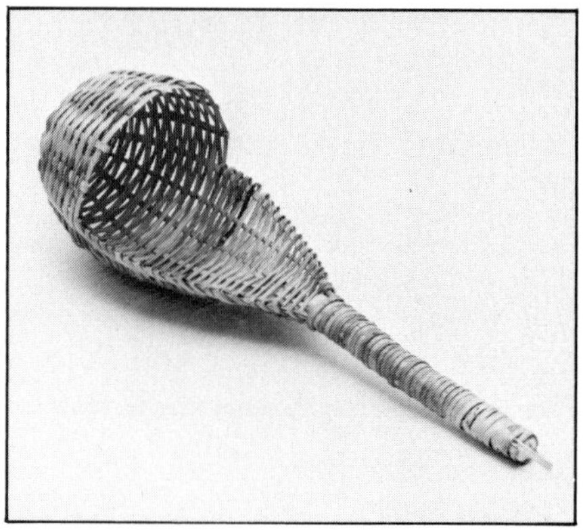

Chinese influence in the Philippines long antedates the Spanish: Chinese settlers may have migrated there as early as the seventh century, and throughout the Western Middle Ages, the Visayan Islands and Luzon were regular ports of call for Chinese traders. They brought porcelain, gunpowder and kite-flying to the islands, as well as their noodles, soy sauce, bean curd, bean sprouts and egg rolls. But today, the Filipinos don't prepare these foods in the Chinese fashion any more than they eat them with chopsticks. Chinese noodles, for example, are often boiled briefly and then sautéed, Spanish-style, in olive oil and garlic. To drain the noodles (*pancit*) between the boiling and the sautéing, a Philippine cook uses a bamboo basket like this one. Ours is 6″ in diameter and 4″ deep, with a long, wooden, bamboo-wrapped handle by which to hang the strainer as well as hold it while shaking the water off the noodles. The sound of noodles against the bamboo is supposed to have given the onomatopoetic sobriquet, *luglug,* to the popular *pancit luglug,* a garlicky noodle dish with shrimp sauce and pork crackling.

Faroy Sales (PIB-60) $3.00

Bamboo Steamer J:44

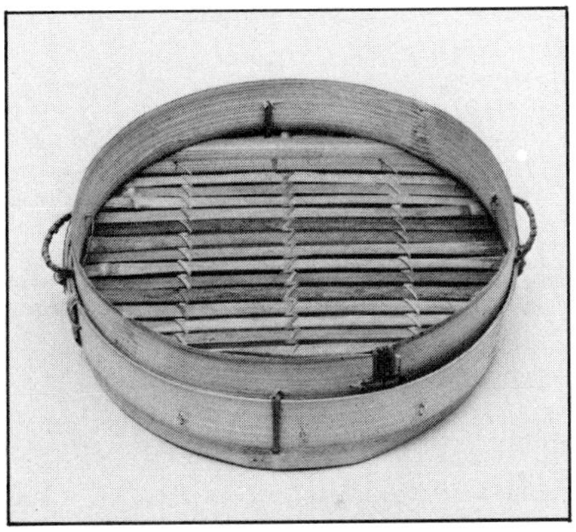

Clearly a device descended from the Chinese kitchen, this bamboo steamer is designed for use over boiling water in a wok. Use it for vegetables and fish, or try the steamed sticky rice sweets that Filipinos prepare for desserts and for their late afternoon *meriendas.* To make *suman maruecos,* wrap a mixture of ground rice, coconut milk and sugar in banana leaves and steam; or line the steamer with cheesecloth to make a cake of the same ingredients, but alternate the rice layers with mashed yam for a colorful contrast. Wide bamboo strips lashed into a 11½″-diameter hoop surround a bamboo-slat steaming tray that sits 2″ down inside the hoop. An extra strip is lashed around the steamer's circumference to act as a shelf on which another steamer can be stacked.

Banana Traders $6.00

Although rice is not sacred in the United States, there remain several rituals in which it figures prominently. The most well-known of these is the tradition of rice-tossing at weddings. Although this was originally done to assure fertility, changing times have made the practice carry the more generalized message of "good luck."

Palayok and Brazier J:45

All Philippine cooking begins with a charcoal fire. Tamed within a metal box or a pit in the ground, it provides the heat for cooking fritters, soups and stews. Here is a set that provides both the fire and the pot: a terra-cotta brazier on which sits the most typical piece of Philippine cookware of all, the *palayok.* Filipinos love to mix and match food, rarely letting any ingredient stand by itself, often putting several together in a slow-simmered soup or stew, and almost always in a *palayok.* Use the casserole to make a rich, savory, but very sour, *sinampalukan:* a fish (or chicken) and vegetable soup that takes its flavor from the leaves—and often blossoms—of the tamarind tree. Our traditionally shaped *palayok* (Tolkien disciples claim that its design is clear evidence of hobbit habitation in the Philippines) is 7½″ in diameter, 2¾″ deep and holds 4 cups. The 2¾″-deep brazier will hold several charcoal briquets and has three holes in its walls to let air in to feed the fire. Both pot and brazier are unglazed.

Bulaklak Marketing, Inc. $6.00

Coconut Ladle J:46

In the Philippines, as elsewhere in Southeast Asia, the coconut palm is not just a source of food and drink: its trunk provides building material for homes, its plaited fronds cover walls and floors, and the husks supply fiber for rope. As fuel, the hard brown shells may be burned directly or processed into charcoal. Or the shells may be made into bowls, cups and kitchen implements: stirrers, dippers, or ladles like this one, depending on the size and curvature of the piece used. Lashed with reeds to a long wooden handle, this piece of roughly finished coconut shell becomes a large, sturdy scoop, 20″ long, useful for ladling a pork, chicken, shrimp and sausage stew over a heaping mound of egg noodles.

H. A. Mack & Co., Inc. $1.25

From a long list of the virtues of coconut: "These Cocus being yet in their husks, may be carried over the whole world, [*and not once hurt or brused*] *and it happeneth oftentimes that by continuance of time, the water within the Cocus doth convert, and congeale into a* [*certaine kinde of*] *yellow apple, which is verie savorie and sweet. The huske beeing taken off, the shel serveth for many uses, as to make ladles with woodden handles, and also certaine little pots, which beeing fastened to a sticke, they doe therewith take* [*and lade*] *water out of their great pots, they make therof also small vessels to beare wine in when they walke into the fieldes, and a thousand other things."*

The Voyage of John Huyghen van Linschoten to The East Indies *from the Old English translation of 1598. Lenox Hill Pub. & Dist. Co. (Burt Franklin), 1970.*

Planting rice in Manila.

Muslim Food Cover J:47

The colorful dress of the Muslim Filipinos—oranges, reds and yellows, enriched by vivid purples and greens—and the brilliant flowers—frangipani, hibiscus, poinsettia, orchids and bougainvillea—of southern Mindanao, where much of the Muslim population lives, are reflected in their basketry. For this Muslim food cover, palm leaves were dyed dark shades of purple, green and russet and woven around natural and purple bamboo slats. Quite large—7½″ tall and 18″ in diameter at the base—it will protect a good-sized tray of sweets for an afternoon's *merienda:* light, crunchy tubes of rice pastry flavored with wild honey; sticky coconut squares; cakes of rice flour and cheese; and glutinous rice steamed in coconut milk and sugar.

Banana Traders $8.90

In Mindoro (the Philippines), laughing while planting corn is forbidden, for such foolishness will result in ears of corn with spaces between the kernels.

Fish Basket J:48

Fish are an important source of protein in the Filipino diet and a popular item on any menu. To carry their catch, Philippine fishermen hang a fish basket like this one over the edge of their small, double-outrigger canoes, to keep the newly-caught fish as fresh as possible for as long as possible. This 14″-high bamboo fish basket will easily keep a one- to two-pound porgy fresh until the last moment before frying it with garlic and onions, and topping it with an egg-and-tomato sauce for a *cardillo;* or frying then braising it in a vinegar-based gravy with garlic, ginger, onions, carrots and green peppers for an *escabeche.* The entrance to the basket is cleverly designed to be one-way only: a cone arrangement of bamboo strips allows the fish to be pushed in, but prevents it from getting out. To remove the fish, one need only press up on the plaited rim and the whole cone lifts out.

Banana Traders $30.00

ESCABECHE

Hot Pickled Fish

To serve 4

A 2- to 2½-pound porgy or other firm, white-fleshed fish, cleaned, with head and tail reserved and the body cut crosswise into 1-inch-thick steaks

1 cup plus 3 tablespoons vegetable oil
4 medium-sized garlic cloves, peeled and cut crosswise into paper-thin slices
1 tablespoon coarsely chopped, scraped fresh ginger root
1 small onion, peeled and cut crosswise into ⅛-inch-thick slices
1 medium-sized carrot, scraped and cut lengthwise into ¼-inch-wide slices, then crosswise into 2-inch-wide strips
1 medium-sized green pepper, stemmed, seeded, deribbed and cut crosswise into ¼-inch-thick rings
1 tablespoon cornstarch mixed with 1 cup cold water
⅓ cup malt vinegar
2 tablespoons dark-brown sugar
½ teaspoon salt

Wash the fish (including the head and tail) under cold running water and pat the pieces completely dry with paper towels. In a heavy 10- to 12-inch skillet, heat the cup of oil over moderate heat until it is very hot but not smoking. Add all the fish pieces and fry them for 5 or 6 minutes on each side, or until they are crisp and richly browned. With a slotted spatula transfer the fish to a platter lined with a double thickness of paper towels. Discard the oil in the skillet.

Wash and dry the skillet, and in it heat the remaining 3 tablespoons of oil until a light haze forms above it. In order, fry the garlic, ginger, onion, carrot and then the green pepper rings in the hot oil, stirring each vegetable constantly for about a minute before transferring it to a plate and frying the next. As you proceed, add more oil to the pan if necessary.

Add the cornstarch mixture, vinegar, brown sugar and salt to the oil remaining in the skillet and stir over moderate heat until the mixture comes to a boil and thickens. Add the fish, garlic and ginger, baste with the vinegar sauce, and bring to a boil again. Add the onions, carrots and green pepper rings and stir for a minute or so.

To serve, arrange the pieces of fish attractively on a deep, heated platter, reassembling them into their original shape if you like. Intersperse the vegetables with the fish pieces or arrange them around the edge. Then taste the sauce for seasoning and pour it over the fish and vegetables.

(From FOODS OF THE WORLD, Pacific and Southeast Asian Cooking, *Time-Life Books, New York. Copyright 1970 by Time Inc.)*

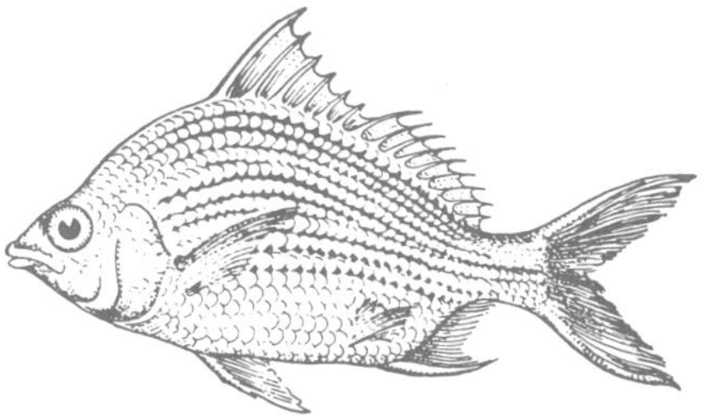

Egg Basket J:49

This 9″-square, woven-bamboo egg basket will hold up to six dozen eggs at once, a quantity that may not last long in a Philippine kitchen. A much-used ingredient, eggs show up in many guises: as a *torta* (meat and egg pancake much like a Spanish *tortilla*), in fritter batter and egg noodles, as a garnish, as a meringue-like topping for *rellenong alimango* (deep-fried crab cakes), or as part of stuffed dishes like *morcon* (braised, rolled flank steak) or *rellenong manok* (an entire boned chicken stuffed with pork, onions, raisins, pickles and eggs). The egg basket is sturdily made, with bamboo slats reinforcing the bottom, and a bent-bamboo hoop holding the mouth of the basket open. We feel compelled to offer the obvious suggestion that our egg basket could just as well store onions, potatoes and the like.

Banana Traders $10.00

Lunch Box J:50

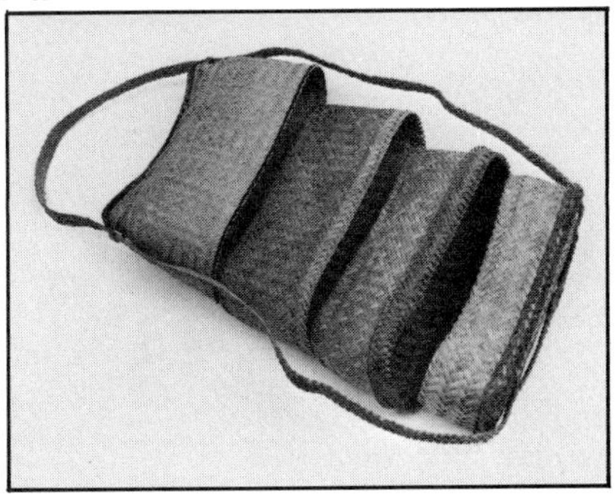

The multi-tiered lunch box is a cross-cultural artifact that does not seem to have made much of an impression in Western European circles. We have seen it, however, in almost every other corner of the world, in an amazingly wide assortment of materials. The concept is always the same: a stack of individual compartments held together by a framework that also serves as a handle; a perfect solution to the problem of assembling and transporting different foods. We have come upon it in stainless steel, in enameled steel, in wood and, oddest of all, in this purse-like woven bamboo example from the Philippines. There are four baskets, each of whose bottom is recessed to fit over the top of the basket underneath. The top and bottom baskets have loops on their sides through which a woven shoulder strap has been strung. When all the pieces are assembled, the satchel forms a rectangle that is 6½″ high, 8½″ wide and 3½″ deep. It's extremely attractive, even if it's not the very first material you'd think of for a lunch box. If you're planning to take last night's soup or a couple of canned peaches and cottage cheese with you for lunch, you would probably look elsewhere. In the Philippines, however, where the transported meal may consist of rice steamed in banana leaves, spicy strips of dried beef (*tapa*), a dried smoked or salted fish, and *carabao* (water buffalo) cheese wrapped in banana leaf, it is a perfectly practical affair.

Knobkerry $25.00

Availability Information

Wholesale sources appear in **bold** type, retail sources in regular type. Please note that wholesale sources will not sell to individuals; but most will supply, on request, a list of local retail sources for their products. Almost all retail sources will accept mail orders. In addition, those sources that have mail order catalogues have been indicated below by an asterisk (*).

ABRAHAM & STRAUSS
20 Elm Place
Brooklyn, N.Y. 11201

A. C. GIFTS NEW YORK, INC.
2642 Central Park Avenue
Yonkers, N.Y. 10710

ALLUMINIO PADERNO S.P.A.
20037 Paderno Dugnano
Milan, Italy

AMERICAN CUTLERY & HARDWARE CO., INC.
184 Bowery
New York, N.Y. 10012

ANNAPURNA
127 East 28th Street
New York, N.Y. 10016

ARABIA, INC.
8300 N.E. Underground Drive
Kansas City, Mo. 64161

ATLAS METAL SPINNING CO.
183 Beacon Street
So. San Francisco, Calif. 94080

BANANA TRADERS
246 East 51st Street
New York, N.Y. 10022
(also retail)

ELI BARRY CO., INC.
P.O. Box F
Kearny, N.J. 07032

BEARD GLASER WOLF INC.
800 Second Avenue
New York, N.Y. 10017

BEIRUT GROCERS, INC.
199 Atlantic Avenue
Brooklyn, N.Y. 11201

BENG-SOLO TRADING CORP.
264 Fifth Avenue
New York, N.Y. 10001

BERARDUCCI BROTHERS MFG. CO., INC.
1900 Fifth Avenue
McKeesport, Pa. 15132

B.I.A. CORDON BLEU, INC.
P.O. Box 627
Burlingame, Calif. 94010

BLOCK CHINA CORP.
11 East 26th Street
New York, N.Y. 10010

BLOOMINGDALE'S
1000 Third Avenue
New York, N.Y. 10022

BONJOUR IMPORTS CORP.
935 Horsham Road
Horsham, Pa. 19044

BOSTON WAREHOUSE CO.
39 Rumford Avenue
Waltham, Mass. 02154

BREMEN HOUSE, INC.*
218 East 86th Street
New York, N.Y. 10028

BRIDGE KITCHENWARE CORP.*
212 East 52nd Street
New York, N.Y. 10022
and
57 West Grand Avenue
Chicago, Ill. 60611

BULAKLAK MARKETING INC.
352 West 39th Street
New York, N.Y. 10018

BURDINE'S
22 East Flagler
Miami, Fla. 33131

CARDINAL CHINA CO.
Cardinal Building
P.O. Box D
Carteret, N.J. 07008

CASA MONEO
210 West 14th Street
New York, N.Y. 10011

CASA RIVERA
40-17 82nd Street
Jackson Heights, N.Y. 11372

CEPELIA CORP.
63 East 57th Street
New York, N.Y. 10022

CERAMICAS PUNTER, S.L.
Apartado 6
Teruel, Spain

HARRIET AMANDA CHAPMAN, INC.
225 Fiftn Avenue
New York, N.Y. 10010

JOYCE CHEN
763 B Concord Avenue
Cambridge, Mass. 02138

C. H. FOOD MARKET
41–05 Union Street
Flushing, N.Y. 11355

THE COMPLACENT COOK
Bridgehampton, N.Y. 11932

CONTINENTAL CRAFTS CO., INC.
145 Portland Street
Cambridge, Mass. 02139

COOKS' CORNERS, INC.
11 Sherwood Square
Westport, Conn. 06880

COPCO, INC.
11 East 26th Street
New York, N.Y. 10010

CORNWALL BRIDGE POTTERY
Cornwall Bridge, Conn. 06754

CRAFT CARAVAN, INC.
127 Spring Street
New York, N.Y. 10012

CREATIVE HOUSE
90 West Ashland Street
Doylestown, Pa. 18901

THE CRITICAL COOK
178 Atlantic Avenue
Brooklyn, N.Y. 11201

CROSS IMPORTS INC.*
210 Hanover Street
Boston, Mass. 02113
(also retail under Cook Things)

CUISINARTS, INC.
1 Barry Place
Stamford, Conn. 06902

TRACY DAWSON IMPORTS, INC.
420 Bernard Street
Los Angeles, Calif. 90012

DEBUYER MANUFACTURE DE FAYMONT
Le Val d'Ajol
88340 Vosges, France

E. DEHILLERIN
18–20, rue Coquillière
75001 Paris, France
(also retail)

DENBY LTD., INC.
41 Madison Avenue
New York, N.Y. 10010

EL MERCADO
510 Broome Street
New York, N.Y. 10013

ETHNIKON GIFT SHOP
22–48 31st Street
Astoria, N.Y. 11105

EUR-ASIAN IMPORTS
225 Fifth Avenue

New York, N.Y. 10010

EVA HOUSEWARES, INC.
P.O. Box 2687
San Rafael, Calif. 94902

EXPOSICION NACIONAL DE ARTES POPULARES
Avenida Juarez #89
Mexico 1 DF, Mexico

FAROY SALES
225 Fifth Avenue
New York, N.Y. 10010

FILIPINÀS INTERNATIONAL, LTD.
528 9th Avenue
New York, N.Y. 10018

FISHER BRUCE & CO.
107 Gaither Drive
Mount Laurel, N.J. 08054

FOODS OF INDIA
120 Lexington Avenue
New York, N.Y. 10016

R. H. FORSCHNER CO., INC.
P.O. Box 846
828 Bridgeport Avenue
Shelton, Conn. 06484

FORZANO ITALIAN IMPORTS, INC.
128 Mulberry Street
New York, N.Y. 10013

JULES GAILLARD & FILS
81, rue du Faubourg St. Denis
75010 Paris X^e, France
(also retail)

GARDEN WAY ASSOCIATES, INC.*
1300 Ethan Allen Avenue
Winooski, Vt. 05404

JOHANNES GIESSER (MESSER) K6
D-7057 Winnenden bei
Stuttgart, West Germany

GILLIES 1840
1494 Third Avenue
New York, N.Y. 10028

GIMBEL'S
33rd & Broadway
New York, N.Y. 10001

GREEK ISLAND LTD.
215 East 49th Street
New York, N.Y. 10017

MILTON GUMPERT
5269 West Pico Blvd.
Los Angeles, Calif. 90019

HAMMACHER SCHLEMMER *
147 East 57th Street
New York, N.Y. 10022

HANDCRAFT FROM EUROPE
P.O. Box 372
Sausalito, Calif. 94965

RUSSELL HARRINGTON CUTLERY, INC.
Southbridge, Mass. 01550

H & E TRADING COMPANY
410 Commack Road
Deer Park, N.Y. 11729

J. A. HENCKELS TWINWORKS, INC.
1 Westchester Plaza
P.O. Box 127
Elmsford, N.Y. 10523

HENRY et FILS
71110 Marcigny, France

HITACHI SALES CORP.
48-50 34th Street
L.I. City, N.Y. 11101

HOAN PRODUCTS, LTD.
615 East Crescent Avenue
Ramsey, N.J. 07446

HOLMEGAARD OF COPENHAGEN, INC.
575 Madison Avenue
New York, N.Y. 10022

HUNG CHONG FOODS INC.
14 Bowery
New York, N.Y. 10013

INDIA NEPAL
233 Fifth Avenue
New York, N.Y. 10016

INTERNATIONAL EDGE TOOL CO.
565 Eagle Rock Avenue
P.O. Box P
Roseland, N.J. 07068

IRANIAN NATIONAL HANDICRAFTS
10 East 53rd Street
New York, N.Y. 10022

THE IRISH PAVILION
130 East 57th Street
New York, N.Y. 10022

IRONSTONE POTTERY
1760 Monrovia Avenue
Building B10
Costa Mesa, Calif. 92627

JANE PRODUCTS, INC.
5 East 20th Street
New York, N.Y. 10003

THE JAPAN MART, INC.
239 W. 105th Street
New York, N.Y. 10025

JAPANESE FOODLAND
2620 Broadway
New York, N.Y. 10025

EDWIN JAY INC.
20 Cooper Square
New York, N.Y. 10003
(also retail, as Hoffritz)

J. P. MARKET
374 Southwestern Avenue
Los Angeles, Calif. 90020

JURGENSEN'S*
601 South Lake Avenue
Pasadena, Calif. 91109

KALAMATA FOOD IMPORTS, INC.
38-01 Ditmars Blvd.
Astoria, N.Y. 11105

KALIAN PRODUCTS CORP.
29 Great Jones Street
New York, N.Y. 10012

KALKUS, INC.
5714 West Cermak Road
Cicero, Ill. 60650

KALPANA
42-75 Main Street
Flushing, N.Y. 11355
(also retail)

KALUSTYAN
123 Lexington Avenue
New York, N.Y. 10016

KAM KUO FOOD INC.
7 Mott Street
New York, N.Y. 10013

KAM MAN FOOD PRODUCTS
200 Canal Street
New York, N.Y. 10013

KARNIG TASHJIAN
380 Third Avenue
New York, N.Y. 10016

KATAGIRI AND CO., INC.
224 East 59th Street
New York, N.Y. 10022

ALBERT KESSLER & CO.
1355 Market Street
San Francisco, Calif. 94103

KITCHEN GLAMOR, INC.*
26770 Grand River
Detroit, Mich. 48240

KNOBKERRY
158 Spring Street
New York, N.Y. 10012

ALFRED E. KNOBLER & CO., INC.
Moonachie Avenue
Moonachie, N.J. 07074

KRISCHER METAL PRODUCTS CO., INC.
Moonachie, N.J. 07074

KUNG'S TRADING CO., LTD.
79 Madison Avenue
New York, N.Y. 10016

LA CUISINIÈRE
867 Madison Avenue
New York, N.Y. 10021

LA PLACETEÑA DISTRIBUTING
5418 Tonnelle Avenue
North Bergen, N.J. 07047

LA TIENDA
210 East 58th Street
New York, N.Y. 10022

LE ROI DE LA COUPE
Coutellerie Chevalerias
La Malaptie — 63250 Viscomtat
France

CHARLES F. LAMALLE
1123 Broadway
New York, N.Y. 10010

H. E. LAUFFER CO., INC.
Belmont Drive
Somerset, N.J. 08873

FRED LEIGHTON IMPORTS, LTD.
763 Madison Avenue
New York, N.Y. 10021

LEYSE ALUMINUM CO.
Kewaunee, Wis. 54216

LION GENERAL
3232 Lurting Avenue
Bronx, N.Y. 10469

LORD & TAYLOR
424 Fifth Avenue
New York, N.Y. 10018

LUCKY GIFT SHOP
20 Bowery
New York, N.Y. 10003

H. A. MACK & CO., INC.
165 Newbury Street
Boston, Mass. 02116

MACY'S
Herald Square
New York, N.Y. 10001

MAID OF SCANDINAVIA CO.*
3244 Raleigh Avenue
Minneapolis, Minn. 55416
(also retail)

MAIN ST. FOODS
41-52 Main Street
Flushing, N.Y. 11355

MALKO IMPORTING CORP.
182 Atlantic Avenue
Brooklyn, N.Y. 11201

MAPROSA S.A.
Calle 1 #295
Mexico D.F., Mexico

DAVID MELLOR
4 Sloane Square
London SWIW 8EE,
England

MEXICAN FOLK ART ANNEX, INC.
23 West 56th Street
New York, N.Y. 10019

MORA & CIE.
13, rue Montmartre
75001 Paris, France
(also retail)

MOROCCO DESIGNS, INC.
1123 Broadway
New York, N.Y. 10010

S. I. MOSS CO., INC.
234 Westport Avenue
Norwalk, Conn. 06851

NEWARK HARDWARE & PAINT CO., INC.
95 Ferry Street
Newark, N.J. 07105

NEW FRONTIER TRADING CORP.
2394 Broadway
New York, N.Y. 10024

NORDISKA*
517 Westport Avenue
Rte. 1
Norwalk, Conn. 06851

NOR-PRO
Nordic Products, Inc.
2211-15 Avenue West
Seattle, Wash. 98119

NORTHLAND ALUMINUM PRODUCTS, INC.
Highway 7 at Beltline
Minneapolis, Minn. 55416

NYBORG & NELSON, INC.
937 Second Avenue
New York, N.Y. 10022

N.Y. MUTUAL TRADING CO.
160 Johnson Avenue
Hackensack, N.J. 07601

CHRISTIAN OOS KG
5530 Gerolstein—Eifel
Postfach 1240, West Germany

OPA OY
c/o Scan Co-op Contemporary Furn.
11310 Frederick Avenue
Paulen Industrial Park
Beltsville, Md. 20705

ORIENTAL COUNTRY STORE
12 Mott Street
New York, N.Y. 10013

ORIENTAL PASTRY & GROCERY CO.
170 Atlantic Avenue
Brooklyn, N.Y. 11201

OSMO HEILA IMPORTS
Podunk Road
Trumansburg, N.Y. 14886
(also retail)

S. OSTROWSKY, INC.
1133 Broadway
New York, N.Y. 10010

OVERSEAS MARKETING CORP.
7008 Marcelle
Paramount, Calif. 90723

JOHN PALMER, LTD.
Victory House
Somers Road North
Portsmouth, Hants P01 1PN
England

PAMPERED KITCHENS
21 East 10th Street
New York, N.Y. 10003

PAN AMERICAN PHOENIX
927 Madison Avenue
New York, N.Y. 10021

PANELLINION GIFTS
29-14 Ditmars Boulevard
Astoria, N.Y. 11105

PAPRIKÁS WEISS*
1546 Second Avenue
New York, N.Y. 10028
(also retail)

PARIS BREAD PANS*
500 Independence Avenue
Washington, D.C. 20003
(also retail)

PILLIVUYT S.A.
18500 Mehun sur Yèvre
France

PORCELAINE de PARIS
10, rue de la Pierre-Levée
75011 Paris, France

THE POTTERY BARN
231 Tenth Avenue
New York, N.Y. 10011

PRIMITIVE ARTISAN
225 Fifth Avenue
New York, N.Y. 10010

THE PROFESSIONAL KITCHEN
18 Cooper Square
New York, N.Y. 10003

QUONG YUEN SHING & CO.
32 Mott Street
New York, N.Y. 10013

RAFU BUSSAN
334 East 1st Street
Los Angeles, Calif. 90012

RAMSEY IMPORTS
P.O. Box 277
Ramsey, N.J. 07446

RECO INTERNATIONAL CORP.
P.O. Box 681
Port Washington, N.Y. 11050

RESTON LLOYD, LTD.
11800 Sunrise Valley Drive
Reston, Va. 22091

E. ROSSI AND CO.
191 Grand Street
New York, N.Y. 10013

H. ROTH & SON*
1577 First Avenue
New York, N.Y. 10028
(also retail)

ROWOCO INC.
700 Waverly Place
Mamaroneck, N.Y. 10543

ROYAL COPENHAGEN PORCELAIN
573 Madison Avenue

New York, N.Y. 10022

G. RUSHBROOKE (SMITHFIELD) LTD.
67-77 Charterhouse Street
London, EC1M 6HL
England

SAHADI IMPORTING CO., INC.
187-189 Atlantic Avenue
Brooklyn, N.Y. 11201
(also retail)

SAM BOK GROCERY
127 West 43rd Street
New York, N.Y. 10036

SAM SIAM CORP.
36 West 34th Street
New York, N.Y. 10001

SCANDICRAFTS, INC.
P.O. Box 665
Camarillo, Calif. 93010

SCHILLER & ASMUS, INC.
1525 Merchandise Mart
Chicago, Ill. 60654

SCHOTT-ZWIESEL GLASS INC.
11 East 26th Street
New York, N.Y. 10010

SCOTTISH PRODUCTS, INC.
24 East 60th Street
New York, N.Y. 10022

SEABON
54 East 54th Street
New York, N.Y. 10022

SERMONETA
740 Madison Avenue
New York, N.Y. 10021
(also retail)

SIAM GROCERY
2745 Broadway
New York, N.Y. 10025
(also retail)

SINDOORI IMPORTS
156 Second Avenue
New York, N.Y. 10003

SPICE & SWEET MAHAL
135 Lexington Avenue
New York, N.Y. 10016

SPRING BROTHERS CO., INC.
218 Little Falls Road
Cedar Grove, N.J. 07008

THE STORE AT SUGARBUSH VILLAGE
Waitsfield, Vt. 05673

NORBERT STRYER
P.O. Box 96
104-20 Queens Blvd.
Forest Hills, N.Y. 11375

SWISSMART, INC.
444 Madison Avenue
New York, N.Y. 10022

TAKASHIMAYA, INC.
509 Fifth Avenue
New York, N.Y. 10017

K. TANAKA AND CO.
326 Amsterdam Avenue
New York, N.Y. 10023

TAYLOR & NG*
P.O. Box 200
Brisbane, Calif. 94005
(also retail)

AUGUST THOMSEN CORP.
36 Sea Cliff Avenue
Glen Cove, N.Y. 11542

TOWN FOOD SERVICE EQUIPMENT CO., INC.
351 Bowery
New York, N.Y. 10003

TRIBAL ARTS GALLERY
84 East 10th Street
New York, N.Y. 10003

TRIPOLI RESTAURANT
160 Atlantic Avenue
Brooklyn, N.Y. 11201

GARY VALENTI
55-72 61st Street
Maspeth, N.Y. 11378

VITANTONIO MFG. CO.
4630 Industrial Parkway
Willoughby, Ohio 44094

WEST BEND CO.
P.O. Box 278
West Bend, Wis. 53095

WHEATON GLASS
1501 N. 10th Street
Millville, N.J. 08332

GEORGE WILKINSON (BURNLEY) LTD.
Progress Works
Burnley, Lancashire BB10 1PB
England

WILLIAMS-SONOMA*
P.O. Box 3792
San Francisco, Calif. 94119

ZABAR'S
2245 Broadway
New York, N.Y. 10024

ZUCCHI OSCAR
Via S. Antonio all'Esquilino, 15
00185 Rome, Italy

Picture Credits

Credits for the illustrations from left to right on each page are separated by a semicolon, and from top to bottom on each page by a hyphen. Abbreviations used in these listings are as follows: NYPLPC (New York Public Library Picture Collection), n.s. (no source), n.d. (no date).

China

2: *Les Plantes potagères,* Paris, 1904—ibid. 3: *Penny Magazine,* London, 1833—A pamphlet of the Chicago Natural History Museum, n.d. 4: *Le Boire et le manger,* Armand Dubarry, Paris, 1884. 5: The Metropolitan Museum of Art, Bequest of Mary Clark Thompson, 1924. 6: The Costume of *China,* George Henry Mason, 1800—n.s., NYPLPC. 7: *Hearth & Home* (magazine), New York, 1873. 9: n.s., NYPLPC. 11. Modern Chinese postcard of work by Ch'en Lin of the Yuan Dynasty, 1301—*The Style of Ornament,* Alexander Speltz, Dover Publications, 1959. 12: *Il Costume Antico e Moderno,* Giulio Ferrario, 1823-38. 19: *La Cuisine chinoise,* H. Lecourt, 1925. 20: *Social Life of the Chinese,* edited by Rev. Paxton Hood, 1868. 23: *Universal Magazine,* n.d.—ibid. 25: *Scientific American,* 1883. 27: *The Chinese Empire,* G. N. Wright, London, 1858—*Il Costume Antico e Moderno,* Giulio Ferrario, 1823-38. 28: *The Chinese Empire,* G. N. Wright, London, 1858—*La Cuisine chinoise,* H. Lecourt, 1925. 29: *Saturday Magazine,* 1833. 30: *The Pictorial Gallery of Arts,* Charles Knight, London, 1845. 31: *Funk & Wagnall's Standard Atlas of the World,* The Firm, New York, 1906—German Drawing, n.s., n.d. 32: *The Chinese Empire,* G. N. Wright, London, 1858. 33: ibid. 35: *La Cuisine chinoise,* H. Lecourt, 1925. 36: The Metropolitan Museum of Art, Gift of J. P. Morgan, 1908. 37: *The Style of Ornament,* Alexander Speltz, Dover Publications, 1959—*A Pictorial History of China and India,* Robert Sears, 1851. 39: *The Style of Ornament,* Alexander Speltz, Dover Publications, 1959.

France

42: n.s., n.d., NYPLPC. 43: n.s., 1900, NYPLPC. 44: *Bohemian Paris of Today,* William Chambers Morrow, 1900; *Graphic Pictures,* Randolph Caldecott, Routledge, London, 1883. 46: *Le Livre de cuisine,* Jules Gouffé, 1874. 47: *Les Plantes potagères,* Paris, 1904. 48: *Handbook of Plant and Floral Ornament from Early Herbals,* Richard G. Hatton, Dover Publications, New York, 1960—*Comment on forme une cuisinière,* (2ème partie), Mme Seignobos, n.d. 49: *Le Livre de cuisine,* Jules Gouffé, 1874. 50: ibid. 51: ibid. 52: *America in the Kitchen: From Hearth to Cookstove,* Linda Franklin Campbell, House of Collectibles, 1976. 53: *Harper's Magazine,* 1869. 54: *Le Livre de cuisine,* Jules Gouffé, 1874. 55: ibid. 56: ibid. 59:*Les Accessoires du costume et du mobilier,* Henry René d'Allemagne, Schemit, Paris, 1928. 60: *Illustrated London News,* November 28, 1871. 62: *Encyclopedia of Practical Cookery,* Theodore Francis Garret, n.d. 64: n.s., n.d., NYPLPC. 66: *La Cuisine de tous les mois,* Philéas Gilbert, 1893. 68: *Une Histoire de la cuisine française,* Christian Guy, Les Productions de Paris, Paris, c. 1962; *Encyclopedia of Practical Cookery,* Theodore Francis Garret, n.d. 71: *Herbst und Winterblumen,* Carus Sterne, 1886. 73: *Les Plantes potagères,* Paris, 1904—*Encyclopedia of Practical Cookery,* Theodore Francis Garret, n.d. 81: *America in the Kitchen: From Hearth to Cookstove,* Linda Franklin Campbell, House of Collectibles, 1976. 82: *Les Accessoires du costume et du mobilier,* Henry René d'Allemagne, Schemit, Paris, 1928. 84: *Traité de pâtisserie moderne,* Emile Darenne and Emile Duval, Editions Lambert, n.d.—ibid. 85: ibid. 90: *The Encyclopedia Britannica,* Cambridge University Press, Cambridge, England, 1911. 92: *L'Histoire, la vie, les moeurs et la curiosité par l'image,* John Grand-Carteret, Paris, 1927-28. 93: *The Pictorial Gallery of Arts,* Charles Knight, C. Knight & Co., London, 1845-47. 94: *L'Orfèvrerie française aux XVIIIe et XIXe siècles,* Henri Bouilhet, Laurens, Paris, 1908; n.s., n.d., NYPLPC. 95: *Groumandugi,* Maurice Brun, 1949.

Hispanic Countries

96: n.s., n.d., NYPLPC—ibid.—*Enciclopedia Italiana di Scienze, Lettere ed Arti,* Instituto Giovanni Treccari, Rome, c. 1929-39. 98: *Illustrated London News,* London, March 1857. 100: *Two Hundred Pictorial Illustrations of the Holy Bible,* compiled by Robert Sears, 1841-42. 101: *Les Plantes potagères,* Paris, 1904—*Handbook of Plant and Floral Ornament from Early Herbals,* Richard G. Hatton, Dover Publications, New York, 1960. 102: The Metropolitan Museum of Art, Purchase 1956, Cloisters Fund. 103: *Penny Magazine,* London, August, 1834—*Les Plantes potagères,* Paris, *1904.* 105: *Penny Magazine,* London, August, 1832. 106: The Metropolitan Museum of Art, Gift of Henry G. Marquand, 1894—*Handbook of Plants and Floral Ornament from Early Herbals,* Richard G. Hatton, Dover Publications, New York, 1960. 110: *Les Plantes potagères,* Paris, 1904. 111: *Alle de wercken van den Heere Jacob Cats,* J. Rotelband, Amsterdam, 1712. 112: *Animate Creation,* John George Wood, Hess, New York, 1885—ns., nd., NYPLPC. 115: Print from the U.S. Library of Congress, Prints and Photographs Division—Drawing by Freeman, in *Le Marchand pittoresque,* 1854. 121: *Pictorial History of America,* Samuel Griswold, Goodrich, House and Brown, Hartford, 1847. 122: The Metropolitan Museum of Art, Gift of Mr. and Mrs. Robert W. deForest, 1911—*Les Plantes potagères,* Paris, 1904. 126: *America in the Kitchen—From Hearth to Cookstove,* Linda Franklin Campbell, House of Collectibles, 1976. 127: *Handbook of Plants and Floral Ornament from Early Herbals,* Richard G. Hatton, Dover Publications, New York, 1960—*Encyclopedia of Practical Cookery,* Theodore Francis Garret, n.d. 128: *Nature Magazine,* American Nature Association, 1940. 129: *Le Boire et le manger,* Armand Dubarry, 1884. 131: *The Life of the African Plains,* Leslie Brown, McGraw Hill and Co., New York, 1972. 133: *Illustrated London News,* London, 1864. 135: The Metropolitan Museum of Art, Gift of Nathan Cummings, 1967. 136: *Le Boire et le manger,* Armand Dubarry, 1884. 137: *The Pictorial Gallery of Arts,* Charles Knight, C. Knight and Co., London, 1845-47.

India

138: *Meyers grosses Konversations—Lexikon,* Leipzig, 1902-13—ibid. 139: ibid.—ibid.; ibid.; ibid. 140: ibid. 142: *Encyclopedia of Practical Cookery,* edited by Theodore Francis Garret; *Funk & Wagnall's Standard Atlas of the World,* The Firm, New York, 1906. 144: *Le Boire et le manger,* Armand Dubarry, 1884. 145: The Metropolitan Museum of Art, The Theodore M. Davis Collection, Bequest of Theodore M. Davis, 1915. 146: *The Style of Ornament,* Alexander Speltz, Dover Publications, 1959. 147: *The American Cyclopedia,* edited by George Ripley and Charles A. Dana, Appleton, New York, 1873-76. 148: Photograph by A. Williamson. 149: The Metropolitan Museum of Art, The Theodore M. Davis Collection, Bequest of Theodore M. Davis, 1915. 150: *The Style of Ornament,* Alexander Speltz, Dover Publications, 1959. 152: *Le Boire et le manger,* Armand Dubarry, 1884. 153: The Metropolitan Museum of Art, Gift of Alexander Smith Cochran, 1913. 157: n.s. 158: The Metropolitan Museum of Art, Gift of Robert W. and Lockwood de Forest, 1919. 159: *Indian Book of Painting,* Ernst Kuhnel and Herman Goetz, Paul, Trench, Trudner Ltd., London, 1926. 160: *Funk & Wagnall's Standard Dictionary of Folklore, Myth and Legend,* edited by Maria Leach, 1949—*Le Pâtissier royal parisien.* M. A. Carême, Second Volume, 1828. 161: *Le Boire et le manger,* Armand Dubarry, 1884.

Italy

162: The Metropolitan Museum of Art, Rogers Fund, 1947. 163: ibid. 164: ibid. 166: *The Encyclopedia of Practical Cookery, edited by* Theodore Francis Garret, n.d.; n.s. 167: *Handbook of Plant and Floral Ornament from Early Herbals,* Richard G. Hatton, Dover Publications, New York, 1960. 168: *Pan American Union Bulletin,* Washington, D.C., n.d. 170: *Le Livre de cuisine,* Jules Gouffé, 1874—Illustrated London News and Sketch, Ltd., 1862. 171: *A Pictorial History of the World's Great Nations, from the Earliest Dates to the Present Time,* Charlotte Mary Yonge, Hess, New York, 1882. 172: *Life in the Roman World of Nero and St. Paul,* Thomas George Tucker, Macmillan, New York, 1910. 173: *The Pictorial Gallery of Arts,* Charles Knight, London, 1845-47. 175: *Le Livre de cuisine,* Jules Gouffé, 1874. 177: *Le Magas in pittoresque, Paris,* 1834. 178: *The London Graphic,* 1872. 181: Undated German rendering. 183: *Herbst und Winterblumen,* Carus Sterne, Freytag, Leipzig, 1886. 185: n.s., NYPLPC. 187: *Les Plantes potagères,* Paris, 1904. 188: "Aubergines," *Larousse Gastronomique,* Prosper Montagné, Librairie Larousse, Paris, c. 1938; *Les Plantes potagères,* Paris, 1904. 192: The Metropolitan Museum of Art, Fletcher Fund, 1946. 193: *Le Vie privée des anciens,* René Joseph Ménard, Morel, Paris, 1880-

83. 194: *History of Rome and the Roman People,* Victor Drury, Estes and Lauriat, Boston, 1890. 195: *Trees and Shrubs of the British Isles,* C. S. Cooper, London, 1909. 197: *Harper's Magazine,* 1860.

Japan

200: *The Hokusai Sketchbooks,* James A. Michener, Tuttle, Rutland, Vt., 1958—ibid.—ibid. 201: Kate Slate. 202: *Riverside Natural History,* edited by John Sterling Kingsley, Riverside Press, Boston, 1888. 204: *Meyers grosses Konversations—Lexikon, Leipzig, 1885-92. 205: ibid.—The Boy Travellers in the Far East,* Thomas Wallace Knox, Harper, New York, 1880-1905. 207: The Metropolitan Museum of Art, The H. O. Havemeyer Collection, Bequest of Mrs. H. O. Havemeyer, 1929. 208: *Meyers grosses Konversations—Lexikon,* Leipzig, 1885-92. 209: *Les Plantes potagères,* Paris, 1904. 210: Kaye Sherry Hirsh. 212: *Household Precepts,* illustrated by Hokusai, 1828. 213: *Les Plantes potagères,* Paris, 1904. 214: *The Hokusai Sketchbooks,* James A. Michener, Tuttle, Rutland, Vt., 1958—ibid. 215: ibid. 217: The Metropolitan Museum of Art, Exchange, 1952, Funds from various donors. 218: Kaye Sherry Hirsh. 219: *Encyclopedia Britannica,* 11th edition, Cambridge University Press, Cambridge, England, 1911. 220: *The Hokusai Sketchbooks,* James A. Michener, Tuttle, Rutland, Vt., 1958. 225: by Emile Bayard after a Japanese painting, NYPLPC. 228: *Le Théâtre au Japon,* Alexandre Benazet, Ernest Leroux, Paris, 1901, Volume 13. 229: The Metropolitan Museum of Art, Gift of Mr. and Mrs. Samuel Colman, 1893. 230: The Metropolitan Museum of Art, Rogers Fund, 1907. 231: The Metropolitan Museum of Art, Bequest of Edward C. Moore, 1891. 232: The Metropolitan Museum of Art, Gift of Mr. and Mrs. Samuel Colman, 1893. 233: *All Around the World,* edited by William Francis Ainsworth, Collins, London, 1869-71. 234: *The Hokusai Sketchbooks,* James A. Michener, Tuttle, Rutland, Vt., 1958—ibid. 235: The Metropolitan Museum of Art, Gift of Suizan Miki, 1952. 236: The Metropolitan Museum of Art, Bequest of Edward C. Moore, 1891; *Harpers New Monthly Magazine,* Harper Brothers, New York, July, 1890. 237: ibid.

Middle East and Africa

234: *Egypt: Descriptive, Pictorial and Picturesque,* George Moritz, Ebers, Cassell, London, 1881-82; *The Style of Ornament,* Alexander Speltz, Dover Publications, New York, 1959. 235: *The Masterpieces of French Art,* Louis Viardot, Gebbie, Philadelphia, c. 1883. 236: *La Guilande de l'Iran,* Flammarion, Paris, c. 1948—*Il Costume Antico e Moderno,* Giulio Ferrario, 1823-38—*La Vie privée des anciens,* René Joseph Ménard, 1880-83. 237: n.s., n.d.—*Nature Magazine,* American Nature Association, Washington, D.C., 1940. 240: *Il Costume Antico e Moderno,* Giulio Ferrario, 1823-38—*Dictionnaire de l'ameublement,* Henry Harvard, Paris, 1887-90. 243: The Metropolitan Museum of Art—*La Vie privée des anciens,* René Joseph Ménard, 1880-83. 246: *The Land and the Book: Lebanon, Damascus and Beyond,* William M. Thomson, Nelson, London, 1886. 247: *Monuments de l'Egyptie et de la Nubie,* Jean François Champollion, Didot, Paris, 1844-89—n.s., n.d., NYPLPC. 250: *Monuments de l'Egyptie et de la Nubie,* Jean François Champollion, Didot, Paris, 1844-89. 251: The Metropolitan Museum of Art. 252: *Faiences decoratives de la vieille Turquie,* Alexandre M. Raymond, Paris, 1930—ibid. 254: *Illustrated London News,* London, August, 1854. 255: Le *Boire et le manger,* Armand Dubarry, 1884. 256: *Illustrated London News,* London, April, 1854. 257: *Amusements philologiques,* Halle, Germany, 1749-50. 258: *The Chefs-d'Oeuvre d'Art of the International Exhibition,* edited by Earl Shinn, Gebbie, Philadelphia, 1878. 260: *History of Mankind,* Friedrich Ratzel, Macmillan, New York, 1896-98. 261: *Nature Magazine,* American Nature Association, Washington, D.C., 1940. 265: *Cyclopedia of Universal History,* John Clark Ridpath, Jones Bros., Cincinnati, 1885—*History of Mankind,* Friedrick Ratzel, New York, 1896-98. 266: From report of the Bureau of American Ethnology, Smithsonian Institute, 1886. 267: n.s., n.d., NYPLPC. 268: Photo by Ed Fitzgerald. 269: *Harper's Bazaar,* January 20, 1872.

Middle and Eastern Europe

274: *Über Land und Meer* (magazine), 1877—*Costume de la Hongroie,* Paris, n.d. 275: *Illustrated London News,* October, 1873. 276: *Kulturgeschichte des deutschen Volkes,* Otto Henne am Rhyn, Grote, Berlin, 1886. 279: n.s., NYPLPC. 280: *Paris illustré,* Boussod, Valadon & Cie., Paris, 1887. 282: *Handbook of Plant and Floral Ornament from Early Herbals,* Richard G. Hatton, Dover Publications, New York, 1960. 283: *Illustrazione Italiana,* Milano, 1933. 284: *Repertory of Patent Inventions,* London, 1795. 285: *Museum des Wundervollen,* J. A. Bergk and T. G. Baumgartner, Baumgartner, Leipzig, 1803-05. 287: *Meyer's grosses Konversations—Lexikon,* Leipzig, 1902-13—ibid.—ibid. 290: *Les Plantes potagères,* Paris, 1904; *Travels in North America,* Peter Kahn, 1753. 292: *Leslie's Monthly Magazine,* New York, 1894. 293: *Kulturgeschichtliches Bilderbuch aus drei Jahrhunderten,* edited by George Hirth, Hirth, Leipzig, 1881-90. 295: ibid. 296: *Les Plantes potagères,* Paris, 1904. 300: *The Style of Ornament,* Alexander Speltz, Dover Publications, New York, 1959. 302: *Le Magasin pittoresque,* Paris, 1854. 303: *Illustrated Weekly,* Charles Clucas & Co., New York, November, 1875. 308: *The Style of Ornament,* Alexander Speltz, Dover Publications, New York, 1959. 310: *International Studio* (magazine), 1908. 311: *Tirggel, ein altes Weihnachtsgeback,* Gottard Schuh, Amstutz, Zürich, c. 1941—*Graphis: Graphic and Applied Art,* Amstutz, Zürich, 1944. 312: *Mon Village,* l'Oncle Hansi, Floury, Paris, n.d. 313: *English Doll Houses of the 18th and 19th Centuries,* Vivian Greene, Batsford, London, 1955. 319: *Handbook of Plant and Floral Ornament from Early Herbals,* Richard G. Hatton, Dover Publications, New York, 1960—ibid. 320: *The Stage and Its Stars Past and Present,* ed by. H. Paul, Gebbie, Philadelphia, c. 1890. 321: n.s., n.d., NYPLPC. 322: *Über Land und Meer,* (Magazine), 1874.

Northwestern Europe

324: Sherwood, Neely & Jones, 1809. 325: n.s., NYPLPC. 328: *Museum des Wundervollen,* J. A. Bergk and T. G. Baumgartner, 1803-05. 330: *History of Rome and the Roman People,* Victor Drury, 1890. 331: U.S. War Department Report on Explorations, 1855-60. 335: *L'Imagerie populaire des Pays-Bas,* Emile Henri van Heurck, Paris, c. 1930. 336: Stockholm Postcard by Aina Stenberg. 337: *Les Plantes potagères,* Paris, 1904. 339: *World Beneath the Microscope,* Wilfred E. Watson Baker, Studio, London, 1935. 341: *Redouté's Fruits and Flowers,* Pierre Joseph Redouté, Ariel, London, 1964. 344: Field Museum of Natural History, 1937. 346: *Handbook of Plant and Floral Ornament,* Richard G. Hatton, Dover Publications, New York, 1960; *Atlas des plantes de France,* Amadée Masclef, Klincksiek, Paris, 1889-91. 348: n.s., NYPLPC. 349: *America in the Kitchen: From Hearth to Cookstove,* Linda Franklin Campbell, 1976—*Handbook of Plant and Floral Ornament,* Richard G. Hatton, Dover Publications, New York, 1960. 353: *Le Boire et le manger,* Armand Dubarry, 1884. 355: *Graphic Pictures,* Randolph Candecott, Routledge, London, 1883. 356: *The Book of Household Management,* Isabella Beeton, Ward, Lock, London, 1909. 359: *The Pictorial Gallery of Arts,* Charles Knight, London, 1845-47. 360: n.s., NYPLPC. 361: *Everyday Things in American Life 1607-1776,* William Charency Langdon, Charles Scribner's Sons, New York, 1946. 364: *British Costume during XIX Centuries,* Emily Jessie Ashdown, Stokes, New York, 1910. 366: *Song of Sixpence Picture Book,* Walter Crane. 367: *Harper's Magazine,* Harper Brothers, New York, July, 1879. 369: *Magazine of Art,* Cassell, London, 1884. 371: *The Queen of Hearts,* Randolph Caldecott, Warne, London, c. 1890. 374: *The House Beautiful,* Clarence Cook, Scribner, Armstrong & Co., New York, 1878. 377: *Illustrated London News,* January 2,1897. 380: *Alle de wercken van den Heere Jacob Cats,* J. Rotelband, Amsterdam, 1712. 381: *Ladies Home Journal,* Curtis Publishing Co., Philadelphia, Pa., 1895.

Southeast Asia

382: *Handbook of Plant and Floral Ornament from Early Herbals,* Richard G. Hatton, Dover Publications, New York, 1960. 388: ibid. 389: *Great Races of Mankind,* John Clark Ridpath, 1893. 390: *Il Costume Antico e Moderno,* Giulio Ferrario, 1823-38. 393: *The Polar and Tropical Worlds: A Description of Man and Nature in the Polar and Equatorial Regions of the Globe,* 1874. 394: *The Saturday Magazine,* London, c. 1832. 395: *A Collection of Voyages and Travels,* Anshaw Churchhill, London, 1744-46. 396: *Florilegium renovatum et auctum,* J. T. de Bry, Frankfurt, 1641. 397: *Henderson's Handbook of Plants and General Horticulture,* Peter Henderson, The Firm, New York, 1910. 398: *Illustrated London News,* London, December, 1857. 399: *The New Cabinet Cyclopedia and Treasury of Knowledge,* edited by Charles Annendale, 1892-95. 402: *Illustrated London News,* London, December, 1857. 403: *How to Cook Your Catch,* Rube Allyn, Great Outdoors Publishing Co., St. Petersburg, Florida.

Index

In the following index, page numbers in **bold** face refer to recipes; numbers in *italics* refer to subjects discussed in essays or in descriptions of the utensils; and numbers in roman type refer to utensils.